Paul McCartney

Printed in the United Kingdom by MPG Books, Bodmin

Published by Sanctuary Publishing Limited, Sanctuary House,
45–53 Sinclair Road, London W14 0NS, United Kingdom

www.sanctuarypublishing.com

Distributed in the US by Publishers Group West

ISBN: 1-86074-486-9

Paul McCartney

Alan Clayson

Sanctuary

Contents

To Garry Jones, singer, composer, bass guitarist and all he should have been

About The Author

Born in Dover, England in 1951, Alan Clayson lives near Henley-on-Thames with his wife Inese and sons, Jack and Harry.

A portrayal of Alan Clayson by the *Western Morning News* as the "AJP Taylor of the pop world" is supported by *Q*'s "his knowledge of the period is unparalleled and he's always unerringly accurate." He has penned many books on music – including the bestsellers *Backbeat*, subject of a major film, and *The Yardbirds* – and has written for journals as diverse as *The Guardian, Record Collector, Mojo, The Times, Mediaeval World, Eastern Eye, Folk Roots, Guitar, Hello!, The Independent, Ugly Things* and, as a teenager, the notorious *Schoolkids Oz*. He has also been engaged to perform and lecture on both sides of the Atlantic – as well as broadcast on national TV and radio.

From 1975 to 1985, Alan led the legendary Clayson and the Argonauts, and was thrust to "a premier position on rock's Lunatic Fringe" (*Melody Maker*). As shown by the formation of a US fan club – dating from an 1992 *soirée* in Chicago – Alan Clayson's following has continued to grow as well as demand for his talents as a record producer, and the number of versions of his compositions by such diverse acts as Dave Berry – in whose Cruisers he played keyboards in the mid-1980s – and New Age outfit, Stairway. He has worked too with The Portsmouth Sinfonia, Wreckless Eric, Twinkle, The Yardbirds, The Pretty Things and the late Screaming Lord Sutch among others. While his stage act defies succinct description, he is spearheading an English form of *chanson*. Moreover, his latest single, 'The Moonlight Skater', may stand as Alan Clayson's artistic apotheosis were it not for a promise of surprises yet to come.

Further information is obtainable from www.alanclayson.com.

"Wings are what The Beatles could have been."
    – Alan Partridge, Travel Tavern, Norwich, 1997

Prologue
"Till There Was You"

> "The number of things that The Beatles are doing gets less
> and less as the years go on."
> > – *Editor Johnny Dean when* Beatles Monthly
> > *ceased publication in 2002*[1]

I've never been able to like Paul McCartney. However, he's not
one of myriad pop stars I love to hate either, and I recognise that
he's realized some extraordinary visions, whether as a rough-and-
ready rock-a-balladeer or as a purveyor of cultured "contemporary"
pop. Furthermore, having glided for so long on pop's strongest
winds, he's become a past master at pulling unexpected strokes –
often just after critics had written him off. He can also be forgiven
almost anything for his stand on animal rights.

Perhaps one of the reasons why I'm not his greatest fan is because,
of all The Beatles, he was the one I most minded girlfriends fancying.
John was married, George was the quiet one and Ringo didn't enter
the equation. Paul also took charge of 'Till There Was You', 'And
I Love Her' and most of the pretty-but-nothings that sent frissons
through female nervous systems. The most cloyingly showbiz of
the four, he scored too with his boyish grin, doe-eyes and stronger
commitment to public relations than rough old John.

Yet I will not indulge in too many cheap laughs at Paul's expense
because, within my limitations, I am a principled wordsmith. As
disgruntled record reissue specialists who have commissioned me
to pen eulogistic sleeve notes will tell you, I never write anything

I don't mean. Moreover, I have to have enough empathy with the artist concerned to even begin any heart-searching contractual arithmetic. As such, Paul McCartney passes muster. If I don't consider him the colossal talent that others make him out to be, I understand that he isn't entirely to blame for being so overrated, and agree with Nick Garvey, bass player on one of the post-Wings albums, that Paul was "more driven than George or Ringo".

Needless to say, this isn't the first literary excavation of McCartney or, indeed, my debut as a chronicler of Beatle-associated matters. For instance, Clayson accounts of George Harrison and Ringo Starr – the "other two" – were completed for another publisher over a decade ago – though they have been thoroughly updated for subsequent editions by Sanctuary.

I have altered my literary approach for the more celebrated McCartney, partly because of too many dissolving outlines and mergers of contents between his tale and those of George and Ringo – as well as that of John Lennon. Rather than dwelling on a straightforward life story and details that every Beatlemaniac or McCartney crackpot knows already, I've focussed on aspects about him that interested me, and attempted to place him in the context of the social, political, cultural and environmental undercurrents that formed him and that he had a hand in changing.

Nevertheless, I am aware that there has developed a too-analytical if respectable form of pop journalism that intellectualises the unintellectual, turns perfume back into a rotten egg, and tells you what Greil Marcus thinks about *Band On The Run* and what Simon Frith thinks he means. Why should I be any different by not dismantling Paul McCartney and sticking him back together again? Yet I wouldn't have embarked on this project if I didn't feel that it was a worthwhile historical exercise, a way of trying to convince people that I'm clever or, as the more cynical amongst you may assume, so I will be paid the remainder of my advance.

I'll shoot myself metaphorically in the foot further by saying that any serious student of McCartney ought to go first and last to Bill Harry's *Paul McCartney Encyclopaedia*[2] that, for raw fact, deals with the bloke as adequately and as accurately as anyone might reasonably expect. Moreover, if you're after constructive analysis of his post-Beatles music, try John Blaney's *Paul McCartney: The Songs He Was Singing*[3].

However, as Horace cautions us, "*quandoque bonus dormitat Homerus*", which loosely translated means "even the cleverest can make mistakes" – even Barry Miles, author of McCartney's official biography, *Many Years From Now*[4], with, say, his propagation of the myth that The Beatles and other Merseybeat groups had the edge over those in other areas because they acquired the discs from which they drew their repertoire from "Cunard Yanks" rather than buying them from local record shops. "Everyone knew someone with a brother, a cousin or a father on the boats," Barry assures us, "and when they returned, they brought with them [hitherto unheard] rock 'n' roll records."

While one of my intentions is to fine-tune, correct and debunk, I want more than this to recreate a feeling of being there – though, ultimately, the litmus test of any musical biography is to compel you to rise from the armchair to check out the records. Whether I succeed in this or not, I hope that I shall utilise your time intriguingly – but remember, however elaborately I dress it up, these are only my opinions – and not always subjective ones either – about items of merchandise available to all. Your thoughts about 'I Saw Her Standing There', 'Give Ireland Back To The Irish', *Liverpool Oratorio* and all the rest of them are as pertinent as mine – and, beyond either of us, the only true approbation an artist needs is from those who buy the albums and pay admission to the shows.

My principal perspective is that of a recording artist, composer, stage performer and writer on musical subjects for more than 30 years. During this period too, I discovered that the music industry, national and beyond, is not so much a small world as a parochial one, which has brought me into contact with many who, however cognisant they were of it, provided relevant information and insight.

Here's an example. You may think I'm making it up, but Denny Laine, awaiting his destiny as Paul's second-in-command in Wings, signed the back of a Lord John boutique card after I'd spotted him emerging from a Carnaby Street tobacconist's in spring half-term 1965, just as his Moody Blues's 'Go Now' was slipping from the charts. I came up to his shoulders then, but he came up to mine when next we met at a charity concert near Farnham on a February afternoon in 1996.

'Go Now' was a highlight of a set that spanned every familiar avenue of a professional career that has switchbacked to the very peaks of pop and down to its most desperate backwaters. Much of this was – and still is – dictated by Denny's restless nature. "That's what I tend to do," he reflected, "get into a band, and then it gets busy, and all of a sudden you want to get away from it all again. That's what happened with the Moodies and Wings with me. Enough was enough. I like to try my hand at other things – things you can't do when you're in a band."

I am grateful to Denny – and also to Cliff Bennett, Rod Davis, Bill Harry, Neil Innes, John Duff Lowe, Gerry Marsden, Ruth McCartney, Tony Sheridan and the late Vivian Stanshall for conversations and interviews that took place before this project was commissioned.

Please put your hands together too for Iain McGregor, Michelle Knight, Laura Brudenell, Chris Bradford, Chris Harvey, Alan Heal, Anna Osborn and the rest of the team at Sanctuary, who went far beyond the call of duty from this biography's genesis to its final publication.

Now let's have a round of applause for these musicians: Frank Allen, Don Andrew, Roger Barnes, Alan Barwise, Dave Berry, Barry Booth, Tony Crane, the late Lonnie Donegan, Nick Garvey, "Wreckless" Eric Goulden, Rick Hardy, Mike Hart, Brian Hinton, Tony Jackson, Garry Jones, Billy Kinsley, Billy J Kramer, Phil May, Jim McCarty, Henry McCullough, Mike Pender, Larry Smith, Norman Smith, Mike and Anja Stax, the late Lord David Sutch,

Dick Taylor, John Townsend, Paul Tucker, Fran Wood and Twinkle. As invaluable were the archives and intelligent argument of my principal researcher, Ian Drummond.

It may be obvious to the reader that I have received much information from sources that prefer not to be mentioned. Nevertheless, I wish to thank them – as well as B and T Typewriters, Robert Bartel, Bemish Business Machines, Stuart and Kathryn Booth, Maryann Borgon, Eva Marie Brunner, Jennie Chamberlain, the late Ray Coleman, Kevin Delaney, Peter Doggett, Katy Foster-Moore, Ann Freer, Gary Gold, Louise Harrison, Michael Heatley, Dr Robert Hieronymous, Dave Humphreys, Robb Johnson, Rob Johnstone, Allan Jones, Barb Jungr, Graham Larkbey, Mark Lapidos, Spencer Leigh, Martin Lewis, Russell Newmark, Mike Ober, Mike Robinson, Jim Simpson, Mark Stokes, Michael Towers, Angela Williams and Ted Woodings – plus Inese, Jack and computer expert Harry Clayson for talking me down from the precipice.

Alan Clayson
May 2003

1 *"Que Sera Sera"*

"There's nothing new – only a new way of doing it."
— *Johnnie Ray on Elvis Presley*[1]

When, in the first flush of their stardom, The Beatles made their stage debut in Ireland – at Dublin's Adelphi Cinema on 7 November 1963 – Paul McCartney announced that "It's great to be home!". Liverpool, see, is known facetiously as "the capital of Ireland" – and three of the Moptopped Mersey Marvels had more than a splash of the Auld Sod in their veins.

Most of Paul's was inherited from mother Mary, whose maiden name was Mohin. Almost as a matter of course, she was devoutly Roman Catholic. Nevertheless, the issue of religion did not label a citizen of mid-20th-century Liverpool politically as much as it had over in Ireland since the Sinn Fein hostilities disturbed the War Office's conduct of The Great War, and led to the secession of all but the affluent north of the country from the United Kingdom in 1921. Mary, therefore, did not take to heart the Catholic Information Centre's boxed warnings in the *Liverpool Echo*'s classified section about the inherent dangers of mixed marriages. Furthermore, while Mary kept the pledge required of the Catholic party in such a union to have any offspring baptised into the faith, her two sons – James Paul and Peter Michael – were not to be educated in Roman Catholic schools or to attend any of the Roman Catholic churches that stood in Merseyside suburbs, but were becoming lost in an encroaching urban sprawl that had spread from central Liverpool since the turn of the century.

Yet the area may be comparable now to Gauguin's South Sea islands or Byron's Italy in its potential to inspire greatness or at least accommodate it. Nonetheless, as far as making headway in showbusiness was concerned, this was nowhere as obvious as it was eastwards to Manchester, which, with its radio and television stations was "Entertainment Capital Of The North", or half a world away in the opposite direction where many of Liverpool's exports (of labour as well as goods) were directed: North America, which Hollywood movies would have you believe was a new-old wonderland of Coca-Cola and the Wild West.

Before the Great Depression, which saw the collapse of all sizes and manner of international business enterprises with attendant multitudes suddenly unemployed, the Mersey had been aswarm with ships bound, however indirectly, for the "land of opportunity". Their voyages had been motivated by the slave trade and then cotton – and it had been during World War I that the 14-year-old Jim McCartney had entered the world of work on the ground floor at a dockside cotton merchants. He had risen to the high office of salesman there by the start of the next global conflict when, as an infinitesimal cog provisioning the bloodshed afar, he did his bit in a local munitions factory. Then, following Hitler's suicide, Jim passed a written test for eligibility to work for Liverpool Corporation.

During those distracted times, he wondered whether his late '30s wasn't a suitable age to look for a wife. He wasn't a bad-looking fellow, was he? He stood straight as a lance and looked over 6ft (180cm) tall in the bowler hat worn when those of his generation walked out with a lady. He was introduced to Mary Mohin by one of his sisters and married her in 1941.

Just over a year later, the remarkable James Paul was born on 18 June 1942, a dry Thursday with alternate warm and cool spells, in Liverpool's Walton Hospital, the nearest maternity ward to the furnished rooms in Anfield where Jim and Mary lived in a forlorn cluster of Coronation Streets.

The "James" was both after his father and in respect of the scriptures, but, from the cradle, the boy was called by his middle name, just as his brother – who arrived two years later – was to be.

From Anfield, the family moved to the south of Liverpool, settling eventually in 20 Forthlin Road, a semi-detached on a new estate in Allerton, ten minutes dawdle from the river, and more convenient for Mrs McCartney in her capacity as health visitor and then a district midwife.

In the living room of this house stood an upright piano. Whilst it suffered the investigative pounding of the infant Paul and Mike's plump fists, it also tinkled beneath the self-taught hands of their father who, to put it simply, loved music. He immersed himself in it as other dads might in do-it-yourself, photography or being so unswervingly faithful to a chosen soccer team that a home game is never missed. As well as listening to artefacts from an impressive sheet music and record collection, McCartney *père* was able to speak with authority about all kinds of elements in North America's musical melting pot, particularly jazz – and his own musical aptitude was judged to be exceptional.

In the 1920s Jim had had no qualms about performing in public, whether extrapolating often witty incidental music as silent movies flickered in city cinemas or performing at parochial entertainments on the 88s – and, for a while, trumpet – with his Jim Mac's Jazz Band. Though still in its infancy, "jazz" had been elevated from slang on 6 March 1913 via its use in a San Francisco Bulletin in a feature concerning Al Jolson, whose 78rpm recording of 'The Spaniard That Blighted My Life' had been released that week. Jim McCartney understood jazz then to embrace both Dixieland and semi-classical items like *Rhapsody In Blue* from George Gershwin, lumped together derisively as "swing" by those who'd automatically switch it off the wireless.

Dapper in immaculately stiff evening dress, Jim Mac's Jazz Band took their places on a palais bandstand to begin the night's selection of dances. In the more unrefined venues, apart from when the high C notes from the trumpet stabbed the air, there was often an underlying noise of boozy chatter until, in the hullabaloo, someone would catch a jazzed-up fragment of melody and an ale-choked mouth would trigger unison singalongs from barrack-room ditties to sentimental ballads about my blue heaven and Ida, sweet as apple cider.

Obliged by economic necessity to focus more exclusively on his day job, Jim cut back on the extra-curricular Charlestons, finally breaking up the band in around 1927. Nevertheless, he continued to play for his own amusement and compose too, though the only extant Jim McCartney opus seems to be 'Walking In The Park With Eloise', an instrumental. He was also the principal accompanist during those "musical evenings" that were a frequent occurrence in many working class households before television became an indispensable domestic fixture.

The sounds that emanated from the McCartneys' front room ranged from sonorous renderings of selections from the latest film musicals like *South Pacific* and *Oklahoma!* to a hymn, nursery rhyme or popular song in an uncertain treble from a child who might have been been led forth, glistening with embarrassment, to the centre of the room to pipe it out prior to being packed off to bed.

Sensibly, while Jim was only too willing to impart hard-won knowledge, neither he nor Mary goaded their lads to over-formalise what were assumed to be innate musical strengths. Of the two, Paul seemed keenest and, from being a fascinated listener whenever Dad was seated at the piano, he progressed at his own speed on the instrument, acquiring the rudiments of harmony, and adding to a repertoire that embraced tunes from cross-legged primary school assemblies and – then quite a new idea – traditional songs from *Singing Together* and other BBC Home Service radio broadcasts to schools.

Three decades before 'Baa Baa Black Sheep' was banned in a London corporation kindergarten, no one had batted an eyelid when the *Singing Together* pupils' handbook required you to sing "mah" for "my" and "wid" for "with" on the few "coon songs" included.[2] Neither were token West Indians or Asians present on the covers of the standard *Oxford School Music Book*, which was distributed to most British primary schools. Preference was given instead to a blazered boy in National Health spectacles trumping a euphonium, a girl attentive and beribboned on triangle, a choir in kilts and rows of young violinists and recorder players in pleated skirts or flannel shorts – all under the baton of a bespectacled teacher.

More exciting than the Home Service's dashing white sergeants, drunken sailors, Li'l Liza Janes and John Barleycorniness was the Light Programme, which interspersed the likes of Educating Archie – comic goings-on of a ventriloquist's dummy (on the radio!) – and *Workers' Playtime* with approved items from the newly established *New Musical Express* record sales "hit parade". Though Sunday lunch has never been the same since the departure of *The Billy Cotton Band Show*, most of the music on the wireless – as in the *NME* charts – before about 1955 was aimed at grown-ups.

Otherwise, there was *Housewives Choice* and *Children's Favourites* – record requests aired by "Uncle Mac" – though Lonnie Donegan, who was to loom large in The Beatles' legend, was to aver, "I first heard blues on *Radio Rhythm Club* on the BBC every Friday night. There'd be one folk song per programme. Sometimes, it was a blues." Generally speaking, however, in between Patti Page's 'How Much Is That Doggie In The Window' – covered by Liverpool's very own Lita Roza – and adult-themed 'Finger Of Suspicion' from Dickie Valentine, there was no middle ground beyond 'Davy Crockett' novelties and lewd outrages like 'Such A Night' by Johnnie Ray, "the Prince of Wails". As in the 1940s, you jumped from nursery rhymes to Perry Como as if the intervening years had been spent in a coma.

This was reflected in the easy-listening permanency of music heard in Britain's dance palais. In Liverpool, however, there appeared to be a more pronounced element of check-shirted country-and-western, ranging from maudlin "sincerity" to clippety-clop propulsion; from stirring songs forged in the cow camps, wagon trains and shotgun shacks of the old frontier to enduring Tin Pan Alley crossovers by the likes of Vaughn "Ghost Riders In The Sky" Monroe, Frankie Laine, Tennessee Ernie Ford, Guy Mitchell and whip-crack-away Doris Day as "Calamity Jane". As the 1950s wore on, Jim Reeves became a name that abided above all these.

"Featured popular vocalists" were brought forward to either specialise in areas thought unsuitable for the usual singer or simply to let them knock back a swift half-pint of beer. A spirit of appeasement might permit maybe two current smashes, including one dip into a new strain of teenage nonsense per night – because, as well as customary demands for 'The Anniversary Waltz' and 'Que Sera Sera', there was always some young smart alec during these days who wanted dance bands – spiritual descendants of Jim Mac-type outfits – to give 'em 'Rock Around The Clock', 'Blue Suede Shoes' or some other "rock 'n' roll" number. What with Kay Starr's crafty 'Rock And Roll Waltz' topping the hit parade, it was going stronger than previous crazes, such as the Jitterbug and the Creep. What were Bill Haley And The Comets after all? They were a dance band like any other middle-aged dance band, except they'd got lucky with this 'Rock Around The Clock' detritus and would have been stupid not to have cashed in quickly.

Now and then, some vocalist or other onstage in a British dance hall would be permitted to gyrate, snarl and roll on his back as if he had a wasp in his pants. Not letting personal dislike of the style stop them either, better-known jazz and dance band musicians also clung onto rock 'n' roll's coat tails. The first record release by Ronnie Scott's former vocalist Art Baxter was 'Jingle Bell Rock'. As a gen-u-ine North American rocker, Chuck Berry was seen derisively duck-walking with his red guitar in *Jazz On A Summer's Day*, a US film documentary. Britain struck back

with The Kirchin Band – whose sixth 78rpm single was 'Rockin'
And Rollin' Thru' The Darktown Strutters' Ball', for a jazz
extravaganza at Butlin's Clacton holiday camp.

As puerile in their way were the twirling sticks of US swing
band drummer Lionel Hampton, whose raucous nod to rock 'n'
roll during a 1955 concert at the Royal Festival Hall prompted
jazz purist Johnny Dankworth to voice his disgust from the
audience. Dankworth must have felt like King Canute when
England's oldest jazz club, Studio 51, closed to reopen as the 51
Club. Its new policy enabled rock 'n' roll and jazz bands to share
the same bill. Well, you have to move with the times – as did
Housewives' Choice idol Lee Laurence, a trained opera tenor, with
his spoof 'Rock 'N' Roll Opera' that same year.

Like all but the most stuffy adolescents of the 1950s, Paul
McCartney would have been thrilled by 'Rock Around The Clock'
whenever it intruded upon Uncle Mac's jingle bells and winter
wonderlands as 1955 drew to a close. "The first time I really ever
felt a tingle up my spine," he gasped, "was when I saw Bill Haley
And The Comets on the telly."[3]

Now a loose-lipped and rather chubby youth, Paul had left
Joseph Williams Primary School, a "bus ride away from Forthlin
Road", after passing the Eleven-Plus examination – as would
brother Mike – to gain a place at Liverpool Institute, which was
located within the clang of bells from both the Roman Catholic
and Anglican cathedrals, along with most of the city centre's other
seats of learning, including the university – opened in 1978 on the
site of the old lunatic asylum – and the Regional College of Art.

Thus far, Paul had proved sound enough, even very able, in
most subjects. He had a particular flair and liking for creative
writing because as well as submitting homework, he would tinker
with fragments of verse and prose for a purpose unknown apart
from articulating the inner space of some private cosmos.

It goes without saying that he shone during music lessons too.
Indeed, while he'd never be able to sight-read faster than the most

funereal pace, he became as well known for his musical skills as the school bully and football captain were in their chosen spheres. However, an attempt to master a second-hand trumpet his father had given him was, let's say, an "incomplete success", put off as he was by the unpredictable harmonics, which jarred his teeth during his first shaky sessions in front of a prescribed manual. "Guitars hadn't come in yet," he'd recall. "Trumpeters were the big heroes then"[3] – even if in Liverpool, you were most likely to be blowing one in a public park or Remembrance Day procession in one of the brass bands that were more prevalent in the north than anywhere else in Britain.

Nevertheless, if Blackpool hosted the Mineworker's National Brass Band Contest every November, Eddie Calvert, Britain's foremost pop trumpeter, was from Preston in the same neck of the woods. If well into his 30s, he'd shown what was possible by scoring a 1954 Number One in the *New Musical Express*'s chart with sentimental 'Oh Mein Papa', recorded at EMI's studio complex along Abbey Road, a stone's throw from Lord's Cricket Ground in London.

Eddie's renown was to infiltrate a Giles cartoon in the *Daily Express* in which an elderly classical musician with a trumpet under his arm is mobbed for autographs by teenagers at the Edinburgh Festival. Three other members of the orchestra watch the frenzy ill-humouredly. "How does he do it?" rhetoricates a cellist. "Signs himself Eddie Calvert. That's how he does it."[4]

How could any British musician become more famous than to be the inspiration for Carl Giles? Young Paul McCartney was impressed, "but I couldn't sing with a trumpet, and I wanted to sing."[3] This wish was granted after a fashion because Paul's musical genesis was ecclesiastic as well as academic, and his then unbroken soprano was put to use in the choir at St Barnabas Church, off Penny Lane, common ground between the raw red council houses of Allerton and, half a class up, the mock-Tudor thoroughfares of Woolton, a suburb that regarded itself as more "county" than "city".

In cassock, ruff and surplice, Paul and Mike cantillated at three services every Sunday and, when required, at weddings and in St Cecilia's Day oratorios. Before his voice deepened, Paul was appointed head chorister. As befitted this office, he was privileged to bear the processional cross as priest and choir filed to and from the vestry. He also doused the altar candles after the General Confession during Matins. Yet the holy sounds he sang every Sunday were novel and intelligible at nine, over-familiar and rote-learnt by thirteen. As it is with every intelligent adolescent, he questioned the motive of adult communicants. Were the rafter-raising votes of confidence and thanks to the Lord once a week to assuage His inferiority complex, to quench His restless thirst for applause or a stockpiling of spiritual ammunition for the defence when the worshippers' cases came up in the afterlife?

Nevertheless, in 1953, with hardly a murmur, Paul had gone along with his father's advice to try for Liverpool's Anglican Cathedral choir. Another supplicant was John Charles Duff Lowe, a boy who was to be in the same class as Paul at the Institute. In middle life, Lowe came upon "a photograph taken when Paul and I both auditioned for the Liverpool Cathedral choir when we were ten, just before we went to the Institute. We both failed on that occasion. I got in six months later – and so, incidentally, did Stuart Slater, later of The Mojos – but Paul never tried again. I think he was recorded as saying he'd tried to make his voice break because he didn't really want to do it. If he had, he'd have got the same musical training that I got: music theory pumped into you every evening and weekends, and services on top of that. As a result, you tended to grow up apart from your mates where you lived. However, in 1958, my voice broke, and I stopped going straight from school to the Cathedral every night."

Whatever Jim's thwarted aspirations for Paul as perhaps a round-vowelled solo tenor setting the Cathedral walls a-tremble with one of Handel's biblical arias, his wife imagined Paul as either a teacher or a doctor. She was, however, never to see either of her children grown to man's estate because, during the summer of 1955, 47-year-old Mary had the removed look of a dying woman – which she was. What she may have self-diagnosed as stomach acidity and non-related chest pains turned out to be terminal cancer.

A photograph on the mantelpiece was to prompt opaque memories of life before the end came on 31 October 1956 – though, in many respects, Mary continued to govern family behaviour patterns from the grave, especially those rooted in appreciation of the value of money, and the notion that hard work and tenacity are principal keys to achievement.

Life without a wife wasn't easy for Jim at first. For a northern male, he was obliged to become unusually attentive to household tasks, particularly cooking. With assistance from relations and neighbours, however, he ensured that his – thankfully, healthy – offspring were as comfortable and contented as his new station as a single parent would allow.

Paul and Mike helped according to their capabilities with jobs on the rotas their father would pin up in the kitchen. Yet though the situation nurtured self-reliance, Paul's childhood was shorter than it needed to be, even though he stayed on at school beyond the statutory age, raised recently to 16. He was a likeable and seemingly unassuming pupil, who walked a tightrope between teacher's pet and the source of illicit and entertaining distraction as some withered pedagogue droned like a bluebottle in a dusty classroom. "Paul was a very amusing cartoonist," laughed John Duff Lowe, "His drawings – maybe one of the master taking the lesson – would appear under your desk, and you'd pass it on."

Before entering the sixth form, Paul had been securely in the "A" stream throughout his sojourn at the Institute, even winning a school prize for an essay. As it was with future Beatle colleagues, Pete Best and Stuart Sutcliffe, distinguishing themselves likewise at Liverpool Collegiate and Prescot Grammar respectively, teacher training college, rather than medical school, was looming larger as the summer examinations crept closer. Paul, however, wasn't keen, half-fancying the idea of being some sort of bohemian artist. One of the two GCE "A" levels he was expected to pass was actually in Art, a subject that – like music – the ordinary working man from the northwest, whether navvy or ledger clerk, saw as having doubtful practical value, an avenue for humorous scepticism as exemplified when an abstract by Arthur Ballard, a Liverpool painter, was exhibited upside-down.

Though Merseysiders might feel quiet pride from personal familiarity with the likes of Ballard, art was less precious a commodity, and its executants were treated less deferentially than in London. As late as 1960, no artist based in Liverpool had been able to rely solely on his work for a reasonable income, owing mainly to the dearth of effective commercial and promotional outlets within the region.

Musicians were in the same boat. If on a business trip to Manchester, moguls from EMI or the kingdom's other three major record companies rarely seized the chance to sound out talent in Macclesfield, Preston, Liverpool or other conurbations within easy reach. In the realm of popular music, it had been necessary for Eddie Calvert as well as Lita Roza and fellow Liverpudlians Frankie Vaughan and Michael Holliday to go to the capital in order to Make It.

Sport too was regarded as a legitimate means of escape from provincial Britain's overall drabness, and dwelling until the grave in the same socially immobile situation as your older relations.

Staring glumly through the lace curtains of the front room, Paul McCartney would have wondered if that was all there was. There was nothing on the horizon to indicate openings other than in secure but dead-end jobs with a gold watch on retirement to tick away the seconds before you went underground.

The view from the city's first tower block – in Huyton – was even more depressing, if perversely spellbinding: the creeping smog, the sulphuric light, the miles and miles of Coronation Streets that multiplied by the year. Looking west, you could just about make out the stadium of a football team stuck halfway down the Second Division.

Yet the city had forged tangible opportunities for cultural development matching those of any in London. It benefitted from the bequeathment of private artistic purchases by John Rankin, James Smith and other enlightened industrialists in its close-knit business community. Such gifts were manifest in all manner of public galleries; some of them purpose-built by the givers. Works could be hung and mounted in the Walker, the Bluecoat, the Academy, the Williamson and in the University. Otherwise, they could be seen in the less rarified atmosphere of arty coffee bars like the Blue Angel, Streate's, the Zodiac and the Jacaranda.

The Jacaranda was a watch repair shop prior to its transformation in 1957 via newly painted walls, bench seats and a dropped trellis-work ceiling with dangling fishnets and coloured balls. A conveniently short stroll from the art college, it had become a rendezvous for its students and staff as well as those with business at the nearby labour exchange. You could sit in the Jacaranda for hours on end for the price of a transparent cup of frothy coffee. Entertainment was usually coin-operated but, as a change from the juke box, musicians were hired to play evening sessions on the minuscule dance floor in the basement.

After its opening in 1959, tutors and students alike could also hold court in the cellar bar of Hope Hall (later, the Everyman). As well as exhibitions of local art, "the Hope" hosted poetry recitals and the kind of films that, having faded from general circulation, were watched as an intellectual duty.

Cinema proprietor Leslie Blond had financed the building of Hope Hall, but the city's most famous commercial patriarch was the late John Moores, instigator of the Littlewoods "football pools" in 1934. Labour party leader Ramsey McDonald had denounced it as "a disease" as it spread across the nation; countless heads of families filling in the weekly coupon that might win them a fortune. By the 1950s, Moores, an adventurous if old-fashioned businessman, controlled a retailing empire that employed 10,000 on Merseyside alone.

The paternalistic firm's art society, 70-strong choir and similar recreational facilities were inspired by the boss himself. Nevertheless, Moores the man was a self-effacing fellow with a harelip and spectacles, who shunned publicity. Yet, in other respects, he might be seen now as a role model for a Paul McCartney in later life, because, if parsimonious in small matters, Moores lent generous support to charities, and was a painter himself on the quiet as well as a collector and connoisseur of modern British art. Indeed, a portion of his millions was tithed to the fostering of art in Liverpool via scholarships and, in conjunction with the Walker Gallery, in 1957 he inaugurated the biennial John Moores Exhibition Of Contemporary Art, one of few British arts institutions known simply by its benefactor's name. Its declared purpose was "to encourage living artists, particularly the young and progressive", justified when the winning of a John Moores prize became one of the proudest boasts a British artist could make.

Quite a few of the artists shown came from Merseyside itself, and noisy argument about the merits of their entries and further aspects of art resounded in Ye Cracke, the pub that was frequented by denizens of the art college – as they did in the Jacaranda outside licensing hours, though the café also attracted the type blamed for what moral crusaders had lately coined "the generation gap".

Yet these youths were fundamentally no different from an archetype that has surfaced in every branch of society down the ages: a "fast boy" oozing sullen introspection, despised by your parents for coming from the wrong side of town. On uncovering your sister's illicit trysts with him, a responsible father would order her to never see him again.

Flighty girls revelled in their disobedience. In the 1950s, they tried either combining child-like naivety and *décolleté* eroticism like Brigitte Bardot, Gallic cinema's "answer" to Marilyn Monroe

– or aligned themselves to Juliette Greco, the Thinking Man's French actress, whose pioneering of white lipstick, coupled with black mascara, tent-like sweater and trousers, made her the vesperal heroine of intellectual adolescent females in dim-lit middle-class bedrooms.

The effect wasn't the same in a Scouse accent – as it wasn't either when the secondary modern yobs who, unlike Paul and Mike McCartney, weren't shackled to homework in the evenings, tried to copy James Dean, the rock 'n' roll rebel prototype who left this vale of misery in his Silver Porsche Spyder at 138kph (86mph) on 30 September 1955. Of Dean's three movies, the posthumously released *Giant* was one of the highest grossing of all time – merely because he was in it for 40 minutes.

1955's *Rebel Without A Cause*, however, remains an all-time favourite – partly through its illustration that you don't have to come from a rough district to qualify as a charismatic wrong 'un. On Merseyside, even boys from Allerton and Woolton mooched down to corner shops with hunched shoulders, hands rammed in pockets and chewing gum in a James Dean half-sneer.

If the attitude was derived from Dean, the appearance of the most menacing teenage cult of the 1950s was almost entirely British. Garbed approximately as Edwardian gentlemen, "Teddy Boys" went around in packs to, say, wreck a Church youth club, snarling with laughter as a with-it vicar in a cardigan pleaded ineffectually. A meek if vulgar reproof – "you flash cunt" – by the victim had sparked off the first Teddy Boy murder in 1954. After that, there'd been questions in Parliament, hellfire sermons, plays like Bruce Walker's *Cosh Boy* – that suggested flogging was the only answer – and films such as *Violent Playground* and 1957's *These Dangerous Years*, both set in Liverpool.

These Dangerous Years – about a teenage troublemaker reformed by a spell in the army – had a title song performed by Frankie Vaughan who, in 1958, had become a bigger pop star than even Eddie Calvert, rivalling Dickie Valentine as Ireland's most beloved male vocalist. There were, nonetheless, perceptible signs of danger for Frankie after the coming of ITV's *Oh Boy!*, a series pitched directly at teenagers, and unmarred by its BBC predecessor, *Six-Five Special*'s frightened dilution of the rock 'n' roll elixir with string quartets, traditional jazz and features on sport and hobbies.

Oh Boy! arrived a year after Bill Haley's first European tour – the first by any US rock 'n' roller. "The ticket was 24 shillings," remembered Paul McCartney, "and I was the only one of my mates who could go as no one else had been able to save up that amount – but I was single-minded about it, having got that tingle up my spine. I knew there was something going on here."[3]

Described by *Melody Maker* as resembling a "genial butcher"[5], Haley was an ultimate disappointment at the Liverpool Empire and virtually everywhere else, though he paved the way for more genuine articles.

Paul McCartney had been approaching his 14th birthday when he first caught Elvis Presley's 'Heartbreak Hotel' on the Light Programme. In a then-unimaginable future, he was to own the double-bass thrummed on this 78rpm single. However, in 1956 he was just one of countless British youths who'd been so instantly "gone" on 'Heartbreak Hotel' that all he could think was that its maker was surely the greatest man ever to have walked the planet.

Listening to this and consequent Presley hits either sent McCartney into a reverie that no one could penetrate or brought on an onset of high spirits that drew in Mike and even a bemused Jim. It was to be the same when Paul discovered Little Richard. In a typically succinct foreword to Richard's 1984 biography, Paul would recollect, "The first song I ever sang in public was 'Long Tall Sally' in a Butlin's holiday camp talent competition when I was 14."[6]

So "gone" was he this time that he started buying Little Richard discs without first listening to them – as you could in those days – in the shop, thus bringing upon himself angered dismay when

"I found this Little Richard album that I'd never seen before. When I played it, I found there were only two tracks by Little Richard. The rest was by Buck Ram and his Orchestra. You needed a magnifying glass to find that out from the sleeve. It's rotten, that kind of thing."[7]

It was, indeed. Yet, having invested an amount of cash that was the equivalent of three week's paper round earnings, Paul intended to spin that long-player (LP) – well, the Little Richard numbers anyway – to dust, sometimes concentrating on maybe only the piano or bass, then just the lyrics. He was determined to get his money's worth. "I didn't have much," he'd affirm, "not enough to chuck about anyway – but most Saturdays, I'd got enough saved to buy a record. It was, like, the highspot of the week, that record. I couldn't wait to get home and play it."[7]

Neither Richard nor Elvis were to visit Britain until they'd shed the qualificative bulk of their respective artistic loads, but a singing guitarist named Buddy Holly did, leaving a lasting and beneficial impression upon one who was to be his greatest champion. Visually, Holly, unlike Presley, was no romantic lead from a Hollywood flick, recast as a rock 'n' roller. To offset an underfed gawkiness, Buddy wore a huge pair of black hornrims. Until he and his accompanying Crickets – guitar, bass and drums – played Liverpool's Philharmonic Hall on 20 March 1958, Paul McCartney had been attracted by "really good-looking performers like Elvis. Any fellow with glasses always took them off to play, but after Buddy, anyone who really needed glasses could then come out of the closet."[8]

Yet it was still a magazine picture of a smouldering Elvis on the bedroom wall that greeted Paul when he first opened his eyes in the pallor of dawn. Presley was also hovering metaphorically in the background during Paul's maiden attempts to make romantic contact with girls who, in the years before the contraceptive pill, had been brought up to discourage completion of sexual pilgrimages until their wedding nights.

McCartney, however, was to enjoy more such conquests than most, his appeal emphasised by paternity allegations after The Beatles left the runway. Among forums for initiating carnal adventures were coffee bars like the Jacaranda where, according to a regular customer named Rod Jones, "there used to be office girls who'd go up there to get laid because all the art students used to hang around there."[9]

2 *"That'll Be The Day"*

"You've got to want to try; win, lose or draw."
— *Clint Eastwood as "Rowdy Yates" in*
"Incident Of The Day Of The Dead",
an episode of Rawhide[1]

Paul knew Rod Jones, but not as well as he did one who'd started his art college course a year earlier in 1957. How had Paul classified John Lennon during the first days of their acquaintance? Was he a friend?

To all intents and purposes, Lennon — nearly two years older than McCartney — had lived with his aunt in well-to-do Woolton from infancy. Soon to die, his mother dwelt nearby with his half-siblings and her boyfriend. After she'd gone, John was not to understand the profundity of the less absolute loss of his father until much later.

The situation with his parents was a handy peg on which to hang all sorts of frustrations. Life had long ceased to make sense for a very mixed-up kid with a huge chip on his shoulder. At Quarry Bank, a grammar school not as liberal as the Institute, he'd undergone often exultant application of corporal punishment for the mischief he made and because he was less an overt bully than something of an emotional fascist as he experimented how far beyond permissible small atrocities he could take mostly non-physical pain and terror with regard to weaker pupils and vulnerable figures of authority. At college, he was loud-mouthed, argumentative and given to bouts of sulking. From breakfast to bedtime, he projected himself as being hard as nails, as hard as his hardened heart.

Despite everything, Paul – like so many others – couldn't help liking John Lennon. For a start, he was hilarious. His calculated brutishness never quite overshadowed a grace-saving, if sometimes casually shocking, wit as well as a disarming absence of a sense of embarrassment, a selective affability and a fierce loyalty towards those few he'd accepted as intimates.

Something else that interested Paul about John was that he was leader of a "skiffle" group called The Quarry Men. He sang and was one of too many rudimentary guitarists. A chap named Rod Davis picked at a banjo, while the rest used instruments manufactured from household implements.

The skiffle craze had followed a hunt for an innocuous British riposte to Elvis Presley. The job had gone to Tommy Steele, a former merchant seaman, but his first chart strike, 'Rock With The Cavemen', had been shut down in 1956's autumn Top 20 by 'Dead Or Alive' from Lonnie Donegan – 'The King of Skiffle', a form born of the rent parties, speakeasies and Dust Bowl jug bands of the US Depression. In Lonnie's lordly opinion then, "rock 'n' roll has no musical value, no variety in sound, nondescript lyrics and a rhythmical beat about as subtle as that of a piledriver. A section of the public likes it – but it's only the youngsters who have to be 'in the swim'. You know, when marbles are the craze, they all play marbles – and rock 'n' roll just about comes into the marbles category. I'm a folk singer, and I intend to stay that way; no rock 'n' roll gimmicks for me!"[2]

When I challenged him about this shortly before his death in 2002, Lonnie Donegan sidestepped by contemplating, "What is 'pure' rock 'n' roll? Its whole essence is that it's impure. It's worse than skiffle to try and pin down as a *mélange* of influences and styles. Rock 'n' roll when she was originally spoke was rhythm and blues, and God knows what that was either. Country blues brought to the city and put through an amplifier?"

Whatever it was, Donegan's first single, 'Rock Island Line' – from the catalogue of walking musical archive Leadbelly – also penetrated a US Top 40 upon which UK acts had rarely encroached. Another was 'Freight Train' by The Chas McDevitt Skiffle Group – with Nancy Whiskey, a Glaswegian lass on lead vocals. It too took coals to Newcastle in that it was an upbeat arrangement that belied the gloomy lyrical content of a 1905 composition by black gospel singer Elizabeth Cotton.

Conversely, Johnny Duncan, a Tennesseean, came to Britain with the US army, but, awaiting demobilisation, stayed on to cause Lonnie Donegan some nervous backward glances during skiffle's 1957 prime. Johnny drew from the same repertory sources as everyone else – blues, gospel, rockabilly, country *et al* – but, being a bona fide Yank, he had an edge over the plummy gentility of most native would-be Donegans.

Yet it was Lonnie rather than Johnny who was the dominant precursor of the 1960s beat boom, given those future stars who mastered their assorted crafts in amateur outfits that followed his example. As well as Cliff Richard, Marty Wilde, Adam Faith and others who received more immediate acclaim, Paul McCartney too had taken on skiffle after buying himself an acoustic guitar. Encouraged as always by his father, he'd taught himself to play after an initial setback on discovering that he needed to restring it to hold down chords commensurate with his left-handedness.

Paul had absorbed pop like blotting paper, and was making what he hoped was a pleasant row on his new acquisition, but Jim would remind him that perhaps it was time to cast aside adolescent follies. He might think that this rock 'n' roll was the most enthralling music ever, but he'd grow out of it. There was no reason why it should last much longer than previous short-lived fads. It just happened to be going a bit stronger than hula-hoops and the cha-cha-cha. Hadn't Paul read in *Melody Maker* that many skiffle musicians were switching their allegiance to less-than-pure traditional jazz, the next big thing, so they said? Unlike skiffle, anyone couldn't do it.

Liverpool's principal bastions of "trad" were contained mainly within the lofty ravines of warehouses round Whitechapel. These included the Cavern, the Temple and – with "no Weirdies, Beatniks or Teddy Boys admitted" – the Storyville (later, the Iron Door). Student union dances at the art college too were generally headlined by a trad band.

Yet no "dads" from Liverpool were to join Acker Bilk, Chris Barber and Kenny Ball in the Top 20 when British trad touched its commercial zenith in 1961 with million-sellers by trumpeter Ball ('Midnight In Moscow') and clarinetist Bilk ('Stranger On The Shore'). See, it wasn't how good you were, it was being in the right place – London or maybe Manchester – at the right time. More than that, it was who you knew.

Paul McCartney didn't know anyone apart from Lennon's Quarry Men and a couple of Institute skiffle combos that trod warily amidst official disapproval. All pop musicians took drugs and had sex, didn't they? In truth, the only stimulant available was in local pubs, where skifflers might be allowed to perform as a change from providing interval music at school and college shindigs.

Feeling the chill of reality, Paul sat his GCE "O" levels – two a year early, the remainder during 1958's rainy June. Two months later, the results alighted on the Forthlin Road doormat. Having passed enough to enter the sixth form, he was able to keep that most noxious of human phenomena, a decision about the future, at arm's length for a while longer, enabling the growth of an *idée fixe* that if he kept at it, he might make a reasonable living as a musician.

He didn't know how Jim was going to take any suggestions about a profession that tended to be treated with amused contempt, unless you'd been born to it – as epitomised by a Mancunian youth named Malcolm Roberts, whose showbiz parents had enrolled him at the Manchester School of Music and Drama. His immediate post-graduate career was multi-faceted. As well as blowing trumpet in the National Youth Orchestra, he also made inroads as an actor, notably via a bit-part in *Coronation Street*. Soon after, he landed leading roles in the West End musical *Maggie May* and a touring production of *West Side Story*.

Paul could have been Malcolm under the same circumstances. That said, it was feasible to climb such an Olympus without coming from a family like Malcolm's, prime examples being Frank Sinatra and our own Matt Monro – who Sinatra was to compliment with "He sounds like me on a good day – or after an early night."[3] A "singer's singer", Monro was appreciated too by the diverse likes of Bing Crosby – and Paul McCartney.

Like McCartney, Matt – born Terry Parsons in 1930 – came from a humble background and had lost a parent (his father) at a young age. When his mother became ill, he spent a year in an orphanage. However, US crooner Perry Como's early records on the Light Programme spurred the starry-eyed Terry's desire to be a singer too. In a voice that would never drop below a strong but soothing light baritone, he started by apeing Como in local concerts where the discovery that responsible adults are actually listening to you singing can create false impressions of personal abilities in an immature mind. Therefore, with more confidence and hope than he could possibly justify, Terry told his mum of a hitherto unspoken intention to make a go of it eventually as an entertainer.

However, though less so than Liverpool, the distance from the Parsons' home, where London bleeds into Hertfordshire, to the storm centre of the British music industry in the West End might as well have been measured in years rather than miles. So it was that Terry Parsons' working life began in a tobacco factory; an unfortunate legacy of which was an inability to stop smoking.

Ten years younger than Terry, Cliff Bennett's background was as lugubrious. He lived along Maxwell Road deep in the heart of West Drayton in outer London suburbia. On leaving school, he commenced an apprenticeship at his father's foundry, "but I didn't enjoy the job and, most of the time, I just listened to music."

Record sessions evolved into attempts at reproducing the unsettling new rock 'n' roll noises, and a 17-year-old Cliff sang in public for the first time at The Ostrich Inn in Colnbrook, Middlesex, accompanying himself on a cheap guitar. Other bookings followed, and if you closed your eyes, with delicate suspension of logic, you could believe that this unlikely looking local herbert had truly got the blues from the Mississippi delta or the ghettos of southside Chicago.

Bennett and Matt Monro were each to have a bearing on Paul McCartney's life years later, but nowhere near as much as Denny Laine, a youth as steeped in showbusiness as Malcolm Roberts. His maternal grandfather had been a music hall trouper, and his elder sister was already preparing for a career as a dancer when Denny was born Brian Frederick Hines during an air-raid on the Birmingham district of Tyseley on 29 October 1944.

As a young teenager, Denny/Brian endured the Draconian rigours of Yardley Grammar School. As he seemed disinterested in academic subjects, Mr Hines enrolled his son in one of the Second City's stage schools, which provided *in situ* training with public presentations such as pantomimes and cabaret at works parties. "I never went in for acting so much," remembered Denny, "the music sort of took over." At the age of 12, he'd already developed into a sufficiently skilled acoustic guitarist to fill intermissions with "Django Reinhardt gypsy-jazz stuff", but an appearance at a prestigious local festival had him singing the skiffle standard, 'Does Your Chewing Gum Lose Its Flavour On The Bedpost Over Night?'.

Like Denny, the rising sap of puberty found Paul McCartney seeking openings among suburban music-makers. That's how he'd come to hear of The Quarry Men during the hiatus between "O" and "A" levels. Prospects didn't seem all that bright for them. Engagements beyond Liverpool were unknown, and the line-up was mutable in state, and yet drawn from the same pool of faces. Neither had The Quarry Men yet received actual money for playing when McCartney saw them for the first time at a church fête in Woolton on Saturday, 6 July 1957.

"I noticed this fellow singing with his guitar," said Paul, smiling at the memory, "and he was playing bum chords, and singing 'Come Go With Me' by The Del-Vikings. I realised he was changing the words into folk song and chain gang words, a clever bit of ingenuity. That was Johnny [sic] Lennon. My mate Ivan knew them, so we went backstage, and after a couple of drinks, we were around the piano singing songs to each other. Later, they sort of approached me on a bike somewhere, and said, 'You want to join?' We used to go around the record shops, listen to the record in the booth and then not buy it. They used to get very annoyed with us, but we had the words by then."[4]

From his first date as a Quarry Man – reckoned to be at a Conservative Club functions room on 18 October 1957 – Paul rose quickly through the ranks, coming to rest as Lennon's lieutenant, and in a position to foist revolutionary doctrines, namely the songs he'd started to write, onto the status quo. The affront to the older boy's superiority was such that Lennon contemplated starting again with new personnel before deciding to try this composing lark himself, and then joining forces with McCartney in what neither of them could even have daydreamed then was to evolve into one of the most outrageously successful songwriting partnerships of all time.

There was no indication of that in 1957. Few, if any, Lennon–McCartney efforts were dared on the boards – probably none at all during slots of three numbers at most in talent contests advertised in the *Echo*, where they'd be up against comedy impressionists, knife-throwers, Shirley Temples and "this woman who played the spoons," glared Paul. "We reckoned we were never going to beat this little old lady as she wiped the floor with us every time. That's when we decided to knock talent contests on the head."[4]

It cost just a little ego-massaging to hire The Quarry Men to do a turn at wedding receptions, youth clubs, parties and "Teenage

Shows" offered by cinema proprietors on Saturday mornings – so that Lennon and McCartney could enjoy fleeting moments of make-believing they were Donegan or Presley.

As well as a singing voice that was on a par with Lennon's, that McCartney had taken more trouble than the others to learn guitar properly made him one of the group's two natural focal points. Lennon got by less on orthodox ability than force of personality. Moreover, unlike everyone but Paul, he wasn't in it for the sake of his health, but as a purposeful means to make his way as a professional musician.

Not exactly the attraction of opposites as some biographers would have it, John and Paul's liaison was now based as much on amity as shared ambition. Nevertheless, they began weeding out those personnel who either regarded The Quarry Men as no more than a hobby or were just barely proficient passengers who made you flinch whenever you heard a difficult bit coming up in a given song.

Those who got by on home-made instruments were the first to go. Among replacements was John Duff Lowe, now a competent rock 'n' roll pianist. Even so, he was subjected to McCartney's quality control. "He asked me to play the introduction to Jerry Lee Lewis's 'Mean Woman Blues'," grinned Lowe. "I did so to his satisfaction, so he invited me to his house in Allerton to meet John Lennon. By then, the repertoire was all Gene Vincent, Buddy Holly, Chuck Berry and so on."

Lowe was present on the day The Quarry Men went to a recording studio in June 1958. They came away from this suburban Aladdin's cave of reel-to-reel tape machines, editing blocks and jack-to-jack leads with a now-legendary acetate that coupled a pointless replica of 'That'll Be The Day' by Holly's Crickets with 'In Spite Of All The Danger', an original by Paul and 15-year-old lead guitarist George Harrison, as new a recruit as John Lowe, who affirms that McCartney was the main writer, qualifying this with "Some say that he was inspired by a favourite record of his, 'Tryin' To Get To You' by Elvis Presley, which, when Paul went to Boy Scout camp in 1957, was Number 15 in the UK charts."

The disc was in John Lowe's possession when The Quarry Men faded away sometime in 1959 – though he'd hear that "John and Paul got together again – and George was playing with other groups." As for Lowe himself, "I joined Hobo Rick and his City Slickers, a country-and-western band. I've got a feeling that George played with us on one occasion. It never occurred to me to become a professional musician – though most evenings, I'd be in either a club called the Lowlands or down the Casbah, Pete Best's mother's place."

3 "It's Now Or Never"

"I don't remember him – or George – being anything special.
They were just mates from school."

– *John Duff Lowe*

Apart from a smattering of offstage lines many acts later, John
Duff Lowe's part in the play was over, but, as the world knows,
George Harrison was there for the duration. He'd been in the
year below Lowe and McCartney at the Institute, but he owned
an electric guitar and amplifier, and his fretboard skills had been
the most advanced of any Quarry Man – "though that isn't saying
very much," qualified Paul, "as we were raw beginners
ourselves."[1] Yet, even before McCartney's sponsorship had
brought Harrison to the group, the idea of an Everly Brothers-
type duo with George may have crossed Paul's mind – and, before
teaming up with John, a McCartney–Harrison songwriting liaison
had borne half-serious fruit.

Overtures from other combos for George's services had been
among factors that had led to the unnoticed dissolution of The
Quarry Men, but, for reasons he couldn't articulate, Harrison was
to commit himself exclusively to not so much a working group as
a creative entity whose principal audience was a tape recorder in
the living room at 20 Forthlin Road.

After Paul had fiddled with microphone positioning the valves
warmed up to this or that new composition, attributed to him and
John regardless of who'd actually written it. Of these works, all
that remain are mostly just titles – 'That's My Woman', 'Just Fun',

42

'Looking Glass', 'Winston's Walk', anyone? One that survived, Paul's 'Cayenne', was, like a lot of the others, an instrumental that took up the slack of The Shadows, very much the men of the moment in early 1960. If backing group to Cliff Richard, a more comfortable British Elvis than Tommy Steele had been, they'd just scored the first of many smashes in their own right.

Perhaps when they'd acquired a more professional veneer (and a drummer) accompanying a Cliff Richard sort was the way forward for Paul, George, John – and Stuart Sutcliffe, an art student who Lennon had stampeded into hire-purchasing an electric bass guitar (a magnificent Hofner "President") for what it looked like rather than its sound.

Michael Cox, a lanky youth Stuart had known at Prescot Grammar, had sung a bit, and his sisters had written on his behalf to an intrigued Jack Good, producer of *Oh Boy!* and later pop showcases on TV such as *Boy Meets Girls* and *Wham!* – on which a majority of male solo vocalists followed each other so quickly that the screaming studio audiences scarcely had pause to draw breath. Thanks to Cox's regular plugs on these transmissions, his third single, 'Angela Jones', was poised to slip into the Top Ten.

It was a shame, thought Paul and George, that Stuart was no longer in touch with Cox. Sutcliffe's arrival in their midst had followed Lennon's proposal that Harrison switch to bass. This had had as much effect as if he'd suggested an Indian sitar. John didn't even bother sounding out McCartney for whom "bass was the instrument you got lumbered with. You didn't know a famous bass player. They were just background people, so none of us was prepared to spend money on something like that."[1]

Paul would maintain that Sutcliffe "was kind of a part-time member because he'd have to do his painting, and we'd all hang out, and Stu would come in on the gigs." Stuart was a gifted painter, then in the style of Britain's post-war "Angry Young Men". Titles from the movement's books, plays and films – *Billy Liar, Look Back In Anger, Room At The Top et al* – are more familiar now than *The Toilet, Milk Bottles, Back Garden* and further in-yer-face executions in oils by such as Edward Middleditch, David Bomberg, Derrick Greaves and John Bratby. Vigour not subtlety was the name of the game. Like Van Gogh, brushwork was conspicuous, and impasto slapped on so aggressively that it stood out in lumps. The subject matters for which these "kitchen sink" artists are most remembered are domestic squalor and sordid scenarios from the inner city – just the thing that you would nail over your mantelpiece.

Yet Bratby in particular was much admired by Sutcliffe – and McCartney, then about to take his Art "A" level. His sole quote in Bratby's biography[2] was to caption its back cover. Inside, there was a 1967 portrait of Paul among those of other celebrities by this self-fixated and faintly unpleasant talent who pioneered an art form that caught a mood of cultural radicalism that would first climax in the Swinging Sixties.

Bratby bypassed Pop Art, predicted as the coming trend, but scorned by the establishment as a novelty. Its British pioneers included Peter Blake, Richard Hamilton and Edinburgh-born Eduardo Paolozzi. Pre-empting Warhol's soup cans, the aim was to bring humour and topicality back into painting via the paradox of earnest fascination with the brashest of junk culture, a mannered revelling in hard-sell advertising hoardings; magazines such as *True Confessions, Tit-Bits* and *Everybody's Weekly* and escapist horror flicks about outer space "Things". Like artefacts of a Coca-Cola century, these were usually disparaged as silly, vulgar and fake for their custard-yellows and tomato-reds. In the interests of research, nascent pop artists listened avidly to Top 40 radio, clogged as it was in the early 1960s with one-shot gimmicks, dance crazes and – just arrived this minute – the well-scrubbed and all-American catchiness of Bobby Vee, Bobby Rydell, Bobby Vinton, Bobby this and Bobby that.

The other horn on the same goat – and one more acutely felt in Art circles on Merseyside – was the beatniks. They tended to consume specific paperback books rather than records. Though not even a pretend beatnik himself, Paul McCartney was caught in the general drift, but actually read some of the literature bought merely for display by others.

Sometimes he got stuck as his brow furrowed over Søren Kierkegaard, the Danish mystic, and his existentialist descendants, chiefly Jean-Paul Sartre. Because their work contained more dialogue, Paul was far keener on Kerouac and Burroughs, foremost prose writers of the "Beat Generation" as well as associated bards such as Corso, Ginsberg and Ferlinghetti. Now a television scriptwriter, Johnny Byrne, one of Merseyside's arch-beatniks, went further: "I fell in with a group of people who, like me, were absolutely crazy about books by the beats. We were turning out our own little magazines. In a very short time, we were into jazz, poetry – straight out of the beatniks – and all around us were the incredible beginnings of the Liverpool scene.'[3]

While this was to become homogeneously Liverpudlian in outlook, beatnik culture in general was as North American as the pop charts. Moreover, in most cases, it was intrinsically as shallow in the sense that it wasn't so much about being anarchistic, free-loving and pacifist as being seen to sound and look as if you were. With practice, you would insert "man" into every sentence, and drop buzz-words like "warmonger", "Zen, "Monk", "Stockhausen", "Greco", "Bird", "Leadbelly" and "Brubeck" into conversations without too much affectation.

A further "sign of maturity" was an apparent "appreciation" of either traditional or modern jazz, but the nearest McCartney, Sutcliffe, Lennon, Harrison and the tape recorder got to it was black, blind and heroin-mainlining Ray Charles who, as "the twisted voice of the underdog", caused the likes of Kerouac and Ginsberg to get "gone" on 'Hallelujah I Love Her So', 'Don't Let The Sun Catch You Cryin'" and the "heys" and "yeahs" he traded with his vocal trio, The Raelettes, during 1959's 'What'd I Say', with all the exhorter-congregation interplay of an evangelist tent meeting. Jerry Lee Lewis and Little Richard were products of the

PAUL MCCARTNEY

same equation, but they didn't punctuate their catalogues of vocal
smashes with instrumental albums and collaborations with such
as Count Basie and Milt Jackson of The Modern Jazz Quartet.

Through John and Stuart, midday assaults on the works of
Charles and other favoured pop entertainers were heard in the life
room at the art college. Another place to rehearse was the flat Stuart
shared in Hillary Mansions along Gambier Terrace within the
college's environs. A large curtainless window, dim with grime,
opened onto a small balcony and a view of not social realist
gasworks, but the vast Anglican cathedral. As bare as the 60-watt
bulb above, the floorboards were pocked with oil paint from the
half-used tubes on the mantelpiece. Like farms always smelt of
manure, so Sutcliffe and Co's bedroom-cum-studio did of the
turpentine necessary for cleaning the brushes and pallet-knives.
Canvasses leaned against walls on which charcoal sketches and the
odd picture scissored from some periodical or other were pinned.

For a while, John dwelt there as well before returning to
Woolton. It went without saying, however, that he and his ensemble
could still use Gambier Terrace, said Rod Jones, another tenant,
"to make a hell of a lot of noise" to the exasperation of two middle-
aged ladies on the ground floor.

It also reached the ears of Johnny Byrne, one of the organisers
of poetry readings accompanied by local jazz musicians at
Streate's. Further jazz-poetry fusions took place at the Crane
Theatre. One presentation there was at the behest of Michael
Horovitz who launched 1959's *New Departures*, a
counterculture poetry magazine: "At the party afterwards,
Adrian Henri, who was the host, said, 'Oh, this poetry stuff is
all right, I think I'm going to start doing it.' Roger McGough
had read with us in Edinburgh – and Brian Patten, who'd sat in
the front row of the Crane gig trying to hide his school cap, was
this marvellous boy who came up and read rather different,
passionate, romantic poems."[3]

While they weren't exactly "jazz", Lennon, Sutcliffe and their two pals from the Institute framed the declamations of Brighton's *vers libre* bard Royston Ellis in the Jacaranda's bottle-and-candle cellar. Afterwards, he introduced them and other interested parties in the Gambier Terrace fraternity to a particularly tacky way of getting "high" with the aid of a Vick nose-inhaler from the chemists. You isolated the part of it that contained a stimulant called benzadrine. This, you then ate.

While each tried not to put his foot in it with some inane remark that that showed his age, Paul and George went along with this and other bohemian practices of the big boys from the college – even though, apart from an interest in art, McCartney and Sutcliffe especially "hadn't much in common, and there was always jealousy within the group as to who would be John's friend. He was the guy you aspired to. Like, you got an Oscar if you were John's friend."

Lennon's personal bond with his college chum was tighter than that with McCartney: "John and Stuart went to this sort of grown-up thing together. George and I were school kids. We were younger – so I think age was something to do with it. The girls at the college were objects of desire etc etc, and they could talk about that. I'm totally guessing now – but I think John was a little bit political, and he might have felt that to let one of us in would be bestowing too many favours – so that Stu might have been a little more neutral than choosing George or me. There was a little separation by the fact that he was John's mate."[1]

Their wonderment at Lennon caused McCartney and Harrison to cut classes for not only rehearsals but simply to sit at one of the kidney-shaped tables in the Jacaranda, proudly familiar as he held court. Revelling in their wickedness, they'd flash packets of Woodbines or a loose handful of a more sophisticated brand filched, perhaps, from parents' walnut cases. The pair pitched in too when proprietor Allan Williams, the latest in a series of Dutch uncles that Stuart would always have, required the painting of murals in the basement.

Services rendered to Williams were in exchange for his acting in a quasi-managerial capacity for Sutcliffe, Lennon *et al* who, observed Colin Manley, guitarist with The Remo Four, "never intended to have ordinary jobs. They just wanted to play music."[4] Though the Four were recognised as Liverpool's top instrumental act, Manley was not prepared then to give up his post with the National Assistance Board for the treachery of full-time showbusiness. Most other local musicians were similarly cautious.

Now calling themselves The Silver Beatles, the more ambitious amalgam of art students and schoolboys were freer than the likes of The Remo Four to accept virtually any engagement offered. Venues ranged from novelist Beryl Bainbridge's house party, which could be heard in all the surrounding streets in an age before phrases like "noise pollution" and "environmental health" were in common use, to a fly-by-night jive hive in Upper Parliament Street where they did battle with a public address system centred on a solitary microphone tied to a broom handle.

The two most willing to picket for more bookings were Paul and, perhaps to mitigate his musical shortcomings, Stuart. With silver-tongued guile, they'd lay on their "professionalism" with a hyperbolic trowel, either face-to-face or in letters when negotiating with this quizzical pub landlord or that disinterested social secretary. To this end, while they spurned the synchronised footwork with which The Shadows iced their presentations, The Silver Beatles were at one with an ancient *New Musical Express* dictum concerning "visual effect". "Some sort of uniform is a great help," it ran, "though ordinary casual clothes are perhaps the best as long as you all wear exactly the same."[5]

On settling for black shirts, dark blue jeans and two-tone plimsolls – strictly off-the-peg chic – all they needed now was the drummer they'd lacked since they were Quarry Men. They secured one of uncertain allegiance in Tommy Moore, a forklift truck driver at Garston Bottle Works. Tommy's frequent night shifts and a very possessive girlfriend bridled him from the outset. At Gambier Terrace rehearsals, "he used to turn up to do the odd thing in the back room," said Rod Murray, another resident, "and he'd disappear early, thank God, because his drums shook the floor."[1] Significantly, the first legal machinations to get the bohemian element out of the flats dated from Moore's recruitment.

Tommy – impossibly ancient at 26 – would suffice until the arrival of someone more compatible with young "arty" types like The Silver Beatles and their coterie with their long words and weaving of names like Modigliani and Kierkegaard into conversations that would lapse into student vernacular. Not over-friendly, Moore preferred the no-nonsense society of Cass and his Cassanovas, Gerry And The Pacemakers and other workmanlike semi-professionals who derided The Silver Beatles as "posers".

To an extent, John, Stuart and, most palpably, Paul played up to the image. The title of 'Cayenne' had been derived from Magritte's surreal 'Daybreak In Cayenne', and, whilst acknowledging that Sutcliffe "contributed an intellectual spirit that we were all kind of happy to pick up on", McCartney was at the forefront of a dressing room incident when someone in another group barged in on a seemingly po-faced reading of Russian poetry: "It was all very beatnik of us. I can't remember any of it now, but it was [gravely] 'Yea, morning shall not be so bright, lest ye look over the...' – and I'm doing this seriously. The rest of the group's like Rodin's *Thinker*. They're all going, 'Ummmm, ummm, yeah, ummmm' – and this sax player starts creeping around unpacking his sax, and whispering 'Sorry to interrupt you.' We could put people on like that."[1]

McCartney and Lennon's pretensions as composers also caused comment when reputations were made much more easily by churning out rock 'n' roll standards and current hits. One of 1960's summer chart-toppers was 'Three Steps To Heaven' by Eddie Cochran, a US classic rock latecomer, whose long-awaited tour of Britain's "scream circuit" was freighted with an indigenous supporting programme made up mostly of clients on the books of Larry Parnes, one of Britain's most colourful pop managers.

On the bill too was Tony Sheridan, a 19-year-old singing

guitarist from Norwich. After the final date in Bristol on 17 April 1960, Sheridan had been "stranded alone in the dressing room when everyone else had gone. For the first and last time in my life, I'd bought myself a bottle of whiskey, and was trying to vent my frustration at being an inferior British musician by getting sloshed. In the end, I smashed the bottle against the wall – but the next day, I was alive and well."

Cochran, however, wasn't, having perished when his taxi swerved into a lamp-post whilst tearing through a Wiltshire town in the small hours. "Sympathy sales" assisted the passage of 'Three Steps To Heaven' to Number One, just as they had 'It Doesn't Matter Any More' by Buddy Holly – snuffed out in an air crash – the previous year. Like Holly too, Cochran was more popular in Europe than on his own soil. In the same boat was one of Eddie's fellow passengers on that fatal journey, Gene Vincent, who paid respects with a heavy-hearted 'Over The Rainbow' when, on 3 May, he headlined a three-hour spectacular at a 6,000-capacity sports arena in Liverpool, supported by an assortment of Larry Parnes ciphers and some first-division Scouse groups procured by Allan Williams.

When the show was over, "Mister Parnes Shillings And Pence" had charged Williams with finding an all-purpose backing outfit for use by certain of his singers for some imminent runs of one-nighters in Scotland. Among those who auditioned successfully the following week were a Silver Beatles that Allan agreed had much improved. He hadn't actually been there, but it had been reported that they'd worked up a wild response from a full house of 300 at the Casbah, a basement club in leafy Hayman's Green, run by a Mrs Mona Best, mother of the drummer in the house band, The Blackjacks.

Therefore, within three weeks of the Gene Vincent extravaganza, The Silver Beatles were north of the border for eight days in the employ of a vocalist with the stage alias "Johnny Gentle".

To use an expression peculiar to the north, Jim McCartney had "looked long bacon" when his son had announced that he was interrupting "A" level revision to go on the road with John Lennon's gang and this risible Gentle man. Like the younger Silver Beatles, Paul was even going to give himself a stage name too – "Paul Ramon", for heaven's sake. All that could be hoped was that the trip would flush this Silver Beatles nonsense out of him.

In the no-star hotels where The Silver Beatles would repair each night, Paul, like all the others, "wanted to be in a room with John"[1]. The week also coincided with Sutcliffe being temporarily *persona non grata* with the mercurial Lennon. Going with the flow, McCartney no longer had to contain his pent-up resentment of Stuart. Teasing became open harangues that were to increase in frequency throughout the tour and beyond.

Spiking it with the diplomacy that would always come naturally to him, Paul would "remember one source of annoyance. This was, I think, the first argument we really had, because we generally got on well, but there were moments when it was definitely me and Stu. We came down to breakfast one morning, and we were all having cornflakes and sort of trying to wake up. Stu wanted to smoke a cigarette, and I think we made him sit at the next table: 'Oh bloody hell, Stu, come on, man! You know we're having cornflakes. Do us a favour.' The joke was that his sign was Cancer. That just happened one morning, and there was a sort of a flare up, but, you know, we soon got back together. There was never anything crazy, and we got on fine."[1]

Tommy Moore, however, had had more than enough of being a Silver Beatle. His resignation after the expedition put paid to the group next going to Scotland to work with Dickie Pride, a diminutive Londoner whose trademark convulsions onstage had earned him the sub-title "The Sheik Of Shake".

Back on the trivial round of suburban dance halls, Paul volunteered to beat the skins before and after the loss of Moore's successor, a picture-framer named Norman Chapman, after only three weeks. Despite hardly ever sitting behind a kit before,

McCartney was quite an adroit sticksman. He would also pound available yellow-keyed upright pianos, amplified by simply shoving a microphone through a rip in the backcloth.

While he was one rhythm guitarist too many as well, his and John's respective tenor and baritone were the voices heard most during any given evening. Paul was genuinely surprised when his singing of ballads caused some of the sillier girls beyond the footlights – if there were any – to make unladylike attempts to grab his attention.

He wasn't impervious to their coltish charms, far from it, but was, nonetheless, aware of how brittle such adoration could be. Symptomatic of the new pestilence now ravaging the record-buying public, a TV series entitled *Trad Tavern* filled the 30 minutes once occupied by *Boy Meets Girls*.

A sure sign of stagnation in pop is adults liking the same music as teenagers. *Trad Tavern* appealed to both – and, while they might not have bought their records, grandmothers warmed to Ronnie Carroll, Mark Wynter, Craig Douglas and others from a mess of UK heart-throbs in the early 1960s who took their lightweight cue from the States. Some breached the Top Ten, but hovering between 20 and 40 was more their mark.

Amidst all the trad and Bobby candyfloss were the kind of big-voiced ballads and singers that had preceded 'Rock Around The Clock'. As much a culmination of all that had gone before as a starting point for what followed (as The Beatles would be), even Elvis succumbed in 1960 with 'It's Now Or Never', an adaptation of 'O Sole Mio', a schmaltzy Italian job from the 1900s – and his biggest hit thus far.

1960 also bracketed Top Ten debuts by Roy Orbison ('Only The Lonely'), Liverpool comedian Ken Dodd (in "serious" mode with 'Love Is Like A Violin') and Matt Monro, whose 'Portrait Of My Love' had been made under the supervision of George Martin, recording manager of Parlophone, an EMI subsidiary, which usually traded in comedy and variety rather than outright pop. "I was convinced that it was the most uncommercial number I had ever heard," Monro would recall, "but within two weeks, it was in the charts and stayed there for months."[6] After falling from its peak of Number Three, it was voted "Record Of The Year" by readers in *Melody Maker*'s annual popularity poll.

Monro, Ken Dodd and Roy Orbison were exceptions, but it was a sweeping adult generalisation that the common-or-garden pop singer "couldn't sing". That was the main reason why they loathed another hit parade newcomer, Adam Faith, the most singular of our brightest post-skiffle stars. Yet his verbal contortions and less contrived wobbly pitch had enough going for it to lend period charm to his 'What Do You Want?' breakthrough and even 'Lonely Pup In A Christmas Shop' – "a ridiculous, stupid thing to do," he'd shrug in his 1996 life story[7], but still a Top Ten entry.

Such was the state of pop affairs when, shortly after the Johnny Gentle jaunt, The Silver Beatles hacked the adjective from their name, and wondered what to do next.

4 *"What'd I Say?"*

"It was one of those constellations at the right time, the right people, the right situation. There was no accident or coincidence to it. The nearest German word for it is *Zufall* – which means literally 'to fall to one'. That's how The Beatles happened as far as I'm concerned: the pieces 'fell' into place."

– *Tony Sheridan*

Trad bands were everywhere, as were places they could play in. With this stylistic stranglehold on many venues, it was small wonder that groups keeping the rock 'n' roll faith were open to offers from abroad – particularly West Germany. In 1959, Mr Acker Bilk's Paramount Jazz Band had been well primed to capitalise on the trad boom after six weeks in a Dusseldorf hostelry where "you just blew and blew and blew," exhaled Acker, "and had 20 minutes off for a drink, and then you were back blowing again."[1] Within a year, however, bastions of Teutonic trad – from Cologne's Storyville to Kiel's Star Palast – had converted to rock 'n' roll *bierkellers*, complete with the coin-operated sounds of Elvis, Gene, Cliff, Adam and the others.

Among difficulties encountered by the Fatherland's club owners was that of "live" entertainment. Patrons were often affronted by native bands who invested the expected duplications of US and British hits with complacent exactitude, a neo-military beat and an unnatural gravity born of singing in a foreign tongue.

Moreover, five years behind the times, German-language chart strikes were principally for middle-of-the-road consumers. There was no plausible domestic "answer" to Elvis or even Cliff Richard – but there were plenty of Dickie Valentines and Frankie Vaughans. Among them were Freddy Quinn, a former deckhand, whose first major hit was with a translation of Dean Martin's jog-along 'Memories Are Made Of This'; Udo Jurgens, omnipresent at every European song festival on the calendar; and Fred Bertelmann, "The Laughing Vagabond". Each one of them was the stock "pop singer who can really sing", and looked about as sexy as your favourite uncle.

Back in Britain, Cliff Richard, Marty Wilde, Dickie Pride and nearly everyone else who'd driven 'em wild on *Oh Boy!* had gone smooth as epitomised by wholesome film musicals from Cliff (once damned in the *NME* for "the most crude exhibitionism ever seen on TV"[2]). Marty was jubilant in his newly married state, and Dickie's 1960 album, *Pride Without Prejudice*, was full of Tin Pan Alley chestnuts with Ted Heath's orchestra in accord with a lodged convention of British pop management that it was OK to make initial impact with rock 'n' roll or whatever the latest craze was, but then you had to ditch it quickly and get on with "quality" stuff so that your flop singles could be excused as being "too good for the charts".

Yet if the average teenager was faced with a choice between Dickie Pride-as-third-rate-Sinatra's 'Bye Bye Blackbird' and Screaming Lord Sutch's 'Jack The Ripper' – "nauseating trash", sniffed *Melody Maker*[3] – it'd be his Lordship every time. The most famous pop star who never had a hit, Sutch and his backing Savages were among few of their sort assured of plenty of work, with or without hits – or trad – and so were Johnny Kidd And The Pirates. The focal point of each was a blood-and-thunder stage act with the performances of Kidd and Sutch themselves as fervently loyal to classic rock as Lonnie Donegan was to skiffle.

The Beatles were more Johnny Kidd than Cliff Richard. Paul McCartney drew the short straw if ever they responded to a request for 'Voice In The Wilderness', 'Please Don't Tease' and other of Cliff's recent chartbusters, but Paul left a deeper wound with Kidd's

'Shakin' All Over' and party pieces like 'What'd I Say?' as a window-rattling, extrapolated finale in which he'd enhance his vocals with knee-drops, scissor kicks and general tumbling about during George's solos. Then about to form The Merseybeats in The Beatles' image, Tony Crane would recall, "McCartney had a guitar that he didn't play slung around his neck. They finished with 'What'd I Say?', and he was madder than any time I've seen Mick Jagger. He danced all over the place. It was marvellous."[4]

This was part of a transformation wrought by a 1960 season in Hamburg's cobbled Grosse Freiheit, a prominent red-light district just beyond the labyrinthian waterfront of the Elbe. A soft "Want business, love?" from a prostitute in Nottingham or Portsmouth might secure a chilled, empty tryst in a darkened doorway, but over the North Sea, bartering in sex was never so furtive. Gartered erotica was openly displayed on the billboards of striptease palaces, and tearsheets exhibited their seamy charms in the perfumed flesh from windows of whorehouses that were to certain Teutonic cities as steel was to Sheffield.

Germany had also clasped British pop to its bosom as a robust bawd would some young dingbat not sure if he was quite ready to lose his virginity. Making tentative enquiries elsewhere, the more out-of-touch impressarios had stretched their eyes at the seemingly extortionate fees for this Presley *schmuck* that all the Fräuleins were talking about. What was the problem? He was actually in the country just then as a soldier in the US Occupation Forces, wasn't he? However, until a cabal of wealthy German promoters commenced, around 1962, a ruthless and costly campaign for US idols to fill spaces in their European tours with engagements in the more capacious clubs, "it was easy," explained the leader of Salisbury's Dave Dee And The Bostons, "to bring British bands in and work them to death, doing two- to three-month stints."[5]

As late as 1968, sending a group over for residencies in German night spots was, reckoned Jim Simpson, a noted West Midlands agent, "rather like training a 1,000m (1,100 yards) sprinter by making him run 5,000m (5,500 yards) courses." Two Birmingham outfits, The Rockin' Berries and Carl Wayne And The Vikings were among those that would make the Storyville and associated Rhineland venues in Heidelberg and Frankfurt thrive again, just after Georgie And The International Monarchs, a Belfast showband, had worked similar magic on the same network.

On the Grosse Freiheit, a haunt called the Kaiserkeller had struck first in June 1960 by enticing some unemployed London musicians across the North Sea to mount its ricketty stage as "The Jets". Their number included Tony Sheridan – with whom The Beatles were to begin their commercial discography.

That lay a year in a future, which Paul, John, Stuart and George couldn't imagine during an endless search for work in and around Liverpool. Then, to cut a long story short, an offer came via Allan Williams of a residency in the Indra, a companion club to the Kaiserkeller, commencing in August 1960. A stipulation about a drummer was satisfied because, at the Casbah, The Blackjacks were about to disband, and, when asked, Pete Best was quite amenable to becoming a Beatle – even if, said McCartney, "he just wasn't the same kind of black humour that we were. He was not quite as Artsy [sic] as certainly John and Stu were."[6]

As Paul had finished his "A" levels, his father supposed it was all right for him to go gallivanting off to Germany like other sixth formers might go back-packing in Thailand. Thus he and the rest boarded Allan Williams's overloaded mini-bus outside the Jacaranda, bound for the night ferry from Harwich to the Hook of Holland.

Hot-eyed with sleeplessness, the Liverpudlians passed through the concrete desolation of the Dutch customs area the next morning. McCartney awoke from one of several brief slumbers with the road buzzing in his ears. As they crossed the German border, quips about spy novels and fake passports ignited nonstop rumbustious banter – with Lennon the central figure – while the bus hurtled through the inky firs of Lower Saxony. Villagers peered incuriously as the elated young Merseysiders wound down the side-windows and shouted insults about *krauts* or thumped out a beat on the bus roof.

Their exuberance died down a little on the outskirts of Hamburg, and had expired completely as they struggled with the first armfuls of careworn equipment into the Indra, pungent still with a flat essence of yesterday's tobacco, food and alcohol intake. With a face like a bag of screwdrivers, Bruno Koschmider, the proprietor, wasn't exactly Uncle Cuddles – but if his manner was cold, he did not seem ill-disposed towards The Beatles. It wasn't in his interest to be. An antagonised group might take it out on the customers.

The Beatles did not complain of any shortage of romantic squalor – well, squalor anyway – after Herr Koschmider had conducted them to three tiny rooms adjoining a lavatory in the Art Deco Bambi-Filmkunsttheater cinema over the road from the Indra. While there weren't enough musty camp beds or frayed old sofas to go round, this was where they could sleep. Like the foul coffee served – as they were to discover – behind the facade of the local police station, it would have sickened pigs, but another Liverpool outfit, Derry And The Seniors, seemed to be making do in two similarly poky holes at the back of the Kaiserkeller.

That evening, the border of light bulbs (not all of them working) round the stage were switched on, and a tired Beatles gave their first ever performance outside the United Kingdom. To their costumes, they'd added houndstooth check jackets, and replaced the plimsolls with winkle-pickers – all except for Pete who hadn't had time to buy the right gear. His gradual isolation from the others had started before they'd even reached Harwich.

After a slow start, Paul had unzipped his toothpaste smile, John's runaway tongue had unfurled and one or two of the glum old men waiting in vain for the usual Grosse Freiheit fare of stripteasers allowed themselves to be jollied along. A more transient clientele of sailors, gangsters, prostitutes and inquisitive youths laughed with them and even took a chance on the dance floor as they got used to the newcomers' endearing glottal intonations and ragged dissimilarity to the contrived splendour of television pop stars.

This was all very well, but, during wakeful periods after they'd retired, the full horror of The Beatles' filthy accommodation reared up in the encircling gloom. Daylight could not pierce it after Paul was jerked from the doze that precipitates consciousness by John breaking wind before rising to shampoo his hair in a washbasin in the movie-goers' toilets.

Up and about by mid-afternoon, The Beatles were recognised occasionally in the immediate vicinity of the Grosse Freiheit. Further afield, they were just anonymous wanderers of the Hanseatic city, one of the oldest municipal republics in Europe and, though 95km (60 miles) from the sea, then the world's third largest port. Its recreational facilities included the Alster yachting lake and promenade; a museum containing the largest model railway ever constructed; a zoo; the mammoth Dom funfair – and, of course, the fun to be had in the Grosse Freiheit mire.

When the '60s started swinging, one of Paul McCartney's paternity suits emanated from the Grosse Freiheit where the night's love life could be sorted out during the first beer break. On initiating conversations with Paul, fancy-free and affectionate females were delighted that he wasn't one to deny himself casual sexual exploits. Though he had a steady girlfriend back home – Dorothy Rhone, a bank clerk – he was perpetually on the lookout for an unsteady one. And if it's salaciousness you're after, Paul and his fellow Liverpudlians' unchallenging appropriation of sexual intimacies was brought to public notice in the first of Pete Best's three autobiographies[7] with its illustrative encounter between the group and no less than eight nubile fräuleins in the murk of the Bambi-Filmkunsttheater quarters. The next day, the five didn't even remember what their faces looked like, let alone their names.

Advisedly, shadowy thighs and lewd sniggering did not leap out of the pages of Paul's letters home during four months away that saw a transfer from the Indra to the plusher Kaiserkeller, where an abiding memory of Horst Fascher, Koschmider's indomitable chief of staff, was of Sutcliffe sketching secretively in a remote corner of the club, and McCartney and Lennon composing in the bandroom where, elucidated Paul, "the only things we write down are lyrics on the backs of envelopes to save forgetting them, but the tunes, rhythms and chords we memorise."[8]

Creative advances did not correlate with personal relationships within The Beatles. John was still prone to antagonising his best friend just to see his hackles rise, but his inner ear ignored the stark truth that Stuart's playing hadn't progressed after all these months. Had Paul expressed a recent willingness to take over on bass before the trip, the group wouldn't have been cluttered still with an unnecessary rhythm guitarist, no matter how contrasting McCartney and Lennon's chord shapes could be. If Stuart hadn't been around, Paul wouldn't have felt so redundant, just singing and gyrating around with an unplugged guitar or impersonating Little Richard at the worn-out Kaiserkeller piano, from which aggravating Sutcliffe would snip wires to replace broken bass strings.

There was no let-up in the tension-charged ugliness, visible and invisible, back in the Bambi-Filmkunsttheater, more loathsome than ever with its improvised receptacles for junk food leavings, empty liquor bottles, overflowing cigarette ash, used rubber "johnnies" and dried vomit.

Yet Germany changed The Beatles and many other British acts forever. Much of it was down to the harsh working conditions. "We started performing every night at 7pm," groaned Bev Bevan, one of Carl Wayne's Vikings, "and did seven 45 minute spots with 15 minute breaks until two in the morning. Each weekend, there were three hour matinees too. Any hopeful beliefs I might have had that pop could earn me easy money were swept away in those weeks in Cologne."[9]

Some were destroyed by the experience. For Twinkle, fresh from a Europe-wide hit with the death-disc 'Terry', "it was a nightmare – mainly because I thought I'd only have to do one set. I did several, doing the same numbers and wearing the same stage outfit. I gave up performing then and there – at the age of 17."

It all but finished The Beatles too when they hadn't even the decency to lie to Bruno Koschmider about spending their rest periods in a more uptown rival establishment, the Top Ten. He was furious to learn that its manager intended to lure them away with better pay and conditions as soon as their extended contract with the Kaiserkeller expired in December. Rather than racketeers and ruffians, the Top Ten attracted young "Mittelstand" adults – a couple of social rungs higher than "youths" – whose liberal-minded parents might drop them off in estate cars. Most of these would be collected just before midnight, owing to the curfew that forbade those under 18 from frequenting Grosse Freiheit clubs past their bedtimes.

The German administration was conscientious too about protecting minors from temptation – though it was too often the case that *Polizei* couldn't be bothered with the paperwork after catching young aliens like George Harrison, only weeks away from his 18th birthday, flaunting the law. However, an ireful Koschmider's string-pulling ensured more intense official interest, and George was sent home before November was out.

The Beatles seemed quite prepared to carry on without him, but the Top Ten was obliged to replace them with Gerry And The Pacemakers (straight from the civil service and British Rail rather than art college and grammar schools) after McCartney and Best were deported too – on Bruno's trumped-up charge of arson.

Though tarred with the same brush, Stuart and John had been free to go after signing a statement in German that satisfied the Polizei that they knew nothing about Exhibit A: the charred rag that constituted Herr Koschmider's accusation that The Beatles had all conspired to burn down the hated Bambi-Filmkunsttheater.

Lennon followed the others back to Liverpool, but Sutcliffe stayed on, moving in with Astrid Kirchherr, a German photographer to whom he was unofficially engaged. She was a leading light of Hamburg's "existentialists" – the "Exis" – whose look anticipated the "Gothic" style prevalent in the late 1970s. Always black with maybe white collars or ruffs like 18th-century dandies, it was predominantly unisex with suede and velvet the dominant fabrics – though you could get by with jeans, windcheater and polo-neck pullover. Exi girls wishing to look more feminine walked the line with ballet slippers, fishnet stockings and short leather skirts. Exi haircuts were *pilzen kopf* – "mushroom head". Though commonplace in Germany, a male so greaselessly coiffured in Britain would be branded a "nancy boy", even if Adam Faith was the darling of the ladies with a similar brushed-forward cut.

Astrid's circle – mostly undergraduates – was a variant of the Parisian existentialists who, since the 1950s, had been stereotyped by period film directors as one of two types of pretentious middle class beatnik: "hot" (incessant rapid-fire talking and pseudo-mad stares) and "cool" (mute, immobile and unapproachable). Both were present at demi-monde parties where table lamps were dimmed with headscarves, and Man Ray hung on the walls. The musical entertainment was scat-singing, bongo-tapping or a saxophone honking inanely. The eyelids of cross-legged listeners stayed closed in ecstasy. With a nod towards the censor, the stimulants and pansexual undercurrents were played down. These weirdos were "good kids" at heart.

"Why kill time when you can kill yourself?" asks a spectral Greco-like woman in 1960's *The Rebel*[10], a Tony Hancock vehicle set in bohemian Paris – all berets, ten-day beards and holey sweaters. *The Rebel* might have been less resolutely banal and probably funnier had the great comedian's flight from respectability taken him to either of the demi-mondes of Hamburg or Liverpool.

It is tempting to imply that the Exis fell for The Beatles like the "Parisian set" in *The Rebel* did for the verbose but artistically cack-handed Hancock. Yet it was more likely that the Hamburg students were tacitly bored with the "coolness" of Dave Brubeck, Stan Getz, The Modern Jazz Quartet and other "hip" music-makers whose LP covers were artlessly strewn about their "pads".

"We had been Dixieland or [modern] jazz fans," explained Jurgen Vollmer, another high-ranking Exi, "and ever since then, we really got into rock and roll, and we never went to the jazz clubs anymore. Our interest developed after we had heard The Beatles, and not only The Beatles but also the other British rock and roll groups – but The Beatles were always our favourite, right from the start."[6]

In content alone, The Beatles were uncannily like all the other groups who could claim *droit de seigneur* over the principally US rock 'n' roll mother-lode. However, Sutcliffe, McCartney and Lennon were all great talkers, using the same reference points as the Exis. "Up north, we'd be reading Kerouac, and they'd be reading Kerouac," affirmed Paul. "We'd be looking at the same kind of things."[11]

The Beatles got to be quite addictive. Exis would neglect their studies, art and day jobs to be near them throughout the watches of the night. "Their natural energy, good humour and wit were seductive," confirmed Vollmer. "We felt at times that we had to force ourselves not to go. Astrid and I went to the movies instead – but we had such an urge to return to The Beatles that we let ourselves go into the doorway of the room, way in the back of the dance floor. The Beatles saw us, and, as soon as they finished the number, broke immediately into 'Stay'[12]. They sang to us."[6]

Of individual Beatles, Pete was a strong-but-silent type in contrast to winsome Paul who, so Horst Fascher would insist, was the "sunny boy"[13] of the group as he scuttled to and from microphones or lilted 'Besame Mucho', one of those sensuous Latin-flavoured ballads that, like 'Begin The Beguine', 'Sway' and 'Perfidia', never seem to go away. Generally, only the title was sung in Spanish when 'Besame Mucho', a frequent *wunche* (request) from the ladies – transported you for a few minutes from the shimmering sea of bobbing heads in the Kaiserkeller to warm latitudes and dreamy sighs – and then the squiggle of lead guitar that kicked off 'Too Much Monkey Business' would jolt you back to reality – either that or Stuart's fluffed run-down into 'It's So Easy'.

A little of Stuart's singing went a long way too, and as an instrumentalist, he was as good as he'd ever get – and that wasn't good enough. Privately, he admitted as much to Astrid, adding that he had only came along for the laugh and because he was John's friend. Whatever was left for Stuart to enjoy about playing with The Beatles was for the wrong reasons. For devilment, he'd deliberately pluck sickeningly off-key notes. If Paul – and George too – thought he was the group's biggest liability, then he'd amuse himself being it. They could get John to sack him for all he cared, even if they'd slain a fire regulation-breaking audience on the last night at the Kaiserkeller.

5 *"Over The Rainbow"*

"Before Paul McCartney gave the bass credibility, the instrument was usually given to the fat boy, who stood at the back and stayed out of sight."
                                    — *Donald Hirst of The Spinning Wheels*[1]

Before they'd departed from Hamburg so ignominiously, Paul had evolved into an outstanding showman, possessed of that indefinable something else – the "common touch" maybe – that enabled him, via a wink and a broad grin diffused to the general populace, to make any watching individual feel – for a split-second anyway – like the only person that mattered to him and his Beatles in the entire city.

Offstage too, he produced the same effect when someone waved at him from across the street, and he creased his face into a bashful half-smile and waved back. There was, nonetheless, a crouched restlessness about Paul, and, however much he might have gainsaid it, he was looking out for any signpost that pointed in the direction of fame.

He was even willing, so he'd intimated already to John, to play bass, even though it was a presence rather than a sound on the vinyl that crackled on the Forthlin Road gramophone, and its executants overshadowed by the higher octaves available to lead and rhythm guitarists.

Such a sacrifice would be to The Beatles' general good because, if Lennon might be closing his ears still, McCartney and Harrison had gauged Stuart Sutcliffe's limitations and could hear what was technically askew – and always would be. They were running out of patience. "We can't go on like this," Gary Bakewell-as-Paul McCartney protests in the 1994 bio-pic, *Backbeat*. "The joke's over. Half the time, he doesn't show up. When he does, he's in the Fifth Dimension. I'm not having it!"

Sutcliffe had become almost literally The Beatles' sleeping partner. Onstage at the Kaiserkeller, he'd been as nonchalantly gum-chewing as ever, but usually miles away mentally. More than ever before, he was physically elsewhere too – so much so that it had been necessary to line up an understudy in Colin Millander, a former Jet who had stayed on as part of a duo in a nearby restaurant. Though three years Stuart's junior – when such a difference mattered – George's exasperation that "he was in the band because John conned him into buying a bass"[2] had shown itself in desultory sabre-rattling with Sutcliffe in safe assurance that Paul would support him when John intervened.

Paul, see, was Stuart's truer enemy. Their animosity boiled over after the latter lost his temper when McCartney, seated at the piano, made some remark about Astrid. Flinging down his bass, Sutcliffe bounded across the boards, mad fury in his eyes, to knock the detested Paul off his perch. Manfully, the others kept the song going as the pair tumbled wrestling to the floor. Used to The Beatles' excesses on the boards, the audience emitted whoops of drunken encouragement and bellowed instruction as the number finished and the irresolute fight ebbed away to a slanging match and the combatants glowering at each other from opposite ends of a huffy dressing room.

Characteristically, Paul would laugh off this proclamation of an open state of warfare as a bit of a lark in retrospective: "Occasionally, we would have our set-to's, not too many really – but the major one was a fight onstage. The great thing about it was it wasn't actually a fight because neither of us were good fighters – so it was a grope! We just grappled each other, and I remember thinking, 'Well, he's littler than me. I'll easily be able to fight him.' But, of course, the strength of ten men this guy had – and we were locked. All the gangsters were laughing at us, and me and Stu are up by the bloody piano, locked in this sort of death embrace. All the gangsters were going, 'Come on! Hit him!' to either of us, and we couldn't do anything."[2]

As events were to demonstrate, McCartney might not have been so jocular had he managed to strike a blow to Stuart's head. Indeed, he might have ended up on a charge of murder before a German judge and jury tacitly prejudiced by his nationality and hirsute appearance. The next day, however, Paul was Mr Nice Guy again, but neither he nor Stuart would forget, and, for weeks afterwards, Paul found himself casting an odd thoughtful glance at Stuart sweating over the bass when Lennon was hogging the main microphone. Who'd have thought it – Stuart sticking up for himself without John protecting him?

Yet almost all the cards were on the table when four-fifths of The Beatles reassembled back in Liverpool – "and then the thing was, 'Well, who's going to play bass?'" asked Paul.[1] As he'd rattled the traps in the absence of Tommy Moore, so McCartney had adapted likewise to bass whenever Colin Millander or Stuart had been indisposed at the Kaiserkeller, but for their first four post-Hamburg engagements, another ex-Blackjack, Chas Newby, was roped in.

Chas was there when The Beatles were a last minute addition to a bill at Litherland Town Hall the day after Boxing Day. A lot of groups would sell their souls for a career, however it ended, that had had a night like that in it. You couldn't refute their impact on a crowd who'd been spellbound from the 'Long Tall Sally' opening until the last major sixth of the final encore. Along the way, The Beatles had stoked up the first scattered screams that had ever reverberated for them.

While there were concessions to the passing joys of the hit parade, they still fell back on olde tyme rock 'n' roll whenever a show dragged – though the catalogue had also been injected with a massive shot of rhythm-and-blues – R&B – via overhauls of The Isley Brothers' 'Shout', 'Money (That's What I Want)' by Barrett Strong, 'Shop Around' from The Miracles and other discs of a kind that would become known as "soul" music (perhaps the most abused term in pop).

Drinking from the same pool were Gerry, The Big Three, Kingsize Taylor, Rory Storm and other personalities who were as much stars on Merseyside as Cliff Richard And The Shadows were nationally. While an element of repertory overlap was expected when, say, The Beatles, Rory and Gerry appeared at the same venue on the same evening, "we took to looking for B-sides, songs that were a little more obscure," recalled McCartney, "in the hope that the other acts wouldn't play them." He contended too that "that is the reason why John and I began writing our own songs. There was no other reason for that other than you knew then that other bands couldn't access your stuff. That's the truth: John and I never sat down and decided we must become composers. We just wrote because it was the only way of saving our act."[3]

Suddenly, there'd been a lot of competition. When Stuart Sutcliffe returned home in mid-January, he was astonished too at how many substitute Beatles, Rories and Gerries had crawled out of the sub-cultural woodwork since he'd been away. From Bootle's Billy Kramer And The Coasters to The Pathfinders in Birkenhead, each district seemed to have an outfit enjoying local celebrity. Even one of Stuart's Prescot Grammar classmates, Neil Foster, was blowing sax with The Delacardoes, who held northeast Liverpool.

Many of these emerging groups had got off the ground by begging elderly promoters for intermission spots to the big bands and jazz combos from which many of their older members had sprung. If allowed, they played between nine o' clock and just after the pubs closed. Then the rock 'n' roll temperature would be lowered for the influx of grown-ups and an interrelated bringing of the evening to a close in squarely "professional" manner. Both the newly arrived revellers and the older musicians fancied that the muck to which their children had been cavorting earlier would fade and die so that "decent" entertainment could reign once more.

Yet the swing towards compact vocal-instrumental (or "beat") groups was unstoppable, and an increasing number of suburban and out-of-town venues were becoming their strongholds. In the city centre too, the Iron Door and the Cavern were no longer prohibiting pop from defiling their hallowed boards.

The Beatles were to become a fixture at the Cavern, making their debut in February 1961 during one of the newly established lunchtime sessions. This was to be Stuart Sutcliffe's only performance at what was destined to become as famous a Liverpool landmark as the Pier Head. Its idiosyncratic reek of disinfectant, mould and cheap perfume was still on his clothes 24 hours later – as it was on those of Colin Manley, among the audience for what must have been an off-day for The Beatles who "still had Stuart with them, and they really weren't very good."[4]

Lennon had been pleased to see Sutcliffe, but to the others their errant bass guitarist's reappearance was like that of the proverbial bad penny now that they'd experienced Chas Newby and then Paul's – and, on one occasion, Johnny Gustafson of The Big Three's – more agile playing. Neither Paul, George or Pete knew how they were supposed to feel when Stuart kept his options open by applying immediately for both a visa to re-enter Germany and for a place on a one-year Art Teacher's Diploma (ATD) course back at the college. Each represented an attempt to "settle down". Either way, it would not bode well for The Beatles.

After he failed to get on the course, Stuart was back in Hamburg by March, but an official colour was given to this by The Beatles, who were pencilled in for a four-month Top Ten season commencing on April Fools' Day. Stuart was to be on hand in negotiations between the club, the West German Immigration Office and Herr Knoop, Hamburg's chief of police. Crucially, he had to support Mona Best's badgering and Allan Williams's assurances that The Beatles were reformed characters, especially fire-bugs Pete and Paul.

While Stuart had proved useful as a mediator, "I believe to this day that he would eventually have been thrown out," said Rod Jones, expressing a commonly held view, "as soon as there was some sort of future. I'm actually surprised that he didn't go before."[2]

Just as it was a case of when rather than if Stuart left the group, the band did not replace him, opting instead for the simpler expedient of transferring McCartney permanently to bass. Years later, Paul would be profoundly disturbed by a suggestion from one Beatles' biographer that his machinations to play bass had effectively squeezed Stuart out: "I thought, 'God, this is a long time ago. This guy might be right.' I mean, he wasn't but you can't help wondering. I rang up George Harrison and I said, 'George, do you remember how I got on bass?', and he said, 'Yeah, we lumbered you with it.' I said, 'Thanks for saying that, because there's this guy who says otherwise.' That was it anyway. It was basically that. Stu lent me his bass, and so we obviously liked each other well enough."[2]

Paul's low-fretted cohesion with Pete's drumming was a subliminal element of The Beatles' intensifying local popularity as word got round, and it became customary for the Cavern to fill long before they followed the trad band or whatever else was in support, to invoke a mood of a kind of committed gaiety, often with cramped onlookers assuming the dual role of accompanying choir and augmenting the rhythm section.

While The Beatles' rowdy style was now not only acceptable but demanded at the Cavern and other recurring engagements, the going was erratic elsewhere, partly because certain parochial agents had no qualms about marrying a loud R&B outfit with, say, the ubiquitous trad band, the C&W (country-and-western) of Hank Walters and his Dusty Road Ramblers and the monologues of comedian Ken Dodd – as took place at a Sunday matinee in a cinema in Maghull, more Lancashire than Liverpool.

The Beatles would arrive too in Birkenhead, Seaforth or – for one fabled night only – Aldershot, over the edge of the world in distant Hampshire, where the cissy *pilzen kopfs* that George, Paul and John would be sporting by the end of 1961 were sometimes a red rag to those for whom an Elvis quiff was not yet a symbol of masculinity.

When Lennon and McCartney had blown a coming-of-age cheque that came from one of the former's well-heeled aunts on a holiday in Paris, Jurgen Vollmer had been there too, and, after getting him, said Paul "to try and cut our hair like his,"[2] the two chief Beatles came back with a heavily fringed variant – almost down to the eyebrows – on not so much Adam Faith as The Kaye Sisters, a corny vocal trio forever on British television variety shows. Nonetheless, while Pete demurred, George steeled himself to do likewise.

A lesser provocation in more unrefined venues was some bruiser's girlfriend's eye being caught by the corporate all-leather uniform in force since the Kaiserkeller stint – particularly the form-fitting trousers, just like the ones Gene and Eddie had worn on that fateful tour.

Apart from a handful cowering near the sanctuary of the stage, The Beatles were, therefore, confronted now and then with a crowd determined to hate them. Within a minute of the first item, a crewcut roughneck, bold with beer, might have to be restrained from being a lion of justice by charging on to strike a blow for decent entertainment for decent folk. Others in the audience, however, confined themselves to howls of derision, sporadic barracking and outbreaks of slow handclapping – though there were instances of grudging applause by those gawping antagonists who tuned into the group's unflagging dedication to their music, and the circumstance's awry absurdity – of which The Beatles themselves seemed be cognisant too.

On the firmer turf of the Liverpool jive-hives where they were rebooked into the foreseeable future, other groups would be copying The Beatles' stagecraft and repertoire, including 'I Saw Her Standing There', an original that had dripped mostly from the pen of McCartney.

Other than that terrible journey to Aldershot, however, campaigns for UK engagements beyond Merseyside yielded next to nothing. So inward-looking was provincial pop that there seemed to be few realistic halfway points between obscurity and the Big Time – and a policy of territorial defence was epitomised by a closed shop of venues in England's westward regions where, visitors of hit parade eminence notwithstanding, work tended to be given only to groups from the area such as The Betterdays, an R&B quintet who were to Plymouth's Guildhall what The Beatles were to the Cavern. The sentiment was why book a group from Liverpool when our own boys can do the job just as well for a fraction of the cost?

A quantum jump could be managed by sending a tape that might prompt someone important from the Promised Land to steer The Beatles to stardom. That was how Cliff Richard had got going. Since him, Shané Fenton And The Fentones from the wilds of Mansfield had mailed a recording of one of their local recitals to the Light Programme and hooked a regular spot on *Saturday Club*, the Light Programme's main pop showcase. Then it was onwards and upwards to a deal with Parlophone and a few modest chart strikes. The combination of a demo and grassroots petitioning had forced a Fontana recording manager to at least listen to The Betterdays.

Paul was keenly aware that his group's present state of marking time was prodding nerves at home, especially as he was still embroiled in hire-purchase payments for his equipment, and income from The Beatles was far less than Mike's as a hairdresser.

Not helping either was the cost of a Hofner "violin" bass that Paul had bought from a Grosse Freiheit shop. This didn't leave much change from his earnings at the Top Ten, which were "OK by English standards," agreed Ian "Tich" Amey of Dave Dee's Bostons, "but didn't go a long way in Germany".

Among The Beatles' duties there was backing Tony Sheridan both onstage – and in the studio after he was offered a recording contract by Bert Kaempfert, a power on Polydor, a division of Deutsche Grammophon, Germany's equivalent of EMI.

As a composer, 36-year-old Bert had contributed to 'Wooden Heart', Elvis Presley's European spin-off 45 from the movie soundtrack of *GI Blues*, a fictionalisation of his military service in Germany. The King acknowledged the melodic debt 'Wooden Heart' owed to the traditional 'Muss I Denn Zum Stadtele Naus', by breaking into German for a couple of verses.

Like nearly everybody else, The Beatles inserted a token song in German into the proceedings in Hamburg. The line of least resistance in this respect was for Paul to sing 'Wooden Heart', but more erudite was his 'Falling In Love Again' from the 1943 Marlene Dietrich movie vehicle, *The Blue Angel*. McCartney excerpts from stage and film musicals also impinged on otherwise frenetic hours on the boards. 'Summertime' (from *Porgy And Bess*) and, when that was dropped, 'Till There Was You' (*The Music Man*) and 'Over The Rainbow' could silence the most rumbustious crowd like a mass bell in Madrid. Inverting the principle that a drop of black makes white paint whiter, neither had The Beatles – and Sheridan – any inhibitions about making a run of the most frantic rock and R&B numbers all the more piquant by hanging fire midway and inserting one deadpanned selection from the perverse and antique likes of 'Beautiful Dreamer', 'You Make Me Feel So Young' and 'We'll Take Manhattan'.

A few Lennon–McCartney efforts were unveiled publicly – two in as many hours by late 1962 – but though 'I Saw Her Standing There' became something of a fixture during The Beatles' later Hamburg seasons, it hadn't the immediacy of 'Twist And Shout' – another from The Isley Brothers – or 'Shimmy Shimmy' by The Orlons, and other more ardently anticipated crowd-pleasers.

Where did songwriting get you anyway? No one paid attention to a home-made song, least of all Bert Kaempfert on the prowl on behalf of Polydor for a bargain-basement "Beat Gruppa" rather than the preferred orchestra for Tony Sheridan's first single.

Bert put his head round the door at the Top Ten during one of many transcendental moments that could not be recreated, that would look impossible if transcribed on manuscript paper. By today's standards, the sound *per se* was puny yet harsh and atrociously distorted as Tony and The Beatles battled with amplifiers of 30-watts maximum that were sent through speakers known to tear, explode and even catch fire because of power surges and the mismatch of British and German ohms. McCartney would recall that, "If we had troubles with our overworked amplifiers – we had to plug two guitars into the same one – I'd just chuck it all in and start leaping all round the stage or rushing over to the piano and playing a few chords."[2]

Despite off-putting technical problems, Sheridan was to remember that "Bert Kaempfert came for several nights. He was impressed by what he thought was our authenticity – which, of course, was second-hand American music infused with elements of our own that were authentic. Afterwards, we discussed with Bert what we ought to record. I'd heard Gene Vincent do 'My Bonnie' – very differently – and later on, a Ray Charles version. Long before we'd even thought about recording it ourselves, we'd done a sort of Jerry Lee Lewis-type arrangement on stage, but without piano. The B-side was the signature tune of my Norwich skiffle group, The Saints."

Tony Sheridan's was the name on the orange Polydor label when these rocked-up versions of 'My Bonnie Lies Over The Ocean' and 'When The Saints Go Marching In' were issued as a single in October 1961. So began Paul McCartney's recording career – helping Tony, Pete, John and George make the best of a couple of so-so numbers intended purely for Germany. It looked like being the only disc on which he'd ever be heard too.

6 *"Some Other Guy"*

"Pete gave Paul competition in the pretty face department."
– John Lennon[1]

As things turned out, 'My Bonnie' wasn't to be the only disc Paul and The Beatles would make. The Tony Sheridan single sold sufficiently to warrant an album containing some other tracks with the group. There was also to be an associated extended-play (EP) disc, also entitled *My Bonnie*.

Import copies were spun by Bob Wooler, one of the disc jockeys at the Cavern, and these consolidated The Beatles' regional fame within a radius of about 25km (15 miles). Now they'd rid themselves of Stuart Sutcliffe, the group epitomised the two guitars-bass-drums archetype of what would go down in cultural history as 1963's Merseybeat explosion. "They improved when Stuart left," noticed The Remo Four's Don Andrew, "but it was a long time before I appreciated what they were doing."[2] There were, however, local music lovers several steps ahead of Don. They were of such a multitude that 'I Saw Her Standing There' occasionally went down as well as some of the non-original ravers. Almost fully mobilised now, The Beatles were at the top of the first division of Liverpool popularity, having won in January 1962 the first readers' poll in a new fortnightly journal, *Mersey Beat*.

They also moved up a further rung or two through their acquisition just before Christmas 1961 of a manager in 27-year-old Brian Epstein, a sales manager at his grandfather's central Liverpool department store, which contained what could be deservedly advertised in *Mersey Beat* as "The Finest Record Selection In The North". Until then, The Beatles had made do with Mona Best, who was efficient enough, but, as she herself realised, didn't have the entrepreneurial contacts and know-how to remove The Beatles from the Liverpool–Hamburg grindstone.

With the advent of Epstein, her say in the group's affairs was diminished to the point of eventual silence, despite vainglorious efforts for it to be otherwise, especially as her handsome Pete was, Mona believed – with much justification – the most effusive fount of the group's teen appeal. Because Mrs Best was of far less use to them now, "John, Paul and George resented her interference," said Bill Harry, editor of *Mersey Beat*. Why couldn't all Beatle women be more like Paul's uncomplaining Dorothy Rhone, who supplied occasional passive glamour when he made her sit on a bar-stool in the midst of The Beatles? Yet for all her apparent acquiescence, it had still been necessary for Paul to suspend his routine philanderings when she and John's future wife, Cynthia Powell, visited Hamburg during the months at the Top Ten.

It was John and Paul, rather than John and Stuart nowadays as, with their girlfriends, they went on picnic excursions by train on hot afternoons to seaside resorts like Ostsee where they would recharge their batteries for the labours of the night. If there was no work that evening, they'd travel further to Timmendorf Strand where it was sometimes mild enough to sleep on the beach.

At the water's edge in hazy sunshine, Paul, Dorothy, John and Cynthia were like children, splashing and yelling in the freezing North Sea surf. Hands dripping sand, they'd direct their artistic endeavours towards the low-tide construction of a tottering castle sinister – all Transylvanian spires, battlements and moat.

The waves had not yet started gnawing at its foundations, and the dying sun was like a lone orange as they simmered down on the empty shoreline to a driftwood campfire and guitar singsongs.

Because there's no Top Ten that evening the idyll slips into a woodsmoke-smelling night of whispered sweet nothings and rhythmic movement beneath blankets and the pale moonlight. The sea sucks at the castle, and it crumbles and falls.

Serenities like this would be few and far between after McCartney and Lennon – and Harrison – could no longer venture into a public place without the pestering of fans and reporters. In unconscious preparation, they took in their stride Brian Epstein's moulding of them into entertainers destined ideally to emerge from provincial oblivion. The Germans have a word for what Brian was doing: *verharmlosen*, to render harmless.

By March 1962, the black leathers – aggressively redolent of Nazi officer trench-coats or motor-bike hoodlums – had been superseded by tweed suits of nondescript design. These, however, were a holding operation for the following year's epauletted jackets with no lapels, which buttoned up to the throat and had no unsightly bulges in the high-waisted trousers owing to the absence of pockets around tight hips. While the basic pattern had been taken from a blue-brushed denim get-up sold in the Hamburg branch of C&A's, that The Beatles had consented to wear it was down to the fastidious Epstein assuring them that it was for the best.

Wisely, however extensive his re-inventions of their visual image, Brian chose not to get very involved in the musical activities of his charges. Unlike Andrew Loog Oldham, soon to be The Rolling Stones' flamboyant man-of-affairs, he would never, for instance, presume to be more than an *éminence grise* behind publicity and further merchandising ballyhoo – or insist on producing their records.

In any case, relaxing in the privacy of his own home, Brian, for all his knowledge and interest in pop, was more inclined to tune into a classical concert on the BBC's Third Programme (later, Radio Three) than the Light Programme's *Pick Of The Pops*. Yet, convinced of something incredible taking place at the Cavern, Epstein had wanted to believe it even if he didn't understand what it actually was any more than his 1970s counterpart would be when looking for a New Sex Pistols. All he knew was that the club was packed, there was an infectious atmosphere and the phenomenon hinged on the enigma of untouchable boys-next-door.

For reasons that included erotic attraction and frustrated aspirations to be a performer himself, he'd made investigative forays into the world of pop long before encountering The Beatles, once worming his way backstage during the interval of a Larry Parnes presentation at the Liverpool Empire. A hall like that with its grand proscenium, velvet curtains and tiers of high-backed chairs, could give you big ideas.

"He remarked on the unusual lighting," Larry would recall, "the pace, individual artists' performances and their clothes. I was extremely flattered"[3] – so flattered that Parnes considered taking Brian on as an assistant. The younger man elected instead to go it alone and he decided that the next titans of teen were as likely to be The Beatles as any other in this new breed of guitar outfits.

If he'd found time to scan *Mersey Beat* and amble over to some of the other clubs, he may have discovered that there were equally capable beat groups in the vicinity. Instead, he persuaded himself that he'd struck luckiest with The Beatles, having stood himself amongst the battalions of iron-bladdered girls positioned stage-front at the Cavern to better gawk at Pete and the other three.

The Beatles had also risen to the challenge of the ballroom circuit, becoming a reliable draw as, courtesy of Brian's persistence via telephone and post, their booking spectrum broadened intermittently to Yorkshire, Wales and as far south as Swindon. As for Hamburg, they were back again in April 1962 to wow 'em at the new Star-Club, which had given no quarter during a ruthless campaign to outflank the Top Ten as the Grosse Freiheit's premier night spot.

Epstein had also signed up Gerry And The Pacemakers, second in the *Mersey Beat* poll. McCartney would "remember all too well sweating the outcome, hoping we could scrape together the necessary points to beat Gerry's band. That's how close it was."[4]

Anyone with the means and tenacity to research Britain's local pop scene then would have discovered that everywhere else had boss groups too. As The Betterdays did Plymouth, Kerry Rapid and his Blue Stars ruled Aldershot (and were playing a rival palais when The Beatles made their solitary foray there). Likewise, Ricky Ford And The Cyclones were supreme in Weston-super-Mare as The Golden Crusaders were in Belfast, The Viceroys in Llanriddod Wells, The Poor Souls in Dundee and Dave Berry And The Cruisers in Sheffield – while in Kidderminster, Shades Five were to weather an intrusion into the town's Playhouse by Birmingham's Denny Laine And The Diplomats.

Before adopting his *nom de théâtre* – "something to do with Cleo Laine and Johnny Dankworth" – Brian Hines had been one of Johnny And The Dominators in which "Johnny could have been anyone because they kept changing the singers". The outfit's Buddy Holly specialist, Brian was also moonlighting as juvenile attraction in a palais big band before leading The Diplomats which, in 1962, also contained Bev Bevan – who was to beat a gradually more splendid drum kit with Carl Wayne And The Vikings, The Move and The Electric Light Orchestra. Among "featured vocalists" that passed through the ranks was Tipton's Nicky James, who'd defied all comers in an "Elvis of the Midlands" contest.

Though the group's catchment area stretched as far away as Oxford, efforts to infiltrate certain territories met organised opposition. Worcester's Lansdowne Agency was, noted regional pop gazette *Midland Beat*, "formed with the sole intention of stopping Brum bands playing at local venues"[5] – an embargo, however, that did not prevent Denny's diplomatic Sunday show at Kidderminster Playhouse in October 1963.

The group were, nonetheless, not in an immediate position to forsake their day jobs like Brian/Denny's as a trainee in the electrical goods section of a department store not unlike I Epstein & Sons. It wasn't exactly showbusiness, but it proved instructive as he was required to both sell and requisition records and musical instruments. He recalled: "I actually got them to buy guitars; they didn't originally."

When Laine And The Diplomats turned fully professional after a year, they sought attention initially by wearing matching suits, peroxiding their hair and making out that they were two pairs of brothers. The repertoire was mostly the current Top 20 and what had become R&B standards like 'Money' and 'Love Potion Number Nine'. "A lot of the bands in Birmingham had the same repertoire as those in Liverpool," noted Denny, "I had a friend called Danny [of Danny King and the Mayfair Set] who had a great collection. He used to put stickers over record labels so that rival groups like us wouldn't know what they were."

The Laine outfit was among a handful in Birmingham that tried self-composed items – though, as everyone knew, these usually caused dancers to sit them out. However, some were more intrigued than the musicians thought. "John Bonham [later of Led Zeppelin] used to watch me and The Diplomats at the Wednesbury Youth Centre," recounted Denny, "Years later, he stayed at my house, and, though I couldn't remember any of the original material the Diplomats did to save my life, he could. We got a bit drunk, and he started singing 'Why Cry', 'A Piece of Your Mind' and others we did. He knew all the words and everything. Unbelievable!"

Rather than any idiosyncracies in their music, it was because the group toed an orthodox line that they made a television debut on topical *Midlands At Six*. As *Saturday Club* – and ITV's *Thank Your Lucky Stars* – were recorded in Birmingham, Denny Laine And The Diplomats were well placed to be booked too for two sub-*Thank Your Lucky Stars* shows – *For Teenagers Only* and *Pop Shop* – and as token pop act on *Lunch Box*, a light entertainment series, built round the personality of Noele Gordon prior to her *grande dame* part in ITV's long-running soap opera, *Crossroads*. Yet, though they also got as far as taping several demos for EMI, The Diplomats and Denny had reached much the same impasse as The Beatles before Brian Epstein had entered the picture.

Thanks to Epstein's dogged prodding of Polydor's UK outlet, 'My Bonnie' by Tony Sheridan and The Beatles was released in Britain on 5 January 1962. *NME* reviewer Keith Fordyce was generous – "both sides are worth a listen for the above-average ideas"[6] – but, unaired on either the Light Programme or Radio Luxembourg, the disc sank without trace.

In June, the same was in store for 'You Got What I Like' by Cliff Bennett And The Rebel Rousers, but Parlophone seemed to regard the group as a long-term investment because it was prepared to risk another six singles before reaping the harvest of its faith in X-factor Bennett, highly regarded as a bandleader, and one of few Britons who imagined that they had a black soul within a white skin that could actually take on black pop without losing the overriding passion.

Yet chart recognition seemed a far-fetched afterthought to Cliff when he and his Rebel Rousers were on the wrong side of the North Sea, putting on the agony night after night at the Star-Club where Paul and John of The Beatles promised to give him a leg up by writing him a song if their group got famous before his did.

Both the Middlesex and Merseyside factions at the Star-Club were mixing socially with Little Richard and Gene Vincent as each disturbed Tony Sheridan's reign as incumbent rock 'n' roll king of the Grosse Freiheit. "I remember how excited The Beatles were to meet Richard," enthused Billy Preston, the Georgia Peach's 16-year-old organist. "In Hamburg, they'd always be with him, asking him about America, the cities, the stars, the movies, Elvis and all that."[7]

Since the most culturally important chapter of his life had closed, Little Richard had recorded little but sacred material following his enrolment in a theological college. In 1961, he'd commenced a gospel tour of the world, but by the time it reached Germany, Richard was giving 'em 'Tutti Frutti', 'Long Tall Sally' and hardly anything else that hadn't been a massive hit for him before he'd got religion.

The billowing drapes of old had been mothballed, and the overhanging pompadour abbreviated severely, but Paul McCartney was still awestruck by the soberly attired, bristle-scalped exquisite he met in the dressing room, and later saw onstage, shrieking his head off and hammering the ivories, just like he had in *The Girl Can't Help It* when it had reached Merseyside cinemas in 1957.

Richard himself would inform his biographer, Charles White, that "Paul [McCartney] would just look at me. Like, he wouldn't move his eyes – and he'd say: 'Oh Richard, you're my idol. Let me touch you.' He wanted to learn my little holler, so we sat at the piano going 'Oooooooh! Oooooooh!' until he got it."[7]

Like Caesar deified by the Gallic peasants, Richard would offend none by refusing gifts pressed upon him – like one of Paul's best shirts after "I developed a specially close relationship with Paul, but me and John couldn't make it. John had a nasty personality."[7]

By the middle of the decade, Richard was to have cause to be grateful to The Beatles when they revived 'Long Tall Sally' on disc. In 1962, however, while he continued to feed off a more glorious past, they could only carry the torch of classic rock – well, their take on it – back to the confines of Liverpool.

Yet more than mere Merseybeat was unravelling there now. Following a lucrative London exhibition, sculptor Arthur Dooley had become a professional Scouser, often on BBC television's early evening magazine, *Tonight*. A protégé of Pop Art pioneer Richard Hamilton, Adrian Henri had reached beyond slapping oil on canvas to performance art and, as he had promised Michael Horovitz, poetry. Other bards and *nouvelle vague* artists of the same vintage included Roger McGough, Brian Patten, John Gorman, Alun Owen (who was to write the script of *A Hard Day's Night*, The Beatles' first feature film), Mike Evans – and Mike McCartney who, with Gorman and McGough, had formed Scaffold, an ensemble that mingled poetry and satirical sketches during the audio-visual and literary events that, walking a tightrope between near magical inspiration and pseudo-intellectual ramblings, were springing up as alternatives to doing the 'Hippy Hippy Shake' with all o' your might down the Iron Door.

The gifted Mike was to adopt the stage surname "McGear" to stay accusations of boarding his more famous brother's bandwagon though, in 1962, the two were on terms of fluctuating equality in their respective spheres. Scaffold were leading what the economist would call a "full life" with regular bookings at Streate's, the Everyman and the Blue Angel, while The Beatles were to be flown, not driven, to Hamburg for a penultimate spell at the Star-Club in November.

While the previous season had been a professional triumph, it had been blighted by the cerebral haemorrhage that had killed Stuart Sutcliffe the afternoon before their arrival. An advance party of Paul, Pete and John hadn't heard the news when they'd taken off from Liverpool. In the skies, they'd been shrill with their first BBC radio broadcast (*Teenagers' Turn* from Manchester's Playhouse) the previous weekend – and in then-unknowing empathy with 'Homesick For St Pauli', the Freddy Quinn million-seller that German milkmen were whistling that spring.

Still raring to go as the aeroplane descended, the three came down with a bump when Astrid Kirchherr, drained of her usual sparkle, met them after their passports had been checked. Paul was at a loss for words. Anything he said or did then wouldn't ring true somehow: "It affected John the most because he'd been closest to him. John was most disturbed by it. For me, it was a distant thing. I can't remember doing or thinking anything – but the main thing for me, that I remember feeling bad about was that he died of a brain thing. It struck me as all being Van Gogh and sort of a wild artistic thing, but I think by then, I'd got a little hardened to people dying. It wasn't like Stu was with us. We'd got used to not being with Stu – but it was a shock."[8]

That night, Paul and Pete grizzled into their beer for a boy they hadn't understood but had liked because, outside the context of all the in-fighting, he'd come to like them. If neither had been over-complimentary about his musicianship, they had to admit that

The Beatles were a better group for Stuart's creative instincts, even if his talents and appetites had proved too much at odds with theirs.

Their eyes were still sore the next day when they went with John and Astrid to greet Brian, George and Stuart's distraught mother at the airport. A few hours later, however, The Beatles were pitching into their opening number with all their customary verve.

They were still at the Star-Club on Maundy Thursday, 19 April when Stuart was interred in Huyton's Blue Bell Lane cemetery. "It was all happening when Stu died," gloomed Paul, "and we were caught up in a sort of whirlwind. John was able to pause in that whirlwind and say, 'Jesus Christ, Stu's died!' – but when you were back in that whirlwind, I don't think we were able to spend much time on it – probably a good thing too."[8]

The next to go – albeit in less absolute terms than Stuart – was Pete Best after the group and manager had netted a hard-won recording contract with Parlophone, having been turned down by virtually every other UK company that mattered. The first session took place on 6 June in the EMI complex along Abbey Road. Like every consequent visit, it was supervised by no less than the head of Parlophone himself, George Martin, who preferred to tape pop groups in cavernous Studio Two where he'd vetoed freshening up the paintwork in case it affected the acoustics that had spiced up the chart entries of such as Eddie Calvert and Shane Fenton.

Martin's only reservations about The Beatles that first day was that he'd heard no unmistakable smash hit within their cache of Lennon–McCartney originals, and that the drummer's lack of studio experience was more pronounced than that of the guitarists. A hireling would have to ghost him when The Beatles returned to record 'Love Me Do', a McCartney opus that, for want of anything better, had been picked as the first A-side.

BBC Radio Merseyside presenter and pop historian Spencer Leigh was to devote an entire book to chronicling the saga of Pete Best's subsequent sacking.[9] One of the lengthier chapters explores divergent theories as to why he was replaced by Ringo Starr, one of Rory Storm's Hurricanes, two months after that initial trip to Abbey Road. One of these suggests that a green-eyed monster had whispered to the other three – particularly McCartney – that Best was the fairest of them all. This was exacerbated by *Mersey Beat*'s report that, during the *Teenagers' Turn* showcase, "John, Paul and George made their entrance on stage to cheers and applause, but when Pete walked on, the fans went wild. The girls screamed! In Manchester, his popularity was assured by his looks alone."[10]

At the stage door afterwards, Pete was almost killed with kindness by over-attentive females from the 400-strong audience while Paul, John and George were allowed to board a ticking-over charabanc after signing some autographs. Jim McCartney was on the periphery of this incident, and admonished the sweat-smeared drummer: "Why did you have to attract all the attention? Why didn't you call the other lads back? I think that was very selfish of you."[11]

Did Mr McCartney have an indirect hand in Pete's dismissal? To what extent did his unfair reprimand – and interrelated exchanges at Forthlin Road – make dark nights of the ego darker still? He rubbed salt into the wound on observing the dismissed Best in the Cavern shadows when a Beatles bash was being documented for the ITV series, *Know The North*. "Great, isn't it!" he crowed. "They're on TV!"[11] Pete bit his tongue and left quietly.

Jim's glee had to be contained as edited footage – of Paul, John, George and the new member doing 'Slow Down' and 'Some Other Guy' – wasn't screened until it had gained historical importance, and the concept of a Beatles without Ringo had become as unthinkable to the world as one without Pete had once been in Liverpool.

"I was a better player than him," protested Starr 30 years later. "That's how I got the job. It wasn't on no personality [sic]."[12] Nevertheless, a session drummer had been on clock-watching stand-by for the recording of 'Love Me Do', but Ringo kept his peace just as Paul did when directed by George Martin to extend the sung hook-line, radically altering the embedded arrangement of the humble little ditty that changed everything.

7 "Don't You Dig This Kind Of Beat?"

"It was fairly innocent then, a bit of a cottage industry. We thought we'd last maybe two or three years."
— *Dick Taylor of The Pretty Things*

The release of 'Love Me Do' in October 1962 meant that The Beatles could be billed as "EMI Recording Artists", and that the glory and the stupidity of being in a 1960s pop group now necessitated being shoulder-to-shoulder in a van for hours on end during a staggered procession of one-nighters that were often truly hellish in an age when England's only motorway terminated in Birmingham.

While local engagements were becoming less frequent, the single shifted plenty in loyal Liverpool, and eventually touched the national Top 20 – just. This followed on from ITV's *Tuesday Rendezvous* on 4 December 1962, which was the first we southerners at large ever saw of The Beatles.

The follow-up, 'Please Please Me', gave more cause to hold on hoping as, before slipping in mid-March, it lingered in a Top Ten in which Frankie Vaughan, Cliff Richard, Bobby Vee and Kenny Ball were also vying to topple Frank Ifield who was at Number One with 'The Wayward Wind'.

If still revolving round clubs and ballrooms, there were even more dates booked than The Beatles could possibly keep. Most burdensome were contracts finalised when the Local Boys Made Good had been only one of many – though the backstage lionising was often quite satisfying: I always knew you'd make it, lads.

Two hits in a row was sufficient to justify a long-player – which The Beatles and George Martin were expected to complete in an allotted 12-hour day with Musicians Union-regulated tea and lunch breaks during conventional London office times and an evening period with a jobsworth locking-up well before midnight.

After Gerry And The Pacemakers, The Big Three, Billy J Kramer, The Searchers, The Merseybeats and The Fourmost notched up respectable chart entries too before 1963's cool, wet summer was out, what was deemed by the media to be a "Mersey Sound" or "Liverpool Beat" gave way to a more generalised group boom, the Big Beat, also spearheaded by John, Paul, George and Ringo – the "Fab Four" – which finished off chart careers of soloists like Mark Wynter. *In extremis*, he was to resort to a Beatles' ballad ('And I Love Her') as a 1964 A-side. After a disturbing hat-trick of comparative misses, Adam Faith took more pragmatic heed of the Big Beat by hiring Chris Andrews, a tunesmith who'd fronted the obscure Chris Ravel And The Ravers but had, nevertheless, put in much hard graft in Hamburg to provide made-to-measure smashes, and The Roulettes, one of the more able also-ran outfits of the mid-1960s, to accompany him. Both on stage and on vinyl, Adam's new repertoire was either derived from Andrews' prolific portfolio, whether both sides of the Ravers' only 45, 'Don't You Dig This Kind of Beat?' and 'I Do' on a 1964 LP, or from plunderings that included a confident 'I Wanna Be Your Man' on the album yet to come.

This, however, was not the way of he who was The Silver Beatles' front man for their 1960 expedition to Scotland. Without a recording contract by 1963, Johnny Gentle joined The Viscounts, a dated harmony trio who popped up on ITV's prime-time *Sunday Night At The London Palladium* emasculating a mildly choreographed 'I Saw Her Standing There'.

They raised a few screams by association. Yet, by 1964, The Viscounts couldn't get arrested, together with The Brook Brothers – self-proclaimed "Britain's ace vocal group" – as well as The King Brothers, The Avons, The Kestrels, The Kaye Sisters, The

PAUL McCARTNEY

Dowlands and similarly dapper non-beat groups who, previously, had buttressed certain wrong-headed music industry moguls' theories that outfits with electric guitars were behind the times. We know these things, Mr Epstein.

Some tried to adjust, usually without getting the point – as did The Kestrels with a xerox of 'There's A Place' from The Beatles' first album. However, The Dowlands' disinclined cover of 'All My Loving' (which, like 'I Wanna Be Your Man', was from the second, *With The Beatles*) was to spend seven weeks in the domestic Top 50 in early 1964, though their 'Wishin' And Hopin'' and 'Don't Make Me Over' were vanquished by The Merseybeats' and Swinging Blue Jeans's respective versions.

If Liverpool had an "answer" to anachronisms like The Viscounts, Dowlands *et al*, it was the all-black Chants, who had been backed onstage by the pre-'Love Me Do' Beatles among others. In 1963, their 'Come Go With Me', the number John Lennon had been singing when Paul McCartney first heard The Quarry Men, surfaced on disc as merely the B-side of a debut 45 – an odd executive decision that kept what might have been a surefire hit from the ears of UK radio listeners.

Adhering closer to the two-guitars-bass-drums Merseybeat archetype, the test case of The Trends made a more obvious attempt to cash in with fleeting changes of name – The Beachcombers, The Beatcombers and The Mersey Men – before their 'All My Loving' lost a Top 40 bout against The Dowlands. The Trends had been as much a fixture at Kirby's Westvale Youth Club as The Beatles at the Cavern – and The Undertakers at Orrell Park ballroom. Among the all-out ravers in The Undertakers' repertoire were 'Mashed Potatoes' and 'Money' but, as it was with The Chants, these tracks were buried on B-sides. Nevertheless, 'If You Don't Come Back', a tale of lovesick insanity, was a "turntable hit" following a plug on *Thank Your Lucky Stars*, which obliged the group to mothball the black crêped top hats and other macabre props and abbreviate their name to "The 'Takers".

Most Liverpool acts who'd breathed the air round The Beatles came within at least a rumour's distance of a qualified fame after convincing this record label or that London impresario that their bass player had sat next to John at infant school, that the drummer had been in the same Boy Scout troop as Paul or that the lead guitarist had danced with a man who'd danced with a girl who'd danced with George. That's not all that much of an exaggeration.

Decca, Pye, Oriele and the other companies who'd turned their noses up at The Beatles in 1962 had read *NME* and *Melody Maker* despatches about the group's first national tours with heart-sinking fascination. Ostensibly second-billed, the four had upstaged Helen Shapiro – Britain's biggest female pop attraction in 1963 – and then Tommy Roe and Chris Montez, North American Bobbies with hits fresh in consumers' minds, who headlined a "scream circuit" package for the first night only.

The next such jaunt was in May 1963 with Roy Orbison – who, bar the remote Elvis Presley, was to command the most devoted British following of any US pop star – plus Gerry And The Pacemakers and various small fry. The Beatles' third single, 'From Me To You', would be a Number One fixture for the entire tour. Shrieking pandemonium and chants of "We want The Beatles!" would greet even compère Tony Marsh's attempts to keep order.

The Beatles' domination of an edition of *Sunday Night At The London Palladium* drew out the agony for Decca *et al*. Worse was to come when they all but stole the *Royal Variety Show* at the Prince of Wales Theatre on 4 November 1963 when, with McCartney's pretty 'Till There Was You' oiling the wheels, the general feeling among adults and others who hadn't wanted to like them, was that John, Paul, George and Ringo were the stock Nice Lads When You Get To Know Them. Ireland's Bachelors – more Viscounts than Beatles – were even nicer lads who, as token pop group in the next year's *Royal Variety Show*, had faced the Royal Box for an amended opening line – "*we* wouldn't change *you* for the wurrrrld!" – of their most recent Top Ten strike.

If The Bachelors and The Beatles put themselves in the way of potentially damaging publicity – like one Bachelor's extramarital amour with a a well-known female vocalist or a Liverpool woman's imputation of her baby's irregular kinship to Paul McCartney – their respective managers would ensure that no nicotine-stained fingers would type out lurid coverage of it for the following Sunday's *News Of The World*. Besides, even if it was true, nothing too sordid was likely to be yet brought to public notice about The Beatles, Gerry, Billy J, The Fourmost and other ostensibly wholesome groups by a scum press who judged any besmirching of cheeky but innocent personas as untimely: save the scandal for The Rolling Stones, who, seized by Decca, were to be a closer second to The Beatles than earlier pretenders like Gerry and his Pacemakers, The Searchers and, in early 1964, The Dave Clark Five.

Perhaps with the Five's – and The Bachelors' – clean-cut, amiable precedent in mind, the Stones' then co-manager Eric Easton had tried and failed to spruce them up with uniform slim-jim ties and waistcoats. While he'd got them to capitulate to photo sessions in which they'd affect what were intended to be smiles, certain Stones would sign autographs with bad grace or refuse altogether. To no avail, Easton would stress the importance of making themselves pleasant to reporters and fans. If a stranger came up to guitarist Keith Richards and said, "Hello Keith. How is your brother Cliff?", Eric – and Decca – would rather a polite lie along the lines of "Fine, thanks. He's keeping well" than Keith telling the enquirer to fuck off. Finally, Easton gave up, deciding instead to leave personal management to his younger sidekick, Andrew Loog Oldham.

As anti-Beatles, the Stones cut appositely sullen figures on the front photograph of an eponymous debut long-player – though anyone awaiting seething musical outrage were disappointed because its content didn't ring many changes. Almost as weighty with R&B standards as the first LPs by The Animals, The Yardbirds, The Kinks, The Downliners Sect, Them, The Pretty Things and

The Spencer Davis Group, it even contained 'Route 66', a set-work that any self-respecting R&B aficionado now heard no more than a mariner hears the sea.

The rise of such groups – principally Londoners – was indicative of the decline of Liverpool as a pop Eldorado by the close of 1963. Too rapid turnovers of personnel within The Merseybeats and The Big Three didn't help either at a time when teenagers needed to identify clearly with a favoured group to the extent that, ideally, the drummer toiling over his kit was as much its public face as the lead singer.

Striking while the iron was lukewarm, all manner of German labels were still rushing out as much associated product as the traffic would allow. Most of it was pressed onto cheap compilations such as 1964's *Liverpool Beat*, an album featuring both Kingsize Taylor And The Dominoes and the more versatile Bobby Patrick Big Six – from Glasgow! – who were to be taken on semi-permanently to back Tony Sheridan. Some were immortalised *au naturel* at the Star-Club, while others were hastened to a studio as soon as the final major sixth of the shift had reverberated so that their adrenalin could be pumped onto a spool of tape.

On the rebound from a night on stage, Kingsize Taylor and his boys thought nothing of banging out an entire LP in four hours from plug-in to final mix. Certainly, they came closest here to capturing the scintillatingly slipshod power forged unknowingly from the Star-Club fracas, day after day, week upon week.

As Taylor did, Cliff Bennett could have continued making a good living in Germany, but he preferred to take his chances at home where he and The Rebel Rousers aroused the interest of Brian Epstein who, encouraged by his runaway success with the cream of Liverpudlia, was eager to diversify. With this entrepreneurial muscle behind them, Cliff's seventh single, a tougher Anglicised copy of The Drifters' 'One Way Love', tore into the Top Ten in autumn 1964, but a second bite at that particular cherry wouldn't present itself for another two years.

Denny Laine went off the boil too after striking even harder a few weeks later. In a last-ditch attempt to shake off provincial fetters, he'd left his Diplomats to fend for themselves in April 1964, the month that Solihull's Applejacks entered the Top Ten. When The Rockin' Berries did likewise that summer, *Midland Beat*'s editorial judgement that "Liverpool started the ball rolling. Now the Midlands is ready to take over"[1] seemed to be proving correct. This first flush of "Brumbeat" peaked when both the Berries and Denny Laine's new group, The Moody Blues, were seen on the same January 1965 edition of *Ready Steady Go*, that most atmospheric of televised pop series of the Swinging Sixties.

If The Moody Blues's name was chosen in vain hopes of sponsorship from Mitchell and Butler, a local brewery, there was also an instrumental by urban bluesman Slim Harpo entitled 'Moody Blue'. "I pushed the group in the direction of the blues- and jazz-based London bands," maintained Denny. "Also, we'd gone to see The Spencer Davis Group, and I was knocked out by them. I thought that if they could get away with it, we could – and that convinced the other lads."

As The Moody Blues had rejected the assembly-line pop otherwise vital for survival in the ballrooms, they came to be appreciated as a "group's group" by the students and bohemians that patronised rhythm-and-blues evenings in, say, the Golden Eagle on Hill Street, or, less regularly, in the nearby Birmingham Town Hall where, on 11 September 1964, ravers could twist the night away to Blue Sounds from Leeds, the jazzy Sheffields and Alexis Korner's Blues Incorporated. Representing the Second City itself were The Spencer Davis Group – and, wrote *Midland Beat*, "the much-improved Moody Blues Five [sic]"[2].

The quintet continued to do so well that they acquired the services of manager Tony Secunda and producer Denny Cordell, who, if Londoners, will be remembered as the Tweedledum and Tweedledee of Brumbeat after they ministered to later Second City acts – including the Move (and died within days of each other in

February 1995). "They were a good team," commented Laine, "who made sure that The Moody Blues didn't do the wrong things."

In the first instance, Secunda negotiated a season of Monday nights at London's Marquee club for the group. From this fêted showcase, they speedily landed a deal with Decca. Despite a *Ready Steady Go* plug and a stunning version of Bobby Parker's 'Steal Your Heart Away' as B-side, the maiden Moody Blues 45, 'Lose Your Money' – penned by Denny and pianist Mike Pinder – did just that.

There were, however, no grumbles from their investors about sales for an overhaul of US soul star Bessie Banks's 'Go Now' – though its abrupt fade provokes visions of Laine being suddenly hooked offstage like a vaudeville warbler getting the bird. "We knew a public schoolboy called James Hamilton," said Denny, "who had a fantastic record collection, and knew a New York disc jockey, B Mitchell Reed. Through them, we got a lot of material that nobody else was doing – like 'Steal Your Heart Away'. 'Go Now' was another one. Bessie Banks did a great slow version, and we bopped it up, put harmonies on it it, made it sort of gospel in our limited way."

Corroboration of this British Number One suffered a setback when 'I Don't Want To Go On Without You' barely rippled the Top 40, dogged as it was by simultaneous covers from The Searchers and The Escorts. Moreover, between session and pressing plant, a flute solo vanished from the master tape. In addition, The Moody Blues looked a motley crew, what with Laine hogging the singing and guitar spotlights on 'Go Now' while general factotum Ray Thomas merely bashed the tambourine and went "aaaaaah" into a microphone.

Ray was allowed one lead vocal on *The Magnificent Moody Blues,* an LP padded with The Hit and stand-bys from the stage act like James Brown's 'I'll Go Crazy' and a fast treatment of Sonny Boy Williamson's 'Bye Bye Bird'. There were also four originals including 'Stop!', flatteringly covered by a singer named Julie Grant. "I formed a writing duo with Mike Pinder because it was an easier way of disciplining yourself," reckoned Denny, "by having another person involved – but Mike didn't really write a lot. He would help me put them together. I would write a song and go to him and ask how we were going to do it with the band, and he'd develop it."

Pinder and Laine's 'From The Bottom Of My Heart' was, perhaps, the most exquisite track any incarnation of The Moody Blues ever made. Laine certainly discharged a remarkable vocal from preludial muttering to a howled, wordless coda as if what was being expressed was too intense for normal verbal articulation.

'From The Bottom Of My Heart' was two months away from release when The Moody Blues secured a slot at the "*NME* Pollwinners' Concert" at Wembley Empire Pool. The predominantly female audience went as indiscriminately crazy over them as it did over all male performers on a bill that embraced what was then the very upper crust of British pop – including The Rolling Stones, The Kinks, Twinkle, The Animals, Them, The Searchers, Georgie Fame, Tom Jones, Wayne Fontana And The Mindbenders, The Moody Blues, Donovan, Herman's Hermits, Dusty Springfield, Freddie And The Dreamers, Cilla Black – and, of course, The Beatles who closed the show.

This afternoon extravaganza on 11 April 1965 encapsulated, I suppose, the beat boom at its hysterical, electric high summer. An act drowned in tidal waves of screams that, while subsiding to mere cheers for Twinkle, Dusty and Cilla, hurled rampaging girls towards crash barriers where they'd be hurled back again by flushed bouncers, shirt-sleeved in the heat, and aggravatingly nearer to Mick, Georgie, Tom, Wayne, Ray, Donovan, Paul and Denny than those who'd give their souls to be. In the boiling mêlée further back, unluckier ticket-holders burst into tears, rocked foetally, flapped programmes and scarves, hoisted inexpertly daubed placards, tore at their hair, wet themselves and fainted with the thrill of it all.

8 "Nobody I Know"

"Paul McCartney came across at the time as being a bit
superficial. I think that he held his cards close to his chest."
— *Dave Davies of The Kinks*[1]

Bing Crosby, that most influential of pre-war singers of popular
song, hadn't realised that The Beatles composed their own material.
Until he did, he shared the view of evangelist Billy Graham – and
every other right-thinkin' North American adult – that they were
just "a passing trend".

A younger elder stateman of pop, Johnnie Ray, was of like
opinion, according to Bill Franklin, his manager: "When The
Beatles first came out, Johnnie said, 'Oh, I give 'em six months,'
and all the things everybody else did, but he got over it. Then we
had a very interesting encounter in London. Johnnie and I were
in a little club called the White Elephant, and Paul McCartney
came over and introduced himself. Paul was very nervous. He was
pawing the ground with his foot, and said some very nice,
complimentary things. Johnnie liked that. It made him feel great."

"I was amazed because he wouldn't talk to me," said Ray
himself. "I said, 'I'm glad to meet you Paul,' and he sort of shuffled
his feet and ran out the door."[2]

Johnnie was sufficiently impressed by McCartney and The
Beatles to record an idiosyncratic 'Yesterday' as Crosby was to
record 'Hey Jude' in 1969, but neither were so anxious to return
to the charts that they were driven to sift through Beatles albums
and, if lucky, demo tapes for a potential smash.

Others of their showbiz proper stamp did, among them, Crosby's favourite vocalist, Matt Monro. While keeping a weathered eye on Britain with scrupulous television plugs of his latest single, it had become convenient for Matt to relocate to the USA in order to commute to an ever-expanding workload there – and also record a body of work that would compare favourably with that of indigenous entertainers like his adolescent hero Perry Como as well as Tony Bennett, Dean Martin and even Sinatra, jackpot of all songwriters.

Among the most conspicuous chart climbers for Monro in the mid-1960s was the first ever cover of 'Yesterday', subject of over a thousand subsequent versions. As early as March 1967, it was approaching 500 – as announced by Dick James, director of Lennon and McCartney's publishing company Northern Songs.

"I just fell out of bed and it was there," divulged Paul. "I have a piano by the side of my bed, and I just got up and played the chords. I thought it can't just have come to me in a dream. It's like handing things in to the police; if no one's claimed it after six weeks, I'll have it."[3] 'Yesterday' was then launched into life with the provisional title of 'Scrambled Eggs' until the tailoring of lyrics that McCartney sang on disc accompanied by his own acoustic guitar strumming – and a string quartet, an early example of The Beatles' augmentation of conventional beat group instruments. Sitars, horn sections, orchestras, tape collage and other resources were yet to come.

Matt Monro's big band rendering of 'Yesterday' made the UK Top Ten in the teeth of a belated rival 'Yesterday' on Decca by Marianne Faithfull – with an accompanying choir – that was advantaged by apparent endorsement by sole composer McCartney ('and I never wished I'd written it,"[4] muttered John Lennon).

First refusal, however, had been given to Billy J Kramer ("it was too nicey-nicey for me") before 'Yesterday' was offered to Chris Farlowe, a white Londoner who was being bruited as "the greatest Blues Singer in the world today"[5]. Marianne Faithfull had dithered over it too. Then Matt Monro's headlining spot on *Sunday Night At The London Palladium* settled the matter – though McCartney's blueprint on the soundtrack album of *Help!*, The Beatles' second movie, scored in the States.

It was George Harrison's task to introduce 'Yesterday' onstage, viz, "For Paul McCartney of Liverpool, opportunity knocks!". George and the others had nicknamed Paul (not always affectionately) "The Star", partly because he seemed to have the most highly developed instinct – and desire – for riding the waves of showbusiness protocol whilst gilding the image of loveable and slightly naive lads from back-of-beyond taken aback by their celebrity – which probably accounts for his behaviour during the chat with Johnnie Ray. Paul's skill for combining necessary ruthlessness with keeping his popularity intact was freeze-framed in an episode centred on him at the window of a chartered aircraft that had just landed somewhere in the American Midwest...

A reception committee of town burghers and their hoity-toity children are waiting on the tarmac. Behind the glass, Paul is waving and smiling. From the side of his mouth, however, he is issuing instructions to Mal Evans, a principal of the road crew, to tell the assembly outside that he – Mal – had decided that, though The Beatles were delirious with joy at the thought of meeting them, they were in need of rest for that evening's show. I'm sorry you're disappointed, but, for their own good, I've had to disappoint the boys too. Thus Evans rather than Paul, John, George and Ringo was the *bête noire* via a strategy worthy of the most battle-hardened public relations officer.

Of all The Beatles too, Paul was the one most abreast with contemporary trends such as the injection of Oriental sounds into pop as originated by either The Yardbirds – or The Kinks on 1965's 'See My Friends' with its plaintive, whining vocal and droning guitars. Their lead guitarist Dave Davies would recall an encounter in a London club, the Scotch of St James, when "McCartney said, 'You bastards! How dare you! I should have made that record.'"[1]

After outlines dissolved, around late 1964, between what outsiders had understood to be the demarcation line of John (rhythm guitar)-George (lead guitar)-Paul (bass)-Ringo (drums), The Yardbirds left their mark on McCartney's lead guitar solo in 'Taxman' (from *Revolver*) on which you can detect shades of the abrasive passagework with which Jeff Beck lacquered 'Shapes Of Things', The Yardbirds then-current hit 45.

Above all, however, Paul listened hard to black music. "Paul loves Motown," Michael Jackson would observe when he and McCartney were friends. "He also loves gut music: early, early American black music like Elmore James – but if you want to see him smile, just start talking to him about 1960s Motown. He says he was a fan like everybody else – and since those years were really important to his career, his memories are very sharp, very sensitive about that time."[6]

Tamla-Motown, a black label based in Detroit, had manoeuvred its first fistful of releases into the US Hot 100 in 1960, beginning with Barrett Strong's 'Money (That's What I Want)'. By the mid-1960s, however, Motown – along with "soul" discs on other labels, notably Stax, its Deep South rival – was being saturation-plugged into the UK Top 50 by pirate radio. Nevertheless, as well as hits by the likes of James Brown, The Supremes, The Righteous Brothers, The Miracles, Nina Simone and Wilson Pickett, McCartney and others in the know were also *au fait* with both the back catalogue and the latest by even old timers such as The Drifters, Ray Charles, Fats Domino, Chris Kenner and Bobby Bland. Newer entries in what had once been called the "sepia" charts in the USA included The Soul Sisters' 'I Can't Stand It', Brenda Holloway's 'Every Little Bit Hurts' and further erudite gems that were infiltrating the portfolios of R&B units in Britain, now looking and sounding dangerously like straight pop groups.

While it was hip to say you preferred the black blueprints (or white in the exception of the "blue-eyed soul" of The Righteous Brothers), all kinds of British recording acts, famous and obscure, were trying on soul for size. 'I Can't Stand It' and 'Every Little Bit Hurts' had been thrust out as consecutive Spencer Davis Group A-sides as James Brown's 'I'll Go Crazy' was for the Untamed, and 'You've Lost That Lovin' Feelin'' for Cilla Black – while The First Gear had a go at Dobie Gray's 'The In Crowd', and The Fourmost heisted The Four Tops's 'Baby I Need Your Loving'. The Hollies were planning to cover the Tops's 'Reach Out I'll Be There' purely for the European market if the original missed – as Cliff Bennett And The Rebel Rousers were to do with Sam and Dave's 'Hold On I'm Coming'.

On the bill of the German leg of The Beatles' final world tour in 1966, Bennett and his band's set contained 'Got To Get You Into My Life', presented to Cliff in a dressing room one night by Paul McCartney on guitar and vocal, and John Lennon dah-dahing a horn section. Whereas The Beatles had attempted soul on disc with such as 'Money', 'Please Mr Postman' and The Miracles' 'You Really Got A Hold On Me' (all on *With The Beatles*) this new offering was a Lennon–McCartney original – "one of Paul's best songs,"[3] said John – in the more ebullient of Motown or Stax's house styles. Produced by McCartney and coupled with Bennett's self-penned 'Baby Each Day', this "best song I ever recorded" was to be Cliff's biggest smash, coming within an ace of Number One in Britain.

"When John and I first started writing songs," conceded Paul, "everything was a nick. Now that's a tip for budding songwriters. We pinched ideas from records all the time. There's nothing immoral or dishonest about it because the imitation's only a way of getting started. Like, you might hear 'Please Mr Postman' by The Marvelettes, and be knocked out by it, and want to do something in that style – so you could start with a line like, 'Sorry, Mr Milkman...' By the time the song's finished, you've probably got rid of the first line anyway. Maybe it doesn't sound even remotely like The Marvelettes either, but it's got you going, acted as the spark. For example, in my mind, 'Hey Jude' is a nick from The Drifters. It doesn't sound like them or anything, but I know that the verse, with these two chords repeating over and over, came when I was fooling around playing 'Save The Last Dance For Me' on guitar."[7]

The circle remained unbroken with Beatles numbers on a Supremes album, 1965's *With Love From Us To You*, and respective revivals of 'Eleanor Rigby' and 'Lady Madonna' by Ray Charles and Fats Domino. In 1967, Charles also did 'Yesterday', which, lasting a month low in the UK Top 50, couldn't have hoped to match Matt Monro's feat two years earlier.

The rainy winter that welded 1965 to 1966 had been party time too for The Overlanders with their Paul Friswell's contention that they "did Lennon and McCartney a favour"[3] via a faithful if unsolicited reproduction of 'Michelle', McCartney's bilingual ballad from The Beatles' *Rubber Soul* album. Friswell's cheek was mitigated when it became the first xerox of a Beatles LP track to top the UK singles chart.

'Michelle' suited the charitable Overlanders, a UK beat group long due a re-assessment as pioneers of folk-rock – and it was attitudes towards this genre that illustrated a major artistic difference between John and Paul. Lennon was fond of Bob Dylan, but McCartney had preferred Paul Simon, a New Yorker then doing the rounds of British folk clubs. 1965's *The Paul Simon Songbook* LP by this singing guitarist caught on with those who'd found Dylan too harsh or were shaking baffled heads now that he was taking the stage with a solid-body Stratocaster and a combo who used to back Canadian rock 'n' roller Ronnie Hawkins. Dylan's records reflected this as Simon's did the "poetic" gentleness that the writer of 'Blowin' In The Wind' had buried in alienating surreality and amplification.

Simon had still been in Britain when 'The Sound Of Silence', an opus with Art Garfunkel, was suddenly at Number One in the States. It almost did the same for The Bachelors in the UK chart, better placed as they were to plug their version on the domestic media. However, Simon and Garfunkel's original 'Homeward Bound' won the day against a cover by The Quiet Five. As this Bournemouth quintet had still spent a fortnight in the Top 50 with it, surely a revitalisation of this trendy songwriter's 'Richard Cory' could restore Them's broken fortunes. Decca even cancelled a single of 'Richard Cory' by The Animals to give their ailing Irish blood-brothers an unobstructed passage, but, with no airplay or actively functioning group to nourish it, Them's 'Richard Cory' flopped.

Them had made hay during what had come to be known as the "British Invasion" of North America, which may be dated from The Beatles' landing in Kennedy airport on 8 February 1964 with 'I Wanna Hold Your Hand' at Number One in the Hot 100. To the chagrin of The Four Seasons, The Beach Boys and other US acts on the same labels John, Paul, George and Ringo had been propelled by one of the most far-reaching publicity blitzes hitherto known in the record industry. While the intruders swamped the Hot 100, The Beach Boys' resident genius, Brian Wilson, had felt, both threatened and inspired artistically.

"I knew immediately that everything had changed, and that if The Beach Boys were going to survive, we would really have to stay on our toes," Wilson wrote in 2001. "After seeing The Beatles perform, I felt there wasn't much we could do to compete onstage. What we could try to do was make better records than them. My father had always instilled a competitive spirit in me, and I guess The Beatles aroused it."[8]

In reciprocation, *Pet Sounds*, The Beach Boys' most critically acclaimed LP, caused The Beatles' nervous backwards glances – with Paul McCartney citing Wilson as "the real contender"[9] rather than The Rolling Stones. Yet, during one Abbey Road session in 1966, Mal Evans was sent out to purchase *Aftermath*, the new Stones album – because, formidable though Lennon and McCartney's head start was, a year after their first original Stones A-side – 1965's 'The Last Time' – Keith Richards and Mick Jagger had penned all 14 tracks of *Aftermath*, which would net as rich a shoal of cover singles as *Rubber Soul* had done, among them one by The Searchers, who, if surviving Merseybeat's collapse, were finding it hard to crack the Top 50, let alone the Top Ten, nowadays.

If nothing else, The Searchers, Gerry, The Beatles *et al* had put Liverpool on the map. In doing so, the city's art scene garnered more attention than it might have done in the course of a less fantastic decade. In return, Liverpool artists remembered The Beatles at least in paintings like Sam Walsh's *Mike's Brother* (ie Paul McCartney) and *Lennon*[10] – as well as John Edkins's *We Love The Beatles* – shown in a posthumous exhibition at the Bluecoat in 1966. Less specific homage was paid in the ritual spinning of Beatles tracks during intermissions after the Cavern was refurbished that same year to host mainly poetry readings and like *soirées*.

Among recurrent acts now was the mixed-media aggregation known as "The Liverpool Scene"[11], founded by Adrian Henri and – epitomising the passing of the old order – ex-members of beat groups, The Roadrunners and The Clayton Squares. Bringing satirical humour as well as pop music to an audience biased against one or the other, The Liverpool Scene drank from the same pool as fellow latter-day Cavern regulars, The Scaffold who, still containing Paul's Brother, were to harry the UK Top Ten via the vexing catchiness of 'Thank U Very Much' – a response, apparently, to Paul giving Mike a Nikon camera – 'Lily The Pink' and 1974's 'Liverpool Lou'.

Over in Hamburg, there was more of a *fin de siècle* tang in the air, whether Kingsize Taylor on the verge of making despondent tracks back to England to become a Southport butcher or the bunkroom above the Top Ten being vacated for a reunion party after a show at the city's Ernst Merke Halle on 26 June 1966 by The Beatles. They and their entourage had completed dates in Munich and Essen before Hamburg where, just as the populace awoke, they arrived at the main station in a train generally reserved for royalty. Then they were whisked away in a fleet of Mercedes, flanked by a cavalcade of police motor-cyclists, to out-of-town seclusion in Tremsbuttel's Schloss Hotel.

A knees-up at the Top Ten had become impractical but a disguised McCartney and Lennon dared a nostalgic amble along twilit streets, and a few old faces such as Astrid Kirchherr and Bert Kaempfert were allowed past backstage security before showtime for selective reminiscences about the group's past that, through its amazing outcome, had attained flashback grandeur.

Along the Grosse Freiheit, the bands played on. As the age of Aquarius dawned, British beat groups still lingered there: doughty anachronisms still giving 'em 'Some Other Guy' and 'Besame Mucho', even as The Remo Four at the Star-Club and on *Smile!*, their 1967 Germany-only LP, crossed the frontiers between R&B and jazz. Not so adaptable, fellow Scousers Ian And The Zodiacs had followed Kingsize Taylor back to England to expire quietly after turning down 'Even The Bad Times Are Good', which, picked up by Essex's Tremeloes, made the Top Five.

During the global aftermath of domestic Beatlemania, John, Paul, George and Ringo had slumped too – at least as concert performers. Much of it was down to the insufficiently amplified music being drowned by screams, but the malaise was also psychological. It was a typical journeyman musician's memory, but Paul, depressed by the monotony of it all, had glowered from the window of a hotel in Minneapolis and wondered if this was all there was, just like he had in Allerton before opportunities beyond a conventional job like his Dad's had knocked. Imprisoned luxury in Minneapolis was just like imprisoned luxury in Milan. The Coca-Cola tasted exactly the same. If it's Wednesday, it must be Genoa. Box-office receipts could be astronomical, even when shows weren't always the complete sell-outs that they had been in 1964, but, essentially, you were in danger of getting stuck on the same endless highway as that travelled by the olde tyme rock 'n' rollers or black bluesmen of a pre-Beatles epoch.

Now you are on a chartered aeroplane to another stadium that could be anywhere in America. Eyes glazed, brain numb, you could fly forever. The highlight of the day isn't the half-hour lethargies of songs on the boards, but whatever restricted larks presented themselves in between. Contrary to what you read in the papers, you're more likely to drink in a what's-the-best-pint-you've-ever-had? ennui that anything resembling either *Satyricon* or a BBC mock-up of an imagined pop group drugs-and-sex orgy with pushers, groupies and loud-mouthed periphery almost smothering the noise of an interminable four-chord turnaround on an improvised stage.

In tomorrow's dressing room, you'll wait in wearied despair as shiftless equipment changeovers keep the second house in Detroit waiting. The stagehands loaf about, eating sandwiches and smoking. Isolated in the midst of it, what was there left to enjoy about such a debasing job in which, like them, you couldn't wait until knocking-off time?

The Beatles were in a protective bubble away from the shabbier aspects of life on the road. Yet enough concern about the delivery of the show lingered to deject Paul McCartney. It wasn't just fear of seizing up as an entertainer either as, when he finally got to bed, stress-related tension in his bones and muscles might have him lying as rigid as a crusader on a tomb. There was also the disturbing subliminal undertow that, according to the laws of averages and superstition, there was bound to be a major calamity whilst getting from A to B sooner or later – as there'd been for Johnny Kidd, killed in a smash-up near Preston, high-flying Buddy Holly and, in 1964, Jim Reeves, whose career also took a turn for the better with a posthumous UK chart-topper.

That royalties were still rolling in for compositions from 'Love Me Do' onwards was comforting in a way for Paul whenever he contemplated the crueller fate of other artistes – or found the creative process sluggish as it often was during endless centuries of self-loathing in interchangeable hotel suites when boredom had him investigating sound without substance on some new gadget or other.

During the 1966 world tour, the main diversions had been of the worst kind – an international incident in the Philippines when The Beatles had been all but savaged by a howling mob or death threats taken more seriously than any received previously when a comment about Christ by John was construed as "blasphemy" by right-wing sloganisers across the USA.

Yet, how could Paul be displeased with his lot? Even before embarking on this latest public journey, he could have dug his heels in and refused to go in the knowledge that he had enough put away for him and his immediate family to never need to work again. As a recent feature in the *TV Times* had stated: "You're a lucky man, Paul McCartney"[12]. This had been a reference not just to his swelling fortune but his proud courtship of a dashing, flame-headed actress named Jane Asher. She was the first daughter of the quasi-dynastic marriage of eminent Harley Street doctor Sir Richard Asher – and the Honourable Margaret Eliot, a professor at the Guildhall School of Music and Drama. Among her students had been Andrew King, future manager of The Pink Floyd, and a young George Martin.

Six years after he was taken on by EMI, George produced 1956's 'Nellie The Elephant', a giggly Parlophone novelty and *Children's Favourites* perennial by Mandy Miller, star of *Mandy*, an Ealing melodrama about a deaf girl. It was significant too as six-year-old Jane Asher's debut on celluloid. Her mother's connections also assisted a maiden appearance in professional theatre in the title role of *Alice In Wonderland* at the Oxford Playhouse while Jane was still completing her education at Queen's College, just round the corner from the Ashers' five-storey home in Wimpole Street.

When she first caught Paul's eye – backstage at Swinging '63, an all-styles-served-here pop spectacular at the Royal Albert Hall – 17-year-old Jane was in transition between minor child star of stage and screen, and more mature parts, having just spent her first week before the cameras in the horror movie, *The Masque Of The Red Death*. Had she wished, Jane could have urged her

PAUL MCCARTNEY

agent to negotiate a recording contract. A combination of personal vanity and a desire to maximise public exposure had already motivated the similarly placed Mandy Miller, Hayley Mills and Lynn Redgrave to preserve their warblings on disc; Mills racking up a US Top 20 entry with 1961's querulous 'Let's Get Together'.

Jane went no further than commenting on new singles as a panellist on BBC television's *Juke Box Jury*, though she'd been aware of The Beatles since seeing them on *Thank Your Lucky Stars*, plugging 'Please Please Me'. By his own account[13], she was more attracted initially to Mike McCartney, but before the Swinging '63 evening was over, Paul had seen her home and asked for a date.

For the first time in ages, he'd done the running. Compared to the skirt that had solicited him since he'd been famous, nicely spoken Jane was as a chained cathedral Bible to a cheap paperback novelette. She had "class", a maturity beyond her years reflected in a wasp-waisted confidence that had charmed every other male she'd ever known since reaching puberty. Suddenly, Paul was escorting her to the ballet, the opera, the classical theatre and other worlds of culture that were once outside a son of a Liverpool cotton salesman's index of possibilities.

Yet he was a hit with urbanely elegant Margaret Asher, who, affirms Andrew King, "was the one who told McCartney that he ought to go and get his clothes in Savile Row rather than Carnaby Street"[14]. She also invited him to move into the top floor at Wimpole Street for as long as it took for him to find a place of his own, now that The Beatles were in the process of uprooting from Liverpool. This, however, turned out to be as much of a social coup – and more – for Jane's brother Peter as it was for Paul.

As a day pupil at fee-paying Westminster School, Peter had formed an Everly Brothers-esque duo with a chap called Gordon Waller. Unlike others of their kind, this was more than a mere flirtation with pop prior to beavering away in the family business for a decent interval before being voted onto the board of directors, and becoming chairman by the time you were 40.

Peter and Gordon were sound enough to be signed to Columbia, another EMI label in 1964. Through knowing Paul, they were tossed 'World Without Love', a number that had been around since he was a Quarry Man. Any song with "Lennon–McCartney" as the composing credits was almost like a licence to print money then, so after 'World Without Love' had been ousted from Number One in Britain by Roy Orbison's 'It's Over', they were back with smaller chart entries – but chart entries all the same – in two more 1964 A-sides, 'Nobody I Know' and 'I Don't Want To See You Again', penned specially for them by Peter's sister's boyfriend.

Two years later, Paul handed them another opus, 'Woman', with the proviso that it be attributed to the fictitious "Bernard Webb" rather than "Lennon–McCartney", just to see if it would succeed on its more intrinsic merits. With his works now on the supermarket muzak bulletin as well as in the hit parade, Paul had leeway for playful financial experiments.

While 'Woman' tickled the Top 30 at home, it scrambled higher in the States where, if another upper-class duo, Chad and Jeremy from Eton, took the edge off their headway there, Peter and Gordon released five albums to every one in Britain. As a measure of their US eminence, Epic Records put out *Dave Clark Five Versus Peter And Gordon*, an LP on which both acts had one side.

The two were, nevertheless, on the wane by 1966 when the Ashers' lodger moved out to take up residence in a large but unostentatious Regency house along Cavendish Avenue, a convenient five minute stroll from Abbey Road. That same year, Paul also purchased – on Jane's recommendation – a rural bolt-hole where fans and media would have some search to find him.

A 50km (30 mile) stretch of cold, grey sea separated the northeast coast of Ireland from High Park Farm near Campbeltown, the principal settlement on Strathclyde's Mull of Kintyre, a desolate peninsula that, through McCartney, was to become known to a wider public than it might have warranted.

Campbeltown was just large enough for an airport to be a worthwhile commercial venture. Certainly, it was handy for Paul's commuting to and from London, even if this involved changing at Glasgow and was not as fulsome a forum for continuous thought as those long-haul flights across the planet's two largest oceans during The Beatles' final tour.

Jetting back to Britain two days after the last hurrah at San Francisco's Candlestick Park on 29 August 1966, Paul wrestled with occupational as well as personal stock-taking. Composition for The Beatles and others seemed the most potentially rewarding direction for him then, and it had been a false economy not to buy himself an expensive reel-to-reel tape recorder, once "too big and clumsy to lug around"[7], so that he could construct serviceable demos of the ideas – not just songs – that were streaming from him. Blessed with an over-developed capacity to try-try again, he grappled with his muse, drawing from virtually every musical idiom he had ever absorbed; some of them further removed from The Beatles' Hamburg core than any Star-Club bopper could have imagined.

For hours on end at Cavendish Avenue, he'd attack melody, rhyme and less specific fragments of lyrics and music from all angles, and some would start becoming more and more cohesive with each take. This escalating engrossment in recording caused him to splash out on a home studio. Soon, it was feasible – theoretically anyway – for every note of an entire album by Paul McCartney alone to be hand-tooled in this electronic den.

9 *"I'm The Urban Spaceman"*

"I'm alive and well, but if I were dead, I'd be the last to know."

— Paul McCartney[1]

As Peter Asher had derived benefit from his affinity, so Barry Miles, editor of *International Times* (*IT*), did when the cash-strapped underground journal was bailed out with cheques from Barry's pal, Paul McCartney, who also suggested that an interview with him in an early edition would attract advertising from EMI and other record labels. Moreover, when *IT* had been sped on its way with a "happening" on a cold October night in 1966 at London's barn-like Roundhouse auditorium, Paul – dressed as a sheik – milled about with both proto-hippies and celebrities like Michelangelo "Blow Up" Antonioni – the artiest mainstream film director of the mid-1960s – and Marianne Faithfull in a cross between a nun's habit and buttock-revealing mini-skirt.

Thousands more than can have actually have been there were to reminisce about the free sugar-cubes that may or may not have contained LSD; the huge bathtub of jelly; the ectoplasmic light-shows that were part of the feedback-ridden act for The Pink Floyd and The Soft Machine (in days before the definite article was removed from their names) – and the latter's recital being interrupted by what amounted to a simple audience participation number by Yoko Ono, a Japanese-American "concept artist", who'd lately left the New York wing of something called Fluxus. Quarter-page notices of her forthcoming exhibitions surfaced like rocks in the stream in *IT*, but, grimaced *IT* associate John Hopkins, "Yoko Ono's happenings were boring. She was the most boring artist I'd ever met."[2]

Thanks in part to sponsorship from Ono and more powerful allies like McCartney, *IT* was to muddle on into the 1970s, joining forces with *Oz* – regarded spuriously as its "colour supplement" – and the sub-*Rolling Stone Frenz* to produce *FREEk*, a daily news-sheet for the 1970 Isle of Wight pop festival. There then followed a few one-off broadsheets pirated under the *IT* banner, and wanting in terms of constructive journalism and artwork.

In its 1967 to 1968 prime, however, *IT* leaked to back-street newsagents in Dullsville as the provincial sixth-former's vista to what Swinging London was thinking and doing. This was disturbing enough for Frankie Vaughan – who, incidentally, had covered 'Wait' from *Rubber Soul* – to launch a campaign to curtail the spread of the hippy sub-culture. "Hippies are leeches on society"[3], he declared at a public meeting, spurning a flower proffered by one such leech in the audience.

Fellow Scouser McCartney begged to differ: "The straights should welcome the underground because it stands for freedom. It's not strange. It's just new. It's not weird. It's just what's going around."[4] Sometimes, however, it was weird, unless, of course, you'd read the books, seen the films – and sampled the stimulants – necessary for understanding. Paul's *IT* interview, for example, was bloated with gaga truisms such as, "It's difficult when you've learned that everything is just the act and everything is beautiful or ugly, or you like it or you don't. Things are backward or they're forward – and dogs are less intelligent than humans, and suddenly you realise that whilst all of this is right, it's all wrong as well. Dogs aren't less intelligent to dogs, and the ashtray's happy to be an ashtray, and the hang-up still occurs."[5] To a readership uncomprehending, disbelieving or shocked into laughter, he also made the commendably honest admission that "starvation in India doesn't worry me one bit – and it doesn't worry you, if you're honest. You just pose. You don't even know it exists.

You've just seen the charity ads. You can't pretend to me that an ad reaches down into the depths of your soul and actually makes you feel more for these people than, for instance, you feel about getting a new car."[5]

After a field visit to Bangladesh in 1968, born-again Cliff Richard, regarded by then as almost as "straight" as Frankie Vaughan, was to concur with an uncomfortable "I don't pretend I felt any heartache for the people in the Third World or anywhere else for that matter."[6]

Via his management, Richard had been requested to articulate the Christian perspective in *The Process*, mouthpiece of the Church Of The Final Judgement, another publication that went the rounds of sixth-form common rooms. Cliff deigned not to reply, but, in issue number five, dedicated to "Fear", Paul McCartney "was not really afraid of people nor of the world ending or anything like that. It's just fear really, a fear of fear". In parenthesis, Jane Asher confided to the same questioner that she "used to be afraid of the world ending and all that five years ago," but has since "learned not to think about it"[7].

Yet, of all underground periodicals, McCartney's first loyalty was to *IT*. With deceptive casualness, he'd entered the life of Barry Miles, bespectacled, taper-thin and of similar bohemian vintage to Royston Ellis and Johnny Byrne, through Peter Asher. Jane's pop star brother had provided finance for Miles – who encouraged people to address him by his surname then – and John Dunbar, Marianne Faithfull's first husband, to open in January 1966 the Indica Gallery and Bookstore, dealing in merchandise of an avant-garde and fashionably mystical bent. A few months later, *IT* was born in its basement office.

Barry's recollections of his first acquaintance with the Beatle whose biography he was to write 30 years later[8], is worth quoting at length: "Paul helped the bookshop out with some loot occasionally. He made us some wrapping paper, a nice pattern. He just produced a big pile of it one day.

"I knew nothing about rock 'n' roll. When I first met McCartney, I didn't even know which one [of The Beatles] he was. The first time I really had a long talk with him was after Indica had just moved to Southampton Row in March 1966. When we were there, we saw a lot of Paul. He was almost mobbed one day, walking down Duke Street. He came beating on the door and we had to let him in, and there was this great horde of people following him. He'd been out looking for some kind of thread for Jane, who wanted it for a dress she was making.

"I thought it would be very good for The Beatles to know about avant-garde music – so I persuaded Paul to come along to a lecture by Luciano Berio at the Italian Institute. We got there and sat down, and almost immediately the press came bursting in with flashlights and so on. That was the kind of thing that happened all the time."[9]

Miles and McCartney became close friends to the degree of an insistence by the millionaire Beatle that he stand every round whenever they, John Dunbar, Peter Asher, John Hopkins *et al* spent an evening in one of few watering holes these days where Paul wouldn't have to listen with heavy patience to any stranger's starstruck twaddle.

As one who'd mixed with fustian intellectuals in Liverpool and Hamburg, McCartney wasn't ignorant of many of the well-read Barry's points of reference, and could hold his own amid the beer-fuelled polemics. Yet, his understanding of what literature was worth reading and what was not became more acute through knowing Miles and the Indica crowd. "Miles was a great catalyst," he agreed. "He had the books. We [The Beatles] had a great interest, but we didn't have the books. Once he saw that we were interested, particularly me because I used to hang out with him, he showed us new things – and I'd had a great period of being avant-garde, going off to France in disguise, taking in a lot of movies, which I later showed to Antonioni: very bizarre, but it seemed exciting at the time."[9]

Whenever he was under no immediate obligation to return to Cynthia and their infant son in the Surrey stockbroker belt, John Lennon would tag along too. Nevertheless, he digested many of the avant-gardenings second-hand. "John was so constricted living out in Weybridge," lamented Paul. "He'd come to London and say, 'What've you been doing?', and I'd say, I went out last night and saw Luciano Berio. That was quite cool. I've got this new Stockhausen record. Check this out. I think John actually said, 'I'm jealous of you'. He just needed to get out of Weybridge, watching telly. It wasn't his wife's fault. She just didn't understand how free he needed to be."[9]

Unhobbled by marriage and fatherhood, Paul's own evenings in at Cavendish Avenue might have found him flipping the three channels on his television before choosing to give the Stockhausen LP a spin. It got him as "gone" as a fakir in a trance. Reports of further self-improvements would raise puffy smiles of condescension from those for whom "culture" was second nature (and "pop music" and its practitioners beneath contempt). Such snobs may have assumed that Paul was exhibiting an observed reverence for what he felt he ought to appreciate, but didn't quite know why. Magnifying the gap between themselves and the common herd, they would not believe that one such as him could glimpse infinity during *Mikrophonie I* and *II*. Yet McCartney's devouring of such new experiences went further than just shallow dropping of names. Indeed, some of it was to infiltrate The Beatles' post-Candlestick Park output.

However, that the group was off the road didn't mean that McCartney was metamorphosing into an emaciated ascetic. His recreational pursuits were both far from sedentary and not always to do with intellectual curiosity. He and the other Beatles were as prone to untoward nonsense involving drugs and girls as any other in an elite of pop *conquistadores* whose disconnection with life out in Dullsville was so complete that their only contact with it most of the time was through personal managers, gofers – and narcotics dealers.

McCartney had been the last Beatle to sample LSD. "Paul is a bit more stable than George and I," explained John, "It was a long time before he took it, and then there was the big announcement."[10] If a latecomer, Paul was the loudest of all the group in the defence of LSD – "acid" – as a chemical handmaiden to creativity: "We only use one tenth of our brains. Just think what we could accomplish if we could tap that hidden part."[11]

You only had to tune in to the music wafting from California where LSD's paranormal sensations were being translated on the boards and on record by Jefferson Airplane, Clear Light, The Grateful Dead and further front-runners of the flower-power sound of the Haight-Ashbury – "Hashbury" – district of San Francisco. Once the musical wellspring of little beyond a few jazz clubs, the city was about to become as vital a pop capital as Liverpool had been.

During its 15-month Summer of Love, the proferring of sex and marijuana "joints" became a gesture of free-spirited friendliness, while the mind-warping effects of the soon-to-be outlawed LSD possessed its "Cavern", the Fillmore West's cavorting berserkers, shrouded by flickering strobes, tinted incense fumes and further audio-visual aids that were part-and-parcel of simulated psychedelic experience.

London sometimes surpassed this with events like the inauguration of *IT* at the Roundhouse, and, another *IT* benefit, the Fourteen Hour Technicolor Dream at Alexandra Palace on 29 April 1967 where The Move, The Pink Floyd, Tomorrow, John Children, The Flies (who urinated over the front row), the omnipresent Yoko Ono, you name 'em, appeared one after the other before tranced hippies and other updated beatniks, either cross-legged or "idiot dancing".

During the merest prelude to becoming a serious chart contender, the most exotic darling of the London underground around this time was Jimi Hendrix, a singing guitarist who'd been "discovered" walking an artistic tightrope without a safety net in New York's half-empty Cafe Wha?, and had been brought over to England to become almost the last major icon to come in from the outside of the British beat boom.

"The very first time I saw Jimi at the Bag O' Nails," recalled McCartney, "it wasn't who, but what is this? And it was Jimi. There weren't many people in the club, but at the next gig, me, Eric Clapton and Pete Townshend were standing in this very packed audience, all come to pay homage to the new god in town."[12]

On Paul's recommendation, Hendrix was booked for a watershed performance at the International Pop Music Festival in Monterey – an overground "coming out" of what was occurring a few miles up the coast in San Francisco and further afield. It was here that the fated Jimi's showmanship as much as his innovative fretboard fireworks – and his English accompanists' quick-witted responses to them – spurred a gallop to international stardom.

A contrasting surprise hit at Monterey was Ravi Shankar, the Indian sitar virtuoso, whose *West Meets East* album with the equally acclaimed violinist Yehudi Menuhin was issued just before 'Norwegian Wood' and 'Paint It Black' brought the sitar to a pop audience – though Shankar had been accused already by longtime devotees of "selling out" and of emasculating his art with Grammy-winning collaborations such as this.

Just as George Harrison had been the principal advocate of the application of Indian musical theories and instrumentation – and spiritual beliefs – to The Beatles' oeuvre, so McCartney was chiefly responsible for at least superficial use of the pioneering tonalities of Berio, Stockhausen *et al* in such as 'Carnival Of Light', a 14-minute tape collage that was the group's contribution to another Roundhouse "happening" early in 1967. The influence of the post serialist composers was evidenced too in 'Tomorrow Never Knows' in which only a repeated tom-tom rataplan and Lennon's battered lead vocal endowment on its trace of melody put it into the realms of pop at all.

On the same album, 1966's *Revolver*, McCartney shone brightest on 'Eleanor Rigby' – "Paul's baby, and I helped with the education of the child,"[13] quipped Lennon. She was, however, destined to die alone – with, seemingly, no one to welcome her through the pearly gates. That was how Eleanor had always lived until she expired in the church that was her only comfort, and was buried "along with her name" with just Father McKenzie, another lonely person, who darns his own socks, in attendance. Old maids would make further appearances in the corporate and solo canon of The Beatles – almost all through the offices of McCartney, who penned the bulk of 'Lady Madonna' and all of 1971's 'Another Day'.

Among acts that covered 'Eleanor Rigby' were The Vanilla Fudge – described in *IT* as "molten lead on vinyl"[14] – and supper-club crooner Johnny Mathis, thus demonstrating how it – and 'Here There And Everywhere', 'Penny Lane', 'When I'm Sixty Four' and further instantly familiar paeons mainly from McCartney – walked a safe and accessible line between the opposing styles of the day. Mellow sunshine rather than mind-zapping thunderstorm, they fitted perfectly into a period in which schmaltz was represented in the charts as much as psychedelia.

Now a vocalist of sub-Engelbert Humperdinck stamp, Malcolm Roberts was to rack up enough readers' votes in the *New Musical Express*'s popularity poll for 1969 to rank just below John Lennon in the "male vocalist" section. Likewise, for all its brush-strokes of surreal imagery, 'Penny Lane' nestled comfortably among easy-listening standards like Stevie Wonder's 'I Was Made To Love Her', Jose Feliciano-via-The Doors's 'Light My Fire', 'Brown-Eyed Girl' by former Them vocalist Van Morrison, Fifth Dimension's 'Up Up And Away', gently reproachful 'Pleasant Valley Sunday' by The Monkees and flower-power anthems like 'San Francisco' from Scott McKenzie.

'When I'm Sixty-Four', a recreation of a Jim Mac Jazz Band-type refrain, was the item that most fitted this brief on *Sgt Pepper's Lonely Hearts Club Band*. The most celebrated of all Beatles' long-players had sprung from late Abbey Road hours of cross-fades, stereo panning, intricately wrought funny noises and similarly fiddly console minutiae when the team were at the forefront of a trend for "concept albums" (which included "rock operas" and like *magnum opi*) – though others weren't far behind.

Mere weeks after *Sgt Pepper* reached the shops, 'Grocer Jack', a kiddie-chorused excerpt from *A Teenage Opera*, composed by Mark Wirtz, once a would-be German Elvis, was in the UK singles list. Nevertheless, while this built up anticipation for an associated album and stage show, the 'Sam' follow-up barely rippled the Top 40, and another 45rpm clip didn't even "bubble under". As a result, investors lost heart and the opera was abandoned.

Joe Average has heard even less of a concept LP that was realised by Paul McCartney late in 1965. As reported in the *Disc And Music Echo* gossip column[15], a few copies were pressed as Christmas presents for just the other Beatles and Jane Asher. It was said to be an in-joking send-up of a radio variety show with the irrepressible Paul as a one-man compère, singer, instrumentalist, comedian and all-purpose entertainer. If it ever existed, the roots of *Sgt Pepper* may lie in this *ultima thule*, this unobtainable prize for collectors of Beatles artefacts.

If one ever turned up in a memorabilia auction, it might bolster McCartney's assertion that it was he who came up with the basic notion of *Sgt Pepper*, "giving The Beatles alter-egos simply to get a different approach"[8], on a return flight from a holiday in Kenya in November 1966 – though he was to aver that "only later in the recording did Neil Aspinall [The Beatles' personal assistant] have the idea of repeating the 'Sgt Pepper' song, and The Beatles and George Martin began to use linking tracks and segues to pull it together."[8]

The *Sgt Pepper* era remains the principal source of countless hours of enjoyable time-wasting for those who collate "hidden messages" in the grooves and packagings of Beatles discs. While this is a subject worthy of 1,000 university theses, we can only scratch the surface here by attending to the most enduring so-called communiqué that supported a rumour that Paul McCartney had been beheaded in a road accident on 9 November 1966 and replaced by a *Doppleganger*. All that actually happened was that he cut his lip that day in a mishap whilst riding a moped, but surely you can hear John say "I buried Paul" in a daft voice in the last seconds of 'Strawberry Fields Forever' – and at the end of 'I'm So Tired' on 1968's "White Album" (*The Beatles*), doesn't he mumble "Paul is dead. Bless him, bless him, bless him..."?

None of them were hits, but there was soon an impressive array of "Paul Is Dead" singles behind counters. Penetrating the crowded airwaves then were the likes of 'Brother Paul' by Billy Shears and the All-Americans, 'Saint Paul' from Terry Knight – future manager of Grand Funk Railroad – and Zacharias and his Tree People's 'We're All Paul Bearers (Parts One And Two)'. In a vocational slow moment after 'Light My Fire' in 1968, Jose Feliciano issued a 'Paul' 45 too. As an ex-Beatle, Lennon's snigger was almost audible when, not content with airing grievances against McCartney in the press, he sniped at him on disc in 1971 with 'How Do You Sleep?' from *Imagine*, confirming that Billy, Terry, Zacharias *et al* were "right when they said that you were dead".

Long before The Beatles' bitter freedom from each other, The Moody Blues had been falling apart too. During a commercially dangerous vinyl silence of not quite a year, Tony Secunda had been replaced as their manager by Brian Epstein, now nowhere as painstaking or energetic as he'd been when he'd taken on The Beatles in 1961. Therefore, with Epstein increasingly less available, and Decca only interested in consistent chartbusters, the group had been obliged to drastically reduce booking fees and soon inevitable cracks had appeared. First out was bass player Clint Warwick "because he was the only one married with a kid," elucidated Denny Laine. "For me, that was the beginning of the end. It changed the whole concept of the band. Because it levelled out with the Moodies – yet another tour of Germany, that sort of thing – it all got a bit insecure."

The vacancy was filled by a former member John Lodge who, according to Denny, "had had the job originally, but his girlfriend didn't want him to move out of Birmingham". Yet so anxious was Lodge for the Big Time that he sold some of his equipment to finance a pending tour of Europe where it was still feasible for the outfit to break even.

The tour took place without Laine who, anticipating Brian Wilson's role in The Beach Boys, was concentrating on writing and studio work before concluding that he couldn't be worse off solo. The ailing Moody Blues, nonetheless, were to be revitalised with 1967's 'Nights In White Satin', the hit 45 from *Days Of Future Passed*, an ambitious concept album with orchestra. From then on, it was plain sailing as album after platinum album refined a magniloquent style so nebulous in scope that such diverse units as Yes, King Crimson, ELO and Roxy Music were all to be cited irregularly as variants of The Moody Blues blueprint.

As for Denny Laine, "I was adrift for a bit. I went to Spain for two years in a village in the house of an American guy who was also studying flamenco. I came back with the idea of doing a folky, acoustic-style thing, but with strings. For a few months, he was backed by The Electric String Band, an amplified string quartet from the Royal Academy of Music – "technicians", Denny called them – plus a drummer and electric bass guitarist. "It was a bit of a nightmare actually," Denny admits now, "because the technicians were all so busy doing other things. It was fun for them, but they didn't find it easy. They were all soloists, really good players. A lot of good ideas came from them."

The advanced nature of Laine's singles with this ensemble, 'Say You Don't Mind' and 'Too Much In Love', was demonstrated when Colin Blunstone's exact copy of the former crept into the Top 20 in 1972. However, getting a satisfactory concert sound for The Electric String Band was problematic. Yet a final engagement, supporting Jimi Hendrix at London's Saville Theatre – in which Brian Epstein had a controlling interest – "went really well," in its leader's estimation, "and a lot of people from the business were there. Then the string players had to go to Russia to tour and things drifted off again."

In need of careers advice, Denny arrived on the off-chance at his distant manager's Belgravia doorstep during 1967's August bank holiday. He received no answer to his knock. Inside, Brian Epstein was expiring in a drug-induced slumber.

He was found on the Sunday afternoon. At around 4pm, eight-year-old Ruth McCartney, daughter of Jim McCartney's second wife, Angela Williams, had been visiting her step-brother and his Beatles in Bangor, a university town where the Welsh mainland nears the island of Anglesey. She and Angela had been bidding him farewell when he'd been requested to take an urgent telephone call. She was to learn its content on arrival back home in Hoylake, over the river from Liverpool, two hours later. The telephone there was ringing too. George Harrison's mum was on the line with an example of how the story had become confused. Brian, she told Angela, had shot himself.

By then, the truth The Beatles had refused to avow had inflicted itself. They could no longer not believe it. An attempt to soothe their anguish had been made by the Maharishi Mahesh Yogi, the Indian guru who'd been running the weekend course in transcendental meditation that, at George Harrison's urging, they'd all been attending at the University of Bangor.

The appeal of a community more enclosed than the innermost pop clique was attractive enough for The Beatles to study meditation further at the Maharishi's yoga-ashram – theological college – in the Himalayas the following spring. Though politicians might covet the pop deity's unlooked-for manipulation of widespread opinion, a charismatic head of a supposed spiritual movement is often on a par with the most adored guitar god – but with a stronger self-certainty about everything he says and does. How else are orthodox religions able to maintain mass subscription to tenets that coming from a street-corner crank would draw only jeers from the few who stop to listen? What else explained the ascendancy of the likes of Sun Myung Moon and, before his disgrace, the US evangelist Jimmy Lee Swaggart over their followers? In a Hindu city, would the notion that communion wafers and wine turn into the body and blood of Christ forestall mockery? Conversely, what is the Christian party-line on the Hindu ascetic's ingenious modes of self-torture? What about tarot cards, not walking under ladders and black cat bones? Spirituality – or, if you prefer, superstition – has less to do with logic than what St Denis held as "perfect unreasonability".

Even prior to his association with Indica, Paul McCartney had explored Buddhism and Hinduism as well as mystical and esoteric Christianity, but had not been completely convinced by any of them. Furthermore, while he continued to practice meditation, even designating a room in his house for that specific purpose, his jet-legged return from India was a fortnight ahead of George and John, and his most piquant memory of the visit one of a solitary session on a flat roof when "I was like a feather over a hot-air pipe. I was just suspended by this hot air, which had something to do with the meditation – and it was a very blissful thing."[16]

Back to the day-to-day mundanities of being a Beatle, Paul was still living down *Magical Mystery Tour*, the made-for-television movie – and their first major post-Epstein project – of which he'd been both the instigator and main producer. To disaffected observers – and, indeed, to John, George and Ringo now and then, his methodology had appeared slap-dash – as if he was making it up as he went along, which he was much of the time. Concordant with the bare bones of the "plot" – summarised by the title – there was much spontaneity, improvisation and scenes that seemed a good idea at the time. Worse, though some clutter fluttered onto the cutting-room floor, its focus still remained vague – but maybe that was almost the point.

The finale was a big-production number, 'Your Mother Should Know', written by Paul, and recorded the week before Brian

Epstein's sudden passing. Like 'When I'm Sixty-Four', it was at one with a fad for olde tyme whimsy that had prevailed in the hit parade since 1966's chart-topping 'Winchester Cathedral' – all vicarage fête brass and posh megaphoned vocals – by The New Vaudeville Band. In its wake came such as Whistling Jack Smith's 'I Was Kaiser Bill's Batman', boutiques like 'I Was Lord Kitchener's Valet' and experiments – by The Beatles too – with dundreary side-whiskers, raffish moustaches and similar depilatory caprices that prompted a Mancunian costumier to manufacture fake ones so those without the wherewithal to sprout their own could still "Make The Scene With These Fantastic New Raves".

On the strength of their debut 45, 'My Brother Makes The Noises For The Talkies', The Bonzo Dog Doo-Dah Band ran in the same pack, but, as it turned out, they defied entirely adequate categorisation – except that, though the outfit's *raison d'être* was centred on getting laughs, they were more Scaffold than Freddie And The Dreamers in that they conveyed in pop terms that strain of fringe-derived comedy that was to culminate with *Monty Python's Flying Circus*.

"In 1966, we decided to expand our style," explained Neil Innes, who was, with Vivian Stanshall, the group's principal composer. "We did 1950s rock 'n' roll, flower-power, anything went – and started writing our own stuff. It only took a year to develop. If it got a laugh, it stayed in the act. On the cabaret circuit and then the colleges, and we were earning as much as any group with a record in the charts. We were liked by people like Eric Clapton as a band most of them would liked to have been in – even though we were never mega recording artists."

Their eventual modicom of Top Ten success – with an Innes opus, 'I'm The Urban Spaceman' – was testament to courage in remaining true to their strange star, but it was, however, secondary to an eye-stretching stage act, which earned them both a cameo in *Magical Mystery Tour*, and a weekly turn on the anarchic ITV children's series, *Do Not Adjust Your Set*.

"I wrote 'Urban Spaceman' in one afternoon," said Innes with quiet pride, "Our producer, Gerry Bron, was fairly strict about studio time, and Viv Stanshall complained about this to Paul McCartney, who he'd met down the Speakeasy. Paul came along to the 'Urban Spaceman' session, and his presence obliged Gerry to give us more time. Paul also had great recording ideas – like double-tracking the drums, and putting a microphone in each corner of the playing area to catch Viv's garden hose with trumpet mouthpiece as he whirled it round his head.

"I was quite keen to do a follow-up that was sort of humorous but still catchy. We selected 'Mr Apollo', which was once like that. Most of it was mine, but Viv got hold of it, and it ended up well over acceptable single length – because it wasn't until 'Hey Jude' that you could get away with it."

10 *"Goodbye"*

> "She wore impeccably applied make-up, including long,
> fluttering false eye-lashes. It wasn't long before she zeroed
> in on Paul."
>
> – *Peter Brown*[1]

In Brian Epstein's final months, the same questions had come up
over and over again. Plain fact was that the contract was up for
renewal anyway, and, according to hearsay, his stake in Beatles'
affairs would have been reduced, though they wouldn't have carried
on totally without him.

Therefore, though Brian might not have approved of Apple
Corps, had he lived, he probably wouldn't have been able to do
much to prevent it. On paper, nevertheless, it made sound sense,
combining a potential means of nipping a huge tax demand in the
bud and a diverting enterprise that could equal profit as well as
fun. This was a common ploy of wealthy pop stars down the ages,
whether Frank Sinatra's Reprise record company, Who singer Roger
Daltry's trout farm, Dolly Parton's "Dollywood" amusement park
or Reg Presley of The Troggs's Four Corners Vision film company.

Apple Corps was intended to house all manner of artistic,
scientific and merchandising ventures under The Beatles' self-
managed aegis. By 1970, however, it had been whittled down to
Apple Records, a label whose releases were monitored by EMI
with all kinds of middlemen taking a cut.

Yet, once upon a time, Apple had been visualised as the most
public expression of the underground's "alternative economy",

but as much its embodiment as the free open-air rock concerts that pocked post-flower power Britain's recreational calendar. So common and large-scale were these altruistic happenings in London – as instanced by the Blind Faith "supergroup" and then The Rolling Stones in Hyde Park's natural amphitheatre and Procol Harum near the tumulus in Parliament Hill Fields – that reaction when scanning billings in *IT* or *Time Out* had shifted from a sardonic "Yeah, but how much is it to get in?" to a jaded "Hmmm, is that all that's on this time?"

Motives, as always, were suspect. The Stones' amassing of an audience of over half-a-million – the largest assembly for any cultural event ever contained by the capital – was, sneered cynics, great publicity, helped sell records and provided raw footage for a TV film. Apple, nevertheless, seemed at first to be genuinely if romantically anxious to give a leg up to deserving causes from the pottering weekend inventor whose converted garage is a grotto of bubbling test-tubes, electrical circuits and Heath Robinson-like devices, to smocked and bereted sculptors chipping at lumps of concrete in upstairs bedrooms, to night porters composing symphonies that would otherwise never be performed.

The Beatles were on such a person's side. They alone understood the difficulties of gaining recognition and finance, having had to struggle for so long themselves before George Martin lent an ear to their efforts. In addition, with Barry Miles the Aaron to his Moses in *IT*, "Paul McCartney asked me to point out that Apple exists to help, collaborate with and extend all existing organisations as well as start new ones. It is not in competition with any of the underground organisations. The concept, as outlined by Paul, is to establish an underground company above ground as big as Shell, BP or ICI, but, as there is no profit motive, The Beatles' profits go first to the combined staff and then are given away to the needy."[2]

If nothing else, Apple was wonderful foolishness. Governed by overweening expressive ambition, it flung indiscriminate cash at the talented, the hopeful and the hopeless until alarming bank statements dictated otherwise. The record company, even with The Beatles as its flagship act, cut back too. Recording manager Peter Asher dispensed straightaway with its Zapple subsidiary for indulgences like George Harrison's knob-twiddling *Electronic Sounds*, and spoken-word items such as a jettisoned 24 album series of in-concert monologues by the late Lenny Bruce who, for those outside his native USA who've ever heard of him, is remembered vaguely for a brand of blue *humor* (not humour) that may appeal to anyone who prefers *This Is Spinal Tap* to *The Glam Metal Detectives*.

Apple's chief non-Beatle triumph was Mary Hopkin, whose records were produced – and, in the case of 1969's 'Goodbye', composed – by McCartney. An 18-year-old soprano, Hopkin was known already in the parallel dimension that is the Welsh pop scene. Until a winning appearance on ITV's *Opportunity Knocks*, her abilities had been directed at the Welsh-speaking market mostly via slots on BBC Wales's weekly pop showcase, *Disc A Dawn*. She began making headway east of Offa's Dyke after fashion model Twiggy brought her to McCartney's attention.

At her father's insistence, some of her B-sides were in Welsh, but her debut Apple A-side, 'Those Were The Days', was in pop's international tongue, and thus began Hopkin's three-year chart run in fine style by spending most of 1968's autumn at Number One after ending the two week reign of seven-minute 'Hey Jude' (which, nevertheless, lasted over two months at the top in the States). Mary's attainment was all the more remarkable in the light of a shorter rival version by the better-known Sandie Shaw, who was still wished "the best of luck" in an Apple press release.

John Lennon had been put in charge of another female vocalist in which Apple had been "interested". Unlike John Hopkins, he hadn't found Yoko Ono boring at all, very much the opposite. As well as taking the place of Cynthia in his bed, Yoko also superseded Paul as a lovestruck John's artistic confrère and filler of the void left by Stuart Sutcliffe as a adjunct personality. She was a mate in every sense; John nutshelling their bond with: "It's just handy to fuck your best friend."[3]

As it had been with Astrid and Stuart, Yoko and John began styling their hair and dressing the same. Paralleling Astrid too, Yoko was the older and, on the face of it, more emotionally independent partner. Through her catalytic influence, the world and his wife were confronted with a John Lennon they'd never known before, one for whom The Beatles would soon no longer count any more than they had for Stuart after he'd made up his mind to return to painting.

Apart from Cynthia, how could anyone begrudge Yoko and John their joy? Many did after *The News Of The World* front-paged the rear cover of *Unfinished Music No 1: Two Virgins*, the couple's first album together. It was a back view of themselves hand-in-hand – and stark naked. The front photograph was too indecent for a self-called family newspaper.

This, like the rest of John and Yoko's many funny-peculiar pranks in the name of art, didn't "give me any pleasure"[4] wrote Paul later, but he showed at least cursory solidarity by accompanying John and his inseparable Yoko to an appointment with EMI chairman Sir Joseph Lockwood to discuss the distribution of *Two Virgins*. He also allowed the inclusion of a shot that almost-but-not-quite revealed all of himself too in the pull-out poster that was part of the "White Album" packaging.

It had been snapped by Paul's new girlfriend from New York, Linda Eastman. Ultimately, he'd been unlucky with Jane Asher – to whom he'd been engaged since January 1968. She'd made an unexpected entry into the Cavendish Avenue master bedroom where another young lady – a New Yorker too – clutched a hasty counterpane to herself. Paul had always been incorrigibly unfaithful; it was one of the perks of his job, but this was the first time he'd been uncovered. Nevertheless, he and Jane weren't over immediately. Indeed, they'd seemingly patched things up when they attended Mike McCartney's wedding in July, but the damage had been done, and was permanent.

A free agent again, Paul chased a few women until they caught him – albeit only fleetingly, but there was no one for the press to take seriously for several months – though it would have been quite a scoop had a tabloid editor got wind of an incident at the Bag O' Nails when McCartney attempted to chat up Rolling Stone Bill Wyman's Swedish sweetheart, Astrid.[5]

It was in the same London night club that Linda Eastman had introduced herself to Paul in 1967, shivering with pleasure at the smile he flashed from the other side of the room. He in turn was to be impressed by a disarming self-sufficiency that would not permit him to be bothered by the fact that she was a divorcée – and the mother of a six-year-old, Heather. In any case, it would have been hypocritical of him not to have been morally generous.

From a family of prominent showbusiness attorneys, Linda was quite accustomed to the company of professional entertainers. This was compounded by her skills as a freelance photographer, and her social intercourse with pop musicians visiting or resident in New York.

Not all such encounters were cordial. Late one 1967 evening in Louie's Bar, a Greenwich Village hang-out with sawdust on the floor and a juke-box, she was one of a clique that included singer-songwriter Tim Buckley, whose introspective melancholy was jazzier than most. He was also something of a boor, bragging later of seducing Linda – who'd taken publicity shots of him in a local zoo earlier in the week – after he'd been boozing heavily that night at Louie's, and had been spectacularly sick as a result. How could she resist?

Apparently, she did – which may be why an ill-natured Buckley also told his guitarist, Lee Underwood, that, following a Rolling Stones press conference in New York, "Mick [Jagger] spent a night with her, and she wrote about it in an American teen magazine."[6] If it ever existed, the article in question has not come to light – nor proof that any liaison between Jagger and Eastman went further than a wistful embrace beneath the stars at the conclusion of a night out.

Linda was on good terms too with The Animals. It was on an assignment at the Harlem Apollo for *Ebony* magazine that she made a lifelong friend of their singer, Eric Burdon. "Linda showed me how to move through that city of cities," enthused Eric. "It was there that we got our first tabs of LSD on the floor of Ondine's night club. Never a participant, Linda was always there to make sure we got home safely after tripping the light fantastic in our favourite place, Central Park. One morning as Barry Jenkins [drummer] and I marvelled at the skyscraper walls that loomed over the city's green sanctuary, Linda snapped away, capturing some of my favourite images of that time."[7]

Another Animal, Chas Chandler had been Linda's escort at the Bag O' Nails for the concert by Georgie Fame And The Blue Flames that was also the occasion she met Paul. Two years later, she was gripping the Beatle arm with a bright, proprietorial grin, and there was less anger than amusement from Heather's father, a geophysicist named Melvin See, when his daughter and ex-wife moved into Cavendish Avenue less than six months after the split with Jane Asher.

Beatles traditionalists did not regard this upheaval as profound an erosion of Fab Four magic as John's estrangement from Cynthia, and the entrenchment of that dreadful Yoko – with whom he was now recording chartbusting singles with an ad-hoc Beatles splinter group, The Plastic Ono Band. Her baleful presence at Abbey Road had exuded too from the needle-time on the "White Album", most notably in 'Revolution 9', dismissed by most as interminable musical scribble. In tacit concurrence, it had been faded out after Paul had been duty bound to mention it without critical comment during his track-by-track discussion of the album – all four sides of it – on Radio Luxembourg on the Friday in November when it was released.

As fans may have expected, Paul had been responsible for the track that mirrored *Rubber Soul*'s 'Michelle' as the biggest-selling cover from the "White Album", namely 'Ob-la-di Ob-la-da', inspired, so one story goes, by the Jamaican patois of Georgie Fame's percussionist, Speedy Acquaye. In March 1969, a Benny Hill television sketch centred on a disc jockey obliged to host an early morning radio show after a night on the tiles. Exacerbating his hungover queasiness was a listener's request for "any platter by Grapefruit, Cream – or Marmalade!" This gag was an illustration of the latter outfit's chart-topping success with a shrewd Yuletide copy of 'Ob-la-di Ob-la-da'. As four of this quintet were Glaswegian, they celebrated by miming it on *Top Of The Pops* in national costume: the Clydeside boys resplendent in sporrans, gorgets, clan tartans *et al* with their English drummer in redcoat gear as a reminder of Culloden.

Each new edition of the weekly programme hammered home to Denny Laine the extent to which his fortunes had declined since 'Go Now'. After Brian Epstein's death, he'd returned to Tony Secunda – "who understood me. Any thing I wanted to do he backed me." So began the great Balls debacle.

This so-called "supergroup" emerged from the ashes of the Ugly's (*sic*), an undervalued Midlands act led by vocalist Steve Gibbons. On its last legs by 1968, it also contained guitarist Trevor Burton whose assets included his standing as an ex-member of the hit-making Move and an effusion of "image" – constant scowl, protuberant eyes and Brooding Intensity. The change of name to Balls was Burton's suggestion. Next came Secunda's directive to migrate to a bungalow in the Hampshire village of Fordingbridge – and, later, to a farmhouse near Reading – as trendy Traffic had to their isolated cottage on the Berkshire Downs.

Though employing the same producer, Jimmy Miller, "getting it together in the country" wasn't without problems for Balls. "A lot of madness went down," growled Trevor, "a lot of drugs too." However, an exploratory bash at a local hall was encouraging, and a lucrative record company advance was promised. By then, Denny had been roped in – so Burton was led to believe – as a bass player, but, according to Laine, "the idea was that we were going to swap instruments around, and bring different people in for different things."

A Burton composition, 'Fight For My Country' – attributed variously to "Balls", "Trevor Burton", "Trevor Burton and Balls" and "Burton, Laine and Gibbons" – surfaced as the only record release after an age of trying out different players; among them Alan White from The Plastic Ono Band. "Some of what became The Electric Light Orchestra were involved," said Denny, "but they weren't worldly enough for me, and I got bored with their lethargic conversation. I wanted guys with energy, who'd been around a bit more."

After an erratic string of college bookings as an acoustic trio – Denny, Trevor and Steve – "Tony Secunda and Jimmy Miller fell out over money," snapped Laine, "and that was the end of that. Then Ginger Baker [former drummer with Blind Faith] came to my house one night and asked me to join Airforce. It was a shambles – too many players all trying to outdo one another, not enough discipline."

As well as percussion, Baker's post-Blind Faith big band was heavy with under-employed Brummies – Burton and Traffic's Steve Winwood and Chris Wood as well as Denny – and Birmingham Town Hall was a fitting debut performance. Most stuck it out for just one more engagement – at the Royal Albert Hall – where a rambling and unrepentantly loud set was captured on tape. From this was salvaged a single, Bob Dylan's 'Man Of Constant Sorrow', sung in Laine's fully developed "hurt" style.

Airforce was one example, but about twice a month from around the middle of 1966, the music press would report a schism in – or complete disbandment of – one group or other; either that or a key member setting himself apart from those with whom he'd been in earshot for every working day since God knows when.

Manfred Mann took formal leave of Paul Jones at the Marquee; Yardbirds vocalist Keith Relf edged into the Top 50 with a solo 45, and the firing of Jeff Beck from the group wasn't far away. Another lead guitarist, Dave Davies, enjoyed two 1967 hits without his fellow Kinks, and Wayne Fontana had cast aside his backing Mindbenders. It was Eric Burdon And The Animals now – just as it soon would be Don Craine's New Downliners Sect.

Georgie Fame had abandoned his Blue Flames, and had plunged boldly into 1966's self-financed *Sound Venture* LP with jazz veterans like Stan Tracey, Tubby Hayes and The Harry South Big Band. The Walker Brothers were to part after a final tour, and Brian Poole and The Tremeloes were recording separately. Alan Price had had several Top 20 entries as an ex-Animal, while Van Morrison had made a less sweeping exit from Them.

All four Beatles were uncomfortably aware that some sort of crunch was coming for them too. John's activities with Yoko and The Plastic Ono Band were bringing it closer by the day. Who could blame Paul, George or Ringo for pondering whether a relaunch as either a solo attraction or in a new group was tenable? Was it so unreasonable for Paul especially to hold in his heart that either way, The Beatles would be recalled as just the outfit in which he'd cut his teeth before going on to bigger and better things?

11   *"Wedding Bells"*

"It was a fabulous band to play with, The Beatles, and we
played together long enough to get very comfortable with
each other on the music side."

– *Paul McCartney*[1]

Weeping female fans mobbed London's Marylebone Registry Office
on that dark day – 12 March 1969 – when Paul and his bride tied
the knot. Next, the marriage was blessed at a Church local to
Cavendish Avenue. To limit the chances of an outbreak of
Beatlemania, neither George, Ringo nor John – who was to get
hitched to Yoko a week later – showed up at either building, and
a police raid on Harrison's Surrey home and the subsequent
discovery of controlled drugs upset his plans to attend the Ritz
Hotel reception.

On the BBC's *Six O'Clock News*, girls who'd witnessed the
newlyweds exit from the registry office were not undismayed by
the last bachelor Beatle's choice, even if most had expected it to
be Jane Asher. Though their views weren't broadcast, some had
speculated whether or not Linda was pregnant.

She gave birth to Mary on 28th August 1969 (yes, I can count
too) in London, though, as it would be with half-sister Heather
and two younger siblings, Mary was to look upon East Gate Farm
near Rye, Sussex, as home. During what amounted to eventual
years of house-hunting, Paul and Linda would restrict themselves
to the southeastern shires. The more wooded trackways of Surrey,

Hertfordshire and Essex may have been considered – though, for the renowned who preferred the bright lights of the metropolis, sufficiently secluded havens were hidden too in Little Venice, Hampstead and Holland Park.

Cavendish Avenue, however, was to remain McCartney's principal address for at least as long as The Beatles endured – though they weren't much of a group anymore by the second half of 1969. Increasingly rare moments of congeniality occurred most frequently when not all of them were present at Abbey Road. The old brusque tenderness between Paul and John, for instance, was caught in a photograph taken during a session when, with the former on bass, piano and drums, they were the only Beatles heard on 'The Ballad Of John And Yoko', the worst A-side since 1964's 'Can't Buy Me Love'. It had been composed by Lennon as he continued painting himself into a corner with Yoko, going so far as to change his middle name by deed poll from "Winston" to "Ono" in a ceremony on the flat roof of Apple's central London office.

This was also the location of that famous traffic-stopping afternoon performance – The Beatles' last ever – with organist Billy Preston, their old pal from the Star-Club. "That idea came from the bottom of a glass,"[2] said Paul of this most captivating sequence from *Let It Be*, the *cinéma vérité* follow-up to *Help!*. Elsewhere on celluloid and in private, you could slice the atmosphere with a spade now that Paul's boisterous control of the quartet's artistic destiny had gathered barely tolerable momentum since John's unofficial abdication as *de facto* leader of the four. A Beatles obsessive could date this from as far back as Lennon's murmured "you say it" before Paul's count-in to the reprise of the title song of *Sgt Pepper*.

It wasn't all smiles at business meetings either. The crux of most disagreements was that McCartney advocated his own father-in-law, Lee Eastman, to disentangle Apple and The Beatles' disordered threads, while Lennon, Harrison and Starr favoured

Allen Klein, a New York accountant who Eastman – and, by implication, Paul – disliked and distrusted.

It was scarcely surprising, therefore, that each Beatle was readying himself for the end after his individual fashion; Ringo, for instance, consolidating his then promising film career, and George attempting, purportedly, to compose a stage musical and the soundtrack to a western, neither of which came to fruition – though it was he who was to emerge in the first instance as the most engaging and commercially operable ex-Beatle after the grand *finale* of Abbey Road.

Because everyone involved understood that there weren't to be any more Beatles after that, a spirit of almost *Sgt Pepper*-ish co-operation pervaded. As healthy too in their way were the flare-ups that replaced the irresolute nods of the "White Album" and *Let It Be*. Of all of them, none was so bitter as the one over Paul's 'Maxwell's Silver Hammer'. This was overruled as a spin-off single in favour of a double A-side of George's 'Something' – and 'Come Together' by John, the most vehement opponent of 'Maxwell's Silver Hammer'. It was, he thought, a glaring example of what he and George derided as "granny music". Yet, while it was suspended over a jaunty, see-saw rhythm, the wordy libretto reveals that homicidal medical undergraduate Maxwell Edison bumps off his date, a reproving lecturer and the judge about to sentence him for murder.

Regardless of content, *Abbey Road* as a whole had a clearer sound than *Let It Be*'s associated album, which had been doctored by US producer Phil Spector, whose muddy bombast and heavy handed orchestration was frowned upon by McCartney, and his poor opinion was echoed by studio engineer Glyn Johns. Yet, issued out of sequence, ie after *Abbey Road, Let It Be* earned another gold disc for The Beatles, albeit a Beatles who couldn't care less anymore.

12 *"Love Is Strange"*

"A curious mixture of the quiet, retiring man and the natural
stage performer."

– *David Gelly*[1]

By 1970, *Beatles Monthly* had ceased publication.[2] From the
same publisher, two more glossy monthlies dedicated to Gerry
And The Pacemakers and The Rolling Stones had fallen by the
wayside long before through falling subscriptions. This, however,
wasn't the case with the Beatles periodical, far from it, but
"because they are not The Beatles," explained the editorial, "but
four separate personalities now."

It seemed silly for those who still styled themselves "Beatle
people" to be anything but pessimistic about a predictable future
that held the group's total disintegration. Yet, if The Beatles
themselves weren't functional as a recording entity, it was a strange
week if a version of a Lennon–McCartney number wasn't among
the supplicatory flotsam-and-jetsam that washed up round a
record reviewer's typewriter.

'It's For You' – one that Paul and John wrote for Cilla Black
in 1964 – had just been exhumed by US vocal group Three Dog
Night, and was a frequent spin on John Peel's *Top Gear* on BBC
Radio One. A highlight of Blonde On Blonde's act at that same
year's Isle of Wight festival was 'Eleanor Rigby', whose sad-sack
verses and baroque arrangement suited the style of this Welsh "nice
little band" admirably. It was also revived by Dozy, Beaky, Mick
and Tich, once Dave Dee's Bostons – while both Wilson Pickett

and a certain Gerry Lockran had had the unmitigated audacity to issue respective cracks at 'Hey Jude' in January 1969 when the original had barely left the charts; Pickett even cracked the Top 30 on both sides of the Atlantic with his.

That same month, Badfinger peaked at Number Four in Britain with Paul's 'Come And Get It' – which did almost as well in the States, despite competition from a xerox by The Magic Christians, named after the movie in which it was heard no less than five times.

The Magic Christian's second male lead was Ringo Starr – for whom McCartney arranged Hoagy Carmichael's 'Stardust' on *Sentimental Journey*, a forthcoming album of showbiz chestnuts. As calculatedly "square" had been Paul's 'Thingummybob', an A-side penned for Yorkshire's Black Dyke Mills Band. He put in an appearance at the recording session in Bradford, having taken on the commission because, firstly, "I still have a soft spot in my heart for brass bands, it's a roots thing for me."[3] It was also as challengingly distant from 'I Saw Her Standing There' as it was from 'Tomorrow Never Knows'.

Eeeeee, my grandad loved bands when he were a lad. Called John Foster and Son Limited Black Dike Mills Band when it took shape from denizens of the Old Dolphin pub in the village of Queenshead, the Black Dyke began with a repertoire that "contained regimental music that inspired England's heroes in the several wars of the French Revolution."[4] In case you're wondering where you'd heard the name, at the Grand Brass Band Competition at Manchester's Belle Vue in 1864, the Black Dyke carried off the cup with The London Victoria Amateurs, The 4th Lancashire Rifle Volunteers and The Holmfirth Temperance amongst runners-up. The greatest day anyone could ever remember concluded – as was proper – with the massed participants blasting up the National Anthem.

By the late 1960s, the Black Dyke were, perhaps, the kingdom's most renowned brass band – though, of similar antiquity, The Brighouse And Rastrick Brass Band had better luck with a treatment of 'The Floral Dance', which all but topped the charts at the apogee of punk, almost a decade after 'Thingummybob' bit the dust. So did the nondescript one-series-only ITV situation comedy, starring Stanley Holloway, for which it was the theme tune.

Yet The Black Dyke Mills Band weathered Apple's subsequent ditching of them as easily as it had all the changes of personnel over the previous century or so. Just as it predated them, so the ensemble outlasted The Beatles for whom the end became publicly nigh when McCartney announced his resignation on 11 April 1970.

"I suppose it ceased to be a working partnership months ago," admitted Paul to journalist Anne Nightingale, "but the Beatles' partnership goes on for seven more years, and this is why I want out now. The other three of them could sit down now and write me out of the group. I would be quite happy. I could pick up my cash and get out. I don't know how much is involved, but I don't want Allen Klein as my manager."[5]

Neither for now did he wish to endure the unpleasantnesses that occur when human beings congregate in a recording studio. During the mild winter that had seen in the new decade, how much more gratifying it had been to tape by multiple overdub enough for an eponymous solo album on four-track equipment in the privacy of Cavendish Avenue and his home-from-home in the Mull of Kintyre. Other than some backing vocals by Linda, Paul – now bearded to the cheekbones – had sung and played every note. With the help of a manual, he had now become sufficiently schooled in the equipment's aural possibilities to commence a day's work with nothing prepared. Without the emotional overheads of working with John, George and Ringo, he layered instrument upon instrument, sound upon sound, for hours on end, anchored by a metronome or retractable "click-track".

Following some fine-tuning in "technically good" Abbey Road and a "cosy" complex in Willesden, *McCartney* was finished to the last detail – or at least the last detail its creator had any desire to etch. "Light and loose" was how he described it in a press release – a "self-interview" – that also got off his chest a lot of feelings about Lennon, Klein ('I am not in contact with him, and he does not represent me in any way') and other issues including the "personal differences, business differences, musical differences" with The Beatles.

Some of its consumers were to find a copy within a package that, after much angered to-ing and fro-ing between Paul and the Klein conclave, reached the shops in April 1970, a fortnight before the valedictory *Let It Be*, and just after *Sentimental Journey*. Without spawning a spin-off 45, McCartney shifted an immediate two million in North America alone, and the general verdict at the time was that it was OK but nothing brilliant. Perhaps it wasn't supposed to be, even if The Faces, fronted by Rod Stewart, thought highly enough of 'Maybe I'm Amazed' to revive it a year later (as would McCartney himself in 1976).

Overall, the album captures a sketchy freshness, even a stark beauty at times. Certainly, it was much at odds with more intense offerings of the day, whether Led Zeppelin, Deep Purple, Man, Black Sabbath, Humble Pie and other headbangingly "heavy" outfits or the "pomp-rock" of ELP, Yes and borderline cases like Pink Floyd and The Moody Blues, castigated for preferring technique to instinct – and *McCartney* couldn't be accused of that.

While the likes of Man and ELP appealed to laddish consumers lately grown to man's estate, self-doubting bedsit diarists sailed the primarily acoustic waters of the early 1970s denomination of singer-songwriters ruled by James Taylor as surely as Acker Bilk had ruled British trad jazz. While there were elements of the same self-fixated preciousness of Taylor, Melanie, Neil Young and their sort, *McCartney* wasn't anywhere as mannered in its embrace of, say, a paeon to its maker's wife ('The Lovely Linda') – and *Let It Be* leftovers ('Teddy Boy') and, the first track ever aired in Britain (on *Pick Of The Pops* one Sunday afternoon), 'That Would Be Something', still being performed by McCartney in the 1990s.

Most of his first true solo effort had resulted from a kind of purposeful mucking about that didn't suggest that Paul McCartney was ready to soundtrack the 1970s as he had the Swinging Sixties with John Lennon, especially after the two's artistic separation was to be confirmed when The Beatles dissolved formally in the Chancery Division of the London High Court on 12 March 1971.

Inevitably, too much would be expected of Paul, John, George and, if you like, Ringo – but whether the much-anticipated *McCartney*, *John Lennon: Plastic Ono Band* and Harrison's *All Things Must Pass* had been tremendous, lousy or, worse, ordinary wasn't the issue for the sort of fan for whom just the opportunity to study each one's sleeve was worth the whole price of what amounted to a new ersatz-Beatle album. It was adequate that it just existed. Nevertheless, like The Rolling Stones, Bob Dylan and Frank Zappa, though McCartney, Lennon and Harrison would rack up heftier sales and honours as individuals, the repercussions of the records they'd made in the 1960s would resound louder. Having gouged so deep a cultural wound collectively, whatever any of them got up to in the years left to him was barely relevant by comparison, no matter how hard he tried.

Paul, in particular, acquitted himself well as a chart contender, made nice music, but none of it made the difference that The Beatles had. His first post-Beatles single, 'Another Day' – as melancholy as 'Eleanor Rigby' – zoomed to a domestic Number Four on 4 March 1971, and began a journey to one position short of this in the US Hot 100 a week later. All that stood in his way to the very top in Britain before the month was out was 'Hot Love' from T Rex, glam-rock giants, whose "T Rexstasy" was as rampant among schoolgirls as Beatlemania once was, and "Rollermania" was to be when Edinburgh's Bay City Rollers – in their gimmick bow-ties and half-mast tartan trousers – were hyped as "the new Beatles". *Plus ça change.*

Lennon's extreme strategies had taken him beyond the pale as an orthodox pop star, while Harrison insisted that he "wouldn't really care if nobody ever heard of me again"[6] after his finest hour at the forefront of the *Concerts for Bangla Desh* in August 1971. McCartney, however, wasn't so happy about someone else having a turn as the teenagers' – or any other record buyers' – fave rave. At the same age – 28 – Roy Orbison had been revered as something of a Grand Old Man of pop during the 1963 tour, but he'd had a receding chin, jug-handle ears and pouchy jowls like a ruminating hamster.

The allure of Paul's yet unwrinkled good looks, his hair remaining on his head and his relative boyishness were belied only by the sorry-girls-he's-married tag that had so irritated the adulterous John before the coming of the second Mrs Lennon when "I really knew love for the first time"[7].

Paul was happily married too, and, like John, intended his missus to get in on the act. Linda had endured piano lessons as a child, but had come to loathe the carping discipline of her teacher. Yet she was sufficiently self-contained to disassociate the music from the drudgery. Indeed, when the dark cloud of the lessons dissolved, she and her school friends had often harmonised *a cappella* for their own amusement in imitation of 1950s vocal group hits such as 'Earth Angel' (The Penguins), 'Chimes' (The Pelicans) and 'I Only Have Eyes For You' (The Flamingos).

Many other outfits of this vintage gave themselves ornithological appellations too – The Crows, The Orioles, The Feathers, The Robins and so forth. It's been said that, with this in mind, Linda, heavily pregnant with a third daughter, modified Paul's original suggestion of "Wings Of Angels" to just plain "Wings" as a name for the group he planned to form for both stage and studio.[8] As with Procol Harum and, since 1969, Pink Floyd, lack of a preceding article was *à la mode*. That there was already a US entity called Wings with a recording contract too was of no apparent consequence.

After recovering from the premature birth of Stella – named after both her maternal great-grandmothers – in London on 13

September 1971, Linda began her diffident tenure in Wings, vamping keyboards as well as ministering to overall effect as a singer. Unlike Yoko Lennon, she was a timid songbird, and wasn't willing initially to walk a taut artistic tightrope with her vulnerability as an instrumentalist. "I really tried to persuade Paul that I didn't want to do it," she protested. "If he hadn't said anything, I wouldn't have done it."[9]

The other more experienced members recruited shared her doubts: "Linda was all right at picking things up, but she didn't have the ability to play freely. If we'd had her and another keyboard player as well, we would have been fine, but Linda was given too much to do. She was a professional though. She got paid like the rest of us."

Thus spake Denny Laine, who had been engaged on an album of his own when summoned to the Mull of Kintyre in August 1971. He'd also been party to a half-serious attempt to put together a "supergroup" drawn from other supergroups with George Harrison, Rick Grech and Eric Clapton from Blind Faith, and Plastic Ono Bandsman Alan White. This was during the interregnum between Balls and the Airforce fiasco. When 'Man Of Constant Sorrow' was issued in autumn 1970, Ginger Baker's post-Blind Faith big band had crash-dived for the last time, thanks mostly to its drummer-leader's heroin dependency – so grave that his "works" had been an established if discreet part of dressing room paraphernalia.

"Ginger had to go away and get better," sighed Denny, "and I was swept under the carpet after Tony Secunda took on T Rex and got them a deal in America. Robert Stigwood wanted me to hang in there, and gave me a retainer. A couple of months later, I got a call from Paul."

McCartney had first met his future lieutenant when Denny Laine And The Diplomats had supported The Beatles at a poorly attended booking at Old Hill Plaza near Dudley back on 11 January 1962. Each had since stayed in the picture about the other's activities, and so it was that "Paul knew I could sing, write and play, and so he called me. It knocked me sideways a little because I wasn't used to being a sidekick, but I admired Paul. That was the first time I'd been with a band with someone more famous than me."

It was also the first time Laine had been in a band with someone of the same Christian name. At the drum stool for several months before Laine's coming was Denny Seiwell, who McCartney had discovered in New York during a thin time in a career that had lifted off when Seiwell completed a spell in a US army band, playing music in an area bordered by John Philip Sousa and The Black Dyke Mills Band. Demobilisation found him in Chicago and then New York, beating the skins in jazz clubs and landing occasional record dates where the versatile Seiwell proved equally at ease attending to "godfather of soul" James Brown's anguished raps as the easy-listening country-rock of John Denver. By 1970, however, he was living a hand-to-mouth existence in the Big Apple where the McCartneys, purportedly, stumbled upon him cluttering a sidewalk along the Bronx. "We thought we'd better not pass him by," recalled Paul-as-Good Samaritan, "so we picked him up, put him on a drum kit, and he was all right."[9] There was another more pragmatic reason for taking him on. "The other New York session guys Paul had approached wanted a lot of dough," elucidated Denny Laine, "and only Denny Seiwell agreed with the amount offered".

As he – and wife Monique – were also amenable to uprooting to Britain, Seiwell seemed to be just what McCartney needed. As well as being an adaptable and proficient time-keeper, his blithe dedication to his craft was refreshing to Paul after the malcontented shiftlessness of certain Beatles in the months before the end. "The important thing is understanding, willingness," judged Paul, "a personality that fits in."[1]

With US guitarists Dave Spinozza and Hugh McCracken – as well as sections of the New York Philharmonic Orchestra – earning their coffee breaks with infallibly polished nonchalance, Seiwell's period in the former Beatle's employ had started with *Ram*, an album that was to be attributed to "Paul and Linda McCartney". Neither presumed to dictate notes and nuances to sidemen with close knowledge of each other's considerable capabilities through working together on countless daily studio sessions, but ran through the basic essentials of every number.

The outcome was a no-frills precision that lent the majority of *Ram*'s 12 selections a dispiriting squeaky-cleanliness as if the hand-picked and highly waged players couldn't accomplish what Paul alone – for all his wispiness and casually strewn mistakes – had committed to tape instinctively on home-made *McCartney*.

This opinion was echoed by contemporary critics – with the *NME*'s "a mixed bag of psychedelic liquorice all-sorts"[10] a prototypical reaction to the compositions *per se*. In what amounted to a personal attack, the now-radical *NME* also denigrated the McCartneys as a smug, bourgeois couple too long and maybe guiltily detached from the everyday ennui of the lengthening dole queues in 1970s Britain.

Yet a public that didn't read the music press were willing to assume that *Ram* and its spin-off singles would grow on them like most of *Sgt Pepper* had after repeated listening. Raw fact is that *Ram* topped the UK album list, though 'Back Seat Of My Car' struggled wretchedly to the edge of the Top 40. That *Ram* stalled at second place in *Billboard*'s Hot 100 was mitigated by its US-only 45, 'Uncle Albert/Admiral Halsey' – freighted with sound effects and stiff-upper-lip vocal – going all the way, despite *Rolling Stone* dismissing the album as "the nadir of rock"[11].

Rolling Stone's perspective was shared with those who imagined themselves sensitive and unopposed to the polarisation of pop in particular styles since the late 1960s as jazz had been for years. "Traditional" could be represented by both Engelbert Humperdinck and Rolf 'Two Little Boys' Harris. "Mainstream" was capacious enough to contain Marmalade, The Faces, James Taylor and, chart newcomers from Indiana, The Jackson Five – while The Jeff Beck

Group and The Moody Blues squeezed in amongst modernists like Traffic and Renaissance. No more providers of teenage entertainment in their way than Engelbert, Soft Machine and Yoko Ono were among brand leaders of the avant-garde.

Formerly "the Tommy Steele of Scotland", Alex Harvey, one of the support acts to Johnny Gentle and the Silver Beatles, was to belong in more than one of these categories as the leader of The Sensational Alex Harvey Band via a discography that embraced both the vile transit camp scenario of Jacques Brel's 'Next' and a revival of Tom Jones's singalong 'Delilah'. Though Paul McCartney planted feet in more than one camp too, Alex hadn't much time for *Ram*: "Do you think McCartney makes records just to annoy me personally, or does he want to get up everybody's nose with his antics?"[12]

Comparisons of Paul's output with that of his former creative confrère were inevitable, and the conclusion of the record industry *illuminati* was that Lennon was cool and McCartney wasn't. Because of a cathartic projection of himself as 'Working Class Hero' on raw and intense *John Lennon: Plastic Ono Band*, Lennon was an executant of "rock" – which only the finest minds could appreciate – while McCartney peddled ephemeral "pop".

In retrospect, the chasm between Paul and John's first efforts as ex-Beatles was not unbreachable, not least because both extolled the virtues of harmony and equality in emotional partnerships – married love, if you prefer – to the level of ickiness. Nevertheless, 'Working Class Hero' contained rude words, and that mighty Cerberus *Rolling Stone* (to whom Lennon had just granted a frank, unashamed and circulation-enhancing two-part interview) had surmised that his singing on 'God' – fifth track, side two – "may be the finest in all rock", and the whole LP was "a full, blistering statement of fury". Thus McCartney and *Ram* were made to seem even more shallow and bland.

As far as John was concerned, Wings was just the latest vehicle for what he still ridiculed as Paul's "granny music". Lennon said as much in his natter to *Rolling Stone*, and was about to exact vengeance on vinyl – in a composition entitled 'How Do You Sleep?' – against what he'd perceived as a lyrical attack on him in 'Three Legs', a *Ram* selection that could have been ditched without any hardship. A McCartney interview in *Melody Maker* headlined "Why Lennon Is Uncool" prompted a bitter riposte from John on the readers' letters page the following week. Adding injury to insult, Ringo – who damned *Ram* with faint praise in print – had drummed on *John Lennon: Plastic Ono Band*, while George had endorsed Lennon's venom by gladly picking guitar and dobro on nasty 'How Do You Sleep?'.

Matters didn't improve with the issue of *Wild Life*, Wings's maiden album, in time for 1971's Christmas sell-in. Four months earlier, engineer Tony Clarke had been summoned to the Mull of Kintyre farmhouse to assist on tracks that were recorded as soon as they'd been routined. What struck him was how much was accomplished in one day compared to the months of remakes, jettisoned tracks and trifling mechanical intricacies that had to be endured from others. Understanding that it was the margin of error that had put teeth into *McCartney*, if not *Ram*, Paul was as jaded with endless multi-track mixing, and made transparent his desire for *Wild Life* to be as belligerently "live" as possible – no arguments, no needless messing about with dials – and on to the next track.

However, for all its brisk finesse, *Wild Life* stalled on the edge of the Top Ten in both Britain and the USA – a tangible comedown by previous commercial standards. It was even less of a critical success than *Ram*, asking for trouble as it did with a capricious revival of The Everly Brothers' 'Love Is Strange' from 1965, and so-so originals that were also pounced upon as symptoms of creative bankruptcy. After a decade on the run – of snatched meals, irregular sleep and pressure to come up with the next Number One – who could blame McCartney for resenting anyone who begrudged a back-street lad who'd climbed to the top of the heap, letting go, stopping trying to prove himself?

"I think I've got some idea of the way he feels about things," reckoned Denny Laine, "because I've been through the same stuff myself. The longer you go on, the tougher it is in lots of ways. People expect more and more of you. For Paul, having been part of the best rock 'n' roll band in history, it must be very heavy. I admire him so much, the way he handles it and doesn't let it interfere with his music."[1]

Just as commendable was that too much convalescent sloth wasn't McCartney's way. "After a few days, I get the feeling I want to be doing something musical," he'd tell you, "so I go and play the piano or guitar for pleasure. It's generally at moments like this that an idea will occur to me – almost as if it's been waiting to come out. The best way to write a song is for it to write itself. Some of the best things I've done have happened like that. They turn up like magic."[1]

"I just don't know how he does it," gasped Linda, but, to paraphrase Mandy Rice-Davies, she would say that wouldn't she? A disaffected listener's angle might be that *McCartney*, *Ram* and *Wild Life* weren't magic, just music – though Paul seemed to have fun on them. Yet you could understand his attitude. Above the tour-album-tour sandwiches incumbent upon poorer stars, McCartney could wait until he felt like going on the road again whilst making music for the benefit of himself rather than a public that would assure a former Beatle at least a moderate hit then, even with something like *Wild Life*.

Paul himself was to say of *Wild Life*, "OK, I didn't make the biggest blockbuster of all time, but I don't think you need that all the time. *Wild Life* was inspired by Dylan, because we'd heard that he just took one week to do an album. So we thought, 'Great, we'll do it a bit like that, and we'll try to get just the spontaneous stuff down and not be too careful with this one.' So it came out like that, and a few people thought we could have tried a bit harder."[8]

Bob Dylan had sunk into an artistic quagmire too by the early 1970s, though his stumblings on disc were shrugged off by sympathetic pundits as writer's block. He was also, they reckoned, a possessor of genius rather than anything as common as the mere talent that was Paul McCartney's. In retrospect, nevertheless, *Wild Life*, if skimpy rather than grippingly slipshod, was enjoyable enough after the manner you'd expect from an album that, like Kingsize Taylor's Hamburg long-player, had next to no time to record – and even 'Bip Bop', *Wild Life* at its most inconsequential was to make more rock 'n' roll sense when Wings oozed rather than exploded onto the stage after a launch party at the Empire Ballroom, Leicester Square, London on 8 November 1971.

A small army of Paul's famous friends – Elton John, Keith Moon, Ronnie Wood of The Faces, all the usual shower – rallied round for the celebration. As the champagne flowed and the paper plates piled up at the buffet, the founder of the feast reserved a little of that well-known charm for every guest that entered his orbit, doling out a few minutes of chat each to witnesses and participants in some of the stirring musical exploits of the past and present, whether John Entwistle – whose Who could no longer take hits for granted – or Jimmy Page with his Led Zeppelin's fourth album yet to be dislodged from Number One in both Britain and the States.

Paul's new hand-made suit hadn't been quite ready that afternoon, but he wore it anyway with the tracking stitches for all to see. Perhaps it was an Art Statement, like. Maybe the entire evening was. Most conspicuously, the entertainment laid on was nowhere to be found on the map of contemporary rock. Seated on the Empire podium was tuxedoed Ray McVay and his Dance Band, lifted by time machine from the pre-Presley 1950s. Their Victor Sylvester-esque duties included accompanying a formation dance team; inserting rumbles of timpani at moments of climax during a grand prize raffle, and providing a framework for those who wished to hokey-cokey the night away or pursue romance to lush stardust-and-roses ballads that wouldn't have been out of place on Ringo's *Sentimental Journey*.

Seizing the opportunity to rewind his life in another respect too, Paul had decided that, while he wasn't intending to hump equipment or coil even his own amplifier leads, Wings were to re-enter the concert arena with small, unpublicised, even impromptu engagements. During the drive back from The Black Dyke Mills Band session, he'd stopped in a Bedfordshire village pub where, in a fit of exuberance, he'd sat down at the saloon bar piano and, without preamble, hammered out some Beatles numbers plus an instrumental that none of the astonished clientele recognised as father Jim's 'Walking In The Park With Eloise'. This wasn't the first or last such episode from one who needed to perform as a drug addict needed his fix.

Nearly all the essential elements were intact to enable Wings to tread the boards. Largely through Denny Laine's urging, another guitarist was roped in. Born and raised in Londonderry, Henry McCullough had cut his teeth in The Skyrockets and then Gene and the Gents, two of around 600 horn-laden showbands operational in Ireland in the early 1960s.

An entertainment institution peculiar to the Ireland, the showband ruled the country's dance halls with a polished mixture of across-the-board favourites, *salvo pudore* in-song comedy and the onstage glamour of braided costumery and neat coiffure. Dressed as if they'd come direct from the set of *Oklahoma!*, colleens sat on strategically placed stools, looking patiently pretty whilst waiting their turns to display synchronised dance steps, add vocal counterpoint or even sing lead as a breath of fresh air in a sphere dominated by Guinness-swilling male bonding.

Changeless and changed after rock 'n' roll, the showbands diverged into ones that stuck to the tried-and-tested guidelines, and ones that aspired to be highly proficient non-stop copyists of whatever North American pop commotions were stirring up the nation. However, such an inordinate amount of the old corn remained that Henry McCullough on the bandstand would wonder if he'd remembered to collect the eiderdowns from the dry-cleaners as he strummed rote-learnt 'Que Sera Sera', 'Sparrow In The Treetop' and 'Noreen Bawn'.

Musicians whose tastes lay in the same rebellious direction marked time too in the payroll of old stagers who thought that you couldn't go wrong with Jim Reeves, and couldn't grasp what had come over these young shavers who were biting the hands that fed them with their constant machinations to include this crazy, far-out music in the show.

There remains bitter division about the showband's influence on both Irish and world pop. It is often too easy to forget that this tight-trousered lead vocalist or that clenched-teeth guitarist may have got his first break by falling meekly into line in a professional showband. Mind-stultifying as it was to them, it was a toehold on showbusiness and, more importantly, a guaranteed income. Yet those veterans predestined to be mainstays of Them, Taste, Thin Lizzy – and Wings – were not so generous in recounting how they'd mastered their assorted crafts in the ranks of The Skyrockets, The Fontana, The Clubmen, The Dixies, The Swingtime Aces *et al*.

Late in 1966, Henry chose to outlaw himself from the stuffy if lucrative showband functions on which he depended for a living to throw in his lot with The People, a combo of psychedelic kidney from Portadown. Being enormous in Armagh wasn't, however, enormous enough, and the group migrated to London where they were renamed Eire Apparent after being taken on by Chas Chandler, now gone from The Animals to behind-the-scenes branches of the music business. As he also had The Jimi Hendrix Experience on his books, Chandler was in a strong position to obtain both a contract for Eire Apparent on Track, the Experience's label, and support spots to Hendrix both in Britain and the USA. Moreover, McCullough was rated as a guitarist by the discerning Jimi, who produced an Eire Apparent album.

Obliged by visa problems to return to Ireland during an Eire Apparent trek round North America in 1968, Henry passed through the ranks of Sweeney's Men, a renowned folk-rock outfit who were about to thrust tentacles into the folk circuit on the other side of the Irish Sea, notably as the surprise hit of that summer's Cambridge Folk Festival. Founder member Johnny Moynihan acknowledged that "Henry put funk into it. He'd just pick up on traditional tunes and they would come out in his playing. One night, we were playing in Dublin, and after the gig, Henry jumped in a car and drove like mad to catch the end of a John Mayall concert elsewhere. This told us what direction he was heading in, and when he was offered a job with Joe Cocker, he took it. He naturally gravitated towards it."[13]

McCullough's arrival in Cocker's Grease Band coincided with Denny Cordell's production of the group's 'With A Little Help From My Friends' wrenching Mary Hopkin from Number One in November 1968. He was backing Joe still when that grizzled Yorkshireman was acclaimed by the half-million drenched Americans who'd braved Woodstock, viewed from a distance of decades as the climax of hippy culture and, via its spin-off movie and albums, the yardstick by which future Cocker performances would always be measured.

For Henry, any Woodstock euphoria was blunted when Cocker ditched the Grease Band to tour the States as *de jure* leader of retinue known as Mad Dogs And Englishmen, but drawn principally from Los Angeles "supersidemen" – including a "Space Choir" and no less than three drummers from that smug élite whose unsparingly snappy jitter was described as "tight", "economic" and by that faintly nauseating adjective "funky".

Back in London, McCullough was one of a Grease Band that were hired to assist on the tie-in double-album to the West End musical, *Jesus Christ Superstar*. This proved to be useful as a bartering tool for a deal with EMI's "progressive" subsidiary, Harvest. Nevertheless, despite a *Top Of The Pops* slot and relentless touring to plug an eponymous LP, the group was no more by the close of 1971.

Henry fell on his feet with Wings for all Denny Cordell's reservations: "When he played well, Henry was a genius, but he could only play in one certain bag, and you had to get him just right. Otherwise, he was very mercurial. He'd just fall out of it."[14]

Paul McCartney was prepared to take a chance on Henry McCullough just as he was on Linda's hit-or-miss keyboard-playing – because, so he reasoned, "Linda is the innocence of the group. All the rest of us are seasoned musicians – and probably too seasoned. Linda has an innocent approach which I like. It's like when you hear an artist say, 'I wish I could paint like a child again'. That's what she's got. If you talk to an artist like Peter Blake, he'll tell you how much great artists love the naivety of aboriginal paintings. Linda's inclusion was something to do with that."[9]

As well as pre-empting punk's more studied guilelessness, Linda McCartney was, according to Eric Burdon, an unwitting pioneer of female visibility in mainstream rock: "I think Linda played a part in paving the way for more female performers to join the boys' club called rock 'n' roll."[15]

For those who prized technical expertise, she served as a bad example of this, beginning with her professional concert debut on Wednesday, 9 February 1972 at the University of Nottingham. The date and venue had been chosen arbitrarily as Wings cruised by car and caravan up the spine of England the previous morning. Turning off the M1 somewhere in the Midlands, they wound up at the university campus and volunteered their services. Room was made for them to do a turn during lunch hour the next day in the student's union auditorium.

Seven hundred paid 50p (81 cents) admission to stand around as Wings strutted their stuff – principally olde tyme rock 'n' roll and excerpts from *Wild Life*. Permitting himself the luxury of apparent self-indulgence, Paul didn't give 'em 'Yesterday', 'Let It Be' or, indeed, any of the good old good ones from The Beatles' portfolio as he took lead vocals on everything apart from reggaefied 'Seaside Woman', penned solely by Linda. Elsewhere, 'Henry's

Blues' was a rambling instrumental showcase for McCullough, while 'Say You Don't Mind' had been rehearsed but left out at the insistence of its composer, who feared disobliging comparisons to Colin Blunstone's elegant resuscitation, then poised to slip into the spring Top 20. A few blown riffs, flurries of bum notes, vaguely apocalyptic cadences and yelled directives were reported, but pockets of the audience felt a compulsion to dance to as nice a little band as Blonde On Blonde – and Paul McCartney's first performance on a *bona fide* stage since Candlestick Park.

The 90 minutes Linda spent to the left of Denny Seiwell's kit passed quickly – surprisingly so – in a blur of *son-et-lumière* heat and audience reaction as remotely unreal as conch murmurs, but for all her panicked vamping in Z minor or whatever key a given number was in, the general feeling as cigarettes were lit and beer-can rings pulled later was that she'd done OK.

Similar casual and unannounced bashes – mostly at other colleges – filled the calendar for the next fortnight. By the final date in Oxford, Linda was solidly at the music's heart, and, for the most part, it had been an agreeable jaunt for a Paul McCartney unbothered by keening feedback bleeps, one of the sound crew blundering on to sort out a dead amplifier, a mistimed falling curtain, audience interruptions or anything else that wasn't in a slap-dash script. While the gear was being loaded afterwards, he'd chatted freely with fans, autographing both copies of *Wild Life* fresh from the pressing plant and a dog-eared *Beatles For Sale*.

Either on piano or at the central microphone too, he'd been joking and swapping banter during proceedings that were epitomised by an amused cheer on the second night – in York – when Linda, crippled with nerves, forgot her cliff-hanging organ introit to *Wild Life*'s title track. Response generally was as heartening as might be expected from crowds enjoying both an unexpected diversion from customary mid-term activities and a surge into the bar afterwards, having participated, however passively in the proverbial "something to tell your grandchildren about".

13 "Mary Had A Little Lamb"

"They smelled of the farm. They brought their kitchen smells
with them – parsley, garlic and the country freshness."
– *Eric Burdon*[1]

While advised by payroll courtiers, McCartney had never been a
corporation marionette. Almost from the beginning – when he'd
been late for the very first business discussion with Brian Epstein
– Paul, for all his apparent conviviality, had been a disquieting and
tenacious presence around Brian, maintaining an acute and
sometimes unwelcome interest in every link of the chain from
studio to pressing plant to market place.

Since their manager's death, the sundering of The Beatles and
the formation in 1969 of what was to become McCartney
Productions and then MPL Communications, whether he made
wise or foolish executive decisions, Paul alone would accept
responsibility for them.

Nevertheless, certain wolves were kept from the door on his
behalf by appointed accountants and lawyers who waded through
mazy balance sheets, computer run-offs and musty ledgers to ensure
that assorted incoming monies would be divided as agreed and
sent via complicated but fixed channels to a frequently disenchanted
client. Taking care of much McCartney business were Eastman
and Eastman Inc, a relationship based not so much on profit as
family affinity – and friendship, particularly with brother-in-law
John Eastman, who had been present at the Mull of Kintyre when
Paul reached his decision to leave The Beatles.

Both on paper and in practice, it was an ideal arrangement. Dignified and quietly besuited – albeit with an occasional penchant for brightly coloured socks – John had acquired the cautious confidence to strike a bellicose stance when necessary in negotiation, and a brain that could, at a moment's notice, spew out dizzying facts and figures. Some eyelids would grow heavy, but at least he had clients' best interests in mind, and Paul would think highly enough of him to ask him to be best man at his second wedding 30 years later.

In 1972, the most immediate concern of McCartney's investors was the mercantile possibilities of Wings's follow-up to *Wild Life*. With this in mind, stadium managers from every major territory were on the line to McCartney Productions, yelling "Klondike!" at the prospect of a round-the-world carnival of Beatles-sized magnitude.

The only snag was that the heavyweight wouldn't fight – well, not for the world championship – yet. As he had with that first low-key sweep round England with Wings, Paul not so much plunged headfirst as dipped a toe *sur le continent* with mainly 3,000 rather than 20,000 seaters over seven summer weeks that covered France to Germany, Switzerland to Finland. The group travelled in a customised double-decker bus, just like Cliff Richard and his retinue of wonderful young people had in 1962's *Summer Holiday*, a film musical of cheery unreality. In keeping with this, McCartney was *éminence grise* behind a film of the tour – for a purpose that was then non-specific – that split-screened in-concert footage with a twee cartoon about a rodent family with human characteristics and a paterfamilias called Bruce McMouse, who dwelt beneath the floorboards of each stage where Wings performed.

Owing largely to publicity that was "non-aggressive" to the point of being nearly as secretive as that for the show in Nottingham, ticket sales were erratic, even forcing a cancellation at a venue in Lyons. It had been quite a while – Barcelona in 1966 with John, George and Ringo – since the peacock had shown his feathers in Europe. In the wings at the Arles Theatre Antique, Zurich's Congress Halle or the Messuhalli in Helsinki, Paul steeled himself to face facts, but he needn't have worried. Barrages of whistling, cheering and stamping greeted him before he sang a bar of the opening 'Bip Bop'.

Attendance figures notwithstanding, Wings were received with affection for what onlookers now understood they ought to expect. The set was longer and, as instanced by a projected array of rural, coastal and lunar scenes on a backcloth during the second half, more elaborate than before. Nevertheless, with the 'Long Tall Sally' encore the only nod towards The Beatles, the audiences heard much the same as their British counterparts plus Leadbelly's "Cottonfields" – subject of a 1970 revival by The Beach Boys – and sides of two recent singles and two yet to come.

First up had been 'Give Ireland Back To The Irish'. Perhaps not really by coincidence, John Lennon had just recorded 'Sunday Bloody Sunday', an album track that was also inspired by the bomb-blasting, bullet-firing malevolence in Northern Ireland rearing up again with the incident in Londonderry that January when 13 were shot dead by British soldiers during a civil rights demonstration.

With increasingly more attention-seeking and deadly tactics from both loyalist and republican cells of fanaticism, both inside and outside jails that were regarded as prisoner-of-war camps, the tension pervaded the whole province, whether it was "Bloody Sunday"; the "dirty" protests in the Maze prison where hunger strikers' eyes burned like coals; frightened customs officials armed with every fibre of red-tape bureaucracy could gather or the jack-in-office malice of the young polytechnic janitor who stuck an "out of order" sign on a working lift to compel a visiting English pop group to lug its equipment up five punishing staircases to the auditorium, and down again when the show finished by the early hour ordained in the curfew regulations.

Allusions to current affairs had been hitherto as rare as winter roses in both Paul McCartney's songs and interviews. In any case, the difficulty with topical ditties is what becomes of them when they are no longer topical or the topic gets tedious? Yet Paul's doctrinal statement about the Troubles, rather than a sidestepping support of general pacifism, topped the hot-blooded Irish lists, while struggling elsewhere in the teeth of radio bans and restrictions, even with an alternative instrumental version on the flip-side.

To redress the balance, Wings followed through with 'Mary Had A Little Lamb' – yes, the nursery rhyme – which, like the National Anthem, turned out to have verses other than the one everyone knew. "It wasn't a great record," confessed McCartney – and in this, he was at one with nearly all reviewers, even if, aided by four contrasting promotional shorts, it rose higher in the domestic chart than its predecessor.

"I like to keep in with the five-year-olds," he beamed, but, six months later, what did this corner of the market make of 'Hi Hi Hi' – which went the scandalous way of 'I Can't Control Myself' by The Troggs, The Rolling Stones' 'Let's Spend The Night Together', 'Wet Dream' from Max Romeo and, climactically, Jane Birkin and Serge Gainsbourg's 'Je T'Aime...Moi Non Plus?'

Excluded from prudish airwaves for sexual insinuation too, offence had been taken when the word "polygon" was misheard as "body gun", interpreted (like "sex pistol') as a euphemism for "prick", "cock", "willy", need I go on? Whether it was or wasn't the wrong end of the stick, the stick still existed – and with none of the clever word-playing double-entendre of, say Cy Coleman's 'The Ball's In Your Court' ('where the competition is stiff'), direct from Broadway. Yet, partly because disc jockeys began spinning the perky, reggaefied B-side, 'C Moon', 'Hi Hi Hi' was Wings's biggest British hit thus far, going flaccid at Number Three as 1972 mutated into 1973.

The new year got underway with Paul tying at 15 – with David Bowie, Van Morrison and Randy Newman – in the "world vocalist" section of the *NME* readers' popularity poll, and the UK issue in March of syrupy 'My Love', a taster for a forthcoming album. If sent on its way with the expected critical rubbishings, the single would be a US Number One whilst just scraping into the domestic Top Ten. Paul's status as a non-Beatle as much as that as a former Beatle was further confirmed by a *Melody Maker* journalist's random survey among schoolgirls shuffling into the Bristol Hippodrome, the first stop on Wings's first official tour of Britain that May. "What's your favourite Paul McCartney song?" "Dunno," replied one moon-faced female before pausing and adding, "Oh yeah – 'My Love'."

No longer the dream lover of old, he had emerged as a cross between admired elder brother, favourite uncle – and, for some, a character from *The Archers*, BBC Radio Four's long-running rustic soap opera. If he wasn't living the so-called "simple life" after he'd moved to East Sussex, he was living it hundreds of miles away on his farm in Scotland. At either, the landscape melted into another endless summer day with not a leaf stirring, a touch of mist on the sunset horizon and a bird chirruping somewhere. Then the seasons changed from gold to marble, and, as they did, the log fire would subside to glowing embers, and the harvest moon in its starry canopy would shine as bright as day over the vastness of the storybook countryside. He, Linda and the girls seemed the very epitome of domestic bliss while they trod the backwards path towards the morning of the Earth.

Even in the bluster of the city, who could fail to adore Britain where female traffic wardens called you "love', cigarettes could be bought in ten-packs, pubs were more than buildings where men got drunk and the humour – as opposed to *humor* – of *Monty Python's Flying Circus* repeats clearing the ground for such as *Fawlty Towers* and *Ripping Yarns* to heave UK television comedy out of the mire of "more tea, Vicar?" sit-coms or half-hours fraught with innuendo about wogs, poofs and tits?

Remaining thus on his native soil, Paul McCartney was flying in the face of the cold and rain, no ice in your Coca-Cola except in the poshest lounge bars, only three television channels and the snarled-up motorways to and from his two principal residencies. Crucially, there were also the burdensome Inland Revenue demands on the rich that had already driven The Rolling Stones to temporary exile in France, Bad Company to Guernsey, Dave Clark to a fiscal year in California and Maurice Gibb of The Bee Gees to the Isle of Man.

While Rye's most renowned addressee was commuter-close to McCartney Productions, only the odd flight overhead from Gatwick airport miles away need remind him of what was over the hills in London, New York and Hollywood. It had left its mark on Paul's songwriting already – in, for example, 'Heart Of The Country' on *Ram*, and would continue to do so in the likes of the imminent 1973 B-side 'Country Dreamer' – actually taped in one of his backyards – and, most memorably of all, 1977's 'Mull Of Kintyre'.

Shrouded by meadows, greenery, exposed oak rafters, stone-flagged floors and Peace in the Valley, Paul had been all for the quietude and fresh air, even penning a feature about the most northerly of his arcadian shangri-las for the newspaper in Campbeltown (for which he was paid the standard National Union of Journalists fee). Whereas they might have pressed ivory or fret, the 31-year-old musician's fingers became hardened from fencing, logging and moving bales.

Yet, while he did not join Ringo Starr on so voracious a social whirl that he'd hide rings under his eyes with the mirror sunglasses that became a standard party accoutrement from that time, what Paul could barely enunciate was that there were times when he missed the limelight as he forwent opportunities to reactivate his old magnetism at dazzling showbiz soirées where a murmur would reach a crescendo as he entered as a signal for all the younger pop stars and their acolytes to drone round him like a halo of flies.

He was to encounter that in macrocosm when mingling with other locals at coffee mornings, jumble sales and parents evenings at the nearby state schools where, unlike the fee-paying Harrisons and Starkeys, he and Linda were to send their offspring. In and about Rye or Campbeltown where nothing much was calculated to happen, year in, year out, the most exciting daily excursion was the uncomplicated ritual of shopping for groceries as Paul and Linda became an everyday sight, hand in hand around the parish. At first, Paul's hesitant smile had not rested on individuals, but had been diffused to the general multitude. He couldn't help but be aware that his arrival once at a barber's in Rye for a self-conscious short-back-and-sides was as profoundly disturbing an experience for others in the queue as noticing the Queen having her hair tortured into a Hendrix Afro in its sister establishment.

Yet soon he was chatting about field drainage, nativity plays, winter farrowing and muck-spreading with the best of them – as demonstrated by him kicking up a fuss when Hibernian stag hunters presumed it was OK to cross his land, and a less justifiable one when staff at the junior school joined a national teachers' strike in November 1986; his disapproval immortalised by one lucky amateur photographer whose back view of a McCartney stamping off in a pique across the playground, front-paged *The Times Educational Supplement*.[2]

At dinner parties with other parents, a relaxed Paul would bring his hosts up to date with Stella's reading, while insisting on one chronicled occasion that they eat in the ambience of the kitchen rather than the less free-and-easy dining room.

In contrast to Mal Evans dashing across busy Abbey Road to the fish-and-chip shop, and as tasty as the repasts of his Rye and Campbeltown circles, was the roast dinner washed down with home-brewed ale at record entrepreneur Richard Branson's new Manor Studios. Half-hidden by woodland some 30km (20 miles) northwest of Oxford, these were used by Wings for two exploratory days that were marked less by the aural results – mostly mixing – than a pointed complaint from a neighbour to police about noise caused when, during a humid night, members of Wings kept opening a studio door otherwise almost permanently shut. During boring mechanical processes at the console, the group also enjoyed facilities that were more agreeable than the clinic-doss house paradox of certain urban complexes they could name – where you got to know by sight individual biscuit crumbs, and followed their day-to-day journeyings up and down a ledge, where an empty can of orangeade might also linger for weeks next to a discarded swab-stick dirtied from cleaning tape heads.

How more civilised it was to be served deferential meals at the huge oak table in the cloistered Manor's ancient hall with its stained glass, crossed swords, exposed beams and half a tree blazing in the fireplace. Alien to a mediaeval baron, however, were the swimming pool and the snooker den – not to mention a studio that had attracted Fairport Convention, Vivian Stanshall and, as American as Stanshall was English, Frank Zappa.

Of British studios, Zappa preferred those few in London that, for all their environmental shortcomings, were several technological steps ahead of the Manor – and so did McCartney, who had fashioned most of the second Wings album, *Red Rose Speedway*, in no less than five different metropolitan locations including Abbey Road. No spectator sport, the recordings themselves were only the most expensive part of a process that, before session time was even pencilled in, had started with Paul rehearsing the material with un-*Wild Life*-like exactitude, balancing ruthless efficiency with the old sweetness-and-light.

With his producer's hat on, McCartney also decreed theoretical apportionment of trackage; the short-listing of devices and effects, and the overall operational definition. Never had he been out on a longer limb, but he kept whatever trepidations he had about his presently maligned skills as a console *savant* in check. Nevertheless, much as at least six engineers employed might have respected the ex-Beatle's learned if sometimes irritating procrastinations over, say, degree of reverberation overspill allowable on the keyboards, Glyn Johns for one had had his apparent fill of being head-to-head with Paul inside the control room.

Partly because he'd been one of McCartney's chief supporters during the *Let It Be* unpleasantness, Glyn had been put in charge of the technological donkey work for the latest effort. Yet Paul's comprehensive logging of production methods since 'My Bonnie' with Bert Kaempfert had ripened in him the self-assertion to issue jargon-ridden instructions, and make recommendations about equalisation, vari-speeding, bounce-downs, spatial separation and so forth that, if not guaranteed to achieve the effect he desired, he considered worth investigating. Tiring of the majestic slowness of conjuring up sounds that may or may not have met McCartney's headache-inducing requirements, Johns, allegedly, washed his hands of *Red Rose Speedway*.

As to the finished product, titles like 'Big Barn Red' and 'Little Lamb Butterfly' were reflective of the maturing McCartney family's rural contentment, and a confirmation that Paul's capacity for "granny music" was bottomless. *Rolling Stone* judged *Red Rose Speedway* to be "rife with weak and sentimental drivel"[3]. The way other detractors laid into it too, you'd think that it made Gareth Gates sound like Zappa jamming with Hendrix. Certainly, Gareth, Will Young, Peter André or some weedy present-day boy band could do as well with a revival of 'My Love' as its originators did in 1973.

Anyway, how could *Rolling Stone*, the *NME* or the newer *Zig-Zag* turn their noses up at a disc that in the USA spent a month lording it over the likes of Dawn, Elton John, Barry White, The Osmonds, The Carpenters, Stevie Wonder plus The Stylistics, Harold Melvin and his Blue Notes and any number of other velvet-smooth acts from trend-setting Philadelphia that kept North American FM radio in tasteful focus with vocal burbling of lovey-dovey mush over limpid sweetening of strings, vibraphone and woodwind plastered over a muted rhythm?

It may have afforded McCartney a wry grin when 'My Love' was brought down at the end of June by George Harrison's 'Give Me Love (Give Me Peace On Earth)', but that lasted only a week before the latest by Billy Preston took over. Ringo's turn would come during the autumn when 'Photograph' – co-written with George – climbed to the top of that same Hot 100. Starr did it again – just – in January when, on knocking off Eddie Kendricks's 'Keep On Trucking', he ruled pop for seven glorious days. Before the year was out, John Lennon would stick it out for a week up there too with 'Whatever Gets You Through The Night' – and so would Wings with 'Band On The Run'.

14 *"Crossroads"*

"It took us ages to become a good band – partly because we kept changing the other personnel."

– Denny Laine

The Wings show that crossed Britain in summer 1972 passed without incident other than a road manager bringing on a birthday cake for Denny Seiwell at Newcastle City Hall where the bill-toppers were joined for the encore by support act Brinsley Schwartz, harbingers of the pub-rock movement.

In the first instance, Wings too had been a reaction against the distancing of the humble pop group from its audience, and the isolation of stardom from the everyday. Empathy with ordinary people going about their business did not extend, however, to police who had appeared backstage with the promptness of vultures after a performance in Gothenberg the previous August. It had come to their ears that controlled substances, to wit 200g (7oz) of marijuana, had been discovered in a package from Britain addressed to McCartney. The tedious wheels of the Swedish legal process had been set in motion, and fines had to be paid before Wings could continue with dates in Denmark, the next country on the itinerary.

Paul passed this off as a farthing of life's small change, even hurling a metaphorical stone after his prosecutors by confiding to a journalist's cassette recorder straightaway that he intended to smoke some more of the stuff as soon as the opportunity arose. Such insolence may have provoked the unwelcome interest of the constabulary local to Campbeltown, who, so a PC Norman McPhee testified at the Sheriff's Court on 8 March 1973, visited High Park for a routine check on the absent owner's security arrangements. Glancing in one of the greenhouses, McPhee, fresh from a course in drugs identification, recognised cannabis plants, cultivation of which was counter to the provision of the 1966 Dangerous Drugs Act, section 42.

Interrupting work on a forthcoming ITV special entitled *James Paul McCartney* to answer the summons, the McCartneys were free to go after coughing up £100 ($160), a mere bagatelle for an ex-Beatle, as there was no question of the narcotic being used for any purpose other than personal consumption. As it had been in Sweden, James Paul McCartney seemed unremorseful, even facetious, as he brushed past the *woompf* of flashbulbs afterwards.

A few hours later, he was back in London, focussing his attention once again on *James Paul McCartney*, under the direction of Dwight Hewison, whose curriculum vitae included Elvis Presley's televised comeback over Christmas 1968. Paul's prime-time spectacular for Britain and the States was among the first such undertakings in which the "rushes" – uncut footage – were filmed on videotape, thereby bypassing the false economy of holding up proceedings for the laborious development of cheaper cine-film.

Sequences included a "voxpop" street scene and some cheery community singing of 'Pack Up Your Troubles', 'April Showers', 'You Are My Sunshine' and further tin-helmeted whimseys and *Sentimental Journey*-type warhorses from the Chelsea Reach, a Liverpool pub, by Paul, Mike McGear and other McCartney relations plus Gerry Marsden and the boozer's regulars. Nevertheless, the greater part of *James Paul McCartney* was excerpts from a late afternoon concert before a studio audience, and staged scenarios, among them an outdoors 'Mary Had A Little Lamb', and a choreographed and moustachio-ed Paul in a white tail suit and pink tuxedo with a high-stepping Busby Berkeley-esque dance troupe. More significant than this blatant concession to showbiz proper was the inclusion of several Beatles numbers such as an acoustic 'Michelle', a passer-by's unique 'When I'm Sixty-Four' and back to Paul for 'Yesterday' just before the closing credits.

While *Melody Maker* sneered at the "overblown and silly extravaganza"[1], it was to run a two-part feature, obsequiously headlined "Wings – Anatomy Of A Hot Band"[2], after according the ensemble's third album, *Band On The Run*, and the single that preceded it, 'Live And Let Die', grudging praise.

Melody Maker noted too the involvement of George Martin in 'Live And Let Die', the first time he'd worked with McCartney – or any Beatle – since Abbey Road. The song had been commissioned as the theme for the James Bond flick of the same name with the lightweight Roger Moore, rather than Sean Connery, in the title role. Martin also served as McCartney's champion when the movie's co-producer, Harry Salzman took it for granted that the Wings version was a useful demo for the use of Welsh *chanteuse* Shirley Bassey or someone like her. "I was completely nonplussed," recalled Martin, "and in my best tactful way, I had to suggest that if he didn't take the thing more or less as it stood, I didn't think Paul would like him to have the song. Eventually, it did sink through and I got the job of doing the film score, but it was a nasty moment."[3]

Martin's soundtrack earned him a Grammy, and *Live And Let Die* was nominated for an Oscar after almost-but-not-quite reaching Number One in the US. While 'My Love' had demonstrated that chart supremacy could give false impression of Wings's standing with the critics, 'Live And Let Die' cut the mustard, and, for the time being, most of them let McCartney in from the cold. They also listened sympathetically to *Band On The Run*, a combination of force and melody that yielded a cathartic send-up of Lennon and his Plastic Ono aggregations in 'Let Me Roll It' as well as hit singles in 'Helen Wheels' (a track remaindered from the UK pressing), 'Jet' and its complex and million-selling title track. Vignettes of around five different melodies to strung-together lyrics, the latter seemed to be a medley, albeit a more marketable proposition than such disparate precedents as 1957's 'One For The Road' – drinking songs by pugilist Freddie Mills – and The Pretty Things' 'Defecting Grey', a dry-run for *SF Sorrow*, the first "rock opera".

Because Paul's favourite Studio Two at Abbey Road had been block-booked already, Wings had chosen to record the album at the only other EMI complex then available – in Lagos, Nigeria – and, even then, they were obliged to transfer to the same city's ARC Studios (owned by Ginger Baker) and endure the scowling disapproval of hired local musicians who resented what they'd perceived as non-African pop stars "plundering" the continent's musical heritage – though, as Michael Jackson was to confirm, this never went deeper in McCartney's case than the sonic possibilities of its instruments: "He goes to hotels in Africa and Jamaica, bringing back different sounds, sticks and some drums."[4]

As well as being accused unfairly of cultural burglary, the McCartneys were mugged in broad daylight by the occupants of a kerb-crawling car not long after Paul had been poleaxed by a respiratory complaint.

It never rains but it pours, and there'd been something rotten in the state of Wings before they'd so much as booked the flight from London. It had set in when Henry McCullough slumped into a glowing huff over what McCartney remembered as "something he really didn't fancy playing"[5]. This was symptomatic of a general antipathy felt by both McCullough and Denny Seiwell towards the group's music, Linda's keyboard abilities and some of the antics in *James Paul McCartney*. Since *Wild Life*, the poisoning of Wings's reputation by pens dipped in vitriol didn't help either.

Five days after the guitarist had resigned by telephone, Seiwell threw in the towel too, mere hours before the rest left for Africa. He'd decided he'd be better off as a freelance sessionman – while McCullough landed a recording contract with Dark Horse, a label founded by George Harrison – who could guess what Paul had been like as a bandleader. By 1977, however, Henry was back on small UK stages in the employ of such as Carol Grimes and Frankie Miller.

Without him and Seiwell, the troubled making of *Band On The Run* had continued with Denny Laine and Paul often finding themselves with headphones on, playing an unfamiliar instrument. Yet from the internal ructions, the tense 'atmospheres', the drifting from pillar to post, from studio to unsatisfactory studio, surfaced the first Wings album that was both a commercial and critical triumph, back and forth at Number One at home and the Hot 100, and the first Wings LP to be issued in the Soviet Union.

The release of the album and its singles hadn't been accompanied by a tour of any description, simply because Wings didn't have the personnel then. Therefore, before they could hit the road again, a search began for a replacement guitarist and drummer. Among those considered for the latter post were, purportedly, Rob Townsend of a now-disbanded Family; Davy Lutton from Eire Apparent, heard already on a 1972 session for Linda McCartney's 'Seaside Woman'; Mitch Mitchell who'd worked for Johnny Kidd, Georgie Fame and Jimi Hendrix and Aynsley Dunbar, whose musical resume was as impressive, having served time with The Mojos, John Mayall's Bluesbreakers, his own Aynsley Dunbar Retaliation and The Mothers of Invention.

Next, Wings were driven to advertise in the music press, thus bursting a dam on a deluge of hopefuls from cruise ships, night clubs, nice-little-bands, pit orchestras, ceilidh outfits, hotel lounge combos, you name it. To accommodate those on a short-list, Paul rented London's Albury Theatre, and hired an existing group to play four numbers with every contender while he, Denny and Linda listened in the dusty half-light beyond the footlights.

It was a long and sometimes mind-stultifying chore that led McCartney, 50 drummers later, to conclude that "I don't think auditions are much use. We won't do it again. We'll just look around quietly, go and see people playing with different bands – but it was quite an experience: 50 different drummers playing 'Caravan' [a mainstream jazz standard]."[8] Yet Paul saw it through to the bitter end, pruning the list down to five, who were to sit in with Wings. Then there were two to be each subjected to a full day – that included an interrogatory dinner – with their prospective colleagues.

There was nothing to suggest that 31-year-old Geoff Britton wasn't the *beau ideal*. He was versatile enough to have coped with stints in both rock 'n' roll revivalists The Wild Angels and East Of Eden, one of Britain's most respected executants of jazz-rock – though best remembered for a novelty hit with 'Jig-A-Jig', a barn-dance reel. Geoff's black belt in karate had been a reassuring asset at the more unrefined engagements that either of these groups played.

Yet, the pop equivalent of the chorus girl thrust into a sudden starring role, Geoff turned out to be living evidence of McCartney's "I don't think auditions are much use". For a start, he was too loose-tongued for Paul's liking when talking to the press, implying, for example, that he was the fittest and most clean-minded member of Wings because, unlike the others, he was a non-partaker of either junk-food or drugs.

He was also unhappy about the financial arrangements, and was at loggerheads almost immediately with both Denny Laine – "a bastard"[5], snarled Geoff – and the new guitarist, Jimmy McCulloch – "a nasty little cunt"[5].

Jimmy's short stature had been seized upon for publicity purposes when he was a mainstay of Thunderclap Newman, the entity responsible for anthemic 'Something In The Air', a post-flower power call-to-arms commensurate with a period when, with Vietnam the common denominator, kaftans had been mothballed as their former wearers followed the crowd to genuinely violent anti-war demonstrations and student sit-ins.

The line-up was completed by singing drummer Speedy Keen and middle-aged multi-instrumentalist Andy Newman, an ex-Post Office engineer, whose heart was in jazz. Though the most conspicuous features of 'Something In The Air' were Keen's nasal tenor and Newman's interlude on piano and saxophone, a particularly enduring visual image was captured in an inspired photograph of Andy dressed as a 'ello-'ello-'ello policeman towering over Jimmy as a short-trousered urchin with a football under his arm.

'Something In The Air' topped the domestic chart for three weeks in summer 1969, and reached the US Top 40 by autumn, a climb aided in part by its inclusion – with Badfinger's 'Come And Get It' – in the soundtrack to *The Magic Christian*. This coincided with the release of the hit's belated follow-up, 'Accidents', which lingered for one solitary week in the British Top 50. Sales were as modest for the associated album, *Hollywood Dream*, even after *Rolling Stone* suggested that Keen was the group's producer, Pete Townshend of The Who, in disguise.

By 1971, Thunderclap Newman was no more, and Jimmy, a working musician since his Glaswegian schooldays, landed a prestigious stint with John Mayall, whose previous lead guitarists had included Eric Clapton, Peter Green and, Brian Jones's successor in The Rolling Stones, Mick Taylor. He then stepped into the shoes of the late Les Harvey in Stone The Crows, fronted by Maggie Bell, a sort of Scottish Janis Joplin but minus the onstage histrionics. The group was, however, on its last legs, and Jimmy had been one of Blue, a nice-little-band connected genealogically with Marmalade, when, on the recommendation of Denny Laine, a friend of several years standing, he was invited to play on 'Seaside Woman'.[6] After he gave as creditable a performance on a Mike McGear solo album at Strawberry Studios in Stockport, Jimmy became a member of Wings in June 1974, two months after Geoff Britton.

Thus reconstituted, Wings continued with sessions half a world away in Nashville, where Paul had already finished a nepotic

'Walking In The Park With Eloise' with assistance from Chet "Mr Guitar" Atkins – co-producer of many early Elvis Presley smashes – Floyd "Mr Piano" Kramer and others of that self-contained caste that could improvise the orthodox "Nashville sound" peculiar to the Hollywood of country-and-western music. By the 1970s, however, Nashville had embraced more generalised pop, though of a kind not uninfluenced by C&W's lyrical preoccupations and melodic appeal. As such, 'Walking In The Park With Eloise' – the one written by Jim McCartney – was issued as a single by The Country Hams and was to remain one of Paul's (and his father's) eternal favourites of all the material he ever recorded.

While the McCartney brood were observed during their six weeks in Nashville, eating regularly at the fashionable Loveless Motel restaurant – famous for its smoked ham, biscuits and peach jam – they slept on a farm outside the city. It was owned by songwriter Curly "Junior" Putnam, who was still reaping a rich fiscal harvest from 'Green Green Grass Of Home', a 1966 global chartbuster for Tom Jones. Otherwise, he'd meant nothing to the world at large, except to those who derive deep and lasting pleasure from studying raw data on record labels – until immortalised by Wings in 'Junior's Farm', issued as a hit single late in 1974 with a strong B-side, 'Sally G', penned by Paul after sightseeing Nashville's red-light district.

In its own right, 'Sally G' crept into the US Top 40, while Paul's production of Scaffold's treatment of 'Liverpool Lou', a sea shanty that had flowered from the same stem as 'Maggie May', fared better in Britain than a crafty 1963 rendering by Dominic Behan, brother of playwright Brendan. Among further items in which the McCartneys were involved during the exploratory period that followed *Band On The Run* were *I Survive*, an intriguing *faux pas* of an album that gained Adam Faith his first *Top Of The Pops* slot in a donkey's age; 'July 4' by Australian vocalist – and protégé of the leader of a now-disbanded Dave Clark Five – John Christie and 'Let's Love', a song by Paul that had more intrinsic value than a bottle of wine when presented to Peggy Lee after the couple joined her for dinner in her suite at London's plush Dorchester Hotel. If not amounting to much in sales terms, that Lee – an international entertainer since 1938 – was "thrilled" by this gift from one she'd perceived to have "loads of class"[5], was as luxuriant a feather in McCartney's cap as her 1965 version of Ray Davies's haunting 'I Go To Sleep' had been for the Kink composer.

During the gaps between records and tours, it was quite in order for lower-ranking Wings musicians to undertake individual projects too – as Denny Laine did with a 1973 solo LP, *Ahh...Laine*, which he'd started when in Airforce, backed by personnel from Stone The Crows. Whatever McCulloch and Britton's plans of like persuasion were – or whether they even had any – are not known, because, at a press conference in New York on 22 October 1974, the McCartneys mentioned that dates were being pencilled in for a tour of ten countries. This, they said, was intended to last over a year, albeit with breaks lengthy enough for the making of an album to follow another one that would be out prior to the first date.

Fans from Bootle to Brisbane were on stand-by to purchase tickets, but, as it was with "the Phoney War" – the lull between Neville Chamberlain's radioed declaration and the first blitzkriegs – the interval between Paul and Linda's announcement and the opening night (at the Southampton Gaumont not quite a year later) was long enough for many to wonder if the tour was ever going to happen.

The most pressing hindrance was centred on the apparently irresolvable antagonism between Britton on the one hand and McCulloch and his less expendable pal Laine on the other. So far, Geoff had kept his fists, if not his emotions, in check, but breaking point wasn't far away. Perhaps a punch-up might have cleared the air. Nevertheless, during sessions in New Orleans's Sea Saint Studios for Wings's fourth album, *Venus And Mars*, McCartney cut the Gordian knot by finding a drummer who'd get on better with Denny and Jimmy.

The job went to Joe English, a New Yorker who had been summoned to assist on *Venus And Mars*, following Geoff Britton's crestfallen return to England. Joe was esteemed by trombonist Tony Dorsey, hired to lead the four-piece horn section being assembled for the tour, mainly on the strength of his experience in the same capacity for soul shouter Joe Tex. Dorsey was also among those with first refusal on numerous studio dates in Los Angeles – which was where he'd entered the orbit of Joe English.

Like Denny Seiwell before him, Joe was, by his own admission, "on the bottom"[7]. This had followed six years of vocational contentment as one of Jam Factory, a unit that had criss-crossed North America, second-billed to the likes of Jimi Hendrix, The Grateful Dead and Janis Joplin. The group's disbandment allied to a messy divorce triggered poverty and general psychological upset, but he'd been thrown a lifeline with a chance to back Bonnie Bramlett, once of Delaney and Bonnie and Friends, drawn from that Los Angeles studio crowd who were the very epitome of that cocksure sexism that informed the stock rock-band-on-the-road in the pre-punk 1970s.

English was spared the monotony of listening to any detailing of the previous night's carnal shenanigans on the Bramlett tour bus when he took up the post with the less aggressively friendly Wings in time for the unleashing of *Venus And Mars* and its first single, 'Listen To What The Man Said', in May 1975.

Because *Band On The Run* had been deemed a commendable effort, both were guaranteed a fair hearing by reviewers – and sufficient advance orders to slam the album straight in at Number One in every chart that mattered. 'Listen To What The Man Said' also went to the top in the States, but, true to what was becoming a precedent, fell slightly short of that in Britain. The 'Letting Go' follow-up traced a similar scent in macrocosm, nudging the US Top 40 while stopping just outside it at home. By a law of diminishing returns, however, a third A-side, 'Venus And Mars' itself, actually climbed higher than 'Letting Go' in the States while missing completely at home, becoming McCartney's first serious flop since The Beatles.

This was but a petty dampener on the overall success of an album that the majority of listeners judged to be pleasant enough, but something of a holding operation, for all its vague star-sign "concept", complete with a *Sgt Pepper*-esque reprise of the opening track, and the penultimate 'Lonely People' – them again – linked to a jaw-dropping version of the contrapuntal theme to *Crossroads*, the long-running ITV soap opera, set in a Midlands hotel and then broadcast during forlorn afternoon hours between the *News In Welsh* and the children's programmes – and, surmised McCartney, "just the kind of thing lonely old people watch"[5].

It was flattery of a sort that the Wings version of 'Crossroads' was churned out over the closing credits before the series – in its original format – finally went off the air over a decade later, following the dismissal of Noele Gordon as central character "Meg Mortimer". Denny Laine may have been the originator and principal advocate of the Wings's cover, having been acquainted with Gordon when she was host of *Lunch Box*, that lightest of ITV's light entertainment shows, on which he and his Diplomats had been resident.

Denny was also lead vocalist on 'Spirits Of Ancient Egypt' as Jimmy McCulloch was on 'Medicine Jar', a number he'd penned with Stone The Crows' drummer, Colin Allen. This corresponded with a spirit of willing concession by McCartney that emanated not only from the grooves of the album, but also during the preliminaries to the long-anticipated tour – for which Laine had also been earmarked to sing 'Go Now' – with Paul tackling Mike Pinder's descending piano ostinati and solo – and a revival of Paul Simon's 'Richard Cory'. Moreover, Jimmy and Denny (playing a twin-necked Gibson) were to break sweat with duelling guitars during controlled "blowing" sections in a couple of numbers elongated for that very purpose.

It had been decided too that the two colours and two orbs that dominated the album sleeve were to be a recurring image in both the tour merchandise and the costumes worn on a carpeted stage in the midst of scenery sufficiently minimal and plain to accommodate back-projections such as the one for 'C Moon' – a reproduction of one of the Magritte paintings Paul had been collecting since 1966. This one depicted a candle with the moon where a flame ought to be.

The props were being constructed while Wings rehearsed five days a week just north of London in EMI's hangar-like film studios, which were surrounded by a wilderness of weeds and coarse grass that was engulfing gear that had outlived its celluloid usefulness – like two flights of ornamental stairs, half a Spitfire and an equally rusty German U-boat.

Inside, as well as the classic two guitars-bass-drums set-up, a grand piano stood on a rostrum for Paul's use, while Linda was now banked by a clavinet, mellotron and mini-moog, new-fangled keyboards that made her Hammond organ seem like a Saxon church in Manhattan. Sight-reading at stage-right behind English's drum kit, the horn players were all-American apart from Howie Casey blowing tenor saxophone just like he had with Derry And The Seniors.

Howie was a comfortable familiar – and so were Linda and Denny, but if Paul was expecting a smooth ride, he was to be disappointed. "No! It's too fuzzy," he shouted, having halted the group mid-song, "The harmonies aren't sharp enough. We've really got to concentrate all the time here, otherwise it'll go limp – and don't scoop up to that last note. Let it fall away naturally."[8] The next half-hour was spent attacking five offending notes from different angles until they matched the boss's "head arrangement".

Gradually, direction and outcome shone through with sharper clarity, specifically when "We got to a point at one time where we were very gloomy, moaning that it wasn't gelling – and that made it worse, of course. So in the end, we had a discussion-cum-argument about the whole thing, and everybody got it out of their system. Each of us would play his own bit instead of looking over his shoulder at the next man – and it seemed to work. That's when we started believing in it. It became real for us that day, and everybody felt much happier."[8]

The litmus-test was an *in situ* bash before an invited audience that included Ringo Starr, Harry Nilsson and others who didn't necessarily want to like it: "record company people and so forth," noticed Paul. "It showed up a lot of holes in the show, bits that needed to be tightened up."[8]

Encouragingly, only those in the know picked up on these in Southampton on 9 September 1975 – though, belying the atrocious sound quality of the trek's first bootleg – a cassette entitled *McCartney In Hammersmith* – a general improvement became perceptible to eight North Americans and a Japanese lady with the resources to attend every stop of the once and, wishfully, future Beatle's passage round the globe.

When his Wings weren't either on an aeroplane or waiting in the departure lounge for the next one, they hurtled along the motorways, freeways and *autobahns* in a state-of-the-art coach as luxurious as a first class railway carriage with attached diner and toilet – so much so that it excited the idle upward stares from traffic-jammed car drivers whose exhaust pipes belched out their envious impatience.

Between the Australian and European legs of the tour, the dramatis personnae convened at Abbey Road to get to grips with *Wings At The Speed Of Sound*, another good rather than great album, on which Paul's delegation of artistic responsibility extended as far as featuring Joe English as lead singer on 'Must Do Something About That' – while Linda's soprano was to the fore on 'Cook Of The House'. Denny and Jimmy were permitted one each too – on, respectively, 'Time To Hide' and, another McCulloch–Allen opus, 'Wino Junkie'. Paul, nevertheless, was loud and clear on the attendant hits, 'Let 'Em In' – and the rather self-justifying 'Silly Love Songs', which, like the album, shot to the top in the USA, Number Two in Britain.

During this and other lay-offs during the tour, the man that *Melody Maker* had front-paged lately as "Just An Ordinary Superstar"[9] made time to attend to MPL, now the largest independent music publisher in the world with 'Happy Birthday To You', 'Chopsticks' – the most recognised (and irritating) piano solo ever composed – and key Broadway musicals (including *Hello Dolly, Chorus Line* and *Annie*) amongst its litter of lucrative copyrights.

Of more personal import, however, were the US rights to Buddy Holly's best-known songs at a knock-down price, owing to comparative indifference to him on his home territory. In Britain, it was a different story. A London Teddy Boy called Sunglasses Ron – so it is fabled – wore his trademark shades day and night from Holly's death until his own in the mid-1990s. The first tribute on vinyl, however, was that of Marty Wilde with 'You've Got Love', a medium-paced jollity whose title said it all, on the 1959 LP, *Wilde About Marty*.

The Searchers, Dave Berry and Peter and Gordon were among those whose pragmatic admiration during the 1960s beat boom had brought forth workmanlike versions of 'Listen To Me', 'Maybe Baby' and the chartbusting 'True Love Ways' respectively, while The Hollies were responsible for a 1980 album that was devoted to Holly.

In the age of the "supergroups", Humble Pie gave us 'Heartbeat', but before that Blind Faith's revamp of 'Well...All Right' was conspicuous for a snake-charmer riff, altered lyrics and a typical instrumental work-out over the fade.

Already, the 1970s had produced Steeleye Span's *a cappella* experiment with 'Rave On' and Mud's Number One in the same style with 'Oh Boy!' – while on the horizon was Wreckless Eric's 'Crying Waiting Hoping'.

Capitalising on this latest evidence of the four-eyed Texan's lasting popularity in the land he visited just once, the 40th anniversary of his birth was marked by the first of McCartney's yearly Buddy Holly Weeks in London. Beginning on 7 September 1976 – midway between two months in the USA and the tour ending as it had begun in Britain – it climaxed with a showbiz luncheon at which guest of honour Norman Petty, Holly's studio mentor, presented a startled Paul with the cuff-links that, so he told the watching throng, had been fastening Buddy's shirt when his corpse was carried from the wreckage of the crashed aircraft.

Later celebrations – in other cities too – would embrace concerts by what was left of The Crickets; rock 'n' roll dance exhibitions; Buddy Holly painting, poetry and songwriting competitions; the opening of a West End musical about him; a "rock 'n' roll Brain Of Britain" tournament – and song contests, although the 1996 winners (a trio with a jungle-techno crack at 'Not Fade Away') at the finals in London's Texas Embassy Cantina had some of their thunder stolen by an "impromptu" jam fronted by Gary Glitter, Dave Dee, Allan Clarke of The Hollies, Dave Berry and – you guessed it – Paul McCartney.

Paul was vocal too in his objection that a 1979 bio-pic, *The Buddy Holly Story*, "was hardly the true story". Putting action over complaint, he financed *The Real Buddy Holly Story*, a documentary screened on BBC2 in 1985 with interviewees that included Keith Richards, Holly's brothers and, using The Quarry Men's scratched 78rpm 'That'll Be The Day' as an audio aid, Paul himself – who also gave viewers 'Words Of Love' to his own acoustic six-string picking. In parenthesis, he was, purportedly, to be supplicated in vain four years later to sink cash in Clear Lake, Iowa's Surf Ballroom – the site of Holly's final performance, and now threatened with demolition – or at least use his celebrity to convince state authorities that the place might be a remunerative tourist attraction.

Back in 1976, however, McCartney's primary Holly-associated concern was supervising *Holly Days* on which Denny Laine, like The Hollies, paid his respects over an entire album. As exemplified by, say, 1960's *I Remember Hank Williams* by rockabilly balladeer

Jack Scott or Heinz's *Tribute To Eddie* [Cochran] three years later, this was not a new idea, but, spawned in Scotland in the same homespun way as *McCartney*, its heart was in the right place, even if it didn't beat hard enough to tempt many to buy either *Holly Days* or its two 45s, 'It's So Easy' and 'Moondreams'.

Nothing from *Holly Days* was trotted out when the tour resumed or on in-concert *Wings Over America*, said to have shut down George Harrison's *All Things Must Pass* and his *Concerts For Bangla Desh* as the biggest-selling triple-album of all time. Moreover, in among its reminders of Wings and the solo McCartney's chart strikes were ambles as far down memory lane as 'Yesterday' and 'I've Just Seen A Face' (also from the non-soundtrack side of *Help!*); 'Lady Madonna' and the "White Album"'s 'Blackbird', and, restored to its raw pre-Spector state, 'The Long And Winding Road' off *Let It Be*. Paul seemed, therefore, to be coming to terms with both his past and present situation as he conducted Wings with nods and eye contact while never sacrificing impassioned content for technical virtuosity. As codas died away or as someone wrapped up a particularly *bravura* solo, he'd direct the adulation of the hordes towards others under the spotlight, and beam as salvos of clapping recognition undercut, say, the opening chords of Denny's 'Go Now'.

Ultimately, Paul McCartney had ensured that his Wings gave the people what they seemed to want – and the consensus in North America was that he'd put up a better show than George Harrison, whose trek round the sub-continent late the previous autumn had also contained a quota of Beatles numbers among the solo favourites – though these had been marred by George's persistent laryngitis, his taking of unpardonable lyrical liberties and unappealing re-inventions such as a 'My Sweet Lord' at breakneck speed. Hardly the last word in mister showbusiness, he hadn't endeared himself to the crowds either with on-mike admonishments like "I don't know how it feels down there, but from up here, you seem pretty dead to me."[10]

John Lennon had sent Harrison a bouquet of first-night flowers, and had attended a couple of the troubled concerts, trooping backstage afterwards to say hello and join in heated inquests into the graveyard hours. He, George and Paul had also contributed songs and lent studio assistance to Ringo Starr's eponymous 1973 album. Though this was coloured as a bastardised Beatles collection, no track had involved all four in the same place at the same time – though 'I'm The Greatest' came close with Starr, Harrison and Lennon at the session in Los Angeles' Sunset Sound Studio. McCartney had wanted to pitch in too, but turgid bureaucracy and his recent run-ins with the law had delayed the granting of a US visa.

Embroiled as they were still in the fiscal turmoils of Apple, it wasn't exactly hail-fellow-well-met between Paul and the others – or, for that matter, between the others themselves – but there was talk of Paul, George, John and Ringo amalgamating again on maybe a casual basis when Allen Klein – now a villain of the darkest hue to Lennon, Starr and Harrison as well – was out of the way. Fanning dull embers for Beatlemaniacs too were reports of at least three out of four ex-Beatles caving in to overtures to do it all again for either a charity or some individual with more money than sense. "God, it's like asking Liz Taylor when she's going to get together with Eddie Fisher again,"[11] Linda cracked back at another broken-record enquiry on the subject – because neither wild horses nor net temptations that worked out at hundreds of thousands of dollars per minute each for just one little concert could drag the old comrades-in-arms together again.

John's public reviling of Paul, and Paul's more veiled digs at John had continued after the 'Three Legs'–'How Do You Sleep?' episode. "'Imagine' is what John's really like," McCartney had informed *Melody Maker*. "There was too much political stuff on the other album."[11]

"So you think 'Imagine' isn't political?," parried Lennon in the same publication the following week. "It's 'Working Class Hero' with sugar on for conservatives like yourself."[11]

Yet no printed or vinyl insult could erase a private mutual affection, cemented together as they were by an extra-sensory understanding of each other's creative appetite, by George and Ringo and by 17 years of joys and sorrows. From New Orleans, McCartney had telephoned Lennon and caught himself asking if John wanted to lend a hand on *Venus And Mars*. John didn't materialise, but Paul did for an evening of coded hilarity and nostalgic bonhomie at the open house that was a well-appointed beach villa in Santa Monica where John was living during a 15 month separation from Yoko.

Not so rose-tinted would be the 1974 night in New York when Paul and Linda fell in with John who was on his way to call on a new-found friend, David Bowie. According to the latter's girlfriend, Ava Cherry, the visit was rather confrontational: "David wasn't really friendly with Paul and Linda. There was this tense feeling. Every time Paul started to say something, Linda would jump in and not let Paul talk. I don't think she liked David very much, and the feeling was mutual."[12] The dialogue deteriorated further when, after listening to the host's new *Young Americans* twice through, Paul snapped, "Can we hear another album?"

His remark was all the more barbed because John had made a pronounced creative investment in *Young Americans*, going so far as to co-write its chief single, 'Fame'. Having absorbed "Philly Soul" deeply, *Young Americans* was as slick as John's other recent sojourns in the studio weren't. These included hacking chords as Mick Jagger emoted 'Too Many Cooks', a Chicago blues obscurity, during shambolic sessions ostensibly for a Harry Nilsson album, *Pussycats*, at Los Angeles' suburban Burbank Studios, whilst taping its demos back at Santa Monica.

Jack Bruce thrummed bass on 'Too Many Cooks', but Paul McCartney elected to man the drum kit when he looked in at Burbank, and ended up on an approximation of 'Midnight Special', once in The Quarry Men's repertoire. A few days later, he was rattling the traps again at a musical "at home" in Santa Monica.

Present too would be Nilsson, guitarist Jesse Ed Davis (Eric Clapton's understudy at the *Concerts For Bangla Desh*), "supersideman" saxophonist Bobby Keyes and blind singing multi-instrumentalist Stevie Wonder – Tamla-Motown's mollycoddled former child-star, who'd been recipient of an affectionate message in Braille on the sleeve of *Red Rose Speedway*.

As there were so many distinguished participants, the results were committed to tape for posterity – and the inevitable bootlegs – on equipment borrowed from Burbank. Paul was most conspicuous with a vocal extemporisation on a go at Santo and Johnny's 'Sleepwalk', an instrumental hit from 1959, but the clouds parting on the gods at play revealed nothing more remarkable than a session crew's meanderings during some tiresome mechanical process at the mixing desk.

Regardless of quality, however, it encapsulated a Lennon and McCartney reunion of sorts, though it wasn't the harbinger of any permanent liaison. "You can't reheat a soufflé,"[13] concluded Paul, who thought no more about sitting in with John and his cronies than he did of similar rambles with Bob Dylan at a party in Joni Mitchell's Californian home a few months later.

Nonetheless, there lingered enough fond shared memories from the days of The Quarry Men, Hamburg *et al* for further get-togethers with John, musical and otherwise, outside the context of the ledgers, computer run-offs, board meetings and the rest of the prevailing business that was taking place over division of the Apple empire.

Lennon and McCartney, however, finished on a sour note on Sunday 25 April 1976 when Paul returned unexpectedly, guitar in hand, to a harassed John's New York apartment after spending the previous evening there. "That was a period when Paul just kept turning up at our door. I would let him in, but finally I said to him, 'Please call before you come over. It's not 1956 [*sic*] anymore. You know, just give me a ring.' That upset him, but I didn't mean it badly."[14]

Without formal goodbyes, the two friends went their separate ways, and were never to speak face-to-face again. How could either have guessed that John had less than five years left?

Wings would be over too by then. Indeed, Jimmy McCulloch and Joe English hadn't stuck around long enough to be heard on the most memorable British hit by a group, that, by autumn 1977, had pared down to just the McCartneys and Denny Laine.

15 *"Japanese Tears"*

> "'Galveston' is about wanting to get back home and now
> the war is over, I can relate the song to 'Mull Of Kintyre',
> which I also do in concert. They have the same feeling
> about them."
>
> – *Glen Campbell*[1]

Perhaps he wasn't the most fitting bearer of sad tidings in this case,
but John Lennon, the "bad influence" from Quarry Bank, heard
about 73-year-old Jim McCartney's death of bronchial pneumonia
in March 1976 before Paul did. From New York, John telephoned
to break the news.

In transit between Copenhagen and Berlin with Wings, Paul
was absent from the cremation, unlike brother Mike, who lived
near his father's Cheshire home. While he'd cried his tears, Paul
had decided that Jim would have understood that the show must
go on. Besides, the tour would serve as occupational therapy, even
if, when the music was over for the day, there'd be heartache.

One outcome of Paul's emotional convalescence was a gradual
estrangement from step-mother Angela and 14-year-old Ruth.
They'd continued living in the house that Paul had bought his
father, but he made it clear that he didn't intend to maintain them
financially anymore. Within a decade Angela had reverted to her
previous surname, Williams, and had told her story to a daily
newspaper. "We don't exist," she was to mope in another periodical
in 1995, "Paul has written us out of his life. I write and send
Christmas cards, but never receive a reply."[2]

Correlated with the beginning of life without her elder step-brother was Ruth's ascent as a professional entertainer. From childhood, she had attended singing and dancing lessons, and was already composing on guitar and piano. Her stylistic determination was what she called "the spectacle": that strata of mainstream pop that embraced the likes of Liza Minnelli, Barbra Streisand and, with a nod to the glam-rock that was still in vogue during her schooldays, Gary Glitter. Indeed, Glitter's tour manager, Mike Mingard, was intermediary in setting up an artists' management company in Birkenhead – with Angela and Ruth as co-directors.

Despite his reluctance to keep these two in the manner to which they'd become accustomed, Paul, like the fated socialite in 'Richard Cory', "spread his wealth around" in other matters. When Wings were in Texas that May, for example, he and Linda bought a horse that had escaped from its paddock and happened to be ambling along the roadside as the tour bus nosed by. Four months later, the US leg of the tour was marked by a no-expenses-spared party on a Beverly Hills estate where celebrity-spotters noted the arriving Mercedes, Bentleys, Porches and Roll-Royces, and speculated about who could not been seen behind their smoked windows.

By contrast, the punk-rock – or, if you prefer, New Wave – storm gathered in Britain, and pub-rock tumbled from its zenith of chart entries for the likes of Ace and Dr Feelgood, and its executants either fell by the wayside or adjusted themselves to changing times – as did Nick Garvey and Andy McMasters of Ducks De Luxe, who resurfaced as half of The Motors. Garvey was also destined for a walk-on part in the life of Paul McCartney, the millionaire superstar epitome of all The Sex Pistols, The Damned, The UK Subs and the rest of them detested.

McCartney was loathed further for a mid-1970s visibility – in Britain anyway – that was comparable to that of a recurring ITV advertisement. There he was with Linda in a comedy sketch on *The Mike Yarwood Show*; grinning and facing the lens in an after-hours cluster of small-talking luminaries at a Rod Stewart concert at London's Olympia, and sharing a joke with Mick Jagger when the Stones appeared at 1976's Knebworth Festival. The McCartneys' pre-recorded personal greetings punctuated the in-person funny stories from the past when Liverpool boxing champion John Conteh – pictured with Kenny Lynch, Christopher Lee and other worthies on the front cover of *Band On The Run* – was subject of an edition of *This Is Your Life*.

More pragmatically, Paul seemed to be omnipresent on *Top Of The Pops*. As well as miming this or that latest single in an official capacity, there were on-camera sightings of him and his wife jigging about amongst the studio audience, sometimes lending manifest if unsolicited support to younger contenders. "By far the nicest thing that's ever happened to me on the show," recollected David Essex, "was back in October 1975 when I reached Number One with 'Hold Me Close'. It so happened that during the number, Paul and Linda McCartney, who were in the audience at that time, actually jumped up and joined in the chorus with me. It was a great moment, very special, and I'll never forget it."[3]

Amused by the memory, presenter Simon Bates would reconjure "one occasion when I was on, and, of all people, Paul McCartney strolled on to the stage. Now this is totally live, and he said, 'Hi, Simon. I'm here to plug my new record.' It was the first time in a long time that a Beatle [*sic*] had appeared live on the show."[3]

Maybe Paul only seemed to put in an appearance every time you switched on prime-time television simply because there were so many sit-coms at the time with central characters that looked like him: John Alderton in *Please Sir*, acrylically garbed Richard O' Sullivan (in *Man About The House* and *Robin's Nest*), the late Richard "Godber" Beckinsale in *Porridge*... Muddling through a weekly half-hour in, perhaps, a classroom, shared flat or, in Beckinsale's case, prison, all sported the neat, dark-haired mop-top, clean-shaven face and aspects of the chirpy persona that was the public image of "Fab Macca", who was, he declared to a waiting press corps, "over the moon"[4] about the birth of his and

Linda's first son – James – on 12 September 1977. Eight days later, he authorised the publication for all the world to see of an official photograph of the little 'un and his enraptured parents.

Elsewhere, however, it was far from fond smiles and baby-talk. Jimmy McCulloch resigned from Wings in September 1977, just prior to their knuckling down to a new album, *London Town*. He preferred to take his chances with a reformed Small Faces, one of few 1960s acts tolerated by leading punk entertainers. Nevertheless, it became rapidly and painfully transparent that all the group's fans, old and new, wanted were the sounds of yesteryear, as poor sales of two "comeback" albums against healthy chart strikes for the reissued 'Itchycoo Park' and 1968's 'Lazy Sunday' testified. With no glad welcome back assured from McCartney, McCulloch was to try again with his own outfit, The Dukes, who bit the dust soon after a 1979 album for Warner Brothers failed to live up to market expectations, and Jimmy being found stone-dead on the floor of his Maida Vale flat with the quantity of morphine, cannabis and alcohol inside his body that led the necessary inquest to record an open verdict.

By then, Joe English was an evangelical Christian, a pop-star-who'd-seen-the-error-of-his-ways, expounding the Bible and preparing a 1981 gospel album, *Lights In The World in Nashville*. He'd lasted fractionally longer in Wings than Jimmy McCulloch before tiresome "months and months sitting in recording studios"[4], waiting his turn to drum, led English to weigh up his self-picture as a musician and the cash benefits of being the last among unequals – behind Paul, Denny and one he considered a poor vocalist and keyboard player – in a group infinite numbers of rungs higher than Jam Factory had ever been.

Joe's decision to slip his cable during sessions for *London Town* – taped in part on board a converted minesweeper bound for the Caribbean – seemed justified in the aftershock of *Rolling Stone*'s condemnation of the finished product as "fake rock, pallid pop and unbelievable homilies that's barely listenable next to Wings's best work."[5] That was the worst review – as disheartening as anything written about *Red Rose Speedway* – but only the most snowblinded McCartney devotees weren't disappointed by *London Town*, for all the meticulousness that hadn't stopped at just music. Hesitation and then annoyance had chased across Paul's face when inspecting a cover on which a tinge of blue marred an otherwise two-tone shot of him, Linda and Denny against a background of Tower Bridge. Upon further reflection, however, he came to quite like it, agreeing maybe with the Confucian adage, "Honour thine error as a hidden intention" as applied to the errant photographer – who, having disposed of the original, was obliged to keep redeveloping the negative until the mistake was repeated.

This subtlety was lost on fans. Their appetites for fresh Beatle-related merchandise unsated by *London Town*, a few fell back on something called *Thrillington* on discovering that, though carrying a logo other than Parlophone, Apple, MPL or Polydor in Britain, it was, nonetheless, a pseudononymous Paul McCartney LP, this track-by-track retread of *Ram* for an orchestra augmented by the cream of London's session players, a recorder ensemble and France's Swingle Singers, a choir best known for addressing itself to jazzy adaptations of Johann Sebastian Bach in a wordless style that has the effect of predetermined mass scat-singing.

The sleeve notes alluded to the fictional life of a Percy "Thrills" Thrillington, the musical jack-of-all-trades responsible for vinyl contents taped in 1971 to be stored away until dusted off to plug a gap for Beatles–McCartney curiosity-seekers between *Wings Over America* and *London Town*.

Paul catered for more mainstream tastes with a vengeance via 'Mull Of Kintyre', a 45 recorded in, well, the Mull of Kintyre during a lengthy respite from the rigours of *London Town*. When spun in the middle of a radio interview in Australia, it prompted the hushed sentence, "Well, I've never heard such a load of crap in my life," from Gerry Marsden. Taking to heart less reactions like this than someone's conjecture that most North Americans wouldn't know what this "mull of kintyre" – or was it "Ma looking tired'? – meant, let alone be able find it on a map, McCartney promoted its coupling, 'Girls School', as the A-side in the States, where it crawled to a modest Number 33.

Yet, as much co-writer Denny Laine's baby, this eulogy to Paul's Hebridean abode was a howling domestic success, replete as it was with the pentatonic skirling of a Scottish pipe band to stoke up a seasonal flavour in keeping with its release in time for 1977's December sell-in with its homecomings, mistletoe and Timex commercials. Ploughing a similar furrow to 'Sentimental Journey', World War II singalong 'Home Town' – the one about "those corny country cousins of mine" – 1969's 'Galveston' from Glen Campbell and the verses before the convict is marched to the gallows in Curly Putnam's 'Green Green Grass Of Home', 'Mull Of Kintyre' was Wings's first UK Number One, shutting down 'She Loves You' as the kingdom's biggest-selling 45. Milkmen from Dover to Donegal whistled it, and there was no finer rendition of 'Mull Of Kintyre' than by a nine-year-old schoolboy named Matthew who, at a fête I attended in a south Oxfordshire village the following spring, clambered onto the makeshift stage, lowered the microphone and delivered it *a cappella* in an impromptu but pitch-perfect treble.

A man's gotta do what a man's gotta do. For Wings themselves, such as they were, plugging 'Mull Of Kintyre' via both a promotional film on location in – you guessed it – and slots on Yuletide TV variety and chat shows, was all in a day's work until well into January. Yet while Paul was thus mutating into as much of a British showbiz evergreen as Max Bygraves, he was to be the only ex-Beatle to figure still in *Melody Maker*'s yearly poll.

London Town also fared better commercially than contemporaneous offerings by both George Harrison and Ringo Starr. As for John Lennon, he had, to all intents and purposes, thrown in the towel since the birth of his and Yoko's only surviving child in 1975, seemingly rounding off his post-Beatles career that October with a self-explanatory "best of" retrospective, *Shaved Fish (Collectable Lennon)*.

Paul succumbed too with 1978's *Wings Greatest*. Padded out with 'Another Day' and 'Uncle Albert/Admiral Halsey', this 12-track compilation embraced further major smashes for Paul as a non-Beatle up to and including 'Mull Of Kintyre'. By its very nature, *Wings Greatest* showed up *London Town*, still only a few months old, in an even poorer light, despite the second of its singles, 'With A Little Luck' tramping a well-trodden path to the top in the Hot 100 and slipping quietly in and out of the Top Ten at home.

It had been preceded by 'Goodnight Tonight', a hit 45 that, like 'Mull Of Kintyre', had nothing to do with either *London Town* or the work-in-progress on the next album, *Back To The Egg*. Less than a fortnight after its release came a remix, which met disco fever, then sashaying towards its John Travolta zenith, more than halfway.

If you sat that one out, you could groove to 'Daytime Nighttime Suffering', buried on the B-side, but rated by aficianados as one of McCartney's most evocative compositions since The Beatles. It was also among the first Wings tracks to feature two new full-time members.

Both were more steeped in all things Beatles than anyone who had gone before. Laurence Juber had started to learn the guitar seriously only after hearing 'I Want To Hold Your Hand', while the first LP that drummer Steve Holly bought was *Sgt Pepper's Lonely Hearts Club Band*. The enthusiasm of these tractable young men was matched by skills acquired mostly on the London studio circuit where they'd crossed paths with Denny Laine. Consequently, each had been procured in summer 1978 by Denny for executive approval by Paul. While Steve was blessed with a talismanic surname, neither posed any limelight-threatening challenge to the high command or were outwardly frustrated songwriters or lead vocalists.

Neither minded being indiscernibly audible on the *Back To The Egg* session for 'Rockestra Theme' and 'So Glad To See You Here', preserved on celluloid because of arrangements that Cecil B de Mille might have approved had he been a late 1970s record producer with the run of Abbey Road and with the biggest names in British rock only a telephone call away. Led Zeppelin's John Bonham alone sent the console's decibel metre into the red, but he was but one-sixth of a percussion battalion that also included Speedy Acquaye and, from The Small Faces, Kenney Jones.

"Keith Moon was going to turn up too, but unfortunately he died a week before,"[6] explained Paul. Nonetheless, fingering unison riffs on electric guitars were Denny, Laurence, Pete Townshend, Hank B Marvin and Pink Floyd's Dave Gilmour. "Jeff Beck was going to come and Eric Clapton," sighed McCartney, "but they didn't. Beck was worried about what would happen if he didn't like the track."[6]

Beck also suffered from tinnitus – which 'So Glad To See You Here' and 'Rockestra Theme' might have worsened when even Bonham's Led Zeppelin cohort, John Paul Jones, one of no less than three bass players, fought to be heard amid the massed guitars, drums, keyboards and horns.

While they made outmoded monophonic Dansette record-players shudder, the two items weren't the flat-out blasts you may have imagined on top-of-the-range stereo. They held their own, however, on *Back To The Egg*, but that isn't saying much as the album for all its diversity was subjected to a critical mauling as vicious as that for *London Town*. If none of them, in their heart-of-hearts, expected it to be astounding, the faithful bought enough copies of lacklustre *Back To The Egg* to push into Top 20s, home and abroad, but the singles, 'Old Siam Sir' and the double A-side, 'Getting Closer' and 'Baby's Request' snatched but the slightest chart honours.

Paul had offered the latter to the venerable Mills Brothers, whose humming polyphony in concert had impressed him during a recent holiday in France. It wasn't, however, a mutual admiration society as it had been with Peggy Lee after she'd gladly clasped

'Let's Love' to her bosom. Perhaps befuddled with jet-lag and not sure which ex-member of those upstart Beatles was actually chatting to them, the Brothers had had the nerve to demand payment for recording what they didn't hear as much of a song – nowhere near the fighting weight anyway of 'Paper Doll', 'Till Then', 'You Always Hurt The One You Love' or any given one of their own hits that had predated the charts.

McCartney's name on the record label would have guaranteed a degree of attention from radio station programmers, just as his achievements prior to any 'Old Siam Sir' folly had sold out Wings's winter tour of England with side-trips to Edinburgh and Glasgow. This coincided with the calculated issue of 'Wonderful Christmastime', which, like 'Mull Of Kintyre', was a hit parade contender during a time of year when the usual rules don't apply. How else had Dickie Valentine's 'Christmas Alphabet' eased 'Rock Around The Clock' from Number One in December 1955? Why did repromotions of Slade's 'Merry Christmas Everybody' keep registering somewhere in the lists years after the disc's optimum moment in 1973? After years of minor entries at most, Gary Glitter was to be back on his Top Ten perch in 1984 with 'Another Rock And Roll Christmas' before falling back on a nostalgia netherworld where current chart status had no meaning.

The Christmas single is, with the "death disc", one of pop's hardiest forms – and Paul's effort in 1979, spurred by a reggae version of 'Rudolf The Red-Nosed Reindeer' on the B-side, and publicity generated by the tour, was guided with almost mathematical precision into the UK Top Ten. Needless to say, music press organs that were still fawning to a person who was once called "Johnny Rotten" despised 'Wonderful Christmastime'.

Mean-minded critics, flop singles, the turnovers of personnel, the arguments, the ultimatums, the eternities in the studio, none of that mattered once Wings kicked off with 'Got To Get You Into My Life', hit their stride with 'Maybe I'm Amazed' and had everyone in this Odeon or that Gaumont involved; fretting when

Paul showed signs of flagging, glowing when he got second wind and giving vent to an ear-stinging bedlam of applause after a particularly fiery 'Band On The Run'. As if they'd all sat on tin-tacks, the volume would rise momentarily to its loudest when, after 'Goodnight Tonight', Paul entered a solitary spotlight with his acoustic six-string for 'Yesterday'. Up there was his reward for working so hard: the acclamation of the great British public. That was better than any filthy lucre or terrible review of his latest LP.

As the artificial show cascaded during 'Wonderful Christmastime', Paul was in his element. The here and now was too important – and magical – to worry about The Mills Brothers and 'Baby's Request' or what the *NME* had printed about 'Wonderful Christmastime'. He had the people eating out of his palm in the way he'd imagined when in a brown study during physics at the Institute.

By way of a dress rehearsal, the group put on a free concert at Paul's old school the day before three nights at Liverpool's Royal Court, his first "home game" since The Beatles played the Empire in December 1964. There's a scene in the 1955 film melodrama *Blackboard Jungle* where a teacher tries to establish rapport with unruly pupils by spinning a disc from his treasured collection. "It's just a guy singing," was the general response. "Guys singing are a dime a dozen."

To Liverpool at large, Paul McCartney at the Royal Court was more than just a guy singing. Veiled in flesh, the Local Boy Made Good was reappearing before his people like Moses from the clouded summit of Mount Sinai to the Israelites.

Yet even some of those who'd paid touts half a week's wages for a ticket were more level-headed – though when Paul piled into 'Twenty Flight Rock' towards the end of the set, the oldest among them might have indulged in knowing nods and inner binges of maudlin reminiscence about a callow bunch called The Quarry Men – or were they The Silver Beatles? – who, through the fantastic outcome of their metamorphosis into the showbusiness sensation of the century, had attained a sort of romantic nobility. While none expected the murky waters of the Mersey to part, the show was on the scale of, if not a Cup Final or Muhammed Ali's last fight in Las Vegas, then the original Animals reunion bash at Newcastle City Hall or The Troggs in the open air of Andover's Walled Meadow in 1977. Only a miracle could have rescued either of them from anti-climax too.

McCartney's whereabouts when not within the Royal Court was a red rag to a media that had decided that if the slightest thing could be sensationalised about his descent on the city, then sensationalised it would be. There wasn't a newspaper editor on Merseyside who wouldn't promise a king's ransom for an exclusive or a candid snapshot, but journalists needed to spin an impossibly likely tale to gain admittance to a suite as protected as Fort Knox after the hiding place was rumbled and its switchboard blockaded with enquiries.

A regional television crew was kept waiting for a rumoured walkabout by the lad from Allerton – though one afternoon, he and Linda (whose forced or otherwise Scouse accent was noted) boarded the Royal Iris, the "ferry across the Mersey" on which The Beatles had twice supported Acker Bilk in the old days.

By the time The Beatles headlined with Lee Castle and his Barons on the selfsame vessel for another 'Riverboat Shuffle', just before lift-off with 'Love Me Do', Bilk had been old hat. Yet via the continuing rotation of the seasons of pop, the Somerset clarinettist had enjoyed an unexpected British Top Ten windfall – with an opus entitled 'Aria' – in the late 1970s when the going was ostensibly hard for all manner of elder statesmen of the Swinging Sixties as The Sex Pistols raced towards Number One with their banned 'God Save The Queen', and countless outfits all over the realm were formed in their image: short hair, ripped clothes held together with safety pins and horrible onstage racket with guitars thrashed at speed to machine-gun drumming behind some ranting johnny-one-note who acted as if he couldn't care less whether you liked it or not.

Even in the teeth of the standing-room-only tour, Paul may have pondered where he fitted into an industry voracious as always for new faces to exploit and discard for a fickle public. Precisely where did he belong in a Britain in which such as the *NME* had been tacitly biased towards the grassroots developments of pub-rock, punk, the Mod revival and whatever was on the way next? Its staff's lampooning of "dinosaur" acts encompassed those it considered either over-the-hill such as The Grateful Dead or wholesomely Americanised like Fleetwood Mac, who were as far from the splendid blues band they once were as Steve Winwood would be from The Spencer Davis Group with 1980's *Arc Of A Diver*, on which more US sound laboratories would receive "special thanks" than humans. Articles about him and his sort would be slotted well towards the back, just before the box adverts for disco equipment.

If McCartney was deemed worthy of as little room too, maybe he wasn't bothered. Most of his following had been disenfranchised by punk, and being mentioned in the same pages as the Pistols, Damned, Stiff Little Fingers and so on was of meagre consequence to him now that he had reached a plateau of showbusiness so unassailable that another single in the British charts or even a US album going platinum would be a mere sideshow.

He didn't need Wings anymore either. No time was better for letting go of the group than after Paul's extradition from Japan on 25 January 1980, following nine days as Prisoner No 22 in a Tokyo gaol. This had put the tin-lid on a tour of the country. He only had himself to blame, though a story persists that Yoko Ono, overwhelmed with spite after a strained telephone conversation with him two days earlier, had prodded nerves to ensure that when Wings threaded their way through the customs area at Narita airport, Paul would be the one instructed to open his suitcase.

Sure enough, a polythene bag of marijuana leaped out from on top of the spare underwear, toilet bag *et al*. Parodoxically, the culprit was suppressing an almost uncontrollable urge to laugh out loud as, handcuffed, he was hustled by uniformed men into custody and hours of circular questioning, as if in a parody of *Midnight Express*. A drama of a US student arrested for possession of hashish, and sentenced to open-ended years in a squalid Turkish prison, it had been *the* hit movie of 1978.

"PAUL IN CHAINS!" screamed a headline on breakfast tables back home while the subject of the report beneath it sank into an uneasy slumber in the detention centre where the local prosecutor had demanded he be sent. Lying there, McCartney groped for reasons why the case – which carried a maximum sentence of seven years hard labour – would or would not be pursued. Bouncing his thoughts off both Linda, John Eastman and a representative of the British Consul during their visits, he built up an damning case against himself before concluding that, while Japanese drug laws were stringent, harsh and effective – in all probability because of the island's position as a vital confluence of southeast Asia's trafficking thoroughfares – the authorities were embarrassed at having such a celebrity *keto* behind their bars, and they didn't know what to do about it.

The tour's promoter – a Mr Udo – concurred with this: "Much loss of face for me," he seethed. "Much loss of face for Minister of Justice also."[7] Yet as the hours dragged by with no word either way about his fate, Paul could either carry on wringing his hands or just shut his mind to the horror of the situation, make at least a half-hearted attempt to be pleasant to the guards and the other prisoners and slide into a routine of sweeping his cell, folding up his bedding and mattress and further compulsory chores. He also began a diary of this extraordinary chapter of his life to occupy hours when he'd otherwise be drowning in despair.

He was responding well to prison life when his belongings were returned to him and he was escorted by a dozen police officers onto the next connecting flight to London. In essence, it wasn't much different to not quite two decades ago when he and Pete Best had been bundled out of Germany for arson.

As he had after the Maharishi's tutorials in 1967, Paul insisted that he was never going to touch narcotics again, whilst either continuing or resuming his habit – as demonstrated by two related if minor run-ins with the law in 1984 when he and Linda were reprimanded and made to pay fines as inappreciable as the amounts of dope with which they'd been caught.

Nevertheless, while the nasty experience in Tokyo was yet to fade, McCartney may have had every intention of staying out of trouble. "I'll never smoke pot again,"[8] he assured one British tabloid the afternoon after his inglorious farewell to the Land of the Rising Sun. Days later, Fleetwood Mac touched down at Narita for a performance at the Nippon Budokan Hall. This was was preceded by a press conference top-heavy with topical discussion about drugs. Next morning, "WE DON'T SMOKE MARIJUANA SWEAR FLEETWOOD MAC!" drew the reader's attention to the front-page of the English-language *Japan Times*.[9]

By then, the McCartneys, weak with relief, were home at last. That Denny Laine – and the two new boys – had left Japan nearly a week earlier may have struck Paul as disloyal. While his glorious leader's freedom was hanging in the balance, Laine had been preoccupied with another solo album. Preceded by a 45 of self-produced remakes of 'Go Now' and 'Say You Don't Mind', the resulting all-original endeavour contained items with Wings that Paul had allowed him to use – as well as another single, 'Japanese Tears', an attempt to come to terms with topical events close to his heart. Issued in May, its sentiments were worthy enough, and the old conviviality between Denny, Linda and Paul hadn't dissipated immediately. Nevertheless, the seeds of Denny's departure and the subsequent demise of Wings had been sown.

16 "(Just Like) Starting Over"

"If I'd have been Paul's manager, I'd have slapped a huge Band-Aid over his mouth for three weeks after John died before I allowed him to speak."

– *Ruth McCartney*

As far as I'm concerned, Paul McCartney's most important contribution to society has been his very pragmatic support of animal rights. Any argument that his celebrity and wealth created the opportunity to do so is irrelevant. Others of his kind were sufficiently hip to understand that, like, cruelty to animals is wrong, and were active after a detached, sweeping, pop-starrish fashion in verbally supporting vegetarianism, anti-vivisection *et al*. Sometimes – because it was trendy – they'd attempted not eating meat for maybe a few weeks before the smell of frying bacon triggered a backsliding. Then they'd be noticed once again in a motorway service station, autographing a table napkin whilst masticating a pork pie; ordering a paté de foie gras to go with a minor Beaujolais in a Montparnasse restaurant – or indulging in new and disgusting passions for huntin', fishin' and shootin' with monied neighbours for whom blood sports had been second nature from childhood.

Though as much a member of the rock squirearchy as anyone else, Paul stuck at vegetarianism, following a road-to-Damascus moment one Sunday lunchtime in the Mull of Kintyre. He was settling down to a main course of roast someone-or-other with the family whilst gazing out at an idyllic rural scene of lambs gambolling round their mothers in a meadow. After at least three decades since he pushed away his plate that afternoon, he's still tucking into non-meat dishes exclusively, preaching the gospel of animal welfare, sinking hard cash into all manner of associated organisations and generally keeping up the good work started by him and his first wife.

The eventual founder of a multi-national vegetarian food company, Linda's picture remains the emblem of the still-expanding, constantly improving and award-winning Linda McCartney range of products stocked in a supermarket near you. Her role model may have been Mary, former wife of Peter Frampton, singing guitarist with *Humble Pie*. Mary's non-meat *Rock 'N' Roll Recipes* was published in 1980, several years before *Linda McCartney's Home Cooking*, still the world's biggest-selling recipe book of its kind.

Both Linda and Paul had tried vegetarianism in the 1960s. He, for instance, had been obliged to do so anyway at the Maharishi's ashram. Yet, when filling in the *New Musical Express*'s "Lifelines" questionnaire early in 1963, McCartney had chosen Chicken Maryland as his "favourite food"[1]. This was a rare treat during that year's travelling life of wayside cafés and snatched and irregular chips-with-everything snacks that coarsened the palate. It had been the same in meat-happy Hamburg where Bratwurst sausage was the equivalent of fish-and-chips, and menus in establishments like Der Fludde, Harold's Schnellimbiss and Zum Pferdestalle – which translates as "the Horses' Stable" – favoured horsemeat steaks, Labskaus – a mélange of herrings, corned beef, chopped gherkins and mashed potato, topped with a fried egg – and *Deutsch bifsteak*. A search for a nut roast would be fruitless as all over Europe a vegetarian was regarded generally as a crank and an inconvenience for dinner party hosts.

None of The Beatles had, therefore, ever considered adopting vegetarianism seriously, even when they had the means to order more than beans-on-toast. On the run around the world, gourmet dishes with specious names – furst puckler, trepang soup, veal

Hawaii, – pampered stomachs yearning for the greasy comfort of cod and chips eaten with the fingers.

By the final months of Wings, however, the catering on the road was, at Paul's insistence, entirely meat-free – though, after the lamentable incident in Tokyo, he wasn't to tour again for years, no matter how hard his various investors pleaded. Among these was CBS, who had joined the queue of major US labels supplicating him for his services as soon as executive washroom whisperings filtered through that he, Ringo Starr and George Harrison were about to shower Capitol Records with writs, alleging breach of contract and money owed.

Looking for a new record company was as chancy as looking for a new girlfriend, and now that the legal professional had insinuated its complex mumbo-jumbo into pop, deals could not be mapped out over lunch as Brian Epstein's had been with Billy J Kramer in 1963. One of the hottest properties in the industry, Paul was in a position to call shots about marketing procedure. If there was the slightest deviation from the ascribed riders, wild horses wouldn't drag him out to utter one solitary syllable or sing a single note on an album's behalf.

It was a tall order but CBS was most prepared to obey, and had also proferred the unprecedented enticement of rights to *Guys And Dolls, The Most Happy Fella* and further musicals containing all manner of showbiz standards by the late Frank Loesser. "That was the only thing CBS could give him that the others couldn't," laughed company executive Harold Orenstein. "Lee Eastman was always copyright hungry."[2] Thus Paul McCartney melted into CBS's caress for the next five years.

His maiden single under the new regime, 'Coming Up', wasn't accepted without comment by a marketing division that preferred the greater depth of sound on an in-concert version by Wings. Nonetheless, for Orenstein and those whose concept of quality was based on columns of figures, the huge advance and the sacrifice of the Loesser catalogue was a sound investment. Indeed, there was an immediate upward turn of the CBS profit graph when Paul bounced back to Number One in the States with 'Coming Up', aided by a promotional video featuring him in various guises as every member of a band. This was an apt taster for the maiden CBS album, *McCartney II*, which returned to his solo debut's homespun and virtual one-man-band ethos.

Such contrivances were not uncommon from the late 1970s. Jon Anderson of Yes had scored in the UK album Top 40 with *Olias Of Sunhollow* in 1976 – while Eddy Grant, former linchpin of The Equals, was to do likewise with 1981's *Can't Get Enough*. Issued, like *McCartney II*, in 1980, the green sleeve of Steve Winwood's *Arc Of A Diver* was as much of a fixture in student halls of residence as Che Guevara's mug had been years earlier. However, it spread out of the campuses and into *Billboard*'s Top Five, and, less instantly, to Number 13 in Britain. As it was with Paul's latest, every note had been hand-woven by Winwood personally via multiple overdubbing in the privacy of the studio he'd had built on his country estate in the Cotswolds.

Winwood, Anderson, Grant and McCartney had each built up instrumental backing tracks using a lot of synthesizers and often adding drums last, when the rhythm had already been invested into a given number. Such methodology prompted antagonism from those who prized the exhilaration of the impromptu from flesh-and-blood musicians to the technical accuracy of a voice floating effortlessly over layers of treated sound.

They could bellyache all they liked – because McCartney left even *Arc Of A Diver* swallowing dust by sweeping straight to the top on both sides of the Atlantic. It was a kick up the backside for John Lennon too, who grinned at his own vexation when hearing himself humming 'Coming Up' when turning a thoughtful steering wheel. Next, a personal assistant was ordered to bring him a copy of *McCartney II*. That it was such a vast improvement on the "garbage"[3] of *Back To The Egg*, reawoke in John the old striving for one-upmanship, and was among factors that spurred a return to the studio to make his first album since reuniting with Yoko in 1975 and becoming her reclusive "househusband".

The resulting husband-and-wife effort, *Double Fantasy*, could almost be filed under "Easy Listening", but its '(Just Like) Starting Over' sold well, and, of more personal import, Paul liked 'Beautiful Boy (Darling Boy)' – track seven, side one – enough to include it among his eight choices when a "castaway" on BBC Radio Four's *Desert Island Discs* in 1982.

This lullaby to the Lennons' only child – and the album from whence it came – had been bequeathed with a "beautiful sadness" because, on 8 December 1980, two months after his 40th birthday, John Lennon had been shot dead on a New York pavement by a "fan" who was Beatle-crazy in the most clinical sense. Like it was with President Kennedy and, in 1977, Elvis Presley, everyone remembers the moment they heard.

In Britain, where we'd been asleep, the morning papers told us nothing – though it seemed to be the only item of news on the radio. By the afternoon, estate agents were wondering who'd be doing the probate assessment; publishers were liaising with biographers; hack composers were working on tribute songs and record moguls were contemplating what tracks by Lennon or associated with him they were entitled to rush-release. Under the editorial lash, pressured denizens of the media cobbled together hasty obituaries and *Help!* was screened in place of scheduled prime-time programmes on BBC1.

Accosted by a television camera crew and a stick-mike thrust at his mouth, Paul, almost at a loss for words, had uttered "It's a drag" and mentioned that he would carry on as intended with a day's work at a studio desk. On the printed page the next day, it seemed too blithely fatalistic, but McCartney was a shaken and downcast man, feeling his anguish all the more sharply for assuming that there'd always be another chance for him and John to talk, face each other with guitars in an arena of armchairs and continue to bridge the self-created abyss that, in recent years, they had become more and more willing to cross. What with Wings in abeyance and John back in circulation again, the notion of Lennon–McCartney – as opposed to Lennon and McCartney – hadn't been completely out of the question.

John's death was both an end and a beginning, simultaneously the most public last gasp and the ricochet of a starting pistol for a qualified rebirth of the Swinging Sixties. Financially, that turbulent decade's principal icons reaped indirect benefits from the tragedy through, say, increases in the already vast amounts of money being poured – mostly by American and Japanese visitors – into the English Tourist Board's coffers for twice-daily guided Beatle tours round London and Liverpool to such golgothas as the Abbey Road zebra crossing and 20 Forthlin Road, which the National Trust was to purchase as a building of historic interest.

Similar tourist facilities were in force in Hamburg – though some old haunts were recognisable only by their names. The Kaiserkeller, for example, was thriving as a transvestite hang-out, but the Top Ten had long gone – as had some of the old faces such as Star-Club proprietor Manfred Weissleder and, also taken a few months before Lennon's slaying, Bert Kaempfert, who had suffered a fatal coronary when on holiday in Spain.

Horst Fascher was still very much at large as an eminence at a Star-Club with a facade just like the old one, but located away from a Grosse Freiheit that was less open-minded about human frailty and the temptations of the flesh as it had been before its brothels were put under government licence, turning their employees into what could be described technically as civil servants with all the attendant by-the-book correctitude.

However embarrassed the mention of its red-light districts in official guidebooks, Hamburg was now displaying pride in its cradling of The Beatles via honorific plaques on significant Reeperbahn walls, and a statue of John Lennon that was unveiled by Fascher, whose affinity to the slain Beatle's birthplace had been strengthened by an espousal to the daughter of Merseybeat

musician Faron of Faron's Flamingos, and the launching of their
son into life with the name "Rory" – as in "Rory Storm". Horst
would be conquering the desolation of the baby's cot death in
1992 when, less than a year later, hell's magnet pulled him down
again when a daughter by his next wife died from a heart
condition despite surgery by specialists flown in from New York
by his old mate, Paul McCartney.

By then, Horst had become a wanted guest at the huge "Beatle
Conventions" that are still annual events in cities throughout the
globe. For many attending these celebrations – including John
Lennon's killer – The Beatles became a craving, almost a religion.
Beyond just fitting a few extra shelves to accommodate more
accumulated records and memorabilia, and combing thinning hair
in a Moptop, certain fans have been known to make a start on the
canons of unconnected acts simply because they recorded on the
same labels as The Beatles, and holiday in a different foreign country
every year just to seek out and buy up Beatle discs issued with an
alien label and matrix number, and, possibly, an additional second
of reverberation on the closing major sixth of 'She Loves You'.

Certainly, an element of posthumous Beatlemania helped propel
'All Those Years Ago', a vinyl salaam to Lennon by George
Harrison, high up international Top 20s. A further incentive for
buyers was the superimposed presence of McCartney and Wings,
such as they were, who'd added their bits when the unmixed tape
arrived from George's Oxfordshire mansion.

For three months, on and off, Paul and the others had been
at George Martin's studio complex on Montserrat, in the distant
Carribean, working on 18 tracks from which to pick and choose
for *Tug Of War*, an album that turned out to be the follow-up
to *McCartney II* rather than the now-disintegrating Wings's
Back To The Egg.

"It was really like going back to Abbey Road," surmised Martin
while work was in progress. "We've been working very closely on
trying not just to get the songs done, but the ideas behind the songs

as well, so that we're playing about with sound, trying to create something new. We've got lots of different instruments on the thing. We used Paddy Maloney of The Chieftains [on uilleann pipes and tin whistle] on one track, and pan-pipes on another."[4]

Steve Holly and Laurence Juber had had nothing to do as Paul called on more renowned if disparate helpmates such as Eric Stewart of 10cc, rockabilly legend Carl Perkins, drummer Dave Mattacks, in and out of Fairport Convention since 1969, and Stanley Clarke, every jazz-rock clever-dick's notion of bass-playing splendour. The sessions were notable too for an artistic reunion with not only George Martin as producer, but also Ringo Starr, fresh from *Stop And Smell The Roses*, an LP with a more pronounced "famous cast of thousands" approach.

To this, Paul had donated the title track and catchy 'Attention', but had decided to cling onto another composition, 'Take It Away', considering that "I didn't think was very Ringo"[5]. Instead, it was the opening track and the fourth of no less than six singles from *Tug Of War* – which went the chartbusting way of *McCartney II*, when released in April 1982. Among other highlights were 'Here Today' – a more piquant tribute to Lennon than singalong 'All Those Years Ago' – and 1982's 'Ebony And Ivory', a duet with Stevie Wonder, which, issued on 45, was another double-first in Britain and North America.

For those who derive deep and lasting pleasure from studying chart statistics, one characteristic of the 1980s was a contagious rash of teaming-ups, some of them very unlikely – none more so than that of Johnnie Ray-era singer Rosemary Clooney and psychotic Los Angeles busker Wild Man Fischer with 1986's 'It's A Hard Business'.

Three years earlier, Cliff Richard had managed a Top Ten strike with Phil Everly. Not raising eyebrows either were alliances by Kenny Rogers and Tammy Wynette, and Queen and David Bowie, but also scrambling up Top Tens in the 1980s would be a Christmas 45 by David Bowie and Bing Crosby, and a Number One reprise of Gene Pitney's 'Something's Gotten Hold Of My Heart' by Pitney himself and crypto-punk vocalist Marc Almond. We Britons had been stunned too to notice gnarled Joe Cocker at Number One in the States with 'Up Where We Belong' and fresh-faced C&W star Jennifer Warnes, not to mention Suzi Quatro and Reg Presley's revamp of 'Wild Thing' for the disco floor; Dave Dee's second 'Zabadak!' with Klaus und Klaus, a German comedy duo – and Van Morrison recording an entire album with The Chieftains, leading ambassadors of Irish folk music.

Morrison and Cliff Richard climbed sufficiently high in the Top 40 to warrant a *Top Of The Pops* slot in December 1989; Van – on the show for the first time since 'Here Comes The Night' with Them – trading perspicatory lines with tall and tanned and young and lovely Cliff. The boy from Hertfordshire was lovely, granted, but Van, to whom nature had been as harsh as it had to Joe Cocker, stood his ground without looking out of place on the televisual flagship of the mainstream pop he thought he'd left behind long ago.

Paul McCartney, however, enjoyed a ten-year singles chart run from 1980 as rich as any thus far – though, after 'Ebony And Ivory' and 'Take It Away', 'Tug Of War' struggled wretchedly to Number 53 in Britain and nowhere in the Hot 100. However, the final 45 of 1982, 'The Girl Is Mine' cracked the UK Top Ten without effort, and nearly went all the way in the USA.

Whereas the 'Ebony And Ivory' liaison had been instigated by Paul, he himself had been solicited by Michael Jackson who, like Wonder, was a former Tamla-Motown child star. Now chronologically adult, he had been in the throes of recording the celebrated *Thriller* in Los Angeles. Paul was among several well-known guest musicians, and his cameo as jovial voice-of-experience to Michael's cheeky young shaver on 'The Girl Is Mine' was the radio-friendly antithesis of Hammer House Of Horror mainstay Vincent Price's as the more agreeable title song's undead, blood-lusting lurker-in-the-night with a rap – about "grizzly ghouls", "hounds of hell" and so forth – that dissolves into maniacal chuckling.

If Price received a fee for his services, McCartney was paid in kind when Jackson pitched in on 'Say Say Say' from 1983's *Pipes of Peace*, Paul's third post-Wings album. It also contained a title track that would be its maker's commercial apotheosis in Britain during the 1980s as 'Mull Of Kintyre' had been in the previous decade. A Yuletide Number One that lingered in the Top 50 for three months, it was helped on its way by a video that re-enacted the mythical and sociable seasonal encounter in No Man's Land between British and German soldiers in World War I. Nevertheless, as George Harrison's 'Isn't It A Pity' – when covered by Dana, a pretty colleen from Londonderry – had been aligned to the Troubles in Ulster, so 'Pipes Of Peace' was to the siting of US cruise missiles on Greenham Common RAF base and the arrival of women with camping equipment from all walks of life to stage a passive protest that continued into the 1990s. While she did not participate, Linda McCartney never failed to send her sisters-in-spirit an annual Christmas hamper from Harrods.

Outside the Knightsbridge department store on the very December day that 'Pipes Of Peace' made its chart debut, an IRA bomb killed six and maimed many more. No one wrote a song about that.

Yeah, well...the previous month, the critics had laid into the album. Surely *Melody Maker* had mistaken *Pipes Of Peace* for *Double Fantasy*, calling it "congratulatory self-righteous" and "slushy"[6] – while the *NME* weighed in with "a tired, dull and empty collection of quasi-funk and gooey rock arrangements"[7]. In retrospect, some of the tracks were rather in-one-ear-and-out-the-other, but, on the whole, it was pleasant enough, even if the stand-out numbers were its two singles.

The first of these, 'Say Say Say', Michael Jackson's returning of the *Thriller* favour, had suffered poor reviews too, but the public thought otherwise, and it shifted millions. It helped that Jackson was still basking in the afterglow of *Thriller* to the degree that even a video about the making of the Grammy-winning album precipitated stampedes into the megastores the minute their glass doors opened.

George Harrison judged *The Making Of Michael Jackson's Thriller* "the squarest thing I've ever seen," adding, "It was a bit off the way Michael bought up our old catalogue when he knew Paul was also bidding. He was supposed to be Paul's mate."[8]

The Beatles portfolio was to become Jackson's property for a down payment of nearly £31 million ($50 million), more than McCartney could afford, when ATV, its previous publishers, were open to offers for this and other bodies of work in 1986. Until then, the ex-Beatle and the superstar 16 years his junior had, indeed, been "mates", renting and watching cartoons like *Dumbo* and *Bambi* whenever Paul visited Michael's Never Never Land ranch in California. When sampling the McCartney's hospitality in Sussex, Jackson had tagged along when the family were invited to lunch by Adam Faith on his farm near Tunbridge Wells. Michael spent much of the time kicking a football about with the children, but over coffee, he'd asked his host, then writer of a weekly financial column, "Faith In The City", in a national newspaper, about how he should invest the fortunes he was earning. Faith suggested music publishing. "The rest is history," chuckled Adam, "Paul says I'm responsible for Jackson buying the rights to The Beatles' music, and then selling them on. He'd snatched them from under Paul's nose."[9]

Neither was McCartney best pleased about how 1984's self-financed and feature-length *Give My Regards To Broad Street* film was received. The initial shard of inspiration for this "musical fantasy drama" had cut him more than two years earlier during an otherwise tedious stop-start drive into rush-hour London. With a screenplay by Paul himself, the interlocking theme was a world-class pop star's search for missing master tapes for an album. This was riddled with *Magical Mystery Tour*-ish sketches in locations ranging from a churchyard to an expensive reconstruction of New Brighton's grand Tower Brighton – which had crumbled in a haze of powdered plaster in 1970. There were also musical interludes of which the majority were refashionings of Beatles and Wings favourites – though 'No More Lonely Nights', an opus fresh off the assembly-line, was the attendant hit single.

Ringo Starr would have nothing to do with the resuscitations of 'Eleanor Rigby', 'The Long And Winding Road' *et al*, but was amenable to providing a romantic undercurrent via his on-screen courtship of his real-life second wife, Barbara, who played "this gorgeous girl reporter from a music paper. Falling in love with your own wife isn't as easy as it looks."[10] Paul also doled out parts to Linda, George Martin and more recent familiars such as Tracey Ullman, a comedy actress who was to take a couple of pot-shots at the charts – and Welsh guitarist Dave Edmunds, who'd been more convincing as the monosyllabic "Alex" in *Stardust*, a 1973 sex-drugs-and-rock 'n' roll flick that was as imbued with tough realism as *Give My Regards To Broad Street* wasn't.

Throughout the six months of shooting, Paul stayed worries about the consequence as director Andros Eraminondas – no, I'd never heard of him either – guided and tempered his endlessly inventive paymaster's designations that, to outsiders, seemed as rash as a good half of *Magical Mystery Tour* had been. Nevertheless, throughout the interminable running of each celluloid mile, McCartney had been impressive for his learned recommendations about rhythm and pacing.

Yet, determined not to like it, certain reviewers looked on jadedly as flash-bulbs floodlit McCartney's anxious entrances to its several premières. While exchanging smirks at each other's cleverness, it was the bane of such people's existence that they had to write about a comparative amateur who was doing something they couldn't do. Paul was such an obvious sitting duck that they felt entitled to claim they'd lost the thread of the plot through scenes they felt should have been rigorously scissored, not laugh at things meant to be funny, snigger during "serious" parts and play safe by concluding that *Give My Regards To Broad Street* was an egocentric caper with precedents in, say, 1969's obscurer and even more self-indulgent *Can Hieronymous Merkin Ever Forgive Mercy Humppe And Find True Happiness*, the brain-child of Anthony Newley, an inverse of McCartney in that he was an actor who had become a singing composer.

Variety, the *Bible* and *Yellow Pages* of the latest cinema releases, shoved aside *Give My Regards To Broad Street* as "characterless, bloodless and pointless"[11]. As they always were, journals local to the towns where it was distributed were kinder, albeit while homing in less on the storyline than the spectacular visual effects that enhanced what was not so much in the tradition of *A Hard Day's Night* – or even *Magical Mystery Tour* in the end – as *Pop Gear, Just For You* and other of those conveyor-belt mid-1960s B-features of diversified and mimed pop ephemera connected by vacuous narrative. That was fine by me, though I preferred McCartney's more bite-sized videos for his singles, especially when he adhered to straightforward synchronisation with a musical performance, rather than project himself – or others – into dramatic situations.

The latter was to be the case with 'Only Love Remains', the principal ballad on his next album, *Press To Play*, which was centred on two elderly actors playing some dingy couple still in love after maybe half a century of wedlock: Darby and Joan who used to be Jack and Jill.

Three years before, McCartney had addressed himself to Jack, Jill and other infant video-watchers with *Rupert And The Frog Song*, 25 minutes dominated by one of the *Daily Express* cartoon character's adventures with voiceovers by sit-com shellbacks Windsor Davis and June Whitfield plus Paul himself, who'd owned the film rights to the checked-trousered bruin since 1970.

He gave *Rupert And The Frog Song* the best possible chance by ensuring it was second-billed to *Give My Regards To Broad Street*, and being a talking head, buoyant with sentiment, on the earlier Channel Four documentary, *The Rupert Bear Story*. Just as Paul's first solo album had beaten *Sentimental Journey* in the battle for chart placings in 1970, so it was in microcosm 14 years on when *Rupert And The Frog Song* defied all comers when both it and the lumped-together episodes of *Thomas The Tank Engine And Friends* – narrated by Ringo – were among BAFTA nominees as 1985's "Best Animated Short Film". Proving what traditionalists toddlers are, it also topped the video charts the previous Christmas. Into the bargain, the soundtrack's principal composition, 'We All Stand Together', sung by the animated frogs, had been high in the UK Top Ten.

Was there no end to this man's talent? He popped up again at Wembley Stadium that summer, emoting a gremlin-ridden 'Let It Be' to his own piano-playing as satellite-linked Live Aid approached its climax. Then he joined the assembled cast for a finale in which he and Pete Townshend bore organiser Bob Geldof on their shoulders.

Geldof was to be knighted for his charitable efforts. Another milestone along rock's road to respectability was the heir to the throne's Prince's Trust Tenth Birthday Gala in June 1986. Paul gave 'em 'I Saw Her Standing There' and 'Long Tall Sally' prior to closing the show by leading an omnes fortissimo 'Get Back'. A handshake from Prince Charles afterwards had less personal significance to McCartney than the fact that he'd just completed his first formal appearance in an indoor venue since Wings's last flap at Hammersmith Odeon in 1979.

If his main spot had been as nostalgic in its way as Gerry And The Pacemakers on the chicken-in-a-basket trail, in terms of audience response, he'd held his own amid Me-generation entertainers like Bryan Adams, Paul Young and, with their whizz-kid singing bass player, Level 42, not to mention Tina Turner, Eric Clapton, the ubiquitous Elton John and all the other old stagers.

Like them, he couldn't take Top 40 exploits for granted anymore, but *Press To Play* hovered round the middle of most international Top 30s, and the singles made token showings in some charts, even drippy 'Only Love Remains' after it filled Paul's entire slot on 1986's *Royal Variety Command Performance*.

He had better luck both critically and commercially – in Britain certainly – with 1987's *All The Best*, his second reassemblage of selected Wings and solo items – including the hitherto-unreleased 'Waterspout' and, of more resonance, 'Once Upon A Long Ago', the UK Top Ten single that was launched a week after the album.

Before the month was out, a similar package, Matt Monro's *By Request* – with a brief tribute by Paul in its accompanying booklet – was in the shops too. Following its use in the soundtrack of *Good Morning Vietnam* that same year, Them's 'Baby Please Don't Go' leapt out of the small screen with a voiceover extolling the virtues of a new make of Peugeot. It would have been foolish not to have put it out as a CD single. Monro, McCartney and Them were the tip of a huge iceberg. With repackaging factories in full production by then, it made as much sense for Monro, Van Morrison – and McCartney when he got round to it again – to include in onstage set-list hits maybe more than 30 years old as well as excerpts from the most recent album.

As commodity began to assume more absolute sway over creativity, the history of pop would be seized upon as an avenue for shifting records beyond simply getting information about compilations inserted in retailer catalogues. Saturation television commercials could hoick up sales from tens of thousands to a quarter of a million a year in the UK alone. In 1987, Steve Winwood's *Chronicles* would see action in the Christmas charts against *All The Best* and other "best of" and "greatest hits" offerings by Van Morrison, George Harrison and Bryan Ferry.

No matter how it was tarted up – as a 12in megamix or pressed on polkadot vinyl – the pop single had become a loss leader by then, a throwaway incentive for adults to buy an album on one of these new-fangled compact discs – on which you could almost make out the dandruff falling from George Harrison's hair on 'My Sweet Lord'. Teenagers, you see were no longer pop's most courted customers in the late 1980s, having been outmanoeuvred by their Swinging Sixties parents. Young marrieds too had sated their appetites for novelty, going no further than buying documentary exhumations of, say, a ragged gospel singalong from 1956 by the "Million Dollar Quartet" of Jerry Lee Lewis, Johnny Cash, Carl Perkins and Elvis Presley – or *Alive She Cried*, a concert by The Doors, which had spent weeks in the UK Top 40 in 1983.

These triumphs of repackaging were to be gilded by younger artists making practical acknowledgement of the lasting influence of old campaigners by contributing to tribute albums of elaborations – and just plain copies – of chosen examples from the portfolios of Syd Barrett, Captain Beefheart, Peter Green and like unforgotten heroes. Most of these were unsolicited, and The Beatles had no control whatsoever over 1988's *Sgt Pepper Knew My Father* on which several new acts depped for the Lonely Hearts Club Band – with Billy Bragg's 'She's Leaving Home' and Wet Wet Wet's 'With A Little Help From My Friends' as its chart-topping double A-side.

There'd be more fleeting *Top Of The Pops* visitations – either on video or in the chicken-necked flesh – with their latest releases by such spring chickens as The Rolling Stones, The Kinks and, a week before his sudden death in 1989, Roy Orbison. Cliff Richard too had shown that he wasn't all *Summer Holiday* and 'Congratulations' by revamping his musical aspirations and, with the aid of sprightlier minds than EMI house producer Norrie Paramor's, arriving in the late 1980s more popular than ever. Indeed, his 'Mistletoe And Wine', out in time for the festive season, was 1988's biggest-selling British single.

As the millennium crept closer, Paul McCartney would also score to a diminishing degree, not so much with songs he could have written in his sleep, but through a combination of stubbornly treading steep and rugged pathways and maintaining a lingering hip sensibility, often justifying the words of John McNally of The Searchers: "You don't have to be young to make good records."[12]

Even on "Sounds Of The Sixties" nights in the most dismal working men's club, The Searchers, The Troggs, Dave Berry and those of corresponding vintage would lure a strikingly young crowd by counterpoising contemporary offerings with the old showstoppers. After disappearing for years, neither was it laughable for others who'd travelled an unquiet journey to middle life to embark on sell-out trans-continental tours as did Paul Simon, Fleetwood Mac, The Grateful Dead, Leonard Cohen – and, after a decade away, Paul McCartney.

17 *"Don't Get Around Much Anymore"*

> "We used to play the same kind of music, American R&B, and we're both from the North. We have the same accent, the same sense of humour."
>
> – *Eric Stewart*[1]

As her distant step-brother readied himself for what amounted to his first tour outside the context of a group, the roar of the crowd seemed far away as Ruth McCartney toiled as a jobbing songwriter. Living in New South Wales in the early 1980s, she teamed up with vocalist John Farnham. Her confidence boosted when their 'New Blood' for Tina Cross reached the Australian Top 20 and Ruth relocated to Los Angeles to better ply her wares before more prestigious customers – among them Randy Crawford for whom she co-wrote 'Cigarette In The Rain', a hit in Scandinavia, South Africa and Italy as well as *Billboard*'s R&B chart.

Paul too had found a compatible collaborator. A telephone call had instigated a link-up with one who he thought initially might be, if not a Lennon, at least another Denny Laine.

Present on guitar and backing vocals in *Tug Of War* and *Pipes Of Peace*, Eric Stewart had also been evident in the videos to the singles 'Take it Away' and 'So Bad', and in *Give My Regards To Broad Street*. He was a Mancunian who'd been almost as much the chief public image of Wayne Fontana And The Mindbenders as Wayne himself. After Fontana and the group went their separate ways in 1965, each blaming the other for declining chart fortunes, the first face you were drawn to in most Mindbinders publicity photographs was that of Eric, lead singer on their first – and most far-reaching – single, 'A Groovy Kind Of Love'. He was also the acephalous outfit's chief creative pivot, though before calling it a day at the Liverpool Empire, on 20 November 1968, this final line-up included Graham Gouldman, one of the great enigmas of British beat: composer of Top 20 strikes for The Yardbirds, Hollies, Herman's Hermits, Dave Berry, Wayne Fontana and Jeff Beck, home and abroad, but unable to get anywhere with his own combo, The Mockingbirds.

While The Mindbenders were no more, Gouldman and Stewart remained business partners. Graham's composing royalties and Eric's solitary hit, 'Neanderthal Man', as one of Hotlegs with ex-Mockingbirds, Kevin Godley and Lol Creme, amassed sufficient capital for the expansion of their Strawberry Studio project, then humbly situated about a Stockport hi-fi shop. Among their clients was Mike McCartney for 1974's *McGear* LP, and it was during these sessions that Stewart and Mike's brother spoke for the first time since The Beatles and Wayne Fontana *et al* had brushed against each other in some backstage corridor in nineteen-sixty-forget-about-it.

Strawberry had already produced a world-class act in 10cc, ie Eric, Graham, Lol and Kevin. Signed to Jonathan King's UK label, the four had had their first chart-topper with 1973's 'Rubber Bullets', a story-in-song of an ill-advised dance at the local county gaol that led to an uprising so beyond control that the governor sent for fire-armed reinforcements. Like its Top Ten predecessor, 'Donna', 'Rubber Bullets' was, even with sociological implications and lines like "it's a shame those slugs ain't real" and "blood will flow to set you free", a borderline comedy disc with neo-"baby" lead singing and deep "fool" bass second vocal.

The laughs came harder in such as 1976's 'I'm Mandy Fly Me' – in which the first-person narrator ended up in the drink via the nosediving of a passenger jet. The charming titular air hostess not only saves him, but seems to walk on the waves to render the kiss of life "just like the girl in Dr No" on top of providing – no, anticipating – every comfort during the flight. Unconscious, he is picked up by the coastguard, but of Mandy, there is no sign. Studying her face on the airline's travel poster shortly afterwards he debates whether it had all been a crazy dream, but, if it had, how come he lived to tell the tale?

As Stewart slung in rhymes, chord changes and 'I'm Mandy Fly Me'-esque twists to the plot as he and McCartney had pieced together possibilities for what became *Press To Play*, the latter considered that he might have procured a Lennon rather than a Laine after all as their liaison first blossomed with 'Stranglehold'. Co-writer of five further selected tracks, an educated guess says that Eric stuck his oar in most obviously in lines like "I think we skip the preamble" and "I'll be happy to lay low, inevitably bound" from 'Stranglehold' or "Ears twitch like a dog breaking eggs in a dish" in 'However Absurd' plus references in 'Move Over Busker' to Mae West and "Nell Gwyn and her oranges" and further instances of a lyricism more peculiar to the wordier 10cc than Wings.

Musically, *Press To Play* was proficient but not adventurous. Many of the lodged conventions of songwriting methodology since the beat boom were, however, thrust aside when McCartney next bonded with Elvis Costello, one of the most successful post-pub rock ambassadors to get anywhere in North America. A series of inspired publicity stunts – and Costello's borrowing of Roy Orbison's horn-rimmed and uncommunicative stage persona – had assisted the passage of his first album, 1977's *My Aim Is True*, and early singles into the UK charts. Backed by The Attractions, he touched a commercial zenith in 1979 with *Armed Forces* as his biggest US seller, and its 'Oliver's Army' spin-off at a domestic Number Two.

For such a prolific and "covered" songwriter, it was perhaps odd that he had since returned to the UK singles Top Ten only with items penned by others, ie Sam And Dave's 'I Can't Stand Up For

Falling Down' (from 1980's *Get Happy*) and 'A Good Year For The Roses', a C&W morosity from the following year's *Almost Blue*. Both were examples of Costello's frequent ventures into unexpected musical areas. A more extreme one was to be 1993's *The Juliet Letters* with The Brodsky Quartet – for which he reverted to his given name, Declan McManus.

One of McManus–Costello's finest recent songs had been 1988's 'The Comedians' for role model Roy Orbison in which the Big O conducted himself with shocked dignity in the teeth of a dirty trick at a funfair whereby he was left dangling all night at the top of a ferris wheel by its operator. The latter's donkey-jacketed virility had, apparently, bewitched Roy's grounded harpy of a girlfriend: "not just that you're never coming back to me/It's just the bitter way that I was told."

Five years earlier, Costello's 'Shipbuilding', penned with guitarist Clive Langer, had been a UK Top 30 entry for Robert Wyatt. In it, an unemployed shipwright longs for the dockyards to open, even though he deplores the purpose of the war vessels – destined for Mrs Thatcher's self-glorifying Falklands conflict – that form his livelihood. Written with Wyatt's "ordinary geezer" voice in mind, it was, said Langer, "the saddest, most brilliant thing I've ever been involved with"[2].

That 33-year-old Costello had finished his formal education in Liverpool – and spent many previous school holidays with relations there – may have lent an element to 'Shipbuilding' that might have been absent had he been similarly connected to Basingstoke or Market Harborough. Elvis was of Irish stock too – another plus point for McCartney, who, a few months earlier, had sent a wreath shaped like a Celtic cross to the funeral of Eamonn Andrews, genial Dublin-born host of both *This Is Your Life* and the children's hour evergreen, *Crackerjack*.

In common with Paul too, Elvis's father was a musician – though, unlike Jim McCartney, Ross McManus had gone fully professional, even gaining a recording deal both as singer with Joe

Loss and his Orchestra and in his own right, albeit with such as an LP of Elvis Presley hits for the Golden Guinea budget label.

Offering hip credibility too, Costello was just what unfashionable McCartney needed, and, after perhaps initial slight misgivings, the two buckled down to "writing a bunch of really good songs," smiled Elvis. "A couple have stuck around in my repertoire, 'So Like Candy' and 'That Day Is Done', which is one that I'm fond of. It was great working with him. Of course it was. I was thrilled."[3]

Five hours a day in a room above Paul's studio in Sussex resulted in 'Back On My Feet' – the B-side of 'Once Upon A Long Ago' – and then items for Paul's *Flowers In The Dirt* and Elvis's *Spike*, albums with respective spin-off singles of which Costello's 'Veronica' figured in the US Hot 100 and the British Top 40.

As it had been when John and Paul had been working together, "his voice is so high so I would end up below him," observed Elvis, "which is a relationship he was familiar with."[3] Moreover, the general thrust of the McCartney–McManus output was the tempering of an abrasive edge with attractive tunes. 'My Brave Face' – a man's bitter freedom from his woman – just about reached the UK Top 20 for Paul – with follow-up 'This One' touching exactly the same apogee – Number 18 – but barely troubling the Hot 100 where 'My Brave Face' had got a look in at Number 25.

These so-so market volleys were incidental to *Flowers In The Dirt* returning McCartney to the top of all manner of album lists, and the ten months of the global tour (including six nights in Tokyo where all had been forgiven) earning an award from a US financial journal as the highest grossing such excursion of 1990 – with a stop in Rio de Janeiro breaking the world attendance record for a pop concert with a paying audience.

Spanning nearly every familiar trackway of Paul's career from 'Twenty Flight Rock' of Quarry Men vintage to 'My Brave Face', he was backed by quite a motley crew consisting of Linda, guitarist

Robbie McIntosh – who'd quit The Pretenders during sessions for a 1986 album – keyboard player and former PE teacher Paul Wickens, drummer Chris Whitten – who'd been with Wickens in a group led by self-styled "pagan rock 'n' roller" Julian Cope – and general factotum Hamish Stuart, founder member of The Average White Band.[4] They were a workmanlike and horn-laden Scottish soul outfit whose focus on the North American market had paid off with a US Number One, 'Pick Up The Pieces', in 1974 and further hits until disbandment in 1982, and Stuart's subsequent earning of credits on albums by, amongst others, Chaka Khan, Melissa Manchester and Adam Faith's managerial and production client, Leo Sayer, and as creator of hit songs for such as Diana Ross and The Temptations.

Stuart picked guitar very prettily on quasi-traditional 'All My Trials', an in-concert single captured in Milan – apparently, the only occasion it was performed by McCartney during this tour, apart from plugs on various TV magazines. In 1989, the number also known as 'All My Sorrows' was – like George Harrison's contemporaneous revival of another skiffle weepie, 'Nobody's Child' – a throwback to days when it slowed things down for The Quarry Men in ping-pong youth clubs, with mordant verses about "you know you're daddy is bound to die" and "carefree lovers down country lanes/Don't know my grief, can't feel my pain". How could Paul have been aware then that the most meaningful phrase for him was to be "my love has gone, left me behind", a parting not from choice, but at death's behest?

McCartney had confessed to Barry Miles that a chord change in 'I'll Get You', B-side of 1963's 'She Loves You', had been purloined from Joan Baez's treatment of 'All My Trials'. From time immemorial, more direct plundering of music in the public domain has been an intermittent ploy of British pop. One potent advantage is that publishers can cream off royalties. Well, who else ought to get them? God? Such mercenary rewards were frequently deserved. In 1963, there was an imaginative rocking-up of the Cornish Floral

Dance by The Eagles, a Bristolian beat group, and the Liverpool children's play rhyme "Johnny Todd" had been transformed most effectively by the late Fritz Spiegl into the theme tune for BBC television's Z-*Cars*. 1970 brought Traffic's daring version of "John Barleycorn" – thought more "authentic" than that of Steeleye Span. In its wake came the likes of the Nashville Teens's spooky 'Widecombe Fair' and Alan Price's 'Trimdon Grange Explosion', written in 1892 as a "whip-around" ditty to gather collections for victims of a County Durham mining disaster.

As well as filling one side of a single, Paul's 'All My Trials' utilised time on *Tripping The Light Fantastic*, a triple-album that was the quaint vinyl souvenir of the round-the-world expedition. Another by-product was the limited-edition *Unplugged: The Official Bootleg* – the sort of thing everyone-who-was-anyone was doing then – from one of the tour's post-scripts – an acoustic recital after the ticket-holders shuffled in from the February chill to the relatively downhome ambience of Limehouse Studios amid London's dockland wharfs. Some would see themselves in a consequent *MTV* broadcast, the first one to be issued on a record.

Nevertheless, no matter how endearing McCartney's wheezing mouth-organ – perhaps his first and most subtle attempt to checkmate the departed John's every artistic move – is on 'That Would Be Something' or how right-on his 'Ebony And Ivory' from behind the electric piano, the loudest ovations throughout these latest rounds of public displays would always be for the many unrevised Beatles selections. Audiences also clapped hard for Paul's olde tyme rock 'n' roll flings – which, in 1989 and 1990, paid homage to Fats Domino as well as Eddie Cochran.

Both Cochran's 'Twenty Flight Rock' and Domino's 'Ain't That A Shame' had just been recorded by Paul[5] among items of similar vintage for *Choba B CCCP* (translated as "Back In The USSR"), an initially Russia-only album of favourite non-originals dating from between Hitler's invasion of the Soviet Republic in 1941 and The Beatles' final season at the Star-Club in his defeated Germany.

From a pool of suitably rough-and-ready musicians, whether Nick Garvey from The Motors or Mick Green of a Pirates reconstituted without Johnny Kidd – and tracks ranging from 'Don't Get Around Much Anymore' (recorded in 1942 by co-writer Duke Ellington) to 1962's 'Bring It On Home To Me' from the catalogue of Sam Cooke, *Choba B CCCP* came out just before the Berlin Wall came down in 1989, and Checkpoint Charlie was rebuilt as a glass-towered conference centre. Perhaps McCartney had recognised that the impending opening up of the eastern bloc – East Germany, the Ukraine, Czechoslovakia and other previously *verboten* regions – would present a new world of possibilities. Few samples of western pop on disc had ever filtered beyond a Berlin where the partitioning of the Fatherland into two distinct cultures and political agendas was never more piquant; the flamboyance of the western Federal Republic contrasting like the Earth to the Moon with the grey Communist utilitarianism beyond the Wall.

With the establishment of a McDonald's fast-food outlet off Red Square not far away, it seemed an expedient exercise to fire a commercial boardside directly at consumers hitherto deprived of music from the very morning of post-war pop. Just as The Beatles' versions of 'Twist And Shout', 'Long Tall Sally', 'Money', *et al* were the only versions for anyone whose *entrée* to pop had been 'Please Please Me', so McCartney's would be of 13 set-works from the annals of classic rock for Russian record buyers until they came upon the originals – and, in the late 1980s, there seemed fat chance of that for a while. Besides, as David Bowie, Bryan Ferry, The Hollies – and John Lennon – were a handful of the many who'd indulged in entire albums of oldies already, why shouldn't Paul?

If nothing else, Paul sounded as if he enjoyed revisiting them. Worth mentioning here are Nick Garvey's memories of both his hand in *Choba B CCCP* and his impressions of its prime mover: "I went to a rehearsal place in Woolwich where Macca ran through and recorded several things with me on bass, him on guitar, Mickey Gallagher on piano and Terry Williams on drums. Linda was there too, but she didn't join in.

"Macca does have this ability to switch into performance mode. It was remarkable to watch it happen – the big smile, the whole thing... He was playing to us! He sang as if it was no trouble at all, though he could be a bit fey. He played too like it was easy as hell, and he knew exactly what he wanted from us, even if it was easy to get the impression that he likes to be in control, and that there's nobody around him to tell him if he's wrong. After all, he hadn't had the opportunity to live in the real world for over 30 years. He couldn't walk down the street because people bother him.

"Overall, I was knocked out by him. It was a lot of fun too. We did 'She's A Woman', all sorts of things. About three months later, I was called down to his studio in Sussex for a second day of recording. I noticed his old Hofner bass in there, with a set-list still stuck on the side. He himself proudly pointed out Bill Black's double-bass on 'Heartbreak Hotel' in the corner, and invited me to have a go on it.

"The line-up was like it was in Woolwich, but with Henry Spinetti – who I'd never met before then – on drums. We did all these old rock 'n' roll songs, most of them in one take with live vocals. There were just a few overdubs for backing vocals. Only three tracks I was on were used, but I got three hundred quid.

"The album was put out in a brown paper bag in Russia, and I thought that was that. However, it generated a certain amount of interest in the rest of the world, and about a year later it was released outside Russia. I wasn't expecting more money as I'd already received a session fee – so it was a real shock when a letter arrived explaining all this. The cheque inside had fallen to the carpet, and I imagined that it was for another 300 quid [$500] so I nearly had a heart attack when it was for £5,000 [$8,000]!"

Paul's reward for his generosity was meagre in hard financial terms in Russia itself, not because *Choba B CCCP* was a flop, far from it, but because – as he realised would be the case – the lump sum (with no performance royalties) he was paid was in roubles that could only be spent within the USSR. Yet he did his duty by the album by agreeing to a live phone-in (with attendant interpreter) on the BBC's Russian Service during a programme with a title that means "Granny's Chest". It was gratifying that more than 1,000 rang, but these were boiled down to 14 – at a cost of approximately £9 ($15) per minute – one of whom was a seven-year-old schoolgirl.

A Hard Day's Night came to Warsaw, and there'd been talk in 1966 of The Beatles crossing the Iron Curtain in person, but they had never been seen on a Russian stage, unlike so many British pop entertainers – including Paul in May 2003 – who have done so since 1989.

Ruth McCartney has been among them too. Pop is a business more riddled than most with chances-in-a-million, chaos theory and seeming trivialities that change everything. Dave Berry attributed his success in continental Europe to an arbitrary gesture with a cigarette butt someone had thrown onstage during his cobra-like act in a televised song festival in Belgium. On the other side of the same coin, PJ Proby's fall from grace was precipitated by his trousers splitting from knee to crotch during a second house at Luton Ritz. Brian Epstein turning up when a support group is valiantly over-running while backstage staff are trying to sober up the main attraction or a radio disc jockey flipping his lid over the B-side of a record and spinning it into the charts – perhaps a variable as unforeseen caused Ruth's self-penned debut album, *I Will Always Remember You*, to follow the footsteps of *Choba B CCCP* by climbing to Number One in *Komsomolkaya Pravda*, the closest you'd get in the USSR to *Record Retailer*.

Paul could wait until he felt like going there, but Ruth couldn't afford to keep the customers waiting, even though all proceeds from her trips to Russia had to be donated to charity until the rouble became an exchangeable currency. Nonetheless, she was well placed to recoup more than golden memories after the fall of communism via a lengthy trek that, in spring 1994, was to embrace reaches of Siberia so remote that they could only be reached by helicopter. When she landed in Salekhard, a fishing town within the Arctic Circle, the electricity turbines were so underpowered that there was no running water for the entire four days she was scheduled to work there – but that, as they often say, is showbusiness.

While Ruth brought the aura of a fresh sensation to Russia, Paul had dyed his greying hair black, having chosen not to go gently into that good night. At least most of it was still on his head – and so was George Harrison's, who, despite swearing that his 1982 album, *Gone Troppo*, had been his last, had pulled an unexpected stroke five years later with million-selling *Cloud Nine* and its singles – which included a US Number One, his first since 'Give Me Love'. Moreover, George's years away from the public at large had turned him too into the latest pop news – particularly now that he'd shaved off a scrappy middle-aged beard – for those young enough never to have heard much of him before.

A major factor in the reactivation of George's pop career was *Cloud Nine* producer Jeff Lynne, once leader of The Electric Light Orchestra, but now with a reputation for steering other faded stars back into the spotlight, notably Roy Orbison, one fifth of The Traveling Wilburys – an impermanent skiffle-like "supergroup" with George, Jeff, Bob Dylan and Tom Petty.

After the ill-starred Roy's fatal heart attack in December 1988, there was much speculation as to who would be his Wilbury replacement. In view of George's comment that "I'd join a band with John Lennon any day, but I wouldn't join a band with Paul McCartney", his "original mate in The Beatles"[6] wasn't in the running. Yet Paul expressed an unreciprocated wish to team up with George Harrison on the grounds that "George has been writing with Jeff Lynne; I've been writing with Elvis, so it's natural for me to want to write with George."[7] Well, it had been a long time since 'In Spite Of All The Danger'.

If there was yet no creative reunion, there were still companionable evenings in a bar or around a dining table – jokey reviling of each other like close friends do whenever they reminisce about the old days as Paul had done for a wider world on *Press To Play*'s 'Good Times Coming' with what I interpret as a veiled reference to two Institute schoolboys deciding on the spur of the moment to hitch-hike across Wales in the lost sunshine of 1958.

These days, it was common knowledge that Paul was prone to disguised nostalgic walkabouts on Merseyside, so much so that one had been mentioned in 1985's ITV sit-com, *The Brothers McGregor*. Apparently, Paul had dropped in at a club called the Blue Cockatoo, formerly the Coconut, for old times' sake. "That was where John Lennon first met Paul McCartney," Cyril McGregor, its resident singer, assured his solicitor. "Asked him for a dance. Used to be bloody dark in the Coconut."[8]

How delightful it was for the former Beatle to mingle anonymously among shoppers in a Wavertree precinct; in a pub garden on the Cheshire plain or browsing in a second-hand bookshop up Parliament Street. Unmolested by autograph hunters and worse, he was conducting himself as if he was a nobody, mooching about beneath an untroubled suburban sky. With the same blithe fatalism, he also chanced being seen by day in London too – pavement-tramping around St John's Wood, Chalk Farm and Ladbroke Grove; in a second-class train carriage to Waterloo; knocking back a quiet lunchtime pint somewhere in Soho; thumbing through scuffed wares in Notting Hill's Record And Tape Exchange; eating in a Camden Town café or taking the air in Regent's Park.

Back in Liverpool, he'd once surprised Tony Crane and Billy Kinsley of a still-functional Merseybeats by walking in on a session at their Amadeus studio in Everton. Luckily, it wasn't one for 'Heaven', a 1991 single by Kinsley and Pete Best.

Out on the streets again, Paul noticed that a Cavern had been reconstructed down Mathew Street next to Cavern Walks shopping mall. On the now-busy thoroughfare's opposite side stood the John

Lennon pub and, halfway up a wall, an Arthur Dooley statue of a madonna-like figure – "Mother Liverpool" – with a plaque beneath reading "Four Lads Who Shook The World", and one of them, like, flying away with wings. Get it?

Civic pride in The Beatles had been emphasised further in 1982 by naming four streets on a housing estate after each of the four most famous members – Paul McCartney Way, Ringo Starr Drive and so forth – in spite of one sniffy burgher's opposition "in the light of what went on in Hamburg and their use of filthy language."[9]

While *Backbeat* – a silver screen perspective on John, Paul, George and Pete in Hamburg – loomed on the horizon, "Beatle conventions" had been fixtures in cities throughout the world for years. Frequent attractions – especially when each August's Merseybeatle festival was on – at both the new Cavern in Mathew Street and the more authentic one in the Beatles museum on Albert Dock were groups whose *raison d'être* was re-enacting some phase of The Beatles' career from the enlistment of Ringo to the end of the Swinging Sixties. Others of their ilk paid homage to solely one Beatle as did Band On The Run, Hari Georgeson, Starrtime and the short-lived Working Class Heroes. By the mid-1990s, there'd be nigh on 200 such tribute bands in Britain alone, virtually all of them encumbered with a right-handed "Paul". The most accurate copycats were – and still are – The Bootleg Beatles, formed from the cast of the West End musical, *Beatlemania*.

While it was said that he procured one of the "Pauls" as a stand-in for a video shoot, McCartney was to raise an objection that, in *Backbeat*, "John" rather than his character sang 'Long Tall Sally', and seemed bemused generally that anyone should make a living impersonating The Beatles.

18 "Come Together"

> "If it moves, I can score it."
>
> – *Carl Davis*[1]

There are some entertainers who regard touring as absolute hell, but Paul McCartney isn't one of them. Within weeks of winding down from his turn-of-the-decade circuit of the planet, he was thinking aloud about doing it all again. Though it wasn't to happen until 1993, he ordered the wheels to crank into motion.

As expected, the next expedition was to be on hold until it could be tied in with an album and plethora of singles, and, when it was actually in motion, *Paul Is Live* (as opposed to *Paul Is Dead*), an in-concert package in time for Christmas. These products were to be in as many formats as the traffic would allow – 7- and 12in vinyl, cassette, picture sleeves, gatefold sleeves, CD, remixes and with or without posters, postcards, tour itinerary and bonus tracks. Such were the hidden costs for the truly dedicated, whether there from the beginning or *Flowers In The Dirt* latecomers, for whom every new McCartney release remains a special event.

The 1993 album, *Off The Ground*, was, however, less special than usual. It was telegraphed by 'Hope Of Deliverance', an instance of blinded-by-science production almost-but-not-quite smothering a mediocre song that died a death, even with Paul, Linda and the boys in the band miming it on *Top Of The Pops*. Though Liverpool poet Adrian Mitchell had been requested to give it and the rest of the *Off The Ground* libretto a once-over, 'Hope Of Deliverance' was a fair indication of what was to come in a collection that was unfettered by the objectivity of an Eric Stewart or Elvis Costello, apart from the latter's 'Mistress And Maid' – which sounded like a *Flowers In The Dirt* leftover – and a 'Lovers That Never Were' that was enjoyable enough, but not up to Costello's reading on his own *Mighty Like A Rose* in 1991.

Paul's animal rights protest number, 'Looking For Changes', was all very worthy too in its speaking up for the voiceless, but, both musically and lyrically, it was one that could have been shelved without much hardship. Yet 'Biker Like An Icon', the third single, did not bely Paul's description of it as "a good little rocky song"[2], though meaning did not take precedent over phonetics.

Perhaps the worst trauma an artist can suffer is a dream coming true. When you're as close as anyone can be to a pain-free existence, maybe there's not much left to say. Your dream became reality, and the feeling you had when you were young and struggling somehow becomes the new dream – more far-fetched than becoming rich and famous had ever been.

With no blues getting bluer, *Off The Ground* was the product of a satisfied mind. Polished and mostly unobjectionable, it was never expected to be astounding – by marginal McCartney enthusiasts anyway – but it sufficed because skillful arrangements and technological advances can help conceal ordinary-sounding songs in need of editing. It nudged the Top 20 in the USA where Beatlemania was always more virulent than anywhere else, and those afflicted bought Paul's records out of habit to complete the set like *Buffalo Bill* annuals. Over here, too many didn't want to like *Off The Ground*, especially during a period when Elvis Costello wasn't cool either, having strayed too far with *The Juliet Letters* from the punk rocker he'd never been.

Who remembered a time when either Costello or McCartney had been called a "genius"? Once upon a long ago, they might have possessed it, but the party line now was that it was soon exhausted. What's a genius anyway? Among the many blessed with that dubious accolade are Horst "A Walk In The Black Forest" Jankowski, Phil Spector, dart-throwing Jocky Wilson and the late Screaming Lord Sutch.

Never mind. As it had been in 1989, the press could slag off Paul's records; latter-day punks could denigrate him as one more bourgeois liberal with inert conservative tendencies and hippies disregard him as a fully paid-up subscriber to what Neil in BBC TV's *The Young Ones* sit-com called "the Breadhead Conspiracy", but there he was again, running through his best-loved songs for the people who loved them – and him – best of all in Melbourne Cricket Ground, Louisiana Superdome, Munich's Olympiahalle and further packed-out stadia designed originally for championship sport.

This time round, there were more Beatles numbers than ever from a portfolio that bulged with more crowd-pleasers than could be crammed into any evening with Paul McCartney, but ticket-holders understood, and were sad rather than angry if he didn't do their favourite. They'd seen it all before anyhow – him pop-eyed at the central microphone with a guitar or seated on a stage-left podium at a piano, the cynosure of perhaps a 100,000 eyes and maybe four sweaty spotlights. Having a high old time up there, he accommodated appropriate gestures and facial expressions as well as off-mike mouthings and momentary eye contacts that probably meant nothing, but made the heart of the recipient – or someone who imagined he or she was – feel like it would burst through its rib-cage.

As always, the mood was light, friendly, but what would have happened had the main set ended with politely brief clapping instead of the foot-stomping and howling approval that brought Paul back on for the encores of 'Band On The Run', 'I Saw Her Standing There' and, finally, everyone blasting up chorus after da-da chorus of 'Hey Jude'?

At last, he'd made a peace between his past and present situation. For form's sake, he stuck in tracks from whatever current album the onlookers may have heard or wouldn't ever hear between the timeless hits. Yet, however slickly predictable his stage show was becoming, he would prove to have much in common in his way with David Bowie, Jeff Beck, Van Morrison and other advocates of the artistic virtues of sweating over something new while Elton John, Phil Collins, Stevie Wonder and like Swinging Sixties contemporaries continued cranking out increasingly more run-of-the-mill albums.

Paul got into the swing of keeping you guessing what he'll be up to next by paying close attention to what made his now-teenage children and their friends groove nowadays. He could relate to much of what he heard, conspicuously that which had grown from a resurgence of unadulterated psychedelia in the 1980s. With Mood Six and Doctor And The Medics showing the way, such as The Sleep Creatures, The Magic Mushroom Band, Green Telescope, Palace Of Light, The Beautiful People, The Suns Of Arqa and Astralasia also garnered a piece of media action then. Their stock-in-trade was "head music for the feet", whereby disco rhythms were married to synthesizer arpeggio, instrumental meanderings, perfunctory and abstract lyrics and evidence of painstaking investigation of early Pink Floyd and Jimi Hendrix as well as The Soft Machine, Hawkwind, Caravan, Magma, Gong, Van Der Graf Generator and other victims of the same passion.

In the bowels of Reading's Paradise, The Fridge in Brixton and Deptford's Crypt, the proceedings were familiar to those aged hippies snapping their fingers within, if not to the majority of attendees who'd been little more than psychedelic twinkles in their fathers' eyes in 1967. As it had been in the *IT* launch and the Fourteen Hour Technicolor Dream, strobes flickered and ectoplasmic *son et lumière* was projected onto the walls as the bands played on and on and on for cavorters with eyes like catherine wheels. Modern trimmings included programmed accelerations of tempo as the night progressed, and, consequently, more dancing than trancing. "Psychedelic music flowered in the 1960s but it is a timeless thing," observed Garry Moonboot of The Magic Mushroom Band. "I love the whole genre because it incorporated so many different styles. Adding that funky beat to it gets a whole new thing going."

When the New Psychedelia was fused with revived interest in modern jazz, "acid jazz" was the result. More symptomatic of the growing bond between the dance floor and a crossover from reality to a wild dream via LSD and its "Ecstasy" descendant were trance, ambient jazz, ambient techno, ambient-pop, hardcore, acid-house, hip-hip, trip-hop, jungle, ragga and further sub-divisions. You had to be sharp to spot the shades of difference, and out-of-touch journalists tended to lump all of them together as "the Modern Dance" after it surfaced in mainstream pop through the chartbusting efforts of The Art Of Noise, The Prodigy, The Shamen, The Orb and The Cocteau Twins, and in rehashes of anthems from LSD's high summer such as Atom Heart's synthesized unearthing of Donovan's 'Sunshine Superman' or The Magic Mushroom Band's alarming reprise of Hendrix's 'Are You Experienced' with quotes from 'Third Stone From The Sun', and Garry Moonboot's wife punctuating her singing with sensual moans.

Exemplifying the form's original material is Astralasia's 'Sul-E-Stomp', a much-requested fixture at the crowded "raves" that brightened Saturday nights in the most unlikely locations. It started almost as a traditional Irish reel before an abrupt segue into a section of more typical fare, ratifying their Swordfish's comment: "There tends to be a mixture of all sorts of culture within our music. We might throw something from Australia in with something from India and try and cross all the cultures over. It's never directed at one vein."

While it is tempting to rationalise the Modern Dance as bearing the same "new broom" parallel as punk had to stadium rock, it was undercut with far greater respect for pop's elder statesmen. A special guest on The Magic Mushroom Band's *Spaced Out* in 1992 was Van Der Graaf Generator's David Jackson on woodwinds. The favour was returned when The Magic Mushroom Band assisted on Jackson's *Tonewall Stands*.

Fleetwood Mac founder Peter Green would be involved likewise in a remake of 'Albatross' in collaboration with Chris Coco, Brighton club disc jockey and mainstay of Coco-Steel-and-Lovebomb, an amalgam of "acid house" persuasion – though the new 'Albatross' was more ambient-techno. Then, in 1995, there was Screaming Lord Sutch's 'I'm Still Raving', another assisted exposition of the Modern Dance that "at over 140bpm [beats per minute]", it says here, "really 'kicks' and will get any club moving." The following year, Eric Clapton – as "X-sample" – had a go at trip-hop with producer and keyboard player Simon Climie, issuing a "bland, colourless album"[3], *Retail Therapy*, as TDF.

More profitable had been Duane Eddy's and Tom Jones's respective returns to the Top 20 via link-ups with The Art Of Noise, electro-pop innovators whose very name was taken from a tract written in 1913 by "industrial music" precursor Luigi Russolo, whose "line note" system of notation is still used by electronic composers today.

Before the group was formed, their Anne Dudley had been hired by Paul McCartney as a string arranger – and it was through her that he was introduced to Martin "Youth" Glover, who had had a prominent hand in an Art Of Noise remix album, 1990's *The Ambient Collection*. Before that, he'd plucked bass in Killing Joke, a post-punk outfit who went in for Searing Indictments of Society. Martin next struck out on his own as a respected Modern Dance producer. Among his clients was The Orb until a disagreement centred on finance in 1993 – which was when Glover became the enabler of Paul McCartney groping his way through a first and foremost essay as a Modern Dance exponent.

Perhaps just in case they looked back in anger at it, McCartney and Glover hid themselves beneath a pseudonym – The Firemen – but the fusion of "downtempo house" and a vague strata of dub-reggae heard on 1994's *Strawberries Oceans Ships Forest* and

1998's more freeform and slow-moving ambient-techno of *Rushes* certainly induced a near-trance-like effect in me – and I wouldn't recommend using either album as in-car entertainment. Maybe not "going anywhere" was almost the intention. With titles like 'Transpiritual Stomp', 'Pure Trance' and 'Fluid', it was almost the music at any given moment that counted instead of rather non-directional individual pieces – and individual players, unless you're a Beatles–McCartney completist.

Antecedents in Paul's body of work are discernable, I suppose, in the aural junk-sculpture of tape-loops that was the instrumental interlude of 'Tomorrow Never Knows' – and the yet-unissued 'Carnival Of Light' for that 1967 "happening" at London's Roundhouse (and my own feeling now is that it was probably meant to be experienced only on that night at that event).

Good old-fashioned guitars reared up among the synthesizers and samples in *Rushes*, and the overall effect was considered tame and old-fashioned by Orb and Youth fans, but if you like, say, Enigma (who superimposed Gregorian chant upon the grid of the Modern Dance) and *The Moon and the Melodies* (a merger of The Cocteau Twins and New Age composer Harold Budd) or maybe Brian Eno and Robert Fripp's *No Pussyfooting* and what David Bowie called his "dreamy stuff" on *Low* and *Heroes*, you'll probably half-like Youth and McCartney's efforts. Otherwise, it's aural wallpaper that you buy with the same discrimination as you would a few kilograms of spuds from the greengrocers.

Nevertheless, it demonstrated that Fab Macca dug the latest sounds – just as *Liverpool Oratorio* had his appreciation of classical music. As Martin Glover was to be the catalyst for The Fireman business, so Paul had leant on Carl Davis, Brooklyn-born and known chiefly as the classically trained composer of television incidental music and film scores, for this maiden venture into what he'd been brought up to regard as highbrow nonsense: "When symphonies came on the radio, my family just went, 'Oh bloody hell!' and switched the station."[4] However, he'd treasured aspirations of symphonic persuasion since penning the soundtrack of *The Family Way*, a 1966 celluloid farce starring Hayley Mills – and it had been Paul, rather than John, George or Ringo, who was photographed, baton in hand, in front of the orchestra during the session for apocalyptic 'A Day In The Life' on *Sgt Pepper*. "Mozart was a pop star of his day," he opined. "Had he been around, he would probably have been in The Beatles on keyboards."[5]

McCartney had first stumbled upon Carl Davis in 1988 via an engrossing feature about him in some "serious" music journal or other. They had a mutual friend in Carla Lane, who, like the McCartneys, had put her celebrity at the disposal of the animal rights movement. Carla, see, was the writer of Liverpool-centred television sit-coms *The Liver Birds* and *Bread*. The latter starred Jean Boht, wife of Davis – with whom Lane had collaborated on a musical drama, *Pilgrim's Progress*. Paul and Linda sent Carl a good-luck message, one of many that papered the walls of his dressing room when he conducted the Royal Liverpool Philharmonic Orchestra at the première. Noticing the McCartneys' note during the *après*-concert party, it occurred to the Orchestra's general manager, Brian Pidgeon, that Davis ought to explore the possibilities about a similar, if more newsworthy, collusion, even if economic potential might outweigh artistic merit, to climax the Liverpool Phil's forthcoming 150th anniversary concerts.

Not long afterwards, Carl's car engine duly died outside a McCartney house party in Sussex. Small-talk didn't become big-talk on that occasion, but Paul rang afterwards, and, during consequent hundreds of hours in each other's workrooms, he stood over Carl at the piano and vice-versa. They fielded all outside interference as one or other paced up and down the carpet, bedevilled by a half-forgotten but brilliant idea that might have jerked him from a velvet-blue oblivion in the still of the previous night. As the oratorio ripened, a companionship beyond a practised but detached professional relationship grew from the liaison of methodical Carl steeped in the formal do's and don'ts of the classical tradition, and the non-sight-reading *parvenu*, six years his junior, with the stylistic clichés and habits ingrained since he'd positioned yet uncalloused fingers to shape that E-chord on six taut strings when he was 14.

After the job had been done, there was a hiccup when Paul insisted that it be officially titled *Paul McCartney's Liverpool Oratorio*, but Carl, if affronted, caved in – as long as he was still paid as per contract, even though McCartney's sleeve notes to the attendant album read "I made the music and someone else wrote it down."

"It's something I have had to learn to live with,"[5] grumped Davis on the subject.

It might have been belt-and-braces self-defence on Paul's part: "It surprised me that some people who knew me quite well asked if I'd written the words and Carl the music," he glowered years later. "I had to explain that I could compose music but was unable to notate it. To me, music is something more magical than simply a series of black dots on a page."[6]

The sidelining of his co-writer was hardly a *Phantom Of The Opera* situation, was it? Yes, and if "world première" meant "last performance", it might be to the put-upon Carl's advantage to be its *éminence grise* rather than anything more resplendent.

As he kneaded the 90-minute work into shape for the big night – at Liverpool's Anglican Cathedral on Friday 28 June 1991 – Davis was not so humble that he couldn't put forward proposals for leading vocal roles. The most illustrious of those who accepted them was Dame Kiri Te Kanawa, a Maori soprano who'd cantillated an aria for millions at Prince Charles's televised wedding ten years earlier. Nonetheless, she was the down-to-earth antithesis of the stock tantrum-throwing primadonna of operatic legend. Furthermore, she'd been keen on The Beatles during her New Zealand girlhood and throughout a four-year scholarship from 1966 at the London Opera Centre.

For all the bel canto purity of Te Kanawa, Sally Burgess, Willard White and the other principal soloists – as well as the cathedral choir – Davis and McCartney elected not to temper the local accent germane to a libretto that, as it often is with first novels too, contained a pronounced measure of autobiography: a wartime genesis; quoting the Liverpool Institute motto in the opening line[7]; 'Headmaster's Song' to the memory of Jack Edwards – Institute headteacher in Paul's day; the death of a parent and "the frail magic of family life"[6]. Into this cauldron, Paul stirred in fictional ingredients such as the central character's birth in the midst of an air raid; his wife being the main bread-winner; his correlated inadequacy driving him to drink and a road accident that nearly causes the pregnant woman to lose the baby before they all live happily ever after.

Within the interlocking eight movements, *leitmotifs*, "second subjects" and all that – less Igor Stravinsky than Miklos Rozsa (or Carl Davis) – were pleasant tunes sufficiently self-contained to be divorced from the oratorio. McCartney thought so too, and authorised the issue of the first of two singles, 'The World You're Coming Into' coupled with 'Tres Conejos', a not altogether relevant number about a Spanish lesson at school. These and other *Liverpool Oratorio* songs might have suited Paul's untrained baritone too, and been capable of shoe-horning, without much adjustment, onto one of his pop albums. Certainly, they were more to do with the Edwardian light operas of Edward German and Gilbert and Sullivan than, say, Schoenberg's *Pierrot Lunaire* – with its complete suspension of tonality – or Edgard Varèse's *Nocturnal* – chromatic menace beneath Dadaist babble and seemingly random phrases from Anais Nin's *House Of Incest*.

Music magazine opined, however, that even the most melodic excerpts from *Liverpool Oratorio* "fell short of the standards set in his finest pop tunes," and suggested that McCartney had "yet to find a distinct 'classical' voice."[6] Nonetheless, while agreeing that it didn't break any barricades, the verdict from other classical organs, if foreseeably condescending and not rabidly enthusiastic, was that *Liverpool Oratorio* was pretty good for a bloke from the unsophisticated world of pop, albeit a multi-millionaire with the services of Carl Davis at his command, and a renown that had obliged him to sign autographs for 200 choirboys after the final rehearsal.

While reaching a lowly 177 in *Billboard*'s pop chart, the album displaced Italian tenor Luciano Pavarotti from the top of the classical list, performing similarly in Britain.

Critical and market response was heartening enough for Paul and Carl to put together *Liverpool Suite* – a nine-minute sequence of the most memorable bits – to follow in its immediate wake, and concert promoters across the continents to underwrite over 100 further performances of the oratorio to date.

Although McCartney didn't thus reinvent himself – as Andrew Lloyd Webber had done – as a sort of nuclear age Sir Arthur Sullivan by juggling milkman-friendly catchiness and Handel-like choral works, *Liverpool Oratorio* was instrumental in narrowing the gap between highbrow and lowbrow, "real" singing and "pop" caterwauling, 'La Donna E Mobile' and 'Long Tall Sally'. With chart strikes for Kiri Te Kanawa and Pavarotti pending, no one was to bat an eyelid when the *Sunday Times* revealed in 1996 that Van Morrison had written music for *Lord Of The Dance*, a multi-media show retelling Celtic folk tales, and centred on high-tech displays of step-dancing that was threatening to eclipse the fêted *Riverdance*.

Of sporadic antecedents, John McCormack – the Pavarotti *du jour* – at the height of his pre-war fame had given a quayside concert of popular ballads for Liverpool-Irish dockers during their lunch hour. More pertinent to this discussion, the University of Ulster had recognised the province's boffin-at-the-high-school-hop by conferring upon the former lead vocalist of Them an honorary doctorate of letters during the summer of 1992. With tasselled cap on his head, and sober grey suit, tie and white shirt covered by the approved red gown, 47-year-old George Ivan Morrison looked the complete antithesis of a hip-shakin' pop demigod – but then maybe he always had.

Bob Dylan's inauguration as an *ex officio* don of Princetown University over 20 years earlier had been a sign that academia had ceased distancing itself from pop – which was soon to begin its infiltration of school curricula. It was remarkable that, unlike film, jazz and other disciplines pertaining to the Coca-Cola century just gone, it had taken until then for higher education to take seriously music that has been recorded for the masses since before the death of Victoria. Nevertheless, by the 1980s, postgraduate research had been encouraged to the extent that the University of Liverpool opened Britain's first Institute of Popular Music – with Mike McCartney among those in its working party. Was it not entirely fitting that a self-contained faculty to centralise existing work should have originated in the birthplace of The Beatles?

The same could be said of the Liverpool Institute of Performing Arts – LIPA – a notion that had come to Paul McCartney shortly before his old secondary school closed in the mid-1980s, and "this wonderful building, which was built in 1825, was becoming derelict"[1]. There was something unstable about Liverpool at that time. Festering unrest amongst the youth in the most depressed districts had exploded during the swimming heat of 1981's summer. From Toxteth and the Dingle, the reek of burning had seeped as far as the city centre, where, for two nights, shops were looted with supermarket trolleys, and torched with petrol bombs.

"After the riots, various people suggested to me that I could help by taking the kids off the streets in some way," recalled Paul in 1994. "Four years ago, I announced the plan to build LIPA, and we started fund-raising. I put in some money to get it going, and we got a lot of help from different people."[1]

It was to be, he said, "like the school in the TV series, *Fame*"[1] in that talented youngsters could be primed for greener pastures via courses that included an artistic conditioning process that, time permitting, might involve songwriting tutorials by none other than the very founder himself – "but I won't be telling the kids how to do it because I think that it is part of my skill that I don't know exactly how to write a song, and the minute I do know how to do it, I'm finished. So I would want to explain that I don't agree that there is an accepted method of writing a song."[1] Perhaps echoing his experiments with Martin "Youth" Glover, he stressed that "the excitement for me would be if I could learn while they are learning."[1]

It was also going to be tenable to receive LIPA training as a road manager, a lighting engineer, a video producer, an A & R executive, a choreographer... but what couldn't be taught was the "bad" attitude necessary before a career in pop became an acceptable option to parents. When McCartney wasn't much older than his students, in dreary middle-class homes in the provinces – where the distance to Swinging London was measurable in decades as much as miles – for a boy to express a desire to make his way in pop was almost the precise equivalent of a girl seeking a post as a stripper. It would preface years of incomprehension, lamentation, deprivation, uproar, assault and oppressive domestic "atmospheres".

As a result, those who'd been psychologically damaged – as I was – by such persecution from so-called loved ones were much more liberal when, as former Mods, Rockers and hippies, they became parents themselves; buying MIDI equipment for 16th birthday presents for children who could con grants out of the government to form a group – even if, in the same defeated economic climate, record companies were no longer chucking blank cheques about as they did after the wheels of the universe came together for The Beatles in 1962 and The Sex Pistols a quarter of a century later.

Regardless, the Institute was to enroll its first students for 1996's spring term in between the preceding media hoo-hah that always went with the McCartney territory and the official unveiling of its plaque by the Queen – who'd been among those who'd dipped into her purse for LIPA – in June.

Though his sojourn at the Liverpool Institute was ignominious, George Harrison's loyalty to the old grey stones (and to McCartney) was strong enough for him to reach for his chequebook on LIPA's behalf too. He had also been amenable to joining with Paul and Ringo in 1994 for the compilation of *Anthology*, a vast Beatles retrospective that would embrace eventually nine albums (in sets of three), a lengthy television documentary – later available on video and DVD – and a group autobiography in the form of edited transcripts of taped reminiscences. "There were one or two bits of tension," smiled Paul, "I had one or two ideas George didn't like."[1] One of these was the project's working title, *The Long And Winding Road*, because it was after one of McCartney's songs. Ringo too blew hot and cold with Paul: "It's a good month and a bad month, just like a family."[9]

Since John's passing, there'd been no successor to him as self-appointed Beatles *paterfamilias* – who'd, purportedly, chastised George for the "incest"[10] of a brief affair in 1972 with Ringo's first wife – but Yoko had remained to the group roughly what the embarrassing "Fergie", the Duchess of York, is to the Windsors. There was no love lost between her and McCartney, who she perceived then as the Salieri to her late husband's Mozart. Yet she and Paul had shared a conciliatory hug at a Rock 'N' Roll Hall Of Fame award ceremony, and she'd spent a weekend that seemed more like a fortnight at the McCartneys when being courted for her co-operation on *Anthology*. Her stay was notable for a session at Paul's home studio in which he, Linda and the children accompanied seven minutes of Aunt Yoko's screech-singing of a one-line lyric called 'Hiroshima Sky Is Always Blue'.

Paul insisted that there was no ulterior motive, that he liked the track, and agreed with Yoko that it was "the result of our reconciliation after 20 years of bitterness and feuding."[9] Before the weather vane of rapprochement lurched back to the old thinly veiled antagonism, Yoko donated stark voice-piano tapes of Lennon compositions for McCartney, Harrison and Starr to use as they thought fit.

Isn't it marvellous what they can do nowadays? Only four years before one of John's demos, 'Free As A Bird', had taken shape as near as dammit to a new Beatles single, there'd been a hit remake of Nat "King" Cole's 'Unforgettable' as a duet by layering his and daughter Natalie's singing over a state-of-the-art facsimile of Nat's original 1951 backing track.

With Jeff Lynne as executive producer, 'Free As A Bird' was likewise doctored with a slide guitar passage from Harrison, Starr's trademark "pudding" tom-toms and McCartney emoting a freshly composed "bridge" as a sparkling contrast to John's downbeat verses. The effect was not unlike an inverse of 'We Can Work It Out'. Yet 'Free As A Bird' stalled in second place in Britain's Christmas list when up against *bête noire* Michael Jackson's 'Earth Song' and an easy-listening overhaul of Oasis's 'Wonderwall' by The Mike Flowers Pops. The Beatles' follow-up, 'Real Love', made the Top Ten more grudgingly, dogged as it was by exclusion from Radio One's playlist of the Modern Dance, twee boy bands and Britpop – ie mostly guitar-bass-drums acts that, like brand-leaders Oasis, borrowed melodies and lyrical ideas from the golden age of British beat.

Who could not empathise with Paul, Ringo and George's mingled dismay and elation when the million-selling *Anthology* albums demonstrated that almost-but-not-quite reaching the top in the UK singles chart was but a surface manifestation of enduring interest in The Beatles that made even their out-takes a joy forever?

The book was a bestseller too; its high retail price mitigated by a weight comparable to that of a paving slab. As for the content, we would like the impossible: videos of the Woolton fête engagement when John met Paul; a rehearsal around August 1962 when the group was about to rid itself of Pete Best; to be a fly on the wall in a dressing room just before *Sunday Night At The London Palladium* or to sample with our own sensory organs Paul's feelings about Yoko's intrusion on The Beatles.

Instead, we got Ringo, George and Paul – and John from media archives – providing not so much new twists in the plot as details about the food they ate, the clothes they wore, the stimulants they sampled, the violence they faced, the hairstyles they adopted – oh, and the music they played – information that the most obsessed Beatlemaniac wouldn't find too insignificant to be less than totally fascinating. McCartney's ruminations, however, were marred by an irritating conversational tic in his over-use of the word "little" – "little guitar", "little studio", "little club in Hamburg", "great little period" (at least twice) ad nauseam. He probably doesn't realise he's doing it.

Events since *Anthology* have demonstrated that it was far from the last word on The Beatles. Not a month passes without another few books adding – like this one – to the millions of words chronicling and analysing some aspect or other of their history. Bootlegs have continued unabated too with their manufacturers intrigued most recently by the emergence in Holland of further hitherto-unissued unforgiving minutes from the *Let It Be* era.

Thus The Beatles endure after the apparent levelling out of Britpop from its mid-1990s apogee. While it was going strongest, the biters were bitten on *Sixties Sing Nineties*, an intriguing 1998 collection in which hits by callow apprentices were given the masters' touch – and delivered with more guts that the originals in the cases of Dave Dee's crack at 'Don't Look Back In Anger' by Oasis, and the circle remaining unbroken with the Wet Wet Wet arrangement of 'Love Is All Around' by composer Reg Presley.

As he had with the Modern Dance, Paul McCartney, well into his 50s, masticated a chunk of Britpop too by combining with 37-year-old Paul Weller – who'd been dating daughter Mary of late – and, more to the point, Noel Gallagher, leader of Oasis, on an Abbey Road reworking of 'Come Together' for *Help!* a 1995 "various artists" album to raise funds to alleviate the war in Bosnia's aftermath of homelessness, lack of sanitation, disease and starvation. Symbolising three generations of pop aristocracy, the trio – naming themselves The Smokin' Mojo Filters – were *Help!*'s star turn, and, almost as a matter of course, 'Come Together' was its loss-leader of a single.

19 "My Dark Hour"

"I'd not have had a day again to equal this, would I?"
       – Sean Connery as Robin Hood[1]

Just as "history" nowadays means mannered costume dramas in six weekly two-hour episodes on television, so "classical music" for many people is what you hear when put on hold to speak to a British Gas sales advisor. When Paul McCartney was young, it oozed in a similar fashion from the BBC Light Programme under the batons of Mantovani, Edmundo Ros, Geraldo and bandleaders of their hue. From *Music While You Work*, it was a short step to Reader's Digest's mail-order record wing with titles like "Music For Reading", "Music For Dining" and "Music For A Solemn Occasion" in its catalogue. 1963 brought *The Quiet Hour* spent with Patience Strong reading verse over holy organ Bach, "offering comfort and solace sorely needed in this hurrying, worrying world."[2]

Such sounds didn't require focus and being able to think, "Yes, that's interesting". There was nothing constructive you could say about it. It was just there, either slushy with strings or inconsequentially plink-plonk, these reductions to musak of *Tales Of Hoffman*, the *Lone Ranger* theme, Ravel's *Bolero*, Handel's *Largo et al*.

Occupying an area bordered by Elgar, Vaughan Williams and Britten, Sir William Walton's lighter pieces might have figured on the Light Programme playlist as well, particularly those written for the "talkies" to suit the conservative demands of Hollywood and Ealing. Walton was responsible too for *Fanfare For Brass* for EMI's celebration of its first 50 years in business, but, for the label's centenary in 1997, Paul McCartney came up with *Standing Stone*, a sonic monument to the very late Ivan Vaughan, the school friend through whom Paul had been introduced to The Quarry Men.

It took the form of a symphonic poem in a traditional division of four movements that the *Music* periodical reckoned "represented a significant leap forward in style and substance, the persuasive outcome of almost four years labour."[3]

Paul had figured out the basic pattern on piano, and drawn a sung narrative from verse he'd written that, addressing both Celtic myths and his Irish ancestry, was his perspective on the Earth's creation, the origins of life and the particular history of an "everyman"-type character named First Person Singular, whose life's journey is a quest for – as you don't need me to tell you – True Love.

While this musical and lyrical bedrock was all his, Paul didn't complete *Standing Stone* entirely on his own. Among helpmates were classical saxophonist and arranger John Harle and composer David Matthews, most vital as a trouble-shooter for McCartney's electronic keyboard, computer and composition software. "We're more or less contemporaries," smiled David, "and I'm a great Beatles fan. Sometimes I regret that I didn't take up the guitar.

"The orchestration he'd created on the computer wouldn't work in real life, and he wanted advice on practical matters, such as the doubling of instruments and balance. I wanted him in every case to make up his mind about what he wanted and not suggest things to him. The difference between what Paul produced on the computer and the finished piece is quite small, but I hope I helped to turn it into a polished work."[3]

To assist with harmonising the four-part chorale that would carry the libretto, Paul called upon the older Richard Rodney Bennett, a composer and concert pianist forever on BBC Radio Three, who'd studied under Pierre Boulez, himself a former pupil of Messiaen and Varèse. Bennett, however, wasn't to inscribe any more of a stylistic signature on the work than David Matthews because McCartney had made it clear from the start "that I wanted *Standing Stone* to be my piece. They understood exactly what I meant, so they kept out of the way while guiding and helping me whenever necessary."[3]

Nearer the beginning, he'd wheeled in jazz keyboard virtuoso Steve Lodder, who, said Paul, "was able to help me keep the flow of ideas by playing back any material I'd written and changing its order. When I finally had its shape, I began to talk with John Harle, who gave me some advice on the overall structure. He would say what he felt about a section and I'd go away for two weeks and work on it – which was a bit like having school homework to do. It was good to have a second opinion on what worked and what didn't. I wanted something to sustain the audience's interest – and mine – since, unlike Beethoven, I was unable to take a theme and develop it in a symphonic way. Whereas other people have been studying classical music for 30 or 40 years, I've seen this stuff only in passing – so I've heard a French horn, liked its sound and used it in a Beatles song like 'For No One'. Also, I used piccolo trumpet in 'Penny Lane' after I'd heard Bach's *Brandenburg Concerto* on television. With *Standing Stone*, I began to put things together in a way I'd never done before."[3]

His mood was one of quiet confidence when settling into a seat for the 300-piece London Symphony Orchestra and Chorus's première of *Standing Stone* at the Royal Albert Hall on 14 October 1997. Pockets of the audience behaved as if it was a rock concert, though they remained silent and not visibly fidgeting during the 75 minutes of grandiloquent music that finished with "love is the oldest secret of the universe" from the choir, prefacing some ticket-holders' exclaimed "yeah!" that set off a standing ovation.

Overnight, the press gathered its thoughts. The reviews weren't scathing, but *Standing Stone* wasn't an especially palpable hit either, now that the novelty of Paul McCartney, classical composer, had faded. Nevertheless, it was received more favourably at New York's Carnegie Hall the following month in a performance that was broadcast to nigh on 400 radio stations across the whole sub-continent. Of later recitals, the most far-reaching was that on British television one Christmas morning when the nation was midway between the children's pre-dawn ripping open of the presents and the Queen's Speech.

The morning after 14 October 1997, however, the critics had tended to overlook the McCartney pieces that had prefaced the main event at the Albert Hall. These were the seven movements of *A Leaf* and another orchestrated piece *Spiral* – for piano – as well as *Stately Horn* for a horn ensemble, and *Inebriation* from The Brodsky Quartet.

Now that he'd acquired a taste for it, Paul would be knocking out more of the same, most recently *Ecce Cor Meum* – "behold my heart" – an oratorio dedicated to Linda, that was the centrepiece of the first concert given at Magdalen College, Oxford's new chapel in November 2001.

Listening to that of McCartney's classical output issued thus far on disc – which includes the 'Andante' from *Standing Stone* as a single – adjectives like "restrained", "shimmering", "caressing" and "atmospheric" occurred to me, and a lot of it has, indeed, a reposeful daintiness that's just, well, nice. The aftertaste is not so much British Gas Showroom as music commensurate with meditation – as implied in *Standing Stone*'s 'Trance' section – improvised dance and other self-improving activities, but heard too in advertisements for mineral water and credit cards as well as in travelogues, painting studios, hip dental surgeries, health food stores, massage parlours and what used to be known as "head shops".

While they adhered to classical form, *Liverpool Concerto, A Leaf, Ecce Cor Meum et al* are avenues of "classical music" effect rather than "classical music" in absolute terms. Maybe the phrase I'm looking for is "New Age" – or, alternatively, "New Instrumental" or "Adult Contemporary Music" – predating the Modern Dance as the only wave of essentially instrumental music to have reached a mass public since jazz-rock in the mid-1970s. Rather than East Of Eden or The Art Of Noise, it connects more with Terry Riley, John Tavener, Morton Subotnik, arch-minimalist Philip Glass, Stomu Yamash'ta – "the Samurai of Sound" – and other "serious" composer-performers who were promoted almost as rock stars by such as CBS, Apple, Island, World Pacific and Elektra subsidiary, Nonesuch.

McCartney need feel no shame either in an affinity to fellow 1960s pop veterans who resurfaced as denizens of New Age. The mainstay of Stairway (probably the best-loved British New Age outfit) is actually Jim McCarty of The Yardbirds – who also penned *Medicine Dance*, a *Standing Stone*-esque opus minus the vocals and orchestral backwash, for a bash in capacious St James's Church off London's Piccadilly in 1993.

Rod Argent of The Zombies – whose trademark was a minor key contradiction of enjoyable melancholy – Eddie Hardin (Steve Winwood's replacement in The Spencer Davis Group) and ex-Georgie Fame sideman Ray Russell are but a few more old stagers who were also reborn as New Age executants – though offerings by both ex-Monkee Mike Nesmith and Todd Rundren never left the runway, perhaps because a perverse public was not prepared to disconnect them from previous incarnations.

If McCartney elects to persist courting the "classical" rather than New Age market, he needs to accept that he'll probably always be a tyro in comparison to someone like Scott Walker, now a kind of Roger Irrelevant of pop, whose infrequent albums are mostly an intellectual rather than aesthetic experience. To arrangements that range in density from everything but the proverbial kitchen sink to a subdued ghostliness, the artist – not *artiste* – seems at times to dart randomly from section to indissoluble section welded to tunes that verge on the atonal, encapsulating fragments of

Schoenberg, Penderecki and composers of that "difficult" persuasion – with only drums and electric bass placing the ilk of *Tilt* and *Pola X* even remotely in the realms of pop.

A more impossible yardstick for McCartney is the late Frank Zappa, perhaps the greatest North American composer of the 20th century or, indeed, any other era. That's not to say he was perfect; his 'Uncle Meat', for instance, was lifted directly from Milhaud's 'Un Homme Et Son Désir', and he lost me when he drifted from the incisive aural imbroglios of the 1960s to the lavatorial *humor* of his post-Mothers of Invention period.

Nevertheless, even the most crass lyrics were supported by complex and frequently beautiful music – and, like Mozart in his final years too, Frank ceased springing for the commercial jugular, and negotiated a complete artistic recovery as a "serious" composer by reconciling severe dissonance and clashing time signatures with serene, lushly orchestrated melody ("electric chamber music", he called it) with a transcendental edge and injection of outright craziness that you won't detect in *Standing Stone*, *Spiral* and all the rest of them. Today, you'll hear Zappa in the "Promenade Concerts" – as you might, for reasons other than musical quality, hear our own dear Paul McCartney one day.

Paul hadn't been so out of his depth – far from it – with 1995's *Oobu Joobu*, a radio series for the same US company that had networked the self-explanatory *Lost Lennon Tapes*. That *Oobu Joobu*'s title was derived from a surreal and burlesque 1908 play by Alfred Jarry may have caused some anticipatory trepidation in listeners, but it was simply eleven one-hour shows (plus a bumper 12th edition) of harmless family fun with records, jingles, funny stories, celebrity interviews, comedy sketches, previously unbroadcasted Beatles and Wings tapes, you get the drift.

There were also what might have been categorised in a more sexist age, "women's features" – mainly recipes – by Linda. The children, however, made only incidental contributions at most. Advisedly, they'd been so removed from direct public gaze that, as teenagers, they were able to walk around Rye and Campbeltown not unnoticed exactly, but without inviting too much comment.

Paul and Linda had instilled into Heather, Mary, Stella and James what ought to be admired about achievement by effort. Taking this to heart, Heather had pulled pints in a local pub, one of several menial jobs that she had held down prior to becoming a potter whose work came to be exhibited as far afield as Tokyo and Sydney.

As talented and as renowned in her way, Mary had followed her mother's footsteps, discovering words like "gate", "field" and "aperture" as applied to the camera as well as the versatility of delayed-action shutters, and what could be done to a negative when, in a darkroom at MPL offices, she began developing and printing her own films. Vocationally, she touched a zenith of sorts in 2000 when commissioned to snap the official photographs of Prime Minister Tony Blair's newborn son Leo. Just over a year earlier, Mary herself had given birth – to her father's first grandchild, Arthur, seven months after her marriage to film director and television producer, Alistair Donald.

Of all the McCartney daughters, however, Stella has thrust her head highest above the parapet. Her surname helped open a door to a flourishing career in fashion design after learning what she could *in situ* as runaround to Parisian couturier Christian La Croix. A chip off the old paternal block, Stella dismissed many preconceptions and introduced fresh ones when studying at Central St Martin's Design School in London, where, at the fashion parade for her "finals", Stella's creations were modelled to a soundtrack by the "proudest dad in the world"[4].

McCartney *père* was prominent too among onlookers at Stella's consequent shows when she landed a lucrative post as head designer at a leading Paris fashion house a mere 18 months after finishing at St Martin's, and was on the way to her first self-made million. This prompted inevitable it's-not-how-good-you-are-it's-who-you-know mutterings, but Stella had a natural flair for cutting the cloth, and, if she had been given any extra pushes up the ladder, the world of glamour benefitted as much as she did.

Stella was said to have crafted her own wedding dress for when she tied the knot with Alistair Willis, former publisher of the "style" magazine, *Wallpaper*, on New Year's Day 2003.

So far, Stella's brother's principal brush with fame – if that is the word – has been when he made headlines in September 1993 after the coastguard was called out by his very worried parents. This had followed James's disappearance from view when bodysurfing in the sea near Rye. Two years later, a misadventure on land left him with a broken ankle when the Land Rover he was driving overturned along a rutted track. In oblique mitigation, however, his co-writing and strumming the chords to 'Back In The Sunshine', a 2001 album track by his father, suggests that the accident-prone young man is turning into an adept guitarist and composer.

James's mishaps had been among few domestic hiccoughs in the mid-1990s, a "great little period" that Paul would remember not only for what happened at the end, but also for the contentment that had preceded it. Nothing was ever the same afterwards.

Lightning struck slowly. In December 1995, Linda recovered from an ostensibly successful operation to remove a lump from her breast. Yet within weeks, she had every appearance of being seriously ill, and was prescribed chemotherapy. That held the spread of what was obviously cancer at arm's length, but X-rays were to reveal malignant cells forming a shadow on her liver.

The ghastly secret became known to a media that noted Linda's absence when Paul was driven to Buckingham Palace on 11 March 1997. As Prime Minister John Major had done on the apparent behalf of Eric Clapton MBE, Van Morrison OBE and Sir Cliff Richard, so his more with-it successor, Tony Blair, a self-styled "guy", had advised the Queen to invest the showbusiness legend as responsible for 'I Saw Her Standing There' as *Liverpool Oratorio* with a knighthood – for "services to music". As it had been when

The Beatles were awarded their contentious MBE's 30 years earlier, Paul was pleased, accepting the greater honour, he promised, "on behalf of the people of Liverpool and the other Beatles."[5]

"A spokesperson" was to inform the *Sunday Times* that "he is very down to earth about being a knight. He doesn't use the title. None of his friends call him Sir Paul. The only time he gets called that is when he is in restaurants or on airplanes."[6] Nevertheless, like Sir Cliff Richard and Sir Elton John, he sealed his status as pillar of the Establishment by paying £3,500 ($5,600) to the College of Arms for the coat of arms that, since the reign of Richard III, anyone considered a gentleman was supposed to keep handy in case he was required to fight for the monarch. On Sir Paul's, the principal symbols are a guitar and a Liver Bird – with beak open as if singing. The design also embraces four shapes resembling beetles, two circles representing records, and the title of the Magdalen College oratorio, *Ecce Cor Meum*.

The guitar signified what was still his principal source of income, and to that end, *Flaming Pie*, his first non-concert album for nearly half a decade, materialised two months after the visit to the Queen. Unlike *Ecce Cor Meum*, it wasn't meant to be taken especially seriously. "I called up a bunch of friends and family and we just got on and did it," he chortled. "And we had fun. Hopefully, you'll hear that in the songs."[7]

Those that did bought *Flaming Pie* in sufficient quantity to ease it up to a domestic Number One and to Number Two in the Hot 100. This – and a nomination for a Grammy – flew in the face of dejecting critiques ("woeful stuff"[8], "rock 'n' roll with its teeth in a glass of water by its bedside"[9]) for an album that conveyed a likeably downhome, sofa-ed ambience, even if most of the 14 songs *per se* weren't much more than sometimes tipsy musings written on holiday or as the conclusion of just messing about. All were by Paul alone apart from 'Really Love You' – born of a jam with Ringo while a tape operator was fixing something or other – and blues-inflected 'Used To Be Bad' with Steve Miller, whose 1969

PAUL MCCARTNEY

single, 'My Dark Hour', had had McCartney on drums and bass. He renewed his professional acquaintance with Paul when his studio in Idaho hosted the bulk of the *Flaming Pie* sessions. "Bulk" is a crucial word here because Steve at 52 had put on weight alarmingly – as marked by a *Top Of The Pops* interlocutor who, damn his impudence, referred to Miller as a "porker" when a 1990 re-release of 'The Joker' topped the UK charts, thanks to its use in an ITV commercial.

Steve warranted a mention in *Many Years From Now*, Paul's authorised biography by Barry Miles. While this tome deals essentially with events up to and including the dissolution of The Beatles, it serves as an intriguing companion to this one, containing as it does more weighing of experience and estimation of motive than you'd expect in a pop life story freighted too with both unfamiliar anecdotes and the old yarns related from the subject's point of view.

He was kind about Jane Asher – from whom "I learned a lot and she introduced me to a lot of things"[10]. Married now to cartoonist Gerald Scarfe, Jane had put her acting career on hold owing to family commitments and those connected with her on-going presidency of the National Autistic Society. However, she had returned to television drama in the 1980s with such as *Love Is Old Love Is New* – a series centred on a couple who wished time had stopped in the 1960s, and containing a generous helping of Beatles songs – and most recently in a resurgent *Crossroads*. In March 2003, she narrated *The Real Cliff Richard*, a Channel Four documentary about the ageing Bachelor Boy.

Jane's aptitude as a home-maker had manifested itself in Jane Asher's *Calendar Of Cakes, Silent Nights For You And Your Baby, The Best Of Good Living* and similar domestic self-help tomes. When mass-produced, her cakes filled shelves in one supermarket chain, but even the most "creative" journalist couldn't make out that they were in competition with Linda McCartney's more savoury merchandise.

Linda was dying by inches. Nonetheless, amid gathering infirmity and awash with medications, she was filling what remained of her life with compiling another cookbook; developing enough film for two more photography exhibitions and battling on courageously with a solo album. More a hospital orderly than passionate *inamorato* now, Paul tried to blow sparks of optimism but resigned himself with wearied amazement that she was still clinging on as he helped attend to her day-long needs.

The flame was low on the evening of Thursday 16 April 1998, and 56-year-old Linda Louise McCartney was gone by the grey of morning. Following a hasty cremation, Paul announced the tragedy, having first endorsed an entirely fictional report that she'd died in California rather than on an Arizona ranch she and Paul had bought in 1979. Without this precaution, today's death bed would have become tomorrow's lapping sea of faces and camera lenses.

The ashes were transported back to England where the family were to mourn Linda publicly at a service of remembrance in central London, complete with celebrity eulogies and readings, someone leading her two Shetland ponies up the aisle, a bagpiper blowing 'Mull Of Kintyre' and renderings by The Brodsky Quartet of McCartney compositions pertinent to Linda. Paul himself was to sing a finale of 'All My Loving' with Elvis Costello during star-studded "Here, There And Everywhere: A Concert For Linda" at the Albert Hall nearly a year to the day after her passing.

Over in California, Eric Burdon had "had no idea how sick Linda had become. The last time I'd seen her was when she and her beloved Paul visited backstage after one of my shows at London's Hammersmith Theatre. Those two were perfect together, woven tight like a many-coloured Shetland sweater."[11]

At a memorial concert in the Sunken Gardens in Santa Barbara – where the press had first been led to believe Linda had died – Eric gave 'em 'The Long And Winding Road' and delivered an insightful oration, abridged thus: "She told me quite seriously that, to become a photographer, one should carry one's camera at all times – just like a soldier carries his weapon – because the action is all around you. She was one of the girls who became one of the boys by becoming a woman upon the road. Go, Linda, go."

20 "She Said Yeah"

> "It would have been very easy for Paul McCartney to have
> retired years ago, but there's this old die-hard thing in him
> that still has so much music to make."
>
> – *Rod Stewart*[1]

Predictably, there were rumours of a lady friend within months of
Linda's funeral. Paparazzi squeezed sleazy mileage from naming
one or two candidates, but there was no evidence to substantiate
a new romance until late in 1999 when Paul was seen in public
with a blonde from Tyne-and-Wear named Heather Mills, whose
artificial leg was of no more account than an earring or a headband.
Nothing could distract from the firm-breasted profile and
timorously pretty but deceptively commanding face.

Heather had never lacked male attention, though the first major
instance of it was at primary school when she and a classmate were
kidnapped by a Mr Morris, their swimming instructor. They
were held for three days before their escape and Mr Morris's
subsequent suicide.

Life *chez* Mills in Washington, County Durham, wasn't happy
either. Heather's father, an ex-paratrooper, would "yell, throw
things and belt Mum over the head," she recalled. "It didn't matter
if we [Heather, brother Shane and sister Fiona] were there or not.
Sometimes, I really believed he was going to murder her."[2] Her
spouse's rages so overwhelmed Mrs Mills that, when her elder
daughter was nine, an affair with a TV actor – from *Crossroads*
of all programmes – who'd been in a play at Newcastle Theatre

Royal, was the trigger for her upping and leaving for London with him. With the initial enthusiasm children often have for onerous household tasks, Heather slipped into the maternal role thus thrust upon her, feeding herself, Shane and Fiona on a miserly weekly budget supplemented with shoplifting.

Inevitably, Heather's schooling suffered, and was unofficially over when her father's shady business dealings led him to being gaoled for two years. The children went to live with a mother they scarcely knew now in Clapham. So rancorously alien was the new situation that 13-year-old Heather ran away to find eventual under-age employment with a travelling funfair. After the friend with whom she shared a caravan died an early death through drug abuse, the glamour of dodgems, candy-floss and shooting galleries palled, and Heather gravitated to London's South Bank to dwell with other vagrants in cardboard-boxed squalor.

She endured this for four months – it was left for others to imagine that it was constant dirt; perpetual mental arithmetic to eke out a few pence; chill from the misty river penetrating clothes that she would uncrumple after a sleepless night; washing in public-convenience hand basins and seeing fellow down-and-outs face down in a puddle of their own vomit.

Not far from her mother's was an off-licence owned by a kindly couple who got wind of Heather's plight, and invited her to move in with them. A local jeweller took her on part-time, but, when accused falsely of pilfering from the stock, she felt she had nothing to lose by actually doing so. Her illicit sale of a quantity of gold chains came home to roost, and an appearance in juvenile court terminated with a stern lecture from a magistrate who placed Heather on probation.

Her 16 years, therefore, hadn't been quiet ones, but, despite – or because of – the distressing odds, she was to emerge from her teens astoundingly self-confident and purposeful. Quite the astute business woman too, she was the brains behind several small if profitable business enterprises. Moreover, the hardships of her first two decades hadn't taken their toll on the good looks that had enabled her to win a *Daily Mirror* "Dream Girl" contest and land jobs as a presenter on *Wish You Were Here, That's Esther* and other television magazine programmes.

It all came tumbling down, however, on 8 August 1993 when Heather was on a Kensington street and in the way of a police motorcycle, which was hurrying to a false alarm. To the agitated oscillations of an ambulance siren, she was hastened to the nearest hospital where surgeons failed to reconnect her severed foot. More of the leg was amputated – fortunately, below the knee – during a lengthy operation.

This might have been the final scene in a 15-act tragedy, but, with her customary and extraordinary resilience, Heather Mills conquered desolation by anchoring herself to the notion that, one way or another, she'd emerge, if not entirely intact, then with hardened mettle. At least she could afford – especially with the out-of-court settlement by Scotland Yard – the thousands of pounds required for a shapely silicone limb with a flexible foot.

She also inaugurated the Heather Mills Trust, a charity for those who had become limbless in global theatres of war, having become horribly aware that "to lose a limb is also to lose your self-worth, your masculinity or femininity. The women no longer feel marriageable, though I saw at least 20 girls among the amputees (in Cambodia) who would have made super models."[2] Her tireless fund-raising was to involve a 1999 Heather Mills single entitled 'Voice' – with a lyric about a disabled girl – and spell-binding slots on chat shows where she provoked shocked laughter by rolling up her trousers and even removing her false leg. Up in the control room, where the producer barked excited instructions to the camera operators, it was fantastic television.

It also had the desired effect of drawing attention to a campaign that was to earn Heather a Nobel Peace Prize nomination and further formal recognitions for her work. Famous enough to warrant a frank-and-unashamed autobiography[3], she was a host at one such ceremony at London's plush Dorchester Hotel on 20 May 1999. Her future husband was there too, clutching the Linda McCartney Award For Animal Welfare he was to give to the founder of *Viva*, an associated movement.

Taking a benevolent interest in Heather's activities, Paul McCartney was to write out a huge cheque for the trust, and contribute guitar and backing vocals to 'Voice'. Then one thing led to another and, after she'd accepted an invitation to a bonfire party at Rye, she and Paul saw in the millenium together and set tongues a-wagging further with a joint ten-day holiday in the West Indies. His name now linked with hers in high society gossip columns, the 59-year-old widower seemed as fondly in love as he could be with a beautiful girlfriend a quarter of a century his junior. That she was a divorcée like Linda – and a veteran of three broken engagements – didn't ruffle him. After all, he'd hardly lived like a monk since the onset of puberty. "What we want most of all at the moment," he outlined to *Hello!*, "is a private life. It's very early days for us, and it's a wait-and-see situation."[2]

Nobody was getting any younger, but the gloom that had followed Linda's final illness had deferred the breezy vitality that had been Matt Monro's when contemplating settling cosily into old age on the consolidated fruits of his success – particularly when there was an unexpected godsend in the rise of *Heartbreakers*, a 1980 Monro compilation, to Number Five in the album chart. Unhappily, retirement was not on the cards for Matt. In 1984, he bid an unknowing farewell to the concert platform with a 'Softly As I Leave You' finale. Just over a year later, he was under the scalpel for an attempted liver transplant when a cancerous growth was uncovered. He was discharged, but returned within two days to die quietly on 7 February 1985.

His doctors blamed his smoking, a habit that George Harrison gave up when the cancer that was to take him too was first diagnosed. After *Cloud Nine* had burst, George had gone to ground again; his only significant return to media focus being inadvertent when he was half-killed in his own home by a knife-wielding paranoid schizophrenic.

Paul had long been concerned about physical attack. Homicidal fanatics were an occupational hazard. In 1971, one such "fan" had jumped onstage at London's Rainbow Theatre and hurled Frank Zappa into the pit, confining him to a wheelchair for almost a year. Not long after John Lennon's slaying, the newly inaugurated President Reagan had taken a bullet from a deranged man trying to impress a Hollywood actor he admired. Two months later, something similar happened to the Pope.

Twenty years after these last two incidents, discreet bodyguards were always around whenever Paul McCartney made formal appearances. One such public venture, however, was made with uncharacteristic stealth.

It concerned his interests in fine art. Even when his studies for A-level Art were far behind him, idle hours on this long-haul flight or in that dressing room had often been occupied with doodling in pencil or felt-tip. A selection of these were included in *Paul McCartney: Composer Artist*, published in 1981.[4]

At home and on holiday, he would unwind too in two- and three-dimensions by painting in oils and doing sculpture, sometimes using driftwood smoothed by decades beneath either the English Channel or the Irish Sea. Most of his efforts were OK, nothing brilliant, but he had those with which he was particularly pleased printed up in a small hardback book for private use, presenting copies to friends.

Other pop stars, however, did not hide such light under a bushel. To some acclaim, Ronnie Wood, now a Rolling Stone, began showing his paintings in the late 1980s during one of progressively longer breaks in the group's touring schedule – while former Kink Pete Quaife – now Peter Kinnes – did likewise in Canada in 1994. His hangings included some autobiographical illustrations such as *Baked Beans*, showing a hand removing a housefly from a plate of the same ("People think we always ate in fancy restaurants. We didn't. All we had time for was beans-on-toast"[5]). Another picture depicts a stern-looking hotel receptionist registering the group members.

An ex-Beatle decided to go public with a Paul McCartney art exhibition at the Kunstforum Lyz Gallery in Hamburg on 30 April 1999. Three years later, he risked displaying "The Art Of Paul McCartney" at the Walker in Liverpool – which was also curating some Turners in an adjacent gallery. This was perhaps unfortunate in its inviting of comparisons between the distinguished Victorian "colour poet" and one who wouldn't be there if not for the Fab Four's long shadow.

While one expert deemed Paul's efforts to be "more interesting than I thought" and another in the same newspaper reckoned they had "promise", a third critic turned his nose up at "wholly talentless daubs. Perhaps endless adulation has made McCartney deaf to the voice of criticism."[6]

Maybe the Beatles' fairy-tale had rendered this particular scribe as deaf to the voice of approbation. Either way, McCartney was in a no-win situation – unless he'd exhibited his art pseudononymously like Pete Quaife. If you'd seen his work like that in a gallery near you, what would you think? Without such objectivity, pop stardom has invested McCartney's hands-on involvement with a similar poignancy to that of such as Bob Dylan, the Prince of Wales, Syd Barrett, Captain Beefheart, David Bowie, The Who's John Entwistle and – yes – John Lennon and Stuart Sutcliffe: goods bought principally as investments for their historical and curiosity value. In fairness, however, Beefheart – as Don Van Vliet – has had over 30 art exhibitions around the world since 1982 when he elected to devote himself to painting. Most buyers were unfamiliar with his pop past.

Yet little intimates that because Paul McCartney was so fully occupied with his musical career, he was a regrettable loss to the world of fine art. As a figure in time's fabric, his period as a Beatle will remain central to most considerations of him.

He'd harked back to the years prior to the 'Love Me Do' countdown with 1999's *Run Devil Run*, a quasi-*Choba B CCCP* album, but with three originals in the same vein. Anyone with the confidence to slot these in without jarring the stylistic flow of such as 'All Shook Up', 'Brown-Eyed Handsome Man' and 'Blue Jean Bop' deserved attention. Give him further credit, Paul's go at Larry Williams's 'She Said Yeah' was almost on a par with The Rolling Stones' 1965 revival, itself as redefining as The Beatles' 'Long Tall Sally' had been to the Little Richard blueprint. Paul's 'She Said Yeah' certainly made a 1964 crack at it by The Animals seem thuggish. Likewise, he improved (though there wasn't much competition) on one of *Run Devil Run*'s comparative obscurities, 'No Other Baby' from Dickie Bishop and his Sidekicks, a sub-Donegan skiffle outfit, but better known – in the USA at least – via a cover by Peter and Gordon's chief competitors in North America, Chad and Jeremy.

The most significant plug for *Run Devil Run* was an end-of-the-century bash at the replica Cavern along Mathew Street to a capacity raffle-winning crowd – including a chap who'd changed his name by deed-poll to "John Lennon" – but with a webcast audience of over three million. Rather than be accompanied by an existing group – as Jeff Beck had been by The Big Town Playboys for 1993's *Crazy Legs*, a Gene Vincent tribute album – Paul pulled together an all-star line-up of Deep Purple drummer Ian Paice, Pink Floyd guitarist Dave Gilmour (who was to also augment The Pretty Things when they resurrected *SF Sorrow* at the Royal Festival Hall in 2002), 1975 one-hit-wonder Pete Wingfield on keyboards and Mick Green, whose dazzling lead-rhythm guitar technique still enlivened a Pirates that had survived pub-rock's fall from favour, and when he was moonlighting in Van Morrison's backing band.

From McCartney's own portfolio, the set contained only 'I Saw Her Standing There' and two of his three compositions on *Driving Rain*. Otherwise, it was wall-to-wall classic rock for 50 minutes that, if you listened dispassionately, sounded fine in a dated sort of way to a dated sort of person.

His fans loved it – just as Ian Dury's did several months later through the release of *Brand New Boots And Panties*. Once described with vague accuracy in the *Daily Express* as "a sort of dirty old man of punk", Dury had spat out in Oi! Oi! Cockney his perspectives on London's seedy-flash low-life; his casually amusing discoveries taking form as musical-literary wit. His death from cancer on 27 March 2000 made the *Six O' Clock News* on BBC1, and the track-by-track exaltation of his most famous album, *Brand New Boots And Panties*, was earmarked for release as near as was feasible to the first anniversary. Backed by Dury's old combo, The Blockheads, McCartney's 'I'm Partial To Your Abracadabra' was as creditable as, say, Robbie Williams's 'Sweet Gene Vincent' or Shane McGowan's 'Plaistow Patricia' whilst swallowing dust behind Madness's 'My Old Man' and a startling re-arrangement of 'Clever Trevor' by Wreckless Eric: "I made it my own rather than doing a kind of karaoke version with The Blockheads playing it just like they used to. I wasn't up for that. I worked hard on that track – so much so that I got a production credit."

Paul had more of a creative role in an album taped after Martin "Youth" Glover reared up again as the producer of Super Furry Animals, formed in Cardiff in the mid-1990s as an amalgam of the Modern Dance, Britpop and olde tyme progressive rock. Like Mary Hopkin before them, they'd become enormous in that area of Welsh pop in which the likes of of Tom Jones, Amen Corner, Dave Edmunds, Man and Catatonia are incidental to acts that sing exclusively in Welsh. Unlike Y Tebot Piws, Edward H Dafis, Y Trwynau Coch and other esteemed predecessors, however, Super Furry Animals did not remain indifferent to the English-speaking market.

The spirit of 1995, therefore, faced the ghost of 1962 at an *NME* awards evening in February 2000. The two factions chatted amiably enough and, through the agency of Glover, McCartney and Super Furry Animals collaborated on *Liverpool Sound Collage*, which was to be up for a Grammy – as 2001's "Best Alternative Musical Album". It had been intended in the first instance as a sort of hi-tech "Carnival Of Light" for "About Collage", an exhibition at the Tate Liverpool by Peter Blake, whose pop-associated pursuits had not ended with his montage for the *Sgt Pepper* front cover.

Neither had Paul's non-pop dabblings with "The Art Of Paul McCartney", though he was on firmer ground with 2001's *Blackbird Singing*, a collection of over 100 poems interspersed with lyrics from some of his songs – dedicated to his and the late Linda's children. As it was with the Walker and his pictures, you wonder if Faber and Faber would have published the manuscript had it been submitted anonymously. "Most artists and musicians are trapped by their own vanity," sneered Billy Childish, himself an artist and musician, "I just don't know how he could allow them to publish his lyrics as poetry, apart from being a foolish big-head. It just says to me that he can't have much regard for himself. I can't believe he would allow himself to be made to look so stupid. Either he is stupid or he doesn't mind looking stupid. I guess either one lets him off the hook."[7]

This was the viewpoint of one who also regarded *The Beatles Live At The Star-Club In Hamburg, Germany 1962* as "their finest album" after the doctoring of the atrocious sound quality of two or so hours on the boards with the newly recruited Ringo, immortalised on Kingsize Taylor's domestic tape recorder. Paul joined forces with George and Ringo in an attempt to nip its release on CD in the bud, but a less onorous professional duty was that by *Driving Rain*, a McCartney solo album that was as freshly state-of-the-art as *The Beatles Live At The Star-Club* wasn't. Sticking mainly to singing and playing bass, he picked 15 of 22 items dashed off in a fortnight with a guitar-keyboards-drums trio of Los Angeles session players whose keeping of expensive pace with him was leavened by technical precision deferring to spontaneity. "We didn't fuss about it," he shrugged. "I'd show them a song, and we'd start doing it."[8]

These songs included 'Back In The Sunshine' (the one co-written by James), ten-minute 'Rinse The Raindrops' – and 'From A Lover To A Friend', the only A-side. It lasted a fortnight in the domestic Top 50, and proceeds were donated to the families of New York's fire service who perished in the aftershock of the terrorist attacks on the World Trade Center.

Just as the previous century had started not on New Years's Day 1900, but 22 January 1901 when Queen Victoria, the personification of an age, shuffled off this mortal coil, so the third millenium began on 11 September 2001 with the collapse of the Twin Towers and its stirring up of further of mankind's destructive instincts and contemptuous treatment of its own minority groups.

That's a generalisation. A lot of people think war is wrong. I mean, like, people get killed, y'know. And how has pop reacted to this? The easiest option, especially in the mid-1960s, was with one-size-fits-all protest songs – 'Where Have All The Flowers Gone?', 'Eve Of Destruction', 'Give Peace A Chance' and so on. The least lyrically complex were sung *en masse* on Ban The Bomb marches, student sit-ins and anti-war demonstrations – though strains of The Kinks's 'Every Mother's Son' were heard outside the White House during the Vietnam moratorium.

It didn't affect decisions made already any more than Killing Joke's set at a CND rally in Trafalgar Square in 1980 – at which the singer introduced one musical comment-on-the-society-in-which-we-live with "I hope you realise that your efforts today are all quite futile."

Understanding this, Paul McCartney – who'd been present in New York when the hijacked aeroplanes tore into the World Trade Center – organised a benefit concert at Madison Square Garden with no political agenda other than raising money for the firefighters and other victims, and to show solidarity against terrorism. Naturally, he wrote a song about it.

As a raw composition, 'Freedom' was convoluted and over-declamatory, certainly nowhere as strong as other anthems on the same subject such as 'Universal Love' by Art "Ski" Halperin, the last "discovery" by the late John Hammond Senior, who'd also brought Billie Holliday and Bob Dylan to a wider world. 'Freedom' wasn't really very good at all, but that didn't matter in the context of the euphoric atmosphere on that October Saturday six weeks after "nine-eleven" – as epitomised in the inevitable video by a manic youth, risen from his seat and, with eyes rolling in his head, oblivious to everything but bawling the raucous refrain as Paul reprised chin-up 'Freedom' with Billy Idol, Destiny's Child, The Who, Bon Jovi, Mick Jagger, David Bowie and the rest of the artistes who'd done their bit on that night-of-nights.

We never see a man. We only see his art. I mean this most sincerely, friends. So how could we ever know if McCartney (once the man for whom "starvation in India doesn't worry me one bit. Not one iota, it doesn't, man"[8]) was seizing an unforeseeable but welcome opportunity to trumpet the November release *Driving Rain* – to which 'Freedom' had been tacked on as a bonus track – or was motivated by a simple desire to help?

He wasn't to perform 'Freedom' when, after assuring enquirers that "We are hoping to bring joy to the world, nothing else,"[9] he commenced putting action over debate with regard to what he was to call his "Back In The World" tour, subtitled "Driving USA" for the country in which it was to be an antidote, said many, to September the 11th as The Beatles' 1964 visit had been to President Kennedy's assassination.

Prior to setting off on this latest jaunt, however, there was something McCartney had to do that was as special in its way as the New York spectacular. On 29 November 2001, George Harrison, no longer able to permit himself the luxury of hope, lost his last and toughest battle. As they had for John Lennon, flags flew at half-mast in Liverpool where there was immediate talk of a concert for George as there'd been for Colin Manley, who'd gilded his fretboard skills with a grinning vibrancy in the ranks of The Remo Four. When he too had died of cancer in 1999, Colin was one of The Swinging Blue Jeans – and both they and surviving members of The Remo Four had been among the cast celebrating his life at the Philharmonic Hall.

George's memorial was to be at the Empire on what would have been his 59th birthday on 24 February 2002. Paul shared a few yarns with the audience and, at the very end, gave 'em a spirited 'Yesterday', just as John McCormack had sung 'Ave Maria' at the concluding Mass of 1932's Eucharistic Congress in Dublin's Phoenix Park.

On the more secular occasion at the Empire (and the one for Colin Manley) you should have been there – because, while no one could pretend that this is what it must have been like in the dear, dead days of Merseybeat, as an atmospheric and companionable evening, it was past objective criticism.

Paul paid homage to George again on more glittering events at the Albert Hall – and on 3 June 2002 at Elizabeth II's "Jubilee Concert" in the grounds of Buckingham Palace during a slot that began with a maiden stage performance of the *Abbey Road* vignette, 'Her Majesty' and reached a climax of sorts in a duet with Eric Clapton of George's 'While My Guitar Gently Weeps' from the "White Album".

Not seen in the televisual coverage was the final number, 'I Saw Her Standing There'. As its coda yet reverberated, Paul was thinking ahead to the following Monday when he was to marry Heather Mills – for whom he'd penned an eponymous song on *Driving Rain* – at a castle hired for that very purpose in the Irish republic.

As Charles Kingsley reminds us, "Love can make us fiends as well as angels." Paul's courtship of his Tyneside paramour had often floated into a choppy sea if stray scum-press paragraphs were to be believed about pre-nuptial agreements; violent quarrels that resonated along hotel corridors and opposition to the match from McCartney's daughters (who "loathed and feared" Heather, according to a *Daily Mail* tittle-tattler[10]). Nevertheless, Heather and Paul's was the fuss wedding of the year after the castle's elderly laird, unused to press encroachment, gave the game away.

Back from the honeymoon, the groom embarked on the second leg of what was now a wartime tour. He was able to charge the best part of £100 ($160) per ticket, more than The Rolling Stones, Cher, Madonna, Elton John, The Who, you name 'em. Most attendees were of, well, a certain age – as they were for a reformed Yes, a stadium-swelling act a little lower in *Pollstar*, the Californian market research company's tabulation of box-office draws. "It seems a lot of our original fans have become professional people," grinned their vocalist, Jon Anderson, "from doctors to astronauts; amazing but logical really."[11]

With this in mind, there was a greater preponderance of Beatles items – including a couple sung on disc by George and John – than ever before – to the extent that "Paul McCartney Sings The Beatles" drew the eye to a *Sunday Times* advertisement that chucked in three-star overnight accommodation on top of the concert when McCartney reached Manchester on 10 April 2003.

Wherever he could – on programmes or the spin-off "live" album – he ensured that composing credits read "McCartney–Lennon" like they had fleetingly before Parlophone and everyone else had made it the more alphabetically correct "Lennon–McCartney", even on the *Anthology*. Paul's attempt then to have it otherwise had been vetoed by John's volcanic widow, and reawoke a dispute that hasn't yet been resolved. You can understand Paul's attitude. On the basis of mostly song-by-song breakdowns by Lennon during one of his last interviews, BBC Radio Merseyside presenter Spencer Leigh figured out that, statistically, McCartney was responsible for approximately two-thirds of The Beatles' output of originals, including 'Yesterday' and 'Hey Jude'.

This was borne out by implication too in John's remarks to an aide in 1979: "Paul never stopped working. We'd finish one album, and I'd go off and get stoned, and forget about writing new stuff, but he'd start working on new material right away, and as soon as he'd got enough songs, he'd want to start recording again."[12] McCartney corroborated this 23 years later in a weighty press statement, fulminating too that "Late one night, I was in an empty bar, flicking through the pianist's music book when I came across '"Hey Jude" written by John Lennon'. At one point, Yoko earned more from 'Yesterday' than I did. It doesn't compute – especially when it's the only song that none of the [other] Beatles had anything to do with."

Was it ever thus? It would be pleasant to think that any number of black bluesmen with a lackadaisical regard for business, received if not royalties then acknowledgement due to them from white rock bands like Led Zeppelin, who rewrote Howlin' Wolf's 'How Many More Years' as 'How Many More Times'. More to the point, a typing error attributed a version of The Yardbirds' 'Shapes Of Things' on an album by The Jeff Beck Group to bass player Paul Samwell-Smith alone rather than drummer Jim McCarty and singer Keith Relf too. Then there was the case of The Animals' 'House Of The Rising Sun'. This joint overhaul of a traditional ballad topped international charts, but as there wasn't sufficient room on the single's label to print all five Animal names, only one was used – that of organist Alan Price, who'd had least to do with the arrangement of the song. The others were placated with the promise that it wouldn't make any difference to shares in the royalties, but insists drummer John Steel, "We never saw any of that money. Alan still earns on it today."

Just as Price was ostracised by the other Animals, so Yoko Ono wasn't invited to either Linda McCartney's memorial service in New York or, apparently, Paul's nine-eleven concert.

While McCartney remains bound to Ono by Beatles business, a woman with closer personal affinity to him has no direct communication whatsoever anymore. Nonetheless, Ruth McCartney cuts a familiar and appealing figure at US Beatles conventions where, if proud of her step-brother's standing as "the Walt Disney of love songs", she has no qualms about airing her views regarding his shortcomings.

While his name, unlike Ruth's, might not mean all that much to Beatles fans in the States, Cliff Bennett could, if he chooses, be a wanted guest at such festivals in Europe, thus accruing a secondary income to earnings on the Swinging Sixties circuit. As McCartney could have told him, a mere Great Voice wasn't enough to sustain contemporary interest. Indeed, a disillusioned Cliff had withdrawn from the music business altogether for many years, but nothing could stop him singing, and, come the 1980s, he'd been back with another Rebel Rousers at a Star-Club Rock 'n' Roll Jubilee with other faces from its pop yesteryears. As soulful as he ever was, the big man with the big voice had brushed aside the millennia since 1962 like so many matchsticks. As the century continued to die, time's winged chariot transported Cliff to Summer Sixties 1999, a weekend wallow in nostalgia at the capacious Brighton Centre with other of the kingdom's surviving entertainers from the decade that had ended with the disbandment of The Beatles. According to a random survey, Cliff and his latest Rebel Rousers stole the show.

Denny Laine did the same when making himself pleasant as one of two pop "personalities" at a charity record fair at the University of Northumbria in 1996. That, however, isn't saying much because the other one was me. This was during a series of one-nighters in the northeast starring Denny and his lone acoustic guitar and my solo turn that defied succinct description.

We became friends, but I couldn't help but feel a frequent sense of wonderment – as if both Denny and the situations in which we found ourselves weren't quite real. Admission was free at the Malt Shovel in Middlesbrough, where my act was interrupted by a woman who kept barging into the playing area and bawling into the microphone at irregular intervals until the landlord threw her out. With this problem removed, I went the distance. A small contingent had been with me all the way, but I only reached the rest during my big finish.

Predictably, Denny went down better by pandering admirably to assumed audience desires with 'Go Now', 'Say You Don't Mind', singalongs (including a 'Mull Of Kintyre' finale) from his decade in Wings, a couple of Dylan numbers, and a 'Blackbird' that would've given Paul McCartney pause for thought had he heard it. For me, however, his finest moment was the unreleased 'Ghost Of The Scrimshaw Carver', a self-penned sea shanty impressive for its instant familiarity.

Denny was also recipient of the most lionising afterwards, both at the Malt Shovel and the following evening at Newcastle's Archer where I still drew uproar from a mixed crowd ranging from undergraduates to "Sid the Sexist" types. Somehow it encapsulated my entire career as a stage performer. Outbreaks of barracking punctuated laughter and applause as I walked an artistic tightrope without a safety net – but with a malfunctioning PA system.

Midway, a strapping lass beckoned me to the lip of the stage to utter an eye-stretching but flattering proposition in my ear. She was probably having a laugh, but this put so much lead in my metaphorical pencil that I was cheered back on for an encore that I did not deliver owing to some hard case clambering up to inform the assembled populace that, to give his foul-mouthed insolence a polite translation, my music was not so good. I retaliated by enquiring off-mike, but loud enough for his mates to hear, about whether he was having trouble with his hormones.

After 'Mull Of Kintyre' just over an hour later, I was stunned when the idol that a provincial schoolboy had encountered in Carnaby Street in 1965 called me from the dressing room to duet with him on his encore, a medley of rock 'n' roll favourites. Twenty-four hours later, this honour was bestowed once more (and with interest) when, following a looser set in which Denny dredged up favourites from as far back as the pre-Moody Blues era, a more subdued recital at Dr Brown's in Huddersfield closed when Chris Kefford, once of The Move, resurfaced as the third member of what one wit present christened the "Beverley Brothers" for 'Roll

Over Beethoven', 'Baby Let's Play House', 'Whole Lotta Shakin'',
'Hound Dog' and so on and so on.

Hurtling home along the M1, I came to the conclusion that
Denny Laine still has everything it takes for another bite – albeit
a qualified one – at the cherry of pop stardom. Yet it had to be
said that *Reborn*, his new album that was pulsating from my car's
cassette player, wasn't quite the means of delivery from the
roughhouses where he and I had been working for most of that
week. Nothing screamed out as a potential single – no 'Say You
Don't Mind' or the 'Ghost Of The Scrimshaw Carver' showstopper
– but he was in fine voice, the playing was polished, the lyrics
erudite and the production lush.

For those very reasons, I found myself wishing, now and then,
for some musical dirt, something a bit crude, to capsize the cleverly
processed stratas of sound. This was exacerbated by arrangements
that hinged on a similar medium tempo that tended to make for
much of a muchness when listening to ten new all-original tracks.

Third from the end, 'Within Walls' (a blues and the only stylised
number present) was the most ear-catching the first time round
– with the preceding 'Fanfare' a close second. Perhaps you have
to get used to the overall drift of *Reborn*. Yet I didn't feel that
because greater effort was needed to "appreciate" individual
tracks that they are somehow "deeper" than anything more
instant. However, I'm glad I possess *Reborn* if only for its promise
of finer things to come.

The next time I saw Denny was in Eastbourne when he opened
the second half of *With A Little Help From Their Friends*, a Beatles
tribute show that you shouldn't have missed but probably did.
Partly because a heavy cold had weakened Laine's voice to a
tortured rasp, the night belonged to The Merseybeats, a working
band for over 30 years, and the most vibrant paradigm of the
Liverpool beat explosion that Joe Average is ever likely to encounter
these days. Ten years before, they were an intermission act in bingo
halls – the legs-eleven patter recommencing while the last cadence

of their encore was still fading – but their dogged pursuit of better things was rewarded in 1996 when they were voted Top Group in a readers' poll in *The Beat Goes On*, then the mouthpiece of the 1960s nostalgia scene. At Eastbourne, this confidence boost showed in The Merseybeats' own delight in being there – a feeling that infected the entire auditorium.

Bantering continuity by mainstays Tony Crane and Billy Kinsley supplemented an affectionate medley of favourites by The Searchers, Billy J *et al*, and Billy and Tony's own cache of lovelorn smashes with the original personnel – 'I Think Of You', 'Wishin' And Hopin'' and so forth. More recent releases like 'Poor Boy From Liverpool' and 1995's revival of Lennon and McCartney's (sorry, McCartney and Lennon's) 'I'll Get You' were received as ecstatically – though, during the latter, the counterpointed quotes from other Beatles items didn't quite come off as far as I was concerned.

Apart from a tendency to over-milk the audience, the effect had been similar at a "Mersey Reunion" tour where The Merseybeats were also required to back a turn by compère Mike McCartney who, if no Ken Dodd, struck a convivial note with 'Two Days Monday' – his Scaffold's debut 45 – during a protracted switchover. With The Merseybeats, he poured out the hits that had elicited little positive response from me when first heard but, at Guildford Civic Hall, I was as captivated as the rest by 'Thank U Very Much' and 'Liverpool Lou'. Even 'Lily The Pink' (with Tony and Billy singing the John Gorman and Roger McGough parts) was nearly tolerable.

Unsubstantiated backstage hearsay had it that Paul was going to roll in from Sussex to cheer on his brother and renew his acquaintance with The Merseybeats and, also on the bill, an entity called Mike Pender's Searchers.

To a more pragmatic purpose than mere socialising, he'd resurfaced in the life of John Duff Lowe, who, in 1981, had let it be known that he proposed selling the worn 'That'll Be The Day'–'In Spite Of All The Danger' relic to the highest bidder. "The acetate lay in my linen drawer for years," recollected John. "Though I played it to one or two people. Then I spoke to Sotheby's to see what it was worth. This got into the newspapers, and Paul immediately put out an injunction because it had an original song of his on it that had never been published.

"A letter from his solicitor's arrived, saying that he wanted to settle the matter amicably. Paul and I had a couple of telephone conversations. He suggested that I come up to London for a chat about the old days, but I said that we ought to get the business about the acetate out of the way first. He sent his business manager and solicitor to see me in Worcester – where I was working at the time. I handed it over, perfectly happy with the deal we agreed, and that was that."

One condition of this was that Lowe was forbidden from discussing – or performing – 'In Spite Of All The Danger' for five years. Furthermore, the mooted chat in London never took place, but John had a close encounter with his old colleague when he was among the 1,000-odd listening to Paul reading his *Blackbird Singing* poems at the annual Hay-on-Wye Literary Festival held over Whitsun in 2001. In the midst of one announcement, Paul directed the crowd's attention to Lowe, who took a bow and even signed autographs later when someone was searching him out in order to bring him to McCartney in the VIP area. However, the bird had flown by the time John was found.

All might not be lost because John Duff Lowe is now – some of the time anyway – in the same profession as McCartney. For a while, Lowe had combined membership of a latter-day Four Pennies with the relaunch of a Quarry Men and the interrelated promotion of their *Open For Engagements*, a 1994 album that most listeners found more *Sgt Pepper* than olde tyme skiffle, despite the inclusion of 'Twenty Flight Rock', 'Come Go With Me' and further items from the 1958 line-up's repertoire.

"Rod Davis came over from his home in Uxbridge to play rhythm guitar on the sessions," said John. "I wrote to Paul and

George asking if they'd like to be on it. Only Paul replied, saying that he couldn't do it, but wished us the best of luck.

"The guitarist and drummer are John Ozoroff and Charles Hart of The Four Pennies – Charles takes one lead vocal, John does the rest – and we have Richie Gould on bass from West Country 'yokel' band, The Carrot-Crunchers."

The flurry of activity continued with my audition to take over from a genial John Ozoroff as lead singer – but that's another story – and Lowe's negotiations for dates at "Beatlefests" in Los Angeles and Chicago, and a tour of Japan.

So far, there's been no follow-up to *Open For Engagements* – at least not by a Quarry Men containing John Duff Lowe – but another with a bit-part in McCartney's life story, Tony Sheridan, has been able to protract a prolific recording career that has included items of greater musical if not commercial worth than the tracks he punched out in three takes at most with John, Paul, George and Pete for Bert Kaempfert.

That Sheridan's journey to his sixth decade hadn't been peaceful became clear after he arrived from Germany for an appearance as one of the advertised "surprise legends" at a "Skiffle Party" in the 100 Club in London's West End on 5 March 1997. He reminded me vaguely of the "Max" character played by John Hurt in *Midnight Express*. His hair was as white as frost, but most of it was still on his scalp above a lined forehead – and, though it might have been a bit of a squeeze, his body looked as if it would still fit into the clothes he'd worn in 1960. Crucially, however, he rocked as hard as ever he did.

After a fashion, much the same is true of Gerry Marsden, omnipresent at all manner of high-profile nostalgia and variety revues such as 1990's Gerry's Christmas Cracker season at Birmingham Town Hall. Beyond Britain, an average of six months a year of international engagements has included spots as celebrity speaker at Beatles conventions such as a Beatlefest in Chicago where his recountings of what Paul McCartney said to Horst

Fascher at the Top Ten in 1961 was punctuated with songs on an acoustic six-string. It was through a suggestion by organiser Mark Lapidos that Gerry came to write his autobiography *You'll Never Walk Alone*[13] with another Beatlefest guest, the late Ray Coleman, former editor of *Melody Maker*.

In this thoroughly diverting account, The Beatles were conspicuous among fellow travellers in the journey that brought Marsden from suburban youth clubs to reliving his past glories in Britain, Australia, North America and everywhere else he's fondly remembered.

Record releases, however, have been sporadic, if often newsworthy. For all his criticism of 'Mull Of Kintyre' in 1977, Gerry selected it for 1985's *The Lennon–McCartney Songbook*. That this vinyl long-player was less Lennon–McCartney than Lennon and McCartney – especially sleeve-note writer McCartney – was the decision of producer Gordon Smith. "He approached me with the idea that I do an LP of John and Paul's numbers," elucidated Gerry. "I never sang any of their songs onstage. Conversely, they never sang mine, sod 'em, but I still liked their music. So I thought, 'Brilliant!'. Gordon sent me a list of the ones he'd like me to do, paid for everything, and I enjoyed the sessions."

That same year, Gerry was amongst principals of The Crowd, the aggregation that reached Number One with a money-raising re-hash of his 'You'll Never Walk Alone' for victims of the Herald Of Free Enterprise shipwreck.

A comparable disaster closer to home was to push Marsden, however unwillingly, to the fore again when Paul McCartney, Elvis Costello and other Liverpool-associated stars, past and present, joined him on 1989's overhaul of Gerry's hit 'Ferry 'Cross The Mersey' – a song that Paul, as he reiterated, had wished he'd written. This was in aid of the Hillsborough Disaster Fund after 95 ordinary people were crushed to death in a swollen stadium during a Liverpool soccer team away match.

After this second 'Ferry 'Cross The Mersey' slid from the charts, the next Britain at large saw of Gerry was in an edition of Channel

Four's *Brookside* soap opera as singing guitarist in a Liverpool "supergroup" with Ray Ennis of The Swinging Blue Jeans, ex-Remo Four bass player Don Andrew – and Pete Best.

Among Pete's most recent attempts to recover scrapings of his stolen inheritance is *Casbah Coffee Bar: Birthplace Of The Beatles*, an album with the teenage Paul McCartney in pride of place on the front cover. Nonetheless, the disc's real star was Billy Kinsley as producer, singer and general factotum in a studio assembly that also encompassed other local luminaries such as saxophonist Brian Jones from The Undertakers, Beryl Marsden – who should have represented Liverpool womanhood in the 1960s charts rather than a lesser talent like Cilla Black – and Roag Best, the youngest brother, as second drummer.

Content was chosen from items on the bar's original juke box – and so are most of the arrangements, though certain idiosyncracies creep in such as the synthesized orchestral backwash that kicks off 'Red River Rock', the fade-in to 'Sea Cruise' and an inspired rethink of 'Sleepwalk' that invokes an ocean dawn from the quarterdeck, and stands head and shoulders above Paul's ragged effort during the 1974 session with John Lennon and his "lost weekend" cronies in California.

Yet the decades of technology that have passed since the Casbah opened in 1958 means that, overall, there wasn't as much grit as I'd have liked – but perhaps that's not the point for incorrigible old rockers with no other cards left to play. If nothing else, *Casbah Coffee Bar* sounds like it was fun to record, even if this particular brand of fun wasn't a thing that money can't buy.

What am I to bid for a review copy of *Produced By George Martin: Fifty Years In Recording*, a lavish box-set retrospective of six CDs? Relevant to this discussion are Martin's self-penned *Pepperland Suite*, a nutshelling of the incidental music to the *Yellow Submarine* movie, and acknowledgement that Paul was the Beatle with whom George had most artistic empathy via the presence of McCartney's contributions to *The Family Way* flick and the

Thingamybob sit-com. There are also four of his post-Beatles efforts on the two discs in this collection that celebrate the later work of the now-retired architect of discs by the showbusiness sensation that made more fortunes than have ever been known in the history of recorded sound.

Epilogue
"Besame Mucho"

"Why don't Paul McCartney and Ringo Starr step into the shoes of John Entwistle and Keith Moon to create the supergroup we've always wanted; say The Whotles or The Bho?"

– GJ Kenna[1]

He'd arrived at the gateway of the next century with more money than sense, and loaded with all manner of honours that he'd accepted with a becoming modesty. Like the other surviving Beatle – not to mention the two still living of the original Who – his prosperity and good works will be sustained into old age, and be subsidised less by new output than the tightly controlled repackagings of classics he'd recorded decades earlier.

Though he acquitted himself admirably onstage as the biggest box-office draw on the circuit in 2003, the days of instant Number Ones and even automatic Top 40 entries have long gone for Paul McCartney. Nevertheless, he's still happy to bask in the limelight of whatever hit records remain in him.

In the immediate wake of Elvis Presley's death in 1977, there was a swiftly deleted tribute single, 'The Greatest Star Of All' by a certain Skip Jackson in which steel guitars weep behind a sort of Illinois Cockney who declares in a flat tone that regrets that "one more great record to make it all complete" hadn't been forthcoming.

On his 50th birthday in 1992, Paul was overcome with similar sentiment, musing a little ruefully that "despite the successful songs I've written like 'Yesterday', 'Let It Be' and 'Hey Jude', I feel I just want to write one really good song. People say to me, 'What's left for you to do?' – but I still have a little [that word again!] bee in my bonnet telling me, 'Hang on. The best could be yet to come. You could write something which could be just incredible.' That keeps me going. Looking at things now, I don't seem to be over the hill."[2]

Nothing of 'Yesterday'–'Hey Jude' quality has come to him since – or maybe it has, but wasn't able to reach enough listeners because of a marketing climate and attitude much changed since The Beatles – and Wings – were around. As Gene Pitney has theorised, "You can't write a great Sixties song now and have it be successful."[3] When was the last time you heard the latest by Paul McCartney or Gene Pitney on Radio One? When was the last time you listened to Radio One? However much he might gainsay it, Paul's target group – like that for this biography – are those who don't buy rap, Britpop, boy bands, *Pop Idol* winners *et al*, whose appetite for novelty is satiated, and who only bother with singles during the Christmas "silly season".

Above all, 'From Me To You', 'Yesterday', 'Hello Goodbye' and 'Lady Madonna' aren't so much vibrations hanging in the air anymore as symbols of the Swinging Sixties – and McCartney has been prevented from soundtracking pop eras that have come after to anywhere near the same degree. While that watershed decade has been over for 40 years, the emotional rather than intrinsic significance of its music lingers, and new songs, however worthy, sung by a Beatle voice can leave a peculiar afterglow. In a parallel dimension, perhaps 'Only Love Remains' by The Beatles is the most covered composition of all time, while 1986's 'Yesterday' by Paul McCartney petered out at a domestic Number 34 before being consigned to the archives of oblivion.

In the real world, all most visitors to the Louvre want to see is the *Mona Lisa*, ignoring what might be essentially finer paintings along the corridors leading to it. Paul McCartney singing 'From

A Lover To A Friend' in concert is regarded as an artistic indulgence, an obligatory lull requiring a more subdued reaction than that for when 'Eleanor Rigby' or 'I Saw Her Standing There' makes everything all right again.

How, therefore, can he ever imagine that "the best could be yet to come'? Another impediment, of course, is that, though hair dye and a soft-focus lens rendered him an old-young creature gripping an electric guitar for the principal *Back In The World* publicity shot, BBC television cameras treated him less kindly in a recurring 2003 trailer for Radio Two – of a solo 'Band On The Run' in which: "He's playing every instrument ever invented," in the sarcastic over-estimation of veteran jazzman Stan Tracey, "and some that are about to be invented. He's mastered them all of course. It's rather touching."[4]

Yet, apart from *choba* jowls and *oobu-joobu* lips, McCartney showed his age here little more than Cliff Richard would have done. Like Richard, too, he remains an irregular chart contender – and an object of admiration by the most disparate people. "I don't think that music has an automatically high value because it's hard to listen to," pontificated modern classical composer Michael Nyman, "and a low value because it's easy to listen to. Give me a Beatles song any time."[5]

To heavy metallurgist and docu-soap personality Ozzy Osbourne, McCartney is "a hero. I met him on *The Howard Stern Show* in 2001, and there were photographs taken of me with him, and I wrote to him and asked if I could have one. He never got back to me and I was kind of disappointed. I mean, The Beatles were the reason I wanted to get into music. I wanted Paul to play on 'Dreamer' [from 2000's *Down To Earth* album], but he didn't want to do it. He said, 'I couldn't play it any better than the bass player that's already playing on there' – but that wasn't the point. The point was to have Paul McCartney playing bass on one of the most Beatle-esque songs I've ever written. He apologised to me and I told him to forget it. Just the fact that he'd sat down and listened to my song was enough for me."[6]

As the subject of sick-making stories of crapulous debauchery and bringing a press conference to a standstill by biting the head off a white dove – and swallowing it – Ozzy's seemingly permanent expression of dazed bafflement might have been been a true reflection of inner feelings when he was granted a one-song spot at the Queen's "Jubilee Concert". Paul McCartney, however, had accepted his longer sojourn on the boards – the last act on – as his due. The dean of British pop, he acknowledged acclaim for merely existing after a comic introduction by Dame Edna Everage.

The intensity of the ovations neither rose nor fell as he completed a polished set consisting of nothing but Beatles numbers. Only if he'd made a complete pig's ear of them, could viewers at home and in the palace grounds have said anything constructive beyond "That's Paul singing 'Her Majesty', 'Blackbird', 'While My Guitar Gently Weeps', 'Sgt Pepper's Lonely Hearts Club Band', 'The End'…"

Then the other acts walked back on and stood in respectful rows when joined by our gracious Queen with the Prince of Wales, who said a few well-chosen words before 'Hey Jude' and its joyous coda sung *ad infinitum* by all the big showbusiness names up there – Shirley Bassey, Tony Bennett, Cliff, Ozzy, Ray Davies, Brian Wilson, Steve Winwood, one of The Spice Girls, Rod Stewart, Tom Jones, you name 'em – and, at the centre of it all, Paul McCartney!

Notes

In addition to my own correspondence and interviews, I have used the following sources, which I would like to credit:

Prologue: 'Till There Was You'

1 *Sunday Times*, 11 January 2003

2 *The Paul McCartney Encyclopaedia* by B Harry (Virgin, 2002)

3 *Paul McCartney: The Songs He Was Singing* by J Blaney (Paper Jukebox, 2003)

4 *Paul McCartney: Many Years From Now* by B Miles (Vintage, 1998)

Chapter 1: 'Que Sera Sera'

1 *Cry: The Johnnie Ray Story* by J Whiteside (Barricade, 1994)

2 *Singing Together* (BBC Publications, 1953)

3 *Who's Who In Popular Music In Britain* by S Tracy (World's Work, 1984)

4 *Daily Express*, 23 August 1955

5 *Melody Maker*, 17 September 1958

6 *The Life And Times Of Little Richard, The Quasar Of Rock* by C White (Harmony, 1984)

7 *The Facts About A Pop Group: Featuring Wings* by D Gelly (Whizzard, 1976)

8 *Buddy Holly: The Real Story* by E Amburn (Virgin, 1996)

9 *Backbeat: Die Stuart Sutcliffe Story* by A Clayson and P Sutcliffe (Bastei Lubbe, 1994), a translation of the original manuscript of *Backbeat – Stuart Sutcliffe: The Lost Beatle* by the same authors (Pan-Macmillan, 1994)

Chapter 2: 'That'll Be The Day'

1. *Clint Eastwood: Film Maker* by D O'Brien (Batsford, 1996)

2 *Picturegoer*, 1 September 1956

3   Quoted in sleeve notes to *The Very Best Of Matt Monro* (Spectrum, 1997)

4   *Who's Who In Popular Music In Britain* by S Tracy (World's Work, 1984)

Chapter 3: 'It's Now Or Never'

1. *Backbeat: Die Stuart Sutcliffe Story* by A Clayson and P Sutcliffe (Bastei Lubbe, 1994), a translation of the original manuscript of *Backbeat – Stuart Sutcliffe: The Lost Beatle* by the same authors (Pan-Macmillan, 1994)

2. *Bratby* by P Davies (Bakehouse, 2002)

3. *The Times*, 24 September 1988

4. *The Beat Goes On*, November 1992

5. *New Musical Express*, 1 November 1957

6. Quoted in sleeve notes to *The Very Best Of Matt Monro* (Spectrum, 1997)

7. *Acts Of Faith* by A Faith (Bantam, 1996)

Chapter 4: 'What'd I Say?'

1. *Acker Bilk* by G Williams (Mayfair, 1960)

2. *New Musical Express*, 19 August 1958

3. *Melody Maker*, 11 March 1963

4. *Let's All Go Down The Cavern* by S Leigh (Vermilion, 1984)

5. BBC Radio Bedfordshire, 29 December 1985

6. *Backbeat: Die Stuart Sutcliffe Story* by A Clayson and P Sutcliffe (Bastei Lubbe, 1994), a translation of the original manuscript of *Backbeat – Stuart Sutcliffe: The Lost Beatle* by the same authors (Pan-Macmillan, 1994)

7. *Beatle!: The Pete Best Story* by P Best and P Doncaster (Plexus, 1985)

8. *Music*, November 1997

9. *Hamburg: The Cradle Of British Rock* by A Clayson (Sanctuary, 1997)

10. US title: *Call Me Genius!*

11. *The Times*, 24 November 1988

12. A 1960 US Number One, and a UK Top 20 entry in 1961 for Maurice Williams And The Zodiacs

13. *Good Day Sunshine*, November 1989

Chapter 5: 'Over The Rainbow'

1. *The Spinning Wheels: The Story Of A Melbourne Rhythm And Blues Band* by D Hirst (Park Fraser, 2002)

2   *Backbeat: Die Stuart Sutcliffe Story* by A Clayson and P Sutcliffe (Bastei Lubbe,

1994), a translation of the original manuscript of *Backbeat – Stuart Sutcliffe: The Lost Beatle* by the same authors (Pan-Macmillan, 1994)

3.   *The Beat Goes On*, November 1999

4.   *The Beat Goes On*, February 1991

Chapter 6: 'Some Other Guy'

1.   *John Lennon: Living On Borrowed Time* by F Seaman (Xanadu, 1991)

2.   *Let's All Go Down The Cavern* by S Leigh (Vermilion, 1984)

3.   *Brian Epstein: The Man Who Made The Beatles* by R Coleman (Viking, 1989)

4.   Paul McCartney's sleeve notes to *The Lennon–McCartney Songbook* by Gerry Marsden (K-Tel, 1985)

5.   *Midland Beat*, No 1, October 1963

6.   *New Musical Express*, 8 January 1962

7.   *The Life And Times of Little Richard, The Quasar Of Rock* by C White (Harmony, 1984)

8.   *Backbeat: Die Stuart Sutcliffe Story* by A Clayson and P Sutcliffe (Bastei Lubbe, 1994), a translation of the original manuscript of *Backbeat – Stuart Sutcliffe: The Lost Beatle* by the same authors (Pan-Macmillan, 1994)

9.   *Drummed Out! The Sacking Of Pete Best* by S Leigh (Northdown, 1998)

10. *Mersey Beat*, 10 March 1962

11. *Beatle!: The Pete Best Story* by P Best and P Doncaster (Plexus, 1985)

12. *Q*, June 1992

Chapter 7: 'Don't You Dig This Kind Of Beat?'

1.   *Midland Beat*, No 1, October 1963

2.   *Midland Beat*, No 13, October 1964

Chapter 8: 'Nobody I Know'

1.   *Kink* by D Davies (Boxtree, 1996)

2.   *Cry: The Johnnie Ray Story* by J Whiteside (Barricade, 1994)

3.   *Behind The Song: The Stories of 100 Great Pop & Rock Classics* by M Heatley and S Leigh (Blandford, 1999)

4.   *The "Playboy" Interviews With John Lennon and Yoko Ono* by D Sheff and G Barry Golson (New English Library, 1982)

5.   On a poster for his appearance at Redhill Market Hall on 30 January 1964

6.   *Nowhere To Run* by G Hirshey (Pan, 1984)

7.   *The Facts About A Pop Group: Featuring Wings* by D Gelly (Whizzard, 1976)

8. *1,000 Days That Shook The World, Mojo Beatles Special*, October 2002

9. *Paul McCartney: Many Years From Now* by B Miles (Vintage, 1998)

10. However, Walsh's most renowned work was a portrait of the late Cuban *guerilléro*, Che Guevara. As a poster print, this became a fixture in student hostel rooms in the later 1960s.

11. They were to record several albums for RCA, tour with Led Zeppelin and be on the bill at 1969's Isle of Wight festival.

12. *TV Times*, 23 October 1965

13. *Thank U Very Much* by M McGear (Arthur Barker, 1981)

14. *Random Precision: Recording The Music Of Syd Barrett* by D Parker (Cherry Red, 2001)

Chapter 9: 'I'm The Urban Spaceman'

1. *Loose Talk* by L Botts (*Rolling Stone*, 1980)

2. *Lost In The Woods: Syd Barrett And The Pink Floyd* by J Palacios (Boxtree, 1998)

3. *Playpower* by R Neville (Jonathan Cape, 1970)

4. *Scene At 6.30* (ITV, 4 March 1967)

5. *International Times*, 16–29 January 1967

6. *Which One's Cliff?* by C Richard (Coronet, 1977)

7. *The Process,* No 5, autumn 1968

8 *Paul McCartney: Many Years From Now* by B Miles (Vintage, 1998)

9. *Days In The Life: Voices From The English Underground, 1961–1971* by J Green (Heinemann, 1988)

10. *Lennon Remembers: The Rolling Stone Interviews,* ed J Wenner (Penguin, 1973)

11. Quoted in *Crazy Fingers* by A Carson (Carson, 1998)

12. *Record Collector,* No 285, May 2003

13. *The Playboy Interviews With John Lennon and Yoko Ono* by D Sheff and G Barry Golson (New Engish Library, 1982)

14. Quoted in *The Yardbirds* by A Clayson (Backbeat, 2002)

15. *Disc And Music Echo*, December 1965 (precise date obscured)

16. *1,000 Days Of Revolution, Mojo Beatles Special,* March 2003

Chapter 10: 'Goodbye'

1. *The Love You Make: An Insider's Story Of The Beatles* by P Brown and S Gaines (Macmillan, 1983)

2. Quoted in *No Sleep Till Canvey Island: The Great Pub Rock Revolution* by W Birch (Virgin, 2000)

3. *Loose Talk* by L Botts (Rolling Stone, 1980)

4. Press release, 17 April 1970

5. *Stone Alone: The Story of a Rock' N' Roll Band* by B Wyman and R Coleman (Viking, 1990)

6. *Blue Melody: Tim Buckley Remembered* by L Underwood (Backbeat, 2002)

7. *Don't Let Me Be Misunderstood* by E Burdon and J Marshall Craig (Thunder's Mouth, 2001)

Chapter 11: 'Wedding Bells'

1. *Who's Who In Popular Music In Britain* by S Tracy (World's Work, 1984)

2. *The Guardian*, 11 March 2003

Chapter 12: 'Love Is Strange'

1. *The Facts About A Pop Group: Featuring Wings* by D Gelly (Whizzard, 1976)

2. Though publication was to be resumed in the 1980s.

3. *Paul McCartney: Many Years From Now* by B Miles (Vintage, 1998)

4. *Brass Bands* by AR Taylor (Granada, 1979)

5. *Chase The Fade* by A Nightingale (Blandford, 1981)

6. *Record Mirror*, 15 April 1971

7. *The John Lennon Encyclopaedia* by B Harry (Virgin, 2000)

8. *Paul McCartney* by A Hamilton (Hamish Hamilton, 1983)

9. *The Paul McCartney Encyclopaedia* by B Harry (Virgin, 2002)

10. *New Musical Express*, 27 May 1971

11. Quoted in *The Illustrated New Musical Express Encyclopaedia Of Rock,* ed N Logan and B Woffinden (Hamlyn, 1976)

12. *Let It Rock*, January 1973

13. *Irish Rock* by MJ Prendergast (O'Brien, 1987)

14. *Joe Cocker* by JP Bean (Omnibus, 1990)

15. *Don't Let Me Be Misunderstood* by E Burdon and J Marshall Craig (Thunder's Mouth, 2001)

Chapter 13: 'Mary Had A Little Lamb'

1. *Don't Let Me Be Misunderstood* by E Burdon and J Marshall Craig (Thunder's Mouth, 2001)

2. *Times Educational Supplement*, 16 November 1986

3. *The Rolling Stone Record Guide,* ed D Marsh and J Swenson (Rolling Stone, 1979)

Chapter 14: 'Crossroads'

1. *Melody Maker*, 17 May 1973

2. *Melody Maker*, 18 and 25 September 1973

3. *The Record Producers* by J Tobler and S Grundy (BBC, 1982)

4. *Nowhere To Run* by G Hirshey (Pan, 1984)

5. *The Paul McCartney Encyclopaedia* by B Harry (Virgin, 2002)

6. First issued as an A-side in 1977, and attributed to 'Suzy And The Red Stripes'

7. *Fab Four* (French fanzine), March 1991

8. *The Facts About A Pop Group: Featuring Wings* by D Gelly (Whizzard, 1976)

9. *Melody Maker*, 5 April 1976

10. *Rolling Stone*, 19 December 1974

11. Quoted in *Behind The Song: The Stories of 100 Great Pop & Rock Classics* by M Heatley and S Leigh (Blandford, 1998)

12. *Stardust: The Life And Times Of David Bowie* by T Zanetta and H Edwards (Michael Joseph, 1986)

13. Quoted in *John Lennon* by A Clayson (Sanctuary, 2003)

14. *The "Playboy" Interviews With John Lennon And Yoko Ono* by D Sheff (Playboy Press, 1981)

Chapter 15: 'Japanese Tears'

1. *Behind The Song: The Stories of 100 Great Pop & Rock Classics* by M Heatley and S Leigh (Blandford, 1998)

2. *Sunday Mirror*, 12 November 1995.

3. *Top Of The Pops* by S Bracknell (Patrick Stevens, 1985)

4. *The Paul McCartney Encyclopaedia* by B Harry (Virgin, 2002)

5. *The Rolling Stone Record Guide,* ed D Marsh and J. Swenson (Rolling Stone, 1979)

6. *Rolling Stone*, 12 December 1979

7. *Chase The Fade* by A Nightingale (Blandford, 1981)

8. *The Sun*, 27 January 1980

9. *Japan Times*, 27 January 1980

Chapter 16: 'Just Like Starting Over'

1. *New Musical Express*, 15 February 1963
2. *Hit Men* by F Dannen (Muller, 1990)
3. *John Lennon: Living On Borrowed Time* by F Seaman (Xanadu, 1991)
4. *The Record Producers* by J Tobler and S Grundy (BBC, 1982)
5. *Club Sandwich*, No 26, 1982
6. *Melody Maker*, 5 November 1983
7. *New Musical Express*, 6 November 1983
8. *Q*, January 1988
9. *Acts Of Faith* by A Faith (Bantam, 1996)
10. *Club Sandwich*, No 35, 1984
11. *Variety*, October 1984
12. *Sunday Times*, 5 May 1990

Chapter 17: 'Don't Get Around Much Anymore'

1. *Beatles Unlimited*, March 1996
2. *Death Discs* by A Clayson (Sanctuary, 1997)
3. To Spencer Leigh
4. By coincidence, The Average White Band's original drummer was also called Robbie McIntosh.
5. As had Elvis Presley's post-army 'It's Now Or Never' for *The Last Temptation Of Elvis*, a charity compilation album.
6. *The Paul McCartney Encyclopaedia* by B Harry (Virgin, 2002)
7. *Q*, July 1989
8. *The Brothers McGregor* by A Wells (Grafton, 1985)
9. *Rolling Stone*, December 1981

Chapter 18: 'Come Together'

1. *Gramophone*, July 1988
2. *The Paul McCartney Encyclopaedia* by B Harry (Virgin, 2002)
3. *All-Music Guide to Electronica,* ed V Bogdonov, C Woodstra, ST Erlewine and J Bush (Backbeat, 2001)
4. *Backbeat: Die Stuart Sutcliffe Story* by A Clayson and P Sutcliffe (Bastei Lubbe, 1994), a translation of the original manuscript of *Backbeat – Stuart Sutcliffe: The Lost Beatle* by the same authors (Pan-Macmillan, 1994)

5. *Classic FM*, August 1997

6. *Music*, November 1999

7. *"Non nobis solum sed toti mundo nati"* ("Not for ourselves alone but for the whole world were we born")

8. *Liverpool Oratorio* (Parlophone LDB 9911301, 1991)

9. *Sunday Mirror*, 23 July 1989

10. *The Sun*, 15 July 1980

Chapter 19: 'My Dark Hour'

1. *Robin And Marion* (Columbia/Rastar Technicolor, 1976)

2. Sleeve notes for *The Quiet Hour* by Patience Strong (Saga STSOC 956, 1963)

3. *Music*, November 1997

4. *Daily Express*, 22 June 1995

5. *Daily Mail*, 1 January 1997

6. *Sunday Times*, 22 December 2002

7. *Daily Express*, 19 May 1997

8. *Independent On Sunday*, 10 May 1997

9. *The Times*, 9 May 1997

10. *Paul McCartney: Many Years From Now* by B Miles (Vintage, 1998)

11. *Don't Let Me Be Misunderstood* by E Burdon and J Marshall Craig (Thunder's Mouth, 2001)

Chapter 20: 'She Said Yeah'

1. *Rod Stewart* by T Ewbank and S Hildred (Headline, 1991)

2. *Hello!* (date obscured)

3. *Out On A Limb* by H Mills and P Cockerill (Little, Brown, 1995)

4. By Pavilion

5. *Beat Merchants* by A Clayson (Cassell/Blandford, 1995)

6. *Daily Mail*, 24 May 2002

7. *Chatham's Burning* (Hangman, 2003)

8. Quoted in *Neil's Book Of The Dead* by N Planer and T Blacker (Pavilion, 1984)

9. *The Times*, 29 March 2003

10. *Daily Mail*, 11 June 2002

11. *Sunday Times*, 12 January 2003

12. *John Lennon: Living On Borrowed Time* by F Seaman (Xanadu, 1991)
13. *You'll Never Walk Alone* by G Marsden and R Coleman (Bloomsbury, 1993)

Epilogue: 'Besame Mucho'

1. Reader's letter to *Viz*, September 2002
2. *The Paul McCartney Encyclopaedia* by B Harry (Virgin, 2002)
3. *The Guardian*, 14 May 2003
4. *The Guardian*, 11 April 2003
5. *The Guardian*, 8 January 2003
6. *Black Sabbath* by S Rosen (Sanctuary, 1996)

Index

Ringo Starr

Printed in the United Kingdom by MPG Books Ltd, Bodmin

Published by Sanctuary Publishing Limited, Sanctuary House, 45-53 Sinclair Road,
London W14 0NS, United Kingdom

www.sanctuarypublishing.com

Distributed in the US by Publishers Group West

ISBN: 1-86074-488-5

Ringo Starr

Alan Clayson

Sanctuary

About The Author

Described by *The Western Morning News* as the "AJP Taylor of pop", Alan Clayson is the author of many books on music, including the best-selling *Backbeat*, subject of a major film. He has contributed to journals as disparate as *Record Collector*, *The Independent*, *The Beat Goes On*, *Mojo*, *Mediaeval World*, *The Times*, *Folk Roots*, *The Guardian* and, as a teenager, the notorious *Schoolkids Oz*. He had also written and presented programmes on national radio and has lectured on both sides of the Atlantic.

Before he became better known as a pop historian, he led the legendary Clayson And The Argonauts and was thrust to "a premier position on rock's Lunatic Fringe" (*Melody Maker*). Today, his solo cabaret act remains "more than just a performance; an experience" (*Village Voice*). "It is difficult to explain to the uninitiated quite what to expect," adds *The Independent*. There is even an Alan Clayson fan club, which dates from a 1992 appearance in Chicago.

Alan Clayson's cult following has continued to grow, along with demand for his production skills in the studio and the number of versions of his compositions by such diverse acts as Dave Berry – in whose Cruisers he played keyboards in the mid 1980s – and (via a collaboration with Yardbird Jim McCarty) Jane Relf and new age outfit Stairway. He has also worked with the Portsmouth Sinfonia, Wreckless Eric, Twinkle and Screaming Lord Sutch, among others.

Born in Dover in 1951, Alan Clayson lives near Henley-on-Thames with his wife, Inese, and sons, Jack and Harry.

"You will tell me no doubt that Mrs Patrick Campbell cannot act. Who said she could – and who wants her to act? Who cares twopence whether she possesses that or any other second-rate accomplishment? On the highest plane, one does not act, one is."

George Bernard Shaw

To Tinkerbelle

Contents

Prologue

"I've Never Really Done Anything To Create What Has Happened"

During a soundcheck in a theatre in Wales, the timpanist of the Portsmouth Sinfonia was addressed as "Oi, Ringo!" by a janitor who wished him to shift his bloody junk away from the safety curtain. In 1984, a British tabloid wrung a news item from a cockroach who'd been named Ringo by the duty officer after it had been brought into a Yorkshire police station by a greengrocer who'd found it amongst his turnips. In countless such trivial occurrences, former Beatle Ringo Starr is fulfilling an early wish to "end up sort of unforgettable".[1]

To the man in the street, his will always be the Beatle name more likely to trip off the tongue than those of John Lennon, Paul McCartney and George Harrison, none of whom assumed a permanent stage alias. Nevertheless, Ringo – born plain Richard Starkey – seemed the least altered of all of them by the scarcely believable years of Beatlemania and its aftermath. Not quite losing the air of an eternal Scouser who'd hit the big time, he'd confess, "I've never really done anything to create what has happened. It created itself, and I'm only here because it did happen."[2]

Yet, however peripheral he might have been to the group artistically, "ex-Beatle" remains an adjective more attributable to Starr than the "mystic" Harrison; McCartney, still basking in the limelight; and Lennon, in the legion of the lost. Back in Liverpool, another ex-Beatle, Pete Best – the one whom Ringo replaced – seemed content until recently as a civil servant, part-time drummer and prized guest speaker at Beatle Conventions.

Pete's first autobiography appeared in 1985. In that same year, it was reported that Ringo was to write one, too. This was not the sole such rumour, nor the only time that Starr had rejected six-figure sums to relate his side of it. "It would take three volumes up to when I was ten," he explained, "and they really only want to know about eight years of my life. So that's why I said no. They want just the juicy bits, just like you."[3]

He's underestimating himself – or he's over-estimating the tired old story of the Fab Four. The sagas of Ringo's sojourn with Rory Storm And The Hurricanes up until 1962 and his career in the 20 years since The Beatles are at least as funny, poignant, turbulent and scandalous as those of that more exalted and chronicled era.

Without much hope, I attempted to elicit Starr's assistance for my account, but all he gave me was a polite refusal via his secretary. This was regrettable but by no means disastrous. After all, a recent biographer of Alfred the Great hadn't interviewed his subject, either. Also, treating Ringo like a historical figure, footnotes and all, I waded through oceans of archive material and screwed myself up to talk to complete strangers about matters that took place up to 40 years ago.

As his profile assumed a sharper definition, Starr surfaced as an admirable man in many ways, although some of my findings shattered minor myths. He was not, for example, the originator of the film title *A Hard Day's Night*, as had been previously supposed.[4] His conscious tendency in interview to "hear myself saying the same things over again"[5] also emerged, and, while it got on my nerves slightly, it was useful for confirmation of personal information and opinions. Unlike Alfred the Great's annalist, I didn't have to arrive at a divergent conclusion but simply choose which of Ringo's remarks about the same matter was most interesting.

For most of my secondary research and consultation, I went first and last to Ian Drummond, who was always at hand at a moment's notice in his capacity as a Beatle scholar of the highest calibre.

I am also very grateful to Peter Doggett for his help with this project, and indeed with other ventures, quixotic and otherwise, over the years.

Special thanks are in order, too, for Susan Hill, Amy Sohanpaul, Carys Thomas, Amanda Marshall – and Helen Gummer, whose patience and understanding went beyond the call of duty as original commissioning editor. The same applies to Penny Braybrooke, who authorised this updated reissue, as well as Jeffrey Hudson, Alan Heal, Eddy Leviten, Dan Froude, Chris Bradford and Michelle Knight. I would also like to say a big hello to Hilary Murray.

Let's have a big round of applause, too, for Dave and Caroline Humphreys for accommodating me whenever I was on Merseyside and for Dave's skill and imagination as a photographer.

For their advice and for trusting me with archive material, particular debts are owed to Pete Frame, Bill Harry, Paul Hearne, Spencer Leigh, Steve Maggs, Allan Jones, Fraser Massey, Steve Morris of *Brumbeat*, Charles and Deborah Salt, Maggie Simpson of *Melody Maker* and John Tobler.

I have also drawn from conversations with the following musicians: Ian "Tich" Amey, Christina Balfour, Roger Barnes, Andre Barreau, Alan Barwise, Cliff Bennett, Dave Berry, Barry Booth, Bruce Brand, Louis Cennamo, Billy Childish, Jeff Christopherson, Frank Connor, Ron Cooper, Pete Cox, Tony Crane, Dave Dee, Wayne Fontana, Gary Gold, "Wreckless" Eric Goulden, David Hentschel, Penny Hicks, Malcolm Hornsby, Garry Jones, Billy Kinsley, Graham Larkbey, Dave Maggs, Jim McCarty, Jill Myhill, Ray Pinfold, Brian Poole, Reg Presley, Mike Robinson, Jim Simpson, Norman Smith, the late Lord David Sutch, Mike Sweeney, Geoff Taggart, John Townsend, Paul Tucker, Val Wiseman and Fran Wood.

It may be obvious to the reader that I have received much information from sources that prefer not to be mentioned. Nevertheless, I wish to express my gratitude towards them.

Thanks are also due in varying degrees to Andy Anderton, B&T Typewriters, Robert Bartel, Colin Baylis, Carol Boyer, Rob Bradford, Eva Marie Brunner, Stuart and Kathryn Booth, Gordon and Rosemary Clayson, Kevin Delaney, Greg and Debi Daniels, Doreen Davidson, Nancy Davis, Helen Drummond, Tim and Sarah Fagan, Kathi and Rick Fowler, Tom Hall (of the Spinning Disk), Sarah

Knake, Yvonne Lambourne, Mark and Carol Lapidos, Brian Leafe, Bill Mielenz, Coy Ness, Carolyn Pinfold, Andrea Tursso and Ted Woodings – plus Inese, Jack and Harry, who preferred Luddite rage at irrecoverable disasters while I taught myself to work a word processor to the incessant clacking of a typewriter by a paterfamilias strung out on Tipp-Ex, man.

Alan Clayson, July 2001

I "I Was Just One Of Those Loony Teddy Boys"

In 1962, the plug was pulled and Richard Starkey was sucked into a vortex of events, places and situations that hadn't belonged even to speculation when, on 7 July 1940 – a week late and a month after the Dunkirk evacuation – he was born in the front bedroom of 9 Madryn Street, a three-up/three-down terrace in the Dingle. As it had been with most of his immediate forebears, unless tempted by the Merchant Navy or compelled by the government to fight foreign foes, nothing suggested that Richard too would not dwell until the grave around this Merseyside suburb that backed onto docklands carved from a plateau of sandstone and granite on the trudging river's final bend before it swept into the Irish Sea.

Since at least the construction of Madryn Street a century earlier, the Starkey name and many of those with whom the family intermarried – Cunningham, Parkin, Bower, Johnson, Parr, Gleave – had been imprinted upon census rolls pertaining to the mean streets of the Dingle-Toxteth area's main thoroughfares, where dray horses still dragged coal for the rusty ships in Gladstone Dock, with its cast-iron bollards. A combination of Victorian custom and hit-or-miss birth-control methods had resulted in many branches of the clan. Particularly prolific were Richard's maternal grandparents, who filled their Toxteth Park home with 14 children. With the port dominating their employment as boiler-makers, tinsmiths, engine-drivers and similar unlettered professions, the Starkey men might have aspired – as Richard would – "to have a semi in a posh part of Liverpool",[1] as his cousins the Fosters did in Crosby.

For the brief time they were together, he and his father were known parochially as Big Richie and Little Richie. Elsie Gleave and Big Richie's eyes had first locked among the cakes and tarts of the bakery where they both worked. Little Richie was the only issue of an unhappy seven-year espousal which began in his Starkey grandparents' house at 59 Madryn Street and ended in divorce in 1943, when Elsie was 29.

Little if any explanation could be offered the boy for why his daddy walked out, but his opinion of the shadowy figure that he was to see henceforth only infrequently was jaundiced to the degree that, on some of the occasions they met, "I wouldn't speak to him. I suppose my mother filled me up with all the things about him."[2] Other than the regular maintenance allowance that he sent, Richard Starkey Senior might as well have been lost in the hostilities that had caused Ministry of Transport officials to remove signposts and direction indicators that might have assisted invading Germans. A few weeks after Little Richie's birth, flares illuminated the sky as the Luftwaffe pounded the docks and the civilian population scurried for shelter.

Sooty foxgloves might have sprung up on the resulting bomb sites, but the Dingle had long been totally unrecognisable as the arcadian meadows where a Viking *thing* ("conclave of elders") had once assembled. One of the seediest districts of the blackened city, it was a huddled land of few illusions – of finger-crushing mangles in communal backyards, rubbish sogging behind railings, outside lavatories, skinny and ferocious cats and corner-shop windows barricaded with wire mesh. Inside the poky brick tangles, naked lightbulbs were coated in dust, damp plaster crumbled at a touch from cold walls, margarine was spread instead of butter and noisy copper geysers hung above sinks in which a wife would both bathe babies and wash up dishes from a Sunday lunch on a newspaper tablecloth. While her spouse slept it off in the cramped living room, the children could be heard beneath sepia skies, hopscotching, footballing and catcalling in the coarsest glottal intonation of a region where even the most refined speakers sounded ambiguously alien and common to anyone south of Birmingham.

"Things were pretty tough for Elsie, as I've always called my mother," Richie would recollect from a decade when a "wacker" accent became exotic. "She tried to bring me up decently. We were poor, but never in rags. I was lucky. I was her only child. She could spend more time with me."[3] Her husband's rancorous departure might have hardened Mrs Starkey's resolve to ensure that Richie was as comfortable and contented as her deprived station would allow. If rather worn, his clothes were always clean, and she'd tuck in his shirt, shine his shoes and brush his hair prior to delivering him to whatever nearby relation or friend was scheduled to mind him while she made ends meet. Four years older than Richie, one such minder, Marie Maguire, became the closest to a sister that he'd ever know while Elsie was busy with diverse menial jobs, such as pulling pints of Tetley's ale behind the bar of the narrow Empress pub, a promontory but a few convenient yards from both 9 Madryn Street and 10 Admiral Grove, where, for its cheaper rent, she and Richie were obliged to move in 1944.

Before overcrowding and subsequent urban renewal caused their borders to overlap, such neighbourhoods saw themselves as a race apart from the rest of Liverpool. *Race* is a crucial word in this most cosmopolitan of settlements, where West Indian immigrants gravitated towards a cluster of Toxteth streets named after Dickensian characters – the Nook pub in Chinatown served the vicinity with English beer, and a Greek Orthodox church stood opposite the Rialto Ballroom in the city centre, then a clattering 20-minute tram ride from Toxteth Dock terminus. The populace was so vulnerable to mixed marriages that the Catholic Information Centre placed boxed warnings in *The Liverpool Echo* about their inherent dangers.

Territorial identity and loyalty sprang from the greater municipal pride that bonded Liverpudlians more firmly than inhabitants of, say, Exeter or Norwich. When a grimy pivot of Victorian commerce, it almost as palpably forged opportunities for cultural development, with Augustus John teaching at the Art School and Dickens giving readings within the imposing Greek façade of the Institute next door. However, by the mid 20th century, a Merseyside artist was regarded as a contradiction in terms, unless a music-hall buffoon like "Big-Hearted Little" Arthur Askey or ukulele-plinking George Formby.

Once pre-eminent in transatlantic and tropical trade, Liverpool had been outflanked economically since the gouging of the Manchester ship canal. With demand for labour at rock bottom in the docks, clerking offices and mills that processed imported raw materials, the only visible reminders of former glory were promenade edifices such as the statue of Edward VII staring towards the hazy hills of North Wales. In between flowed the Mersey, which more than ever lived up to the Old English translation of *Liverpool* as "the place at the pool with thick water", as it was suffused with a soup of industrial pollutants and sewage. A species indigenous to the river was a brown, floating lump known euphemistically as a "Mersey trout". It was often encountered on day trips on the ferry to New Brighton, when, as well as a whirl at the fair, a pleasure-seeker yet chanced a dip in the dung-coloured waters.

Like every other British conurbation, Merseyside was a realm of queues as the country paid for its war with "Utility goods" and rationing that lasted well into the 1950s. Food tablets were available for families like the Starkeys, for whom a meal with chicken – before the grim advent of battery farms – was a most unlikely luxury. Some items were so scarce that you could only get them with weeks of saved-up ration coupons. A Mars bar, for instance, was such an expensive treat then that a knife would divide it between maybe five slavering children.

Less inviting were the third-pint bottles of lukewarm milk provided at morning playtime at school, courtesy of the Welfare State, which also encouraged a massive advertising campaign – centred on Norman Wisdom, the peaked-capped "little man" of British film comedy – to get people to drink more of the stuff for its calcium and vitamins. One of the most loathed desserts of many a late-1940s childhood, milk pudding was very much part of each week's menu.

With geometrically-patterned linoleum the only hint of frivolity in many homes, this drab era was epitomised in Liverpool by the middle-class male from Woolton who, after hours at a ledger in a dark business suit, would relax over a post-dinner crossword in quiet cardigan and baggy trousers. Through lace curtains, his adolescent – *not* teenage – son would glower and wonder if this was all there was. No parent or careers advisor had ever intimated that there might be openings other than in secure but dull jobs like Dad's, with El Dorado a bonus in your wage packet. Perish the thought, but you might be better off as the offspring of some unrespectable Toxteth navvy who didn't frown should you ask to go to the cinema on Sunday and wouldn't disinherit you if you dared to come downstairs in an American tie.

GIs on passes would burst upon the fun-palaces of Liverpool in garb in which, until the foundation of their base at Burtonwood, only blacks, London spivs and the boldest homosexuals would be seen dead – padded shoulders on double-breasted suits with half-belts at the back, "spearpoint" collars, black-and-white shoes and those contentious hand-painted ties with Red Indians or baseball players on them. To the ordinary Scouser, the United States seemed the very wellspring of everything glamorous, from the Coca Cola "Welcoming A Fighting Man Home From The Wars" – so its hoarding ran – to The Ink Spots, whose humming polyphony would enrapture the Liverpool Empire in April 1947. Priscilla White, a docker's daughter who knew the Starkeys, was typical of many young Liverpudlians who "lived in a world where the model of all that was good in life was in a Doris Day movie".[4]

As well as Barkis remarking that Mrs Peggotty "sure knows her cookin'" in a US cartoon-strip edition of David Copperfield, almost as incredible were the Wild West films that Richie came to absorb up to three times a week. He was certain that no one in the Dingle, even in the whole of England, ever talked *thataway*. Neither would an Empress barmaid not bat an eyelid if some *hombre* was plugged full of daylight in the lounge bar. A god descended on Liverpool once when "Singing Cowboy" Roy Rogers rode Trigger from the Adelphi

Hotel down Lime Street to the Empire, but Richie's hero was Gene Autrey, "the Yodelling Cowboy", who was "my first musical experience as a kid. I remember getting shivers up my back when he sang 'South Of The Border'. He had three Mexican guys behind him singing 'Ay-yi-yi-yi...' and he had his guitar."[5]

Cowboy music was more prevalent on Merseyside than anywhere else in England, probably because of the transatlantic seamen, who, as well as importing crew-cuts, "classics" in comic form and Davy Crockett mock-coonskin hats, were as knowledgeable about the Red Foleys, Webb Pierces, Ernest Tubbses and Cowboy Copases of North America as the better known Slim Whitmans, Tennessee Ernie Fords and Tex Ritters. Keeping abreast of new developments in country and western, the Dansette record players of Liverpool crackled with Hank Snow's 'I'm Movin' On', 1952's 'The Wild Side Of Life' by Hank Thompson And His Brazo Valley Boys and 'Down On The Corner Of Love' from Buck Owens, while the rest of the country were still coping with the Davy Crockett craze, 'The Yellow Rose Of Texas', Doris Day riding the Deadwood stage and the clippety-clop offerings of Frankie Laine and Vaughan 'Ghost Riders In The Sky' Monroe.

'Ghost Riders In The Sky' was definitely more exciting to Richie and his St Silas' Church of England Primary School classmates than any native music aired on the British Broadcasting Corporation's three national radio stations, which – with limited needle time – meant Kathleen Ferrier, *The Pirates Of Penzance* and *Melody Time* with the Midland Light Orchestra. Apart from junior geography, the only trace of Americana within the school's Victorian portals was in 'Git Along Little Dogies', 'Polly Wolly Doodle' and other selections from the *Singing Together* pupils' handbook distributed by the monitor during cross-legged music lessons around the upright piano in the main hall, which also served as gymnasium, dining room and for religious assemblies, which were conducted either by the head or by the vicar of the church – also named after the first-century minor apostle – in which Richie's parents had been wed.

The school was a five-minute dawdle from Admiral Grove. Mid-morning passers-by would catch multiplication tables chanted mechanically *en masse* by the older forms, perhaps to the rap of a bamboo cane on a teacher's ink-welled desk. Richie found arithmetic the most trying subject of all the "rubbish shoved into you at school – all those figures".[6]

He didn't endure St Silas' infants for long because of the first serious manifestation of the digestive maladies that were to blight his life. Possibly this delicateness was hereditary, for, like Big Richie, he would always be nauseated by any dish with the vaguest tang of onion or garlic. One afternoon, when he was six, "I felt an awful stab of pain. I remember sweating and being frightened for a while,"[7] when, to the agitated clang of an ambulance bell and clutching his abdomen, he was hastened to the Royal Children's Infirmary on the junction of Myrtle Street, beneath the shadow of the Roman Catholic cathedral, where most of the city's chief medical, penal and higher-educational establishments were clotted.

What was diagnosed initially as a ruptured appendix led to an inflamed peritoneum. In the thick of the inserted tubes and drips after the first operation, there seemed almost no hope of survival as Richie subsided into a coma in the intensive-care cubicle. However, although that pitiful, helpless life could have been taken without effort, Death decided to spare Richard Starkey, although his waxen face would remain pale and silent for nearly two worrying months afterwards. As parental visits were restricted, he was not spoon-fed with familiar sounds, and from more anaesthetised sessions under the scalpel and their painful aftermaths, he surfaced as a persistently poorly old-young creature whose surroundings seemed to fill him with melancholy reflections. Inwardly, however, "I didn't mind too much. I made a lot of friends. Too bad they always got better and left me alone."[7]

His formal education was hampered through the difficulties of running a school in hospital where blackboard work was generally impractical for immobile patients of different ages and abilities, and no new activity could be instigated without a doctor's permission. Much the same applied to the continuance of organisations such as Wolf Cubs and Brownies, as well as occupational therapy like basket-weaving, sketching and participation in the ward band. Richie's would, apparently, be the first hand to shoot up when the teacher sought volunteers to hit a drum as rhythmic pulse to 'Donkey Riding' or 'Down In Demerara'. He'd also be recalled once rat-a-tat-tatting a tin drum in an Orange Day parade. "When he was very young, he always wanted to make a noise on something, empty boxes and suchlike,"[8] Elsie would tell you when the myth gripped harder.

While she visited Myrtle Street whenever she was allowed, his father "came once to see me in hospital with a little notebook to ask me if I wanted anything".[2] On his seventh birthday, and with discharge in sight, Richie – with Grandad Starkey gazing fondly – unwrapped a bright-red toy bus "and drove it 'round and 'round my huge, high bed. When he left, the boy in the next bed looked so sad and lonely, I thought it would be nice to give him my red bus to cheer him up."[9] Leaning over, Richie tumbled to awake from concussed oblivion with burst stitches and the prospect of the rest of 1947 in hospital intensifying his growing inferiority complex.

Back in time to enter St Silas' junior department, he was nicknamed "Lazarus" by some of those who didn't mistake him for a new student. He was still virtually illiterate and would suffer the eventual indignity of being taught with children a year his junior. Among them was a Billy Hatton and – fleetingly – Billy's best friend, Ronnie Wycherley, who was destined to confinements in hospital with rheumatic fever and the damaged heart that would kill him.

Even the Dingle's most godless accorded an outward respect for its priesthood, and if neither St Silas nor his mother turned Richie into a devout churchgoer then he would adhere to a belief in life after death, even when he no longer "prayed and sung hymns. I've done everything our religion talks about, but it doesn't mean all that for me."[10] In a word-association game years later, Richie's reaction to "Christmas" was "happy times...food and drink... It doesn't mean anything religious to me".[11] Without the usual companionships nurtured during an uninterrupted school regime, he grew pensive and rather solitary, weeping when scolded or emotionally moved. His appearance suited him – shortish and hangdog, with flexible thick lips, crooked nose, droopy Pagliacci eyes and grey streaks in his brown hair and right eyebrow. His appearance was also more than faintly comical, and that also suited him. Like Tommy Cooper and Ken Dodd, "I have a face which seems to make people laugh."[1] Verbally, he was comparable to Dr William Spooner, in that he didn't have to try to be funny. Rather than conscious narrative jokes, his attempts to nutshell oral discussions in class and on the playground were often inadvertently hilarious because, although his wits would creak, quiver and jolt into life, his thoughts would emerge from his lips almost as mangled as a Stanley Unwin monologue. People amused themselves by getting him to talk.

At St Silas' and, next, Dingle Vale Secondary Modern, he was as well known for this quirk as bullies and cricket captains were in their spheres. Elsie had paid Marie Maguire to help him catch up with his reading with twice-weekly exercises from a primer, but, despite her conscientious efforts, Richie – by no means bookish and forever an unorthodox speller – had still been ineligible to even sit the Eleven Plus examination to determine whether he'd move up to a grammar school or instead go to a secondary modern, where the "failures" went.

As laughable as it was that he should sit with clever Billy Hatton at the Bluecoat Grammar School in Wavertree, unblinking in the monotony of Euclid's knottier theorems and Caesar's Gallic Wars, Richie found his own level at Dingle Vale, where he was judged "a quiet, thoughtful type, although working rather slowly. Academic work will no doubt improve in time, as he is trying to do his best."[12] Positioned academically around the middle of the lowest stream, he was poor at music, which was then taught as a kind of mathematics, in which a dotted crotchet was expressed diagramatically by "three of the little milk-bottles you have at school".[13] However, Starkey of 2C wasn't too bad at art, while at drama he "takes a real interest and has done very well".[12] He was also discovered to possess an aptitude for mechanics, so much so that later he'd have no qualms about dismantling a car engine and putting it back together again.

In one 1952 term, Richard was absent on 34 occasions, not all of which were through illness. His "A" standard for conduct implies that teachers were ignorant of his bouts of truancy with their *leitmotifs* of petty shop-lifting and smutty stories over communal cigarettes. Indeed, a legacy of these delinquent days was the smoking that he'd never have the will to stop. He'd already promoted his first alcoholic black-out "when I was nine. I was on my knees, crawling drunk. A friend of mine's dad had the booze ready for Christmas, so we decided to try all of it out. I don't remember too much."[14] An appalled Elsie would always remember, but she never knew then that he sometimes spent his dinner-money on "a few pennyworth of chips and a hunk of bread and save the rest for the fairground or the pictures".[7]

Revelling in his wickedness, Richie and his cronies would seek refuge in cinemas outside Dingle Vale's catchment area. While denouncing Roy Rogers, Hopalong Cassidy *et al* as "kids' stuff", there was still much to please Starkey in this escapist post-war epoch of Martians, robots and outer space things, although he inclined towards the more thought-provoking movies of this genre, such as *The Day The Earth Stood Still*, in which spaceman Michael Rennie lands in Washington, DC, to curb the Earthlings' self-destructive tendencies. During other idle hours, an acned youth would slobber over Hollywood's platinum blondes and identify with lonesome anti-heroes like narcissistic and defeatist James Dean or the more mature Victor Mature, whom Richie preferred as "tough but likeable – a guy for the lads of 15 to look up to".[15] With an intelligent rather than intellectual passion for the flicks, he "admired people like Elizabeth Taylor, Marlon Brando, Burt Lancaster and Fred Astaire. They never give bad performances."[15]

In another field of entertainment, Richie was also a fan of "Prince of Wails" Johnnie Ray, who anticipated the exhibitionism that would pervade rock 'n' roll. The intrinsic content of his stage repertoire, however, was much the same as that emitted from lustier throats during the merrier evenings in the Empress, when drinkers would be drawn into 'Sonny Boy', 'Bye Bye Blackbird', Doris Day's 'Sentimental Journey', 'Night And Day' and more cosy unison singalongs about roses and stardust. Furthermore, like contemporaries such as Cab Calloway, Jo Stafford, Guy Mitchell and The Platters, who also included Liverpool Empire on their European tour itineraries, Ray's spot was preceded by jugglers, trick cyclists, comedians and other variety turns. Nevertheless, in his mid 20s, Johnnie was the wildest act going in an age when popular vocalists were generally approaching middle life before achieving worthwhile recognition.

Against the heavily masculine images of the Tennessee Ernie Ford school of singers, frail Ray was as unlikely a star as, well, Richard Starkey; but, with his hearing-aid visible from the audience during the 'cry-guy' hamminess of 'The Little White Cloud That Cried' – his own composition – and the thwarted eroticism of 'Such A Night', women had hysterics and circle stalls buckled wherever he went. Nonetheless, Johnnie became dismayingly human to Richie, who was among the rapt crowd watching him *sip coffee* in a window of the Adelphi. "He was eating in fancy restaurants and waving at people from big hotels, and I thought, 'There! That's the life for me.'"[16]

Sucking on a Woodbine with either Johnnie Ray crackling from the Dansette or Vic Mature before him on the fleapit screen, Richie might have declared, had he read Wordsworth, that "to be young was very heaven" – although not for long, even if domestic conditions had improved after Elsie was able to give up work on marrying – with her son's approval – a painter and decorator from Romford whom she'd met via the Maguires. Of mild disposition and steady character, Harry Graves came to be accepted by a community not that removed from what he'd known back in the Cockney end of Essex.

During a half-term holiday in 1953, the new "stepladder" – so Richie in his gobbledegook dubbed Harry – took his wife and stepson over the edge of the world for a few days with his parents in Romford, where the obstinate 13-year-old refused to don a raincoat when caught in a thunderstorm of Wagnerian intensity. A simple sniff chilled to chronic pleurisy and another spell in Myrtle Street before lung complications necessitated Richie's transfer to the cleaner air of Heswall Children's Hospital in the rural Wirral.

Again, his schooling suffered, and it was officially over by 1955, when he'd regained sufficient strength to go home (where there was now a black-and-white television). All that remained was the formality of returning to Dingle Vale "to get the certificate to prove I'd left. You needed that to get a job. They didn't even remember I'd been there."[17] More humbling was an interview at the Youth Employment Office, where, if he agreed to a secondment to Riverside Technical College to complete basic education, there was a vacancy for a delivery boy with British Rail. It wasn't exactly the Pony Express but, if he stuck at it, he could finish up half a century later as a retired station master with a gold watch.

Whatever the secrets behind doors marked "Private" on every main platform, little intrigued Starkey after a week or so of errands that a child could run. Vanity demanded a uniform to be worn with negligent importance, but, in order to signify that here was a man engaged in man's work, he was given a mere *kepi*, as "you had to do 20 years to get the rest. Anyway, I failed their medical and left after a couple of months."[2]

In the regulation-issue, two-tone jacket of a barman/waiter, his next job was on a passenger steamer pottering between George's Landing Stage and New Brighton. He bumped up his wages of £3 and ten shillings wages with tips picked up mostly during peak hours, when he had hardly a second to himself, dashing from table to table with a trayful of drinks.

He played hard, too, especially when someone's parents were away for the weekend and "we had parties [where] everyone gets drunk and passes out".[18] With all but miniatures beyond individual pockets, spirits were not so much in evidence as Newcastle Brown and Devon cider in living rooms transformed into dens of iniquity by dimming table lamps with headscarves and pushing back armchairs to create an arena for smooching as a prelude to snogging and attacks of "desert sickness".[19] The soundtrack to this effused from the 78rpm discs that would be scattered around the Dansette in the corner.

Not so brittle were the plastic 45s that started to supersede 78s in 1955, a streamlining that was an apt herald of the "teenager", a word now coined to donate all those 'twixt twelve and 20 who were deciding whether or not they wished to grow up. Yet, even after the generation gap widened and the new breed received as independent "consumers", the BBC – as a universal aunt with its stranglehold over the nation's electric media – gave the public only that music that it ought to want, hence *The Black And White Minstrel Show*, the veletas and tangos of Victor Sylvester's *Come Dancing*, *Spot The Tune* with Marion Ryan and Cy Grant's calypsos during his slot on Cliff Michelmore's topical *Tonight* magazine.

Some supposed that the "square" sounds they picked up on the Light Programme were because they were listening on a cheap wireless, but from new Braun transistor to cumbersome radiogram it was the same on all of them, for also directed at the over-30s were shows monopolised by such as The Beverley Sisters and Donald Peers ("The Cavalier Of Song"), as well as musical interludes in those built around the ilk of ventriloquist's dummy Archie Andrews, "Mr Pastry" and Lancastrian "schoolboy" Jimmy Clitheroe. "Not one of my favourite comedians,"[16] said Richard Starkey.

The search for anything teenage was just as fruitless on Independent Television (ITV) when it began in 1956 with weekly spectaculars headlined by North America's Patti Page ("The Singing Rage") and, straight from fronting some palais bandstand, Dickie Valentine in stiff evening dress. While *Round About Ten* was a bit racy in its embrace of Humphrey Lyttelton's Jazz Band, the inclusion of The Teenagers – a winsome boy-girl troupe – in Vera Lynn's *Melody Cruise* was something of a false dawn.

Bandleader Ted Heath didn't "think rock 'n' roll will come to Britain. You see, it is primarily for the coloured population."[20] However, penetrating the BBC and its rival's snug little kingdoms as 1955 mutated into 1956 was a cover version of black rhythm and blues combo Sonny Dae And The Knights' 'Rock Around The Clock' by Bill Haley And The Comets, a paunchy US dance group. "When [Haley] came out," noticed Richie, "he was about 28, but when you're about 14 or 15 anyone at 28 is like your dad."[21] Nevertheless, the record was a hit with teenagers after adult blood ran cold at its metronomic clamour. Incited by the newspapers, girls jived in gingham and flat ballet shoes while pen-knives slit cinema seats when

Haley's movie of the same name – "the old backstage plot spiced with the new music",[22] quoth *Picturegoer* – reached these islands. Priscilla White was "told off for getting my school blazer ripped. Everybody was going mad and jumping about the aisles, and that was only for a film. I put sugar and water on my hair to get a Bill Haley kiss-curl. I tried milk as well, because that is supposed to dry the hair up. It was quite big, wasn't it, that kiss curl cut?"[23]

Haley would tender apologies at press conferences for his Comets' knockabout stage routines, but what with this "rock" nonsense going so well it'd have been bad business not to have played up to it, wouldn't it? Anyway, one of the band had served under Benny Goodman. Even with five concurrent entries in the newly established *New Musical Express* record-sales chart (or "hit parade"), Bill was more harmless than Johnnie Ray had proved to be. However, even as "the Creep", hula-hooping and the cha-cha-cha were proffered as the next short-lived fads, rock 'n' roll put forward a more suitable champion in a Tennessean named Elvis Presley, who dressed as a hybrid of amusement-arcade hoodlum and nancy boy. With an electric guitarist shifting from simple fills to full-blooded clangorous solo, Presley's first single had been a jumped-up treatment of a negro blues. From then on, his embroidered shout-singing and sulky balladeering had become both adored and detested throughout the free world.

Reports of Presley's unhinged go-man-go sorcery in concert caused Methodist preacher (and jazz buff) Dr Donald Soper to wonder "how intelligent people can derive satisfaction from something which is emotionally embarrassing and intellectually ridiculous".[24] Of the new sensation's debut UK release, 'Heartbreak Hotel', the staid *NME* wrote, "If you appreciate good singing, I don't suppose you'll manage to hear this disc all through."[25] What more did Elvis need to be the rage of teenage Britain? "It was all so new and exciting," enthused Richie. "No one believes what an effect that had on my life, just this lad with sideboards and shaking his pelvis and being absolutely naughty, [although] if you look back on those photos now he had big baggy trousers and it was all a bit weird."[26]

Although Tin Pan Alley's nose was put out of joint at the proportionally meagre sheet music sales, when it transpired that 60 per cent of the RCA record company's output for 1956 was by Elvis the hunt was up for similar money-making morons. Needless to say, these sprouted thickest in the States, where countless talent-scouts thought that all that was required was a lop-sided smirk and gravity-defying cockade. Many saw Jerry Lee Lewis as just an Elvis who substituted piano for guitar and hollered arrogance for hot-potato-in-the-mouth mumbling. While Capitol was lumbered with a pig in a poke in crippled, unco-operative Gene Vincent ("The Screaming End"), Acuff-Rose would snare two for the price of one in The Everly Brothers. There were black Presleys in Chuck Berry and shrieking Little Richard, female ones like Wanda Jackson and Janis Martin and a mute one in guitarist Duane Eddy. After Carl Perkins – an unsexy one – came bespectacled Buddy Holly and unsexy and bespectacled Roy Orbison with his eldritch cry and misgivings about the up-tempo rockers he was made to record by Sam Phillips, owner of Sun, the Memphis studio where Elvis had first smouldered onto tape.

Just as uncomfortable an Elvis was Tommy Steele, his innocuous English "answer", who, before abdicating to make way for Cliff Richard, had his effigy waxed for Madame Tussaud's and was sent up by Peter Sellers – of BBC Radio's *Goon Show* – as "Mr Iron", who "doesn't want to bite the fretboard that fed me". Despite finding rock 'n' roll objectionable, powers at the BBC were obliged to cater for Steele, Presley and their sort's disciples when the continental commercial station Radio Luxembourg began broadcasting pop showcases in English and ITV broke the tacit "toddler's truce" by filling what was previously a blank screen between 6pm and 7pm. The Corporation countered with *Six-Five Special* to keep teenagers out of trouble between the football results and *Dixon Of Dock Green* while their parents put younger siblings to bed.

Dr Soper might have watched it "as a penance"[24] but *Six-Five Special* sought to preserve a little decency by employing such upstanding interlocutors as disc jockey Pete Murray – who abhorred Elvis – and former boxing champion Freddie Mills. Comedy sketches, string quartets and features on sport and hobbies were inserted between the pop, which – as well as "rock 'n' roll" by such as trombonist Don Lang and his Frantic Five – was made to encompass Dickie Valentine, Joe "Mr Piano" Henderson plus traditional jazz and its by-product, skiffle – which was ruled by singing guitarist Lonnie Donegan, an ex-serviceman who reviled rock 'n' roll as "a gimmick. Like all gimmicks, it is sure to die the death. Let's hope it will happen soon. Nothing makes me madder than to be bracketed with those rock 'n' roll boys."[22]

Despite himself, Lonnie would be remembered as a more homogenously British equivalent of Elvis than Tommy Steele through his vibrant fusion of black rhythms and the music hall, especially after he broadened his appeal with 'Have A Drink On Me' and other gems from the golden days of the Empire. Moreover, anyone who'd mastered basic techniques could attempt skiffle. In fact, the more home-made your sound the better, for no one howled with derision if an amateur skiffle group included broom-handle-and-tea-chest bass, washboards tapped with thimbles and perhaps dustbin-lid cymbals. These and chords slashed on acoustic guitars were at the core of its contagious backbeat. Over this, certain outfits found a unique style even with 'The Grand Coolee Dam', 'Midnight Special' and other set works. "That's where half the enjoyment lies," pontificated one of skiffle's lesser icons, Bob Cort, "in experimenting with ideas."[27]

You had to be sharp to discriminate between them, but there evolved regional shades of skiffle, with Merseyside leaning – as might be expected – towards country and western. As well as an emulation of Nashville's Grand Ole Opry at Liverpool's Philharmonic Hall in 1955, there would be more than 40 local cowboy groups operational in what was christened "the Nashville of the North" by the late 1950s. All looking as if they'd cut their teeth on a branding iron, the likes of Johnny Goode And His Country Kinfolk, Phil Brady And The Ranchers and – still going strong 40 years later – Hank Walters And His Dusty Road Ramblers plundered the North American motherlode, covering all waterfronts from Slim Whitman's falsetto "sweetcorn" to the hard country of Hank Williams, with its unusual absorption with rhythm.

Also with names as homely as hitching posts, there grew younger splinter groups, many defying licensing laws concerning minors when playing the 300-odd venues affiliated to the Liverpool Social Clubs Association. Not old enough to quaff even a cherryade in these taverns, Billy Hatton moonlighted in such a band while his friend Brian O'Hara was guitarist in Gerry Marsden's Skiffle Group, an outfit connected genealogically to Hank Walters' bunch. Modelling themselves more on Flint McCullough, scout with BBC's *Wagon Train*, or half-breed "Cheyenne" Bodie over on ITV, some traded under fiercer nomenclatures: Clay Ellis And The Raiders, The James Boys – after pistol-packin' Jesse – and, later, Johnny Sandon and The Searchers (from a John Wayne movie).

With National Service soon to be abolished, "everyone took up guitars instead of guns",[10] generalised Richie, and too real was the boom in demand for the instruments in central Liverpool music shops like Rushworth's and Hessy's. Even Eddie Miles, the Starkeys' next door neighbour's teenage son, had purchased one. Nevertheless, as Richie had lost interest when once a member of an accordion band that practised in the drill hall opposite St Silas Church, so he lacked the application to teach himself to strum a guitar – although from somewhere or other he'd absorb a rudimentary three-chord trick in A major, and the same on piano, but in C. Such a knack was, however, incidental to his self-image as "just one of those loony Teddy Boys standing on the corner".[28]

Undersized, homely and of depressed circumstance, he was ripe to "run about with gangs in the Dingle as a tearaway with a Tony Curtis haircut, crêpe shoes and drape with a velvet collar".[3] Along with the sports coat and sensible shoes, mothballed forever were the cavalry twills, as around his legs now were circulation-impeding drainpipes tapering into fluorescent socks with a rock 'n' roll motif. His short back and sides now only a recollection, his longer tresses were now teased into a quiffed glacier of Brilliantine.

Out for more than boyish mischief these days, he was typical of many formerly tractable young men who, bored silly by slide-shows and ping-pong, would get themselves barred from church youth clubs by either brandishing a blatant Woodbine or letting slip a "bloody" in front of some cardiganned curate. Chewing gum in an Elvis half-sneer, they'd take to the streets of desolate housing estates or the hinterland near the docks, where decent folk would cross over to avoid a swaggering phalanx of Teds with brass rings decorating their fists like knuckledusters.

Saying "bloody" and even ruder words unreproached, Richie tagged along with seedy-flash louts of more powerful build and sideburns like the boot of Italy as they barracked in cinemas (except during the sexy bits, when they'd go all quiet) and, without paying, barged *en bloc* into dance halls, particularly ones where Teds – "and coloureds" – were refused admission. Once inside, they'd be studied – not always surreptitiously – by girls with ruby-red lips, tight sweaters, wide belts and pony-tails who – in their imaginations, at least – were as elfin as Audrey Hepburn in *Roman Holiday*. If pursuit of romance was either unsuccessful or not the principal mass objective of the expedition, Teds would seek more brutal sensual recreation. If you so much as glanced at them, the action could be *you*. A meek reproof by the victim had sparked off the first Teddy Boy murder on a London heath in 1954. Nevertheless, Merseyside was the setting for *These Dangerous Years* and *Violent Playground*, 1957 films supposedly reflecting the corruptness of the "new" cult, with local boy Freddie Fowell playing a gang leader.

Although runtish, Richie tried to look the part with a belt studded with washers stolen from work. "But I wasn't a fighter," he reflected. "More of a dancer, really, though that could be dangerous if you danced with someone else's bird."[6] Yet it wasn't in a ballroom where he paired off with a bird of his own, Patricia Davies, who was three years younger, fair and sufficiently *petite* not to tower over him. At the same secondary school – St Anthony of Padua's in Mossley Hill – she'd become friendly with red-head Priscilla White when both cherished ambitions to be hairdressers. "The soul of patience",[4] Elsie Graves was a Wednesday-evening guinea pig for the giggling would-be stylists as, after cooking them a tea, she allowed Pat and Cilla to "bleach her hair and do terrible things to it".[4]

When Pat was superseded by another local spinster called Geraldine, she may have consoled herself with the submission that, if you were after a man for his money, Elsie's lad wasn't much of a catch, especially after he was sacked from the ferry when, on clocking in direct from an all-night party, he was emboldened enough by booze to impart pent-up home truths to his supervisor. However, Harry was able to persuade Henry Hunt & Sons, an engineering firm specialising in gymnasium and swimming pool equipment, to take on his stepson as a trainee joiner, as it had Eddie Miles.

Richie's overalled apprenticeship began badly when he bruised his thumb with a hammer on the very first day and vertigo stranded him tremulous with terror on a high diving board during an installment job in faraway Cardiff Public Baths. But he wasn't as infinitesimal a human cog at Hunt's as he'd been with the railway. By doggedly cranking and riveting from 8am until 5.30pm day upon day for the next seven years, the road to self-advancement and that "semi in a posh part of Liverpool" would be clearer.

2 "Well, I Thought I Was
The Best Drummer There Was"

Against the odds, Liverpool spawned a generous fistful of hit-parade entrants during the 1950s. Like Arthur Askey *et al*, they'd had to head south to Make It because moguls from Britain's four major record companies (centred in London), if obliged to visit Manchester, "the entertainment capital of the North", rarely made time to also negotiate the 36 miles west to sound out talent. Besides, why should Merseyside's ratio of pop artists be larger than that in any other port, or indeed anywhere at all? After all, Hull had produced only million-selling David Whitfield and Bristol pianist Russ Conway, heart-throb of BBC's *Billy Cotton Band Show*. Liverpool had had more than its fair share with Lita Roza and her chart-topping copy of Patti Page's 'How Much Is That Doggie In The Window' and Frankie Vaughan, who was to oust Dickie Valentine as Britain's most popular male singer in 1958's *NME* readers' poll.

Civic pride in these triumphs was dampened by a poor showing on the rock 'n' roll front with merely Russ Hamilton – beforehand Ronald Hulme of Everton – on *Six-Five Special* with his gentle, lisping croon.[1] Only a rocker by affinity, too, was Edna Savage, a Liverpool lass who became a 1956 one-hit-wonder on Parlophone, an EMI subsidiary, through the ministrations of her producer, George Martin, with whom some too linked her romantically. However, in 1958 she married Terry Dene, another *Six-Five Special* regular. In an enormous polkadot bow tie and hair dyed shocking pink, the best man was Wee Willie Harris, who was bruited by his

34

manager as London's – and, by implication, the entire kingdom's – very own Jerry Lee Lewis.

Liverpool had no Jerry Lee, but there were myriad aspirant Donegans, from The Hi-Hats – formed within the Mercury Cycle Club – to Crosby's James Boys, who, from intermission spots, were now main attraction at dances held at that suburb's "Jive Hive", otherwise known as St Luke's Hall. As The Two Jays, Billy Hatton and another guitarist, Joey Bower, had landed a six-week residency in a club on the Isle of Man.

Northwest of the Dingle, and then almost on the city's perimeter, Stoneycroft threw down a gauntlet in 1957 with The Texan Skiffle Group, led by Alan Caldwell, a tall youth with a wavy blond tousle and lean frame, whose parents, Violet and Ernie, supported his and his older sister Iris' activities with a zest that other mums and dads might have thought excessive. In the Caldwells' tidy Victorian house off the leafy Oakhill Park estate, the children's friends were welcome at all hours, Violet often rising from slumber to make them snacks.

She had much to boast about in Iris and Alan. The daughter had passed the Eleven Plus and, if less academically distinguished, Alan was extrovert champion of many a school sports day and football match. He'd brag that he held the "unofficial" British underwater record of 73 yards, but more verifiable was his swim one summer holiday across Lake Windermere, as much a feat of his, Ernie's and Violet's will as stamina.

The Caldwells also encouraged more glamorous endeavours, applauding the personable Iris in her choice to transfer from her city centre grammar to Broad Green School of Dancing, within walking distance of home. As their son had progressed at his own pace on the family's upright piano, he merely had to ask for a guitar when it became associated less with flamenco than with Lonnie Donegan. Like the late King George VI, Alan was cursed with a stammer, but it was noticed that this vanished whenever he sang with his group, which – to the consternation of sensitive neighbours – was allowed to rehearse in the front room. When the unit was ready for engagements, Mrs Caldwell would act as its agent, ordering a gross of business cards emblazoned with the legend "Presented By Downbeat Promotions" from a Wavertree printer.

With Violet's blessing, too, 16-year-old Alan opened the Morgue Skiffle Cellar in March 1958. With appropriate skeletons painted in luminous white on black walls, it was located in the starkly lit basement of a huge semi-derelict house – originally a home for retired nurses – in Oak Hill Park. Up to 100 customers would tap their feet twice a week to Caldwell's and other local combos, such as The Hi-Fi's and The Quarry Men, until a raid just over a year later by police acting on (not groundless) allegations that the Morgue was a place of ill repute where boys smoked and girls got pregnant.

Whatever he got up to in his spare time, Alan's day job – in a cotton mill – wasn't exactly showbusiness, but it would do while he looked for opportunities beyond youth clubs and parties to become a professional entertainer. The Group, therefore, took part in every talent showcase advertised, whether it be in village hall or at the Rialto Ballroom, right in the heart of Liverpool. Twice in three months, they turned out at Garston's Winter Gardens auditorium, where the days were won by, respectively, "rock 'n' roll comedian" Jimmy Tarbuck and Ronald Wycherley, who was making a go of it as a singer. For as little as a round of fizzy drinks, The Texan Skiffle Group could be hired for such salubrious venues as Old Swan's Stanley Abattoir Social Club.

Meanwhile, Caldwell's aptitude for athletics didn't wither, as he often elected to sprint home rather than wait for a bus, even after relatively distant bookings such as the Casbah in Hayman's Green. In spring 1958, he was picked for the Pembroke Harriers team for a cross-country event in London. After finishing, Alan couldn't go home without sampling an evening at Chas McDevitt's Skiffle Cellar in Soho, once Tommy Steele and Terry Dene's stomping ground. Still a prestigious showcase, even skifflers in the sticks considered a booking either here or, in the same square mile, the 2I's, the Gyre and Gimble and Trafalgar Square's Safari Club to be worthwhile, in case foremost pop impresario Larry Parnes or a svengali like him spotted them. The Saints, a group formed by pupils at a Norwich grammar, ran away from home and slept in doorways in order to audition there. Two members of the band – guitarists Kenny Packwood and Tony Sheridan – stayed on to back Marty Wilde, a more successful testee. As well as Wilde, Adam Faith and others who received more immediate acclaim, hit-makers from later eras of British pop – among them Spencer Davis, Gary Glitter and, all the way from Glasgow, Alex Harvey – also entertained at McDevitt's.

On the night that he was there, Dame Fortune smiled on Alan Caldwell, who, after giving an impromptu performance, was able to solicit a one-song spot – with 'Midnight Special' – for The Texan Skiffle Group on Radio Luxembourg's *Skiffle Club*, which was recorded in Manchester. Historically, they were the first such Merseyside act to broadcast in this manner, a fact not greatly appreciated at the time.

Of more pragmatic import was the Group's victory in a talent contest instigated by *The People* newspaper and holiday camp potentate Billy Butlin. With this placing them a cut above others of their kind, Iris – now earning £7 a week as a circus showgirl for a summer season in the Welsh holiday resort of Rhyl – was able to whisper in the right ears before she moved south to more lucrative work at a Butlins camp in Pwllheli. Through Iris, her brother's band secured a place low on the bill of a presentation back in Rhyl headlined by Marion Ryan. Ernie and Violet drove down to catch their golden boy's biggest moment thus far.

A mainstay in his Group's constant flux of musicians was John Byrnes, who, with a more transient guitarist, Paul Murphy (who would later assume the stage surname Rogers[2]) – a pal of Richard Starkey – had actually spent several hours in a local recording studio taping an Everly Brothers-style version of Charlie Gracie's 1957 hit 'Butterfly'. Like Alan, John wasn't a musician for the sake of his health. Indeed, Byrnes and Caldwell were all that remained of the band when it was decided to hack the word "Skiffle" from its name for a relaunch as Al Caldwell's Texans, because groups who still used instruments made from household implements had become *passé* and, worse, insufferably square, after physics professors with clipped beards conducted "experiments with skiffle" at London University; Sunday School teachers seized upon it as a medium through which to promote youthful Christianity; and Dickie Valentine covered 'Putting On The Style', Donegan's second Number One. None of them quite got the point. Into the bargain, washboard players had trouble joining the Musicians' Union, and were thus prohibited from defiling the stage at some venues.

The more "sophisticated" skiffle acts that hadn't fallen by the wayside switched to traditional jazz, but most backslid, via cautious amplification, to rock 'n' roll and an increasingly more American UK hit parade. Not alone in the practice of magnifying his volume by simply shoving a microphone through the hole in his acoustic six-string was the lead guitarist with Seaforth's Bobby Bell Rockers, who had been in existence since Bell (né Crawford) had seen Freddie Bell And The Bellboys in Bill Haley's *Rock Around The Clock* movie in 1956. Nonetheless, it wasn't wise to disagree when "Kingsize" Taylor – burly front man with The Dominoes, formerly The James Boys – argued that "we were the first rock group in the city, but around the same time there were two other groups – Cass And The Cassanovas and The Seniors – who also claim to be first".[3] No Russ Hamilton, either, was The Cassanovas' ambidextrous percussive aggressor, Johnny Hutchinson, who wielded reversed sticks so that the heavier ends battered his drum kit. Not to his taste was the lighter touch necessary to emphasise vocal polyphony in such as Ian And The Zodiacs – The Dominoes' rivals as north Liverpool's boss group – and Gerry And The Pacemakers, led by Gerry Marsden.

Before re-entering the lists, The Texans held exhaustive auditions which, because of the space required for electronic paraphernalia and drums, spilled into the Caldwells' hall. There but not participating was Jimmy Tarbuck, to whom one supplicant – a guitarist called George Harrison – was already familiar, having attended the same primary school. Also too young and inexperienced was a Graham Bonnet from Manchester, where the fame of the boys who'd been 'guest stars' to Marion Ryan had spread, thanks to Alan's mum's publicity machine and the local press.

With the chastening knowledge that Kingsize and his boys had just recorded ten numbers in Crosby's Lambda Studio, a glorified garage, Alan and John elected to make up lost time by plunging in with Texans drawn from a mutable pool of players shared with other groups, such as guitarist Charles O'Brien from The Hi-Fi's and the drummer with The Darktown Skiffle Group. His name was Richie Starkey.

For beer money and a laugh, Starkey and Eddie Miles had started The Eddie Clayton Skiffle Group in early 1957. As well as its more down-home connotations, "Clayton" rolled off the tongue easier than "Miles" and looked better, symmetrically. Augmented by three of Hunt's other employees – notably Roy Trafford, a singing tea-chest bass plucker – and someone with a telephone acting as their "manager", the Group moved from canteen concerts at work to a debut at Peel Street Labour Club in Toxteth and entering a skiffle contest at St Luke's Hall. Although they weren't placed, the lads weren't that dismayed because they, like most amateur skifflers, saw the group as a vocational blind alley. No one took it seriously.

No better or worse than any other tin-pot combo taking its cue from Godhead Donegan, The Eddie Clayton Skiffle Group also adhered to Bob Cort's *New Musical Express* dictum concerning "visual effect",[4] although Starkey, with his woebegone countenance, might have been hard pressed by the bit about "however worried you are, never let it show".[4] In bootlace ties and shirts of the same colour, the Clayton outfit were as one, too, with Cort's "some sort of uniform is a great help, though ordinary casual clothes are perhaps the best as long, as you all wear exactly the same".[4]

From the onset, it was decided that Richie should play drums, "because it was the only thing I could do".[5] Apart from rattling about on biscuit tins (with Cadbury's Roses the most authentic snare-drum sound), the cheapest option was a "Viceroy skiffle board" – an *NME*-advertised "tapbox" with miniature drum, washboard, cowbell and hooter that, for 39 shillings and sixpence, was "ideal for parties and playing with radio or gramophone". However, a combo of Eddie Clayton's calibre deserved at the very least a Broadway "Kat" snare-and-cymbal set costing £10 4s.

While visiting Romford, Harry Graves paid slightly less for a second-hand drum kit[6] of indeterminate make for his stepson. This was lugged onto the train and Harry sat with it throughout the journey back to Lime Street, where he dragged it over to the taxi rank. He wondered how much gratitude he could expect from Richie, who – so the tale goes – had been furious when Elsie, with the best of intentions, had arranged for him to attend an exploratory rehearsal on hearing that someone in the next street was in a "proper" band. "You can imagine how I felt," he snorted, "when this turned out to be a silver band playing old Sousa marches and all that in a local park."[7]

Richie was, however, delighted with Harry's gift, even if he'd become rather scornful of Teddy Boy rock 'n' roll recently, even giving away his collection of 78s to one of his foster cousins. Although it was finding favour more with collegians as a sign of maturity, Richie too had been infected with an apparent appreciation of traditional jazz, but then "that got boring, and I went through modern jazz – Chico Hamilton, Yusuf Lateef, people like that – but there's no great urge in any of them".[8] After a short while, he ceased striving to drop buzz-words like "Monk" and "Brubeck" into conversations, but a legacy of this phase was Starkey's purchase of 1958's 'Topsy Part Two', a 45 based on a 1930s standard and focused on a solo by virtuoso American drummer Cozy Cole, although "I've never been one to buy drum records".[8]

Cole stood on the sidelines of the NME's Top 30, and – to the disgust of veteran drumming aesthetes from Jack Parnell to Buddy Rich – other jazz- and swing-band percussionists were also making records that bordered on pop, twirling their sticks gratuitously and forming contingent rock 'n' roll combos in which subtle cross-rhythms and dotted bebop crochets on the ride cymbal – *ching-a-ching-ching* – had no part. In Britain, such lapsed jazzers as Tony Crombie – who would accompany Wee Willie Harris – and Rory Blackwell were now socking a crude but powerful offbeat less like that of Haley – whose 'Rock Around The Clock' rim-shots were actually quite tricky – than those of Louis Jordan, Bill Doggett, Big

Joe Turner and other late-1940s R&B exponents, possibly so that their gold-digging could be justified because "blues is the main content of jazz",[9] according to skiffle scribe Brian Bird.

With no such pretensions, US drummers such as Preston Epps and Earl Palmer were less ashamedly jumping on the rock bandwagon. Chief among them was Sandy Nelson, a Californian who was the percussion equivalent of Duane Eddy in that his hits – like 'Teenbeat' and a revival of such as The Bob Crosby Orchestra's 'Let It Be Drums' of 1940 – were pared down to monotonous beat against a menacing guitar ostinato. He even had the nerve to refashion thus 'Big Noise From Winnetka' by Gene Krupa, who was then such a jazz legend that he was to be the subject of a 1960 biopic.

Britain struck back with Tony Meehan from Cliff Richard's backing quartet The Drifters – later The Shadows – in LP tracks like 'See You In My Drums', underlined with bass pulsation. A *protégé* of Rory Blackwell, Jimmy Nicol – a former Boosey & Hawkes drum repairer – replaced Crombie behind Wee Willie and then backed Vince Eager. Next, he was sent on tour by Eager's manager, the celebrated Larry Parnes, with his own New Orleans Rockers, who planted feet in both the trad and rock 'n' roll camps.

While Nicol's path would interweave briefly with that of Starkey's, a less shooting-star destiny awaited Burnley's Bobby Elliott, who drummed for a local mainstream jazz orchestra and splattered patterns and accents across bar-lines in a club trio that supported visiting instrumentalists like saxophonists Harold McNair and Don Rendell. Although modern jazz was "all I ever listened to and all I ever watched",[10] he capitulated to the rock 'n' roll and higher engagement fees of the town's Jerry Storm And The Falcons.

Compared to Elliott, Starkey's passion for jazz was scarcely more than a sudden flirtation that ran cold when he realised that, for all his natural sense of rhythm, life was too short to tolerate carping tutorials and "go 'rump-a-bump'"[8] for hours daily to be like Krupa – although he initially attacked his new kit with gusto, showing no signs of ever stopping. Finally admitting to himself that he – like Johnny Hutchinson – was an unadulterated rock 'n' roller, he developed his hand-and-foot co-ordination, accurate time-keeping and even the beginnings of a naïve personal style by trial and error, but "because of the noise",[11] which irritated the entire terrace, his mother – who was no Violet Caldwell – allowed him only 30 minutes of crashing about per evening upstairs in number 10's small back room "and I got really bored just sitting there banging because you can't play any tunes".[8]

In the kitchen, when he'd finished, Elsie would object to him smiting the furniture with his sticks to music from the wireless, "and that was it for me, practising. Drumming's simple. I've always believed the drummer is not there to interrupt the song."[12] Later, he'd liken it to "painting. I am the foundation, and then I put a bit of glow here and there, but it must have solid substance for me. If there's a gap, I want to be good enough to fill it. I like holes to come in."[8]

Drum solos were tedious to him, and if ever he had a pet hate amongst their perpetrators it was bandleader Buddy Rich, who was every smart-alec's notion of percussive splendour because "he does things with one hand I can't do with nine, but that's technique. Everyone I talk to says, 'What about Buddy Rich?' Well, what about him? Because he doesn't turn me on."[13] Furthermore, "I couldn't tune a drum to save my life. They're either loose or tight,"[14] and, despite Dingle Vale's "little milk bottles", Starkey would speak with quiet pride of getting by without ever being able to read a note of standard music script, let alone a drum stave. Neither could he ever manage a clean roll faster than moderato. On listening to Rich, Krupa or – later – even Elliott, "I know I'm no good on the technical things but I'm good with all the motions, swinging my head, like. That's because I love to dance, but you can't do that on the drums."[5]

He would lay himself open to misinterpretation and derogatory *bons mots* with comments such as "I like to make mistakes",[8] with regard to his chosen instrument, but with self-tuition impractical when he began, the only advice he'd be qualified to offer other budding drummers would be, "Get in a group as fast as you can.

You'll learn more in one day than you can hope to in six months stuck in a little room. Make your mistakes on a stage in front of an audience. You'll realise them more quickly."[15]

With the Clayton outfit often a player or two short, his errors hung in the air more flagrantly, especially when he and John Dougherty – the most consistent of its washboard players – were at rhythmic loggerheads. Moreover, as he couldn't carry heavy objects far and had to rely on buses to reach Garston's Wilson Hall and like palais on the outer marches of the group's booking circuit, he'd sometimes arrive with only half his equipment. Nevertheless, the unit was a comparative rarity in that it had a sticksman with a full kit for all to see during what amounted to a residency at Boys' Club meetings in the Dingle's Florence Institute, a Victorian monstrosity near enough for the drums to be walked there.

For all of this parochial renown, recitals elsewhere were infrequent, and Starkey's fealty to Clayton was tried by Miles' imminent departure to the marriage bed and its resultant casting aside of adolescent follies.[16] According to Wally Egmond of The Hi-Fi's, Richie was "not an exceptional drummer",[17] but there came overtures from other skiffle groups for him to join them, especially since – with his own savings and the balance donated by his grandfather – he'd bought a brand-new black Premier kit with "lapped" pigskin, rather than plastic heads. Although there was still little he could do to prevent the cymbal stands from keeling over on rickety stages, he cured the bass drum's inclination to creep forward by fitting it with heavy-duty "disappearing" spurs. On the basis of owning this customised possession, rather than how he played it, he recalled, "Well, I thought I was the best drummer there was, better than all the other drummers. Maybe I was just convincing myself."[18]

Contacted via Admiral Grove's corner newsagent's telephone, the great Richie sat in non-committally with other outfits, once drumming for three in the course of one shattering evening. A kindly conductor on the number 61 bus route to central Liverpool had eased considerably his transport problems by arranging for him to store the kit overnight at the Ribble bus depot whenever he needed, as he did in March 1959 at the Mardi Gras, a stone's throw from Myrtle Street hospital, on the occasion of his first engagement with Al Caldwell's Texans. Although the Darktown mob "turned over fast to rock 'n' roll, changing their name to The Cadillacs",[7] prospects with The Texans – soon to add the adjective "Raving" to their name – seemed rosier, particularly as they now received actual money for playing.

The Raving Texans – still with no fixed line-up yet – were tormented by an identity crisis. They mounted one evening stage decked out in Hawaiian shirts and sunglasses while, to gain a booking at the Cavern – a jazz haven in central Liverpool – they performed as The Jazzmen, their opportunism backfiring when they deviated from manager Ray McFall's purist designations about what should and shouldn't be played there. The club's clientèle put up with skiffle, but with Jerry Lee Lewis' 'Whole Lotta Shakin' Goin' On' The Texans invited enraged booing and even the hurling of chairs stagewards. For daring to rock the Cavern, McFall felt entitled to deduct 10s from the culprits' already meagre pay.

With such foolhardiness behind them, leader Caldwell reflected that his true vocation was to cut up rough with the rock 'n' roll elixir that an increasingly large following would swallow neat. As Byrnes' rhythm-guitar chopping was more than adequate, Alan – an indifferent player anyway – left his guitar at home so that he could concentrate on lead vocals, Presley-esque gyrations and pumping the piano, if one was available. He was also toying with a new group name that – like Marty Wilde And The Wildcats – differentiated between star (him) and accompanists. They could be The Hurricanes while, initially, he called himself Al Storm. The surname was a common *nom du théâtre* for, as well as Burnley's Jerry, there was Southampton's Cliff Richard lookalike Danny Storm and Tempest Storm, a notorious strip-teasing acquaintance of Elvis Presley. He'd also heard of a Billy Gray And The Stormers, who would land a season at a Butlins in Filey. By 1959, Caldwell was Jett Storm, named after the character played by Marty Wilde in his silver-screen debut. Caldwell settled ultimately for the forename Rory, a genuflection towards Rory Blackwell, who'd lately broken the world record for non-stop drumming. With the approbation of his adoring parents, who'd rename their house "Stormsville", he became Rory Storm by deed poll.

Richard Starkey pledged himself to Rory Storm And The Hurricanes in November 1959. With him at the kit, they'd come second to Kingsize Taylor And The Dominoes out of more than 100 groups during the previous month's heat of a "Search For Stars" tournament at the Empire, organised by ITV's Canadian starmaker Carroll Levis to counter the rival channel's *Bid For Fame*. In the final round, at Manchester's Hippodrome, although neither Dominoes nor Hurricanes or Bobby Elliott's new band, The Dolphins, were able to seize the prize of exposure on Levis' television series, all emerged with a more promising date schedule in which a list that had once signified a month's work became a week's. "After that, you were on your own," elucidated Cilla White. "Agents never saw themselves as more than bookers."[19] it might not have been sufficient for Richie to think seriously of resigning from Hunt's, but The Hurricanes would next appear in Liverpool in uniform black-and-white winkle-pickers (gold for Storm) and starched white handkerchiefs protruding smartly from the top pockets of bright-red stage suits for the group (light pink for the lovely Rory).

Bespoken by Duncan's, a city-centre tailor, this sharp corporate persona was assumed because the unit's turnover of personnel had abated with the recruitment of Starkey, lead guitarist Charles O'Brien – whose prowess as a boxer was a reassuring asset at less refined venues – and fellow Hi-Fi Wally Egmond on electric bass guitar. Although Salisbury's Johnny Nicholls And The Dimes had acquired one of these new-fangled instruments via a "Cunard Yank" in as early as 1956, it was only after Freddie Bell's Bellboys appeared at the Empire with one in 1957 that Kingsize Taylor stampeded his bass player, Bobby Thompson, into buying a Framus model when Hessy's imported a few. Not only were they more portable but they also radiated infinitely greater depth of sound and volume than a broomstick bass.

Rory Blackwell And His Blackjacks had been using a Fender bass in the Rock and Calypso Ballroom at Butlin's during one of Alan-Rory's fraternal visits to Pwllheli. As well as Alan ingratiating himself with the famous Blackwell, a more concrete outcome of the trip was the sensation that Egmond caused later when throbbing his new Fender for the first time at the Jive Hive.

United by artistic purpose and mutual respect, Merseyside's semi-professional outfits were civil enough to each other when queueing after an evening's engagements at Morgan's fish-and-chip shop if in Birkenhead or likewise unwinding in a graveyard-hour coffee bar – that light catering epitome of the late 1950s – such as the Zodiac just off China Town or the Jacaranda, within spitting distance of Central Station. However, easy offstage camaraderie became sly competitiveness when each individual group went back to work. Some vocalists' dedication was such that they'd cry real tears during agonised *lieder* with the aid of an onion-smeared handkerchief. They might also resin their hair with paraffin wax, which served the dual purpose of lending extra sheen and, as it ran down to soak shirts, making it look like they'd worked up a hell of a sexy sweat. Those bands that could afford a tape recorder would rig it up in the most acoustically sympathetic corner of a dance hall to capture an audible gauge whereby performances could be measured against those of the opposition.

A Rory Storm And The Hurricanes extravaganza generally felt tremendous when watching Rory's on-stage cavortings with the other four bucking and lunging about him, but as sonic vibrations *per se* you should hear it on tape afterwards! Although akin to an Irish showband in terms of band-audience interplay, The Hurricanes and Storm were also forerunners of more abandoned mid-1960s acts such as The Rolling Stones and The Pretty Things. Like the Stones, the group were coalesced by a forceful rhythm guitarist, but a given number seemed sometimes to be about to fall to bits in a flurry of meandering tempo, jarring three-part harmonies, blown riffs and bawled directives from Byrnes. More capable of musical effect rather than music, The Hurricanes could manage no more than an approximation when certain hall regulations obliged them to conclude an evening's proceedings with the National Anthem. The group were also immoderately fond of the key of G major.

For all of that, however, by 1960, the charismatic Storm was a hard act to follow. His singing voice might have been dull, but – indefatigable self-publicist as he was – his nickname of "Mr Showmanship" was no overstatement. A man of extreme strategy, he outraged heterosexual chauvinists with his gigolo wardrobe – which, from mere pink nylon, would stretch to costumes of gold lamé and sequins – and peacock antics. To illustrate Carl Perkins' 'Lend Me Your Comb', he'd sweep an outsized one through a precarious pompadour which kept falling over his eyes, but this was nothing to what he did when the group played venues attached to swimming baths, where, in the middle of a song, he was likely to push through the crowd, clamber to the top board, strip to scarlet swimming trunks and dive in.

If not conventionally handsome, he became the darling of the ladies for his grinning vibrancy, and was, therefore, not immune to the bellicose resolves of their possessive boyfriends. On mercifully few occasions, however, the Storm quintet discovered what it was like to get themselves and their equipment damaged by disgruntled yahoos in real- or imitation-leather windcheaters and jeans, their Brylcreemed ducktails in direct descent from the Teds. When he later squeezed even harder on the nerve of how far he could go, Rory's injuries were sometimes self-inflicted as he plummeted from the glass dome of New Brighton's capacious Tower Ballroom and fractured his leg or was concussed on an equally rash climb to a pillared balcony stage left at Birkenhead's Majestic.

Although Storm fronted The Hurricanes, the others didn't skulk to the rear, exchanging nervous glances. Maddened by someone's incessant whistle-blowing during one engagement,

Richie slung a stick towards the offender, striking instead a hulking local gang leader who, mistakenly, enacted a reprisal against Rory. A rowdy bunch with impressive self-confidence, The Hurricanes would sometimes swap instruments for comic relief in which notes chased haphazardly up and down fretboards amid feedback lament and free-form percussion. Both to restore order and to let Rory take a breather, Richie was bullied into 'Big Noise From Winnetka', which necessitated his commanding the stage virtually alone under his own voodoo spell for minutes on end – and he had to admit that "the audience love it. If there's a drum solo, they go mad."[20]

Sandy Nelson had also been on the recording session for The Hollywood Argyles' 'Alley Oop', which was one of the first items that Starkey sang with The Hurricanes, who, like many other Liverpool groups, had "featured vocalists" who specialised in areas not thought unsuitable for the chief show-off. Able to swoop elegantly from bass grumble to falsetto shriek in the space of a few bars, Egmond was the balladeer who stopped the show with breathtaking treatments of Peggy Lee's sultry 'Fever', The Everly Brothers' 'Let It Be Me' or Gershwin's 'Summertime', from *Porgy And Bess*.

With the humorous semi-spoken lope of 'Alley Oop',[21] Starkey was in charge of less demanding material. By *bel canto* standards, he had a horrible voice, devoid of plummy enunciation and nicety of intonation. Instead, you got slurred diction – perfect for 'Alley Oop' – and gravelly ranting as he got through a number any old how, frequently straining his disjointed range past its limits. In context, the effect of spontaneity over expertise was not unattractive, even gruffly charming, because "I'm more of a personality. It's a fun-loving attitude to life that comes across. I have a good time."[22]

It was incumbent upon Merseyside groups to exude a happy, smiling on-stage atmosphere, as well as action-packed rock 'n' roll, to defuse potential trouble amongst the customers during, say, February 1960's "Gala Rock Night" at Litherland Town Hall with

The Hurricanes, Dominoes, Bobby Bell Rockers and Ian and his Zodiacs, then constituting the upper crust of Liverpool pop. Yet, however peacefully this event passed, the Merseyside constabulary were still called out to suppress a wave of brawling and vandalism afterwards when over-excited adolescents with hormones raging wondered what to do until bedtime.

However, as long as the teenagers handed over the admission price and behaved themselves while inside, their deeds of destruction in the streets were of no concern to palais promoters, who hadn't let private dislike stop them clasping rock 'n' roll to their bosoms, either. Turning such a hard-nosed penny were the managements of Liscard's Grosvenor Ballroom, St Helen's Plaza and the Neston Institute, all of which degenerated into roughhouses on pop nights. At West Derby's Locarno, the city's first disc jockey, Mark Peters, was installed. However, after Peters devoted himself more to singing with a group, Billy Butler and Bob Wooler would surface as the city's most omnipotent masters of ceremonies, with selections from their vast record collections being borrowed by musicians eager to surprise dancers with more than the obvious Top-20 favourites.

Some, such as Kingsize Taylor, went directly to source. On the mailing lists of remote record labels like Aladdin, Chess, Imperial and Cameo Parkway, The Dominoes were able to perform selections "before anybody had heard the records. We had them sent over from the States."[3] Among precious few other native rock 'n' rollers regarded with anything approaching awe were Johnny Kidd, Vince Taylor and Ronnie Wycherley, who, as 'Billy Fury', was being groomed for fame by Larry Parnes. As for wholesome Cliff Richard, a self-respecting rocker like Richie Starkey would have "never bought one of his records in my life".[23]

Reflecting Liverpool's general cultural isolation, its groups came gradually to drink from a repertory pool singular to the region, including early Tamla-Motown and Atlantic singles, US Hot 100 smashes that failed everywhere else and songs buried on B-sides and "side two, track four" on LPs, such as Ray Charles' treatment of

'You'll Never Walk Alone' from *Carousel*. Numbers by Chuck Berry – then without major British hits – cropped up more than anyone else's, but other Merseyside cult celebrities included Dr Feelgood And The Interns, Richie Barrett, The Olympics and Chan Romero. Filling the Jive Hive and Wavertree's Holyoake Hall – where Wooler presided – well before filtering to the rest of the country were Scouse arrangements of 'Dr Feelgood', 'Money', Willie Dixon's 'My Babe', The Jive Bombers' 'Bad Boy' and other discs that, not immediately obtainable from high-street retailers, had wended their way over from a more exotic continent. "The music we liked took a different direction from the rest of the country," commented Cilla White, then completing a secretarial course at Anfield Commercial College. "We had our own versions of everything, and no one thought for a minute that they were inferior."[19]

In Rory Storm And The Hurricanes, where form overruled content, most songs were common property of scores of other groups. The traditional opener was Vince Taylor's spirited 'Brand New Cadillac' and the core of the set was drawn likewise from the Valhalla of classic rock, with Warren Smith's 'Ubangi Stomp' featuring among the more obscure choices. During Ray Charles' 'What'd I Say', Rory would, ideally, trade "heys" and "yeahs" with participating onlookers, take it down easy, build the tension to the verge of panic and, to round it off, flounce into the wings, leaving 'em wanting more.

Perhaps the Rory Storm And The Hurricanes story should have ended there, because arguably they were as good as they were ever going to get. Routining new numbers speedily and incompletely before ennui set it, Storm was averse to formal rehearsals, and so they'd venture but rarely beyond the boundaries of their stylistic definition. The consolidation rather than development of this was to be their downfall.

This, however, lay three years ahead. The first business of any pop group is simply to be liked, and none could deny that Rory and his Hurricanes were in the top division of Merseyside popularity. As a measure of their wide appeal, their fan club was situated at an address in faraway Anfield, where its secretary, Julie Farrelly, would answer letters of undying love for Rory, for whom female screams were already reverberating.

3 "I Took A Chance And I Think I've Been Lucky"

Six-Five Special's less pious successors – *Oh Boy!*, *Drumbeat*, *Boy Meets Girls*, *Wham!* and the short-lived *Dig This!* – produced a worthier strain of British rock 'n' roller by the end of the decade. You wonder how some might have evolved, had they not acquiesced to their handlers' suggestions to follow the Tommy Steele path as all-round entertainers. As well as Cliff Richard's film musicals of cheerful unreality, Vince Eager – as "Simple Simon" – would dip his toe into pantomime in Southport Floral Hall's *Mother Goose* in 1960 while Marty Wilde announced his wish to "do the real class stuff like Sinatra".[1] Even Johnny Kidd, the hardest UK rocker of them all, would soften towards country and western when his sporadic hits dried up.

Others, however, remained hostage to the beat. With his Horde Of Savages, Screaming Lord Sutch – a more enduring clown than Willie Harris – was prevented by his image from going smooth while Vince Taylor, clad in studded biker leathers, kept the faith in France. Another example was Tony Sheridan, now much changed from the absconded schoolboy in McDevitt's Skiffle Cellar. After serving Wilde and then Taylor, Tony struck out on his own, leading a trio with drummer Brian Bennett and, on bass, Brian Locking, both of whom were foreordained to join The Shadows. However, although 19-year-old Sheridan – a guitarist/singer of unusual flair – created a ripple before 1959's *Oh Boy!* cameras, an invitation to do likewise on an edition of *Boy Meets Girls* headlined by Gene Vincent was cancelled when, in his own publicist's words, Sheridan "went haywire, failing to be on time, arriving without his guitar, etc".[2] Television was therefore closed to him, and only on sufferance did Larry Parnes allow Sheridan just under ten minutes on an all-British supporting bill – including Billy Fury, Joe Brown (from the *Boy Meets Girls* house band) and Georgie Fame – to Vincent and Eddie Cochran, an Oklahoman Elvis then in the British Top 30 for the fourth time, on an around-Britain package tour, beginning on Elvis Presley's birthday, 8 January 1960.

Naturally, the host descended upon the Liverpool Empire, where, after the show, Rory Storm and John Byrnes nattered familiarly with Tony Sheridan and Larry Parnes talked with Allan Williams, proprietor of the Jacaranda. This enterprising Welshman arranged another Merseyside spectacular for the two Americans on 3 May at a 6,000-capacity sports stadium between Exchange Station and Prince's Dock. Lower on the bill, the expected smattering of Parnes' lesser creatures were interspersed with some of the city's top acts, including Cass and his Cassanovas, Gerry And The Pacemakers and, with The Hurricanes, Rory Storm, who was as much a star in Liverpool as Cochran was in the hit parade. Two more parochial outfits would also be added to that Tuesday evening's sold-out programme after Eddie died from his injuries in a road accident between the Bristol Hippodrome and London Airport on 17 April.

Bigoted old Teds threw contemptuous pennies at them, but Vincent was almost upstaged by the local boys, whether Gerry Marsden with his moving 'You'll Never Walk Alone' or Rory stunning 'em with 'What'd I Say' and Carl Perkins' insidious 'Honey Don't' with Walter and Starkey – shifty in sunglasses – anchoring its understated shuffle. When embers of excitement were being fanned too briskly, as Gene's grand entrance neared, it was stuttering Rory, rather than Gerry, whom Williams sent forth again to the microphone to douse flames of open riot with a nonplussing "S-s-s-stop it, y-y-y-you k-k-k-kids!"

A tape recording of the greatest night anyone could ever remember was, unhappily, erased, but the impact of the Liverpool groups on

Larry Parnes was sufficient for him to charge Williams with the hurried task of assembling a selection of them from which could be chosen an all-purpose backing band for use by certain Parnes signings who'd been earmarked to tour Scotland. As amplifiers buzzed into life and string-calloused fingers fluttered prelusively on fretboards, Storm *sans* Hurricanes sauntered into the afternoon auditions in Slater Street's Corinthian Social Club[3] not intending to leave until he'd had his picture taken with Billy Fury, who was to string along with his manager to provide a second opinion.

In the photograph of the pair standing on the club's threshold, Billy in daylight appeared stunted and unimposing next to Rory, an Adonis in Italian suit and hair lacquer who had somehow acquired a tan during a wet spring. It was because he looked such a pop star of a man and Fury – whose Top Ten success was not yet consolidated – didn't that Parnes threatened to call off the Scottish undertaking if Williams or Storm published a single copy of the shot. God knows what might have happened if Storm and his boys had bothered to play for Parnes that day and he'd been foolish enough to pick them. What could have prevented flamboyant Rory in Aberdeen or Inverness from shoving the cipher that The Hurricanes were backing into the wings so that he could commandeer the central mic himself?

This was mere hypothesis, however, because Rory had passed up this potential passport to a wider work spectrum, having committed himself and his band to an imminent and lengthy residency at Pwllheli's Butlin's, gained though the influence of sister Iris. Rory might have been able to pack his case with Ernie and Violet's approval, but other parents grumbled about the chances that their Hurricane sons were wasting by being silly to themselves in such a risky business as this pop music. Elsie Graves had been to see Richie perform with The Hurricanes and "thought he would eventually find a place for himself in an ordinary dance band",[4] meaning one as part-time as The Eddie Clayton Skiffle Group had been, because she didn't want him to throw away his four years' worth of apprenticeship at Hunt's. Amused by the memory, Richie would reconjure how "Elsie and Harry tried everything to persuade me to stay. 'Get your trade,' they told me, 'and you'll never be stuck for a job.' It's good advice for any lad."[5]

In the unquiet twilight of his adolescence, however, Richie's mother "talked an awful lot of rubbish. I didn't believe a word she said."[6] He was more in thrall of his Geraldine, who had so monopolised his plain charms that they had become engaged. In alliance with her parents-in-law-to-be, she prevailed upon him to be sensible and withdraw from The Hurricanes even as Storm called at Admiral Grove – as he'd also had to do at the Egmonds' in Broad Green – to affirm his own faith in the group. Its immediate future was "as good as a holiday and you get paid for it".[7] You couldn't argue with £25 pounds for a 16-hour week, could you, when eight was then considered an ample wage for a young executive slaving from nine to five every day?

"If Rory hadn't twisted his arm," opined John Byrnes, "I don't think he'd have done half the things he did."[8] Sensing that Starkey needed only courage to chuck Geraldine, Byrnes and Storm had laid on with a trowel spicy imagery of the saucy, fancy-free "birds" with whom it was feasible to fraternise at the holiday camp, even in a pre-birth pill age when a nice girl would tolerate no more than a fumble at her bra-strap while still unwed – and when Butlins' rules forbade staff from entertaining anyone with a different set of hormones in their assigned chalets. Its ballrooms – where fluorescent lighting made all look sun-tanned and fit – were hunting grounds, see, for souls aching for romance. The procurement of this was often easier for a player on the bandstand than the pimpled Average Joe mooching about with a sense of defeat in the gloom past the burning footlights. A strong enough motive for even the most ill-favoured youth to be a rock 'n' roll musician was the increased licence it gave to make eye contact with gawking young ladies fringing the front of the stage. A tryst during a beer break could be sealed with a beatific smile, a flood of libido and an "All right, then, I'll see you later".

On top of illicit perks were career opportunities at Butlin's in Pwllheli, where Georgie Fame had been enlisted into Rory Blackwell's Blackjacks in the previous year. Russ Hamilton had been a Redcoat – hearty blazered motivator of sports and social activities – at Blackpool's outpost and Cliff Richard had got his break in the Rock 'n' Roll Ballroom at Clacton, while Joe Brown had twanged guitar for Clay Nicholls And The Blue Flames at Filey before Parnes, *Boy Meets Girls* and a recording contract. If the worst came to the worst, Butlin's even had its own label, which had just issued a single by The Trebletones, its Bognor Regis band.

On resigning from Hunt's, Richard "took a chance and I think I've been lucky".[9] Starkey was one for whom Butlins was not, overall, a hellish experience, "but I hated a lot of it at the time."[10] The camps were a reflection of Billy Butlin's personality, which, before his knighthood, was that of an effervescent ex-fairground hoopla huckster. With borrowed capital, the first manifestation of his radical scheme for a walled and communal family holiday site was at bracing Skegness in 1936. From this blueprint, there grew an empire of knobbly knees contests; good-natured cheers from entire sittings of diners whenever a butter-fingered waitress let fall crockery; Olympic-sized swimming pools; noisy team games with Redcoats jollying everyone along; children lining up for ride after free ride on the deliciously terrifying Wild Mouse – and campers grousing about the food, the accommodation, the band and, of course, the meteorological whims of British Augusts.

1960's weather was indeed something to grouse about. From July to September, it was unseasonably cool in Wales, with the highest rainfall figure since before the war. This had compensations for Richie, who, more prone to burning than most, would sunbathe in dark glasses, long-sleeved shirt, jeans and improvised nose-protector. As pale as he'd been when he first exposed himself, he'd stroll back to a dwelling a good deal grubbier than those of the holidaymakers, with their new lino, bright wallpaper and chalet maids.

Starkey didn't like you taking the mickey out of him when girls were around, but when in his usual good humour, Egmond affirmed, "He was the life and soul of any party."[11] Sometimes it was unintentional. When O'Brien was teaching Starkey to swim, "He seemed to be doing fine until he realised he was in the twelve-footer.

Then he just yelled and vanished from sight. Three of us dived in and pulled him out. We had a good laugh about it afterwards."[11] On the one occasion that he went on a pony trek at Pwllheli, his nag bit him. More shocked than hurt, he chose to dismount and walk back to camp. This was not to be his only altercation with a horse.

Richie and Rory were the most reluctant of all the group to rise before midday, groaning expletives when the camp Tannoy system crackled at seven with 'Zip-A-Dee-Doo-Dah', 'Oh What A Beautiful Morning' or a tune as oppressively perky. Richie especially would be surly over breakfast if there'd been more than this ritual disturbance. "The first sign of him waking," observed Egmond, "took the form of one open eye staring 'round the chalet. Then it would be an hour before he'd stir properly."[11]

Another trait that was not always endearing was his insistence on sloping off to the Dingle – no matter how inconvenient it might be for the group – to celebrate birthdays and other anniversaries. (He could counter that Storm did likewise for the Liverpool soccer team's home matches.) Neither was he enamoured with Rory bestowing colourful stage names upon each Hurricane, just as Lord Sutch had with his Savages. As films and TV series such as *Rawhide*, *Gun Law* and *Wagon Train* were popular,[12] the Wild West was Storm's principal theme as Byrnes became "Johnny Guitar" after a 1954 Western, while saturnine O'Brien was "Ty Brien", a nod towards Ty Hardin, then famous for his title role in BBC's *Bronco*, a poor man's *Cheyenne*. Egmond metamorphosed into the less specific "Lou Walters". The group also accrued apposite accessories, such as gold cowboy boots, saloon cardsharp fancy waistcoats and the stringy desperado beards that came and went on Richie and Charles/Ty's mugs.

Not wishing to be awkward, Starkey gave in and let Rory introduce him as "Rings" – and then "Ringo" – "Starr", which he emblazoned on his bass drum in stick-on lettering. A mythical gunslinger had already lent his name to one of the younger Merseyside singers, Johnny Ringo, leader of The Colts, but Richie's new forename was for his lingering Teddy Boy habit of adorning each hand with three or four increasingly splendid rings. When

"Ringo" was juxtaposed with his run-of-the-mill last name, it sounded "a bit funny. 'Starr' was a natural. It made sense to me and I liked it. It stuck."[13]

It also better facilitated Storm's build-up to "Starr Time", a section of the show in which his drummer could now resort to more than 'Big Noise From Winnetka' and 'Alley Oop'. With vocal cords beyond remedy by the end of the season, Ringo/Richie was rewarded with scattered screams for three other selections, which included – in a lower key and with the others on the *bwap-doo-wap* responses – 'Boys', a B-side by New York's Shirelles, a female vocal group of ingenuously fragile conviction. He tried Johnny Burnette's ambulant 'You're Sixteen' less often, because Rory generally kept that one for himself.

Backing the competitors in the camp's pop-singing and jiving contests – sponsored by a tobacco firm – as well as delivering the music night after night in the Rock and Calypso Ballroom, Ringo would claim later to have been "educated at Butlin's".[13] What had once been casual was now stylised, and when they returned – rebooked for next summer – to the trivial round of Merseyside engagements Storm and The Hurricanes "couldn't have had better practice for a stage career. Those [Pwllheli] audiences really used to heckle us, and when they wanted requests it was usually for some square song that we'd hardly heard of before, so it was up to us to keep things going. We simply had to ad lib and try not to take any notice of the remarks they slung at us. And, even more important, we had to play without any sort of arrangement, most of the time."[10]

While at Butlin's, a visiting Rory Blackwell had tried to poach the much-improved Johnny Guitar for his Blackjacks, and Guitar may have regretted his folly in not taking up the offer, because the pestilence of trad jazz – springing from Bristol, where clarinettist Bernard "Acker" Bilk was king – was ravaging Britain to the detriment of rock 'n' roll. It had spread beyond the earnest obsession of the intellectual fringe and ban-the-bomb marches to a proletariat where "ACKER" was studded on the backs of leather jackets where "ELVIS" or "GENE" once were, and girls fainted to the toot-tooting of Humphrey Lyttelton. Bilk, Chris Barber and Kenny Ball each breached the Top 20. After Bilk came within an ace of a Number One with 'Stranger On The Shore', a Manchester disciple wrote to ask him if it was about Jesus.[15] As Acker's Paramount Jazz Band went in for striped brocade and bowler hats, so matching Donegal tweeds, Confederate Army regimentals and even legal gowns and barrister wigs would be the uniforms of lesser units with bland banjo players, a confusion of front-line horns and "dads" who thought that a hoarse monotone was all you needed to sing like Louis Armstrong.

In some numbers, the jazz content was frequently negligible because, if some black dotard from New Orleans had recorded a particularly definitive solo, it was considered prudent to learn it note for note for regurgitation at every public performance. The Massed Alberts (a sort of English Spike Jones and his City Slickers) and the chart-topping Temperance Seven (produced by George Martin) were only jazz marginally but still appeared on programmes like BBC's opportunist *Trad Tavern* and at jazz strongholds such as West London's 100 Club, Uncle Bonnie's Chinese Jazz Club(!) down in Brighton and, in Liverpool, the Temple, the Cavern and – with "No Weirdies, Beatniks or Teddy Boys admitted" – the Storyville (later the Iron Door), all contained within the ravines of lofty warehouses around Whitechapel.

The Liverpool Echo would advertise and review trad concerts while disregarding lowbrow rock 'n' roll. Nevertheless, possibly because queues formed round the block whenever The Temperance Seven – a pop group by any other name – were on, it made financial sense for the Iron Door and the Cavern to tentatively slip in a little out-and-out pop between the trad, even when the Cavern became "the Club Perdido" every Thursday for modern jazz. Without Ray McFall threatening to fine anyone now, Rory Storm And The Hurricanes had been one of the highlights of his club's first all-pop events, just before they left for Pwllheli.

Despite this breakthrough, the majority of such venues that counted on Merseyside remained stubbornly biased towards local trad outfits like The Joe Silman Dixielanders and Noel Walker's

Stompers, and so it was that Rory Storm's Hurricanes responded to demands from West Germany for cheap rock 'n' roll labour. It was to be a worthwhile experience, for, in as late as 1968, sending groups to the Fatherland for a three-month stretch was still considered a foolproof way of separating the men from the boys. Black Sabbath's manager, Jim Simpson, reasoned that it was "rather like training a thousand metre runner by sending him on 5,000-metre courses".[16] Nine years earlier, Acker Bilk had been well primed to capitalise on the trad boom after six weeks in a Dusseldorf bierkeller, where "you just blew and blew and blew and had 20 minutes off for a drink, and then you were back blowing again".[15]

Walking an uncomfortable line between trad and pop, Garston's Swinging Blue Jeans would discover the hard way that jazz had been old hat with West German teenagers since 1960. From Kiel's Star Palaast to Cologne's Storyville, bastions of Teutonic jazz had converted within days to rock 'n' roll bierkellers. The new policy was, however, most rampant in Hamburg, Germany's largest port, after *Oh Boy!* refugee Tony Sheridan and a motley crew of other unemployed London musicians were imported in June 1960 and christened "The Jets" by impresario Bruno Koschmider to reclaim the many patrons who had drifted away from his Kaiserkeller club, affronted by its clumsy local band's attempts to copy American pop.

Until lured away after a month by one of Koschmider's richer rivals – Peter Eckhorn, of the newly-opened Top Ten – The Jets made the Kaiserkeller thrive again by not bothering to duplicate recorded arrangements, choosing rather to pile up a sweaty intensity during indefinitely extended extrapolations of 'What'd I Say', 'Whole Lotta Shakin'' and even 'When The Saints Go Marching in'. The beauty of pieces with such loose, simple structures was that they required little instruction past the rare "No, not dum-dum-de-diddly-*dum*; try dum-dum-de-diddly-*dah*".

After fuming over the loss of The Jets, Bruno remembered an encounter with another rockin' Briton, Brian Casser, in the 2I's. Although a Londoner by upbringing, Casser was actually the "Cass" in Cass And The Cassanovas. He could be contacted by telephone – so he informed Koschmider – at the Jacaranda, where all the Liverpool groups congregated because it was near the dole office. A story goes that it was not Casser but Allan Williams who answered the ring from one of Koschmider's underlings. No, Brian and The Cassanovas are north of the border with Johnny Gentle, one of Larry Parnes' clients. Can I help at all? Perhaps we could discuss it next time Mr Koschmider and yourself come to London? Through the quick-thinking Williams, a couple of Scouse groups who weren't in either Scotland or Butlin's were sent across the North Sea to Hamburg, and in October 1960 it was Rory Storm And The Hurricanes' turn. They were to replace Derry And The Seniors – who'd been there since July – and work split shifts with The Beatles, a group traceable back to The Quarry Men. Although official stipulations had them there only until December, Bruno's advertisements stressed that they'd see the New Year in at the Kaiserkeller. Comparing the relative sizes of their respective names on its wall posters, "RORY STORM AND HIS HURRICAN [sic]", as Butlins veterans, were judged to be a bigger attraction than the small-lettered Beatles.

On this first occasion that Starkey had ever breathed foreign air, he travelled alone and had to change in Paris. During the usual scramble, he lost track of his drum kit. His attempts to explain his predicament in sign language led to the arrival of gendarmes. Fortunately, one of these understood English, but the kit was still not located until the next morning.

As he hurtled through the forests of Lower Saxony, hot-eyed with sleeplessness, tell-tale twinges of homesickness and anxiety about the mess he might now be in took their toll. Hamburg had been as torn by war as his own city, but if Ringo anticipated seeing parking lots formed from bomb sites, as you still could back home, he found instead a bustling modern metropolis – as Liverpool wouldn't be for years – fully recovered from the attentions of the RAF. The gaunt buildings on the Elbe waterfront were a link with home, and so were the cobbled streets of St Pauli, where the Kaiserkeller stood. There, instead of some dirty cellar like the

Cavern, he unloaded his equipment outside a place plusher than even the Rock and Calypso.

Whereas the Pwllheli ballroom had a touch of the Caribbean, the Kaiserkeller had a nautical theme – mock-fishermen's nets hanging from its capacious ceiling, boat-shaped dining alcoves *et al* – as befitted a port, albeit one 60 miles inland. It was but one such establishment around the Grosse Freiheit, however, a tributary of the Reeperbahn ("Rope Street"). This glum translation belied a notoriety as the neon starting point of innumerable languid evenings of perfumed wantonness, living tableaux of flesh and late-evening temptation by doorstep pimps. I am prohibited by inbred propriety from entering into distressing detail, except to state that, an erotic Butlins since the days of three-mast clippers, St Pauli's brothels and strip-tease palaces were eye-openers to anyone who assumed that humans could be sexually gratified without mechanical complexity and only with other humans.

As Tony and The Jets had guided Hamburg's first musical Merseysiders around the Salome strip club, the Roxy transvestite bar, Der Fludde, the shocking "Street of Windows" and other of the district's diversions, so the information was passed on to Rory's Hurricanes by The Seniors – who were staying on briefly in another club – and The Beatles. *Wurst* sausages, *Korn*, *Apfel Küchen* and other German foodstuffs and beverages might have been recommended, but Storm's group were more grateful when told that "*Cornflakes mit Milch*" was served in one Freiheit cafe. Like Storm, Sheridan was fond of swimming and was the original advocate of excursions to Timmendorf Beach, on the North Sea.

The prodigal Tony had no right to expect one, but Rory Storm And The Hurricanes were recipients of a testimonial from Koschmider praising their nightly entertainments. They were also paid more than both The Seniors and The Beatles; enough to lodge in the British Seamen's Mission – where lunch was something with chips and a cup of tea – along Johannis Bollwerk, rather than in the two dingy rooms with no bedding at the back of the club with which The Seniors had made do. The five Beatles still lived in some dungeons adjoining a cinema toilet.

Sardonic about the privileged Hurricanes, who were also speaking of making a recording whilst in Germany, The Beatles were particularly indifferent towards "the nasty one with his little grey streak of hair",[17] a reference to Ringo by George Harrison, the same lead guitarist who'd been too young for The Texans. There was also some open unpleasantness when Rory reneged on a promise to advance the quintet's leader, John Lennon, the cash he still needed for a guitar that he'd been drooling over in a shop window in central Hamburg. Nevertheless, the ice broke and The Beatles found the newcomers intrinsically friendlier than the rather supercilious Seniors had been. According to Pete Best, then their drummer, "That's where their friendship with Ringo began."[18]

Three Beatles – Harrison, Lennon and general factotum Paul McCartney – would be on hand when The Hurricanes recorded within a fortnight of opening at the Kaiserkeller. The sum total of all their big talk, however, was three of Wally's ballads – one take each – in Hamburg's tiny Akustik Studio, into which extraneous sounds from the main railway station would infiltrate if the door was left ajar. Financed by Storm and Allan Williams, Eymond warbled 'Fever' and Kurt Weill's 'September Song' – à la Johnnie Ray's 1959 treatment – while accompanied by the other Hurricanes and 'Summertime' with Richie and The Beatles. As evidenced by the ambitious Storm not actively joining in, the session was purely exploratory, a treat for the lads and a confidence boost for the bespectacled Wally.

Starr's teen appeal wasn't obvious, either, but his harmless jocularity, saucer eyes and air of bewildered wistfulness incited a protective instinct from a fair cross-section of Reeperbahn *frauleins* that they couldn't feel for Wally, even though he sang like a nightingale. After ogling the drummer all evening, one girl's bottled-up emotions bubbled over and she had to be forcibly dragged from the club, shrieking, "Ringo! Ringo!", even as she was pushed into the street.

Sending palpitations through more feminine nervous systems were The Beatles, particularly Pete, but Ringo for one would remember a time less than a year before when they'd been far outside the league of Liverpool's leading groups, who had known them by sight just as Jacaranda riff-raff. Only on noticing Harrison in its basement teaching another Beatle, Stuart Sutcliffe, the stock rock 'n' roll root notes on a new bass guitar had Starr understood that they were an actual group under Williams' wing.

All of them were ex-grammar-school pupils. Fresh from the sixth form, McCartney was wondering if his GCE "A"-level results had alighted on his Allerton doormat yet, while the older Lennon and best mate Sutcliffe had, to all intents and purposes, quit art college to go to Hamburg and Best had cancelled plans to become a trainee teacher. Stuart, Paul and John would insert the odd long word and names like Kerouac and Kierkegaard into conversations that would lapse into student vernacular and their own Goonish restricted code. They'd once been involved in a fusion of poetry and rock with *vers libre* bard Royston Ellis, who'd judged them to be "more of the bohemian ilk than other young northerners at the time, and their pleasant eccentricity made them acceptable".[14] He'd been astonished that "they didn't even know about getting high on benzedrine strips from nose inhalers",[14] a gap in their understanding that he rectified.

Partly because of their arty affectations and Lennon and McCartney's pretensions as songwriters, The Beatles were derided as unprofessional "posers" by no-nonsense musicians like Johnny Hutchinson. Nonetheless, he'd often step in on occasions when they were without a drummer, as they were when one of Best's predecessors, Tommy Moore, was very late for Larry Parnes at the Corinthian. They'd got through nine days in Scotland backing Johnny Gentle, despite mutterings from the tour manager about their slovenly turn-out. A pop fan of Cilla White's discernment complained that she "couldn't bear them. I thought they were scruffy and untidy. Their dress was horrible. They wore these terrible motorbike-type jackets. I didn't want to know."[19]

The tragedy of The Beatles was that they didn't care how awful they were. In fact, they rejoiced in it. "It seemed an incredible time before they actually started a number," averred Keith Hartley, a novice Merseyside drummer, "as if they were just messing about."[20] Sutcliffe could barely manage the simplest bass run and, as Cilla had noticed, McCartney broke strings "so often that I used to think one of us in the front row would sometime get an eye knocked out".[19] While they'd learned much from seeing Tony – nicknamed "the Teacher" – at the Top Ten, on the creaky Kaiserkeller stage you'd never know if they were going to play while perched on amplifier rims, smoking lazily, or else, infused with the fizz of readily available chemical stimulants, leap into an onslaught of endlessly inventive caperings, improvised comedy sketches and skylarks crazier (if less physical) than Rory's.

Some items might stop abruptly after a couple of confused verses, but one such as 'Whole Lotta Shakin" could last a full half-hour, during which Paul might abandon his instrument to appeal to dancers to clap along to what they recognised as Pete's *mach schau* beat, which embraced pounding hi-hat, snare and bass drum in the same lone four-in-a-bar rhythm, chorus after chorus, amid shouts of encouragement, until the levelling guitars surged back in again and, generally, the snare reverted to the usual offbeat and the hi-hat to eight quavers a bar, while the bass drum continued to hit fours rather than its standard rock 'n' roll onbeat.

Although The Beatles had no specially designated frontman like Storm or Sheridan, the greater emphasis was on vocal selections, which ranged from slow solemnities – usually from Paul, the group's Wally – to the blood-curdling dementia of one in the throes of a fit whenever John attacked 'Money', although McCartney was just like Little Richard when he raced through 'Long Tall Sally'. At least it wasn't weak, and neither were they faking it. Far away in Liverpool, they'd endured a baptism of barracking, heckling and catcalls, but they'd gamely retaliated and so, rapidly and grotesquely, a camaraderie of turmoil accumulated between The Beatles and their antagonists so that ugly moments were bypassed as everyone tuned into their awry absurdity – especially as the five themselves conveyed the impression that they, too, were aware of it. The anarchic antithesis of the slickness that was the synchronised footwork of The

Shadows, who were now nearly as famous as Cliff Richard himself, The Beatles walked a highly strung artistic tightrope without a safety net but still stoked up a wildly enthusiastic atmosphere, even from St Pauli's small-hour *demi-monde* of prostitutes, gangsters and *Schlagers* picking fights.

Much of the Beatle attitude rubbed off on Rory Storm And The Hurricanes during the two outfits' shared workload of alternating 30- to 90-minute sets from dusk until the grey of morning. Soon, they too would see nothing amiss in cigarettes dangling from their lower lips whilst on stage, nor in serially consuming Koschmider's gratis nightly allowance of beer and salad between numbers. Ringo also altered his drumming to *mach schau* specifications while hitting solidly and defiantly behind the beat by a fraction both to invest material with stronger definition and to increase tension. It would not be too presumptuous to say that the subtleties of Best and Starr's rhythmic developments while in the Kaiserkeller were to alter pop drumming procedures forever.

Tales of what The Beatles and The Hurricanes did and said when fermenting in Hamburg are still elaborated by so-called "insiders". During that initial sojourn, the most documented incident stemmed from their joint conspiracy to render the Kaiserkeller's unstable stage irreparable via an excess of stamping and jumping so that Koschmider would be compelled to get a new one. It actually caved in during an over-lively 'Blue Suede Shoes' by Storm and The Hurricanes, who compounded their infamy by vacating the club with suspicious haste. Already unsure of the loyalty of his squad of waiter/bouncers since their supervisor, Horst Fascher, had defected to the Top Ten, it would also have been a false economy for Bruno to have ordered them to take revenge with fist and cosh against the English wrongdoers. Instead, he made an example of Rory with a hefty severance from his pay packet and an extra-legal dismissal for "breach of contract".

Storm had set no Deutschmarks aside for such an unthinkable eventuality and, rather than seek repatriation from the British Consulate, roamed St Pauli aimlessly. As he hadn't the means to continue rooming at the Seamen's Mission, he was found a bunk in Sheridan and The Jets' dormitory above the Top Ten until his reinstatement by a calmer Koschmider.

Bruno may also have feared that Eckhorn would take advantage of the situation and entice away the rest of the Kaiserkeller's British contingent, as he had Sheridan. Impervious to their employer's intimidations, The Beatles and Hurricanes' trips to the Top Ten had already gone beyond commiserating with Rory and watching the band; now they were getting up on stage and playing. Acting swiftly, Koschmider gave The Beatles a month's notice, which he shortened even more by arranging the deportation of 17-year-old Harrison for violation of the red-light curfew and two more of them on a trumped-up charge of arson. Storm and The Hurricanes were informed that they wouldn't be seeing in the New Year in Germany after all – although, if he'd so desired, Starr could have stayed on, as he was being headhunted by Sheridan, who – soon to be bereft of the other Jets, when their contract expired – was on the look-out for at least the skeleton of a backing combo (to be called, at various times, The Beat Boys and The Wreckers).

If it finished on a sour note, this first collective encounter with the Fatherland had wrought a more workmanlike Rory Storm And The Hurricanes, toughened for less demanding if more reputable tasks in England. Theirs was a common outcome of having to *mach schau* for hours on end. Through playing for three months at the Top Ten, Dave Dee And The Bostons – Wiltshire equivalent of Storm's unit – found that, "when you come home, you aren't half tight – musically tight. You don't know it's happening to you, because you get tired."[21]

Back in Liverpool, Storm and The Hurricanes reached a rapid zenith, exemplified by their being accosted in the street to sign autographs and imitation when a Bill Hart from Bootle "got a £15 drum kit. I was Ringo".[22] Moreover, Starr's cousin John Foster became "Johnny Sticks", emulating what was onomatopoeically known as Ringo's (and Pete Best's) "atom beat" in Crosby's Roy Brooks And The Dions. Part of the attraction was The Hurricanes' implied bloke-ish camaraderie of all boys together, and – with Starr and Walter in mind – the notion that you didn't have to be Charles Atlas to be in a group. With the alibi of a stage act, a mousy boy had an excuse to make himself look other-worldly as Starr did now with his rings, boots, shiny turquoise suit, gold lamé shirt and strip of hair that, silver under the spotlight, had led a few Germans to insult him unknowingly by inquiring if he dyed it.

Many British towns now appeared to have their own Rory Storm And The Hurricanes. Clacton, for instance, had a Dave Curtiss And The Tremors and Dagenham its Brian Poole And The Tremeloes. If less conveniently placed to strike at the heart of the country's pop industry, Shane Fenton And The Fentones were the toast of glum Mansfield, and tambourine-rattling Wayne Fontana And The Jets were soon to be that of Oldham, where the last chip shop closed at 10.30pm. There was also a growing preponderance of outfits – like, for instance, Bristol's Eagles (winners of a national Boys' Club talent competition) or The Hellions from Worcester – who, with no demarcated leader, were amassing substantial grass-roots followings. Although some local pretty boy might be invited on stage to be Cliff or Billy for a while, he was no longer regarded as an integral part of the group. Most broke up within months of formation, but the concept that an acephalous group could be a credible means of both instrumental and vocal expression had been established.

In Liverpool, for every group that threw in the towel – the Bobby Bell Rockers and Cass And The Cassanovas – a dozen sprang up. As well as Johnny Hutchinson's remarkable Big Three, 1961's harvest included The Hot Rods, The Konkers, The Dronetones, The Albany Four, The Katz, The Zeros, The Lonely Ones, The Quiet Five, the all-girl Cockroaches and – named after the new fortnightly journal devoted to Merseyside pop – The Merseybeats, who, in common with The Moths, The Keenbeats and others, worked the word *beat* into their titles or used insectile appelations to be more like The Beatles, who, with Gerry's Pacemakers and The Remo Four, were about to topple Storm and The Hurricanes as the area's most popular draw – although which would play at the optimum moment when any combination of them were on the same bill was still a matter for conjecture that spring. In February, Storm lorded it over The Beatles and Kingsize's Dominoes at Litherland Town Hall, but before the month was out Gerry headlined over The Hurricanes there and The Beatles did likewise at the Cassanova Club.

Rory himself had cause for more pointed nervous backward glances with the coming of further outstanding showmen such as Freddie Starr (formerly Fowell of Violent Playground fame), Lee Curtis and Faron (alias Bill Russley), a performer disposed towards knee drops and scissor kicks and whom Gerry And The Pacemakers would take to Hamburg as guest vocalist.

Consolation for private anxieties and dark nights of the ego was a full work schedule within easy reach and – in those days – only instruments, puny amplifiers (30 watts at most) and drums to transport. From *Mersey Beat*, the reader could select an evening out from a wide array of venues, from a suburban pub's functions room with The Zeros to an "Operation Big Beat" at the New Brighton Tower with Rory, Kingsize, Gerry, The Beatles and The Remo Four from 7.30am to 1am. Without an alcohol licence and below ground, the Iron Door could stay open until daybreak, as it did in March 1961 when, breaking fire regulations, 2,000 attended its twelve-hour "Rock Around The Clock" event. A more typical night's work for Rory Storm And The Hurricanes, however, was an arrival at the Jive Hive at 8.15pm for a half-hour set, then on to the Cavern to do 45 minutes before returning to the Jive Hive to play last and then home by midnight.

Their name would not be synonymous with any particular club or palais, as The Swinging Blue Jeans were to their manager's Downbeat, The Undertakers to Orrell Park Ballroom or The Delacardoes (two smart chaps in glasses) at the Green Dolphin. The Beatles were a fixture at the Cavern which would see no more Club Perdido Thursdays and was putting the remaining vestiges of its jazz dignity into booking trad acts to warm up for The Beatles. Despite its sodden, choking blackness, the Cavern had become a lunchtime haunt of those who eked out a living or fed off college grants in studio flats in crumbling Victorian townhouses to the east of the Anglican cathedral. The Beatles had fascinated a similar "existentialist" crowd in the

Kaiserkeller. To Cilla White, they were "just as scruffy as ever. They were sort of clean and scruffy, if you know what I mean. Then I started listening to their sound. They were better than I thought."[19]

Not everyone adhered to this view. For such as The Remo Four's Colin Manley, "they really weren't very good".[24] All the same, "They were loud," admitted a Swinging Blue Jean. "They had presence."[23] Sometimes they made the mistake of airing a home-made Lennon-McCartney opus, but, as a Helena Joyce moaned, "We much preferred them to belt out the old Everly Brothers numbers."[22] Nonetheless, soon the massed humanity milling about in the Cavern for The Beatles would embrace not only the beatnik set but older schoolchildren, shop assistants and office employees like Cilla, who was in a typing pool at a Stanley Street firm that manufactured insulated cable.

Cilla's reward for her incurable record buying and club going was a position as *Mersey Beat*'s peanut-waged fashion columnist. Since finding herself microphone in hand one frolicsome night at the Iron Door, she'd also become one of a handful of freelance female vocalists who performed with several different Merseybeat groups. With dance troupes like The Shimmy-Shimmy Queens and occasional suppliers of sex interest like Dot Rhone, who simply sat on a stool in the midst of The Beatles, girls like Cilla were either an aberration or a breath of fresh air in a male-dominated sphere. Like beauty queen Irene Hughes and the younger Beryl Marsden did with The Merseybeats and The Undertakers, respectively, "Swingin' Cilla" granted most of her favours to Kingsize Taylor (then her boyfriend) and The Dominoes. However, only token persuasion was needed to get her to sing with other bands with whom she and her pals hobnobbed. Among these were The Big Three, Faron's Flamingos – and Rory Storm And The Hurricanes.

In their beloved key of G ("It could be a Yale key, for all I cared"[19]), Cilla unfurled a supple – if rather nasal – richness onto the sophistications of such as 'Autumn Leaves' and 'When I Fall In Love', but she wasn't above ravers like 'Hound Dog' and 'Boys'. Wally wasn't bothered about her borrowing his 'Fever' and 'Summertime' now and then, but Ringo was damned if he was going to let her have his 'Boys'. A compromise was reached and "we did it as a duet, and even then he didn't concede anything. He had a microphone over the drums and I used to have to sing it bent over his kit."[23] Ostensibly overwhelming her with matey affection, he'd cattily dub her "Swingin' Cyril" and – a pot calling the kettle black – criticise her broad "wacker" tongue, even if it lent her the common touch with audiences, absolving himself by saying, "I'm the drummer. I don't have to talk, but you do."[19] Starr's sage, seen-it-all-before air often irritated Swingin' Cyril as much as it did many others, and yet, beneath it all, Cilla and Richie had a deep and lifelong friendship and an almost sibling pride in each other.

As Rory was keen on bringing Cilla to Hamburg's Top Ten as Gerry would Faron, Ringo was dispatched to sound her out. Rather than talk to her with her rather intimidating father within earshot, Richie tapped on the side window near her desk in Stanley Street. She'd have to ask her dad, she said, and she'd only been a few weeks here. Predictably, Mr White, as self-appointed guardian of his daughter's job (and innocence), wouldn't hear of it.

From the family home along grimy Scotland Road, Cilla's dad would walk to work down Boundary Road, which ran directly to the docks. At number 56d, a council flat, Maureen Cox, Richie's "steady", lived with her mother, Mary, while her father, Joe, was at sea much of the time as a ship's steward. With the candour of middle age, Maureen – "Mo" – would describe herself as being "thick as two short planks"[24] when she left school at the minimum age of 15 to begin as a junior hairdressing assistant at the Ashley du Pre beauty parlour, which necessitated evening classes and jolting morning rush-hour bus journeys to a stop or two before the Pier Head terminus. Whatever her way with shampoo, curlers and banal chit-chat, she was a good advertisement for the salon in that, shedding her puppy fat, she'd blossomed into a pocket Venus with an urchin cut – usually a natural brown – that emphasised the raw drama of her fashionably high cheekbones, bold blue eyes and assured if impersonal poise as she titivated some aged virago's tortured curls.

En route to one of her hairstyling lessons, she'd seen Ringo emerge from the old Ford Zodiac that he drove unqualified and asked for an autograph. From the perspective of a club stage, Mo was at first no different from any of the other pale-faced "Judies" in suede, leather or fishnet who chattered excitedly until the group was announced. On one evening, however, Johnny Guitar gave her a second glance and they "walked out" a few times. Later, at the Blue Angel, it was Ringo who started a conversation with Mo and a stout friend, offering them a lift home. The girls seemed to have some vice-like grip on each other, or maybe Mo didn't wish to show unmaidenly eagerness, for her and Richie's cinema date the following week was as a threesome. In an attempt to separate them, Starr screwed himself up to telephone Maureen at work – where personal calls were frowned upon – and, for the next assignation, the friend got the message and Ringo and Maureen got better acquainted to the extent of public tendernesses, like his lighting two cigarettes at once and passing one to her.

To some, it was inconceivable that a bird like Mo was going out with Ringo. Backstage gossip assumed that it was an attraction of opposites, the fascination that women sometimes have for the pathos of the clown. Also, celebrity – even if only parochial – can be a powerful aphrodisiac. Her sense of humour was more barbed than his but as dry and, while she was forthrightly capable of sticking up for herself, Mo was content to be an adjunct to his self-image as a renowned and much-travelled man about Liverpool, a bit of a card and more than able both to keep down his drink and to stand his round.

Richie, Mo and intimates like Cilla, Paul Rogers and Pat Davies would hold court most frequently in the Zodiac cellar (now licensed), where a jam session by personnel from The Hurricanes, The Pacemakers, The Beatles and The Big Three was still dinning long after milk floats had braved the cold of sunrise. It had been enlivened by the unveilings of Nicola, a French stripper with whom one spectator became overly and demonstratively entranced. On another night, the door was bolted hastily when a drunken rabble converged outside. With no telephone inside, staff and members – including Maureen and Ringo – quaked to the noise of gleeful ramming and savage oaths as the mob tried to break in, only tiring of their sport hours later.

During more tranquil booze-ups in the Zodiac, the Cabin, the Blue Angel and similar musicians' watering holes, bands would brag of imminent tours of outlandish countries and even record releases; but, while yet to deteriorate into a cauldron of back-stabbing, underhandedness and favouritism, Mersey Beat's *ésprit de corps* was such that it wasn't uncommon for, say, Faron to vault on stage for a couple of numbers with The Dominoes or Rory Storm to stand in for a laryngitic John Lennon. Although Ringo wouldn't feel that he knew The Beatles well enough to invite them to his uproarious coming-of-age party at Admiral Grove,[25] he deputised likewise for Pete Best when the latter was poleaxed with bronchitis and on later occasions. Once, Neil Aspinall – a ledger clerk who supplemented his income by driving and unloading for The Beatles – dared to rouse Starr before noon to fill in for Best at the Cavern, "but I had no kit. I got up on stage with only cymbals and gradually Pete's kit started arriving piece by piece."[26]

If Rory Storm imagined that he was on terms of fluctuating equality with The Beatles, *Mersey Beat* editor Bill Harry was there to take him down a peg or two – literally. When tabulating the newspaper's first popularity poll, Bill – an Art School chum of Lennon's – counted "more votes for Rory Storm And The Hurricanes than The Beatles, but I put The Beatles at Number One because I'd heard that Rory was buying bundles of copies and a lot of Rory Storm entries were in the same green ink. About 20 or 30 would arrive from the same postal area at the same time, so I discounted those." Flying in the face of rancour "about you writing about The Beatles all the time" from no less than Bob Wooler, Bill placed Storm and The Hurricanes fourth, behind The Remo Four, Gerry and, of course, John and co. Looking back on 1961, *Mersey Beat* would tip The Beatles, Mark Peters and new face Karl Terry for national acclaim.

On some fronts, even Harry's darling Beatles were being overtaken. Paul Rogers had had his single '42,000 Kisses' issued, and discs by both The Seniors (with Freddie Starr) – a 45 and an album – and Scouse folk quartet The Spinners wouldn't be far behind it.

Then domiciled in England, Gene Vincent was pressing Gerry And
The Pacemakers to accompany him on a tour of Israel while,
grabbing the bull by the horns, Steve Bennett And The Syndicate
spent much of the latter half of 1961 in a tent in rural London.
Sniffing around the record companies, they failed a recording test
with Pye because their diction was "too northern" but still netted
lucrative engagements at US air bases in the Home Counties. Lest we
forget, gone beyond altogether was Billy Fury, of lesser years than
Storm and most of The Hurricanes, who was snapped consorting
with royalty at Ascot.

The Beatles had lately signed with *bona fide* manager Brian
Epstein. More than just a bloke with a phone, he ran North End
Music Stores (NEMS), which – so its regular *Mersey Beat* box ad
read – was "The Finest Record Selection In The North". As well as
prodding his contacts in the business on The Beatles' behalf, he was
sinking hard cash into them and, if nought else, getting them off the
Liverpool-Hamburg treadmill with a booking schedule that reached
as far south as Swindon.

Rory Storm was still in much the same rut, marking time with
Butlin's and Germany. In 1961, the cream of south Lancashire had
been represented in Hamburg by Gerry, The Seniors, Rory Storm
And The Hurricanes, The Big Three – and The Beatles, who, all but
Best, adopted the *pilzenkopf* ("mushroom head") hairstyle, as worn
by Klaus Voorman, Peter Penner and other of their bohemian – or
"exi" – admirers in Hamburg. Pidgin German left its mark in the
Mersey groups' on-stage dialogue past the expected *danke schoens*
and *prosts*. A frequent *wunsche* ("request") for the ladies was the
langsome *lied* ("ballad") 'Besame Mucho' while the men clumped
tables to Wilbert Harrison's 'Kansas Stadt'.

Conversely, the English of club staff and exis might have been
riddled with Scouse slang, but there were rumblings that, if you'd
heard one Mersey Beat group, you'd heard the lot. As a consequence,
other UK counties had been scoured for acts that could offer more
than the two-guitars-bass-drums music that was fast becoming
prototypical of Liverpool. Half of the dialects of Britain resounded

around the Reeperbahn in 1961, from the countrified Cockney of Kent's Bern Elliott And The Fenmen to the trill of Glasgow's Isabelle Bond to the flat vowels of Walsall's Tanya Day to the Cornish burr of Dave Lee And The Staggerlees.

Rory Storm And The Hurricanes replaced a Nottingham outfit, The Jaybirds, at the Top Ten, and, with Tony Sheridan – now the Elvis of St Pauli – shared its sleeping quarters. Although The Hurricanes accorded Tony – still without a permanent band – competent accompaniment during their stint, he'd select The Beatles for the honour of backing him on a German 45 and half of its attendant LP.

Some of the tracks – notably 'Let's Slop' – would allude to the Twist and its variations. This "most vulgar dance ever invented"[29] was as much the latest rave worldwide as trad had been in Britain alone. Its Mecca was New York's Peppermint Lounge, where, to the sound of Joey Dee And The Starliters, socialites and middle-aged trend-setters mingled with beatniks to do the Twist, in which you pretended to towel your back whilst grinding out a cigarette butt with your foot. Its Acker Bilk was Chubby Checker, but all manner of unlikely artists were recording twist singles, from Sinatra and Elvis downwards. Worse, it wouldn't go away, probably because you were too spoilt for choice with alternatives like the Fly, the Locomotion, the Slop, the Mashed Potato, the ungainly Turkey Trot, the Mickey's Monkey, the Hully Gully, the Hitch-Hiker, the back-breaking Limbo, the Bristol Stomp, the Madison and even a revival of the Charleston. Little dates a 1960s film more than the obligatory Twist sequence, and to this day the elderly will slip unconsciously into the Twist whenever the music hots up at a dinner and dance.

Dance-craze records in the charts generally indicate stagnation in pop, and Britain in 1961 was certainly heaving with that. On pop TV in those days were insipidly handsome boys next door such as Ronnie Carroll and Mark Wynter with slop ballads that your mum liked. The Mudlarks, spiritual descendants of *Melody Cruise*'s Teenagers, were voted the UK's Best Vocal Group in the *NME*. Young England responded by packing out clubs that had gone over to the depraved

Twist like Birmingham's Moat Twistacular and Ilford's Twist at the
Top, which had its own Joey Dee And The Starliters in The Seniors,
who would name their LP after the place.

Mersey Beat's rhetorical question "Has Trad Jazz Died On
Merseyside?"[30] was answered tacitly in the volume of twist
exhibition teams – The King Twisters, Mr Twist And His Twistettes,
ad nauseum – that utilised time where a trad band once might have
done. When the headliners went on, group members like Mel "King
of Twist" Turner of The Bandits and – to the Judies' delight – an
embarrassed Pete Best would be thrust to the front to demonstrate
the dance. Classic rock was elbowed aside for renderings of 'Twist
And Shout' (and just plain 'Shout') by The Isley Brothers, Dee Dee
Sharp's 'Mashed Potato Time' and, from The Orlons, 'Shimmy
Shimmy' and 'The Wah-Watusi'. The subject matter was less directly
to do with mobility, but the beat was essentially the same in such as
The Marvelettes' 'Please Mr Postman', The Contours' 'Do You Love
Me' and 'I'm Gonna Knock On Your Door', sung originally in the
"baby" counter-tenor of Eddie Hodges. The hipper Mersey Beat
bands were also rifling the catalogues of Benny Spellman, Barbara
George and other Americans unbeknownst to the ordinary Scouser
or, indeed, the ordinary anyone else. Ringo Starr swore by Lee
Dorsey, a black soul singer from New Orleans, to whose albums he
would turn as regularly as a monk to the Bible.

The order of the day back at Pwllheli, however, was not Lee
Dorsey or The Orlons but the passing joys of the British hit parade
– The Marcels' mauling of 'Blue Moon', Bruce Channel's 'Hey Baby'
and – when some idiot's girl wanted it – the much-covered 'Sucu
Sucu'. More palatable to The Hurricanes was Ray Charles' 'Hit The
Road, Jack', which was rasped out during Starr Time with Wally
prominent on the skittish, gospel-esque backing responses. As
Saturday was changeover day, the Rock and Calypso Ballroom was
at its most untamed on the preceding night, but during Rory Storm
And The Hurricanes' second Butlins stint it seemed more frenzied,
the laughter shriller, the eyes brighter. Some Fridays, security
officers would have to rescue Rory as he lost tufts of hair to clawing

females while The Hurricanes made their escapes with mere autographs, Richie scribbling, "Best wishes from the sensational Ringo Starr."

4 *"I Had To Join Them As People,*
   As Well As A Drummer"

"RORY STORM BACK SOON!" proclaimed *Mersey Beat*'s front page, and when he was, Bill Harry was one of the first to know. "He was always plugging and plugging," he remembered. "I was in bed in my flat in Mount Street and, about four in the morning, there was this furious banging on the door. All the people in the other flats were hanging out their windows and a cop car came, shining its lights. 'What's going on?' It was Rory with some photos of himself for *Mersey Beat*." Ensuring that his birthdays, too, were public events, Storm seemed to think that everything that happened to him was worth communicating to the whole of Merseyside. Nevertheless, his talent for self-promotion was such that many were convinced that he was always about to soar to the very summit of pop. He could do just that whenever he felt like it. But why should he? He was the greatest already.

If second-billed now to Gerry, The Beatles and other acts that had once supported them, Rory and The Hurricanes made up for long absences in Germany and Pwllheli by packing in as many local engagements as the traffic would allow before they had to vanish again. In a month underscored with run-of-the-mill club dates, there'd be some prestigious presentations like a "Rock And Trad Spectacular" at Southport's tiered Floral Hall, a St Patrick's Night "Rock Gala" at Knotty Ash Village Hall or the "Cavalcade Of Rock And Twist" at the New Brighton Tower, where, wrote schoolgirl diarist Sue Evans, there were "thousands. Danced with four gorgeous Beat Types."[1] When Jerry Lee Lewis was on at the Tower or The Shadows at the Cavern, Mr Showmanship would be noticeably present, if not actually performing, as if to infer that, but for a hit record or two, he was their equal.

Sometimes, Rory would cause upset, as he did by declaring two Hurricane girlfriends as victors of a "Miss Merseybeat competition"[2] that he was judging; but, with work as far away as Italy for the taking, things were looking up again, although not as much as they were for The Beatles, now that Epstein had spruced up both their behaviour and appearance. Nowadays, they'd forsaken Hamburg leathers and *mach schau* for mohair suits and were playing to a fixed routine and not swearing or horsing around on stage half as much. In other words, Brian was reshaping them into what a respectable record-company executive in 1962 presumed a good pop group to be.

The very day before they and Epstein entered into agreement, The Beatles had played to only 18 patrons on a wintry Saturday in a palais within the military borough of Aldershot, way down in Hampshire. This booking had been arranged by Sam Leach, the most adventurous of Merseyside promoters and a great friend of Rory Storm, who, with The Hurricanes, drew via word of mouth over 200 at the same distant venue the following week. Although Leach then turned his back on Aldershot, Storm and his group continued this southern offensive on their own. Largely through Mrs Caldwell's telephone badgering, they even ventured as far east as Norwich. However, such expeditions were sporadic, for, unlike The Beatles, they hadn't the clout to get themselves attached to some big leisure corporation like Mecca or Top Rank.

A feather in their cap, however, was that 1962's Butlin's foray would be at bracing Skegness, the Lincolnshire camp that was the oldest and largest in Sir Billy's network and the setting of the latest Billy Bunter book, in which he'd been pleasingly portrayed. Earlier that year, the group had spent a sunnier spring than most Liverpudlians with their first residency in a club in Marbella where the Spanish would soon debase their culture by permitting the construction of pubs, fish-and-chip shops and further home comforts for British holidaymakers.

To keep Rory Storm And The Hurricanes on the boil back home, the news was leaked to *Mersey Beat* by his mother that Rory had, apparently, saved three – including Ringo – from drowning in the Mediterranean. However, although they'd be welcomed back with the usual warmth, a Rory Storm publicity stunt was now as commonplace as a whist drive. The Swinging Blue Jeans, The Beatles and The Big Three had all had London recording tests, and with *Mersey Beat*'s demand "London, Take A Look Up North"[3] yet unheeded, unless Storm pulled a more palpable stroke than being nabbed by a porter spray-painting "I Love Rory" on a Bootle railway station wall, he and his Hurricanes were going to miss the boat.

From other regions, some groups more electrifying than they were likewise breaking loose of parochial orbits and were even invading Liverpool clubland. The Hellions' Iron Door debut was yet to be, but frequenting it now were Bern Elliott's Fenmen, Sheffield's serpentine Dave Berry And The Cruisers, Gerry Levene And His Avengers from Birmingham (soon to have its own *Midland Beat* gazette), Blackburn's Lionel Morton Quartet and, from Manchester, The Hollies and Freddie And The Dreamers, whose spindly, four-eyed singer would fling off all his garments bar a pair of vivid "short shorts" during a Hollywood Argyles ditty of the same title.

Kent's Sounds Incorporated were constantly on the move around Britain and Europe, more often than not backing Gene Vincent, while The Eagles – after appearing in a B-feature about Bristol youth movements – had snared a weekly showcase (*Meet The Eagles*) on Radio Luxembourg. Shane Fenton And The Fentones, meanwhile, had made a higher quantum jump to a regular spot on the Light Programme's two-hour-long pop show *Saturday Club* and a modest stack of Top-30 hits on Parlophone. Their opposite numbers at Decca were to be Brian Poole And The Tremeloes (who'd been at Butlin's in Ayr in 1961 when Rory Storm's Hurricanes were at Pwllheli).

Certain Hurricanes were disturbed that the fish weren't also biting for them. Obliged too frequently to sign on at Renshaw Hall labour exchange, they may have been piqued by their leader's shameless habit lately of appearing without them for some dates as the *ad hoc* aggregation "Rory Storm And The Wild Ones". Egmond had been the first to slip his cable for a spell in The Seniors, who were about to release another 45 from their Fontana album. *Mersey Beat* gossip had it that Ringo was to join him. Instead, in January 1962, Starr threw in his lot with Tony Sheridan at the Top Ten in Hamburg after Peter Eckhorn (with Sheridan) had flown to Liverpool to be disappointed by the price that Epstein had now put on The Beatles. So that he'd have something to show for his journey, Peter tantalised Starr with £30 a week – huge for the time – and use of a flat and car.

The Top Ten would soon be losing trade irrecoverably to the Star-Club. The newer and more extensive venue's owner, Manfred Weissleder, had already out-bid Eckhorn for Horst Fascher as manager, a checkmating augmented when this compound Hercules secured The Beatles – and Sheridan – to open the place in April 1962. In anticipation (and to Eckhorn's annoyance), Sheridan named his group "The Star Combo" as he worked his notice period in tandem with Roy Young, a Little Richard type from Oxford. With a pedigree stretching back to *Six-Five Special*, Young would also desert to the Star-Club.

Ringo, however, would not be drumming before its stage backdrop of skyscrapers when Sheridan and The Beatles supported and proudly socialised with visiting US idols – including Ray Charles, Little Richard,[4] Pat Boone and the ubiquitous Vincent – who'd plug gaps in their European itineraries with nights at the Star-Club and, round-robin style, at Weissleder-controlled engagements in Stuttgart and Hanover. While Ray Charles might have thought, "That boy [Sheridan] sings with a lot of soul,"[5] Ringo had become disenchanted with Tony, who, on closer acquaintance, was given to provoking arguments, sulking and impetuously launching into songs not in the *modus operandi*, unhelpfully leaving the panicking Combo to busk behind him. Like, what key's this one in, man? Like, Z minus, man.

With more than his fill of both Hamburg and "the Teacher", Starr had gone home to his mother and Rory Storm And The Hurricanes, who had spent an expensive few months with Blackpool drummer Derek Fell whenever he wasn't required by his usual group,

The Executives. It was accepted without question that Ringo, like the equally perfidious Wally, would return to the fold. Although neither could be trusted not to stray again, it was outwardly as if nothing had happened, as they got into trim for Skegness in the Majestic, the Iron Door and other too-familiar haunts, as well as a short series of mess dances for US airmen in France. If Rory could square it with Elsie and Harry, Richie promised to see out the contract with – so Rory had assured *Mersey Beat* – "the only group to make the grade at Butlin's for three years in succession".[6]

While Starr had been away, blasé Storm had developed into even more of a ritualist. If he wasn't to be an Elvis in the wider world, he'd limit himself to remaining adored as one locally. He was now captain of the recently formed Mersey Beat soccer eleven, for whom he'd later score a hat-trick in a charity match against Liverpool FC. Moreover, he still ran for Pembroke Harriers and fronted both The Hurricanes and The Wild Ones. "He never wanted to make it nationally," his sister would insist after he didn't, "as he was happy being King of Liverpool."[7]

There didn't appear to be much future in music anyway. Fontana's patience with The Seniors was snapping, as neither of their singles had had enough airplay to near the charts, and The Big Three and the other latest contenders had got nowhere with their auditions. The studio audience on ITV's new show *Thank Your Lucky Stars* still screamed indiscriminately at male pop idols but, as much pin-ups as they were nowadays, TV and film actors like Ed Byrnes (jive-talking "Kookie" of *77 Sunset Strip*), Sean Connery (in his first Bond movie) and even Peter Sellers (star, with Leo McKern, of 1962's *The Mouse That Roared*, a topical Cold War satire).

It had occurred to Starr that he stood more chance of a livelihood as a musician than any two-a-penny singer. Even further from the core of UK pop than Liverpool, Derek Fell had nevertheless once been a temporary Shadow. From Burnley, Bobby Elliott was now in Shane Fenton's Fentones, having distinguished himself in a short-list that included a lively London sticksman named Keith Moon. Other of Starr's percussive contemporaries had roamed beyond rock 'n' roll. Having taught himself to read the relevant dots, Jimmy Nicol had been in the ranks of David Ede And The Rabin Rock, whose upbeat muzak was an apt prelude to his next post, under the baton of light-orchestra conductor Cyril Stapleton. Nicol was also hired for a session with Cleo Laine, who was as much a *grande dame* of jazz as presenter Noele Gordon on ITV's *Lunch Box*, lightest of light entertainments, in whose studio band Pete York – beetle browed and gifted – drummed for the money he could not yet earn in various Midlands pop and jazz outfits.

While these players opted for grey facelessness outside the main spotlight, Ringo Starr pondered. As it had been just before Pwllheli in 1960, he'd reached something of a crossroads. Even in Germany, he'd tried to telephone Maureen daily, and when at home he was now foregoing carousing away many of his nights off in the Liverpool clubs, preferring instead to stay in spinning records with Mo or in front of the television. From his armchair in Admiral Grove, he became a lifelong watcher of *Coronation Street*, a soap opera as ingrained with northern working-class realism as the BBC's police series *Z-Cars*, also home produced but of grittier substance than gorblimey *Dixon Of Dock Green*.

As far as censorship would allow, these programmes emphasised what might be in store for Richard Starkey, should he choose to pack in drumming. After his grandfather's funeral in 1961, "It took a long time to get over it," sighed he. "We'd always been close, and I worshipped him."[8] Still mournful a year later, Richie would wonder whether 22 wasn't a good age to settle down. The old man had twisted the plain gold wedding ring from his hand when his grandson had been engaged to Geraldine, and "I always reckoned I'd wear it when I got married".[9]

As Harry and Elsie often reminded him, it wasn't too late for him to resume his Hunt's apprenticeship. While taking exasperated stock, he contemplated wedding Maureen and uprooting altogether for the less humdrum USA, even going as far as writing to the Chamber of Commerce in Houston, simply because it was at the heartland of the Wild West – although Texans were more likely to be in oil than bronco-bustin', these days – and was the nearest city to Centerville, birthplace of Lightnin' Hopkins, a post-war blues artist to whose grippingly personal style an enthralled Ringo had been introduced by Tony Sheridan one Hamburg afternoon around a record player.

Houston's reply was quite heartening, but the thickness and aggressive intimacy of the application forms for emigration were too offputting. Hunt's seemed to be beckoning still; but, while removed from parental pressures about a proper job, Richie in Skegness received a letter from Kingsize Taylor offering £20 per week for him to fill the drum stool soon to be vacated by Billy Hatton's friend Dave Lovelady, who had bowed to his parents' wishes that he complete his degree course in architecture. As Taylor was a bandleader of steadier stamp than Sheridan or Storm, Ringo gave tentative assent to be a Domino as soon as he was free. The personnel of The Dominoes and Hurricanes had overlapped already in the past year when the former's Bobby Thompson had stood in during Egmond's furlough with The Seniors, and so, as one professional to another, Storm was dispassionate about Richie's decision, issuing an open invitation for the drummer to re-enlist one day. Neither regarded this eventuality as improbable.

Able to suspend the question of Starr's replacement until they were back in Liverpool, Rory and The Hurricanes carried on with a season that was not passing without incident. The Wars of the Roses had not, apparently, been forgotten as two gangs of young millworkers from, respectively, Wigan and Wakefield fought each other on every possible pretext for the entire week that they were there. Several other Friday evenings were also enlivened with punch-ups. Storm was once forced to pick his way across a railway line to throw off some hard-cases riled by his narcissistic endeavours on the bandstand. On the horns of a similar dilemma, Johnny Guitar elected to take his medicine and be swung in full stage gear into a swimming pool in which an Indian elephant had lately expired and bobbed about in the chlorinated water for three days until a crane could be found to shift it. For a contravention of the Butlin edict about who could and could not enter staff chalets, Guitar and Starr were banished beyond the camp walls, except when they were needed in the ballroom, where every other request from the dance floor seemed to be for Pat Boone's 'Speedy Gonzales'.

Last but far from least, rumour has it – right or wrong – that Starr, with over a fortnight to go, decamped midweek, still owing Johnny his half of the rent for the shabby caravan they'd leased for the period of their expulsion. Possibly to thumb his nose at the authority that had willed this disgrace, Ringo was off to join The Beatles almost immediately after Lennon and McCartney had driven through a windy night to bang on the trailer's door at 10am on an August Tuesday, offering a fiver more per week than Kingsize Taylor. They'd told Brian Epstein to fire Pete Best, who "didn't even have the opportunity of discussing it with the rest of the group".[10]

Now that The Beatles had gained that elusive recording deal – with Parlophone – Pete had been of no more use to them. They'd been glad enough to recruit him in 1960, however, when Allan Williams wouldn't have let them go to Hamburg without a drummer. Back on Merseyside, Best's volcanic mother, Mona, had served them as Violet Caldwell did her boy's group. As Stormsville was the hub of The Hurricanes' operation, so the Bests' 15-room home in Hayman's Green was that of The Beatles. "She was a strong, dominant woman," Bill Harry described Mrs Best, who did much of her shy son's talking for him. "I think she was responsible for getting them their first radio gig. She was why Neil Aspinall was brought in. He was Pete's best friend and he lived with the Bests." Even after they'd clicked with Epstein, she still saw herself as patroness of the group, who, according to Bill, "didn't want her interference".

Although the imperceptible isolation of her son from the others had started during that first trip to Hamburg, Mona was victim of a more intensifying character assassinations by Harrison, McCartney and Lennon than Pete over venomous pints in a pub's murkiest corner. Stuart Sutcliffe had had no hand in this, as he'd left the group in 1961 to recommence his art studies in Hamburg.[11] The Beatles had not replaced him, favouring the simpler expedient of transferring Paul to bass.

Horst Fascher would swear that McCartney was what he called the "sunny boy"[12] of the group, although, as far as Southport promoter Bill Appleby was concerned, "Pete was definitely the big attraction and did much to establish their popularity during their early career."[13] A lot of what Best did was passive, because girls melted just beholding his athlete's physique and sultry Cliff Richard handsomeness. However, unlike Paul, he was genuinely bemused at the interest of the Judies, whose cow-eyed efforts to grab his on-stage attention had teased his dark eyes from the drums. They'd shiver with pleasure at his rare bashful grins and squeal with ecstasy when he took an even rarer lead vocal on 'Boys', Carl Perkins' 'Matchbox' and, especially, Presley's 'Wild In The Country', which exuded the breathy sentience of a man who has been sprinting.

Pete wasn't allowed to sing when The Beatles made that first radio broadcast in Manchester, but when they were mobbed afterwards he was unjustly berated by Paul's father for inadvertently stealing the limelight. Mr McCartney[14] might have preferred the group to ditch Lennon, who had the cheek to call him by his Christian name and who – as he'd once warned his son – was the proverbial bad influence. However, he acknowledged that Paul and John were the quartet's creative muscle and, like them – and young George, swimming with the tide – took exception to Best always being singled out for a front-page photo in *Mersey Beat* and on posters ("Hear Pete Best Sing Tonight!"), and when Bob Wooler whipped up an encore with "Let's hear it again for John, Paul, George—" pause "—and *Pete!*" the volume of screams rising to its loudest.

This partiality might not have mattered so much, had the softly spoken drummer not been such a being apart from the other three, a Tony Curtis among the *pilzenkopfs*, a non-partaker of benzedrine and Preludin and a swain whose intentions towards his Marks & Spencer's girlfriend were honourable. Only on the periphery of their private jokes and folklore, and as reliable as he was mature, there was no denying that, to his fellow Beatles, Best was a bit...well, you know. Anyway, he had to go.

The final nail in his coffin was a try-out for Parlophone in one of

EMI's studios down at Abbey Road in St John's Wood. As rock 'n' rollers in concert tended to accelerate and slow down *en bloc* to inconsistencies of tempo caused by the mood of the hour, it wasn't uncommon for drumming on record to be ghosted by someone more technically accomplished than a given act's regular player. In the early 1960s, among those earning Musicians' Union-regulated tea-breaks in this fashion were ex-Kenny Ball Jazzman Ron Bowden, Jimmy Nicol, Bobbie Graham, Clem Cattini of The Tornados and 32-year-old Andy White from The Vic Lewis Orchestra, whom George Martin would bring in – with no slight on Pete Best (and, next, the untried Ringo) intended – on the session for 'Love Me Do', written by McCartney and Lennon as The Beatles' debut single.

Some would recall the Lord of Parlophone denying that there was anything fundamentally wrong with Pete as a drummer and then contradicting himself a couple of years later. Locally, Best was rated highly by no less than Johnny Hutchinson, who had been advocated by Epstein as Pete's successor during the horrid conspiracy. Precursors of the late-1960s power trio, Johnny's Big Three was the most forceful outfit on Merseyside, a characteristic reflected in its members' hard-living behaviour off stage, crystallised by one of them downing a whole month's allocation of free beer at the Star-Club in the space of an evening. It was the likelihood of conflict involving fisticuffs with John Lennon that precluded Hutchinson from being the most serious candidate for the new Beatle. The real thing, Johnny wouldn't have tolerated a pretend tough guy like Lennon poking ruthless fun at him to anywhere like the degree that had driven the gentler Tommy Moore from the group in 1960.

Besides, as he'd already resisted inducements to join Johnny Kidd And The Pirates, why should Hutchinson give up The Big Three for The Beatles? Nonetheless, he consented to dep for Pete Best, who, for some reason, wouldn't fulfil two Beatles bookings that couldn't be postponed in the interregnum between his sacking and Ringo's arrival for two hours' rehearsal before his debut as an official Beatle in front of an audience of 500 at a Horticultural Society dance in Birkenhead on Saturday 18 August 1962.

Determined upon the utmost correctness, Epstein had telephoned Stormsville to inform Violet that The Beatles were prepared to wait for Ringo to finish at Skegness. Nevertheless, when not in possession of this intelligence, Rory had fulminated against The Beatles for so inconveniently purloining his drummer. However, he turned a thoughtful steering wheel while dashing back to Liverpool to find a substitute. Collecting his mother, he hastened to Hayman's Green to present sympathies to the Bests. Did Pete want to be a Hurricane? He could start right now. No, said Mona, he was too depressed. Facing the music back at Butlin's, The Hurricanes in desperation had taken on Anthony Ashdown, an actor[15] who fancied a go on the drums for one dreadful week before Norman McGarry from Johnny Sandon And The Searchers – another unit in disarray – took over. Time was when drummers were falling over themselves to work with Rory Storm.

Matters mended to an extent when The Hurricanes poached The Memphis Three's 16-year-old Gibson Kemp, who, it was hoped, would grow into the bulkier Starr's stage suit. Brian Epstein had advised Ringo that, under the circumstances, it might not be politic to press Storm or Kemp for the £15 it had cost him, as things were ticklish enough as it was. The horticultural show had been the quiet before the storm. At the Cavern on the following evening, there'd been a near riot when The Beatles had entered with their new member, with Harrison, his main champion, being punched in the face. Flanked by bodyguards, Brian ignored bawled abuse and – like Ringo – several poison pen letters from incensed Best devotees.

Later, the tyres of Epstein's brand-new Ford Zodiac were let down as further proof that, as a self-effacing Starr lamented, "they loved Pete. Why get an ugly-looking cat when you can get a good-looking one?"[16] To be fair, Ringo had shaved off his scrappy beard and, on Brian's recommendation, had had his hair resculpted at Horne Brothers to a heavy fringe that, after a decade of quiffing, wouldn't cascade naturally into a Beatle cut for nearly a year. Neil Aspinall dropped off the result at Admiral Grove, where Elsie's surprise at her son's new look was parried with, "It's no different change, really," registered by Aspinall as the first Beatle Ringoism. His mother might have liked his neater, shorter style, but when a photo of Richie was printed in *Mersey Beat* it took a while for readers to become accustomed to this changeling in The Beatles, a frog where there'd been a prince. His supplanting of Best had been represented in its pages as the amicable if sudden consequence of scarcely more than a mild disagreement between the parties, but the hostility at the Cavern demonstrated that the truth was known in the street.

Pete would remain a Beatle morally to some who heard him drum with the group, but most fans – if fickle in affections towards its individuals – found it in them to maintain overall loyalty. "It will seem difficult for a few weeks," admitted Harrison, "but I think that the majority will soon be taking Ringo for granted."[17] After an uncomfortable few minutes when the set opened at the Cavern – especially when George, with a black eye, publicly welcomed Ringo – the four were cheered by the seething crowd. Other than turn from The Beatles altogether, there was nothing for it but to accept the new situation, and by November onlookers were yelling to the now-unchallenged front line to let the underdog behind them sing a number. It was, calculated *Mersey Beat*, his "wonderfully shy personality which appeals to the fans".[13] In short, he was a Pete Best without good looks, a Beatle for girls to love more as a brother than a demon lover.

Musically, Ringo's coming made no pronounced difference. An up-and-coming Bootle vocalist, Billy Kramer didn't "think The Beatles were any better with Ringo Starr. I never doubted his ability as a drummer, but I thought they were a lot more raw and raucous with Pete."[18] Often inclined to close his eyes while playing, Ringo was hardly less reticent than Best on stage. Subordinate to even George – himself very much the junior partner – in the group's power structure, he'd been only too glad to take a back seat during the Pete Best furore. So began the typecasting of him as the one who'd "play it smoggo. I don't mind talking or smiling. It's just that I don't do it very much. I haven't got a smiling face or a talking mouth."[19]

When history was rewritten in the first authorised Beatles biography,[20] Ringo became not merely a hired hand but the chosen one, the *beau ideal*, but in 1962 there was nothing to suggest he wasn't as expendable as Pete had proved to be. The trickiest hurdle during Best's removal had been retaining the services (and the van) of Aspinall, who'd been disgusted by the group's underhandedness. After much heart-searching, he stayed on as their road manager while still lodging for a time at the Bests', with whom he would remain in regular and affectionate contact.[21] Initially, he was civil but not over-friendly towards Ringo, who was not yet one of the Beatle clan, as shown by his non-attendance on the Saturday after he joined at Lennon's dutiful wedding to a pregnant Cynthia Powell.

Ringo didn't belong then any more than Jimmy Nicol – another chosen Beatle – would years later, when "the boys were very kind but I felt like an intruder. You just can't get into a group like that. They have their own atmosphere, their own sense of humour. It's a little clique and outsiders just can't break in."[22] Just a satellite of their inward-looking firmament, Starr would draw on a cigarette and nod in agreement with whomever had spoken last as, not purposefully snubbing him, group and road manager spoke of parties he hadn't attended, venues he'd never played, people he didn't know. "It was like joining a new class at school," he'd deduce, "where everybody knew everybody but me."[23] He was also the oldest Beatle and the only one without a splash of the Irish blood that tinged the rest with variable qualities of leprechaun impishness. Neither was it practical for him – even if he'd been up to it – to add his voice to their three-part vocal harmony, which, perfected over hundreds of hours on stage, "seemed to fall into place quite naturally".[24]

While striving not to put his foot in it with some inanity, Ringo had ample opportunity to log the characteristics of each longer-serving Beatle. He felt most at ease with the selectively amiable Harrison, who, although a better guitarist than either, had been made to feel intellectually as well as chronologically inferior to the other two, whose songwriting alliance was a fount of emotional confusion for him. Unable to penetrate McCartney and Lennon's caste within a caste, George hero-worshipped the heedless John, to whom he was "like a bloody kid, hanging around all the time",[25] while George's greater familiarity with Paul since their Liverpool Institute schooldays had provoked in him an attitude similar to that of a youngest child viewing a middle sibling as an insurmountable barrier to prolonged intimacy with an admired elder brother.

To a lesser extent, Ringo would also be caught up in Harrison's wonderment at Lennon, who was a pretty raw guitarist but a driving rock 'n' roll vocalist with instinctive – if indelicate – crowd control when he brutalised himself to give "the impression of being so hard",[26] as Bob Wooler scoffed. This was at odds with his rather strait-laced, middle-class upbringing in Woolton, the village-like suburb that was more Lancashire than Liverpool. At art college, he'd been a lecture-disrupting wit, made more provocative by an illusion of perpetual mockery in the amblyopic eyes that he was too vain to protect with spectacles. While a fair if messy cartoonist, he was also a scribbler of surreal stories and nonsense verse, which Starr, in his earliest sentences to the national music press, described as "the weirdest you ever saw, but it stops him going mental".[27] Ringo also giggled politely when John outlined his invention of the group's name: "We thought of crawly things and then added the beat."[27]

However, for Johnny Hutchinson, the crawliest thing in The Beatles was McCartney, whom he vilified as "a grade-A creep",[7] while with more diplomacy Ringo would judge Paul "pleasantly insincere".[28] He had, however, a certain right to be, as he, of all The Beatles, was blessed with both the most innate musical talent and a moon-faced resemblance to Elvis. A most heterosexual young man, McCartney also got away with more romantic conquests than most, which might have led green-eyed monsters to whisper to his detractors. Those within the group would cite Paul as the most frequent originator of its intrigues and discords, but this had been mitigated by his silver-tongued willingness to picket wary landlords and entertainments secretaries on The Beatles' behalf.

Paul was the most prolific in his and John's liaison, of which 'Love Me Do' was but the tip of the iceberg. Of course, Liverpool pop composers were not unprecedented; Russ Hamilton had been one, and Mersey Beat had brought with it many more, some with the confidence to submit items to other artists, as Stuart Slater of The Mojos did to Faron's Flamingos and Lee Curtis did to Russ Conway, albeit in vain. None, however, was as formidably commercial as Lennon and McCartney were to be by 1963. A favourite of Starr's, their vibrant 'I Saw Her Standing There' was superior to many of The Beatles' non-originals. As well as inserting more of their own material into the stage set, John and Paul had started canvassing others to perform songs that they felt were unsuitable for the group. Beryl Marsden, for example, was promised 'Love Of The Loved', until Epstein insisted that it go to Cilla White, who'd be Cilla Black when she and other Liverpool performers – including Gerry And The Pacemakers, The Big Three, Billy J Kramer, and Billy Hatton's Fourmost – were signed to Brian Epstein's NEMS Enterprises management company

However profitable these acts became, The Beatles would forever be Brian's administrative and personal priority They hadn't been in complete agreement about his fastidious transformation of them into smoother pop entertainers, but outbreaks of mutiny had lessened after he'd set the ball rolling for George Martin to contract them for two singles with an option on further releases if these gave cause for hope.

As Martin's humble beginnings in a north London back street were not detectable in his refined elocution, so only the most discerning could spot the Scouser in Brian Epstein. Worlds from the Dingle, his cradle days had passed in Childwall, a district even more select than Woolton. When malevolent Nazi shadows fell over Liverpool, the Epsteins fled to rented accommodation in Southport until 1944. Out of short trousers by then, Brian was to endure the rigours of several expensive boarding schools at which undercurrents of anti-Semitism and homo-eroticism would help to make him what he was. So, too, would a curtailed term of national service and a more constructive year at the Royal Academy of Dramatic Art.

In 1961, as far as he was able, Brian was dragging the family firm into the 20th century in his capacity as a director and, more specifically, as sales manager of the city-centre branch of NEMS' record department. What must have been a potent combination of vocational boredom and frustrated artistic ambition took the 27-year-old – in his sober attire and smart haircut – to the suffocating fug of the Cavern and a desire to steer The Beatles out of it to success. Although Ringo wasn't a full Beatle yet, Brian still took it upon himself to call on Elsie and Harry – as he'd done on the guardians of John, Paul, George and Pete – to allay any reservations that they might harbour about their son's continued showbusiness career. The Graves were still wringing their hands about Hunt's but were reassured that The Beatles had at their helm such an orderly, nicely spoken gent like Mr Epstein, who was charming, open-handed, straight as a die and devoid of all the complicity of a Violet Caldwell or Peter Eckhorn.

His feelings about the new Beatle might have been as lukewarm as Neil's, but Brian had assimilated that Starr was unlikely to rock the boat for Lennon and McCartney, who began treating him as a mascot, "a faithful spaniel"[20] and sometimes a metaphorical whipping boy. "If anything goes wrong," sniggered Lennon, "we can all blame Ringo. That's what he's here for."[29] Acquiescent and exploitable, he didn't at first express indignation at John's sarcasm and Paul's condescension. More than just studiously avoiding confrontation, he attempted to ingratiate himself with them beyond simply being punctual and learning their songs.

Less endearing a trait was his nervous habit of trying to recapture the sensation of something that had raised a laugh but didn't bear him periodically repeating it. Once, to amuse his new colleagues, he sacrificed one fan's good opinion of him by churlishly dishevelling her carefully arranged blonde beehive, and, during a fierce argument with Lennon, McCartney and Epstein versus Sam Leach over payment prior to one local booking, the waiting customers nudged each other and tittered as Ringo strutted around the hall with a banner inexpertly daubed with the legend "No Pay No Play".

Happily for The Beatles, he would not be as crass when talking to those scattered newspapers who began to take an interest in them after 'Love Me Do' was released in October 1962. Nevertheless, he had a tendency to protest too much, telling interviewers the exact number of fun-packed weeks that he'd been in the group, impressing on them that he was as "offbeat"[27] as any other Beatle and – in as late as 1964 – stressing how lucky he was "to be on their wavelength. I had to be, or I wouldn't have lasted. I had to join them as people as well as a drummer."[23]

When their second 45 crept past the 'Love Me Do' high of Number 17 in the hit parade, many fears that he'd go the way of Pete Best were dispelled and he'd hear himself uttering crisp rejoinders to Paul and John's jibes. Less self-consciously, too, he'd enter into the spirit of the little comedy playlets that provided diversion during squalid time-killing in van and bandroom. By then, The Beatles had introduced their own one-song "Starr Time", which would be written-up as "one of the most popular spots of the evening".[30] For him to take on Best's sensual] 'Wild In The Country' might have invited ridicule, but 'Boys', with its joyous verve, and – later – jaunty 'Honey Don't', would more than do. Although it was never implemented, there was debate about a Starr dancing display. "But only for certain audiences," mused McCartney "We all mess around on drums a bit, and we could take his place now and then."[18]

Ringo had still been a Hurricane when viewers' letters had goaded the producer of ITV's topical *Know The North* to check out The Beatles at a Southport booking. On that crucial night, morbid inquisitiveness found their drummer glooming under the Cavern's damp arches when the group with Ringo faced cumbersome television cameras for the first time. On 22 August 1962, these were lugged into the club to film The Beatles performing in uniform waistcoats. His head exploding, Pete Best made for the exit after some unfortunate remarks from a jubilant Mr McCartney.

Exacerbating Pete's misery was that "somehow I and a lot of other people up in Liverpool had a feeling they would make it – nationally, at any rate".[31] He and his mother had made it a vain point of honour to get a single out with him on it before 'Love Me Do'. He'd turned up his nose when a chance to become a

Merseybeat was put his way by Epstein. Instead, room was found for him in Lee Curtis and The All-Stars.

Pete's tenure as an All-Star began during a Monday-to-Friday residency at Birkenhead's Majestic. A solo singer in an age of groups, Lee Curtis aspired towards big-voiced ballads which, if recorded, would rely more on massed strings than electric guitars, but for now he pandered to assumed audience desires with many of the same songs that Pete had known with The Beatles. *Mersey Beat* would note "the extent to which the magnetic personality of Pete Best appeals to girls",[12] but in his heart Pete "was continuing in a group not as popular, doing the same old gigs I'd done up to August with The Beatles".[32]

Before The Beatles transcended Liverpool's scruffier jive hives, there were excruciating backstage moments that lasted forever when they and Pete affected not to recognise each other, although John supposedly once murmured a few guilt-ridden platitudes. Having shuffled past, each faction, weak with relief, would unstiffen and empty his lungs with a whoosh. Such awkward junctures were not unique on Merseyside now, as "the friendliness and comradeship between different groups seems to have lessened," observed Johnny Sandon, now parted from The Searchers. "Groups don't help each other now. If one group suffers misfortune, others are glad."[33] At the root of many other such schisms was Brian Epstein, who would divide outfits by granting, say, only the vocalist a fixed wage – as he did to Billy J Kramer and The Coasters – and reproach The Beatles for obligingly backing a vocal-harmony act called The Chants.

Conspicuous losers in this serious game of musical chairs were Rory Storm And The Hurricanes, who would just scrape into the 20 groups listed in *Mersey Beat*'s 1962 poll, a true comedown. Nevertheless, Storm had been attractive in his phlegmatic – and, possibly, tactical – forgiveness, wishing The Beatles and Starr all the best when 'Love Me Do' began its yo-yo progression up the charts. In turn, The Beatles hadn't let him down when they were among the five bands at the Tower to fuss over him on his September birthday. Brian – and Ringo – were to make more pragmatic amends later.

On a first-come-first-served basis, Epstein would not attend to the recording careers of his other charges until The Beatles had got off the ground with theirs. He ensured that *Mersey Beat* knew that they'd been genuinely and importantly airborne when they went from Speke Airport to London to tape their single almost three weeks before the Rory Storm bash.

At 7pm that day, Andy White arrived at Abbey Road for the three hours allocated to this Liverpool shower. Ringo – who hadn't been told – was already timorously aware that he lacked even the other three's lean recording experience. All that he'd notched up was the Akustik lark with Wally and 40 ragged minutes with Rory, The Hurricanes and a reel-to-reel machine in an otherwise-deserted Cavern. As White assembled his kit, Starr bit back on dismay as Martin explained, "I simply didn't know what [Ringo] was like and I wasn't prepared to take any risks."[34]

While White was then married to one of the hit-making Vernons Girls,[35] Martin was of greater celebrity to The Beatles, who were less round-eyed at his puffing oboe at Sadler's Wells than him producing the disparate likes of The Goons and Shane Fenton (whom the group had met socially, as he was currently spooning with Iris Caldwell). Martin would remain awesome for several more years, but never more so than at that first session, when he imposed drastic alterations on their rehearsed arrangement of 'Love Me Do', made them record a "professional" song ('How Do You Do It') that he'd picked from a publisher's office to be the follow-up and, finally, required them to return the following week, as he wasn't much pleased with the evening's work.

Martin was actually one of the least dogmatic of British producers, and at some point during the recording of 'Love Me Do' he waved in the dejected Ringo, seated quietly beside a white-coated console engineer, not to the drums yet but to a tambourine to be struck every third beat in the bar. He was to thump it with a maraca on the B-side of 'PS I Love You', but on several later takes of 'Love Me Do' it was he and not White behind the kit as the team edged nearer a satisfactory result.[36]

Regarding him as a mediocre musician at most, George Martin didn't appreciate that Starr was in a different rather than lower bracket to someone like White, and that, given a choice, Ringo's fills were "like a giant walking. My breaks are always slow, usually half the speed of the track."[37] One who understood was Clem Cattini, who "always admired Ringo. So many people knock his ability, but he was always ideal for The Beatles' sound."[38] As Starr had acquitted himself adequately enough on the 'Love Me Do' outing, he was trusted to execute the "intricate drumming effects"[13] that were in Martin's recipe for John and Paul's 'Please Please Me', that had surfaced as a better bet for the next single than 'How Do You Do It'.

On consulting with the high command of Lennon, McCartney and Epstein, Martin also decided that, from his selection of their Cavern crowd-pleasers, George and Ringo could be allowed one lead vocal each on the hasty album EMI wanted from The Beatles to cash in on 'Please Please Me', that topped the charts in March 1963. The drummer had "a voice I was uncertain about",[39] but, beefed up with double-tracking and hyperactive reverberation, 'Boys' – if not the most euphonious – was, along with Paul's 'I Saw Her Standing There' and John's 'Twist And Shout', the LP's most exultant encapsulation of The Beatles' early glory, not least because of its producer capturing it in one take. "Otherwise you'd never get the impact."[39]

Parlophone now had "a male Shirelles",[40] reckoned Martin, and a sure sign that The Beatles were to go places – and even match The Tornados and the precious Shadows – was sour grapes from such as Joe Meek, for whom The Beatles had "nothing new about their sound. Cliff Bennett And The Rebel Rousers have been doing the same thing for a year now, and so has Joe Brown."[41] Meek had been on the crest of a wave himself in 1962, when his production of The Tornados' 'Telstar' had been Number One in the States, where no UK pop act had ever made sustained headway nor was likely to again, if you agreed with *The New York Times'* dismissal of Billy Fury in *Play It Cool* as an Elvis duplicate without "the stamp of an original personality".[42] In the same 1963 film, Helen Shapiro – voted the *NME's* most popular British female singer – attained the dubious accolade of peaking at Number 100 in US music trade paper *Billboard*'s "Hot 100", the highest US entry for any of her singles.

Technically, Helen had been the main attraction when The Beatles had embarked on their first national tour that spring, but audience reaction was more subdued than she'd come to expect. Possibly, this was kindled by dispiriting press articles which discussed whether she was "A Has-Been At Sixteen"[13] but The Beatles – buoyed by their 'Please Please Me' victory – were, she noticed, evoking more than passive attention from boys as well as girls for their unpolished enthusiasm and self-created musical resolution. Quite a few felt the urge to scream, probably because they were as sick as the group were of the polished patter and quasi-Shadows legwork that had been the norm since 1960.

A-twitter with excitement and childish swagger at their abrupt fame, the Liverpudlians were full of themselves on the tour coach, their conduct stopping just short of open insolence towards certain others in the cast. Not yet sure of where he stood in all of this, Ringo became – so fellow travelling minstrel Barry Booth asserted – "a law unto himself", more placid, even-tempered and in need of less hand-holding than the other Beatles. He was also readier than they to blend into the jovial, laugh-a-minute ambience of the bus as it hurtled around trunk-road England.

If not household names yet, The Beatles were now recognised in wayside cafes and cornershops and were to close the first half on the next tour, for which only Americans could possibly headline over them. Negotiations for The Four Seasons and Duane Eddy began, but two of their more perishable compatriots – Chris Montez and Tommy Roe – were sent instead and the bill underwent a merciless readjustment as crowd response dictated that The Beatles play last.

During this jaunt, one local journal mentioned Starr's "tremendous hypnotic beat".[44] Although he'd had still to be directed via nods, foot-stamping and eye contact through their more ambitious numbers, he'd got the hang of The Beatles' rhythmic *oeuvre* and had, related Cliff Bennett, "fully settled in" by the end of a reluctant Yuletide season at the Star-Club. (Ironically, the tune that

German milkmen were whistling in 1962 was a hit song from the Berlin musical *Homesick For St Pauli*.) As resentful as the others that their UK chart campaign had been disturbed, and about being away from Admiral Grove on Christmas Day, Ringo was sometimes discovered missing seconds before showtime, excusing himself with a joke when the frightening Horst Fascher, jabbing at his watch, came upon him pedantically "collecting sticks or changing cymbals, so I would tell him that, if he wasn't on stage in time, I would kick him up the arse".[11] Nevertheless, this, The Beatles' most onerous obligation to Hamburg, had hidden blessings. "By the time they came back with Ringo," even Colin Manley had to admit, "they were different altogether. They had matured, found their timing, and you could see they were going to happen in a big way."[38]

5 "I'm Happy To Go On And Play Drums – And That's All"

The rest, as they often say, is history. 1963 alone brought the conquest of Britain via hit-parade Mersey Beat, Beatlemania and *The Royal Variety Show*. The year ended with seven Beatles records in the singles Top 50 – including three on more expensive extended plays (EPs) – and the top two positions in the LP list. Lennon and McCartney had tossed spare chartbusting songs to Cilla, Billy J and The Fourmost, and their bank balance had been swelled further by the first shoal of unsolicited cover versions. Their music was also to be used for a West End beat ballet *Mods And Rockers*, and although Ringo would confess that "we didn't understand what all this stuff about Aeolian cadences was about"[1] a prosy *Sunday Times* article lauded John and Paul as "the outstanding composers of 1963".[2]

To balance circulation, The Beatles had been superimposed upon the grid of a Fleet Street that had been relentlessly overrun with "serious" news of the Profumo scandal, the nuclear test ban treaty, the Great Train Robbery, racial unrest in Alabama and, to cap it all, the West Indies beating us at cricket. Between radio reports of England's shame and East/West-black/white tension came the sinless strains of 'From Me To You', The Beatles' third 45. While they gestured with cigarettes during TV interviews and let loose the odd mild expletive like "crap" and even "bloody", "they were regarded as clean-living lads during the time they were getting established", confirmed Harold Wilson, leader of Her Majesty's opposition, "whatever may have gone on later"[3] – or before.

Innocent scamps like Just William's Outlaws, The Beatles' much-copied mid-air leap on their 'Twist And Shout' EP sleeve was the epitome of antidotal Mersey Beat, that shook theatres with healthy, good-humoured screams. There were also the asinine poems written and sent by subscribers to glossy monthly magazines dedicated solely to both The Beatles and, briefly, Gerry And The Pacemakers, then tussling with each other for chart supremacy. A Pacemakers show in Bristol was halted by Authority after repeated warnings about rushing the stage, while queues formed outside a Lincoln box office a week before Beatles tickets went on sale. A girl crushed her spectacles in her fist because her view of The Searchers was blocked, while her brother debated whether or not he liked The Merseybeats, and deb of the year Judy Huxtable was snapped clamouring for Ringo Starr's autograph like everybody else.

Scouse was now the most romantic dialect in the country, and the bigger chain stores were stocking Beatle wallpaper, 22-carat Beatle bracelets and Fab Four powder compacts. Woolworth's had moptop wigs and Sayer's had guitar-shaped cakes, "the cake for SWINGING parties". The jacket of their collarless Cardin stage suits was "the Liverpool Look for you to knit for the man in your life" as a cardigan, its pattern obtainable via an order form in *Fabulous* magazine. Learning that the manufacturers of NEMS-sanctioned Beatle boots could barely cope with demand, an enterprising Sussex company marketed "Ringo, the new Beat Boot", which also boasted elastic gusset sides and rounded toes. Less prosperously opportunist were the makers of Applejack smocks – after a Solihull sextet whose hits included Lennon and McCartney's 'Like Dreamers Do' – and shirts designed by the drummer/manager of Tottenham's Dave Clark Five immediately after their 'Glad All Over' dislodged The Beatles from a long reign at Number One in January 1964.

Girls getting used to mini-skirts would trim their newly cut fringes with nail clippers to "identify with these characters as either other girls or as sexual neuters",[4] so A Psychiatrist had it. Boys would be suspended from school for also grooming their locks to a style and length previously associated with effeminacy and crazed intellectuals – although, as Ringo pointed out, "If you took at early pictures of ourselves with long hair, we had nothing, [but] everyone – especially in America, where it was Crewcut City – they all said, 'These long-haired creeps.'"[5] After 'From Me To You' became their Top Ten debut in Australia in 1963, a prim Sydney headmistress barred not only the wearing of *pilzenkopf*s but also the carrying of Beatles pictures in satchels and membership of their fan club.

Further antagonism to the group was expressed by a Tory MP bleating that "we must offer teenagers something better".[6] He did not say what, but causing more comment in the House of Commons was the cost to rate-payers of the extra policing and stewardship compulsory at Beatle concerts. "We're rate-payers too,"[6] protested Starr.

Even middle-class fathers disparaging them in breakfast rooms knew the individual names, none better than that of Ringo, the only Beatle to adopt a *nom du théâtre* as well as the additional gimmick from which it had been born. Despite there being a French pop singer also called Ringo, the Liverpudlian's would be the Beatle name known in continental Europe long before those of John, George and Paul. "It's had a lot to do with my success and acceptance," he'd admit. "It might sound mad, but people remember it." Cornered by some foreign Beatles fans a couple of years later in Cannes, Lennon dryly signed himself "Ringo Starr" and they went away quietly

That your parents had figured out which one was which was an indication of how cosy Beatlemania became before 1963 was out. *Daily Express* correspondent Derek Taylor – later the group's press officer – could only praise them after being briefed to do a hatchet job after the quartet had agreed to play their allotted four numbers to the Queen Mother in November 1963, but "that meant they couldn't be any good",[8] according to younger pop consumer David Cook (later 1970s pop star David Essex, but then an amateur drummer). For many, The Beatles had matured too quickly and, like Tommy Steele, they'd be soft-shoe shuffling before you could blink, wouldn't they? There'd been a taste of that when they'd waved a jovial goodbye during the finale of ventriloquist's dummy Lenny the

Lion's BBC television show and – like many a British showbiz evergreen – appeared on ITV's *Blackpool Night Out*, taking part in comedy spoofs and, alongside hosts Mike and Bernie Winters, crooning 'I Do like To Be Beside The Seaside'.

More the meat of Cook and his sort were the belligerently unkempt Rolling Stones and later hairy monsters detested by adults, like The Kinks, Yardbirds and Pretty Things. Plundering Chicago and Mississippi negro ethnicism, these had sprung from the college circuit and cells of blues archivist/performers onto the new BBC chart showcase, *Top Of The Pops*. "Their scene was strictly teenage rebels," noted Ringo, "but we went from four-year-old kids to 90-year-old grandmothers. Their scene was violence. We never created violence, even in the start."[9] Yet, while you wouldn't catch them yukking it up with Mike and Bernie, the Stones had reason to be grateful to The Beatles for the endorsement that led to a Decca recording deal, as well as John and Paul's gift – as a stabilising second single – of 'I Wanna Be Your Man',[10] bestowed prior to its selection for autumn 1963's *With The Beatles* LP. They'd completed the track virtually on the spot while looking in on a vexing Stones' rehearsal in a Soho club.[9]

Lennon taught Ringo 'I Wanna Be Your Man' as his drummer's lead vocal on the album. Although Starr sang and played simultaneously on the recording, five separate sessions and an overdub of maracas were needed for an acceptable take, and even this lacked the hungry drive that the Stones had invested into their improvement on a slapdash composition – and, if it was a compliment, it was they who'd be aurally caricatured on The Barron Knights' 'Call Up The Groups' comic medley of 1964.

Sometimes he'd be overlooked, but a token Starr song towards the close of the first side on every LP or as an EP makeweight came to be as anticipated by Beatle traditionalists as the group came to be Number One every Christmas. "We weren't going to give him anything great,"[11] guffawed John, and often Lennon and McCartney gave him nothing at all beyond accompaniment on an unrevised twelve-bar rocker of yore. Both of 1964 vintage were Ringo's 'Honey

Don't[12] for *Beatles For Sale* and 'Matchbox', another Carl Perkins opus, on the 'Long Tall Sally' EP.

"While the others created musical works of art," contended NEMS publicist Tony Barrow, "he was left in the cold and merely brought in when they wanted some percussion."[13] Although The Beatles' early Parlophone albums were conceived technologically during recorded sound's late mediaeval period, they heralded a new attitude towards a product that had regarded not been as a rounded entity but as a cynically throwaway patchwork of tracks hinged on a hit 45. Testaments to commercial pragmatism rather than quality, these were targeted – especially in the States – at fans so beglamoured by an artist's looks and personality to be rendered uncritical of frankly sub-standard, haphazardly programmed output, excused as an exhibition of "versatility" but of no true cultural value.

The first Beatles LP was padded with a brace of singles, but each that followed was to be a conscious musical progression, with an increasing ratio of tracks the equal of single A-sides, in terms of effort and imagination. Having proven themselves proportionally as sound an investment for EMI as Presley for RCA, the four would be allowed unlimited Abbey Road time and the freedom to requisition all manner of auxiliary instrumentation and, later, musicians to enhance a Lennon-McCartney stockpile that could fulfil the group's contractual commitments many times over.

With The Beatles was a tentative exercise in such experimentation, as, like unrestrained children in a toy shop, the four fiddled about with whatever weird and wonderful implement was either lying about their favoured Studio Two or staring at them from one of the complex's storeroom shelves. For Ringo, this would lead to swatting a packing case in place of snare on one number; on another, the Cuban tom-tom that The Shadows had used on 'Apache'; and to pep up 'Don't Bother Me' – George Harrison's first published solo composition – an Arabian bongo. Soon, he would feel no less odd tapping something as straightforward as a cowbell on 'I Call Your Name'[14] as rattling a *chocalho*[15] for 'She's A Woman'.

Little would seem odd by then, and in any case Ringo would be devoid of resistance to the force that had effectively finished off his old life. He was, nevertheless, aware that he was just a link in the chain but that it was to his advantage to stay malleable, as he "let the others do all the worrying. I'm happy to go on up there and play drums and that's all."[16] While he'd been awarded a small percentage of shares in Northern Songs, Lennon and McCartney's publishing company, Starr's main source of income was his quarter of Beatles Ltd, a budgetary receptacle for all net takings from concerts from which "even our accountant doesn't know how much is ours alone. Myself, I never give it much thought, money. I just always think of myself as having plenty."[17] Being the poorest Beatle was better than being the poorest Hurricane, but he'd have tenacious bouts of circular and only half-understood discussions with an affable Epstein about Beatle finance and why he didn't get as much as even George, but at least he was no longer on a hireling's wage.

Perhaps to imprint further his uncertain importance to the group, he'd even put forward a song he'd made up for consideration as an LP track, originally for Paul to sing. Shyly, he'd first demonstrated it on a piano in the BBC's Paris Theatre while The Beatles were waiting to make a broadcast, continuing "to push it on them every time we make a record".[18] Called 'Don't Pass Me By', the lyrics were his own but the tune was an unconscious plagiarism, so he was informed, of a Jerry Lee Lewis B-side. As he might have expected, it was greeted with affectionate derision, McCartney once burlesquing its chorus on air and *Saturday Club* presenter Brian Matthew dubbing Starr "the Dylan Thomas of Liverpool".[19]

While his attempt at composing for them – and his infrequent huffs and objections – remained ineffectual, Ringo felt less vulnerable a Beatle now that he was receiving as much fan mail as the rest, and there was, therefore, less occasion for NEMS publicity sheets to maximise such of his subsidiary skills as poker and billiards. Neither was he now the newest member of the crew since the appointment of ex-Cavern bouncer Malcolm "Big Mal" Evans as assistant to an overworked Aspinall, who needed all of his wits about him to cope with the tactical problems of moving the operation from A to B.

Once at B, he and Mal would buttonhole promoters, organise security, shoo unwanted company from dressing rooms and attend to the group's food, sleep and overall health requirements, both before and after they bounced onto the boards to face the ear-stinging decibels that greeted even the compere's attempts to keep order.

In the chemistry of the four interlocking public personalities, Ringo was seen as a catalyst in a grey area inhabited by glum clowns and moral agents. Admitted into a backstage sanctum, a local reporter might raise a puffy smile on glimpsing near the washbasin a bottle of Yardley's Shampoo For Men with a label on which a hand had taken the trouble to scrawl the addenda "and Ringo". The victim would also chuckle along to hearty twitting about his hospitalisations, slum background and scholastic deficiencies. "Ringo doesn't know the meaning of fear," joked John, "or any other word of more than three letters."[20] Meaning no harm, either, was a symbolic Lennon present to Starr of a pathetic stuffed dog in a glass case. "We're never serious," grinned Paul, indicating Ringo. "Just look at him. How could we be serious?"[7] On one hilariously ad-libbed *Saturday Club*, Starr himself would decline to read a cue-card because he was "the one who doesn't say anything".[21] And besides, he laughed, "I can't read."[21]

A tendency for Lennon and McCartney to butt in when Starr was about to answer an interviewer's question was often as misunderstood as their witticisms at his expense. Nowadays, they and George seemed to be forming a protective cordon around Elsie's only child, as if remorseful about earlier indifference and the ignoble reason for which their eyes had alighted on him in August 1962. More often than not, he'd pair off with Paul for joint holidays and when the group had to double up in hotel suites, but "no matter which one I'm with, it's like being with your best friend. We're like brothers. Me and whoever I'm with are really dead close."[7]

They'd make an educated guess that Pete Best hadn't his usurper's natural thespian qualities, which became plain when, striding up and down banks of hairdriers, Ringo played a salon proprietor to noteworthy effect in *The Mersey Sound*, a documentary commissioned by the production body of *Tonight*. He reverted to being The Beatles' mute Harpo in the mostly unscripted non-musical turns that they acted out beneath screams during 16 days of "The Beatles Christmas Show" at London's Astoria Cinema. This season was broken only by the kindly Epstein ordering an aeroplane to fly the Scouse majority of the cast home to spend Christmas Day with their families, with a limousine delivering Ringo to his normally sleepy street, where a crowd of children swooped from nowhere to see the smile and wave that was diffused generally as he hurried indoors.

There were mixed emotions about The Beatles in Liverpool, although it was hardly their fault that they couldn't play the city's small clubs any more. Nevertheless, because they'd once paced it, the Cavern's very stage was to be sawn up and sold at five shillings a fragment to the over-abundance of those daft enough to want one. The first coachloads of Beatle worshippers had pulled up in May 1963 and, before the high summer of Mersey Beat ran its course, "Those of us who hoped for their success now resented it," gritted one who'd once spent lunchtimes with the so-called Fab Four, "since we could no longer see them at the Cavern. What a sense of betrayal! They had been just another group of lads that everybody knew."[3]

Others front-paged by *Mersey Beat* as "hit parade Scousers"[22] were only condescending to be seen at the Empire or the Odeon now that it was commonplace for Rolls Royces to disgorge famous sight-seers – Lionel Bart, Ken Dodd, Chet Atkins, Nancy Spain – to, say, The Searchers Fan Club convention at the Iron Door in January 1964. You couldn't move, either, in the Mandolin, the Peppermint Lounge, the Sink and all the other venues that had sprung up along with the London-type boutiques now operational in the city centre.

Like Vikings of old, metropolitan record-company scouts had come for plunder. The slowest witted held the view that all pop groups are the same – "Let's sign as many as we can, see which racket catches on and hammer it hard. Make a fortune, eh? [pause] Where exactly *is* Liverpool?" With the disbandment of The Eagles indicating that there was to be no offsetting "Avon Beat", some shyster from Bristol had wanted to hedge his bets by contracting every group in Liverpool, in the hope that one might be a New Beatles who would hold sway over the rest like a baron over villeins. In the first month of 1963, the more cautious Decca made off with Billy Butler, The Big Three, Beryl Marsden – and the Lee Curtis All-Stars, who, because they had Pete Best, had been a close second to The Beatles in the 1962 *Mersey Beat* poll.

Hardly a week would go by without another Merseyside act being thus thrust forward, or so it seemed. Suddenly, someone who'd cadged cigarettes off you the previous month would be seen in the *NME* with his or her outfit posing round a fire escape or on brick-strewn wasteland. From nowhere, Jeannie And The Big Guys (formerly The Tall Boys, it says here) were in *Record Mirror*'s review column with a version of 'Boys'. It wasn't transmitted up north, but The Fourmost had been on that new *Ready, Steady, Go!* on ITV, while a *Look At Life* cinema newsreel was devoted to Billy J Kramer, Cilla opened for Gerry on his latest UK tour and The Swinging Blue Jeans were in an edition of *Z-Cars* that had been given a beat-group slant.

The Jeans had had an altercation in a BBC canteen with The Rolling Stones, whom the *NME* believed were "a London group with the Liverpool sound",[22] as were, supposedly, The Dave Clark Five, whose unseating of The Beatles was seen by some press organs as a sign that the "power" had returned more conveniently to the capital. As black rhythm and blues smashes had been automatically covered (and usually diluted) for the white market in the States, so some recording managers saved themselves a trip to Liverpool by getting groups within a closer proximity to London to steal a march on their northern counterparts by taking first grabs at the R&B motherlode, hence the Clark quintet and Brian Poole And The Tremeloes' respective vanquishing of Faron's Flamingos' 'Do You Love Me' and Bern Elliott And The Fenmen's 'Money' making the Top 20 simply because – Barrett Strong's original apart – it was the first. The Kinks, however, were unable to duplicate this feat with the two Mersey Beat-tinged singles that preceded their chart-topping 'You Really Got Me'.

As production exercises only, Joe Meek flavoured a couple of other London outfits with Liverpudlia, but while the going was good other producers would set up mobile recording units in Merseyside ballrooms to tape as many unsigned units as could be crammed onto a cheap compilation album with a title like *Group Beat '63* or *This Is Merseybeat*. Included on Decca's *At The Cavern* were Lee Curtis And The All-Stars, who were to lose Pete Best after their first two singles missed; they had no placing in 1963's *Mersey Beat* poll. By then, it had dawned on Decca that ex-Beatle Best was wasted as a sideshow. A variation on The Beatles blueprint via closer vocal harmonies and "a slightly heavier beat",[23] Pete Best's Original All-Stars were therefore budgeted for a trial single and, in collusion with Mona, pop periodical journalists sought to jot down Pete's considered replies to questions like, "Have you ever met Ringo?"[24] "Do you ever see The Beatles these days?"

To the last question, Lennon's shame-smitten mumblings to him might have given expediential leeway for Pete not to qualify to *Melody Maker* his "yes, occasionally, but we're all on the move so much, we don't have a lot of time to talk".[23] His outfit, you see, was also "going well. We're not making as much money as The Beatles, but we're working all the time, all over the country."[23] As if they were still the best of mates, he would "wish them the best of luck, and I mean it. I don't know to this day why we parted company."[23] The only tang of acidity was his wish "to clear my slurred name in Liverpool and prove to all the people who made my name mud that I have a good group".[23]

Whatever false impression readers of *Melody Maker* had of Pete's impending ascent to stardom, there was less doubt about that of Rory Storm And The Hurricanes. To his diary, even Johnny Guitar had to confide, "Group not very good these days. No new songs. Will have to improve. Not much work. Another three months in France cancelled."[25] Although still enough of a local treasure to be prominent in ITV's *Beat City* rebuttal to *The Mersey Sound*, Rory's group had become also-rans, having to their credit only a flop single with 'Doctor Feelgood' and a track on *This is Merseybeat* recorded crudely in a Rialto hallway. Their new drummer, Jimmy Tushingham, was the latest in a growing number who'd squeeze into Starr's old and fading stage suit after Gibson Kemp left for Germany and Kingsize Taylor. "They reckon that anyone who lasts more than a week is something of a phenomenon,"[26] griped Keith Hartley,[27] who, from Preston's Thunderbeats, actually served five months.

Worse than a too-rapid turnover of drummers was that Inland Revenue officials were also on Storm and The Hurricanes' trail after Ringo had had to disclose his earnings when he was in the group. Nevertheless, for old time's sake, and to salve his conscience for leaving them in the lurch, it was he who threw down a lifeline by settling the tax bill and, over a few drinks in the Blue Angel, nodded along with Brian Epstein's suggestion to pressure The Beatles' booking agent to sign them and to underwrite a 15-hour London recording session.

For Brian's only venture into disc production, he relied much on the judgement of the studio engineer as Rory and The Hurricanes ran through 'Ubangi Stomp', Bobby Darin's, 'I'll Be There'[28] (then much requested in Liverpool clubs) and the two that Parlophone – in Epstein's half-nelson – would get round to releasing in late 1964. The perfectionist Brian insisted on over an hour of retakes until he was satisfied with Wally's vocal cadence in 'Since You Broke My Heart', an Everly Brothers opus from 1960. Its A-side was a mock-Latin adaptation of Leonard Bernstein's 'America' (from *West Side Story*), that had captured Storm's imagination while the group were in Spain. Through his persistence, "we shortened it, used some of our own words, and it goes like a bomb".[29] Well, it wasn't bad, and, although the bulk of its disappointing sales were in loyal Liverpool, the publicity reminding the average Joe of the group's Beatle connection put them – as it did Pete Best's new outfit – in a stronger negotiating stance for engagements that now stretched to the very edge of Swinging London – but no further.

Much was also made of the backing singers, "America", which – as well as Wally – included Ringo, Iris Caldwell and her husband Shane Fenton, with whom she was also conjoined professionally in a song-and-dance act. Confronted by the rearing monster of the group boom, Fenton had made a protracted withdrawal from the pop mainstream after declining a management offer from Epstein. Speculating in the administrative side of the music industry, among those he aided in this capacity were The Hollies, who had absorbed his old drummer Bobby Elliott into their number. Paralleling Fenton's retreat, Paul Raven (later Gary Glitter) was biding his time as *Ready, Steady, Go!*'s floor manager, because "things were getting impossible for me as a performer. The Beatles had turned the pop world on its head. I couldn't fit into a group and I wasn't from the north and I stood as much chance as a mongrel at Crufts."[30]

Cliff Richard, too, had been rendered as old as the hills by Mersey Beat, but, smiling indulgently, he plunged deeper into pantomime and evangelical Christianity, while Adam Faith swapped *pizzicato* strings for clanging guitars and walloping drums on his records. As he steeled himself for cabaret, Billy Fury was gratified to discover that, unaffected by London *sangfroid*, northern girls still screamed at him, although at the Liverpool Empire date on one of his final headlining package tours some of those screams had been for The Beatles, who'd slipped in incognito and were slipping out again when a particularly piercing female shriek of recognition caused them to be nearly killed with kindness. Their lips moving mechanically as they hastened from the *mêlée* with as much grace as they could muster, one of Ringo's favourite quips of the time might have been overheard: "Yes, I went to school with Billy Fury, but I don't remember which day."[31]

Fury then lived around the corner from Abbey Road in Cavendish Avenue. Number seven would be Paul McCartney's first official London address, after his berth with actress girlfriend Jane Asher's family in Wimpole Street became common knowledge. With the Lennons ensconced in a bedsit off the Cromwell Road and Epstein in a new block near Hyde Park – handy for West End nightclubbing – The Beatles had found it a false economy to remain a Liverpool-based organisation while attending to an increasing broadcasting and recording workload 200 miles south. His mother was already complaining in print that "I don't see much of Richie nowadays – not half as much as I'd like to",[32] but, wrenching himself from Admiral

Grove, Ringo bedded down in a small hotel near NEMS' first London office, at the top of Shaftesbury Avenue. While looking for somewhere less temporary, he became pally with property developer Roger Shines, and by early 1964 Starr and Harrison were sharing an apartment below Brian's in Whaddon House, William Mews.

Initially, Starr could "move about in London like an ordinary bloke. If you behave sensibly and plan where you go, you can be OK."[7] In sunshades, cloth cap and non-descript overcoat supplemented with hunched shoulders and a limp, he'd hazard a journey as far as Southend to catch an Everly Brothers tour (with The Rolling Stones among the package's small fry), but there was no need for any disguise when all four Beatles went to Ronnie Scott's supercool jazz cellar in Soho to hear blind multi-instrumentalist Roland Kirk. They'd long been nightbirds by then. After late-afternoon corn flakes, they weren't found wanting when scrutinised through the spy-hole of "in" clubs like the Cromwellian, the Bag O' Nails off Carnaby Street, the Speakeasy or the cloistered Scotch Of St James, a bee-line from Buckingham Palace. Ringo retained most hedonistic loyalty to the supercool Ad-Lib off Leicester Square, but he was often seen in other pop-star hangouts attractive for their strict membership controls, tariffs too highly priced for the Average Joe, lighting more flattering than that in a Butlins ballroom and no photographers admitted.

"When we first made it," he would recollect, "I lived in night clubs for three years. It used to be a non-stop party."[33] In a discotheque's deafening dark, where nobody Twisted any more, Ringo would lend truth to reports in teenage journals that "he can do all the rave dances, including a few that haven't been invented yet".[24] Partnered by a black girl attached to a US vocal group that had just come from *Ready, Steady, Go!*, he held his own as the star dance-floor attraction when necks craned to watch him do the Banana, the Monkey and other dances that no Briton was supposed to have mastered yet.

Back in the second-string Beatles' untidy sitting room, with LP covers scattered everywhere, the hi-fi would pulsate to modern US

R&B, better known as soul music. As well as those that were plugged into the lower rungs of the charts by Britain's new pirate radio stations, Ringo and George were *au fait* with eruditions like Chuck Jackson, The Marvelettes, Brenda Holloway and The Soul Sisters, the latter of whose 'I Can't Stand It' and then Holloway's 'Every Little Bit Hurts' were quickly covered by Birmingham's Spencer Davis Group (with Pete York), who were loudly admired by Ringo for sounding American. Nonetheless, he preferred Chan Romero's original 'Hippy Hippy Shake' to The Swinging Blue Jeans' more definitive treatment.

"Our music is second-hand versions of negro music," he'd theorise. "Ninety per cent of the music I like is coloured."[7] And who could quibble when he bought two copies each of such as Kim Weston's 'A Little More Love', The Miracles' 'I've Been Good To You', Little Stevie Wonder's 'Fingertips' and – more familiar to most other Britons – The Supremes' 'Where Did Our Love Go?'. When asked about the other ten per cent, he'd tell you how he "really enjoyed good country and western",[7] being particularly fond of Buck Owens and Roger Miller. In his purchase of albums by such as Woody Guthrie and early Bob Dylan, Ringo also showed a liking for that strain of modern American folk music that mixed traditional and self-composed material. On BBC's *Juke Box Jury*, his verdict on Bobby Vinton's smoochy 'There I've Said It Again' was that it was ideal, "if you're sitting in one night and not alone".[31]

While Maureen Cox would visit him as often as work would permit, she was not the only girl in Ringo's life, according to "friends" and the press gossip. She could discount a lunatic fringe exemplified by an 18-year-old Huyton girl whose parents had to place an advertisement in the local paper stating that, contrary to rumour, she was not marrying Ringo Starr.[34] However, his nights on the town with various Quant-cropped dolly-birds were supported by concrete evidence, especially as women outnumbered men five-to-one in clubs like the Scotch and the Ad-Lib. A talkative model named Vicki Hodge was remarkable for her indiscretion about a dalliance with Richie – and Yul Brynner and society photographer

David Bailey – and was still kissing and telling in *The News Of The World* years later.

In his own eyes, Richie was faithful to Mo, in that his casual romantic adventures did not adulterate his emotional allegiance to one who "knows the moment I face her what's wrong and what to do about it, and I'm happy again in a minute".[35] If he'd so desired, Richie needn't have wandered far beyond Whaddon House to take his pick of "a lot of scrubbers and exhibitionists who hang around, shout outside all day and night, ring the bell and all that. If I get out the car and refuse to sign autographs, they shout four-letter words at me and everybody near here hears it. It's not very nice."[17] The other occupiers weren't amused, either, that the environs were also a focus for Beatle-related graffiti.

One or two of these scratches made no bones about Brian's homosexuality, which sometimes reflected on Ringo. Vicky Hodge might stay for breakfast, but "I've been called a queer before, you know. You just can't win."[1] Fuelling the whispers were the William Mews Beatles' good-natured attendances at Epstein's all-male parties, despite his worries that they might guess his inclinations. They'd known from the beginning.

Mo had no worries about Richie's virility, but there were times when the wretchedness of her devotion cut keenly. In an age when a pop star would lose fans if he wasn't a bachelor and, therefore, "available", he'd been instructed "to pretend I didn't know Maureen and wasn't in love. Can you imagine what it must have been like for her reading in the papers that I didn't know anyone called Maureen Cox?"[36] That too many jealous Liverpudlian girls did had already forced his full-time girlfriend to quit her Ashley du Pré job, what with customers levelling none-too-pleasant stares and even physical threats at her. Once, as she sat waiting in his car outside a West Derby ballroom, varnished fingernails had shot through the open window and raked the side of her face to the accompaniment of screeched curses.

Unnerving though such incidents were, Mo did not yet escape to London, suspecting as she did what her parents' reactions would be to the very idea of a daughter of their living in sin. If pressed about Richie, she and he were the stock "very good friends".[37] For a change, she might say that she was his "private secretary",[37] because the highlight of many a dull day without him was arriving at Admiral Grove to ease Mrs Graves' writer's cramp as she ploughed through sackfuls of correspondence that, as well as ordinary letters, might as easily include a life-sized sketch of Richie or – because he'd said somewhere that he liked science fiction – another tea chest of paperbacks. Back from work, Harry would address the answers and, twice a week, Freda Kelly from the northern wing of the Beatles Fan Club would cart them away for stamping.

Often, admirers would call personally and *en masse*, a brigade of 200 once needed much convincing that Ringo wasn't inside before leaving his stepfather suddenly alone on the doorstep. "Mum was frightened when we first got famous," recounted her son. "She was always getting people telling her I'd been killed or had an accident. Rumours got around and the press would get on to her."[36] Nevertheless, pestering from journalists and fans was not so uncontainable that the Graves could not still be "perfectly happy living in Admiral Grove",[38] even now that Richie had the means to grant them a dotage rich in more substantial material comforts than his present of a movie camera to Harry, who "gets such pleasure out of it, putting it back in the case when he's finished and cleaning it. Me? I just leave mine lying about any old place."[33] All other Beatle parents had been uprooted to up-market housing, but for the time being Harry and Elsie would not presume as much upon Richie's good fortune. However, no one in the family could deny completely the benefits of kinship to a Beatle. With Ringo's cousin John Foster at the drums, The Escorts were one up on scrimmaging rivals envious of their Blue Angel residency and their winning of a contract with Fontana Records in the Lancashire and Cheshire Beat Contest.

Suffering now for his own and his relations' future luxuries and sinecures, Ringo had vomited with nerves just before The Beatles topped the bill of ITV's *Sunday Night At The London Palladium*, the central height of British showbusiness. Tormented with earache, he was not left in pained quietude but dressed in an oversized coat, sunglasses and low-crowned trilby and hustled to the nearest hospital for emergency treatment. Marooned on his podium that evening, Starr's knuckles whitened around his sticks and 'I Wanna Be Your Man' was sung with razor-sharp poignancy.

His humble but specific dietary predilections were frequently frustrated by platters uncovered for him on tour by well-meaning gourmet chefs. Turning queasily from caviar or onion fritter rings, his stomach would yearn for chips and overdone steak, chicken sandwiches or the lardy solace of a mixed grill. If he couldn't wash these down with either light ale or whisky and Coke, he'd order pink Mateus Rosé, the only wine he was sure about. It was a red-letter day, anyway, if the group were allowed to eat a restaurant meal in solitude.

As well as autographing table napkins while masticating a sausage, Ringo also had to put up with disobliging comments about his nose, which, if you read magazine articles without knowing what he looked like, you'd believe resembled that of Cyrano de Bergerac. "Have you ever considered plastic surgery?"[7] dared a thick-skinned *Melody Maker* reporter. In an episode of a BBC television comedy series, Eric Sykes and Hattie Jacques triggered bursts of canned laughter with a comparison of Starr and General de Gaulle's respective conks. *The Jewish Chronicle* rang NEMS to enquire if he was one of them, and an apologist in *Boyfriend* – a schoolgirl comic – defended it as "a sign of distinction, one of the things that makes him attractive".[39] As taunts about it would even be scripted in The Beatles' first movie, *A Hard Day's Night*, Ringo had little choice but to desensitise himself and get "used to anything you'd say about it. I've come to terms with my own nose. It's the talking point when people discuss me. I have a laugh, and it goes up one nostril and out the other."[7] However, his hooter was to be less unfairly eye catching after The Who, with their trowel-prowed Pete Townshend, and Dave Dee, Dozy, *Beaky*, Mick and Tich each made their *Top Of The Pops* debuts in 1965.

Even as their luck held while other groups came and went, The Beatles still expected it to run out. "It's been fun, but it won't last long," avowed Lennon. "Anyway, I'd hate to be an old Beatle."[40] To Ringo, who'd come in on point of take-off, it had happened with the spooky deliberation of a dream, but he wasn't so dazzled as to think that pop stars – contrary to definition – were immortal, or that he'd never have to wonder about Hunt's again: "A couple of Number Ones and then out 18 months later won't make you rich. You'll be back on the buses."[41]

If nothing else, he'd recoup golden memories of adulation, although he'd be the only Beatle who'd sigh for the uproarious tribal gatherings that would degrade their musicianship. "I can't take it when they just sit there and listen to you," he'd reflect from a year when they might have done, had the group still existed. "I think it gives you that 'I'm here to be appreciated', attitude which is really a drag. They don't have to keep quiet at shows. If they want to hear the music, they can buy the records and listen to them."[42]

Income from million-sellers meant that even Ringo could afford well-deserved breaks in faraway places. With Harrison and McCartney, he'd limbered up for The Beatles' 1963 tour with Roy Orbison by spending twelve days staying with German friends in Tenerife. Four months later, he was in Greece with Paul "to get my toenails tattooed".[43] Like any poor boy who'd never signed a cheque or called hotel room service from a bedside telephone before, his consumption was more conspicuous than those born into wealth: "When the money first began to pour in, I'd go and buy ten suits, a dozen shirts and three cars. I spent money like it had just been invented."[44]

Coveting Billy Fury's drummer's blue-grey pearloid kit (made by Ludwig, a US firm), Ringo shelled out for a brown one with Swiss-made Paiste cymbals.[45] In doing so, he inflicted untold injury on home trade as every other stick-wielder, from schoolboys to chart-riding professionals like Chris Curtis of The Searchers and Dave Lovelady (now in The Fourmost), started beating a Ludwig, too. Because it travelled with The Beatles, the Ludwig became the standard group drum set for most of the 1960s. Nevertheless, some such as Bobby Elliott and Bernard Dwyer (of Freddie And The

Dreamers) favoured Trixon equipment from Germany, and eventually so would Dave Clark, after his trademark Rogers kit was raffled for charity.

Dave would finish 1964 as the second most famous drummer in the world. The first, of course, was Ringo Starr.

6 "Over In The States, I Know I Went Over Well"

The Beatles' subjugation of the rest of the world was a large-scale re-run of the hysteria they'd long known at home but with even more presentations to civic heads, louder screams every stop of the way and longer queues of handicapped unfortunates wheeled deludedly down backstage corridors for the group's curative blessing. From dismissal by an Italian radio broadcaster as "a band without a future",[1] the four were swamping foreign Top Tens five or six singles at a time. The Indonesian Minister of Culture outlawed Beatle hairdos and *A Hard Day's Night* came to Warsaw. Back home, Ringo had been proposed as president of several higher-education establishments and had been house guest at Woburn Abbey at the invitation of the Duke of Bedford's swingin' son, Rudolph. While he'd still been able to do so without too much fuss, Starr had visited Dingle Vale Secondary one open day, "and they were charging people to look at my desk"[2] – or, at least, one that might have been once been his.

A *Daily Express* cartoon had Harold Wilson and Macmillan's successor, Sir Alec Douglas-Home, soliciting The Beatles for their votes in the post-Profumo general election, thus lending credence to the homily, "I care not who makes a nation's laws as long as I can write its songs." The quartet had also been earmarked for a cameo appearance in *Coronation Street*, although this was precluded by their tight work schedule. More than just another pop group as transient and gimmicky as any other, they were now part of the national furniture, and would be honoured as such by Prime Minister Wilson.

"Our appeal," ruminated Starr, "is that we're ordinary lads",[3] which, as it had in Britain, did the corrective trick in a United States depressed with its own traumas – the Kennedy assassination, vehement opposition to the Civil Rights Amendment and the first boy soldiers blown to bits in Indochina. Into the bargain, its Top 20 was sodden with unmemorable instrumentals, drivelling ballads, a declining Presley and wholesome anthems like The Beach Boys' 'Be True To Your School'. To the chagrin of The Beach Boys, The Four Seasons and others on Capitol – The Beatles' US label – the Merseysiders were launched with one of the most far-reaching publicity blitzes hitherto known in the record industry North America was, therefore, theirs for the taking when they arrived fully mobilised in February 1964 for *The Ed Sullivan Show*, the sub-continent's *Sunday Night At The London Palladium*. Surely nothing should have topped the Palladium, but, after Sullivan and their US concert debut at the Washington Coliseum, "they could have ripped me apart," raved Starr, "and I couldn't have cared less."[4] Even after they flew out, 'I Want To Hold Your Hand' remained at Number One, while hurtling up were all their singles that in the previous year had been aired to negligible listener reaction by the more lurid disc jockeys such as Wolfman Jack and New York's Murray the K ("the fastest talker I've ever met,"[5] said Ringo). Beatles chewing gum alone netted millions of dollars within months.

As is their wont, the Americans, convinced of the incredible, exhibited an enthusiasm for it that left more reserved British Beatlemaniacs swallowing dust. Our colonial cousins were devouring the grass on which the group had trodden and the retrieved jelly-beans that had rained as votive offerings onto the stage on which the idols had played.[6] "I enjoy it at the back," said Ringo, "and when they start throwing things, it's a good place to be."[7] Girls would faint on fingering the guitar autographed by all four and owned by some pensioner in a moptop wig who'd declared himself "the oldest Beatles fan". The whingeing of their children would cause well-off parents to interrupt European holidays for a flight to Liverpool where back copies of *Mersey Beat* would fetch hugely inflated prices and the chair on which Ringo had always perched when in the Cavern band room would be kissed like the Blarney Stone.

A US "tribute" single, 'My Boyfriend Got A Beatle Haircut' by Donna Lynn, was issued by Capitol in March 1964. As sure as fate, there followed a cartoon group in *Shindig* comic called 'The Beadles' – who used imagined Scouse colloquialisms like "blimey, guv'nor" and "blighter" and addressed each other as "mate" – and hastily assembled soundalike discs were released by such as The American Beetles, The Bug Men, John And Paul, The Merseyboys, *ad nauseum*, mostly by Los Angeles session musicians who probably bitched during coffee breaks about this Limey combo everyone's talking about. Local outfits found that it paid to break up and reform as soon as they'd either grown their hair or acquired wigs and rehearsed tortuous Liverpudlian accents and slang – "wack", "gear", "fab" and so on – for on-stage continuity during a set consisting wholly of yeah-yeah-yeah Beatles-Mersey Beat imitations. Some tried passing themselves off as genuine Britons, while those in redneck areas – such as San Antonio's Sir Douglas Quintet – dared not sport a *pilzenkopf* off stage for fear of disapproval expressed in designs stronger than people simply bellowing, "Get yer 'air cut!" from a passing car.

'Lies' by New York's Knickerbockers was the most precise duplication of the salient points of The Beatles sound[9] while The Byrds' more enduring career was founded on less frenzied aspects of Mersey Beat. Modelled to breadwinning UK specifications, too, were the likes of The Ramrods[10] (who covered 'I Wanna Be Your Man'), The Standells, The Wackers, The Manchesters, The McCoys and, far behind them all, a Big Apple stage-school unit with the nerve to call themselves The Escorts – and otherwise notable only because they contained a Richard Perry whose life was to cross that of Ringo Starr in the next decade.

North to Massachusetts, The Barbarians recorded a pragmatic "Mersey Beat" 45 entitled 'Are You A Boy Or Are You A Girl', although their drummer, Victor Moulton, loathed "14-year-old girls from the Bronx who go to Mod shops and say, 'What can we get that's English to walk around in today?' and, at 11pm, they have to take off their John Lennon hats and go home."[11] Many US musicians who would loom large in the lives of certain Beatles – notably Starr – were those who'd largely defied the British onslaught. While admitting that Ringo was "instrumental in making the drums what they are today",[12] Jim Keltner – from an Oklahoman family of drummers – served Gary Lewis And The Playboys, the proudly American exception during that 1965 week when the *Billboard* Top Ten was all British. Helping to keep surf music alive in the Top 30 that year was 'New York's A Lonely Town (When You're The Only Surfer Boy)' by The Tradewinds, a "four-strong group from Providence", according to their press release, but actually Vini Poncia and Pete Anders, a multi-tracked professional team from a Big Apple songwriting factory.

For such craftsmen, jumping on bandwagons did not sate them with pride, but it nevertheless kept the wolf from the door. Donna Lynn's was not to be an isolated Beatle-related yuk-for-a-buck. When directing such a disc at an individual member, compilers were more likely to single out Ringo than John, Paul or George. John, Paul and George who? Kennedy? Revere? Washington? Who didn't know who was meant by Ringo, or thought they did? Just the title of Lorne Green's re-released 'Ringo', although an entirely unconnected dramatic monologue of the fictitious Old West pistolero, was sufficient to elevate it onto radio playlists and all the way up the Hot 100. There was, however, no doubt about who the man was in Penny Valentine's 'I Want To Kiss Ringo Goodbye',[13] which was released the week before The Beatles returned to London, or 'Ringo For President' by Australia's Rolf Harris and aimed at the States; 'Bingo Ringo' in the Deep South drawl of Huckleberry Hound; and even Beatle-Christmas crossovers in The Four Sisters' platonic 'I Want Ringo For Christmas' and 'Santa Bring Me Ringo'[14] from Christine Hunter.

"I Love Ringo" lapel badges outsold all associated merchandise, but Starr was not thus hallowed solely because he was easily identifiable. He had also stolen the show from the others in a society that was later to concede to the adoption of Cabbage Patch dolls. Promoted in like fashion, The Beatles had in Ringo something as lovably affecting, a little boy lost, a snare-drum Cinderella, the diminutive sad sack toiling on his lonely pedestal and engaging boundless sympathy for being the most inconspicuous one. As if the audience had all sat on tin-tacks, the volume of screams would climb to its loudest when Lennon moved his microphone over to the kit for Starr Time. A wave of groaned pity would filter across cinema rows during the *Hard Day's Night* scene in which Ringo received but one fan letter against the others' thick wads, with a delighted cheer issuing when a whole mailbag is belatedly produced for him alone. On his birthday, a Jeri Fannin of Xenia, Ohio, threw a celebration as an excuse to display her collection of nearly 1,000 photographs of her – and everyone's – most beloved Beatle. Perhaps George, Paul and John should have hung on to Pete Best.

In Britain, the level of applause had not risen at the Royal Command Performance when, delayed by his descent from the drum riser, Ringo had taken his curtain call a few seconds after the guitarists, "but over in the States I know I went over well. It knocked me out to see and hear the kids waving for me. I'd made it as a personality. Who wouldn't be flattered?"[15] As a consequence, he overcame many earlier inhibitions and grew more verbally self-assured as nicotine-stained digits scribbled down quotable Beatle repartee.

North Americans, you see, were accustomed to their pop stars being more devoid of independent opinion than any Larry Parnes cipher. Since the demobilisation of Elvis as a sergeant and all-round entertainer, a smooth-running, insipidly handsome youth (usually with a blow-wave and the forename Bobby) would be set in motion by his manager as a walking digest of Presley's more palatable, all-American aspects. Subliminally, through the medium of teen magazines and even in the piffle he was given to sing, the Bobby would parrot stolid middle-aged dictums – your parents' word was law, don't talk dirty, *et al* – and parade a dearth of private vices. With the gentlest humour, he'd answer enquiries about his favourite colour, preferred foodstuffs and the age at which he hoped to marry.

Having flexed their muscles with the European press, The Beatles capsized this cautious regimen through a combination of effusive zaniness, bluff unsentimentality and sarcastic one-line debates about inflammable issues and Beethoven's poems. "We were the first ones in rock 'n' roll that didn't kid the kids about drinking milk, and America was shocked," elucidated Starr. "'A scotch and Coke?' they'd ask, and we'd go, 'Yes, a scotch and Coke!' We were just honest lads, and it got us into trouble sometimes, but we didn't give in to the hypocrisy."[16] The equal of the others now, he was as instant a pundit as they, cracking back as snappily and impudently to banal, ill-informed questions – such as the classic "How did you find America?"[17] – as repetitious as a stuck record from circling media hounds. "Do you like being Beatles?" "Yes, or we'd be Rolling Stones."[18] When are you going to retire?" "In about ten minutes." "Have you any brothers?" "My brother was an only child."[7] "Did The Beatles come to America to get revenge for the Revolution?" "No, we just came for the money"[19] "Has success changed your life?" "Yep." "Don't you ever say anything but 'yep'?"' "Nope." "Why don't you sing?" "I can see you haven't heard our LPs."[20] "What about Senator Barry Goldwater?" "Not much fun, is he?"[21] "What would you be if you weren't a Beatle?" "The Beatles' manager." "What's the difference between English press conferences and those held in America?" "They're the same – people asking questions."[7]

In cold print, Ringo's remarks often seemed inane and pedestrian, but it was the poker-faced, what-are-you-laughing-at way he said 'em. In *A Hard Day's Night*, after a peppery, waxed-moustachioed rail commuter's clichéd moan about fighting a war for your sort, he humbled, "Bet you're sorry you won." In this stylised celluloid account of The Beatles' eventful preparation for a television showcase, Starr seized critical attention not with the deadpan sentences he enunciated with unprecedented clarity[23] but in non-speaking sequences that gilded his public image by bringing to light what Brian Epstein called "the little man's quaintness".[24] Less Harpo Marx than Charlie Drake, he exuded elements of that lip-trembling, doe-eyed pathos that some find endearing as a forlorn wanderer who had been badgered into thus "goin' paradin'" by "Paul's grandfather" (Wilfred Brambell[25]), a mischief-maker who'd ascertained from group banter that Ringo was its butt. Soon, Starr is seen advisedly unrecognisable in tramp's rags moping along a canal bank to George Martin's woebegone, harmonica-led orchestration of The Beatles' 'This Boy', now re-titled 'Ringo's Theme'. Among incidents *en route* are Ringo spreading his coat over a puddle *à la* Sir Walter Raleigh for a dolly-bird who, wrongly apprehending it to be shallow, promptly vanishes beneath a fathom of mud. In turn, Ringo is almost bowled over by a car tyre pushed by a grubby urchin who begins a description of his gang of four – an expanded metaphor for The Beatles.

Ringo-as-tramp's dramatic impact was not marred by the fact that he'd come "straight from the Ad-Lib out of my brain and feeling really down because I'd been drinking all night. I was incapable of saying a line, so Dick [Lester, director] had to use me somehow, and he kept making me walk 'round and look at the kid and that. So that's how that scene came off, and suddenly they say, 'Oh, you're a fantastic actor.'" Hungover as he was, "to make you laugh is not hard for me on film. I can do the funny walk, the funny looks. I can pull a few faces and limp a bit."[26]

Although Starr was designated most frequently by reviewers as the one with a likely destiny as a tragi-comedian, the group was praised collectively for its contribution to a project that ushered in a tougher, more realistic approach to pop movies. *A Hard Day's Night* was produced by Walter Shenson, a Californian whose past had included *The Mouse That Roared*, Acker Bilk's 1962 vehicle *A Band Of Thieves* and other British flicks that did not extend the boundaries of the avant garde. He did not regard Starr as "the greatest intellect in the world"[27] but nevertheless saw in him "a superb actor, an absolute natural. He can take direction from a director, which is a very difficult thing to do. You might even call it an art."[28]

Ringo's truant afternoons gawping at Hollywood hadn't been wasted in other respects, either. He'd become quite a film connoisseur by the mid 1960s, with Paul Newman – anti-hero of *Sweet Bird Of Youth* and *Hud* – as admired now as Victor Mature. Furthermore, the drummer was sufficiently intrigued by the filming process to roll up earlier than the other Beatles on the set of *A Hard*

Day's Night – if he hadn't over-indulged at the Ad-Lib – and being the most obviously thrilled at "seeing myself on that 20-foot screen, doing it and pretending".[26]

A layman's interest in still photography had been mirrored during his *Hard Day's Night* walkabout by a ludicrous attempt to take a snap of himself, but "when we were making the film, I had my own Pentax and I just kept clicking all the time".[28] As Lennon's stabs at literature had been collated into two slim best-sellers, so a tome of Starr's photos was allegedly planned for publication, initially for the USA, and he was looking forward to being "able to plug it".[28] However, all that the public saw were the two dozen or so shots captioned in *Rave* magazine's "Picture Scoop Of The Year". More were promised to *Mersey Beat*, but, shrugged Bill Harry, "I never got any of them."

Now sub-titled "Britain's leading beat paper", *Mersey Beat* was dying like a sun going nova, its final burst of energy unleashed in full-colour illustrations, articles on non-Merseyside acts and a circulation that sprawled as far south as Leicester. In March 1965, it was swallowed by *Music Echo*, in which coverage of the Liverpool scene was confined to a solitary page commensurate with faded interest – even in the city itself – in any more groups with sheepdog fringes who could play 'Twist And Shout' – although who hadn't come out when, for *A Hard Day's Night*'s northern première, The Beatles had passed in triumph through rapturous streets where chants of "We want Ringo!" outnumbered all others and a girl almost hurled herself under the group's Rolls Royce because she couldn't see him properly. They belonged to Liverpool and Liverpool let everyone know it. During the US tour that followed, a placard was hoisted in the midst of the shrieking masses in a Detroit stadium. It read, "We Are From Tue Brook.[29] We Are Proud Of You."

On the 1965 evening that The Beatles performed before nearly 6,000[30] – a new world record – at New York's Shea Stadium, Rory Storm And The Hurricanes were on at Orrell Park ballroom, with Storm as daredevil and hip-swivelling as ever. Throughout the hardship and disappointment that he had borne, Rory had not begrudged Richie his luck and had been unruffled by a gradually more tenuous contact with his old drummer. Nevertheless, Harry Graves had been there on the afternoon that centre-forward Rory and Wally scored three goals for the Mersey Beat XI against Florence Albion. One ex-member of his Hurricanes was accorded the *NME* headline, "Ringo Man Records!"[34] when his next outfit made a 1964 single, but Rory Storm's links with The Beatles had, nevertheless, not been as exploited by the press as much as they might have been.

Storm's rival bandleader Kingsize Taylor – who, but for The Beatles, would have been Starr's employer – had modestly come into his own on the Star-Club circuit of Hamburg, Kiel and Berlin, where "they are still a bit behind the times. They go for the old Little Richard gear and stuff like that."[31] Agreeing that he'd been "out of the country at the wrong time"[31], Kingsize made occasional forays to Britain, where a booking at the Iron Door sparked off a commendatory write-up in *Melody Maker*, a UK tour with Chuck Berry, a spot on *Ready, Steady, Go!* and the protraction of a prolific if generally unsuccessful recording career into 1967.

The only representative of Mersey Beat womanhood in the UK hit parade, Taylor's old flame, Cilla Black, had also been the first female to reach Number One since Helen Shapiro. On a tour with The Fourmost and Sounds Incorporated, she came to close the show after the headlining PJ Proby – "someone who is silly to himself",[4] opined Ringo – was harried from British theatres following an on-stage trouser-splitting episode. Despite her compromising casting in 1965's *Ferry Across The Mersey*, a period film whose evocative title song was Gerry And The Pacemakers Top Ten farewell, Cilla survived Mersey Beat's collapse via a lengthy and well-received season at the Palladium supported by The Fourmost, who'd portrayed the *losers* in a "battle of the bands" contest in *Ferry Across The Mersey*.

A real-life loser was now the cornerstone of The Pete Best Four (as Dave Clark was in his Five), but neither the Four's Decca 45 – a revival of Eddie Hodges' 'I'm Gonna Knock On Your Door'[32] – nor Pete's spot as mystery guest on US television's *I've Got A Secret* netted as much as his 1964 libel suit against Ringo, who'd discovered that nothing was "off the record" to some journalists. Nonetheless, it was galling for Best – who'd denied himself the amphetamines consumed by the other Beatles – when, during an interview with the soft-porn magazine *Playboy*, Starr had added a stupidly antiphonal "he took little pills to make him ill" after Lennon had explained, "Ringo used to fill in sometimes if our drummer was ill. With his periodic illness."[33] Although the case would drag on for four years, Pete would win a bitter and undivulged victory that, after legal fees, was sufficient to pay for renovations to his new house in West Derby.

A more physical dispute with Best – a punch-up in a St Pauli alley – would be recalled by Tony Sheridan during a 1964 media junket in a brave attempt to lift his new *Just A Little Bit Of...* LP off the ground. Although well placed to grow fat on Beatlemania, Sheridan had been resident in a Reeperbahn club when one of his 1961 singles with the Best Beatles was reissued to spread itself thinly enough to be registered as a million-seller without making that much of a dent in either the UK or the North American charts. Drawn from his exile by pragmatism, Tony had brushed his grey-flecked hair forward, had been "guest star" on a tour with The Searchers and Roy Orbison and had been invited to appear on British TV again. He'd also renewed his acquaintance with The Beatles, meeting them at Whaddon House after a *Hard Day's Night* shoot for "talk of the old times, laughs about some of the German raves and best wishes for the future".[35]

This hail-fellow-well-met reunion was not, however, repeated when the group and Sheridan were benighted in the same Australian hotel a few months later. It has been since chronicled that this leg of The Beatles' 1964 world tour was little more than a heavily subsidised debauch, which is why it was opportune that George and Ringo's respective parents decided not to come along for the ride. Indeed, with the intelligence that it was to be winter Down Under, Ringo had exclaimed in London, "No birds or beaches or anything? The trip's off. I'm not going!"[35] The other three had nonetheless gone on without him, after he'd been spectacularly sick in the toilet during a late-morning sitting for European publicity shots in a Putney portrait studio. Still off colour, he'd been examined by a local doctor, who diagnosed tonsillitis and pharyngitis; but it was a high temperature that necessitated an immediate removal to University College Hospital, near Covent Garden.

With the tour to commence in Copenhagen the next day, the three functioning Beatles, their manager and George Martin gathered at Abbey Road to try and resolve the quandary. Harrison was all for cancellation, as "playing without Ringo is like driving a car on three wheels".[36] Nevertheless, even he was persuaded by Epstein that their only choice was a substitute. Who? Tony Meehan? Clem Cattini? Tony Newman, from Sounds Incorporated? Andy White? What was Pete Best doing these days? "The difficulty," expounded Brian, "was finding someone who looked like a Beatle and not an outcast."[37] Martin mentioned Jimmy Nicol, who, since finishing with Cyril Stapleton, had been one of the workman-like but individually uncredited Ghost Squad on *Beatlemania*, a cheap Pye LP of *This Is Merseybeat* bent on which – at the standard Musicians' Union rate – 14 Beatle hits had been copied.

The Beatles would remember that Terry Heneberry, producer of both their 1963 radio series *Pop Go The Beatles* and The Rabin Band's forgotten *Go Man Go Show* three years earlier, had also thought highly of Nicol. From the Liverpudlians' own circle, so too did singer Tommy Quickly, after Jimmy had drummed on one of his Pye singles and with Georgie Fame, in whose Blue Flames Jimmy was presently working. Moreover, he'd also made a couple of singles with his own – and now dispersed – outfit The Shubdubs, who'd each adopted a severe moptop.

On that strange Wednesday, 24-year-old Nicol was stirred from an after-lunch nap in his Barnes living room by a ring from George Martin. No, it wasn't another session job. Well, not of the kind he might have expected. Could he be at Studio Two by three o'clock to rehearse with The Beatles? Behind Ringo's famous Ludwig kit, Jimmy ran through five items with them over two hours with curt tuition mainly from John and George and "no music script, but that didn't matter. I already knew the numbers from *Beatlemania*."[38]

Reeling with disbelief at this amazing assignment, he telephoned an understanding Georgie Fame and dashed home to pack for Denmark. On every stage, Lennon "gave me a great build-up",[39] but by the second day a banner calling for a "Ringo Quick Recovery!" (sic) was hauled up during The Beatles' regal progress along the canals of Amsterdam.

Despite a secrecy exemplified by the false name ("Mr Jackson") on the door of his private ward, Starr's whereabouts had been rumbled and Covent Garden exchange jammed with concerned calls. Many were from the States, where, even as they spoke, 'What's Wrong With Ringo?' – a 45 by The Bon-Bons – was being pressed. In Australia, an Adelaide radio station was carrying regular bulletins on the likelihood of him rejoining the group for opening night in the city's Centennial Hall. Over in Sydney, another presenter was whimpering that, rather than Nicol, The Beatles might have given an Aussie musician a chance. From a McCartney quip at the city's Mascot airport – "We're going to give him a gold watch, shake his hand and tell him it was nice"[40] – grew alarmist hearsay that Starr had had enough and was intending to retire, and some went on believing this, even as he countered that "the word 'retire' clicks off a little picture in my mind of a chap digging up the garden and planting seeds. Well, that's not the life for me yet."[41]

Rather than remain huddled under his bedclothes contemplating a free buss pass, Ringo had been touched by a telegram of the "miss you" variety from the other three and, not wishing to inconvenience anyone more than necessary, nor miss any of what was still great fun, he rose after not much more than a week in bed, the minimum time recommended by the doctor. Armed with a bottle of medicine "in case I get any twitches"[43] and compelling a motorcyclist to speed from Heathrow to collect the passport he'd left in his jacket pocket, he let Brian bundle him onto a flight to Sydney via San Francisco, where his transfer from Pan Am to Qantas was accomplished after the usual press conference and fan riot. A toy koala was thrust into his arms as he disembarked and the grinning Sydney media let him go after he'd itemised every piece of personal jewellery he was wearing and knocked back a goodwill glass of Australian lager. When he caught up with The Beatles in their Melbourne hotel, a vast police inspector piggy-backed him through a crowd of thousands. Pale and shaking, he ordered a stiff drink even while heading towards the lift to his suite. He may have needed another after the illuminating experience of watching the group strut their stuff that night with Nicol at the city's Festival Hall.

Afterwards, there was a party to welcome Ringo back and thank Jimmy, for whom a plane from Brisbane had been booked for the next morning. By cruel contrast to his twelve days as a Beatle when "it seemed that the whole population had turned out to meet us",[43] he'd be greeted by only his wife and infant son when he landed back in London. As well as a fair rather than markedly generous cheque, Jimmy had come out of it with an inscribed gold Eternamatic wristwatch that had been presented to him by Epstein, who had, reputedly, taken tacit umbrage at his comments to the press, such as an over-frank "I don't think he [Starr] can play in time",[44] and what was seen as rash sight-seeing, shopping sprees and, once, sitting in with singer Frances Faye and her band in a Sydney nightclub.

These excursions were partly because Nicol had never been entirely comfortable socialising with The Beatles and had sought instead the company of Sounds Incorporated,[45] The Phantoms and other of the package tour's small change who were likewise free to take the air after breakfast without being mobbed. When The Beatles and Jimmy later found themselves booked one night at the same British theatre, neither party made the effort to pop over to the other's dressing room for a chat.

Back with The Blue Flames, Nicol would be signing as many autograph books as Georgie Fame. As a further barometer of his unlooked-for fame, he was contracted to regroup The Shubdubs to take the place of The Dave Clark Five for a Blackpool summer season after Clark developed a stomach ulcer.

The Five had been the first beat group to undertake a full US tour in the wake of The Beatles, who, some would argue, they shut down fleetingly as Uncle Sam's top British act. During one 1964 week, two-thirds of *Billboard*'s Hot 100 was British in origin as more of our major pop icons (and some minor ones) made headway in the unchartered States. This was especially true of Freddie And The Dreamers and Herman's Hermits, whose respective lead vocalists looked as if they needed even more mothering than Ringo.

Top US record-business folk – songwriters like Clint Ballard Jnr and Jackie de Shannon, producers Jimmy Miller and Phil Spector[47] and manager/accountant Allen Klein – became as wasps around the jam-jar of Albion just as the island's own big-shots had lately been around Liverpool. Conversely, Jack Good, the brains behind *Six-Five Special*, *Oh Boy!* and other ground-breaking pop shows, was now inflicting similar wounds on American television. Other Britons who were penetrating North America via pop-associated styles and trends included John Peel (*né* Ravenscroft), who, because he happened to have been born near Liverpool – posh Heswall, actually – was engaged as resident "Beatle expert" by a Dallas radio network. Among less parochial celebrities were two of Ringo's London friends: designer Robin Cruikshank, with his Robin Ltd company, and photographer Terry O'Neill, who became one of Hollywood actress Faye Dunaway's husbands. "It was just like being part of an international team,"[47] said O'Neill. Another Londoner who "arrived" in the States was *haute couture* Diaghilev, Mary Quant, who, pressed by some to autograph her creations, "began to feel rather like a Beatle".[48]

One of her willowy models, Pattie Boyd, felt even more like one when, after landing a bit part in *A Hard Day's Night*, she was charmed away from her then-boyfriend by George Harrison. By 1964, she was cohabiting with the guitarist in a bungalow on his wooded estate in Esher. George's life at Whaddon House with his flatmate had been cordial enough, and they'd even composed together after a desultory fashion when "he was playing my guitar and I had the tape on, so we tried something".[49] During the filming of *A Hard Day's Night*, "the height of luxury" for Victor Spinetti (who played a neurotic television director) was to repair to their apartment "and have bread and butter and chips and watch television".[50] Outside, the marathon vigils held by tatty girls with laddered tights and someone else's love bites was tiresome, and even boys were trying to kiss the Knightsbridge Beatles as they came and went, but it was a burglary of the flat on 19 April – while the group were recording a Jack Good TV special – that had been the last straw for George and Ringo (and Brian), who decided to evacuate to dwellings less exposed to public attention.

City lights had not lost their allure for Ringo, who, unlike George and Pattie – and the Lennons, too – did not flee into Surrey. Instead, through the agency of genteel Brymon Estates, he installed himself on the opposite side of Hyde Park in a leased one-bedroom apartment on the ground floor of Montagu Square, a long Victorian block near the Swiss Embassy. He'd suffer muffled giggling from fans who'd winkled out his ex-directory telephone number but, this and worse inconveniences went with the job, and he couldn't crab about its perks. The most tangible of these was the easy money that had facilitated the purchase of a Facel Vegal so ornate that it "gets more looks than I do".[15] Because George had one, next came a silver, six-door Mercedes 600 with contoured seats, for which he'd have a chauffeur on call "because if you haven't you can't park anywhere or go out and get drunk".[51] However, it was somehow soothing to sit behind the wheel himself. "If things got me down, I'd just get out the car and drive away into the night. It sort of got me out of myself."[52] This habit would intensify after 8 October 1964, when he'd slipped furtively from Abbey Road to take – and pass – his driving test.

Both alone on a moonlit ride and switching from scotch to bourbon down at the Ad-Lib, Ringo was prone to plunging into orgies of maudlin reminiscences. You could stand him a feed in the Ritz, but he'd still be sentimental about when he used to small-talk on the pavement with The Hurricanes while chomping Morgan's newspapered fish and chips. To one who'd berate his Mercedes dealer with "but they only cost £11,000 new",[53] a gold Cadillac now could not compare to the Dingle days of his first car, "a red and white Vanguard which I bought for £75 from some guy down the road. Second gear didn't work, but I loved it."[51]

Now that he was of world renown, the past was never far away, especially when relations and family friends he hadn't realised existed turned up at stage doors, where the very security guards paid to keep riff-raff out could often be bribed to let them in. Three teenage girl "cousins" in New Zealand had – said the eldest – emigrated from Liverpool in 1963. Ringo couldn't locate where their lineage crossed with his own, but, as warlords were entertained at mediaeval banquets by jesters, he let them stay to amuse him as they span again what must have been a very likely tale to have gained them entry to a dressing room theoretically as protected as Howard Hughes' Las Vegas penthouse.

Starr and Harrison had been present in the NEMS office where, 17 years after his reported desertion of his family, Alfred Lennon had suddenly re-appeared for a short conversation with John. If less dumbfounded, Starkey *père et fils* had been "strange together"[54] when they'd been likewise re-united, but Richie's more self-esteeming sire had not had his hands as open for any bounties that might trickle from the Beatle's coffers. This was perhaps just as well, because, during a 1965 visit to his son – the last occasion they ever met – Ringo's natural father, escorting his second wife, had "got the feeling we weren't wanted. He never paid our train fare."[55]

Starkey junior would not risk discomforting his mother by being chummy with her long-lost ex-husband, especially as she was so overtly enjoying her second-hand celebrity. From the Cavern, she'd joined other Beatle relatives in a costly telephone link-up with Radio WROD in Florida, to be transmitted throughout the USA the next day. "I'd love to go to America. I believe it is a lovely place you have there,"[55] she'd enthused, as if it were the Isle of Wight.

Hardly the scoop of the century, either, was Elsie's refuting that Richie had a steady girlfriend. According to *Confidential*, Hollywood's most scurrilous showbiz gossip rag, he had plenty of unsteady ones, from Marlene Claire – captain of New York's Peppermint Lounge go-go dancers – to actress Ann Margret. He'd allegedly "bent her shell-pink ears with an hour of long-distance oogly-googling, all in a special type of Teddy Boy lingo that left little

Annie limp".[56] From the organ that assured readers that timid Cynthia Lennon had once been considered as The Beatles' lead singer, such deathless claptrap could be disregarded, as could assumptions that the sap had been rising beyond a joke when a shapely woman journalist had asked, "What subject do you not want to talk about?" "Your husband,"[15] Ringo snapped back, eyeing her with exaggerated lasciviousness. However, with countless hordes of a certain type of female admirer aspiring to an orgasm at the mere sight of a Beatle, members of the road crew were not astonished when instructed to bring the more personable up to one or other of their masters' hotel suites. In the lobby of Miami's Deauville Theater, Starr cut out middlemen and perfunctory chivalry by snatching one such girl by the arm and manoeuvring her into the nearest lift for tea and biscuits upstairs.

If in more gregarious a mood, he'd often be seen holding court in the bar area with a Southern Comfort close at hand as night drew on. He'd evidently discovered this brew's short-lived magic while in the States. When The Beatles were in Australia, a promoter at McCartney's 22nd birthday party in Sydney would witness "how absolutely rotten drunk Ringo got. At about 3am, he passed out on his feet and just slowly sank to the ground where he stood."[39]

It was a trifle unsettling for the spirited Maureen to imagine that her Richie's waking hours between one concert and the next weren't spent innocently shuffling cards, shaking a dice or slapping a table-top in time when John and Paul played their latest opus on acoustic guitars. Like his mother, Mo was still required to keep up the "just good friends" farce, even though half the world knew that they'd holidayed together with Paul and Jane in the Virgin Islands, albeit with the open-minded skipper of their hired yacht as chaperone. It was possibly a disgruntled fusion of work taking him away from her and the group taking him for granted that made him dig his heels in and refuse to leave the Admiral Grove hearth for The Beatles' first concert in France until Brian made ill-affordable time to talk him around.

Matters between Mo and Richie came to a head when he was re-admitted to University College Hospital for the extraction of tonsils that – after he'd dredged up a croaky 'Boys' in Australasia – had become so troublesome that no Starr lead vocal would be heard on some dates of their subsequent American tour. While he lay on the operating table, there was media speculation about the future of the gruesome excisions. Was it true that they'd be sent to a fan who'd requested them? Were they to be auctioned? In a Carl Giles newspaper cartoon, a girl off to keep watch outside the infirmary was commanded, "You're not bringing 'em back here!"[57] by her father.

Her patience might have been rewarded if she'd been there when George and Paul visited, bearing grapes and sympathy to their drummer's bedside. They were sent on their way with screams, but Maureen passed to and fro unnoticed by most star-struck loiterers. Legend has it that Ringo proposed matrimony during the sweet nothings of one of her visits, but some say that, surrounded by a chuckling throng, he actually went down on bended knee to her one woozy night at the Ad-Lib.

One of Starr's familiars among the Swinging London ravers was Keith Moon, now with The Who. A known prankster and exhibitionist, Moon would create mayhem from nothing, the most documented example being his disruption of a party in Chertsey by steering a Rolls Royce Silver Cloud into the host's swimming pool. However, although his antics necessitated extreme sanctions by the group, this was balanced by his principal asset: he drummed like a rhythmically integrated octopus. Much of his technique – too quick for the eye to follow – had been learned from The Pretty Things' Viv Prince, who deputised when Keith was indisposed and, in 1966, recorded a solo single entitled 'Minuet For Ringo'.

This dedication was yet another indication of how famous rather than how skilful a drummer Ringo had become. Within professional circles, he was deemed less worthy of respect than lapsed jazzmen like Bobby Elliott, The Rolling Stones' Charlie Watts ("the only drummer who leaves out more than I do"[58]) and Pete York, with his regular column in *Midland Beat* and its valuable tips from his own strict practice rota, plus learned critiques of the latest kit accessories. While esteeming Keith Moon as "the Elvin Jones of the pop world",[59]

York twitted Dave Clark – as most of the industry's intelligentsia did – for the crude percussive hooks that were clearly the selling points on any one of the Five's early hits.

There were claims that Clark didn't beat the skins on his own records, although he was a competent enough instrumentalist on the boards. Similarly, through a leak about Andy White, and on the more oblique grounds that garrulous New York session drummer Bernard Purdie had apparently been employed by Tony Sheridan when his German Beatle recordings were tidied up, allegations were made by the ignorant that Ringo didn't play on his group's discs. With Nicol in Australia, Paul might have been protesting too much by saying, "This fellow is fine, but we just can't afford to be without Ringo on a real recording session, because the kids would know that that record was the one without him."[37]

Any uniqueness in The Beatles' drum sound was partly down to George Martin's miking experiments with varying degrees of acoustic overspill and technique of swathing the tom-toms in dishcloths and even blankets to achieve the "pudding effect", as it was jargonised. "It makes me, like, thuddy," explained its prime exponent. "I've always wanted my snare to sound like a tom-tom with a snare on, never just like a snare – you know, those fast jazz snares."[60]

If the antithesis of Prince and Moon, Ringo's style – like that of Charlie Watts – was becoming outstanding for the frugality, whereby "I try and not move at all throughout a whole song, embellish or decorate it at all, keep it really, really simple".[60] Like a vicar shy of sermons, "Drum breaks still bring me out in a cold sweat. I have mental blackouts."[60]

No matter who might have been as capable of thumping The Beatles' drums, it was Ringo who bound them morally as well as within tempo. While John, Paul and George were hesitating over a marijuana cigarette rolled by Bob Dylan after they and the fêted protest-singer-in-transition were introduced in 1964, Starr had had no qualms about trying it, his blissful smile on inhaling being an indication to the other three that this narcotic was seemingly harmless. When Lennon was poised to march out of a ghastly flag-waving British Embassy reception in Washington, it was Ringo who cajoled him to "get it over with". Appearing freakish to patronising Foreign Office males with conservative suits and short-back-and-sides haircuts, the group were jostled, politely insulted and hailed like taxis; but, even after a woman had scissored off a souvenir lock of his hair, Starr seethed only inwardly when requested to present the raffle prizes to these nicely spoken if "silly people, because they hate to admit they like you, too. They think it's wrong."[61]

Just as hoity-toity, sometimes, were the mayors, beauty queens and showbiz "personalities" who were falling over themselves to have their pictures taken with these common-as-muck Scousers who were influencing the minds of millions. Despite his mystified "Vivien who?" when he'd been asked to meet her, publicity-conscious Vivien Leigh had bounded forward to pump Ringo's hand furiously before the shutters stopped clattering. It gave The Beatles deep pleasure to snub people like those many rainbow-shirted, yapping US disc-jockeys who'd dubbed themselves "the fifth Beatle". Because Noël Coward had been waspish about them, "We thought he was a spiteful old man," related Ringo, "so we behaved like spiteful little boys. You know, 'We won't see you because you didn't say nice things about us.'"[61] When classical pianist Artur Rubenstein invited them to his suite in the Sydney hotel opposite theirs, Starr sarcastically suggested the compromise of a get-together halfway across the street.

Naturally enough, the most welcome (and least transparent) of the illustrious who wanted to breathe the air around The Beatles were those who'd been central to a Merseyside adolescence, including Carl Perkins – who'd been an observer at Ringo's 'Matchbox' session – and tough-guy film stars such as Burt Lancaster, at whose Hollywood home Paul, George and Ringo had relaxed one evening, watching Peter Sellers' newest *Pink Panther* movie. Before they left, the hospitable Lancaster promised to send Ringo some Wild West six-guns, if he could get Mr Epstein to arrange an import licence. Later, Elvis Presley would give Starr holsters for them.

Brian would convince his boys that it might be bad form to back away from all of the big-names-in-good-cause galas that were now being held in their honour. You'd see Zsa Zsa Gabor, Shirley Temple and Tuesday Weld piling their paper plates high with salad. Bing Crosby and Edward G Robinson might be unbuttoning themselves in adjacent urinals to yours in the gents. On a staircase, Cassius Clay would spar playfully with Ringo. Don't look now, but isn't that Groucho Marx? That young man that no one recognises – my daughter has a pin-up of him in her school locker. Interestingly, it had struck Starr that "it's the one-shot characters who can be nasty, like the people who make one record and think they're the greatest thing ever to hit showbusiness. Deep down, they know they've got no real talent and that they've had a lucky break."[61]

Well, so had he, but every silver lining has a cloud. Waking up in a luxurious cage of claustrophobic torpor, Starr would almost expect to yawn and stretch to a standing ovation, so intrusive was the world's adoration. Where was the world? "It's great being here in New York!" Ringo had called to the crush barriers as The Beatles were herded from train to limousine in Washington's Grand Central Station. "I've heard that you've got a bridge here," he'd chortled in Sydney. "No one tells me anything. They just drag me out of bed to look at rivers and things."[61] There were photographs of him performing in every continent, but, like an insect – a beetle, perhaps – he could see only his immediate environment. He'd guess he was in Canada only by Mounties that patrolled the besieged hotel. The Earth's richness and immensity lay beyond an ocean of faces and flashbulbs, and his only bleary eyed glimpses of it would be, say, a sunrise in Indianapolis after an obliging state trooper sneaked him into a squad car for breakfast in an empty roadhouse out on the freeway.

Less pleasant a memory was someone tearing a St Christopher's medallion – an aunt's coming-of-age gift – from his neck as he struggled through a *mêlée* of New York fans. Then there was the telephoned death threat taken so seriously that a detective hunched beside the drum rostrum throughout a stadium show in Montreal (to catch the bullet, perhaps) as Starr "played low" like Pete Best, with cymbals positioned straight up, *à la* Buddy Rich. Nobody minded that his posture impaired the group's performance, because who could hear it anyway? "By 1965, we were turning into such bad musicians," groaned Ringo. "There was no groove to it."[62] For devilment, the front line would slam sickening dischords while Starr just as deliberately stamped the bass drum on the offbeat.

For the wrong reasons, tours could still be a laugh, but onlookers would wince at the hollow of Ringo's hands where one range of monstrous callouses touched the next as he fastened a life jacket. He'd scan the Atlantic for sharks while the aircraft with peeling paint that had been chartered for the group bounced through turbulence. Maybe retirement hadn't been such a ridiculous notion after all, he'd think, while sinking into an uneasy oblivion.

7 "I've Been Thinking And Wondering Where It's All Going"

After he'd asked Mr Cox formally for his daughter's hand, Richie and 18-year-old year old Maureen tied the knot on 11 February 1965. To confound the anticipated crowds, the ceremony took place midweek and minutes after the 8am opening of Caxton Hall, the registry office nearest to Montagu Square. George dared to arrive on a bicycle, looking surprisingly alert, considering that he and John had been up most of the night, polishing up two of his compositions for possible inclusion on the soundtrack of *Help!*, the next film. With the groom's stepfather, Harrison was an official witnesses, although neither Lennon nor McCartney had been informed about the ceremony until Brian Epstein telephoned the previous afternoon. "The first thing I thought," recounted Lennon, "was, 'What a sneaky thing to do,' [but] if it was a public wedding, half of America would have come across."[1] From his holiday in Tunisia, Paul brought an exquisite gift – a silver apple – for the happy couple.

Brian gave them a magnificent dinner service. If "a bit shocked"[2] when he'd heard of Ringo's intentions, he was a solicitous best man. The wedding was celebrated with a lavish breakfast in his Belgravia townhouse, and it was Brian who arranged the seaside honeymoon in the Sussex home of The Beatles' solicitor, David Jacobs.[3] By the weekend, the newlyweds were back at Montagu Square, because this secluded crescent in Hove had remained secluded for just three short hours before it was clogged with a babbling mass of well-wishers and doorstepping hacks. The latter were bought off with a press conference on the back patio, where Ringo exhibited quiet good taste in matching polkadot shirt and tie and Maureen, in a twin-set, showed off her wide gold ring with its criss-cross design and explained that her baptismal name was actually Mary.

The most depth that reportage on the event contained was speculation as to whether it would affect the popularity of the group in general and Ringo in particular. Lennon alone knew that "there might be a shuffling of fans from one Beatle to another – at least, that's what happened when news that I was married was 'revealed'."[1] George would be the next to go, but, although his Pattie had also been a salon assistant, she was used to the trappings of inherent wealth and wasn't a poor-honest-girl-from-back-home like Mo or, I suppose, Cynthia Lennon. Like Jane Asher, Pattie combined care of a Beatle with a separate career and income, and could not, therefore, be regarded with the same affectionate approval as the other wives or be the subject of a US novelty single in the vein of The Chicklettes' 'Treat Him Tender, Maureen'.

This plea was taken to heart by the new Mrs Starkey, who continued answering fan correspondence and was patient when, voluptuously weary from another time-zone, Richie would dump his luggage in the hallway and trudge straight into the bedroom for some shut-eye, leaving travel-stained clothes on the carpet. If no Fanny Craddock, she'd always prepare a full meal – Lancashire hot-pot, say, or roast beef and Yorkshire pudding – no matter how late he returned from Abbey Road sessions – which were now running over into the graveyard hours – although she "didn't hold with" trays in bed. Even in the heart of emancipated Swinging London, Mo was still a very northern woman and Richie a northern man. "I don't think women like to be equal," he confided flatly. "They like to be protected and, in turn, they like looking after men."[4]

By Christmas 1966, Maureen would have a bigger house to mind when she, Richie and Tiger – a peach-coloured poodle and wedding present – moved to St George's Hill, the same Weybridge stockbroker estate as Cliff Richard and, more recently, Tom Jones and the Lennons. Slightly dearer than John's mock-Tudor Kenwood, Sunny

Heights had actually been purchased in June, but, while it was an uninhabitable no-man's land of planks and rubble during extensive refurbishing, the Starkeys lingered at Montagu Square, which they decided to keep on, first as a *pied à terre* and then for letting. Overlooking a golf course, Sunny Heights stood in three acres, but, unlike Kenwood, it was approached not by a long drive but by three steep flights of stone steps from a four-car garage.

Ringo loved marshalling the contracted builders and master gardeners who'd dine out later on the jaw-dropping information that he talked like an ordinary bloke, just like that "randy Scouse git" in *Till Death Us Do Part*.[5] With the reckless indulgence of many a fellow from the pub who'd come into a sudden fortune, Starr treated this veritable mansion as "a toy",[6] an outlet for all manner of structural idiosyncrasies. If he liked (and he did), he'd have a go-kart track weaving in and out of the tree-lined landscaping. In a hoop-shaped alcove was his bar, The Flying Cow, replete with mirrors, tankards, counter, fruit machine and even an antique metallic till. He even started painting a mural on a wall in the Games Room, but when he abandoned it halfway through guests were free to add to it as they wished.

This extension was dominated by a pool table. After becoming hooked on snooker in the States, he'd ordered NEMS' general manager, Alistair Taylor, to obtain the necessary equipment. US Forces' officers clubs were tried to no avail, but, hanging the expense, a table, cues and a triangle of balls wended their way over from Germany, along with two fitters. When the other Beatles disappeared to foreign climes on weeks off, the Starkeys stayed put, savouring both the initial rapture of married life and a house that no son of Elsie Graves had ever dreamed of owning until he collected his cards from Rory Storm.

Some corners of Sunny Heights were given over to gold discs and mementoes of a past that, through its unbelievable outcome, had attained a certain romantic grandeur. Appropriately, a portrait of John and Paul loomed over the main mantelpiece. Interestingly, while no vestige of a drum kit could be found anywhere ("when we don't record, I don't play"[7]), the building would be well stocked with electronic gadgets that were technological steps ahead of the Joneses, as well as the Lennons, McCartneys and Harrisons. In nooks and crannies all over the place were light machines, tape recorders, stereo record players and – even in the toilet – televisions, on which the BBC's new second channel could be seen. Screened on either of two projectors were feature films and home movies, like 20 coloured minutes centred on close-ups of Maureen's eye and another shot from the swing that had been bought for the use of children.

The Starkeys' eldest boy was born at London's Queen Charlotte's Hospital on 13 September 1965. Journalists who could count were told that he was one month premature. Boys' names are generally the most difficult, but there were still ripples of sanctimonious opprobrium when Ringo announced that the baby was to be launched into life with the name Zak. Having always dreaded the abridgement of his own to Dick, Zak was, parried Ringo, "a nice strong name, and it can't be shortened. That was something I didn't want at all."[2] In obsequious support, a few young parents in the States also gave their sons this "mad cowboy name that had been spinning 'round in my brain at the time".[8]

Zak would rue "being described as my kid" when Starr's prediction that, "by the time he's grown-up, I won't be playing rock 'n' roll drums"[9] proved false. Nevertheless, he'd received more paternal attention than most, for – heeding Elsie's advice, for once – Ringo made the most of his offspring's cradle days. As he played inexhaustibly with Zak, most of Ringo's intimates agreed that fatherhood suited him, although he'd attended personally to only one nappy-change before engaging a matronly nanny until The Beatles elected to cease public engagements in 1966.

As well as freeing him from the more nauseating aspects of child-rearing, this appointment also enabled the Starrs – like the Lennons – to accept with an easier conscience evening social engagements in London, such as attending Walthamstow Granada with George for The Walker Brothers and Roy Orbison – performing with an ankle in plaster – or the première of *Alfie*, with Cilla singing the title theme.

Sundown usually brought to Ringo an onset of high spirits, and it was sad to sink them into a sofa when they cried out to be shared with others. Therefore, there was no immediate let-up, either, in his frequenting of West End clubland, as in Weybridge "we had lots of acquaintances but few close friends because of our position, I suppose".[10] Once, he skidded across the country from a concert in Cardiff – the last in The Beatles' final UK tour – to avoid missing a Christmas party at the Scotch of St James.

An alternative to cutting a rug there or at newer watering-holes like Tiles or Sybilla's – in which George Harrison had a financial slice – was to breeze down to the Revolution in Mayfair to hear Lee Dorsey or The Ike And Tina Turner Revue. Slumming it, he might troop over to Wardour Street's Flamingo, Marquee or Crazy Elephant to mingle amongst Mods up too late to pester anyone for autographs. Instead, they'd be grooving to Zoot Money's Big Roll Band, Chris Farlowe, The Spencer Davis Group, The Graham Bond Organisation or – less often since his 1964 Number One with 'Yeah Yeah' – Georgie Fame,[11] all of whom would back visiting black Americans such as Dionne Warwick, Stevie Wonder or Rufus Thomas. If touted as "The Swinging Club Of Swinging London",[12] the Flamingo wasn't the Harlem Apollo but it was the nearest to it that Ringo was ever likely to experience, as in the States "we really can't get out. It's too much of a problem. We'd like to see The Supremes at the Copa, and I'd even like to go to Nashville, and to Harlem, especially."[13]

Sometimes he'd need little coaxing to get up and have a blow himself. On a crowded Soho stage one summer evening, he and Denny Laine of Birmingham's Moody Blues, on bass, were the bedrock of "probably one of the worst bands I've ever been in".[11]

After kicking up this sort of row or dancing 'til dawn up the Ad-Lib, Sunny Heights was more restful than the incessant background churn of traffic around Montagu Square. Nevertheless, city dwellers by instinct, the Starkeys understood that Weybridge wasn't forever. Despite Ringo's developing fascination and expertise in film, no cinema room had been constructed or even a proper screen unfurled when a bare wall would suffice. Neither did they bother with a swimming pool, maintaining that it was "not worth it when John's is just up the road".[13]

In regions further beyond the pale of London, the 1950s were only just ending, and the mildest excesses of the capital – wearing hipster flares or combing your hair in bouffant Small Faces style[14] – were a big deal. Mod clothes that no Londoner had been seen dead in since 1964 would be worn by bumpkins at every village-hall dance until they outgrew them. Now and then, certain areas would align with the capital and sometimes even supersede it. The junk shops of Aldershot, for example, prospered during a craze for Victorian military uniforms. Olde-tyme whimsy prevailed in the hit parade, too, with 1966's 'Winchester Cathedral' by The New Vaudeville Band – all vicarage fête brass and megaphoned vocals – and Whistling Jack Smith's 'I Was Kaiser Bill's Batman'. To no avail, both The Mojos and The Fourmost drew out the agony with respective quaint revivals of 'Goodbye Dolly Gray' from the Great War and George Formby's 'Aunt Maggie's Remedy'.

The Beatles had been the only representatives of Mersey Beat in 1966's *NME* poll-winners concert, their swan song on a British stage. Now that they were to stop touring, after honouring existing contracts, the group's music became even harder to reproduce in concert by using conventional beat-group instrumentation. While the backwards-running coda of the 1966 B-side 'Rain' – one of Ringo's eternal Beatles favourites – was yet to come, for 'Yesterday' from the *Help!* LP Paul would sing to solely his own guitar strumming, as there was little to be gained in taking to the road with the string quartet hired for the recording. Had it too been flung into the screams, John's flute-garnished 'You've Got To Hide Your Love Away' would have been even more like feeding a pig strawberries.

Ringo's number on this album, 'Act Naturally', however, was sufficiently uncomplicated to feature in the stage act for a while. A US country-and-western chart-topper for Buck Owens in 1963, it was to be virtually The Beatles' last recorded non-original, as no Lennon-McCartney opus had been suitable for Starr Time on *Help!*. Some of the lines of their 'If You've Got Troubles' had stuck in his throat, and

– epitomised by his distrait yell of "Rock on, anybody?" at the guitar break – this mediocre effort did not ignite in the studio and was abandoned for something in an idiom untried by the group on disc. Roger Miller's 'Husbands And Wives' was a fixture then on the Sunny Heights turntable, but it was decided that the perkier 'Act Naturally' was more Ringo. With Harrison's choicest country picking and McCartney singing the harmony part once double-tracked by Owens, 'Act Naturally' was pressed as a 45 in territories such as Australia, where it got as far as Number Three.

In Britain, Ringo's "grinchy"[15] voice had been praised in a letter to *Melody Maker* which also urged The Beatles to let him sing more. Sufficiently flattered to reward the writer with an LP ("tell him to send the bill to the *MM* and I'll pay it"[15]), Starr replied that he was "quite happy with my one little track on each album".[15] Nevertheless, there were times at Abbey Road when merely spectating until the last phase of each piece grated more than usual, and time-consuming card games with Mal, Neil and anyone else similarly redundant became unendurably yawnsome. That he was the most expendable Beatle, musically, also fed thoughts that he was being cold-shouldered like Best had been. He was not present when the other three assisted on a folkier treatment of 'You've Got To Hide Your Love Away' by The Silkie, duffle-coated university students much like they themselves might have been had they never heard rock 'n' roll. John, Paul and George were also the only Beatles heard on 'Norwegian Wood', destined for *Rubber Soul*, the LP released after *Help!*.

Starr reputedly "had it out" with the others about his growing sense of isolation. No one ever consulted him about anything or considered whether he had any opinions or aspirations, did they? Concerned that their dogsbody drummer should think they'd been ignoring him, Paul and John made amends by granting him a composing credit on 'What Goes On', an unremarkable pre-Beatle creation by Lennon that he'd "resurrected with a middle eight thrown in with Paul's help to give Ringo a song".[16] Well, with their works now covered by everyone from international stars like Matt Monro and Peter Sellers to banjo bands and barbershop quartets, John and Paul had space for generosity.

'What Goes On' was also given pride of place at the start of side two of *Rubber Soul*, and John's 'Norwegian Wood' was remade with Ringo's interjections of finger-cymbals, maracas and tambourine. Along with the Stones' 'Let's Spend The Night Together' and 'I Can't Control Myself' by The Troggs, this smokescreening of an extra-marital affair was excluded from prudish airwaves. "You can read obscene lyrics into any song," said Ringo, shaking his head sagely. "Those people are living in the past."[17]

"Those people" might have read something shocking in *Help!*, too, had they known that The Beatles had giggled their way through much of its shooting in a marijuana haze. Even more unchallenging than *A Hard Day's Night*, Ringo confessed, "It wasn't really acting. We didn't know what we were doing. We just said the lines as they were. We'd read them and then just go out and say them in front of the camera."[18] Walter Shenson had made a reportedly reluctant Ringo the central figure of the film's flimsy narrative – Oriental religious cult plus nutty professor chase after priceless ring that has ended up on his finger. Presumably because they were all new to the overseas market, some of the self-referential jokes he and the others had to utter dated back to 1963.[21] The more vitriolic reviews also gloomed that The Beatles had been overshadowed by a distinguished supporting cast that included Eleanor Bron, Roy Kinnear, Leo McKern and, once again, Victor Spinetti.

For me, Ringo's big moment in *Help!* was his flat "hullo" when George uncovers him rolled in a blanket in a car's boot. This deed also earned Harrison his one vote against Starr winning with 60 a *Melody Maker* poll asking, "Which Beatle wins the honours in *Help!*?"[20] He was worthy of the accolade if only for the cellar scene featuring him, Eleanor Bron and an unchained and full-grown tigress a yard away, with a keeper – clenching a shotgun – just out of lens range. To Ringo's relief, the movie's insurers had stipulated that a stunt-man lookalike by the name of Hans Pretscherer had to be used for the Alpine skiing sequences, but the price of this precaution was Maureen, from a distance, once mistaking Herr Pretscherer for her husband and running to embrace him.

Although both of their films were, drawled Shenson, "big-grossing because they weren't too costly to make",[21] The Beatles were adamant that, in the next one, they wouldn't be happy-go-lucky funsters any more – in fact, they wouldn't even be Beatles. After they'd dithered too long over a screenplay of lightweight comedy Western *A Talent For Loving*,[22] Shenson perceived that, "to find a good enough storyline, which has four leading men, is very difficult".[21] He hadn't visualised any Beatle appearing in a movie without the others, but by autumn 1966 Richard Lester had Lennon as "Private Gripweed" in *How I Won The War*, a curate's egg of a World War II satire. On location in Spain, John told a visiting Ringo how swiftly his enthusiasm for this acting lark had evaporated, but Ringo wasn't as sympathetic as he might have been. He'd have jumped at the chance to play Private Gripweed.

John passed idle hours off camera composing his magnum opus, 'Strawberry Fields Forever', and Ringo regrew a beard that had made headlines several months earlier, when he'd been photographed with it boarding a plane for the West Indies with Maureen and the Lennons. Bound by common ordeal and jubilation, The Beatles, their aides and most of their relations "were one big happy family", Cynthia would remember, "because we were thrown together because of circumstances but luckily enough we all got on very well together".[23] Her mother would be Montagu Square's first tenant, and decades later Paul McCartney would remember the widowed Harry Graves when sending special invitations to the première of his oratorio in Liverpool Cathedral. While an allegation that Ringo had had to ask the group's permission to marry was the brainchild of a bored journalist, Starr liked the notion "that I would do that because of our close ties".[24]

Their uniformity on stage applied when they were off duty, too, as they attended the same openings, listened to the same records and sampled the same stimulants. If George, say, had a garment that the others admired, they would acquire one like it within a week. It was no coincidence, either, that, after Ringo had led the way, Paul, George and John – and the road crew – each experimented with dundreary whiskers, pointed Imperials and similar depilatory caprices. By 1967, all were sporting raffish moustachios.[25]

No one, however, had been in complete agreement over the controversial issue of their investiture by the Queen – on Mr Wilson's vote-catching advice – as Members of the British Empire. Paul cut short his holiday in order to attend the press conference necessary to flesh out the newsflash of the forthcoming decoration, while John sauntered in 20 minutes late after Brian had had to send a car to fetch him. To John, their acceptance of it was as absurd as a demand in one of Screaming Lord Sutch's political manifestos that they should be knighted. Meanwhile, McCartney was delighted with his MBE. Not knowing what to think, Ringo smiled and waved like he was supposed to as The Beatles were driven through cheering crowds to Buckingham Palace on 26 October 1965. His strongest motive for going through with it was that the medal would be something big to show his parents, but he didn't propose ever to wear it.

For a laugh, he'd affix "MBE" after his name on a 1973 album sleeve".[26] The only other use he made of it was when The Beatles and Epstein were among those celebrities who signed a petition – published as a full-page petition in *The Times* – calling for the legalisation of marijuana. He'd been slightly put out about learning from an interviewer of the others' intentions, but had been perfectly willing to be on the list, because "even in hospitals now they can't get into it, as they're not allowed to have it for research, which is silly".[7] He would not, however, be trapped into advocating its use as a herbal handmaiden to creativity, even if he reckoned that "it gave people more scope and more things to talk about".[7]

Extremes of drug experience beyond mere reefers were implied in the self-consciously "weird" debut singles by new bands like The Move and The Pink Floyd, as well as the transition of The Pretty Things, The Small Faces and other established groups from boy-meets-girl songs to musical insights that were not as instantly comprehensible. Lysergic acid diethylamide – LSD – had been "turning on" factions within London's in crowd for almost a year before it was outlawed for recreational use in 1966. Nevertheless, the pop industry's association with acid had led The Troggs' manager to confine his clean-minded lads to provincial bookings in Britain in order to minimalise the chances of illegal drug publicity sticking to them.

Ringo didn't "turn on" in London, however, but in the eight-bedroomed Beverly Hills villa that was the nerve-centre of 1965's US tour. It was George and John's second "trip", the first having been the result of downing spiked drinks by an irresponsible middle-class swinger. For Harrison, its mental distortions had been akin to a mystical reverie, while it began Lennon's incredible journey to unknown – and upsetting – realms of inspiration. Stimulating though it was, LSD was not all it was cracked up to be for Ringo and made no appreciable difference to him beyond hallucinations and surreal sensations that lasted only until he came down. While the others spoke openly about their psychedelic escapades, he hadn't much to add. After a few more trips, he decided that he'd had enough.

Sharpening paranoia as they did, drugs – always obtainable from local narcotics dealers – did not make touring any more bearable. From stadium dug-outs, The Beatles slouched rather than rushed pell-mell towards the stage. Up there, even Paul was forcing his customary exuberance, while John roared purgative off-mic obscenities into the constant bedlam. Afterwards, withdrawn George would inscribe autographs with bad grace or refuse altogether while Ringo would carry on with his game of patience.

In the final dinning weeks of The Beatles' most public adventure, he'd been as a fish beneath stormy waves. While bemoaning the group "not playing properly but nobody hears anyway",[27] Starr made the best of the pleasanter lulls in the itinerary, such as a reunion with old St Pauli comrades backstage at Hamburg's Ernst Merck Halle. There was little else to enjoy. The four performed for three evenings in the Nippon Budokan Hall with the disquieting knowledge that, outside, there were frenzied demonstrations of protest about pop-singing *ketos* polluting this temple of martial arts. However, this was nothing to the naked malevolence at Manila International Airport, where, in official retaliation for unwittingly snubbing the Philippine president's wife, The Beatles entourage underwent an ordeal of red tape in the customs area and, reportedly, the pushing and shoving of a jeering mob. Assured of leniency or even a commendation, however, they behaved in "the roughest reception we've ever had", recalled Starr, who purportedly weathered the brunt of their aggression: "They really had it in for us."[28]

A psychological rather than physical battering awaited them in North America, where sections of the media had sensationalised a story of how Lennon had "boasted" that his Beatles were more popular than Christ. The possible in-concert slaughter of the artists by divine wrath – or someone acting on the Almighty's behalf – improved attendances but did not forestall public bonfires of Beatle records, picketing of shows by Ku Klux Klansmen or attempted peltings of the Fab Four with decayed fruit and more odious projectiles.

The Beatles downed tools as a working band at San Francisco's Candlestick Park on 29 August 1966 after a half-hour no better or worse than any other slew of stale, unheard music they'd dished out for ticket-holders that year. After 'Yesterday', Paul announced "a special request for all the wonderful back-room boys on the tour". Behind him, Ringo then piled into the rote-learnt 'I Wanna Be Your Man', and even that was fluffed as he repeated its first verse rather than remember the second. "Nice working with you, Ringo," called John just before he, Paul and George catapulted themselves into the wavering *a cappella* intro to 'Nowhere Man'.

Starr was "convinced we gave up touring at the right time. Four years of Beatlemania was enough for anyone."[29] In 1963, the pretend faints and good-humoured ecstasies had been harmless and even amusing, but now the antics of fans frightened him as, in straits of emotional blackmail, they'd dangle from ledges, gulp down poison and slash wrists to simply be noticed by a Beatle dashing past those close enough to maul him. Leo McKern would never forget the terror that chased across Ringo's countenance when a simpering, Bermuda-shorted tourist, garlanded with cameras, had waddled towards them for autographs while they were routining a *Help!* scene amid sand dunes: "At a moment of apparent security, deep in the work in hand, he'd experienced an unexpected and unlooked-for assault."[30]

Pondering an uncertain future, Ringo imagined that such intrusions would tail off "when the records start slipping, as they're bound to one day. Then I look at Elvis, who's 30, and I wonder how he keeps on. Some of the old rockers thought they were the living end at the time, then one day the public didn't want to know. I suppose the best thing to do is roll along and say, 'Well, let it happen as it does,' but I've been thinking and wondering where it's all going."[9]

Studying the charts as a stockbroker would a shares index, he'd been defensive about a recent single, 'Daytripper', not leaping as quickly to the top as previous Beatles singles. There to see the *Melody Maker* Pop 30 compiled, he masked his disappointment with "coming into the *MM* at Number Three is quite something".[31] Exacerbating the indignity of coming third to The Rolling Stones in the *NME*'s yearly chart points table, its 1966 popularity poll had The Beatles second to The Beach Boys as World Vocal Group, but "good luck to them. We haven't been doing much, and it was run at a time when they had something good out."[27] The impetus had slackened elsewhere, too. In Germany, the influential *Bravo* magazine's Golden Otto award was won in 1966 by Dave Dee, Dozy, Beaky, Mick And Tich, with The Beatles as mere runners-up.

Pop was a fickle mistress, but Ringo, if not yet a millionaire, was so amply set up now that there was small danger of him having to scratch a living again. Nowadays, he was lunching with the likes of Paul Getty. Midway through a holiday in Corsica, Maureen had more than her fill of sun, but it was no trouble for Ringo to ring Alistair Taylor to lay on a private jet to take them home.

An earlier aspiration to own a chain of hairdressing salons would be forgotten, but he'd started investing guardedly if providently in land securities recommended by Beatle financiers. His boldest step was the founding in 1966 of the Brickey Building Company Ltd, which utilised the supervisory wisdom he'd accrued during the remodelling of Sunny Heights. Most of the new firm's business was in decoration and architectural adjustments to the houses of its proprietor's showbusiness contacts – including John and George – but it also probed into property development. Nevertheless, although

Brickey "sold quite a few flats",[32] it would be credit-squeezed out of existence in less than a year by a government fighting a formidable balance-of-payments deficit. "It was impossible with Harold Wilson," snarled Richard Starkey, MBE. "We got left with five houses and two flats, what with the freeze."[33]

Starkey's grasp of political matters was hesitant. Broadly, his Dingle roots were socialist, but by 1966 his wallet might not have been. In this, he paralleled Cilla Black, but now their paths were diverging. She'd been disgusted, for example, by his and the other Beatles' advocacy of the narcotics that were already destroying Tommy Quickly and Brian Epstein. Nevertheless, their friendship would withstand this and similar ethical crises. The Graves and the Whites still dwelt in close proximity to each other, albeit in more salubrious circumstances. Through Richie and Cilla's prosperity, all had been able to retire early and leave their council terraces for a dotage on the other side of Woolton. Elsie and Harry, the last Beatle parents to move, chose a bungalow in a tucked-away cul-de-sac on Gateacre Park. While Harry would contemplate what to do between breakfast and bedtime, Elsie – pensive at the bedroom window – would peer down on her sprawling city of overlapping towns.

Liverpool still had beat groups, plucky anachronisms unknown beyond Lancashire battling through the old 'Money' and 'Hippy Hippy Shake' warhorses to those for whom Mersey Beat had become a dim recollection. In 1965, Cilla, Richie and Mr Epstein had been on a panel judging the northwest heat of the last "All-Britain Beat Contest". The outfit who came second were The Connoisseurs, who in the following year would take Vince Earl from Rory Storm And The Hurricanes. Earl had stood in Wally's shoes after that elastic-larynxed bass player had left Storm to form The Combo, a septet on the frontier of jazz and pop and notable for its sensational horn section.

It was fitting that Storm and his current Hurricanes had headlined at the creditor-beleaguered Cavern hours before bailiffs came to close it down. As incorrigible an old rocker as ever was, Rory knocked 'em dead with the same old material. He was so far behind that he was ahead of the first traces of 1968's rock 'n' roll revival, but he was too indolent to do anything about it by taking up his apotheosised former drummer's standing offer of monetary assistance whenever he was ready to record a belated follow-up to 'America'.

At the invitation of a New York record executive, The Pete Best Combo had actually been over there to tape a US-only album and for concert dates concentrated mainly in Canada. Containing saxophonists, Pete's latest campaign to recover scrapings of his stolen inheritance evoked only the sweet torment of screams by association. Back home, his career wouldn't plummet like it did almost straight away in North America simply because it had never left the runway, and Pete fastened onto the excuse that he hadn't been cut out for "the swinging scene of those times. I'm not the type that can be swayed by fashion."[34]

The life of Lee Curtis would also be clouded by not making it, but he'd got by as a singer in Germany and had been made welcome at The Beatles' after-hours party in the Ernst Merck Halle. Down at the Star-Club, The Remo Four were wowing 'em with jazz-rock these days, but not so adaptable was Kingsize Taylor, who had reached the end of the line. Largely through the bad faith of the gangsters that controlled the venues at which he worked, he'd been left destitute and had to apply for an assisted repatriation. As The Beatles jetted overhead, Kingsize heaved his guitars, amplifiers and suitcases into a second-class compartment. Miss the last train and you'll wait on the platform for ever.

8 "They More Or Less Direct Me In The Style I Can Play"

How I Won The War had been but one factor hinting that The Beatles were growing apart. There was also George's soul-cleansing safari to India, ostensibly to study sitar, and Paul's incidental music to the 1967 movie *The Family Way*. While it was yet to come to fruition, a film role for Ringo alone was likely, as soon as he and Brian felt sufficient heat from one of the "scripts sent in every day, but most of them are so bad".[1] As they'd been within earshot of each other for every working day since God knew when, it was refreshing, noticed Starr, "to choose when we're together instead of being forced together – and you need to break up a bit to relax, man".[2] The separateness of their individual projects, he felt – to coin a music-business cliché – Enriched The Group As A Whole. Marital fetters counted for less than Beatlehood then and, he guessed, for always. Maureen, Cynthia, Pattie and Jane were all pale blonde by 1967, but the men "have a strange hold on each other", Ringo reassured himself. "At one time, we never went out, even with our own wives and girlfriends, unless another Beatle went along, too."[3]

Not long after the armoured car had whisked them from Candlestick Park, he and Lennon's nerve-wracking pint in a roadside pub had been an exploratory brush with the outer world. Nevertheless, withdrawal from it to a private Beatle commune had been discussed. In pursuance of this subsequently abandoned scheme, the Harrisons and Starr had flown out to the Greek island of Lésvos in July 1967, although he had to leave early to be at Maureen's side in the final months of a planned second pregnancy.

During this transitional year, there'd be other such searches for both physical and spiritual utopias, most of them made possible by the day-to-day mundanities of shifting records. As the expiry date of Epstein's management contract with The Beatles crept closer, once-merry rumours darkened to a certainty that, perturbed by the unresolvable bungles he'd made while learning his craft, the group were to reduce their old mentor's cut and say in their affairs and wheel in a third party. Most fingers pointed at Allen Klein, whose reputation as "the Robin Hood of pop" stood on his recouping of disregarded millions for his clients from seemingly iron-clad record-company percentages. Through hovering over British pop as a hawk over a partridge nest, his administrative caress had come to encompass The Dave Clark Five, The Kinks and the uncut rubies – including The Animals, Herman's Hermits and Donovan – that had been processed for the charts by freelance production whizz-kid Mickie Most. The Rolling Stones had also bitten, grinned Most, after they'd "seen me driving around in the Rolls and owning a yacht, and started wondering where their money was going. Allen got them together and gave them money."[4] Klein also bet Mrs Most that he'd also be superintending The Beatles by 1967.

Klein started sniffing around them. "Allen tried to come in when Brian was there, just as a business manager, and not run our lives," Starr would recall, "and Brian would have nothing to do with him."[5] Klein wasn't the most popular among record-industry moguls, but, wasting no time with small-talk while driving hard and unrelenting bargains, one accountant with no reason to love him believed, "He revolutionised the industry. You've heard lots of terrible stories about him, most of which I concur with, but he was a tough American cookie, and he came over here and negotiated for the artists he was involved with."[6] Paul McCartney had been particularly impressed by his wheedling of an unprecedently high advance from Decca for the Stones in 1965.

Paunchy, short haired and an observer of a routine ruled by the clock, Klein had framed family photographs on his desk within the panelled top floor of a Manhattan skyscraper. For all his methodically blunt stances on the telephone and in the boardroom, he was an impassive, reflective, pipe-and-slippers sort at home and liked to distance himself from the office. Everything that painfully committed Brian wasn't, you wouldn't catch Allen nibbling afternoon scones at Sunny Heights, because he didn't "bother that much with artists, but you have to develop some sort of rapport – although it's important that you stay away. Otherwise you can really get on each other's nerves."[7] When his wooing of The Beatles moved into top gear, he – like a certain Oriental mystic they'd encountered – underwent a crash-course in their music to better butter them up. Nonetheless, the latest stock-market quotations were infinitely more engrossing. For Allen Klein, pop music was simply a commodity to be bought, sold and replaced when worn out.

In 1967, he'd been only fractionally more than a name to Ringo, who'd have been quite happy – as long as the other three were – to keep things the way they were with Mr Epstein, if only because, throughout her marriage thus far, Maureen couldn't "think of any time when we didn't do something because of the money. We never gave consideration to the cost."[7] Habit still motivated her collection of spittled books of trading stamps, but she had but to ask her husband's NEMS secretary, Barbara, if ever she wanted more than the several thousand with which Richie regularly transfused her bank account. On a self-confessed "fund-spending brainstorm" at least once a year, she'd been known to consign entire racks of newly purchased clothes to the dustbin because they hadn't looked as impressive in front of a Weybridge mirror as they had in Harrod's. With customised tailgate, Rolls Royce parts, electric windows and walnut on fascia and doors, Richie's Mini Cooper S had worked out five times more expensive than an ordinary one.

Having never had much back on Merseyside, both were immature about cash. In Greece, blithe ignorance about exchange rates led to a panicked cable to London and a Beatle hanger-on in Athens contacted to get Ringo out of a mess that almost left him without a bed for a night whose blackness would be his sole shield against the excrescent havoc that would accumulate round him. Since 1963, he'd never had to prove identity to sign a bill, and had become unused to actually paying for anything with actual bank notes. Even small change was as unnecessary to him as eyesight to a monkfish – or so he thought. Motoring home from a party in London, his petrol ran dry and, stranded without a penny, he was obliged to hitch a ride with a man from nearby Thames Ditton who, in the ensuing conversation, chilled Starr with the information that he wrote for a national daily. However, a week of trepidation slid by, not a line crept into the newspapers and he was soon able to breathe again. There hadn't been any need to be so ingratiating when, on arrival at Sunny Heights, he'd presented his dangerous but, as it turned out, honourable rescuer with an autographed copy of The Beatles' most recent gramophone record, *Sgt Pepper's Lonely Hearts Club Band*.

However much its content has been devalued by reassessment, this syncretic work was technically an improvement on the preceding LP, *Revolver*, which had contained 'Yellow Submarine', the only British Number One with Ringo as lead singer. With a suggestion or two from Donovan, a crumpled Scot who'd started as a UK "answer" to Dylan, this had been contrived by Paul and John as an ideal children's song for Starr that would simultaneously capture a flavour of nautical Liverpool,[8] with the one-shot novelty of such as 'The Runaway Train', The Singing Dogs or The Southlanders' 'I Am A Mole And I Live In A Hole' plus a topicality in its spoken prologue while referred obliquely to Dr Barbara Moore's hike from Land's End to John O'Groats. This would be cut, partly because today's news is tomorrow's guinea pig hutch liner.[9]

More and more decisions of this magnitude were being made in the studio now that ten hours – the time spent recording The Beatles' first LP – was no longer considered adequate for one track these days. "We're quite big with EMI at the moment," understated Ringo. "They don't argue if we take the time we want."[10] A brass band inserted for two bars, sea-faring sound effects and the inclusion of Pattie Harrison and Rolling Stone Mick Jagger's singing paramour Marianne Faithfull in the *omnes fortissimo* chorus were among mere touch-ups on this kitsch *meisterwerk* that, coupled with McCartney's contrasting 'Eleanor Rigby' – the 'Yesterday' of *Revolver* – nipped in the bud a cover version by fellow Parlophone act The She Trinity, fronted by Beryl Marsden. It also foreshadowed a later-1960s practice whereby a 45 was a spin-off from an already successful album, as well as being the blasting charge for 'Purple Aeroplane' – a parody by Spike Milligan – and a Maurice Chevalier mistranslation in 'Le Sous-Marin Vert'.

Joe Brown, The Beach Boys, Barbra Streisand, Richie Havens and Jeff Lynne were five of many who recorded 'With A Little Help From My Friends', the jogalong Starr Time on *Sgt Pepper*.[11] The song had started life as 'Badfinger Boogie', with "What would you do if I sang out of tune/Would you throw tomatoes at me?" its original opening couplet. Bearing in mind the jelly-babies of yore should The Beatles ever go back to the stage, Ringo said, "'I'm not singing this song,' so it was changed to 'Will you walk out on me?' [*sic*]"[12]

A segue from the album's title track,[13] 'With A Little Help From My Friends' had a sung introduction announcing Ringo in his Lonely Hearts Bandsman alter ego, "Billy Shears", because, as he explained at length, "the original concept of *Sgt Pepper* was that it was going to be a stage show – you know, we start with the clapping and people shouting and then I come on – and we were going to do it like in a theatre; we'd do it in the studio and simulate it. We didn't in the end. We did it for the first couple of tracks and then it faded into an album, but it still made it a whole concept. It was as if we did a few tracks and suddenly there was a fire and everyone ran out of the building but we carried on playing."[5]

A multi-million-seller, the LP vied with their 45 'All You Need Is Love' – issued on Starr's 27th birthday – to top the Australian singles chart, but in 1987 Ringo – unlike the other living Beatles – declined to appear in the celebratory *It Was Twenty Years Ago Today*, Granada Television's two-hour invocation of psychedelic times past that *Sgt Pepper* had unquestionably inspired. Neither had he put forward any choices of characters for the album's fabled montage cover. For Ringo, it "wasn't our best album. That was the peak for everyone else, but for me it was a bit like being a session musician."[5] But wasn't it always? A print from one of the last occasions when press photographers could enter Studio Two easily while The Beatles were there had Paul at the piano, George and John on guitars and Ringo also in hippy get-up – all beads, chiffon, crushed velvet and Afghan fluff – standing aside as if awaiting orders. "They've usually got a rough idea of how the drum goes as well as the guitar and the organ and the 40-piece orchestra," he explained. "They say, 'I'd like that bit to do that.' They more or less direct me in the style I can play."[14]

Almost invariably, he'd be the first to arrive at Abbey Road. Once, while looking for something to do until the others rolled up, he was drawn gladly into Studio One to add handclaps to a number being recorded by Solomon King, a portly American balladeer. When The Beatles got down to work at last, Starr might go home after they'd finished without having done more than cudgel up a scarcely-heeded opinion about a playback only marginally different from the first 54 takes of it that he'd heard. He'd clang tubular bells on Paul's 'When I'm 64', but for George's one *Sgt Pepper* opus, 'Within You Without You', Ringo looked on as an Indian tabla player tackled its three switches of time signature.

Starr might have been nearer the centre of events if he, too, could have come up with a convincing composition of his own. It wasn't as if he wasn't prepared to give songwriting a half-hearted go, but "They're all just ching-a-lings. There's no great tunes come out as far, as [far as] I'm concerned."[14] Through the perseverance of Klaus Voorman (at this time bass guitarist with Manfred Mann), he became slightly more dextrous a guitarist, "and with not knowing, I just jump into strange chords that no one seems to get into. Most of the stuff I write is twelve-bar, anyway."[15]

Twelve-bar songs would have been out of place during this, The Beatles' fleeting "classical" period that would straddle forms as diverse as music hall and John Cage electronic collage. However, Ringo had been permitted creative input, in a piecemeal manner. On *Revolver*, for example, his chance remark caused Lennon and McCartney to change the title of its eerie omega, 'The Void', to 'Tomorrow Never Knows'. A sound-picture of LSD's inner landscapes, its backing track included a melange of tape-loops realised by all four Beatles, Ringo's extract possibly from the wordless soundtrack of his cine-film study of Maureen's eye. Registered as joint-Lennon-McCartney-Harrison-Starkey efforts would be the avant-gardenings of 'Carnival Of Light', in a similar vein to 'Tomorrow Never Knows' but devoid of lyrics and its trace of melody, which was threaded onto a tape recorder during a "happening" at London's Roundhouse; and 'Flying',[16] an infinitely more conventional instrumental first heard on Boxing Day 1967 during *Magical Mystery Tour*, the group's television extravaganza.

Whatever hand he'd had in these pieces, Ringo's principal contribution to that year's epoch-making cache of records was by complementing McCartney and Lennon's patterns of chords and rhymes with percussive subtleties. As the corrupted snare sound on David Bowie's *Low* LP would be in 1977, so Starr's loose-skinned tom-toms and non-resonant snare – first evident on *Revolver* – were copied until then. Praise indeed had been George Martin's acknowledgement that, in *Sgt Pepper's* fragmented finale, 'A Day In The Life', the distinctive scuffed drum section was entirely Ringo's idea.

The Beatle recording of which he would be proudest, 'A Day In The Life' was the valedictory spin on pirate Radio London as it closed in August 1967, while Ringo's recorded farewell on behalf of The Beatles also penetrated the ether on the final day of operation. If *Sgt Pepper* had been this illegal station's most plugged album during that flower-power summer, the single was surely Procol Harum's 'A Whiter Shade Of Pale'. The abstract libretto and adaptation of a Bach fugue in its arrangement would not have been envisaged as pertinent to a chart hit before 1967, when – thanks in part to The Beatles' remorseless prodding of cultural nerves – pop became "relevant", a viable means of artistic expression rather than an ephemeral tangent to more egghead activity. Three of The Pink Floyd had met during a degree course at Regent Street Polytechnic from which they – like Procol Harum, Soft Machine, Cream, The Sam Gopal Dream and the like – had surfaced as darlings of London psychedelic clubs such as the Spontaneous Underground[17] and The

Night Tripper (later The UFO), where an act's appeal to a tranced-hippy clientèle, either cross-legged or "idiot dancing" with catherine wheel eyes, depended less on looks and tight trousers than on the dazzling atmosphere that thickened during incessant extrapolation of tracks from both their album debut and the unfamiliar successor being "laid down" during a studio block-booking of weeks and months. The Beatles hadn't been above sticking their noses around the door of adjacent Studio One during a Pink Floyd session or Lennon breaking into 'A Whiter Shade Of Pale' as men of the moment Procol Harum trooped into the Speakeasy one evening.

The music press had been full of how "mellow" John was now that he was in his late 20s. "It's a groove, growing older,"[18] he told them. It was also a groove to attend hippy happenings without an outbreak of Beatlemania obliging a hasty departure. Shouting, "It's John Lennon!" if he sidled past you wasn't "cool" in the capital nowadays. Without fuss, he'd absorbed a 14-hour "Technicolour Dream" at Alexandra Palace, in which the paranormal effects of LSD were emulated via the contrast of flickering strobes and ectoplasmic *son et lumière* projections on the cavernous walls and bands – not groups – played on and on and on and on. One after another, they appeared on platforms erected at either end of the exhibition centre – The Pink Floyd, The Move, Tomorrow, John's Children (with a guitarist called Marc Bolan), The Flies, you name 'em. During one of the few intermissions, the promenading audience was treated to a turn by a Japanese-American named Yoko Ono, who would conjecture that "you don't need talent to be an artist".[19]

Over in more clement San Francisco, then just as vital a pop Mecca as Merseyside had been, performance artists like her similarly bridged gaps between bands at the "be-ins", "freak-outs", "mantra-rock dances" and "love-ins" that were held in the city's parks, in its transformed ballrooms and – with Derek Taylor on its steering committee – nearby at the Monterey International Pop Music Festival, where the UK was represented by The Who and – on Paul McCartney's recommendation – The Jimi Hendrix Experience, whose Seattle-born singing guitarist had been adopted as Britain's own.

Ringo possessed Hendrix's *Are You Experienced?*, as well as albums by such as Jefferson Airplane, The Doors, Captain Beefheart And His Magic Band, Buffalo Springfield and other new US combos who captivated him briefly as "one sort of takes over from the other".[14] Finding them "nice people"[18] when they visited London, his taste was sufficiently catholic for him to also be a fan of the pre-packaged Monkees, who, aimed at pre-teens, had been thrust together to play an Anglo-American pop group of *A Hard Day's Night* Beatles vintage in a worldwide TV sitcom.

Monkees LP track 'Cuddly Toy' – later castigated for its sexism – had been penned by Harry Nilsson, a Brooklyn-born bank clerk of Scandinavian extraction. Stocky, light skinned and blond, he looked it, too. He was also prey to sudden mood swings, commensurate with the classic artistic temperament. If no Modigliani, he was a fair semi-professional songwriter and, after co-writing 'Readin' Ridin' And Racin'' – a paean to hot-rodding – for California's Superstocks, he'd placed two more of his compositions with The Ronettes, whose svengali, Phil Spector, would introduce Nilsson to Richard Perry in 1968.

Although a US Escort no more, Perry had gained more than a toehold in the record business as producer of cult celebrities like Captain Beefheart and Tiny Tim. His stylistic yardstick was George Martin's output with The Beatles, who, since *Revolver*, "represented the highest examples of recorded art from every standpoint".[20] Nilsson was fond of them, too – in fact, maybe too fond, because, "as soon as I saw what they were doing, I just backed off".[21] Nevertheless, while gaining promotion to computer-department supervisor at the bank, his brace of RCA albums – *Pandemonium Puppet Show* and *Aerial Ballet* – became, with *God Bless Tiny Tim* and Beefheart's *Safe As Milk*, the toast of the London in crowd after Derek Taylor had mailed the collected works of Nilsson to Brian Epstein with the testimonial that "he is the something The Beatles are". The group itself agreed, perhaps flattered by the *Aerial Ballet* single, a medley of Lennon-McCartney songs under the umbrella title 'You Can't Do That', one of their 1964 B-sides. Nicknaming him "the fab Harry", John took the initiative by telephoning Nilsson at the bank, while Ringo would meet him through Klaus Voorman. This began a lifelong amity between the two oldest Beatles and a man whom future fanzines would refer to as a "quasi-Beatle",[22] so much would their lives interlock.

While Nilsson's 'You Can't Do That' scudded up Australia's Top 40, Pete Anders and Vini Poncia did likewise in *Billboard*'s Hot 100 with 'There's Got To Be A Word'. Best exemplifying the passing of the old surf/British-invasion regime was their change of name from The Tradewinds to Innocence, with its hint of flower-power leanings and *à la mode* lack of preceding article.

Paradoxically, 1967 was also a boom time for schmaltz, with ex-palais crooner Engelbert Humperdinck's 'Release Me' keeping The Beatles' double A-side 'Strawberry Fields Forever'/'Penny Lane' from Number One in Britain, just as his 'The Last Waltz' would do with Traffic's 'Hole In My Shoe' a few months later. Down Under, 'All You Need Is Love' was slung from the top by Slim Whitman's 'China Doll'. Supported by smashes of the same persuasion by the likes of Tom Jones, Solomon King and Petula Clark, as well as Sinatra, this counter-revolution of "decent music" was tacitly applauded by such as the *NME*, whose alley-cat tittle-*Tatler* continued to fawn over the coups of ancient Tin Pan Alley executives while crowing, "This year, Yardbirds absent from Top 30."[23]

In view of the sub-culture's supposed bartering system of narcotics and promiscuity, you could understand the establishment attitude; but, with the hoo-hah over the famous Rolling Stones drugs bust and, later, the *Oz* corruption trial, "The news is all over everywhere," was Ringo's homespun reasoning, "so they're spreading it. They think it's great if the police raid a place, but 50 million people have read about it again, and a couple of thousand will say, 'I'll try drugs.'"[24] However, he recognised that the Summer of Love was no more the dawning of the age of Aquarius than the Twist had been. Amused, he ascribed the supplanting of flower-power in Britain by slouch-hatted, tailboard-riding Al Capone chic to "those lightweight clothes. You'd freeze to death. So flower people are putting on their overcoats again."[14]

However, via the account that everyone who was anyone had at the Indica bookshop off Piccadilly, he'd thumbed through hardbacks of mystical, religious and fashionably aerie-faerie nature – *Autobiography Of A Yogi*, *The Golden Bough*, Tolkein, *et al*. His clear expositions during interviews of karma, the transmigration of souls and the world of illusion was evidence of more than cursory poring over these tomes, which looked as well on Sunny Heights' shelves as did the fresh lick of emulsion on its walls.

Along with bouts of highbrow reading and getting the house repainted, the Starkeys' undertaking of numerous hobbies of late was symptomatic of the triumph of sedate Surrey domesticity over nightclubbing, since the arrival of Zak's brother at London's Queen Charlotte's hospital on 19 August. Maureen named him Jason, thereby thwarting her husband's desire "to give him initials – JR or something like that. My gardener said, 'You're not a man 'til you've had a little girl.' That flattened me out, and now I want a little girl."[3]

A week after Jason's delivery, Richie was not ready to tear himself away from his home to a meeting of the International Meditation Society, to which the Harrisons dragged along Paul, Jane and the Lennons. How much more gratifying than either the Ad-Lib or the latest Beatles fad was a curtained evening on St George's Hill spent oil painting, clay modelling, watching TV or cooing over the babies. The Starkeys might have been any commuting executive's family at leisure, and in a sense Ringo would become just such a person during the group's period of self-management after Mr Epstein's unexpected death, on 27 August, precipitated "a strange time for us, when it's someone you've relied on in the business, where we never got involved".[15] Come winter and he'd be rising at nine to "drive in with John and see Paul and George in town. I get home about half past seven, have my dinner, chat, do whatever you do and then go to bed."[14]

A hiccup over the costing of some landscaping by a Mr Gregory had involved legal proceedings,[25] but otherwise all of Starr's problems seemed to be little ones. As well as children, there were the mental debates before the shaving mirror over whether the dagger beard he'd been cultivating to go with his moustache gave him a touch of the corsair or was just plain silly.

Aesthetics aside, his growth as a photographer was blighted by a technological naïveté, but, gleaning what he could from trial and error, he discovered words like *field*, *gate* and *aperture*, as applied to a camera; the versatility of delayed-action shutters; and that "there's a lot you can do with a negative",[4] when he started developing and printing his own films in a newly created darkroom at Sunny Heights. Here, at least, was an area in which he was an authority, as far as McCartney, Harrison and Lennon could see, "and I had all these funny lenses".[26] Billed as its Director of Photography, he showed what these and the rest of his equipment could do in a lot of *Magical Mystery Tour*, such as "a scene with George where I put him in my living room and projected slides on him. It's nothing new – it was done back in 1926 or so – but I happened to be a camera buff, and I think it came out fine."[26]

Second to Paul, Ringo was the Beatle most active in *Magical Mystery Tour*'s editing process in a cramped Soho cutting room while tossing morsels to a slavering press over scampi and chips washed down with hock in an adjacent restaurant. In *Magical Mystery Tour*, he informed them, he was the badgered nephew (in a trendy Al Capone suit) of a fat lady who joined a variegated cast of holidaymakers on a charabanc to undertake a journey of no known destination or outcome. It had been Paul's idea to make it up as they went along. Who needed a screenplay, especially one like they'd had in *Help!*? Who wanted a tenth-rate Marx Brothers? The only guide that they'd devised for this film was "one sheet of paper with a circle on it, and it was marked like a clock, only there was one o'clock, five o'clock, nine o'clock and eleven – something like that. The rest we had to fill in."[5]

He'd quell forebodings about formless eccentricity with phrases such as "aimed at the widest possible audience", "children, their grandparents, Beatle people, the lot" and "interesting things to look at, interesting things to hear".[27] On the last point, few could say that its music was a let-down, as demonstrated by a double *Magical Mystery Tour* EP – costing three times more than a single – almost topping Britain's Yuletide chart. The laboured surrealism of the film, however, wasn't quite the ticket for a nation in the hiatus between a cold-turkey teatime and mid-evening insobriety. It was not damned immediately by underground periodicals who'd been determined to like it, but elsewhere, "It just freaked everybody out," groaned Starr years later, "which was a pity. If it came out today, it would be more accepted. I always loved *Magical*."[18]

"We all did"[18] was his loyal addendum, knowing full well how uncomfortable John and George had been about it from the beginning. From an admittedly prejudiced perspective, Pete Best was even more scathing in retrospect about *Magical Mystery Tour* and "the psychedelic stuff. After that, as far as my own taste was concerned, it was waning."[28] Not the same, either, was the Cavern, now re-opened to host poetry readings and similarly arty *soirées*, although Rory Storm And The Hurricanes would still perform there on occasions. Nevertheless, soon after Ty Brien's untimely demise at the age of 26[29] and an inglorious attempt at a relaunch with two ex-Mojos and Karl Terry, Rory and Johnny Guitar finally threw in the towel. Wally Egmond's Combo – as well as Pete Best's – also packed it in around this time, so that Wally could complete his training as a psychiatric nurse.

No Mersey Beat performer of the old school had forgotten four callow lads who'd had a run of luck in 1962. Away from all this reefer-smoking music, The Beatles were probably just the same as they were – especially Ringo, who, so they'd read, remained "just a guy from Liverpool. Maybe I have changed, but only in little ways. I'm still what I was."[30] What was this transcendental meditation caper they'd cottoned on to now? To Cilla Black, "It's somebody who goes to the loo with a big pile of papers and sits there and reads them all."[31]

She could cackle, but it had been a spiritual unguent for The Beatles after Mr Epstein's lonely life had been taken by what the coroner had concluded had been "incautious self-overdoses" of the tablets, potions and draughts that had been over-prescribed to combat both his real and imagined maladies. He might not have had to rely on them, implied Starr, had both manager and group been aware of the benefits of meditation "on those tours. We got very little sleep, and some form of mental relaxation is what we missed."[32] However, it might not have cut much ice in the fleshpots of Hamburg.

On the very weekend of his passing, Brian had half-promised George that he'd join The Beatles at the International Meditation Society's initiation course at a university faculty in the Welsh seaside town of Bangor. "That's how it used to be," Starr would reminisce. "If someone wanted to do something, all we'd do was follow them."[5] Maureen was still recovering from Jason's birth, but Ringo would relay to her the enlightening nectar from the lips of the robed and ascetic Mahesh Prasad Varma, who, styling himself as "Maharishi Mahesh Yogi", had founded the British branch of the society in 1959.

Through short daily contemplations, the Maharishi had said while toying with his silver beard, the regenerative result of meditation was that all human vices would be eradicated bit by bit, until a pure state of bliss was achieved. There was also a greater alertness, increased productivity and sharper differentiation between the trivial and the important. As Starr comprehended, "People in nine-to-five jobs can use it, because it can be done anytime."[32]

Nevertheless, The Beatles had curtailed their indoctrination in Bangor so that they could assimilate their manager's death in the privacy of their own homes. A few days later, Ringo would be beside John's sombre swimming pool where his considered response to the tragedy was chronicled by a correspondent from *Disc* magazine. The Maharishi had "told us we mustn't let it get us down, [because] Brian would be able to feel our feelings in his spiritual state. If we try to spread happiness, then Brian will be happy too" – so would Ty Brien – "but the thing is not to get too selfish about it. If you get depressed about it, it is a form of self-pity, because you are only sympathising with your own loss."[32]

Out of respect to Mr Epstein's mother, The Beatles did not – as they'd intended – wear flower-power finery at the memorial service but instead turned up in dignified suits. Ringo's white shirt sleeves were fastened with the diamond cufflinks given to him on a 24th birthday spent recording a spot for *Top Of The Pops* by "a generous man. We owe so much to him. We have come a long way with Brian along the same road."[33]

Mr Epstein hadn't been sure that he wholly approved of this Varma, and in the end Ringo "couldn't believe 100 per cent in the Maharishi. He's a very high man, but he wasn't the one for me."[34] An uncle's cynical warning that "He's after your money, lad"[14] had reinforced Starr's misgivings about – for example – the guru's argument that The Beatles ought to tithe a sizeable fraction of their income into his Swiss bank account. His Grace also had pious hopes of a recording career, having already been nominal "producer" – with pride of place on its cover – of *Cosmic Consciousness*, an album by flautist Paul Horn, one of his European disciples.

Varma's advent, however, was at a juncture when Starr might well have been ripe for religion, "at a point," as he himself construed, "where I wondered what I was and what it all was."[14] A year earlier, his flippant reaction to *God* in "Think In", a *Melody Maker* word-association column, had been, "Somebody must like Him."[35] In the following year, the Starkeys' approach to Him appeared too insolently sudden to those who would assume that, in February 1968, they'd accompanied the other Beatle couples to Varma's *yoga-ashram* ("theological college") in India simply because they hadn't wanted to be excluded from another new activity. This scepticism was supported by the pair's return to Weybridge after less than a fortnight of study.

There is, however, much to suggest that the expedition was a well-meant attempt at self-improvement by Maureen and Richie, who embraced a few weeks of vegetarian meals – more baked beans and mash or egg and chips than nut roasts or samosas – "because we knew there wouldn't be any meat over in India".[2] Ringo also took off with George for a day's preparatory conference with the Maharishi in one of his Scandinavian academies.

The Harrisons and Lennons had been the advance guard when the Starkeys, Paul and Jane travelled a long, bumpy route from New Delhi to a plateau above the forested foothills of the Himalayas, where a member of the staff of 40 conducted them around not a compound of mud huts but a sunny encampment of stone cottages (each with five rooms and a four-poster bed), a swimming pool, a laundry, an open air amphitheatre, a post office and a dining hall that served a 7am breakfast of cornflakes, toast and coffee. Other seekers of nirvana at the ashram that spring ran a gamut from a Woking hairdresser to Hollywood film star Mia Farrow and Mike Love of The Beach Boys,[36] who Ringo said "goes on and on like Spike Milligan" and was the life and soul of the party. New songs poured from John, George and Paul, many of them observations of other students. Lennon's 'Dear Prudence', for instance, was dedicated to Mia Farrow's reclusive sister. For his wife, Cynthia, the stay in India was an opportunity to save their deteriorating marriage, but – like Paul and Jane's fading passion for each other – there was no help for it.

When his Grace wasn't looking, The Beatles' lofty ideals would sometimes wobble a little. A "Meditating: Do Not Disturb" notice would be pinned on a door so some could, purportedly, come up for a breath of foul air in hands of poker and firewater wine smuggled in by Mal Evans from the shanty town of Rishikesh on the opposite bank of the Ganges. Well, after all, part of the attraction of the Maharishi's creed was that you didn't have to forsake earthly possessions or – within reason – earthly pleasures. "Of course, there were lectures and things all the time, but it was very much like a holiday," summarised Ringo, who also found the place "a bit like Butlin's",[37] a comment that probably raised a derisive laugh in Stormsville when it reached *The Liverpool Echo*.

The Caldwells mightn't have been that astounded by the news that, just before lunch one morning, Mo and Richie announced their immediate departure for England to the Maharishi, who "suggested that perhaps we should go off somewhere and then come back but we wanted to come home. It was like a hundred reasons which formed into one thing." Mostly, they were homesick for the children, but – for Ringo, particularly – the prickly heat had not been mitigated by the peaceful balm of the campus, nor the spicy dinners by the supply of tins of beans and cartons of eggs he'd brought with him.

He promised to parcel George, John and Paul some more cine film as he and Maureen left by hired car for Delhi and a flight home that was largely untroubled, bar an ugly moment at Tehran Airport, where someone asked if he was "one of The Beatles. I said, 'No,' and he just walked away. I guess we're not too big in Tehran."[2]

Back at St George's Hill, the Starkeys decided to sidestep the inevitable barrage of press attention by escaping with the boys for a couple of days at a location deep in the home-counties countryside. "At the moment, I meditate every day," he'd assure waiting interrogators. "Well, I might skip the odd day if I get up late or arrive in town late or something."[38] No one doubted him for a second.

9 "I Suppose I Seem Fairly Straight"

If Mr and Mrs Average had been alienated by *Magical Mystery Tour*, the Maharishi and some of The Beatles' marijuana-smoking music, Ringo surfaced as the group's anchor of normality during the eye-stretching aeon between the Rishikesh escapade and 1971's disbandment amid the flying buttresses and quizzically raised judicial eyebrows of London's High Court.

Before Paul and Jane and then the Lennons and Harrisons came home in dribs and drabs from the all-too-human Varma, Ringo had been the only Beatle on the spot at NEMS' new Mayfair storm centre to excuse their latest error and plug the new single, 'Lady Madonna', on which singer Paul – via a nasal affectation – was mistaken for him by many. The lad himself had shuffled wire brushes for a rhythm track reminiscent of Humphrey Lyttelton's trad jazz instrumental 'Bad Penny Blues' from 1956. Yet, with reissues of 'Rock Around The Clock' and Buddy Holly's 'Rave On' in the UK Top 50, rock 'n' roll revival had "suddenly hit the headlines", noted Ringo. "Because this one is a rocker – a slight one, anyway – people are saying it's a rock 'n' roll record."[3] Like The Move, who'd invested their 'Fire Brigade' with an antique Duane Eddy twang, The Beatles were accused of regression as well as bandwagon jumping. "It's not a backwards step," Starr protested. "It's just another type of song from The Beatles."[3]

To his interviewers, Ringo looked very well after his foolhardy travels. More relaxed and articulate than before, he was weaning himself off booze – "just the odd bourbon or beer"[1] – with coffee and chain-smoked American Larks. The zenith of depravity nowadays was "the odd bet on a horse, but no bookie will ever get rich on my bets".[2]

Although extravagant in other matters, his wife was as circumspect about the children's "few bob pocket money each week". Said Ringo, "Once it's spent, that'll be that, though I guess I'll be like most dads, buying them something when they ask for it, then getting a row from Mum."[5] Maureen was annoyed too when Richie still dumped his clothes on the bedroom floor but gladdened by his diminished ardour for nightclubbing – "I sort of expect it to be like it used to be but it never is"[3] – and his contentment (while it lasted) with the sedate domesticity of Brookfields, their new home outside Elstead, a village near Farnham where Surrey bleeds into Hampshire. Rather than the huntin', fishin' and shootin' traditions of those born into privilege, the Elstead acres' natural lake, orchard and forest were enlivened with the new residents' practice of go-karting.

"Why should we be lonely?" was Ringo's rhetorical demand of the final edition of *Rave*. "We have each other, and we never knew anyone in Weybridge",[4] where Sunny Heights – like a few remaining Brickey Builders properties – was still unsold. With the desires of such magazines' subscribers in mind, he threw in cosy anecdotes about Tiger's new-born puppies and the harshly truncated fairy tales he related to Zak ("a bloody terror") and Jason: "There was Father Bear, Mother Bear and Baby Bear, and Mother Bear made some porridge – but a thief broke in and stole it."[5] In the short months when rural quiet and isolation from the capital were refreshing, he swore, "We couldn't live in town again – too much noise and too much going on. I suppose I get bored just like anybody else, but instead of having three hours at night I have all day to get bored in."[4]

Out-buildings around the centrally heated 16th-century manor house included stables, a garage and – exotic for even the home counties then – a sauna cottage. Within the ivy-clung walls, with their exposed rafters, the Starkeys had a cinema and a snooker room, where Ringo would "put the videotape machine on and film myself playing".[4] Owner, too, of the first privately purchased cassette recorder in Britain, his butterfly concentration now embraced all manner of soon-exhausted hobbies involving "thousands of pounds' worth of equipment. I call them my toys, because that's what they are."[6] Often, he'd lose interest while merely glancing at instructions for setting up a newly delivered gadget. When winter gloom descended, he warded off ennui with more familiar pastimes such as "a week when I'll just play records. Then I might spend a day just playing with my tape recordings."[4]

Excitedly, he'd sometimes drop everything to develop some flash of musical inspiration but, after strumming or pounding a bit, it would become too much like hard work and he'd hope the phone would ring. If not, his egg and chips would be getting cold or *M*A*S*H* just starting on television. Maybe he'd have another go tomorrow. His songwriting methodology is worth quoting at length: "I usually get a first verse and then I find it impossible to get anywhere else with the song. I can't say, 'Now I'm going to write.' I just have to be around a guitar or piano and it just comes. Usually, what I do if I'm in the mood is put the tape on, if I've got a tune, and then I play the same tune like a hundred times with different words. Then I take the tape off and get it all typed out and then I pick the lines out that I'll put together."[7] To give himself more scope, he even took guitar lessons for a while in a praiseworthy attempt to progress beyond "my famous three chords"[8] of A, D and E major.

For one incomplete 1968 ditty, 'It Don't Come Easy', he sought help with arrangement from George, who was more malcontented a victim of The Beatles' ruling composers' frequently disheartening indifference to the efforts of colleagues. For another item, 'Three Ships In The Harbour' ("which had 93 verses"[8]), Ringo called on Harry Nilsson, who had lately been gratified by a royalty-earning version of his 'One' by Three Dog Night.

Similarly lucrative was this North American vocal group's cover of Lennon and McCartney's 'It's For You', using Cilla Black's 1964 UK hit as a helpful demo. A legacy from Brian Epstein which put the lady more directly in the news was *Cilla*, a weekly 50-minute series negotiated before his death. Its huge budget could be justified by record-breaking viewing figures, bolstered by Paul McCartney's Top-Ten signature tune and guest stars of the magnitude of Tom Jones, Harry Secombe, Tony Bennett, fiery chart newcomer Julie Driscoll – and a delighted Ringo, whose invitation was at his old mate's own instigation.

On BBC1 on 6 February 1968, he became the first Beatle to sing without the others on another artist's show as unseen millions watched the inauguration of Ringo Starr's solo career, even though "without John, Paul and George I feel vulnerable, like a sultan with 300 wives who, one day, goes out to buy an ice cream for himself".[9] His pre-performance puffing of several fretful cigarettes was interrupted by a comforting telegram "from all your big brothers".

Black and Starr's scripted patter was far from 1961, when she'd had to lean over his kit to share the mic for 'Boys' at the Aintree Institute. Ringo sported a period trilby for their duet of coy 'Do You Like Me Just A Little Bit', suggested by Paul's father from his 1920s dance-band repertoire. The following week's guest, hip Donovan, had intended to simply sing his latest single, 'Jennifer Juniper', but, bragged Cilla, he'd been so taken with the Liverpudlian duo that "he wanted to do something similar".[10] In baggy black suit, shirt and white tie, Ringo's likeable disposition had also come to the fore with a solo rendition of 'Act Naturally' before he proceeded to do just that as a "ventriloquist" – with Cilla as the dummy – in a brief sketch.

Since proving himself as instant a hit in *A Hard Day's Night*, Starr (via the late Brian) had been courted by movie moguls on the look-out for new talent – or was it with cynical expediency that "they sort of stuck on me as Ringo the Film Star because I don't write or anything"[11]? Hardly a week went by in the mid to late 1960s without some pop icon fancying him or herself as a "proper" cinema attraction; Dave Clark, Manfred Mann's Paul Jones, Mick Jagger and even Cilla needed to have a go. What did the world miss when eternal Geordie Eric Burdon allegedly failed a screen test to star in a film treatment of Evelyn Waugh's *The Loved One* with Rod Steiger?

After Lennon had tested the water with *How I Won The War*, Ringo had also accepted a modest part – and his first screen kiss – in a non-Beatle film. ("Best thing around at the time, I thought."[12])

In the advisedly X-certificate Italian-French production *Candy*, he dominated the screen for a few minutes as Emmanuel, a Mexican gardener preparing for holy orders but unsuccessfully sublimating his very worldly lust. He was perceived by Starr as "a very nervous sort of fellow. I was nervous, too, as it happened, and that's how I played the part."[13]

"I'd never have got it if I hadn't been a Beatle,"[12] he admitted, but whither boxing champion Sugar Ray Robinson or Gallic *chanteur* Charles Aznavour also landing parts in *Candy*? In the title role, hitherto-unknown Swedish 17-year-old Ewa Aulin was stunned by "the chance to work with Ringo Starr"[14] during his five-day shoot in Rome, but critical accolades were to be saved for James Coburn, Marlon Brando (as an Oriental guru) and Richard Burton for their more substantial skills in this adaptation of a *risqué* novel – with long-range echoes of Voltaire's *Candide* – by Mason Hoffenberg and Terry Southern, one of Ringo's favourite writers and author of *Dr Strangelove* and the screenplay for *The Loved One*.

Certain passages – like Candy's aunt employing a clothes peg to prevent male entry to her clitoris – were deemed too indelicate for depiction on the silver screen. Even so, a projectionist was arrested for daring to show the film in one American state. Not in the book was Emmanuel's confounded attempt to undo innocent, adolescent Candy on a billiard table. With Zapata moustache and broken English ("ees a-no good"), Ringo served, in retrospect, as an untutored and more sinister model for Andrew Sachs' portrayal as a Spanish waiter in the anarchic 1970s sitcom *Fawlty Towers*.

Most press notices mentioned Starr only in passing. Neither did Starr then "see myself more as a film star than as a Beatle, or vice versa".[15] The follow-up to *Help!* that the group still owed United Artists had not yet passed beyond shallow and arrogant talk of persuading Fellini to direct and sounding out Groucho Marx, Mae West and Jimmy Durante for non-specific bit parts. Someone's brainwave of trying Tolkein's *The Lord Of The Rings* was scotched by its originator's disapproval and the argument of Ringo (pencilled in as Bilbo Baggins' confrere, Samwise Gamgee), who argued that "it will take 18 months to mount and, by that time, we will all go off the idea. What we must do is to start something on the spur of the moment, otherwise we will never get it done. We are always into other things."[15]

Among these "other things" was George's incidental music for an oddity of a movie entitled *Wonderwall*. Its soundtrack – with percussion by an Indian ensemble, The Remo Four's Roy Dyke and an uncredited Starr – was the first album to be issued via EMI by Apple, The Beatles' own record company, a division of Apple Corps, a name registered in 1963 as an eventual umbrella term for maverick artistic and scientific ventures. Also to be financed under the quartet's naïve and self-managed aegis was a Lennon-formulated plan for a school for the Beatle children. "We saw it [Apple] housing all our ideas, and we believed it would all go well," groaned Ringo when it didn't. "But we weren't businessmen, and we aren't now."[15]

Some of their pop peers had also diversified for fun and profit, off-the-cuff examples being Chris Farlowe's military memorabilia shop in Islington; Merseybeat Tony Crane's stake in a Spanish night club; Monkee Davy Jones' New York boutique; and Reg Presley's patenting of his fog-dispersal system. With what was assumed to be wealth past calculation, The Beatles could be more altruistic. According to clever newspaper advertisements, a kindly welcome awaited not just those who'd nurtured a connection with the group's inner circle but any old riff-raff who wished to solicit Apple for finance for pet projects. Impetuous cash was flung at such as a so-called "electronics wizard"; two unprofitable shops; a troupe of grasping Dutch designers trading misleadingly as "The Fool"; film-makers who wouldn't make films; poets who didn't write poems; and, remembered Ringo, a tent for "another guy to do a Punch and Judy show on a beach. They'd take the money and say, 'Well, maybe next week.'"[16] When 3 Savile Row was established as Apple's permanent address, sackfuls of mail would overload its postman; pleading voices would bother its switchboard; and supplicatory feet would ascend its steps from morn 'til night before a narrow-eyed doorman was appointed to shoo them off. Yet, to loitering pavement fixture Alex Millen, his fallible idols "did strengthen the belief that Joe Soap was important and, yes, you too could have something to say".[17]

In the white-walled, green-carpeted offices, it was a boom time for Apple's staff, too, when they'd assimilated the heedlessness of their paymasters' expenditure. A dam burst for a river of wastefulness to carry off gluttonous restaurant lunches; bottle after bottle of liquor, illicit trunk calls to other continents; and wanton purchases of trendy caprices swiftly to lie forgotten in desk drawers. With a stroke of a pen, a bold executive could award himself a Rolls Royce, a house extension and even a whole house. His secretary would conceal his thefts to better hide her own.

Out of his depth, Starr saw the organisation as another expensive toy to be disregarded, if not jettisoned altogether, when he grew tired of it. Soon he was "only involved in Apple as much as I have to be. If there's a decision to blow up the building, I'll go along and raise my hand and say, 'Aye.'"[18] Whenever he was in the mood, he'd lean forward on the hard-backed Regency chair in his office and play company director. For a while, he shrugged aside the disgusting realities of the half-eaten steak sandwich in a litter bin; the receptionist rolling a joint of best Afghan hash; the typist who counted paperclips and span out a single letter (in the house style of no exclamation marks!) all morning before "popping out" and not returning until the next day. A great light dawned. "We had, like, a thousand people that weren't needed, but they all enjoyed it. They're all getting paid for sitting around. We had a guy there just to read the tarot cards, the *I Ching*. It was craziness."[19]

Apple Records was the only department that "didn't let us down".[16] With guinea pigs like ex-Undertaker Jackie Lomax, soprano Mary Hopkin (a regular on BBC Wales' *Disc At Dawn*) and former James Brown *protégée* Doris Troy, Harrison and McCartney cut their teeth as record producers, with Mary's debut Apple single knocking The Beatles' 'Hey Jude' from the top of the British charts. She was then ousted in November 1968 by a funereal-paced 'With A Little Help From My Friends' by bellyaching Joe Cocker, an ex-East

Midlands gas fitter whose producer, Denny Cordell, had – with Keith Moon and Manfred Mann – been proposed for a freelance commission during Apple's optimistic genesis. Intrigued by Cordell's sweaty if less attractive overhaul of his *Sergeant Pepper* moment, Ringo volunteered his eager services for Cocker's subsequent album, although his contribution was scrapped.

Within Apple, Ringo had founded on 16 July 1968 his Startling Music publishing concern, initially to gather royalties should any of his pedantically wrought compositions ever warrant release. Eclipsed by the other Beatles' more tangible activities, he was, nonetheless, happy to rattle the traps for Paul and George's clients – mostly in Savile Row's new basement studio – and, after he'd got used to her, for Yoko Ono, who had now replaced McCartney as John's artistic collaborator as she had Cynthia in his bed.

Yoko had once sniffed around Ringo for his patronage for her "concept art", but he was unmoved by her wrapping Trafalgar Square statues in brown paper, her inane *Grapefruit Book*, her *Four Square* (a remake of *Bottoms* that consisted of what you think it did) and anything else she considered necessary to win his sponsorship. His bemusement with Yoko contrasted with John's jealous imaginings, after he brazened it out by escorting her to the Old Vic to catch a stage adaptation of his slim 1964 volume, *In His Own Write*. A perturbed *Beatles Monthly* passed her off as his "guest of honour", but nothing could cover up the genital display on the sleeve of *Two Virgins*, which was published in *The News Of The World* months before the eventual release date of the disc, which had been postponed while Lennon's appalled advisors tried to talk him out of it. *Two Virgins* was the first of a trilogy of Ono-Lennon albums filled with sounds not generally thought of as pop entertainment. Although they didn't "dig their records",[20] the Starkeys of all the other Beatle couples swooped most unquestioningly to Lennon's defence. Of the unclothed 'Two Virgins', Ringo commented, "It's just John being John. It's very clean."[21] Yoko became "incredible". No one else doubted it, either. "We'll be pleased when people realise that she's doing something [and] that she's not trying to be the fifth Beatle."[21]

Waiting to console Yoko just before Lennon's cremation twelve years later, Starr's muttered "it was her who started all this"[22] indicated an adjustment of his stated opinion, in as late as 1971, that her and John's amour had not taken priority over group commitments. "Ringo was a little confused," deduced Klaus Voorman, "because John's closeness to Yoko was sad to him. John and Yoko were one person, which was difficult for him to accept."[23]

When The Beatles next convened at Abbey Road, Yoko's constant and baleful adherence to John in both control room and playing area entitled Paul to bring along his current American girlfriend and then the one who succeeded her, Linda Eastman, from a family of showbusiness attorneys. Although Linda and Yoko had both attended school in the same smart New York district, they didn't have much else in common, although they'd each marry their respective English *beaux* during the same month in 1969.

Lukewarm rapport between the chief Beatles' immovable women was one of Ringo's "little niggly things that cropped up"[24] while he sat on the fence as the group muddled through a double album that, in its prosaic name alone, justified George Martin's observation that *The Beatles* was "sort of businesslike",[25] as engineers grew accustomed to two or even three Beatles missing at any given session. As the four's emotional and professional solidarity shredded, a combination of self-interest and acquiescence permitted ear-catching pieces like 'Back In The USSR' (which spurred Zak Starkey to "zoom around like an aeroplane"[26]), 'While My Guitar Gently Weeps' and jarring 'Revolution Nine' to be flanked by inconsequential filler: one-line librettos, pretty-but-nothing lieder, excerpts from raucous jamming and self-referential musical jokes like 'Glass Onion'. Ringo's chief memory of 'Birthday' was, "Anyone could shout a line...the roadies, the tea lady. If anyone had a line, it would be used."[27]

This ersatz rocker also bracketed the nearest that Starr would ever come to a recorded drum solo. Although his new wooden Drum City kit had two hanging tom-toms, neither were hit for eight petulant bars of kick-bass, snare and hi-hat bashed simultaneously on the beat, *mach schau* style.

Anything went. More catalytic familiars and guest players than ever were assembled to add icing to the cake. Mal Evans blasted trumpet on 'Helter Skelter' and Yoko was loud and clear on 'The Continuing Story Of Bungalow Bill' and 'Revolution Nine'. Because such moonlighting was frowned upon by his record company, Eric Clapton's solos on George's numbers had to be attributed to 'Eddie Clayton' – Ringo's idea – just as they'd been on *Wonderwall*. Jack Fallon – a Canadian emigrant who'd promoted Beatles bookings in the West Country during the Pete Best era – was hired to scrape country and western violin on 'Don't Pass Me By', the exhumation of which – although a personal triumph for Starr – illustrated the depth to which standards had fallen.

The track had withstood attempts to alter its title, but only several structural changes to its mediocre melody convinced McCartney, Martin and Lennon that 'Don't Pass Me By' no longer resembled the work of another. Even so, its twist-in-the-tale lyric was too nonchalantly morbid and clumsily expressed, but as no one expected little Ringo to be a genius composer that very fact would render this slight, laughable novelty – buried towards the middle of side two – endearing to Beatle diehards. "Ringo's best ever,"[28] grinned one reviewer before savaging 'Revolution Nine', which prefaced the valedictory 'Goodnight', Starr's other lead vocal on *The Beatles*.

Lennon's lullaby to his neglected son, 'Goodnight', was banked with slushy strings and The Mike Sammes Singers. Like 'Yellow Submarine', it had borne George Martin's removal of a spoken preamble – of the "toddle off to beddie-byes, kiddies!" bent – but Ringo's plaintiveness rather than John's edgy inflection better conveyed the necessary – and too apt – air of over-tiredness before the last run-out groove.

Ringo would not look back on *The Beatles* with much affection, although there'd been no discernible animosity at first. However, to engineer Ken Scott, under Paul's instructions during brass overdubs for 'Mother Nature's Son', "Everything was going really well, and then John and Ringo walked in – and, for the half hour they were there, you could have cut the atmosphere with a knife."²³ Since the advent of Yoko, and John's co-related passiveness, McCartney's attempts to motivate the other personnel had backfired, his boisterous purpose translated as barely tolerable bossiness.

An irksome lecture from *bête noir* Paul about a fluffed tom-tom fill had been the delayed-action spark that had fired Ringo to stalk out of Abbey Road mid-session. Sooner than any Beatle imagined, he'd testify in court, "Paul...is very determined. He goes on and on to see if he can get his own way. While that may be a virtue, it did mean that musical disagreements inevitably arose from time to time." Starr added that such tensions had stimulated the group's creative resources. Nevertheless, he'd had a surfeit of Paul's schoolmasterly perseverance – and the withdrawn John letting him get away with it – during the making of *The Beatles*.

Treated as but a tool for Lennon and McCartney's ebbing collective genius, "things were getting a bit rough"³⁰ for Ringo. After motoring the long and gradually more loathed miles from Elstead, his hackles would rise further as it became usual for the studio receptionist to see him facing her and "reading a newspaper. He used to sit there for hours, waiting for the others to turn up."³¹ When a quorum of Beatles finally got to work, he'd be on the edge of agitated debates that would scale such a height of vexation and cross-purposes that console assistants would slope off for embarrassed tea breaks until the flare-up subsided to a simmering huff. Then, in his isolation chamber, Ringo's ears in the headphones would tingle after hours spent thumping out take after rejected take, his concentration split through straining to decipher the drone of murmured intrigue amid the tape spools and blinking dials. Crowned by Paul questioning his very competence as a musician, "I couldn't take it any more."³⁰

That their weary drummer's resignation was more than a registered protest or one of his infrequent fits of pique became clear with his verbal notice to John and then Paul. Yet neither they nor George dared credit this extreme strategy by the standard-bearer of group stability. The matter was hushed up and they endeavoured to carry on as if nothing was wrong. Actually, Ringo's departure –

although regrettable – was by no means disastrous, as Paul, George and John managed a composite drum section for 'Back In The USSR'.

They were about to minister likewise to 'Dear Prudence' when the prodigal returned after a fortnight in the Mediterranean on Peter Sellers' yacht. Out of The Beatles' reach, he'd calmed down enough to jot down the basic structure of a new Starr original, 'Octopus' Garden', following the vessel's chef's fascinating discourse one lunchtime about life on the ocean floor. Tight coils within had unwound and, for all that had driven him from the group, it abruptly made sense to ring up and report for duty again. Half expecting a row, he was greeted with a drum-kit festooned with remorseful flowers and "welcome back" banners.

This conciliatory and even amicable mood persisted for what was left of the sessions. Because they meant one less pole of alliance for Ringo and George, Lennon's increasing absences helped, as he and Yoko hurled themselves into a ludicrous world peace mission, headline-hogging espousals of favoured minority causes and, regardless of cost, an elaborate yet slap-dash array of arty demonstrations. "John has always been freakish," explained Ringo, as much to himself as anyone. "Now that he has married Yoko, it shows more."[20]

Much of the Lennons' behaviour – especially their penchant for nudity – tarred their associates with the same brush. The riotous closure of Apple's Marylebone boutique – when all remaining merchandise was given away – touched off a *Daily Mirror* cartoon set near the queues. "Ringo got carried away, officer," says McCartney to a constable confronting a naked Starr.

While this may or may not have set Ringo hooting with hilarity, not so funny were repercussions of a narcotics squad pounce on his Montagu Square maisonette, where Yoko and John had found a temporary refuge from self-aggravated media attention. Unacceptable to the plain-clothes sergeant in charge was their plea that the cannabis his men had dug out was the lost property of some earlier tenant. While he was above shifting the blame onto his former mother-in-law, Lennon let out the raw information that Jimi Hendrix and beatnik novelist William Burroughs – a former drug addict – had both stayed there.

Stung by this unwelcome publicity, Brymon Estates Limited instigated civil proceedings against Starr to bar the Lennons and other undesirables from using the premises. Although their battle was lost before the Queen's Bench in February 1969, the affair left such a nasty taste in Ringo's mouth that he sold his freehold interest in the place.[32]

Most reports on the case pointed out that the landlords had no gripes about the Starkeys residing there. When The Beatles had publicly renounced consumption of illegal drugs, Starr was the only one who neither continued nor resumed the habit (well, not immediately), although he qualified this in saying, "Who says that booze and cigarettes aren't as much of a drug as pot?"[33] Nevertheless, in as late as 1973, he agreed without hesitation to broadcast an anti-narcotics appeal on US radio. He had his head screwed on, see, not like those other weirdos. Guilty of cocaine possession not long after the Lennons' bust, George seemed just as screwy as John on the quiet, with rumours circulating that he was to become a full-time Hare Krishna *bhakta*, bald head and all. Since Linda had moved in with him, even Paul – once the personification of narcissism – had become whiskered and scruffy.

No matter which journal still canvassed its readers on the most popular Beatle – Paul in *Jackie*, John in *Disc* – Ringo was invariably second. Seeming a beer-and-skittles sort who rejoiced in his married state, "I suppose I seem fairly straight and a family type, so people do associate more with me than, say, John."[6] When ATV bought a majority stake in Northern Songs in 1969, Ringo got shot of his holding for £80,000 but otherwise he didn't have more money than sense nowadays, because, "If I think I'm being conned, I do without."[34] Although long removed from the everyday, he was bereft of the guilt and concerned indolence of others who also had "more money than I ever dreamed of".[2] Begging letters were sifted by his secretary and "I usually give the genuine ones a hand, but the scroungers get nothing."[2] Another occupational hazard of The Man With Everything was being spoilt for choice: "My friend Ray in Liverpool has got this collection of just 40 records, and he knows them all and loves each one. I've got maybe 1,000 and I never really know which one to put on."[6]

He did not, however, hanker after the old days of Dingle poverty, as it was "so black up there. I'm not sure I could ever live there again. I haven't turned into my dad like so many of those I knew in Liverpool, [but] it's difficult if you live on the same street as those you grew up with; you think twice about putting on, say, a green suit with yellow dots."[6]

His idiosyncratic finger adornment was moderated, but, in anticipation of the decade that elegance forgot, he took to dressing in such eye-torturing garments as a *very* red shirt, a custard-yellow cravat with a jewelled pin, a white-striped green suit and knee-high fur boots. The acme of gentility, "I went up to a cousin's wedding in an old gold suit, not very startling, and some gate-crashers had a go at me."[6]

For sit-down meals on these occasions, there were no special pre-requisites (apart from his known dislike of onions) for the Starkeys, whose first try at vegetarianism had lasted just a few weeks – although Ringo didn't "really like killing anything, not even a fly".[33] Distant teenage kin jockeying to exchange self-conscious familiarities with their famous relation were often discountenanced at how like their fathers – and even grandfathers – he was. He was, nevertheless, *au fait* with recent "rock" developments across the Atlantic, but he preferred mainstream, musicianly artists like Canned Heat; Blood, Sweat And Tears; and bottleneck guitar exponent Ry Cooder, whose sticksman, Jim Keltner – from Gary Lewis And The Playboys – "really pleases me more than some incredible jazz drummer who can flit 'round them like a jet plane".[19]

He was also partial to Bob Dylan's Band's True West blend of electric folklore on *Music From Big Pink*. In perverse mood, he'd try Tiny Tim, an ineffable entertainer with a castrati warble, but the furthest-out limit of Starr's taste appeared to be the cartoon voodoo of *Doctor John The Night Tripper* – alias Los Angeles session player Mac Rebennack – with its zombie wails and throbbing murk. That Rebennack's image was not entirely contrived became evident when, on meeting him, Ringo was charmed by his "weird language, which is half English, half cajun and half rhyming madness".[23]

More a record collector than listener, "I don't play much pop, but Maureen does."[26] Nevertheless, Tamla-Motown at full blast could transport Starr – however temporarily – from the suffocating calm of Brookfields, and concerts by Frank Sinatra and Hank Snow were taken in during escapes to London. *Sotto voce*, he'd croon such sparkling "standards" in embryo as 'For Once In My Life', 'Little Green Apples' and 'What The World Needs Now Is Love'.

Ringo wasn't so square that he couldn't be reprimanded for the excessive volume of his portable record player by haughty holidaymakers sunbathing by the same hotel swimming pool. Neither was he an advocate of the Marine Offences Act that killed off the competitive pirate radio stations that had "helped to keep the scene alive. We're left now with the monopoly of the BBC and what seems like half a dozen terrible bands playing for most of the day."[1] With Radio Luxembourg's shows still hosted by leftovers from the 1950s Light Programme clique, the cautious programming by the corporation's two national pop outlets had certainly hastened *Top Of The Pops'* shallower and less subversive in content, which brushed its nadir one schmaltzy 1968 week when the only group presented was The Tremeloes (now *sans* Brian Poole), who were – with Marmalade and Love Affair – a prong of a grinning triumvirate that were hopeless pretenders to The Beatles' throne during this silver age of British beat, constipated as it was with their retinue of disposable and harmless purveyors of popular song – The Casuals (albeit veterans of Hamburg), Cupid's Inspiration, Pickettywitch, Liverpool's Arrival and all the rest of them – who faltered after maybe two Top-30 entries.

Because it exposes a point of view, even the lovey-dovey couplets contained in Marmalade's 'Lovin' Things' or The Casuals' 'Jesamine' and even 'Don't Pass Me By' might be construed as political, but, after 19th nervous breakdowns, dead-end streets and strawberry fields, composers were wringing apocalyptic drops from GIs missing presumed dead in Indo-China, slaughter at anti-war demonstrations and Ireland, bloody Ireland. The latter issue would be addressed by Ulster *colleen* Dana in a poignant version of George Harrison's 'Isn't It A Pity', written in 1969. More direct was Edwin Starr's just plain 'War'. Nonetheless, war and terrorism on the *Nine O'Clock News* was commonplace enough to horrify viewers as much as a shoot-out in a gangster movie.

When asked about Vietnam and other inflammable topics, Ringo was sufficiently hip to understand that killing people is wrong. He wouldn't join together – as Mick Jagger did – with militant anti-Vietnam War protesters outside the US Embassy, nor come up with even an irresolute anthem like Lennon's 'Revolution', but he was as active – in a detached, sweeping, pop-starrish fashion – in verbally supporting pacifism, although, "Just at the moment, we can say what we feel, but it doesn't really change anything. I can't trust politicians. They're all liars, you know. And when the younger generation get the vote, it will be very interesting to see what they decide to allow and exactly what they don't. The young people all want peace, and they'll get it if they just wait, because they're going to outlive them all."[33]

The Starkeys' own offsprings' upbringing was undramatic and as free of major traumas as the restrictions of the paterfamilias' fame would permit: "I don't want people interested in them just because they are my children."[26] Nonetheless, Zak and Jason could not help but become aware of their indulgent dad's wealth and the celebrity that he would always enjoy. Four-year-old Zak's daub of a beetle-like creature would grace the cover of 1969's Christmas flexidisc for the fan club. "Like any kid," grinned Ringo, "he wants to play with his own toys and mine as well."[6] As his father had scorned drumming lessons, Zak was restricted to just one tutorial. "Then he just told me to listen to records and play along with them."[35] Given a free choice, Zak was more likely to thunder along to The Who than The Beatles.

Like his brother after him, Zak was found a piano teacher. He'd also begun to learn recorder at the local Church of England state primary. When the family moved to London, the children would attend more exclusive seats of learning, but Starr in Elstead was reluctant to send his boys to a fee-paying boarding school. "Not unless they tell me they definitely want to go. If I can only see them as much as one hour a day, then I want that hour."[26] When he progressed from his bit part in *Candy* to co-starring with Peter Sellers in *The Magic Christian* in early 1969, he risked bringing the family to his place of work. "But this can prove to be tricky, because the kids get bored and start fiddling about with all the equipment. It can also be very embarrassing if one of them shouts out, 'Daddy!' whilst we're doing a take."[4]

Ringo's infants were not to be in evidence on the long-awaited third Beatles film, *Let It Be*. For the inter-related LP, they'd developed the "mock rock" of 'Lady Madonna' with a production criterion so shorn of gratuitous frills that it sounded *au naturel*: Cavern rawness married to advanced technology. After insisting that they'd never do so again, they were captured portraying themselves infinitely more than ever before in this documentary, in which – without premeditated *Hard Day's Night* zaniness – The Beatles rehearsed, recorded, jammed and gave an unpublicised performance under a leaden sky on Apple's flat roof, clothed against the biting wind. Public-address speakers aimed at the street below provoked the downing of measuring tapes in neighbourhood outfitters, a swelling crowd to clog the pavement and police from the station nearly half a mile away to curb the breach of the peace, MBEs or not. The most repeated off-camera joke was Ringo saying, "For the first time in years, we give a live show. Is it our fault only 500 people turn up?"[36]

Both before and during *Let It Be*, a more formal concert comeback – perhaps a full-scale tour – had been discussed with dwindling fervour. John with Yoko had set a precedent of sorts backed with the *ad hoc* AN Other on the hitherto-unscreened *Rock 'n' Roll Circus* television spectacular headlined by The Rolling Stones, who had themselves returned to the boards earlier that year with ten sensational minutes at the *NME* poll-winners bash, the same venue at which, in 1966, The Beatles had vanished from the British stage forever.

From "I can't see why we shouldn't"[37] with San Franciscan screams still ringing in his ears to "No, I don't think I ever would",[3] Ringo blew hot and cold about The Beatles' availability for bookings in 1969. In April, an Apple spokesman could not be induced to comment, whilst "Ringo and John are so obviously in disagreement"[13] over a blurted Lennon statement that the quartet "will give several public shows this year".[13] Starr would never be against performing *per se*, "but it's the whole operation of getting there that's the drag".[14] Also, he was afraid that, after tax and other deductions, "[we'd] be left with a fiver and a packet of ciggies each".[15]

Nonetheless, he'd elect as usual to go along with whatever the majority – by implication, John and George – decided. His proposition of a format "where you'd have one camera, just step in and do your bit, like the *Grand Ole Opry*"[38] went unheeded as the fly-on-the-wall wheeze took root. As Lennon, McCartney and, especially, Harrison had new songs to squeeze onto the album, Ringo's 'Octopus' Garden' fell by the wayside, too, although George and then John (on cack-handed drums) chucked in some amused ideas when he plonked it out on the Apple ivories.

This condescending levity and episodes such as an affectedly surreal exchange between John and Ringo – the film's "only true individualists"[39], wrote *The Morning Star* – were oases of borderline comedy during the frayed celluloid miles of Paul's prodding of nerves, testy George's walk-out, Yoko's screech-singing, masked bickering and all of the subtle discords discernible to anyone who has ever suffered being in a pop group, particularly one on its last legs. Like Andy Warhol's interesting-but-boring *Flesh*, with its improvised dialogue and frowsy scenarios, the tedium was nearly the idea. Viewers could, for example, sense eyes glazing over to McCartney's chatter. Nevertheless, The Beatles went the distance with *Let It Be*, largely through the introduction of a revitalising element in jovial Texan organist Billy Preston, an old acquaintance from the Star-Club who'd been taking up an invitation to drop in at Apple when Harrison "just grabbed him and brought him down to the studio".[40]

Years before they let him, the self-important Phil Spector had asserted that he wanted to produce The Beatles, and he – rather than the disinclined George Martin – was the mug drafted in to edit, spruce up and mix the "new-phase Beatles album" (as it would say on the *Let It Be* package) and its single, 'Get Back', which was peculiar to Ringo – who seemed to have forgotten The Dave Clark Five's 'Bits And Piece' – as "the only record where the drummer's the hook" and for Lennon sliding a bottleneck guitar solo "like an amateur, but it comes off".[24]

Although heard merely toiling behind his drums, dogsbody Starr's musical appetite was the least ruined by the harrowing *Let It Be* sessions. Therefore, it was he who'd sit most often beside Phil at the mixing desk whenever a second opinion was required. Past his best, the fastidious New Yorker was in poor humour after a recent car accident. So histrionically did Spector throw his weight about in Apple's basement that Ringo took loyal pity on the hectored engineers – among them an old Merseyside friend George Peckham[41] – and, pulling Spector aside, asked him to "cool it".

In the first instance, Spector's doctoring – overseen by Starr – satisfied McCartney, who, over the phone to Ringo, "didn't put it down, and then suddenly he didn't want it to go out. It was two weeks after that he wanted to cancel it."[19]

On the strength of his short cameo in *Easy Rider*, the hit movie of 1969, Spector had been recommended to the receptive Beatles by Allen Klein, whose prophecy that he'd one day represent the group seemed to be fulfilling itself. To Ringo, Allen came across as "a powerful man, and also, no matter what anyone says, he's fair".[19] Despite warnings from some of his previous clients and associates, John and George were also yielding to the Robin Hood of pop's contractual sweet-talk that he illustrated with flattering quotes from their lyrics. However, once his champion, Paul preferred to believe his lawyer-in-laws' tittle-tattle of Klein's sharp practices, high handedness and low cunning. *L'affaire Let It Be* was a handy bone of contention, and Klein – not Spector – would be the recipient of Paul's written plea – to little effect – that the *Let It Be* album be stripped of the superimposed orchestral and choral grandiloquence that contradicted the original endeavour to hark back to the Mersey Beat womb.

The Beatles' dissolution became more than foreseeable when John announced that he'd be leaving soon and yet agreed that it should not be public knowledge yet, for fear that it would unman Klein's bellicose negotiation of a more advantageous royalty deal with Capitol. Nonetheless, a hint of what lay ahead could be fathomed by journalists in Lennon's reported crack that "the circus has left town but we still own the site".[42] Those journalists uneasily in the know – such as fellow Merseysider Ray Connolly, of *The Evening Standard* – did not betray the deeper confidence, unsure of how seriously anyone could take John, who had become a laughing stock since falling in with that frightful Yoko. "John is crazy like that," chuckled Ringo. "He will say one thing one day [and] the opposite the next."[15] Only a handful of fans outside Abbey Road caught Ringo's sally as he ambled across Abbey Road car park for a session on 26 August 1969: "I'm going back to the circus."[43]

10 *"I Couldn't Believe It Was Happening"*

Of each Beatle's preparations for the end, Ringo's were the most pragmatic. Before *Let It Be* nestled uneasily in the album lists – among *Led Zeppelin II*, Andy Williams' *Greatest Hits*, Black Sabbath and the latest from Crosby, Stills, Nash And Young, The Who and Simon And Garfunkel – he'd struck out on his own again with *The Magic Christian*, technically his second non-Beatle film.

Terry Southern's short novel did not contain anyone called "Youngman Grand", but this rather superficial main character was, nevertheless, inserted into the script for the screen version of *The Magic Christian* at the first hint of publicity-gaining Beatle involvement. The production's press department would now be able, for instance, to instigate a *Fab 208* Ringo Competition[1] to win seats at the royal world première in December, with *Magic Christian* T-shirts awarded for the runners-up. Moreover, as well as Starr's acting, there'd be a cameo by John and Yoko and soundtrack donations by a new Apple signing, Badfinger, whose two-year chart run was stabilised with McCartney's catchy 'Come And Get It', sung five times during the picture.

While accepting that he was being "used for the name",[2] Ringo had sought the part as an admirer of Southern and as a further opportunity to discover more about what now seemed one reliable indicator of future direction, even if "I've had no special tuition but I've learned a lot from watching other people."[3] As well as *in situ* expositions by distinguished fellow thespians, he noted how lengthy periods hanging around during retakes, camera repositioning *et al* were best spent. Rather than "stand there waiting like a mummy, I relax and do things – act naturally, you might say"[3] Other than the familiar shuffle of playing cards, his hands were also occupied with newer dressing-room pastimes, notably with "my enamelling kit. I was always enamelling things or doing something with paints and coloured pens."[4]

Another lesson logged for future use by Ringo was how a product's lack of substance could be disguised with a large budget and employment of the famous. Although less prominent than Ringo, *The Magic Christian* was also blessed with – among others – Raquel Welch whipping female galley slaves and Yul Brynner in drag crooning Noël Coward's 'Mad About The Boy' to Roman Polanski. Nearer to the tale's main thrust were Sir Richard Attenborough as a rowing coach, Laurence Harvey as a Shakespearian actor, traffic warden Spike Milligan and John Cleese, a supercilious art dealer, who, respectively, are bribed to sabotage an Oxford-Cambridge boat race; outrage an audience with a striptease; swallow a parking ticket; and allow the defacing of a Rembrandt.

With others in his Monty Python gang, Cleese also left his mark on the Anglicised screenplay which was described as "an essentially genial indictment of British capitalist society".[5] Today, it surfaces as one of Sellers' lesser comedies, with Starr serving mostly as witness to his appropriation of the funniest lines as the much-altered original plot dissolves into a series of themed sketches – about folk who'll do anything for money – with predictable outcomes. To Ringo, in his lead as a Liverpudlian vagrant adopted by "Grand" (Sellers), "they were just saying, 'Be yourself'"[6] by permitting the occasional sub-*Hard Day's Night* flat truism. "To keep my ears warm" was his reply to "Why are you wearing a deerstalker?" during a scene on bleak scrubland for which he'd been kitted out in ridiculous Victorian hunting tweeds and clumsy climbing boots.

As expected, the most sympathetic reviews came from the pop weeklies – "his 'This Boy'-type pathos is particularly strong" (*NME*[7]); "first class with the facial expressions" (*Disc*[8]). Elsewhere, the general conjecture – with the artist in agreement –

was that Ringo had coped well enough with an undemanding role "as heavy as a bucket of feathers".[9] *The Daily Express* was the most vitriolic: "His sad, spaniel expressions of wide-eyed innocence suit the character and he delivers his lines competently if monotonously".[10]

Nevertheless, the project had been fun for Ringo, who had at least been among friends. As well as working alongside veterans of Beatles movies such as Patrick Cargill and Denis O'Dell, he'd welcomed George Harrison as an intrigued observer at a railway location shoot back and forth between Wargrave and Henley-on-Thames, where the Harrisons were soon to purchase the grandiose Friar Park mansion. Meanwhile, Paul and the new Mrs McCartney (plus Princess Margaret) had been present at a studio sequence in Twickenham. The Lennons' attempt to join the team for a crossing on the *QE2* to finish the movie in the States was nipped in the bud when John was denied a US visa because of his marijuana conviction. Sellers' commiserations with Lennon's plight were genuine, for, as speaker at an Oxford Union debate, the ex-Goon had been cheered for his admission that he too had dabbled with outlawed drugs.

Nervous on the first day before the cameras, Ringo had been taken aback by Peter, who "I knew quite well, but suddenly there he was going into character and I got confused."[11] Nevertheless, the bond between Starr and Sellers – previous owner of Brookfields – tightened through hedonistic joint ventures like booking Mayfair's Les Ambassadeurs for a celebrity party – a rare occurrence for Ringo in those days – that, in keeping with the film, climaxed with hundreds of dollar bills fluttering from the ceiling. There followed a fortnight together in the south of France and then Paradise Island in the Bahamas, after completing their immediate *Magic Christian* obligations in New York. In the build-up to its London première, both were forever on television talk programmes.

During BBC1's *David Frost Show*, the two sang a number from *Abbey Road*, The Beatles' latest LP. Unconvincing in embryo during *Let It Be*, 'Octopus' Garden' – Richard Starkey's second published solo composition – had passed muster when the group convened for what was tacitly assumed (by John and Paul, anyway) to be the vinyl finale. A simpler companion reverie to 'Yellow Submarine' and with a country and western tinge, 'Octopus' Garden' stood as tall as most of McCartney's sugary *Abbey Road* offerings and was easier on the ear than, say, Lennon's stark 'I Want You (She's So Heavy)'. It wasn't, however, a masterpiece of song. Against nearly 200 for George's 'Something' (the album's attendant single), it spawned not one cover version known to me. Nevertheless, the requisite breezy, infantine effect was fully realised via Paul and George's emollient backing harmonies and Ringo's sound-effect idea of a blowing through a straw into a close-miked tumbler of water.

More indicative of John, George and Paul's disinclination than their producer's artistic regard for the budding Schubert was Ringo's good-natured appearance as token Beatle among The Hollies, Pan's People, Cilla Black and other guests on *With A Little Help From My Friends*, a Christmas Eve tribute to George Martin on ITV. Obeying Musicians' Union dictates, he re-recorded the lead vocal to mime 'Octopus' Garden', gripping a trident with a few children at his feet.

Flickering into decorated living rooms at an optimum yearly moment of homecomings and Timex commercials, Ringo's reputation as the straightest Beatle had been further strengthened by recent family events as "normal" as susceptible fans might have imagined them. At Queen Charlotte's as usual, Maureen's third pregnancy had on 17 November produced Lee Parkin, the daughter that she and Richie had so desired, her second name being a restoration of a Starkey family name. Home for the baby was a six-bedroom spread along leafy Compton Avenue on the exclusive Glentree estate in Highgate, rather than rural Elstead, which was "too far away"[4] for her father to commute to Apple in his new six-door black Mercedes. As with Sunny Heights, Ringo endured a long wait for a buyer, eventually letting Brookfields go for £100,000 to Steve Stills from Crosby, Stills, Nash And Young, who declared that he intended to have the libretto of 'Within You Without You' carved in stone for display in the garden. Although "it wasn't until after The Beatles folded that I started to do a lot of session work",[1] Starr was listed by Stills – omnipresent at Apple Studios then – among the illustrious assistants on his debut solo LP, listed on the sleeve as "Richie".

Big names who saw the New Year in at Ringo's Highgate housewarming included next door neighbours Maurice Gibb of The Bee Gees and his first wife, singer and media personality Lulu. Sharing the same profession, it would have been odd if the Gibbs and Starr hadn't collaborated informally in the privacy of their respective home studios. With Lulu's brother, Billy Lawrie, Ringo knocked together 'Rock And Roller', which surfaced as a 1973 single when Billy trod briefly in his elder sister's footsteps. One evening, Maurice "sang" on 'Modulating Maurice', a track from an album's worth of woofing and tweeting that Ringo had concocted on one of these new-fangled monophonic synthesisers. "They take control of you, those machines," he confessed. I turn all the dials and press buttons and get excited and put a few mics out and put it through amplifiers into my Revox. We found this riff on the machine and I was playing with it, and [Gibb] started humming words and read the dials, like [the] modulator and envelope shaper, things like that."[12] Another item featured drums with "lots of echo, and it just sounds strange. I love it. Some of the tracks are just incredible."[12] Though pre-empted somewhat by George's *Electronic Sounds*, the self-explanatory solo album that followed *Wonderwall*, Starr's more calculated twiddles were earmarked for consumption by a dwindling public still uncritical of any goods branded "Beatle", until "I got involved with John Tavener, who was doing *The Whale*, which was more far out."[12]

During pop's fleeting "classical" period, when *Sergeant Pepper* and its syncretic ilk had ushered in concept albums, rock operas such as The Who's *Tommy* and other questionable "works", CBS promoted American minimalist composers such as Steve Reich and Terry Riley as if they were rock stars, while Britain's Island label saw similar potential in French electronics boffin Pierre Henri and "Samurai of Sound" Stomu Yamash'ta, a percussion virtuoso awarded a classical Grammy for an album of pieces by Henze and

Maxwell Davies. In tall, long-haired John Tavener, perhaps Ringo of all people had stumbled on some sort of English equivalent.

Tavener had attended Highgate School before gaining a scholarship at the Royal Academy of Music, where he ditched his keyboard studies to concentrate solely on composition. Pop passed him by because, he said, "It hasn't got much to do with what I'm doing."[13] At the Royal Albert Hall Proms in 1968, his first major works, *The Whale* and the BBC-commissioned *The Alium* were applauded rabidly, thus establishing Tavener as a behemoth of what Ringo called "underground classical music"[12] when, via the local grapevine, he listened to a cassette of a BBC broadcast of *The Whale*. Contacted at his parents' Wembley address, a bemused Tavener – only vaguely aware of The Beatles' stature – was invited to Compton Avenue, where in his enthusiasm Ringo had set up a meeting at Savile Row with Lennon and Ron Kass, manager of Apple Records, with the intention of discussing a record deal.

More than even the *Wonderwall* soundtrack, *The Whale* was an intellectual challenge rather than entertainment to the common consumer. Juxtaposing the Jonah story with laudable anxiety about ills perpetrated against sea mammals by humans, Tavener's frame of reference embraced the pioneering tonalities of the post-serialists – unorthodox tone clusters, free choral babbling and a sound painting of Jonah being vomited onto the shore. Not Gilbert and Sullivan, either, was 'Melodrama And Pantomime' with its explosions and megaphone shrieking, although another movement, 'The Storm', was surprisingly subdued, an unlikely link with 'Octopus' Garden' and its "we would be warm below the storm/in our little hideaway beneath the waves".

Sales of *The Whale*, its creator's "serious" credibility and guaranteed Radio 3 exposure were just enough to make a second Tavener album – of three shorter and more theatrical pieces – a worthwhile exercise. Its main track, 'Celtic Requiem (Requiem For Jenny Jones)', had been scored for the London Sinfonietta in 1968. Tavener's observations of "a very strong connection between children and death"[14] were underlined musically with a preoccupation with E flat, as Riley's 'In C' was with its implied key. Nevertheless, recurrent children's play rhymes (by Little Missenden Primary School pupils) were suspended over instrumental ensembles and a soprano tackling a mainly Irish and Latin libretto. Also taped at St John the Evangelist Church, a cavernous Islington edifice, were 'Nomine Jesu' and 'Coplas', both more stubbornly chromatic and of more obviously Christian bent than 'Celtic Requiem'.

Discounting drivel like *Electronic Sounds* and the Lennons' self-centred soul-baring, Ringo's discovery was responsible for Apple's most adventurous releases. Tavener's commercial downfall, however, was less to do with his music than with Derek Taylor's retrospective confession, "We didn't promote it. We really couldn't."[15]

At just over £30,000, Ringo's was but the smallest individual Beatle overdraft now harrying the company ledgers. Overnight, glib unconcern deferred to pointed questions – "as business men, not Beatles,"[16] verified Ringo – regarding the whereabouts of the colour television and fitted carpet that vanished from the Lennons' room and questions such as, Which typist phones Canberra every afternoon? Why had so-and-so given himself a rise of £60 a week? Why is he seen only on pay day?

After Allen Klein proved his worth by procuring the promised higher royalty rate for The Beatles, John had persuaded Ringo and George to support the official appointment of the New Jersey go-getter to steer the ship back on course. Even Paul – who didn't want to trust Allen – had to applaud the cessation of all of the embezzlements and fiddles. Suddenly, it was beans on toast in the office kitchen instead of Beluga caviar from Fortnum & Mason.

Something of a pop personality in his own right these days, Allen was not above granting interviews to relevant organs. "I intend to make [Apple] financially successful and tailored to The Beatles' own specifications," he vowed to *Melody Maker*, "but when you get a lot of energy wasted, it doesn't make for an efficient organisation."[17] As old retainers were cast adrift, sinecures discontinued and a clocking-in system installed, Starr concurred with Klein: "We used to keep everyone on until our new business manager came along and showed us the real facts of what they were all doing. A lot of them got sacked because they weren't doing their jobs, and that's fair. They would usually hate you for it, but that doesn't bother me."[18]

Even the enterprise's only true money-spinner, Apple Records, was subject to cuts as unviable releases were cancelled and contracts unrenewed. "If you have a big tree with a thousand million roses," pontificated Ringo, "prune it down and you'll get maybe ten fantastic roses. That's what's happening."[19] Starr and Harrison, components of the most fantastic rose of all, teased both journalists and themselves with talk of a follow-up to *Abbey Road*: "There's nothing wrong with The Beatles," chirped Ringo in as late as March 1970. "When we've got something to do, we'll do it. We're all in touch."[20] A return to the stage was "unlikely, but you can never tell with us",[21] he winked. Ere 1969 was out, however, he hedged his bets with a planned solo LP, which – unlike *Two Virgins*, *Electronic Sounds et al* – was to be marketed as if it was a *bona fide* group record.

When John Citizen read the "shock" announcement in December that the LP *Ringo Starrdust* was to be recorded for issue in 1970, three tracks were actually already in the can, while the rest would be cut in time for rush-release in March. While the concept of collecting every disc that The Beatles ever made was not yet economically unsound, buyers still scanned the provisional track listing with trepidation – 'Whispering Grass', 'Love Is A Many Splendoured Thing' and 'Autumn Leaves'. "The only good thing to come out of the break-up was the opportunity to buy four Beatles albums a year," reckoned a future member of post-punk act Squeeze, "and then I heard Ringo's first album. I left it at a party one night."[22] Many other home fans would also be listening to successive Starr records *before* purchase.

"I really dug all that old music," Ringo explained, "because that was the first I ever heard, and I thought, 'My mum'll be pleased if I sing all those songs.'"[23] Apparently, the notion had been fermenting for a couple of years and, with the group in abeyance, time hung heavy. Like the man who paid to conduct the London Symphony Orchestra at the Albert Hall for just one night, Ringo had the wherewithal to fulfil a dream.

While *Ringo Starrdust* was as self-indulgent in its way as mucking around with a synthesiser, at least a Beatle was taking on "decent" music instead of any John-and-Yoko crap. EMI retailers' attention could also be directed to its George Martin production and Starr's hire of arrangers of the calibre of Quincy Jones, Count Basie's Chico O'Farrell, Johnny Dankworth and some of his own musical cronies, such as Klaus Voorman and Maurice Gibb. Because he'd impressed Ringo with his orchestrations on the *God Bless Tiny Tim* album, Richard Perry was chosen to frame a version of Doris Day's 'Sentimental Journey', which he invested with a new American device called a Vocoder.

To stress the selling point of nostalgia, the cover and full-page advertisements would show a dapper Ringo in front of a mock-up of the mean junction on which the towering Empress pub stood. Some of his Liverpool relations would gaze from the windows. In its bar, all of the aged standards on the record had once poured from ale-choked mouths and flushed, happy faces. Indeed, the promotional shot – directed by Neil Aspinall – would be of Ringo backed by The Talk Of The Town Orchestra crooning 'Sentimental Journey', which had been seen to make greater sense as the album's title than *Ringo Starrdust*.

'Autumn Leaves' and a version of 'I'll Be Seeing You' were also rejected. You wonder what they were like when assessing the numbers that did survive. The immaculate scoring was exemplified by the few bars of fluid saxophone busking that leaped from the horn riffing on O'Farrell's 'Night And Day', the glissando swoops of Voorman's violins in Ted Daffan's 'I'm A Fool To Care' or Elmer Bernstein's witty 'Have I Told You Lately That I Love You?' *leitmotifs*.

"He sings better than you'd expect him to,"[24] wrote a

particularly snowblinded reviewer. Unchanged to the pressing plant went a misjudged note on the coda of 'Bye Bye Blackbird' and some brief but dubious scatting in Fats Waller's 'Blue Turning Grey Over You'. *Sentimental Journey* certainly contained material tried by the likes of Crosby, Sinatra and Matt Monro, but none were so deluded to think Starr a quality vocalist any more than Johnnie Ray – an entertainer, incidentally, whom I am perverse enough to admire. Who cares if *Sentimental Journey* isn't real singing? Admittedly, on more than one outing, it could have been a faceless anyone, but otherwise, as Ringo would assure you himself, "Once my voice comes over on the radio or record, you know it's me."[24]

Those touchy about the original 78s of the LP selections may not acquiesce, but, although I'd never have bought corny *Sentimental Journey* myself, I felt that Ringo's humble vocal endowment, with its hit-or-miss pitching and untutored phrasing, compounded a mesmerically hideous charm common to certain singers who superimpose a disjointed range and eccentric delivery onto a given song's melodic and lyrical grid. Others in this idiosyncratic oligarchy are asthmatic Keith Relf, laconic Dave Berry and Reg Presley, with his Long John Silver burr. Nonetheless, the hoisting of *Sentimental Journey* high up Top 40s throughout the world testified less to this virtue than to the value of showing the title clip on such as *The Ed Sullivan Show* and a media jaunt made by Ringo in the flesh. "The great thing was that it got me moving," said the artiste, "not very fast, but just moving. It was like the first shovel of coal in the furnace that makes the train inch forward."[25]

Although it was announced that there were "absolutely no plans"[26] for its release, 'It Don't Come Easy' was typical of many Starr compositions that studio onlookers like Richard Perry would "hear grow until it becomes a real song".[27] Under George Harrison's supervision, three versions of 'It Don't Come Easy' were recorded during the graveyard hours on 18 January at Apple with help from a movable feast of musicians that included Stills, Eric Clapton – and Voorman, with whom Ringo would become associated "like Bill and Ben"[11] as a competent rhythm section on numerous records for a cabal of musicians, mostly expatriate Americans on the make.

Ringo would plead that they "only want me because of the way I play",[11] but, as most had endured an age of anonymous studio drudgery, perhaps they'd also ascertained that breathing the air around The Beatles was a springboard, if to not fame, then to a stronger negotiating stance for more extortionate session fees. Some had arrived with Delaney And Bonnie And Friends, an amalgam from Los Angeles' 'Blue-Eyed Soul School' to whom Eric Clapton had rendered practical endorsement with finance for a European tour and a place in their ranks as lead guitarist. Harrison, too, was roped in after he and the Starkeys attended the troupe's London concert in December.

If not indulging himself on the boards, Ringo was overwhelmed by the Friends' ebullience and flattered to be requested to help out on this demo or that backing track. Phonetically pliant as he was, keeping such company affected his vocabulary. Suddenly, a "guy" – not a bloke – "balled" a "chick", instead of a bird. You didn't go to the toilet any more but to the "john". He was loud, too, in praise of the Friends' drummer, Jim Gordon, and his successor, Jim Keltner, who, on a par with Hal Blaine, now, echoed Starr's eternal opinion that "drummers don't need to be so tricky. The best ones for me are the ones with less technique to show off."[28]

Ringo didn't always practise what he preached. On a take for a Doris Troy session, "I forgot what I was doing and made a lot of noise just to cover up. [I] never forgave myself."[28] Such aberrations aside, he earned an accolade when rattling the traps on an eponymous LP by multi-instrumentalist Leon Russell, whose perpetual on-stage top hat and star-studded LP credits were symptomatic of in-crowd acknowledgment that he was the epitome of the smug sexism and "funky" rhythmic jitter of the interchangeable Delaney And Bonnie "super sidemen", who, crowed their saxophonist, "went on to back all the players that really do have a lot of influence".[29] You didn't need to hear a self-

absorbed Friend's "laid-back" solo album to know what it was like
– maybe four songs on each side, all delivered in a nonchalantly
"raunchy" caw and bloated with hip restricted code and dragged-
out fades, it would dwell on balling chicks, "toking" and being on
the road with a rock 'n' roll band. Yet Ringo was willing to play
with them. "I'll play with anyone, but I like to know at least one
person there."[11]

After over six hours spent labouring with Harrison and The
Grease Band's bass guitarist for *Leon Russell*, Ringo "amazed the
shit out of me"[30]. Russell was especially impressed that his versatile
Beatle assistant was up to "that New Orleans syncopation"[30] on
'Shoot-Out At The Plantation', shrill 'Pisces Apple Lady' (about a
Savile Row employee with whom Leon had "got it together") and
'Delta Lady', a retread of a single by Joe Cocker, who – with Russell
and other former Friends – would form the cumbersome Mad Dogs
And Englishmen.

Considerably more prestigious than aiding Russell was Ringo's
part in albums recorded in London by BB King and the late Howlin'
Wolf. Since the blues boom of *circa* 1968, many revered black
practitioners in the evenings of their lives had been advised to gear
their music for a wider forum by reprising their classics with some of
the renowned white musicians that they had inspired. Although Wolf
had been disappointed with the US outfit used on *Electric Wolf*, his
first album of this persuasion, the deferential humour and glad co-
operation of producer Glyn Johns' British volunteers for 1970's
London Sessions was more satisfactory – although, with Starr,
Voorman and Clapton, "Monday's session wasn't too successful at
all," growled Wolf, "but yesterday we managed to get four sides cut,
and it was really great."[29]

After initial awe in their wizened presences, Ringo concluded
that working for Wolf and, later, BB King (alongside personnel that
also included Charlie Watts, Alexis Korner and Dr John) was "no
more important to me than sessions with John or George".[11] He was
also among stalwarts reeled in by Harrison for his *All Things Must
Pass*. According to Ringo, "he paid his dues"[19] on this triple album,

the first evidence that George had broken cover as a true solo artist. The album absorbed an immortalisation of its participants' arrogance in 'Apple Jam' – a whole two sides of meandering extemporisations that Ringo "didn't play much"[19] – and a less tedious majority of George's accumulated songs, including 'Behind That Locked Door', which addressed itself to hopes and apprehensions about Bob Dylan's first major engagement since his motorcycle mishap. Dutifully, the Harrisons, Starkeys and Lennons turned out for this set (with The Band) at the Isle of Wight Pop Festival in September 1969.

Later that month, because he'd just left Middlesex Hospital after three days' observation for an intestinal complaint, it wasn't Ringo but session drummer Alan White who'd been asked along when a new Lennon composition, 'Cold Turkey', was previewed by a hastily rehearsed Plastic Ono Band at a Canadian event similar to Dylan's comeback. If uxoriously shy-making at times, Lennon's outpourings were leaner and tastier meat than Harrison's, and Starr had not been tardy in offering his services for a studio remake of 'Cold Turkey', John's second hit 45 without The Beatles. With Maureen, Ringo had also deputised for John and Yoko – recovering from a road accident – at the Chelsea Town Hall press launch of its predecessor, 'Give Peace A Chance'. In return, while no fellow Beatle had metaphorically held Ringo's hand for the unveiling of *Candy*, the Lennons had been there on for *The Magic Christian* charity première, albeit bearing a placard daubed with the slogan of another cause they'd been incited to support.

As far as Starr was concerned, McCartney's absence on these occasions was of his own choosing, rather than ostracism by the other Beatles. He and Linda had been invited to the New Year celebration at Compton Avenue, and the Starkeys had joined them as spectators on the opening night of Mary Hopkin's season at the Savoy. It seemed to be all smiles professionally, too, with Ringo's rataplans still detectable on Hopkin records and Paul arranging Hoagy Carmichael's 'Stardust' for *Sentimental Journey*.

Starr was to inform his solicitor that *Sentimental Journey* was one bone of contention to which McCartney alluded, late one afternoon at Cavendish Avenue, during a tongue-lashing of such violence that Ringo could no longer imagine that The Beatles would regroup. "We'd gone as far as we could with each other."[31] As well as the lines drawn over Klein, there loomed a market collision detrimental to the sales of all if, as scheduled, *Sentimental Journey*, *Let It Be* and Paul's eponymous solo LP all reached the shops in the same spring month. Separate letters from each of his colleagues supplicating Paul to postpone *McCartney* were awaiting delivery, and Ringo, brusquely scribbling autographs while hurrying down Apple's steps to his waiting Mercedes, "didn't think it fair that some office lad should take something like that 'round".[11] At Paul's place, he identified himself on the intercom and was welcomed for what began as a friendly chat until underlying tension came to a head when Paul "told me to get out of his house. He went crazy. He just shouted and pointed at me. I couldn't believe it was happening."[11]

Outside that banged front door, Ringo strove to detach himself from this unprecedented upset: "It's only like a brother. You mustn't pretend that brothers don't fight, because they fight worse than anybody."[11] *En route* to an immediate conference with George and John, he decided on the line of least resistance: *Sentimental Journey* would be brought forward, "which makes me seem like a good guy, but I wasn't really, because I needed to put it out before or else Paul's album would have slayed me. And it did."[24] Half a million sales for *Sentimental Journey* seems quite healthy, but you can understand why Ringo might have eaten his heart out when McCartney garnered two million in US advance orders alone.

That June, Starr elected to strike while the iron was lukewarm with a long-mooted album of country and western, then the squarest, most right-wing genre in pop. Nevertheless, it had started to remove itself from earlier association with lowbrow redneck antagonism towards commies, niggers, queers and hippies – even if, in 1970, a Houston radio station had been twice fire-bombed by some good ol' boys who begged to differ with its radical, anti-draft slant.

Taking their cue from the popularity of spaghetti westerns and Nashville's spellbinding gaudiness, multitudinous licensed premises of the early 1970s had been transformed into parodies of Dodge City saloons. Barging through the swinging half doors of an Edinburgh pub or Auckland bar, you'd bump into Calamity Jane lookalikes and stetsoned quaffers of Southern Comfort. Belying daytime guises as janitors or computer programmers, conversations would be peppered with Deep South slang – "mess of grits" for "plate of food" – picked up from Merle Haggard albums. On a nicotine-clouded stage, the band would crank out 'Okie From Muskogee', 'Crystal Chandelier' or 'Polk Salad Annie'. If these mightn't have made the charts, they were at least as well known as many that had.

Another sound fiscal argument for Starr's intention was that, lately, The Byrds, Neil Young and – as Ringo had observed first hand, at a London showcase – ex-Monkee Mike Nesmith had all "gone country", while Keith Richards and Gram Parsons (of Byrds offshoot The Flying Burrito Brothers) had discussed possible fusions of country and classic rock for an audience still biased against one or the other. Furthermore, both Jerry Lee Lewis and Charlie Rich had managed recent comebacks in the *Billboard* Country And Western chart.

The first choice as Ringo's producer was Bob Johnston, who'd been at the console for Dylan's austere *John Wesley Harding* and its *Nashville Skyline* follow-up. Johnston satisfied busy Starr that the album could be completed as quickly as one Beatles track, without fussy overdubs and retakes. Bob was also amenable to cutting it in England, "but he wanted a lot of bread, so I decided not to do it with him".[19] Instead, Ringo gave the job to the steel guitarist on the Dylan records, Pete Drake, a 39-year-old virtuoso equally at ease improvising the orthodox "Nashville sound" for entertainers as diverse as Elvis, Perry Como, The Monkees – and George Harrison, who'd had him flown to London's Trident Studios for *All Things Must Pass*. Ringo remembered, "I had to fetch him from the office one day, and he was in my car and I had all these country tapes, and we got talking about country music."[19]

Drake advocated Nashville's Music City complex as the most fitting setting to cut the kinda tunes folk like a-tappin' their shoe leather to. They could begin next week. Starr had started an opus, 'Band Of Steel', which namechecked Hank Williams and lesser country legends in much the same manner as Cowboy Copas' 'Hillbilly Heaven'. It was not, however, among those selected from more than a hundred new copyrights grubbed – possibly over-hastily – from demo tapes in offices clotted round 16th Avenue, the Tin Pan Alley of Nashville. As Buck Owens sang in 'Songwriters Lament', there were "songwriters under every rock". Ringo "was with a few guys with guitars, and we were picking out the songs I liked".[19] To be published by Startling Music, those shortlisted were mostly lachrymose ballads, often just a few degrees from schmaltz, with titles such as 'Silent Homecoming', 'Loser's Lounge' and 'Love Don't Last Long'. All bar 1968's 'Wine, Women And Loud Happy Songs' had been written in 1970, mostly by either Sorrells Pickard or Chuck Howard, guitarists on the sessions.

This pair also belonged to the pool of city musicians whose close knowledge of each other's capabilities grew from playing together as accompanists at the Grand Ole Opry and on countless daily record dates. Some of these craftsmen were recording artists in their own right. Drake himself had won a gold disc for a 1963 single, 'Forever', and was planning *The Steel Beatle*, an instrumental LP of Lennon-McCartney numbers. Just as distinguished were Buddy Harman – the bass player on Roy Orbison's biggest hits – and guitarist Jerry Reed, composer of Presley's 'Guitar Man', the 1968 smash that convinced many that the King had returned to form. Other Presley associates enlisted by Drake for Starr were the celebrated Jordanaires vocal quartet, engineer Scotty Moore – more familiar as a guitarist – and, regarded with sentimental reverence by Ringo, drummer DJ Fontana.

With brisk finesse, 20 tracks – for trimming down to a strong but soothing single album – were ready within three days, although for much of the first morning Ringo "was really nervous, and Pete would say through the glass, 'Hoss, if you don't get loose, I'm going to come in there and stomp on your toes.'"[20] So lacking in conviction – and accurate pitching – was he at first that a Jordanaire was instructed to sing along in unison over the headphones. Even so, suspect high notes – such as that which concluded 'Without Her' – remained and had to be veiled in reverberation.

The mood, nevertheless, relaxed sufficiently to bring forth perhaps the most adept singing of Starr's career. Soon, he was joining in whenever someone kicked off a bout of informal jamming while warming up for the next track. All inhibitions gone, he even strummed one-chord acoustic guitar and ranted perfunctory lyrics for a 25-minute work-out. Ebbing zeal for issuing this as one side of a future LP still resulted in an excerpt appearing as 'Coochy Coo' on an Italian A-side – and a US flip-side beneath the album's title song, 'Beaucoups Of Blues', which, in a swirl of fiddles and Drake's metallic careen, crept into the lower half of the Hot 100.

Among brighter choices for a fanfare 45 were the episodic 'Love Don't Last Long'; 'Fastest-Growing Heartache In The West', a rootin'-tootin' narrative about a corrupted Beverly Hills housewife and her tired hillbilly husband; or 'I Wouldn't Have You', a virtual duet with Jeannie Kendal. As well as sustaining the ambiguous atmosphere of enjoyable melancholy, 'I'd Be Talking All The Time' had Ringo as a homespun prairie Plato, while he was cast as the prodigal, guitar-pickin' scion of a wealthy family for '15-Dollar Draw'. Even better suited to his hangdog voice, 'Woman Of The Night' was the *cri du coeur* of some poor, uncomplaining fool in love with a tearsheet.

A flawed but altogether reasonable record of its kind, *Beaucoups Of Blues* deserved more than a wretched struggle to Number 65 in the States and no chart placing whatsoever at home, where more vivid memories lingered of the pig in a poke that was *Sentimental Journey*.

What else could he do? A Beatle fan – if not member – for life, Ringo "was not interested in being in a new band. I was bigger than any band I could have joined."[21] Bolstering all of his objections in principle, an album of drum solos was out of the question, because abler technicians such as Jon Hiseman – another *Leon Russell* helpmate – or Ginger Baker could wipe the floor with Ringo Starr. Besides, Cozy Powell, fresh from The Jeff Beck Group, was about to fill what he'd perceived as a market void for a Sandy Nelson of the 1970s.

As for films, Ringo vacillated between a desire for "a serious role that calls for some real acting to show I can do it"[16] and "to be a character actor sort of like Peter Sellers. I wouldn't mind doing a musical. When I'm 45, it would be kidding myself to try to be a pop star, but you can make films when you're 50."[32] Founded in wishful thinking, too, was a Hollywood Western, and his acquisition of a script "for a science-fiction film which I'm trying to get together", although he could not divulge its title. "There's a big part for me, the biggest I've done. Apart from that, I've no other film waiting at the moment."[33]

As his small-screen guest spots increased, the quality of Ringo's performances so improved that he was accepted in comedy circles as both a joker and a fair "feed" (a straight man who reacts to phoney insults). During a *Magic Christian* publicity blitz in the US, he'd made cameo headway with a sketch on the cult comedy series *Laugh In*. "Sometimes they don't catch me," was his doleful riposte to Joanne Worley's remark about how wonderful it must be for him when girl fans chased him.

During this trip, Ringo's presence was announced from the stage at one of Elvis Presley's cabaret pageants at the International Hotel in Las Vegas. "There wasn't a lot of the old stuff," moaned Apple executive Peter Brown. "He left us old rockers wanting more."[34] When Brown and the Starkeys wormed their way backstage to pay respects afterwards, so began weeks of speculation that Ringo, Elvis and Raquel Welch were to team up for an imminent TV spectacular, but, sighed Starr, "It was just dragging on too long, what with the preparations and the talks and Elvis having other commitments. I told Elvis I couldn't wait – it was holding me up – and he could see my point."[35] With Ringo as proud guest of honour at the Cannes showing of *Woodstock*, Presley's private abhorrence of this and other movies' glorifying of hippy sub-culture (of which he saw The Beatles as a part) was probably at the root of his dilatoriness.

In the wake of *Sentimental Journey*, Ringo had already been approached to entertain diners for a season in Las Vegas *à la* Elvis. His deep thought before declining – "I wouldn't mind, but it would mean putting an act together"[36] – demonstrated the appeal of mainstream showbusiness. The Fourmost, The Swinging Blue Jeans, Billy J Kramer and lesser lights of dear, dead Mersey Beat were attempting to tread that path, too. Even tongue-tied Rory Storm had hung up his rock 'n' roll shoes and was commuting as a disc jockey between engagements in Benidorm, Amsterdam and the Silver Blades ice rink back in Liverpool. At another extreme, 1970's Television Personality Of The Year, Cilla Black, was starring in the extravaganza *Way Out In Piccadilly* with Frankie Howerd. Up in the West End, too, Starr and Lennon had been there on the night that Gerry Marsden had gladly taken over the male lead from Joe Brown in *Charlie Girl*, which ran and ran.

After a fashion, Paul McCartney – with his sketchy "granny music" and irrepressible spirit when in the limelight – awaited a destiny as a showbiz evergreen. By late 1970, he'd set irreversible wheels in motion for the official dissolution of The Beatles. "Suddenly your brain gets twisted and you do strange things," lamented Ringo. "I just kept thinking, 'What's he doing it to me for?', but then I realised he's got to do it to get what he wants, so I don't put him down for that. [But] you'd get lawyers coming 'round day and night, millions of affidavits, too many problems that I didn't want to do because I just wanted to play. We got a bit catcalling, which really wasn't right, but we had to go through it."[11]

While clouds of litigation gathered, all four parties were "tight, nervous, everyone watching everyone else",[37] noticed the forgiving Cynthia Lennon, who, with her new spouse, was "at home" one day for well-wishers that included her increasingly distant Beatle pals and ex-husband. "Everyone was wondering," recalled Ringo, "and I was the one who wondered longest."[38]

At a Hollywood press binge for *The Magic Christian*, Ringo had sidestepped questions about The Beatles, as he'd deemed them irrelevant to the function's purpose, and also because he didn't want the painful truth to hang as a vibration in the air. A year later, when the case was declared in Paul's favour and Apple's finances placed under the Official Receiver's scrutiny, Ringo Starr could no more not believe it was happening: "I felt so absolutely lost. I went into hiding to escape the pressures. You just sit around the house like everyone else does. You go to London or you go shopping or to see a film or watch telly."[21]

11 "I Love It When They Let Me Go Off On My Own"

Even when weakened by the after-effects of pneumonia in 1972, Elsie Graves continued to sort out and pass on the hundreds of letters that still arrived for Richie, who still spent Christmases in Liverpool, among those who loved him best. Long resigned to how he made his living, Elsie was overjoyed to fuss over her famous son and his family for a few uninterrupted days. Paying duty calls on elderly relations and his mother's intimates, he seemed the same as ever on the surface.

Many of his old stomping grounds, however, were much changed. The Rialto was now a warehouse, the Locarno a sports club and the Mardi Gras flattened to create space for a multi-storey car park. Although Ringo and others had put their eminence at proprietor Roy Adams' disposal, this only drew out the ultimate agony when the sinking of an underground railway shaft would necessitate the demolition of the Cavern, too. Since its 1966 facelift, the club had kept a ritual weekly "Beatle Hour" of records spun in regretful affection for the departed "Four Lads Who Shook The World", as a plaque in Mathew Street would read after the English Tourist Board latched onto its cradling of The Beatles when pop's history became as lucrative as its present.

A pop memorabilia auction had been held in New York in as early as October 1970, with Pete Townshend's broken guitar and a Cadillac that had once transported The Beatles its dearest lots. Already, there was a sense not so much of nostalgia as impending hangover after the Swinging '60s. On the cards were "British

Invasion" reunion tours of the States, which gave a welcome cash transfusion to many old acts, among them The Searchers and Billy J Kramer. Although *a* Big Three would cut a 1973 album, Ian And The Zodiacs had thrown in the towel after turning down 'Even The Bad Times Are Good', which later cracked the UK Top Five when picked up by The Tremeloes.

Other unlucky Mersey Beat brethren had returned to secure anonymity via application form or beseeching telephone call. Like demobbed servicemen, they'd often find their old jobs waiting for them. Some would reappear at the parochial venues from whence they came, but real or imagined horrors about this unmarried mother or that outraged Mr Big from Germany obliged certain ex-beat group musicians to renege on their past and jump at shadows.

Dame Fortune granted a few another bite at the showbusiness cherry. Billy Fury's former pianist, Lancastrian Peter Skellern, made it in his own right with 1972's 'You're A Lady', although Ringo qualified that its homely brass-band backing "was more of a hook than he was".[1] Closer to home, Tony Waddington and Wayne Bickerton, former "Lennon-McCartney" of The Pete Best Combo, created the chartbusting Rubettes from session players in 1974. Best himself had gone "into a different kind of lifestyle"[2] as a civil servant.

Another denied the acclaim he may have merited was Rory Storm, who died in his Stormsville bedroom in September 1972 after an injudicious quantity of whiskey washed down tablets prescribed for a respiratory infection. A lay verdict on Violet Caldwell's suicide the next morning was that her golden boy's demise was too grievous to be borne, coming as it did so soon after that of her husband in May.

A couple of the national tabloids that headlined the tragedy carried a quote from Shane Fenton – now back in the Top Ten as Alvin Stardust – comparing his brother-in-law favourably with Rod Stewart. Ringo had also been tapped for his feelings about his old boss, with whom he'd long lost touch. No, he wouldn't be at either the cemetery or the wake, because "I wasn't there when he was born, either."[3] Pressured newshounds who'd never heard of Storm seized on another big-name link in Cilla Black, who had just sacrificed a day's break from a Blackpool variety season to tape – with Starr and George Harrison in attendance – 'When Every Song Is Sung', a Harrison song meant originally for Shirley Bassey.

Because his debut on *Cilla* had gone down so well, Ringo had been chosen for a spot in the second series. Shot on location at a Scandinavian ski resort, it was not a particularly enjoyable chore, marred as it was by a Professor Thorolf Rafto selling a chance conversation with the ex-Beatle as an exclusive to a Norwegian newspaper and another report of a tipsy Starr's facetiousness in refusing to cough up even a symbolic coin to a World Refugee charity until the English football results were obtained for him.

Now that the protective bubble of Beatlehood had burst, there'd be further evidence that Ringo wasn't Mr Normal after all – but probably he never had been in the first place. He'd still imply that a typical evening *chez* Starkey was spent slumped in front of the colour TV, and he switched on the old Fab Four charm when required, as he did when doggy eyes, a grin and autographs settled the matter when police pulled him over for suspected drunken driving. When in his cups, he would dismiss his chauffeur and try to win bets with Maureen over how quickly he could race the Mercedes to some fashionable London niterie – usually Tramps in Jermyn Street – where whirring Nikons would herald their skidding arrival. On one such dash, Starr took a bend too speedily. A tree ricocheted him back onto the road.

Richie's private sweetness remained apparent to Cilla when, unknown to her, the Starkeys had, by coincidence, booked a bungalow in the same hotel grounds in Antibes. He jumped out from out behind a rock, roaring like a lion as Cilla, her husband and their push-chaired son were taking the air one morning. This good-natured ambush precipitated a pleasant holiday for the two families. The only sour note was struck during the Starkeys' farewell dinner for the Blacks. After Ringo had turned his nose up at more exotic fare on the menu, the French waiter uncovered his order of fried egg and – so the chef had understood – crisps. No one at the table could prevent Starr, his rage sharpened with Dom Perignon, from berating the hotel manager, whose kitchen had "ruined my friends' last evening here".[5]

Once bitten, he emphasised to the galley cook that with every meal was to be served "*pommes frites* to you, not chips, because those are crisps in your language"[5] when the Blacks and Harrisons were among guests on *SS Marala*, the luxury yacht – with original masterpieces on its walls – that Ringo had hired for the duration of 1971's Cannes film festival. As 'Octopus' Garden' had been born at sea, so he and George pieced together an opus entitled 'Photograph' with, recalled Cilla, "everyone on board chipping in with bits for it".[5] Some months afterwards, Ringo proffered a newer opus, 'Back Off Boogaloo', when Cilla was shortlisting material for her next single. She preferred 'Photograph', but her plea for a demo had already been met with Ringo saying, "No, it's too bloody good for you. I'm having it myself."[5]

He could be as less affectionately rude to entertainers he didn't know, too, especially the latest teen idols, such as The Osmonds, Jackson Five, Bay City Rollers and "that lumberjack",[1] David Cassidy. Although Rollermania was rampant among schoolgirls for several months, none of these callow newcomers shaped up remotely as either new Beatles or new Elvi,[6] but they did not warrant Starr's disparagement of them as "no-talent bands or talent that's been forced".[1] Under pressure, he'd admit to listening to The Jackson Five for their precocious youngest member, Michael – "the only kid I really like in that respect. Usually, a kid in a show gets all the sympathy applause: 'He's only two foot eight and he got up there and sang that song.' It's a load of rubbish."[1]

Starr's uncharitable surliness and increased alcohol intake were detectable in the immediate aftermath of The Beatles. He had taken the group's messy finish the hardest and, for longer than the other former members, "would not rule out that one day we might play together again. Just say the feeling is based on my natural optimism."[7] In the event, however, he would hope that "no single

Beatle could ever again dominate the others".[7] With McCartney the fly in the ointment, a rumour spread that Ringo, John and George were to try again with Klaus Voorman, as The Ladders.

When both were guests at Mick Jagger's San Tropez wedding in May 1971, Ringo had nattered awkwardly with Paul, whom he hadn't seen since the McCartneys had left London for their Scottish home from home shortly after the unpleasantness at Cavendish Avenue. A fortnight later, Ringo received a copy of his old chum's second post-Beatles LP. As skimpy as *McCartney*, *Ram* was worthy for only "a couple of lines, that's all", in Starr's opinion. "It's like he's not admitting that he can write great tunes. I just feel he's let me down."[8]

Blunter still was John's view that his estranged colleague's efforts were "rubbish".[9] From watching helplessly as the two pilloried each other in the press and even record grooves, Starr's allegiance to the Lennon camp was strengthened by McCartney's social and professional boat-burning and John's need of a drummer with whom he'd "played together so long that it fits"[9] to keep unostentatious pace on the two "his and hers" Plastic Ono Band albums that resulted from the Lennons' course of primal-scream therapy under American psychologist Dr Arthur Janov. "There's no real toe-tappers on it,"[8] was Starr's understatement on John's bald personal exorcisms and regurgitant confessions – 'Mother', 'Isolation' and so forth – as well as the spurning of former ideals and heroes (notably in 'God') and self-projection as 'Working-Class Hero', a track without percussion that was banned from BBC airwaves for its use of the f-word. It was "an all-time great" to loyal Ringo, who could "sit with some people and they swear and you think, 'Christ, stop it!', and you can sit with people who swear because it's a word, and that's how it was on the album."[8]

However gravely cathartic the released result, the sessions were more fun than *Abbey Road* and closer to the spirit of Mersey Beat than *Let It Be* had ever been, as Voorman and Starr reacted instinctively whenever guitarist Lennon warmed up, as always, with ancient rockers half remembered from the Cavern. Surfacing on later bootlegs were Lennon's knockabout reclamations of 'Honey Don't' and 'Matchbox' from Ringo.

Whatever avant-garde changes her improvisations rang, not even the slowest-witted fan hoped for ersatz Beatle magic from Yoko. With a musical past not accordant with that of her accompanists, Yoko's looser jamming on her *Plastic Ono Band* outing and its *Fly* follow-up were less governed by common time and rote-learnt chord patterns. Just as pre-ordained were the wordless orgiastic moans and nanny-goat vibrato as "OK Yoni" – so *Private Eye* lampooned her – ululated free-form like a front-line jazz horn over Ringo's patient beat.

If inwardly baffled by her, Ringo – like hundreds of other celebrities asked – contributed to Yoko's hastily organised "Water Event" at New York State's Everson Museum of Art, set to run for three weeks from 9 October 1971, her spouse's birthday. Starr's green plastic bag filled with the correct liquid was found a place among the steam engines, test-tubes, blotting paper, fish tanks, *et al* – not to mention the toilet customised to emit 'Working Class Hero' when flushed – and other banal exhibits that filled three halls. For Ringo and every other guest who didn't know much about art, the occasion climaxed at John's post-preview party, at which – with Phil Spector its heart and soul on a makeshift podium – the *omnes fortissimo* choruses of olde-tyme rock 'n' roll were mixed up with Beatles hits (including a 'Yellow Submarine' with Starr befuddled over the words) and *in absentia* "tributes" to Harrison and McCartney.

After an ITV chat show a month earlier, John had slipped across the Atlantic and, in the teeth of attempts to deport him for his drug conviction, was to reside in the States for as long as he lived. Among purported vocational tangents during his final months in England was writing and producing 'Four Nights In Moscow' for consideration as Ringo's maiden solo 45. However, Starr shied away from appearing as beholden to Lennon as he had been as a Beatle, arguing, "What I have to combat is the original image of me as the downtrodden drummer. You don't know how hard it is to fight that."[10]

Association with a non-melodic instrument to the rear of the stage prejudices the acceptance of pop drummers as serious composers – and even serious musicians – by those who imagine that any fool can bash drums. An off-the-cuff case is that of Yardbird Jim McCarty, who, despite co-writing his group's most enduring songs and his subsequent formation of Renaissance and lesser-known but equally adventurous outfits, suffered from years of categorisation as an incorrigible R&B swatter before recognition in the 1980s as a colossus of new age music, with pieces as innovative in their way as any in the Yardbirds/Renaissance canon. Other talents from behind the kit who were up against similar undervaluation include Thunderclap Newman's Speedy Keene, David Essex and – on the tail end of Mersey Beat – comedian Russ Abbott.

Rather than 'Four Nights In Moscow' (if it ever existed), Ringo Starr chose to blow the dust off 'It Don't Come Easy', which was his greatest work as a commercial songwriter – but perhaps I'm only saying that because it had once gone down well as a request in a grim metropolitan palais when I was singer with a quintet called Turnpike in the early 1970s. With only the vaguest clue about the verses, I had to make most of them up as I went along. Any meaning in Ringo's hard-won but sloganised lyrics had less importance than the cumulative effect of this sub-Spector production's prelusive fizz of cymbal; Harrison's clanging guitar arpeggios; the fat gusto of the horn section; Mal Evans' tambourine beefing up Voorman and Starr's moderato punch; gospel-esque backing harmonies; and the lugubrious carriage of a tune that the milkman could lilt on his round.

Helped on its way by *I-never-knew-he-had-it-in-him*-style reviews, 'It Don't Come Easy' deservedly outsold then-current offerings by George, John and Paul. While more intrinsic virtues swept it into Top Fives across the planet, those for whom The Beatles' regrouping was seen then as sure as the sunrise focused instead on the topical B-side, 'Early 1970', which would have gone in one ear and out the other had it not been possible to guess the identity of the distant comrades to whom its main subject – an instrumentalist of limited ability – alludes, one with "a brand-new wife", another "with his mama by his side, she's Japanese" and a third who's "always in town playing for you with me".

Ringo had been at so desperate a loss after *Abbey Road* that, to his own six-string tinkering on 'Early 1970', he'd wondered whether Paul, John and George were still going to "play with me". However, million-selling 'It Don't Come Easy' and its afterglow of instant self-esteem was buoyed with the inauguration of the first fan club devoted to Starr alone and his placing as Top Drummer in *NME*'s 1971 popularity poll, in which The Beatles had been superseded as Top Group by Creedence Clearwater Revival. (Just prior to his hit, he'd been at a lowly 13 place in *Beat Instrumental*'s tabulation.)

On 1 August that year, the *NME*'s Top Drummer had belied previous insistences that "personally, I don't want to play in public again"[11] by smacking the skins alongside Jim Keltner in George Harrison's spectacular at Madison Square Garden in aid of Bangladesh, prostrated as it was by disease and famine in the wake of a cyclone and an invading Moslem army. With *All Things Must Pass* its principal source of repertoire, George had drawn together the ex-Delaney And Bonnie minions, a small choir and – on acoustic guitars – three members of Badfinger to accompany more illustrious peers. Of these, only Starr and Billy Preston were punctual attendees at a rehearsal studio near Carnegie Hall. With two sold-out houses to entertain, as well as consumers of the event's movie and triple-album spin-offs, Harrison knocked together a disciplined presentation embracing nothing that hadn't been a smash for someone in the band or wasn't sufficiently well known for a spatter of clapping to swell and subside over its unannounced introduction. "We weren't out to just entertain each other," concurred Ringo. "It's no good just standing there with your guitar, freaking yourself out."[1]

On the night, Ringo "was crazy with nerves beforehand, [but] I enjoyed myself immensely. It was nice, anyway, because we had a lot of good pals around."[9] A sort of bloated 1970s equivalent of a "scream-circuit" package, it was held together by an adaptable combo common to a cache of "featured popular vocalists". These included Harrison himself; Preston, who supplemented his Apple hit 'That's The Way God Planned It' with some fancy footwork; and Ringo, who was loved for a distracted, breathless 'It Don't Come Easy'. He also rattled an apprehensive tambourine in the trio behind Bob Dylan, whom George had talked into a 20-minute spot before the big finish. As Dylan had been in hibernation since the Isle of Wight, George spoke for everyone when he said, "It was great to have him in it at all."[12]

Overlooked in the next morning's newspapers was the fact that it had also been Ringo Starr's first true stage show since Candlestick Park. Nevertheless, the barrage of cheering, stamping and whistling after 'It Don't Come Easy' had dissipated lingering twinges of disappointment about The Beatles' break-up. From the purposeless time-killing that followed *Beaucoups Of Blues*, he had made an indelible mark as a non-Beatle – as opposed to ex-Beatle – and now there were even handsomer dividends inherent in the work put his way these days.

That "it gave Ringo an opportunity"[12] had been one incentive for Allen Klein's underwriting of *Blindman*, an Italian-made spaghetti western that xeroxed the salient points of those that had recently hoisted Clint Eastwood, Lee Van Cleef and Charles Bronson to international acclaim. Indeed, like Eastwood's *A Fistful Of Dollars*, its plot was an Occidental rewrite of a Japanese picture.[13] Two a-penny then, cowboy films were also much in vogue for pop stars wishing to extend themselves. Bob Dylan's economic acting abilities, for example, would be realised with an apposite role as "Alias" in Sam Peckinpah's *Pat Garrett And Billy The Kid*, for which he also penned incidental music. Ringo, too, had donned spurs, "because it was so far from anything I'd ever done",[1] despite elements of *déjà vu* compounded in his part of a Mexican named "Candy" whose dastardly deeds embraced the ravishing of a pulchritudinous blonde played by a Swedish actress.

Although he disliked unnecessary sex and violence in the cinema himself, Klein thought it prudent to stress the more gory aspects of *Blindman* on posters. But, however much it reflected plebeian taste, the new picture would wait years before a rigorously scissored general release in Britain. One day, Ringo would see the censor's point. "It was over the edge," he later admitted. "There's a scene where all these women are running through the desert, trying to escape from us Mexican bandits, and we're just sitting on our horses picking them off."[14]

Resplendent in sombrero and dyed jet-black beard, Starr as Candy was proudly "evil from start to finish"[14] as psychotic brother of a chief bandido who kidnaps the intended brides of 50 Texan miners from a wagon train guided by The Good Guy. The word "guided" is crucial here, for the gringo in question was sightlessly feeling his route by relief map. However, his responsibility for many Boot Hill burials – including Candy's – would be testament that blindness was no barrier to his gunfighting expertise.

This risible plot was mitigated by the sands, cacti, stony hills and seas of dry mesquite grass around Almeria, the Spanish location of *Blindman*, just as it had been for *The Good, The Bad And The Ugly* and the two *Dollars* movies. Authentic, too, were the unwashed, olive faces of beggars hovering outside the town's Grand Hotel, where Ringo – muttering his lines over and over again – was joined by Klein and Mal Evans, both of whom would serve as extras when shooting began.

His watch and all but one of Starr's trademark rings were locked in the hotel safe so that the pallid circles of skin round his wrist and fingers could tan. Another headache for director Ferdinando Baldi was the homely Scouse intonation that simmered just beneath Latinate Candy's broken English, even if he was otherwise "real slimy"[15] or, at least, the film's investors wanted badly to believe he was. However, Ringo's performance – even when dubbed for the première in Rome on 15 November 1971 – actuated not vicarious loathing but mirth from paying customers, although "playing a cowboy" had made the butt of their humour "a hero to my children for the first time".[16]

He'd decided to "start every scene fairly straight and end up as an out-and-out madman".[1] His dementia might have verged on genuine at times, for – as well as the prickly heat and Baldi bragging later of keeping "the great Ringo waiting five hours for only one shot"[14] – he'd grown heartily fed up – and saddle-sore – with riding a horse so herculean that aid was required each time he mounted. Into the bargain, the main title song he'd written and produced (with Voorman) had been turned down. Instead of booming from the silver screen, it would B-side 'Back Off Boogaloo', tardy successor to 'It Don't Come Easy'.

Starr's most menacing creation, 'Blindman' ("best film part I've ever had"[17]), smouldered from a monochordal narrative verse, gathering tension via a bass-drum thud and a two-note synthesiser motif simulating a tuned guiro-castanet effect, the chorus springing from a sudden tacet. If not a precursor, neither was it dissimilar to 'Baby's On Fire', a minimalist "standard" by Brian Eno, then the thinking man's glam rocker. Certainly, it was more of an intellectual experience than straightforward 'Back Off Boogaloo', with Ringo's voice almost drowned in a unison chorus that went on and on and on. "Play me a pop song that isn't,"[3] he retorted when taken to task over how repetitious it was.

Supposedly a put-down of Paul McCartney, 'Back Off Boogaloo' was no profound insight into the human condition. On one Sunday, Starr had woken up with the melody in his head as he hunched over a guitar downstairs. "It just all came out, all the verses part, and then I was watching the football on the telly in the afternoon and [commentator] Jimmy Hill said, 'That was a tasty goal' about someone, and I said, 'Tasty! What a nice word!' and rushed over again, and that's how I got the middle."[18]

Quasi-military drum tattoos that punctuated its arrangement were also a feature of 'Amazing Grace' by the Scottish regimental band, which kept 'Back Off Boogaloo' from topping the UK charts in spring 1972, just as T Rex's 'Hot Love' had with McCartney's 'Another Day' a year before. Both of T Rex's next two Number Ones – 'Get It On' and 'Telegram Sam' – and 'Back Off Boogaloo' were characterised by a hard rock chug and pseudo-cryptic lyrics, so much so that T Rex devotees – and the group's self-glorifying leader, Marc Bolan – would make waspish and spurious allegations that Bolan had ghosted 'Back Off Boogaloo' for Ringo.

T Rex's grip on singles charts in most territories – with North America a glaring exception – evinced a swing back to the flash and cheap thrills of the big beat era as Bolan, Slade, Alice Cooper and The Sweet paved the way for the theatrical glam-rock excesses of Gary Glitter, David Bowie, androgynous Eno's old group Roxy Music and Suzy Quatro, clad in biker leathers while reviving 'I Wanna Be Your Man' with no lyrical revision. Woodstock Nation denim and cheesecloth was chic no more. In the ascendant were sequins, lurex and mascara'd gentlemen dressed like ladies.

Glam rock was not denigrated by Ringo to the same degree as The Osmonds and their bland kind. Nevertheless, Slade – who were the Black Country's as The Beatles were Liverpool's – were another "no-talent band, but they have created an image and a way of life for a lot of people. But I can't see them lasting."[1] In his lordly view, too, "Bowie is a step beyond what Marc is doing, and then you've got Alice somewhere in between."[1]

From a chequered past as a child actor, fashion model and underground celebrity, Bolan's dogged quest for renown and his garrulous conceit when he achieved it had infuriated older contemporaries. When he boasted of being now on an artistic par with Lennon – which he might have been – after visiting pop's Grand Old Man in New York, his host warned him, via the press, to watch his step. When Bolan implied that the squealing "T Rexstasy" that attended his recitals was one in the eye for The Rolling Stones, Jagger sneered that he was "not interested in going back to small English towns and turning on ten-year-olds"[10] – or, presumably those under ten, like Zak and Jason Starkey, who were – so their Dad comprehended – as spellbound by T Rex as he had been by Little Richard. An admirer of Marc's stagecraft – "he knows how to sway the atmosphere and that's a great skill"[1] – Ringo telephoned his Kensington flat with "this idea. See what you think, yes or no."[19]

The ensuing meeting between the down-to-earth Scouser and foppish Marc was one of these Momentous Encounters when, reported Bolan, "It's always the people I least expect to get close to that I end up friends with."[20] Before Marc's magnificent certainty about everything he said and did grated, Ringo was presented with a splendid Les Paul electric guitar from one to whom he became "almost a father. He has been through it all before, and there's so much he has taught me."[20]

As well as his unlikely counsellor snapping Bolan for the sleeve of T Rex's *The Slider* album, another concrete cause for gratitude emanated from Starr's desire to venture beyond merely acting in films, as "the easiest thing is being in them. It's harder when you start producing and getting them together."[18] His first – and most abiding – essay as a director was to be *Born To Boogie*, a full-colour cinema picture about T Rex, financed by Apple. An artist of Marc Bolan's calibre deserved nothing less.

Its centrepiece was a T Rex bash on "the day pop came back",[21] 18 March 1972, when tidal waves of screams hurled rampaging girls towards the stage at the Empire Pool, Wembley. There in 1966, with the cadence of 'I'm Down' yet reverberating, Ringo had had to bolt pell-mell to a ticking limousine which fans quick off the mark had chased as far as Harrow Road. Six years on, he was in the orchestra pit presiding over operations, oblivious to the commotion. It must have been a strange sensation to be completely ignored by crazed females to whom he was just some bloke nearer than they were to darling Marc. Afterwards, the *mêlée* outside was so uncontrolled that a camera was demolished and Mal Evans had to heave Bolan bodily to an armoured getaway car.

At least one lens had been focused constantly on the crowd during the show. In the cold light of a Twickenham Studios' cutting room, an intrigued Starr found that, rather than just screaming, "everyone in that audience was getting something different. That's why we used all those close-ups. There's one guy and his chick and they're just sitting very still watching it. Then there's the chicks who are going completely insane."[18]

On further examination, "I wanted to do some more. You see, my theory about filming concerts is that you can't create the atmosphere that's in the hall. We got [Bolan] to write a few things and set up a couple more days' shooting."[18] Set mostly at a small airfield and Tittenhurst Park – the Lennons' vacated 80-acre estate in Berkshire – the additional footage was reminiscent of *Magical Mystery Tour*, with contrasting scenes threaded together with a deadpan catchphrase – Ringo's suggestion – taken from Wanda Jackson's energetic 'Let's Have A Party' from 1958. Just as arbitrary was the random casting, which included Ringo himself (as the Dormouse to Bolan's Mad Hatter in one sequence), a bearded nun, a dwarf that gnaws offside mirrors from cars and Elton John, who, prior to his chart debut in 1971, had been Reg Dwight, pub pianist and jobbing tunesmith.

The *Born To Boogie* music – T Rex's hits and showstoppers – plus the infectious Wembley excitement could not be overwhelmed by any superfluous visual silliness, and Ringo was to be commended for his long weeks of daily scrutiny – 9.30am until late evening – of each reel, frame by frame, even though "I don't want no editor's trip where it's all fast cuts, because I get bored. I like to use a large proportion of straight shots."[18] Marc, at his elbow, and the studio technicians were astounded by his learned recommendations about rhythm, pacing and camera angles. He also cut an impressive movie-mogul figure during the publicity jaunt, which took in children's television and – for what it was worth – a trip to the States, where 'Get It On' had clawed up the Hot 100 in time for the world première on 14 December 1972.

Ben Hur it wasn't, but Starr had cause to be elated by critical compliments – even back-handed ones, like the sniffy *Morning Star*'s "directed(?) by Ringo, this is the best teeny-bopper entertainment since The Beatles succumbed to insecticide".[22] Excited after an EMI executive told Marc that his daughter had tried and failed to get into her local ABC to see *Born To Boogie*, Starr and Bolan "drove down there together just to look at the queues forming up outside the cinema".[23]

Yet, as if it were one of his hobbies, Ringo's passion for film direction had cooled, not with its creative labour but with the mind-stultifying legal and budgetary mechanics of post-production clearance and distribution. Like a gymkhana pony refusing a fence, he now balked at the project he'd first put to Marc of a TV series documenting the day-to-day lives of famed personalities.

Always stimulated by the celebrity of others, Starr had banked on the co-operation of such as footballer George Best, Marc, Cilla and Elizabeth Taylor, for whose 40th birthday the Starkeys had jetted to Budapest – the location of her current movie, *Bluebeard* – to celebrate. The editing block at Twickenham was no fun whatsoever compared to being a desired guest at so many glittering occasions. As well as Liz's knees-up, vibrantly gregarious Ringo would be photographed sharing a joke with Mick Jagger, Barbra Streisand, Princess Grace of Monaco – you name 'em – at Cote D'Azur launches of new record companies, gala award ceremonies and on/off shindigs like David Bowie's lavish "retirement" do at the Café Royal in July 1973. Through George Harrison, Starr's self-endowed leisure also facilitated a spectator's enthusiasm for Formula One racing. The VIP treatment that was automatically theirs at these buzzing panoramas found both ex-Beatles on celluloid toasting Jackie Stewart – winner of 1970's Monte Carlo Grand Prix – in Polanski's *Weekend Of A Champion*.

Ringo's companions in revelry were of a world more cultivated than that of a Scotch of St James raver *circa* 1965, but his renewed zest for the social whirl was so voracious that he'd hide rings around his eyes from the previous *soirée* with the mirror sunglasses that became standard party accoutrement during that period.

A soulmate during these roisterings was Keith Moon, Zak's hero and another *Born To Boogie* starlet, just as Starr would be a minor commentator in *The Kids Are Alright*, a 1979 film portrait of The Who. Seven years earlier, in 1972, he was most effective as perverted, spivvy "Uncle Ernie" in Lou Reizner's soundtrack of a stage presentation of *Tommy* at London's Rainbow Theatre. When commitment to a new film, *That'll Be The Day*, prevented Ringo's participation in the actual show, an obvious substitute was 25-year-old Moon, his new drinking partner (with brandy the favoured tipple).

In a lucid moment, Keith had confessed that his role as The Who's newsmaker was purely for publicity. However, that he maintained his maniac persona throughout his short life infers a less sound motivation. Perpetuated by the easy money that had fallen into his lap since gatecrashing the group in 1963, his tomfoolery – like parading around West End clubs in Nazi attire – would often deteriorate into a nonsensical, attention-grabbing frenzy of explosives in hotel bedrooms; breaking into an aeroplane pilot's cabin while airborne to rap his drumsticks on the control panel; slashing his wrists at the drop of a hat; and applying a cigarette lighter to his £150 pay-packet for a day's film work. Since accidentally killing his chauffeur in 1970, Moon had become even more lost, afflicted with worsening black-outs – both on stage and off – through punishing up to four decanters of spirits within an hour of waking "just to get things moving".[24] On his final tour with The Who in 1977, his fee would be a paltry £40 after deductions for depredations he'd inflicted *en route*.

The older Ringo tended to laugh at Moon's larks rather than be drawn into them. Although only a passing role was provided for him in *That'll Be The Day*, Keith made a disproportionate impression off camera by hiring a helicopter to touch down on the roof of the Isle of Wight hotel allocated to the cast so that he could emerge from this conveyance in full Red Baron flying rig. "It's the only way to travel, man."[17]

On one night, back at the hotel's ballroom stage, there was an extraordinary assembly of "Ringo on lead guitar, me on bass", recalled David Essex, along with "Graham Bond on drums, Harry Nilsson on tambourine and Honky Tonk(?) on drums – and we had

Billy Fury as singer. You never heard such a noise in your life, because we were all playing about with instruments we don't normally play, just for the fun of it."[17] By 4am, enough guests had complained about the row that police materialised in their midst and the music terminated. Less ruinous of others' sleep was the night on which the funfair scenes were shot. "Ringo and I were in T-shirts, pretending to have a good time when all the time it was pouring rain" – Essex again – "[but] that was great, because we had the run of the fair all night. Years ago, I used to work on a funfair, and I had to teach Ringo how to balance as we went 'round, collecting money from the punters."[17]

Pleasurable, too, was the extravagant party that Moon threw on completing his part as drummer in Bickerstaffe Happy Holiday Camp's Blue Grotto's resident rock 'n' roll combo for 1959's *Stormy Tempest And The Typhoons*. Ray Connolly's screenplay had plagiarised Rory Storm's group at Butlins in more than name. In silver jacket and hair stiff with lacquer, Tempest was played by Billy Fury, a touching instance of typecasting for the ailing rock-a-balladeer, soon to undergo a second heart operation.

With his days on the Mersey ferry holding him in good stead (especially when required to carry a tray of glasses), Ringo-as-Grotto-barman's scripted comments on Tempest's band included a description of their off-duty carnal pastimes and – considering his real-life career, post-Hurricanes – an ironic "but there's no future in being a Typhoon. I mean, where does it get you?" From director Claude Whatham, he'd been given *carte blanche* "to ramble on all I wanted, because people write lines for you that you'd never say. So I did my own dialogue. I love it when they let me go off on my own."[25] This may invoke howls of derision, but I think that Ringo's second lead in this poignant evocation of provincial England in the late 1950s stands as his most powerful artistic statement. Through improvising around his own character and personal history, his role as Mike Menarry blew away like dust his previous and future efforts in records and films. Any argument that *A Hard Day's Night*, 'It Don't Come Easy' *et al* created the opportunity to do so is irrelevant.

The promotional spiel that it was "a strong dramatic part laced with humour"[1] was justified. As Sinatra had begged for his Oscar-winning part in *From Here To Eternity*, because he "might have been"[26] Joe di Maggio, so Ringo Starr was Mike Menarry – or, at least, aspects of him were. "My part as Mike is total flashback," he observed, "since he's very much me as I was in the late 1950s."[17] A Liverpudlian Ted, Ringo/Mike dons "my own actual velvet-collared jacket. Everyone reeled back from the smell of mothballs when I put it on. I wear a pair of socks I used to wear in those days, too."[17]

The unlettered Menarry's sole reading matter is comics. He is otherwise preoccupied with getting off with birds – "a quick tickle to see if they go, then it's 'round the back and getting me end away" – but unbothered and philosophical about any repulsions. Less brazenly, but just as unashamedly, he fiddles the Grotto customers' change. When boasts of prowess in any given field is disproved, he blames anything but himself. For his two left feet in a Grotto jiving contest, "it was the band, you know. No one can dance to that noise." The "sodding cue" loses him a round of snooker.

Shabbily likeable though he is, Mike/Ringo does not immediately impress his chalet mate, Jim MacLaine, David Essex's big-screen debut. Jim is a good-looking Somerset youth who, although earmarked for university, had left a sheltered life on impulse on the morning of his "A"-levels to the dismayed confusion of his mother, with her middle-class values. At Bickerstaffe, the would-be rakish Mike's unwitting machinations lead MacLaine to lose his virginity in a haze of cheap perfume, Australian wine and grubby bedsheets. "From then on," sniggered Ringo, "he'll have anything. He doesn't care. I introduce him to the naughty side of life."[1]

Mike next finds his doubtful friend a job as his assistant operator on the dodgems with a travelling fair, inducting him into the routine procedure of how to "work and sweat and work and fiddle". However competent a tutor he is, Mike inadvertently cheats one rider too many, and after a bloody reprisal by the aggrieved party's motorbike gang is left with a limp for the sequel, *Sooner Or Later* –

retitled *Stardust* by autumn 1973 and with Adam Faith assuming the role of Menarry – now road manager and confidant of MacLaine as he becomes a 1960s pop star. Ringo felt that his continuance as Menarry would be to condone a storyline too close for comfort to that of The Beatles. More specifically piquant for him than the tough realism of behind-the-scenes drugs and sex was the fact that a mainstay of Jim's group, The Stray Cats, is underhandedly replaced just as they crack the charts.

Although Faith delivered a portrayal of Menarry as convincing in its way as Starr's, Essex would always speak fondly of his previous co-star, who'd "really knocked me out. One of the biggest thrills of my life was working with Ringo,"[27] two of whose "sculptures" – a milk and a Coca Cola bottle – would be among ornaments in David's 16th-century Essex home. Their mutual appreciation of Dr John's Creole psychedelia and the research for *That'll Be The Day* combined to inspire Essex's first Top-Ten strike, 1973's 'Rock On', which aligned itself to 1950s rock by namechecking "Jimmy Dean" in its hook.

Further signs of disassociation with contemporary pop was that same year's *American Graffiti*, with its recreation of 1962 in a small Midwestern town. Rock 'n' roll revival acts abounded, like Sha Na Na and Shakin' Stevens And The Sunsets, and forgotten Mod classics would shortly be attempted during The Sex Pistols' exploratory stumblings. These regressive trends and the snowballing of specialist fanzines chronicling them encouraged many hearts to pound in anticipation while squeezing between jumble-sale hags blocking passage to a pile of scratched 45s and brittle 78s on white-elephant stalls. Such expeditions for overlooked artefacts from earlier musical eras helped to hold a ghastly present at arm's length.

In this respect, Ringo's sterling acting – if it *was* acting – in *That'll Be The Day* could not efface his compromising elitist connections – however remote – with such as *All Things Must Pass*, the overblown *Tommy* rehash, Leon Russell's triple *Live* album and disc jockey John Peel's chortling that Starr's was "one 'superstar' family that still makes it"[28] on 'Back Off Boogaloo'. Ringo's future actions would take no account of adverse reactions towards the distancing of the rock star – forever, in the States – from a home audience that would soon be ripe for the shouting and banging of punk, a movement that by original definition precluded stardom. Other territories, especially North America, would stay amenable to Ringo Starr's output for a while longer, and – commercially, anyway – the best was yet to come. But otherwise, his tide was already ebbing.

12 "I Can't Wait To Go, Half The Time"

For a while, he didn't trouble to wash off the Teddy Boy tattoo – or, rather, the transfer – on his right ear. He may have also kept the Cupid and heart that had likewise adorned Mike Menarry's buttocks – as seen in a chalet scene – but these were not revealed on the chat-shows he undertook at the time. As well as pushing *That'll Be The Day* and drumming behind Jimmy Tarbuck and Tim Rice's 'impromptu' 'Singing The Blues' on ITV, he used the exposure to promote steel, glass and plastic furniture purchasable from "Ringo Or Robin Limited", who were exhibiting at Liberty's department store, off Regent Street, during the last fortnight in September 1971.

Among keen patrons of Starr's collaboration with Robin Cruikshank was Prime Minister Edward Heath, who received a specially designed mirror – on which was inlaid his own image over a postcard English landscape – for Christmas 1973. With Cruikshank in charge of the technological donkeywork, Ringo's mechanical turn was given its head with the likes of a coffee stand fashioned from Rolls Royce radiator grilles, circular fireplaces and flower-shaped tables. Like vintage champagne, these goods were available for any citizen to buy. From the shop in Rathbone Street, near Oxford Circus, you could spend your loose change on, say, a £600 sofa or – a snip at £40 – a smallish mirror with either a Bambi or Apple logo.

While art deco was still fun for him, Ringo had a particularly glowing newspaper review of the firm's latest creations blown up and displayed in Apple's front windows, but – his dilettante's attention flitting elsewhere – the business would be up for sale by 1976. Nevertheless, there was a time when a livewire ex-Beatle stuck to office hours, during which "we have a lot of hassles and we have a lot of fun. It depends who comes to see us."[1] In this less hectic phase of his celebrity, however, many plans progressed no further than discussion. He formed Wobble Music Ltd and the Reckongrade production company, but for what purpose was anyone's guess. He also spoke of financing a film with one of the Smothers Brothers – a kind of US Mike and Bernie Winters – and "one with a guy about models, which I think is a saleable thing".[1] Dating from this time, *Adventure: Ring Of Fire* was a documentary – with incidental music by George Harrison – about Lorne and Lawrence Blair's expedition to the Indonesian archipelago. This would be screened at last in summer 1988 – albeit in seven parts on BBC television – with Ringo as Executive Director.

Even with excellent notices for *That'll Be The Day*, Starr never got around to acting in another movie halfway as appealing, sticking instead to mainly minor roles that required little preparation. There was, however, mention of a silent movie, which "would be great, [because] I wouldn't have any lines to learn. It's the words that get in the way all the time, in many films."[2] Neither would he have minded "a costume drama – that's the ultimate fantasy. Something like *The Three Musketeers* or *The Knights Of The Round Table*, where I could wear a suit of armour and do a bit of swordfighting."[2]

At one point, he approved Michael Pertwee's screenplay for *The Biggest Dog In The World* and his choice of producer in Walter Shenson, from The Beatles' days, but eventually Ringo let this children's comedy slip from his grasp, possibly because it would follow too soon after *That'll Be The Day*. Furthermore, as well as his finding memorising lines and the demanding schedules with their early mornings onerous, "There's all the steps they have to take after you agree to do it. I have said yes to a few things, but they're still out there looking for the money I find it very hard to make the sort of commitment you need in movies. It's such a long-time situation."[3]

Just prior to *That'll Be The Day*, Ringo's marking time between more challenging projects had been typified by his part in *200*

Motels, the only major film by Frank Zappa, leader of The Mothers Of Invention, whom Ringo had considered "a real weirdo but, once you get to know him, he isn't. He's probably one of the straightest men I've ever met."[3] Via a rapid turnover of personnel and changes in his stylistic determination, Zappa's records were attracting – for better or worse – a wider audience in their drift from incisive aural junk-sculptures towards lavatorial "humor".

This strain was lamentably palpable in *200 Motels*, which, while praised for its spectacular and pioneering visual effects, was stamped by *The New York Times* as being "a subjective *A Hard Day's Night* in desperate need of the early Beatles".[4] Actually, it was as close to *Magical Mystery Tour* as The Mothers' *We're Only In It For The Money* had been a cursory send-up of *Sgt Pepper*, from its parodic sleeve to the 'Day In The Life' piano omega. *200 Motels* also absorbed traces of *Candy*, to which Mother Howard Kaylan actually makes delicate and pointed reference when discussing pornographic literature.[5]

Perhaps *200 Motels* might have been more like *A Hard Day's Night* had one of its principal hirelings, Wilfred Brambell, stayed the course. Instead, Paul's ex-"grandfather" despaired of ever understanding – let alone learning – his part as The World's Oldest Bass Guitarist in a script riddled with "balling chicks"-type slang for Zappa's sluggish "fantasy opera" of his Mothers' sleazy adventures when their tour reaches Centerville – not Lightnin' Hopkins' birthplace but a mock-up of a surreal US town inhabited by "just plain folks".

Busy behind the cameras, Zappa elected to appear only in musical segments with The Mothers and a put-upon Royal Philharmonic Orchestra. Therefore, as well as playing a character called "Larry the Dwarf", Ringo – in straggly black wig and dagger beard – doubled as an ill-at-ease Zappa, who composed songs around his recorded eavesdropping on the discord and intrigues that make pop groups what they are. One inducement to burden himself with these peculiar roles was the fact that Keith Moon was in it too, as a nun, as well as The Mothers' own august percussionists, Jimmy Carl Black and latter-day Mojo Aynsley Dunbar. By one of Zappa's chance operations, involving the first person to enter a particular room, Ringo's current chauffeur and former Apple errand-boy, Martin Lickert, was given a rewrite of Brambell's part.

As the fragile storyline was lost to in-jokes, cartoon sequences and Frank's ructions with his co-director, it hardly mattered that Ringo made no effort "to other be" as either Zappa or Larry. Too much for the common movie-goer, 200 Motels faded swiftly from general circulation to be shown occasionally only in film clubs and "alternative" cinemas, where it was watched as a duty by those who'd wished for time to stop in the late 1960s.

By 1973, whatever was left of hippy conviviality at Apple had contracted into a unity of darting suspicion when – uncool though it was – turgid examination of Allen Klein's handling of Messrs Harrison, Lennon and Starr's divergent affairs could not be postponed, especially with the expiry date of the contract approaching. The mustering of legal forces to compile evidence of an increasingly distant manager's transgressions was motivated by a new willingness to credit provocative but not completely fictional tales by their friends and various of Klein's incensed former associates of his shifty and senselessly blunt stance in negotiation.

For all the fear that spread from him like cigar smoke, Klein was not as greedy as he might have been. Compared to some of his peers, who were entitled to half of everything that their clients earned regardless, the Robin Hood of pop took only a fifth of that which he'd actually secured for his artists. As John, Ringo and George became more adept at dealing directly with third parties, so the counter-suing Klein was dyed a villain of the darkest hue by October 1974, when he lost the case and Apple's complex finances were unfrozen. With its original ideal of bucking the bourgeois system long forgotten, "All Apple does is collecting," said Ringo. "We have no artists. We have nothing to push, but it looks after the films. It owns The Beatles' name, so, in fact, collects The Beatles' royalties."[6] These would now pour along defined streams towards the deltas of each separate ex-Beatle's business executor – that is, John's Yoko, George's Denis O'Brien and Paul's Eastmans.

Ringo's counterpart was Hilary Gerrard, a former Apple executive who'd also act as personal retainer on the mighty rough road that lay ahead. To those outsiders who twigged that he was Ringo's manager and not merely some companion, Gerrard's name would for years be as synonymous with that of his flamboyant charge as Colonel Parker's with Elvis.

Missing the team activities and glamour of The Beatles, Gerrard's man was still making the most of his fresh lease of life since 'It Don't Come Easy' by seldom turning down a worthwhile opportunity to promote himself, whether discoursing about his favourite records on Radio 1's *My Top Twelve* or dressing up as a pope with twirled moustachios in *Lisztomania*, directed by the outrageous Ken Russell, fresh from immortalising wretched *Tommy* on celluloid. One of Starr's favourite directors, his film biography of the prolific Hungarian composer was as true to life as a comic strip. Playing a Scouse "Urban IV" with the same disregard for authenticity as he had "Frank Zappa", Ringo's big moment was imploring Liszt – The Who's Roger Daltrey – to focus his talent towards exorcising the devils from Richard Wagner (Paul Nicholas, straight from *Stardust* and *Tommy*).

After acting and directing, Starr had had a stab at producing, too, when it was agreed that he should be head of Apple Films, as he was the only ex-Beatle then to make strides in that direction. Initially, he ruled in fact as well as name from a plush office (with bar alcove) near Horse Guards Parade. Visitors could deduce what the division would be up to next from macabre props dotted among the spindly potted trees and smaller ornaments in the executive suite, as well as the plaque on its door reading "HQ Dr Baron Frankenstein, Brain Specialist". Ringo was going to make a horror movie.

He'd seen himself in the title role of *Count Downe* – or, as it was renamed, *Son Of Dracula* – but pragmatism prevailed and, like Zappa, he plumped for a smaller part to concentrate better on administration and supervision. To direct, he'd appointed Freddie Francis, whose *curriculum vitae* bulged with good, honest British trash like *Dr Terror's House Of Horrors*, *The Evil Of Frankenstein* and – also starring Peter Cushing – 1965's *The Skull*. For Ringo's updating of the Dracula legend – the impending ascent of his lovestruck son (who yearns to go straight) onto the throne of the netherworld – Francis recommended such genre shellbacks as Suzanna Leigh and Dennis Price while, at his employer's insistence, fitting in last-minute cameos for show-offs like Keith Moon. He didn't put his foot down, either, when the old-pals act extended to Nilsson, for whom Ringo was "now a very dear, close friend and I love him".[7] With no theatrical experience but in the public eye then with the million-selling single 'Without You', Nilsson consented to be Count Downe in what was now "like a non-musical, non-horror, non-comedy comedy," quipped Starr, "or it's a horror-horror, musical-musical, comedy-comedy."[8]

It wasn't all smiles, however, when shooting began in late 1972 within the foggy, slip-slapping wharfs and gilded bridges of London's docklands. The novice producer was soon beset with "such a headache. Everyone shouts at you. I didn't know that, if you didn't get the crew home and in their beds by midnight, you couldn't work them the next day, because, you see, I'm a musician, and if we start working and it starts to cook, we'll keep it rolling for three days, if necessary."[9]

As well as learning the hard way about union dictates, Ringo had become disagreeably aware that the plot *per se* was too feeble to go the distance as a full-blown epic. Like other scenes featuring the Wolfman, Frankenstein and other stock characters, his own – in robes and long white beard as 200-year-old Merlin the Magician – was not altogether relevant to the basic yarn but was necessary to both regain wandering audience attention and justify the printing of the words "Ringo Starr" in large letters on the lobby placard inside the Atlanta cinema, where – like *Gone With The Wind* 35 years earlier – *Son Of Dracula* was premièred in May 1974.

Too early for the gothic craze that afflicted a faction among post-punk British adolescents, Ringo's effort was seen only in the States, to the chagrin of a less fervent home following; for many, the exclusion provided an absolute cure for Beatlemania. Yet, for the lucky Yanks, even personal appearances by Starr and Nilsson when the film opened elsewhere could not prevent its relegation to "all the little villages because, if we put it on in a town, it got slated".[10] The soundtrack, too, could not be rescued from deletion by wringing monetary drops from the presence within its grooves of Ringo, George Harrison (on cowbell) and guitarist Peter Frampton from Humble Pie, whose album *Wind Of Change* – with Billy Preston and Starr on some tracks – was the small beginning to solo success in North America later in the decade.

Frampton and Starr had also been present at Soho's Trident Studios for the recording of *Son Of Schmilsson*, which, by apparent coincidence, had Nilsson-as-Dracula on its front cover (and with a dummy in his mouth on the rear). This LP, like its bigger-selling predecessor, *Nilsson Schmilsson* – containing 'Without You' – was produced by Richard Perry, whose long residence in California and frequent working trips to England had not tempered his East Coast twang. From overseeing Captain Beefheart, Tiny Tim, the blues singer Taj Mahal and Theodore Bikel (later a *200 Motels* star), the emergence of Perry as the most fashionable record producer of the next decade began with 1972's *No Secrets* and its attendant 'You're So Vain' hit for Carly Simon. With his very name a selling point, Perry then moved closer to middle-of-the-road pop with customers like Johnny Mathis, Barbra Streisand, mushy Percy Faith and, purring Mister Wonderful, Andy Williams. A conspicuous feather in his cap was a London album with Ella Fitzgerald.

In truth, although grandiloquent in style, Perry was nowhere as inventive as Joe Meek, George Martin or even Phil Spector, but he'd acquired the knack of injecting just enough of prevailing fads into an easy-listening artist's music to avoid turning off older fans. Hence we were blessed with Mathis' adaptation of 'My Sweet Lord' and Faith's 'Sun King' for the supper clubs and Streisand recording at Keith Richards' French villa. There was even a period in 1974 when it was cool to dig Williams' *Solitaire* album, because he'd been backed by musicians hip enough to be listed on its back cover.

Among these was Klaus Voorman, whom Perry had also called upon for *Nilsson Schmilsson*, and it was through that elegant Teuton that George Harrison became sufficiently intrigued to look in on an Ella Fitzgerald session and Ringo to actually drum on *Son Of Schmilsson* and, just prior to this, on a solo 45 by Righteous Brother Bobby Hatfield, after Perry – damn his impudence – had considered Starr "good enough to play sessions for me".[11]

Basking in his 15 minutes of fame, Perry took the Other Two Beatles' flattering surveillance in his stride, while acknowledging the group's influence in his "knowing what they did and why it was great and applying it to other situations".[12] The concord when taping one Nilsson track was such that, relaxing in Tramp afterwards, Perry was emboldened to offer Starr his console favours, if or when he was ready to commence another album. However, although fascinated by Richard's visionary notion for selecting "a certain song and create visual for it, instead of the other way 'round, as it is traditionally done",[12] a sceptical Starr decided to put his first "proper" post-Beatles album on ice.

Above the tour-album-tour sandwiches incumbent upon poorer pop aristocrats, Starr would wait until he felt like making a new record while picking and choosing the studio dates that were earning him legion (if usually pseudonymous) LP credits. At Trident, Olympic and Apple, he did his bit for such as Grammy-winning songwriter Jim Webb, as well as this or that "super sideman" for whom it had become convenient to migrate to Europe to fulfil a rewarding workload. For saxophonist Bobby Keyes, his augmentation of The Rolling Stones had been a springboard to his own boring, boring album, in which "a lot of the tracks just came about from jamming",[13] with stellar assistance from pals that included the Tweedledum and Tweedledee of such occasions. Harrison and Starr also applied their touch to 1973's *Brother* by Lon and Derrek Van Eaton, Apple's last signing. On their 'Sweet Music', Ringo tapped out that changeless 4/4 next to another drummer, Jim Gordon, whose drug-related problems had led to the recent cashiering of him by Traffic. He ended up in an asylum for the criminally insane for matricide, an incarceration attributed to the chemicals that were common currency when, from Delaney And

Bonnie's Friends, he'd muscled in among that superstar elite that exchanged smirks with ol' George across the mixing desk at Trident.

Starr did not always assume that records could only be made with the same smug oligarchy, for in 1972 he tried again with John Tavener. Although in the throes of composing an opera based on the life of St Theresa, the clever young man put his mind to "a bit for some pop record they're producing – just something for the middle, different from the rest. Ringo just said, 'You write whatever you want to write.'"[14] It must have been rather too "different", however, because, if Tavener ever finished it, his musical bridge has not been heard to this day in connection with any disc by Starr, who in the following spring finally got around to commissioning a thrilled Richard Perry to go ahead with *Ringo*, which would stand forever as the artist's best-selling solo album and Perry's apotheosis as a producer, "one which I may never top".[15]

This dark self-judgement might have been wavered had Ringo adhered to "this great plan of doing a world album: you know, two tracks in Nashville, a couple in London, some in Peru or wherever".[3] Instead, a compliance with Perry's request for him and Nilsson to compere a Grammy-awards presentation in Nashville enabled the finalising of details and a decision to cut corners by block-booking Los Angeles' Sunset Sound Studio for five exploratory days when Starr was to be in the city anyway for a meeting about the Klein business with Harrison and Lennon. It was also the involvement of these two during a second week of *Ringo* sessions that marked the closest that The Beatles would ever come to an artistic reunion before the 'Free As A Bird' single in 1995.

On the five tracks – including a 'Photograph' with strings, choir and Bobby Keyes sax solo – that were dispatched during the initial sojourn, some were propelled by guitar sections too singular to have been played by anyone else but George. For Perry, the overall outcome had been most pleasing, "right from opening night. We had to keep the tape going because, as soon as we'd start the playback, they'd go into a jam which didn't sound like a jam [but] a new song, which was totally different from what we were playing."[12] "We" embraced a mutable pool of familiar cohorts, from the Van Eaton siblings to Marc Bolan to pianist Nicky Hopkins on the rebound (like Starr) from Harrison's *Living In The Material World*. Yet, of all the negotiable names that would be annotated on the *Ringo* back cover, none was more so than all four former Beatles.

Staying on in Los Angeles to promote his wife's new double LP, *Approximately Infinite Universe*, John socialised with Starr and Perry, stringing along with them to a screening of the prurient *Last Tango In Paris*. He also listened hard to *Ringo* thus far and was prompted to submit a song himself. Grown from a weak hook but two tough riffs, 'I'm The Greatest' was a semi-autobiographical opus made to measure for Starr, mentioning specifically his birthplace, his part in "the greatest show on Earth", his age and his "kids". The Lennons' so far unrequited longing for children was casting a shadow over their marriage, and this may have contributed to the bite inherent in John's demo that was missing on *Ringo*'s slicker retread, with its over-larded applause.

'I'm The Greatest' had been lacking only a middle eight, which Ringo, Lennon and Perry were puzzling out on the studio's concert grand when Harrison telephoned to invite himself along. If John was still huffy about the specific exclusion of Yoko – and, indirectly, himself – from the Bangladesh extravaganza, he and George were inclined not to bicker in their old drummer's presence and, therefore, "You could really tell that they were excited!" gushed Perry. "There was such a fantastic energy coming out of the room!! It was really sensational!!!"[12]

Not sending him into quite the same verbal paroxysms as this coup were less pronounced instances of ex-Beatle creativity during the *Ringo* sessions. With The Band, George backed Ringo on 'Sunshine Life For Me', a hootenanny hoe-down that had been composed and then shelved when the Harrisons and Donovan were holidaying in Ireland in 1969. Its sub-title, 'Sail Away, Raymond' pertained to a creature of Klein's. With Mal Evans, George also penned 'You And Me (Babe)', which, although tuneful and riven with a deft fretboard obligato, was a vehicle through which Starr could close the album with a monologue that thanked everyone – famous and obscure – who'd taken part.

His juxtaposition in this of the words "John", "Lennon", "Paul" and "McCartney" could only have been deliberate, although neither had played on the same tracks. More objective about Apple's legal turmoils as well as John's public insults, Paul had been amenable to pitching in on 'I'm The Greatest', but he was refused a US visa owing to a recent fine for possessing narcotics, which had been seized during a European tour with Wings, a new group built around himself, ex-Moody Blue Denny Laine and Linda – now his occasional songwriting collaborator – on keyboards. This setback did not, however, stop Paul from contributing his mimicking of a saxophone *à la* The Fourmost on Johnny Burnette's ambulant 'You're Sixteen', his pursed-lips roughness mitigating Nilsson's too-pat multitracked backing responses. Paul's digits were also employed in the latter's compilation – also at Abbey Road – of a backing track for a new number, 'Six O'Clock', for editing as necessary by Perry, who was taking a breather from Sunset Sound to help supervise a McCartney television special in London.

Notable for its snotty synthesiser ostinato, 'Six O'Clock' could have been made up by McCartney in his sleep. It was certainly commensurate with the wispy lyrics and syrupy jingles that comprised *Red Rose Speedway*, Wings' 1973 album. However, its intrinsic value mattered less than its use – with Starr's added drums and vocals – in a campaign that would colour *Ringo* as a bastardised Beatles collection, supplemented too by Voorman's *Sgt Pepper*-ish lithograph on its sleeve and the teasing insertion of the odd Lennon-McCartney song title into its lyrics. Whether they conjured up magic or mere music wasn't the issue; that the Fab Four were theoretically together on the same lump of plastic was sufficient to feed hope that soon everything would be OK again, just like it was before John went funny in 1968, and that The Beatles would regroup officially to tour and record the chart-toppers that John and Paul – all friends now – would be churning out once more.

In 1973, whether these four mortals as individuals sold records or not did not yet depend upon commercial viability As Paul demonstrated, an ex-Beatle was guaranteed at least a minor hit, even with sub-standard produce. In the States, both he and George had clambered as far as Number One, and, after the climb of 'Photograph' up the same Hot 100 that autumn, Ringo's turn came too – just – when, on knocking off Eddie Kendricks' 'Keep On Truckin', he ruled pop for one glorious week.

The lead voice apart, 'Photograph' would not have been out of place on one of its co-writer's discs. Like a lot of Harrison items, something about it was infuriatingly familiar, its very introit invoking both 'Let's Spend The Night Together' and The Lemon Pipers' 'Green Tambourine'. Nevertheless, its fetching aftertaste of "beautiful sadness" – broadly, a yearning for an absent loved one – made it a much-requested radio spin for a nation still awaiting the return of many of its sons from Vietnam following the January cease-fire. Similarly, long after tumbling from its domestic high of Number Four, 'Photograph' lingered as a home thought from abroad on Radio 2's *Two-Way Family Favourites* as Britain scoffed its Sunday roasts.

Although 'Photograph' was half George's, this single represented Ringo's peak as a composer in hard financial terms, especially as its B-side, 'Down And Out', was all his own work. This leftover from 1972 was unsuitable for *Ringo*, living only in its stabbing horns, Gary Brooker's piano and producer Harrison's bottleneck solo. If its lyrics were almost as perfunctory, 'Step Lightly' – another attributed to Richard Starkey alone – reconciled more easily with the album's pervading climate. With clarinets and the syncopated clattering of Starr's own feet lending it a 1930s dance-band feel, it was selected as the second track on side two, just where 'When I'm 64' – in the same vein – had been on *Sgt Pepper*.

Just as savoury an ingredient in the *Ringo* cauldron as its Beatles affiliations was Starr's songwriting liaison with Vini Poncia, a bond that proved to be more lucrative than that of Poncia and Peter Anders with The Tradewinds and Innocence. Since 'There's Got To Be A Word', the duo's entry into Richard Perry's trendy orbit had resulted in an LP under their own names and Vini's production of

Melissa Manchester and other of Richard's clients. Ranking, I suppose, as Perry's lieutenant on *Ringo*, Poncia was fumbling one evening for a key to suit Starr's larynx for one number "and I had lots of bits of songs and I played some to him, and then he had a few bits and we found we could write together. That's how we got together, and we've been together ever since."[16]

The first harvest of the Poncia-Starkey team reaped the catchy 'Oh My My', with a fake party atmosphere infectious enough to warrant its release as a US-only Ringo 45 and a hit to boot. Had its "get you into bed" line been altered, that honour might have gone to 'Devil Woman', which, with its standardised title, had a guitar lacerating it with clichéd heavy metal fuzz. It was, however, peculiar for Starr, hitting a different rhythm to that of the less heavy-handed Jim Keltner, who was otherwise heard on another four tracks, mainly clumping along in unison with Ringo in a like manner to the percussion artillery in Gary Glitter's Glitter Band.

Starr's reliance on Keltner – increasing in years to come – invites speculation both about Starr's self-picture as a musician and his preferred studio methodology. As Sly Stone and, I suspect, Dave Clark did, he and his producer – head to head in the control booth – appear to have sometimes employed the disciplined Keltner for the backing track, with Ringo layering his own more idiosyncratic drumming only after the beat had already been invested. Ringo's technical input was also guided by instinct. Engineer Stephen Lipson recalled that, because Starr liked the look of a certain microphone, "We tried it on the drums. He was happy. They sounded like Ringo Starr."[17]

One of the strengths of *Ringo* was that no participant was expected to suppress his individuality. Harrison's vocal harmony on 'Photograph' and Lennon's on 'I'm The Greatest', for example, were not "depersonalised" in the mix. Neither was Bolan's pulsating 'Telegram Sam' guitar buried in the descending piano inversions and booting saxophones on a version of Randy Newman's 'Have You Seen My Baby?'.[18]

Tending to drive his T Rex underlings hard in the studio, Bolan was not conditioned to Perry and Starr's laid-back attitude. This expression was taken almost too literally on some of Ringo's vocal takes, when onlookers made bets on "which side of my face I'd fall on after a whole fifth of bourbon".[19] Through interpolations like a vignette from 'What Shall We Do With The Drunken Sailor?' on the fade-out of 'You're Sixteen', ordinary fans might also have ascertained their hero's giggling intemperance. Even so, his singing was more consistently and clinically accurate than it had been on *Beaucoups Of Blues*.

In an industry where sales figures – especially North American ones – are arbiters of success, the proof of the pudding was the rise of *Ringo* to the top of *Billboard*'s album tabulation. In its singles chart, triumph chased triumph when, with 'Photograph' still in the Top Ten, 'You're Sixteen' likewise lasted seven days at Number One, until dragged down by Barbra Streisand, of all people. 'You're Sixteen' was not a Starkey original, but only McCartney had also hit the jackpot twice. To Lennon, who hadn't managed it at all, it appeared that the Beatle least likely was "doing better than any of us".[20] However, if signs were not yet perceptible, Ringo was about to fritter it away to all but the very dregs.

He'd anticipated the profits from *Ringo* and its offshoots by purchasing Tittenhurst Park within a fortnight of the Lennons' putting it on the market in September 1973. A compromise between remote Elstead and metropolitan Highgate, the Starkeys' new spread off Ascot's main thoroughfare to London was the opposite side of "Hollywood-on-Thames" to the Harrisons in olde-worlde Henley. Nearer neighbours who were also Starr's *nouveau-riche* equals in the hierarchy of pop included Rod Stewart in Bray, Jimmy Page of Windsor and Rick Wakeman in Camberley To a man, they were now inhabiting a world as exclusive as that of Berkshire's other landed gentry, and as far removed from whatever back-street terrace or middle-class semi-detached they came. Sunny afternoon idylls were blighted mildly by the whoosh of an occasional Concorde from Heathrow miles away, but otherwise only cascading pylons towards the horizon reminded them of the 20th century

Ringo's 26-room white Tudor mansion and some of the outhouses were buildings of historical importance that he was obliged by law to maintain and to permit National Trust inspectors "reasonable access". Alien to an Elizabethan squire, however, were many allowable alterations, such as the sauna, the swimming pool and – behind stained-glass windows – the inevitable snooker den. John had recorded his second solo LP, *Imagine*, in the eight-track studio that had supplanted all but the pipe organ in what had once been a private chapel. Renamed "Startling Studio" by its new owner, it was made available for public hire via the Reading area's classified telephone directory; nuisance calls from Beatle fans were rewarded only with an answerphone or manager/engineer Mike O'Donnell lifting the receiver. Nor was Ringo ever seen more than rarely among the seed trays of Tittenhurst Nurseries' market garden.

As the family settled into the new home, a strange question occurred to Maureen: would she lose the place if she and Richie split up? If in the midst of even more material comforts now, their partnership – of two old friends who used to be lovers – was not proportionally blissful.

A man suddenly preoccupied with success is likely to be an inattentive husband, but the road to the Starkeys' divorce could not be ascribed to such a tidy cause. Prior to *Ringo*, each had holidayed separately, with Ringo seizing the chance to get foxed without disgusted reprimands from her. Roaring drunk on champagne *en route* to the Bahamas, he, Marc Bolan and Bolan's missus had guffawed so hysterically and often at the in-flight comedy film that an irate fellow passenger batted their heads with his paperback and summoned the chief steward. The ensuing altercation had turned into a real-life farce.

Back at Tittenhurst Park, not so funny was George Harrison's after-dinner outburst before other guests that he was deeply in love with Mrs Starkey. As he and Pattie had also drifted into open estrangement, he had not intended so much to bewilder Maureen as to offend Pattie, who tore from the table to lock herself in the bathroom. Although Ringo's immediate reaction had been token anger, this tense evening had not concluded with any showdown, and he was astonished at how easily he could make light of it the next day and, worse, how slightly his pride smarted at the thought of Maureen reciprocating George's affection.

Any bad blood between Harrison and himself was soon diluted, and he'd always drum on George's records whenever he was asked and was available. Together, the two also considered buying up and relaunching Apple, until it made more sense for Harrison to found his own Dark Horse record label. Its releases included a rescued Apple project, *The Shankar Family And Friends*, on which Starr and other Western rock 'n' rollers blended with the Indian orchestra – bamboo flutes, sarods *et al* – that Ravi Shankar had assembled to support George on an unhappy 1974 tour of North America.

His pressured preparations for this trek had meant that Harrison could pluck not one stinking note on Starr's *Goodnight Vienna*,[21] the album calculated to snap at the heels of *Ringo*. Paul was fresh out of songs for Ringo, too, busy as Wings were with what many would regard as their leader's *pièce de résistance*, *Band On The Run*. History would repeat itself when Paul's LP – released just after Ringo's – would wither its sales potential.

The commercial inconvenience of George and Paul's desertions was cushioned by John, whose attendance on the *Goodnight Vienna* sessions in Los Angeles would be more insidious than it had been on *Ringo*. He had time to spare, because he'd left Yoko to hurl himself into a 15-month "lost weekend" in California in the company of Keith Moon, Mal Evans, and Nilsson, hard drinkers suffering from a premature male menopause, marital difficulties or both. With his own marriage floating into a choppy sea, Starr flopped onto the next stool for three-in-the-morning bar-hopping and late-afternoon mutual grogginess by the pool. Staying the phantoms of middle age, the *côterie* – bar Mal – jointly rented a well-appointed beach villa on Stone Canyon Road in smart Santa Monica beneath the cedared sweep of the Hollywood hills.

With Keith as likely to fling a bottle at the television screen as rise from an armchair to switch it off, more than a formality – until he moved next door to a nervous Steve McQueen – was the proviso that they meet costs of all repairs to the premises and its contents, which included the gold discs of more regular tenants like Carole King and portraits of John F Kennedy. From his frames, the late president gazed reproachfully at rooms littered with junk-food debris, empty crates of liquor, overflowing ashtrays and drunken layabouts. Now the house that had once belonged to his family was liberty hall for its present occupiers' circle of friends of friends, as well as redundant super sidemen, members of Rick Nelson's Stone Canyon Band and more fabled and fleeting callers, like Alice Cooper, ex-Monkee Mickey Dolenz, Phil Spector and ace guitarist Joe Walsh,[22] a New Yorker who had lately joined The Eagles.[23] Fanning dull embers for Beatle watchers, McCartney and – more frequently, from a Beverly Hills *pied à terre* – Harrison popped by, too.

Hollywood breeds many insecurities, but the cardinal sin is to show them. Visible desperation is too nasty a reminder of the impermanence of stardom and wealth. With artificial adrenaline pumping, the gang and their hysterically chattering hangers-on would saunter into topless clubs; gatecrash parties, race by moonlight to the Malibu surf; and kerb-crawl in phallic Lincoln Continentals with deafening sound systems. It wasn't uncommon for any one of them to stir with a hangover in a strange bed, unable to recollect the circumstances that led him there. Lennon, with his immigration woes, was afraid to fly off on whimsical side trips to London, where his boozy boys would lark about in Apple, Tramp and pubs like the Pheasantry in King's Road, where their roistering was tolerated.

If futile and public, their escapades were mostly harmless and stories of what they got up to have been improved with age. Revelling in his wickedness, Ringo was photographed with a cigarette inserted up his nose in Sunset Strip's Playboy Club, but that was nothing to his jumping three red traffic lights and a subsequent court order to attend a two-nights-a-week course on the US highway code. Then there was Lennon's ejection – with a sanitary towel fixed to his forehead – from west Los Angeles' Troubadour, where he and Nilsson had been heckling The Smothers Brothers. Less widely reported was an excessively worshipful and inebriated audience with Jerry Lee Lewis. For John's birthday celebration, Ringo secured Cherry Vanilla – a singing actress much given to exposing her bust – to recite Shakespeare in her New York whine, while on 7 July 1974 Moon had splashed out on a skywritten "Happy Birthday, Ringo!" across Tinseltown's rind of smog. A more practical gift to the Starkeys was the $7,000 drum set Keith had no clear memory of buying a visiting Zak, for whom Moon was the god of percussion, "the very best in the world".[24] If prompted, he'd concede, "My old man's a good timekeeper, but I've never thought of him as a great drummer."[24]

Zak's old man indulged himself with a kit of greater antiquity, handmade in 1926 and unusual for its steel-bottomed tom-toms. No recent hedonistic extreme had been "more satisfactory than playing. It still feels magic to create something with somebody in the studio."[25] In the same interview, he referred to "a pretty weird group" of himself, Carly Simon and Dr John on a track on *Playing Possum*, Richard Perry's latest production for Carly. For Ringo, more typical artistic tangents were albums by Nilsson and Moon, as well as *Harry And Ringo's Night Out*, a jettisoned 1974 film.

There was nothing too interesting or original on either Nilsson's *Pussycats* – produced by Lennon – or his swift follow-up, *God's Greatest Hits*, renamed *Duit Où Mon Dei* to placate his record company. The first had come simply because he and John "were sitting around with nothing to do, so we said, 'Let's do an album.' We picked songs off the top of our heads and just did them."[7] With Ringo, Klaus, Bobby Keyes and Moon – all the usual shower – he and Lennon wrapped up *Pussycats* in New York after Los Angeles sessions had collapsed.

Both Sides Of The Moon was a more mischievous fiasco. From out of the woodwork, Keith had drawn the likes of Dick Dale ("King Of The Surf Guitar") and Spencer Davis – a quieter member of the Hollywood Raj – to help out, but although their names looked well on the album's cover nothing could save Moon – who didn't compose – from desecrating his own heritage with laughable remakes from the repertoire of The Who and selections from that of his previous group, Wembley's Beachcombers, who'd gone in for surf music. Even purposefully amusing items like 'Solid Gold' – with Ringo as an announcer in a crossover routine – palled on replay, as recorded comedy often does.

The laggard of the pack, Mal Evans had needed little cajoling to arrange a horn section for Moon's version of a Lennon B-side. Having gained nothing from deserting his family to trail along with his former masters, 40-year-old Mal's slaughter by gun-toting police after a fracas in his flat with some mean-minded tart he'd picked up was said by some to have been a sort of suicide.

Marc Bolan was to perish in a car crash in 1977. The Grim Reaper was coming for Keith Moon, too, and many who knew "the Madman" – as best friend Starr knew him – were not entirely surprised at his body's final rebellion in 1978, after a lifetime of violation. By coincidence, the stretcher carried him from Ringo's old Montagu Square flat, which no later tenant had troubled to strip of its psychedelic decor.

As he hadn't bothered with Rory Storm, why should Starr stir himself to attend Bolan, Moon and other old mates' funerals, when "I totally believe your soul has gone by the time you get in the limo"[26]? Not as enigmatic as it might have been was his dejected aside, "I can't wait to go half the time."[26] Although Moon's mindless bravado was peculiar to himself, faintly disturbing to Ringo in retrospect was Nilsson's remark, "Pete [Townshend] protects Keith. I always think John would defend Ringo in the same way."[7]

Mastering his inner chaos, albeit temporarily, Starr pulled back from the abyss. As the madness subsided, he'd realised, "I just got caught up in that strange belief that, if you're creative, you've got to be brain-damaged."[27] With Nilsson's first shipwreck as a sea mark, Starr steered *Goodnight Vienna* using *Ringo* as his map. A spliced-up medley of Lennon's title song and its reprise was a minor US Top-40 entry as a single. To preserve a rough-and-ready edge, each kicked off with tempo announcements, and the second version closed the album like some cocktail-lounge combo with an accordion winding up for the intermission. Banked by a riff reminiscent of 'Money', 'Goodnight Vienna' was more complete an opus than 'I'm The Greatest', particularly in lyrical touches like "I felt like an Arab that was dancing through Zion".

The affable Lennon also stuck around to play guitar on 'All By Myself', one of three *Goodnight Vienna* efforts by the Starr-Poncia team. Its "fool" bassman grumblings were quite compelling, but 'All By Myself' – plus 'Oo-Wee' and the plodding 'Call Me' – sounded like the merely competent output of a couple of blokes who fancied themselves as songwriters. The album's backbone, therefore, was what Ringo called the "foreign tracks" by such as Nilsson, whose 'Easy For Me' – mixed feelings about a dowdy spinster – discharged the same drawn-curtain menace as that wrought by Jacques Brel. It was more the stuff of Scott Walker – the fiercely emotional Belgian composer's foremost interpreter and a proverbial "pop singer who can really sing" – than a painstaking croaker like Ringo Starr, who was ideal for the less wracked 'Snookeroo'.

Engaged in some tedious household task, I was vexed at hearing myself humming 'Snookeroo', which, although soothing, was the work of Elton John, one of myriad artists I love to hate. In the 'I'm The Greatest' tradition, 'Snookeroo' was tailored by Elton's wordsmith, Bernie Taupin, as an authorised overview of a squandered youth in Liverpool. As well as one of Starr's school reports featuring in advertisements for *Goodnight Vienna*, the old days were addressed more obliquely on the record's front cover, which reproduced the cinema poster for 1951's *The Day The Earth Stood Still*, with Ringo's mug pasted over that of Michael Rennie in space-suited salutation.

The ancient ditty 'Skokiaan' was the source of 'No No Song' by folky Hoyt Axton, a Jamaican-flavoured litany that warned – probably sardonically – of the horrors of whiskey, cocaine and so forth against the paradise of total abstinence. Unreleased as a British 45 for fear of Radio 1 programmers getting the wrong (or right) end of the stick, 'No No Song' came within an ace of duplicating the feat of 'You're Sixteen' in the States.

Recommended by Lennon, an overhaul of the evergreen 'Only You' was less of a US hit, but a hit all the same, and as unsuitable for Starr as 'Easy For Me'. Wisely, he did not try to compete with the soaringly lovesick lead tenor on The Platters' original. Instead, Ringo's inability to attack higher registers without sounding querulous was supposed to convey the impression that his devotion was too intense for satisfactory melodic articulation. It was a joke, all the same.

Roger Miller's creaky 'Husbands And Wives' was comical not for Ringo's singing but for a mawkishness comparable to anything on *Beaucoups Of Blues* and its tune's too-close affinity to Miller's 'Little Green Apples'. Quirkier but more credible, 'Occapella' from the Lee Dorsey catalogue held the ear with a sparkling arrangement that nodded towards Dr John, and was flexible enough to switch smoothly from verses jittery with timbales to a wordless choral passage that might have been lifted by time machine from some mellow new age compact disc.

Highlights like 'Occapella' and 'Goodnight Vienna' itself balanced 'Call Me', 'Only You' and other *faux pas* on an album that was as likeable, after its fashion, as *Ringo*. During 1974's Yuletide sell-in, its crawl to a *Billboard* Number Eight, while abiding just a week in the UK Top 30, signified less a deterioration in quality than its dimmer "Beatle reunion" aura, plus a generally smaller quota of famous guests. Furthermore, Richard Perry's star was on the wane, as his much-touted 1974 LP for Martha Reeves – a former Tamla-Motown *grande dame* – failed to live up to market expectations.

Goodnight Vienna might have fared better if Starr had realised that a few half-page adverts in the music press and a round of interviews in same were no longer sufficient to incite readers to consume his latest record. You had to howl it a bit louder in apocryphal 1974, when the "high-energy" entertainments of roving minstrels like Led Zeppelin, Peter Frampton[28] and Grand Funk

Railroad packed out US stadiums and European outdoor festivals. Despite its potential value in stabilising his wobbling winning streak, "Touring right now is not my cup of tea. I just don't need it right now."[29] After doing his minimal duty by the new album, he couldn't wait to "get back to the drinking and partying".[29]

13 "Wherever I Go, It's A
Swinging Place, Man"

After *Goodnight Vienna* and 'Only You' slipped from modest
apogees in their respective charts, Ringo never had another solo hit
in Britain. Any ex-Beatle's television slots were always special, but
home viewers began to care less about them as personalities. More
intriguing nowadays was the flowchart of titbits – true and untrue –
that splattered vivid and often scandalous hues onto their private
lives. Second to John – now a permanent US resident – Ringo, say,
plugging his album on Radio 1's *Rockspeak*, was regarded as a
phantom from the recent past who'd returned to haunt moth-eaten
Mods and Rockers saddled with mortgages and a daughter at art
college who couldn't stop talking about some group called The Sex
Pistols. Her cousin in the police cadets could reel off the personnel
on the latest Return To Forever, Billy Cobham and Weather Report
jazz-funk albums. For Top Drummer in *Melody Maker*'s 1975 poll,
he'd probably favoured technique over instinct by voting for either
Cobham, Bill Bruford, Phil Collins of Genesis or Alan White, who,
after *The Plastic Ono Band*, had replaced Bruford in Yes.

What was a minor sales territory like the United Kingdom to
Ringo, now that Mammon had spirited him away to the New World?
If on an irreversible slide elsewhere as a mere pop star, he was
lionised almost as if he was an Artist in the States, with its "different
atmosphere to anywhere else in the world. And I love television over
there."[1] His sojourn in Santa Monica had caked his speech with
words like "gotten", "sidewalk", "candy" (for "sweets"), "pants"

(for "trousers") and "elevator", and it became his habit to celebrate Thanksgiving – for the secession of the American colonies from his native land.

US tax laws were slightly less harsh than Britain's, but more of a magnet for Starr was its scope for playing the field. To one of many "friends" who sold his story to the *paparazzi*, Ringo "had been labelled for so long the least significant member of The Beatles that he was desperate to assert himself, if only by pulling beautiful girls".[2] His infidelities in California climaxed when a romance with Nancy Andrews – a Hollywood maid-of-all-work – took a serious turn. As much part of the furniture at Stone Canyon Road as Nilsson's Irish girlfriend and May Pang, Lennon's Chinese secretary and extra-marital paramour, Nancy – a wasp-waisted brunette eight years Ringo's junior – was worth more than a second glance. Since graduating, she'd travailed on the periphery of showbusiness as a model, publicity agent and pursuant of other occupations that relied similarly on keeping up appearances and creating a favourable impression.

More Linda than Yoko, she would put her talents – some of them previously unrealised – at Ringo's disposal during her six years, on and off, as his "constant companion". Whilst proving no stranger to many of the commercial and economic machinations of his calling, Nancy's photographs were published on his album sleeves and press hand-outs, and the Andrews-Starr composition 'Las Brisas' was recorded on Ringo's *Rotogravure*, the album that appeared after *Goodnight Vienna*.

At first, Ringo's new love was known only to the Santa Monica set. When Maureen saw him on his infrequent flying visits to England, she explained away his worn-out moodiness as a combination of jetlag, vocational pressures and Los Angeles' ordeal of conviviality. While wishing that he'd unwind a little and actuate an unstrained conversation with her, she kept in her heart the hope that their present separation was but a temporary setback. As her advocate would tell the judge, "She doesn't want divorce. She is fond of her husband and would like nothing better than to make a go of it."[3] Sometimes, Maureen would blame her own shortcomings, but he seemed more abstractedly tolerant of – or indifferent to – her accumulation of eye-stretching bills on his Apple account for costly objects she couldn't see without wanting to possess them. Neither she nor Richie were lovestruck and irresponsible Cavern dwellers any more, but still she was not beyond extreme strategies, if not to rekindle the flame of their lustful courtship then to remind him of what it had been like.

She may have also feigned aloofness to retain composure, but Maureen's frank nature could not allow her to stay silent about stray mutterings that she'd read in gossip columns. Recalling his cheery promiscuity as a London bachelor in 1963, she wasn't so naïve to presume that her "sodding great Andy Capp"[3] of a husband hadn't been tempted into a fling or two while in another hemisphere for all those months. What was she complaining about? He'd provided her with everything she could possibly want, hadn't he? Anyway, he still loved her, didn't he, in hand-squeezing farewells and in the respect accorded the mother of his offspring? After all, he reasoned, "Someone has to look after them."[4]

The mist of resigned despair shrouding Tittenhurst Park thickened with the tightening of Richie's attachment to this Nancy Andrews. More quizzical than angry, the eclipsed Maureen implored him to help her grasp what it all meant, so he "gave me the names of two or three solicitors".[3] He'd admit adultery, and she could name Nancy as co-respondent, if she so wished. Maureen would have preferred him to have shouted back or grope for some excuse for his conduct, some avenue for forgiveness, but he reckoned that "it comes to the point when it doesn't work. You try all these different rooms, and 'Let's do it for the children' and all that, and in the end you have to say, 'It's not working anyway. Why am I doing this? Why is she into that? She's probably into that because I'm into this' – and then it's the breakdown." Like his father before him, "I'm northern, so once it's broken, I cut it off as fast as I can. It's just an attitude I have. Once it's gone, it's gone."[5]

He endured her incessant circular arguments and cliff-hanging silences for a decent interval before leaving – eyes bloodshot with emotional fatigue – for Heathrow and the next flight to California and Nancy. Prior to the hearing for the decree nisi on 17 July 1975, Ringo flaunted his shame across two continents by squiring his girlfriend at the West End première of *Tommy* while treating her to her first Grand Tour of Europe. Maureen saw their photograph with his bow-tied tuxedo and her tanned cleavage in the newspaper.

With pale, drawn cheeks and clasped hands, Maureen gave evidence on that comfortless summer morning in the London Divorce Court, where each bewigged forehead prickled with sweat. The extent to which the humidity might have affected the sitting's financial ordinances was not immediately obvious. Ringo's ex-wife did not face the prospect of earning a crust again, as long as she wasn't too frivolous with a generous award of a yearly lump sum, with increments and a side-serving of assorted sinecures and life policies. On top was Starr's continued support of her parents and Maureen's custody of the children, who would move to the mansion he'd bought her[6] in London's Little Venice, overlooking the canal.

For a while, Ringo was unable to fully exercise his right of access "*pour des raisons fiscales*",[7] as *Paris-Match* had it, that permitted tax exiles only 90 days per annum in the United Kingdom. The ravages of the Inland Revenue had already driven Maurice Gibb to the Isle of Man, The Rolling Stones to France and Tony Sheridan to apply for Irish nationality. However, it was the loosening of family ties as much as his desire to shield those monies not annexed by Maureen that unleashed the gypsy in Ringo's soul, and he "went wandering".[8] With a mountain of keepsakes and memorabilia in storage, and Nancy gripping his arm proprietorially, he roamed the Côte D'Azur and around Los Angeles from hotel to rootless hotel, where he'd be conducted to the best seat in the restaurant and the switchboard or room service would relay complimentary tickets and social invitations, offering flattery without friendship to one whose every workshy action was worth half a page in *The Sun* or *The Los Angeles Times*. At the reception desk, his thick Scouse articulations would draw muffled titters from those to whom opulence had always been second nature.

While an onyx cigarette-holder protruded from his lips and gold and precious stones festooned his neck, chest, wrists, fingers and ears, depilatory whims also became more vital a subject of discussion than his artistic substance. "To see what it looked like and to make sure I didn't have boils or anything on my scalp",[9] he upset his mother – already dismayed about the divorce – by shaving every hair from his head, including his eyebrows. To please her, he let it thicken to a kind of tonsured stubble. In 1991, after a decade with a full beard and moustache, he would grin at a lucky tabloid photographer while dashing through Heathrow with a face planed of all but what he called a "third eyebrow"[10] beneath his lower lip. It looked comical, but credulous Beatle followers would lap it up as the prerogative of glamour.

"You wonder about getting up," he sighed, "and there is nothing special to do, so you delay it. Finally, you do get out of bed, and you just try to fill the day."[11] Fleeing from boredom, if he wasn't on an aeroplane he'd be in the departure lounge waiting for the next one. With the ease of a daily commuter on the 8.23 to Waterloo, he'd jet from Monaco to Amsterdam for dinner with The Three Degrees – the Prince of Wales' favourite vocal group – and Rod Steiger; from Amsterdam to Johannesburg to watch some tennis match; from Johannesburg to New York just to buy shoes from Ebony; from New York to Las Vegas for a calamitous evening of blackjack or roulette; from Vegas to London for Wimbledon; and from Heathrow back to Monaco for some rich gadfly's wedding. There he'd queue for the buffet with such as Rudolf Nureyev, Christina Onassis and the principality's own Princess Caroline. When he described himself as "a jet-setter – wherever I go, it's a swinging place, man",[12] it was a statement rather than a boast.

The most swinging place of all was Monte Carlo, where, instead of breaking the bank, he gambled for small stakes in Loews, a casino recommended by Peter Sellers. With London less than two hours along the air corridor, he began to regard the resort as a base when, putting a brake on a life of suitcases, he purchased a penthouse suite in one of its "neo-brutalist" modern blocks. To Loews' manager, Paul

Maser, "He's still a little outrageous sometimes – like, he turned up here with his hair in a ponytail – but, overall, he seems to be exactly like someone who is now sitting back, enjoying the fruits of success."[2]

As travel had brought him weariness without stimulation and souvenirs without wisdom, so a pampered but empty semi-retirement led him to sometimes shun the sun, the beautiful people and evening meals in restaurants frequented by expatriate gentlefolk nearing middle age. Instead, he'd have a quiet night in, wallowing in episode after episode of *Coronation Street* and other videoed and soapy links with all that he'd left behind.

Bathed in tedium, he might put down his schooner of white wine, apple cider or brandy – depending on the hour – to mess about on piano or guitar and maybe sort out a *chanson* for the next album. More often than not, days would trudge by without a glimmer of a tune or lyric, or else everything that he attempted would sound the same. Nancy would think so, too, and intimate that a change of scene might make a world of difference – or half a world, anyway, if he took her to his bungalow, rented from Nilsson, high in the hills above Los Angeles. At an address that included the rather iconoclastic street name Haslem Terrace, Richie and Nancy would extend a gladder welcome to callers whose drawling ebullience was more comfortable than the stilted "Franglais" of the Monaco socialites they hardly knew.

Although the Starkey children would spend school holidays there, it was also open house for "all the old faces"[13] from the dissipated *Pussycats* era. "Once the bars close," he calculated, "they'll all drive up here," to be greeted with Starr's expansive "'Hi, man! Yeah, come on in!' If I'm really wrecked, I say, 'You know where everything is. I'm off.' You can actually leave your guests and they don't mind if you're there or not. So that's LA for you. It is a great town, because of the passing strangers."[13] In Ringo's "matured" contemporary abode, visitors would be armchaired with a drink before the open grate, or – if wishing to stretch their legs after a car ride – they would peruse walls lined with framed photographs, platinum discs and other relics of their host's distinguished past. In a playroom, their host had assembled a drum kit for anyone who fancied flailing around.

He would have no need ever again to rattle the traps – or sing, for that matter – because, by 1976, his nine-year EMI/Capitol contract would have run its course. The easiest option was to do as Lennon would and take "a year off, with no obligations to anybody. He's his own man for twelve months, and he's never been that."[14] Nevertheless, the company submitted to Ringo – via Hilary Gerrard – a tantalising bid (albeit one much less than those by other labels) for Starr to re-sign, as he was still hottish property in the States, even if only as good as his latest record elsewhere. On the scorched streets of Monte Carlo – and, by implication, the rest of Europe – "people notice him and point him out," observed Paul Maser, "but they don't go rushing up to him for autographs like they used to. Let's face it, he's hardly a sexy young pop star any more, is he?"[2]

Indeed he wasn't. Although he sported earrings and wore his hair as short as it could be, the newly radical *NME* categorised Starr and those of similar 1960s vintage as pop dinosaurs. If the Pistols dismissed The Beatles as "Scouse gits"[15] and later fired Glen Matlock for liking them, a lot the older outfit's public postures – particularly Lennon's – both before and after Beatlemania had been wilder than those of any punk group. Among salaams to them within the new regime were revivals of 'Help!', 'I Wanna Be Your Man' and 'Twist And Shout' by, respectively, The Damned, The Rezillos and Siouxsie And The Banshees. Chasing punk was a hyped fad for "power pop" (punk minus the loutish affectations), of which the Great White Hope was the winsome Pleasers, blue-grey-suited propagators of "Thamesbeat" who shook their moptops and went "oooooo" as well. Rick Buckler, drummer with The Jam, and The Damned's Rat Scabies acknowledged Ringo's influence, while Roag Best – rehearsing with his Watt Four in the Hayman's Green basement – was given a few pointers by his big brother.

One day, Pete would make the best of a bad job by appearing with a reconstituted Combo at the "Beatle conventions" that were now becoming annual fixtures in cities throughout the free world.

Further entertainment at these functions came courtesy of guest speakers, archive films, weird-and-wonderful exhibitions and sets by bands who, even more intensely than The Pleasers, had cloned The Beatles' image, complete with big-nosed sticksmen, unsmiling lead guitarists *et al*, plus handles like "Walrus", "Cavern" (whose Paul Garrigan was rated "best Beatle drummer since Ringo"[16]), "Abbey Road" and mild sensations of Merseybeatle '90 at Liverpool's Adelphi Hotel, the Soviet Union's own "Beatles Club", managed by Allan Williams. After a record-breaking season at the Everyman Theatre, *John, Paul, George, Ringo – And Bert* – a stylised musical play about the Beatles saga by William Russell, a teacher at Dingle Vale secondary school – moved to London's Lyric. Perhaps its most poignant moment was "Pete Best" dirging 'With A Little Help From My Friends', sacked and alone beneath the proscenium. From the slicker *Beatlemania*, also up the West End, The Bootleg Beatles – the most accurate imitators of all – were formed from the cast.

Because EMI/Capitol still owned the genuine article's master tapes, it was able after 1976 to run riot with posthumous million-selling double albums, such as the up-tempo *Rock 'n' Roll Music*, which in the States spawned a smash 45 in 'Got To Get You Into My Life', culled from *Revolver*. In the interests of expediency, the compilers had ignored offers of help and even injunctions from Lennon and Starr, who were powerlessly sour-faced about its running order, reversion to the pre-1967 royalty rate and the "craphouse"[17] packaging, which, scowled Ringo, "made us look cheap, and we were never cheap".[17]

As a prelude to the campaign, the old firm had recycled "greatest hits" collections by those ex-Beatles about to fly the nest. A few weeks after John's *Shaved Fish* and a year before *The Best Of George Harrison*, Starr's *Blast From Your Past*, with its muzzy sleeve portrait, almost missed being shipped to Christmas shops owing to delays at the pressing plant and the artist's own intervention when its five tracks per side were being selected. As well as giving short weight, this predictable ragbag – the last Apple album – offered little stimulus for the hunter of Beatle rarities.

Giving Ringo more than just a financial return was the chart-swamping aftermath when all 20 of "the finest pieces of plastic around that no one has done anything beyond yet"[13] were reissued on the same spring day in 1976, almost a quarter of a century after 'Love Me Do'.[18] Perusing the UK Top 40, a *Time* correspondent enquired rhetorically, "Has a successor to The Beatles finally been found? Not at all – it is The Beatles themselves."[19] Just before The Sex Pistols shaped up as if they might, Ringo pleaded doubtfully for "a band that gets up there and wipes us out".[13]

A perennial alternative, of course, was for The Beatles themselves to deliver the *coup de grâce*. Not a week passed without some twit or other asking Ringo when the group were going to reform. Now and then, there'd be reports of his tentative agreement to recitals on closed-circuit television for $50 million, or as a surprise on the Rolling Thunder Tour that – with Bob Dylan and a pot-pourri of guest performers – was traversing North America with an itinerary publicised only locally. However, only one Beatle – Ringo – put in an appearance when Dylan and The Band headlined a benefit night in Houston for imprisoned boxer Rubin "Hurricane" Carter. In 1985, rumour would be rife among the multitudes at Wembley for Live Aid that their segment of the international spectacular would culminate with a spot by Julian Lennon and his father's three old comrades. Of that "get-together stuff",[20] Starr regretted that "it doesn't matter how many times we deny it, it'll still go on. Even if there's only one of us left, they'll say he's getting it together with himself."[20]

The four were tempted to call the bluff of Lorne Michaels, producer of *Saturday Night Live* (a TV satire transmitted from New York), who said that he'd squeeze them onto the show if they'd accept the prescribed Musicians' Union fee of $3,200. He didn't mind, apparently, if John, Paul and George wanted to "pay Ringo less".[21] In this playful slight, Michaels showed his ignorance of Starr's higher average of US singles chart placings than the rest, prior to the comparative failure of the 'Goodnight Vienna' medley.

When found guilty in September 1976 of "subconscious plagiarism" in the most notorious civil action of the decade, George was sagging on the ropes as Paul basked in rave notices for his *Wings Over America* concert album and Ringo teetered on the edge of the *Billboard* Top 30 with 'A Dose Of Rock 'n' Roll', harbinger of his *Rotogravure*. With Marc Bolan informing him that "a girl asked him about that new artist, Ringo Starr",[17] he was puffed up enough to demand that Dutch fanzine *Beatles Unlimited* retitle itself *Starr Unlimited* for the edition for which he had deigned to be interviewed, "because we're not The Beatles any more. We're trying to get away from that."[22]

Ringo's pride before the fall might have been aggravated when his visit to Amsterdam in March 1976 was front-paged by *De Telegraaf*. He was merely sight-seeing, he told Holland's most popular newspaper, but only an incurious press would not have got wind of more portentous reasons for a former Beatle's descent into their midst. When he later purchased a stately 19th-century house, it transpired that he'd been shown around properties along the canals. In the gabled Hilton Hotel's Presidential Suite, he'd also been honoured with a party bountiful with topless go-go dancers, a lake of Bols (Dutch gin, that he didn't like) and Manke Nelis, a crippled accordionist bribed in from the *straat* outside.

Footing the bill was Ahmet Ertegun, goateed supremo of Atlantic Records, with whose destiny Starr would be bound until 1981, although Ertegun, as its embodiment, was "not going to control my artistic life. I can give them the records and they can sell them, if they can."[2] As its snatch of The Rolling Stones when they fled Decca in 1971 attested, Atlantic – and its Stax subsidiary – had long been a receptacle, as Ringo knew well, for "a lot of good acts",[22] from The Coasters and The Drifters back in the 1950s to a bevy of chart-busting black soul singers, among them Wilson Pickett, with whom Starr had a fast friendship. Moreover, the guitarist with Stax house band Booker T And The MGs was Steve Cropper, who'd been one of those twanging the wires on both *Ringo* and *Goodnight Vienna*. Therefore, Ringo, at his lawyer's urging, let Germany's Polydor pick the bones of the less important "rest of the world", while Atlantic took charge of selling him throughout North America.

It was to be quite a job, and Starr's easy-going shiftlessness didn't help. "I never work on anything," he confessed. "Dedication is such a weird word, after Albert Schweitzer and people like that. No one dedicates themselves to anything now."[13] Knowing him of old, Tony Barrow – now a senior executive at Polydor – would complain, "We had many offers for TV specials and whatever for him, but he was always totally unavailable to do them."[2] In the studio, too, "Ringo just seemed content to let the producer lay down some backing tracks for him and then he would pop in from Monte Carlo and just stick on his vocals."[2]

In fairness, his drum fills were heard on all bar one track on *Rotogravure*, even if these were anchored as usual by Jim Keltner. However, a break from precedent was the replacement of "busy"[14] Richard Perry with Arif Mardin, a Turk like Ertegun, who – in elevating him to Atlantic's vice presidency – gave practical recognition of the combined musical and supervisory skills that Mardin had perfected through his studies at the Schools of both Economics and Music in London and New York, as well as his dexterity as a bebop pianist as much at ease with the mainstream euphoria of Duke Ellington as the textural complexities of Dizzy Gillespie. It was through arranger Quincy Jones – then in Gillespie's employ – that Mardin came to Atlantic as a producer on emigrating from Istanbul in 1958 at the age of 26.

He saw himself as "a catalyst to bring the administrative situation together – all the musicians, the atmosphere, the happiness in the studio – and then to get the sound and edit and splice".[23] As such, the calm and flexible Arif was much praised by clients as diverse as Wilson Pickett, Dusty Springfield, King Curtis, Aretha Franklin and Petula Clark. Trusting his artists instincts, he was rewarded with a Grammy in 1975 for guiding the talents of The Average White Band – brassy Hibernian soul – and The Bee Gees, who, on *Main Course*, had been in transition from 1960s teen idols to paladins of the disco fever that by 1976 was sashaying towards its John Travolta zenith.

Main Course struck Ringo as "too squeaky – it's like brown music, not black music",[20] but he agreed to meet Mardin in London "to see if we could sit together for an hour".[13] There grew a practised but rather detached professional relationship between the parvenu who "didn't know an E flat from an F demented"[14] and the wine-sniffing jazz connoisseur. While understanding – as Ertegun did – that Starr's economic potential outweighed any artistic merits, Mardin still enjoyed The Beatles enough for 'Glass Onion' to be the title theme of one of his own rather specialist instrumental albums.

At Los Angeles' Cherokee Studios and, later, in Atlantic's own New York complex, sessions ran smoothly, with rarely more than a few takes for each track. Ringo needed time to adjust to Mardin hardly ever expressing either distaste or excitement verbally. By gazing up at the glass-fronted control room, Starr learned to gauge his producer's reaction: "If I see Arif dancing, then I know we're getting a take, but if he's just looking around the room, someone must have played wrong."[13]

Ringo liked "a party atmosphere if we're working well. We all sit around and drink and really have a good time."[14] There might, therefore, have been plenty of scope for squiffy errors within the small army of famous friends that had rallied around to – hopefully – recreate that *Ringo* miracle, for "there isn't a player I know or have heard of who I don't feel I could call and they'd come and play for me".[14]

Satisfying every musical and lyrical qualification required of an evergreen like 'Yesterday' or his own 'Something', George Harrison's 'When Every Song Is Sung' had had a chequered career since Cilla Black's abortive recording in 1972. Retitled 'I'll Still Love You', it was then attempted by Mary Hopkin and, in 1974, by Cilla again, who felt that "even then it didn't have the magic it deserved".[24] Mainly via George's thrillingly ponderous obligato, with its shades of Jeff Beck, some "magic" crept into Ringo's shot at this "big ballady thing I've always loved",[14] but not enough to prevent its burial on side two, among makeweight bagatelles like 'Spooky Weirdness' – a concluding collage of funny noises and electronically doctored utterances – and, driven by a guttural bass throb, 'This Be Called A Song', which, if Hilary Gerrard's favourite *Rotogravure* number, remains a shallow lunge at pseudo-reggae selected from out-takes of Eric Clapton's *No Reason To Cry* LP.

Like Clapton, John Lennon flew to California "just to play on his song".[14] His self-satisfied donation, 'Cookin' (In The Kitchen Of Love)', was premonitory, as he was to extend considerably his "year off", since his position as Yoko's reclusive house-husband in New York's snooty Dakota block had been complicated by the arrival of Sean. Not a note would be heard commercially from John for the next four years. "He's really into that now, cooking,"[14] noticed Ringo during conversations whenever those on the Lennon number took five.

Leaving behind their own cosy domesticity on a Sussex farm, the McCartneys were in the throes of the Wings Over America tour, which, on reaching Los Angeles, was thrown into confusion by an incapacitating hand injury sustained by the group's guitarist. Time hung heavy, so Linda and Paul dropped into Cherokee Studios, where several tankards of cider oiled the wheels of their reunion with Ringo. As Mardin didn't need Ringo for a while, the three continued reminiscing in a nearby restaurant. During a further carouse after dessert, the McCartneys capitulated to Starr's persuasion "and we wandered round to the studio, and they decided they were ready to sing",[25] backing him on 'Pure Gold', a slop-ballad with plinking piano triplets and a limpid sweetening of violins that he had already received from Paul's assembly line.

Starr and Poncia had some mush of their own in 'Lady Gaye',[26] which – avoiding the George Harrison mistake – was an authorised rewrite of 'Gaye', a UK Top-Ten entry for Kidderminster schoolteacher Clifford T Ward in 1973. In their Americanised clutches, 'Gaye' surfaced as "more universal, so it's about a lady who's vaguely a hooker".[22] As token country and western morosity, their 'Cryin" – nothing to do with Roy Orbison – was more elegantly resigned, a feathery bank of strings stripped away in favour of a lonely and lachrymose pedal steel guitar, played by "Sneaky" Pete Kleinow, who had likewise serviced The Bee Gees.

The only other Starr composition thought worthy of his

Rotogravure was 'Las Brisas', which was a memento of a furlough in Acapulco with Nancy. By straying from formula, the couple – now engaged – hadn't struck gold, exactly, but this was the album's most arresting outing. Its instrumental core was 'Legend Of Xanadu' trumpets, Ringo's own maracas and the cantering propulsion of Los Galleros, a mariachi combo recruited from a Mexican eaterie in downtown Los Angeles. Completing this pastiche was the artist's Costa Del Dingle emoting of his holiday romance.

Nancy had impinged further on his act by duetting with her intended on 'By Your Side', but this – along with another Lee Dorsey cover ('I Can Hear You Calling'), an obscure Dylan song ('I Didn't Want To Do It') recommended by Harrison and other items[27] recorded over the three weeks in Cherokee Studios – still moulder unreleased in, presumably, Atlantic's vaults. Perhaps the same fate ought to have befallen the album's singles, especially 'A Dose Of Rock 'n' Roll', which was not anything of the sort but a laid-back, loping concession to disco that borrowed indirectly from the lyrical thrust of 'A Shot Of Rhythm And Blues'. Of the same inspirational vintage and as over-vocalised was a rehash of Bruce Channel's 'Hey Baby', Ringo's US Hot 100 swan song, while just as much of a *moderato* muchness as 'Pure Gold' was 'You Don't Know Me At All', which, aided by a promo film shot on the Reeperbahn, entered chart listings all over Europe.

That all of these A-sides were "foreign" tracks confirmed much of Tony Barrow's assessment of Starr, as well as the present aridity of the ex-Beatle's songwriting well. His principal creative input to the album was in its title – from a line in a Judy Garland movie[28] that he'd caught on television – and cover. Because "the tracks were like pictures",[22] this contained a liberal smattering of Ringo's snapshots of his children, Lennon, McCartney and so on: "All these people are eating and I'll just be drinking."[22] The concept had come to him when this was precisely the scenario at one New York session.

Other personal touches were the assignment of publishing for some *Rotogravure* compositions to his own new set-up, Zwiebel, German for his detested "onion". Further mention of gastronomic preference was evidenced in his "no garlic, thank you" remark on the fade of 'Cookin'' and the inclusion on the back cover of a photograph of the front door at 3 Savile Row, which, since The Beatles had vacated the premises, had been defaced by felt-tip and blade with an *imbroglio* of fans' graffiti. By so doing, Starr stole a march on Lennon, who might have "had it on his – and, as he's not got a record coming out, I thought I'd get in fast."[9]

Ringo may have been unconscious of the irony of the release date of *Rotogravure* – 17 September 1976 – coinciding with the final closure of the Cavern. He was, however, cognisant that his own undertakings weren't what they used to be, either – although he might have once imagined that he couldn't go wrong with George, John and Paul all on his latest album, which, if not first rate, was at least superficially enjoyable. As always, the record industry was voracious for new faces to exploit and discard for a fickle public, and the danger of Ringo being left behind in this soul-rotting race was perceptible even in the States, now, where *Rotogravure* clawed to Number 28, a true comedown by previous standards.

To achieve this, he and Gerrard had hired Los Angeles publicity firm Brains Unlimited to organise his most intense media expedition since The Beatles, covering the USA, Japan and Europe. Patiently sipping Mumm Cordon Rouge – he knew better than to mix drinks – Ringo would give unblinking copy, but his handlers would exchange frequent fretful glances at his commendably frank appraisal of his singing ("the range of a fly, but a large fly"[13]) and how he approached it ("you try it drunk, you go back sober and do it for real – some takes you use when you're drunk"[13]). Mention at the Paris stop of Cliff Richard's contemporaneous LP, *I'm Nearly Famous*, drew the self-denigrating remark, "I used to be."[29]

However, he had high hopes of those he'd signed to his Ring O'Records, inaugurated on 4 April 1976 and destined to peter out just like Ringo Or Robin Limited and the rest of his entrepreneurial sideshows. Depressingly familiar was one Polydor helmsman's observation that he was "using it like a toy",[17] as epitomised by the label's greater specialisation in transitory singles because "they reminded him of his youth".[30] Typical of these were the one-shot likes of 'Cokey Cokey', coupled with 'Away In A Manger' – also with a reggae arrangement – by "Colonel" (alias a Douglas Bogie). Contrary to sound legal advice, Starr chose to settle contracts with a simple handshake rather than chain anyone – himself included – to small-print mumbo-jumbo.

Apple in microcosm, Ring O' had to lease its output to a parent company – Polydor, and then Mercury – until that unreached day when it could afford to declare its independence, without any middlemen claiming a slice. To help the venture on its way, the renowned proprietor's endorsement of its artists and hints that he might add himself to its roster ensured airplay – if not sales – of products that reflected Ringo's musical preferences rather than their inherent marketability, as demonstrated in his reissue of Tavener's *The Whale* to forecasted approbation by "quality" journals but few takers from among the great unwashed.

These days, Ringo also tapped his feet to a conservative assortment of old and new: Led Zeppelin ("they're the tops!"[9]), Clapton, 10cc, Bryan Ferry and – rebutting his earlier dim view – Slade. He was delighted to see that his beloved country and western was now tickling the fancy of a younger audience, thanks to the unhurried emergence of a new tradition of performers who swept a new broom while upholding the genre's down-home lores and veneration for its elder statesmen. Presaging the kd langs and Dwight Yoakhams of the 1980s were Guthrie Thomas, gauche Kinky Friedman and his Texas Jew-Boys and Gary Stewart, who impressed Ringo as "simply amazing, and he'll come through like a teenage Jerry Lee Lewis".[9] He didn't, but he may have given cause for Ringo and label manager Barry Anthony to rub their chins while talent-spotting for Ring O'.

Initially, Starr had sought an established star – a friend, if given the choice – to be the company's flagship act in order to mitigate insolvencies encountered while launching unknowns. However, after failing to outbid RCA when Harry Nilsson was up for grabs, he looked around for "a new one to make him that big".[31]

Unfortunately for Ring O', nobody on its books amounted to much, in spite of what was on paper the fullest distribution network and promotional support around. Mostly too appropriate to the blander end of the mid-1970s pop spectrum, Johnny Warman (no, I've never heard of him, either), Stormer (the label's very own 10cc), Suzanne (its Olivia Newton-John, but blonder), Bobby Keyes (that man again) and all the rest of them were deserved flops, or else were drowned in the riptide of punk.

"Works" were very much the order of the day, then. With 1973's *Tubular Bells* rather than *The Whale* as precedent, Yes, Jethro Tull and Hawkwind were three prominent outfits who cut florid albums with an overall unity teeming with interlocking themes, links and *leitmotifs*. Even Dave Dee – several worlds from 'Legend Of Xanadu' – sang on one (*Few And Far Between* by Jean Musy, an intensely bearded Frenchman), while Steve Winwood had a bigger say in the overblown *Go* by Stomu Yamash'ta. Glutted with EMI producer Parsons' famous associates, The Alan Parsons Project boarded the "works" bandwagon in 1976.

Ring O' responded with *Startling Music* by David Hentschel, a console engineer and keyboard player who'd been engaged by McCartney, Carly Simon, Jim Webb, Elton John and Rick Wakeman, amongst others, before advancement to plum production jobs for the progressive likes of The Nice and Genesis. Through Sussex-born Hentschel's own co-producer, John Gilbert, and via Neil Aspinall, a demo tape of his arrangement of Richard Strauss' *Also Sprach Zarathustra* was identified as the 2001 tune by a "knocked out"[9] Ringo, who suggested a retread of "the most successful thing I've done since The Beatles, which we thought would give it a certain familiarity".[9] When could David bring his machinery down to the Ascot studio? Already there for his use was a state-of-the-art ARP 2500 synthesiser.

In its track-for-track interpretation of the entire *Ringo* album for this instrument, plus slight help from session guitarist Ronnie Caryl and Genesis drummer Phil Collins, Hentschel's technological feat was – despite jazzy and pompously "symphonic" interludes – as lightweight, after its fashion, as James Last. During what was to him but a production assignment, Hentschel found Starr "just like a normal bloke", who, if a little over-fond of a wee dram, did not exercise any executive control whenever he dropped in to review progress – and provide finger clicks for 'Step Lightly'. Nevertheless, despite this blessing and Hentschel's spate of radio and newspaper interviews, *Startling Music* was soon lost to the archives of oblivion.

Next came Graham Bonnet, who, undaunted by his audition with Alan Caldwell's Texans, had bided his time before achieving qualified fame as half of Marbles in 1968 with a version of a Bee Gees song, 'Only One Woman', at Number Five in the UK. Four years of scrimmaging later, he'd landed both the title role in Lou Reizner's stage production of *Tommy* and the managerial acumen of comedian Bill Oddie. Although a gritty vocalist, Bonnet's parameters as a composer were limited to royalty-earning B-sides during his stint as a Ring O' recording artist. After another of his Bee Gees covers and a Hall And Oates opus both bit the dust, the label soldiered on with Bonnet's ambitious disinterments of 'Rock Island Line', 'Danny' – a then-unissued Presley film song[33] – and Dylan's 'It's All Over Now, Baby Blue'. However, as the similarly placed Joe Cocker – and, indeed, Suzanne, with her retread of hoary old 'You Really Got A Hold On Me' – could have told him, a mere Great Voice wasn't enough – although, after a spell fronting Deep Purple splinter group Rainbow, Bonnet finally cracked the charts under his own name in 1981.

Carl Groszman, an Australian singing guitarist of Cat Stevens' stamp, didn't get very far with Ring O', either. Having written 'Down The Dustpipe' – a hit for Status Quo – within a year of his arrival in England in 1969, Groszman had ticked over for a while with such as 'A Dose Of Rock 'n' Roll' for Ringo, who vouchsafed the pressing of his debut 45, 'Face Of A Permanent Stranger'.

This promising young songwriter was also allowed to tape "an album which got wasted. I mean, it didn't surface"[22] after Ringo "wound up going to all these meetings. I was getting nutsy [*sic*] and there was nothing happening. Artists always try to run a record company like it isn't a business."[31] On top of mind-stultifying meetings to decide about the next meeting, Ringo and Anthony were disquieted about Polydor's lack of faith in Ring O' and its related unhelpfulness in securing releases in continental Europe. Starr's company, therefore, laid low until the Polydor deal expired in August 1978.

Cutting back, Ring O' re-emerged on a smaller scale as Able Label Productions, which – while keeping a grip on creative initiative – leased its product to bigger organisations via new director Terry Condon from freshly-painted Mayfair offices not a few hundred yards from where Ringo used to run Apple Films. Before Ring O' also became an albatross, he approved the retention of Warman, Suzanne, Groszman and Stormer and the massing of manipulative force behind records by newcomers like a highly rated singer (another one) in Scotland's Rab Noakes, as well as Colonel-type novelties such as Dirk And Stig,[33] whose 'Ging Gang Goolie' – the Boy Scouts campfire singalong – had been Able Label's first release as Noakes' 'Restless' was its last.

Fed up with trying in vain to tease hits from often dispirited and malcontented artists, Starr terminated the operation in December 1978. "If you don't sell records, then it costs you money," he observed. "You have to look at it straight and say, 'What's going on?', and you either turn it around or you do as I did yet again [and say] that it is time for it to end."[2]

14 "If I Don't Get You, The Next One Will"

It was some kind of back-handed compliment when Ringo heard that up-and-coming film actors John Belushi and Dan Akroyd with Joe Walsh and other members of The Eagles had unwound on an after-hours club stage in Chicago with a long extrapolation of 'With A Little Help From My Friends', rather than 'It Don't Come Easy' or 'Photograph'. Ringo was, however, probably unconscious of bobsleigh rides through 'Boys' and 'I Wanna Be Your Man' by The Milkshakes, who in the early 1980s presided over a Medway town's group scene that was as self-contained in its quieter way as Mersey Beat.

Whether in Chatham, Alice Springs or Centerville, the muzak dribbling from supermarket Tannoys was more likely to be 'Yellow Submarine' than 'Back Off Boogaloo' or even 'Octopus' Garden'. Tune into an easy-listening radio station and The Beatles orchestral medley you'd hear would be all Lennon and McCartney, who could have "made it" with any competent drummer and second guitarist.

Nevertheless, Ringo Starr had proved himself no slouch without them. Now that the halcyon days of *That'll Be The Day* and *Ringo* were gone, who could blame him for doing nothing in particular? It was no sin to make a fortune by providing harmless entertainment, was it? A disadvantaged back-street lad who climbed to the top of the heap, who could begrudge him a secluded but cosseted retirement in his mid 30s? Look at Lennon. With Harrison his heir apparent as the Howard Hughes of pop, he was sighted less often than the Loch Ness Monster nowadays.

What Starr could not articulate was that he adored being in the limelight, seldom missing opportunities to be the focal point of eyes grateful to him for just existing. How would he have felt if politely brief clapping rather than a howling, foot-stomping ovation had greeted him when he mounted his drum podium for just the finale of The Last Waltz, The Band's farewell to the road after 16 years, that had begun in hick Canadian dance halls just as The Beatles had in the jive hives of Merseyside? At San Francisco's 5,000-capacity Winterland auditorium on Thanksgiving Day 1976, it was a Pacific coast "answer" to the Bangladesh concert in its array of the famous and semi-famous – Muddy Waters, Van Morrison, Dr John, Emmylou Harris and Bob Dylan to name a few – individually bowling on to sing a couple of numbers with the departing Band and joining in the *omnes fortissimo* 'I Shall Be Released' from *Music From Big Pink* and – kicked off by Ringo – the dinning instrumental work-outs that followed.

A few months earlier, at the Los Angeles Forum, Ringo could not restrain himself either from sauntering on when Wings were called back for an encore to present Denny Laine – not "obvious"[1] Paul – with a bouquet after "just going to the concert like anybody else".[2] Words are cheap, but after similar wistful attendances at the metropolis' Roxy Theater for Bob Marley And The Wailers and in Den Haag with Vini Poncia for The Hollies – chin-wagging with their Allan Clarke afterwards – he "got 'round to thinking that I want to do it. I'd like to go out with a circus – not elephants, but a circus. Dylan's [Rolling Thunder] and Bangladesh [were] that way"[3] A year later, he was still dithering: "It'll be like a revue, not like Paul and Wings, but Ringo and other people. More theatrical."[1]

With such innovations as graphic equalisers, programmable desks and even synthesised drums to do battle against adverse acoustics, Ringo wasn't alone in feeling that touring with a backing group was attractive enough to erase flashbacks of how dreadful it had been in the distorted epoch when vocal balance had been achieved by simply moving back and forth on the microphone. Riding a so-called Mod revival, The Who – with Kenney Jones on drums – were on the boards again, and so soon would be diffident Steve Winwood, bankrupt Gary Glitter and others from quiet fastnesses where the only manifestations of the squalid holocaust over the hills in London, New York and Hollywood were gold discs lining balustraded stairwells.

As the 1980s loomed, his spirit might have been willing, but he lacked financial motive. It was less grief to get smaller kicks with short, one-off events like The Last Waltz and a Labour Day telethon in aid of medical research in 1979 from Las Vegas, where – at the request of Bill Wyman's agent/girlfriend – he beat the drums on 'Twist And Shout', 'Jumpin' Jack Flash' and, appropriate to the occasion, 'Money' in an all-star assemblage called "Superjam" and, with Bill, lent an hour answering telephoned pledges.

To a less charitable end, he'd present a white horse to Julian Lennon at that fledgling pop star's 19th birthday celebration amid the gold-diggers and brattish swells in London's faddish Stringfellow's night club. All that he had to do to upstage founders of such feasts was to simply go to them. Glam-rock latecomers Queen[4] began 1976 with 'Bohemian Rhapsody' at Number One and EMI International's dazzling party in their honour at the Cunard Hotel. Petals from the very flower of UK pop in the 1970s were there – Bowie, Rod Stewart, Bryan Ferry – sipping posed cocktails that looked like melted crayons, when a buzz filtered through the 300-odd guests that Ringo Starr had arrived. This wasn't television or a picture in *Jackie*; that impossible yardstick of teenage escapism and aspiration – a Beatle – was actually within, asserting his old power in abundance in his involuntary lure for the younger conquistadors and their acolytes who buzzed around him like bees around a jam jar.

Ignored at his side was Lynsey de Paul, to whom he had given a fishing rod, because she was always angling for compliments. Some of these were deserved, for, although her five-year chart run was about to end with a British Song For Europe entry, singing in public was secondary to Lynsey's songwriting skills. 1972 had been her red-letter year, with a Top Five debut ('Sugar Me') and The Fortunes showing class in the US Hot 100 with her 'Storm In A Teacup'.

Her confidence boosted by this syndication, Lynsey crossed to

Los Angeles to better ply her wares before more prestigious customers than this lucky Birmingham combo. A tangent of this expedition was her romance with actor James Coburn, and it was on her return to London after breaking with him that she embarked on a more light-hearted affair with Ringo for several months. Possibly, this was an antidote to the vulnerable de Paul's protracted and harrowing legal wrangling with her ex-manager. As well as the new boyfriend's masculine charms, she was also beneficiary of his tambourine-bashing and image in the publicity photo for 'Don't You Remember When', a ballad she produced for aging "Forces' Sweetheart" Dame Vera Lynn. If not a hit, it was an excuse for another EMI beanfeast at the Dorchester, in Park Lane, where its composer had no complaints about any shortage of compliments. When Starr's 90 days in the United Kingdom were up, so, more or less, was their amour, Lynsey penning 'If I Don't Get You (The Next One Will)' as its requiem.

Over in California, Nancy might have supposed that the main purpose of her fiancé's 90 days a year in England was to make a fuss of his children. She was, therefore, taken aback by reports of his supposed satyric exploits in UK tabloids[5] and reported airy comments such as "there are girls in my life because I still have all the normal urges".[6] Nevertheless, although there were frank exchanges in their Los Angeles bungalow, she held onto the belief that her ex-Beatle was worth keeping and that his intentions remained honourable. She tried, therefore, not to hear any more of his other attachments and clung onto her dignity as his official lover by devoting herself, as always, to the enhancement of his neglected career.

It may have pleased her to think that it was the ante-start agonies of the sensitive artist that impeded his knuckling down to another album. He seemed to be holding it at arm's length by accepting more record dates for friends. Although not confining himself as much to the established, it was a reversion to that trough between *Beaucoups Of Blues* and *Ringo*: nothing too strenuous – "a couple of days, only three or four tracks, because I don't want to get stuck in to do the whole album, because I don't even want to do my own album".[7]

While he grappled with his depressed muse, a Starkey original, 'Band Of Steel' – the one from the *Beaucoups Of Blues* period – was resurrected by Guthrie Thomas on his *Lies And Alibis* LP. Its inclusion – with the composer on drums and, with Thomas and Steve Cropper, lead vocals – was more to stoke up airtime from curiosity-seeking disc jockeys beyond Guthrie's usual orbit than its worth as a song. The stylised blue yodels on its fade-out hinted that 'Band Of Steel' – an all-purpose country and western item stuffed with negative symbolism – might have been just end-of-session badinage.[8] If it was, far funnier were earlier send-ups of the form, such as The Rolling Stones' 'Dear Doctor', 'Rameses II Is Dead (My Love)' from The Fugs and – a few months after *Lies And Alibis* – 1977's 'Men's Room LA', an attempt by to see if God could take a joke by Kinky Friedman, who was blessed with Ringo as "The Voice Of Jesus" on its spoken passage, which was personalised with references to Liverpool and France.

With Friedman on Dylan's Rolling Thunder wayfaring was The Alpha Band, who – via Friedman's owlish guitarist Joseph "T-Bone" Burnett – got Ringo to play on a brace of tracks (including Dylan's 'You Angel You') on their US-only *Spark In The Dark* album as a change from their own jazzier drummer. Often flanked by cronies like Jim Keltner and Dr John, Starr was roused to serve likewise Manhattan Transfer – who, with Bette Midler, spearheaded an injection of archly kitsch cabaret into pop – and Keltner's own Attitudes, a loose convention of "funky cats" who performed for their own delectation in venues local to Los Angeles, until Jim's pal George Harrison underwrote and issued their two albums and a pestilence of singles on his Dark Horse, a label only marginally more lucrative than Ring O'.

The most interesting – and disappointing – of these diversions was Adam Faith's cluttered Los Angeles production of *Puttin' On The Style*, an album on which, at Paul McCartney's suggestion, Lonnie Donegan remade some of his skiffle smashes – as Howlin' Wolf had his blues set-works – with a host of famous lifelong fans like Ringo, Elton John, Faith's *protégé* Leo Sayer and Queen's guitarist, Brian May, sitting in with Donegan's regular band. With only one barely remembered US hit, Lonnie might bring much of the aura of a fresh sensation to that majority of young Americans who'd never heard of him.

Everyone had heard of Ringo Starr, but this appeared to be to his cost now, as shown by the album that he'd eventually finished – *Ringo The Fourth* – faring worse than even the Lennons and Harrison's *avant-garde* abominations of the 1960s. As some English history primers start with the Battle of Hastings, so when numbering his new solo LP Starr excluded the two released during the Dark Ages of The Beatles. Significantly, this was also his first effort since the group's sundering that was bereft of any aid from John, Paul or George – although, even without this omission, I doubt that *Ringo The Fourth* could have risen much higher than its dismal Number 162 in the States. As Starr's name on the sleeve of Attitude's *Good News* and Harrison's on Splinter's *Two-Man Band* could not forestall tumbles into the bargain bin, so it was understood that having an ex-Beatle on board – even on another ex-Beatle's record – was no longer a licence to print banknotes in that watershed year of 1977.

Most of Starr's old retainers – including Keltner – were also missing from *Ringo The Fourth*. Instead, he left it to Mardin to pick and choose from the slickest supporting musicians on Atlantic's files, as well as layer an icing of contemporary celebrities such as Bette Midler, Luther Vandross, Jim Gilstrap and Melissa Manchester, whose latest 45, 'Monkey See Monkey Do', was a much-demanded radio spin.

Belying this ominous preamble, *Ringo The Fourth* was in theory Starr's most courageous musical statement, in that the bulk of its ten tracks were from the Starkey-Poncia songbook, even if two were cast-offs from *Rotogravure*. However, other than 'Gypsies In Flight' as the country-and-western weepie, most were gorged with an over-generous helping of a *moderato* soul style – smoother than Stax or Motown – that was then just ceasing to waft from trend-setting Philadelphia as the likes of Gilstrap, The Stylistics, The Three Degrees and MFSB neared their sell-by date and such as Vandross, Chic and Tavares took

RINGO STARR

up the slack – a word well chosen, because still exhaling from late-night stereos were routine "Philly soul" duplications, all synthesised string backwash, clipped *chukka-wukka* guitars and prominent backing chorale lowing an over-stretched coda as the main vocalist's hopes of imminent sexual congress increased. For good measure, there might be bursts of beefy horn riffing or a key change whenever you started to doze off.

Left off *Ringo The Fourth* but a B-side common to both of its US singles, 'Just A Dream' – original in its unoriginality – utilised this yawnsome formula as well as a lyrical juxtaposition of unconscious reverie and agonised waking reality, as pre-empted in Roy Orbison's 'In Dreams' from 1963. On the album, neither 'Simple Love Song' nor the McCartney-esque 'It's No Secret' are about anything much, 'Out In The Streets' – in which he was less dockland Ted than Bowery switchblade-wielder – being Ringo's most specific self-projection. He was, however, more attractive as a rueful pipe-and-slippers survivor of school and adolescent trauma in 'Gave It All Up'. Its narrative underlined with street-corner mouth-organ, this was the collection's most poignant stroke, if marred by a weedy chorus and sub-Philly production.

Rather than scourings from the archives of his youth or specially commissioned songs, Mardin and Starr consumed needle time with reworkings of 1970s items that walked a tightrope between *bona fide* songs and fine-quality disco fodder. Because Ringo's version of La Seine's 'Tango All Night' had permeated the dance floor in as recently as 1976, the *Ringo The Fourth* single on which Atlantic pinned its hopes was 'Drowning In The Sea Of Love', composed for Joe Simon in 1971 by Gamble and Huff, the very Lennon-McCartney of Philly soul.

Of slightly greater antiquity was 'Sneakin' Sally Thru' The Alley', a Lee Dorsey effort from the previous year that had been revived by Robert Palmer, Yorkshire's highbrow soul connoisseur, then on the verge of a Frampton-sized US triumph. Its clichéd re-arrangement for Ringo's album absorbed the processed handclaps, flatulent clavinet and "twanging-plank" bass lines that would plague pop for the next decade.

As Palmer gained a toehold in the US charts in 1975, so – more gingerly – did Gold Rush with 'Can She Do It Like She Dances'. With a hookline of ascending semitones as lewd as the verses, Ringo coped well with its feverish lechery, but essentially he wasn't cut out to sing most of the material on *Ringo The Fourth* because, however much he attempted to hack it as a fervid blue-eyed soulman without affectation, he was no Cliff Bennett or Steve Winwood. Although he tried hard, the voice was raucous rather than passionate when he extemporised. While it might have been enchantingly ludicrous for, say, *Sentimental Journey*, Ringo's ingrained Scouse pronunciation – "I love you so mooch", "our uffur [affair] is over" – was often just ludicrous on *Ringo The Fourth*.

His accent may have stuck out like a sore thumb to his all-American session crew, but only its Californian gloss made it conspicuous back in Liverpool, where some still saw him not as a gilded ghost but as a scrawny drummer from Rory Storm's Hurricanes who'd hit the jackpot and had stayed lucky. By his own admission, "I don't know why it happens to me half the time."[3] All they knew was that, if he hadn't joined The Beatles, he'd probably be in a job where he had to metaphorically touch his cap, as they did.

By keeping his nose clean, Pete Best had worked his way up to deputy manager at Garston Job Centre. On leave, he'd bank extra brass by answering questions about the old days and beating his drums at Beatle-associated events and – less often but more lucratively – on US television. His autobiography was on the cards, too, but whatever this earned him would be peanuts against the millions he missed. Some childish Beatle fanzines mocked his resentment, calling him "Mr Sour Grapes" and suchlike for being the spectre at their revels, an impurity who must have deserved their heroes' cowardly purging as well as "heartache, grief, financial embarrassment – you name it. Now and then, something comes up – a bill or something – or, when it snows, you'd like to disappear off to the Bahamas. Then you think, 'If I'd been a Beatle, I wouldn't have had any worries.'"[9]

One day, Pete would regard himself as more fortunate than poor John – and Ringo, too. With a happy marriage and two lovely daughters, he was certainly better off than Tommy Moore, who, since The Beatles, had been more contented with his lot, a job with the Liverpool Corporation while playing in a jazz band some evenings. An apoplectic fit would take him at the age of 47.

Nothing could alter the less professional affinity of another long estranged from The Beatles, but all that Ringo's natural father – a Bolton window-cleaner, these days – had to show for it now was a signed photograph of the group. He'd stopped sending unacknowledged presents to his grandchildren, but could only be proud of his son: "He's done well, the lad, and good luck to him. He owes me nothing."[10]

The eldest of Richie's brood, was proving a bit of a handful. With his dad's gallivanting absences and "Count Dracula hours"[11] setting no good example, Zak's truancies and disruption of classes were causing anxiety at his private academy in Maida Vale. With an open invitation to bolt to "Uncle" Keith Moon's West End apartment, what chance had the unhappy youth had? "See, during my puberty, Moonie was always there with me," he explained, "while my old man was far away in Monte Carlo or somewhere." Although he took after his dad facially and in his manner of speaking, "Being Ringo's son is a total pain," he'd grimace. "I'm always written about as Ringo's son, always classed with him in every single thing I try to do."[12]

Like all but the most serious-minded teenagers of the late 1970s, Zak had been excited by punk and, while still modelling himself on Keith Moon, was a fan of The Ruts, a sub-Pistols bunch from north London. From merely looking the part (earring, zippered bondage trousers, black leather bomber jacket), Zak became the youngest member of The Next, who, from weekend rehearsals, risked engagements at parties and then alternating with El Seven and The K9s, as well as a group formed around the sons of late Yardbird Keith Relf and other local outfits at South Hill Park Community Centre, the rougher Bridge House and like venues within spitting distance of Tittenhurst Park, where Zak would occupy a lodge cottage on leaving school. Eventually, Sarah Menikides – a girlfriend five years his senior – would live there too.

As well as his prowess as a percussionist, Zak's supplementary importance to The Next was his procurement of free time at Startling Studio, despite his insisting, "I don't want any help from my dad. I want to prove that I can do it by myself. He hasn't done a thing to help me, and I don't want him to."[13] Source of much envenomed discussion was Ringo's wariness about his boy drumming for a living. Dad did not "envy him the challenge".[14] Besides, The Next might not be able to use the studio for much longer, because Ringo had just put the manor up for sale through Chancellors, an Ascot estate agency.

Windsor and Maidenhead Council's concern about its state of repair – a lot of dampness, apparently – brought forth contemptuous offers of less than half of its six-figure asking price, and thus it was taken off the market, even though its peripatetic owner flitted between California and Monte Carlo most of the year and was actively looking at properties elsewhere in Europe. As Amsterdam was fast becoming one of the music industry's storm centres, two floors of Mr Starkey's house there had been converted to white-furnitured offices to deal with the fingers he'd poked into various pies.

He'd also looked over likely looking buildings in Hamburg of fond memory. After so doing, he couldn't push off without looking in at the Star-Club, now, could he? An erotic cinema was on its old site, for it had relocated – as a discotheque featuring occasional live acts – to the Grossneumarkt, further from the disreputable heart of the Reeperbahn, which, now under government licence, was not as open-minded about human frailty as it had been. While there were many new auditoriums, such as the Fabrik (once a factory), some old haunts still bore their original names, if nothing else. The Top Ten had long gone, as had Peter Eckhorn and Manfred Weissleder, but the Kaiserkeller was still in business as a transvestite bar.

Although he'd kept in touch with acquaintances from that distant chapter, Ringo couldn't help but visualise them in some fixed attitude, doing what they did then. Sure enough, when he and George looked in at a Star-Club anniversary show, there was Tony Sheridan – who'd been rumoured to have been killed while entertaining US troops in Vietnam – slaying 'em on stage. Backed by former Presley sidemen, he brushed aside the millennia since 1962 like matchsticks. On sale in the foyer was his new so-so LP, *World's Apart*, produced by Klaus Voorman, who had also made a prodigal's return to Germany.

Nature hadn't been particularly kind to grey-haired, grizzled Tony, but ex-bouncer Horst Fascher was in rampant good health. The proprietorship of the place and marriage to Bill "Faron" Russley's daughter obviously agreed with him. For Horst, Starr and Harrison ambled on to shake hands with "the Teacher", but, if bubbly before the flashbulbs, Ringo left soon afterwards, harassed by the general onslaught of the German media – that had buttonholed him the second he'd stepped off the 'plane – and by Sheridan's manager harping on about The Beatles doing a concert for the Vietnamese boat people.

There seemed fat chance of anything of the sort as George went on to the next stop on the promotion campaign for his newest album and Ringo tooled back to Monte Carlo. Unlike the other two, he was still close enough to John to persuade that home-keeping mister to donate a drawing to another Big Apple Beatlefest raffle (for UNICEF), even though "we don't live in each other's pockets any more. After Paul was busted for carrying pot in Tokyo, I didn't even have his phone number."[14] Putting the kybosh on that leg of Wings' world tour, the detainee's week pondering his folly in a Nippon gaol elicited a sympathetic telegram from Harrison and "flowers and a packet of candy"[14] from Starr.

As any creative reunion appeared more and more untenable, the group's hardcore fanatics fragmented into separate camps, subscribing to, say, Wings' Fun Club, the Harrison Alliance or – through a *Record Collector* small ad – the Ringo Starr Fan Club, instigated by an enthusiast from Chesham, Berkshire. Whether scorned, admired or just tolerated in this new phase of Beatlemania, Ringo was still perturbed that "being an ex-Beatle or being Ringo Starr sometimes doesn't allow you to be yourself when you walk into a room full of people, but I am pleased that I was what I was, and I am happy that I am me."[2]

Others weren't as happy with him as they used to be. To Klaus

Voorman, excluded from *Ringo The Fourth*, "He's changed. He's not as reliable and he's not so nice."[15] Other musicians hadn't a bad word to say about Starr, but "they only see me on a nice day".[3] One who did was *Beatlefan*'s London correspondent, Andrew Matheson, who, at the Queen gathering, found him "chatty, funny and natural".[16] Waiting outside for a taxi after his new-found friend had departed, our man Matheson's favourable opinion was enhanced when Ringo's limousine glided back from the Dorchester to give him a lift home.

However, there was no mistaking the steel underneath the happy-go-lucky exterior whenever he had matters to discuss at Atlantic's Los Angeles headquarters. "I wouldn't say he's rude," estimated one employee, Kristen Gunderson. "Let's say you're not left in any doubt what he wants. If it's to do with his recordings, then he wants it dealt with first. He's no different in that respect to every other artist; it's just that, in Ringo's case, you don't quite expect it."[17]

More than anyone, Elsie Starkey understood that "he doesn't want to be thought of as a clown any more. He's more serious than most people realise, and he can be forceful when he needs to be. More than anything, he wants to become successful as an actor."[18] A US go-between, Alan Pariser, was on the look-out for such an opportunity, but the route to any role as strong as that of Mike Menarry was fraught with potholes such as the *NME*'s not-unfounded jibe that, other than his records, Starr had spent most of the years since 1970 in "duff movies and heavy-duty ligging".[19]

He couldn't resist the proverbial "something to tell his grandchildren about" of a not especially ample part in Mae West's final movie, *Sextette*, no matter how disappointing the reviews that caused its fade with indecent haste from general circulation after a midnight première in Atlanta in July 1978. In this bawdy farce, Miss West – wisecracking in her sexy serpentine husk – was in character as Marlo Manners, a Hollywood screen goddess who'd just plighted her troth to her sixth husband.

Ringo played Laslo Karozny, a temperamental European film director who'd also been so manacled to her. At first, as with Peter Sellers and *The Magic Christian*, Starr "felt completely out of things"[20] in the presence of a celluloid legend who'd "never needed Panavision and stereophonic sound to woo the world. I did it in black-and-white on a screen the size of a postage stamp. Honey, that's talent."[21] However, comforted perhaps by the knowledge that she was a Beatles fan,[22] "by the second day, I would have stayed for as long as she wanted me. She's old enough to be my grandmother, so it's sort of embarrassing to say, but she's bloody attractive. And Mae's no Garbo. Mae doesn't want to be left alone."[20] Doddering she might have been, but she turned out for the post-production blow-out to receive the plaudits of male co-stars, which also included Tony Curtis and George Hamilton. Also on hand were bit-part players like Alice Cooper and – as a camp dress designer – Keith Moon. As well as being a mediocre epitaph for Mae West, *Sextette* was also Keith Moon's last film.

More certain an indicator of future direction for Ringo than *Sextette* was his effortless lead in *Scouse The Mouse*, a concept album of a children's story by distinguished old stager Donald Pleasence, under the musical direction of Roger Brown. As a poor consolation to Starr's UK following, chagrined at so much US-only product, this soon-deleted record of late 1977 and its affiliated illustrated book[23] and painting-competition entry form was exclusive to Britain and the Commonwealth. However, although an ITV animation of *Scouse The Mouse* was proposed, the powers that be procrastinated until the advent of the grander Roland Rat brought the curtain down on Pleasence's rodent.

Rat would be to Scouse what a Sherman tank is to a Mini. Like Tony Hancock, he'd abide none of the doe-eyed winsomeness that some – including Scouse's investors – deemed touching. If crass and insensitive, Rat was further favoured by a more colourful supporting cast and funnier plots than that which launched – and finished – *Scouse*, a mouse's progress from pet shop to cage in a Liverpool household, where he learns English from the television. Inspired by a vocal group called The Jollys, he learns to compose, sing and dance. Aflame with ambition, he escapes and, after various adventures, sails on the QE2 into New York harbour, intending to take the land of opportunity by storm.

Hmmm. With Ringo at the taping in Soho's Berwick Street Studios were members of narrator Pleasence's family and a motley assortment of stars that included Barbara Dickson (from *John, Paul, George Ringo – And Bert*), Adam Faith (the other Mike Menarry) and, just blown in from the Windy City, comedienne Ruby Wax. It was produced by Hugh Murphy, who was about to shine with an international hit in Gerry Rafferty's 'Baker Street' – but not with 'The Taster', (Alan) Clayson And The Argonauts' debut single.

In our yokel innocence, we were too unsure of ourselves for open mutiny when, during the session with Mr Murphy, our keyboard player's triplets were ghosted by one of Rafferty's men, Tommy Eyre, who was also among those musicians that Murphy called up for *Scouse The Mouse*, a most polished album in its crossfading of sound effects, songs and dialogue. If swallowing chaff behind later efforts in the same mould by Roland Rat, The Mister Men and Rupert Bear (under Paul McCartney's aegis), Murphy's raw material was tolerable and pertinent to imagined visuals – particularly 'Caterwaul' (a "cats' choir" waltz), Faith's gorblimey 'America (A Mouse's Dream)' and 'Scousey' by Lucy Pleasence, whose clear soprano was worthy of a Maddy Prior or Jane Relf.

Within Ringo's lion's share of eight numbers, 'Scouse's Dream', 'I Know A Place' (a duet with Polly Pleasence) and the hootenanny 'Running Free' stuck out, but the ace in the pack – although it's not saying much – was the nautical lament, 'SOS'.[24] Far less objectionable than *Ringo The Fourth*, this album for infants was a suitable vehicle for Starr's unforced urbanity, always a handy resort when the going got rough, which it would with growing frequency

Adapted from 'A Mouse Like Me', the *Scouse The Mouse* finale, A Man Like Me' (watered-down Kurt Weill), concluded *Bad Boy*, Starr's seventh solo LP. As he couldn't get a hit to save his life now, Ahmet Ertegun had let him go to Portrait, a CBS tributary. It was, therefore, a matter of pride for Ringo and Portrait to ensure that *Bad Boy* left more of a wound in the US charts than *Ringo The Fourth* had. Who needed Mardin and his layers of treated sound when aiming for home-made passion with Vini Poncia at the helm in studios in far-flung Canada and the Bahamas?

That was the theory, anyway, and *Bad Boy* certainly clambered fractionally higher in *Billboard*'s tabulation than its predecessor, thanks largely to a leg-up from a US television special, chat-show spots and – for the inventive Beatle rumour-monger – the enigmatic and pseudonymous listing of auxiliary musicians on its sleeve.[25] Balancing these manoeuvres were the paucity of critics who went ape over *Bad Boy* and, crucially, that mighty watchdog of pop propriety *Rolling Stone*, kicking Starr when he was down with "not even passable cocktail music. Ringo isn't likeable any more, and that truly is depressing."[26]

This was a harsh dismissal because, pin-pointed in the crash of exasperated cymbals that jerked you from 'A Man Like Me', *Bad Boy* was a more idiosyncratic if warmer work than either of Mardin's squeaky-clean Atlantic albums. Nevertheless, now a stale songwriting team, Vini and Ringo had virtually shed their creative load on *Ringo The Fourth*, for only two more Poncia-Starr compositions were ever released, both on *Bad Boy*. 'Who Needs A Heart' was its punchy opener, and lame 'Old Time Relovin'' was just one degree removed from country and western by its staccato organ obligato and jammed *accelerando* coda. As insignificant an opus was the *Bad Boy* UK single 'Tonight', offered to Ringo by author John Pidgeon and Ian McLagan,[27] a beau of Keith Moon's widow and a jobbing musician since leaving Rod Stewart's Faces.

A sense of simply going through the motions once more was evident in Ringo's strained and often uninvolved singing on merely workmanlike overhauls of 'Monkey See Monkey Do', Gallagher And Lyle's 'Heart On My Sleeve' and 'Hard Times', a wittily observed piece that had been suggested by George Harrison, who'd played on Peter Skellern's 1975 album of which it was the title track. Older items rehashed on *Bad Boy* included a Benny Spellman single from 1962 ('Lipstick Traces On A Cigarette') and 1957's 'Bad Boy'[28] by The Jive Bombers, covered lately by both Mink De Ville and Sha Na Na, as was 'Heart On My Sleeve' by Bryan Ferry. Likewise,

Manhattan Transfer's 'Where Did Our Love Go?' may have nudged Ringo's revival of this revival of The Supremes' 1964 smash, which was infused on *Bad Boy* with that strutting boogie rhythm synonymous with Canned Heat but programmed on an aberrant sequencer. Now that he was free from the constraints of sustaining a chain of chart entries, Ringo would be sating himself with many more too-premeditated reconstructions of the ancient hits of others after *Bad Boy*. Although he'd never succumb to drum machines, with their robotic exactitudes, the latest studio gimmick would intrude upon guts and – especially if the original versions of the likes of 'Where Did Our Love Go?' had emotional significance for the listener – leave a queer aftertaste.

So, too, would *Ringo*, the TV tie-in, which was a vehicle for him to mime to pre-recordings of his best-loved songs with and without The Beatles and – implying by association that they were just as eternal – excerpts from *Bad Boy*. These were hung on an approximation[29] of Mark Twain's *The Prince And The Pauper*. Set in Hollywood rather than Tudor London, it begins with George Harrison's cameo explanation about two identical babies born at the same moment. One grows up as Ringo Starr, idol of a world shortly to watch him perform in a satellite-linked concert. He swaps places with his doppelgänger, "Ognir Rats" (get it?), a pitiable sandwich-boarded pedlar of sightseers' maps of Beverly Hills. Seen along the way as both changelings get into various scrapes are such as Vincent Price, Angie Dickinson and *Star Wars'* Carrie Fisher (as Ognir's girlfriend). Nonetheless – you guessed it – all ends well in the nick of-time, with Rats taken on as highly waged road manager to the proper Ringo, who wows 'em – as evidenced by heavily overdubbed screams – in the bounced broadcast.

Despite this element of wishful thinking, *Ringo* was a splendid if dear means of publicising *Bad Boy* and Starr's back-catalogue, and – with Ringo playing both himself and Rats – as an elaborate general audition for any suitable film roles going, because "no one is going to offer Ringo Starr a top role these days just because I used to be in The Beatles. I've got to be able to do the job. That's much more demanding, but much better, too. I could end up with egg on my face but, succeed or fail, it's all down to me standing on my own two feet as an actor."[14] It could have been *Ringo* that brought him his first solo top billing – "I'm the hero, you know, the king of the castle"[20] – in a family movie in preparation since 1977 called *Caveman*. "When you need a small, suave, funny, awkward, unprepossessing leading man," elucidated its director, Carl Gottlieb, "there aren't a lot to choose from: Dustin Hoffman, Dudley Moore, Robin Williams – and who else is there who's also a star? There's Ringo."[30]

As an afterthought, *Ringo* was shown elsewhere five years after North America. In the lonely Sunday hour after the God-slot, it induced a glaze over many British eyes maddened already with the prospect of an evening sabotaged by snooker. Back in 1978, even in the States the impact of *Ringo* had abated quickly, and people who read of his personal desolations over the next year felt sorry for him, but not sorry enough to buy his records, not even the albums that had now been made available on budget labels.

When seated by the fireside on one November evening in Haslem Terrace, Starr had been alarmed by sparks belching suddenly from the chimney, where a stray shard of flame had already ignited the roof and the attic, where he'd stowed cherished memorabilia, from gold discs to his first pair of drumsticks and the shoes he'd worn for that official maiden booking with The Beatles at Port Sunlight. On dashing to investigate, he rang the fire brigade before singeing his hair in the process of grabbing what he could from the spreading inferno. No one was hurt, and half an hour's hosing by six engines saved most of the bungalow and Ringo's costly musical equipment, but little remained of the blackened attic's contents.

To journalists, who'd had no inhibitions about quizzing him as the building still smouldered, he'd wailed, "Money could never replace those things."[31] A more deliberate blaze had long ago incinerated further links with Ringo's past when Iris Caldwell threw most of her deceased brother's remaining possessions onto a bonfire instead of putting them under the hammer at the auctions of pop artefacts that were so beyond a joke as to concern Christie's and other top salerooms. However, Iris' drastic clear-out had uncovered a 1962 tape of a Rory Storm And The Hurricanes engagement, with Ringo, at the Jive Hive, and there was talk of finding someone to hire a studio to clean up its atrocious sound quality for release as a tardy 1979 supplement to a double LP, out two years earlier, that had improved digitally a similarly hand-held recording on Kingsize Taylor's tape machine of a night during The Beatles' last season at the Star-Club.

If documentary rather than recreational, The Beatles' *Live At The Star-Club, 1962* was more engrossing to most people than anything current by Ringo Starr. Nevertheless, as Elvis Presley had demonstrated in as recently as 1977, a death in pop could still revive a flagging chart career, and certain record-business moguls wondered what Starr tracks they'd be entitled to rush-release if he didn't survive an emergency operation on 13 April 1979 in a Monte Carlo hospital. Five feet of blocked intestine had to be removed by laser surgery after he'd been carried in doubled up with the tell-tale abdominal pangs of his old ailment, peritonitis. As it had been when he was six, "Everything twisted up inside me."[32] However, although he'd told the convalescing Ringo that "another minute or two and it would have been curtains",[32] a surgeon was able to inform both well-wishers and a press corps itching to relay obituaries that the patient was "a courageous man and responded well to treatment. A lot of sick people tend to be miserable after an operation, but Mr Starkey was very cheerful and able to swap jokes and banter with the nurses. The doctors are very pleased, but work is out of the question for the time being."[32]

Although still green about the gills, Ringo was sufficiently recovered to pass a medical examination for United Artists' insurers on the postponed *Caveman*. As a legacy of McCartney's arrest in Tokyo, Starr and his luggage would be searched thoroughly by customs officials desirous of a dope-free Mexico, but, assuming that he was cleared, the initial shoot was scheduled for February 1980 in the rocky sierra surrounding Puerta Vallarta, near Durango. He was to play "Atouk", chief of a rebel tribe, in this prehistoric comedy with no highbrow pretensions. Neither were there qualms about authenticity as Atouk tames dinosaurs who were extinct aeons before humankind commenced its deplorable sovereignty of the planet. While *Caveman* swiped gently at 1966's *One Million Years BC* in the Raquel Welch coquettishness of shapely Barbara Bach (as "Lana") and, in a more overall sense, the apemen section of *2001: A Space Odyssey*, it was closer in spirit to earlier stabs by Buster Keaton, Charlie Chaplin and Laurel and Hardy at the Neanderthal sub-genre of film in its slapstick simplicity and jokes about dung. Apart from a 15-word language created by the community's Chinese wise man (*ca-ca* for "excrement", *zug-zug* for "copulation" – you get the drift?), the dialogue consisted mostly of grunts and moans accompanied by much gesticulation, body talk and face-pulling. It definitely beat having to learn lines. As a sop for Beatle freaks, the tale begins in one zillion BC on 9 October, John Lennon's birthday.

For the first few reels, Ringo appeared in the same guise he had striven to hurl aside since *Help!*, as a Chaplin-esque underdog – although one more lively and engaging than before – but he was in no mood to care about that. In his eagerness, he'd have cheerfully dusted off his *A Hard Day's Night* character.

Treated like dirt by the other tribesmen, who use their womenfolk as fishing poles, Atouk becomes a vagabond who, while gathering about him his own warriors, trains himself to walk upright, discovers fire (and barbecued chicken) and, in the film's most diverting sequence, makes music with his band, one of them thrusting a dotard's hand rhythmically into the flames so that he screams in time. After defeating hefty tribal bully Tonda (American footballer John Matuszak), he wins Lana, the object of his desire, but, chuckled Barbara Bach, "I'm the bitch. In the end, the girl next door wins out. I get thrown in the dinosaur dung."[30]

How frightfully funny. Gottlieb's credentials as co-scriptwriter of 1975 blockbuster *Jaws* and saturation advance publicity guaranteed *Caveman* a fair critical appraisal in a society that had taken Benny Hill's saucy inanities to its heart. Indeed, US press comment is worth quoting at length. Against the *Chicago Tribune*'s "not so much a bad movie as it is a tedious one with a slight script",[33] there was "nicely whimsical"[34] from *The New York Times*, "enchanting"[35] (*Village Voice*) and "infantile but also playful and appealingly good-natured"[36](*Newsday*). Although hardly Marlon Brando as Don Vito, Ringo didn't come out of it too badly, either. *The Washington Post* might have turned its nose up with "going 'round pointing and saying 'ca-ca' is not what one would have expected from a legendary Beatle",[37] but to sweeter-natured reviewers he was "better here than he's been in anything since The Beatles' films",[37] "a delight"[31] and – possibly a double-edged accolade – "as puppy-dog charming as ever".[33]

With all of the attributes of a box-office smash but none that actually grabbed the public, *Caveman* was soon booming out in half-empty Midwestern drive-ins, and on its second night in London's West End it drew all of six customers in one cinema. Some even stuck it out to the National Anthem.

However its shortcomings affected Starr professionally, his participation in *Caveman* was also one of far-reaching private import – at least, as private as one whose every waking hour was chronicled was allowed. Tongues wagged about Ringo and leading lady Shelley Long in the teeth of his stock assurance that they were "very good friends but that's as far as it goes",[14] but of infinitely more substance were rumours about him and Barbara Bach, which provoked "confirmed reports" that they were to wed as soon as her divorce to Italian industrialist Augusto Gregorini was finalised. There was no reason not to believe that this "B-Movie Queen Might Turn A Beatle Into Prince Charming",[30] as, holding hands, they seemed never to be off US television throughout the spring of 1981 while plugging *Caveman*. Next broke the distressing news that the pair were co-habiting a leased house off Sunset Strip, while a Los Angeles estate agent was under instructions to go up to $2 million for a more permanent dwelling spacious enough to contain her two and his three offspring as well. Contradicting the gossip, Barbara – like Ringo – could not "imagine why I would ever get married again. The way I am now, if I want to be with someone, I'll be with that person, but I see no reason to carry his name as well."[30]

Lana and Atouk's on-camera flirtations (prior to the

unpleasantness with the dung) had, he admitted, "just spilled over nicely into real life".[38] Their social circles in Hollywood had overlapped before *Caveman*. "It wasn't love at first sight," reflected Barbara; "it began to grow within days of meeting each other."[38] In Durango, she'd been touched when he chose to sport with local children between takes, and he'd admired her stoicism as John Matuszak hurled her time and again into the Maguey River when one scene had to be re-shot until Gottlieb was satisfied.

Underneath a brash outer shell, Ringo came across as "so interesting, a very nice guy",[30] and she was quite happy when he escorted her both to a St Valentine's dance held during the last week of filming and on a trip to the Mexican Grand Prix. His wooing of her was consummated "when Ringo invited me to his home in Monte Carlo to watch the Monaco Grand Prix. I didn't hesitate [for] a second. It seemed totally natural."[38] On his part, Starr was as besotted and full of jaunty vitality as a middle-aged man could be with a stunning starlet eleven years his junior: "I haven't been this happy in years. I'm ecstatic."[39]

All of this was mortifying for both Nancy Andrews and Barbara's boyfriend, cinematographer Roberto Quezada, who gallantly withdrew. Nancy, however, was not prepared to be so acquiescent. Via the US legal system, Richie would pay. Although his alien status was among pleas for the quashing of her case against him (a kind of updated breach of promise), a precedent had been set by showbusiness attorney Marvin Mitchelson, whose eloquence had won Michelle Triola a sizeable chunk of her ex-lover Lee Marvin's assets and established the right in California for unmarried partners to sue for property division. Securing Mitchelson to speak for her, too, Nancy sought "palimony" of several million dollars' share of communal property and a percentage of Ringo's earnings for her toil on his behalf to the erosion of her own vocational prospects. However, bar the shouting, she was reduced to just a memory in Ringo's mind, as he only had eyes for his new love, now.

Her surname having been shortened from Goldbach when she left her all-girls convent school on Long Island at 16 to become a model,

Barbara's high cheekbones, hazel eyes and avalanche of silver-blonde hair betrayed more of her mingled Austrian, Irish and Romanian ancestry, although she and sister Margerie were raised in Queens, New York's predominantly Jewish suburb. While she "never felt I was a fantastic beauty",[30] she had been in a younger but comparable league to Twiggy, Celia Hammond and Pattie Boyd on the catwalks and before the shutters, after a cover picture in *17* led to assignments in Europe. Through a casual encounter along a Roman via, Barbara was featuring in Italian TV commercials when she was noticed by director Franco Rossi, who gave her a part in a film treatment of Homer's *Odyssey*, despite her amateur standing as an actress.

Although she could have pursued this opening, Barbara had committed herself to Gregorini and subsequently the rearing of Francesca – born in 1969 – and Gianni ("Johnny"), whose emergence four years later had been complicated by the umbilical cord coiling around his neck and briefly but crucially cutting off his oxygen supply. A sufferer from cerebral palsy, Johnny was, nevertheless, fortunate in that his rich father paid for the best therapy that money could buy and a corrective operation in the States.

With the children still babies, Barbara was an active campaigner for reform in staid Italian legislation on abortion and divorce until, with the souring of her relationship with Augusto, she moved to Los Angeles to dip her toe back into movies with pot-boiling parts in minor chillers such as *The Island Of The Fish Men*, *The Humanoid* (as evil Lady Agatha) and a remake of 1945's *The Unseen* (where she met Quezada), as well as professionally humiliating and very American satires like *Mad Magazine Presents "Up The Academy"*, in which "I could have been a stuffed doll".[38]

Despite submitting eventually to a nude photo spread in *Playboy*, "I did not want to be known as a sex symbol. I had different films offered to me where I was to play attractive, sexy people, but I was not interested."[38] Without realising what it would entail, she auditioned for television's *Charlie's Angels*, but was bypassed for looking "too European, too sophisticated. I'm afraid I didn't take them seriously enough when they asked questions like, 'What brought you to Hollywood?' I'd often wondered myself. Somehow, I sensed that the problem was not whether I could act but whether I could be fluffy enough."[38]

In 1977, she compromised between thespian aspiration and natural radiance with the role for which she will be best remembered: Major Anya Amasova in *The Spy Who Loved Me*. This tenth James Bond excursion was a rewriting of an old plot, with Anya – an added character – as Roger Moore's Russian opponent and bedmate. Barbara's reluctant voluptuousness here was vindicated in the following year, when she starred with Edward Fox and Robert Shaw as a severely uniformed Yugoslav resistance fighter in *Force Ten From Navarone*, the sequel of sorts to Alistair Maclean's *Guns Of Navarone*.

At the opposite extreme to this taut espionage drama was *Caveman* and blossoming romance with Ringo Starr, ex-Beatle, who seemed an odd choice to her family, because he was so different from her previous sweethearts. Also, Barbara was not a pop consumer. If pressed, Ray Charles and Aretha Franklin were about her limit. As for Ringo and The Beatles, "I don't think I could have named five of their songs a year ago. I was never really into music, though I am now, up to my ears. I'm surrounded by it, because Richard is making another album."[30] The one-line lyric of a new Starkey composition, 'Can't Fight Lightning', was dedicated to Barbara. On the hitherto-unissued recording, she and Francesca had shaken maracas.

15 "I Knew I'd Had This Problem For Years"

Whereas Paul McCartney was accorded 41 lines in the *Who's Who* social register, Ringo Starr was squeezed between Kay Starr and Steppenwolf in *Whatever Happened To...?*, a publication purporting to be "the great rock and pop nostalgia book".[1] As Paul gave a speech of thanks for another Ivor Novello statuette, 40-year-old Ringo was almost artistically inoperative, as "by 1980 I could not write any more and I was just that personality person. I would be at all the parties with my bow tie on. If you listen to the records, you can hear them going downhill."[2] While *McCartney II* and its 'Coming Up' single were each Number One virtually everywhere, the Lennons were almost ready to return to the fray with a new album, *Double Fantasy*, and a willingness to impart to the weightier journals pearls of beatific precepts and wisdom that they'd accumulated during their five years away.

When prodded whether he had a message for the 1980s, Ringo's reply was as nihilistic as any punk rocker: "Message? I'm not a post office."[3] His Chesham fan club advertised no more in *Record Collector*, but, just as much "Mr Showbusiness" as McCartney, he was the ex-Beatle most likely to host award celebrations, accept plaques on behalf of the group[4] and be amusing on chat shows when prompted to retell one of the old, old stories. "Nobody ever asks about Rory Storm or The Eddie Clayton Skiffle Group," he lamented. "They were good bands, too."[5] Like other 1960s has-beens, he'd also answer perfunctory and unnoted enquiries about whatever current record his interviewer would or wouldn't ever hear. Then everyone would clap and the case would close again on Ringo Starr.

He'd let go, stopped trying to prove himself. Unlike Paul, "I don't want to put a band together and play every night. I just don't want the hassle."[3] Instead, he went on more holidays than the Duchess of York. What was escapism for most was the world in which he lived. When in Paris, no waiter's eyebrows would rise if he ordered sausages and chips to go with a minor Beaujolais in Montparnasse restaurants where only such as Bardot, Dali, Fellini, Warhol, Hemingway and Jackie Kennedy could afford to clatter fork on plate.

Borabora, in the Tahitian archipelago, was so remote a tropical paradise that it could only be reached by boat. Yet, on its beach, his lilo would be adjacent to that of, say, Charlton Heston or Raquel Welch.

In common with the dolphins he might have sighted there, Starr seemed to be devoting his life to the pursuit of pleasure, much of which was derived from staying in the public eye. "Most of the time," he'd pronounced, "I do things because I want to do them, which isn't necessarily right, but I like to have a good time."[6] The 20th anniversary of 'Love Me Do', for example, would be an excuse to drum and sing an ill-advised medley of 'Honey Don't' and 'Blue Suede Shoes' with the house band – and Barbara cavorting in the foreground – on Michael Parkinson's Australian chat show.

It wasn't as if he needed the cash, but he became the first – and only – former Beatle to palm some for endorsing merchandise on television, when he extolled the virtues of a make of leisurewear in a series of seven Japanese commercials. He also appeared in dubbed sketches, composed four short ditties (all entitled 'Simple Life') and – relaxing on a sofa – ruminated generally about Renown T-shirts, slacks, *et al.* Yen had also beckoned aesthete David Bowie into the spheres of Oriental advertisements, but he'd pulled back after just recording a soundtrack to one for a brand of sake (rice wine).

Although not the Sir Henry Irving he may have presupposed himself to be, Bowie had also been more circumspect about his availability for dramatic projects than Starr. A pretext for Ringo's trip to two of his favourite European capitals were his respective

discussions about his next movie with X-certificate writer Harold
Robbins at Amsterdam's Amstrel Hotel and then on to Vienna and
Robert Altham, producer of 1975's Academy Award-winning film
Nashville. As vibrantly purposeless was the noise made about Ringo
playing a "way-out psychiatrist"[7] in an aborted comedy – but,
although films seemed a rosier basis for optimism nowadays, "I do
want to make one rock 'n' roll album a year. Once a rock 'n' roller,
always a rock 'n' roller."[7]

If 1978's *Bad Boy* was classified thus, Ringo was rather behind
schedule when, on 15 September 1980, he spent Thanksgiving with the
Lennons in New York's Plaza and picked John's brains for feasible
numbers for a new LP because "he knows me better than anybody else
in the world, better than the other two, so he really becomes involved
– playing, singing, doing everything he can."[8] For self-designated
Beatle patriarch John, "It was like a brother relationship," May Pang
would recollect sadly. "It's so hard to explain, but it was just that he
had great love for all of them – for George, for Ringo...and for Paul."[9]

As well as tossing his former drummer demos of four new songs
– including 'Life Begins At 40' and 'Nobody Told Me' – and
promising to be there when recording began in January, John
sounded out Ringo about Portrait's efficiency as distributors, as he
was wondering about issuing the one after *Double Fantasy* on his
own label. Starr seemed rather disgruntled with Portrait then. With
Bad Boy a disheartening speculation, the label had insinuated that
he'd be better off with someone else. Furious, too, that CBS had
denied him both adequate funding and use of the company jet for
promotion of the record, Ringo had been hawking his talents around
other labels before coming to roost on Boardwalk – a subsidiary of
Neal Bogart's Casablanca corporation – in the States and RCA for
other territories. His maiden album under the new regime would
bear the title *Stop And Smell The Roses*, having exhausted several
others such as *Stop!*, *Ringostein*, *Can't Fight Lightning* and *Private
Property*. The latter was also the name of the lesser of two
McCartney contributions, as Ringo had fallen back on his "famous-
cast-of-thousands" approach.

Paul had decided to cling onto 'Take It Away', considering that "it would suit me better, the way it went into the chorus. I didn't think it was very Ringo."[10] However, less a Wings cast-off than 'Private Property' and its synthesised brass,[11] 'Attention' was typical of many McCartney creations to which Ringo's first reaction – like mine to Elton John's 'Snookeroo' – had been, "No, not this time. Then I've been in the hotel lift and his song comes out of my mouth as a whistle, and I think, 'Sod him. He writes bloody catchy tunes.'"[12]

'Attention' hinged on a clever-but-simple two-note tiff honked by saxophonist Howie Casey, who, since leading The Seniors, had become a denizen of the London session scene and had been hired by Paul to augment Wings in the studio and on tour. In the Superbear complex in the Nice mountains, Paul also produced 'Can't Fight Lightning' – left off the album in the eleventh hour – and a countrified Starr treatment of Carl Perkins' jogalong 'Sure To Fall', once a McCartney lead vocal with The Quarry Men. He was also loud and clear, now, in the vocal unison sections – with Casey's wife, Linda McCartney and Barbara Bach – and in his backchat with double-tracked Ringo over Lloyd Green's steel-guitar solo.

The album would touch on Western swing, too, in George Harrison's supervision in Paris of a vicariously delightful version of Jo Stafford's 'You Belong To Me'. Expressive of Harrison's own re-creations of childhood preferences on his recent *Somewhere In England* collection, Ringo sang the 1952 million-seller more or less straight. He also made a credible job of George's solemn gambol 'Wrack My Brain', deservedly the LP's only single. Another Harrison piece for *Stop And Smell The Roses* had been 'All Those Years Ago', but Starr couldn't pitch its higher notes. When a hit 45 for George in 1981, it had been re-invented as a requiem to John Lennon, who hadn't been able to manage the subsequently cancelled January sessions after all.

"John who?" her shaving husband in the bathroom had spluttered when Kathy Best had shouted the news from the wireless that creepy December morning on Merseyside. Meanwhile, the drummer that Lennon had rescued from having to get up to go to work was far from the differing greynesses of Liverpool and New York when he was told by Barbara's Francesca. He knew which John had just been slain on the sidewalk outside the Dakota by a former hospital security guard – henceforth referred to by Ringo as "the arsehole"[6] – who was mad about The Beatles in the most clinical sense.

In Maida Vale, it was dawn when Maureen and Cynthia Lennon – who chanced to be sleeping there – were woken by his call from the Bahamas. Next, Richie, as fearful as George and Paul of a copycat shooting, summoned the tightest security net for his and Barbara's immediate flight to New York via Miami to offer condolences to Yoko. The hundreds of air miles across the Atlantic seaboard was the only opportunity for continuous thought, the final sanctuary in which he could catch and hold happier images of the intimate that horror had swallowed so mercilessly.

From the aircraft, the couple were shepherded by five minders to a purring Cadillac. Through its one-way windows, they glanced at chalked headlines on newspaper stands and electronically transmitted images of Lennon on TV sets in electrical goods shops pocking the stop-starting drive from Kennedy Airport to the city centre. Suntanned amidst the cold, they were self-contained spectators with no stake in the tragedy until, with no parking space in the Dakota forecourt, shock impinged itself on them as they hastened past clutching hands (some flapping autograph books), winced at the pitiless *whoomph* of flashbulbs and stepped over the self-same paving stones that had been wet with Lennon's blood. Although he apprehended the massed grief behind that corridor of police barricades, Ringo "was not very happy with the vigil. Those people showed very little respect for either John or Yoko. It was disgusting."[13]

Once inside, the compulsory journey appeared even more foolhardy when the widow insisted at first on speaking to only Ringo. Barbara could wait in another room. Biting back on his anger, Ringo persuaded Yoko gently that, as she and John had been – sorry, still were – one, so it was with him and Barbara now. After defusing what might have developed into an untimely flare-up, Ringo played for a while with Sean, the Lennons' son, bringing a smile to the five-year-old's face before leaving – but, commented one of her friends, "Yoko was not forgiven. Oh, Ringo was nice. He always was nice."[14]

"When we came out," Starr explained later, "I didn't need to hear people telling me how much they loved The Beatles, because I wasn't there to see a Beatle. I was there to see my friend."[15] That it had been a rite by which the "Beatle generation" – if rendered wrinkled, balding and old by the speed of events – was saved by the sacrifice of its leader in his prime was one analogy that may have appalled him, but, while between planes in Miami, he'd perceived some fatuous truth in a youth's comment, "'At least the rumours that you're getting together will stop now.' But, of course, they probably never will. There's already this crap going down about us doing a memorial album for John."[6]

Actually, it was only a single, 'All Those Years Ago', on which Ringo and Wings had backed George, but otherwise the surviving Beatles and fellow travellers – like Tony Sheridan, who hadn't spoken to Lennon since 1964 – behaved much the same as any outsider who kept, at Yoko's request, the worldwide ten-minute silence for John on the Sunday after the shooting. Ringo "just stayed at home and I thought, 'John's dead.' That was probably the best way to pay my respects: by keeping quiet."[15] To this day, he has forbidden himself to record the songs that John had given him at the Plaza and from any media comment far beyond suppositions as uninformative of deeper feelings as any in the rash of "tribute" discs that were being composed while the corpse was still warm. According to Starr, Lennon had transcended to some meritocratic pop heaven "up there with Jimi Hendrix and Elvis and all the rest of them".[15] For years, eyes would stretch when he began interviews by tweely addressing an unseen Lennon, before assuring others present that "he's watching over us, you know".[6]

Whether these performances were designed to be funny or not, dreadfully serious were the fangs of Alsatians tugging at leashes gripped by a squad of sentries on 24-hour surveillance around the Starkey residence in Los Angeles. Like some Mafia don, their employer was edgy when approached by even the mildest of strangers. Visitors would not he admitted, therefore, unless they'd telephoned well beforehand with the precise hour of arrival. "Suddenly I felt I could be a target for the next madman."[16]

Without premeditation, death had already come close at dusk one spring evening in 1980 when Ringo and Barbara were motoring to a Surrey party from the Dorchester. At 60 miles an hour, Ringo swerved to avoid a collision with a lorry on the dual carriageway of a Kingston bypass made slippery by a downpour. After ramming two lamp-posts while riding out a 50-yard somersaulting skid, he ignored a leg injury and pulled his passenger clear before calmly limping back to the upside-down 1973 Mercedes 350 SL for his cigarettes. As he tended to a shaken Barbara, curtains were drawn back in nearby windows and someone dialled for the police and an ambulance. Surrounded by flashing blue lights and rain-coated watchfulness, Ringo comforted Barbara while a grim-faced constable jotted down facts and elected not to charge him. His "We had a crash; it's cool"[17] was the most-quoted remark, after he and Barbara – with her cuts, bruises and hurt back – were rushed to Roehampton Hospital, where they were discharged before the rest of the world woke up.

If made temporarily wary of powerful automobiles, Starr still found the emotional detachment to purchase the same model a month later. By then, a crusher had pummelled the wreck to a cube for plinth display as a Ringo Or Robin-type conversation piece in Tittenhurst Park. Ringo also decreed that splinters of the windscreen be mounted in a heart-shaped broach each for himself and Barbara, whose resolve to stay together had hardened *en route* to the casualty ward.

Their courtship had been assumed to be stormy by those who perused one tabloid hack's scoop of the two's violent quarrel outside Tramp as they clambered into a taxi. As the vehicle sped their fist-shaking ravings off into the neon night, the scribbling newshound saw no reason why the incident could not be portrayed as a common occurrence. Nevertheless, any gleeful hopes of pursuing the couple's turbulent separation were thwarted when, three weeks after the Kingston accident, Barbara announced to her father that she intended to marry the boy.

Originally, they'd planned to plight their troth in Malibu, sending a video of the service to the groom's parents, who, while they could manage the occasional outing to Ascot for his and the grandchildren's birthdays, didn't fancy venturing overseas from Woolton. Possibly, it was John's slaughter in gun-totin' North America that caused Richie's switch of location to Marylebone Registry Office on 27 April 1981. By coincidence, not only had registrar Joseph Jevons officiated at the McCartneys' nuptials in the same town hall but the bride in the ceremony preceding the Starkeys' that windy afternoon was the daughter of former Apple engineer George Peckham, whose own espousal Ringo had attended.

These fascinating snippets – and, indeed, the wedding itself – was less interesting to *The Daily Express* than "The Reunion"[20] that it splashed across its front page the next day. The photograph that Terry O'Neill had flown from New York to take was later syndicated throughout the globe for a tidy sum. The three surviving Beatles were shown together in public for the first time since John's passing. The second set of faces that drew the viewer were those of their American wives, especially the new Mrs Starkey, who, mixing metaphors, "had always believed in Prince Charming if ever he came riding up on his charger".[18]

In her joy, she was as flushed as the roses that decorated her plunging ivory silk wedding dress. Designed by David and Elizabeth Emanuel, who'd likewise served the Princess of Wales, Barbara's get-up clashed with that of Ringo, all black with Teddy Boy bootlace tie and sunglasses unnecessary beneath the leaden skies outside, where his and Paul's exits to non-descript taxis were hailed by screams from an 800-strong crush of fans, who'd divined what was going on. More averse than his former colleagues to adulation, George – with Olivia Harrison – contrived to shuffle out almost unnoticed.

At the wedding party for the first Mrs Harrison and Eric Clapton in 1979, George, Ringo and Paul had pitched in with an *ad hoc* combo – that embraced various Rolling Stones, Denny Laine, the reunited Cream and Jeff Beck – on a makeshift stage to hammer out mostly classic rock and the peppier *Sgt Pepper* songs. While queueing for a go on the drums with Ginger Baker, Jim Capaldi, classical-turned-pop percussionist Ray Cooper and Zak of The Next, Starr was struck with the notion of doing "one like that again with just the four of us [Beatles], once Sean is five and John starts playing again, [because] it didn't seem strange at all. We were having a booze-up and a laugh. It felt pretty good to me."[19]

Of course, a few twitches of a trigger had put paid to that; but, at the Starkeys' wedding reception at Rags, a Mayfair club, a car-rental firm had deposited amplifiers, two guitars and a bass should any among those present feel an urge to entertain in what was described by Roger Shine – one of the witnesses on the certificate – as "a knees-up Mother Brown and lots of dancing, with people playing spoons and overturned champagne buckets".[20] Although Ray Cooper rattled the cutlery, others stuck to conventional instruments, with Nilsson and McCartney taking turns at the piano while Harrison and Starr plucked guitars. The strains of 'Strawberry Fields Forever' were, allegedly, heard as a homage to poor John. Other than the five-pointed, solid-silver star given as a keepsake to each of the 70 guests, it was a very down-home affair, with a high percentage of relations and old chums from Liverpool, a wedding cake – star-shaped, naturally – and, with 20-odd youngsters up past their bedtimes, all over by midnight. The happy couple had left already in a white Rolls for a decoy honeymoon "in California". Actually, it was spent in London, the last place any prying reporter would expect to find them.

For the 161 days per annum that the Department of Immigration permitted Ringo to reside in the States, the family could make itself comfortable in a rented mock-Georgian dwelling in Beverly Hills with obligatory swimming pool and orange grove. Although the refinement of the owner's Picassos was mitigated by Starkey touches, such as the strands of twinkling Christmas lights around the front door in April, the USA was less than a second home, now, as Ringo's first "American period" had terminated effectively with Lennon's murder. For several years, there'd be but flying visits on business, for TV promotions and social duties such as a pal's New York wedding in May 1962. With an attempt on President Reagan's life by another "arsehole" that year, "What chance do other people have? I always loved living in England."[21]

He would regain little lost native popularity and he'd miss the Californian sunshine, but the weeks arranging the wedding had made him understand how homesick he'd become during his six years of globe-trotting. Back at Tittenhurst Park, he could develop tolerance towards the local council's officiousness in refusing him permission to modernise "antiquated"[21] Startling Studios with video facilities. They also turned down his cheeky application for a grant of a few hundred quid to improve the riding stables, now that, with Barbara's enthusiasm for equestrianism, he was over his antipathy to horses, galloping his acres on "Dolly Parton", a beast more his size than the *Blindman* stallion.

Spoken of as if an old nag out to grass himself, the fellow was never seen to do a stroke of work. As in the "happy ending" of a Victorian novel, with all the villains bested and the inheritance claimed, he'd settled down to a prosperous lassitude where nothing much was calculated to happen, year in, year out. Beneath an untroubled sky, "Squire" Richard and his lady would stroll around the grounds with their dogs – a labrador, a spaniel and an alsatian – and children, of which they'd decided enough was enough. For balance, there was the occasional hiccough, such as the eye that bled when the alsatian bowled him over. It was serious enough for Ringo's transference from Heatherwood Hospital, on Ascot's main roundabout, to the optical unit at King Edward VII's in Windsor, but in his usual shades he was able to keep a tea engagement later that afternoon, where the day's misfortune provided something to chat about.

Too arcane a subject in some southern parlours were tidings specific to Merseyside. However, like several other British cities, the festering unrest in its most depressed districts had exploded during 1981's humid July. From Toxteth and the Dingle, the reek of burning had seeped as far as central Liverpool, where, for two nights, shops were looted with supermarket trolleys and torched with petrol bombs. Alarm bells and sirens executed a discordant threnody as the

Rialto Ballroom – where all the groups used to play – crumbled in a haze of smoke and powdered plaster.

Ringo had remained *au fait* with south Lancashire affairs through his study of the *Liverpool Echo* and other local journals that were mailed to him at Tittenhurst Park. Although he thought it "good that students are actually into the music that much, rather than the Great War",[23] he wouldn't go as far as Paul in patronising the University's Institute of Popular Music, although he would be – along with Virgin magnate Richard Branson – in a consortium bidding for the cable television music franchise in Merseyside.

In its battle against recession, the area had fallen back on its potential for sight-seers through its then-near-invincible football team – and its cradling of The Beatles. As well as twice-daily guided tours to such golgothas as Admiral Grove and conferring Beatle-connotated nomenclatures on the shops and watering holes newly operational around redeveloped Mathew Street, Liverpool further stressed its pride in the group by naming four streets on a Wimpey Homes estate[24] of raw red brick after each of them – Ringo Starr Drive, Paul McCartney Way and so forth – despite one sniffy councillor's earlier objections that, in the light of Allan Williams' published memoirs[25] of "what went on in Hamburg and their use of filthy language", "The Beatles should in no way be linked with the civic name of Liverpool."[26]

Although it dominated national news bulletins for a day, there wouldn't even be a "Billy Fury Mews" when – like he knew it would – a heart attack finished Ringo's fleeting classmate in 1983. As he might have wished, Fury passed away with a single in the Top 50, although unable either to begin his comeback tour of Britain or complete *The Only One*, his farewell album. His fans' sorrow was either exorcised or exacerbated by a special edition of *Unforgettable*, a Channel 4 nostalgia romp, on which he was seen running through his best-loved songs for the people who loved them – and him – most of all.

Unlike Fury, Cilla Black had no need to dwell on past glories. Genial hostess of ITV's *Surprise! Surprise!* and, next, *Blind Date*, her shrill giggle would also infiltrate 1980s situation comedy. The highest-paid woman on television, her generation's Tessie O'Shea, a defiant wearer of genuine fur coats and now an evangelical Tory, she said that she planned to retire at 50 to her Buckinghamshire manor.

Pete Best had no such expectations, but he was employed gainfully during one break from the Job Centre in publicising *The Complete Silver Beatles*, a 1982 release of the group's Decca test 20 years earlier. This had been purchasable for years as a bootleg, which, defying all copyright laws, was a commodity abhorrent to Ringo – although John had built up quite a collection.

Perhaps Pete's maligned sense of humour was more acute than Ringo, John, Paul and George had realised, as, during this jaunt, he autographed one of Ringo's gold discs that was up for auction at a Los Angeles Beatles convention. On similar occasions, both the Starkey and Harrison family's Liverpool lavatories were displayed and sold as solemnly as Duchamp ready-mades. Like a splinter from the True Cross, one of Ringo's ties fetched the highest bid at a Methodist fête in Wolverhampton.

Money matters of greater portent were on the agenda whenever the living ex-Beatles and Mrs Lennon met to discuss the dividing of the empire and, later, long-running litigation against EMI/Capitol over royalties. At one such council in Starr's usual roof-garden suite at the Dorchester, one of Yoko's gofers observed that "nothing was accomplished",[14] but, when she wasn't around, the three who'd travelled a longer road with John loosened up with selective reminiscences about the struggle back in Liverpool and Hamburg, when the Earth was young.

Time would never heal totally, and there'd always be traces of sibling rivalry, but none of them were feigning indifference about the other two's activities any more. Liverpool City Council would have to wait forever "for sentiment to work the oracle [*sic*] that showbiz millionaire entrepreneurs have tried in vain", as they refused to reform without Lennon "in an effort to launch Merseyside as a major tourist centre".[26] That would be up to others. Nonetheless, the outlines between Paul, George and Ringo's recording endeavours had merged a little more since the jolt of 'All Those Years Ago'. McCartney was also back in the harness with George Martin, and it was at the latter's newish Air Studios on the Caribbean isle of Montserrat that Ringo – with Barbara – had eluded a few days of an English winter on a working holiday, at Paul's behest, to drum in tandem with *Ringo The Fourth* veteran Steve Gadd on 'Take It Away', which, ratifying McCartney's earlier judgement, would be the hit spin-off from the follow-up to *McCartney II*, *Tug Of War*.

After a companionable French holiday with the McCartney brood, the Starkeys were there in fancy dress for the rock 'n' roll dance championship during one of the annual "Buddy Holly Weeks" that had taken place since Paul's acquisition of the bespectacled Texan's publishing rights. For the laugh, too, Barbara, Ringo and Zak turned up at a complex in northwest London to be in the 'Take It Away' video before an invited audience, who were thrilled with the post-shoot jam session, which included requests for ancient Cavern standbys like 'Searchin'' and 'Lucille'.

The video's director, John Mackenzie, was also the grey eminence behind *The Long Good Friday*, a gangster flick whose greyer eminence was George Harrison, executive producer of HandMade Films. As with Alfred Hitchcock, the sharp-eyed might espy George playing bit parts in these. With Ringo behind the kit, for instance, George was one of The Singing Rebels band during a concert sequence in *Water*, starring his Thames Valley neighbour Michael Caine.

If he was only too pleased to assist Harrison and McCartney, who could blame Starr – once the most engaging and arguably, if briefly, commercially viable ex-Beatle – for eating his heart out with Paul still an international chart assailant and George – with music of less prevalent significance – a paladin of British cinema? With no such negotiable strings to his bow, what was Ringo nowadays?

His wilderness years were by no means over, but *Stop And Smell The Roses* had sidled to the outskirts of the US Hot 100 on the back of 'Wrack My Brain' – his first Top-40 entry since 1976 – and the associated aftershock of Lennon, who was presumably one of the "three brothers" thanked by Ringo on the album jacket. He needed every marketing device he could procure, what with the chaotic effect on Boardwalk of the death of Bogart – Starr's principal champion on its board – and one influential journal voting *Stop And Smell The Roses* the "worst record of 1981".[26]

With pioneering essays in the brutish *braggadocio* of rap behind counters in that year, Ringo's album wasn't truly as awful as all that, but, as *The Toronto Star* pointed out, "There's lots of sludge, stuff no one except, perhaps, an ex-Beatle could get away with."[27] The weirdest outpouring of all was when – like the late Gene Vincent, The Hollies, The Nashville Teens, The Dave Clark Five's Mike Smith and other shameless stars *in extremis* – he revamped one of his old hits. There'd been no half measures with 'Back Off Boogaloo', either. As producer Nilsson had with 'You Can't Do That' in 1968, Starr squeezed in vignettes of Beatles numbers, as well as the circular riff of 'It Don't Come Easy'.

Quotes from hits by Rod Stewart, Otis Redding and David Bowie[28] broke up the monotony of Nilsson's song for Ringo, 'Drumming Is My Madness',[29] which would not have been out of place on *Both Sides Of The Moon* in the ambulant, blaring broadness of the instrumentation behind its nonchalant, slightly camp vocal that also pervaded Nilsson and Starr's 'Stop And Take The Time To Smell The Roses', with Ringo's burlesque spoken passages.

'Brandy' and 'Waking Up' were two duller Starr-Nilsson items that suffered the same fate as 'Can't Fight Lightning'. Not even taped by Ringo was 'How Long Can Disco On?', the only other known handiwork of this half-serious collaboration. A weedy joke underpinned with downbeat reggae, it had already fed 1980's *Flash Harry*, on which Nilsson had taken a leaf from Ringo's book by mobilising illustrious contemporaries, among them Lennon, Little Feat's Lowell George and lyricist Van Dyke Parks, who was also called upon to arrange 'Back Off Boogaloo '81'.

A side-effect of Ringo's pattering tom-toms on 'Heart Of Mine', for Bob Dylan's *Shot Of Love* album, was a concurrence with another present, latter-day Rolling Stone, guitarist Ron Wood.[30] From their tinkerings between takes came 'Dead Giveaway', which lifted the ear only with Wood's over-dubbed saxophones and Eddie Cochran-ish bass twang. More sweat had been invested by Steve Stills – the last of five *Stop And Smell The Roses* producers – and co-writer Mike Stergis into gentle 'Nice Way', which, other than Starr's singing, might have been a Crosby, Stills And Nash out-take.

Apart from a short article about Ringo's return to recording in the *NME*, his patchy album was all but ignored in a Britain where Adam Ant was 'Prince Charming', if not king. Not reaching a particularly wide audience, either, were its promotional films, *Wrack My Brain* and *The Cooler*, a musical psycho-drama that was screened in the Short Subject category of 1982's Cannes Festival. As it was underwritten by his MPL Communications, it was to be expected that McCartney's three *Stop And Smell The Roses* concerns would be at its heart. Beginning to fill for Starr the void left by John, Paul himself appeared in various guises throughout the clip, which – borrowing a little from an episode in BBC2's Monty Python offshoot comedy *Ripping Yarns* – had Ringo as an inmate in a prison camp guarded entirely by women (one of them Linda McCartney). His perpetual machinations to escape – punished by spells in the said "cooler" – are tempered by deteriorating sanity and resultant ambivalent feelings towards the commandant, played – as was proper – by Barbara.

Despite the polish of Godley and Creme, then the apex of pop video direction, *The Cooler* "wasn't suitable" to Walter Shenson at Universal, who passed on the most tenable scheme for its general distribution – a pairing with his *A Hard Day's Night*. He considered the film to be "too depressing and surrealistic. We want to preserve the innocence of *A Hard Day's Night* as much as Paul."[31] That it starred Ringo mattered less than the much more bankable McCartney being "only seen in it briefly".[31]

Wrack My Brain was shown and the LP plugged on some of the US television spots – *Good Morning America*, *The Johnny Carson Show*, *et al* – that Starr's handlers had been able to negotiate in spite of his "taking less and less interest in recording or promoting them".[32] Nevertheless, on a parallel channel, Pete Best with *The*

Complete Silver Beatles in *Whatever Became Of...* put up a more sedate if less morbidly breath-taking dispatch than Ringo, who was the worse for liquor on *The John Davidson Show*. Prior to similar routine interviews, he'd often knocked back more than he should have, but had always got a grip on himself. He'd never been as far gone as he was then, when "those nights when you drink more than you remembered had become almost every night".[32]

His entourage watched him anxiously if indulgently from the wings, but to the coolly professional studio cameraman it was fantastic television as the fuddled subject with the pale, puffy complexion repeated his perplexed and then outraged host's questions as well as his own answers and fiddled around with a Polaroid on his lap. Starr's usual mannerisms were exaggerated as he raised his voice almost to a shout and then dropped it to near inaudibility. It was necessary to splice together two segments of the pre-recorded programme as Davidson stormed off and, recalled a contrite Ringo, "They had to convince him to come back – but I was in the dressing room, having a few more cognacs."[23]

Footballer *manqué* George Best would likewise make a clown of himself before millions. Less publicised, however, was PJ Proby who, incoherently outstaying his welcome on an early evening magazine programme on UK provincial television, had staggered from the Plymouth studio to busk on a carelessly strummed guitar in the foyer of the nearby Drake Cinema. Similarly chewed upon and spat out by the Swinging '60s, the likes of Tommy Quickly, Wayne Fontana, Keith Richards and The Bonzo Dog Band's Viv Stanshall were bobbing like corks on seas as shoreless. Heroin, tranquillisers, scotch, beer – whatever the drug of choice, it was but a temporary analgesic, an alleviation of the pangs of despair.

To Tony Barrow, Starr's addiction – once a private matter – had intensified because he felt himself to be "a second-class Beatle".[33] Whatever the cause, he confessed, "I knew I'd had this problem for years,"[34] and, although not a Latin scholar, Ringo ineffectually, started practising Seneca's maxim *pars sanitatis velle sanari fruit*[35] by replacing spirits – even his customary afternoon Remy Martin brandy – with the less toxic wine. With no ill effects, this had accompanied lunch and dinner for Barbara when in Italy, where she "didn't drink to get drunk".[21] However, by emptying 16 bottles a day, her second husband would be resigned to a self-imposed house arrest, as going anywhere else "meant I'd have to be in the car for 40 minutes without being able to have a single drink".[21] Barbara held no steadying sway over him as she "fell into the trap because of me. She used to go to bed at ten at night and get up at eight in the morning until we met. Then her career went the same as mine."[34]

A part in *Dallas* was dangled in front of him, but, while he had no objection to being in a TV soap opera almost beyond parody, he'd wait until 1983, when a US mini-series of Judith Krantz's novel *Princess Daisy* had him and Barbara as a jet-setting couple denying themselves no expensive whim. It didn't require much acting, although Ringo – ever the professional – had to force himself to eat caviar in one scene, washing out his mouth between each take.

Since *Princess Daisy*, Barbara has been seen but rarely on either the small or silver screen, as "no work has been offered to me that is worth two to three months' separation from my family".[27] Nevertheless, over a drink – and another and another – in an Ascot pub, a chat with Harry Nilsson led an eavesdropper to spread the spurious tale that he and the Starkeys were to finance a movie entitled *Road To Australia* with a screenplay by Norman Panama, who'd written the Bing Crosby/Bob Hope/Dorothy Lamour *Road* comedy films in the 40s. Ringo would be Hope, with Barbara providing romantic interest in the Lamour role.

She'd tell you, "We've always thought of work as an extension of marriage,"[17] but as the 1980s slipped into gear theirs had degenerated into an open state of warfare. It was simpler for her to go with him than go against him, but the mean slanging-match outside Tramp wasn't an isolated occurrence after all, as threats and quarrels frothed and fumed. Next came shabby paragraphs in gossip columns stating that the Starr fairytale had gone wrong. There were more subjective worries, too, that one or other of them would attempt suicide out of spiteful bravado. At home, Richard and

Barbara would "sit around for hours and talk about what we were going to do – and, of course, I'd get so bleeding drunk I couldn't move. The result was nothing happened."[34]

Ringo made no long-term plans. How could he? All the same, only new diversions would save his marriage, and possibly his life, so he cast about vainly to find some; but, from Nilsson to Elizabeth Taylor – pictured portly and plastered on the cover of Kenneth Anger's *Hollywood Babylon* exposé[36] – Ringo kept the company of only those united by a taste for liquor. "If you were straight, I wouldn't have you in my house. And, in the end, I couldn't even get a record deal. I wasn't hungry any more."[3]

16 "Please, God, I Have To Stop Living This Way"

With a New Year's Eve engagement at the Fulham Greyhound the ceiling of its ambition, The Next had thrown in the towel by 1981. From its ashes arose Monopacific. Zak Starkey would protest, "I'm every bit as hard up as the rest of the band."[1] Poor lad, his moneybags of a father had given him only a hi-hat cymbal for Christmas. When Startling Studios were booked, Monopacific battled with their equipment in a disused lodge on Tittenhurst estate, but whenever Zak was staying with his mother – who'd given him a jumper – "I have to get a train from the station"[1] the same as everybody else.

It was a tough old life but, unlike Julian Lennon and other acquaintances he could – and did – mention, Zak preferred the quainter hostelries of Ascot among old friends, because "even if I get successful, I don't want to live like my old man. I'm not into all that. I want to be respected for my drumming with the rest of the guys than earn a million pounds."[1]

The ease with which nightclubbing Julian secured a recording contract was a howling example of a surname opening doors, and Zak deserves respect for his musicianly self-image for attempting to actively earn a living and for not kowtowing to those music industry bigwigs who "talk to me just because of who my dad is".[1] Nevertheless, it was through his connections with Keith Moon – whose picture adorned the wall of the Tittenhurst lodge – that Monopacific acquired a manager in the late outrager's personal assistant, Peter Butler, and the attention of The Who's John Entwistle, Roger Daltrey and Pete Townshend, the latter of whom considered young Starkey's to be "the most accurate emulation of Keith's style",[1] qualifying this with, "Luckily, Zak also has a style of his own, but many have been moved when listening to his explosive solos to say, 'My God! It's him!'"[1] Obviously, Zak's shadowing of Moon hadn't been wasted, for at the few venues Monopacific played before going the way of The Next his performance – if gratuitously busy – still maintained a precise backbeat, as his sire would have expected.

While assisting on Ringo's new LP, *Old Wave*, at Startling Studios, Entwistle found time to produce Zak's next ensemble, Nightfly, who, smiled Starkey Snr, were "heavy and hard, but I'm not allowed to call it 'heavy metal'".[2] It was a step up, professionally, in that Zak was now hitting in time for battle-hardened ex-members of Bad Company, Status Quo and Whitesnake. Largely through Entwistle, he was employed for what he did rather than what he was on many lucrative sessions, notably for Denny Laine's *Lonely Road* and – its title track a nod to Zak's mentor – Daltrey's *Under A Raging Moon*. In conjunction with ageing keyboard *wunderkind* Eddie Hardin – who, in 1967, replaced Steve Winwood in The Spencer Davis Group[3] – Zak recorded his debut album, their *Musical Version Of Wind In The Willows*. For all Zak's desires to be accepted on his own merits, pragmatism ruled, and he'd acceded to his father's trick of giving the record more than an even break by garnering a shoal of whatever well-known names could be trawled to sing on it, with Donovan, Entwistle and Joe Fagin[4] being the biggest that could be legitimately printed on the sleeve. There were mutterings about staging this work in a London theatre in 1986, but the album's sales had been too discouraging.

To his exasperation, Zak's music made less of a splash than press muckraking about his relationship with Ringo, in which, essentially, he reacted as most temperamental adolescents – especially eldest sons – might, under the circumstances. Allowing himself one grand gesture of defiance against a nosy world, he kept his registry-office hitching to Sarah Menikides on 22 January 1985 a secret to even his parents – even though, in all conscience, neither disapproved of either Sarah, their cohabitation or of young marriage. Once over his deceived surprise, Ringo characteristically wished them all the best by throwing a small celebratory party for family and friends at Tittenhurst Park.

He'd do the same when Zak came of old-fashioned age – 21, not 18. By then, Starr had become the first Beatle grandfather, as Sarah, after an induced labour, had given birth to seven-pound Tatia Jayne that same September a week year earlier in a private ward at Heatherwood, near enough for twice-daily visits by one whom the baby would be taught to call "Grandad", a diminutive that had been good enough for his own immediate forebears. Zak would prove equal to his new responsibility, as would an elated Ringo to his less stressful one, whereby "you can have all the pleasures, give all the chocolates, then go home when the baby gets sick".[5]

"Grandma" Maureen's rapture was compounded by her imminent wedlock to another affluent man with a beard. Taller and much younger than her first husband, Isaac Tigrett had made his loot via the founding of the worldwide Hard Rock Cafe chain, which he sold in 1988 for an eight-figure amount. While Starr was pleased for Maureen – and himself, because he'd no longer be liable for alimony – there had been a *soupçon* of recent discord. Tigrett had bought one of Starr's drums to put on display with other pop artefacts in his New York branch after it had found its way to an auction. However, since the Haslem Terrace fire, Ringo's fevered replenishing of Beatle memorabilia led to a telephoned plea to Maureen to restore the drum to his possession. He'd love to have it back. Upset by her disinclination to pull strings on his behalf, he straightaway got onto Harry Nilsson, then in the Big Apple, to go around to the diner and, if need be, prise the desired object from its hanger. His bosom buddy was so fraught that Nilsson set off on the (ultimately failed) mission immediately.

When Maureen and Ringo spoke next, he seemed resigned to – even amused by – her intransigence over the drum, as their atrophied affinity continued to mellow into a remote cordiality epitomised by his congratulations when she presented Isaac with a daughter – Augusta – in 1988. With the Tigretts abiding mostly in Dallas nowadays, and with Barbara's children spending part of their time with Gregorini, the offspring of the extended family were never in the same place at the same time; Richie and Barbara's children, for example, didn't meet until just before the wedding. Nevertheless, at Tittenhurst Park, all subdivisions of kindred dwelt in harmony, accepting that there were perks to domestic complexities. However, Zak's emotions might have been mixed at Ringo's obliging and solicitous pointers when Johnny – charmed by the sound of his big stepbrother's thrashings – wanted to play the drums too. Perhaps Ringo had already gauged that Johnny had no aptitude for rhythm, and that his enthusiasm would falter when he became taken with another boyhood craze. As it turned out, Johnny would follow his natural father's footsteps, after graduating from a US university with a degree in Business Studies.

The most wayward adolescence was endured by Jason, who rounded it off by falling foul of the law for possessing cannabis. If Ringo dared lecture his second son on any aspect of this misdemeanour, apart from the stupidity of getting caught, he had as brittle a leg to stand on as he had when Zak shacked up with Sarah. His boozing was getting out of control, and the only ace up his sleeve was his narration for US radio of a heroin caution for "today's kids" which, to synthesised accompaniment in waltz time, excused his past psychedelic escapades with "but that was then" and invoked 'Yellow Submarine', 'Blue Meanies' ("more of them than ever before") and Lennon, who'd known the drug well. His views on the subject were further clarified when he gave John Cleese, Bill Oddie and Michael Palin – radical balusters of British comedy – percussive assistance and the run of his home studio to produce the satirical 'Naughty Atom Bomb' for the *It's A Live-In World* LP, which – with such as Paul McCartney, Paul's cousin Kate Robbins, The Thompson Twins and Zak lending a hand, too – would benefit London's Phoenix House drug rehabilitation centre.

From the starting line of The Concerts For Bangladesh, pop by the

1980s pop had cranked into top gear while hurtling along the road to respectability and, after Live Aid gained The Boomtown Rats' Bob Geldof a knighthood, Ringo – who'd received an MBE for less – was seen, like everyone else of late, to be involved in quite a few good causes. These ranged from passive attendance with Olivia Harrison and Barbara at a Fashion Aid event (associated with live Aid) at the Albert Hall to tagging onto a queue[6] of the famous – plus those who'd like to be and some who were no longer – at London's Sarm Studio, where he sang – without the affectation of many of the others – one line over a craftily sampled backing collage of jungle noises in one of the more scintillating charity singles of the 1980s, 'Spirit Of The Rain Forest', proceeds of which went towards protecting same. Both Ringo and Zak would demonstrate solidarity on the matter of racism by taping at Ascot an unobtrusive contribution to the post-Live Aid *Sun City*, a recording project that would aid anti-apartheid movements in South Africa and the Americas.

The recording was masterminded by guitarist Steve Van Zandt, who used to back New Jersey's Bruce Springsteen, whose bit in 'Sun City' was more pronounced than Starr's. Bruce was renowned for his Yogi Bear vibrato and an energetic stage act – that Ringo proclaimed "unbelievable"[7] – sharing similarities of style with Nils Lofgren, another of the ex-Beatle's East Coast songwriting acquaintances.[8] Lofgren's best-known opus was 'Shine Silently', co-written with Alice Cooper's guitarist Dick Wagner and covered – with a riveting *a cappella* introit – by The Hollies.

Lofgren's friend Springsteen was abetted by his E-Street Band, whose animated saxophonist, Clarence Clemons, had once been in James Brown's more disciplined Famous Flames and was also in the horn section for the 'Sun City' bash. However, he was not introduced to Ringo (by Springsteen's drummer Max Weinberg) until later. This cordial encounter – like Starr's with Lofgren – was to have a more than incidental bearing on the future professional activities of all three, not least of which would be Starr's singing on 'Bein' Angry' – a track from Nils' 1989 *Silver Lining* album – and appearing with Springsteen and Clemons in a later Lofgren video.

Another of Ringo's more philanthropic cameos had already produced a remunerative side-effect – or so it seemed when it began. Bill Wyman had been among those persuaded by multiple sclerosis sufferer and ex-Small Face Ronnie Lane to make up a supergroup at a London gala in aid of ARMS (Action for Multiple Sclerosis). Shouldering much of Lane's load, Wyman organised further ARMS concerts, which spawned a more fixed set-up, with guest players around a nucleus of Wyman, Charlie Watts and singing guitarist Andy Fairweather-Low concentrating on olde-tyme rock 'n' roll as Willie And The Poor Boys. In a half-hour-long video of the same title focused on a show at Fulham Town Hall, Starr was brought in to sweep up afterwards as a janitor-cum-middle-aged Teddy Boy

Bill was, as much as Charlie, Ringo's opposite number in The Rolling Stones, and it was these two who cemented a Beatle-Stone business liaison when American architect and property speculator John Portman and London hotelier Alan Lubin were scouting around for financial support to open a posh restaurant in the Peachtree Center, an Atlanta commercial development. Through his brother Len, Lubin cultivated an association with Starr, who was counted in, and – like Wyman – put forward his own eminence for the partnership's use.

So it was that he and Bill boarded a chartered flight from Heathrow to Atlanta with a prattle of Radio 1 disc jockeys and competition winners for the official opening of "the Brasserie" on 5 October 1986. Although doomed to closure within two years, the place got off to a flying start, with the bulk of US media folk homing in on Ringo, who required police protection. Bill's was a relatively calm corner of the proceedings, despite the Stones being between world tours, as well as his semi-public intrigue with an under-age girl. This publicity binge concluded with a self-conscious and oddly matched jam session, with the Englishmen presiding over front-line rollicking by Jerry Lee Lewis, Stax soulman Isaac Hayes and Jermaine Jackson, whose more acclaimed brother Michael had sung with Paul McCartney on two hit singles.

Concrete proof that Wyman's appetite for feeding his peers was not dampened by the failure of the Brasserie was his Kensington eaterie "Sticky Fingers" – after a Stones album – which, so some bored journalists made out, was in direct competition with Lennon's, which served dishes like "Penny Lane pâté" and "Rubber Sole and chips" over in Covent Garden, next to Stringfellows. Joining owner Cynthia and her son Julian for a meal, a chat and a comparison of catering procedures one evening were Maureen Tigrett and her daughter, Lee. Maureen and Cynthia's younger selves would have just about recognised the well-dressed divorcees nibbling at Lennon's.

No matter how far their wanderings had taken them, all Merseysiders looked homeward when hearing of the Hillsborough disaster, in which 95 ordinary people were crushed to death in a swollen stadium during a Liverpool soccer team away match in 1988. On the following Saturday, the entire city observed a two-minute silence for their lost neighbours. Nowhere was it more absolute than in the Anfield ground, where tears ran down the cheeks of elderly supporters. For some, Gerry And The Pacemakers' 'You'll Never Walk Alone' – the Kop Choir anthem – was the only pop record they'd ever bought. Three years earlier, Gerry had led The Crowd – another all-star aggregation that included Zak Starkey – to Number One with a cash-raising remake of this plaintive showstopper for victims of the *Herald Of Free Enterprise* shipwreck.

With Paul McCartney and members of Frankie Goes To Hollywood, The Christians and other newer Scouse bands among those joining him, Marsden was back on top following Hillsborough when his 'Ferry 'Cross The Mersey' was likewise used in aid of a Liverpool FC relief fund, which had been already buoyed with a vast whip-round from local factories. Ringo also dipped into his purse and, with Cilla Black, recorded a comforting message on *The Sun*'s prompt emergency hotline "to help those families try to rebuild their lives".

It was Cilla who tipped off a "very angry"[9] Ringo when their names – and photographic images – were taken in vain in an ingenious advertising campaign by Security Omega Express, the crux of which was the correlation between success and Richard Starkey, Priscilla White, Harry Webb and other entertainers' rechristenings.

"He personally and The Beatles," gritted a Starr aide, "are always getting ripped off."[9] Who knew, for instance, where income generated from Beatle records issued lately in the Soviet Union went? How about Ringo's blue suede shoes appreciating by several thousand per cent, or his 1966 Mini Cooper – including its Richard Starkey log book – fetching a fortune for some Londoner 20 years later? A five-carat diamond ring stolen from Starr in Paris changed hands several times at an increasingly inflated price before finding its way back to its rightful owner when gendarmerie swooped on a shop in the city's St Quen district.

Sometimes it appeared that the ex-Beatles were being cheated by each other, too, during the perpetual unscrambling of Apple lucre. This was demonstrated by Starr, Harrison and Mrs Lennon's lawsuit against McCartney over a deal whereby the last six albums he'd delivered to Capitol had rewarded him with what was interpreted as an increased royalty increment for Beatles output.

While he couldn't be reproached for more personal animosity towards McCartney, Pete Best had now found it in him to "harbour no bitterness over what happened". Via the same Sotheby's sale that flogged off a pair of Starr's drumsticks, he'd disencumbered himself of much accumulated booty from his Beatle days, but "I'm keeping my drums and the clothes we wore when we first started out and the gifts we gave each other, like bracelets and little trinkets, because they still have a very great sentimental value." With brother Roag supplementing his drumming, the forgiving Pete would dust off his kit and, with an eponymous group, play a set – which would even embrace a Beatles B-side – in a John Lennon Memorial Concert at Liverpool Philharmonic with other Mersey Beat musicians belying their daytime occupations as pen-pushers, charge-hands and captains of industry.

Neither Best's combo, The Undertakers, Earl Preston and his TTs nor any other of the old hands up there on that night of nights would be invited to perform at a televised and international tribute from Liverpool's Pier Head, sanctioned and partly compered by Yoko, who, since her husband's slaying, had not retreated from public life.

George Harrison would have nothing to do with her Liverpool extravaganza, but while they declined to show up in person Ringo and Paul each sent a filmed piece, with Ringo's "Hi Liverpool!" and supergroup rendering of 'I Call Your Name' – a minor Beatles track from 1964 – bridging a gap between Philadelphian duo Hall And Oates and Welsh guitarist Dave Edmunds' John Lennon Tribute Band.

After his own manner, Starr had tampered with The Beatles legend as much as Yoko when, in 1983, the man who'd shied away from *Stardust* because it was too near the knuckle had been inveigled into a 26-part series entitled *Ringo's Yellow Submarine: A Voyage Through Beatles Magic* by a US radio syndication network whose vice president, Willard Lochridge, had crowed of him being "the DJ, working intimately with ABC on the content and presentation".[10] As disappointing to fans as Ringo's undignified decision to participate, his pre-recorded and scripted commentaries – plus a culminant live phone-in from Tittenhurst Park – were peppered unthinkingly with tiny factual errors[11] as he endorsed the group's function as a commodity that could be recycled indefinitely.

Perhaps I've misread his motives. His surrender of no fresh anecdotes or weighing of experience might have been quite deliberate. Maybe they'll be revealed if he authorises a biography or, more unlikely, writes one himself. Certainly, the *Beatle Magic* nonsense was no bone to be picked, any more than the resolved Capitol wrangles with Paul whenever the three survivors of one of the most singular human experiences of that Coca Cola century met – as they did more frequently than ever, these days – for hotel-bar or dinner-table evenings that bred coded hilarity, matey abuse and retrospection about days gone by. "Sure, we keep in touch," confirmed Ringo. "With Paul, it's a good month and then a bad month, just like a family. I see George more often, because we live closer to each other."[12]

As George and Ringo were each sorrowfully aware, it was no longer so easy for new albums by old heroes to be passed without comment by record-label quality controllers. Neither ex-Beatle was sufficiently "current" in either output or "attitude", with Ringo expressing doubts about the advent of compact discs, which were "a bit too clean for me. I'm from the old school. I like a bit of dirt on the record."[13] His favourite modern group were New York's archaic but exhilarating Cramps, who specialised in psychobilly – a collision of rockabilly and psychedelia – and were as dirty as they come.

George had employed a drum machine to toughen his 1982 album *Gone Troppo*, but at heart he too was "from the old school", so much so that, sickened, he told the whole fair-weather music business to get knotted by announcing – wrongly, as it happened – that *Gone Troppo* was to be his vinyl farewell. In that year, Starr – with *Old Wave* mastered – was in no position to make such unrepining calculations.

However, prior to Ringo's leaving, the label's A&R department had harkened to Joe Walsh's hunch that Ringo still had "a good rock 'n' roll album in him".[14] Brought in to draw it out of him, Walsh "beefed up"[14] *Old Wave* by spicing certain numbers with his over-amplified guitar clichés, developing likely fragments of song computed in his old friend's oft-sozzled mind and persuading him to invest in harder drumheads, which certainly lent the kit a tarter drive – but, with the project's very title (and sleeve photograph, of a teenage Richard Starkey) indicating how seemingly out of touch Starr was, Boardwalk might have feared a tarring with the same brush.

A subtext to Boardwalk and British RCA's dumping of Ringo Starr – the only ex-Beatle to be thus cast adrift – was Walsh's "allowing me to have one party – and then he tried to stop it, but it was too late then. He had to wait until the next day."[15]

With a composing credit granted to all participants, 'Everybody's In A Hurry But Me' was the too-apt title to one of three excerpts from instrumental rambles onto which Starr and the harassed Walsh superimposed whatever lyrics could be strung together. Much superfluous blowing on more substantial songs – and, on the fade-out of 'Alibi', some half-baked scat singing – also padded out the album, but the meeting of its deadline was rendered irrelevant by RCA and Boardwalk's action after hearing the result, an extremity that was validated when Ringo was then unable to kindle any worthwhile interest in *Old Wave* from any other British or US companies, who all seemed to have too vivid a recollection of *Stop And Smell The Roses*. He was, therefore, at more of a loose end than usual when his name cropped up as Paul McCartney and his production staff planned *Give My Regards To Broad Street*, MPL's first feature-length flick.

A romantic undercurrent of this much-criticised and egocentric caper was Ringo – drummer in Paul's band – and "this gorgeous girl reporter from a music paper" (Barbara) who "get friendlier and friendlier as the movie progresses. Falling in love with your own wife isn't as easy as it looks."[16] The main story was a hybrid of an atypical day in the life of MPL and aspects of *The Wizard Of Oz* and *Magical Mystery Tour*. Ringo wanted originally to be its villain, but Paul had him down merely as rather cantankerous, sniggering, "which we all know is different to his usual sweet-natured self"[17] – or it used to be.

Although (or because) it was "more like family than work",[16] on locations as varied as a Victorian graveyard and a reconstruction of New Brighton's Tower Ballroom – destroyed by fire in 1970 – Ringo insisted on pauses, however inconvenient, so that he wouldn't miss the goings-on in *Coronation Street*. Possibly afflicted with an unquiet conscience about his *Yellow Submarine faux pas* of the previous year, he was also pernickety about what songs he'd drum on when Paul got to grips with the soundtrack, with a large helping of refashioned Beatles items, on which Starr would not let himself be accommodated. However, Paul didn't need Ringo like Ringo needed Paul.

Beyond film set and console, McCartney's social attachment to Starr was strong enough for each to sit together at an Everly Brothers reunion show in London. Worship of pop's greybeards would extend beyond such acts of faith and garrulous praise. The 60th birthdays of both Chuck Berry and Fats Domino would each be sanctified on purchasable video with famous younger helpmates in sight giving them a contemporary seal of approval – and buttressing their own standings with credible influences. An array of British stars – including Screaming Lord Sutch, Brian May and The Kinks' Dave Davies – would pay homage to a truculent Jerry Lee Lewis during one of the Killer's recitals at Hammersmith Odeon, and a link-up with The Art Of Noise had delivered Duane Eddy back to the UK Top 20 in 1986. Backed by George Harrison, Jeff Lynne and others who'd grown to manhood to his twanging, Eddy was also able to cut a new album, which – for those who hadn't listened to him since the early 1960s – was much how they might have imagined him to sound as his pension beckoned.

On 21 October 1985, it was *Carl Perkins And Friends: A Rockabilly Special*, commissioned for Channel 4 at Limehouse Studios in London's West India docks. Its genesis lay in *Homecoming*, Perkins' album of earlier that year with three other chicken-necked campaigners – Jerry Lee Lewis, Roy Orbison and Johnny Cash – at the now much-modernised Sun Studio in Memphis, where opinionated console sage Sam Phillips had primed four country boys for greener pastures *circa* 1955. Pre-empting George Harrison's Traveling Wilburys, many *Homecoming* tracks were communal efforts, with verses and middle eights apportioned more or less equally between all four vocalists, in rough-hewn harmony on the choruses. Among auxiliary musicians on the LP's eight-minute party number, 'Big Train (From Memphis)', was Dave Edmunds, whose adolescent imagination had been fired by rockabilly.

Fifty-three-year-old Carl had been a contributor – as had George Harrison – to Edmunds' production of the soundtrack for *Porky's Revenge*, a US teen-exploitation movie, and it was Edmunds and his regular band who'd be stage fixtures in the *Rockabilly Special* and Harrison the foremost Friend. Ringo, too, was another to whom Carl sent a "video letter" with a reply slip and stamped, self-addressed envelope. On jumping at the chance, Ringo secured seats in the studio audience for Hilary Gerrard, Barbara (with a camera), Jason and Lee, so that they could see him breathe the air around one of his old idols. Paul McCartney declined to appear, but other delighted invitees – such as Eric Clapton, Rozanne Cash (daughter of Johnny), two of The Stray Cats and *Double Fantasy* guitarist Earl Slick – also squeezed names onto the guest list.

The rest of the 250 tickets were snatched by Teddy Boys who

queued, freezing and iron-bladdered, in their garish regalia until admitted to a homely auditorium, where grey-haired Carl would be close enough for everyone to watch his fingers create that terse resonance that was rockabilly guitar-picking at its most refined. Unswerving in their fidelity since the 1950s, the older Teds would push past ex-Beatles to besiege Perkins for autographs. What was it to them that this was the first time George Harrison's light baritone had been aired in front of a British audience since 1966?

Before the fond smiles of backstage staff, George and Ringo had bear-hugged each other, united forever by common ordeal and jubilation, as well as the unbearable excitement of the task that lay immediately ahead. It was "one of the magic nights of my life", so Starr's handwritten note to Carl afterwards would attest. If not as "pure" as it could have been, and flawed at times by the egos of some involved, the show was a joy because everyone wished it to be. Judicious editing would decimate a lot of the tedium – mainly the interminable extrapolations that Edmunds had to curtail – before the New Year's Day broadcast.

When Dave's group and Carl had warmed up, Ringo was first out of the wings. Not bothering with Ted rig-out, he was, apart from a grin, more a shifty bebop drummer – dark glasses, pink tie, black shirt – as he positioned himself behind the kit for an elongated 'Honey Don't' that he sang with more bite than when going through the scream-rent motions at *Another Beatles Christmas Show* in the Hammersmith Odeon almost exactly 20 years earlier. As its last cadence died, he gasped, "It's been a long time."

Obliquely advertising Clapton's recent authorised biography,[18] the continuity between Starr and Perkins that heralded the guitarist's walk-on was worthy of *Cilla*. Sharing the verses of 'Matchbox' with Carl, neither of the two Britons disgraced themselves before tolerant Teds who might have wished for a more traditional rendition. At a cracking pace, 'Matchbox' was triumphant rather than despondent in 1985, and onlookers were struck by Starr's obvious pleasure in performing again, even if just tapping tambourine when, after quenching his thirst during the intermission, he sat with the others in a devout horseshoe around Perkins' high chair as they were guided through a final rampage which included 'Big Train', 'Sure To Fall' and obscurer byways of rockabilly.

Onto the cutting-room floor would cascade George's plug for HandMade Films, but the company's turn would come three years later with a televised hurrah for its first decade in business, for which Perkins returned the *Rockabilly Special* favour by keeping 'em cutting a rug in the dancing area. With a renewed if fleeting taste for the roar of the crowd, Harrison allowed himself a stake in the proceedings, too. A few months earlier, he'd taken a more formal plunge into the limelight before 12,000 for each of two evenings at Wembley Arena in a package show for one of Prince Charles' charities. For many, Elton John's proclamation that Harrison "and Ringo Starr!" were about to play a short set rode roughshod over Level 42, Go West and all the rest of the synchronised frenzy that had gone before.

Although he merely backed George's nervous 'While My Guitar Gently Weeps' and was thwacking indistinguishably between Phil Collins and Big Country's drummer during the finale on the first night, Ringo brought the house down the next day when, stepping down from his rostrum, he clasped the central microphone to trigger the audience and assembled cast's responses and choruses as, with voice in finer – and deeper – fettle than imagined, he prodded the right festive nerve with a rough-and-ready 'With A Little Help From My Friends', going the distance with workmanlike pitching shorn of any sticky extemporisation. To the relief of those wincing as the coda's perilous high C – "friiieeends" – approached, he was steered out of danger by both the participatory unison and an almost palpable wave of goodwill that continued to wash over him on the play-out when, uttering Arthur Askey's nasal "I thang yew" catch-phrase, he rattled a tambourine while shuffling off with a jaw-dropping flicker of Billy Preston-like dancing. At 47, who'd have thought that the old boy still had it in him?

With Ultravox's Midge Ure (on bass) the exception, only other elder statesmen – Elton John, Eric Clapton, Jeff Lynne – had been chosen for George – and Ringo's – slot at Wembley. Predictably, rumour abounded that, subtracting Ure and adding Julian Lennon, these had decided at Friar Park rehearsals to form less *ad hoc* a supergroup, but the most that transpired was that some of its *dramatis personae* made themselves useful during George's unhurried contradiction of his 1982 "retirement" statement with a new album, *Cloud Nine*. Perhaps we ought to be thankful, because, according to Ringo, "the worst band I ever played with in my life had Eric Clapton, Elton John, Keith Richards, Ronnie Wood and I all playing in my studio in Tittenhurst Park in 1985. Too many leaders. It just didn't work."[19]

Clapton had been on hand for *Old Wave*, which no US or British company whatsoever had been prepared to issue, but Hilary Gerrard's dogged country-by-country pursuit of contracts yielded pressings in Canada, Brazil and – most lucrative of all – West Germany, where its wing of Boardwalk was sufficiently enthused to risk a promotional 45 with 'In My Car', the weightiest of the "jammed" numbers. Within the record's remaining originals, there was hardly a tune, although 'Hopeless' came close to it and 'Be My Baby'[20] almost smokescreened its melodic pedantry with gimmicky vocal effects.

The fake effervescence of phasing and a lead-guitar section fattened with an Echoplex pedal polluted Starr's already dodgy cover of 1960s soul balladeer Chuck Jackson's 'I Keep Forgettin'', but more effective through its lack of artifice was a competent if pointless copy – bar contrived Dixieland interludes – of The Sir Douglas Quintet's wondrously dim 'She's About A Mover'. A synthesised orchestra with "trumpets" to the fore jutted from 'As Far As You Can Go', a forgettable *lied* by guitarist Russ Ballard, who, in sunglasses more perpetual than Ringo's, had journeyed through the previous two decades in Adam Faith's Roulettes, Unit 4 + 2, Argent and as a soloist, before concentrating on the possible as a jobbing composer. Another "professional'" piece as inappropriate to Starr's pipes as 'Easy For Me' from *Goodnight Vienna*, 'Picture Show Life' – describing flashes of Hollywood *demi-monde* – was, nevertheless, the album's strongest opus, although against the challengers that's no great accolade.

Ringo himself vetoed the release of a follow-up to *Old Wave* that had been born of a Christmas holiday in the Bahamas, where he bumped into "Chips" Moman, a proficient rather than brilliant US producer with a fast mouth. A southerner, Moman had gained some recent prestige in "outlaw" country-and-western circles via his ministrations to Waylon Jennings and Willie Nelson, who appealed to both rednecks and the newer country consumers who – scorning the form's rhinestoned tackiness but not its down-home maturity – adhered to the leaner, more abandoned approach of Nelson, Jennings and younger entertainers like The Sweethearts Of The Rodeo, Randy Travis and kd lang, with her spiky hair-do and artlessly laddered stockings. For Starr, another point in Moman's favour was his previous reputation for reactivating waning stars such as Tommy Roe, Paul Revere And The Raiders and The Boxtops.

Theoretically, he was just what Ringo needed, and after initial misgivings "because we didn't understand each other's accents"[21] the two spoke eagerly of cutting no fewer than three albums together, with Ringo's input much the same as it had been for *Beaucoups Of Blues*. The first of these got under way in the Three Alarm complex in Memphis one afternoon in February 1987. Without the safety net of a record-company advance, Chips agreed to meet studio costs ($150 per hour), supply a core of musicians and grub around publishers for material. Starr, meanwhile, would pay his own expenses while in the sprawling industrial city beside the ugly Mississippi. The area resembled Merseyside in spirit, too, in that it had cradled – just as Liverpool had The Beatles and Mersey Beat – the nascent talents of Presley, Perkins, Jerry Lee, Orbison and others who flowered momentarily in their wake.

During a US tour, The Beatles had made hush-hush designs to record at Sun, the one-storey studio that was the shrine of rock 'n' roll, but exposure by a Memphis radio station had necessitated an enraged cancellation to avoid fan besiegement. Now that the screaming had abated, a contrasting vexation when intelligence of Ringo's presence at Three Alarm leaked was the *Memphis Commercial Appeal*'s insulting leader that "an ageing Beatle is yesterday's news".[22] As a result, Starr, supported by Barbara, was threatening to transfer the entire operation to Los Angeles. This was only prevented when Moman whistled up a hundred-strong picket outside the errant newspaper's offices and the city council, desirous to humour a majority of its electorate, rushed through a hasty resolution to honour their visitor's contribution to culture and extend an official welcome. Appeased, the Starkeys organised one of their parties for councillors and showbiz periphery on a riverboat shortly after the album was "90 per cent ready"[15] in April.

Because "it might be an historic moment",[21] Ringo had requested that specific sessions be videoed, especially the ones where Clapton, Edmunds, Perkins and, purportedly, Dylan had dropped by. Two Perkins numbers were reported to be in the can, as were Starr treatments of Billy Swan's 'I Can Help' smash from 1974, as well as two items shortlisted from proffered demos: 'Shoobedoo' and 'Whiskey And Soda'.

For all of Moman's later claims that no session was tainted with alcohol, there is small cause to doubt Ringo's allegations that "certain nights we were all under the influence" of wine, tequila "or whatever else we felt like drinking".[21]

After only one of the three mooted albums, Ringo had had his bellyful of Chips, with whom he "ceased to communicate"[21] on returning to England. Two years on, he was still umming and ahing about the LP, which, in the harsh light of day, "I began to think that maybe it was not my best shot. Maybe we could find some better songs."[21] With his ambivalence justified when only one major company – MCA – came close to taking it on, he was game enough to want to try again at London's Mayfair Studios, with Elton John in the chair, but the four-week block-booking in August 1987 had to be reallocated when Starr acknowledged finally that he was no more a serious pop recording artist.

Come 1988, the only album of his that most retailers considered worth stocking was *Starrstruck*, a "best of" compilation by Californian reissue specialists Rhino Records, who had rejected his suggestion that it include the unreleased 'Can't Fight Lightning' as a bonus track for Beatle completists.

If his career as a hit-parade entrant was spent, Ringo still had tinier fish to fry. With *Scouse The Mouse* a dry run, he addressed himself more to youngsters by succeeding the more expressive Johnny Morris in 1984 as narrator of the adventures of moveable models known to infant ITV watchers as *Thomas The Tank Engine And Friends*. From a misconception that children's hour was "all *Star Wars* and high technology",[15] it occurred to him what little traditionalists toddlers are when Thomas became Tatia Jayne's favourite programme, "more because she's into the action than because it's her grandad's voice on screen".[24] To Ringo, "It's just mind-blowing that Thomas is so big in this day and age. It used to be 'Look! There's Ringo' in the street. Now it's 'Look! There's Thomas.' Would you believe there's hordes of screaming three-year-olds outside the house?"[23]

As a Dingle urchin, he was "more a Beano man",[23] never to be among the eight million predominantly middle-class families who'd come into possession of one of the Reverend Wilbert Vere Awdry's books of railway stories that – set in the imaginary land of Sodor – had been originated in 1945 to enthrall his measled son, Christopher. "There's something about a steam train. Unlike diesels, they have their own personalities,"[23] deduced this wizened Gloucestershire cleric, who created his engines – all with boys' names – to haul anonymous female coaches.

Although in direct opposition to BBC1's *Postman Pat*, viewing figures for *Thomas* were heartening enough to warrant both more series and the manufacture of 26 re recorded episodes on cassette/text packages – by Pickwick Records' Tell-A-Tale subsidiary – to keep the brats quiet throughout the Empire. It was also nominated as 1985's Best Animated Film in the British Academy Awards, along with *Rupert And The Frog Song*, with its Paul McCartney soundtrack. No more than old pop icons' complicity in TV commercials, there was no shame in them entertaining the pre-teens, either. Among Ringo and Paul's Merseyside predecessors in this sphere were, on ITV alone, Freddie Garrity as general factotum of *Little Big Time*, Billy J Kramer compering *Lift Off* and Gerry

Marsden a *Junior Showtime* regular. Each – Starr included – relied on forthright but amiable impudence and, like every northern comic from Askey to Tarbuck, the conveyance of a feeling that everyone knew him and he them.

Unlike a campaigning politician recoiling inwardly at kissing babies, Ringo genuinely enjoyed the company of children, "because I used to be one".[24] Therefore, as well as attending to more orthodox *Thomas* promotional duties, such as an interview on *Good Morning* Britain (mitigated by his hearty guzzling of a speciality prepared during the magazine's cookery spot), he gladly responded to a request by *Dreams Come True* – a benevolence sponsored by ITV – to brighten a day out for two seriously ill nippers – to whom he was the *Thomas* man rather than a pop singer – by conducting them around the Bluebell railway in Sussex. With his own desolations on hold, "Ringo was smashing – a really nice guy," beamed the charity's co-ordinator, Margaret Hayles. "When little Theresa had a relapse, he sent her flowers." He charmed Margaret as he had Barbara in Durango, when "he played with the children and teased them all the time".[23]

The New York Post pronounced him "the most likeable children's TV host since Captain Kangaroo"[25] when Thomas was attuned in 1988 for the US market as *Shining Time Station*, seen by many reviewers as on a par of quality with internationally popular *Sesame Street*. Rather than use models, its makers had hired actors such as Leonard Jackson (star of *The Color Purple*), Brian O'Connor (*Beverly Hills Cop*) and – as "Mr Conductor" – Ringo Starr, who'd be up for an Emmy award as Outstanding Performer In A Children's Series. Another outcome of *Shining Time Station* was his role as the Mock Turtle – with what was nearly a mid-Atlantic accent – in a two-part dramatisation of *Alice In Wonderland* for coast-to-coast transmission that autumn.

After his required month filming the *Shining Time Station* tales in the Big Apple, he publicised it as he had *Thomas*, but was often sidetracked onto less savoury issues, such as Albert Goldman's morbid biographical portrayal of Lennon, which Starr hadn't read. For all his monochrome garb and matching hair dye, he cut a smaller, mousier, more vulnerable figure than anticipated when, on *Entertainment Tonight*, he made the surprising boast, "It's three months to yesterday that I haven't had a drink. Ninety days."[24]

Regarding his public activities nowadays, he admitted that, other than *Thomas*' US equivalent, "Lately, I haven't been doing much at all."[24] Nowadays, he and Barbara were merely famous for being famous, wanted and ever-present guests at every high-society shindig, club opening, after-dinner laudation, *et al*. Often they attracted more attention than those with better claim to it, such as David Hentschel, who – with Startling Music just a memory – had penned the incidental music for 1988's *Educating Rita*. He'd be seated behind the Starkeys at the première.

There they were, the Ringo Starrs, in fancy dress at the Chelsea Arts Ball in a cluster with Cilla, Pattie Harrison-Clapton-as-was, actor John Hurt and Cathy McGowan, or sharing a joke with Terry O'Neill at the Hamilton Gallery on the publication day of that photographer's folio. Wasn't that Ringo drumming on an interminable blues jam with Clapton and members of The Police at Island Records' 25th anniversary do? And again behind Harrison, Dylan and Jagger's "spontaneous" 'I Saw Her Standing There' at The Beatles' induction into the rock 'n' roll Hall Of Fame at New York's Waldorf-Astoria? Didn't we see him – and her – at the Variety Club luncheon in honour of Tommy Steele, and the party for Goldie Hawn, and God knows how many Elton John birthdays? With Elton and all the usual mob, Mr and Mrs Starkey piled onto Concorde to zoom to New York when, in 1988, George Harrison was suddenly at Number One in the Hot 100 for the first time in 15 years. "So he's inviting all his mates over to celebrate,"[26] explained Ringo into a stick mic at Heathrow.

Even Barbara was outshone by Fergie, twittering and pregnant in bright orange, for the first night of *White Mischief*; but she and Richard – and the McCartneys – had been everyone's darlings over drinks at the Hippodrome just before the London screening of *Give My Regards To Broad Street*. They'd also cut a dash at *The Mission*, and so had Johnny with them for *Dark Crystal*.

Extensions of these finger-fluttering entrances and exits included Ringo serving as host on an edition of *Saturday Night Live* and as mystery guest of blindfolded panellists on *What's My Line?*, where he was identified after only eight questions. Off the television, the most unique public stint of either of Ringo's or Barbara's career was joining a celebrity team – representing Parisian jewellers Cartier – in Nepal for the world elephant polo championship. Although "pretty sceptical when it began",[27] they were drawn into the spirit of the occasion, despite elimination in an early heat.

For profit as well as fun, Ringo warbled 'When You Wish Upon A Star' – eerie in a *Sentimental Journey*-esque way – amid other reinterpretations of Walt Disney film songs by such odd bedfellows as Sun Ra and Sinéad O'Connor on *Stay Awake*, an album masterminded by New Yorker Hal Willner, on the rebound from a preceding artistic knock-out with *Lost In The Stars*, a similar salute to Kurt Weill.

Ringo also banked a huge cheque for five days in the Bahamas for a Sun County wine commercial, the first and last he'd ever undertake for an inebriating beverage because, as he'd implied on *Entertainment Tonight*, he and Barbara had taken the pledge. It hadn't been a moment too soon, either. While denying that their alcoholism was critical, Barbara would "try to straighten us out every couple of months, but then we'd fall straight back into the trap. I knew I should be doing something to get help, but I just never got around to it."[28] Friends would suggest that they "sort of cooled it a bit"[28] and, waking up thick-tongued and red-eyed after another bender, they'd swear not to touch another drop; but, sinking three fingers of hair-of-the-dog spirits within half an hour of getting dressed, "You're powerless to do anything about it. You get to the point where there's no choice left. You're at the point where you say, 'Please, God, I have to stop living this way.'"[29]

Already, Viv Stanshall, Alice Cooper and – decisively – Harry Nilsson had or were sweating away the blue devils, with Cooper using his experiences in a clinic as the theme for a comeback album. When obliged by law, Keith Richards had kicked heroin by acupuncture, while – through the love of a good woman and a spell in a Manchester nursing home – Wayne Fontana had overcome his dependence on valium and was no longer a booker's risk.[30] Not so strong minded was Dennis Wilson, who had been suspended from The Beach Boys until such time as he weaned himself off the drugs and alcohol that had an important bearing on his professional unreliability. In 1983, he drowned in a Californian marina, his judgement of the water's temperature and his own fatigue impaired by too much vodka. Ringo featured in the pool of drummers that got the group through an eponymous 1984 album and existing stage dates.

Not as capable of such kindnesses by the later 1980s, he and his missus took steps to dry out under supervision but, unlike half-forgotten Nilsson, for an ex-Beatle to so do required decoy tactics, false names and secret destinations as much as spare underwear. Without these precautions, today's private hospital would become tomorrow's sea of faces and camera lenses outside the building. For that very reason, Ringo didn't search for a cure anywhere – especially in England – where "creative" scribes would disguise themselves as staff to get some sordid scoop. Instead, in October 1988, he and Barbara checked into an exclusive rehabilitation centre 20 miles across rugged Arizona crags from the nearest town.

Possibly, it was Ringo's own fault that the cover was blown because, at Tucson airport, "I landed as drunk as a skunk. I drank all the way and got off the plane totally demented. I thought I was going to a lunatic asylum."[28] The game was up, and so were the headlines as a flow-chart of the Starkeys' mutual unhappiness unfolded: Ringo And Wife In Booze Hell! Wife-Beater Ringo!! Shame Of Crazed Beatle!!! Starr's Vicious Secret!!!! Fodder for tabloid cartoons was his drumming driving other inmates to drink. Ha! Ha! Very funny.

From the clinic, Ringo telephoned Derek Taylor to blunt journalistic quills, but he was too late to stop one newspaper from making a mountain of George Harrison's mild remark, "I'm really glad he's sorting out his problems."[31] Its Sunday edition would carry

Tony Barrow's pessimistic assessment of Ringo's chances of beating the booze.[31]

During a five-week limbo, the Starkeys – sleeping apart – confronted and wrestled with their inner and unknowable conflicts. Jerked from slumber, dawn would seem a year away. Nevertheless, help was but the press of a buzzer away when phantoms of eddying imaginations threatened to engulf them.

Accosted by enquirers after her clinic's famous patients, vice president Judy Schieb fogged by expounding the basic tenet of its "Minnesota method", whereby it was understood that "it's a disease of the mind, body and spirit. We assist people in dealing with their feelings [and] they start seeing some of the reasons why they are not willing to face life on life's terms. We ask that they take a look at their family of origin and how that might have transferred into their adult life."[32] What else could have brought Richard Starkey from being "crawling drunk"[28] in 1949 to the hour when he was poured into Tucson?

From this unpromising beginning, "Eight days in, I decided I am here to get help because I know I'm sick, and I just did whatever they asked."[28] As well as counselling – much of it from recovered sufferers – treatment included detoxification, compulsory exercise, group therapy, confinement to the premises and no sex. In cold print, it reads like prison, but Starr interacted well within the orderliness of the regime: "You get so safe in the clinic. I didn't want to leave."[29]

Their ways changed, Barbara and Ringo re-encountered the outside world, knowing their "trigger points" – ie the places, people and circumstances conducive to relapses. If tempted, either could snatch up the telephone and dial a sympathetic Alcoholics Anonymous ear at their behest "any time of the night or day and say, 'I feel shaky. Can you help me?' You just worry about getting through 24 hours at a time, but living in the present is so simple. We've been given our lives back."[29]

Many would find themselves excluded from Starr's social affairs: "Now, if any of my friends can't deal with me being sober, then I just don't bother with them, because, for me, to live is more important than a friend getting uptight just because I won't have a drink."[28] Evangelical in their new sobriety, he and Barbara would quit parties at godly hours "when everyone else starts getting rocky"[29] – except ones they held themselves. At a celebration in Cannes of their first year on the wagon, they were toasted in fruit juice. They'd always be alcoholics, but, affirmed Ringo, "My intention is never to drink again."[33]

A bout of pneumonia and then the death of his mother had poleaxed him soon after his sojourn in Arizona, but, although Ringo still looked a little haggard, no one doubted him when he said he felt "a lot better than I have for ages",[33] least of all Zak, Jason and Lee, to whom he gave books on his condition, as the clinic had instructed him, because "statistics say children of alcoholics are more inclined to become alcoholics themselves".[33] They were also encouraged to attend AA programmes at the centre attached to a Chelsea church hall, their more even-tempered father's main resort when things got tough.

At least he hadn't died in hell like Elvis, and it wasn't as if he was on the same endless-highway dilemma as a rock 'n' roller or black bluesman of a pre-Beatle epoch, with singing and playing an instrument his only saleable trade. Nevertheless, inactivity was Ringo's worst enemy, but it was more the example of other still-stagestruck 1960s contemporaries that prompted him to think aloud about hitting the road again: "I didn't want to front a band. I wanted to have fun. I wanted to be with good players, and I wanted to be with friends."[18] No one who listened was sure whether to believe him or not.

17 *"Now I Just Stay Nervous"*

When Ringo Starr watched the video of a 'Beatles Movie Medley' single – a splice-up of old clips – on *Top Of The Pops*, it seemed so far away, almost like another life. Sometimes, he could scarcely credit that it had been him on those records, in those films, at those stadiums. Was it truly him that once conquered the world? Such a feeling may have been anticipated, as, back in 1965, he'd predicted, "I wouldn't go on tour as a rock 'n' roll drummer with a group if I was 30. I'd feel so old and out of it."[1]

In a then-undreamable future, he'd retract these sentences when pop's history was seized upon as an avenue for selling as many – and, often, more – goods as its present. With repackaging factories in full production as the end of the century rolled around, it made sense for mature artists – supported by saturation television advertising – to plug "greatest hits" collections of recordings up to 30 years old as heavily as a latest album. Sometimes, the plugging of singles was done for them via the kind of unsolicited snippet coverage in TV commercials and movie soundtracks that sent The Hollies, The Righteous Brothers and, for gawd's sake, The Steve Miller Band to the top of the UK charts in the late 1980s, when at one stage the Top Ten contained but one entry that wasn't either a reissue or the revival of an old chestnut.

As Ringo could have done with 'She's About A Mover', it was a common if generally unviable practice for veteran stars to attempt a relaunch with a single of a cover from the hit repertoire of a contemporary. In 1988, for instance, Dave Berry fired a splendid pot-shot with Chris Farlowe's 'Out Of Time', while Farlowe himself had tried with Long John Baldry's 1968 Number One, 'Let The Heartaches Begin'. There was also such as Sandie Shaw with Cilla's 'Anyone Who Had A Heart', and Alice Cooper's go at Love's 'Seven And Seven Is'.

A more successful strategy was that of combining with another – often unlikely – artist. Not raising an eyebrow were alliances by Kenny Rogers with Tammy Wynette, Buck Owens with Emmylou Harris and Queen with David Bowie, but also scrambling up Top Tens in the 1980s were a Christmas single by Bowie and Bing Crosby, a UK chart-topping reprise of Gene Pitney's 'Something's Gotten Hold Of My Heart' by Pitney himself and crypto-punk vocalist Marc Almond and BB King's blistering obligatos tearing at a 1989 ditty by U2.

In the March of that year, Buck Owens had been in London for the Wembley Country Music Festival and sacrificed some free time to meet Ringo at Abbey Road, the ex-Beatle – absent for 14 years – expressing his amazement that the complex now had a restaurant in its basement. If it added little to either Owens' solo blueprint or the version of *Help!*, the pair's duet in Studio Two of 'Act Naturally' would be the title track of Owens' next album and, as a 1990 single, would cross over from the US Country charts into its pop Top 40, aided by a video shot in a restored Wild West town just outside Los Angeles.

In the same month that 'Act Naturally' was taped, Brian Poole, Reg Presley, Tony Crane and others of the same vintage – known collectively as "The Corporation" – rehashed The Showstoppers' 'Ain't Nothing But A House Party'. Even that tip-toed into the lower marches of the British lists.

Teenagers were no longer pop's most courted consumers, having been out-manoeuvred by their Swinging '60s parents and young marrieds who had satiated hunger for novelty. A humble US provincial journal caught the mood by defining rock 'n' roll as "a type of music preferred by adults aged 13 to 60".[2] These days, it was not laughable for those with "good" foreheads, crow's feet and double chins to slice into the hit parade with a newly-recorded 45 – like Alice Cooper with 'Poison' in 1987 – or, after vanishing for years, embark on sell-out transcontinental tours, as did Paul Simon, Fleetwood Mac, The Grateful Dead and, in his 50s, Leonard Cohen. Words being cheap, even George Harrison had let slip the "possibility" of him doing so, too, during the *Cloud Nine* junket, although those in the know realised that he had no such intention, there being little point in further publicising a million-selling album.

With Harrison's Bangladesh grand slam and the Carl Perkins TV special being the outstanding examples, Ringo had kept a facile hand in as a stage performer but had never put himself out on a limb as George had in 1974 and, to a greater degree, Paul still did. Nevertheless, not long out of the clinic, Starr had sat in on a couple of numbers when Bob Dylan's 1989 world tour reached Frejus, a few miles down the coast from Monaco, which was now more home than tax-prohibitive England since the sale of Tittenhurst Park in January 1988.

Taking a leaf from George's book, he was scouting around for a domain in Hawaii, while maintaining a toehold in London with a hideaway in Kensington. On one visit to the old country, he'd attended a show in a Dylan season at Hammersmith Odeon which included an ad-libbed cache of iconoclastic non-originals like 'She's About A Mover' and Kyu Sakamoto's 'Sukiyaki'(!). Rose-tinted memories of his groundbreaking concerts with The Band in the salad days of *Blonde On Blonde* had blinded many critics to the quality of his performances in the late 1980s, which were far more fun than those of his now more fêted commercial rivals. Also, while The Beach Boys, The Troggs and others worked a passage of the past around the globe, each new Dylan release was still a special event.

A new album by Ringo wasn't, but he could still clean up in North America if ever he wanted to take a band out there, maybe – as he'd long considered – one along the lines of Dylan's "Rolling Thunder thing, with no big production at all".[3] With resilient fatalism, he was no more in such fear of arseholes with firearms and the lurking of death around the next bend of the highway – or in the skies. Contradicting an earlier dictum, he had attended the funeral of guitarist Stevie Ray Vaughan, lost in a Wisconsin helicopter mishap while on tour with Eric Clapton.

The likes not of Stevie Ray Vaughan but certainly Clapton, Fleetwood Mac, Steve Winwood, Dire Straits and similar purveyors of cultured adult-orientated pop will always find habitual buyers for their reassuringly more ordinary albums from among those who'd matured with them. If you hadn't, you sought diversion in musical realms that you couldn't have imagined yourself ever liking – opera, 1930s dance bands, Gregorian chant – or else you regressed to adolescence by submerging yourself in another netherworld where current chart status has no meaning.

While it frequently lent credence to Adam Faith's assertion that "the worst thing in the world is to be an ex-pop singer doing the clubs",[4] at least no 1960s relic grew old there any more. An old hit-parade entrant was still a legendary hero, who – like an updated Caesar deified by the Gallic peasants – would offend none by refusing to autograph a dog-eared EP cover depicting him with most of his hair still on his head.

Incorrigible old mods, rockers and hippies would now be in compulsory ties or smart casuals, as these garments were often the norm at Blazers in Windsor, Caerphilly's Double-Diamond, the '60s Club in Marbella and other citadels of "quality" cabaret where there were rarely less than capacity crowds for "Sounds Of The '60s" nights. Promoters raked in loot via the customers' punishment of pricey liquor, while a sunken orchestra sight-read discreetly before some buffoon of a compere regaled all with gags that would shock a drunken marine. Then it'd be, "Without further ado, ladies and gentlemen, I'd like to bring on a *grrrrrreat* entertainer I know you're all going to enjoy – well, my late grandmother was quite fond of him..."

To utilise onlookers' time interestingly, a grrrrreat entertainer was no longer obliged to forge a *vita nuova* as a third-rate Sinatra. As everyone from The Swinging Blue Jeans on the chicken-in-the-basket trail to the Stones packing out the Hollywood Bowl had proved, all an act still intact from the 1960s had to do was to become an archetypal unit of its own, spanning with differing emphases every familiar trackway of its professional career – all of the timeless hits, each change of image, every bandwagon jumped. Nevertheless, at Reading's

Top Rank Bingo Hall in 1990, even the most susceptible of the elderly ravers bopping round their handbags could not have pretended that this was what it must have been like down the Cavern when The Merseybeats – with only Tony Crane left from the old days – gave 'em more than they paid for between games.

With a solo star like Freddie Garrity, who cared about the identity of The Dreamers behind him, in their collarless suits, Chelsea boots and three-piece Ringo drum kit? However, where there was no demarcation line between group and singer, it was often not quite the full shilling – the travesty that was the 1989 Byrds, with only the drummer a direct link with the 'Mr Tambourine Man' hitmakers; Herman's Hermits minus Herman; Dozy, Beaky, Mick And Tich with Mick and Beaky too youthful and no Dave Dee. A social secretary had to be careful about which Searchers he'd be booking, because, as well as the ones with the most valid legal claim to be the genuine article, there was "Mike Pender's Searchers" and – also led by another who'd been on 'Sweets For My Sweet' – Tony Jackson And The Vibrations.

As some groups on the circuit consisted wholly of slim-hipped herberts for whom 'Love Me Do' antedated conception, it seemed that, in order to find work, you needed just the rights to an old name, no matter how obscure. Roaming Britain in 1991 were Joe Brown's old backing group, The Bruvvers, who got by with one original member and his son, and Barry Noble and his Sapphires, who – with a certain logical blindness – could make out that they'd "achieved a couple of minor hits".[5] What was true was that Barry's bunch contained all of its "chartbusting" school of '62, which is more than can be said of a Hedgehoppers Anonymous, formed by four blokes with no connection whatsoever with the 1965 one hit wonders.

No matter how legitimate the set-up, nothing would coax builder Johnny Hutchinson or Birkdale butcher Kingsize Taylor back into the fray, although ambulance driver Johnny Guitar was fronting a reformed Hurricanes at Merseyside venues, mostly on the strength of renewed fascination with the original quintet stoked up since the mid 1980s by no less than two locally presented plays – *The Need For Heroes* and *The King Of Liverpool* – centred on the character of Rory

Storm. With ex-Merseybeat Billy Kinsley as lead vocalist, Pete Best, too, was no longer kicking against going the whole hog. Although his most recent single, 'Heaven' (penned by Rick Wakeman), had been attributed uncontroversially to "Kinsley and Best", Pete was, by 1991, quite blatantly calling the group after his now very collectable 1965 album, *The Best Of The Beatles*. Best of luck to him.

For a solitary charity engagement in 1989, Best had replaced the late John Banks in The Merseybeats. In that year, too, it was whispered that Ringo would likewise drum for Keith Moon in The Who's 25th anniversary tour. With no new LP in the shop, they were taking the States, in particular, for every cent that they could get by fixing solely and unashamedly on their back catalogue – even *Tommy*. Suddenly, their aficionados could not refute the suggestion that The Who were in the same bag as other huge but stagnant headliners like The Beach Boys and the reconstituted Monkees.

With another 20 episodes of *Shining Time Station* to be done, Ringo had shown that there was more to him than trying and failing to recapture chart glory. Having broken into the children's world without any trouble, why shouldn't he also provide entertainment as harmless for their elders by mining the same seam as The Beach Boys? Like their Brian Wilson, he was *compos mentis* again after an age of having "your brain all twisted in some way".[6] Nowadays, with hands no more a-tremble or nose enpurpled, he was eating regular meals, quaffing Adam's Ale and keeping daylight hours, even acquiring a tan – "And what happens? The doctors come along and say it's bad for you."[7]) He was also accepting studio sessions again, mostly in Los Angeles, where, for instance, he drummed for blues singer Taj Mahal on an album that emerged in 1991 on Private Stock, an independent company best known for its new age portfolio.

Happily persevering with teetotalism, Ringo was not, however, as voluble about its merits as Barbara, who, while sanctioning a bid for stardom by Francesca, had eschewed showbusiness herself, except when it provided a platform on which she could emphasise the horrors of alcoholism and appeal for cash to establish a Self-Help Addiction Recovery Programme (SHARP) centre in Britain offering the Minnesota Method. Her persistence paid off in the 1991 opening of such a clinic in London and hopes that treatment might be made available on the National Health one day. Against her former career, her commendable efforts in this direction had "more meaning – and, in the future, I'll probably do some counselling".[6]

He wasn't Maureen's "sodding great Andy Capp" any more, but Ringo's rise from his pit became most perceptible in 1989, when, no longer represented by Hilary Gerrard, he delegated day-to-day administrative responsibilities so that he could set about the clear-minded organisation of a show with a hand-picked "All-Starr Band", as the wheels for an autumn tour – with Barbara its official photographer – creaked into motion. It would take in the States, Canada and, lastly, Japan, embracing a concert at Tokyo's precious Nippon Budokan without any of the external antagonism that had blighted The Beatles' show there.

The logistics of shunting the show over to Europe were mulled over, but, as well as the distractions of the World Cup, there were tacit doubts about whether Starr could still pull the crowds there. After all, he wasn't Cliff Richard, who had recent smashes to slip in among the strolls down Memory Lane. If it was any yardstick on Beatle terms, a trudge around its concert halls by Yoko Ono a couple of years before hadn't broken even, not even out of sympathy or morbid inquisitiveness. While it might have been standing room only for a fortnight – possibly a whole month – at Blazers for Ringo, it might have been unwise for him to take on Wembley, even if he, too, had just come back from hell.

"The honest truth," as he perceived it, "is that I would not have been able to manage the rehearsals, let alone the tour, if I was still drinking."[7] Enforcers of their own order, bandleaders like John Mayall and *avant-garde* jazzer Annette Peacock would not tolerate boozing by their employees, and God help you if they caught you with drugs. Although by no means such a killjoy, it was Ringo's wish that his All-Starrs behave themselves off stage: "I explained to the band that I'd just come out of a clinic, and I'd like the hotel rooms to be left as we found them; but, after the show, if some of the members liked to drink, I couldn't be in charge of that – and you could always spot the ones who'd had a night out, when we got up the next morning for the plane."[8]

Casting about pop's old boy network, he'd been seeking not so much an abstemious backing group than a merger something like a less heavy-handed Bangladesh band, in which all participants were capable of either handling a lead vocal or otherwise being cynosure of the spotlight while the rest took a back seat. Ringo's All-Starrs would be the first of this strain of supergroup – that most fascist of pop cliques – to tread the boards in the 1980s, for neither The Corporation nor The British Invasion All-Stars – a producer's throwing-together of various members of The Yardbirds, The Nashville Teens, Creation and The Downliners Sect – would be heard outside the studio.

Formed as casually for recording purposes only were The Traveling Wilburys: Harrison, Dylan, Jeff Lynne, Roy Orbison and Tom Petty, the latter a singing guitarist whose style had been determined by hard listening to The Byrds. After the completion of 1988's *Volume One*, the Wilburys had returned to individual projects, but, bound by their "brotherhood", each implemented services for the others. Dylan, for instance, wrote a track for an Orbison album, although this was never recorded, owing to the ill-starred Texan's sudden death that December.

Through George, Ringo drummed on 'I Won't Back Down', a 45 lifted from Petty's *Full Moon Fever*. He was also present on its video, although he was unable to make the final day's shoot, thus necessitating the employment of a lookalike.[9] Petty – with Lynne, Joe Walsh and Jim Keltner – had accompanied Starr on 'I Call Your Name' for Yoko Ono's Pier Head spectacular, and was a likely candidate for the All-Starrs. On the cards, too, were Peter Frampton, former Traffic guitarist Dave Mason – another who'd made his qualified fortune across the Atlantic – and, at tour co-ordinator David Fishoff's suggestion, bass player Jack Bruce, who in 1972 had been canny enough to shelve more ambitious labours for two dull albums and attendant tours with two members of Mountain – who'd been spoken of as "the new Cream" – in order to cash in on his old trio's reputation.

Whether or not Ringo asked him to be an All-Starr, Bruce preferred to coerce Ginger Baker into joining him on a trek around the US with a band that broke the ice each night with an hour's worth of old Cream numbers. For Starr, an equivalent coup would have been turns by McCartney and Harrison, who were both sent his itinerary, but this long-shot would result in only Paul – or someone who looked like him – hovering in the backstage disarray at one stop.

Two – or three – ex-Beatles for the price of one would have been a most delectable treat for the fans, as would the handful of Rolling Stones that – judging by stepped-up security precautions – were half expected when The All-Starrs appeared near the Connecticut settlement where Jagger *et al* were readying themselves for another global money-spinner. However, how few would have recognised Buck Owens, had he accepted his invitation to duet with Ringo on 'Act Naturally'? A year later, more might have done when the Owens-Starr recording of this was up for a Grammy as Best Country Vocal Collaboration.

Beatle diehards, nevertheless, would have still clapped harder after the drum roll heralding the main attraction's "long-lost daughter", Lee, who took a bow the night the Stones didn't bother to show up – and she'd be viewed dancing around the front row in the domestic laser disc video, edited mainly from two shows at Los Angeles' Greek Theater, where the US tour wound down. On both of these evenings, Zak Starkey sat in with his father's methuselahs. He might have managed more such performances, had he not been so busy with Ice, the group that succeeded Nightfly, in which he played "heavy"[10] guitar as well as drums. "Rough and ready with a dance groove,"[10] they'd been in Japan that summer and had notched up some radio sessions back in Britain.

The Band's Garth Hudson was at the Greek Theater, too, as was actor Gary Busey, star of a 1979 film portrait of Buddy Holly, singing along to 'With A Little Help From My Friends' in a set that had been flexible enough to allow for other guest appearances *en route* by such as comedian John Candy (on keyboards), Nils Lofgren's guitarist brother Tom, Brad Delp from hard-rockin' Boston (named after their home locality), Max Weinberg and – after The All-Starrs had spent the day at his New Jersey house – Bruce Springsteen, who flashed smiles, plucked at his guitar, wrinkled his nose, clenched his teeth and mouthed the words others sang before monopolising the central microphone himself for a busked 'Long Tall Sally'.

While presiding over these comings and goings, the ultimately all-American All-Starrs' cordiality was such that any upstaging during working hours provoked no friction. According to Ringo's band introduction, it was Jim Keltner[11] rather than himself who was "the greatest drummer in the world". Between them, Starr would admit to "no sense of competition. We have a rule: if I do one fill, he gets the next one."[12] At California's Pacific Auditorium, the outfit interrupted the proceedings for the community singing of 'Happy Birthday To You' for a damp-eyed Billy Preston, whose 'That's The Way God Planned It' was cut after the second show in favour of 'Get Back'. He was also allowed 'Will It Go Round In Circles?' and 'Nothing From Nothing' from the hat-trick of US million-sellers that he'd scored since Bangladesh. Although the last of these was long ago, Billy could still whip up the rabble with his soulman antics.

An anti-climax, therefore, was Nils Lofgren's bit, during which he usually emoted 'Shine Silently' and – while Ringo took five – Buddy Holly's 'Raining In My Heart'. He'd then over-reach himself with a new number, 'Being Angry Is A Full-Time Job'. It didn't have a prayer in the midst of an equilibrium of everyone else's biggest smashes, even Joe Walsh's 'Desperado' from The Eagles' songbook, itself an arresting choice as it pre-dated his period with them. Rather than bore 'em stiff with excerpts from his latest LP, *The Confessor*, Walsh pleased the audience by pleasing himself with nothing that hadn't already proved a showstopper for him.

Ringo had been lucky to procure Joe, who, contacted in New Zealand, was waiting for confirmation of a support spot on The Who's journey across America – possibly his belated reward for producing 1981's *Too Late The Hero*, John Entwistle's last solo album. After Starr's more enticing offer, however, he wriggled out of all prior commitments. So, too, did Mac Rebennack – announced by

Ringo as "the only doctor in the house" – who had rather diluted his Night Tripper dread through compromising assistance in diverse TV commercials, from milk to American Express cards, as Dolly Parton's pianist, and in the non-sardonic title and evergreen content of his newest album, *In A Sentimental Mood*. Nonetheless, he lugged his feathered, beaded head-dress and the rest of his old Dr John stage costume from its mothballs and reminded himself of the words of 'Iko Iko' (into which would be integrated the percussion interlude 'Right Place Wrong Time') – the nearest he ever came to a hit – and, the most up-tempo excerpt from *In A Sentimental Mood*, Johnnie Ray's intense 'Such A Night'. He wouldn't let Ringo down, and in 30 cities he'd pound his Yamaha grand, beat auxiliary drums in 'Back Off Boogaloo' – the 1972 arrangement that was supplanted on the second night by 'I Wanna Be Your Man' – and, for his ordained time in the limelight, belt out the old magic, even if nobody was getting any younger.

Almost without fail, too, Rick Danko and Levon Helm would uphold the retrospective criteria of each evening with 'The Weight', 'Cripple Creek' and 'The Shape I'm In', just as they had in The Last Waltz and Danko had continued to do in solo tours across Canada and Australia. Since The Band, he and Helm had made separate headway as film actors, although both were cast in a 1985 remake of *The Man Outside*. The prolific Danko had also marketed an instructional video on the intricacies of the electric bass.

Whereas The Band had employed a horn section for their final romp, thrifty Ringo settled for Clarence Clemons alone with whatever hi-tech device could fatten his saxophone sound when required. His *A Night With Mr C* album was then current, but he didn't push it with The All-Starrs, electing instead to embellish overall effect, as he'd done with Springsteen.

If The All-Starrs' *de jure* leader, Starr had had the least recent experience of the road. During weeks of rehearsals with all the most advanced cordless radar equipment on a Los Angeles soundstage and in the Park Central Amphitheater near Dallas, scene of the opening night, "the great discovery was that I could still play at all. I

rediscovered the dream I'd had when I was 13 and which, in a haze
of alcohol, I'd gradually forgotten. The others had to be very patient
with me, because I had to learn all my songs again. I'd sung a tune
like 'Yellow Submarine' on the record, but I'd never played it live."[8]

Likewise unaccustomed to singing for so long, George Harrison's
1974 tour had become even more harrowing when every battered
nuance had been rasped from his inflamed vocal cords. Learning
from George's misfortune, Starr hired recommended Californian
voice coach Nate Lam, "not to turn me into Pavarotti, but more to
show me the tricks of breathing, pacing myself and not just
screaming. But that's another reason for having people who are not
just musicians but also singers."[8]

After thrusting aside doubtful starters like 'Drumming Is My
Madness' and 'In My Car' (in short, anything from *Goodnight
Vienna* onwards) Ringo's lion's share of The All-Starrs' lead vocals –
from the lower chest now, instead of the throat – boiled down to
about ten "songs you know and love",[13] as he'd tell those who would
nearly – but not quite – swamp his tutored singing, after his Max
Miller cry of "all together now!" brought in the choruses. He'd lean
down to direct his microphone at the lips of those congregated
around the apron of the stage for responses, like John's nautical
quips in 'Yellow Submarine'. Although its *Abbey Road* counterpart,
'Octopus' Garden', was missing as well as 'Don't Pass Me By', Starr
did not renege on other set works that he'd recorded "a long time
ago with those other chaps" by fracturing the emotional intent of,
say, 'With A Little Help From My Friends' with any revision bar a
brief Walsh solo, although on 'Honey Don't' – which didn't count as
much – Clemons' sax was where Harrison's guitar had once been.
Furthermore, the subject of the rapid-fire lyrics was not "steppin'
around" any more but, let's face it, "sleepin' around". Minus its
banks of strings, 'Photograph' came over more forcefully, too. Other
minor changes littered the remaining mixture of Beatles items
peculiar to himself[13] and a smaller amount of his 1970s smashes, but
most were improvements when heard in arenas that were also
designed for sport.

While the boys in the band sharpened the show's focus, blizzards of dollars subsided into wads in David Fishoff's office, where telephones rang with merchandising deals, advances against takings, franchises and estimates spewed out at a moment's notice to promoters in Nevada, Maryland and wherever. All of them were yelling, "Klondike!" at the prospect of a carnival of at least a quarter the magnitude of a Beatles *blitzkrieg*, albeit – as Brian Epstein had once promised – "not in the context of the previous terms".[14] All had signed cast-iron contracts guaranteeing that poor box-office receipts meant cancellation. There was, nevertheless, no cause for despondency, what with Pepsi Cola's sponsorship of the tour and the trusted capabilities of Fishoff, who'd handled The Monkees' second coming after water-testing tours since 1983 by The Association, The Turtles and other old groups wanting another bite at the cherry. Sniffing the wind, he'd written to Ringo with a similar proposal in as early as 1987, and the ex-Beatle's eventual affirmative was – so it'd read in the tour programme – "my most exciting, satisfying and biggest success yet".

This presumption would be corroborated by *Pollstar*, a trade magazine that estimated Ringo's average ticket sale at 7,000 to 8,000 per venue, with over 20,000 at New York's Jones Beach mitigating losses at half-empty stadiums in Buffalo and Sacramento. The total gross was reckoned to be in excess of $5 million. If modest compared to the dough amassed by the Stones, The Who and McCartney, $5 million was still impressive, as was the care taken to ensure customer satisfaction. For this "Tour For All Generations", children under seven were allowed in to minimise babysitting costs and facilitate a family atmosphere of picnics and deckchairs, weather permitting – which it didn't, at a lot of engagements. Thanks to soundchecks lasting hours and two gigantic video screens on either side of every stage, never had Ringo or any of the others – not to mention the local heroes who'd cornered the 30-minute second billings – been heard or seen so well by so many in the given setting.

Prominent at the official proclamation of the tour on 20 June 1989 at the New York Palladium, Ringo made sure that even more knew about it with further in-person plugs on *Good Morning America* and *The David Letterman Show*, going as far as inviting Letterman's band leader to play with The All-Starrs on any evening that he felt the urge.

At the Palladium press conference, he noted that, while The Beatles had played many of the auditoriums a quarter of a century earlier, others lined up by Fishoff were in "towns that weren't built the last time I did this".[15] He bemoaned the fact that there were so few All-Starrs dates below the Mason-Dixon line but hoped to remedy this "maybe next time".[15]

Both on and off stage, he'd refer to his new-found sobriety. Correspondents admitted to his inner sanctums would not be offered as much as a shandy, even at the knees-up to celebrate Ringo's first Canadian booking since The Beatles played Toronto in 1966. "I used to drink when I got nervous," he told them. "Now I just stay nervous."[7] It took some getting used to, as well: "For the first week it felt real strange to be playing, because I'm an old rocker so, after these shows, half of my brain was going, 'Let's go crazy!' and the other half was going, 'We don't do that now.'"[8]

Savouring every unclouded moment, he was quite tickled by the standing ovations that were his before he'd sung a crotchet. Prancing on, he'd wave good-humouredly while advancing stage centre. When he hit the prelusive "got to pay your dues if you want to sing the blues" of 'It Don't Come Easy', he'd already be hostage to the beat of its introductory fanfare that had been counted in while he waited in the wings and the tension mounted.

As the matrons in his worldwide fan club would ritually mob beanpole Johnnie Ray after every performance until the month of his death in 1990, so – like a parody of Beatlemania – libidinous middle-aged women rushed down aisles towards the little fellow "like Yasser Arafat impersonating a Krishna"[16] in his ponytail and the sunglasses that he'd declared were "from Elton's safe". For the second half, he'd steal on in a different jacket from a wardrobe that included ones in bright pink, silver lamé (with tails) and Chinese silk, all dragons and tassels.

From his acned years as a would-be Teddy Boy, he still believed that you wouldn't guess that he was no Mr Universe, if his apparel was sufficiently gaudy. His emergence up-front from behind the kit with The All-Starrs demonstrated that he was no Mick Jagger. However, neither was he a cosmic clown like Freddie Garrity. Even so, he got the giggles occasionally and effected a "champion" handclasp above his head whenever a number went down especially well.

Like his "keep it rollin'", "take me to heaven, Clarence" and similar mid-song yelps of encouragement, much of his patter became predictable to the syllable as every recital yielded "the best audience yet", particularly after they'd bought the badges, T-shirts and other durables that he'd always inform them were for sale during the interval. Charming some and sickening others, he'd enquire, "What do you think of it so far?" and, several times, "What's my name?", raising a titter with "I love that bit" when everyone bawled "Ringo!" back at him. When the entourage traversed the North Pacific, this question mutated to "*Watushi no namae wa nandeseuka?*" for the Japanese leg.

Because he was Ringo, he got away with these enthusiastic inanities and deporting himself as if he had all the time in the world. The *LA Times* critic rubbished him at first, but then concluded, "Ringo was a smiling, delightful neo-vaudevillian who capered about joyfully while making all the hokey moves that fell flat earlier seem somehow full of life."[17] Like some old ham in a musical, he talked rather than sang bits of the songs, but apart from the odd painful note his lessons with Nate Lam hadn't been in vain, although he attacked each opus "like a drummer by shifting his weight from side to side and singing each word on the beat".[15] Getting braver as the tour progressed, he began to experiment with diction and phrasing, but not enough to mar the good old good ones played in approximately the good old way, despite feet-finding false starts, cluttered middles and miscued endings. Yet, for all the carefree mistakes that only old pros could make, The All-Starrs went about their business without pomposity, "a little loose, a little ragged and a whole lot of fun".[18]

Johnnie Ray hadn't liked "the word *talent*. Talent is what Einstein had. What I do is communicate with the audience."[19] As shown by the full and lucrative cabaret workload that he enjoyed throughout his life, Ray was never found out. Neither was Ringo as he carved once more a deep niche across the heartland of North America. If he'd sometimes been as corny and gawky in his way as Ray in Uncle Sam's baseball parks, well, it was almost the point. Once, I arrived late at an anti-seal hunt rally in Trafalgar Square. Craning my neck, I couldn't make out who was on the podium in front of Nelson's column for, undeserving of the ensuing uproarious laughter, were the speaker's innocuous stabs at black humour. At one particularly fatuous *bon mot* involving a rude word, everyone but me became quite overcome with thigh-slapping mirth. When he stepped down, I discovered that I'd been listening to a famous comedian.

The moral of this fable – if it has one – could also be applied to others who'd sustained the momentum of public favour since shedding most of their artistic load. Some would adopt an "emperor's new clothes" technique by intimating that what they had could only be appreciated by the finest minds. In Ringo's case, it was roughly the opposite. To frantic applause in the States and – at a guess – an amused cheer in Britain, he seemed to imply with a wink that he wasn't a genius musician or, indeed, a genius anything, but that didn't matter, because he had an indefinable something else.

On the grounds of his light, friendly mood on and off the boards, he'd come to terms with his past and present situations by concentrating on the possible with what *The New York Times* lauded as "the better kind of nostalgia tour",[20] and although some of his antics had been a bit crass he hadn't milked audiences as much as some might have anticipated. Of course, he'd have been lynched if he hadn't done Beatles numbers, but he'd practised a grace-saving constraint exemplified by equating 'Honey Don't' with Carl Perkins – not *Beatles For Sale* – in its preamble and in his refusal of a big-time chauffeured ride to Vancouver's Pacific Colosseum from the airport in the psychedelic Rolls Royce that had once belonged to John.

He'd select only one Lennon-McCartney composition ('I Wanna Be Your Man') for the concert album issued by Christmas 1990 – by EMI, of all labels – to combat bootleggers who still profiteered from anything on which an ex-Beatle even breathed. All the same, The All-Starrs had been unable to cut a studio LP because, flying in the face of vigorous supplication from Ringo, "no one would take a chance on us. It was as if they didn't trust us any more. They still think we're a bunch of crazies. They kept saying things like, 'What kind of music are you going to do?'"[21]

Ringo Starr And His All-Starr Band came out in the same month as *Traveling Wilburys Volume Three*. Such a clash didn't drain revenue from each faction as it would have done in days of yore. Indeed, the borders between them had already dissolved when 'With A Little Help From My Friends' from the Greek Theater turned up as a bonus B-side on a pressing of the Wilburys' 'Nobody's Child' charity single and on a compilation LP of the same title for Olivia Harrison's Romanian Angel Appeal, following her shocked inspection of an orphanage near Budapest. Of the other Beatle wives in collusion with Olivia, Barbara was the most active in checking that the funds reached their target. Back in England, she was gratified to report, "It's made such a difference. In one orphanage I visited, the walls have been cheerfully painted with flowers and the alphabet, and there are sinks and toilets."[6] She and Mrs Harrison also tithed some of their time and money to the Parents For Safe Food campaign.

Inevitably, Barbara's warm-hearted voluntary work bred invasions of privacy by the media nuisance brigade with the same mind-stultifying questions. "Will The Beatles reform?" "Yes," snapped Barbara, "in heaven."[6] While this ultimate reunion had yet to come to pass, the principal liaison between any combination of ex-Beatles remains that of Ringo and George, who, with a left-handed bass guitarist dressed as a walrus, appeared together in the promotional video of 'When We Was Fab' from *Cloud Nine*. In keeping with this invocation of The Beatles, the two donned the *Sgt Pepper* uniforms that Jason and Lee had been borrowing for fancy-dress parties. Harrison and Starr also had walk-ons in the 1988 movie *Walking After Midnight*, starring James Coburn.

Ringo was also seen as himself with Jeff Beck and The Pink Floyd's Dave Gilmour in a promotional film of 'Too Much To Lose' by Czechoslovakian jazz-rocker Jan Hammer. His own All-Starrs video was shown at a trade fair in Cannes, which led to intermittent screenings on satellite TV, but negotiations for more taxing parts never got past a stray newspaper report that it was probably possible that Starr might be in a flick about pre-revolutionary China as Morris "Two Gun" Cohen, the Guevara to Chiang Kai-Shek's Castro. However, the sudden demise in 1987 of its producer, Tony Stratton-Smith – founder of Charisma Records – effectively finished it off, if it had been ever more than hot air.

Starr was perpetually "about to" get to grips with a US situation comedy, too, as an ageing pop singer and widower left in charge of the offspring in *The Flip Side* (directed by Don Johnson); as a club promoter in *Ringo's Rock Riot*; and as guest voice in *The Simpsons*. In December 1990, *TV Guide* had him procrastinating about another series: "I am English, and we don't want the show written for an American, because there'd be a difference in the humour and in the delivery."[22]

"I'm afraid the teenage roles are gone for me,"[22] he added, but he was well qualified to play the father of one in an Oldsmobile commercial, which obliged him – or a stunt man – to slide down a banqueting table, out of a twelfth-floor window and into a Cutlass car driven by Lee, now quite a late-20th-century young adult, with dyed-purple hair. In common with stepsister Francesca – not to say the likes of Moon Unit Zappa, Donovan Leitch Jnr and other scions of showbiz families – Lee's acting career was furnished with the best and worst start by her dad's long shadow both keeping her feet on the ground and creating pre-conceived ideas about her abilities.

Assumptions that Ringo would never feel his way out of his Beatles-nostalgia rut were strengthened as, one by one, reissues of his solo albums on compact disc were deleted. Nonetheless, the spectre of Chips Moman persisted in its haunting of him, despite a 1990 ruling by an Atlanta magistrate which thwarted plans for the issue of the Memphis album by Moman's own CRS firm. The prosecution had argued that CRS could not oversee its distribution and publicity "in a manner befitting an artist of Starr's stature".[23] Into the bargain, Moman was to surrender – in exchange for less than half of his demanded recording expenses – the Three Alarm master tapes to the plaintiff, who'd given a most diverting account of himself in the witness box.[24]

While there was written and taped evidence[25] corroborating that the resurrection of the record to coincide with the All-Starrs tour – as well as a mooted out-of-court financial settlement – had crossed Ringo's mind, he'd been disconcerted by the expedient Moman's endeavours to "blackmail" him into rush-releasing it, ignoring his desire to overdub drums "to get more of my personality on it".[23] Moreover, in the light of his late victory over the demon drink, Starr would also feel uncomfortable about endorsing an opus entitled 'Whiskey And Soda'.

There'd been little point in Ringo putting out even a single in 1990, as, despite the pencilling-in of dates in Europe, he postponed another All-Starrs adventure until the following August amid rumours that Todd Rundgren and Keith Emerson had been drafted in to replace those unavailable from the 1989 personnel. Scheduled to perform in Fishoff's good ol' US of A "in the same places",[21] Starr advocated for this market consolidation a prudent change of format, with probably 'Octopus' Garden' and other favourites excluded from 1989, plus a track or two from a brand-new album. Because he'd shown that he meant business by his willingness to reach his public again – even if it was the same public as last time – someone had finally seen no harm in "taking a chance on us" in the form of a 1991 recording deal with Private Stock, signed largely because Ringo had got on well with Taj Mahal's producer, Skip Drinkwater, who ventured forth on an immediate quest for songs for his new client, before being superseded by Jeff Lynne, who had steered both George Harrison and Roy Orbison back into the charts.

Thus Ringo's life settled into the next stage of what has become almost a set pattern for biographies of famous 1960s pop musicians. After the years of struggle, the climb to fame, the consolidation, the decline and the "wilderness years" comes, hopefully, the qualified comeback. In nearly all examples, too, the repercussions of the initial breakthrough – in Ringo's case, the flush of chart strikes with The Beatles – yet resound, having gouged so deep a wound on pop that it gives the decades left to the artist a certain irrelevance, regardless of latter-day commercial or artistic windfalls.

Ringo Starr was to have a necessary hand in an excavation and even a surprise exhumation of The Beatles, but other than that his professional undertakings in the 1990s and since have stemmed, more or less, from that first nostalgia trek with The All-Starr Band. Certainly, there have been no more films ("No one's asked me, and I'm not interested right now"[26]), although he drummed on Little Richard's remake of 'Good Golly Miss Molly' for *King Ralph* and was the voice on middle-of-the-road 'You Never Know' from the soundtrack of a flick entitled *Curly Sue*; and, of course, there was his "appearance" in US cartoon series *The Simpsons* in 1991.

No, I haven't seen either *King Ralph* or *Curly Sue*, but if you're the type who finds nothing about The Beatles too insignificant to be intriguing then you probably have. Furthermore, you may have discovered already *Beatlefan*, the journal that chronicles all things to do with the Fab Four, together and apart. Otherwise, if you think you'd derive deep and lasting pleasure from studying and comparing, say, on-stage utterances of each concert Starr has played since 1989, write to *Beatlefan* at PO Box 33515, Decatur, GA 30033, USA.

Well, that's the Yanks for you. Where would the world be without them? More to the point, where would Ringo and The Beatles be? What about the all-important personage of Alan Clayson, too? Thanks to *Straight Man Or Joker*, *The Quiet One: A Life Of George Harrison* and *Backbeat* – the latter essentially a biography of Stuart Sutcliffe – I've been an honoured guest at many US Beatlefests, where I've met some interesting people, several of whom I would now regard as close friends. That any given Beatlefest in the States dwarfs even the Merseybeatle event puts us and them into perspective. This is a silly analogy, but, if Beatlemania lasts a lifetime for British devotees, it's for all eternity for their US counterparts.

That may be why the second phase of Ringo's world tour with his All-Starr Band in 1992 covered North America more extensively than any other territory. Keith Emerson didn't join him, after all, but Todd Rundgren did, along with Nils Lofgren and Joe Walsh from the old troupe. Further full-time newcomers included Zak Starkey (all pals with Dad, now), Dave Edmunds and Burton Cummings, a mainstay of The Guess Who, a Canadian outfit who, in around 1970, had racked up half a dozen US million-sellers but made far less impact in Europe.

When The All-Starrs crossed the Atlantic in summer 1992, perhaps the most eagerly anticipated stops were those at the Montreux Jazz Festival(!) for the recording of a second live All-Starrs album, the Stadtpark in Hamburg, London's Hammersmith Odeon and, especially, the Liverpool Empire, after Cavern City Tours announced limited weekend package trips to see him there. BBC Radio 4's early-morning magazine *Today* made a big fuss (although my bit was cut, blast their impudence), and the show was to be filmed for the Disney Channel, along with location sequences in the city centre. By one of these coincidences that occupy many an idle hour amongst Beatle disciples, Pete Best and his group were working the new Cavern on the very evening – 6 July – that The All-Starrs were on at the Empire.

Although McCartney – with and without Wings – had been back a lot, this was Ringo's first home game, so to speak, since The Beatles. For a few, therefore, it was more than just entertainment by a pop singer. Veiled in flesh, the Local Boy Made Good was re-appearing before his people like Moses from the clouded summit of Mount Sinai to the Israelites. Others were more level headed, but, while no one expected the waters of the Mersey to part, the show was on the scale of a cup final or Muhammad Ali's last hurrah in Las Vegas.

Although a roaring ovation brought him back for 'Act Naturally' and 'With A Little Help From My Friends' – encores he'd done throughout the entire expedition – only a miracle could have rescued the performance from anti-climax. A disaffected onlooker's angle might have been that, other than a few local references during announcements and Ringo dedicating an opus to his mother, it was just like any other evening on the tour. Although Starr rattled the traps as expected, he was more like a featured singer than anything else, sometimes vanishing into the wings as one of the others took over with an item, often half remembered at most by the audience.

Give him credit, though. Ringo wasn't playing it so safe this time around. Mixed in with the yellow submarines and help from his friends – and a bold instrumental version of 'Lady Madonna' – were items from the new studio album, *Time Takes Time*, recorded in Los Angeles for Private Stock. As well as a high calibre of hired musicians and arrangers at his disposal, there were star appearances by such as Brian Wilson and Tom Petty and a moveable feast of top producers: Jeff Lynne, Phil Ramone (who'd also worked with Paul McCartney and Julian Lennon), Don Was and Peter Asher[27] (also involved in the taping of 'You Never Know').

Among tracks shortlisted were a Lynne original ('Call Me'), Rick Suchow's 'What Goes Round' (picked as the singalong finale), a version of Elvis Presley's 'Don't Be Cruel' and songs written by Ringo either alone, with Paul McCartney (the remaindered 'Angel In Disguise') or with Johnny Warman, the principal source of new material, with no fewer than three selections: catchy 'Don't Go Where The Road Don't Go', similarly autobiographical 'All In The Name Of Love' and the social commentary 'Runaways' – a bawled audience request at Hammersmith.

As Ringo had aged, so had most of the topics tackled by either him or his wordsmiths. In a realistic conversational flow, parenthood (in 'Golden Blunders'), the passing time, regrets about past foolishness *et al* were filtered through clever arrangements and technological jiggery-pokery that somehow made the LP too pat, too dovetailed, too American for my taste, but that's the feeling of someone who would far prefer to find some scratchy old 45 by The Troggs in an Oxfam shop to receiving, say, the latest CD by Bruce Springsteen as a Christmas present.

What the hell do I know? A million Bruce Springsteen fans can't be wrong. Nor could a million fans of Ringo Starr back in 1973. However, moving the clock forward nearly 20 years from 'Photograph' and 'You're Sixteen', was either *Time Takes Time* or its spin-off single, 'Weight Of The World', a hit? You guessed it. However, its failure probably had less to do with its polished quality than with a chart climate that begs the question, who wants proper songs any more – even those as unremarkable (if pleasant) as 'Weight Of The World', with its Byrds-like jingle-jangle? Catch me in full philistine rant about virtually all of the major rap executants and any new Boyzone-type boy band, and I sound just like some middle-aged dad *circa* 1966 going on about The Rolling Stones. Nevertheless, if I'd gone to an All-Starrs recital, what would I have wanted to hear? Ringo didn't become a contemporary challenger again partly because his fans, old and new, will always clap loudest for the sounds of yesteryear.

George Harrison's understanding of this was apparent when, at a few days' notice, he performed at the Royal Albert Hall in 1992, doing nothing that wasn't in either The Beatles' or his solo repertoire of smashes. Not missing a trick, he waved in Ringo for the encores: 'While My Guitar Gently Weeps' and a 'Roll Over Beethoven' that incorporated a drum battle with other percussionists present.

Ringo had never been averse to special guests, either. In 1992, he'd got Harry Nilsson – another bit-part player on *Time Takes Time* – to be an All-Starr for one evening only in Las Vegas. Once well known for never singing in public, Nilsson also appeared that August at a Chicago Beatlefest for a question-and-answer session on stage and to give 'em a set that included 'Without You', backed by the house band, Liverpool. At the hotel, his was the room next to mine. My acquaintance with him got off to a bad and unknowing start when I telephoned the front desk to request them to ask what turned out to be Nilsson's two children to turn down their bloody video as I was trying to sleep off jetlag. However, when formally introduced, he and I got on well, possibly because, frankly, I'd never been impressed with many of his records. This meant that I wasn't fawning over him like nearly everyone else. During a chat on songwriting methodology, we exchanged demo tapes[28] and a promise to meet up when either he was next in England or I in California. We also discussed me penning his biography.

Some say that he was an inconsistent genius while others dismiss him as a tiresome *bon viveur*, but I liked Harry Nilsson because, for some reason God alone knows, he liked me. After all, I'd never been over-complimentary about him in either *The Quiet One* or *Straight Man Or Joker?*, the latter of which he'd scrutinised in my presence. Nevertheless, I felt that, as long as his painfully obvious poor health improved, some kind of return to prominence was not entirely out of the question for him, although one of his parting sentences lingers with me still: "I'm not as sure of my tomorrows as I used to be."

Harry Nilsson died in January 1994, and a few months later Harry Graves passed away at the age of 87. Shortly after his stepson attended the funeral in Liverpool, another with a principal role in the Ringo Starr story was gone, too. Despite a bone-marrow transplant from her elder son, leukaemia took Maureen Tigrett – Starkey as was – in a cancer-research clinic in Seattle in December. Her children and their respective fathers were all present at the final moments.

Tragedy almost struck the family again when Ringo interrupted an All-Starr tour that August after Lee – diagnosed as hydrocephalic – was rushed from the London garden flat that she shared with Jason[29] to an operating theatre, where keyhole surgery relieved the pressure of excess fluid on the brain and thus saved her.

Ticket-holders were sympathetic rather than angry about the cancelled dates of what was – for the US faithful, at least – the most value-for-money All-Starrs thus far, containing as it did Billy Preston, Felix Cavaliere from The Young Rascals, Grand Funk Railroad's Mark Farner, Randy Bachman – whose Bachman-Turner Overdrive had risen from the ashes of The Guess Who – and, on bass, John Entwistle, The Who's second-string composer. His taciturn stage presence belied a love of performing, expressed earlier in his fronting of Who splinter groups in the 1970s, as well as his bellowing of 'Twist And Shout' with the latter-day Who.

In an *NME* interview in 1966, John's colleague Pete Townshend had discussed which members were the equivalents of John, Paul, George or Ringo – for The Who, like many other mid-1960s outfits, had boiled down to The Beatles' blueprint as much as certain Britpop acts did later. Indeed, the notion of the self-contained beat group had been instilled from the cradle for Oasis, Pulp, The Bluetones, Supergrass and all the rest of those regarded by tidy-minded (or lazy) journalists as modern equivalents of whatever 1960s group they could be seen to resemble, however superficially.

Yet arguments that Oasis were first today's Rolling Stones and then today's Beatles – with leader Noel Gallagher its Lennon *and* McCartney – do not hold water because of radical changes in economic, sociological and technological atmospheres over the past 30 years. Being in a pop group is, for example, a much more acceptable career option to those parents who, when children of the 1960s, had been victims of repressions epitomised by short hair and long hem-lines.

You may dismiss this as a too-sweeping generalisation but, after escaping the clutches of those who didn't understand, former Mods, Rockers and hippies were much more liberal with their own offspring, buying synthesisers as birthday presents for teenagers who could even con grants out of the government to form a band – even if, in the same defeated climate, record companies were no longer chucking huge advances about, as they had when the wheels of the universe came together for The Sex Pistols in 1976, as vital a watershed year as 1962 or 1967.

Cemented together by the joys and sorrows of their heyday – and the opportunity to make an easy fortune – the Pistols reconvened in 1996 for a world tour. This included an appearance on *Top Of The Pops* that was, to me, as touching in its way as an occurrence in the previous autumn, when the surviving Beatles embodied the truism articulated by John McNally of The Searchers: "You don't have to be young to make good records."[30]

The perpetual to-ing and fro-ing of rumours had intensified with the runaway success of *Live At The BBC*, a collection of early broadcasts ("a really cool album," reckoned Ringo[31]) and an official announcement of an anthology of further Beatles items from the vaults being compiled by Starr, Harrison and McCartney themselves. These were to be released over the period of a year on nine albums (in sets of three) and linked to a six-hour documentary film spread over three weeks on ITV and presented likewise on foreign television.

Next came talk of the Fab Three recording new material for the project. When asked to participate in a connected news feature for London's Capital Radio, I ventured the opinion that all they'd be doing was incidental music. Writing in *The Daily Mail*,[32] the late Ray Coleman[33] hoped that it wouldn't go any further than this, arguing – with none to disagree – that it wouldn't be the same without Lennon and fuelling Ringo's truism, "There were four Beatles and there are only three of us left."[31]

After a fashion, Starr, McCartney and Harrison's efforts weren't without Lennon. Sessions at Paul's studio in Sussex and George's in Oxfordshire yielded the grafting of new music onto stark performances of 'Free As A Bird' and other compositions by John on home tapes provided by his widow after Paul's conciliatory embrace of her at a Rock 'n' Roll Hall Of Fame award ceremony. "It was just a natural thing which gradually evolved," explained Ringo. "It actually took about three years for all this to happen."[31]

Isn't it wonderful what they can do nowadays? Precedents had been forged in the 1960s by the respective superimposition of accompaniment onto the sketchiest demos by Buddy Holly[34] and Jim Reeves. In 1981, Nashville producer Owen Bradley's skills with sampler, varispeed and editing block had brought together Reeves and Patsy Cline on record with a duet of 'Have You Ever Been Lonely'. Ten years later, there arrived an international smash with 'Unforgettable', a similar cobbling together of Nat "King" Cole and daughter Natalie's voices over a state-of-the-art facsimile of Nat's original 1951 backing track.

With Jeff Lynne as console midwife, 'Free As A Bird' took shape as near as dammit to a new Beatles record, complete with Ringo's trademark "pudding" drums, a 'Let It Be' bottleneck-guitar passage from George and Paul emoting a freshly composed bridge as a sparkling contrast to John's downbeat verses, The effect was not unlike that of a mordant 'A Hard Day's Night'. Although it was 'Ticket To Ride' that he was describing as "uplifting and sad at the same time",[35] Beatles admirer (and imitator) Noel Gallagher could have said the same about 'Free As A Bird'.

"It's great, and I'm not just saying that because I'm on it,"[36] enthused Ringo. Well, to quote Mandy Rice-Davies, he would say that, wouldn't he? However, it was certainly better than 'Can't Buy Me Love' and 'The Ballad Of John And Yoko', A-sides issued by The Beatles when Lennon was alive. Yet, for all the accumulation of expectation via no sneak previews, a half-hour TV special building up to its first spin over a remarkable video and the multitudes willing it to jump straight in at Number One, 'Free As A Bird' stalled at second place in Britain's Christmas list when up against Michael Jackson's 'Earth Song' and an easy-listening overhaul of Noel Gallagher's 'Wonderwall' by the amazing Mike Flowers Pops. The follow-up, 'Real Love', made the Top Ten more grudgingly, dogged as it was by exclusion from Radio 1's playlist of Britpop, boy bands and chart ballast from the turntables of disco and rave.

Who couldn't empathise with Ringo's mingled disappointment and elation when the million-selling *Anthology* albums demonstrated that almost but not quite reaching the top in the UK singles chart was but a surface manifestation of enduring interest in The Beatles that made even their out-takes a joy forever?

Then there was the money. Revenue from every aspect of the *Anthology* project certainly swelled the participants' bank accounts. Well before 1996 was out, Starr would be indexed among Britain's richest 500 in an annual survey conducted by *The Sunday Times*.

In deference to the years before the coming of Ringo, the first *Anthology* package contained items with Beatles who had left the fold one way or another before 1962. Such inclusions did not benefit Stuart Sutcliffe, mouldering in Huyton parish cemetery these past 35 years, but Pete Best could foresee that these were to earn him what Derek Taylor had estimated as "a decent amount of money."[37] – decent enough, at least, for Pete to resign from the civil service and concentrate fully on being *de jure* leader of Best Of The Beatles now that *Anthology* had helped to broaden its work spectrum to a busy 1996 schedule covering 18 countries, as well as bigger UK venues than before – Margate Winter Gardens, London's Bottom Line, Southport Floral Hall, Barnsley Civic, Sutton Secombe Theatre, you name 'em.

Like Ringo does with The All-Starrs, Pete employs a close relation – brother Roag – as second drummer and takes on board Beatles numbers and the livelier crowd-pleasers from his latest album. While *Back To The Beat* spotlights his ensemble's reworkings of 1960s classics, Pete has since composed some numbers of his own. Interviewed by a national newspaper just prior to the uncaging of 'Free As A Bird', he said, "They're like what The Beatles would sound like if they were around in the 1990s."[38]

18 "I'll Be Fine Anywhere"

For the past five years, it's been more or less business as usual for Ringo – and quite big business, too. In spring 1996, for instance, he banked half a million pounds for uttering just one line in a Japanese television commercial for Ringo Suttar natural juice. Into the bargain, he didn't even have to go to Japan to do it, merely board a first class flight to Vancouver to be filmed in front of a photograph of Mount Fuji.

Not so lucrative, however, would be Starr's hitherto-unissued revival of 1971's 'Power To The People', John Lennon's fourth solo 45, sharing vocals with Billy Preston and, apparently, Eric Burdon for the soundtrack of *Steal This Movie*, a biopic of 1960s political activist Abbie Hoffman. Ringo agreed to do it out of the goodness of his heart, because all that he had to do these days was sit back and let the royalties from the ongoing Beatles industry roll in.

Rather than his customary million pounds or so per annum from his cut of sales of the four's back catalogue, dividends from 1996's renovated *Yellow Submarine* – with additional footage, remixed soundtrack CD, video and DVD and associated clothing, memorabilia and toys – reduced even the Ringo Suttar money to a sideshow. More was to come – up to £5 million more in a single tax year via the publication of The Beatles *Anthology* autobiography[1] in 2000. Despite a £35 cover price, this accrued enough advance orders to slam straight in at Number One in *The Sunday Times*' book chart, a feat duplicated across the world.

With its weight on a par with that of a paving slab, this de luxe

"Beatles story told for the first time in their own words and pictures" had been several years in its gestation. Transcriptions of recent ruminations and fallible reminiscences by Harrison, Starr and the lately knighted McCartney and archive spoken material by Lennon – plus a treasury of photographs, documents and further memorabilia – were edited by Genesis in consultation with fellow travellers of the ilk of Klaus Voorman, Sir George Martin and, until his death in 1997, Derek Taylor.

Overall, a likeable and sometimes courageous account – and an intriguing companion volume to this one – passed the litmus test of any pop life story, in that it provoked a compulsion in the reader to check out the records. Nevertheless, it was flawed, mainly because there is little if any anchoring text for that Tibetan monk who still hasn't heard of the wretched group, and while the surviving Beatles were often painfully honest about events that occurred up to 50 years earlier it was an autobiography aimed at fans who prefer not to know too much about what kind of people their idols are in private life. Too many illusions will be shattered, and the music may never sound the same.

As serious a fault was that, like the televisual *Anthology*, it lacked the perspectives of other living key *dramatis personae*, such as Pete Best, Tony Sheridan, Kingsize Taylor, Cilla Black – you name 'em. But where do you draw the line? By including all of the acts on the same label? Everyone who ever recorded a Beatles song? The factory hands who pulped the trees to make the paper on which they were written?

Anthology remained a best-seller while, with 60-year-old Neil Aspinall still at the helm, a four-strong team at Apple – now run from one of the white townhouses encircling central gardens in Knightsbridge – helped co-ordinate EMI's biggest-ever marketing campaign. Its budget was between £1 million and £2 million in Britain alone, and eight million copies of *1* – titled originally *Best Of The Beatles*, a compilation of The Beatles' 27 UK and/or US chart-toppers – were shipped around the world.

The fastest-selling CD ever, *1* was just that in Britain, Japan, Spain, Germany and Canada within a week of its issue in autumn

2001, with over 400,000 customers stampeding into Japanese record shops during the first day. At home, it outsold the latest by Oasis four to one.

Whether looking forward to the past is a healthy situation for any artist is open to conjecture, but it was hard fact that Joe Average was more intrigued by the corporate Beatles than Ringo Starr or any other individual locked in their orbit.* If Paul and George weren't yet ready to go gently into that good night, Ringo's acceptance of the situation was manifest in his continued trans-continental treks with The All-Starr Band and the first twelve-track volume of *The Third All-Starr Band Live*, with all of the usual suspects delivering their vintage goods, notably US Number Ones in The Rascals' 'People Got To Be Free' and – all from 1974 – Billy Preston's 'Nuthin' From Nuthin'', Bachman-Turner Overdrive's 'You Ain't Seen Nothing Yet' and Grand Funk's rehash of Little Eva's 'The Locomotion'. Britain held her own, however, with John Entwistle doing creepy 'Boris The Spider' (the discerning Jimi Hendrix's favourite Who opus) and new recruits Simon Kirke – once Free's drummer – giving 'em 'All Right Now' and Procol Harum's Gary Brooker 'A Whiter Shade Of Pale', 'Conquistador', 'The Devil Came From Kansas' and 'A Salty Dog'.

Although his portfolio bulged with more crowd-pleasers than any of them, the All-Starrs' leader understood, too, that few – apart from regular readers of *Beatles Monthly*, *Beatlefan* and suchlike – could speak with any authority or interest about a cossetted life divided domestically between Monaco, California and – for however many weeks per annum ordained by Britain's tax laws – a country estate in Cranleigh, Surrey. These days, Ringo Starr's name was far less potent an incentive to hold the front page, unless he pulled some eye-stretching stroke such as getting half killed, like George Harrison would be by some Beatlemaniac (from Liverpool, of all places) late in 1999. That had been far bigger news than any new or recycled disc by any ex-Beatle that a journalist might or might not have been aware as he cobbled together an editorial tirade about the government's vacillation about curbing the increase of violent crime in these distracted times.

369

Slotted somewhere towards the backs of most national newspapers in May 1998 was a story concerning the most successful of Ringo, George and Paul's attempts to contain the industry of illicit Beatles merchandise, which was thriving as if the *Anthology* albums had never been. There was even a US magazine – *Belmo's Beatleg News* – devoted solely to unforgiving hours of everything (and I mean everything) on which The Beatles, together and apart, ever breathed. Germane to this discussion is an item like *Lost And Found*, which contained the Chips Moman sessions and, rubbing salt in the wound, an excerpt from Ringo's spell in the witness stand during the hearing in Atlanta to stop their over-the-counter release.

At what sort of lunatic were such products targeted? Who had the patience to sit through six takes of the same backing track, a fractionally shorter edit of some Italian B-side, a false start of 'Act Naturally', one more fantastic version of 'It Don't Come Easy' and then spend infinitely less time actually listening to something like *Lost And Found* over and over again than discussing how "interesting" its contents were?

The overall effect of eavesdropping on such conversations was akin to overhearing a prattle of great aunts comparing ailments. Yet, to The Beatles' most painfully committed fans, the intrinsic worth and high retail price of a bootleg hardly mattered and, displayed between, say, *The Koto Music Of Japan* and *Aznavour Sings Aznavour Volume Three*, it serves as a fine detail of interior decorating and a handy conversational ice-breaker.

Beatles talk became more animated among the faithful in 1998, when a borderline case – *The Beatles Live At The Star-Club, Germany, 1962* – reared up again when Lingasong, a company of no great merit, announced its intention to reissue it on lavishly packaged CD. Reviewing it the first time round, a now-defunct UK pop journal had noted contemporary implications in the back-cover photograph of 1962 teenagers congregating beneath the club's attributive neon sign, "Treffpunkt Der Jugend" ("youth rendezvous"), before concluding waspishly, "The Beatles couldn't play, either." That's as may be, but Billy Childish, a leading light of the 1980s Medway Town's pop scene, had considered it "their finest LP". The artists concerned, however, lacked Billy's objectivity about both the alcohol-fuelled playing and a muffled sound, despite further expensive studio doctoring.

So it was that, on a midweek day in May 1998, The Beatles and Apple forced Lingasong before the High Court in London. Leaving his Southport butcher's shop to take care of itself for the day, Kingsize Taylor would swear that he'd been granted verbal permission by John Lennon to immortalise The Beatles' late shift at the Star-Club, "as long as I got the ales in". Lennon's go-ahead meant – so Taylor had assumed – that it was OK by the others, too. The judge decided that it wasn't, and the mutton-dressed-as-lamb press-packs of the CD that had been distributed by Lingasong in false anticipation of victory became instant prized rarities.

While Starr, McCartney and Harrison presented a united front against Lingasong, team spirit wasn't as pronounced on their return to individual activities. George, for example, was to slide some bottleneck on an overhaul of Kitty Lester's 'Love Letters' on *Double Bill* by Bill Wyman's Rhythm Kings, but had been less inclined to do so on in-one-ear-and-out-the-other 'I'll Be Fine Anywhere' and pleasantly funeral 'King Of The Broken Hearts' during sessions for Ringo's album of summer 1998, *Vertical Man*.

"He wasn't in the mood," sighed Ringo. "Two weeks later, I phoned him up from LA just to say, 'Hi,' and, 'What are you doing?'

"'Oh, I'm in the studio, playing with the dobro.'

"I go, 'Oooh, a dobro would sound good on my album.'

"So he goes, 'Oh, all right. Send it over, then.' I really wanted that slide guitar. His soul comes out of that guitar. It just blows me away."[2]

Produced by Mark Hudson, singing guitarist with The Hudson Brothers – a US act signed to Casablanca in the mid 1970s – 13-track *Vertical Man* embraced what Beatle-ologists might have interpreted as more than a little offhand breast-beating. Was its very title a reference to Ringo's recovery from alcoholism, or to Atouk the *Caveman* becoming Homo erectus when, inadvertently, he cracks his bent spine into an upright position? Furthermore, for unmitigated audacity alone,

Starr's trundling and artistically pointless retread of 'Love Me Do' – with Aerosmith's Steven Tyler on harmonica – deserved attention.

"I think I've got the hang of it now,"[2] laughed Ringo. Perhaps it was a symbolic laying to rest of the ghost of Andy White, now aged 71 and a resident since 1983 of New Jersey, where he teaches children to play in Scottish-style pipe-and-drums bands. As he was on the same land-mass at the same time as Starr, maybe he should have been hired for the new 'Love Me Do' to please the more perverse amongst us. Instead, Ringo stuck with more negotiable studio guests such as Brian Wilson, Tom Petty, Steve Cropper, Alanis Morrisette – a young Canadian whose debut album, 1995's *Jagged Little Pill*, had sold millions – and, crucially, Paul and George.

Paul was loud and clear on 'What In The World', one of the majority of items co-written by Ringo himself. Conspicuous among the exceptions was his 'Drift Away', a US smash in 1973 for Dobie Gray, best known previously for Mod anthem 'The In Crowd'. 'Drift Away' was also tried by The Rolling Stones early in 1974, but it wasn't included on their then-current LP, *It's Only Rock 'n' Roll*, probably because, like Ringo's version, it wasn't up to the fighting weight of the original; partly because Starr chose to hover in the background of what amounts to a duet by Alanis Morrisette and Tom Petty, both technically more proficient but less distinctive vocalists.

When to the fore and singing his own lyrics, Ringo comes over as a kind of Scouse Socrates in the sloganising optimism of 'Minefield' and the title track, although he's not quite so chirpy on ambitious 'Without Understanding', with passages scored for a fusion of operatic contralto with tablas and wiry sitar. A breath of the Orient is exhaled for two bars only in 'Minefield', which, while alluding to Dylan, actually mentions the Maharishi. Similar biographical references crop up more subtly in period "pudding" tom-toms throughout; psychedelic babble in 'I Was Walkin'', embracing possibly the most delightful drum fill in Starr's entire career; 'I Am The Walrus'/'Fool On The Hill' mellotron peeping out on 'King Of The Broken Hearts', along with George's fretboard careen; 'Free As A Bird' *blat-blat* snare to kick off 'Vertical Man' itself; and a 'She's

Leaving Home'-esque string arrangement for 'I'm Yours', a ballad as uxorious in its way as any of Lennon's paeans to Yoko.

Elsewhere, you can pick out a riff reminiscent of the early Kinks in 'What In The World' and respective touches of Cropper's Booker T And The MGs and Elvis Presley's 'Got A Lot O' Livin' To Do' in 'Puppet' and 'I'll Be Fine Anywhere' – but, welded together, the contents of *Vertical Man** were more absorbing than any Starr album since *Ringo*. However, so counter was it to the turn-of-the-century pop climate of rap and interchangeable boy bands that it begged the question, who wants proper songs any more? Least of all ones like *Vertical Man*'s first spin-off single, 'La De Da'?

While the libretto to this lightweight but attractive ditty was *a propos* of nothing in particular, that was fine by me. 'La De Da' certainly sounded like a hit, and I should imagine that Ringo would have had no trouble working it up into a rowdy singalong with All-Starrs audiences. Yet it wasn't considered a worthwhile marketing exercise in Britain, and its promotion in the United States was dogged by ill luck. A planned video shoot at Shea Stadium at a convenient moment during a major-league baseball match was scrubbed when rain stopped play. Undeterred, Ringo and the camera crew then took to the sidewalks of New York with Hanson, a blond trio, then the latest pre-teen sensation.

The resulting clips were seen in North America on *Entertainment Tonight* and *MTV News*, and Ringo was there in person on other programmes, such as a sofaing beneath sweaty arc lights on *The Regis And Kathie Lee Show* and on ABC TV's *The View*, actually giving 'em 'La De Da', 'Photograph' and – over closing credits – 'With A Little Help From My Friends'. 'La De Da' alone was intended for the more prestigious *Tonight* show with Jay Leno (a sort of US Terry Wogan), along with a pre-recorded interview with both Ringo and Paul during a break in the *Vertical Man* sessions. Even if

---

* Remaindered *Vertical Man* numbers 'Good News' (notable for yodelled backing vocals), 'Every Day' (nothing to do with either the 1957 Buddy Holly song or a UK Top-50 entry for The Moody Blues in 1965), rockabilly 'Mr Double-It-Up' and C&W-tinged 'Sometimes' were saved for selection as B-sides for spin-off singles 'La-De-Da' and 'King Of Broken Hearts'. Trivia freaks will be fascinated to learn that 'Sometimes' was the US B-side of 'La De Da', although 'Love Me Do' was on the back of the German single and, with 'Mr Double-It-Up', 'Every Day' turned up among bonus tracks on the Japanese pressing of *Vertical Man*.

the black carnival in the immediate wake of Frank Sinatra's sudden death – the US equivalent of that of the Queen Mother – in Los Angeles on the day of transmission hadn't put paid to this, Ringo Starr still couldn't have got a hit with 'La De Da' to save his life, partly because the USA's love affair with British pop was now at its most distant since Sinatra's optimum Hot 100 moments in the 1950s.

Two days before the passing of Old Blue Eyes, Ringo had fronted The Roundheads at New York's Bottom Line on 12 May 1998, his first club date since The Beatles. As the presence on the boards of Joe Walsh and Simon Kirke indicated, outlines dissolved between The Roundheads – centred on Mark Hudson and his brothers – and the latest incarnation of The All-Starr Band, although this time Starr monopolised the lead vocals, giving 'em all the expected favourites plus highlights from *Vertical Man*.

With the promptness of a vulture, this recital was made available on CD straight away by Mighty Fishy Records. It was less a roots-affirming engagement – similar to those to which the Stones were partial in the midst of global stadium tours – than a dress rehearsal for the next day's filming of *Storytellers* at Sony Studios for VH-1 television. This special concert spawned a damage-limiting official album, but this was less important than the broadcast itself, the heftiest push there'd ever be for *Vertical Man* and 'La De Da'.

Neither were mentioned a week later when Ringo attended an auction in aid of Elizabeth Taylor's AIDS charity in the Moulin De Mougins restaurant as part of the Cannes Film Festival. His on-stage spot with Elton John and actress Sharon Stone was memorable for someone pledging $90,000 if the three would perform 'Great Balls Of Fire'. Capping this, another pudgy millionaire – carried away by the jubilee atmosphere but unsure which member of that English combo everyone used to talk about was up there – promised a further $90,000 if they did 'Twist And Shout'.

The next two months were filled with preparations for the next All-Starr Band tour. The mid-August agenda included the Moscow Sports Complex on 25th August 1998 – when Starr became the first

Beatle to chance a performance in Russia* – and London's Shepherd's Bush Empire, which was poignantly appropriate, given that the All-Starrs now contained the highest percentage of Britons thus far, namely Peter Frampton, Simon Kirke, Gary Brooker and Jack Bruce. Putting his more *avant-garde* leanings on hold, Bruce – Cream's former bass player – replaced John Entwistle, who, with Zak Starkey now on drums,† was embroiled in Who projects.

If not as constant a travelling minstrel as Bob Dylan, forever on the road with his appositely named Never Ending Tour, Ringo – finding the pace energising – had an All-Starrs on the road for each subsequent year, mostly back and forth across the Land of the Free.

It was to US consumers only – or, perhaps more specifically, to watchers of repeats of *Shining Time Station* and those too tough to admit that they did – that Ringo's last album to date was pitched. Out in time for 1999's December sell-in, *I Wanna Be Santa Claus* was a perennial record-industry strategy. The tradition stretched back to the very dawn of 33rpm long-players. Since Bing Crosby shifted a million of his *Merry Christmas* in 1947, the disparate likes of Mantovani, Elvis Presley, The Beach Boys, The Partridge Family and Max Bygraves have been among countless artists trying their luck with albums freighted with seasonal evergreens.

On paper, Ringo seemed no different from everyone else, in his commandeering of 'Rudolf, The Red-Nosed Reindeer', 'Little Drummer Boy' (as inevitable, as Valentino's recording of 'Kashmiri Song') and all the rest of them. He even exhumed 'Christmas Time Is Here Again', doggerel from a Beatles fan club flexidisc disguised as a "proper" song (with bagpipes), and dared to take on 'Blue Christmas', an Elvis Presley A-side from 1964. Nevertheless, Ringo and his team clothed these in idiosyncratic musical vestments such as a quasi-military Gary Glitter-ish drive to 'Winter Wonderland', a pseudo-reggae jerk and Hawaiian guitar solo on 'White Christmas' and a spoken interlude in 'Rudolf...'.

There were also a commendable number of cleverly arranged Starkey-Hudson, originals including 'Christmas Eve' (albeit

---

* Where, incidentally, Ruth McCartney, Paul's stepsister, has made impressive headway as an entertainer.

† Zak was also working with guitarist Johnny Marr, founder member of The Smiths.

expressing the same downbeat sentiments as 'Blue Christmas'); charitable 'Dear Santa'; 'The Christmas Dance', which veered from an ostinato on loan from Elvis via Arthur Crudup's 'My Baby Left Me' to an ersatz Viennese waltz; and the finale, 'Pax Um Biscum (Peace Be With You)', in which a tuning-up orchestra segues into lyrics as succinct as a *haiku* and backing that emulates a celestial Indian *bhajan*.

Although he acquitted himself admirably on *I Wanna Be Santa Claus*, Ringo's non-Beatle income hinged mainly on earnings on the road with the All-Starrs. While the troupe was to reach Australasia in 2000, it was for North America that it was always designed. Sponsored by something called the Century 21 Real Estate Corporation, the last tour was 29 US cities long and began with a press conference in New York's Plaza Hotel, where The Beatles had been under siege prior to their *Ed Sullivan Show* debut in 1964. Now there was no shrieking tumult kept at bay by mounted policemen outside but, instead, a few dozen journalists and fans unscreened by security, receiving a sober greeting from besuited Steve Salvino, senior vice president of marketing, who introduced the firm's next TV commercial – in which Ringo (in cameo, as part of the deal) spoke two lines – and pointed out that proceeds of century21.com's online auction of artefacts donated and autographed by the stars would be donated to charity.[3] To help him keep abreast of this and other matters – such as a series of real-time web chats from various stops – to do with the tour, Ringo was presented with a laptop computer with Internet access, but confessed, "I've sent three emails in my life, and my wife, Barbara, typed two of them."[4]

When Salvino unveiled the 2000 edition of the All-Starrs, the most famous new face – in New York, anyway – was Eric Carmen. Four years after his Ohio garage band, The Choir, warmed up for The Yardbirds in 1966, he'd formed the more prosperous Raspberries. On leaving the group in 1974 – that year again – he scored a global million-seller in 'All By Myself' and a two year run of lesser US hits but hits all the same. While his stint with the All-Starrs was "an honour, a wonderful thing",[4] it was also an avenue of welcome exposure for his latest album, *I Was Born To Love You*, which, if not adventurous, was at least competent. The same could be said of nearly every disc by another member of the entourage, Dave Edmunds, both before and after the Carl Perkins *Rockabilly Special*.

Commensurate with this was Ringo's promise that the band would be "out there doing the songs that people know and love. That's what the All-Starrs is all about. We go out for a couple of months, have a lot of fun and do all the hits. We've more or less settled on 90 per cent of what we're going to be doing. For me, the rehearsal part is always the worst. We all have to get to know each other again so that I'm really comfortable when we do the show."

Epilogue
"I Go Along With Whatever Is Happening"

Ringo himself once agreed that, "If I hadn't taken the chance and gone to Butlins and then joined The Beatles, I'd still be on the shop floor as a fitter. I'm not really a strong-willed person. I go along with whatever is happening."[1] Possibly, he'd have stuck with Rory Storm to the bitter end or else joined some luckier local outfit, thereby recouping more than golden memories from the Mersey Beat craze before drifting back to Liverpool, privately relieved, perhaps, to return to normality.

What if King Harold had won the Battle of Hastings? What if Adolf Hitler had been strangled at birth? What if Elvis had been cross-eyed? What if The Beatles had passed their Decca audition? Let's concern ourselves with facts. When the graph of Richard Starkey's life gave a sharp upward turn in 1962, he blossomed as if made for the success that, in the long term, denied him maturity. In the teeth of the uncritical adulation of Beatlemania, never was his character tested more thoroughly and found sound. More important to The Beatles than his drumming, acting and certainly his singing was his graduation from passenger to the one who kept them on the rails. To Bob Wooler, he was their "only working-class hero. That lad was still living in the Dingle when he was a hit parader. Lennon, on the other hand, was a very privileged person.[2]

With his millions, Ringo behaved much like any other disadvantaged lad who'd won the Pools: the Rolls, the flashy clothes, the diamond rings, the champagne, the sexy model, the tax exile in Monte Carlo. When The Beatles went sour, he spent less time on anything constructive than on just mucking about – albeit "with extraordinary panache"[3] – becoming but a footnote in social history.

If it matters to him, he can die easy in the knowledge that his will remain the name most likely to trip off the tongue whenever pop percussionists are discussed by lay people – and, if ever a ballroom is built on Mars, you can bet even money that soundchecking drummers there will still be hailed "Oi, Ringo!" by its janitor.

Notes

In addition to my own correspondence and interviews, I have used the following sources, which I would like to credit:

Prologue: "I've Never Really Done Anything To Create What Has Happened"

1. *Confidential*, August 1964
2. *Rave*, March 1969
3. Atlanta press conference, 5 April 1986
4. This expression was coined obliquely by Eartha Kitt in her self-composed 'I Had A Hard Day Last Night', B-side of 1963's 'Lola Lola' (Columbia BD 7170)
5. New Musical Express, 23 March 1968

Chapter 1: "I Was Just One Of Those Loony Teddy Boys"

1. *Rave*, March 1969
2. Beatles Monthly, December 1986
3. *Sunday Post*, 9 November 1969
4. *Step Inside* by C Black (Dent, 1985)
5. *New Musical Express*, 14 October 1976
6. *Sunday Express*, 9 March 1969
7. To Billy Shepherd
8. *Melody Maker*, 3 September 1964
9. *TV Times*, 9 October 1984
10. *Daily Mirror*, 29 November 1969
11. *Melody Maker*, 15 January 1966
12. Mr S Roberts' report (1952)
13. *The Oxford School Music Book* (OUP, 1951)

14. Sun Day, 1 October 1989
15. *The David Essex Story* by G Tremlett (Futura, 1974)
16. *Melody Maker*, 8 January 1966
17. To Hunter Davies
18. *News Of The World*, 6 October 1977
19. A pre-1970 euphemism for fondling (desert sickness = wandering palms)
20. *The History Of Rock*, volume one, number five (Orbis, 1982)
21. *Rolling Stone*, 30 April 1981
22. *Picturegoer*, 1 September 1966
23. *New Musical Express*, 23 March 1968
24. *Melody Maker*, 29 March 1958
25. *New Musical Express*, 24 February 1956
26. *Disc*, 16 December 1972
27. *New Musical Express*, 1 November 1957
28. *Melody Maker*, 15 January 1966

Chapter 2: "Well, I Thought I Was The Best Drummer There Was"

1. I must pass on the raw information that, despite having a voice like Piers Fletcher-Devish of ITV's *The New Statesman*, Hamilton had a 1957 million-seller with 'We Will Make Love'. Its B-side, 'Rainbow', reached Number Seven in the US charts
2. Murphy/Rogers was not Paul Rodgers, the Middlesbrough vocalist who was a founder member of Free in 1968
3. *Melody Maker*, 1 August 1964
4. *New Musical Express*, 1 November 1957
5. *Beatles Monthly*, December 1986
6. The kit used by the first rock 'n' roll drummers was a standard dance-band set, which, by the mid 1950s, was bass drum and pedal (right foot), small tom-tom (mounted on bass drum), floor tom (right hand), snare drum for the off-beat (right hand), two cymbals (crash [for sudden accentuation] and ride [for continuous playing]) mounted on stands. To the left, the hi-hats (two cymbals facing each other) are brought together with a snap by a left foot pedal to provide a matching but more unobtrusive offbeat to the snare. Later, the hi-hat stand was heightened to be within easy reach of the stick. The drum shells were usually of wood. Throughout the 1950s, US drums could not be imported because of government trade embargos to protect Premier, Carlton and other British makes
7. To Billy Shepherd
8. *Melody Maker*, 7 August 1971
9. *Skiffle* by B Bird (Robert Hale, 1958)
10. *New Gandy Dancer*, undated (*circa* 1984)
11. *Mersey Beat*, 3 September 1964

12. *Melody Maker*, 2 October 1976
13. *Disc*, 16 December 1972
14. *Melody Maker*, 12 April 1975
15. *Melody Maker*, 14 November 1964
16. Miles would, however, return to the stage as a member of Hank Walters' Dusty Road Ramblers
17. *Mersey Beat*, 18 July 1963
18. *Daily Mirror*, 29 November 1969
19. *Step Inside* by C Black (Dent, 1985)
20. *New York Times*, 21 June 1989
21. The "look at that caveman go" hook line of 'Alley Oop' was adapted by David Bowie for his 1973 hit, 'Life On Mars'
22. *Creem*, October 1976
23 *Melody Maker*, 8 January 1966

Chapter 3: "I Took A Chance And I Think I've Been Lucky"

1. *New Musical Express*, 12 December 1959
2. Polydor press release, 1962
3. Later in 1960, it was re-opened as the Blue Angel, a cabaret night club much frequented by showbusiness folk visiting Liverpool. As a yardstick of its exclusiveness, Judy Garland would be ejected from the Blue Angel for not paying for her drinks
4. *Mersey Beat*, 3 September 1964
5. *Sunday Post*, 9 November 1969
6. *Sun Day*, 3 November 1985
7. An unnamed Liverpool local newspaper, 25 August 1960
8. To Spencer Leigh
9. *Melody Maker*, 17 April 1965
10. To Billy Shepherd
11. *Mersey Beat*, 18 July 1963
12. These programmes also introduced many young Hollywood actors to the general public. Among these were Clint Eastwood, Lorne Green and, later to share a girlfriend with Ringo Starr, James Coburn
13. *Melody Maker*, 14 November 1964
14. To Charles Hamblett and Jane Deverson
15. *Acker Bilk* by G Williams (Mayfair, 1962)
16. *Brum Beat*, December 1989
17. Quoted in *The Quiet One* by A Clayson (Sidgwick & Jackson, 1990; Sanctuary, 1996; 2001)
18. *Melody Maker*, 28 March 1964
19. *Fabulous*, 15 February 1964
20. *Beatles Monthly*, October 1982

21. Dave Dee on Radio Bedfordshire, 29 December 1985
22. *Sunday Times*, 27 February 1983
23. *The Beat Goes On* number five, April 1991
24. *Daily Mirror*, 3 November 1987
25. For this celebration (which fell on a Sunday), Rory Storm And The Hurricanes returned from Pwllheli to live it up with around 70 guests that included Sam Leach, Cilla White, The Big Three, Joey Bower, Billy Hatton, Gerry and all his Pacemakers
26. *Love Me Do* by M Braun (Penguin, 1964)
27. *Melody Maker*, 16 December 1962
28. *Mersey Beat*, 6 December 1962

Chapter 4: "I Had To Join Them As People, As Well As A Drummer"

1. Sue Evans' diary, 3 February 1963
2. Unconnected with *Mersey Beat* newspaper
3. *Mersey Beat*, 15 February 1962
4. Whose band included 15-year-old organist Billy Preston, who'd be seen playing with The Beatles in 1970's *Let It Be* movie
5. Polydor press release, 1962
6. *Mersey Beat*, 19 April 1962
7. To Spencer Leigh
8. *Sunday Post*, 9 November 1969
9. *Melody Maker*, 6 January 1966
10. *Mersey Beat*, 15 August 1963
11. But not for long. Within a year, Sutcliffe would die at the age of 21 of a cerebral haemorrhage
12. *Good Day Sunshine*, November 1989
13. *Mersey Beat*, 1 August 1963
14. Who, in parentheses, shared the same birthday as Ringo Starr
15. Ashdown had just finished a role in the 1962 film drama *The Loneliness Of The Long-Distance Runner*
16. *Sunday Times*, 30 September 1971
17. Harrison's letter to a fan named Jenny (sold at Sotheby's, December 1981)
18. *Beatles Monthly*, August 1983
19. *Love Me Do* by M Braun (Penguin, 1964)
20. *The True Story Of The Beatles* by B Shepherd (Beat, 1964)
21. When, in the late 1970s, Pete Best's drumming brother formed The Watt Four, Neil Aspinall was prominent in the campaign to find the group a recording contract. He also attended Mrs Best's funeral in 1987
22. To Glenn A Baker
23. *Melody Maker*, 14 November 1964

24. George Harrison to *Fabulous*, 15 February 1964

25. To Jan Wenner

26. To Ray Coleman

27. *Disc*, 24 November 1962

28. *Barbara Walters Special* (US TV, 31 March 1981)

29. *Beatles Monthly*, December 1986

30. *Disc*, 12 November 1963

31. *Melody Maker*, 28 March 1964

32. To G Pawlowski

33. *Mersey Beat*, 12 November 1962

34. *All You Need Is Ears* by G Martin and J Hornsby (St Martin's Press, 1979)

35. A troupe of choreographed singers recruited from amongst employees of Liverpool Football Pools company

36. Although the White and Starr takes became so similar as to be interchangeable, it is believed that White's drumming is heard on the 45 and Starr's on the album version of 'Love Me Do'

37. *Melody Maker*, 7 August 1971

38. *The Beat Goes On*, April 1991

39. *Rolling Stone*, 15 July 1976

40. *Mersey Beat*, 3 January 1963

41. *Melody Maker*, 7 May 1963

42. *New York Times*, 3 August 1963

43. Quoted in *Sunday Times*, 27 February 1983

Chapter 5: "I'm Happy To Go On And Play Drums – And That's All"

1. *Beatles '64* by A Royl and C Gunther (Sidgwick & Jackson, 1989)

2. *Sunday Times*, 27 December 1963

3. *Sunday Times*, 27 February 1983

4. *Confidential*, August 1964

5. *Melody Maker*, 23 November 1964

6. *Here Are The Beatles* by C Hamblett (Four Square, 1964)

7. *Melody Maker*, 14 November 1964

8. *Melody Maker*, 2 November 1971

9. *Melody Maker*, 8 September 1971

10. In Ken Colyer's Studio 51 Club in London's Great Newport Street, Lennon and McCartney offered The Rolling Stones 'I Wanna Be Your Man' as a follow-up to their minor hit treatment of Chuck Berry's 'Come On'. The Stones' 'I Wanna Be Your Man' (released in November 1963) reached Number Twelve in the UK charts. The *With The Beatles* version was their first to be taped on four-track equipment

11. To David Sheff

12. Once a lead vocal by Lennon but surrendered to Starr circa August 1963, 'Honey Don't' was also notable as the first Beatles recording to namecheck a member of the group, ie Starr's cry of "Rock on, George – one time for Ringo!" just before the guitar solo. The Beatles' arrangement of 'Honey Don't' was "covered" by Liverpool's Rhythm And Blues Incorporated on Fontana in January 1965

13. *Sunday Mirror*, 13 November 1988

14. This 1964 composition by Lennon and McCartney had been a B-side for Billy J Kramer And The Dakotas. The Kramer arrangement was cloned by The Beatles on their 'Long Tall Sally' EP in 1964

15. A cylindrical metal shaker containing peas or lead shot

16. *Melody Maker*, 16 November 1963

17. *Melody Maker*, 17 April 1965

18. Wellington (New Zealand) press conference, 23 June 1964

19. *Top Gear* (BBC Light Programme), 16 June 1964

20. *Beatles Monthly*, July 1988

21. *Saturday Club* (BBC Light Programme), 4 April 1964

22. *Mersey Beat*, 1 January 1963

23. *Melody Maker*, 28 March 1964

24. *Fabulous*, 5 February 1964

25. Extract from Johnny Guitar's diary, September 1962-January 1963

26. *Beatles Monthly*, October 1982

27. Hartley and a later Storm drummer, Aynsley Dunbar (also an ex-Mojo), would each garner a greater celebrity with first John Mayall's Bluesbreakers and then as bandleaders, while Trevor Morais, formerly of Paten's Flamingos, who could also claim a brief stint as a Hurricane, came up trumps as one of The Peddlars, who made the UK Top 20 in 1969. Yet, for every famous ex-Hurricane, there was a Brian Johnson, an Ian Broad, a Carl Rich...and a Jimmy Tushingham

28. A version by Gerry And The Pacemakers reached Number 15 in the British charts in 1965

29. Storm quoted in NEMS press release, November 1964

30. To George Tremlett

31. *Juke Box Jury* (BBC television), 7 December 1963

32. *Mersey Beat*, 13 February 1964

33. *Sunday Express*, 9 March 1969

34. *Huyton And Prescott Reviewer*, 14 November 1963

35. *Radio Luxembourg Record Stars* (Souvenir, 1965)

36. *Woman's Own*, December 1969

37. *16*, December 1964

38. Elsie Graves to Mersey Beat, 30 July 1964

39. *Boyfriend* annual (Trend, 1966)

40. *New York Times*, 20 December 1964

41. *Melody Maker*, 2 December 1967

42. *Scene And Heard*, 3 January 1973
43. Beatles Monthly, September 1963
44. *Sunday Post*, 9 November 1969
45. 18- and 20-inch cymbals plus 15-inch hi-hats. Later, he switched to Zildjian 22-inch bass drum, 16-inch snare and 13-inch hanging floor toms. Starr would eventually own three Ludwig kits – a Super Classic and two of the Downbeat variety (with bass drums modified to 20 inches)

Chapter 6: "Over In The States, I Know I Went Over Well"

1. Italian Broadcasting Company, *circa* autumn 1963
2. *News Of The World*, 21 October 1977
3. Milwaukee press conference, 4 September 1964
4. *Melody Maker*, 8 January 1966
5. *Love Me Do*, by M Braun (Penguin, 1964)
6. Because George Harrison had mentioned publicly that he was partial to jelly-babies, this practice had started during 1963 in Britain. To The Beatles' consternation (and discomfort), it was continued in the USA with jelly-beans – as different from jelly-babies as hailstones to snow
7. *Beatles Unlimited*, July 1976
8. Whose hit 45 'She's About A Mover' of 1965 was later recorded by Ringo Starr. At the time of its release, however, it was covered in Britain by Buddy Britten And The Regents, who'd known The Beatles and Rory Storm And The Hurricanes in Hamburg
9. So much so that it fooled most of the people (well, me, anyway) when presenter Spencer Leigh announced it as a Beatles out-take during an April Fool's Day edition of his Radio Merseyside show in 1989
10. Not the British instrumental group of the same name
11. *History Of Rock* volume three, number 35 (Orbis, 1982)
12. *Beatles Unlimited*, July 1976
13. Not the journalist who wrote for *Disc* in the mid 1960s
14. Covered in Britain by television string puppets Tich and Quackers
15. *Melody Maker*, 14 November 1964
16. *Beatles '64* by A Royl and C Gunther (Sidgwick & Jackson, 1989)
17. "We went to Greenland and took a left turn," replied Ringo. Quoted in *Rock Explosion* by M Bronson (Blandford, 1986)
18. *Beatles Monthly*, August 1988
19. Washington press conference, 11 February 1964
20. *Cincinnati Enquirer*, 28 August 1964
21. Toronto press conference, 7 September 1964
22. *Record Songbook*, June 1964
23. When faced with untrained thespians with thick accents, it was common for

directors to make them act with ear-plugs, thereby obliging them to speak louder and pronounce their lines more clearly. This practice might not have been applied to any Beatle, but it was certainly the case with members of The Dave Clark Five in John Boorman's *Catch Us If You Can* (1965)

24. *A Cellarful Of Noise* by B Epstein (Souvenir, 1964)

25. Then at the height of his fame in the BBC television comedy *Steptoe And Son*. He and his co-star, Harry H Corbett, performed in 1963's Beatles' Royal Command Performance

26. *Melody Maker*, 6 June 1971

27. To Ray Coleman

28. *Mersey Beat*, 30 July 1964

29. A suburb of Liverpool

30. Including a schoolgirl named Barbara Goldbach, who had a more-than-incidental bearing on Ringo Starr's later life. She was chaperoning her younger sister "because she was a Beatle freak. I wasn't." (*Playboy*, January 1981)

31. *Melody Maker*, 1 August 1964

32. In 1974, Little Jimmy Osmond climbed to Number Eleven in the British charts with his rehash of 'I'm Gonna Knock On Your Door'. Two years earlier, this pint-sized Mormon had reached Number One with 'Long-Haired Lover From Liverpool', composed by Christopher Dowden during the zenith of US Beatlemania

33. *Playboy*, February 1964

34. *New Musical Express*, 20 March 1964

35. London press conference, 31 March 1964

36. Copenhagen press conference, 4 June 1964

37. *Beatles Down Under* by GA Baker (Wild & Wooley, 1982)

38. *Disc*, 27 June 1964

39. To Glenn Baker

40. Mascot airport press conference, 13 July 1964

41. *Top Pop Stars* (Purnell, 1964)

42. San Francisco press conference, 13 June 1964

43. *Melody Maker*, 20 June 1964

44. To Ernie Sigley

45. In their ranks then was Trevor White, who was destined to play Ringo Starr in the Australian production of the *Lennon* musical in 1988

46. Spector produced 'Ringo I Love You', a 45 by a Bonnie Jo Spears, alias the "Cher" in Sonny And Cher. Without Sonny, she continued to enjoy a successful recording career, but also became well known as a film actress

47. *TV Times*, 14 May 1988

48. *Quant On Quant*, by M Quant (Cassell, 1966)

49. *Mersey Beat*, 13 February 1964

50. *Beatlefan*, Dec 1981

51. *Sunday Express*, 9 March 1969

52. To Billy Shepherd

53. Sunday Post, 9 November 1969

54. Daily Express, 12 March 1981

55. Radio WROD, 3 September 1964

56. Confidential, August 1964

57. Daily Express, 3 December 1964

58. Melody Maker, 12 April 1975

59. Midland Beat, May 1966

60. Melody Maker, 7 August 1971

61. Sunday Express, 7 December 1969

62. Q, January 1991

Chapter 7: "I've Been Thinking And Wondering Where It's All Going"

1. Melody Maker, 20 February 1965

2. Woman, December 1969

3. Not the BBC presenter of the same name

4. Beatles Monthly, February 1988

5. A controversial new BBC television comedy. However, like Z-Cars and Top Of The Pops had been, Till Death Us Do Part would be accepted as part of mid-1960s Britain's social fabric

6. Rave, March 1969

7. Melody Maker, 2 December 1967

8. Sun Day, 3 November 1985

9. Melody Maker, 17 April 1965

10. Daily Mirror, 5 November 1987

11. In whose Blue Flames Jimmy Nicol did not re-enlist after The Shubdubs. On 29 April 1965, Nicol was declared bankrupt. Later, he emigrated to South America

12. Where To Go In London And Around, 27 October 1966

13. New Musical Express, 25 June 1966

14. The ultimate Mod group, The Small Faces' coiffure emphasised the cult's solidarity in the mid 1960s as the moptop had earlier. It involved a centre parting to the crown and a bouffant back-combing the rest of the way, with the sides brushed straight over the ears

15. Mark Radford's letter to Melody Maker, 10 April 1965

16. To David Sheff

17. Melody Maker, 14 August 1966

18. Music Echo, 5 April 1969

19. Like one from The Beatles' first in-person appearance on Ready, Steady, Go! (4 October 1963), when Dusty Springfield read out a fan's postcard inquiring why Starr wore so many rings on his fingers. "Because I can't get them through my nose," he replied

20. *Melody Maker*, 14 August 1966

21 *Melody Maker*, 7 May 1966

22. From a Richard Condon novel. After The Beatles rejected the film, it was directed for 1969 release by Richard Quine and starred Richard Widmark, Genevieve Page, Topol and Cesar Romero

23. *Beatlefan* volume IV, number three, April 1982

24. *Radio Luxembourg Record Stars Book* (Souvenir, 1965)

25. Thus prompting a Manchester costumier to market fake ones with 'side-pieces' so those without the wherewithal to sprout their own could still "Make The Scene With These Fantastic New Raves!"

26. 'Step Lightly' on 1973's *Ringo* would be "Featuring The Dancing Feet Of Richard Starkey, MBE"

27. *New Musical Express*, 25 June 1966

28. *Disc*, 23 July 1966

29. *Disc*, 16 July 1966

30. *Just Rest* by L McKern (Methuen, 1983)

31. *Melody Maker*, 11 December 1965

32. *New Musical Express*, 25 June 1966

33. *New Musical Express*, 23 March 1968

34. Rotterdam Beatles Convention, 12 April 1985

Chapter Eight: "They More Or Less Direct Me In The Style I Can Play"

1. *New Musical Express*, 31 December 1966

2. *New Musical Express*, 23 March 1968

3. *Woman*, 7 December 1969

4. *Disc*, 22 March 1969

5. *Melody Maker*, 7 August 1971

6. Roy C Smith of accountants Comins & Son Ltd, who were employed by The Rolling Stones (*Q*, March 1989)

7. *Daily Express*, 5 November 1987

8. In 1968, it would be the title theme to the full-length cartoon movie depicting the group in a surreal "modyssey" from Liverpool to "Pepperland". The negotiation of its release with United Artists would be Brian Epstein's last major service as The Beatles' manager

9. And possibly because the recording of marching feet that accompanied this passage might have also been used on 'Crusader', a recent LP track by The Hollies, who incidentally were recording with The Everly Brothers in the next studio during the 'Yellow Submarine' session

10. *Melody Maker*, 9 July 1966

11. Joe Brown's cover reached Number 32 in the UK charts and Number Eleven in Australia. There was also a version issued before the *Sgt Pepper* release date by a duo called The Young Idea which got to Number Ten in the British hit parade

12. *New York Times*, 21 June 1989
13. Although attributed to "Lennon-McCartney", there have been rumours that the song 'Sergeant Pepper's Lonely Hearts Club Band' was actually composed by McCartney with assistance from Mal Evans
14. *Melody Maker*, 9 July 1966
15. *Melody Maker*, 31 July 1971
16. Originally titled 'Aerial Tour Instrumental'
17. Held every Sunday afternoon at the Marquee from February 1966
18. *Disc*, 16 December 1967
19. Excerpt from Yoko Ono's opening address at her exhibition at the Everson Museum of Art, 9 October 1971
20. *Melody Maker*, 31 March 1973
21. *Melody Maker*, 1 February 1975
22. *Beatlefan* vol II, number six, October 1980
23. *New Musical Express*, 16 December 1967
24. *Weekend*, 14 July 1967
25. Gregory's original estimate had been £2,500, but he apparently asked for £8,000 more before the job was completed. Starr refused to pay and the matter went to court
26. *Rolling Stone*, 30 April 1980
27. *Rolling Stone*, 14 December 1967
28. Rotterdam Beatles Convention, 12 April 1985
29. Of complications arising from an operation to remove his appendix
30. *Radio Luxembourg Record Stars Book* (Souvenir, 1965)
31. *Melody Maker*, 25 May 1968
32. *Disc*, 3 September 1967
33. *Melody Maker*, 3 September 1967
34. *Daily Mirror*, 29 November 1969
35. *Melody Maker*, 8 January 1966
36. With whom Varma would tour the USA in the summer of 1968
37. *Melody Maker*, 16 March 1968. This remark also inspired a *Sunday Express* cartoon (4 March 1968) in which the Maharishi enquires of Lennon, "This Butlin guru that Ringo speaks of. What's he got that I haven't?"
38. *Disc*, 16 March 1968

Chapter 9: "I Suppose I Seem Fairly Straight"

1. *Disc*, 23 March 1968
2. *Sunday Post*, 9 November 1969
3. *Melody Maker*, 16 March 1968
4. *Rave*, March 1969
5. *TV Times*, 14 May 1987
6. *Sunday Express*, 9 March 1969
7. *Scene And Heard* (Radio 1), April 1972

8. *New York Times*, 21 June 1986
9. *Newcastle Evening Chronicle*, 8 December 1971
10. *Disc*, 13 January 1968
11. *Melody Maker*, 2 December 1967
12. *Melody Maker*, 24 July 1971
13. *Music Echo*, 5 April 1969
14. *Daily Express*, 7 December 1969
15. *Daily Mirror*, 27 June 1969
16. *Rolling Stone*, 18 November 1976
17. *Sunday Times*, 27 February 1983
18. *Music Echo*, 19 April 1969
19. *Melody Maker*, 7 August 1971
20. *Daily Mirror*, 8 November 1968
21. *Daily Express* (date obscured)
22. *Chicago Tribune*, March 1981
23. *Rolling Stone*, 27 August 1987
24. *Melody Maker*, 31 July 1971
25. *Rolling Stone*, 15 July 1976
26. *Woman*, 7 December 1969
27. *Modern Drumming*, December 1981
28. *New Musical Express*, 9 November 1968
29. *Sunday Times*, 24 February 1971
30. *Rolling Stone*, 30 April 1981
31. Ron Richards to Mark Lewisohn
32. However, Brymon Estates Ltd's good name was to be further besmirched – if that's the word – when, at 34 Montagu Square in 1974, Mama Cass Elliott died of debilities not unrelated to drug abuse
33. *Daily Mirror*, 29 September 1969
34. *Sunday Express*, 7 December 1969
35. *Sun*, 23 September 1982
36. *Radio Times*, 15 May 1969
37. *New Musical Express*, 11 November 1966
38. *Rolling Stone*, 9 July 1970
39. *Morning Star*, 21 May 1970
40. George Harrison to Anne Nightingale
41. Former guitarist with Earl Royce And The Olympics and then The Fourmost
42. *Melody Maker*, 19 July 1969
43. To Ian Drummond

Chapter 10: "I Couldn't Believe It Was Happening"

1. *FAB 208*, 7 November 1969
2. *Melody Maker*, 6 June 1971

3. *Music Echo*, 5 April 1969

4. *Sunday Express*, 7 December 1969

5. *Films And Filming*, December 1969

6. *Melody Maker*, 24 July 1971

7. *New Musical Express*, 13 December 1969

8. *Disc*, 13 December 1969

9. *Daily Sketch*, 16 December 1969

10. *Daily Express*, 9 December 1969

11. *Melody Maker*, 31 July 1971

12. *Sunday Express*, 9 March 1969

13. *Daily Express*, 12 March 1972

14. Sleeve notes to *Celtic Requiem* (Apple SAPCOR 20)

15. To Peter Doggett

16. *Sunday Post*, 9 November 1969

17. *Melody Maker*, 19 July 1969

18 *Sunday Mirror*, 29 November 1969

19. *Melody Maker*, 7 August 1972

20. *New Musical Express*, 14 October 1976

21. *Daily Express*, 17 July 1971

22. Difford to *Rolling Stone*, 16 February 1984

23. *Scene And Heard* (Radio 1), 3 January 1973

24. *New Musical Express*, 28 March 1970

25. *Circus*, November 1976

26. An Apple spokesperson to *New Musical Express*, 14 March 1970

27. *Melody Maker*, 31 March 1973

28. *Melody Maker*, 2 October 1976

29. *Melody Maker*, 16 May 1970

30. Russell to *Rolling Stone*, 30 January 1970

31. *Rolling Stone*, 30 April 1981

32. *Woman*, December 1969

33. *New Musical Express*, 12 February 1970

34. *Melody Maker*, 7 February 1970

35. *New Musical Express*, 21 February 1970

36. *Daily Mirror*, 3 October 1970

37. To Ray Coleman

38. *Melody Maker*, 6 April 1973

Chapter 11: "I Love It When They Let Me Go Off On My Own"

1. *Disc*, 16 December 1972

2. Rotterdam Beatles Convention, 12 April 1985

3. *Special Pop* (French), November 1972

4. Unidentified London tabloid

5. *Step Inside Love* by C Black (Dent, 1985)

6. I'm not certain whether the plural of Elvis should be Elvi or the second declension, Elves. What do you think?

7. *Daily Express*, 21 July 1971

8. *Melody Maker*, 31 July 1971

9. To Jan Wenner

10. Quoted in *The Wit And Wisdom Of Rock And Roll*, compiled by M Jakubowski (Unwin, 1983)

11. *Melody Maker*, 19 February 1972

12. *Melody Maker*, 6 August 1972

13. As *A Fistful Of Dollars* was derived from *Yojimbo*, so *Blindman* was from *Zatoichi* (about a blind swordsman)

14. *Daily Express*, 21 July 1971

15. *Melody Maker*, 6 June 1971

16. *Music Echo*, 17 July 1971

17. *The David Essex Story* by G Tremlett (Futura, 1974)

18. *Scene And Heard* (Radio 1), 3 January 1973

19. *Melody Maker*, 6 May 1972

20. Marc Bolan to John Blake

21. *New Musical Express*, 24 March 1972

22. *Morning Star*, 15 December 1972

23. *The Marc Bolan Story* by G Tremlett (Futura, 1975)

24. To Margaret Nicholas

25. *Rolling Stone*, 30 July 1981

26. Frank Sinatra to Tony Scaduto

27. *Melody Maker*, 12 October 1974

28. *Disc*, 17 March 1972

Chapter 12: "I Can't Wait To Go Half The Time"

1. *Scene And Heard* (Radio 1), 3 January 1973

2. *The David Essex Story* by G Tremlett (Futura, 1974)

3. *Circus*, November 1974

4. *New York Times*, 11 November 1971

5. Kaylan uttered the deplorable sentence, "Emanuel the gardener thrust his mutated member up her slithering slit."

6. *Beatles Unlimited*, 14 December 1976

7. *Melody Maker*, 6 December 1975

8. *Rolling Stone*, 23 May 1974

9. *Rolling Stone*, 30 April 1981

10. Ringo Starr to Bob Woffinden

11. To John Tobler
12. *Melody Maker*, 31 March 1973
13. *Melody Maker*, 4 December 1971
14. *Daily Express*, 20 March 1972
15. Quoted in *The Record Producers* by J Tobler and S Grundy (BBC Publications, 1982)
16. *Beatles Unlimited*, 14 December 1976
17. *Making Music*, May 1987
18. Originally recorded under the working title of 'Hold On'
19. *Creem*, October 1976
20. *Tomorrow* (US television chat show), 28 April 1975
21. Nothing to do with Eric Maschwitz and George Porford's pre-war operetta of the same title but a north of England expression meaning, "I'm getting out of here"
22. Not the same Joe Walsh who was in Lee Curtis And The All-Stars
23. Not the British beat group but a US soft-rock act whose *Greatest Hits* would be in *Billboard*'s album chart for most of 1976
24. *Sun*, 23 September 1982
25. *Melody Maker*, 12 April 1975
26. To John Blake
27. *Q*, January 1991
28. In 1978, Frampton would be among the stars in a musical film based on *Sgt Pepper's Lonely Hearts Club Band*
29. *Melody Maker*, 23 November 1974

Chapter 13: "Wherever I Go, It's A Swinging Place, Man"

1. *Melody Maker*, 7 August 1965
2. To John Blake
3. *Daily Mirror*, 4 November 1987. Maureen's reference in the same report to "Andy Capp" is an allusion to a beer-swilling, womanising cartoon character in the same newspaper
4. *Melody Maker*, 23 November 1974
5. *Daily Telegraph*, 6 November 1987
6. It was worth nearly £500,000 in 1986, when Starr appealed against an order backdating an increase in his alimony payments to his ex-wife. In the following year, she sued her solicitors for not wringing enough money from Ringo to allow her to live in the manner to which she had become accustomed before the divorce. Mr Justice Bush threw out the case, leaving Maureen with a six-figure bill for costs
7. *Paris Match*, 3 May 1976 (translation: "for financial reasons")
8. *Weekend*, 24 February 1984
9. *Melody Maker*, 2 October 1976
10. *Sun*, 20 February 1991

11. *Sunday Mirror*, 23 July 1989

12. *Scottish Weekly News*, 28 March 1987

13. *Creem*, October 1976

14. *New Musical Express*, 14 October 1976

15. *Pebble Mill At One* (ITV), 4 January 1977

16. Merseybeatle '90 programme, August 1990

17. *Rolling Stone*, 18 November 1976

18. Andy White was heard on the re-release of 'Love Me Do', as the master with Ringo's drumming had been mislaid. However, demand was such that the Starr version was taped for pressing from a pristine original Parlophone single to appear on a twelve-inch issued later in 1977

19. *Time*, 21 May 1976

20. *Rolling Stone*, 30 April 1981

21. *Beatles Unlimited*, March 1977

22. *Beatles Unlimited*, December 1976

23. *Melody Maker*, 26 May 1973

24. To Spencer Leigh

25. *Circus*, October 1976

26. Originally titled 'Birmingham'

27. Including 'Wild Shining Stars', 'Out In the Streets', 'It's No Secret', 'The Party' and 'Lover Please'

28. 1948's *Easter Parade*. The line in question was Judy Garland's "You'll find my picture in the *Rotogravure*" (a journal)

29. *Special Pop* (French), October 1976

30. *News Of The World*, 16 October 1977

31. Ring O' Records press release

32. *Rolling Stone*, 18 November 1976

33. It was 'Danny' that Presley recorded for (but that did not feature in) 1958's *King Creole*. It was also the B-side of Marty Wilde's 'Teenager In Love' in 1959

34. Alias Eric Idle from the *Monty Python's Flying Circus* team and latter-day Beach Boy Rikki Fataar. Both starred in *All You Need Is Cash*, a spoof Beatles film, with Dirk as the "Paul" figure, and Stig as "George"

Chapter 14: "If I Don't Get You, The Next One Will"

1. *Beatles Unlimited*, 14 December 1976

2. *Circus*, November 1976

3. *New Musical Express*, 14 October 1976

4. In 1988, Ringo (and Barbara Bach) spoke about Queen in *Live Killers In The Making*, volume two of *Queen: Magic Years*, a set of three one-hour videos by Picture Music International

5. *Sun*, 18 March 1981

6. *Scene And Heard* (Radio 1), 4 April 1972

7. *Scene And Heard* (Radio 1), 5 April 1972

8. Starr's musical association with Guthrie Thomas continued. In 1983, for example, he appeared on another Thomas album, *Like No Other*

9. Pete Best at Rotterdam Beatles Convention, 12 April 1985

10. *Daily Express*, 23 April 1981

11. *Sunday Mirror*, 23 August 1989

12. *Sun*, 23 September 1982

13. To Simon Kinnersley

14. To Paul Connew

15. New York Beatlefest, 24 February 1979

16. *Beatlefan*, September 1985

17. *News Of The World*, 6 October 1977

18. To John Blake

19. *New Musical Express*, 10 December 1978

20. *Rolling Stone*, 30 April 1981

21. *Loose Talk* compiled by L Botts (Omnibus, 1980)

22. Mae West had recorded Lennon-McCartney songs and had been delighted to be included on the *Sgt Pepper* sleeve photo montage

23. The illustrations were by Gerald Potterton, who'd also worked on the *Yellow Submarine* film animations

24. Not the Abba hit, nor the Manhattan Transfer album track, on which Starr drummed

25. Push-a-lone (lead guitar), Git-ar (rhythm guitar), Hamish Bissonette (synthesisers) and Diesel (bass) were probably musicians who appeared in the Ringo TV special. These included Dr John, Dee Murray (Elton John's bass player), Lon Van Eaton and Jim Webb

26. *Rolling Stone*, 5 April 1978

27. Starr returned the favour by drumming on 'Hold On', a track on McLagan's 1979 *Troublemaker* album. *Troublemaker* was, allegedly, also the title of a film Ringo intended to make with Nancy Andrews

28. Not the Larry Williams composition of the same title that was covered by The Beatles

29. By US scriptwriters Pat Proff and Neil Israel

30. *Playboy*, January 1981

31. *Western Evening Herald*, 29 November 1978

32. *Beatlefan*, August 1979

33. *Chicago Tribune*, 18 April 1981

34. *New York Times*, 13 April 1981

35. *Village Voice*, 18 April 1981

36. *Newsday*, 14 April 1981

37. *Washington Post*, 18 April 1981

38. Weekend, 24 April 1984
39. *Beatlefan*, June 1980

Chapter 15: "I Knew I'd Had This Problem For Years"

1. *Whatever Happened To...* by J Brunton and H Elson (Proteus, 1981)
2. *Q*, January 1991
3. Chicago press conference, April 1991
4. For example, on 10 May 1979 at the World Music Awards in Monte Carlo, he represented The Beatles by receiving their award for Outstanding Contribution To Pop
5. *The Aspel Show* (ITV), 5 March 1988
6. *Rolling Stone*, 30 April 1981
7. *Daily Express*, 23 April 1981
8. *Circus*, November 1976
9. *Beatlefan*, (August 1983)
10. *Club Sandwich* number 26, 1982
11. A steel-guitar obligato was edited from this recording, probably because this instrument also dominated another track, 'Sure To Fall'
12. *Melody Maker*, 2 October 1976
13. New York press conference, March 1981
14. *Yoko Ono* by J Hopkins (Sidgwick & Jackson, 1987)
15. *Barbara Walters Special* (US television), 31 March 1981
16. *Daily Star*, 18 December 1981
17. *Weekly News*, 14 March 1981
18. *Playboy*, January 1981
19. To John Blake
20. *Daily Express*, 28 April 1981
21. *Weekend*, 24 April 1984
22. Fulton County Superior Court (Atlanta) statement, 15 November 1989
23. *New York Times*, 21 June 1989
24. Opened in 1982 by Michael Heseltine, MP, for Henley-on-Thames, where in 1986 George Harrison would be campaigning against the demolition of the town's Regal Cinema to make room for a shopping mall. Heseltine was, reportedly, unmoved by Harrison's lobbying
25. *The Man Who Gave The Beatles Away* by A Williams and W Marshall (Elm Tree, 1975)
26. *Rolling Stone*, December 1981
27. *Toronto Star*, 21 December 1981
28. For example, a line from Bowie's 1975 US smash 'Fame', co-written with John Lennon and guitarist Carlos Alomar
29. Possibly the title may have been inspired by 'Drums Are My Beat', a 1962 single by Sandy Nelson, whom Nilsson may have known during his earliest days as a professional songwriter

30. Wood had also composed with George Harrison, notably 'Far East Man', which was heard on both Harrison's *Dark Horse* and Wood's *I've Got My Own Album To Do*, each released in 1974

31. *Beatlefan*, June 1982

32. *Sunday Mirror*, 23 July 1989

33. *Sunday Mirror*, 13 November 1988

34. *Sun Day*, 1 October 1989

35. "The wish to be cured is the first step towards health" (Seneca)

36. Seen as a documentary on British television in April 1991

Chapter 16: "Please, God, I Have To Stop Living This Way"

1. *Sun*, 23 September 1982

2. *New Musical Express*, 12 December 1984

3. Later, Hardin, like Jim McCarty, became an exponent of new age music, elements of which were present in *Musical Version Of Wind In The Willows*

4. Once Joe Feegan of The Strangers, who were active if hitless before and during the Mersey Beat boom

5. *Sun Day*, 3 November 1985

6. Including Kim Wilde, Brian Wilson, Johnny Warman (of Ring O' Records "fame"), the B52s, Kate Bush, Belinda Carlisle, Andy Fairweather-Low, Richie Havens and LL Cool J

7. Chicago press conference, March 1981

8. Lofgren recorded a version of The Beatles' 'Anytime At All' on his 1981 album *Night Fades Away*

9. *People*, 9 December 1990

10. *Beatles Monthly*, February 1983

11. For example, he mentioned that 'I'm Down' was the opening number at 1965's Shea Stadium performance when it was actually the finale

12. *Sunday Mirror*, 23 July 1989

13. New York press conference, 23 June 1988

14. *Beatlefan*, April 1982

15. *New York Times*, 21 June 1989

16. *Club Sandwich* number 35, 1984

17. *Club Sandwich* number 34, 1984

18. *Survivor* by R Coleman (Sidgwick & Jackson, 1985)

19. *Q*, January 1991

20. Penned by Walsh alone, this was not The Ronettes' 1963 hit of the same title

21. Fulton County Superior Court (Atlanta) statement, 15 November 1989

22, Memphis Commercial Appeal, 9 March 1988

23. *TV Times*, 14 May 1988

24. *Entertainment Tonight* (US television), 6 January 1988

25. *New York Post*, 6 January 1988
26. *Daily Mirror*, 21 January 1988
27. *Beatlefan*, December 1985
28. *Sun Day*, 1 October 1989
29. *Woman's Own*, 10 December 1990
30. In 1991, Wayne was back in business, backed by a new set of Mindbenders (alias Manchester's Mike Sweeney And The Thunderbyrds)
31. *Daily Mirror*, 6 October 1988
32. *Sunday Mirror*, 12 October 1988
33. *Sunderland Echo*, 25 November 1988

Chapter 17: "Now I Just Stay Nervous"

1. *Melody Maker*, 17 April 1965
2. *Wink Bulletin*, 8 December 1988
3. *Melody Maker*, 2 October 1976
4. *Evening Post*, 23 June 1986
5. *The Beat Goes On*, February 1991
6. *Woman's Own*, 10 December 1990
7. *Sunday Mirror*, 23 July 1989
8. *Q*, January 1989
9. A Jack Lee Elgood from Hampshire
10. *Beatles Monthly*, January 1989
11. Keltner's brother Eric was drum technician for the tour
12. *New York Times*, 21 June 1989
13. Although there were instances of brief singalongs of the main refrain of 'She Loves You'
14. Brian Epstein to Murray the K on WORFM, April 1967
15. New York press conference, 20 June 1989
16. *San Francisco Chronicle*, 2 September 1989
17. *LA Times*, 3 September 1987
18. *Las Vegas Review*, 31 August 1989
19. *Daily Telegraph*, 31 March 1990
20. *New York Times*, 6 August 1969
21. *Beatlefan*, April 1991
22. *TV Guide* (US), December 1990
23. Fulton County Superior Court (Atlanta) statement, 15 November 1989
24. Beginning when he tapped the microphone on the stand and asked, "Is it rolling, Bob?"
25. The principal exhibit was a letter from Starr to Moman. There was also Ringo's statement at the New York press conference (see note 15) that "we may do a number from [the Memphis album] just to promote it"
26. To Allan Kozinn

27. Sister of Paul McCartney's ex-fiancée, Jane Asher, and half of Peter And Gordon, his portfolio as a producer includes albums by James Taylor, Linda Ronstadt, Tony Joe White and Bonnie Raitt
28. Nilsson's tapes were of a proposed 1993 album containing a huge helping of comic songs and a rediscovered duet with John Lennon of The Platters' – and Ringo's – 'Only You'
29. Now following in his father and brother's footsteps as a drummer
30. *Sunday Times*, 5 May 1990
31. *Beatles Monthly*, July 1995
32. *Daily Mail*, 24 June 1994
33. Former editor of *Melody Maker* and biographer of both Lennon and Brian Epstein
34. Most recently – and aptly – by The Hollies
35. *Sunday Times*, 15 January 1995
36. *Guardian*, 21 October 1995
37. *People*, 29 October 1995
38. *Guardian*, 2 October 1995

Chapter 18: "I'll Be Fine Anywhere"

1. Published by Cassell, 2000
2. *Mojo*, August 1998
3. Inner-City Games, a non-profit organisation "dedicated to providing enrichment opportunities for inner-city youth"
4. *Daytrippin'* (US Beatles fanzine), issue eleven, summer 2000

Epilogue: "I Go Along With Whatever Is Happening"

1. *Sunday Express*, 3 September 1969
2. *Sunday Times*, 22 February 1983
3. *The NME Encyclopaedia Of Rock* compiled by N Logan and B Woffinden (Star Books, 1976)

Index

Basie, Count 201
Bassey, Shirley 215
Bay City Rollers, The 216
Beach Boys, The 120,
153, 160, 171, 336,
341, 344, 375
Beachcombers, The 251
Beat Boys, The 67
Beatles, The 61, 62, 63,
64-5, 66, 67, 68, 69,
69, 70, 72, 73, 74, 75,
78, 79, 81, 85, 86, 87,
88, 89-90, 91, 92, 93,
94, 95, 96, 97, 98, 99,
101, 102, 103, 104,
105, 107, 108, 109,
110, 111, 112, 115-6,
117, 119, 120, 121,
122-6, 127, 128, 130,
131, 134, 135, 137,
138, 139, 141, 142,
144, 145, 146, 148,
149, 150, 151, 152,
153, 155, 156, 157,
158, 159, 160, 161,
162, 163, 164, 165,
167-8, 169, 170, 172,
173, 175, 178, 179,
181, 182, 184, 185,
187, 188, 189, 190,
191, 192, 195, 196,
198, 199, 200, 205,
206, 211, 212, 213,
216, 219, 221, 224,
226, 231, 234, 235,
236, 237, 240, 241,
242, 249, 253, 256,
259, 261, 262, 263,
264, 266, 269, 271,
274, 275, 279, 281,
282, 284, 289, 290,
291, 296, 298, 301,
302, 305, 307, 310,
322, 323, 324, 325,
327, 330, 334, 345,
350, 352, 354, 355,
358, 359, 361, 363,
364, 365, 366, 367,
368, 369, 370, 371,
374, 374-5, 378
BEATLES ALBUMS
With The Beatles 103,
104
A Hard Day's Night
(and film) 12, 116, 119,
123, 124, 125, 126,
128, 132, 148, 164,
176, 189, 194, 229,
235, 292, 311
Beatles For Sale 104,
354
Help! (and film) 141,
146-7, 148, 152, 167,
177, 292, 340
Rubber Soul 147, 148
Revolver 159, 160, 162,
164, 262
*Sgt Pepper's Lonely
Hearts Club Band* 159,
160-1, 162, 180, 197,
235, 242, 244, 304,
354, 389, 394, 396
The Beatles 181, 182,
183
Yellow Submarine (and
film) 323, 367, 396
Abbey Road 195, 196,
200, 217, 220, 350
Let It Be (and film)
189, 190, 191-2, 193,
195, 206, 217, 383
Beck (Group), (The) Jeff
210, 266, 304, 356
Bee Gees, The 197, 265,
267, 272
Beefheart, Captain (And
His Magic Band) 164,
239
Beethoven, Ludwig van
124
Bell, Freddie (And The
Bellboys) 38, 45
Belushi, John 274
Bennett, Brian 52
Bennett, Cliff (And The
Rebel Rousers) 97, 98,
281
Bennett, Steve (And The
Syndicate) 74
Bennett, Tony 176
Bernstein, Elmer 201
Bernstein, Leonard 110
Berry, Chuck 29, 50, 127,
325
Berry, Dave (And The
Cruisers) 80, 202, 339-
40
Best, George 227, 312
Best, Kathy 300
Best, Mona 85, 88, 94,
109
Best, Pete 11, 12, 63, 64,
65, 65, 67, 73, 85, 86,
87, 88, 89, 90, 94-5,
106, 108, 109, 110,
123, 127, 128, 129,
139, 155, 168, 182,
214, 261, 281, 308,
311-2, 322, 344, 359,
365-6, 368
Best, Roag 261, 322, 366
Beverley Sisters, The 27
Bickerton, Wayne 214
Big Country 328
Big Three, The 68, 70, 72,
74, 80, 82, 87, 92, 108
Bikel, Theodore 239
Bilk, Acker 58, 59, 60,
75, 125
Bird, Brian 41
Black (*née* White), Cilla
19, 28, 32, 33, 50, 64,
65, 70-1, 72, 92, 100,
108, 127, 144, 154,
168, 175, 196, 211,
215, 216, 227, 266,
307-8, 321, 327, 334,
340, 368

152, 153, 156, 161,
162, 166, 167, 168,
169, 170, 171, 172,
173, 175, 176, 178,
179, 180, 183, 184,
188, 190, 195, 196,
197, 200, 202, 203,
204, 205, 206, 207,
215, 217, 218, 219,
220, 221, 227, 234,
236, 239, 240, 241,
242, 244, 245, 247,
248, 249, 263-4, 266,
268, 269, 274, 278,
279, 284, 288, 289,
299, 300, 301, 302,
304, 308-9, 322, 323,
324, 326, 327, 328,
329, 336, 341, 346,
347, 350, 355, 356,
357, 361, 363, 364,
368, 369, 370, 371, 372
Harrison (née Arias),
Olivia (George's second
wife) 304, 319, 355
Harrison, Wilbert 74
Harry, Bill 73, 78, 85, 126
Hart, Bill 67
Hartley, Keith 64-5, 110
Harvey, Alex 37
Harvey, Laurence 194
Hatfield, Bobby 240
Hatton, Billy 22, 23, 31,
35, 84, 92
Havens, Richie 160
Hawkwind 271
Hawn, Goldie 334
Hayes, Isaac 320
Hayles, Margaret 333
Heath, Prime Minister
Edward 27, 233
Hellions, The 68, 80
Helm, Levon 349
Hemingway, Ernest 298
Henderson, Joe "Mr
Piano" 30

Hendrix (Experience),
(The) Jimi 163, 164,
184, 302, 369
Heneberry, Terry 129
Henri, Pierre 197
Hentschel, David 271,
272, 334
Henze, Hans Werner 197
Hepburn, Audrey 32
Herman's Hermits 132,
157, 343
Heston, Charlton 298
Hi-Fi's, The 36, 43, 39
Hi-Hats, The 35
Hill, Benny 292
Hill, Jimmy 223
Hiseman, Jon 210
Hitchcock, Alfred 309
Hitler, Adolf 378
Hodge, Vicki 113-4
Hodges, Eddie 127
Hoffenberg, Mason 177
Hoffman, Abbie 367
Hoffman, Dustin 290
Hollies, The 111, 196,
275, 310, 319, 339
Holloway, Brenda 113
Holly, Buddy 29, 173,
347, 348, 364, 373
Hope, Bob 313
Hopkin, Mary 179, 205,
266
Hopkins, Lightnin' 84,
235
Hopkins, Nicky 242
Horn, Paul 170
Hot Rods, The 68
Howard, Chuck 208
Howerd, Frankie 211
Howlin' Wolf 204, 278
Hudson Brothers, The
371
Hudson, Garth 347
Hudson, Mark 371, 374,
375
Hughes, Howard 134

Hughes, Irene 70
Hulme, Ronald 34
Humble Pie 239
Humperdinck, Engelbert
165
Hunter, Christine 122
Hurt, John 334
Hutchinson, Johnny 38,
41, 64, 68, 87, 91, 343
Huxtable, Judy 101

Innocence 165, 244
Irving, Sir Henry 298
Isley Brothers, The 76

Jack, Wolfman 120
Jackson Five, The 216
Jackson, Chuck 113, 329
Jackson, Jermaine 320
Jackson, Leonard 333
Jackson, Michael 216,
320, 365
Jackson, Tony (And The
Vibrations) 343
Jackson, Wanda 29, 226
Jacobs, David 141
Jagger, Mick 159, 176,
188, 217, 227, 334,
347, 353
Jam, The 261
James Boys, The 31, 35,
38
James, Jesse 31
Janov, Dr Arthur 217
Jaybirds, The 75
Jazzmen, The 44
Jeannie And The Big Guys
108
Jefferson Airplane, The
164
Jennings, Waylon 330
Jethro Tull 271
Jets, The 60, 62, 67
Jevons, Joseph 304
Jive Bombers, The 50,
288

McFall, Ray 44, 59
McGowan, Cathy 334
McKern, Leo 82, 148, 152
McLagan 288
McNair, Harold 41
McNally, John 363
McQueen, Steve 249
Meehan, Tony 41, 129
Meek, Joe 97, 108-9, 239
Memphis Three, The 88
Menikides, Sarah 282, 316, 317, 318
Merseybeats, The 68, 70, 101, 178, 343, 344
Merseyboys, The 121
MFSB 279
Michaels, Lorne 263
Midler, Bette 278, 279
Mike Flowers Pops, The 365
Milkshakes, The 274
Millen, Alex 179
Miller (Band), (The) Steve 339
Miller, Jimmy 132
Miller, Max 350
Miller, Roger 113, 147, 253
Milligan, Spike 160, 171, 194
Mills, Freddie 29
Mink De Ville 288
Miracles, The 113
Mitchell, Guy 24
Mitchelson, Marvin 294
Modigliani, Amedeo 164
Mojos, The 92, 146, 168, 235
Moman, "Chips" 330, 331, 356-7, 370
Money, Zoot 145
Monkees, The 164, 178, 207, 249, 344, 351
Monopacific 315-6
Monro, Matt 147, 202

Monroe, Vaughan 20
Montez, Chris 98
Moody Blues, The 145, 243
Moon, Keith 82, 136, 137, 180, 227, 228, 229, 235, 238, 248-9, 250, 251, 282, 286, 288, 315, 316, 344
Moore, Dr Barbara 159
Moore, Dudley 290
Moore, Roger 296
Moore, Scotty 208
Moore, Tommy 64, 87, 281-2
Morris, Johnny 332
Morrisette, Alanis 372
Morrison, Van 275
Morton, Lionel (Quartet) 80
Most, Mickie 157
Moths, The 68
Moulton, Victor 121-2
Move, The 150, 163, 173
Mudlarks, The 75
Murphy, Hugh 287
Murphy, Paul 37
Murray the K 120
Murray, Pete 29
Musy, Jean 271

Nashville Teens, The 310, 346
Nelis, Manke 264
Nelson, Rick 249
Nelson, Sandy 41, 48, 210
Nelson, Willie 330
Nesmith, Mike 207
New Vaudevile Band, The 146
Newman, Paul 125
Newman, Randy 245
Newman, Thunderclap 219
Newman, Tony 129

Next, The 282, 283, 305, 315, 316
Nice, The 271
Nicholas, Paul 237
Nicholls, Clay (And the Blue Flames) 56
Nicholls, Johnny (And The Dimes) 45
Nicol, Jimmy 41, 83, 87, 90, 129-30, 131, 137
Nightfly 316, 347
Nilsson, Harry 164-5, 175, 228, 238, 239, 240, 241, 248, 250, 251, 256, 260, 270, 305, 310, 313, 314, 317, 335, 336, 361-2
Noakes, Rab 273
Noble, Barry 343
Nureyev, Rudolf 259

Oasis 363
Oddie, Bill 272, 318
O'Brien, Denis 236
O'Connor, Brian 333
O'Connor, Sinéad 335
O'Dell, Denis 195
O'Donnell, Mike 247
O'Farrell, Chico 201
O'Hara, Brian 31
O'Neill, Terry 132, 304, 334
Olympics, The 50
Onassis, Christina 259
Ono, Yoko 163, 180, 181, 182, 183, 184, 189, 192, 193, 201, 205, 218, 236, 242, 248, 256, 267, 301, 302, 308, 322, 323, 345, 346, 373
Orbison, Roy 29, 117, 128, 144, 208, 267, 280, 326, 330, 346, 357
Orlons, The 76
Osmonds, The 216, 224

John Lennon

Printed in the United Kingdom by MPG Books Ltd, Bodmin

Published by Sanctuary Publishing Limited, Sanctuary House, 45-53 Sinclair Road,
London W14 0NS, United Kingdom

www.sanctuarypublishing.com

Distributed in the US by Publishers Group West

ISBN: 1-86074-487-7

John Lennon

Alan Clayson
Sanctuary

About The Author

Born in Dover, England, in 1951, Alan Clayson lives near Henley-on-Thames with his wife, Inese, and sons, Jack and Harry. His portrayal in the *Western Morning News* as "the AJP Taylor of the pop world" is supported by *Q*'s "his knowledge of the period is unparalleled and he's always unerringly accurate". He has written many books on music, including best-sellers *Backbeat* (subject of a major film) and *The Yardbirds*, as well as for journals as diverse as *The Guardian, Record Collector, Mojo, The Times, Mediaeval World, Eastern Eye, Folk Roots, Guitar, Hello!, The Independent, Ugly Things, The Times* and, as a teenager, the notorious *Schoolkids' Oz*. He has also performed and lectured on both sides of the Atlantic, as well as broadcast on national TV and radio .

From 1975 to 1985, he led the legendary group Clayson And The Argonauts and was thrust to "a premier position on rock's Lunatic Fringe" (*Melody Maker*). As shown by the formation of a US fan club – dating from a 1992 *soirée* in Chicago – Alan Clayson's following has continued to grow, as has demand for his talents as a record producer and the number of cover versions of his compositions by such diverse acts as Dave Berry – in whose Cruisers he played keyboards in the mid-1980s – and new-age outfit Stairway. He has also worked with The Portsmouth Sinfonia, Wreckless Eric, Twinkle, The Yardbirds, The Pretty Things and the late Screaming Lord Sutch, among others. While his stage act defies succinct description, he is spearheading an English form of *chanson*. Moreover, his latest album, *Soirée*, may stand as his artistic apotheosis, were it not for the promise of surprises yet to come.

Further information is obtainable from www.alanclayson.com.

Contents

To Valdis Eriks, Laura and Anika

"He's dead but he won't lie down"
– Old music-hall song

Prologue

"I Only Learnt To Play To Back Myself"

Just what the world needs, eh? Another book about John Lennon.

You probably know at least the bare bones of the story backwards, but for that aged Tibetan monk who still hasn't heard of him, Lennon is recognised generally as the leader of a 1960s pop group called The Beatles, who sold – and still sell – millions of gramophone records. If Lennon – arguably, the group's chief creative pivot – had shed most of his artistic load by 1968, he'd left such an ineradicable impression on the complacency of post-war pop that certain of his more jaw-dropping public activities were dismissed initially as the prerogative of celebrity.

Although the world become wiser to his failings – mainly via a decidedly erratic post-Beatles career – his omnipotence is such that veneration has yet to fade for countless fans in a languid daze from the fixity of gazing – figuratively, anyway – at the Dakota Building, the luxury apartment block in New York that was his family home for the final years of a life that was as triumphant as it was tragic. As a 1960s myth, rather than the mere man who was shot dead by a nobody called Mark David Chapman on 8 December 1980, John Lennon was built to last.

As early as 1963, a certain Billy Shepherd was preparing his *The True Story Of The Beatles*, the first of more biographies of The Beatles – together and apart – than anyone could have imagined then. Described by BBC radio presenter John Peel as "the engine room of The Beatles",[1] Lennon has been particularly well served. Indeed, the principal events of almost every day of his life since 1962 have been accounted for in some publication or other, and even as sources of "new and rediscovered facts" continue to dry up, there are presently nearly 70 books concerning him alone still in print. How many have you read already?

Even before his hasty cremation, publishers were liaising with authors about posthumous explorations of every nook and cranny of John's four decades on this planet. Raw information has been chronicled over and over again, whether cornucopias of listings – say, the 700 pages of Keith Badman's day-by-day diary, *The Beatles After The Break-Up* – or Bill Harry's vast, meticulous and culminant *John Lennon Encyclopedia*, which deals with people, places and things concerning the subject as accurately and as adequately as anyone might reasonably expect.

While these books cater for the devotee who derives deep and lasting pleasure from studying basic data, more opinionated tomes have ranged from near-hagiographies – such as *Lennon* by Carole Lynn Corbin – aimed at those for whom the former art student sits at the right hand of God to the likes of *Every Sound There Is: The Beatles' Revolver And The Transformation Of Rock And Roll*, a collection of essays pitched at the consumer who attends a concert in order to chat about how "interesting" it was in licensed premises afterwards. In the privacy of his own home, he reads a lot, thinks a lot, but does nothing. Perhaps the word I'm looking for is *intellectual*. Dripping from the pens of college academics from across the globe, titles like "A Flood Of Flat-Sevenths", "Premature Turns: Thematic Disruption In The American Version" and "Rearranging Base And Superstructure In The Rock Ballad" telegraph that you might need to have a dictionary of musicological terms – or at least a plain dictionary – close to hand.

At another point on the spectrum is *The Lives Of John Lennon* by the late Albert Goldman, a best-seller that depicted Lennon as barking mad after a lifetime of incredible human frailty. Forgive my xenophobic paranoia, but I've read few books concerning British pop written by North Americans that have come anywhere near capturing the peculiarities of being British. I'm not even sure whether a non-Liverpudlian like myself is qualified to write about a Beatle, but I don't waste sentences explaining what I mean by "winkle-pickers" and "not half". I do not revolt readers by juxtaposing imagined British colloquialisms like "all of a blessed sudden" with hip Americanisms such as referring to a sex orgy as a "fuckfest". I don't think Ascot is a suburb of London. Crucially, anyone who refers to John Lennon's "cockney chirpiness" – as a *Rolling Stone* journalist did in a biography of Paul McCartney – is a bit suspect.

In Canadian Geoffrey Giuliano's *Dark Horse*, a "secret life of George Harrison", Pete Best's dismissal in 1962 is over in half a sentence, and not long afterwards The Beatles are winding up a world tour in San Francisco four years later. Furthermore, did John really shout, "Sieg heil, you mothers!" at the Kaiserkeller audience? And what's all this about "after leaving Quarry Bank High School For Boys in 1953, George was enrolled at the Liverpool Institute"? Maybe Giuliano thinks "high school" means "primary school" over here. In any case, it was Lennon, not Harrison, who went to Quarry Bank. That was among Giuliano's more glaring gaffs, but with self-interested vigilance I stumbled on a few other testaments to Rudyard Kipling's "what should they know of England who only England know?" but, overall, *Dark Horse* was an untaxing read with little that was particularly new or significant revealed.

Yet, when I was approached to write this present account, I wondered how difficult it would be for me too to say anything fresh or valuable about John Lennon without taking liberties with the old backstage plot, treating his most flippant remarks as gospel or squeezing paragraphs from, say, drummer Jim McCarty's observations when his Yardbirds secured a support spot with The Beatles' during their 1964 season at Hammersmith Odeon. During an intermission, he saw Lennon standing at the top of a fire-escape at the back of the building in the teddy-bear costume he wore for one of the comedy sketches, which then filled part of the show. John was considering the purchase of one of a fleet of limousines from a London showroom. As it was inconvenient for the pop star to visit the garage during opening hours, its bowing, scraping proprietor had arranged for the vehicles to nose past the twilit foot of the metal stairway.

Another problem I had is this: I don't know about you, but Lennon's more orthodox music – both solo and with The Beatles – has become so embedded by 40 years of availability and airplay that I hear most of it nowadays no more than a sailor hears the sea. To ask my opinion about 'She Loves You', 'Strawberry Fields Forever' or 'Imagine' is like asking me about railway lines or donkeys' false teeth because I can't say anything objective about them any more. They're just there.

For reasons connected vaguely with this, and for psychological stimulation, I Blu-Tacked a picture of John Lennon on the wall. It hung there until I got sick of the wretched fellow gazing reproachfully at an untidy room that my piano and writing desk dominate like twin castle sinisters while, like a medieval scribe at his parchment, I deciphered exercise books full of scribble and transcribed interview tapes. While I was still establishing an order peculiar to myself, Lennon witnessed too the occasional wild-haired search for some mislaid jotting or other that had me ready to kill someone.

Bear in mind also that, as a soldier going over the top in the Great War, I have to screw myself up before talking to various members of the *dramatis personnae* about events that took place up to half a century ago – although over the years, I've become more desensitised about asking incisive questions that stop just short of open impertinence. If some of my interviewees here were politely evasive on occasions, that very silence often illuminated the back stairs of John Lennon's life as surely as if they'd actually named names and told tales.

You see, I'm determined that this will be the last word on Lennon – or at least the last word on those aspects of Lennon and his associates that intrigue me. However, in a dark and lonely corner of my mind, a still, small voice tells me that it won't be, because all publications to do with The Beatles and John Lennon remain such sound marketing exercises that I wonder if there's ever going to be a cutting-off point. Apparently, someone's at work on a biography of Mal Evans, one of the group's road managers. Will there also be a book each from every act on the same label? Everyone who ever covered or revived a Lennon–McCartney song? The foresters who felled the trees to make the paper on which they were written?

I'll stop being facetious for long enough to state that interest in John Lennon – for what he was and for what consumers think he has become – will endure because his influence as a vocalist and composer is and has been acknowledged by every pop artist that has mattered, and his lyrics are still quoted like proverbs.

During the four-year sabbatical before the brief re-emergence that climaxed in his sudden death, Lennon had become as unreachable an object of myth as Elvis Presley. There wasn't a newspaper editor in the world who wouldn't promise a fortune for a Lennon exclusive or an up-to-the-minute photo. Rock stars passing through the Big Apple made at least token efforts to gain an audience with the Grand Old Man, despite his many dubious antics in the past and the hearsay circulating about peculiar goings-on in the Dakota.

Having gouged so deep a wound in pop culture, it might not have mattered if, in the years left to him since the sundering of The Beatles in 1970, Lennon had not continued even a sporadic recording career, let along one containing odd sparks of the old fire that used to power him when The Beatles were stuck on the Liverpool–Hamburg treadmill. At that time there had been so many ideas – and not only musical ones – chasing through his mind that it was all he could do to note them down. Flames of inspiration would kindle during a 20-minute dawdle to Hamburg's main railway station to buy yesterday's *Daily Express*. Others jerked him from a velvet-blue oblivion back into the dungeons where The Beatles slept during their maiden visit in 1960.

Even after the group made it, tomorrow would seem a year away as with McCartney, more often than not, John would figure out a chord sequence to fragments of melody or rhymes to form a couplet. From a mere title, the ghost of maybe a sketchy chorus would smoulder into form and a red-eyed objectivity and private quality control might engross him and Paul until evening became morning with the two surrounded by cigarette butts, smeared coffee cups and pages full of scribbled verse and notation peculiar to themselves.

As he'd never learned to sight-read or write musical script, John was untroubled by the formal dos and don'ts that traditionally affect creative flow. There were only the stylistic clichés and habits ingrained since his teenage self had positioned as-yet-uncalloused fingertips on the taut strings of his first guitar. "I only learnt to play to back myself,"[2] he'd admit later.

On 9 December 1980, a BBC television reporter asked George Martin, The Beatles' producer, if he thought that the deceased was a great musician.

"He was a great man," replied the diplomatic Martin.[3]

John Lennon wasn't a virtuoso, far from it, but he functioned fully (most of the time) according to his capacity within the context of The Beatles and was able to cross the demarcation line of John (rhythm guitar), Paul (bass guitar), George (lead guitar) and Ringo (drums) when it was necessary to cut corners. He played lead, for instance, on both 'The Ballad Of John And Yoko' – on which neither Harrison nor Starr were present – and 'Get Back'. He was no slouch on keyboards, either, having been hunched over a Vox Continental organ when necessary – admittedly, unheard above the screams – during The Beatles' final tour.

Yet John Lennon hadn't had all that much going for him when he trod the boards as an amateur with the skiffle outfit The Quarry Men in 1957. While he could just about find his way around his instrument then, he aroused little fervour for either his singing or his first attempts at composition. On the surface, he wasn't that brilliant at anything then. And yet...

Alan Clayson
December 2002

1 "Who Am I To Regard As Mother?"

At 6:30pm on Wednesday 9 October 1940, John Winston Lennon was prised into the world at Liverpool's Oxford Street Maternity Hospital. The BBC Home Service weatherman had forecast that the night and the next day would be dull but mild, which they were. Dull but mild it remained for more or less the next fortnight. But one evening before the baby was brought home, wailing sirens and flares illuminated the sky as the Luftwaffe dropped ton upon booming ton of death and destruction in and around the slip-slapping wharfs of the docklands where the Mersey sweeps into the Irish Sea.

The following morning, brick dust crunched beneath the hooves of dray horses dragging coal through mean streets to rusty ships, but Julia Lennon's firstborn was destined for a comfortable middle-class home – with a fitted dining-room carpet, not lino – in Menlove Avenue, one of the main thoroughfares of Woolton, a village-like suburb that aligned itself more with rural Lancashire than Merseyside, embracing mock-Tudor colonies, golf clubs and boating lakes.

After his father, Freddie, a seaman of Irish extraction, vanished to all intents and purposes when John was five, so soon did the concept that there is no God but Mummy, and Daddy is the prophet of Mummy. With Freddie represented – perhaps unfairly – as the villain of the piece, the subsequent complications of his wayward mother's love-life and domestic arrangements made it more convenient for the child to grow up in Mendips, the semi-detached villa of Julia's childless sister, Mary Smith (whom John would always call by his cradle articulation "Mimi") and her ex-serviceman husband, George, once an infinitesimal cog in the global hostilities but now running his late father's dairy business. George was to die suddenly when his nephew by marriage was 14.

As John was to discover, Julia lived nearby with her second family, and bound by the invisible chains that shackle child to parent he used her council house as a bolthole whenever strait-laced Mimi's rearing methods became oppressive. The innate confusion of "Who am I to regard as mother?" affected John's ability to trust adult authority figures, whom he mocked and abused as a defence against being rejected by them – particularly after Julia was killed in July 1958 by a car with a policeman, late for his shift, at the wheel.

Moreover, despite the extenuating circumstances, he felt that he'd been cast out by his mother as well as by Freddie, having had enough experience of her to know what he was missing, hence the bitterness inherent in outbursts against teachers, friends and his devoted aunt. She usually blamed doubtful company for John's mischief when, short-trousered and gaberdine-raincoated, he began his formal education on 12 November 1945 in the kindergarten at Moss Pits Lane Infant School, a few streets' dawdle from Mendips.

The following April, John was expelled for disruptive behaviour and, chastened by this disgrace, commenced a less wild career at Dovedale Road Primary School. For a while, he modelled himself on "William Brown", Richmal Crompton's outrageous 12-year-old from a well-to-do rural family, whose first exploit, *Just William*, was published in 1917.[4] Lennon, however, was to go beyond the rough-and-tumble of acceptable boyhood larks on passing his 11 Plus and gaining a place at Quarry Bank, a grammar school nicknamed "the Police State" by the Liverpool Institute, Prescot Grammar, the newer Liverpool Collegiate and other more liberal seats of learning for its pretentious affectations and Draconian rigmarole. An Eton-like house system was in full force there and so was corporal punishment, administered as often as not with the swish of a bamboo cane on buttocks or outstretched palm.

John might have fared better at a secondary modern, where 11 Plus "failures" went, or better still a comprehensive, had one been established on Merseyside by the early 1950s with the schools' more pronounced "education for all" concept theoretically enabling children to follow what best suited their abilities and inclinations as they developed. As it was, it didn't take long for John to transform from a capable if uninvolved pupil to a C-stream hard case, hanging onto his place at Quarry Bank by the skin of his teeth. By the end of his second year there, he had become a sharer of smutty stories and magazines of female lingerie and a mainstay of the smoking club behind the bicycle sheds. Indeed, the adult Lennon would be tearing the cellophane off up to three 20 packs a day.

As well as overt offences, John was a more insidiously bad influence on others via his insulting "politeness" to teachers, his red-herring time-wasting tactics in class, his copied homework and his dumb insolence when directed to spit a sweet into the litter bin during lessons.

Similarly leading by example outside school, Lennon had some kind of vice-like grip on his allies in delinquency, some of whom weren't so much friends as disciples whom he could usually persuade to do almost anything. Among them was the type of specimen that might be lured into some shaming *faux pas*, sent on a fool's errand, driven to near-suicide with mind games and slapped hard on the back or around the face under the flag of aggressive friendliness so that he'd have to grin at John with tears in his eyes. He'd want to join the gang, but he'd be a figure of fun at best, at worst the arbitrary object of aggression, and in between an outsider denied the social intercourse that king-bee Lennon and his alpha-boys took for granted. Outwardly unbothered and faithful, he struggled not to put his foot in it when John threw down a few words like small change to a beggar, before that butterfly concentration alighted elsewhere.

Some of Lennon's "victims", however, either weaned themselves off him or started to snap back. A few went so far as to put up their fists and look fierce, noting how swiftly their antagonist would back down. "I used to beat them up if they were small enough," John was to admit, not especially ruefully, "but I'd use long words and confuse them if they were bigger. What mattered was that I stayed in charge."[5]

Not standing when he could lean, hands rammed in pockets and chewing gum in a half sneer, the attitude of that Lennon boy – lazy, destructive, narcissistic and, as far as he dared, a bully – was also reflected in further extra-curricular activities that had little bearing on what he was supposed to be learning at school. Absorbing a hidden curriculum, he'd developed a messy aptitude as an illustrator and writer of comic verse and stories since Dovedale Primary. On a par with this at Quarry Bank, however, was his interest in the guitar, the instrument that Elvis Presley hung around his neck. Lennon didn't only like Presley; he worshipped him – no other word would do. John Lennon worshipped Elvis Presley – the Hillbilly Cat, the Memphis Flash, the King Of Western Bop – from the moment he heard 'Heartbreak Hotel', the Tennesseean's debut entry in the newly established *New Musical Express* record charts, and saw the first photograph of him published in Britain[6] as a hybrid of nancy boy and amusement-arcade hoodlum. As far as John was concerned, Elvis was to die metaphorically when manager Colonel Tom Parker's smoothing of his rough diamond began in 1958, with the stressing of an uncomplaining diligence while the young star was on National Service in the US Army.

Other of the Quarry Bank schoolboy's rock 'n' roll heroes went down, too. Little Richard, a chart fixture with such set-works as 'Rip It Up,' 'Long Tall Sally' and 1958's 'Good Golly Miss Molly' – all dominated by his vamping piano and declamatory vocals – eschewed pop for the Church. Whilst at theological college and a subsequent ministry, he was to issue little but religious material for several years.

Jerry Lee Lewis, meanwhile, was also prone to vigorous bouts of evangelism, but he continued to play the devil's music after 1957's 'Whole Lotta Shakin' Goin' On', and attendant electrifying appearances on US television catapulted him to international attention. The momentum was sustained with such as 'Great Balls Of Fire' and 'High School Confidential' before a tour of Britain brought to light his bigamous third espousal to an under-aged cousin.

Chuck Berry would be off the air, too, after 'Roll Over Beethoven', 'Sweet Little Sixteen', 'Johnny B Goode' and other self-penned items, which celebrated in song the pleasures that were available to American teenage consumers. In 1959, Berry was to serve the first of two jail terms, which put temporary halts to his career. Nevertheless, this incarceration served to boost his cult celebrity status in Britain where he'd been seen "duckwalking" derisively with a crotch-level guitar only in *Jazz on A Summer's Day*, a film documentary about the Newport Jazz Festival.

Buddy Holly And The Crickets also wrote their own songs and this ability, plus the compact sound of two guitars, bass and drums on the group's only UK tour, was one of the major elements that coalesced to produce the British beat boom. This 1958 visit was in the wake of a string of international smashes, which began with the previous year's 'That'll Be The Day'. However, in the aftershock of his fatal aeroplane crash in 1959, US obituarists tended to write off Holly as a has-been in professional as well as absolute terms.

It was no coincidence that, after Buddy's British trek and subsequent death, sales of guitars boomed at Frank Hessy's music shop in central Liverpool. John Lennon, however, had acquired one as a result of an earlier craze traceable to "king of skiffle" Lonnie Donegan being permitted to sing one or two blues-tinged North American folk tunes to the accompaniment of washboard, double bass and his own guitar strumming while a member of Chris Barber's Jazz Band. "Really, it was me doing impressions of Big Bill Broonzy, Leadbelly, Josh White and Lonnie Johnson," confessed Lonnie when I interviewed him two years before his death in November 2002, "as well as Woody Guthrie, Hank Snow, Hank Williams...but they came out as Lonnie Donegan."

From a 1954 Barber album on Pye Records, there were sufficient BBC Light Programme airings of Lonnie's 'Rock Island Line' to warrant its issue as a grudging spin-off single in autumn 1955. Its alarming climb into the sleepy Top 20s of both Britain and the United States made it expedient for the 24-year-old to go solo. "I didn't see success in the USA as long term," estimated Donegan. "I had every intention of coming back and rejoining Chris Barber, but the agent booked me for all sorts of rock 'n' roll shows all over America. The first one was with Chuck Berry in Cleveland. I was doing very well, but then I received a telegram from Pye saying, 'Come Home. "Lost John" at Number Two.' I was shocked at all the skiffle clubs that had opened everywhere and the thousands of guys trying to imitate Lonnie Donegan. It was uncanny how much John Lennon sounded like me on that Quarry Men tape that turned up a few years ago."

When 'Rock Island Line' boomed from the loudspeakers just before the main feature in a Grantham cinema, Roy Taylor, a member of The Harmonica Vagabonds with fellow members of the YMCA, claimed, "I couldn't believe my ears! Next morning, I bought the record. Then I bought a guitar and started a skiffle group called just The Vagabonds. For our repertoire, Lonnie couldn't turn out records fast enough."

Future Trogg Chris Britton in The Hiccups in Andover, Van Morrison with Belfast's Sputniks, Peter Smith (later Crispian St Peters) of Swanley's Hard Travellers and other hitmakers-in-waiting listened hard to Donegan, who bossed the ensuing craze throughout its 1957 prime and beyond. Backed by his own Skiffle Group, Donegan's driving whine and vibrant personality lacquered further adaptations of similar North American material, which, if failing to further his cause in the land from whence it came, kept him in domestic smashes, even after he offended purists by tilting for wider acceptance with chestnuts from the golden days of Empire, such as chart-topping 'Putting On The Style' and 'My Old Man's A Dustman', an adaptation of the Merseyside folk ditty 'My Old Man's A Fireman On The Elder–Dempster Line'.

"The platform for working at that time was the variety theatres to a very general public," explained Lonnie. "You could work half the year, and spend the rest doing nothing. I was headlining over dancing girls, comedians, jugglers, whatever, and couldn't just stand there like one of Lowry's Matchstick Men, because I had to learn to back-project, announce and get laughs. You had to perform, not just play. Otherwise, you died and got no more work."

No skiffle purist, John Lennon didn't mind Lonnie thus broadening his appeal. After a fashion, he too was extending himself beyond US folk songs. At first, he hadn't played his new guitar much, although Julia – who plinked a banjo – had taught him a few less-than-full chords before she died. Rather than progress beyond these, he'd focused more on cultivating a lustrous, brilliantined pompadour tapering to sideburns like scimitars, even going through a phase of flicking back his quiff just like Elvis, pretending that it wouldn't stop falling over his eyes.

Sometimes, in a time-honoured ritual of thwarted eroticism, he'd place a Presley single on the record player in his bedroom and arrange himself in front of the wardrobe mirror, standing there with his guitar. From the opening bars to the coda, he'd curl his lip and pretend to slash chords and pick solos with negligent ease. He'd mouth the lyrics, *yeah*-ing and *uh-huh*-ing to thousands of ecstatic females that only he could see.

Once, an only-too-real female burst in. Gaping at the arched eyebrow and crooked smile in the doorway, John felt no end of a fool. Then Aunt Mimi gazed into the middle distance and spoke in generalities. The gist was that it's heartbreaking to see people struggling desperately to be something they can never hope to be. Their vain attempts to scale the heights of their dreams give glimpses of high comedy to someone watching but bring themselves nothing but misery. Tragi-comedy is only truly funny to the truly heartless – but there's no tragedy in being untalented if you've no knowledge of it. It's a bearable state, even a happy one, until someone opens your eyes to it. Ignorance – or arrogance – can be a very protective shell.

This embarrassing episode may have goaded John to make a more cursory go at learning his instrument properly, bringing him to realise that certain basic chord cycles recurred over and over again in skiffle and classic rock. Yet the fascination of holding down an E major chord didn't interfere with his work on the visuals, getting all the Elvis Presley moves off too, even though there wasn't room in the bedroom for feigning a collapse and crawling to the edge of a imaginary stage. The chief motivation for his efforts, of course, was connected with the fleeting flashes of knicker as girls jived in gingham whenever he went to a dance.

A hard-won mastery of basic musical and choreographic techniques, combined with the rising sap of puberty, therefore found him at the central microphone – indeed, the only microphone – with The Quarry Men, as a perk of being in a pop group was, so he understood, readier licence to talk to girls, at least, than most of the other chaps who'd paid to shuffle about in the gloom beyond the stage with a built-in sense of defeat.

Almost as a matter of course, John had a walkover in whatever power struggle there was in The Quarry Men. As well as an ingrained bossiness, he could claim real and imagined genealogical links with showbusiness. There was, apparently, a Liverpool-Irish grandfather, Jack Lennon, who'd emigrated to North America and been in a touring revue called Andrew Robertson's Kentucky Minstrels prior to returning to Merseyside as a pub entertainer. However, John kept quieter about The Lennon Sisters –

Dianne, Peggy, Kathy and Janet – who came to national attention in the USA as featured vocal group on light orchestral supremo Lawrence Welk's weekly television show, all scripted grinning and harmless fun. And when they were signed to Coral – Buddy Holly's label – in 1955, they became known as singers of catchy tunes with jaunty rhythms, as demonstrated in their US novelty hit a year later with 'Tonight You Belong To Me'.

This Lennon sisters had no place in John's index of possibilities as a Quarry Man. In the burning glare of the footlights – if there were any – at what posters then billed as "swing sessions" in this village institute or that social club, he sometimes incurred the dislike of the expected cluster of teddy boys and other male riff-raff on one side of the hall, keeping up a baleful barrage of catcalls and barracking, whilst the girls danced round each other's handbags opposite. Narrow-eyed with frustration and alcohol, if they could get it, their objective for being there might metamorphose into more brutal sensual pleasure than the pursuit of sex.

Such attention was partly self-inflicted because of John's visible and omnipotent hold over the other Quarry Men, just like Lonnie Donegan had held sway over his Skiffle Group. If Lonnie looked like a used-car salesman offstage, the King of Skiffle could be mesmeric in concert, creating true hand-biting excitement as he piled into numbers that the Group didn't know, taking on and resolving risky extemporisations and generating a sweaty, exhilarating intensity never before experienced in British pop. In retrospect, it's not silly to put Lonnie Donegan on a par with Jimi Hendrix.

More typical of the genre than either hitmaking Donegan or raw amateurs like The Quarry Men was Ricky Richards' Skiffle Group, resident in the Skiffle Cellar, a stone's throw from the 2 I's, central London's more renowned shrine of British pop. After nearly half a century, their entire recorded output – 12 hitherto-unissued tracks, taped mostly in the double-bass player's Wembley home – was made available for public consumption on a small record label in 2002.

In all conscience, I cannot resort to cheap laughs at Ricky and his ensemble's expense because, as well as being a slice of cultural history, the CD entitled *Shake It Daddy* is also entertaining, but not because it's so bad it's good; as well as making a fair lo-fi fist of numbers that were common property of other outfits all over the country, the lads turn in two Richards originals – including the title song – which stand as tall as their workman-like versions of 'John Henry', 'Wreck Of The Old '97', 'Putting On The Style' *et al*.

Give him credit, too. Ricky's fretboard picking was held in high regard by the discerning Tony Sheridan, then emerging – albeit briefly – as one of Britain's most sensational rock 'n' roll guitarists. Both were destined for walk-on parts in Lennon's life after he left Quarry Bank in July 1957.

When the predictably poor results of John's GCE O-levels fluttered onto the doormat a few weeks later – he'd failed all of them, albeit by only one grade – Aunt Mimi made an appointment to discuss her charge's future with the headmaster, Mr William Pobjoy, who informed her that John's most legitimate contribution to school affairs had been when The Quarry Men performed during the interval at the sixth form's end-of-term party.

Mimi hadn't realised until recently, she said, that John's wretched skiffle group even had a name, let alone gone beyond just messing about with guitars. His fooling around on the Spanish model she'd been badgered into buying him was all right as a hobby, she'd told him, but she'd thought she'd die of shame if he ever appeared onstage with a pop group. He'd answered back that a boy he knew called George Harrison only had to ask for one of these electric guitars and it was his. Well, that's as may be, but showbusiness isn't a reliable living, is it? You couldn't see it as a career unless you'd been born into it.

Even then, Mr Pobjoy chipped in, if you were a vocalist in the popular style, you had to "mature" with an output that veered between sentimental ballads and singalong ditties. Look at Lonnie Donegan and, before him, indigenous entertainers like Max Bygraves, Ronnie Hilton, Donald Peers ("the Cavalier of Song") and the neo-operatic Lee Laurence.

Again, that's as may be, replied Mimi, but John's nonsense about wanting to make his way as a "pop star" was nearly as appalling as a girl announcing that she wanted to shake her backside in a burlesque troupe. In the perceived moral decline of the country since the war, such a viewpoint was to remain the norm in decent provincial households, where patterned wallpaper was the only hint of frivolity and where the 1950s wouldn't end until about 1966.

That was one reason why John was a nuisance at school. That he was one, Mimi had suspected from the beginning, if only because his behaviour there impacted at home in constant turmoil over his choice of friends, his insolence, his speech, his manners, his slouch, those crude drainpipe jeans and him sculpting his hair in that stupid quiff-and-ducktail style, with side-whiskers like one of these teddy boys: secondary modern ne'er-do-wells who, garbed in seedy flash finery, prowled the evening streets in packs, looking for things to destroy and people to beat up.

Lately, Mimi continued, she'd started to position herself at the front window whenever she'd deduced that John was about to leave the house. He didn't have to catch her eye; even sensing her glaring, quivering and tight-lipped disapproval was enough for him to return and change out of the more ridiculous clothes he'd got past her quality control.

When he next got a word in edgeways, Mr Pobjoy – who had given the boy a kinder written testimonial than either he or Mimi might have expected – suggested that the Youth Employment Centre might not find John beyond redemption and that an apprenticeship of some kind wasn't out of the question. Alternatively, he recommended that John could do worse than join the Regular Army.

However, as Aunt Mimi wouldn't hear of her fallen angel entering the world of work before she considered he'd completed his "education", the outcome of a rather fraught discussion was that John was to be enrolled at Liverpool's Regional College of Art that September. Entry standards for the establishment were particularly lax, to the point of being non-existent beyond evidence of a slight artistic turn.

The Quarry Men survived their leader's transfer to the higher-education establishment in the city centre, although by then he had come to seek the particular company of a lad named Paul McCartney, enlisted into The Quarry Men in July 1957. The fact that his elder son was joining a group fronted by that John Lennon was a severe test of paternal support, but McCartney's widowed father accepted Paul's case for the defence, that John had been a square peg in a round hole at Quarry Bank and that he was a fine fellow when you got to know him.

Moreover, for all his loutish affectations, Lennon knew how he was supposed to behave when introduced to other boys' parents. McCartney, forever rejoicing in his council-estate origins, "never realised John put on this 'working-class hero' stuff. Nobody had a set of Winston Churchill books. Nobody had an aunt, 'cause we called 'em 'aunties'. 'Aunt' was very posh. Nobody had relatives who were dentists or worked at the BBC, as two of John's Scottish relatives did. Nobody had relatives in Edinburgh, my dear! This was a middle-class structure in which John was very much part of. When symphonies came on the radio, my family just went, 'Oh bloody hell!' and switched the station."[7]

The Quarry Men's new pianist, John Duff Lowe, was in the same form as Paul at Liverpool Institute and met John in the McCartney living room in the city suburb of Allerton. "It wasn't a particularly momentous encounter," he recalled, "though when you're 16, anyone 18 months older is often a bit intimidating. John also used to dress in what you'd loosely describe as teddy-boy gear. Paul's father – like all parents – was paranoid that his children were going to turn into teddy boys, pushing bottles into people's faces and creating mayhem in the clubs. The uniform indicated someone who was looking for trouble. John gave the impression of being like that but was actually quite a nice guy.

"George Harrison came into the group a week or two after me. Prior to us, the band had Rod Davis on banjo, Pete Shotton on washboard, Eric Griffiths on guitar, Colin Hanton on drums, Len Garry on tea-chest bass, John Lennon and, right at the end of the skiffle era, Paul McCartney."

Without the others, Paul and John began to practise and even write songs together, sometimes truanting to do so. They even lugged their instruments with them when, on the spur of the moment, they went hitch-hiking in the south of England one Easter holiday. That was when they'd really become friends.

Although their style was based on blues, hillbilly and further subdivisions of North American folk music, the pre-McCartney Quarry Men also embraced rock 'n' roll, and it was this element that had impressed Paul when he'd attended a performance in 1957 at Woolton summer fête (which someone taped for then-unimagined posterity, as well as the ears of an elderly Lonnie Donegan). So began one of the most crucial liaisons in pop. Not long afterwards, George Harrison deputised for and then superseded original lead guitarist Eric Griffiths, who, like most of the other personnel, regarded skiffle as a vocational blind alley, a trivial pursuit to be thrust aside on departure to the world of work, marriage or National Service.

John Duff Lowe's growing disinclination to remain a Quarry Man, however, was mostly because of geography: "I lived in West Derby, on the opposite side of Liverpool to all the others. Whereas Paul could easily bike round to John's house, it was a journey on two buses for me. I didn't tend to get involved during the week. We'd rehearse on Sunday and perform the following Saturday if anyone would have us. Also, whenever we turned up anywhere, the quality of the hall pianos varied so much. They were often either out of tune or had notes missing. This especially annoyed John, as the guitars had to be retuned to the piano."

Hundreds more than could actually have been there were to reconjure a night within the Mersey hinterland at maybe a church youth club with a wholesome, self-improving reek about it. They'd handed over the sixpence (2 ½p) admission to a with-it vicar in a cardigan, who'd booked The Quarry Men to perform in a playing area with a solitary white bulb as the lightshow and a microphone and two of the three guitars plugged perilously into one amplifier via two shared jacks. The other was fed through something soldered together from a kit advertised ("with a ten-watt punch") in *Melody Maker*.

This latter arrangement was the work of George Harrison, a bus driver's son, happy just to be around the beery breathed John, three years his senior and a fully fledged rock 'n' roller who boasted about how he'd tilted successfully for the downfall of some girl's underwear. An educated guess, however, is that John Lennon at 17 was probably still a virgin, like the vast majority of his adolescent peers. In days before the birth-control pill and the Swinging '60s, pre-marital sex was a much bigger issue. To sceptical cronies, a changing-room lothario at Quarry Bank would boast of carnal capers that everyone guessed were tall tales. He might have got to "third base" after a lot of effort, but only a "cheap" girl didn't "save herself" for her future husband. Until recently, John had imagined that girls went all the way only if they really loved you, and even then a true daughter of the 1950s would have none of it while yet unwed. Nevertheless, through some undignified fumblings, Lennon discovered that even a youth club's most arch proto-feminist – the sort who looked as if she couldn't wait for a game of ping-pong, followed by a chat about life after death over an orange squash – her whole tweedy, earnest being was screaming for sex just as much as any bloke.

Although George Harrison was the most heterosexual of males too, his heart would feel like it had burst through its ribcage whenever the great Lennon lowered himself to actually speak to him, no matter how nastily. Once, George brought a friend to be introduced to Lennon, but without looking around the cocky so-and-so outstretched his fingers over his left shoulder for the newcomer to shake. Had John then offered anything other than slights, exploitations and jokes at his expense, George might have been worried about his position as the lowest of the low in The Quarry Men hierarchy. Unaware that Lennon was an inwardly fearful youth whose successful promotion of himself as a physical and verbal fighter had brittle substance, it gave young Harrison a feeling of belonging.

Yet while George was looked down upon by John, this was balanced by the former's freshly acquired skills as a trainee electrician, notably ensuring that overloaded amps with naked wires were rendered less lethal and less likely to cut out halfway through a number. George had also taught himself ripostes to counter John's sarcasm, his callous teasing and, more recently, the near-impossibility of having a sensible conversation with him.

Of all The Quarry Men, John Lennon was the loudest in praise of BBC radio's *The Goon Show*, a development of the offbeat humour and topical parodies of an earlier series, *Crazy People*, which starred Spike Milligan, Peter Sellers, Michael Bentine and Harry Secombe, veterans of entertainments organised by the armed forces from their own ranks. Incongruous parallels, casual cruelty and stream-of-consciousness connections not only made *The Goon Show* different from mainstream series like *Educating Archie* and *The Clitheroe Kid*, but also ushered in that stratum of fringe-derived comedy that culminated in the late 1960s with *Monty Python's Flying Circus*. Aspects of The Goons became apparent, too, in the stylistic determination of such as Scaffold, The Bonzo

Dog (Doo-Dah) Band and, less directly, The Beatles, particularly in their first two films. It was also evident in Lennon's associated slim volumes, *In His Own Write* and 1965's *A Spaniard In The Works*. Many of the assorted oddments that filled these books dated from the first broadcasts of *The Goon Show* and John's habit of scribbling nonsense verse and surreal stories supplemented by Milligan-esque cartoons and caricatures, a habit that intensified with exposure to the programme.

John was also among those irritating people who re-enacted *Goon Show* sketches the next day during the programme's high summer, which was reflected in spin-off double-A-side hit-parade entries in the UK in 1956 for 'I'm Walking Backwards For Christmas'/'Bluebottle Blues' and 'The Ying Tong Song'/'Bloodnok's Rock 'n' Roll'. While these singles were released on Decca, solo records by Milligan, Sellers and Bentine, as well as two album anthologies entitled *The Best Of The Goon Shows*, came to be issued by Parlophone, a subsidiary of EMI, another of Britain's four major record labels. The discs were produced by George Martin, elevated to headship of Parlophone in 1954 at the age of only 29.

To The Quarry Men, George Martin was an unknown figure in an unknown future in 1958, when the group was a vehicle for John Lennon's self-projection as an aspirant Donegan or Presley. Because John imagined himself a firm enforcer of his own discipline at rehearsals, there had been disenchantment amongst certain of the others, exemplified by premature departures motivated by his ruthlessness in sticking to the job in hand. Over-sensitive souls walked out, mortally offended, to dissect his character and musical ability with bitter intensity.

Yet middle-aged ex-Quarry Men from the Woolton Fête era would reunite and perform again for fun and profit. Moreover, hardly a day would go by without them remembering with doleful affection one who had been the Woolton Flash as surely as Elvis had been the local equivalent light years away in Memphis.

2 "There Was Something Slightly Worrying About Him"

"The Quarry Men wasn't that special a thing," reckoned John Duff Lowe, "and I was getting fed-up with the hour-long journey from West Derby to rehearsals, and my girlfriend used to moan. Also, A-levels came along, plus parental pressure."

Among the principal assets of a fragmenting Quarry Men was the vocal interplay between Lennon and McCartney. Yet, while composition was then an eccentric diversion, at most, to nearly all working British pop musicians, the power structure whereby George Harrison was to be subordinate to John and Paul for as long as they stayed together was founded on the handshake that had now formalised the Lennon–McCartney songwriting partnership – or so you'd read when the myth gripped harder.

Unlike such composer/lyricist teams of the Gilbert and Sullivan or Andrew Lloyd Webber and Tim Rice persuasion, the functions of McCartney and Lennon were never so cut and dried. Even non-fans would be able to differentiate eventually between the work of either, especially after a sea-change *circa* 1967, after which they tended to compose separately, or at least present each other with numbers in more advanced stages of completion than before.

Yet it was an apparent McCartney–Harrison opus, 'In Spite Of All The Danger', that was to grace one side of the first Beatles-associated record, an ego-massaging pressing taped and cut on while-you-wait shellac in a studio customised on the ground floor of a terraced house in Liverpool's Kensington district. A quarter of a century later, a cluster of new streets in the area would be named in three of the participants' honour – John Lennon Drive, Paul McCartney Way, George Harrison Close.

Such a venture by an amateur skiffle outfit wasn't uncommon, of course; following a qualified triumph in a national skiffle competition in 1957, an echo-drenched and plummily inhibited single by Roy Taylor's Vagabonds exhausted an unrepeated self-financed run of 50 copies. However, The Quarry Men – by this time John, Paul, George, John Duff Lowe and Colin Hanton – shelled out for only one copy of 'In Spite Of All The Danger', which was coupled with an unimaginative reworking of 'That'll Be The Day', with Lennon as Buddy Holly.

"We rehearsed quite a long time for the session," recalled Lowe, "'That'll Be The Day' was the A-side. It was John's idea, but we all chipped in to pay for it. The studio was just a back room with these huge machines on the table, no overdubs, one microphone in the middle of the room and a piano. The guy, Percy Phillips, cut the acetate out there and then and we walked out with one copy. It didn't even have a proper sleeve; it was put in a 78rpm Parlophone sleeve. Nobody used it for any other purpose than lending it round. I ended up with it. Even after The Beatles had become well known, none of them then bothered to try and get it back."

The disc's existence alone was a bartering tool for engagements that were few and far between, and often undertaken for as little as a round of fizzy drinks. Moreover, Lennon's preoccupation with The Quarry Men – soon to rename themselves Johnny And The Moondogs – took its toll on his art studies. What did stereoplastic colour, tactile values and Vorticism matter when the group was filling the intermission spot that evening at, say, Stanley Abattoir Social Club or the Morgue Skiffle Cellar in Oak Hill Park?

A new-found college friend of Lennon's by the name of Bill Harry "put forward the proposal that the Students' Union used its funds to buy PA equipment for John's band to use". This seemed a practical suggestion as Lennon, McCartney, Harrison and a turnover of other musicians were also being engaged as a recurring support act at college shindigs headlined by the likes of The Merseysippi Jazz Band, then Liverpool's pre-eminent combo, and fully mobilised a decade before traditional jazz permeated the Top Ten via the toot-tooting of Acker Bilk, Kenny Ball *et al.* "In 1958,

28

it was all jazz bands," sighed John Duff Lowe, "and we played mostly intervals during their beer breaks. We were always warned not to play too loudly."

The Quarry Men's only concession to the impending trad-jazz craze was Louis Armstrong's 'When You're Smiling', albeit with John singing in Harry Secombe's "Neddy Seagoon" voice and inserting cheeky references to college staff into its lyrics. Otherwise, nearly every item in the metamorphosing Quarry Men's repertoire now was a *salaam* to Elvis Presley, Gene Vincent, Jerry Lee Lewis, Chuck Berry, Little Richard and further behemoths of classic rock. "John wanted to put even more rock 'n' roll into it," recalled John Duff Lowe, "which meant that Pete, Rod and Len had to go because you didn't have washboard, tea-chest bass and banjo in rock. When I first became a Quarry Man, John was already squeezing out the skiffle-type music."

As it had always been, Lennon tended to be singled out as "leader" by both the casual listener and those Quarry Men still in terrified admiration of one who, as Philip Hartas, in charge of foundation sculpture, soon realised was "like a fellow who'd been born without brakes. His objective seemed to be somewhere over there that nobody else could see, but he was going, and in that process a lot of people got run over. He never did it to me, but he had this very sarcastic way of talking to people."[7]

When Lennon, in his first term at art college, attempted to change from a lettering course to graphics like Bill Harry, the head of that department, George Jardine, a pruny looking gentleman in sports jacket and patterned tie, wouldn't have it. Like some other members of staff, Jardine regarded Lennon as a nightmare of a young man, although it was recognised that many fellow students vied for John's attention, just as they had at Quarry Bank. Partly, it was to do with his strong personality, but also because The Quarry Men, if not the wildest act going on Merseyside, were starting to be noticed outside the comparative security of Students' Union bookings, having become adept at bypassing potentially ugly moments, often via Lennon's instinctive if indelicate crowd control.

With the music itself, the bars that linked choruses and bridges were cluttered and arrangements often shot to pieces, despite bawled off-mic directives. Yet every now and then, the group would be home and dry long before they reached the final number, in which either Lennon or McCartney on lead vocals might pull out every ham trick in the book, guarding a *pro tempore* stardom with the passionate venom of a six-year-old with a new bike.

However, it was enough that The Quarry Men/Johnny And The Moondogs survived at all at a time when talent scouts from London – where the country's key record companies were clotted – rarely found the time to listen to what was going on in other regions. Although it's true that most British regions had spawned at least one hit-parade entrant apiece during the 1950s, so parochial was provincial pop that there seemed to be few realistic halfway points between obscurity and the Big Time. But if you weren't to be a big name in a wider world, you could limit yourself to being cherished as one locally.

A hick outfit's transition to going semi-professional was usually assisted by the growth of a substantial fan following via regular performances in youth clubs, coffee bars, pub functions rooms and so forth. From one of the toughest districts in Liverpool, Gerry Marsden's Skiffle Group had worked a similar circuit to The Quarry Men, although Gerry confessed, "I didn't see them until Paul joined. Their sound was rubbish, but he and John stood out as talented. Somehow whatever John did was just *different*. He seemed to have absorbed all the rock 'n' roll influences and then come out the other side with entirely his own variation on them."

At a higher position in the local pop hierarchy than Lennon, Marsden's outfit had slipped into a routine of maybe two or three bookings a week within easy reach and with the occasional side trip into the next county. Meanwhile, the outer reaches of Johnny And The Moondogs' stamping ground didn't extend beyond the environs of Liverpool, at least until autumn 1959, when the group – which had by now boiled down to just John, George and Paul – made it through to the final regional heat of Carroll Levis's *Search For Stars* – the spiritual forerunner of *Opportunity Knocks* – under the proscenium at the Hippodrome Theatre in Manchester, "Entertainment Capital of the North", some 50km (30 miles) to the east.

The ultimate prize was the spot on Levis's ITV series, just as The Vagabonds had gained one on BBC TV's *Come Dancing* after being merely runners-up in the World Skiffle Championship the previous year. However, an obligation to catch the last train back to Lime Street Station in Liverpool put the tin lid on Lennon, McCartney and Harrison's chances, as it left too early for the three to be judged (by volume of applause) at the show's finale. Yet, while he didn't harp on about it at Mendips – advisedly – this crestfallen headway mattered more to John than any progress he was making at college.

To Mimi's dismay, John's career there was seeming to trace much the same ignominious trajectory as it had at Quarry Bank. Failure seemed inevitable from the start. In preparation for The Entrance on the very first morning, John had risen early to spend an inordinate amount of time combing his hair into a precarious quiff, gleaming with Brylcreem. For quick adjustments, he stuck a comb in the top pocket of a concessionary sports jacket buttoned over a lilac shirt that Mimi detested. He walked to the bus stop in approved Cavalry twills, but when he alighted he had a slightly pigeon-toed gait, having changed somehow during the jolting journey into the contentious drainpipe jeans, so tight that it looked as if his legs had been dipped in ink. Thus attired, he stood at the college portals and narrowed short-sighted eyes. He was too vain to be seen wearing the spectacles he'd needed for chronic short-sightedness since Dovedale Primary.

The undergraduate's self-image was at odds with the only subject he kept quiet about: his privileged upbringing in Woolton. An inverted snob, he'd already embraced the *machismo* values of both teddy boys and proletarian Merseyside males and generally came on as the Poor Honest Wacker – a working-class hero, in fact, although the only paid work he ever did, apart from as a musician, was as a labourer at local waterworks Scaris & Brick for a month during a summer recess. Nevertheless, by the end of his first term at college, he had started speaking in florid Scouse, laced with incessant swearing.

He'd also latched onto the notion that northern women were mere adjuncts to their men. John's overwhelmed new girlfriend – and future wife – Cynthia Powell seemed to tolerate this role, as well as the jealous anxieties that made him turn pale, clench his fists and make exasperating scenes if she said as much as a civil hello to a male not

JOHN LENNON

on his mental list of those that he considered to have no romantic
interest in Cynthia.

And yet, however much he showered her with kisses and sweet
nothings in private, Cynthia, a lass from over the river in Cheshire,
was otherwise just one of an entourage in danger of being lost in his
shadow as he continued to establish himself as a lecture-disrupting
clown, and lunaticked around the city centre with his Moondogs and
college sidekicks. Often, she and John would emerge from lectures
for an intended tryst in, say, Rod Murray's bedroom in Gambier
Terrace, just around the corner from the college, but they wouldn't
have walked far before, say, George greeted them with his trademark
whistle. With him and others in tow, endeavouring to monopolise her
boyfriend, Cynthia's heart would sink to her boots – but then, from
time to time, she'd catch John eyeing her in an uncharacteristically
lovelorn fashion, perhaps because he had finally noticed that she'd
allowed her blonde perm to go to highlighted seed so that she now
looked a bit like Brigitte Bardot, who had emerged as France's national
femme fatale thanks to a combination of unruly sexuality and doe-
eyed ingenuousness.

Cynthia observed too that, when John was in the public eye, he
played the fool as if on cue. "He worked so hard at keeping people
amused, he was exhausting," said Rod Murray, another student. "One
day, I saw him running down the street, holding a steering wheel – no
car, just the wheel. He said he was driving down to town."[7]

Lennon's buffoonery would sometimes deteriorate into a nonsensical
(and frequently alcohol-fuelled) frenzy and soon would come the antics
that would get him barred from pubs. "I just knew I'd never see him
grow old," remarked Gerry Marsden with the benefit of hindsight. "Even
as a young guy, there was something slightly worrying about him. It was
like he was racing through life. He didn't have the look of a man who'd
be happy in maturity."

Back in class, John's tutors could not help but imagine that he did
very little reading. "You had the feeling that he was living off the top of
his head," said Philip Hartas.[7] It was a veneer of self-confidence, rather
than any heavily veiled air of learning, that enabled John Lennon to bluff

his way through prolonged discussion on art. His bluff was often called by the late Arthur Ballard, an artist who might have gained national renown had he chosen not to remain a big fish in the small pool of Merseyside culture. A painting lecturer and general tutor at Liverpool College of Art for over 30 years, Ballard, who "looked for new ways forward while respecting tradition",[8] came to be both a figurehead and *éminence grise* of the regional art scene. However, he was just one of many, including Arthur Dooley, future creator of Mathew Street's "Four Lads Who Shook The World" statue, erected after The Beatles became famous, and the instigator of a spectacular punch-up with the pugnacious Ballard over elitism in art education.

Germane to this discussion, too, are Ballard's swim across the Seine for a bet, as well as his Art College seminars conducted in a nearby pub. A strategy regarded as unorthodox even now, in the early 1960s it verged on lunacy – as to a lesser degree did Arthur's defence of Lennon in the faces of those who wanted his expulsion. Ballard insisted that, if John was "a bloody nuisance and totally uninformed in every kind of way",[7] he possessed more than mere talent. "You could see in his written output the heritage of Lewis Carroll," reckoned Bill Harry. "John also reminded me of Stanley Unwin – his malapropisms, etc – but there was an Englishness about it when everyone else was copying the Americans."

Located within earshot of the bells of both the Anglican and Roman Catholic cathedrals, bohemian Liverpool was, so Harry reaffirmed, "a pallid imitation derived from what the Americans were doing". Nevertheless, it was enough like Greenwich Village, New York's vibrant beatnik district, that newshounds from the muck-raking *Sunday People* were sent there and to other supposed centres of romantic squalor on a crusade to root out what would be headlined "THE BEATNIK HORROR!". Lashing those present in Rod Murray's flat in Gambier Terrace with drinks, the journalists assured everyone that it was to be a feature on the difficulties of surviving on student grants.

It certainly was, agreed John Lennon, who didn't actually live there – although he was trying to persuade Aunt Mimi that everyone who was anyone had their own studio flat near college. Yet, as Mendips – his official address – was technically within the city limits, he didn't qualify

33

for a maintenance grant for living expenses, anyway. While he would breathe in the atmosphere of coloured dust, palette knives and hammer-and-chisel at Gambier Terrace for weeks on end as a "hiding tenant", there was always the safety net of Mimi's home cooking and clean sheets if he needed to get his nerve back for another round of pooling loose change for a trip to the off-licence to see him and his intimates through palavers that turned afternoon into gone midnight.

Mostly, these sessions constituted dialogue for the sake of dialogue, with subjects ranging from the transmigration of souls to the symbolism of dreams to what Sartre wrote about the Soviet intervention in Hungary in 1956 and what Camus thought he meant. Then there were charades, word games, character assassinations of college staff, free-association poetry, séances and shy making soliloquys about the participants' lives, their souls and their aspirations, replete with asides about the masterpieces they were going to paint, the avant-garde films they were going to direct, the ground-breaking novels they were going to get published and the marvellous music they were going to compose...

As their nicotine-stained fingers scribbled, the hacks from *The Sunday People* steered such discussions towards more pragmatic matters, smiling in sympathy when – so Rod Murray remembered – John told them that "he had to go home and scrounge food off his relatives". Inwardly, however, they were feeling dubious about the assignment. The situation wasn't up to scratch – or, to be precise, down to scratch. Murray's room, in which they were sipping coffee, was mildly untidy but quite clean and agreeably decorated. One so-called beatnik flatmate had just come home from an honest day's toil in a suit, while a female tenant had said she had no qualms about inviting her parents around for a candlelit dinner.

Nevertheless, with others eager to get their pictures in the paper, John Lennon obeyed an instruction to dress down and make the place more higgledy-piggledy, chucking some household waste about to make it more photogenic. You want the readers to think you're poor, starving students, don't you?

On 24 July 1960, two million people read *The Sunday People*'s beatnik piece, which was printed alongside a photograph, the first Britain at large saw of John Lennon.[9] With sideburns now past his earlobes and sporting

34

sunglasses, Lennon had pride of place, lolling about on the littered floor amongst Bill Harry, Rod Murray and other self-conscious "beatniks". He looked as if he probably slept in his vest.

A paragraph beginning, "They revel in filth..." consolidated further received wisdom about students for middle-class fathers in slippers, baggy trousers and "quiet" cardigans brandishing patriotic pokers in breakfast rooms whilst deploring the impending abolition of National Service – especially on reading of how one beatnik from Leeds had avoided it "by posing as a psychiatric case". These stalwart heads of families would welcome a return to the days when a sound thrashing would have turned these layabouts from the road to hell, along with every other wastrel across the country living on the grants paid for by the taxes on their elders and betters, and attempting – so it said here – "to seek happiness through meditation". What's meditation when it's at home?

The Sunday People's investigation only served to confirm what had been already guessed about what was described in its pages as "not really orgies – but they do get very naughty", as well as the sordid scenes of the fish-and-chip paper in the fireplaces, the overflowing ashtrays, the peeling wallpaper, the drunk lying face-down in a puddle of vomit on the stairwell and the fresh avalanche of plaster that the door-knocker's rapping thunder had dislodged in the hallway. Outside, rubbish sogged behind the railings of the inner city's crumbling town houses, holding each other up like the drunk and his pals rolling homewards after chucking-out time.

"An awful lot of the stuff in that article was either blatant untruths or so distorted," protested Rod Murray. "All right, we did do silly things. Everybody does when they're young, don't they? I don't think we were quite that odd. Or that bad."[7]

From THE BEATNIK HORROR! surfaced the enduring legend that John Lennon slept in a coffin at Gambier Terrace, although he actually roughed it there only for brief spells, until it made abrupt sense to look homeward again to Mendips, where the sugar was in its bowl, the milk in its jug and the cups unchipped on their saucers and set on an embroidered tablecloth. There he would make short work of the meal

Aunt Mimi prepared for him as he watched a cowboy film on television prior to soaking himself in the hot, scented water of the aqua-coloured bath before going to sleep in his own little room again.

3 "His One Saving Grace Was That Stuart Liked Him"

There was a new mood at college – for a while. It was pleasing for both Aunt Mimi and his tutors to note how industriously a suspiciously subdued Lennon was applying himself to at least aspects of his coursework. John's yardstick of "cool" was now as much Amedeo Modigliani as Elvis Presley or Gene Vincent. The Italian painter's post-Impressionist portraits of fragile females with long necks were perceived as masterpieces. Nevertheless, the Modigliani personality cult hinged more on the hand-to-mouth existence of this gifted but neurotic and improvident bloke whose noble visage effused melancholy and poor health (like Gene Vincent's). These traits were aggravated in part by a proneness to alcoholic blackouts. In 1920, he promoted one of such depth that he never regained consciousness. This was followed immediately by the suicide of his young wife, who had loved him to distraction.

Lennon's new wonderment at Modigliani was down to a new best friend, Stuart Sutcliffe, a gifted painter whose lecture notebooks were as conscientiously full as Lennon's were empty. Indeed, when written or practical assessment was pending, John would cadge assistance from Stuart – and Cynthia – just as he would a Woodbine. "Lennon's no hero of mine," glowered Johnny Byrne, now a TV scriptwriter but then one of Liverpool's arch-beatniks. "His one saving grace was that Stuart – who I respected enormously – liked him, and Stuart knew Lennon in a way that perhaps no one else did at the time."

It was certainly through Sutcliffe that what Paul McCartney would describe as the hitherto self-suppressed "closet intellectual" surfaced in

John. "John debunked a lot of intellectual analysis," judged Stuart's sister Pauline, "particularly when people found in his output roots in all sorts of literary and artistic figures that he would claim never to have been familiar with."

So it was that Lennon shook off enough ingrained indolence to manage at least his transfer from lettering to painting, and actually even to do a bit of painting. Largely because of Sutcliffe too, he became less disinterested in the theory of art to the extent that lectures were often approached as venues for either illicit relaxation or exercising his wit at the tutors' expense.

There will remain division over whether Stuart was gifted – even brilliant – in absolute terms or whether he was just a minor talent peripheral to the fairy tale of John, Paul, George and Ringo, after his purchase of one of these new-fangled electric bass guitars enabled him to be in Lennon's group from 1960 until just the wrong side of the 'Love Me Do' watershed.

Sutcliffe might not have been much of a bass player, and his earliest output as a Liverpool art student, if technically astounding, leaned on the ideas of others, most conspicuously the kitchen-sink realism of John Bratby, Edward Middleditch and other post-war Angry Young Men, themselves derivative of Van Gogh. Nevertheless, in the final months of his life, Sutcliffe produced abstracts that had little obvious precedent. We can speculate forever about whether he'd have gone on to be another Picasso, a designer of Christmas cards, a teacher or on The Beatles' payroll again. According to Astrid Kirchherr, German dress designer, photographer and Sutcliffe's fiancée, "Stuart was a genius and would have been a very, very great writer and painter."[7] Well, to paraphrase Mandy Rice Davies, she would say that, wouldn't she? A more objective view of his work is that of John Willett, a respected art critic and organiser of a Sutcliffe retrospective at Liverpool's Walker Gallery in 1964, who held that it was "a good deal more than merely 'promising'".[10]

In a contemporaneous newspaper article entitled "The Arts In Liverpool,"[11] Willett noted, "the embryonic and still-unconscious relationship between the visual arts, jazz and the rock groups. We shall become more aware of this when the late Stuart Sutcliffe's pictures are shown here in May."

The concept of a firm link between rock 'n' roll and art-college coursework was exemplified by The Beatles' conscious musical progression, and this itself was traceable to Sutcliffe. "Because of his influence," attests Pauline Sutcliffe, "they became more self-consciously 'arty' – not just in the way they looked and sounded but the whole package. After Stuart's death, they achieved something quite extraordinary, in the sense of developing pop music as an art form whilst retaining mass appeal." What cannot be denied is that, with Astrid Kirchherr, Stuart anticipated much of the look – including the gimmick haircuts – adopted by the Moptopped Mersey Marvels before their emergence as pop stars.

It's intriguing to note how many other important British acts from every phase of the mid-1960s beat boom contained members who may once have aspired to pursuing a career in fine art with music merely an extramural pursuit in which personal popularity and financial gain were irrelevant. Off-the-cuff examples are The Rolling Stones, The Yardbirds, The Kinks, The Rockin' Berries, The Animals, The Pretty Things, The Bonzo Dog Band, The Move and Pink Floyd, while Roxy Music, The Portsmouth Sinfonia, Deaf School, The Sex Pistols and Ian Dury And The Blockheads were among those that informed pop undercurrents in the following decade. Culture has been too quick to forget that, after the coming of Beatlemania, many such dabblers let themselves be sucked into a vortex of events, places and circumstances that hadn't belonged to speculation before record-industry talent scouts began to scour the country for, if not *the* New Beatles, then *a* New Beatles.

The Old Beatles' primary artistic emphasis dwelt in sound, but visuals were a good second, whether the Midwich Cuckoo uniformity that first brought them to global attention or the hiring of illustrious pop artist Peter Blake for 1967's *Sgt Pepper's* montage – on which Stuart's image was touchingly included, among more fabled celebrities.

By that time, the Fab Four's long shadow had already furnished Stuart Sutcliffe's posthumous career with its best and worst start. In 1964, the first major retrospective of his work – the one at the Walker – was attended by coach loads of Beatle fans with only the vaguest notion of what they'd come to see. They may have shared the *Liverpool Daily Post* reviewer's opinion of it being an "impressive and moving experience",[11] but to them Stuart was less a legitimate artist than "the fifth Beatle" – auburn-haired when the others were dark – and The One Who Died.

The most authoritative Beatle annals pinpoint a punch-up after a booking at Seaforth's Lathom Hall on either 30 January, 4 February or 6 February 1961 as the ultimate cause of Stuart Sutcliffe's death just over a year later. 2001, however, saw the publication of *The Beatles Shadow: Stuart Sutcliffe & His Lonely Hearts Band*, Pauline Sutcliffe's subjective rewrite of the tie-in biography to the *Backbeat* biopic movie of 1994. The lady now claimed that John and Stuart's mere scuffle in the movie was actually a full-blooded assault that climaxed with Sutcliffe sustaining a kick in the head, which "was what eventually led to Stuart's death". In parenthesis, Pauline also theorises that Stuart and John had oral sex on a bunkbed during The Beatles' first trip to Germany but, if it happened, she didn't witness it. Indeed, her source of this story was Geoffrey Giuliano's *Lennon In America*, and Giuliano was guessing too.

The *Backbeat* book blamed drugs for Stuart's demise, while the film accused some thugs who set upon him and knocked him unconscious outside some Liverpool pub on an unseasonably warm winter's evening in 1959. This incident – portrayed in the opening scene – is worth extrapolating at length, not for its historical accuracy but as an encapsulation of the personal dynamic between the two pals.

We're deep in Liverpool's dockland.

"Kiss me, honey-honey, kiss me…" The amplified song stabs the night air outside a Tetley's pub. Full and noisy, it's a Victorian monstrosity that retains a shabby pre-war grandeur. Through a nicotine haze, we see its sight-reading resident band – piano, sax, bass and drums played by aged semi-pros who always sound as if they're winding up for the night. At the microphone, the "Featured Popular Vocalist" is a pert little madam giving it all she's got. In her imagination, she's Shirley Bassey at the London Palladium. Her exhortation to seduction does not interrupt the chattering tumult of mostly middle-aged drinkers, shutting off – however briefly – the dingier realities of lives led in a huddled land of few illusions.

"Thrill me, honey-honey, thrill me..."

Perhaps making some sort of Art Statement by being in such a place where you'd be least likely to find them, two teenage bohemians, barely old enough to quaff a cherryade on the premises, are dissolving their usual Walter Mitty fantasies in low-life reality. Instead of Ban The Bomb duffle-coats, they're sham-tough in leather jackets, drainpipe jeans and teddy-boy quiffs. One of them looks like a young John Lennon mainly because he is a young John Lennon, while a watered-down James Dean – the Hollywood actor who was the prototype rock 'n' roll rebel – is Stuart Sutcliffe, sketching on the pad that never leaves his side.

At another table, conversation is petering out for Nello, Gral, Spak and Nigel, brawny Player's Navy Cut seamen all. The past ten minutes have been spent knocking back the Tetley's and dragging on cigarettes whilst nodding in guffawing appreciation of Nigel's lying account of how he'd got the bra off Marie-Christine, a hoity-toity Irish-Catholic barmaid who'd never give any of them a second glance. You can see in his leer that Nigel had stowed plenty of ale on board since opening time. Looking around, it seems that all of the judies worth being seen with are spoken for. There is, therefore, nothing for it but the frustrated strategy of a nasty piece of work who wants to make everything else nasty too.

Those skinny lads over there. They'll do. What's more, they don't belong. Everybody else here thinks that Elvis Presley is a nancy boy with his girly haircut – just like theirs. If one of them so much as glances in Nigel's direction, the action will be him. Seconds crawl by as he watches them like a lynx.

Stuart and John consider themselves right desperadoes. En route from the city centre to Injun territory, what a time they had that afternoon. John asked a particularly crabby tobacconist for *"20 Players vagina, please."* Next, they were thrown out of some desolate amusement arcade for potting the prizes rather than the ducks in the shooting gallery. Ending up in this tavern, they are surfacing as an unscheduled addition to the cabaret.

"Don't care even if I blow my top..."

Their mocking parroting of each line is turning a few heads. The girl's getting the giggles. Tired of waiting, Nigel decides he'll be a lion of justice, striking a blow against these disturbers of decent entertainment for decent folk. He stubs out his cigarette and nudges Nello, who is concluding a debate about Everton's chances of relegation. Bold with beer and the promise of exultant brutality, Nello and the rest scrape back their chairs with Gunfight At The OK Corral deliberation and follow their leader over to the trouble. Nigel has already weighed things up. He'll concentrate on the weedier one. The other one with the loudest mouth looks as if he might be able to take care of himself.

Nigel shapes up in front of Stuart, legs apart, thumbs hooked in his belt. Stuart is too involved in the drawing to raise his head.

"Hey, you! You don't like this number?"

"Ask him. It's his sister."

Stuart hands Nigel over to John, who is better at outfacing hard cases. He's the sort that people laugh at rather than beat up. Yet this new situation will not yield vintage Lennon.

There's nothing yet to justify picking a fight, even if the girl's no more his sister than Brigitte Bardot. A second line of attack comes swiftly into play as Nigel alights on Stuart's discarded picture. It's of the female singer, nude. "What's this?"

"Nothing," shrugs Stuart. Then, foolishly, "What do you think it is?"

"I think it's filth!" Nigel shouts as a sudden campaign plan stirs in his mind.

John, hopeful of transforming the slit-eyed and deadly seriousness into light banter, says, "That's art, not filth."

"Art, eh?" chuckles Gral in a manner that is not unfriendly. Maybe the danger will pass.

Nigel isn't going to let it. "Call that art?" he sneers. "What else?"

At last one of the crew cottons on. "Says it's his sister," says Nello, copying Nigel's fathomless gaze at Stuart.

"That's not his sister."

"No?"

The prattle immediately surrounding them drops to half its volume. In this corner of the pub, Nigel has taken over as the star turn. This is the thrill divine, and there isn't a second to be lost.

"That's my fuckin' wife!"

The two boys – and that's all they are – realise that nothing will stop Nigel and his thugs, types who half-kill you to impress girls. Well, if it's inevitable, John's going to stick a pin in first.

"She never is! She wouldn't throw herself away on crap like you. You're too fuckin' ugly!"

"Right!"

It's time to go. Oblivious to everything but the need to escape, John and Stuart are off like greyhounds. Indeed, they make most of their exit on all fours, scrambling through forests of under-the-table limbs. In the drink-slopping uproar above, their pursuers become a cursing search party. Although too shrill for a couple of bars, the singer is a trouper beyond her years and the show goes on.

"But honey-honey, don't stop."

The boys blunder through a sudden side door, then across a yard and over a wall into a back alley. It stinks of piss. Taking grinning stock, it seems like any one of a few such close shaves they've known since falling in with each other at art college. They're feeling lucky – but today isn't their lucky day. From hostile shadows emerge a sauntering phalanx, glistening with malicious glee.

His throat constricting, his skin crawling and his heart pounding like that of a hunted beast – which he is – Lennon forces a shaky smile. "OK, fellows. A joke's a joke."

"Here's another joke," Nigel snarls. "See if you get a laugh out of this." But before the punchline comes, the victims flee in two directions. Neither gets very far. Within yards, Stuart is seized by the shoulders, swivelled around and brought down with a knee in the balls. Meanwhile, Gral has John by the collar and hurls him against the wall. In a frenzy of terror, John lets fly a wild jab that sinks into Gral's stomach and crumples him into a heap, gasping for breath.

If it had been any other bloke but Stuart, John would probably have scarpered. There's no point in getting hurt too, is there? As it is, he wades in to even up hopeless odds. Stuart is squirming around on the cobbles to amused jeers as he tries to shield his head and genitalia from steel-capped boots. With no pause for careful thought, John lands some indiscriminate punches and even manages to grab Nigel's belt *and pull with despairing triumph before losing his grip via a sock in the mouth from Spak.*

Stuart is yelling in panic and blood cascades from his face, but that isn't enough. On and on it goes, even after one kick catches him just above the left ear and he loses consciousness. Finally, it stops being fun and he's rolled over into a pile of garbage.

When he comes to, there's no tranquil numbness but an ache of needle-sharp piquancy, quivering in the very centre of his brain. Cracked and rusted cathedral bells crank into reluctant and unintended motion, emitting stark tolls of angry, dischordant clanging. Through a force-field of distortion and pain, he picks up the fading clack of footsteps and John bawling in impotent rage, "I'll get you! I'll get the lot of you! I'm gonna bring a mob down here and beat the crap out of you! I'm gonna get you all!"

The unendurable noise in Stuart's skull vanishes, as mysteriously as it will when it recurs in later years, and the shuddering agony subsides to simply the mother of all headaches. John's features swim into grisly focus in the yellow light of a street lamp. He'll have a fat lip by morning.

"You OK?"

"How do I look?"

"Put it this way: you'll get better. They'll always be ugly."

In an Andy Capp cartoon in *The Daily Mirror*, Capp – a beer-swilling, womanising Geordie – is dissecting the character of his best friend, Chalky, over a venomous pint. A chap on the next barstool adds a disobliging comment of his own about Chalky. Capp's response is not grim agreement but an uppercut that sends the other sprawling: "That's my mate you're talking about!" The amity between Stuart Sutcliffe and John Lennon embraced territory just as forbidden and often inexplicable to outsiders. How else can be explained abrupt reconciliations after hours of verbal and emotional baiting, a tacit implication in a seemingly innocuous remark sparking off a slammed front door and jokes side-splitting to nobody else?

If Lennon and Sutcliffe weren't exactly David and Jonathan, June Furlong, one of the life models at Liverpool's Regional College of

Art, believed that she'd "never seen two teenagers as close as those two". Moreover, their friendship provoked in George and, especially, Paul an apprehension akin to that of a child viewing another sibling as a barrier to prolonged intimacy with an admired elder brother, and for a similar reason Lennon was to be dismayed, initially, when Sutcliffe and Astrid Kirchherr became an item – although this might have been simple jealousy because he fancied her himself.

What is indisputable is that, during the turbulent adolescence that prefaced a turbulent manhood, hardly anyone – as Johnny Byrne deduced – knew Lennon as intimately as Stuart. Nonetheless, the Sutcliffe saga prior to his 1959 encounter with John is, arguably, as interesting as the over-exposed story of his chum. Born on 23 June 1940 in Edinburgh, Stuart had been the first issue of a union that had stunned his father's relations. Charles Sutcliffe had wed a Roman Catholic, Millie Cronin, at a time when papism was still on a par with fascism in many quarters of Scotland. It was, however, the dissolution of a previous marriage that caused the couple to flee to England for several years before returning to Edinburgh for the arrival of Stuart and, in 1942, his sister Joyce. Within a year, however, the fever of mobilisation found them in Huyton, near the Merseyside shipyard, where marine engineer Charles had been posted. The family would never live in Scotland again, and Stuart, Joyce and a second daughter, Pauline, would each catch and hold a Lancashire drawl.

At Prescot Grammar School, Stuart discovered that he could duplicate any known two-dimensional form and had the naïve beginnings of a personal style, as well as a fancy that he'd like to make his way as some sort of visual artist. Nevertheless, although Arthur Ballard drank socially with Mr Sutcliffe, for all Arthur's capacity for holding down the beer, painting wasn't a man's trade, somehow, to Stuart's father. As Millie predicted, "Daddy was shocked. We'd hoped he'd become a doctor. 'My son a painter!' said Daddy. 'I'll never live it down.'"[12]

Stuart held out against his father – who was, in any case, almost permanently away at sea – and enrolled at the Art College a year below normal admittance age, surfacing as a *Wunderkind*. "He could have become a sculptor just as effortlessly as he became a painter," maintained

Philip Hartas, while Arthur Ballard, now Stuart's and Lennon's general tutor, had "met other gifted students, but few, if any, had that particular kind of spark that was genius".

Stuart's abundant output there was the culmination of much painstaking preparation. Bill Harry was immortalised in a Van Gogh-type portrait by Stuart. "First he did about 40 sketches," recalled the subject, "and then he started the painting proper on a piece of board, and he completed it in one afternoon. I was surprised at how easily it came to him. It just sort of flowed."

One of Stuart's course essays, "The Function Of A Door", betrays his preference for working by himself rather than in the chattier ambience of class: "I find in the silence of isolation the element in which all great things fashion themselves." Other philosophical confidences in his writings would coincide with the enlightening nectar that The Beatles would hear from the lips of the Maharishi Mahesh Yogi ten years later.

Ahead of his time sartorially, too, Sutcliffe was notable for combining aspects of the beatnik (such as a transient, wispy beard) with seedy flash "cat" clothes. "James Dean was his hero," said Ballard, "and he looked like him, too." He distanced himself further from others by his taste in music, as Rod Murray recalled: "He was the first to bring rock 'n' roll records into college, even when most people still thought pop was rubbish."

This was a point in Stuart's favour, as far as John Lennon was concerned when, with deceptive casualness, they entered each other's orbits through the auspices of Bill Harry. By early 1959, Bill had been editor and main (some would say sole) contributor to some short-lived and narrowly circulated magazines, one of which was for Frank Hessy's music store, "which Hessy crippled," said Bill, "with the terrible name of *Frank Comments*." Undaunted, Harry's next plan was more ambitious: he was going to write a book about Liverpool. Stuart could illustrate it and John could throw in a few of his funny poems. The project had been motivated through Bill being "very annoyed and frustrated that, whenever I had to go to the cinema, it was all American films. The best comics were supposedly American comics, too, but I personally liked the *Eagle* and things. I was staunchly liking British things, and in particular a Liverpool thing. I said, 'Why can't we do something about Liverpool?'"

An informal working party convened in a students' pub, Ye Cracke in Rice Street, to mull over Bill's latest wheeze. It was a cordial discussion, which ultimately led nowhere, but Stuart and John's friendship began in the bar's smoky recesses. Neither had any inkling then of the extent to which their lives – and deaths – would interweave.

Although they were the same age, John was in the academic year below Stuart. Because of this and their greatly contrasting standpoints over coursework, many college lecturers were surprised later that they even knew each other, let alone became the best of mates. "Stuart was a totally different character in the sense that he was a very reflective chap," maintained Philip Hartas. "He would fall into quiet moods and he'd be thinking a lot or he'd go off and he'd come back in, that sort of thing. There were things going on in his head, and he wasn't living at the tempo that Lennon was living at."[7]

While the differences between Stuart and John consolidated their friendship, so equally did all that they had in common. For instance, they both needed spectacles and neither had an omnipresent father as a guiding (or restraining) force. Each found vague enchantment in the *idea* of aping self-destructive Modigliani – starving in a garret apartment, burning his furniture against the cold of a Parisian winter and going to an early grave for his art. However, a less uncomfortable option might have been the happy(ish) ending in *The Horse's Mouth*, a light film comedy – based loosely on a Joyce Cary novel – that the pair saw at the Jacey Cinema in Clayton Square in 1958. Starring Alec Guinness and with kitchen-sink sets designed by John Bratby, the movie was about an obsessive artist, a social liability who might have been Modigliani's frightfully refined English cousin. He's frightful to live with too, but his friends stick by him. In a way, this antedated what one college contemporary was to say of Lennon: "He was a terrible fellow, really, but I liked him."

John had learned at least as much about self-immolation from his drunken exploits with more footloose lads from college than from his discussions about Modigliani with Stuart. Furthermore, unlike Modigliani, *The Horse's Mouth* character and, indeed, Sutcliffe, John was basically lazy. Yet, with Stuart showing him how, he grew less cautious about the marks he made on the canvas. "It was Stuart who nurtured an interest in John to want to know more about things than he knew," said Arthur Ballard. "In other words, he was educating him. Lennon wouldn't have known a Dada from a donkey. He was just so ignorant."[7]

Conversely, Stuart was often content to be a passive listener as John, angry or cynically amused by everything, held forth during their wanderings along street and corridor, giving his lightning-bright imagination its ranting, arm-waving head.

Occasionally, Stuart would let slip a seemingly uncontroversial comment, which might spark off a sudden and inexplicable spasm of rage in John. He'd take a long time to calm down. Then again, Lennon would mock his comrade for no tangible reason at all. "Hanging's too good for it" was his view of one of Stuart's early abstracts.

"I can imagine John taking the mickey out of Stuart mercilessly in private," reflected Bill Harry. "He'd try it on, and if you stood up to it, fine. If you put up with it, he'd keep on." Although Stuart struck back occasionally, nothing John said or did could belittle him in Stuart's eyes, and vice versa. Outlines dissolved and contents merged. They started to dress similarly and copy each other's mannerisms; John, for instance, took to flicking his cigarette away just like Stuart always did. Without purposely snubbing anybody, they evolved a restricted code that few outsiders could crack. Ballard would cite Stuart as source of "a lot of that goofy kind of…Dadaist sort of humour. It's entirely Stuart's influence on John Lennon that introduced that Dada element."[6]

In turn, Sutcliffe's fascination with Lennon extended to spectating during his rehearsals with George Harrison and Paul McCartney whenever the college's Life Room was vacant. Alternatively, John, Stuart and the other two might sit at one of the kidney shaped tables for hours in the local Jacaranda coffee bar, a convenient stone's throw away. The café was owned by Allan Williams, who began acting in a quasi-managerial capacity for Johnny And The Moondogs not long after one of Stuart's canvases, "Summer Painting", won a junior prize at the second of John Moores' biannual exhibitions at the Walker and was subsequently bought by the son of Moores himself, founder of the Littlewoods Pools empire and Merseyside's foremost philanthropist.

This gave Sutcliffe the wherewithal to make the down-payment on his Hofner President bass at Hessy's. With John, Stuart also originated a more attention-grabbing name, The Silver Beetles, although John added that it should be spelled Beatles, as in beat music.

What they needed more, however, was the drummer that had been lacking since the last days of The Quarry Men. Early in 1960, they found one in Tommy Moore – although it was assumed that, with his heart in jazz, 26-year-old Tommy would suffice only until the arrival of someone more suitable for an outfit derided as "posers" by certain personnel in fellow local bands Cass And The Cassanovas, Rory Storm And The Hurricanes, Derry And The Seniors and other more workman-like city outfits. John and Paul's pretensions as composers caused comment, too, because neither a teenager in a dance hall nor the BBC Light Programme's director would be interested in their home-made songs.

Nevertheless, The Silver Beetles were developing into a more credible attraction than The Quarry Men, having moved up from youth clubs and Students' Union supports to welfare institutes, far-flung suburban palais, Lancashire village halls, working men's clubs and, indeed, any venue that had embraced regular "beat" sessions.

Moreover, Lennon had spat out the nicely spoken Lancashire plum in his singing as well as in his speaking and now had a baritone that was bashed about and lived-in – in other words, the voice of a great rock 'n' roll vocalist. By European *bel canto* standards, the adult John Lennon couldn't sing – not "real singing", as sonorous as Roy Orbison's supple purity or Elvis Presley when he tried hymns. Lennon's voice had lost all vowel purity and nicety of intonation, probably because he had been endeavouring consciously to sound like the classic rockers he admired while it was either still breaking or just freshly broken. As Gene Pitney's polished tenor would be warped to an electric-drill-like whine – albeit an oddly appealing one – so John's uncertain treble had been corrupted for all time by, say, hot-potato-in-the-mouth Presley, the hollered arrogance of Jerry Lee Lewis, neo-hysterical Little Richard and Gene Vincent, "The Screaming End".

John's voice grew more strangled as he broke sweat and his adolescent spots rose through the lacto-calomine lotion and turned red. He was probably nothing without the PA system, but when he became intense, every sound he dredged up was like a brush-stroke on a painting. Backing off until the microphone was at arm's length, just a sandpapery quiver during a dragged-out note could be as loaded as a roar with it halfway down his throat.

Yet The Silver Beatles failed to feature among the local fare advertised low on the bill when, on 3 May 1960, Gene Vincent headlined a three-hour extravaganza at Liverpool Boxing Stadium, promoted by Allan Williams and celebrated pop Svengali Larry Parnes. The principal studs in the latter's stable of male performers were Tommy Steele, Marty Wilde and Billy Fury, while he also handled the equally charismatic Vince Eager, formerly Roy Taylor of The Vagabonds.

Roy/Vince had been on the bill of a 1960 UK tour by Eddie Cochran, a multi-talented Presley type from Oklahoma, which ended in a road accident on 17 April between the Bristol Hippodrome and Heathrow Airport. "Larry Parnes rang to say that I ought to get down to the hospital in Bath, where Eddie was on the danger list," recalled Eager. "There, the surgeon told me that Eddie was unlikely to survive. I was extremely upset, but when I emerged from the hospital, there was Parnes with the press and half his bloody pop stars, ready for a photo opportunity. I just drove off and refused to speak to Larry, who even before Eddie died had told the newspapers (a) about the 'irony' of Eddie's latest release, 'Three Steps To Heaven' – which was in fact the B-side then – and (b) that I was off to fly back to America with the coffin."

Any bonhomie of old between Parnes and Eager degenerated to probing suspicion, but Gene Vincent – also pulled from the wreckage – had insisted on honouring existing British dates, such as the one in Liverpool where Larry had ensured that Lance Fortune, Julian X and other of his lesser stars were also included. A last-minute addition to the bill, Gerry Marsden's ensemble – now rechristened Gerry And The Pacemakers – arrived in the first division of regional popularity.

In the Jacaranda after the show, Parnes thought aloud about a further, less ambitious joint venture with Allan Williams. He wanted, he explained, an all-purpose backing outfit for use by certain of his singers. Names he kept mentioning were Marty Wilde – then sagging on the ropes but bound to have another big hit soon – and Billy Fury, a Liverpudlian then on the crest of his first Top Ten breakthrough.

As ordinary Ronald Wycherley, Fury had first met Parnes in Marty Wilde's dressing room at Birkenhead's Essoldo Theatre in 1958. Ronald had recovered recently from rheumatic fever but, enthralled by his prominent cheekbones and restless eyes, Larry gave him his familiar stage alias and levered him into the package show that night. The proverbial overnight sensation, Fury was then dressed by Parnes in gold lamé and his metamorphosis from a nobody to a teen idol was set in motion. Billy/Ronnie rarely spoke to fans, as at that time he was apparently self-conscious about his "wacker" accent, which to anyone south of Birmingham sounded simultaneously alien and common then.

Nevertheless, Fury was more comfortable as an English Elvis than either Tommy Steele or Cliff Richard, who had both entered the 1960s by following the wholesome all-round-entertainer path. Nonetheless, Richard's backing ensemble, The Shadows, were respected generally as Britain's top instrumental act – although not by John Lennon, who affected to despise the showbiz polish and now-period charm of their big smiles and intricately synchronised footwork. Larry Parnes told Allan Williams that Billy Fury was looking for an outfit who could rival The Shadows as he did Cliff, and that Larry would bring Billy along if Allan could hurriedly assemble some Liverpool groups for him to see.

Although John Lennon was also present in the Jacaranda that night, he couldn't summon the courage to approach the Great Man, but two nights later he asked Williams if The Silver Beatles could audition for the job. Allan assented, but he pointed out that they'd be up against Cliff Roberts and his Rockers, Derry And The Seniors, Cass And The Cassanovas, Gerry And The Pacemakers, you name 'em – the very upper crust of Liverpool pop.

That morning, John fiddled with his hair prior to donning the current group-costume of jeans, short-sleeved black shirt, two-tone tennis shoes and apposite mock-silver pendant. Then he and the other Silver Beatles – minus a latecoming Tommy Moore – joined the midday queue of hopefuls at the Wyvern Social Club, with its essence of disinfectant and faint whiff of last night's alcohol, tobacco and food.

Although some of the other groups wore sewing-machined tat, worn and torn with frayed cuffs and indelible stains born of sweat and spillage, The Silver Beatles felt grubby beside those with starched-white handkerchiefs protruding smartly from the top pockets of their matching bespoke suits cut by city centre tailors.

George tried to locate the source of a buzz from an amplifier while John paced up and down, smoking furiously and cursing the still-absent Moore. Abruptly he stopped midstep, having decided to take up a post near the door through which he reckoned Billy and Larry would enter. It was as if he'd forgotten the emergency of the situation as he kept muttering to himself what he was going to say and the cool way he'd say it.

John and everyone else were brought up sharp when Allan Williams shepherded Billy – head down, collar up – and Larry Parnes across the dance area to wooden seats in its most acoustically sympathetic spot. During a break in the subsequent proceedings, John Lennon was among those approaching Billy Fury for an autograph. Paul, George and Stuart had never seen him this way before, so spellbound and humble. It was as he was enacting a parody of hero-worship, but it was too obvious that he wasn't. "Thanks, Billy – if it's all right to call you that," he grinned after Fury signed the proffered scrap of paper. "I...um...I'm John. I sing with a group!"

"Keep singin', man," replied Billy with a – possibly insincere – grin, "don't let it die." That was how a true star behaved.

Perhaps John had half an idea that, if Fury and Parnes didn't like The Silver Beatles, he was going to somehow ingratiate himself with them, join the payroll to fix Billy's drinks, light his cigarettes, laugh at his jokes. Maybe he'd be taken on as a clapper boy. Clapper boy? Gene Vincent used to have these two who just...well, clapped their hands, sang backing vocals and generally leapt around to get everyone raving.

After this rapt interlude, John resumed his hard-man persona as if nothing had happened, and then it was The Silver Beatles' turn to show what they could do. Unable to wait any longer for Tommy Moore, Lennon implored Johnny Hutchinson of the Cassanovas to step in until the interruption of Tommy's eventual arrival and the consequent delay while he settled behind the kit.

Yet The Silver Beatles gained the day, insofar as Parnes scribbled on his notepad, "Silver Beetles [*sic*] – very good. Keep for future work." Less than a fortnight later, John, Paul, George, Stuart and Tommy were off on a string of eight one-nighters in Scotland, backing not Billy Fury but Johnny Gentle, a Parnes luminary less likely to give Cliff Richard cause for nervous backwards glances. A year younger than Lennon, Gentle had once been John Askew, a merchant seaman who sang semi-professionally before he was spotted and rechristened by Parnes. Beginning with 1959's 'Boys And Girls Were Meant For Each Other', this square-jawed hunk's 45s all missed the UK chart, but he was often seen on British television pop series such as *Oh Boy!* and *Drumbeat* and was, therefore, guaranteed a period of well-paid one-nighters with pick-up groups who'd mastered mutually familiar rock 'n' roll standards and the simpler sides of Johnny's four singles.

Travelling to Scotland with Gentle, as each Silver Beatle's small wage dwindled the spurious thrill of "going professional" manifested itself in John purportedly assisting Johnny with the composition of a song entitled 'I've Just Fallen For Someone'. Lennon was to be uncredited, however, when the number was issued by Parlophone in 1963, when Gentle had assumed another *nom du théâtre*, 'Darren Young', and when it was recorded by Adam Faith on his eponymous debut album two years earlier.

This creative diversion was atypical of the prevalent mood of stoic cynicism during the trek around Scotland, particularly following an engagement noted for Tommy Moore drumming with his head in bandages, the sole casualty of an accident that left their van crumpled into a stationary car that afternoon. He had also become a prime target of Lennon's poking of ruthless fun, especially now that George had started to stick up for himself. Moreover, via shameless manoeuvring, John eased himself between the sheets of the only single bed available at one bed and breakfast while Tommy and anyone else out of favour spent as comfortable a night as was feasible in sleeping bags on the floor.

Well before they steamed back to Liverpool, a disgusted Moore – with only £2 left to show for his pains – had had enough of washing in streams, shaving in public-convenience hand basins, staring across a wayside café's formica tabletop as that loathsome Lennon tunnelled into a greasy but obviously satisfying chips-with-everything fry-up – and especially the van, that mobile fusion of lunatic asylum and death cell.

A beat group without a drummer was no use to anyone. Into the bargain, Britain's take on traditional jazz was now midway through a golden age, bracketed by Chris Barber's million-selling version of Sidney Bechet's 'Petite Fleur' in 1959 and Chris and his band framing Ottilie Patterson's ebullient singing over the closing credits of the 1962 movie *It's Trad, Dad*. This trend had spread across the English Channel, where The Dutch Swing College Band, Germany's Old Merrytale Jazz Band and other pre-eminent outfits on the continent had absorbed their music from British 'dads' like Barber, Kenny Ball and Acker Bilk rather than its US originators.

Trad-jazz bands were therefore more numerous than they'd ever been when John, Paul and George were Quarry Men, and so were the places in which they could play. In the Cavern, for instance, Liverpool's main jazz stronghold, there were specific designations about what should and shouldn't be heard there. Watching enthusiasts were likely to know more about the music than many of the entertainers, and it hadn't been unknown for purists to express their displeasure with slow handclapping and a shower of pennies cascading onto the stage if, say, a trad outfit deviated from prescribed New Orleans precedent by including saxophones.

While Cavern manager Ray McFall could understand that efforts to expand a given act's work spectrum must involve a degree of hyperbole and opportunism, he believed that he was entirely justified in making substantial deductions to the already minuscule fees of any young group who, having misrepresented themselves as maybe "a jump-blues outfit" to procure an interval slot there, committed the cardinal sins of amplification and creation of music in which the jazz content was negligible. The Cavern had put up with skiffle in the past, but what could not be tolerated was lowbrow rock 'n' roll. It was, he scowled, detrimental to the club's reputation.

4 *"Aggressive Restraint, A Brando Type"*

Bruno Koschmider owned the Kaiserkeller and the Indra – night clubs off the Reeperbahn ("Rope Street") in the heart of Hamburg's Grosse Freiheit ("Great Freedom"), where a red-light district had developed since the pillaging French had passed through in 1814. He had been one of the first German impresarios to put action over debate with regard to *Englander* pop. The entertainment in the Kaiserkeller had been mostly coin-operated, but a German group had been hired for the evening when, on an visit to Hamburg in spring 1960, professional interest found Allan Williams seated at one of the club's tables. When the music got under way, he moaned quietly to his companion, Lord Woodbine, another figure whose association with The Beatles eventually made him better known than he might have otherwise been.

As plain Harold Phillips, Woodbine arrived from Trinidad in 1948 to settle in an area of central Liverpool where Scouse Bohemia intermingled with a Scouse Harlem. Ennobling himself with a lordship named after the cheap cigarettes he chain-smoked, he was established quickly as "one of a great line of Liverpool characters," smiled Bill Harry, "full of cheek and audacity, but fun to know." Among his many occupations were builder and decorator, calypso singer and barman in the rougher parts of Toxteth, where he defused any unrest by brandishing a cutlass.

Woodbine was a reassuring presence at Allan Williams' side in the Kaiserkeller, where the native combo were actually quite proficient in a complacent kind of way, but Williams – abetted by Woodbine – was soon spieling in top gear about the marvellous Liverpool outfits he could procure for the fellow in charge. Outside the USA, whose rock 'n' rollers Bruno Koschmider couldn't afford, Allan's groups were rated as the finest by no less than Larry Parnes, manager of Billy Fury, who was the English Elvis as surely as The Old Merrytale Jazz Band were Germany's "answer" to bands led by "trad dads" like Monty Sunshine and Chris Barber.

The parley ended, nonetheless, on a sour note when it transpired that Allan's tape of the acts under discussion had been rendered a cacaphonous mess, possibly through demagnetisation somewhere *en route*.

Yet, following Williams and Woodbine's deflated departure, Bruno had to sample British pop for himself. Not in Liverpool, however, but Soho, the closest London came to having a red-light area. Specifically, he was looking for the 2 I's coffee bar, where this Larry Parnes person had "discovered" Tommy Steele and Marty Wilde. Familiar smells of multi-mega-tar tobacco, real coffee and Greek and Italian restaurants were lacing the evening air when, down Old Compton Street, he found what he'd been assured was still the epicentre of British pop.

The coffee bar was small, smaller than the Indra, and there was an immediate tell-tale sign of it having known better days in a yellowing photo display in the window of Tommy, Marty, Cliff, Adam and others who probably hadn't been near the place since they'd scented chart success. Nevertheless, Koschmider snatched a ragbag of London-based players – including singing guitarists Tony Sheridan and Ricky Richards, the *Shake It Daddy* man – to be reassembled as the Kaiserkeller's house band, named The Jets and put to work six nights a week on the club's rickety stage for an exploratory period.

On their opening night, the Englishmen's devil-may-care exuberance – pleasing themselves rather than the customers – brought them safely into harbour. "We had a Midas touch," said Sheridan with quiet pride. "There was no question of failure. It was nothing like we'd ever experienced in England. Our repertoire was about 50 per cent rocked-up skiffle, 50 per cent rock 'n' roll." This combination embraced a wide spectrum, from weepy 'Nobody's Child' to torrid workouts of Ray Charles' 'What'd I Say', which sometimes finished with Tony's collapse after up to 30 minutes of trading heys and yeahs with an enraptured crowd left wanting more.

However, by the late summer, the Kaiserkeller needed a comparable draw to The Jets, who were now administering their powerful elixir at a rival establishment, the Top Ten. Bruno remembered and made contact with Allan Williams, who sent Derry and the Seniors. Within days, the Kaiserkeller was thriving again and Koschmider's thoughts turned to his sleazier Indra. With few customers for its gartered erotica most evenings, it could be only more profitable to put on pop there too.

Koschmider then requested another Derry And The Seniors from his man in Liverpool, who wondered about the group now trading as just plain Beatles. The Scottish expedition with Johnny Gentle hadn't elevated the band from being a kind of pop equivalent of a stock chorus girl to instant West End stardom; on the contrary, they'd hit rock bottom as accompanists to the cavortings of Janice, a Mancunian stripper at the New Cabaret Artistes club, a fly-by-night dive run under the aegis of Williams and Woodbine.

This booking passed without incident, but there was trouble when, in June 1960, The Beatles gained a mercifully brief weekly residency at the corporation-owned Grosvenor Ballroom in Liscard, a suburb of Wallasey at the mouth of the Mersey, on the opposite bank to Liverpool. Although the group weren't mentioned in no less than two local journals' *exposés*, The Beatles played against prolonged outbreaks of hooliganism involving assault, actual bodily harm and criminal damage. These and other disturbances enhanced the district's notoriety as a scene of rowdyism, with teenagers pouring in to join the fun from as far away as Runcorn, nearly 30km (20 miles) downriver.

The venue degenerated into fist-flying roughhouses whenever delegations from enemy gangs attended. When someone was concussed by a projectile one Saturday night, a mass reprisal against his supposed assailants concluded with a broken nose and sprained wrist for one of the "bouncers" – security officers employed by promoter Les Dodd. More serious was the stabbing of a boy on a Beatles night at another of Dodd's concerns, the Institute in nearby Neston. The injured boy was rushed to hospital for treatment, requiring 24 stitches.

The musicians weren't safe, either. The drummer in one of the other groups was scragged behind his kit by "fans" who rolled him on the

JOHN LENNON

floor and ran off with his sticks. As for The Beatles, their own conduct – especially that of Lennon – did not defuse unrest. Yet despite purported instances of unpunctuality, slovenly stage attire and arriving a player short or with only half their equipment, they became a reliable draw. "For today's teenagers, the most basic musical standards are acceptable," one anonymous parish councillor was quoted, "as long as the song is recognisable as rock 'n' roll or fresh from the Top 20 pops. I don't object to how or what these groups play as long as it's within the bounds of propriety and that they can make a go of the 'National Anthem' at the end if hall regulations require it – which they seldom do these days."[13]

Among the Wallasey Corporation's listed complaints were smashed windows, defaced lavatory walls, countless dents to the pinewood floor by stiletto heels and – beggaring belief – persons unknown removing the piano from one of the auditoriums and abandoning it on a distant railway bridge, where it remained for almost a fortnight while two borough councils debated responsibility for locating its owner. Closer to home, a wrought-iron gate was lifted from its hinges and dumped in Grosvenor Street, causing burst tyres to the car of an elderly gentleman, who lost his spectacles in an altercation after he remonstrated with watching youths whom he suspected were responsible.

Less specific grievances from residents were the noise from motorcycles and hordes of rowdies taunting and threatening passers-by. Moreover, neighbourhood gardens were used as receptacles for cigarette butts and broken liquor bottles, while the sexton of Trinity Church, at the junction of Grosvenor Street and Manor Road, reported the finding of used condoms and discarded underwear in the long grass around the graveyard.

Les Dodd, too, acknowledged that matters were getting out of hand now that he was taking more than 300 admissions every Saturday. Yet, while these "big-beat" sessions were profitable, they had become, he agreed, a magnet for disorder beyond someone merely letting off a fire extinguisher on the way out. Therefore, he said, he was reverting to his old policy of admitting only the over 20s and keeping the music to a strict tempo – no jiving, no rock 'n' roll and definitely no teenagers.

On being told of the loss of the Grosvenor nights one afternoon in the Jacaranda, Lennon shook a frustrated fist in the direction of London, which was only maybe four hours away on the train but might as well have been on Mars. A showcase engagement in the capital was the key to going onwards and upwards. Like that clichéd movie sequence of dates being ripped off a calendar to a background of clips, a slow dazzle would preface the final Grosvenor-type bookings, then package tours with big names...sessions on the BBC Light Programme's *Saturday Club*...recording contracts...Number Ones...*Sunday Night At The London Palladium* on ITV...

Then John's reverie was brought up short. The fly in the ointment was that no one could get a booking in London until they got a booking in London. Confused? So was John. If a band made contact with an agency there, they'd be told that a representative would turn up the next time they played in London. The band would then explain that they hadn't got anything coming up in London because every time they rang a London agency, they were informed that someone would go and see them next time they played in London. At this point, the agent would say he was sorry but he couldn't do anything until they landed a booking in London.

Lennon had also heard reports that Rory Storm And The Hurricanes were going down an apposite storm during their weeks at a Butlin's holiday camp in north Wales. All the future seemed to hold for The Beatles was the trivial round of recurring and diminishing local engagements. It was likely that the battle to stay afloat would force them back to the youth clubs from whence they'd come, particularly as they hadn't yet recruited a full-time drummer since the exit of Tommy Moore.

For every door that opened, two closed – but hire-purchase debts were among principal reasons why certain Beatles couldn't really quit the group, no matter what, even when, at one of the Grosvenor evenings, of the £45 in net takings only £10 had been split between three acts.

Out-of-town trips weren't a consideration, either, mainly because there were so many new outfits being formed that the jobs went almost always to locals. Why bring in outsiders when your own can do the job just as well for a fraction of the cost?

Another worry was the continuing trad-jazz craze. The Tony Osborne Sound's 'Saturday Jump' was the opening and closing theme to *Saturday*

Club and females were fainting to such as Bilk, Barber, Ball, Humphrey Lyttelton and The Temperance Seven, even if it was as much to do with the boozy atmosphere generated as the personalities and the sounds they made – ie plinking banjos, endless tootling by front-line horns and a Louis Armstrong impersonator singing like he'd been gargling with iron filings, all set off by barrister wigs and legal gowns, Roman togas, Confederate Army uniforms or some other ridiculous take on the striped waistcoats and bowler hats that Bilk and his Paramount Jazz Band wore.

So The Beatles loitered in city centre pubs and cafés with other rock 'n' rollers in the same boat, small-talking, borrowing equipment, comparing notes, gossiping, giving away secrets. Out would pour lies about how close they were to their first single coming out and how they were a sure-fire certainty to support Screaming Lord Sutch when his never-ending string of one-nighters next reached the North, carrying on as if these possibilities were still on the cards long after the trail had gone cold, if they ever existed in the first place.

On top of that, there was a rumour that a girl was expecting Stuart Sutcliffe's child and was pressing him to do the decent thing voluntarily upon pain of her brothers manhandling him to the registry office. A spell outside The Beatles' usual orbit might have appeared a fine notion to Stuart, despite Arthur Ballard seething about his star pupil abandoning hic art course for John Lennon's beat group.

It was small wonder, therefore, that the lads were open to an offer of work in Germany, on the proviso that they could enlist a drummer. At the Casbah, a teenage haunt where they'd played as Quarry Men, they understood that proprietor Mona Best's handsomely saturnine son, Pete, was beating the skins with the club's resident quartet, The Blackjacks. With the information that The Blackjacks were about to disband, there was no harm in The Beatles asking if he fancied a trip to Hamburg. Pete packed his case with Mona's full approval, but 19-year-old John had to jump the highest hurdle of parental opposition. Nevertheless, tight-lipped Mimi washed her hands of the whole business, although she would not acknowledge – as her son did – that his Art College studies were over.

On 17 August 1960, John breathed foreign air for the first time when the night ferry docked at the Hook of Holland and Lord Woodbine took over at the wheel of an overloaded minibus carrying the five Beatles, Allan Williams, his wife and brother-in-law – who was to snap a much-syndicated photograph of the passengers, minus Lennon, too comfortable in a prime seat – at the Arnhem War Memorial.

Williams and Woodbine's eyes were bloodshot with nigh-on two solid days' driving when youths and adults climbed down from the minibus outside the Kaiserkeller, which was plusher than any palais they'd played on Merseyside. However, after Bruno took charge of his human freight, he conducted them around the dingy Indra and then to three small, windowless rooms adjoining a toilet in a cinema over the road. This was where The Beatles would sleep. Even Woodbine and Lennon were too nonplussed to joke about Stalag 13, Red Cross parcels and forming an escape committee.

After a couple of hours of convalescent sloth, The Beatles rose to give their first ever performance outside the United Kingdom. How could they have imagined then that, six years later, they'd be giving a scream-rent concert at the now-demolished Ernst-Merck-Halle – a Hamburg equivalent of the London Palladium – to which they'd be driven in state in a fleet of Mercedes with *Polizei* outriders?

In 1960, however, nearly all newcomers from Britain wished that they were in hell rather than Hamburg at first, but they couldn't wait to get back there when their sojourn was over. There might have been better ways of breaking a group in, but The Beatles didn't know of any. Being on the road and staying in bed-and-breakfast establishments for eight days in Scotland was one thing, but being up each other's armpits in the dungeons in which they lived when working for Koschmider was another. All of them – including middle-class Lennon – discovered within themselves instincts that they hadn't known existed for living together in their foul quarters, which soon became fouler with the remains of junk food, empty beer bottles, overflowing makeshift ashtrays and general sock-smelling frowstiness.

Musically, too, John, Paul, George, Stuart and Pete came to know each other in an almost extra-sensory way whilst ascertaining how to "read" an audience. Thus at the Indra – and, a few weeks later, at the plusher Kaiserkeller – John's runaway tongue unfurled and the sailors, gangsters, prostitutes and tourists on nights out and teenagers who'd stumbled in from the street laughed with him and even took a chance on the dance floor as they got used to the newcomers' ragged dissimilarity to the contrived splendour of television pop singers. The five scruffy Liverpudlians had good and bad nights, of course, but there were moments when they were truly tearing it up, the most wailing combo on the planet.

After hours, they had been guided around the city's diversions by members of both The Seniors and, nearing the end of their Top Ten run, The Jets. Ricky Richards had accompanied John Lennon to the Musikhaushummel shop for the handing-over of crumpled deutschmarks for a short-armed Rickenbacker Model 1996 guitar.[14] Later, on a flying visit to Hamburg in 1961, Richards was to join The Beatles onstage, borrowing John's expensive instrument to give 'em his 'I Go Ape' and 'C'mon Everybody' party pieces.

While the band fraternised with dyed-in-the-wool rock 'n' rollers like Richards, as well as the Kaiserkeller's formidable team of waiter-*cum*-bouncers, the fact that the five Beatles who'd arrived in Hamburg were ex-grammar school and, therefore, supposedly of Britain's academic elite might have been a subliminal lure for Hamburg's existentialist crowd – the "Exis" – of which Jurgen Vollmer, Klaus Voorman and Astrid Kirchherr were leading lights. This was in spite of George Harrison's confidence to a scribbling journalist in 1967 that he thought The Beatles, overall, were "academic failures". And indeed, when the need arose, Sutcliffe, Lennon and McCartney were capable of inserting into conversations long words – in English, mind, but long words all the same – plus studentish vernacular, along with mention of the likes of Modigliani and Danish philosopher Soren Kierkegaard. With Harrison, they'd once been involved in a fusion of poetry and rock with Sussex beat poet Royston Ellis, who'd judged them to be "more of the bohemian ilk than other young northerners of the time". To a certain degree, Stuart, John and Paul – and, indeed, Pete and George – played up to it. In one incident, they dumbfounded a member of another outfit in the dressing room by pretending to be reading Russian poetry to each other, each intoning and murmuring appreciatively in mock seriousness.

Perhaps via some complex inner debate, this general arty aura enabled Hamburg's young aesthetes – who, bragged Vollmer, "spoke pretty well English that we had learned at school"[15] – to give in to a self-conscious conviviality as they tuned into the epic vulgarity taking place on stages in the Kaiserkeller, the Top Ten and elsewhere in the Reeperbahn mire. Some detected a strength of personality in John that was lacking in the rest. "Lennon, the obvious leader, was like a typical rocker," estimated Jurgen Vollmer, "cool, no gestures except for pushing his body slightly in rhythm to the music. Aggressive restraint, a Brando type."[7] Yet Lennon wasn't all sullen magnetism, as he had few qualms about using coarse language in heated moments on the boards and would attack, say, 'Hound Dog' with the blood-curdling dementia of one in the throes of a fit.

The bass player to Lennon's left, however, was no one's idea of a genius entertainer. That, however, didn't matter to Astrid Kirchherr, because during one Kaiserkeller evening she and he had crossed the boundary between inferred companionship and declared love. However odd a choice this Englishman, there were no old-fashioned looks *chez* Kirchherr after Astrid and Stuart began to share the same bed.

Ken Horton, an old schoolfriend of Stuart's, would receive written details of the moment when Stuart proposed to "my too-wonderful little angel. I'm her church and she's the bells that ring!"[7] John, a more volatile pal, thought that there were bats in his belfry, and, therefore, so did Paul, George and Pete. As self-appointed guardian of Stuart's moral welfare, Lennon dictated the party line: Astrid is a great-looking bird, granted, but fancy tying yourself down when great-looking birds are available in every corner of the Grosse Freiheit.

The subtext, of course, was that Astrid had loosened John's bond with Stuart. These days, just the subtlest inflexion in Sutcliffe's voice would send Lennon into a paroxysm of virulent bad temper, especially when Astrid was around. When she wasn't, he'd ease up, happy to have Stuart's undivided attention once again. Yet, present or absent, Astrid was often in direct line of fire when Lennon exercised an unappealing tendency – that he would never curb – to blurt out what his mind hadn't formulated in simple terms.

The astounding boorishness that would explode like shrapnel all around the Kaiserkeller could be funnelled to more concentrated effect in less public situations. Still stereotyping Germans after all these weeks, an aside like "Rudolph Hess asked me to tell you he was quoted out of context" would issue from the side of Lennon's mouth when simply ordering a lager from a barmaid. At first, Astrid couldn't imagine why she'd been singled out for worse and more relentless treatment. She'd answer back, but just as disconcerting as his tirades were John's intermittent retreats, as if to a prepared position.

To see the two people he cared about most rearing up at each other cut Stuart like a sharp knife. As if watching a tennis match, his eyes would dart from bride-to-be to best friend as harmless jesting swung in seconds to open trading of insults. He couldn't even fight for the woman he worshipped in this, the severest test ever of the mutual and reciprocal loyalty that was the bedrock of his relationship with John. As Lennon stormed off after another excruciating round with Astrid, Stuart would empty his lungs with a whoosh and begin the case for the defence – as John would do for him were the position reversed. Whether beside herself with rage or weak with relief, Astrid would receive the old placatory reassurance that John was a fine fellow when you got to know him.

Astrid's assumption that Lennon loathed her, however understandable, was actually false. She was just the sort of bird he'd have liked for himself – closer to a well-mannered Brigitte Bardot than Cynthia – but he felt that she was out of his league. Indeed, it was inconceivable initially that a girl like that was going out with Stu. Maybe he – John – wasn't so much in a lower league as a different one. If he'd been brave enough to chuck Cynthia and Stuart hadn't been interested, John might have sniffed around Astrid himself. As it was, there were long, dangerous moments, even at the height of antagonism, but like many so-called extroverts he covered a sensitivity with respect to women by brutalising himself – in his case, by coming on as the rough, untamed Scouser.

He was childish and a right bastard to boot, but both Astrid and her mother found it hard to hide a fascination with Lennon, whom both perceived to be probably the most seethingly angry person in the world. On visits to her home in the prim suburb of Altona, he would scan the bookshelves and Astrid's record rack, making few exceptions in a string of derisive comments about every author – Cocteau, Sartre, Genet ("all that Left Bank shower"[7]), Poe, Wilde, Nietzsche, de Sade – and composers like Wagner and Stravinsky, whose works he may or may not have heard.

One day, however, the tempest dropped and he stopped fighting the situation. His manner towards Astrid became not genial, exactly, but brusquely urbane. The exchange of a civil word or two gave way every so often to what might be construed as a compliment. Although his lips never moved upwards, his eyes began to smile almost gently upon her. She was Stuart's and, if she was his, he'd feel the same way about her. Suddenly, he was pleased for Stuart. He'd done all right there.

Of course, he wouldn't have been the John Lennon of popular acclaim if he'd moderated the barbed invective, but with Astrid, at least, it was delivered with much the same lurking affection that he also reserved for Stuart. Gradually, Astrid grasped the social contradiction of rudeness and bonhomie that was Lennon. This paradox in his nature was exemplified during a memorable first encounter in Hamburg with Frank Allen, one of Middlesex's Cliff Bennett And The Rebel Rousers. "Ah yes. It's Frank, isn't it?" acknowledged John after being introduced, "I've talked to other people in the club and it seems that, next to Cliff, you're the most popular member in the band. I don't know why. Your harmonies are fucking ridiculous."[16]

The concordat between Stuart, John and Astrid did not lessen the growing antipathy towards Sutcliffe shown by the rest of the outfit, long-faced from the start about his lackadaisical bass playing. Paul's summary was that "he'd fallen madly in love with [Astrid], and it peeved us like mad that she hadn't fallen in love with any of us: this great blonde chick that we'd never seen the likes of. Stu was really mad on her. We all fancied her a bit but it was, kind of, 'Hands off, I'm serious.'"[7]

Romantic entanglements aside, as the weeks slipped by, Paul, John, Stuart and George stretched out the 15 or so numbers they'd cobbled together with the newly recruited Pete until the monotony of duplicating them over and over again caused the group to insert even the most obscure material that could be dug from their common unconscious. Few

Lennon–McCartney items were unveiled then, but a typical waiter/bouncer's memory was of the two composing in the bandroom during intervals between sets rather than joining the others at the bar.

Yet the scenes in the Kaiserkeller dressing room and the cinema dormitory weren't always how susceptible fans might have imagined – John and Paul running through their latest opus with Pete slapping a rhythmic idea on a table, George tuning his guitar, Stuart sketching in the corner. I'm not sure how many people know this, but connections between pop music and sex are much more distinct than those between pop music and higher artistic expression. Indeed, the strongest motive for most red-blooded lads to be in beat groups was the increased opportunities it presented to fraternise with girls.

In Europe's premier erotic playground, 'fraternising' embraced more than the awkward fumblings that Lennon had known with the demure damsels he'd pursued when a gawky church youth-clubber. Such moments soon belonged to a previous existence.

The younger Beatles might have half-imagined – as he did – that John knew it all, but a visit to the Hippo Bar, where women grappled in mud, or the shocking Street of Windows down Herbertstrasse soon made him realise that sex was in its infancy on Merseyside as he looked the whores up and down like a farmer at a cattle auction. "You couldn't see into it," said Ricky Richards of the latter establishment, "because of great big iron doors either end like the entrance to a concentration camp."

If you liked it plain and simple, sundry orthodox corruptions – street-corner hookers, peep shows, bordellos – were to the Reeperbahn as steel to Sheffield but, as the flow-chart of immorality unfolded further, a veritable Pandora's box of kinky proclivities would open, too, and be celebrated rather than submerged as they were for the tired businessmen – fearful of identification – who indulged their fantasies in the clandestine brothels of Soho.

Before British pop musicians became commonplace on the Reeperbahn, there was usually no question of financial transaction as there would have been for unlovely old rascals purchasing fleeting respite from sexual loneliness. Now, with neither Aunt Mimi nor faithful Cynthia looking, John Lennon became quite accustomed to casual and unchallenging procurement of sexual gratification from almost any one of the girls ringing the stage apron, tits bouncing, to better ogle him and the others with unmaidenly eagerness. All he had to do was let one of his infrequent smiles rest on the front row, and then on a specific girl – maybe a pocket Venus like Astrid – for a split-second that lasted 1,000 years.

In gregarious mood, one such as Lennon would be sighted, rum and cola within reach, surrounded by a bevy of sisters-in-shame aspiring to an orgasm at his thrust in a convenient alcove via a knee-trembler that could be over in seconds or stretched out like toffee, depending on how much effort it took for his legs to give way – or how much time he thought he had. Sometimes, a group might have to fill in with, say, an instrumental until its flushed vocalist – now an expert at dressing while running – panted onstage, zipping himself up.

However, amatory pushovers could come home to roost later in an appointment at the appropriate hospital department for, say, a Wassermann test for syphilis, because a lot of the females involved weren't too fussy about whom they obliged when showtime was over, as long as he was British and in a beat group. "It was funny to witness tearful goodbyes," chuckled the late Colin Manley of The Remo Four, "only to see someone's sweetheart holding hands with a member of the next group to arrive fresh from England."[15] When cognisant of the situation, it became easy to transgress the unwritten machisimo rules lodged in Liverpool, as eager young lads learned not to spoil a no-strings dalliance by getting sulky with a woman who needed someone who didn't care any more than she did. Indeed, on departure, musicians might proffer their bedmate of the previous few weeks to a new arrival as an Eskimo might invite a house guest to "laugh" with his wife.

The Reeperbahn was also a narcotic ghetto as well as a sexual one, and, alas, it's true that British pop musicians there partook of drugs not available over the counter in pharmacies. Cocaine was mentioned in 'I Get A Kick Out Of You' and amphetamines were the subject of Bo Diddley's 'Pills' long before pop stars and drugs became as Tweedledum to Tweedledee in late-1960s newspaper headlines, and "getting high" was used as a reference by such disparate and often doomed heroes as Charlie Parker, Johnny Cash, Keith Richards, John Lennon, Eric Clapton,

JOHN LENNON

Jimi Hendrix, Janis Joplin, Peter Green, Lou Reed, Syd Barrett, Gram Parsons, Phil Lynott and Boy George – plus certain members of the 1960 edition of The Beatles, whose "cool" was enhanced by promoting a drug habit deemed necessary to keep the Dracula hours of their profession rather than combat domestic exhaustion in the manner of the tablet-swallowing housewife in The Rolling Stones' 'Mother's Little Helper'.

The most common sources of artificial energy in the Grosse Freiheit were beer and the amphetamine – "speed" – content of Preludin (phenmetrazine) and, to a smaller degree, Captigun, a brand of suppressants for dieters. Unlike comparatively harmless pick-me-ups such as caffeine-based Pro-Plus – legal in Britain and favoured by sixth formers and undergraduates for all-night assaults on coursework – Preludin and Captigun had been outlawed in 1957 in the UK and were, professedly, available only on prescription in Germany. Nevertheless, unauthorised caches could be procured with ease. It was no hanging matter if you were caught with "Prello", anyway; most police officers in the Reeperbahn couldn't be bothered with the paperwork.

Some of the students with whom The Beatles fraternised dosed themselves with more Preludin than that recommended by doctors, leaving them feeling worse than dog-tired unless they got hold of more. Supplies came to be stocked, too, for the use of employees in nearly all late-night Hamburg premises that featured jazz or rock 'n' roll in order to ensure that the final session in the grey of morning by a given resident act would be as energetic as the first at dusk. Behind the bar in one such establishment appeared a photograph autographed, "John Lennon, King of Prello." Ricky Richards, however, insisted, "You didn't need drugs in Hamburg. The whole place was a buzz." Even when you had to be onstage for four and a half labour-intensive hours Monday to Friday, six on Saturday and Sunday.

It hadn't been immediate but, while pouring an increasingly gargantuan quantity of amphetamines and alcohol into himself, John Lennon became the life and soul of the party (more so than he'd been at college) as whatever little was left of his ingrained Woolton gentility flowed out of him as the liquor flowed in – and flowed out again as toilet-talk about knickers and tits. He was determined that nothing was going to show him up for the nicely brought-up *Mittelstand* boy he was. His voice got louder, his jokes got cruder, his eyes got brighter and his face got redder before he staggered off to puke. The grid of a drain fogging in and out of focus might have been the last image to penetrate his brain before he slumped into the whirling pits and woke up with a worse hangover than ever before.

Lennon's off-duty rampaging gave foundation to many of the embellished tales that would unfold in later trips to Hamburg, such as when he halted a poker game with Gerry Marsden and other Liverpudlians to pour a malevolent glass of water over the slumbering drummer of The Graduates, a group of South Africans. His victim's reciprocation in kind moments later prompted the devil in John to advise him that, if he swallowed the insult, his tough-guy veneer would be cracked forever. Leaping to his feet, he seized hold of an empty bottle and brought it down on the Boer's head. The latter's pride smarted more than his cranium, but further blows were not exchanged owing to a misapprehension that the rest of the players at the table were going to swoop unquestioningly to a fellow Scouser's defence. Had he known how sickened they were by John's behaviour, he might not have been so hasty in slinking back to a damp bed with as much dignity as he could muster.

There were other occasions just as lamentable. Golden rain squirted from Lennon's bladder onto the wimples of three promenading nuns, and foul-mouthed "sermons" were preached by him from the same balcony. While he was a popular leader rather than a follower, even his customary Rosencrantz and Guildenstern, Paul and George, cried off at the last fence during an attempt to mug a pie-eyed sailor who'd just stood them a meal. John was also full of *sieg heils* and "You zhink you play games mit der Master Race!" and so forth, goosestepping with a Hitler salute and a finger across his upper lip.

Another apocryphal story to do the rounds in Hamburg was that, one evening at the Kaiserkeller, some local Al Capone tugged at John's trousers while he was onstage and requested 'Shakin' All Over'. Lennon cracked back, "*Donner und Blitzen*! You're the *Schweinhund* that bayoneted my uncle!" There was no answer to that – not in words anyway – and Bruno Koschmider was suddenly an abject, frightened man, wringing his hands.

It was "all a terrible misunderstanding, Herr Albrecht...never forgive myself". In a way, John was in more danger then than he'd be after the famous "We're more popular than Christ" incident in 1966.

Whether this yarn was true or false, as 1960 drew to its close, it wasn't all smiles anyway with Koschmider, who had grown rather leery of The Beatles of late. "*Ist gut*," he'd exclaim – with a scowl that said it wasn't – after interrogating them about a tale he'd been told about them planning to defect to the hated Top Ten. The Jets' contract there was about to expire and the retinue set to scatter like rats disturbed in a granary, with Tony Sheridan opting to stay on with no fixed backing unit, using instead whoever happened to be around – such as The Beatles.

Acting swiftly, Bruno gave the Liverpudlians a month's notice while withdrawing whatever immunity he'd sorted out with the police concerning the youngest Beatle's nightly violation of a curfew forbidding those under 18 from frequenting Grosse Freiheit clubland after midnight. George Harrison's deportation was arranged by late November.

As for the others, who had decided to muddle on without Harrison, Bruno looked into the middle distance and intimated that an open-all-night city crawling with human predators might not be safe for them if they dared to commence the Top Ten residency. *A propos* nothing in particular, he mentioned a Danish prostitute who had incurred the recent wrath of another club owner and whose corpse was discovered floating on the Weser in Neinberg by the River Police. The coroner had recorded an open verdict.

The two underlings flanking Bruno shook their heads and sucked on their teeth to feign sadness rather than anger at the sin that required such a harsh rebuke. You could tell from the thrust of their cruel and battered faces – cauliflower ears, Neanderthal foreheads, noses as flat as door knockers – that, when schoolboys, many of the Kaiserkeller's waiter/bouncers had been known for their persecution of the helpless. Still grinning with sheer glee at the pain of others, they were at Koschmider's beck and call if he decided that a degree of correction was required for any erring British musicians.

At a distance from safety measurable less in the miles from England than how they were going to get back there, while serving their notice at the Kaiserkeller, The Beatles pondered whether the journey might begin in an ambulance or a hearse. Violence, however, proved unnecessary – within a fortnight of George's removal, Bruno had Pete Best and Paul McCartney handcuffed, bundled into a *Peterwagon* (Black Maria) and, after questioning, ordered out of the Fatherland on a trumped-up charge of arson.

So then there were two and both were forbidden to seek employment as freshly unearthed paperwork revealed that The Beatles had had no work permits for their months at the Kaiserkeller. While Stuart remained in the house of his betrothed, John had little choice but to go home.

He dumped his luggage in the hallway of Mendips and tramped straight upstairs with a mumbled "Never again". To Mimi, he looked just like a refugee from the war-torn Europe of the 1940s. Yet he seemed fundamentally undamaged the next morning, as he lay propped up in bed, stuffed with his favourite "cowboy's breakfast" of bacon and beans and basking in winter sunshine and the sound of a faraway pneumatic drill.

The way he told it, time that hung heavy between one night onstage and the next had been spent just resting and practising guitar. On days off, he'd seen the sights, boated on the lake and visited the zoo, art galleries, museums and a couple of folk fayres. The way John told it, the only thing he'd missed was doing brass rubbings in Hamburg's older churches.

Mimi wasn't impressed. Uncle George had served three wartime years in the army, and she had gleaned that travellers' tales about the fleshpots of Germany were hard fact. Nevertheless, she imagined that she knew her John well enough to understand that his hand in any off-duty frolics had been a duty rather than a pleasure. At any rate, you should have seen the way he and Cynthia fell into each other's arms – love's young dream!

John had written to Cynthia most days while overseas and, after over three months apart, she arrived on the doorstep to coo over her unshaven, bleary eyed Heathcliff. One long kiss vaporised all the endless centuries of anguish. Later, in more private surroundings, John led the unbuttoning, buckle-searching, finger-sliding way. He was a man now, rough, earthy and confident. Cynthia couldn't ask how or why, but she may have guessed what he'd been up to from signals that penetrated the tacit vow of silence that has persisted among bands of roving minstrels for as long as *omertà* has among the Mafia.

Stray mutterings about amorous adventures in Germany were unsettling for anyone's steady girlfriend, particularly if she had to keep up a just-good-friends farce to protect the "available" image of groups that had set their sights higher than local jive-hives. Frank exchanges over tablecloth or counterpane brought near to the surface both her noisome home truths about him and his disobliging comparisons of her with unforgotten *frauleins* so self-possessed that they weren't bothered about anything as tedious as the girl he'd left behind at home.

Nevertheless, John told Cynthia that sex had been on tap in Hamburg but didn't go into detail. Finally, she came to understand that, if you're truly in love, it's better that secrets remain concealed. It meant that she also had to fool herself that John had been, like he said, so weary each night after playing at the Kaiserkeller that all he wanted to do was sleep.

In any case, the group's future was more important than what might or might not have happened abroad. They had turned into a hard act to follow. It was there for all to see on the first post-Hamburg date back at the Casbah, promoted via Mona Best's posters – boasting the "Return Of The Fabulous Beatles" – and via word-of-mouth. The full house remained spellbound until the final chord, and there was a long moment of shell-shocked hush before clapping crescendoed to a bombardment of whistling, cheering, stamping pandemonium.

Something that John, especially, had picked up from watching the likes of Derry Wilkie, Tony Sheridan and Ricky Richards was microphone technique and how to capitalise on, rather than shrink from, any inabilities to pitch a high note without cracking. The transformation was most apparent when he pitched into ravers such as 'Money' and 'Dizzy Miss Lizzy', ad-libbing huskily almost like a jazzer, pop-eyed and workman-like but sounding world-weary, cynical and knowing beyond his years – which he was after Germany. They all were.

5 "Which Way Are We Going, Boys?"

Pulling out all the stops and unfettered by slickness, The Beatles continued to dole out nonchalantly incendiary performances that their lengthy sojourn in Germany had wrought. Well before the first encore at the Casbah, all there had homed in on the new sensation's primaeval rowdiness and contagious backbeat. Half the time you couldn't hear much more than thump-thump-thump, but even in days before onstage monitors and graphic equalisers, when vocal balance was achieved by simply moving back and forth on the microphone, the three-part harmonies of John, Paul and George had been hard won but perfected in readiness for what lay ahead for them, if not for Stuart and Pete.

It might have defied Elvis Presley to have stolen the show from the post-Hamburg Beatles – although that might not be as outrageous a statement as it seems, as the King had caught the overall drift of an era dominated by boys next door with well-scrubbed good looks (Bobby Vinton, Bobby Vee, Bobby Rydell *et al*) with Italianesque ballads, lightweight tunes with saccharine lyrics and infrequent self-mocking rockers. He was now getting on with "quality" stuff, as did his idol Dean Martin, one of Frank Sinatra's Rat Pack, who put in a back-slapping representation on a demobbed Presley's homecoming television spectacular from Miami, one of his last appearances before vanishing into the wings for nigh-on eight years.

Theoretically, as a solo entertainer Presley was answerable only to himself, in contrast to the five Beatles, who, in close proximity to each other in Hamburg, offstage as well as on, had initiated explorations of territory beyond the public intimacies of on-mic comments and momentary eye contact. This was epitomised by Stuart and Paul attempting to score catty points off each other – now not even having the grace to do so behind John's back. The tacit implication in a seemingly innocuous remark from either might spark off the other's hastily unplugged guitar and a slammed backstage firedoor.

Yet Lennon too was prone to antagonising Stuart just to see his hackles rise, and Stuart in turn articulated what the others would deny even if they inwardly concurred: that John's running commentary that had filled every unforgiving minute in Hamburg could be intensely irritating. Why wouldn't he shut his mouth for a bit? You'd fall asleep within earshot of his twittering, sometimes, and yawn and stretch to it too.

As there was no let up either in the general underminings and sly machinations that make all pop groups what they are, Sutcliffe was now shilly-shallying about whether to quit the group and resume his career as a painter. With John sitting on the fence, flare-ups between Stuart and Paul – and, to a smaller extent, Stuart and George – had increased in frequency after the bass player's return to England in mid-January 1961. John was pleased, but, to the rest, his reappearance was akin to that of the proverbial bad penny now that they'd got used to Paul's more agile bass playing. "Stuart wasn't sharing the same commitment to The Beatles as the others were," agreed his younger sister, "he was absent from rehearsals, and he didn't practise the bass. If you're in a group that wants to go places, you're not going to be very happy with a member who isn't as serious about it."

Stuart kept other options open by applying immediately for both a visa to re-enter the Fatherland and for a new course back at the Art College. Each represented an attempt to "settle down". Either way, it did not bode well for The Beatles – especially as John, for all the occasional sport that tormenting his best friend provided, had now issued the naked threat: if he goes, I go.

For Stuart, however, it made no odds now if he was a Beatle or not as he counted the minutes to Astrid's impending fortnight in Liverpool the following month. Proud beyond words, he showed her off round college where even some of the lecturers were impressed. Yet a little humility might have helped Stuart at the interview to re-join what he

called "the old jeans-and-sweater gang with a pencil and sketchbook".[7]
Art history lecturer Nicholas Horsfield, one of his referees, "lost patience
with him. Perhaps 'aggressive' is the wrong word – but he didn't go about
it in the way one usually goes about getting a recommendation."[7]

That finished him with Liverpool anyway. Stuart didn't even stick
around long enough to honour existing Beatles engagements, and he and
Astrid fell into each other's arms amid the gusting engine steam at
Hamburg-Hauptbahnhof station. Through her, Stuart became the first
Beatle to emulate the brushed-forward Exi *Pilzenkopf* – "mushroom
head" – haircut, commonplace in Germany, even if a male so greaselessly
coiffured in Britain would be branded a nancy boy. When Sutcliffe rejoined
the group for a second Hamburg season in April at the Top Ten, John's
howl of derision led him to betray Astrid by restoring his hair fleetingly
to its original brilliantined pompadour. Yet, before the night was out, it
was back the way she liked it.

For Sutcliffe, stretches onstage were now going by as total blurs like
some run-of-the-mill job he'd done for years. Every note sounded the
same, a mere vibration hovering over a backbeat that an idiot couldn't
lose. Emitting an almost palpable air of self-loathing, he'd slouch on to
unacknowledged applause, and glazed listlessness would set in by the first
chorus. His mind would drift off further than ever before from the task
in hand. Astrid's presence in the audience would split his concentration,
and, to the further chagrin of his fellow musicians, he thought nothing
about abandoning the bass mid-set to go over and speak to her.

He couldn't envisage being a Beatle for much longer as he was now
going to recommence his studies at Hamburg's State School Of Art. After
not so much an interview as a discussion in the assistant director's office,
it had been agreed that he was to be exempted from the foundation
course, and was to go directly into a master class supervised by no less
than Eduardo Paolozzi, regarded as an heir to Arp, Tzara, Braque, Bacon
and other gurus of contemporary art.

Before Sutcliffe had marshalled his thoughts and told John, McCartney
and Harrison's sniping at his musicianship and overall indolent attitude
towards the group became, alternately, more subtle and less courteous.
As well as cold looks and cold shoulders, the various protagonists had

cottoned on to badgering each other with trivia and irritating old wounds. "Bet Stuart makes a hash of it!" Harrison once shouted to all and sundry when Sutcliffe was about to deliver his solo vocal outing, 'Love Me Tender'.

Most of the other music the customers heard from The Beatles too were items – both up and down tempo – from the annals of classic rock, the current Top 20 – and US smashes from what used to be called the "race" or "sepia" charts, but obtainable easily enough in Britain.

It was replicated in moderately crude fashion, partly because the massed bowed strings on, say, The Shirelles' 'Will You Love Me Tomorrow' would prove difficult to even approximate on electric guitars. Indeed, if anything, smooth edges had been roughed up rather than *vice versa* when they'd chanced their arm back at the Grosvenor on Christmas Eve 1960.

On the day after Boxing Day, they'd not so much dipped a toe as plunged head first into new depths at the Town Hall in Litherland – with John half shouting the opening shot, and a cigarette dangling from Paul's lower lip. There wasn't an obvious stage act, and they did all-out rock like other local outfits, but the idea was to keep 'Money', 'C'mon Everybody', 'Little Queenie' and all the rest of them almost open-ended while the lead vocalist – usually John or Paul – covered a waterfront from full-blooded screech to whispery and intimate, and then back again as he piled on the pressure.

The Beatles played their guts out that night, and were a howling success. Yet it seemed silly for them – for any provincial group – to feel then that there was any kind of future, what with so many others nearer the core of the British music industry, battling likewise for record contracts and just encores.

Furthermore, even if you were able to break through nationally, you had to accept a second-hand and, arguably, counterfeit status to North American stars such as, say, New Yorker Brian Hyland, Tommy Roe from Atlanta, Georgia and others from places as outlandish and unreachable. Following the climax of classic rock and the establishment of the "Bobby" regime, the hit parades of North America and, by implication, everywhere else became even more constipated with fly-by-night dance crazes, inconsequential but maddeningly catchy one-shot novelties and further assembly-line youths with doe-eyes, hair-spray and bashful half-smiles. Their looks were commensurate with merchandise like Roe's 'Piddle De Pat' and, even harder to live down, Hyland's 'Itsy Bitsy Teenie Weenie Yellow Polka Dot Bikini'.

A domestic case study is that of Surrey-born Jimmy Justice, who, in July 1962, was to be booked for the Cavern, which had gone over almost completely to mainstream pop while The Beatles were in the midst of their first residency in Hamburg. If not as insipidly handsome as any of the predominant Bobbies, Justice was one of a mass of UK heart-throbs in the early 1960s who took their cue from North America. At the height of his fame in 1962, he breached the Top 20 with a hat trick of two US covers and one by a jobbing English tunesmith. Therefore, the Cavern was full when Jimmy appeared there, direct from a tour of Scandinavia, with his backing combo, the Jury – containing musicians from nearby Blackpool. They were supported by up-and-coming local heroes, Billy Kramer And The Coasters. Tony Sanders, the Coasters' drummer, noticed Jimmy and Billy chatting in the dressing room: "Kramer looked every inch a star, but Jimmy Justice didn't, although he was then the big event and Billy was a nobody."[17]

Yet the girls screamed loudest at Jimmy Justice that night. Before the year was out, he'd figure too in the *New Musical Express* readers' popularity poll – in which London's Helen Shapiro would emerge as the kingdom's top female singer. Her reworkings of US hits may be seen now as on a par with (and, in the case of Dionne Warwick's 'Walk On By', superior to) templates by such talents as Connie Francis, Brenda Lee, Carole King, Mary Wells, Skeeter Davis, you name 'em – and anyone with the nerve to even attempt 'Are You Lonesome Tonight' in 1962 while the Elvis Presley treatment was fresh in his fans' memories, deserved attention. Nevertheless, like Jimmy Justice, she was to leave the Top 50 forever by 1964 as a solo artist in an age of groups.

When the beat boom was two years away, however, it was sufficient for the act destined to spearhead it to be on a par with Rory, Gerry and other of Liverpool's most popular rock 'n' rollers – and for Pete Best's mum to co-ordinate the operation from the telephone in the hallway at Hayman's Green. She was now general runaround and bottle washer, conducting negotiations on The Beatles' behalf with this quizzical landlord or that disinterested social secretary – just like Rory Storm's mother, Violet Caldwell, did for him and The Hurricanes.

It was thanks largely to Mona's dogged efforts that The Beatles became fixtures at the Cavern. Otherwise, their stock-in-trade were regular one-nighters at the Casbah, Aintree Institute, the Cassanova Club and like venues that were pocking every vicinity of the city. If finding these guitar combos and their followers personally objectionable, it made sense for some middle-aged entrepreneurs to turn a hard-nosed penny by ripping the insides out of disused warehouses, mucking out cellars or extending licensed premises to make room for a stage and an – invariably standing – audience.

The same scenario was being repeated in other northern cities – as exemplified by Halifax, cradling a scene that was as self-contained as that in Liverpool. Indeed, there are parallels with the Cavern in that the opening of the Plebians Jazz Club in 1961 was motivated too by quasi-evangelical zeal to further the cause of jazz – mostly trad – regardless of financial gain. Then pop crept in and eventually took over the subterranean club in its ravine of town centre warehouses.

Halifax was to spawn no 1960s hitmakers – and seemingly impossible visions of breaking free of parochial fetters appeared before, say, Dave Berry, Jimmy Crawford, Joe Cocker and other entertainers who "coming from out-of-the-way Sheffield, are shackled before they start". Thus spake *Top Stars Special*, created in 1960 as a supplement to the *Sheffield Star*. This daddy of all pop gazettes, which covered local music, predated by a year the first independent newspaper of its kind, the celebrated *Mersey Beat*, brainchild of Bill Harry, John Lennon's college chum.

Among *Mersey Beat*'s aims was the fostering of Liverpool musicians' self expression beyond just hammering out 'Dizzy Miss Lizzy' down the Cavern. As well as John Lennon's Goonish early prose, the bi-weekly journal was responsible for innovations later adopted by the national music press – including the first "gig guide" and photographs taken on location or onstage rather than posed studio shots.

Bill's account of the journal's origin is worth quoting at length: "Since I was a kid, I'd been putting together magazines. I was planning a new one called *Storyville And 52nd Street*, divided between trad and modern jazz. Yet I remember walking down from the college one lunchtime, and thinking why do a jazz thing when there's John's band, Cass And The Cassanovas, Rory Storm And The Hurricanes and all the other groups I'd got to know?

"Soon I began making notes of what was happening locally because people didn't seem to be aware of it. Bob Wooler, the Cavern's MC, and I got together and worked out that there were over 300 groups in Liverpool of every variety – not just four-man guitars-bass-and-drums outfits, but duos, trios, octets, all girl bands and all black vocal. Incredible!

"One group might have known about a couple of venues or promoters – while another would know of different ones, but no one knew how many there were in the whole city. Every youth club, town hall, even ice rinks and swimming pools had rock 'n' roll on. Some outfits were playing seven nights a week, three or four gigs a night!

"The word got round what I was up to, and a civil servant called Jim Anderson lent me 50 quid to start *Mersey Beat*. The first issue was out on July 6th 1961. I did all the distribution myself. First, I went to the three main wholesalers – including WH Smith – who took some. Then I arranged for all the different venues to take copies. Next, I went to see the managers of the music stores.

"One of the things I was trying to do with *Mersey Beat* was get the musicians to express themselves, and bring a flavour of their world across to the readers, what it was like on the road, playing the gigs and so on – because I was always interested in dragging the potential out of creative people. That's why I used to have John writing his 'Beatcomber' columns – the first published examples of his prose – members of groups who were cartoonists...Stuart Leithwood of The Koobas was one. We had illustrations by The Remo Four too. The Roadrunners did little pantomimes for Christmas."

That each of the first pressings of *Mersey Beat* sold out within a morning demonstrated the strength of demand for venue information and news coverage as well as other activities, professional and otherwise, of a veritable host of key personalities who were as much stars in Liverpool as Cliff Richard, Helen Shapiro and Jimmy Justice were in the charts.

Nevertheless, *Mersey Beat*'s plea, "London Take A Look Up North" on 15 February 1962, was to be unheeded in the first instance.

During the previous unseasonably cold summer, its second issue had made a lot of a Beatles record date that had taken place in Germany. Among their duties at the Top Ten was backing Tony Sheridan, who'd become the city's undisputed rock 'n' roll king – and he remains the name that trips most readily off the tongue whenever British musicians in Hamburg are discussed. "I was an ingredient in the pudding," the man himself would concede. "I don't think that I was any more important than anyone else – except that I was a bit more experienced. That was my plus point."

Learning the tricks of the trade from one now nicknamed "The Teacher", Gerry And The Pacemakers had preceded The Beatles at the Top Ten – where their front man's fretboard skills had been fine-tuned through paying acute attention to Sheridan. Indeed, Gerry – and John Lennon – were to share the same high-chested guitar stance with Tony.

John and three other Beatles – Pete, Paul and George – were hired by Bert Kaempfert, freelance producer for Polydor, Deutsche Grammonphon's pop subsidiary, to accompany Sheridan on half his debut album, *My Bonnie* – including the title song which, as a spin-off single, was to enter the German chart briefly. The remaining tracks were taped with other UK musicians in Hamburg.

"Bert had been trying rock 'n' roll with young Germans," Tony explained, "but it had sounded ludicrous. He was impressed by what he thought was our authenticity. It's a shame no one taped any of the Top Ten gigs. I was doing most of the lead guitar – though if John, say, took a solo, it was halfway good because it came out of the rawness of him. George was young, inexperienced and a bit over-awed by the whole thing – but very keen to learn. Because the drummer wasn't that good, rhythm guitars had to compensate for the lack of a strong beat. Bert made no comment about this and was quite happy to leave it the way it was when we recorded."

In a perhaps wrong-headed attempt to capture the *au naturel* power they and Tony generated on the boards, The Beatles were hastened to a session mere hours after the last major sixth of the night at the Top Ten had reverberated so that their adrenalin could be pumped more profitably onto a spool of tape, a phonographic equivalent of bottling lightning – albeit adulterated by the clinical exactitudes of the studio.

All the numbers were punched out in three takes at most, and there was time in hand for Kaempfert to lend critical ears to items from The Beatles' repertoire without Tony. He was impressed particularly with their arrangement of the ragtime standard 'Ain't She Sweet' – with John on lead vocal – and 'Cry For A Shadow', a Harrison–Lennon instrumental.

Neither would be issued outside Germany until they had acquired historical interest. After fate had taken The Beatles' hand, Bert would recall that, "It was obvious to me that they were enormously talented, but no one then – including the boys themselves – knew how to use that talent or where it would lead them."[15]

Never mind, even being a backing group on a foreign disc was a yardstick of achievement for The Beatles back home – and, after so beginning their commercial discography, Lennon would assume Sheridan's lead vocal when it was incorporated into the act when, describing themselves for a while as "Polydor Recording Artists", he, Paul, George and Pete recommenced an itinerary in and around Liverpool. The spectrum of work had broadened – and they'd always have Hamburg – but there was a creeping sense of marking time. They'd taken their impact on Merseyside to its limit, but no one understood how to advance to the step between consolidation of a regional following and the threshold of the Big Time. "Which way are we going, fellows?" Lennon would shout when spirits were low.

"To the top, Johnny!" was the Pavlov's Dog response.

"What top?"

"To the toppermost of the poppermost!"

Progress to that goal had been slight since 'My Bonnie'. As well as venues where they'd gone down well before, there were forays to such disparate locations as the Merseyside Civil Service Club and New Brighton's grand Tower Ballroom, the most capacious seaside dancehall in the northwest outside Blackpool. There were two evenings at the Three Coins in Manchester, and a ghastly loss-making one-shot odyssey with amplifiers on laps in the van to Aldershot, the first ever engagement in the south.

Far closer to home, on the day of a booking 30km (20 miles) up the coast in Southport, heavy rain had persisted well into the evening; there was something good on the television and the local paper was on strike. This meant that a poster outside – with "No Weirdies, Beatniks or Coloureds admitted" along the bottom – was the sum total of the advertising. John didn't bother to tune up properly, and soon gave up making a show of it after taking the stage in front of a miniscule crowd. He also kicked off 'Three Cool Cats' before George had finished announcing it, causing the younger player to sulk all the way home.

On aggregate, an individual Beatle's income was a fraction of that of a dustman, even after they won the first readers' poll in *Mersey Beat*. Unless a bigger stroke than this was pulled, the group was soon likely to be figuratively twitching and thrashing like an aged dray-horse that'd collapsed in its shafts, lugging coal to the docks. A Beatles bash in Liverpool, see, was as commonplace as a whist-drive. They were in peril of being overtaken by newer groups like The Undertakers, Carl Vincent's Counts and Billy Kramer And The Coasters – and some not so new. The Big Three, for instance, had risen like a phoenix from the ashes of Cass And The Cassanovas.

You'd see John Lennon and one or two of the others mooching about the town centre, calculating what the one-shilling-and-sixpence they had between them could do. A plate of beans on toast washed down with a cup of liquid smoke? It was as if they'd never got drunk with Ricky Richards, made a record with Tony Sheridan, played Aldershot – only 65km (40 miles) west of the Eldorado that was London – or invoked sporadic screams from girls in the Top Ten for a particularly bravura 'Roll Over Beethoven'. Down in the dumps because of a letter from the HP firm threatening to repossess his amplifier, John looked up from filling in all the "Os" on the front page of yesterday's *Daily Sketch* to speak half-seriously of packing it in. Hessy's was always buying back instruments and equipment that they'd sold a couple of years before to a bunch of young sprogs with the world at their feet.

Stuart had sold his bass to Klaus Voorman, and had written from Hamburg to say that he'd sent off for an application form and prospectus from a teacher training college in Leicester. "Going to Germany was a bit like a student taking a year out to do VSO," reckoned sister Pauline. "It was presented like that to his mother – that he'd come back to do his post-graduate work and settle down. No one could predict that he'd fall for a German girl and base himself in Germany. The paradox was he did in Germany what he didn't do in England – complete his studies, become responsible, drop the pop, and start to make some sort of career in Art. I don't think he particularly wanted to do the teacher training course at all. It was only to placate his mum."

For much the same reason, John started thinking aloud to his aunt that a steady job, a mortgage, maybe wedding bells might be worth considering as The Beatles were on a road that was obscure, a dusty, wearisome road that didn't look as if it led anywhere important – but there was always a chance that it might.

You only had to be in the right place at the right time, hadn't you? Look at The Jaybirds – a Nottingham group who'd worked at the Top Ten too – who were actually under contract to Embassy, admittedly, a label of no great merit – but, hey, what about Cliff Bennett and his Rebel Rousers who had had a proper single out on an EMI label – Parlophone – earlier this year? Some of the other acts with whom he'd compared notes in Hamburg and elsewhere were going places too, and it disturbed John that the fish weren't biting for his Beatles as well.

Aunt Mimi often reminded him that it wasn't too late to make a proper go of it as a commercial artist. Recently, she'd undergone a descent down the worn, slippery stairwell to the Black Hole of Calcutta that was a Beatles lunchtime session in the Cavern, fighting a desire to flee the enveloping fug of mould, perspiration and cheap perfume, not to mention the prickly heat that grew by the minute as more jabbering teenagers joined the massed humanity bobbing up and down before a wooden stage beneath bare light bulbs.

Minutes after her arrival, John and the rest of those dreadful fellows sauntered on – and he was smoking! – to hit all their instruments at once to a staccato "Right!". Mimi clapped her hands to her ears with a moan of agony. What first struck her in every sense was the deafening din, and how dissimilar it was to anything pop she'd ever seen on television. Cliff Richard had indulged in a little scripted playfulness on *Sunday Night At*

The London Palladium. This was fine, but John was belching into the microphone, and saying things like the f-word. Indeed, she was more profoundly shocked by his language than she was by the "music".

Nonetheless, she restrained herself – or was prevented – from wriggling through to the front to drag John off the stage and out. Instead, Mimi contented herself instead with trying to glare him out of countenance, but then Paul stepped up for a sentimental ballad, something she actually recognised. Moreover, his pleasant-enough warbling stayed in key, and a *claque* screamed when he finished. Amongst them when John waved George Harrison forward to sing Buddy Holly's 'Crying Waiting Hoping', a jocose, middle-aged woman was clapping and cheering as voraciously as everyone else.

When the sweatbath was over, this person – who turned out to be George's mother – was there already when Mimi decided to confront John with this latest and most heinous folly the minute that he stumbled into what might be described as a changing room.

"Weren't they great!?" enthused Mrs Harrison.

Mimi was glad someone thought so. If that was entertainment, let's have a great deal less entertainment, said she.

More insidiously, John drove his mystified aunt nervous for weeks by dirgeing "A-wimoweh a-wimoweh a-wimoweh a-wimoweh..." round the house, *sotto voce* like a mantra. It was the background chant of 'The Lion Sleeps Tonight', a song that milkmen were whistling as incessantly towards the end of 1961.

Surprisingly, the British cover version, albeit using a different title – by The Karl Denver Trio – had risen higher in the Top 20 than the US template by The Tokens. That there were further signs of resistance to the dominance of North American pop was one reason for The Beatles, in optimistic moments, to at least pretend that they'd ascertained from a buzz in the air that they were almost there.

Another was that they'd acquired someone with more clout than Mona Best. If he wasn't a born manager, Brian Epstein was as determined as her to do whatever willingness and energy would do to push The Beatles further up the ladder of success, all the way up if the time came. Unlike others of his age – 27 – he didn't behave as if all he liked about

pop was the money it could generate. Neither was he intending to sell
The Beatles like tins of beans – with no money back if they tasted funny.

He was also too much of a gentleman to stand outside on the pavement
and bark the show to passers-by. Neither would he demean himself by,
say, sitting with the back of the chair against the stage, holding up the
central microphone on the end of a broomstick as Cynthia Powell had
done in the first flush of wonderment at John, when once a mic-stand
hadn't been available.

This Mr Epstein had been lost in wonder too. The group had been
vaguely aware of him as a privately educated Jewish businessman who
had followed his father into the family firm, which had grown since the
turn of the century into a prominent Merseyside department chain,
specialising in electrical goods and furniture. By 1961, Brian was a bored
and frustrated sales manager at the city centre branch of NEMS – North
End Music Stores – and heir apparent to the prominent firm that had
sprung from a grandparent's small suburban shop.

In a hidden history of pop, the true *éminences grises* and some of
the figureheads are Jewish if you consider how many were the movers
and shakers of rock as businessmen, composers of 'Hound Dog', 'Twist
and Shout' and so many more standards – and chart contenders, notably
Abe Zimmerman's boy, Robert, the most famous Jew since Charlton
Heston. That's Bob Dylan to you, mate, just as Liverpool's own late
Frankie Vaughan's surname was actually Abelson. Furthermore, Lou
Reed is also Lewis Rabinowitz; Carole King is Carole Klein, and Doc
Pomus is Jerome Solon Felder, though his songwriting partner, Mort
Shuman – like Phil Spector, Paul Simon, Leonard Cohen and Graham
Gouldman, hit composer and founder member of 10cc (three-quarters
Jewish) – stuck with his given surname in the teeth of the anti-Semitism
that still lingered in the psyche of even the most vehement foes of the
Nazis. As late as 1966, Brian Epstein was to complain that because he
was a Jew, he'd not been included on the Queen's birthday honours lists
as his Beatles had been.

By coincidence, NEMS's young Mr Epstein had been attending a
seminar in record retailing management in Hamburg the same month
that his future clients were working at the Top Ten, but The Beatles first

impinged on his consciousness via *Mersey Beat*. "At NEMS, Brian Epstein took a dozen," confirmed Bill Harry, "but he rang me, astonished, to say they'd all gone just like that, and ordered a gross of the next issue – which had on the front cover a picture and the complete story of The Beatles recording in Germany. He couldn't believe it when those sold out virtually in a day – so he asked me to come and have a sherry in his office to tell him what was happening. He was avid for information, and asked if he could write a record review column.

"He knew all about The Beatles months before a reputed guy came into NEMS and asked for 'My Bonnie', and Brian asked me to fix for him to go down the Cavern to see them."

Epstein didn't feel quite so out-of-place in the Cavern as Aunt Mimi, but he went through a brief phase of dressing down from his usual conservative suit, shirt-and-tie and sensible shoes to go there and to other venues where he was observed looking round so frequently to assess how well The Beatles were going down that observers guessed he had a vested interest. Funny, no one had ever noticed him around them before.

Much has been written about Brian's homosexuality – often the butt of unpleasant jibes by John over the years[18] – and his erotic attraction to The Beatles, particularly Lennon. Yet in his first autobiography, *Beatle!*, Pete Best states that Brian propositioned him one evening in 1962, "but there had been nothing nasty about it, nothing obscene, nothing dirty. It was a very gentle approach."

When the group – then without Pete – took a fortnight's break from a hectic schedule between 27 April and 11 May 1963, Brian – godfather to John and Cynthia's new-born son, Julian – persuaded Lennon to join him for a 12-day break in Spain. Paul McCartney's notion about the acceptance of such an invitation from a known homosexual was "John, not being stupid, saw his opportunity to impress upon Mr Epstein who was the boss of the group. He wanted Brian to know who he should listen to. There was never any hint that he was gay."[19]

Some within The Beatles' circle, however, imagined that the two holidaymakers had an affair – which John denied emphatically at the time, to the point of a drunken attack on Bob Wooler for a remark about "the honeymoon". Brian too insisted "It is simply not true," when asked about the matter by Don Short of the *Daily Mirror*. In any case, as it was with Pete Best, Epstein "wouldn't have done anything to frighten John off," stressed Brian's personal assistant, Wendy Hanson. "John was a womaniser – and Brian was a very sensitive person. He'd never push himself on anyone."[19]

Nevertheless, ever the iconoclast, Lennon, routinely unfaithful as both a boyfriend and husband, may have decided to experiment for much the same reason as French sex symbol Serge Gainsbourg, who admitted in print that, yes, he'd once had a homosexual experience, "so as not to remain ignorant".[20] In a 1983 memoir, *In My Life*, Lennon's childhood pal and fellow Quarry Man Pete Shotton wrote that John himself had confessed that there had been a half-hearted attempt at non-penetrative sex on one occasion in Spain, perhaps lending credence to Lennon's rationalisation that, "Well, it was almost a love affair, but not quite. It was never consummated – but it was a pretty intense relationship."[21] This was also implied in 1991's *The Hours And Times*, a 60-minute celluloid dramatisation of the trip – with Lennon played by Ian Hart, the same actor who portrayed him in *Backbeat*.

After the Spanish jaunt, however, there was no other indication that what passed between John Lennon and Brian Epstein was anything beyond friendship and business.

Who cares anyway? Back in 1961, Brian's first task had been to transform the four louts into what a respectable London agent or record mogul in those naive times expected a good pop group to be. As he'd been a leading light in school plays, and had once spent not quite a year as a student at the Royal Academy of Dramatic Art, Brian was only too glad to give a few pointers with regard to presentation and professional conduct.

Some thought him too old to understand what made teenagers tick, but he'd kept abreast of popular culture, partly via *Mersey Beat*, and partly via a continued interest in the gossip and goings-on within showbusiness proper. If his membership of Equity had lapsed, he still subscribed to *The Stage* and had glanced occasionally at *Melody Maker* and the *New Musical Express* – which he was now studying as a stockbroker might the Dow Jones index.

Brian had decided from the onset that The Beatles needed a smarter, more corporate image. Despite John's forceful arguments to the contrary, he visualised them, he said, in stylish but not too way-out suits plus all the accoutrements. He'd pay for these just as he'd paid off all outstanding HP debts on their equipment.

There were shows of resistance too when he insisted that they played to a fixed programme with no patter that embraced swearing – meaning anything stronger than "bloody" or "crap", then the vilest oaths cinema censorship would permit. Neither was John to insert rude words in songs as instanced by "All my life, I've been waiting/Tonight there'll be no masturbating" in Buddy Holly's 'Oh Boy!'. Luckily, they were intending to drop that number anyway.

The Beatles had to be taught to bow when they'd finished a song, and smile in a gentlemanly way. They had to rest that smile not on individuals but on the general populace. Had they ever come across the term "back projection"?

In short, Epstein wanted to instil into them poise, and charm, not to mention clear diction during continuity. However, John wouldn't take any such tutorials seriously, and kept staring at Brian in a disconcerting and penetrating manner, full of Brooding Intensity that promised nothing but mockery.

A Professor Higgins job on Lennon proved, therefore, to be too Herculean an effort. After he changed the subject when Brian pondered whether the group ought to dispense with stage dialogue altogether, bar "Thank you very much" and "Goodnight", there was no choice in the death but to let him cuss, sneer, tell off-colour jokes, spit out chewing-gum, give front row scrubbers the eye, and generally be just the sort of exhibitionist yob that Brian had been brought up to despise.

Yet some of what his manager had tried to do had rubbed off after a superficial fashion – or maybe John had become so desperate to Make It that he was prepared to mellow out as required to achieve the desired end. When that was done, and he was a showbusiness treasure like Cliff Richard, he could revert to type – or whatever the type had become.

Lennon couldn't bring himself to be extravagant with praise, but, for all the fussing around with suits and bowing, he acknowledged how

Epstein kept his cool in any kind of difficulty more effectively than Allan Williams or Mona Best might have done, even when in the midst of some tightwad of a promoter and his shirtsleeved hitmen – who were shouting and swearing that the contract wasn't worth the paper it was written on, and The Beatles were in breach of it anyway. Not raising a bland voice, Brian's reasoned contentions would be riven with phrases like "If you'll pardon my correction" and "Excuse me, but five minutes ago, you said something about…" that wore them out, and made them pay the agreed fee – which was, nonetheless, still small enough for the lads to piss it away at the nearest pub within the hour.

These days, "the lads" was tending to mean just John, George and Paul, now that Pete's mother wasn't around as much anymore, cramping everyone's style, and Pete himself was becoming a being apart from the other three, a Tony Curtis among the *Pilzenkopfs*, a non-partaker of Preludin and a swain whose intentions towards his girlfriend, Kathy, were honourable.

At least Stuart Sutcliffe had jumped before he was pushed. Casting The Beatles aside as adolescent foolishness, he'd since got his hair cut "almost respectable". He told sister Pauline ruefully, "I think I must be growing up." The emotional and physical cost of being a Beatle and then making up for lost time as a painter, however, incited fears for his health as dizzy spells, convulsions, chronic indigestion and other maladies he'd been suffering for some time became more persistent.

Correspondence with John was in aptly glum existentialist vein, dwelling at length about how pointless everything was, and upon esoteric issues in which Lennon assumed the role of "John the Baptist" and Sutcliffe that of "Jesus Christ". The most quoted and evocative lines from these letters came to be John's poetic "I can't remember anything without a sadness/So deep that it hardly becomes known to me/So deep that its tears leave me a spectator of my own stupidity."[22] Picking at these oblique lines for meaning, they are reminiscent of "True lowliness of heart/Which takes the humbler part/And o'er its own shortcomings weeps with loathing" from 'Come Down O Love Divine', a Whitsuntide hymn that both boys from church-going upbringings would have been familiar with.

Inspired perhaps by these dialogues, Stuart began an ultimately unfinished autobiography-*cum*-novel entitled *Spotlight On Johnny*. Describing himself in the third person (as "Nhoke"), Stuart disclosed that "when he stood up, he complained of a blackout and tremendous headaches". As this was happening in real life, he consulted German doctors who recommended treatments that could only retard rather than arrest the progress of what he could only refer to as "the illness".

Some can take amphetamines every day without paying a price, but Stuart Sutcliffe couldn't. The rocky road to his fatal cerebral haemorrhage was signposted by classic drug withdrawal symptoms. As well as the ailments he'd mentioned to Pauline and John, there were panic attacks, irritability, hyperactivity and long wakeful periods in bed. More sinister was muttered trepidation building to Hitlerian scream; muzzy eyesight as a harbinger of temporary loss of vision; swaying and staring vacantly as a prelude to a convulsive fit; nightmare hallucinations ("the horrors") and other disturbances that reduced Sutcliffe to a pathetic isolate.

He'd be seen sitting with Astrid at a Grosse Freiheit club's most secluded table, lost in melancholy and paranoia, his fingers pressed against his forehead, and his lips pressed together as if holding back pain. When his eyes weren't screwed shut, she'd notice that their twinkle had gone, and a burned-out look was emphasised by purple-black blotches beneath them, like mascara that had trickled and dried.

To those back home who could not see the sickness he radiated, the only indication that anything was amiss was in letters that flitted too fitfully from topic to unrelated topic, and were riven with unfathomable but disturbing sentences like, "Actually, I'm an acute migraine worker accompanied by my bloodiness so you can try and catch me from there."[7] His handwriting had become noticeably larger and more spidery, deteriorating to near-illegibility like Captain Scott's log as its writer died by inches in the Antarctic blizzards.

On Tuesday, 10 April 1962, death took Stuart Sutcliffe without effort on the stroke of 4:45pm. In the ambulance, Astrid's face was his last vision before he passed over.

A Dr Peter Hommelhoff, Director of Medicine in a Hamburg hospital, who'd examined Sutcliffe the previous June, had concluded that the patient's poor state of health was the legacy of too much alcohol – and, especially, amphetamine – and "cerebral paralysis due to bleeding into the right ventricle of the brain" was noted in the post-mortem report as an apparent confirmation of Hommelhoff's diagnosis rather than any purported blow to the head by John Lennon or anyone else.

John learned of Stuart's death directly from Astrid when he arrived in Hamburg the day before The Beatles opened at a new venue, the Star-Club, soon to be the most famous landmark in the Grosse Freiheit. The terrible news struck home, and Lennon struggled not to lose his cool. He strained his wits for some hilariously appalling remark to show how unaffected he was. He ought to combust with laughter or at least shrug his shoulders indifferently, not turn an eyelash. At the end of that briefest of pauses, he could manage neither of these pretences. For once at a loss for words, he buried himself in Astrid's embrace.

The next day, however, he stood apart from the bear-hugging outbursts when he, Astrid, Paul and Pete greeted Millie, Stuart's mother at Hamburg-Fuhlsbuttel Airport. He seemed too calm to her – like a detached spectator with no interest or stake in the tragedy. Since yesterday, he'd made up his mind to be the hard man again: too tough to cry.

Within hours, The Beatles were pitching into their first number at the Star-Club with all their customary verve. However, when all the stupid songs about fast cars and girls were over, John could no longer not believe it. During the expected after-hours carousing, he was as free with his uncouth tongue as he was with pouring a gargantuan quantity of booze and pills into himself. He appeared to be quite himself again, but, now and then, he fell silent as shards of disjointed memories pierced an already over-stimulated mind. So often they were of trivialities – Stuart flicking away a cigarette end along a college corridor, buying his Hofner "President" bass at Hessy's, catching his eye momentarily during that first night at the Indra… What amounted to an unspoken wake for Stuart ended with a now-forgotten altercation with somebody or other that you could hear all over some six-in-the-morning bar.

Beneath it all, John Lennon was a shaken and downcast man, feeling his anguish all the more sharply for realising how many functions his best pal could no longer fulfil for him: careers adviser, father confessor, straight man in their double act, healer of some of the psychic wounds of his childhood, and someone he could bounce his ideas off and be rewarded with honest, constructive answers. There would never be another like Stuart. Would there?

Stuart Sutcliffe, the boy who'd had everything it took, was buried in Grave No 552 in the 1939 section of Huyton parish cemetery after a service in St Gabriel's Church where he'd once borne the processional cross as head chorister. Owing to work commitments, The Beatles had been unable to attend. They'd last seen him in February 1962 during his last visit home. He was emaciated and corpse-grey in the face, but in other ways, he was still the Stu they remembered.

"Wearing your mum's suit then?" Paul had quipped when he turned up at a Beatles bash in a lapel-less outfit, buttoning up to the throat – one of Astrid's creations. Stuart laughed too – but not at himself. A lot of the lads watching The Beatles had their hair combed like the *Pilzenkopfs* John, George and Paul were now sporting. He'd bet even money that it wouldn't be too long before they'd be copying The Beatles' lapel-less, high-buttoned stage costumes too.

6 "I Don't Know – What Do You Think?"

More than half of John Lennon's life was over when The Beatles made their next escape attempt from the Merseyside–Hamburg treadmill. Acting swiftly, their new manager had laid on with a trowel NEMS's position as a major retailer in the northwest to cajole Decca recording manager Dick Rowe to try out his group on New Year's Day 1962 over the edge of the world in London.

After scoring a Number One with 'Broken Wings' by The Stargazers in 1953, this Mr Rowe had become recognised as a leading producer and talent spotter of the UK record industry. Later 1950s singers who also thrived under his wing as Decca's head of A&R (Artists and Repertoire) included Tommy Steele, Anthony Newley and Billy Fury. For a while, he left Decca to work for Top Rank for whom he procured a chart entrant in John Leyton, albeit, via independent console boffin Joe Meek. When the label folded, he returned to Decca to minister to further smashes such as Jet Harris and Tony Meehan's 'Diamonds' of 1963. However, for all his Top Ten triumphs, Rowe has earned a historical footnote as The Man Who Turned Down The Beatles on the grounds that "groups with guitars are on the way out".[22]

Rowe had delegated the task of auditioning The Beatles to Mike Smith, his second-in-command, intimating that it was probably a waste of time, but you never know.

Listening to the results today, the overall impression is that The Beatles weren't at their best when, for a man who was half an hour late, they ran through numbers predetermined by Brian to demonstrate their prowess as "all-round entertainers". Paul seems too eager to please, while John's lead vocals have about them an unnatural politeness. All in all, it's rather solemn. As an illustration of how solemn, it's George who comes across as having the most "personality", a prime consideration in an age when groups had to have a token "leader" – though the concept of "George Harrison And The Beatles" flashed only fleetingly across Mike Smith's mind.

Neither did Dick Rowe think that these Liverpudlians were all that brilliant. They could find his way around their instruments, but were merely competent singers, and their sound conjured up back-of-beyond youth clubs with soft drinks, ping-pong and a presiding vicar who, like Rowe, was yet unaware of Merseybeat's distant thunder. Outfits like The Beatles could be found in virtually every town in the country.[23] Only last month, he'd snapped the tape machine off before the end of something similar by The Zircons – Spalding's winners of a pan-Lincolnshire "battle of the bands"-type contest in 1961, if you're wondering where you'd heard the name.

Decca wasn't the only company to reject The Zircons – and The Beatles. Pye, Philips and three of EMI's four labels did on receiving a second-generation copy of the Decca tape: all John, Paul, George and Pete had to offer apart from the faded second-hand celebrity of 'My Bonnie'. Each label never failed to apologise in writing for any delay in replying, excusing itself with the backlog of similar packages that arrived every week. The general feeling was that, while Mr Epstein's boys did have talent, there were sufficient guitar outfits under contract already. The tape was, therefore, being returned with best wishes for future success and blah blah blah.

A despondent mood was encapsulated by Lennon sparking earnest discussion about soliciting budget labels like Embassy and Top Six, where bargain-bin acts were hired to crank out workman-like xeroxes of other people's hits, sometimes squeezing half-a-dozen such tracks onto an EP – extended play – disc. "Can you tell the difference between these and the original sounds?" was Embassy's rhetorical question on one such tacky sleeve. Indeed, you could – but only the occasional misjudged timbre of the lead vocals or a butter-fingered riff made such merchandise so-bad-it's-good.

Now that the honeymoon was over, Brian was one scapegoat for The Beatles' marking time. Another was the Bests, whose house was, nevertheless, still used as an assembly point. That Mona no longer held The Beatles in the palm of her hand was manifested in the way the others started treating Pete – whose isolation became more and more perceptible. Now and then, he'd find himself straining his ears to catch murmured intrigue when, say, Harrison and McCartney, speaking in low voices, froze him with the inadvertent malevolence of their glances – or when McCartney and Lennon tinkered on secretive guitars in a backstage alcove.

While John was handsome after a funfair bumper-car operator fashion, it was hardly Pete's fault that he was the darling of the ladies for his more conventional good looks as well as an unobtrusive content in posing no deliberate threat to the front line except when he was required to surrender the kit to Paul in order to sing and demonstrate Joey Dee And The Starliters' 'Peppermint Twist'. He did so with all the endearingly flustered poise of an otherwise desk-bound head of accounts dancing with some voluptuous typist at the office party. In the watching throng, he'd see his mother, Kathy, and brother Rory, their eyes shining with pride, but there was no such encouragement from George, Paul and John these days.

Amicability was in short supply generally as the encircling professional and personal gloom thickened. As they hadn't become stars overnight, The Beatles were less a bunch of mates out on what amounted to a subsidised booze-up than one more deadbeat group, lurching from gig to gig. At the same venues time and time again – even the Casbah, for God's sake, until it closed in June 1962 – they could be bought for fees that (on Merseyside anyway) were often static at best. Promoters, then as now, took little account of inflation.

The music was becoming static too. Why bother with anything new when praise indeed was information that the show a customer missed was just like the one he saw the time before? No one was getting any younger; performing onstage was The Beatles' only saleable trade, and they were travelling the same long-road-with-no-turning as olde-time rockers like Gene Vincent and Screaming Lord Sutch with no choice but to go right on doing it, just to break even.

One of the only perks of the job was exemplified supposedly by the witnessed aftermath of a booking at the Aintree Institute, where John was holding court outside to two girls, one squawking, "Oooo, 'e's lovely!" and the other conspicuous for a huge bosom and a turned-up nose. After a while, Lennon forwent even cursory chivalry by seizing both by the arm and manoeuvring them into the darkness.

Being central figure in a gleesome threesome, however, wasn't sufficient material reward for a night's work. John and the others started focussing more sharply and unfairly on painfully committed Brian, who, admittedly, had been responsible for one or two major blunders already whilst learning his craft – such as the choice of songs for the Decca date – and would be responsible for many more to come. His principal failing then was that he was a salesman rather than an uninhibited hustler. He was also honest and painstaking to the point of arousing suspicion from an industry that was blighted more than most by time-serving incompetence, fake sincerity, backstabbing and the contradiction of excessive thrift and heedless expenditure.

There was no one else but Brian for The Beatles to blame for the apparent petering out of interest, apart from each other. Besides, bickering helped pass the time. Yet, thanks to their learner manager dialling his finger to a stub, The Beatles were leading what the economist would call a "full life" in a way. A list that had once signified a week's work became a day's. A lunchtime session at the Cavern might be followed by a few hours convalescent sloth until an early evening session at the same venue. Before onlookers realised that they'd left the building, The Beatles' van would be halfway down the street on a dash to a town hall over the river in Birkenhead.

As for Hamburg, the latest visit in April had found them supporting and socialising with Fats Domino, Gene Vincent, Little Richard and other visiting heroes of their school days that, unlike the Top Ten, the Star-Club could afford. George Harrison hit it off immediately with Billy Preston, Little Richard's 15-year-old organist, but Lennon had made up his mind to exercise an observed disrespect towards the ineffable Richard himself. Calling him "Grandad" and telling him to shut up was the least of it, but John was as diligent as everyone else in making myriad private observations of his old idol's performance for incorporation into his own.

The previous month, Epstein had negotiated both an engagement in Stroud, a market town almost as far south as Aldershot – and Pete, George, Paul and John's first BBC radio broadcast – three numbers on *Teenagers' Turn* from Manchester's Playhouse. Even this was no indication that The Beatles were anything more than a classic local group, despite an enthusiastic response – embracing screams – from the studio audience during the show, that translated to a stylised mobbing outside.

Reaction had been similar when Birmingham's Denny Laine And The Diplomats had made their debut on the ITV magazine *Midlands At Six* – and, as it had been when The Beatles' visited Decca, nothing had come of EMI convening the outfit at its Abbey Road complex in London's St John's Wood to tape a few demos.

On the outer fringes of the capital, The Dave Clark Five ruled Tottenham's Royal Ballroom as The Beatles did the Cavern. "It was pandemonium," gasped their singing organist, Mike Smith, "crash barriers and all that. The police station opposite used to get leave cancelled whenever we were on." Everyone had a great time on Dave Clark Five nights at the Royal, but not great enough to buy in chart-busting quantities any of the three singles the Five had released by 1962.

As it was with Clark in the Five, Pete Best was the recipient of most of the fuss from fans on rare occasions like *Teenagers' Turn*. However, he proved to be ostensibly the least promising member of The Beatles when George Martin, still recording manager of Parlophone, summoned them to Abbey Road on Wednesday 6 June 1962. Accustomed to on-stage inconsistencies of tempo caused by the mood of the hour, drummers were most prone to behind-the-scenes substitution in the studio. Though he was sound enough behind the kit in concert, rumours abounded later that even Dave Clark didn't actually rattle the traps on his own discs.

"The reasons were purely financial," elucidated ex-Johnny Kidd sticksman Clem Cattini, the first dyed-in-the-wool rock 'n' roller to emerge as a familiar figure on the capital's recording scene. "You were expected to finish four tracks – two singles – in three hours. A group might take a week to do two titles, not because they were incapable, but because sessions are a different mode of thinking to being on the road. You can't get away with so much. You need more discipline."

Having someone like Cattini ghost his drumming, would, therefore, have been no slight on Pete Best, but the mere suggestion that it would be necessary was sufficient to compound the doubts, justified and otherwise, that the others had about him, and precipitate his heartless sacking a few weeks later.

How different would Pete's life – and the cultural history of the world – have been if Brian Epstein hadn't come into the life of George Martin when The Beatles were midway through their seven weeks at the Star-Club? What Brian had decided would be a final assault on the record industry had ended in a victory of sorts during an appointment with George Martin in EMI's Manchester Square offices. What Martin had heard of this Mr Epstein's group wasn't particularly enthralling, but it would do no harm, he supposed, to see how they shaped up in the studio.

If he hadn't, we can safely say that, at the very least, the chances of Martin receiving a knighthood decades later would have been the same as those of Wally Ridley, Norrie Paramor and John Burgess, EMI label chiefs of the same vintage, all good men and true but, like George, possessing simple proficiency rather than genius. Certainly, it's unlikely that Martin would have been the subject of such a six-CD celebration to his half-century in the business – *Fifty Years In Recording* – as he'd be in 2001.

At the height of the trad-jazz craze, he'd scored his first Number One with The Temperance Seven's 'You're Driving Me Crazy', a camp 1961 recreation of a 1920s dance tune, complete with stiff-upper-lip vocal refrain. Before that, however, Parlophone had been responsible for few smashes compared to rival labels. It thrived mostly on dance bands, choirs, children's favourites – epitomised by Mandy Miller's 'Nellie The Elephant' – film themes, televisual spin-offs and easy-listening outings, some attributed to The George Martin Orchestra: releases that sold well enough without actually penetrating the Top 20.

Those that did were usually short-lived novelties such as 'Robin Hood' by Dick James, Charlie Drake's 'My Boomerang Won't Come Back' and 1962's 'Right Said Fred' from Bernard Cribbins, some under the supervision of George Martin – while perhaps the biggest feather in his lieutenant, Ron Richards' cap had been overseeing an Ella Fitzgerald session.

If Martin and Richards emerged subsequently as among the least dogmatic of the British record business's backroom boys, they were both long steeped in the unbending formality and cold professionalism of ordained working hours with no extra time or favours done, and the Musicians' Union springing to the defence of any pedant who yelled a malicious "Time's up!" in the middle of a take.

The Beatles were to challenge this by running over into the small hours and creating what George Harrison was to describe as "new meanings on old equipment". Before their arrival, however, Martin and Richards' provisioning of Parlophone with some sort of equivalent to whatever chart contenders rivals had snared had been barely more than cursory – with Ron drawing the short straw for such discoveries as Shane Fenton And The Fentones, guitarist Judd Proctor, Paul Raven (later, Gary Glitter) and The Clyde Valley Stompers. As usual, Richards was also directed to take charge of the recording debut of the pop group booked for 6 June, but an intrigued Martin assumed responsibility after looking in to check progress.

Before the Great Man grinned cheerfully and waved goodbye to them as they commenced the long drive back to Liverpool, The Beatles had been less round eyed at learning of his hand in 'Robin Hood', 'Right Said Fred' *et al* than Martin's serving as console midwife to a forthcoming album by the team of BBC television's satirical *That Was The Week That Was* series as well as The Goons, together and apart. By coincidence, the last solo Goon to scurry into the hit parade with a disc specifically designed to be funny was Peter Sellers in 1965 with his cod-Shakespearean recitation of The Beatles' 'A Hard Day's Night'.

One of Sellers's lesser film comedies, 1969's *The Magic Christian*, was to co-star Ringo Starr, once of Rory Storm's Hurricanes, who had replaced Pete Best in The Beatles in August 1962, cheating him unknowingly of his "inheritance" in the 11th hour. The new recruit wasn't the most versatile drummer in Liverpool, but he was a Pete Best for girls to adore more as a brother than dream lover, and bright enough not to ask too many questions yet. Even after the shared experience of the Kaiserkeller, Starr hadn't felt he'd known The Beatles well enough to invite them to his 21st birthday party. Nevertheless, they became closer during subsequent Hamburg seasons and on the Merseyside circuit. Despite his hangdog appearance, Ringo turned out to be blessed with a ready wit that was as guileless as John's was cruel. "Ringo was a star in his own right in Liverpool," asserted John. "Whatever that spark is in Ringo, we all know it, but we can't put our finger on it. Whether it's acting, singing or drumming, I don't know. There's something in him that's projectable."[21]

The new recruit was, however, the least significant participant in September when The Beatles recorded their maiden Parlophone single, 'Love Me Do'. EMI's executive body were to be in two minds about it during their weekly scheduling conference where, before committing themselves, the more obsequious underlings tried to gauge the opinion of each label's head of A&R. Thus after the customary "I don't know – what do you think?" discussion, it was decided that 'Love Me Do' would be cast adrift on the vinyl oceans in the first week of October.

7 "Pinching Our Arrangements Down To The Last Note"

John's euphoria at this latest development had been undercut by a grave domestic complication. Pregnancy wasn't what happened to nice girls like Cynthia, but one afternoon in the summer, she'd announced that her period was a week overdue – and she'd been sick in the morning, though that might have been through stomach-knotted anxiety. That her waist measured one inch bigger may have been nothing either, but her wrists, armpits and ankles felt peculiar.

She was seeing prams and pregnant women everywhere, in the streets, in public parks and on television. In an episode of *Dr Kildare* – the ER of its day – there'd been an unmarried mother. Her boyfriend smiled like John. The screen couple had separated and the baby was adopted – but perhaps there'd be a delightful romantic scene with John proposing on one knee, and promising to love Cynthia forever. Gruff pragmatism ruled, however, and she may have been left with the impression that, if the lyrics to some of The Beatles' numbers – about mister moonlight and words of love – were anything to go by, John and she were being conned out of something.

John's courtship of Cynthia had been fraught much of the time, but that was when they'd been closest because, as far as John – torn between resentment and panic – was concerned, the minute they left the registry office on 23 August 1962, they were already over somehow. The heart, the essence of what they had been, was wrapped up by the time they arrived at the reception – at which Aunt Mimi was pointedly absent – in an unlicensed restaurant. Yet, while marriage wouldn't blinker his roving eye, Cynthia at least felt hopeful during that hiatus between the wedding celebrations – interrupted by a Beatles booking that evening at some ballroom in Chester – and the issue of 'Love Me Do'.

Initially, the sales territory of the record was limited to loyal Liverpool – where it went straight in at Number One in *Mersey Beat* – until scattered airplay began humbly with a solitary spin crackling from Radio Luxembourg between the National Anthem that concluded the evening's viewing on BBC television and the pre-dawn shipping forecast on the Home Service.

Next, 'Love Me Do' slipped into the *NME* list at Number 21 on 8 December, and hovered on the edge of the Top 20 until just after Christmas, outselling on aggregate the latest by Chris Montez – the most recent US Bobby – and an expedient revival of 'Love Me Tender' by Richard "Dr Kildare" Chamberlain. At Number One was Frank Ifield, a new pretender to Cliff Richard's crown, with an exhumation of a 1949 country-and-western million seller, 'Lovesick Blues'. He'd headlined over The Beatles earlier that month on a mismatched bill at Peterborough's Embassy Cinema.

The local paper reported that they'd "made far too much noise".[24] Adding insult to injury as 'Love Me Do' continued to lose its tenuous grasp on the British charts, The Beatles were back at the Star-Club, supporting Johnny And The Hurricanes, a saxophone-dominated combo from Ohio, nearly all of whose hits – and there hadn't been any of late – were rocked-up treatments of old chestnuts.

Yet, all told, The Beatles had done well for first-timers, but who would assume that they wouldn't be back doing Liverpool-Hamburg piecework by this time next year, even as Brian Epstein negotiated their maiden national tour, low on the bill to Helen Shapiro?

However, the rip-tide of Merseybeat that was to overwhelm Helen, Johnny And The Hurricanes and Frank Ifield swept closer as the new year got under way. Ifield would be performing in venues where current chart standing had no meaning within 18 months of *Mersey Beat*'s announcement in January 1963 of the impending release of a second Beatles single, 'Please Please Me'. Hinged loosely on 'Please', a Bing Crosby ballad from the 1930s – which Frank Ifield had sung at Peterborough – it had been written mostly by John, and conceived initially in the style of Roy Orbison, a US balladeer typecast as a merchant of melancholy.

Similarly, 'Love Me Do', had been as dirge-like in embryo, presented as, recalled Lennon, "a slower number like Billy Fury's 'Halfway To Paradise', but George Martin suggested we do it faster. I'm glad we did." He was also to confess later, "We all owe a great deal of our success to George, especially for his patient guidance of our enthusiasm in the right direction."[25]

Martin's efforts "represented the highest examples of recorded art from every standpoint," fashionable 1970s producer, Richard Perry would gush.[26] Yet the Knight of Parlophone's position as The Beatles' artistic enabler was earned in large part for what he *didn't* do. After the first exploratory session, he'd dismissed the notion of singling out one of the group as nominal "leader". Neither had he foisted his own compositions on them as, say, Pye's Tony Hatch would on The Searchers or Decca's Tommy Scott on Twinkle and Them, taking advantage of a young act still too much in awe perhaps of the voice calling them to order via the control-room intercom to splutter, "We'd rather not, sir."

From the beginning, Martin had involved the group in the technical side of studio methodology. He'd also been prepared to accommodate the most radical suggestions – initially, The Beatles' preference for 'Please Please Me' to the perky and "professional" non-original 'How Do You Do It', once earmarked for Adam Faith, which Martin considered ideal as a follow-up to 'Love Me Do'. On the producer's instructions, nonetheless, the arrangement of 'Please Please Me' was accelerated and simplified with tight harmonies and responses behind Lennon's lead vocal.

Even at this early stage, George Martin had discovered that John, immodest about other matters, was genuinely unconceited about his singing to the point of insisting, "I can't say I ever liked hearing myself."[27] It made him wary of compliments about such contrasting items on The Beatles' first LP, *Please Please Me*, as downbeat and sensitively handled 'Anna' to 'Twist And Shout' on which he almost ruptured his throat with a surfeit of passion.

"I could never understand his attitude," sighed Martin, "as it was one of the best voices I've heard. He was a great admirer of Elvis Presley's early records, particularly the 'Heartbreak Hotel' kind of sound, and he was always saying to me, 'Do something with my voice. Put something on it. Smother it with tomato ketchup. Make it different.' He was obsessed with tape delay – a sort of very near-echo. I used to do other things to him, and as long as it wasn't his natural voice coming through, he was reasonably happy – but he'd always want his vocals to get special treatment. However, I wanted to hear its own natural quality."[27]

The timid songbird and his new bride were living at Mendips when 'Please Please Me' was released. Children would swoop from nowhere to see John Lennon, Woolton pop star, answer the door or be collected by road manager Neil Aspinall in the van for transportation to a palais maybe six or more counties away. Wherever "the newest British group to challenge The Shadows"[28] went nowadays, it always seemed to be one week after Cliff Bennett And The Rebel Rousers and one week ahead of Johnny Kidd And The Pirates in Chatham's Invicta, Tamworth's Assembly Rooms, the El Rio in Macclesfield and like venues played by every group that expected its run of luck to fizzle out at any minute.

Nevertheless, a sea change was taking place as epitomised by the actions of a certain Peter Stringfellow, awaiting his destiny as the self-proclaimed "world's greatest disco owner". Fresh from spinning the latest sounds in Nottingham's Dungeon, he had, with his brother Geoff, opened Sheffield's Black Cat – alias St Aidan's Church Hall – where one florin (10p) would buy admission. In February 1963, the Stringfellows had caved in to repeated requests by girl fans to book The Beatles. After wringing their hands over the seemingly extortionate fee demanded by Brian Epstein, a show was pencilled in for The Black Cat but, on police advice, this was moved to the more capacious Azena to limit the danger of scream-rent riot.

Back on Merseyside, heads turned when Ringo Starr's old Ford Zodiac stopped at a zebra crossing, but no Beatle yet attracted the beginnings of a crowd, despite a quote attributed to Lennon: "Our fans like us. They know that that whenever possible, we'll meet them, talk to them and sign their autographs."[29]

Yet even dates at the Cavern soon became quite ticklish operations. While Helen Shapiro was, technically speaking, the main attraction on the current round-Britain tour, she'd been upstaged by The Beatles and, on two dates when she was indisposed, so had Danny Williams and Billie Davis – British vocalists with a backlog of hits and a current chart strike.

On the very opening night (2 February) in Bradford, 'Please Please Me' had, according to *Record Mirror* – and the *Record Retailer* trade journal – entered at Number 16 in the charts. The following week, it jumped 13 places to hold the same position for a further seven days before reaching its apogee of Number Two. It was checkmated by Frank Ifield's 'The Wayward Wind', featuring his trademark yodel. A fortnight later, it was down one place, but returned to Two on 16 March with only 'Summer Holiday' from Cliff Richard in the way. Then it was downhill all the way – 5, 7, 11, 17 and out.

The pattern was similar in the other charts – except that *Melody Maker* had 'Please Please Me' lording it over 'The Wayward Wind'. In this respect, The Beatles were the first Merseybeat act to reach Number One in Britain – as proclaimed by Bob Wooler one lunchtime at the Cavern.

With a little logical blindness and retiming of the truth, The Beatles might be said to have tied at the top with Frank Ifield, but we must add the raw information that *The Guinness Book Of Hit Singles* – the Yellow Pages of such matters – has 'Please Please Me' at Two, and confirms that the first disc by a Liverpool group to unarguably top all UK singles charts was 'How Do You Do It' from Gerry And The Pacemakers (also on Parlophone) in April 1963. Yet what was becoming supposedly discernable as the "Mersey Sound" or "Liverpool Beat", would germinate the following month when The Beatles' 'From Me To You' eased 'How Do You Do It' from the top.

Moreover, in less than a week after the Shapiro jaunt, The Beatles had supported Tommy Roe and Chris Montez on another "scream circuit" trek where these boy-next-door North Americans had been obliged to conduct themselves with studied good humour when, right from the first evening, the running order was reshuffled as crowd reaction dictated that the home-grown Beatles play last, even on the three stops where they appeared as a trio, owing to John being huddled under bedclothes at Mendips with influenza.

Yet Decca and other of EMI's rivals thought they smelt a perishable commodity. What about The Beatles and Gerry And The Pacemakers' tour in May with the long-awaited Roy Orbison – who, bar the remote Elvis, commanded the most devoted British following of any US pop star? He'd be no lamb to the slaughter like Montez and Roe. Toughened by more than a decade in the business, Roy proved still able to work that old magic without obvious effort, enough to disconcert any Merseybeat group, chart-riding and frantic, on the same bill.

All he had to do was stand his ground with his black guitar and emote the nine hits he'd racked up since 1960. Indeed, at the Adelphi Cinema in Slough, he was required to reprise 1961's 'Running Scared' midway through his preordained quarter of an hour, while the sustained and rabid cheering – rather than screaming – after his 'In Dreams' finale was such that impresario Tito Burns at the back of the hall bore witness that "after 30 minutes, we still couldn't get The Beatles on. This was the first time I'd seen a standing ovation in Slough."[30]

Thus was set the pattern for the rest of the three weeks that the sonorous Orbison came on after Gerry and preceded The Beatles onstage. Alighting on this with false hope, those with axes to grind liked to imagine that the peril from the northeast was in retreat. Indeed, to Joe Meek, Merseyside had always been following rather than setting trends as instanced by a Liverpool "answer" to Screaming Lord Sutch in a new act called The Mersey Monsters. As far as Meek could see too, "The Beatles have nothing new about their sound. Cliff Bennett And The Rebel Rousers have been doing the same thing for a year."[31]

It was business as usual, therefore, for Joe with his productions of Bennett's cover of The Shirelles' 'Everybody Loves A Lover' – a Merseybeat "standard" – and Sutch's 'Jack The Ripper', vilified in *Melody Maker* as "nauseating trash".[32] All the same, Meek paid heed to what he regarded as a passing trend via 'You've Got To Have A Gimmick Today' by The Checkmates in March 1963, and a Beatles–Frank Ifield crossover in 'I Learned To Yodel' from The Atlantics, fronted by a vocalist with the negotiable name of Jimmy *Lennon*.

Nevertheless, "What's this Liverpool outfit everyone's talking about?" was a question asked with increasing frequency by elderly executives in

London record company offices while office juniors discussed whether The Beatles had got into a rut what with their next A-side, 'From Me To You', having the same overall melodic and rhythmic thrust as 'Please Please Me'. Next, talent scouts from the capital came sniffing round Merseyside just in case the word about a "Liverpool Sound" carried any weight – especially as other Epstein clients (Billy J Kramer, The Fourmost and Cilla Black) had been tossed Lennon–McCartney songs almost as licences to print money long before the dissimilar ilk of Bernard Cribbins, Ella Fitzgerald and Celine Dion dipped into the same portfolio.

Though only amateurs then, Kramer and his Coasters, had found themselves two places behind The Beatles in *Mersey Beat*'s 1963 poll, their individuality lying in Kramer's boyish charm and pleasant croon – which, if required, could turn into a mannerly growl. Recognised as the one that mattered, Billy alone was covered by Epstein's management agreement, and The Coasters replaced by The Dakotas, a more accomplished quartet from Manchester. Under George Martin's direction, the pairing's debut 45 was a crack at The Beatles' album track, 'Do You Want To Know A Secret', the work of Lennon.[33] At the composer's suggestion, Kramer's name on the Parlophone record label was split with a non-signifying "J". John also supplied 'Bad To Me' – penned during the Spanish holiday with Epstein – Kramer And The Dakotas second hit. Seeing out 1963 in fine fashion was another Beatles-associated smash – this time by Paul McCartney – 'I'll Keep You Satisfied', as well as an instrumental Top 20 entry, 'The Cruel Sea', for the Dakotas only.

Neither Billy nor the Dakotas were able to recapture the success they enjoyed in 1963 and 1964 – and the same was true of the second string to Epstein's bow. It was almost a matter of course that, prior to Kramer, Gerry And The Pacemakers would melt into Epstein's managerial caress, even though, on a first-come-first-served basis, he did not attend to their recording career until The Beatles had left the runway with theirs. So it was that a few months after 'Love Me Do', Gerry's lot had gained an EMI contract too.

Before 'How Do You Do It' was dragged down, Gerry had joked, "How does it feel to be Brian's number two group then?" when bumping into John at NEMS. Around the same time, joint press interviews were convened in a London hotel for Marsden and Lennon as principal spokespersons for the Merseybeat movement.

Shortly after the first *Beatles Monthly* was published, a similar periodical devoted solely to Gerry And The Pacemakers was considered a worthwhile market exercise for a while. Both outfits remained on terms of fluctuating equality as Gerry's second offering, 'I Like It', wrenched 'From Me To You' from the top. After The Searchers did likewise to the latest by Elvis Presley in August, they, Gerry, The Beatles and Billy J Kramer slugged it out for hit parade supremacy for, more or less, the rest of the year.

The first signs of danger were to rear up in spring 1964 when Gerry's 'Don't Let The Sun Catch You Crying' stalled at Number Six, a true comedown by previous standards. By then, however, he was already considering – as so many of his kind were to do – pantomime, charity football matches and children's television, and was tracing Tommy Steele's scent as an "all-round entertainer". This aspiration had, I suppose, become apparent initially on 1963's *How Do You Like It* LP when the expected Merseybeat was mixed with orchestrated evergreens, notably 'You'll Never Walk Alone' – which infiltrated folklore as the Liverpool Football Club anthem.

Most other Merseybeat entertainers with the faintest tang of star quality had at least a moment of glory when London got in on the act. Having mastered individual crafts in the ranks of outfits like The Thunderbeats and The Midnighters prior to their formation in April 1963, a debut single was a long time coming, but 'Magic Potion' was issued shortly after Brian Epstein saw Beatle-like potential in The Koobas. Through him, they were to land nine dates supporting The Beatles, going down so well that a golden future was predicted by both the music press and the in-crowd that frequented the Scotch of St James, the Speakeasy and other metropolitan clubs.

The Remo Four weren't amateurs either. Connected genealogically with Jimmy Justice's Jury, Liverpool's most esteemed instrumental unit were seized likewise by Epstein and, through him, Pye, though they functioned principally as all-purpose accompanists on disc for such as Gregory Phillips and Tommy Quickly, and on nationwide package tours.

Pye also hooked the biggest non-Epstein fish in The Searchers. Their saga is a cautionary tale of how it might have been for John, Paul, George and either Pete or Ringo. As The Beatles reigned in the Cavern, so the similarly mildewed Iron Door was the fiefdom of The Searchers, following much hard graft in Hamburg where the group developed the tidy chorale and unique fretboard interaction that would influence later acts (notably The Byrds).

The Iron Door was also the location for The Searchers' after-hours taping of 11 tracks that secured them their deal with Pye in June 1963. By August, they were home and dry when an exuberant reading of The Drifters' 'Sweets For My Sweet' booted Elvis from Number One – as 'Sugar And Spice', the soundalike follow-up (composed by Tony Hatch) nearly did 'She Loves You', The Beatles' fourth 45. Yet, foreseeing only fleeting prosperity for Merseybeat, Pye was disinclined to risk promising group originals as A-sides, preferring to stampede the boys into its Marble Arch studio for *Meet The Searchers* and, less than four months later, *Sugar And Spice*. On each of these LPs, The Hit was padded with items from tunesmiths based in Denmark Street – Britain's Tin Pan Alley – and stand-bys from the stage repertoire.

With respect to the latter, while they could rock as hard as anyone, The Searchers were exceptional for less frantic versions of standards like 'Twist And Shout', preferring calm precision to then lead singer Tony Jackson risking damage to his vocal cords, Lennon-style, on what was only doggerel about an already outmoded dance.

The Searchers' approach paid dividends with lighter selections too. Like The Beatles, they were particularly adept at stealing the show from wilder co-stars by adapting songs by The Shirelles, The Ronettes and other US female vocal groups of ingenuously fragile conviction. From The Orlons' catalogue alone, 'Shimmy Shimmy' and May 1964's chart-topping 'Don't Throw Your Love Away' were conspicuous on *It's The Searchers*, their third Pye album in less than a year.

Provoked even more by EMI's infuriating success with The Beatles, a chastised but cynical Decca adopted a more scattershot approach by flinging numerous discs by beat groups from Liverpool at the public, albeit by being "excessively thrifty" over the publicity needs of all but the most consistent best-sellers. In January 1963 alone, the label made off from Liverpool with The Big Three, Beryl Marsden, new Cavern master-of-ceremonies Billy Butler, and (because their drummer was now *ex*-Beatle Pete Best) Lee Curtis And The All-Stars.

On George Harrison's recommendation, Dick Rowe signed The Rolling Stones in May. Dave Berry And The Cruisers, Surrey's Nashville Teens, Macclesfield bluesman John Mayall, Them from Belfast, The Moody Blues (a sort of Birmingham "supergroup"), Unit 4 + 2 (likewise in Cheshunt), The Applejacks from Solihull and The Zombies (pride of St Alban's) were among later acquisitions but for each such hitmaking act, there was a Beat Six, a Bobby Cristo And The Rebels, a Gonks, a Falling Leaves – and a Lee Curtis And The All-Stars.

A dependable draw both in Liverpool and Hamburg. Curtis "was delighted that he (Pete Best) joined me because he was such a personality on Merseyside. To have Pete Best drumming behind you was a tremendous attraction. I'd seen him with The Beatles and it was absolutely amazing because the girls screamed like hell for Pete to sing."[34] Nevertheless, it was the start of something small. During one of their residencies at the Star-Club, Astrid Kirchherr commiserated with Pete, but her sympathy wasn't sufficient to mitigate "continuing with a group not as popular," he sighed, "doing the same old gigs I'd done with The Beatles".[2]

Along with other companies, Decca lugged mobile recording equipment up to Liverpool to tape as many acts from the city of overlapping towns as could be crammed onto a compilation LP with a title like *This Is Merseybeat* or *At The Cavern*. Acts selected for any additional attention had, preferably, to have won their spurs in Hamburg or scored in *Mersey Beat*'s latest poll. The Big Three were advantaged further by being managed by Epstein, while The Mojos had a rich stockpile of their own songs into which other combos dipped. Others were fronted by outstanding showmen like Kingsize Taylor, Rory Storm, Derry Wilkie, Freddie Starr – and Bill "Faron" Russley who led his Flamingos through a British take on The Contours' 'Do You Love Me', the sure-fire smash that, purportedly, he'd let slip through his fingers in 1963 when he dictated its lyrics to Essex's visiting Brian Poole for the price of a double whiskey. Unable to extend much beyond being adored locally too, Beryl Marsden, rather than a lesser singer like Cilla Black, should have represented Merseyside womanhood in the 1960s charts.

The Escorts' elegant 'The One To Cry' and the arresting 'Lies' by Johnny Sandon And The Remo Four were among other undeserved flops – not to mention sterling tries at 'Fortune Teller', 'Some Other Guy', 'Twist And Shout', 'Let's Stomp' and other set-works that went down a storm on the boards by also-rans who more than bore out Bill Harry's gloomy comment to me that "the cream doesn't necessarily come to the top in this sort of business".

According to one story – probably apocryphal – the entire personnel of one picked-to-click Merseybeat outfit wound up stacking and loading auto parts in the same warehouse by autumn. That was when they saw a picture of The Merseybeats in the same issue of *Music Echo* in which some southern ponces were duplicating both the sheepdog fringes and the mid-air jump against brick-strewn wasteland patented by The Beatles on the cover of July 1963's *Twist And Shout* EP. Moaning about it to *Melody Maker* in August, John Lennon had noticed that Gerry And The Pacemakers suffered "terrible copying" too, but far more groups had been formed in The Beatles' image, "pinching our arrangements and down to the last note at that."[35] While some used insectile appellations – Termites, Moths, Grasshoppers *ad nauseum* – others would work the word *beat* into their titles – Beatstalkers, Counterbeats, Beat-Chics, Fourbeats, Beat Boys, Beat Merchants, Beathovens and so on.

Youth club combos in the sticks wore collarless suits and moptops that resembled spun dishmops whenever they shook their heads and went "oooooo", and there'd be continuity in tortuous Liverpudlian accents by either "John" or "Paul", and an unsmiling lead guitarist who, in imagination at least, played a black Rickenbacker through a Marshall amplifier, just like George Harrison, the most androgynously hirsute of the four.

Was it only last year that a Billy Fury quiff was a sure sign of a cissy? Today's pony-tailed navvy might take heed how contentious the issue of long-haired males could be then in households in which, with increasing frequency, grandmothers pleaded for calm amid blazing rows between parents and once-tractable children over the teenage noise issuing from transistor radio, Dansette record player and black and white television, not to mention the wearing of winkle pickers – "Are your feet really that shape?" – thigh-huggingly "crude" drainpipe jeans, eye-torturing ties, and haircuts. A nasty rumour was soon to be filtered round provincial Britain that Mick Jagger of The Rolling Stones, whose hair was girlier than that of The Beatles, was to undergo a sex-change operation so that he could marry one of the others.

Mersey Beat reckoned that the Stones were "a London group with the Liverpool sound" – in common with Brian Poole And The Tremeloes maybe? The latter's 'Twist And Shout' reached the UK Top Ten in 1963 – and they were chosen to launch the first edition of ITV's *Ready Steady Go*, remembered as the most atmospheric pop showcase of the decade. Next up was 'Do You Love Me' causing Decca to cancel a xerox by Kent's Bern Elliott And The Fenmen so that Brian's boys could have a clearer run and the edge over those by Faron's Flamingos (relegated to a B-side by Oriole) while the more dangerous enemy, The Dave Clark Five, just signed to Parlophone's sister label, Columbia.

London talent scouts, see, were sparing themselves a trip to England's crowded northwest by getting pop talent from different areas to steal a march on the Merseysiders. Fanning out from the Holy City, they'd discovered that numerous other acts had been rifling the same classic rock and R&B (rhythm and blues) motherlode too. Some were also coming up with originals of similar persuasion. Glaswegian beat groups, for example, had matured in a similar fashion to their Scouse counterparts through years of isolation from the main sequence of British pop. Though the high summer of Scottish rock was to be a long time coming – peaking in 1969 when Marmalade scored a UK Number One with a Beatles cover – Dean Ford and his Gaylords, the outfit from which Marmalade sprang, appeared regularly at the Picasso (Glasgow's "Cavern") where they shared the limelight with The Alex Harvey Soul Band, The Golden Crusaders, Chris McClure's Section and other performers with the strongest possible local reputation.

After leaving their scotch-and-cokes half-finished in the Picasso, some A&R representatives then crossed the Irish Sea where, say, Dickie Rock and the Miami Showband were coaxed into releasing a version of 'Boys', Ringo's solitary lead vocal on the *Please Please Me* LP, for the Pye man, as the beat boom pushed even the most up-to-date showbands – a phenomenon peculiar to Ireland – out of the picture. A few would weather the storm, but, shortly, the showband was to be an anachronism.

Like everywhere else nowadays, the republic was deemed to have a form of pop music peculiar to itself, namely "Blarney Beat" as propagated by such as The Creatures, The Four Aces, The Chosen Few and, from Dublin, Dominic Behan, brother of playwright Brendan, who was signed to Pye for a crafty 1963 single of 'Liverpool Lou', a shanty that had flowered from the same stem as 'Maggie May', 'Heave Away' and 'Row Bullies Row'.

Thus, as the close of 1963 loomed, Liverpool's leading pop executants – most of them as good as they'd ever be – were no longer as sure as they had been only a few months earlier that accident of geography would facilitate the procuring of a slot on ITV's *Thank Your Lucky Stars* next month that would kick off a week-by-week scramble into the Top Ten. Yet there were a few that were still clinging onto that as a certain hope even as the hire-purchase company carted off their equipment, following, say, desperate strategies such as the lead vocalist pooching-out his lips like Mick Jagger's – or the enlistment of a saxophonist and organist as a nod towards The Dave Clark Five, who were ahead of The Beatles for a split second early in 1964.

The Beatles, The Searchers and The Mojos had been among far-sighted Scouse musicians who had uprooted themselves to become London-based concerns. The Koobas had done likewise, following three triumphant weeks at the Star-Club in December 1963, even if Britain was no longer crying out so loudly for four-man beat groups with Beatle haircuts and assumed or genuine "wacker" accents, who could crank out 'Twist And Shout', 'Hippy Hippy Shake', 'Money' and the entire Chuck Berry songbook.

Yet, heard on Oriole's *This Is Merseybeat* centuries ago that summer, Rory Storm would insist, with his hand on his heart, that he'd never harboured any desires about becoming nationally famous – although he could have been any time he liked. Lee Curtis, however, would "envy all those people who made it. I'd loved to have made it, and I think about it every day of my life."[17]

Curtis dismayed his female following when he appeared on a *Mersey Beat* list of performers thought to be married. Heading this was John Lennon, but the image of him held by most lovestruck pubescent girls in Inverness or Penzance was born of the pages of Catherine Cookson-esque romantic chivalry and grown to man's estate as a Poor Honest Northern Lad Who'd Bettered Himself as a pop singer with an electric guitar. How many of them wondered what his penis was like (or whether he even had one)? Ignorance was bliss – and worship of an idol without vice or blemish was, I suppose, less harmful an analgesic than most to an otherwise mundane provincial existence of school, homework and youth club.

John was married, true enough, but it was to Cynthia, known then – erroneously, as events were to prove – as the shrinking violet of The Beatles' clique. The speed of events after take-off with 'Love Me Do' had not, however, overwhelmed her as she coped with marathon fan vigils outside her, John and the baby's Kensington bedsit; stifled giggles from those who'd winkled out the ex-directory number, and even an attempted kidnap of Julian. Disguises, decoy tactics and secret destinations were to be as essential as spare underwear whenever the Lennons went on holiday. On one occasion, Cynthia had to be smuggled out of a hotel in a laundry basket.

She knew nothing of John's fleeting assignations with "scrubbers", which took place in the seclusion of, say, a backstage broom cupboard, or the cursing that marinated the air after the van broke down, and Neil Aspinall's new helpmate, Malcolm "Big Mal" Evans, once a Cavern bouncer, located the problem and knew that it'd be a long and messy botch job. This he'd explain patiently just as heavy drops of rain spat on the windows and pummelled the roof, and he began tinkering under the bonnet to the necessary accompaniment of an engine spluttering like an old man coughing his guts up after a lifetime of 60 cigarettes a day. Fifteen, twenty minutes later, the downpour eased, and suddenly Lennon was glooming over Mal's shoulder, goading him with sarcastically useless suggestions.

John had been singled out as "leader" in the lyrics of 'We Love The Beatles', a 1964 single by The Vernons Girls, recruited originally from employees of the Liverpool Football Pools firm. Weeks prior to all four Beatles comprising the panel in a special edition at the Liverpool Empire, he was also token member on BBC television's *Juke Box Jury* – and the main feature of the opening edition of *Midland Beat* in October 1963 was an interview with "John Lennon of The Beatles, but otherwise the entire content is restricted to Midlands items" – for, according to editor Dennis Detheridge, "Liverpool started the ball rolling. Now the Midlands is ready to take over."

As a Birmingham pop picker might scan *Midland Beat*, so her country cousin could the pages of Torquay-based *South-West Scene* and more local sources where too were so many beat groups that amid the *Andover Advertiser*'s reports on jumble sales and winter farrowing, its "Teen Scene" section would be summarising 1964 as "the year of the groups. The Record Charts were inundated with them and so was Andover!"[36] The town was to cradle The Troggs, who were to work the country bumpkin angle in 1966: *ooo-arrr* Long John Silver-isms and media hacks quoting "I" as "oi", "us" as "we", "we" as "us", you get the idea... The only stroke they didn't pull was "be" instead of "am", "is" or "are".

Back in autumn 1963, however, Scouse was still the most alluring dialect in the kingdom, and from its slang, words like "fab", "gear" and "grotty" filtered through the pages of teenage comics and into the mouths of the most well-spoken young Britons. Yet, though every other dance floor request seemed to be for 'Twist And Shout' or, when some idiot wanted it, 'She Loves You', Horsham's Beat Merchants were typical of a strain of groups that ditched Beatle-esque winsomeness and stage suits for a motley and belligerently unkempt interpretation of "authentic" R&B when they supported The Rolling Stones, shortly after The Beatles had headlined both at *Sunday Night At The London Palladium* and, before that, at a recital for the seated young toffs and their with-it headmaster at Stowe public school in Buckinghamshire.

John, Paul, George and Ringo had also been seen in May 1963 waving a cheery goodbye during the closing credits on ventriloquist dummy Lenny The Lion's show on BBC TV's *Children's Hour*. Then there was a prime-time evening sketch involving the donning of boaters and a singalong of 1912's 'On Moonlight Bay' with comedy duo Morecambe and Wise. Whatever next? Would there unfold a Gerry-esque flow-chart of pantomime, soft-shoe shuffling and charity football after they were overtaken – as they surely would be – by a newer sensation?

Offstage, The Beatles were hanging around with the likes of Alma Cogan, bubbly singing perennial of television variety. She had been endeavouring to recoil from the lightweight, tulle-petticoated jauntiness that had made her – 'Banjo's Back In Town', 'Twenty Tiny Fingers' *et al* – by sifting through the sheet music, LPs and, if lucky, demo tapes of beat groups. The most glaring expression of this policy was to be her cover in 1964 of 'Eight Days A Week' by The Beatles who liked her well enough to accept an open invitation to the liberty hall that was her Kensington flat. She was also omnipresent on the pilot series of *Ready Steady Go* in autumn 1963 – which also featured then a besuited interlocutor in his thirties and occasional send-ups of current hits by comics of the same age. Alma developed an on-screen soft spot for near-neighbour John Lennon, once cuffing him playfully on *Ready Steady Go*, following some – possibly scripted – ad-libbing between cheeky young shaver and jovial voice-of-experience commensurate with The Beatles' apparent toeing of a winsome line of pseudo-rebellious behaviour. Well, we're all a bit wild when we're young, aren't we?

It was, however, The Beatles' spot in *The Royal Variety Show* at London's Prince of Wales Theatre that November that prompted the *Daily Express* to brief its Liverpool-born showbusiness correspondent, Derek Taylor, do a "hatchet job" about their yielding to showbusiness proper, even if Lennon raised a laugh with the larger-than-life bluntness of his "rattle yer jewellery" announcement. Taylor, however, could only praise them – and be rewarded with a post as Brian Epstein's right-hand man and ghost writer of his *Cellarful Of Noise* biography.

Though located in the same city, the distance from the pearly cleavages and bow-tied tuxedos of the Prince of Wales theatre might have been measurable in light-years from the frayed jeans, CND badges and beatnik beards in the Marquee, Studio 51 and and other R&B clubs from whence had sprung The Rolling Stones as well as The Yardbirds, Kinks and Pretty

Things – all groups to enter the charts in 1964 without much compromising their long-haired images, and by sticking to their erudite guns musically. Running in the same pack, The Downliners Sect were well placed to do likewise as they too started to sound and look alarmingly like a pop group, but they surfaced instead as patron saints to legion also-ran provincial combos like The Beat Merchants.

Taking the same cue as the Sect and The Merchants, Joe Meek wheeled in North London's Syndicats to see if they could make numbers by Howlin' Wolf, Chuck Berry and Ben E King *not* sound like The Beatles.

By 1964, the Olympic torch of both Merseybeat and Home Counties R&B had been carried to every nook and cranny *sur le continent* where 'Money', 'You'll Never Walk Alone', 'The Hippy Hippy Shake' and further set-works had been worked into the repertoires of every other domestic pop star from Johnny Halliday – a sort of Gallic Elvis – downwards after France dropped territorial defences to import British pop talent by the ton. Former solo vocalists in Italy, say, or Spain were now integrating themselves into beat groups, and a venture into Teutonic Merseybeat had been made already by Manfred Weissleder, proprietor of the Star-Club. Guided by him, four Hamburg teenagers became The Rattles, a name with the same scansion as "Beatles" and an implication that here was the German wing of the movement – especially since there'd been a cultural "twinning" of the two cities as exemplified by Bill Harry's organisation of an aeroplane trip for Cavern regulars to Hamburg in 1963.

In parenthesis, loitering at the airport with passport at the ready, Lord Woodbine occupied a last-minute spare seat. He spent most of the subsequent weekend buying up contraband to sell at inflated prices back home. On the return flight, he spread his booty amongst pliant fellow passengers, retrieving it after they'd passed through customs.

Though everyone from The Rattles to The Beatles continued to turn to US R&B as monks to the Bible, North America's domination of post-war pop was over for the time being – in Europe anyway – now that the British beat boom, spearheaded by John, Paul, George and Ringo, the "Fab Four", had set new commercial and artistic yardsticks for schoolboy groups (including my own Ace And The Crescents) engaged in shambolic garage rehearsals, but daring to dream of Beatle-sized renown.

British pop musicians in general had been moving up in highbrow circles too following Adam Faith's intelligent and eloquent showing on BBC television's inquisitorial interview programme *Face To Face* in 1960. Adam was the first from the world of pop to experience such a grilling, and, because he gave a good account of himself, he paved the way for further "articulate" pop pundits such as ex-Oxford undergraduate Paul Jones, Spencer Davis with his BA in German – and John Lennon.

However, the notion of pop music as a viable means of artistic expression wasn't taken seriously amongst prominent intellectuals until the coming of The Beatles, unless you counted the earnest fascination of Andy Warhol, Peter Blake, Eduardo Paolozzi, Richard Hamilton and other pioneers of Pop Art in Top 40 radio from the late 1950s onwards.

Initially, "quality" newspapers like *The Times* and *The Observer* were preoccupied almost exclusively with the hysteria that accompanied Beatles performances on the "scream circuit", putting condescending inverted commas around their name, followed by "the Liverpool 'pop' group" or similar explanatory phrase.

Then William S Mann – who covered classical music for *The Times* – entered the fray on 27 December 1963. The day after a prosy end-of-year cultural overview (credited to "Our Music Critic") was published, John Lennon – not revelling in pretend ignorance as usual – confessed truly that he had no idea what Mann meant by phrases like "Aeolian cadences", "sub-mediant key switches", "chains of pandiatonic clusters" and "melismas with altered vowels". Neither was John aware of a similarity between the chord progression in 'Not A Second Time' (from *With The Beatles*, the second LP) and those in the coda to Mahler's *Song Of The Earth* (*Das Lied Von Der Erde*). He was, nevertheless, vaguely flattered by Mann's laudation of Lennon and McCartney as "the outstanding composers of 1963".

Two days later, Richard Buckle of the *Sunday Times* had them as "the greatest composers since Schubert". Nor far off were a random Beatles B-side, 'Yes It Is', analysed in *Music And Musicians* magazine, and Fritz Spiegl's *Eine Kleine Beatlemusik*, a 1965 album of their hits arranged in the style of Mozart.

Although McCartney and Lennon would still be damned with such faint praise as "reasonable good 'amateur' composers, greatly assisted by the poverty of British composing standards" in the *Sunday Times* as late as 13 November 1966, the die had been cast, and the elevation of The Beatles from dealers in ephemera to attracting the sort who read the likes of Mann and Buckle as gospel, was about to become unstoppable.

In a world beyond *Times* subscribers and, indeed, Britain's entire population, penetration of North America by The Beatles seemed an impossible dream in 1963 – though they'd entered the US Hot 100 by proxy when, during a break in a British tour, Del Shannon, a US pop vocalist of similar kidney to Roy Orbison, booked a London studio and some session players for a cover of 'From Me To You', purely for the US market. It was issued on the Bigtop label, and had slipped in at Number 86 on 6 July, climbing nine places over the next fortnight.

Progress for Beatles records in their own right was negligible. The first four singles and the *Please Please Me* long-player (minus two tracks and retitled *Introducing The Beatles*) were not deemed worthy of release by Capitol – EMI's regular US outlet – as, declared Jay Livingstone, a senior executive, "We don't think The Beatles will do anything in this market", unmindful as he was of whatever was gripping a backwater like Britain.

That's why 'Love Me Do' was issued by Tollie; 'Please Please Me', 'From Me To You' and the album by Vee-Jay, a Chicago company of slightly more importance; and 'She Loves You' by Swan. Thanks in a perverse way to Del Shannon's version, 'From Me To You' crept by association to Number 116 towards the end of the summer, and that appeared to be that for The Beatles in the USA – so much so that George Harrison was able to spend three pleasurable weeks as just an English relation at married sister Louise Caldwell's home in Benton, a small Illinois mining town. "That's the only experience", reflected Louise, "any one of The Beatles had of living in the States as a normal human being. Nobody had ever heard of him."

An interview on local radio – by WFRX's Marcia Raubach, the first presenter to spin a Beatles disc on US airwaves – and even a stage appearance with The Four Vests, Benton's boss group, had the impact of a feather on concrete, and Harrison was to return to Britain with a funny story about the aftermath of his bash with the Vests when someone told him that "with the right kind of backing, you could go places". This judgement proved correct, and the next the good people of Benton saw of Mrs Caldwell's brother was on the nationally networked *Ed Sullivan Show* the following February.

8 "Kids Everywhere Go For The Same Stuff"

By the middle of 1964, news of The Beatles and everything else that was gripping young Britain had spread to the other side of the world. In every Australasian city, you'd come across many an outfit that had reinvented itself as an ersatz British beat group. There were also instances of domestic talent checkmating the originals in the charts – for example, a New Zealand ensemble, Ray Columbus and his Invaders, whose version of Lennon and McCartney's 'I Wanna Be Your Man' sold more than those by both The Beatles (on a New Zealand-only A-side) and The Rolling Stones.

On the mainland, a bunch of skiffle latecomers in Melbourne found a Mick Jagger soundalike in future accountant Rod Turnbull and bowlerised the Stones' name. What's more, The Spinning Wheels hired Roger Savage, the lately emigrated engineer of the Stones' first Decca session, and worked up a repertoire as rife with – often the same – Bo Diddley, Chuck Berry, Howlin' Wolf and Muddy Waters favourites and unoriginal "originals" as that of their role models. Most spectacularly of all, however, Sydney's Bee Gees mutated from an updated Mills Brothers into quasi-Beatles.

Over in Japan, the most renowned "answer" to the Fab Four was The Spiders while Los Shakers – Caio, Hugo, Osvaldo and Pelin – cornered Latin America. The latter outfit came closest to copying both the Look and the Sound, while The Spiders jettisoned their covers of 'Please Please Me', 'She Loves You' and so forth soon to develop an in-built and charmingly naive originality lacking in most other acts of their kind, even if lead vocalist Masaaki Sakai hadn't much notion what he was singing apart from those self-composed items that, if dependent on what was going on in Swinging London, were delivered in Japanese with an abandoned drive, all the more piquant in the light of government disapproval of pop – to be manifested in frenzied protest demonstrations about those Beatle *ketos* polluting the Budokan Hall, Tokyo's temple of martial arts, for three evenings in summer 1966.

In reciprocation, The Spiders undertook a tour of Europe. Los Shakers, however, chose to consolidate their standing at home. Yet their take on British beat was more melodic than a lot of the genuine articles. Moreover, the pronunciation of their all-English lyrics is so anonymously precise that they wouldn't have been out of place in the Star-Club or the Cavern, *circa* 1963 – just as all-American Her Majesty's Coachmen – with bowler hats their gimmick, and 'Money' their first single – would have been quite comfortable depping for The Searchers in The Iron Door, judging by their second 45, jingle-jangling 'I Don't Want To See You'.

The Coachmen rivalled the comparably Anglophile St George and his Dragons as Sacramento's boss group – and The Creatures from Maryland could have filled in for The Zombies at St Alban's Town Hall, despite an electric organ tone like someone piddling into a metal bucket. There were also familiar-sounding rings to Michigan's Flowers-Fruits-And-Pretty Things and The Merseybeats (of Kentucky!). Likewise, The Gants from Mississippi grew out their crew-cuts and wore vestments of visual and musical personality bespoken by The Beatles and, especially, The Dave Clark Five – to the extent of Xeroxing two successive Five US A-sides – with singer Sid Herring as *norf* London on these as he was Scouse on a treatment of The Beatles' 1966 B-side, 'Rain'.

Northeast to New Jersey, The Redcoats' singing drummer, John Spirit had been one of The Ran-Dells, who, in 1963, reached the US Top 20 with the novel 'Martian Hop'. Then John heard The Beatles, and formed The Redcoats with himself as Lennon and guitarist Mike Burke as McCartney. Next, they enlisted a George Martin in Steven Rappaport, producer of 'Martian Hop', and proved as capable of sounding as much like mid-1960s Beatles out-takes as a luckier regional quartet, The Knickerbockers, did with 1966's chartbusting 'Lies'.[37]

No such luck befell more hastily assembled discs by the likes of The American Beatles, The Bug Men, John And Paul, The Manchesters, The

Wackers and The Beatlettes – some of whom had no physical form beyond television and recording studios, being the work of session musicians who probably bitched during coffee breaks about this Limey unit everyone's talking about.

Of more committed entities attempting to likewise cash in on The Beatles and British beat, the usual summit of short careers was recurring parochial engagements and sporadic regional airplay for one, maybe two singles that demonstrated musical ability at odds with overweening expressive ambition until the perpetrators were able to come to terms with the world of work, the marriage bed and Vietnam, and stop yearning for the next feedback-ridden, drum-thudding evening at the local hop.

Until what has passed into myth as the "British Invasion", no UK pop act, let alone native copyists, had ever made sustained headway in North America. The most recent instance had been Billy Fury's backing group, The Tornados racing to Number One in the US Hot 100 with 1962's aetherial 'Telstar'. Also produced by Joe Meek, an attendant LP had sold well too before further US advances were checked by executive politics causing the cancellation of a coast-to-coast tour.

Yet our sceptr'd isle had become the sub-continent's – indeed, the world's – prime purveyor of pop after The Beatles' messianic descent on 7 February 1964 onto what had been called Idlewild Airport a few months earlier. It had now been renamed "Kennedy Airport" because, on the same November day in 1963 that British newspapers had announced The Beatles' forthcoming US trip, President John F Kennedy had been assassinated in Dallas, "a place not known for war". So would sing Jerry Lee Lewis in 1966's 'Lincoln Limousine', a breezy, Macgonagall-esque album filler that remains my all time fave rave of requiems to any dead celebrity – especially with its inane "Oh Lord, it would have been better if he had stayed at home" line, and another about the "20 dollar rifle" that "took the life of this great man" as Lewis leads up to the truism that "you never know who's your enemy or your friend".[38]

Jerry Lee himself received composer's royalties for "Lincoln Limousine", but the Joseph Kennedy Jnr Foundation For Mental Retardation was the beneficiary of profits from budget-priced *John Fitzgerald Kennedy: A*

Memorial Album (which included his inaugural speech in its entirety). Produced and broadcast by a New York radio station within half a day of the shooting, it shifted four million copies in less than a week.

The late JFK waded in with a second hit LP, *The Presidential Years*, after a 45, 'The Voice Of The President', nestled uneasily on juke box selection panels between Bobby ballads – and the Californian surf music that dominated the pop airwaves in North America then. Ruling the genre were The Beach Boys, who celebrated surfing and its companion sport, hot-rod racing with chugging rock 'n' roll backing overlaid with a chorale more breathtaking than that of The Beatles.

To the chagrin of the Boys and others on Capitol, John, Paul, George and Ringo were to be launched with one of the most far-reaching publicity blitzes hitherto known in the record industry. Then 'I Want To Hold Your Hand' (the first Beatles disc the company had been prepared to release) reached the US Hot 100 on 1 January 1964 – and, within months, it and repromoted 'Love Me Do', 'Please Please Me' and 'She Loves You' had all risen to Number One. Even the B-sides of the first two made the Top 40 too. However, 'From Me To You', the one that had climbed highest of all before 1964 – though that's not saying much – could only manage Number 41.

While the intruders so swamped the Hot 100, The Beach Boys' resident genius, Brian Wilson, felt both threatened and inspired artistically. "I knew immediately that everything had changed, and that if The Beach Boys were going to survive, we would really have to stay on our toes," Wilson wrote in 2001. "After seeing The Beatles perform, I felt there wasn't much we could do to compete onstage. What we could try to do was make better records than them. My father had always instilled a competitive spirit in me, and I guess The Beatles aroused it."[39]

"I do my best work when I am trying to top other songwriters and music makers," he'd remarked to a journalist in 1964. "That's probably my most compelling motive for writing new songs: the urge to overcome an inferiority feeling."[40] While 1965's *Beach Boys Party!* LP was to include three Beatles covers, "When 'Fun Fun Fun' came out the previous year," assessed New York producer Phil Spector, "Brian wasn't interested in the money, but how the song would do against The Beatles."[40]

Whatever Wilson, Spector and others in the US record business thought, sages in the media had predicated that The Beatles' North American walkover had been an antidote to both an unexciting Hot 100 and the depressing winter that followed the Kennedy tragedy. "Kids everywhere go for the same stuff and, seeing as we'd done it in England, there's no reason why we shouldn't do it in America too,"[41] had been John Lennon's more forthright judgement on why most of the UK's major groups – and many minor ones – made progress to varying extents in the unchartered United States and Canada.

After The Beatles, the New World had gone almost as crazy about The Dave Clark Five, Freddie And The Dreamers – fronted by a kind of Norman Wisdom of pop – and Herman's Hermits. The more introspective Zombies – who'd struggled to Number 11 with their solitary UK Top 20 entry, 'She's Not There' – all but topped the US Hot 100 with it. In 1965, 'Tell Her No', which faltered outside the Top 40 at home, came to rest high in the US Top Ten too, aided by The Zombies' mild-mannered, scholarly image and regular visits to the States where 'She's Coming Home' and 'I Want You Back' were less spectacular hits but hits all the same.

To adult North America, The Zombies – like the combos led by Dave Clark, Freddie and Herman – were a palatable compromise to "hairy monsters" like The Rolling Stones, The Pretty Things, Kinks and Them. In tacit acknowledgement, US immigration authorities temporarily refused visas in 1965 for more Limey longhairs wishing to propagate their degenerate filth in Uncle Sam's fair land. Nevertheless, alighting on mid-west towns, even in the graveyard hours, a British group might be greeted by hundreds of hot-eyed teenagers, a large percentage chaperoned by parents who hadn't chastised them for squandering their allowances on, say, a six dollar can of 'Beatle Breath', or 'My Boyfriend Got A Beatle Haircut' by Donna Lynn.

This first US Beatle-related 45 was not to be the last. However, as well as anthems of adoration – 'Santa Bring Me Ringo' from Christine Hunter, The Beatlettes' 'Yes You Can Hold My Hand' *ad nauseum* – there were others such as 'To Kill A Beatle', a single of unconscious presentiment by someone called Johnny Guarnier. Its lyric was from the perspective of a US teenager, insanely jealous because every other girl at high school had lost her marbles over the new sensations from England.

Less sinister in retrospect are the likes of 'Beatles You Bug Me' and 'The Beatles' Barber' directed at those posses of "manly" types – in Australasia[42] as well as the USA – who expelled much hot air planning raids on the group's hotel quarters to hack off their girly locks, knowing that such an assault would be applauded by right-thinkin' folk who also frowned on male hairstyles longer than a crewcut.

Such an attitude bolstered the integrity of British beat amongst the hippest of the hip. The Animals' hit arrangement of traditional 'House Of The Rising Sun' confirmed folk singer Bob Dylan's resolve to "go electric", and Andy Warhol sneaked backstage at the Brooklyn Fox auditorium because "I wanted to be in the presence of The Yardbirds". To a more practical end, many US music industry bigwigs, correctly anticipating further demand for UK talent, crossed the Atlantic to stake claims in the cultural diggings.

Fascination with all things British peaked most conspicuously in that 1964 week when two-thirds of the Hot 100 was British in origin, and The Beatles occupied *nine* positions in the Canadian Top Ten. So insatiable was demand for anything on which any of the Fab Four had even breathed that Tony Sheridan was brought to a wider public than he may have warranted in the normal course of events after a repromoted 'My Bonnie' sold a purported million in 1964. Other releases by Sheridan might have been of greater musical worth, but the the tracks he smashed out on that bleary eyed 1961 morning with John, Paul, George and Pete better enabled him to protract a prolific recording career up to the present day.

"For a short time, there was a bit of interest in Britain and the States," shrugged Sheridan, "even if nobody was pushing me very much. I also went to Australia at the same time as The Beatles. Then I returned to England where, for a while, I played one night stands – but I never made anywhere near the money that could be made in Germany."

Meanwhile, The Beatles' cast-out drummer had already milked his affinity to the group via a six month run of sell-out dates in North America – principally in Canada – with his Pete Best Combo. For many, Pete will always remain "the Fifth Beatle", but less plausible candidates for this ludicrous honour had already included New York disc-jockey "Murray The K" (also "the Sixth Rolling Stone") – because he almost-but-not-quite blagged his way into rooming with George Harrison during that first US visit – and Cynthia Lennon after *Confidential*, Hollywood's most scurrilous showbiz gossip magazine, assured readers that she had once been considered as the group's lead singer.

This deathless claptrap apart, there *was* a Cynthia Lennon US Fan Club that found plenty to fill the pages of a monthly newsletter. "They wrote about about what I wore to film premieres, and what I said," elucidated Cynthia to me in 1996. "They were really sweet. I was only a housewife, but a very special housewife to them until divorce divorced me from The Beatles."

As the formation of such an organisation demonstrates, the British Invasion as a phenomenon had less to do with the main participants themselves than the behaviour of the North American public, who, once convinced of something incredible, exhibited a fanaticism for it that left the British themselves, even the most passionate Beatlemaniacs, at the starting line.

Back home, however, the Fab Four's renown was such that any direct connection with them was a handy bartering tool to rake in a bit of loot. After 18 years as the most shadowy figure in John's life, Freddie Lennon, then a kitchen porter in a Surrey hotel, had reappeared with his hands open in March 1964 on the Twickenham set of *A Hard Day's Night*, The Beatles' first movie. After a short conversation with a bemused John, he left and some money was – through John – mailed to his place of work. Freddie capitalised further by selling his life story to something-for-everybody *Titbits* magazine and then recorded a self-written single, 'That's My Life' (My Love And My Home), coupled with 'The Next Time You Feel Important' (a revival of a Vera Lynn number) for Pye late in 1965 – on which he was accompanied by some former Vernons Girls and, glad of the session fee, Folkestone's Loving Kind, veterans of poorly waged spots low on the bill of round-Britain package tours on which they were never sure of sleeping in proper beds each night.

Because of its singer's talismanic surname, 'That's My Life' received a modicom of airplay and was said to be "bubbling under" the UK Top

50. Allegedly, Brian Epstein – at John's instigation – then prodded nerves to curtail further headway. Freddie was determined to tell the boy about what must surely be some mistake, and arrived at "Kenwood", the mock-Tudor mansion in nearby Weybridge in which John, Cynthia and Julian now lived. Outside a banged front door, Freddie would be at a loss to understand his son and heir's deafness to his pleas. So began a family feud that would never quite resolve itself.

Many others better qualified to board The Beatles bandwagon were finding the going rough too. The Fourmost had secured an eight month season in a 1964 variety presentation at the London Palladium – at which John Lennon was a frequent attendee. Though their *raison d'être* was centred on comedy, there was a lake of offstage tears. Guitarist Mike Millward had been diagnosed with cancer which was alleviated with radium treatment during which it was discovered that he also had leukaemia.

With the-show-must-go-on stubbornness, he wouldn't let the lads down. If a huge, scalp-revealing tuft of his hair fell out the very moment the compère spoke their name, he'd stick it back on with Sellotape. When he could no longer keep such a level-headed grip on himself, he asked bass guitarist Billy Hatton if he ought to throw in the towel. "I said yes," remembered Hatton, "and it was the hardest yes I've ever had to say."[17] In a Cheshire hospital, nothing more could be done for Mike, and he died peacefully on 7 March 1966.

The following month, A Night For Mike took place at the Grafton Rooms in Liverpool 6. "A Host Of Top Show Business Stars" was promised, but most of these consisted of those who'd missed the boat in 1963: ghosts from the recent past, still battling through 'Twist And Shout', 'Hippy Hippy Shake' and all the other anachronisms. When the *Titanic* was sinking too, its house band carried on playing even as the waters covered their heads. On a calm mid-Atlantic night, you might hear them still as a spooky drift as if through a seashore conch.

On the evening in 1965 when The Beatles performed before nearly 60,000 at New York's Shea Stadium, Rory Storm had been hip-swivelling in front of his Hurricanes in a Seaforth ballroom.

Possibly because Rory was such a flamboyant showman, there'd been no place for him in that same year's *Ferry Across The Mersey*, a belated period film starring Gerry And The Pacemakers, in which the main thrust of the plot was a Battle of the Bands contest. Among the losers were The Koobas. Adding insult to injury, their sequence ended up on the cutting room floor. This might have been a blessing in disguise because it would have drawn attention to the group's compromising origins at a time when the Merseybeat ferryboat was grounding on a mudbank. Indeed, the belated flick's evocative title theme was Gerry's UK Top Ten farewell – and a requiem for Merseybeat's passing.

In the States, Billy J Kramer's fourth single, 'Little Children', was his biggest smash there, but momentum was lost through ex-public schoolboys Chad and Jeremy's US-only cover of Billy's next single, Paul McCartney's 'From A Window'. Into the bargain, Kramer's desire to update his image was thwarted by prior commitments to pantomime and like engagements – and 1965 began with his first serious flop in 'It's Gonna Last Forever' and the co-related departure of most of the original Dakotas. Finishing eight places below composer Burt Bacharach's version, 'Trains And Boats And Planes' was Kramer's final hit.

By then, The Beatles were the only Liverpool act that could still take chart placings for granted. *Mersey Beat* was finished too, having been absorbed in March 1965 into *Music Echo* in which the Liverpool scene was confined to a solitary page commensurate with faded interest – even in the city itself – in any more quartets who shook their moptops and went "oooooo".

"It was always a struggle to keep *Mersey Beat* going," grumbled Bill Harry, "but we persevered. Eventually, we'd built up circulation to 75,000 a week and gone national. The first ever front cover of The Rolling Stones was in *Mersey Beat* in 1963. Then Brian Epstein became involved. At first, he kept things as they were – with me having complete editorial control. Then he started doing things like commissioning a gossip column by some London writer, and insisting that bog standard record company photos of whoever was Number One had to be on the cover rather than anything more atmospheric.

"The first week we did that, the same picture – of The Kinks – appeared in both *Disc* and *Record Mirror*, but Brian insisted we keep on doing it. I told him it was mad, and that I wasn't going to do any other of his stupid ideas either. Then I walked out of the office and never went back."

Whereas they had frequently graced *Mersey Beat*'s front page – and those of national music journals – The Searchers were soon to leave the UK Top 20 forever with 'Take Me For What I'm Worth' – which lent its title to their final LP of the Swinging '60s – and one with a commendably high quota of sturdy group originals. Most of these dripped from the pen of drummer Chris Curtis, whose exit in 1966 exacerbated further the *volte-face* of The Searchers' fortunes.

Yet even in the spooky era after their chart adieu, The Searchers continued delivering goods that at least *sounded* like hits – and could have been if the group's very name hadn't become a millstone round their necks. "We were groping in the dark then," shrugged Frank Allen – who'd replaced Tony Jackson in 1964 – "and we'd lost the knack of picking hits."

While The Searchers floundered, The Beatles continued to flourish – by fair means or foul. Straight in at Number One in Britain during 1964's cold, wet December, 'I Feel Fine' began with a buzz like an electric shaver: mid-range feedback. The following summer, The Kinks would approximate this at the start of 'I Need You', B-side to 'Set Me Free'. At the same time, The Who were enjoying their second hit, 'Anyway Anyhow Anywhere' – and, lubricated with feedback too would be The Yardbirds' 'Shapes Of Things' and its flip-side 'You're A Better Man Than I' in 1966. Each made a most effective melodrama of what was merely implicit in the mild gimmick had that kicked off 'I Feel Fine' – a rival group's idea that The Beatles had picked up so fast that, as was often the case, the general public assumed that they'd thought of it first.

Months before 'I Feel Fine', The Yardbirds, The Kinks and The Who had all been featuring guitar feedback on the boards as a deliberate contrivance to sustain notes, reinforce harmonics and, when necessary, create severe dissonance. This strategy had been logged by Lennon when The Kinks were low on the bill to them at Bournemouth's Gaumont Cinema on 2 August 1964. In the teeth of audience chants of "We want The Beatles!", Dave Davies, The Kinks' lead guitarist, began 'You Really Got Me', their recent chart breakthrough, by turning up his amplifier to feedback level, "and the high-pitched frequency cut right through the screams of The Beatles' fans" his brother was to write in his autobiography, *X-Ray*.[43] Ray Davies noticed too that John Lennon was watching from the wings.

Come Christmas and Lennon had composed 'I Feel Fine'. "That's me completely," he was to insist. "The record with the first feedback anywhere. I defy anyone to find a record – unless it's some old blues record in 1922 – that uses feedback that way. So I claim it for The Beatles before Hendrix, before The Who, before anyone – the first feedback on any record."[21]

Though John played the tricky ostinato of 'I Feel Fine' on the record, George learnt it parrot-fashion for regurgitation onstage as The Beatles travelled a world that was becoming an intrusive and frequently dangerous place; its immensity and richness lying beyond a barrier of screeching hysteria and the pitiless *woomph* of flash-bulbs – particularly during an exceptionally stressful world tour in 1966. The Coca-Cola tasted just the same, but they'd guess they might be in, say, Canada by Mounties patrolling the besieged hotel – or Chicago because pizza is the city's equivalent of fish and chips.

Wherever they were, John, George, Paul and Ringo dished out a routine 30 minutes-worth of unheard music through a usually inadequate sound system at what were more tribal gatherings than concerts now. Prior to each, they sometimes had to field the stock questions about haircuts and when Paul was going to marry, at press conferences where certain of the local media took umbrage that the Fab Four seemed vague about what country they were actually visiting, having long ceased to care about the glimpses they caught of the places where their blinkered lives had taken them.

The Beatles and their retinue would, however, be made to care in Manila, capital of Luzon, the largest island of the Philippine Archipelago. They'd managed two performances – to 30,000 in the afternoon, 50,000 in the evening – on 4 July 1966 at the city's Rizal Memorial Football Stadium. At the hotel, Brian Epstein received an invitation for them to be guests of honour at a party to be thrown by Imelda, wife of Philippines' autocratic President Ferdinand Marcos, at Malacanang Palace on the morning after the Rizal shows, for the families of the totalitarian government and military junta. Not appreciating that it was less a request than an order, Epstein let the weary entourage sleep on.

The following day, Beatle fans at Manila International Airport were puzzled that they could have ventured close enough to touch their idols had it not been for a jeering, jostling wall of flesh formed of the enraged dictator's creatures, assured of official leniency and even commendation no matter how they behaved towards the departing foreigners.

Open malevolence stopped just short of naked ultra-violence as the agitated Beatles hauled their own baggage up switched-off escalators, and shuffled through a customs area pulsating with pushing, shoving and snail-paced jack-in-office unpleasantness. Out on the tarmac, the party scuttled for the aeroplane where they fastened seat-belts, weak with relief. Final escape was delayed, however, when, no sooner had they unstiffened and emptied their lungs with a *whoosh*, Mal Evans and press secretary Tony Barrow were summoned back to the terminal to be questioned over some freshly unearthed red-tape.

Sent on their way by the boos and catcalls of the mob, never had arguments – particularly from John and George – against The Beatles continuation of touring made more sense.

As a post-script to this episode, when The Zombies dared eight concerts in the Philippines a few months later, "We did all these long interviews," recalled their Rod Argent, "and they asked us what we thought of The Beatles. Then all the papers the next day said 'Zombies Say Beatles Are Louts And Hooligans For Attacking Our First Lady!' We didn't know anything about all that stuff that had happened before."[44]

Hot on the heels of The Beatles' experience of The Philippines, a battering psychological rather than physical had awaited them on the North American leg through John Lennon's off-the-cuff comments about the increasing godlessness of our times during an interview with the London *Evening Standard*. When reprinted in the US teenage magazine *Datebook*, his opinions that The Beatles "are more popular than Jesus right now" and that "Christianity will go, it will vanish and shrink" were interpreted by a more general media as boastful "blasphemy" in a land that, until the British Invasion – and with Colonel Parker's manipulation of Elvis setting the sir-and-ma'am standard – had been used to a pop star being relatively devoid of independent opinion, having been put in motion by his handler as a walking digest of truth, justice and the American way.

Subliminally through the medium of teen magazines and even in some of the piffle he released on disc, he would echo stolid middle-aged dictums – your parents' word was law, don't talk dirty *et al* – and parade an apparent dearth of private vices. With the gentlest humour, he'd answer questions about his favourite *color*, preferred foodstuffs and the age at which he hoped to wed.

Lennon's nearer-the-knuckle ruminations were a particular red rag to "redneck" whites from the Deep South, caricatured as clannish, unsophisticated and anti-intellectual, thanks to incidents like the beating-up of black entertainer Nat "King" Cole in 1954 by racist extremists during his act before a mixed audience in Birmingham, Alabama. Soon to come was the firebombing of a Houston radio station by some good ol' boys who begged to differ over its radical anti-Vietnam policy. Their right-wing militancy was laced with pious fear of not so much "God" as "the Lord", "the Man In The Sky", "the Boss Of The Riders" or, if one of them had swallowed a dictionary, "The Big Architect". He was entreated as the need arose as either a homespun prairie philosopher, a sort of divine pimp – or an enforcer of redneck prejudices, which included the ongoing disapproval of long hair on men as it was written in 1 Corinthians xi 14: "Doth not nature itself teach you that, if a man have long hair, it is a shame unto him?"

It was here, in the heart of the Bible Belt, that thousands of Beatles discs were being ceremonially pulverised in a tree-grinding machine to the running commentary of a local disc jockey. Other mass protests were just as demonstrative. The group's new LP, *Revolver*, was removed from 22 southern radio playlists, and hellfire sermons preached of the fire and fury that would fall from above on any communicants who attended forthcoming Beatles concerts – though the sub-text of the casting out of this pestilence by one Memphis station was that it was as much in a kind of inverted vengeance for Brian Epstein's dim view of its exposure of a hush-hush (and subsequently scrubbed) Beatles' session at the city's Sun

Studios, where country boys like Elvis, Jerry Lee and Roy Orbison had been groomed for greener pastures.

Radio blacklisting and hostile audiences, however, were trifling problems compared to the possible in-concert slaughter of Lennon by divine wrath – or someone acting on the Almighty's behalf – even if hard-nosed US promoters considered this insufficient reason for cancellations. After all, even as 'To Kill A Beatle' had been making its deserved journey to the bargain bin, nothing had happened when two earlier death threats had been directed at The Beatles. On 20 August 1964, an anonymous telephone caller informed the management of the Convention Center in Las Vegas that a bomb had been planted somewhere in the building after the group's matinee performance at 4pm, but this was not taken seriously enough for the second show at 9pm to be nixed.

Eighteen days later, the switchboard operator at The Beatles' hotel in Montreal put through a call to Brian Epstein from someone who said that a bullet would have Ringo Starr's name on it when he perched behind his kit that evening at the city's Forum auditorium. Better safe than sorry, Epstein arranged for a detective to hunch beside the drum rostrum – to catch the slug, maybe – as Starr "played low" like Pete Best, with cymbals positioned straight up *à la* Buddy Rich. Nobody minded that his posture impaired the performance because who could hear it – or gunfire – anyway against the bedlam?

As the ripples of the "holy war" spread in August 1966, the danger was more omnipresent than ever. "The *Evening Standard* piece was by a very responsible journalist, Maureen Cleave, and the quote was put in its correct context," cried Tony Barrow. "John was making a statement on the world at that moment, and the fact that a pop group seemed to be drawing more attention than God. Certainly, there were more people going to pop concerts than attending Churches. It was lifted completely out of context and, in that respect, it was a terrible thing for a PR man to have his client say."[45]

A final attempt at damage limitation took place at a press conference hours before opening night in Chicago. There, John was trotted out to make a statement that most took as an apology. "It was the first time I had seen him really nervous at a press conference," observed Barrow, "probably because he didn't really know what to apologise for."[45] Lennon said as much to the assembled media, though adding "I'm sorry I opened my mouth…"

Engagements in the north passed without unanticipated incident, other than picketing by Ku Klux Klansmen outside Washington's DC Stadium. Below the Mason Dixon line, the anti-Beatles ferment was counterbalanced by "I love John" lapel badges outselling all associated merchandise. Nonetheless, a promise was made to Epstein from a pay phone that one or more Beatles would die on the boards at the Mid-South Coliseum in Memphis. Yet, though a firework that exploded onstage gave all four a horrified start, the show was delivered. The next morning, The Beatles slipped smoothly away into a temporary airborne respite from what was becoming an uneasy existence.

More insidious a worry had been – and was still – one German *fraulein*'s strong claim that one of The Beatles had fathered her child. That was a main reason why the group didn't work in the federal republic between 1962's final Star-Club residency and the Ernst-Merck-Halle show in 1966, despite losing out on lucrative appearances on *Beat Club*, a televisual pop showcase as vital in its fashion as *Ready Steady Go*. It was the means whereby Salisbury's Dave Dee, Dozy, Beaky, Mick And Tich became more popular in the Teutonic market as they were at home, to the extent of beating The Beatles by over 3,000 votes to win the German pop periodical *Bravo*'s Golden Otto award in 1966 – the equivalent of being Top Vocal Group in the *NME* poll.

However, for all the professional and personal problems whirling round The Beatles' protective bubble, the Hamburg stop on 26 June 1966 had been one of increasingly rarer oases of calm during their troubled trek around the globe. In a mellow mood, John doled out bite-sized chunks of unspoilt-by-fame attention to each of the old pals allowed into a backstage area that was as protected as Fort Knox. Yet for all Lennon's mateyness, Astrid Kirchherr sensed that he wanted to but couldn't invite her back into his life once more. He wanted to but couldn't rewind to 1961 and moments when…

Abruptly, there was a lull when Astrid, Lee Curtis, Bert Kaempfert *et al* fell silent and stared, wondering if John was real. After that, the atmosphere loosened up between them before he risked being confronted with Stuart Sutcliffe's spectre during a late night amble round some of the old haunts still standing down the Reeperbahn.

Then it was back to the party where a lot of the guests had decided that The Beatles had done enough showing-off for one night, and were keeping the watches of the night by joking around, yarning about what Rory Storm had said to Bruno Koschmider at the Kaiserkeller in 1960, and skirting round any old bitternesses that simmered still. It seemed so faraway now: the Indra, Lord Woodbine, Ricky Richards, the Top Ten, The Graduates, Pete Best, 'Ain't She Sweet', Johnny And The Hurricanes...

Two months later, The Beatles played their last concert – in San Francisco's Candlestick Park – and, for all their common ordeals and jubilations, the ties that bound them began to loosen. While mere sideshows to his pivotal role in The Beatles, among solo projects undertaken by John already were *In His Own Write* and *Spaniard In The Works* – two slim but best-selling volumes of verse, stories and cartoons – and he was to be seen as "Private Gripweed", a bit-part in *How I Won The War*, a movie on general release in the period between Brian Epstein's untimely death in August 1967, and December's interesting-but-boring TV spectacular, the self-produced *Magical Mystery Tour*. After that, the only direction should have been down, but Beatles discs continued to sell by the mega ton.

9 "Controlled Weirdness"

The journey to a John Lennon all but unrecognisable from the Merseyside beat merchant of 1962 had commenced weeks before the last date of the 1966 tour with a drug experience beyond, say, some speed to wire him up for the show and a "spliff" to unwind tense coils within afterwards.

Lennon had had, so he was to say, several spliffs – marijuana cigarettes – about his person when, soberly attired, he, Starr, McCartney and Harrison had been driven in a black Rolls-Royce through cheering masses to Buckingham Palace for their investiture as Members of the British Empire on 26 October 1965. "Taking the MBE was a sell-out for me," Lennon growled later, "one of the biggest jokes in the history of these islands."[2]

That the whole business was anathema to him was reflected further when he contended that, whilst waiting to be presented to the Queen at 11:10am, he and the other three had retired to a palace washroom to light up and pass round one of his spliffs. Yet Lennon's recollections may have been an attempt to beef up an image of himself as a rebel rocker – and his story was to be refuted by George Harrison, who maintained that nothing more narcotic than ordinary cigarettes were smoked. Certainly, none of the national treasures seemed noticeably under the influence of marijuana's admittedly short-lived magic when either talking to the sovereign or discussing the morning's events with the media at the Savile Theatre up the West End.

Perhaps no ordinary newshound would have noticed anyway. Not yet versed in the effects, paraphernalia and jargon of illicit drugs either, the BBC would pass The Small Faces' 'Here Comes The Nice' single – dealing with the dazzling effects of amphetamine sulphate ("speed") as it had already Bob Dylan's 'Rainy Day Women Nos 12 & 35' and its "everybody must get stoned!" chorus. 1966's 'Heroin' by The Velvet Underground, however, hadn't a hope of a solitary Light Programme spin, and the Corporation frowned on The Byrds' 'Eight Miles High', and, later, even Beatles tracks like 'Tomorrow Never Knows', 'A Day In The Life', 'Lucy In The Sky With Diamonds' and 'I Am The Walrus' as the "us and them" divide intensified with the Fab Four among celebrities advocating the legalisation of marijuana, and assisting on 'We Love You', the Rolling Stones 45 issued in the aftershock of the famous drug bust in guitarist Keith Richards' Sussex cottage.

In 1967 too, the spoof 'LS Bumble Bee' by Peter Cook and Dudley Moore was symptomatic of a general knowledge if not use of lysergic acid diethylamide 25 – LSD. To a degree, the effects of "acid" were simulated via light shows and other visual effects in renowned "underground" venues like Middle Earth in London, Amsterdam's Paradiso and New York's Fillmore East, where "bands" – not groups anymore – played on and on and on and on for hippies in a cross-legged trance and whirling dancers, their psyches boggling with paranormal sensations and surreal perceptions.

On the USA's west coast, LSD was far more prevalent than in Europe. It underpinned the music of Jefferson Airplane and The Grateful Dead, brand-leaders of the "flower-power" ethos of the Haight-Ashbury district of San Francisco, a city about to become as vital a pop Mecca as Liverpool had been – while down in Los Angeles, Brian Wilson's now acid-drenched visions were to be made tangible in *Smile*, a jettisoned masterwork – though excerpts were to serve as selling points on later Beach Boys albums.

Though Wilson studied the British opposition's output assiduously – as it did his – he had caught individual tracks on the radio but did not listen to the US pressing of *Rubber Soul* (The Beatles' last pre-LSD album) in its entirety until several weeks after its release in December 1965 – when a friend arrived at Brian's Laurel Canyon home with a copy. "When I heard *Rubber Soul* for the first time," recalled Wilson, "I was so blown out, I couldn't sleep for two nights."[40] He was particularly impressed with John's 'Girl' and Paul's 'Michelle', and overall aspects that he was to perceive as "religious, a white spiritual sound".[40]

After *Rubber Soul* had spun its little life away four times, Wilson told his wife, Marilyn, "I'm going to make the greatest rock 'n' roll album ever made."[40] Almost straightaway, he started work on what was to become *Pet Sounds*, which was to vie with 1967's *Sgt Pepper's Lonely Hearts Club Band*, the follow-up to *Revolver*, as "greatest album of all time" in turn-of-the-century assessments by broadsheet newspapers.

Brian commented during a 1995 television documentary, "We prayed for an album that would be a rival to *Rubber Soul*. It was a prayer, but there was no ego involved – and it worked. *Pet Sounds* happened immediately."[39] It wasn't up to *Rubber Soul*'s fighting weight commercially, but *Pet Sounds* was The Beach Boys' most critically acclaimed LP, causing The Beatles' nervous backwards glances – with Paul McCartney citing Wilson as "the real contender"[46] rather than The Rolling Stones.

Exacerbating the indignity of coming third to the Stones in the *New Musical Express*'s yearly chart points table – and second to Dave Dee, Dozy, Beaky, Mick And Tich in *Bravo* – the *NME*'s 1966 popularity poll had The Beatles second to The Beach Boys as World Vocal Group. "Good luck to them," grinned Ringo Starr, "We haven't been doing much lately, and it was run at a time when they had something good out."[47]

Starr was referring not only to *Pet Sounds*, but also 'Good Vibrations', Brian Wilson's chart-topping "pocket symphony".[40] This was part of *Smile*, which Brian Wilson reckoned would surpass both *Rubber Soul* and *Pet Sounds*, but the advent of *Sgt Pepper's Lonely Hearts Club Band* was among factors that caused its abandonment. "When I heard it," recalled Brian, "I knew that The Beatles had found a way to really take rock in a new direction. It scared the heck out of me."[39] It also kick-started Wilson's wretched LSD-fuelled journey across a terrible psychological desert for the next two decades.

John Lennon too had come to know acid well, and was to be The Beatles' most avid consumer. It had been part of the anything-goes – some would say "nihilistic" – spirit of Swinging London for many months before John was "spiked" by one of George Harrison's passing acquaintances in January 1966. Dick Taylor, The Pretty Things' lead guitarist, recalled, "The students above me when I lived in a flat in

Fulham in 1966 organised these lock-out nights – 'raves' you'd call them now – at the Marquee when LSD was legal. Personally, I was extremely wary of it."

"I had a good time on acid," parried the group's singer, Phil May, "but other people had problems." John Lennon did not include himself amongst them, and his reasons for continuing to take LSD were once much the same initially as those of Eric Burdon of The Animals: "I want to take a piece from every book. I want to learn from everything. That is why I originally took LSD. No, that's not right. I took it just to get stoned."[48] This was a bone of contention between Burdon and a new-found friend, Frank Zappa, leader of The Mothers Of Invention, who hissed, "The general consensus of opinion is that it's impossible to do anything creative unless you use chemicals."[49] Yet the "psychedelic" mental distortions of LSD were to transport John Lennon to untold heights of creativity – and further from 'Twist And Shout' than any Cavern dweller could have imagined.

More knowingly, again largely through George Harrison, he was now more open to the music of other cultures – what would be termed "world music" – though The Beatles weren't by any means the first pop stars to do so. Rolf Harris, for example, had woven the didgeridoo into the rich tapestry of Western pop in 1963, and Serge Gainsbourg issued *Percussions*, a 1964 LP that indicated a stark awareness of African tribal sounds. Moreover, Rosemary Squires, omnipresent on BBC radio light entertainment programmes even before Alma Cogan, listed Tibetan music among her extra-mural pastimes, becoming secretary of Britain's Tibetan Society from 1972 to 1975.

The Beatles were notable for their corresponding fascination with India. As with LSD, one individual's reaction to the sub-continent's classical tradition can be markedly different to that of another. Lennon found the droning ragas transfixing, and complementary to his more celestial acid reveries as well as his current reading of *The Golden Bough*, *Autobiography Of A Yogi* and further hardbacks of philosophic and aerie-faerie bent, purchased from the hip Indica bookshop off Piccadilly. He also bought a sitar – but, unlike George, he never got further than treating it like some fancy guitar.

John and the other Beatles' interest was gratifying news for stockists of Oriental merchandise in the West. Moreover, the most seemingly unlikely musicians latched on to it as well. Mainstream jazz drummer Buddy Rich, for instance, was to team up with tabla player Alla Rakha on a 1968 album – though, because he composed and conducted most of the written (as opposed to improvised) music, *Rich À La Rakha* was as much the work of Ravi Shankar, the master sitarist under whom George Harrison was to study.

Another catalyst in this collaboration was jazz flautist Paul Horn, a European disciple of the Maharishi Mahesh Yogi, whose international profile – like Shankar's – was to be heightened by the patronage of The Beatles, but not until later, in the watershed year of 1967, when music, passing hastily through its own "classical" period, was elevated from ephemera to Holy Writ, and the notion of pop as an egghead activity intensified. The most lasting effect was that "bands" began demanding public attention for "concept" albums and similar epics that couldn't be crammed into a ten-minute spot on a package tour with Helen Shapiro.

Instead of screaming hysteria, there was now knotted-brow "appreciation" as a working band's appeal became reliant not so much on big smiles and tight trousers as stamina to sustain lengthy extrapolations of items from both its last album and the unfamiliar successor being "laid down" during a studio block-booking of weeks and months, much of it impossible to reproduce onstage using conventional beat group instrumentation.

Naturally, The Beatles, though no longer stage performers, were at the forefront of this new attitude towards recording, notably after George Martin declared his independence of EMI in 1965 via the formation of his Associated Independent Recording (AIR) production company, taking Ron Richards with him – and then reaching his professional apotheosis through the making of *Sgt Pepper*.

As much Martin's baby in its way as The Beatles', it was judged to be a milestone of pop: "a milestone and a millstone", qualified George Harrison.[50] Many – especially in the States – listened to The Beatles' latest gramophone disc in the dark, at the wrong speeds, backwards and even normally. Every inch of the label and sleeve montage was scrutinised for concealed communiqués which would turn listeners into more aware, more creative human beings, truly at one with John, Paul, George and Ringo.

Nothing would be the same, not even the past. The "come on, come on" call and response in 'Please Please Me', for example, was, estimated a member of Clayson And The Argonauts in 1977, John Lennon's vain plea to Cynthia to menstruate and thus assuage fears about an unwanted pregnancy. Such banal argument still provides hours of enjoyable time-wasting for Beatle freaks, old and new – despite, say, a lyrical error ("two foot small" instead of "two foot tall") on 1965's 'You've Got To Hide Your Love Away' that Lennon decided should be uncorrected because "The pseuds'll love it."[51] More pointedly, his 'Glass Onion' in 1968 denied that there were ever any secret sub-texts to be found anywhere in The Beatles' *oeuvre* in the first place, whilst inserting false clues – like "the Walrus was Paul" – and misleading self-quotations, "just to confuse everybody a bit more".[51]

Perhaps 'Glass Onion' was a double-bluff – because there's no reason for the list of "uncovered" hidden meanings to ever end. The most conspicuous insertions as the Swinging '60s drew to a close were based on clues traceable to *Sgt Pepper*, which supported a widespread rumour that McCartney had perished in a road accident, and had been replaced by a *Doppelgänger*.

Very much alive in 1967, Paul, more than John, had been prime mover on an album that had been conceived as less a regular LP with about a dozen separate tracks than a continuous work with no spaces between songs. This was to be the artistic climax of EMI's liaison with The Beatles, which had heralded a new budgetary commitment towards the long-playing pop record, a product that had been, more often than not, a testament to market pragmatism rather than quality, and targeted – particularly in the USA once more – at fans so beglamoured by an artist's looks and personality to be rendered uncritical of frankly substandard, haphazardly programmed output, excused as an exhibition of "versatility", but of no cultural value. Brian Wilson was to heap further praise on *Rubber Soul* with "It was the first time in my life I remember hearing a rock album on which every song was really good."[39]

The Beatles' first LP had been padded with a brace of singles, but each that followed was a conscious musical progression, with an increasing ratio of tracks the equal of A-sides. Moreover, by the close of the decade, it had become common procedure to issue a 45 off an already successful album – as 'Something'/'Come Together' was to be from 1969's *Abbey Road*.

Nonetheless, the absence of the usual Christmas single in 1966 had made it necessary to release 'Penny Lane' coupled with 'Strawberry Fields Forever', tracks intended originally for the forthcoming *Sgt Pepper*. This was regrettable, but not disastrous – even if George Harrison was to admit, "There are some good songs on it, but it's not our best album."[50]

With its expensive and syncretic precedent, record companies found themselves underwriting albums of like persuasion (eg The Rolling Stones' *Their Satanic Majesties Request* and *Days Of Future Passed* by The Moody Blues) plus "rock operas" (The Pretty Things' *SF Sorrow*, The Kinks' *Arthur*, and The Who's *Tommy* – all, technically, song-cycles) and other *magnum opi* (John Mayall's *Bare Wires*, *The Crazy World Of Arthur Brown* LP and The Small Faces' *Ogden's Nut Gone Flake*).

Yet *Sgt Pepper* may be seen – albeit with a certain logical blindness and retiming of the truth – as not the first time such an idea had been attempted in pop. This may be a silly analogy, but perhaps all albums are concept albums in the sense that all pop songs expose a point of view.

Is being thematic the same as having a concept? Was 1965's *The Sect Sing Sing-Songs*, four repulsively amusing ditties about death by The Downliners Sect, a concept EP? What about 1963's *Little Deuce Coupe*, on which The Beach Boys string together a bunch of songs about hot-rod cars, whether lauding the record-breaking 'Spirit Of America' or weeping over 'Old Betsy', maybe one oil-change away from the breaker's yard? Certainly, in its unsubtle way, *Little Deuce Coupe* created more of a specific and recurring mood than *Sgt Pepper*.

The same is true of Joe Meek's *I Hear A New World Part One*, a narrowly circulated 1960 EP of mood music to help audio dealers demonstrate these new-fangled "stereo" gramophones in 1960 – and its cancelled *Volume 2* [*sic*] follow-up. As you might gather from titles like 'Orbit Round The Moon', 'Magnetic Field', 'Love Dance Of The Saroos' and 'Dribcots' Space Boat' – not to mention the wordless "little green men" vocals and overall electronic aetheria – it was a sound painting concerned entirely with Joe's almost child-like fascination with outer space. Part of Meek's reputation as a record producer rested for decades on *I Hear A New World* – as *Smile* still does for Brian Wilson – until all 30 minutes of the two *I Hear A New World* EPs were made available as a CD album in 1991, courtesy of reissue specialists RPM Records.

While it did contain various seques and links, plus the reprise of the title theme, *Sgt Pepper* wasn't "about" anything as *I Hear A New World*, *Little Deuce Coupe* or, more germane to this discourse, *SF Sorrow* and *Days Of Future Passed* were – and only at the beginning and near the end were you reminded of what was supposed to be Sgt Pepper's show. "It was as if we did a few tracks," said Ringo Starr, "and suddenly there was a fire, and everyone ran out of the building, but we carried on playing."[52] Yet, regardless of its diverted intention, *Sgt Pepper* is tied forever to psychedelic times past – and perhaps that's the lasting "concept". Listening to it decades later, a middle-aged hippy would almost smell the joss-sticks and see its fabled jacket being used as a working surface for rolling a spliff.

Technically, *Sgt Pepper* improved on *Revolver* as close-miked vocals floated effortlessly over layers of treated sound, and gadgetry and constant retakes disguised faults, if impinging on grit. These days, a mere ten hours – the time spent recording the four's first *LP* – was no longer considered adequate for one Beatles *track*. For example, in 1968, 'Not Guilty', a George Harrison number, ran to a marathon 100-odd takes.

A year earlier, 'Strawberry Fields Forever' and 'Penny Lane' had also travelled mile upon mile of tape, week upon week of studio time, but had been kept from Number One in the UK by Engelbert Humperdinck's schmaltzy 'Release Me', thus allowing Decca and Dick Rowe a moment of revenge. Though he'd continued to strike lucky with outfits like The Small Faces, The Animals – who'd defected from EMI – Marmalade and, for Decca's new "progressive" Deram subsidiary, The Move and Procol Harum, Dick was more at home with "real singers" like some of his pre-Beatles finds had been – and so it was that Humperdinck and Tom Jones led a counter-revolution of "decent" music when signed up by the late

Rowe in the mid-1960s before his calculated withdrawal from a business in which his critical prejudices no longer fitted.

The Beatles were to prove ultimately more sound an investment for EMI than Humperdinck and Jones put together for Decca. Accumulated since their partnership began in the late 1950s, Lennon and McCartney's ever-swelling stockpile of hit songs could – even by 1962 – fulfil EMI's contractual requirements many times over, and even allow a "Lennon–McCartney–Starkey" credit for *Rubber Soul*'s unremarkable 'What Goes On' ("resurrected with a middle eight thrown in with Paul's help to give Ringo a song" explained John[21]). With their works being covered now by everyone from international stars like Matt Monro and Peter Sellers to banjo bands and barbershop quartets, John and Paul could afford to be generous.

They and the other two had long been granted unlimited studio time, and the freedom to requisition all manner of auxiliary instrumentation and musicians – as instanced by the highly waged Mike Sammes Singers, a mixed sex aggregation – more a choir than a vocal group – whose living hinged principally on up to three studio sessions a day. Among more renowned employers were The Beverley Sisters, Tommy Steele, Cliff Richard, Anthony Newley, Matt Monro, Helen Shapiro, Tom Jones, Engelbert Humperdinck – and The Beatles, for whom the Singers were equally at ease with Lennon's psychedelic 'I Am The Walrus' as 'Goodnight', his lushly orchestrated lullaby to five-year-old Julian that was to close 1968's *The Beatles* (alias the 'White Album').

EMI smiled fondly too as John, Paul, George and Ringo, like unrestrained children in a toy shop, fiddled about with whatever weird-and-wonderful implements were either lying about their favoured Studio Two or staring at them from one of the Abbey Road complex's storerooms. In this workshop–playroom ambience, George Martin had been quite acquiescent to, perhaps, an Arabian bongo pepping up 'Don't Bother Me' on *With The Beatles*; Ringo swatting a packing case in place of snare on 'Words Of Love' from 1964's *Beatles For Sale*; and the hiring of a string quartet for 'Yesterday' the following year.

Engineers muttered darkly but said nothing out loud when console dials went into the red during *Sgt Pepper* sessions or George Martin razored a tape of Sousa marches to pieces and ordered someone to stick it back together any old how for the instrumental interlude in John's 'Being For The Benefit Of Mr Kite', the item that was to round off side one.

According to Martin, it was Lennon who first coined the term "flanger", which entered general technical vocabulary for an electronic strategy whereby two signals in a slightly out-of-time alignment were deployed as automatic double-tracking. It was used to enhance The Beatles' vocals – for example, John's on 'Lucy In The Sky With Diamonds' – but is more noticeable when applied to percussion, as in the effervescent drumming on The Small Faces' 'Itchycoo Park', Eric Burdon's 'Sky Pilot' and throughout 1968's *Strictly Personal* LP by Captain Beefheart.

The likes of The Small Faces, Burdon and Beefheart were, however, unable to attract the same financial outlay from their respective investors as The Beatles, whose *Sgt Pepper* vied with their most recent 45, 'All You Need Is Love', to top the Australian *singles* chart. Fittingly, *Sgt Pepper*'s 'A Day In The Life' epilogue was also the valedictory spin on Britain's pirate Radio London when it went off the air in August 1967.

If *Sgt Pepper* had been the station's most plugged album, the single was surely Procol Harum's 'A Whiter Shade Of Pale', which John Lennon started singing playfully as members of the group – sorry, band – trooped into the Speakeasy one evening. He remembered Procol Harum under a less abstract appellation, The Paramounts, supporting The Beatles when they last played the Hammersmith Odeon in 1964.

The selectively amiable Lennon, however, wasn't all smiles when Pink Floyd were conducted in from the adjacent studio at Abbey Road to see the masters at work. He was the only Beatle not to return the call on hearing reports of the otherworldly sounds emitting from the less sophisticated four-track lair where the Floyd were recording their first LP, *Piper At The Gates Of Dawn*. Could it be that the younger quartet were achieving what The Beatles were still chasing? After all, composer Syd Barrett – their biggest asset and biggest liability – had, with the other personnel keeping pace, gone further into the cosmos than they had on 'Astronomy Domine', and disconnected with our solar system altogether on 'Interstellar Overdrive'. Moreover, 'Gnome', 'Matilda Mother', 'Flaming' and his mock-medieval 'Scarecrow' had cornered pop's gingerbread-castle hour more effectively and instinctively than had 'Lucy In The Sky With Diamonds'.

In Abbey Road, too, The Pretty Things were completing their transition from a Home Counties R&B group to operating ambiguously with chart-directed singles and increasingly more erudite "musicianly" fancies on albums. Issued in November 1967 after much prevaricating from EMI, 'Defecting Grey' was a 45rpm medley of five pieces that paved the way for *SF Sorrow*, unquestionably the first rock opera. "What we were after," elucidated Phil May, "was an album that didn't have tracks but musically was just one piece. That's why it had a story – the only way we could give it continuity. What was also relevant was that *SF Sorrow* was made on acid."

If you want my opinion, *Sgt Pepper* – on which LSD played its part too – remains a lesser work than *SF Sorrow* and *Piper At The Gates Of Dawn*. Nevertheless, The Beatles' album, rather than The Pink Floyd debut and the relatively poor-selling Pretty Things offering, had been the more manifest trigger for countless beat groups from The Rolling Stones downwards to mutate into a "band" of self-absorbed pseudo-seers, exchanging smirks across the mixing desk at one another's cleverness. Thus *Their Satanic Majesties Request* appeared in the shops, complete with a fold-out sleeve as freighted with symbolism as *Sgt Pepper*'s. A month after 'All You Need Is Love' came 'We Love You', coupled with 'Dandelion', a piece of similar pixified scenario as 'Lucy In The Sky With Diamonds'.

Absorbing the signals as they came from a greater distance, Caio, Hugo, Osvaldo and Pelin adjusted to *Sgt Pepper*-esque psychedelia without quite getting the point, judging by 'The Shape Of A Rainbow' and 'I Remember My World', which occupied the dying minutes of a "concept" album that might be all most UK record buyers will need to experience of the latter-day Los Shakers.

Back home again, The Koobas also recorded a "work" with dialogue *et al* filling space between tracks. Taped at Abbey Road with Geoff Emerick, The Beatles' usual engineer these days, this was to be The Koobas' only long-player, released belatedly and appreciated only in retrospect despite the efforts of Brian Epstein and a more committed Tony Stratton-Smith, who became the group's manager (and occasional lyricist) in 1966.

After four years of following trends set by others, The Koobas were becoming their own men at last. Conversely, when 1967's Summer of Love climaxed on 25 June with The Beatles' satellite-linked televisual broadcast of their 'All You Need Is Love' flower-power anthem, others moved in quick. Direct from Denmark Street, 'Let's Go To San Francisco Parts 1 & 2' was spread over two sides of a single by The Flowerpot Men – who mimed it on *Top Of The Pops* and went on the road in beads, chiffony robes and like regalia, tossing chrysanthemums into the audience.

The Flowerpot Men were not among the more superficial pop newcomers who captivated John Lennon, but his taste was sufficiently broad-minded to appreciate The Monkees, four youths put together by a cabal of Californian business folk for a networked TV series based on the *Hard Day's Night*-period Beatles. Their hit records were merely part of the package of one of the most ruthless marketing strategies the entertainment business had ever known.

When The Monkees visited Britain, John was amenable enough towards them when introduced, but was to have a deep friendship – comparable to that he'd known with Stuart Sutcliffe – with one of the four's hired songwriters, Harry Nilsson, then a semi-professional who kept body and soul together as a Los Angeles bank clerk.

There remains division over the late Nilsson. Was he an inconsistent genius who defied categorisation or a tiresome *bon viveur*, content to have fulfilled only a fraction of his potential? Artistically, the second half of his career was certainly less impressive than the first. An impressive number of tracks on Nilsson's quaint *Pandemonium Puppet Show* were subject to cover versions, among them Billy J Kramer's of semi-autobiographical '1941', singing disc-jockey Kenny Everett of 'It's Been So Long', and 'Without Her' by Engelbert-ish Jack Jones. Other items from this debut LP and 1968's *Aerial Ballet* were tried later by The Turtles, Rick Nelson, Mary Hopkin, The Yardbirds, Herb Alpert, Andy Williams, Blood, Sweat And Tears, actor George Burns – and, most spectacularly, Three Dog Night – with a million-selling treatment of the latter album's 'One'.

A lot of the syndications sounded tame when up against what were more than useful demos. The most transforming ingredient was Nilsson's supple three-octave vocal daredevilry, encompassing trumpet impersonations, scat-singing and further idiosyncrasies. Despite bouts of overdone grandiloquence, neither did Brooklyn-born Harry disgrace himself on his own reshapings of such as Ike and Tina Turner's 'River Deep Mountain High' and Fred Neil's 'Everybody's Talkin'', a Grammy winning chartbuster when used in 1969's *Midnight Cowboy* movie. Thus evolved the enigma of Nilsson as the acclaimed composer whose most enduring releases were penned by others.

One of his most immediate personal characteristics was that Nilsson was prey to sudden mood shifts, commensurate with the classic "artistic temperament". A closer parallel with John Lennon was that, when he was young, his parents had separated, with Harry choosing to remain with his mother. They moved to San Bernardino, California, where, until they acquired a proper house, they made do with a mobile home where "gangs of Hell's Angels would encircle the trailer late at night and harass the people."

Later, Harry went back east to attend high school at Long Island, New York, where he emerged as a promising baseball player. More cerebral activities included painting and sculpture, and he taught himself to play the piano when captivated by Ray Charles ("he made me want to do something with music"). Finished with formal education at the age of 15 in 1956, he hitch-hiked to Los Angeles, where he worked as a cinema usher, rising to assistant manager before being made redundant when the place closed.

The priesthood was among vocations that beckoned next, but he landed a post as a night-shift computer operator with the Security First National Bank (where he was known as "Harry Nelson") whilst writing songs and hawking the results round Hollywood by day. 'Groovy Little Suzy' was accepted by Little Richard, who, stunned by the young man's vocal range and mastery of "scatting", suggested that Harry might make it as a pop star in his own right, despite an ingrained dislike of singing in public ("I just wanted to be a record person"). He ticked over with television jingles and demos for music publishers, and, backed by the cream of Hollywood session musicians, released unviable singles as 'Johnny Miles' and as 'The New Salvation Singers' (ie his voice multi-tracked up to 90 *times*).

Still semi-pro, he became recognised around Los Angeles studios as a reliable session vocalist and jobbing tunesmith. After co-writing 'Readin' Ridin And Racin'' – a hot-rod opus – for The Superstocks, and 'Travellin' Man' for The New Christy Minstrels and Slim Whitman, he placed two more of his compositions with The Ronettes, and another with The Modern Folk Quartet. A liaison with these acts' producer, Phil Spector, promised much, but three songs recorded by Harry with the "Svengali Of Sound" remained unissued for ten years. Though the Spector connection opened doors, Nilsson contemplated a withdrawal from the music business altogether on experiencing The Beatles ("As soon as I heard what they were doing, I just backed off"). Now married, and promoted to computer-department supervisor, he seemed to be on the verge of "settling down".

After The Monkees had selected his 'Cuddly Toy' – later castigated for its "sexism" – for 1967's *Pisces, Aquarius, Capricorn And Jones Ltd* album, Nilsson was offered a contract by RCA and surfaced as the toast of the London In-Crowd after Derek Taylor – now publicist for The Byrds, The Beach Boys and other US acts – mailed *Pandemonium Puppet Show* to Brian Epstein with the testimonial that "he is the something The Beatles are". The group itself agreed, perhaps flattered by the spin-off 45, a medley of 11 Lennon–McCartney songs, under the umbrella title, 'You Can't Do That', which climbed the Australian Top 40.

Nicknaming him "The Fab Harry", John Lennon was prompted to nominate the new cult celebrity as his "favourite American group"[53]. John next took the initiative by telephoning Nilsson at the bank ("Hello, this is John Lennon." "Yeah, and I'm Uncle Sam."). Invited to drop by when in London, Harry was to meet Lennon in 1968 – and thus begin a lifelong amity.

Attempts to add the talented Harry to NEMS's galaxy of stars proved futile as he had decided to take care of business himself on resigning from work: "That job gave me insight. You gain a business experience that helps you understand why companies make such decisions." Besides, Brian Epstein's stake in Beatles' matters – and those of his remaining Liverpool artists – was becoming more and more detached as the expiry dates of his five-year contracts with them crept closer – as did his association with them in more absolute terms.

Brian's often severely tested loyalty to his principal charges had extended to proffering in vain his personal fortune to compensate promoters if they consented to cancel the final US tour in the light of real fear for John's life after his "We're more popular than Christ" remark. Yet once-merry rumours darkened to a certainty that, perturbed by some of the irretractable mistakes he'd made whilst learning the job, the group were at the very least to reduce Mr Epstein's cut and say in their affairs.

In an interview given to *Melody Maker* on 9 August 1967, however, he'd been "certain that they would not agree to be managed by anyone else". Television chat-show appearances – frequent these days – also assured fans that he was as much The Beatles' clear-headed mentor as he'd ever been. Indeed, on their behalf, he was in the midst of setting the wheels in motion for a *Yellow Submarine* cartoon fantasy about them as Sgt Pepper's bandsmen.

To David Frost on ITV, however, he'd spoken less of the Fab Four than the Savile Theatre, in which he'd had a controlling interest since 1965. The current Sundays At The Savile pop presentations, which sometimes mitigated the poor takings for the drama and dance productions during the week, had been Brian's brainwave. However, his preoccupation with this and other projects were but analgesics, alleviations to the pangs of despair, general insularity and an essentially guilt-ridden homosexuality. These had been symptomised by Brian's interrelated and increasing apathy towards the needs of those still on his books, even Cilla Black, his main concern after The Beatles. She was so disenchanted that she'd been on the point of leaving him until moved by both a tearful plea for her to reconsider, and a consequent swift negotiation of a weekly TV series.

Cilla was going from strength to strength, but Gerry And The Pacemakers had thrown in the towel by 1967. After unfruitful bids for solo chartbusters, Gerry bounced back to a degree as the "all-round entertainer" he'd always aspired to be. He was host of ITV's *Junior Showtime*, broadcast from Manchester, where he was in his element with his unforced Scouse backchat. Next, he secured the male lead in the West End musical *Charlie Girl*, which ran and ran after an opening night dignified by the presence of John and Ringo in the audience.

Similarly, Billy J Kramer kept the wolf from the door as a compère on children's television whilst try-trying again with '1941' and a patchwork of other diverse styles on releases that included one attributed to "William Howard Ashton". While his tenacity is to be admired, all his post-Epstein attempts to get back on his perch pointed in the same direction: the 1960s nostalgia circuit, belying the title of a 1983 single, 'You Can't Live On Memories', freighted with a reference to his former svengali.

Billy's feelings about Brian as a businessman were not indicative of any loss of personal affection. The same was true of Cilla Black, who was among the few to whom Epstein confessed his private anxieties. Another was Pattie, George Harrison's wife, who warned Brian of the dangers inherent in the over-prescribed tablets that he took to sleep, to stay awake, to calm his nerves, to lift his melancholia.

During the last month of Brian Epstein's life, another messiah had risen for The Beatles as he himself had at the Cavern eons ago in 1961. His Divine Grace the Maharishi Mahesh Yogi seemed at first glance as different from Brian as he could be. He was, he replied, a dealer "in wisdom, not money" when pressed about how his International Meditation Society was financed.

To Cilla Black, this meditation caper he propagated was akin to "somebody who goes to the loo with a big pile of papers and sits there and reads them all".[39]

She could cackle but The Beatles were serious enough about meditation to undergo the Society's initiation course, conducted by his Divine Grace at a university faculty in Bangor during the Bank Holiday weekend in August 1967. Once, it might have been the last bolt-hole anyone might have expected to find them. Yet fans and the media had were out in force at Euston railway station for what one tabloid named "The Mystical Special", the mid-afternoon train to the north Wales seaside town that was a short drive from Gerry Marsden's recently purchased home-from-home in Anglesey.

"I was there that weekend that made such a change to our lives," recalled Gerry, "and it didn't register that they were only a few miles away with the Maharishi – but I wasn't interested in all that."

Brian Epstein was interested but not convinced about all that either – and, in the end, neither, collectively, were his principal clients. Both Epstein and The Beatles' misgivings had been reinforced as much by the satirical magazine *Private Eye* dubbing the Maharishi "Veririchi Lotsamoney Yogi Bear" as the fellow's own submission that they ought to tithe part of their income into his Swiss bank account.

Brian had, nevertheless, half promised that he'd join his boys at Bangor. "That's how it used to be," Ringo would reminisce. "If someone wanted to do something, all we'd do was follow them."[52] The wives and girlfriends – John's Cynthia, Ringo's Maureen, George's Pattie and Paul's Jane Asher – were the same, as exemplified by the uniform pale-blond hairdos they were all sporting by the middle of 1967.

That's as may be, but as Ringo and Maureen's second child, Jason, had been born on 19 August – and, by sickening coincidence, Ty Brien, guitarist with Rory Storm And The Hurricanes, had died onstage that same month – the Starrs hadn't been ready to tear themselves away from their Surrey acres to a lecture by the Maharishi the following week at the Park Lane Hilton to which George and Pattie had dragged along Paul, Jane and the Lennons.

Their attendance there was traceable to the previous February, when Pattie had attended a lecture on "Spiritual Regeneration" at London's Caxton Hall. The doctrines advanced that evening were imperatively appealing, although the orator had stressed that his words were but a vague daub, and that his guru – the Maharishi – could paint a more pleasing verbal picture.

Born plain Mahesh Prasad Varma, the robed and ascetic Maharishi – "Great Soul" – had founded a British branch of the International Meditation Society in 1959 and had worked up around 10,000 initiates by the time Pattie – and George – relayed to the rest of the gang the sweet flowers from his silver-bearded lips. It seemed that, through short daily contemplations, all vices would be eradicated bit by bit until a pure state of bliss was achieved. Moreover, such washing of spiritual laundry was possible without forsaking material possessions (bar the Society's membership fee).

This seemed an excellent creed to a supertaxed Beatle as he stole into the Hilton's hushed functions room. The Great Soul so lived up to the Harrisons' spiel that, directly afterwards, George, John and Paul buttonholed him and wound up promising to join him in Bangor.

While packing, they rang others who might want to go – and boarding the Mystical Express too would be Ringo, Mick Jagger, Marianne Faithfull and Pattie's sister, Jennie. Waylaid by "What's the Maharishi like?", "Do you think you'll all be changed by next Tuesday?" and other bellowed questions, Jagger dismissed the outing straightaway as "more like a circus than the beginning of an original event".[39] Unable to shove through the mob, Cynthia Lennon missed the train – and one of the last opportunities to save her deteriorating marriage.

The rest of the party crammed eventually into the same compartment as the Maharishi. The uproar at Euston had brought home to him what a catch he'd made. Previously, he'd been unaware of The Beatles' stature, but he made a mental note to try to insert quotes from their lyrics into his talks about karma, the transmigration of souls – and the world of illusion.

For pop stars who'd lived in more of a world of illusion than most since 1963, it was perhaps too much of an adventure. Hard cash had become as unnecessary to them as eyesight to a monkfish, and, after a communal meal in a Bangor restaurant, George Harrison was the first to realise why the waiters kept hovering around the table. And it was he, too, who settled the bill with a roll of banknotes he chanced to have – as you do – in the hollow sole of his shoe.

Neither this incident nor the hard mattresses in the student hostels on the campus were as disconcerting as the press conference that Varma's public-relations agent had set up in the main hall, where most newsmongers appeared to regard The Beatles' preoccupation with meditation as flippantly as Cilla Black did. Hard to take seriously by those who thought they knew him was rough old John Lennon becoming a mystic.

One or two sick jokes circulated among the press corps on Sunday afternoon. Brian Epstein's lonely life had ended suddenly in London the previous night. Pattie Harrison's disquiet had been justified, because, as Westminster Coroner's Court would conclude, Brian had been killed by "incautious self-overdoses" after he'd become bored with a dinner party at his country home and chosen to drive back to his London flat. The doors to his bedroom were forced open the next morning and an ambulance called, but there was nothing the paramedics could do.

The expected rumours went the rounds before the day was out. The most absurd was that he'd been bumped off by a hitman connected to a New York syndicate who'd offered Brian millions for The Beatles three years earlier. The most commonly held notion, however, was that he'd committed suicide. There'd been a purported attempt late in 1966, followed by a spell – not the only one – in a London clinic in May 1967 to combat combined depression, stress and exhaustion. He was visited by Larry Parnes and John Lennon sent flowers and a note ("You know I love you. I really mean that"), which caused the tortured Brian to burst into tears.

Just over a month later, his 63-year-old father was taken by a heart attack, but Brian was unlikely to have added to his beloved and newly widowed mother's grief by doing away with himself. Moreover, in keeping with the *Melody Maker* interview, a letter he sent the previous week to Nat Weiss, The Beatles' US attorney, was quite upbeat, ending, "Be happy and look forward to the future."

As in the "happy ending" in a Victorian novel, with all the villains bested and the inheritance claimed, Brian at 32 could have retired, rich in material comforts and enjoying the fruits of his success. Money, however, can't buy you love – at least, not the love that Brian was wondering if he was losing since the armoured car had whisked his Beatles away from Candlestick Park. Suicide or accident, perhaps Brian Epstein was past caring.

Inside the college at Bangor, the Great Soul had consoled his famous devotees. Nevertheless, as twilight thickened, The Beatles brushed past the stick mics, note pads and flashbulbs as they strode from the university building into a black Rolls-Royce. For all the dicta they'd just absorbed that trivialised death, they were visibly shaken. "I knew we were in trouble then," John was to state with retrospective honesty. "I didn't really have any misconceptions about our ability to do anything other than play music, and I was scared. I thought: we've fucking had it."[5]

So it was that The Beatles became as kites in a storm and the man-in-the-street started raising quizzical eyebrows at their increasingly wayward activities – beginning with *Magical Mystery Tour*.

Nearly two years after their second film, *Help!*, The Beatles were discussing the third one they were contractually obliged to deliver to United Artists. *Yellow Submarine*, apparently, didn't count. After they'd turned their noses up at suggestions ranging from a Western to an adaptation of *The Lord Of The Rings*, Paul McCartney came up with a plan to make something up as they went along.

Like many Beatle ideas – particularly after Epstein's death – it was more intriguing conceptually than in ill-conceived practice. Less than a fortnight after the funeral, journalists were pursuing a charabanc, which, with "Magical Mystery Tour" emblazoned on the sides, was trundling through the West Country containing, reportedly, The Beatles and a supporting cast as variegated as a disaster movie's.

As well as the chaos that their very presence summoned, the 40-seater bus – now divested by a disenchanted Lennon of its too-distinctive trappings – failed to negotiate Devon's twisty country lanes, thus ruling out such potentially stimulating locations as Berry Pomeroy Castle and Widecombe Fair.

Though the bulk of *Magical Mystery Tour* was drawn from this troubled excursion, many interior sequences were shot elsewhere, mainly back in London where The Beatles also began six weeks in a darkened cutting room, wading through the formless celluloid miles of improvised dialogue and scenes that had seemed a good notion at the time. As Paul was less uncertain about the finished picture, John, George and Ringo elected to leave him to it. Unless called to give second opinions, they whiled away hours in an adjacent office with such diversions as inviting in and clowning around with "Rosie", a Soho vagrant who'd been immortalised in a recent hit by street busker Don Partridge.

A completed *Magical Mystery Tour* was premiered on BBC1 on Boxing Day for the majority of Britons still with black-and-white TVs, and repeated in colour on BBC2 on 5 January prior to general big-screen release across the Atlantic. While it wasn't *Citizen Kane*, 35 years of celluloid extremity later *Magical Mystery Tour* is less the hybrid of turn-off and tedious cultural duty it used to be than an occasionally intriguing curate's egg. Witness The Bonzo Dog Doo-Dah Band accompanying the cavortings of a stripper, and the visuals for The Beatles' own songs – which were, according to Paul McCartney's biographer, Barry Miles, "the vehicle for a number of prototype rock videos, some of which, like 'Fool On The Hill', could be shown on MTV and look as if they were freshly made".[46] Finally, when divorced from the film, the soundtrack – 'I Am The Walrus', 'Flying' and the rest of the double-EP that all but topped the UK singles chart – is still a winner.

Yet, as 1967 mutated into 1968, apart from predictable plaudits from the underground press and the *New Musical Express* – and a less foreseeable one in *The Guardian* – *Magical Mystery Tour* as a film was almost universally panned. Most common-or-garden viewers agreed too that it wasn't the most suitable viewing – especially in black and white – for a nation sleeping off its Yuletide revels. You can't help wondering too how many would have watched it to the bitter end if it had starred The Koobas or Los Shakers.

Though uneasy about it from the start, John Lennon hadn't said much at the time, passively attempting to quell media forebodings by not contradicting the others when they spoke of *Magical Mystery Tour* being full of "interesting things to look at, interesting things to hear" and "aimed at the widest possible audience" namely, "children, their grandparents, Beatle people, the lot".[54]

In other matters, however, he seemed his usual plain-speaking self, cracking back at critics with faultless logic and calm sense laced with the quirky wit they expected of him. When the group and its creatures repaired to Rishikesh, the Maharishi's *yoga-ashram* (theological college) on the Ganges, for further study in February 1968, it was John who was to perceive that his Grace was all too human, telling him so to his face after a Beatles hanger-on accumulated enough tittle-tattle to speak to Lennon about Varma's apparent clandestine and earthly scheming for the seduction of a lady student, propositioning her with the forbidden meal of chicken as other cads would with a box of chocolates. Deaf to protestations of genuine innocence after confronting the Great Soul with his infamy, Lennon announced his and Cynthia's immediate departure.

When they got back to England, rock 'n' roll revival was in the air, and The Beatles took heed with their next chart-topper, 'Lady Madonna', reminiscent of Fats Domino. After being sucked into a vortex of experiences deeper than just plain folks could ever have imagined, John had surfaced with the certain knowledge that rock 'n' roll was healing, inspirational. It had saved Lennon's soul more often and more surely than any amount of sermonising from vicar or guru.

It was on John too that the truth about their post-Epstein business affairs – a truth that he and the others had refused to avow for too long – most inflicted itself. It was he who was chief advocate of calling in Allen Klein, one of the bigger apes in the US music business jungle, to sort out the mess that was the so-called "controlled weirdness" of their multi-faceted Apple Corps, a blanket term for artistic, scientific and merchandising ventures under The Beatles' self-administered aegis when the company was launched in April 1968 – the beginning of the tax year.

Some of their pop peers diversified for fun and profit too, random examples being Chris Farlowe's military memorabilia shop in Islington on earnings from his 1966 Number One, 'Out Of Time'; Merseybeat Tony Crane's stake in a Spanish night club; Monkee Davy Jones's New York boutique; and The Troggs' Reg Presley patenting of his fog-dispersal device. The far wealthier Beatles could be more altruistic. According to eye-catching newspaper advertisements, actively encouraging people to send in tapes, a kindly welcome awaited not just those who'd nurtured a connection within the group's inner circle, but any old riff-raff who wished to solicit Apple for finance for pet projects.

When 3 Savile Row was established as Apple's permanent address, sackfuls of mail would overload its postman, pleading voices would bother its switchboard, and supplicatory feet would ascend its stone steps morning, noon and night until a burly doorman was appointed to shoo most of them away. "We had every freak in the world coming in there," groaned George Harrison.[55] Yet to loitering pavement fixture Alex Millen – an "Apple Scruff" – his fallible idols "did strengthen the belief that Joe Soap was important and, yes, you too could have something to say".[55]

With this in mind, impetuous cash was flung at such as two unprofitable shops that closed within three months; "Magic" Alex Mardas, the one who blackened the Maharishi's name in Rishikesh, who was also a so-called "electronics wizard" yet whose wondrous inventions advanced little further than him talking about them; a troupe of grasping Dutch designers, trading misleadingly as "The Fool"; poets who couldn't write poems; and film-makers who didn't make films.

While Apple Films was to produce a handful of worthy if rather specialist labours of love like *Messenger Out Of The East*, a documentary of Ravi Shankar and the land that bore him, Apple Records was the organisation's only lasting success. It was subject to a leasing deal (and Parlophone catalogue numbers) with parent company EMI, who were to refuse to release the likes of one-man-band Brute Force's 'The King Of Fuh' (containing a chorus that ran, "I'm the king of Fuh/I'm the Fuh king") and worse. Nevertheless, the founding of an ostensibly independent label reduced the number of middlemen and increased The Beatles' own quality control of product.

None of the – sometimes critically acclaimed – records that Ronnie Spector (Phil's missus), ex-Undertaker Jackie Lomax and New York soul shouter Doris Troy made for Apple would make them rich, but Welsh soprano Mary Hopkin began a three-year chart run when her 'Those Were The Days' debut knocked inaugural Apple single, The Beatles' own 'Hey Jude', from the top of the British charts – and both Billy Preston and Badfinger, a Merseyside act spotted by Mal Evans, had hits too. The Modern Jazz Quartet and classical composer John Tavener also reached a bigger audience through Apple Records.

An Anglo-American "supergroup" containing ex-Byrd Dave Crosby, Steve Stills from Buffalo Springfield and Graham Nash, late of The Hollies, were approached to sign with Apple, but as no member of Crosby, Stills And Nash could extricate himself from existing contracts, the deal fell through – as did that with another promising outfit, Fleetwood Mac. A lesser star in embryo, James Taylor, was taken on, but 20-year-old David Bowie slipped through The Beatles' fingers after a chat with Paul McCartney. So also did Freddie Garrity, front man of Freddie And The Dreamers, and The Remo Four, who mutated into one-hit wonders

Ashton, Gardner And Dyke. While a one-shot Apple single by Hot Chocolate was issued in 1969, did The Beatles commit the Dick Rowe error by auditioning and then rejecting Bamboo, a Swedish outfit that would connect genealogically with Abba?

While the record division was profitable, Lennon saw quickly that the rest of Apple was as dodgy as Rafferty's motor-car. In the kingdom of the brainless, the half-wit is king. That's how good intentions came to cradle deceit – with personality masquerading as principles, and power intrigues as crusades.

In his memoir, *As Time Goes By*,[56] Derek Taylor, an obvious choice to organise the press department, likened his two years at Apple to being "in a bizarre royal court in a strange fairy tale". Derek's urbane, sympathetic manner won many important contacts for Apple, but John Lennon's was, ostensibly, the loudest voice of reason amid the madness. The music press had been full of how "mellow" he was in his late 20s too. "It's a groove growing older," he told them.[57] He therefore gave the outward impression of a person completely in command of his faculties, an affluent and happily married family man in perfect health, smiling and laughing, with no worries.

Actually, he was deeply worried.

10 "The Change In Him Was Like Jekyll And Hyde"

By the end of 1968, Joe Average thought John Lennon was as mad as a hatter. In restaurants in which fame hadn't prevented The Beatles from dining, strangers on other tables would speak in low voices and glance towards him. Some insisted they could sense an aura of lunacy effusing from Lennon as others might the "evil" from the late child murderer Myra Hindley's eyes.

Was he really off his rocker? Had he – like Friedrich Nietzsche – lost his mind during an unremitting contemplation of his own genius and glory?

Previously, he had seemed to teeter on the edge of insanity – or, if you prefer, craziness – as epitomised by Merseyside polymath Adrian Henri witnessing him lying on the floor of a local pub, pretending to swim. Told by the landlady to stop, Lennon replied that he daren't because he'd be sure to drown. Some of his scrapes later in Hamburg and after he'd taken acid were on a par with this – but he seemed lucid enough in interview, and, in all respects, he appeared sane to Cynthia.

Neither of them were infatuated teenagers any more, holding hands around Liverpool. Now all such pretty fondnesses had long gone. Circumstances had obliged him to marry her – though, had he been reading Nietzsche in 1962, Lennon may have stumbled upon and agreed with the German philosopher of irrationalism's personal credo: that marriage and family are incompatible with a life of constant creativity. In other words, domesticity is the enemy of Art. Beatle John the rock 'n' roll bohemian didn't believe in wedlock, but Woolton John the nephew of Aunt Mimi went ahead with it. For him and Cynthia, therefore, there had never been much hope. He could have, but didn't make enough of their relationship.

That isn't to say he didn't care about the mother of his child – for all the confusion there had been since 1963 between Lennon the husband and father and Lennon the "available" pop star. Neither was he immune to twinges of conscience as the enormity of what he was about to do sank in – but, by mid-1968, he had no apparent option but to burn his boats as far as he was able and either instigate a new beginning or anticipate a fall from grace by destroying his former self. In the end, he did both.

To a journalist's tape recorder, he had declared his love for Yoko Ono, a Japanese–American who many still see as walking evidence of her own conjecture: "You don't need talent to be an artist."[58] As some mug with a pocketful of money, John had been introduced to her on 9 November 1966 during a preview of her *Unfinished Paintings And Objects* display at the gallery attached to the Indica bookshop. Charmed by the bewildering exhibits, he was the anonymous sponsor of Yoko's *Half Wind Show* at another London gallery, taking a benevolent interest in her activities, past and present. Because she was doing a turn there, he was among promenading onlookers at the "Fourteen Hour Technicolor Dream", a mixed-media extravaganza – all flickering strobes and ectoplasmic light projections – at Alexandra Palace on 29 April 1967.

Yoko had captured his heart during a period when, according to Barry Miles, a vulnerable John was in the throes of a nervous breakdown, informing Miles later that "I was still in a real big depression after *Pepper*. I was going through murder."[46] Yoko – who'd made the more non-committal statement that she was then "very fond"[59] of John – was a most unlikely Morgan le Fay-esque figure. If it was a *Carry On* film, you'd see an ecstasy of off-camera bodice-ripping that fateful night in May 1968 when Yoko was invited by her secret admirer to Kenwood when Cynthia was away. Just before the closing credits roll, Yoko turns a furtive key on the bedroom door and winks at the camera to maybe a melodramatic flash of lightning.

If it was a romantic novel, however, there'd have been an abrupt and inexplicably tearful reconciliation with Cynthia – followed, no doubt, by nature taking its course – but things don't happen like that in books. At least, they didn't to Cynthia.

Lennon's behaviour was to puzzle and then infuriate what was left of the Cynthia Lennon Fan Club after he left her and Julian to move into a London flat with his new love – and at this point, the story becomes as much Yoko's as John's, and the enigma of their liaison has only deepened since.

Like most of their fans, The Beatles' authorised biographer, Hunter Davies, blamed – and continues to blame – "the arrival in John's life of Yoko Ono"[22] for the end of the group. At the time, a perturbed *Beatles Monthly* had passed her off as John Lennon's "guest of honour"[60] after he brazened it out by escorting her to London's Old Vic on 18 June 1968 to catch a National Theatre adaptation of part of *In His Own Write*. *Two Virgins*, the Bed-Ins and further "happenings" were to follow swiftly.

"The change in him was like Jekyll and Hyde," sighed a still saddened and perplexed Cynthia in 1997. "John would have laughed at himself years before if he could have seen the future. Before he met Yoko, there was an item in *The Times* about her film, *Bottoms*" – myriad naked human buttocks in close-up – "and John said, 'Look at this mad Japanese artist. What will they print next?!' So his attitude then was she was a nutcase – and I agreed. I'm not a conceptual artist. When I look at things, I like to understand what I'm looking at."

For schoolgirl subscribers to *Beatles Monthly*, Yoko was destined to turn into pop's cross between Wallis Simpson and Beryl Formby, who watched her henpecked husband, George, the Lancashire music-hall entertainer, like a hawk, and ruled him with an "iron petticoat". However, in the world of Art – and music – Ono was already a Tracey Emin *du jour* via exhibitions that embraced, say, an all-white chess set and an apple with a £200 price tag, and an event in Liverpool's Bluecoat Chambers, where she'd had different paying customers picking up pieces of a jug she'd just smashed. Other escapades included wrapping Trafalgar Square statues in brown paper, the writing of *Grapefruit* – a self-help book of stultifying inanity – and, of course, *Bottoms* (remade as *Four Square*).

Yoko had also tried to make it as a pop singer, actually sending demos to Island, a record label that went in for oddball ethnic material. She had, however, found a niche in the distant reaches of the avant garde through vocal gymnastics that owed much to the free choral babbling and odd tone clusters of modern "serious" composers Schoenberg and Penderecki as well as stubbornly chromatic *seitoha* (Japanese classical music).

Moreover, in the company of free jazzers, notably Ornette Coleman, she used her voice like a front-line horn – as she did at a performance on a Sunday in March 1969 at the University of Cambridge with musicians of the same kidney as Coleman. With Lennon at her feet, back to the audience, either holding an electric guitar against a speaker – causing ear-splitting spasms of feedback – or twiddling with some electronic device to create bleeps, flurries, woofings and tweetings to complement the peep-parps from Danish saxophonist John Tchikai, the clatterings of drummer John Stevens and Yoko's screeches, wails and nanny-goat jabberings.

They were cynosures of an unnerving stare from what looked like a gigantic photograph of silent and undemonstrative students. A minority absorbed it in a knowing, nodding kind of way, whilst blocking out an impure thought in the tacit question, "How could anyone like this stuff?" Everyone onstage, even Beatle John, was an artist after all, and it became obvious that the greater the effort needed to appreciate this squiddly-bonk music, the more "artistic" it must be.

After clapping politely when the row ceased, the highlight of the night was the opportunity afterwards to babble about how "interesting" it all was, this "spontaneous music" that was an avenue to drop names like Ornette, John Cage, Edgard Varèse and Luciano Berio. Once, when so many venues had been closed shops to The Beatles because of jazz, that had been the sort of attitude John couldn't stomach: that air of pitying superiority towards those who didn't like it – or enjoyed it for what was derided as "the wrong reasons".

It was sweet, however, to have checkmated McCartney in the game of hipper-than-thou one-up manship that had persisted between them since time immemorial. Once The Beatles had moved south, Paul had held the winning hand what with living in the heart of London while John dwelt on on his Weybridge stockbroker estate. This was exemplified by Paul being in thicker with, well, Berio after sitting through his electronic avant-gardenings at London's Italian Institute on 23 February 1966.

That evening, it had been too much effort for Lennon to drive the long and gradually more hated miles from Surrey.

His hand in that crazy, far-out music at Cambridge had been one in the eye for McCartney, but nowhere as much as Lennon and Ono's *Unfinished Music No 1: Two Virgins*, not least for its sleeve photographs of the pair naked, back and front, that pledged John to Yoko more symbolically than a mere engagement ring ever could. After a macabre fashion, it paralleled the front picture of 1963's *The Freewheelin' Bob Dylan*, showing the artist in casual attire ambling down a wind-swept New York street, arm-in-arm and happily in love with his then-girlfriend. Lennon and Ono too demonstrated that they didn't look much different from anyone else, but the intention of *Two Virgins* was more to do with magnifying the gap between its makers and the common herd – or in their mind, "us two and you lot" – which would soon include Ringo, Paul and George as well.

When auditioning unsuccessfully to join The Texans – later, Rory Storm And The Hurricanes – in 1957, Harrison as a 14-year-old had played and sung Gene Vincent's arrangement of a song from the 1920s, 'Wedding Bells'. Its hookline ran, "Those wedding bells are breaking up that old gang of mine."

"The old gang of mine was over the moment I met Yoko," concurred John Lennon. Forgetting about both previous *amours* and Cynthia, he continued, "It was like when you meet your first woman, and you leave the guys at the bar and you don't play football anymore and you don't go play snooker and billiards. Maybe some guys like to continue that relationship with the boys, but once I'd found *the* woman, the boys became of no interest whatsoever, other than they were like old friends – but it so happened that the boys were well known and not just the local guys at the bar."[2]

As well as an expression of this, *Two Virgins* was also, so he and Yoko explained, an Art Statement. Joe Average was, however, too bewildered to give an Art Reply.

On a rare visit to London just before Christmas that year, I noticed the back cover – you could see their bums – in the window of One Stop Records, a small West End record store renowned for being first with the latest sounds. Inside, I pretended to thumb through the wares nearest the window whilst squinting discreetly. The previous autumn, I'd bought the edition of *International Times* (*IT*), Britain's foremost underground organ, that had first impinged on the general populace via a minor media fuss about a centre spread of Frank Zappa stark naked on the toilet, but with his modesty strategically hidden. Partly as a result of this, both *IT* and its companion journal, *Oz*, had been subject to intense and unwelcome attention from the police. *IT* was raided mostly for its for sex contact ads, and the *Oz* saga climaxed at the Old Bailey after the notorious "Schoolkids" edition (to which my teenage self contributed four articles).

That lay two years in the future of when my eyes were searching for the front of *Two Virgins* in One Stop. I'd heard that San Francisco's groovy *Rolling Stone* – not yet readily available overseas – had dared to print both sides of the sleeve. Nevertheless, it is difficult to articulate how extremely shocking that first sight of Lennon's flaccid Beatle willy was to a 17-year-old product of a strait-laced, church-going upbringing – not unlike John's own ("Sunday School and all that"[27]) – in a Hampshire country town where the 1950s didn't really end until about 1966. John Lennon, the Moptop Mersey Marvel, couldn't have done it, but, by God, he had! How could he have been so rude? Whatever did his auntie think?

When *Two Virgins* appeared, the "hippy" musical *Hair* had opened in London. Its murkily lit "nude scene" was there for all to see the very day after stage censorship was abolished in 1968's Theatres Act. This would also allow a presentation by a band from Leicester, Black Widow, that featured a bare lady prostrate beneath singer Kip Trevor's sacrificial sword amid chilling screams and abundant spilling of fake blood.

Generally speaking, however, even the most scantily clad female on the jackets of the budget label Hallmark's *Hot Hits* series of carbon-copies of then-current smashes wore more than girls did then on a summer's afternoon on Margate beach.

Yet a *Hot Hits* photo (especially the one in which a blonde in a bikini grips a phallic fishing rod) was far more erotic than *Two Virgins*, as was *Oh Calcutta!*, a post-*Hair* revue that ran at the Roundhouse in Chalk Farm, embracing nakedness in clear light – and also, incidentally, an apposite comedy sketch about schoolboys masturbating together, penned by John Lennon, whose career summary in the printed programme ran, "Born October 9, 1940. Lived. Met Yoko 1966." In London's Underground stations at the same time, a poster promoting a newly released flick, *Till Death Us Do Part* – based on the BBC comedy series[61] – had an unclothed Warren Mitchell as Alf Garnett in pride of place (albeit covering up his genitalia with hands and tobacco-pipe) and a caption thanking John Lennon for "pioneering this form of publicity".

It resonated too at the reception following Cilla Black's wedding in 1969 to her longtime fiancé, Robert Willis. Reading a congratulatory telegram from John and Yoko, the bride got a cheap laugh by adding the addendum "Stay nude!" (the same scansion as 'Hey Jude' – get it?).

On 1 March that year too, whilst fronting The Doors at Miami's Dinner Key Auditorium, 'Lizard King' Jim Morrison's ritualised cavortings ended with his arrest for "lewd and lascivious behaviour". According to the group's keyboard player, Ray Manzarek, the former Albuquerque public schoolboy was sending up his sex-symbol status with a routine involving a towel, and may have accidentally exposed himself. Backstage opinion intimated that the consequent charge was trumped-up by local authorities, anxious to strike a blow for common decency against another anti-establishment icon that, since 1966, had been corrupting their children – who had often been as disgusted as their parents by his behaviour.

John Lennon's intimates had not associated penis display with one who, only three years earlier, had seethed, "You don't do that in front of the birds!" when he, Cynthia and the Harrisons had been confronted by a drunken Allen Ginsberg wearing only underpants – on his head – at a London *soirée* held on the beatnik bard's birthday.[62]

That was before LSD entered Lennon's life. *Two Virgins* might have been rooted in too much acid triggering onsets of self-imposed humiliations. He and Yoko were also to start on heroin, now a more popular chemical handmaiden to creativity for certain songwriters than hallucinogens. 1969's chart debut by David Bowie, 'Space Oddity', was regarded in some quarters as a paean to heroin, and a sense of longing rather than self-loathing emanated from the addict in 'Sister Morphine' by Marianne Faithfull, whose wretched bouts of heroin addiction would blight periodic comebacks now that 1965's 'Summer Nights' had waved her out of sight of the UK Top Ten forever. A newer female star, Linda Ronstadt, would brag that "I can sing better after shooting smack [heroin] in both my arms."[63] Yet there was strong hostility to drug culture from many musicians, both in interview and record grooves – such as those of Frank Zappa's later 'Cocaine Decisions', a swipe at a stimulant in more general use within the music industry in the 1970s.

It was feasible that, as well as consumption of hard drugs, John Lennon's conduct also had a connection with St Francis of Assisi, who was given to sometimes preaching the gospel in the nude as an act of self-abasing godliness. Though it was the sort of statement he might have made, it was not St Francis but Lennon who assured *Melody Maker* editor Ray Coleman, "I try to live as Christ lived. It's tough, I can tell you."[27] Furthermore, a few months prior to the cloak-and-dagger release of *Two Virgins* – and the day before he consummated his desire for Yoko in Weybridge – it was said that Lennon had summoned McCartney, Harrison and Starr behind closed doors in an Apple board room in order to proclaim himself the Messiah. He wasn't being funny ha-ha either.

Paul had been persuaded to write a commendation (if it was one) that called Lennon and Yoko "saints" for the *Two Virgins* cover, but he and his new girlfriend, Linda Eastman – a showbiz photographer from a family of US attorneys – were, reportedly, most offended by the entire affair.

Of all the other Beatle couples, Ringo and Maureen swooped most unquestioningly to Lennon's defence. The *Two Virgins* sleeve was, concluded Ringo, "just John being John. It's very clean."[64] Yoko became "incredible". No one doubted it either. "We'd be pleased when people realise that she's not trying to be the fifth Beatle," Starr continued[64] – though, when waiting to console Yoko before Lennon's cremation 12 years later, he was supposedly overheard to mutter, "It was her who started all this."[65] This indicated an adjustment of his previously stated opinion, as late as 1971, that her and John's *amour* had not taken priority over group commitments. "Ringo was a little confused," deduced Klaus Voorman, "because John's closeness to Yoko was sad to him. John and Yoko were one person, which was difficult for him to accept."[66]

George Harrison, however, wasn't confused at all. One day at Savile Row, he could no longer contain his resentment, particularly as Yoko was now taking an active hand in the running of Apple. She'd been the one, for example, who'd interviewed Freddie Garrity (!). George burst into the couple's office and came straight to the point. Naming Bob Dylan among those with a low opinion of Yoko, Harrison went on to complain about the present "bad vibes" within The Beatles' empire, which were correlated with her coming. "We both sat through it," said John, "and I didn't hit him. I don't know why."[2]

Soon, John's extreme broadness of gesture – which extended to changing his middle name by deed poll from "Winston" to "Ono" – was an embarrassment to the world outside The Beatles clique too. Perhaps the more resolute gentlefolk of the press got wind of the "Messiah" nonsense, because early in December 1969 it was reported in the *Daily Express* and then in several other domestic newspapers that John was "considering" an offer to play the title role in a forthcoming musical, *Jesus Christ Superstar*, but only on condition that Yoko star too as "Mary Magdalene". All this was a surprise to composer Andrew Lloyd Webber and his lyricist, a former EMI production assistant named Tim Rice, who issued a terrified denial straightaway.

The *Express* feature was, allegedly, the first John heard of the matter too, but he didn't mind. It gilded the image of him as the coolest cat ever to walk the planet, the most messianic symbol of hipness since Bob Dylan, the most way-out star in the firmament – though not a star in the sense of sending teenage girls into paroxysms of screaming ecstasy any more. *Two Virgins* had put paid to that – as articulated in the hookline of the topical disc "John You Went Too Far This Time" by Rainbo, alias Hollywood starlet Sissy Spacek: "Since I saw that picture, my love will never be the same."

A special "Groupies" edition of *Rolling Stone* in 1969 concerned female music-lovers renowned for evading the most stringent security barriers to impose themselves on rock stars. The more free-spirited of these "groupies" (not "scrubbers" anymore) remained interested in John Lennon sexually – "It'd be a privilege for him to even notice me," said one[67] – but others were wary of one who had mutated from object of desire to not so much a spoken-for all-father as a universal batty uncle: not a clown prince of pop like Freddie Garrity had been – far from it – but a Holy Fool, a sort of clown godhead of pop.

In reciprocation, a fur-coated woman had shouted, "You are a very holy man," when he and Yoko had emerged on 28 November 1968 from Marylebone Magistrates Court , where John had been fined after pleading guilty to possession of substances contrary to the provisions of the 1966 Dangerous Drugs Act, section 42.

He and a pregnant Yoko had been recipients of a Narcotics Squad pounce the previous month after they'd found a temporary refuge from self-aggravated media attention in a rented maisonette a few blocks from Regent's Park. Unacceptable to the officer in charge was John's excuse that the cannabis he and his men – and a sniffer dog – had discovered was the lost property of some earlier tenant, maybe Jimi Hendrix or novelist William Burroughs.

The first Beatle of three to be "busted", Lennon was no longer above the law, MBE or not. The rip-tide of the drama – "an offence of moral turpitude" – was to wash over his attempts in the next decade to settle permanently in the United States , but in 1968 he accepted it as part of life's small change and he didn't find the furore completely unwelcome.

He seemed so bound up in himself and Yoko that every occurrence and emotion was worth broadcasting to as wide a forum as possible, just as it happened – just as, in microcosm, Rory Storm was prone to do in the old days, ensuring that his birthday celebrations were public events, and being nabbed by a porter spray-painting "I Love Rory" on a wall at Bootle railway station.

With the means to go infinitely further, John Lennon ordered the issue on Zapple, Apple's short-lived "experimental" subsidiary label, of his second LP with Yoko, *Unfinished Music No 2: Life With The Lions*. The back cover was a *Daily Mirror* photograph of him with his arm around a distressed Yoko in the midst of policemen and morbid inquisitiveness outside the Marylebone court room. The disc's content, however, was concerned principally with Yoko's subsequent miscarriage – and included the dying foetus's heartbeat, which was offered to and rejected by *Student* magazine as a giveaway flexidisc.

Most self-obsessed of all was autumn 1969's *Wedding Album*. One side of this feast of entertainment was the two's repeated utterances of each other's name suspended over their own pounding heartbeats – though there was a blurry link, I suppose, with Marcel Duchamp's "ready-made" art and the provocation of Dada just after the Great War.

If that was the case, then *Self-Portrait* paralleled Duchamp's *Fountain*, a urinal with "R Mutt 1917" painted on it ("which is just out of this world", gasped John[2]). *Self-Portrait*, a 42-minute movie starring Lennon's famous cock – and some fluid that dribbled from it – was screened at London's Institute of Contemporary Arts in September 1969 as one of several British premieres of Warhol-esque films of similar non-events made by John and the more seasoned movie director, Yoko. Like other Ono–Lennon artistic collaborations during this period, most of them were laboured, inconsequential and generally misconstrued comedy. The chief exception was *Rape*, a disturbing hour or so of an obtrusive cameraman following an increasingly alarmed foreign student around London. *Rape* aside, however, some viewers tried to fool themselves that Yoko and John's celluloid ventures were quite absorbing in parts, even as others fidgeted in their seats.

Rape was broadcast on Austrian television on 31 March 1969, as just-married Yoko and John were completing their first "Bed-In for Peace". Now with centre-parted hair splayed halfway down his back, bearded to the cheekbones and defiantly round-spectacled, John had smoked a cigarette during a quiet, white-costumed wedding in Gibraltar on 20 March. It was followed at the Amsterdam Hilton's luxurious honeymoon suite by the Bed-In. They hoped that lying about for a week whilst entertaining the press would stop the atrocities in Vietnam and Biafra more effectively than any post-flower-power protest march or student sit-in.

Both the ceremony and the Bed-In were mentioned in 'The Ballad Of John And Yoko', The Beatles' final British Number One. That each chorus began with the interjection "Christ!" – him again – restricted airplay, and the entire narrative confirmed the Lennons' status as a Scandalous Couple on a par with Serge Gainsbourg and Jane Birkin, makers of that summer's 'Je T'Aime...Moi Non Plus', on which an easy-listening arrangement seeped incongruously beneath their grunts, moans, whispers and half-crooned lines like one that translates as "You are the wave: I, the bare island. You go, you go and you come between my loins" as prospects of imminent sexual climax increased towards the fade. In spite of an outright BBC ban, it ended Creedence Clearwater Revival's reign at Number One in Britain, and reaped even fatter harvests *sur le continent* (though it wilted at *Position Soixante-Neuf* – if you'll pardon my French – in the US Hot 100). 'Je T'Aime…' sold an eventual million copies and continued to fill dance floors with groping smoochers as surely as 10cc's 'I'm Not In Love' after it.

Ono and Lennon's canoodling went beyond the bounds of generally acceptable ickiness too. Moreover, to say things most people didn't want to hear or understand, they'd made their headline-hogging lives an even more open and ludicrous book with further eye-stretching pranks such as press conferences from inside kingsize white sacks; the slapdash letter to the Queen that would accompany John's renouncement of his MBE; sending acorns to world leaders; his scrawly lithographs of themselves having sex; and ordering the plastering of billboards proclaiming "War Is Over!" all over 11 city centres. The Ancient Greeks had a word for such conduct: *hubris*, which defies succinct translation, but alludes to a heroically foolish defiance rooted in a feeling that one is beyond the reaches of authority and convention.

In response, a lot of the "War Is Over!" signs were defaced within a day of their appearing. However, something those who did so could comprehend more readily, if not sympathise with, had emerged from another crowded "Bed-In" – this time in Toronto – where Lennon's 'Give Peace A Chance' was taped. Though "Lennon–McCartney" was given as the composing credit on the record label, this was his first smash – Number Two in Britain, 14 in the USA – without Paul, George and Ringo, attributed as it was to the ad hoc "Plastic Ono Band". The subsequent full-page advertisement in the music papers informed readers "*You* are The Plastic Ono Band!" Yet, over 30 years later, I still haven't received any royalties for 'Give Peace A Chance'. Have you?

Never mind, it was a catchy effort, even if the verses were just syllables strung together to fill enough 2/4 bars to separate each instantly familiar *omnes fortissimo* chorus – which if nothing else carried the message of the title across.

The contradiction between Lennon's twee projection of himself and Yoko as "Mr and Mrs Peace" and his beery unpleasantness towards members of The Terry Young Six, another act on the Helen Shapiro tour, raised a derisive laugh from the Six's keyboard player, Barry Booth, who recalled him as "a nasty bastard then". Moreover, prior to the Bed-Ins, John had been active only after a detached, pop-starrish fashion in verbal support of pacifism, sharing the general disenchantment with the hippie counter-culture following the Sharon Tate bloodbath and the general dissipation of flower-power idealism. He said as much in an interview with *Student*'s editor, Richard Branson, a former pupil at Stowe Public School, where The Beatles had played that curious recital in 1963.

Lennon had earned the approbation of *Student*'s leftish readership partly through the B-side to 1968's 'Hey Jude', 'Revolution'. However irresolute it would seem in retrospect, it was John's most far-reaching assessment in song of any of the cultural, political and other undercurrents pertinent to the culmination of the Swinging '60s – though there was also an abstraction of this in 'Revolution 9', the longest track on The Beatles' eponymous first Apple album – a double – which may be heard as a rendering in sound of one of Stuart Sutcliffe's latter-day paintings in that it was trying to express a unconscious emotion.

Selected at the insistence of Lennon, who created almost all of it with Yoko, only the recurring "number nine" announcement lends 'Revolution 9' even vague orthodox form – though Lennon was to aver that "It has the basic rhythm of the original 'Revolution' [a different take of the B-side that begins side four of *The Beatles*], going on with some 20 tape loops we put on, things from the archives of EMI. There were about ten machines with people holding pencils on the loops. I did a few mixes until I got one I liked. I spent more time on 'Revolution 9' than I did on half the other songs I ever wrote."[21]

This patchwork of noises that the man in the street wouldn't think of as musical is comparable to Varèse's *La Pòeme Électronique*, a montage commissioned to accompany an exhibit at the 1958 World's Fair in Brussels. This too was assembled literally second by second from seemingly random sources. 'Revolution 9' was lauded too by Barry Miles in the *International Times* as a send-up of John Cage's 'Fontana Mix', an 11-minute "chance operation" tape collage recorded in 1958 and a classic of its kind, like his more famous "silent piece", '4'33"', which requires a pianist to sit before a keyboard without touching it for that length of time. Coughs, the rustling of programmes and the huff of footsteps walking out of the auditorium are part of the performance.

'Revolution 9' ("an aural litmus of unfocused paranoia", concluded *Rolling Stone*[68]) reached a far, far larger audience than all its avant-garde antecedents combined – antecedents of which most of its buyers were unaware. Hence its dismissal as "rubbish" by those who were bored, irritated and, now and then, inadvertently amused by what they heard only as scribble between 'Cry Baby Cry' and 'Goodnight'. Others, including me, weren't so sure, and listened again – and again and again – until 'Revolution 9' reached out and held them forever.

The outlines between The Beatles and Lennon's undertakings with "Mrs Peace" were fast dissolving and yet widening the chasm between him and his old comrades. "I don't think you could have broken up four very strong people like that," countered Yoko. "There must have been something that happened within them – not an outside force at all."[21] The disbandment of The Beatles would connect with their own inner natures and desires – and when it dawned on them that not everything they did was great – but the new brides of John Lennon and Paul McCartney were among catalysts that enabled it.

With all pretensions of The Beatles' four-man brotherhood now gone, Yoko's constant and baleful adherence to John at Abbey Road entitled Paul McCartney to bring along Linda Eastman, soon to be Linda McCartney. While she and the older Yoko had both attended school in the same well-to-do New York suburb, they didn't have much else in common, although they were both to marry their respective English *beaux* during the same month. There were moments of congeniality, but generally the lukewarm rapport between the chief Beatles' immovable women was just one of Ringo's "little niggly things"[69], which cropped up as the group worked through *The Beatles* and then *Let It Be*: "the most miserable session on Earth", scowled John.[2]

Yoko and Linda, however, were but two guest participants as the group vacillated between the colour-supplement artwork of *Sgt Pepper* and a vain endeavour to get back to their Merseybeat womb. They were trying too not to alienate those for whom pop meant little until a belated admiration for a disintegrating Beatles' "joyful music-making that only the ignorant will not hear". Thus read a King's New Clothes-ish critique of the 'White Album' in *The Observer*.[70]

Perhaps the least "joyful" music they'd ever made, *Let It Be* was intended as purposeful veering away from the string quartets, backwards-running tapes, horn sections, sitars and Mike Sammes Singers of yore. The idea had been to tape nothing that couldn't be reproduced onstage. "It would be honest," so George Martin had understood, "no overdubbing, no editing, truly live, almost amateurish."[7]

It was, therefore, to be The Beatles pared down to just vocals, guitars, bass and drums, plus keyboards where necessary. These were fingered by Paul – and Billy Preston, whose joviality and energetic instrumental dexterity had first impressed The Beatles in 1961, when he was Little Richard's organist at the Star-Club.

No matter how deferential they were towards Billy during the making of *Let It Be*, The Beatles subjected George Martin – no longer the imposing figure he'd been in 1962 – to the same oafish discourtesies they were rendering each other. This was among reasons why he became as fed up with the project as they were.

Therefore, rather than a disinclined Martin, Phil Spector was drafted in to edit, spruce up and mix what was to be described as a "new-phase Beatles album".[71]

Of all of them, John Lennon and George Harrison had been the keenest on the record productions of this undersized if self-important New Yorker. He'd been hot property in the early 1960s for his spatial "wall of sound" technique, whereby he'd multi track an apocalyptic *mélange* – replete with everything, bar the proverbial kitchen sink – behind beehive-and-net-petticoat vocal groups The Crystals and The Ronettes and other artists who'd submitted to his masterplan.

In the wake of the British Invasion, he let it be known that he wanted to work with The Beatles – and several years later, they let him.

As heard on numerous bootlegs, Spector's raw material for *Let It Be* had resulted from weeks of loose jamming, musical ambles down memory lane and hitting trouble whenever John, Paul and George came up against each other's new compositions.

In keeping with a flagrant spirit of self-interest, discord and intrigue, anything that needed too much thought got a thumbs-down. The strained atmosphere had alleviated slightly with the wheeling-in of Preston, who also joined in the celebrated, and unannounced, afternoon performance – The Beatles' last ever – on the flat roof of 3 Savile Row on 30 January 1969.

Afterwards, the participants, their musical appetites ruined by the project as a whole, were tempted to jettison the frayed miles of *Let It Be* tapes, but the fastidious Phil's doctoring satisfied even – at least, in the first instance – Paul McCartney, albeit not the keenest Spector fan. Yet Paul was to demand – to little effect – that the *Let It Be* album be divested of the superimposed orchestral and choral grandiloquence he regarded as gratuitous frills that both attempted to smother ugly moments (such as Lennon's poor bass playing on 'The Long And Winding Road') and contradicted George Martin's original uncluttered production criterion. In the pungent words of Abbey Road engineer Glyn Johns, Spector "overdubbed a lot of bullshit all over it, strings and choirs and yuck".[12]

Johns – and McCartney – may have considered this the case with 'Let It Be' itself and 'The Long And Winding Road', but in a statistically commercial sense, these songs were triumphs in that, like the comparatively unvarnished 'Get Back', they both topped the US Hot 100 as spin-off singles.

Nevertheless, Spector was out of the picture when the team – Lennon, McCartney, Harrison, Starr and Martin – rallied for the *Abbey Road* finale, which the discerning Frank Zappa regarded as "probably the best mastered, best engineered rock 'n' roll record I've heard," albeit adding, "which has nothing to do with the material on it".[73]

When *Abbey Road* was hot off the press, John was approached to compère an open-air pop festival in Canada with a majority of olde-tyme rock 'n' rollers – Fats Domino, Little Richard, Chuck Berry, Gene Vincent and Bo Diddley – on the bill. Instead, he, Yoko and some hurriedly rehearsed Plastic Ono Bandsmen – guitarist Eric Clapton, drummer Alan White (from The Alan Price Set) and, on bass, Klaus Voorman – performed at midnight on Saturday 13 September 1969. Issued as *Live Peace In Toronto 1969*, their ragged set consisted mainly of 1950s classic rock, a nascent arrangement of 'Cold Turkey' – a forthcoming new Plastic Ono Band single – 'Give Peace A Chance' and Yoko's screech-singing.

Manning the barricades in front of the stage, the Hell's Angels stewardry called Ono and Lennon dirty names. In the wings, however, Gene Vincent was weeping with emotion as, overweight and in a grey-faced, boozy haze, he tried to forget both a worrying demand for maintenance from a former wife and certain knowledge that his now steadfastly painful crippled leg would have to be amputated.

The ill-starred Gene's appearance at Toronto astonished those who thought that he was already dead – and he would be within a month – but the bigger event for most was the Plastic Ono bash. Regardless of its content, it was enough for most of the 20,000-odd onlookers that it happened at all. If not on the scale of Moses re-appearing before the Israelites from the clouded summit of Mount Sinai, it was the proverbial "something to tell your grandchildren about": John Lennon's first major concert – the first by any Beatle – since the showdown at Candlestick Park.

For all that, the album sold but moderately, ie less than a million, while 'Cold Turkey' touched a high of between 10 and 30 in most charts by Christmas. Its B-side was Yoko's 'Don't Worry Kyoko (Mummy's Only Looking For Her Hand In The Snow)' – which could have been about anything – or nothing. However, a Beatle-ologist might conjecture that it was an exaggerated commemoration of John missing a bend and rolling over a hired Austin Maxi somewhere in the Scottish highlands during a brief holiday the previous July. Only one passenger – six-year-old Julian – escaped uninjured; Yoko, John and Kyoko, Yoko's daughter by a previous marriage, needed stitches.

Lennon found 'Don't Worry Kyoko' as potent as his adolescent self had Little Richard's 'Tutti Frutti'. Indefatigable work-outs of 'Don't Worry Kyoko' and 'Cold Turkey' filled his last stage appearance in Britain – with a Plastic Ono *Supergroup* containing the bemused likes of George

Harrison and The Who's madcap drummer, Keith Moon – at London's Lyceum ballroom in December 1969.

They'd done it for charity, even though no one was sure or not if Lennon was joking in a recent interview that he was "down to my last 50,000".[74] If ever he'd believed that his means were infinite, a letter from The Beatles' accountants had disabused him of this. His overdraft on the corporate account was £64,988 – and those of the other three were of comparable amounts. Worse, they'd lost control of Apple, where embezzlement and more open theft – such as that of the television and fitted carpet in the room the Lennons had commandeered at Savile Row – was rife.

Matters improved with the arrival and consequent purge by go-getting Allen Klein – "like the archetypal villain in a film", according to Ray Davies.[43] Klein's reputation as the "Robin Hood of pop" stood on his recouping of disregarded millions for his clients from seemingly irrefutable recording company percentages. Grateful clients included Bobby Vinton, Bobby Darin – and Phil Spector.

When the '60s started swinging, he'd made himself as useful to The Dave Clark Five, The Kinks and the uncut rubies – including The Animals and Herman's Hermits – that had been processed for the charts by freelance producer Mickie Most. The Rolling Stones had also bitten, grinned Most, after "they'd seen me driving around in a Rolls and owning a yacht, and started wondering where their money was going".[75]

Then Klein sought to win the biggest prize of all. He began hovering over John, Paul, George and Ringo like a vulture over a horseless cowboy with an empty canteen staggering across the burning desert. The subject of a small wager between Mickie's wife and Allen was that he'd be superintending The Beatles by Christmas 1967. Indeed, he'd gathered that Paul McCartney had been particularly impressed by his wheedling of an unprecedently high advance from Decca for the Stones two years earlier.

"Allen tried to come in when Brian was there, just as a business manager, and not run our lives," Ringo Starr would recall, "and Brian would have nothing to do with him."[52] Klein wasn't popular amongst other moguls as he wasted no time with small-talk while driving hard and unrelenting bargains on the telephone and in the boardroom. Nonetheless, though no love was lost between them, EMI chairman Sir Joseph Lockwood said, "In fairness to Klein, I ended up doing deals that I have never regretted."[76]

To Lockwood and the rest of EMI's executive body, Klein was everything that Brian Epstein wasn't. An observer of a routine ruled by the clock, he was an impassive, reflective type at home, who liked to distance himself from the office – and his clients because "otherwise you can really get on each other's nerves".[77] Yet, though to him pop was simply a commodity to be bought, sold and replaced when worn out, he wasn't self-deprecating about his knowledge and love of it, and when his wooing of The Beatles moved into top gear, Klein – like a certain Eastern mystic they'd encountered – underwent a crash-course in their music to better butter them up and, by 1969, his prophecy that he'd one day represent the group seemed to be fulfilling itself.

One of many bluff homilies attributed to Klein was "What's the point of Utopia if it don't make a profit?"[77] – and Apple was living proof. In its white-walled, green-carpeted headquarters, it had been a boom time for the more self-serving members of staff after they'd assimilated the heedlessness of their paymasters' expenditure and guessed – erroneously – that their means were limitless. A dam burst for a river of wastefulness to carry off gluttonous restaurant lunches; bottle after bottle of expensive liquor; illicit trunk calls to other continents; and wanton purchases of trendy caprices to lie swiftly forgotten in desk drawers. Not far from the truth would be a scene from 1978's spoof Beatles bio-pic *All You Need Is Cash*, in which a thinly disguised Apple Corps is pillaged by its employees while in the foreground its press agent chats to a television news commentator (played, incidentally, by George Harrison).

Out of his depth, John Lennon, with Yoko, had stuck to conventional office hours and played company director until the novelty wore off. Initially, he'd looked away from the revolting realities of the half-eaten steak sandwich in a litter bin; the receptionist rolling a spliff of best Afghan hash; the typist who span out a single letter (in the house style of no exclamation marks!) all morning before "popping out" at noon and not returning until the next day.

A great light dawned, but as neither John nor any other individual Beatle felt responsible for straightening out a venture that had taken mere weeks to snowball into chaos, the task had fallen to Allen Klein. Yet, though Lennon, Harrison and Starr yielded to Allen's contractual seduction, McCartney, once his champion, preferred to believe his lawyer brother-in-law's tales of Klein's sharp practices, high-handedness and low cunning.

McCartney, however, had to applaud the purge that discontinued sinecures and unviable ventures. Among the first within the organisation to go had been The Fool and Magic Alex – and there'd be no more "Unfinished Music" on Zapple, which "seized up before it really got going", grimaced George Harrison, "as with so many things at Apple". With commendable honesty, Harrison confessed that "both of the Zapple albums that did come out were a load of rubbish"[78] – namely *Life With The Lions* and George's own self-indulgence, *Electronic Sounds*.

Even Apple Records, starkly the enterprise's only money-spinner, was to be subject to inevitable cuts as unviable releases were cancelled, contracts unrenewed, and retainers stopped. After Mary Hopkin, Billy Preston and Badfinger's chart strikes for Apple were over, all that remained were The Beatles, together and apart.

In the offices too, personnel were subject to Klein's pruning stick; a clocking-on system was installed and the fiddling curbed. Overnight, glib unconcern had deferred to pointed questions. Why does that typist ring New Zealand every afternoon at 5:15pm on the dot? Why has so-and-so given himself a rise of £60 a week? Why is he seen only on pay day? Suddenly, lunch meant bringing in sandwiches instead of ordering a taxi to a fancy *brasserie* up West.

The Beatles had to bite back on sentiment when the ruthlessness also meant the casting adrift of old retainers by Klein, who, becoming something of a pop personality in his own right – as Epstein had been – confirmed in a *Melody Maker* interview his scheme "to make Apple financially successful and tailored to The Beatles' own specifications, but when you get a lot of energy wasted, it doesn't make for an efficient organisation".[79]

However, Allen Klein's streamlining of Apple was nothing compared to his renegotiation of a royalty rate with Capitol that amassed millions for The Beatles – albeit a Beatles that would disband within months.

11 *"An Escape Valve From The Beatles"*

In 1969, John Lennon won an *NME* poll in which other famous vocalists had each been asked to nominate their own three favourites. He was, debatably, as adept as he'd ever be by the late 1960s – as illustrated by the coda of the White Album's 'Happiness Is A Warm Gun' when he swerved cleanly into falsetto, having already built from muttered trepidation to strident intensity earlier in the song, tackling its surreal lyrics without affectation.

Yet self-doubt about his singing skills was to persist as an ex-Beatle who allowed Phil Spector and a later producer, Jack Douglas, to smother his vocals in what became a trademark echo, not only in the mix but even as he sang onto tape, refusing to open his mouth unless this was so. "After he left me, he did all his own distortion to his heart's content," lamented George Martin, "and I didn't like that. After all, the raw material was so good."[27]

With vocal vehemence taking precedent throughout over nicety of intonation, the studio version of 'Cold Turkey' was issued, so Lennon put it, "as an escape valve from The Beatles",[2] from whom he'd cast his net furthest. He was also absenting himself from press calls, business meetings and record dates just as the similarly lovestruck Stuart Sutcliffe had stints on the Top Ten stage in Hamburg.

As if in prophecy, John wasn't around for what seemed to be The Beatles' final recording date on 3 January 1970. In skittish mood during this tying-up of a *Let It Be* loose end, George Harrison – whose progress as a composer was among other factors that had led to the present state of affairs – indulged in a little taped tomfoolery at John's expense: "You all will have read that Dave Dee is no longer with us, but Micky, Tich and I would like to carry on the good work that's always gone down at (Studio) Number Two."[80]

On hearing of this, John grinned askance and told the wife – and Allen Klein, now his official manager. As fatigued as everyone else was of the fraternal animosity, Lennon had been relieved that the atmosphere during the making of *Abbey Road* was more co-operative than it had been for *Let It Be*. The subtext, of course, was a tacit agreement that *Abbey Road* was to be the last LP, and they might as well go out under a flag of truce.

Of each Beatle's preparations for the end, John's had been the most lucrative – on vinyl anyway. Even *Two Virgins* had inched into the lower reaches of the US album list. Yet, while *Let It Be* – issued out of chronological sequence after *Abbey Road* – lorded it over the likes of *Led Zeppelin II*, Andy Williams' *Greatest Hits* and the latest from The Who, Crosby, Stills, Nash And Young and Simon And Garfunkel in May 1970's charts, Paul McCartney's eponymous solo debut and Ringo's *Sentimental Journey* were in there too – though neither spawned a spin-off 45.

Like children of parents who stay together just because neither has yet quite enough motivation to leave, Ringo and George – who'd both quit briefly already – were waiting for one of the other two to marshall his words and dare the speech everyone knew he'd been agonising over for months. While *McCartney* was still at the pressing plant, Paul had been preparing a press release that almost, but not quite, proclaimed the end of The Beatles. Behind closed doors, he'd also been setting wheels in motion for the formal dissolution of Messrs Harrison, Lennon, McCartney and Starkey as a business enterprise. Yet months before the writs were served, John had slipped a teasing "...when I was a Beatle" into an interview with *Disc*,[81] and, feeling as little regret, had announced privately his own exit well before Paul – though this had been hushed up, mainly for fear of it cramping Allen Klein's bullying of Capitol.

Having said it at last, much of the tension of the preceding months had flowed from John Lennon. An unsettled chapter in his life had just ended. If a lot of his problems had been self-aggravated, it had been a stressful and demanding time that he wouldn't wish on anyone else. Now he could get on with the rest of his life. How could he have known then that he had only ten years left?

Moreover, having soundtracked the 1960s, he and the others wouldn't be able as solo stars and ex-Beatles to so minister to the next decade when all but the most snowblinded would understand how ordinary, even disagreeable, the mere mortals behind the myth could be. "George was the most normal and friendly of men," said Richard Reed, the architect who restored Harrison's newly purchased mansion in Henley-on-Thames. "He introduced me to John Lennon. He was shorter than I expected and not as pleasant as George. He just shook my hand and turned away."[82]

In the wake of February 1970's echo-drenched 'Instant Karma' – recorded and mastered within a day of its composition – I discovered quite early on how yawnsome Lennon was becoming via an associated interview headlined "Shut Up And Listen!: The Thoughts Of Chairman John" in *Record Mirror*.[83] What I could not articulate to myself then was that I was being tested by a horrified realisation of being unendurably bored by his pontifications about The Plastic Ono Band, his and Yoko's new short haircuts, his peace mission and an oscillating commitment to other worthy (or not) causes – the *Oz* trial, say, or the clearing of convicted murderer James Hanratty – he was espousing with varying degrees of pragmatism at the rate of roughly one a week.

Readers paid attention, however, because, even as 'Power To The People', his first 45 as a *bona fide* ex-Beatle, penetrated the UK Top 40 on 20 March 1971, somewhere in such discussions Lennon might fan the dull embers of The Beatles' future, which were becoming duller by the day. While clouds of litigation gathered, he and the others had been "tight, nervous, everyone watching everyone else", noticed the forgiving Cynthia, who, before her ostracism from that most innermost of 1960s in-crowds, was "at home" one afternoon for guests that included her increasingly distant Beatle pals and ex-husband.

Yet the illusion of reconciliation that was *Abbey Road* had tricked the general public into believing that The Beatles weren't over. Indeed, until well into the 1970s, not a week would pass without some twit or other asking John, George, Paul or Ringo when the four of them were going to get together again in the studio. It was seen as almost inevitable by even the most marginally hopeful outsider for whom the concept of collecting every record The Beatles ever made was not yet economically unsound. Thus an ex-Beatle was assured of at least a minor hit, even with substandard merchandise.

In 1976, when all four happened to be on the same land mass at the same time, they would be tempted to call the bluff of Lorne Michaels, producer of *Saturday Night Live* (a TV satire transmitted from New York), who said that, if they agreed to play together before his cameras for the prescribed Musicians' Union fee, he'd squeeze them onto the show. Depending on whose account you read, unfortunately – or, perhaps, not so unfortunately – Lennon and McCartney ordered a taxi, but decided they were too tired. Alternatively, Paul, Ringo and George arrived for the show, but John's chauffeur drove to the wrong studio, thereby capsizing what might have been the ultimate practical joke.

As things turned out, a Ringo Starr album of 1972 would be the nearest the living members would ever come to a reunion on disc, embracing as it did compositions and active participation by all four, albeit not at the same time. Lennon's main contribution, 'I'm The Greatest', came close as it featured himself, Starr and Harrison at Los Angeles' Sunset Sound Studio. McCartney had been amenable to pitching in too, but was refused a US visa owing to a recent conviction for possessing narcotics, which had been seized during a European tour with Wings, his new outfit, in which Linda fingered the keyboards.

Entitled *Ringo*, the LP was coloured, therefore, as a bastardised Beatles collection, supplemented as it was by Klaus Voorman's *Sgt Pepper*-esque lithograph and Starr's teasing insertion of the odd Lennon–McCartney song title into its lyrics. That the Fab Four were theoretically together on the same piece of plastic was sufficient to feed fans' expectations that soon everything would be OK again, and The Beatles would regroup formally to tour and release the chart-toppers that John and Paul – all friends again – would be churning out once more.

Pressed on the subject, glam-rock overlord Gary Glitter hit the nail on the head: "They'll have to come back as a bigger creative force than before, which will be very difficult indeed."[84] As difficult had been

Muhammad Ali regaining his world heavyweight title in 1975. Possibly, The Beatles might have regained theirs, even though the world had become wiser to their individual weaknesses – and the fact that, after picking and choosing from both illustrious chums and the trendiest and most nonchalantly squeaky-clean studio musicians, none of them would ever accomplish what The Beatles, for all their casually strewn errors, had committed to tape instinctively and without complacency.

With their wealth now secure, John, Paul, George and Ringo were all above the tour-album-tour sandwiches incumbent upon poorer stars, and each could wait until he felt like going on the road again or making a new record. However, an unkempt-looking Lennon still took the trouble to plug 'Instant Karma' – a "live" vocal over a backing tape – twice on *Top Of The Pops*, with that creepy Yoko next to him on a stool, either blindfolded and holding up her scrawled signs with PEACE, SMILE, BREATHE and other cryptadia on them, knitting a jumper, or mouthing silently into a microphone. Weird, eh?

Yet George Harrison, the former Beatle least addicted to the limelight, had been first off the starting line after sifting through a backlog of around 40 compositions for a new LP, a double, even a triple if he felt like it – which he did. This he titled *All Things Must Pass*, which was completed with more than a little help from an insufferably smug cabal of "heavy friends" and Phil Spector applying his spent "genius" to the console.

The first *All Things Must Pass* single, 'My Sweet Lord', sold millions, certainly more than 'Instant Karma', but both were reflective of a turn-of-the-decade fad for spirituality. Born-again fervour saw evangelical marches up high streets, the Bible on hip bookshelves, the Scriptures quoted at parties, and record deals for outfits like The Water-Into-Wine Band, from England's West Country, whose come-to-Jesus output was epitomised by 'Song Of The Cross', a 1971 album track that was quite moving in a *Ben Hur*-ish sort of way. On the other side of the same coin, Graham Bond led an early 1970s unit, Magick, which focused on his fascination with the occult and was as different from The Graham Bond Organisation, once the toast of London's mid-1960s in-clubs, as the Moon from the Earth.

The same comparison might be made between Lennon's first post-Beatles album and *Abbey Road*. Like its vinyl companion, *Yoko Ono/Plastic*

Ono Band, John Lennon/Plastic Ono Band was the cathartic outcome of a course of Primal Scream therapy under Los Angeles psychologist Dr Arthur Janov. Its basic premise, that all neuroses stemmed from deprivation of parental love, enabled John to look up from the bottom of his 30-year-old pit and imagine that he saw a strip of blue sky with God peering over the edge. It wasn't Him but the good doctor who made a half-hearted attempt to film a sitting with the famous pop star for use, he said, in a documentary – presumably to rope in further well-heeled patients.

John would be smiled in and smiled out of such consultations, which overflowed with extravagant lamentations and, ideally, rejoicings too. All the pain John had been carrying since the departure of his father and the death of Julia was supposed to disappear like the sack of woe falling from Christian in *The Pilgrim's Progress*.

With the starkest instrumentation, and the exhilaration of the impromptu prized more than technical accuracy, the Primal Scream experience came to a head in the songs he'd written for *John Lennon/Plastic Ono Band*. There was also a point of contact with Sleepy John Estes, Lightnin' Hopkins and other black bluesmen who trafficked in individual visions of an immediate world, about which they strove to say enough without too much lingering intimacy or any of that "oh gawd!" tweeness that characterised Melanie, Nick Drake and any other precious post-Woodstock balladeer, seated singing to a guitar and beaming a small, sad smile every now and then.

John's personal exorcisms, like 'Mother' and 'Isolation', mingled with stark rejections of former heroes and ideals – notably in "God" – and 'Working Class Hero', an acoustic ballad that railed against the mysterious "they", and got itself banned from most daytime radio stations for its use of the f-word, even if Lennon was no more the salt of the earth than Mick Jagger, also a scion of privet-hedged suburbia. He came on even more falsely as a workin' class 'ero, albeit in an affected raw Cockney instead of thickened Scouse.

Ripe language and soul baring were apparent in Lennon's newspaper interviews too – as was the almost audible snigger whenever he sniped at McCartney. His old comrade was pilloried further in 'How Do You Sleep' from 1971's *Imagine*, though the two had still been on speaking terms, with John ringing Paul when the track was on point of release. By contrast, *Imagine* also contained paeans of uxorious bent (such as 'Oh Yoko', 'Oh My Love' and the apologetic 'Jealous Guy') as well as a utopian title track, fairy-dusted with strings, that, for better or worse, was to endure as Lennon's most memorable post-Beatles opus.

'How Do You Sleep' had had George Harrison in support on lead guitar – and the month before the release of *Imagine* in September 1971, George was to invite John to participate in his Concerts *For Bangla Desh* in New York, but only on the understanding there'd be no place in the set for a number or two from Yoko as well. As the evil hour when her husband was actually going to perform without her crept closer, the humidity in New York thickened to what The Lovin' Spoonful had sung about in 'Summer In The City'. No breeze blew, and Yoko's forehead and upper lip was bestowed with pinpricks of sweat. It was weather that breeds maggots in dustbins and Ono's tantrum was so violent that, crushing his spectacles in his fist, John had slammed out of their hotel for the next flight back to Europe.

Harrison's giant step for Bangla Desh took place regardless and, in one throw, he outshone all the Lennons' more mystifying tactics to right the wrongs of mankind. Perhaps in a spirit of resentful competitiveness, John spoke briefly of a Wembley show for a worthy cause with him, Yoko and their sort of people instead of George and his crowd.

No time was better for Lennon to be charitable on such a scale. With *Imagine* soon to be at Number One in the States, no time was better either for him to make hay with a world tour too, but both ideas – if they were ever even considered seriously – had been jettisoned by the time he left his country of birth forever for the United States on 3 September 1971.

The first album – a double – from his "American period" was 1972's *Sometime In New York City*. He and Yoko were backed by Elephant's Memory, a local band fresh from a maiden Hot 100 strike. This joint venture also embraced excerpts from both the Lyceum extravaganza and a guest spot at the Fillmore East with Frank Zappa's Mothers Of Invention. Nevertheless, apart from the odd inspired moment, notably a driving revival of The Olympics' 'Well (Baby Please Don't Go)' with

Zappa, the kindest critics agreed that *Sometime In New York City* was documentary rather than recreational.

The essence of it was slogan-ridden musical journalism that had less in common with 'John You Went Too Far This Time' than the likes of 'He's Gonna Step On You Again' and 'Tokoloshe Man', UK hit singles the previous year by John Kongos, a South African – and a *Wedding Album*-period John Lennon lookalike – who freighted his songs with uncompromising lyrics born of the socio-political situation back home.

The music was strong enough for Kongos to ride roughshod over the principal worry about topical ditties: what becomes of them when they are no longer topical or the topic becomes tedious? That's how it was with John and Yoko's statements about the National Guard shooting rioting convicts in an upstate "correctional facility" ('Attica State'); a bloke receiving a ten-year gaol sentence for possession of an inappreciable amount of dope ('John Sinclair'); the troubles in Northern Ireland ('Sunday Bloody Sunday', 'The Luck Of The Irish'); and further current – and, generally, very North American – events and scandals.

Lennon was the central figure of one such *cause célèbre* himself. Though respected – or at least patronised – by powerful allies, his attempts to settle on US soil were hindered by, purportedly, ceaseless official harassment provoked by anti-government sentiments on *Sometime In New York City*, and his and Yoko's active part – an acoustic set – in a concert-*cum*-political rally in Ann Arbor, Michigan, on 10 December 1971 on behalf of marijuana miscreant John Sinclair, who was freed three days later.

The following August, the Lennons hosted a bigger spectacular, *One To One*, at Madison Square Garden for a children's charity, but that didn't serve as *quid pro quo* for the quashing of John's "moral turpitude" offence back in 1968. How can we ever know whether his splendid *One To One* effort – and a personal donation of $60,000 on top of the nigh-on $2 million dollars raised – was prompted by a simple desire to help or an ulterior motive? It was the same equation as those pop stars who pranced before the world at Live Aid in 1984.

Whatever the reason, it wouldn't wash with the US Immigration Department. This meant that John still had to keep reapplying for an extension of his visa to stay in the USA.

For all *Sometime In New York City*'s display of marital and artistic unity, the deportation notice that hung like a sword of Damocles over Lennon was among factors that were causing trouble in his marriage – so much trouble that he left Yoko in New York in 1973 for a 15-month "lost weekend" in California, where he lived with May Pang, her Chinese secretary, in a well-appointed ocean-side chalet, once owned by the Kennedys, in Santa Monica beneath the woodland sweep of the Hollywood hills. The place was open house for his circle of friends and friends of friends as well as callers like Alice Cooper, once and future Monkee Mickey Dolenz – and Paul McCartney.

Far more permanent a guest was Harry Nilsson, whose pop-star mystique had accumulated since *Aerial Ballet*, owing to out-of-focus publicity photographs and a reluctance to be interviewed. After Grammy -winning 'Everybody's Talkin'', more (mostly US) hits followed. The first of these was 'I Guess The Lord Must Be In New York City' from *Harry*, a third album that had been lauded in *Stereo Review* as "America's equivalent of *Sgt Pepper*".[85]

Surprisingly, Nilsson chose an interpretation of ten Randy Newman songs for his next album. After the market failure of *Nilsson Sings Newman* and an overlooked score for the film *Jenny*, he signed briefly – and never again – with a management company who procured him a role as a wandering folk singer in an episode of the television series *The Ghost Of Mrs Muir,* but "it was awful". He was of the same opinion of Otto Preminger's *Skidoo*, "possibly the worst film ever", but sodden with big names such as Groucho Marx, Mickey Rooney and George Raft – and a Nilsson soundtrack. Next came his "treatment" for *The Point*, the first ever feature-length cartoon film for television. It won many awards, and yielded another US chart entry in 'Me And My Arrow'.

Then Nilsson enjoyed a major international breakthrough (if mixed reviews) with 1971's *Nilsson Schmilsson*, recorded in London in June 1971 with help from famous mates. This contained three hit 45s, 'Without You' (a British and US Number One, written by two members of Badfinger), 'Coconut' and 'Jump Into The Fire'. He liked England enough to live there for a while, dwelling in the exclusive metropolitan flat where John and Yoko had holed up during the divorce from Cynthia – and where Keith Moon was to die. Some 50 old folk from a nearby Darby and Joan club would be featured as the choir on 'I'd Rather Be Dead' on *Son Of Schmilsson*, which, Nilsson's commercial tide-mark, brought another US Top 30 single, 'Spaceman'. The album was promoted in Britain via *Nilsson In Concert*, which, on the proviso that there would be no studio audience, was taped and shown on BBC2 – along with *The Point* – on New Year's Day 1972.

He failed to consolidate his success owing to an unsound decision to record *A Little Touch Of Schmilsson In The Night*, an album – possibly satirical – of orchestrated standards like 'Over The Rainbow', 'Makin' Whoopee' and 'As Time Goes By'. Produced by Derek Taylor, rejected tracks included 'Auld Lang Syne', 'I'm Always Chasing Rainbows' and 'Hey Jude'. Nilsson also overhauled selections from his first two LPs – as *Aerial Pandemonium Ballet*. I dare say it's heresy to say so to those in a 1960s repetend, but in nearly every case, it was a change for the better.

Yet, however much his critical standing had, on balance, improved, Nilsson's marriage, like John Lennon's, was failing. In much the same boat, Ringo Starr also strung along with John and Harry for three-in-the-morning bar-hopping followed by late-afternoon mutual grogginess by the Santa Monica swimming pool. Joining in the fun too was Keith Moon, The Who's chief show-off, whose buffoonery would often deteriorate into a nonsensical frenzy and, eventually, it would make headlines: explosives in hotel suites, slashing his wrists at the drop of a hat, and applying a lighter to his £150 pay packet for a day's film work (in days when £150 was worth something).

After accidentally running over and killing his chauffeur in 1970, Keith began punishing up to four decanters of spirits a day. More likely to fling a bottle at a television screen as rise from the armchair to switch it off, his fee for his last UK tour with The Who would be a paltry £40 on subtracting compensation for damage he'd inflicted along the way.

The instant fortune that had come his way since insinuating his way into the group in 1963 permitted Moon to think nothing of such costly indulgence. Mal Evans, however, was obliged to be more circumspect when, missing the activity and reflected glory of being a Beatles runaround, he left the family home in Surrey for sunny California, where, imagining his former masters needed him still, he rented an apartment near Santa Monica.

With Mal on board, the gang and its hangers-on were regular frequenters of topless bars, and were prone to gatecrashing parties and kerb-crawling. It wasn't uncommon for any one of them to wake with a hangover in a strange bed, unable to recollect the circumstances that had brought him there. Just as stories about Lennon in Hamburg had improved with age, so too did those of the Santa Monica coterie's escapades. Among these was one evolving from Moon coming across his boyhood hero, surf guitarist Dick Dale, at the Whiskey-A-Go-Go. "I was in the middle of a song," related Dick, "when he walked up on stage with Mal Evans. He was stoned, and he grabbed the mike right out of my face and said, 'Dick Dale, I'm Keith Moon of The Who.' Who? I'd never heard of The Who, but he told me – and everyone else – that he'd got John Lennon and Ringo on his solo album, *Both Sides Of The Moon*, and if Dick Dale didn't play on it, he'd junk the whole project."

As dilettantish were projects like Nilsson's slovenly *Pussycats*, which got underway simply because he, his Irish girlfriend, Lennon and May Pang "were sitting around with nothing to do, so we said, 'Let's do an album.'" With Starr, Moon and all the usual shower, he and producer John wrapped up *Pussycats* in New York after the sessions in Los Angeles had collapsed in a fog of drug abuse, which was discernible on a record that veered fitfully from long, leaden melodies to strident but oddly flat cracks at such as Dylan's 'Subterranean Homesick Blues', a mickey-taking 'Loop-De-Loop' – a fly-by-night rival to the Twist by one Johnny Thunder[86] – and a 'Rock Around The Clock', which was "speedy" in every sense of the word.

On the swift follow-up, *God's Greatest Hits* (retitled *Duit On Mon Dei* to placate the record company), Nilsson and his accomplices were also audibly half-seas over in an assortment of sub-'Without You' *Lieder* and unfunny gabblings on such as 'Good For God' and other perpetuations of an arrogance that encapsulated at its most loathsome the self-destructive disdain of the "superstar" for the record-buying public.

Further endeavours to stay the phantoms of middle age included Ringo securing an actress much given to exposing her bust, to recite Shakespeare during John's 34th birthday celebrations, and John's excessively worshipful and inebriated audience with Jerry Lee Lewis – whose own over-indulgence, brushes with the law and extreme domestic ructions had only enhanced the legend.

More widely reported was Lennon's ejection on 12 March 1974 – two years to the day after his US visa was revoked – from west Los Angeles' Troubadour, where, whilst drinking heavily, he had been constantly interrupting a show by The Smothers Brothers with interjections that included swearing and a recurrent "I'm John Lennon!" There were also allegations that he had assaulted both the comedy duo's manager and – with a sanitary towel attached to his forehead – one of the night club's waitresses, who was to file a complaint against him to the city's district attorney. Once outside the building, Lennon instigated another scuffle with a waiting photographer.

John managed to keep a civil tongue in his head the following night, when he and May Pang attended an American Film Institute dinner in honour of James Cagney, and a few weeks later, when he got together with Paul McCartney for a chat in the light of appeals from the United Nations for them, Ringo and George to do their bit for the Vietnamese boat people. There'd also been someone with more money than sense who was ready to shell out $50 million for just one more Beatles performance, even if there was a danger that what he'd hear might not be magic, just music.

Lennon was then in the throes of producing *Pussycats* at Los Angeles' suburban Burbank Studios, whilst taping demos back at Santa Monica. "We picked songs off the top of our heads and just did them,"[21] he shrugged. This strategy was very much in force when McCartney, staying at the Beverly Hilton Hotel, looked in – with Linda – at what were becoming fiascos at Burbank on Thursday 28 March 1974. Paul helped in trying to salvage an arrangement of 'Midnight Special', which was once in The Quarry Men's skiffle repertoire, and was invited to a musical evening the following Sunday at Lennon's house.

Present too would be Nilsson, guitarist Jesse Ed Davis – Eric Clapton's understudy at the Concerts *For Bangla Desh* – "supersideman" saxophonist Bobby Keyes and blind singing multi-instrumentalist Stevie Wonder, Tamla Motown's cosseted former child star, who'd notched up his first US hit, 'Fingertips', in 1963. He'd been on the bill with Lennon for both the John Sinclair benefit and the One To One concert.

As there were so many distinguished participants at Santa Monica, it was decided to keep a tape rolling for posterity – and the inevitable bootlegs – on equipment borrowed from Burbank. With McCartney choosing to beat the drums, they cranked out an interminable quasi-reggae version of Ben E King's much-covered 'Stand By Me', a slow and raucous 'Lucille' and, with Wonder to the fore, a medley of Sam Cooke's 'Cupid' and 'Chain Gang'.

These were punctuated by various meanderings during which were heard the intermittent strains of Bobby Byrd's 'Little Bitty Pretty One' – revived two years earlier by The Jackson Five – and, beneath, improvised lyrics by Paul, Santo and Johnny's 'Sleepwalk' instrumental from 1959, as well as blues-derived chord cycles over which Lennon, who bellyached throughout about the low volume of his voice in the headphones, kicked off an extrapolation that touched on his immigration woes.

None of the sung or spoken dialogue was anywhere as entertaining as that on the fêted "Troggs Tape" (an illicit recording in London of a cross purposes studio discussion riddled with rude words) and, musically, the clouds parting on the gods at play over in California revealed nothing more remarkable than what you might hear whenever any idle session crew warms up with loose jamming not intended for public ears.

Regardless of quality, however, it – and 'Midnight Special' at Burbank – amounted to a Lennon and McCartney reunion of sorts, though it wasn't the harbinger of any permanent amalgamation. Yet, if time hadn't healed, there lingered still memories of the struggle back in Liverpool and its unbelievable consequence. McCartney let slip that he wouldn't mind working with Lennon again on a less casual basis, while John was now saying how wrong it had been for the group to have split so decisively.

What's more, though the lines drawn over Allen Klein were among reasons for it, all the ex-Beatles were now of the same mind about one who'd overseen the solo careers of Lennon, Harrison and Starr until 1973. That's when their mustering of legal forces supported a new willingness to credit provocative tales – not all of them true – by their friends and various of Klein's incensed former clients of shifty manoeuvres and artful transfer of cash into his own account, passed off later by Keith Richards as "the price of an education".[87]

Klein was, nevertheless, not as greedy as he might have been – on paper anyway. Compared to some of his peers, who'd made themselves entitled to over half of everything their artists earned, the Robin Hood of Pop took but a fifth of what he'd actually secured. Yet, as John, George and Ringo unravelled enough supposed evidence of "excessive commissions" from Klein's mazy balance sheets to justify a court case, so the counter-suing Allen, once a hero, had been dyed a villain of the darkest hue by the time the blizzard of writs settled the various incoming monies into complex but defined financial streams running towards the respective deltas of Klein and each involved ex-Beatle's present and separate business executor – that is, George's Denis O'Brien, Ringo's Hilary Gerrard and John's Yoko.

Yet, while administrative matters were being resolved, Lennon, McCartney, Harrison and Starr's very vacillation over a reunion in the studio and, less likely, on the boards, indicated neither destitution nor any real enthusiasm. John and Ringo went back to the woozy vortex of Santa Monica, Paul to Wings and the simple life on his Sussex farm, and George to an ill-judged North American tour.

John was the only former Beatle to send George a bouquet of first-night flowers, and the two had nattered affably enough at one post-concert party. At another, however, everything turned red as hell for Harrison, and he saw himself rounding on Lennon and the flat of his hand shooting out in an arc to make glancing contact with John's spectacles. These clacked onto the ground and, while John was grubbing for them, George was loud enough to be heard in Liverpool. The subsequent tongue-lashing streamlined what had become, in Lennon's estimation, "a love-hate relationship of a younger follower and older guy. I think George still bears resentment towards me for being a daddy who left home."[21] This time, the "hate" sprang specifically from John's procrastination over signing some papers relating to The Beatles – and that John hadn't taken up an open invitation to join George onstage one night during the troubled tour to do a turn as a surprise treat for the fans.

No more the tough guy that he'd never been, Lennon "saw George going through pain – and I know what pain is – so I let him do it".[27]

The hatchet was never quite buried, and, as the months turned into years, only infrequent postcards filtered between Harrison and Lennon. Other than that, they knew each other only via hearsay and stray paragraphs in the press – and John was to be wounded by the "glaring omissions"[21] of him from George's pricey autobiography, *I Me Mine*.[88]

This volume was published early in 1980 when a musical, *Beatlemania*, shattered box-office records in London's West End and a sign appeared outside Mendips – from which Aunt Mimi had long gone – reading OFFICIAL NOTICE. PRIVATE. NO ADMISSION. MERSEYSIDE COUNTY COUNCIL for the benefit of foreign visitors, mostly from the USA and Japan, pouring huge amounts into the English Tourist Board's coffers for conducted treks round Liverpool to such shrines.

By 1980 too, Beatles conventions had become annual fixtures in cities across the globe, complete with guest speakers, archive film and forums for fans to reveal "My Beatles Experiences" as well as trivia quizzes, "celebrity" discussion panels, showings of ancient film footage, sound-alike contests and continual community singing to acoustic guitars. Life-size displays of LP covers might enable you to "be photographed with the Boys", and a mock-up of Abbey Road studio plus 40 pre-recorded Xeroxes of Beatle backing tracks may cater for less tangible fantasies. Along a single corridor at one such extravaganza, I passed a Cynthia Lennon lookalike, a high-buttoned moptop and a Sgt Pepper bandsman.

All the major conventions hire groups that are, if anything, even more contrived than Los Shakers, The Beatlettes, The Monkees *et al*, with their big-nosed drummers, moon-faced bass players; handles like "Walrus", "Cavern", "The Blue Meanies", "Abbey Road" and "The Beetle Brothers"; and *raisons d'être* centred on impersonating the founders of the feast, note for note, word for word, mannerism for mannerism. On a global scale, the most famous are The Bootleg Beatles, formed from the cast of *Beatlemania*. Maybe the most accurate copycats anywhere, they cover every phase, from the coming of Ringo to the end of the Swinging '60s, via cleverly co-ordinated costume changes.

While the ex-Beatles themselves have proffered saleable artefacts for charity auctions at these events, none – bar Pete Best – has ever attended one. Instead, "special guests" have been drawn from old colleagues, former employees – and, scraping the barrel, authors of Beatle biographies. A typical example is Sam Leach, an unsung hero of Merseybeat when compared to the Brian Epsteins and Bill Harrys of this world. However, as perhaps the era's most adventurous promoter – the one responsible for John, Paul, George and Pete's terrible journey to Aldershot – Sam cut a popular figure at a 1992 convention in Chicago. The Yanks couldn't get enough of him retelling anecdotes from the old days in his lush wacker dialect, and presenting well-argued theories about the Liverpool beat explosion and its aftermath, whether on the podium in the ballroom or whilst signing books and posters at his stall in a memorabilia fleamarket, which dwarfed any in Britain, even Liverpool's *Merseybeatle* weekend.

Customers covered a waterfront and ranged from babes-in-arms to pensioners, but mostly young marrieds disenfranchised by post-*Abbey Road* pop and older individuals who once might have been part of a screaming mass as amorphous as frogspawn at this or that stop on a Beatles US tour. Since then, they'd settled into jobs and parenthood – but while 'She Loves You' or 'I Feel Fine' yet spins its little life away, balding Weybridge stockbrokers and face-lifted Minneapolis hairdressers will become irresponsible Swinging '60s teenagers again.

Nothing by The Beatles had ever been delcted, and because EMI/Capitol still owned the master tapes, it had been able to run riot with posthumous million-selling double albums like the all up-tempo *Rock 'n' Roll Music*, which, in the States, spawned a smash 45 in 'Got To Get You Into My Life', culled from *Revolver*. Meanwhile, Britain experienced the chart-swamping aftermath of 20 Beatles singles being repromoted on the same spring day in 1976, almost a quarter of a century after 'Love Me Do'. Perusing the UK Top 40, a correspondent from *Time* magazine enquired rhetorically, "Has a successor to The Beatles finally been found? Not at all – it is The Beatles themselves."[89]

12 "Who'd Want To Be An 80-Year-Old Beatle?"

Guest speakers at Beatles conventions are two-a-penny compared to the diehard fan who can tell you at a second's notice, say, the B-side of the Australian pressing of 'Cry For A Shadow'. Many doctors regard such a skill as a mental disorder, even giving it a name, Asperger's Syndrome. Being mad about The Beatles, however, is a more socially acceptable pastime – even obsession – than, say, accumulating information about donkeys' false teeth, collating the reference matrixes of electricity pylons or, as is the case of a lady from Sunderland, believing that, by entering the loins of her (now estranged) husband, the ghost of a certain country and western entertainer whose records she collected had impregnated her with the son she would have baptised "Jim Reeves".

How did yours start? Was it because your first remotely romantic encounter – a chaperoned kiss under the mistletoe – was soundtracked by The Dave Clark Five's 'Do You Love Me'? Maybe a patrol leader you had a crush on at Girl Guides mentioned that she was keen on Bolton Wanderers or Sean Connery. You plan your life and bank balance around a soccer team's away matches. You watch the same movie so often that you can recite the script by heart. You holiday in a different overseas resort every summer just to seek out and buy your favourite group's discs issued by an alien company. Attic floors groan beneath the weight of memorabilia.

The worst aspects of Beatles idolatry are likely to be represented forever by the homicidal Mark David Chapman – but, as Bob Dylan reminds us in 'The Times They Are A-Changin'', we shouldn't criticise what we can't understand. When John, Paul, George and Ringo landed in New York in 1964, Chapman was eight and living with his parents and younger sister in Atlanta, Georgia. He compiled the first of many scrapbooks that kept track of The Beatles' ever-unfolding career. By the time Mark's voice broke, every nook and cranny of his bedroom was crammed with Beatles' merchandise: pictures of them all over the walls, and piles of records with label variations, foreign picture sleeves and the canons of associated artists: the Word made vinyl in the comfort of his own home. His function then was to remain uninvolved directly, just to absorb the signals as they came.

For hundreds, thousands of hours, he'd file, catalogue and gloat over his acquisitions, finding much to notice, study and compare. Discs by The Beatles, corporate and solo, from different countries made the same sounds, but there were visual differences. When 'I Feel Fine' was released in the Netherlands, Dutch Parlophone was in the final months of using the old logo – with the firm's name in large capital letters across the top of the label, and an additional "45" prefix at the start of the catalogue number. The second pressing stuck to the same fundamental design, except that it was printed in a more compact typeface. This is most noticeable on the song title. Another intriguing feature is that "McCartney" is misspelt in the composing credits. The Dutch 'I Feel Fine' also had a push-out rather than solid centre.

Should you express polite interest, Mark would probably explain apologetically that nobody got to *look* at it, much less *hear* it. The Beatles wasn't about enjoyment any more, but being addicted as surely as someone else can be to heroin. Wanting to learn everything possible about them, no piece of information was too insignificant to be less than totally absorbing. Mark could dwell very eloquently and with great authority on his interest, but couldn't grasp why fellow pupils at Columbia High School were not as captivated. The ones kind enough not to look fed up regarded the rather pudgy youth in round John Lennon glasses as otherwise "just a real quiet, normal guy".[5] Descriptions of him by others ranged from "slightly eccentric" to "a creeping Jesus", but Mark had taken his Beatles' fixation too far now to care any more than a chimp in the zoo does about what the people looking through the bars think.

When he graduated in 1973, the Fat Owl of Columbia High had experienced both LSD and, fleetingly, the glory and the stupidity of being in a pop group. In keeping with a mood of the early 1970s, he was now professing to be a born-again Christian. Two years later, Mark was working amongst Vietnamese refugees on a reservation in Arkansas, pleasing his superiors with his diligence and aptitude for the most onerous of tasks. Through the love of a good woman, he was contemplating enrolling at a theological college. No longer outwardly living his life through The Beatles, it was a period that he'd recognise as the nearest he'd ever come to contentment.

Chapman's future victim, however, was in a bad state. Flitting between California and New York, John Lennon had grown fatter, if less publicly ridiculous. Glassy-eyed musings and vocational turbulence also slopped over onto albums like *Pussycats* and Ringo's *Goodnight Vienna* – with a title track by Lennon. Because both he and Ringo were enthusiastic listeners to Johnny Winter, a boss-eyed and albino Texan bluesman who'd had been catapulted from regional celebrity to the front page of *Rolling Stone*, Lennon contributed 'Rock 'n' Roll People' for 1974's *John Dawson Winter* album, a delayed reaction to a captivation with 1969's Grammy winning 'The Thrill Is Gone,' the only mainstream pop hit by BB King, one of the few surviving links between post-war blues and mid-1970s rock.

John's own *Mind Games* in 1973, however, was as so-so as *Goodnight Vienna*; yet *Walls And Bridges*, if rehashing some old ideas, still effused potent singles in ethereal 'Number Nine Dream' – which, as usual, climbed far higher in North American charts than anywhere else – and, also in 1974, the US Number One 'Whatever Gets You Through The Night'. This was recorded with help from Elton John, a now famous singing pianist, who had first become known to Lennon when Xeroxing the hits of others for EMI's *Music For Pleasure* budget label (to which *Mind Games* was to be consigned one day) before metamorphosing into a cross between Liberace and a male Edna Everage.

Another British star omnipresent in the States then was David Bowie, no longer a glam rocker, but touring as a blue-eyed soul man, a fair indication of the direction he was to pursue on his forthcoming *Young*

Americans album. It was through this that John Lennon made his most iconoclastic contribution to 1970s popular culture. As his "lost weekend" approached its Sunday evensong, he'd been invited to a Bowie session for a resuscitation of 'Across The Universe' – from *Let It Be* – in New York. There, he ended up co-writing 'Fame', *Young Americans'* infectious US chart topper, with David and an awe-struck Carlos Alomar, a highly waged guitarist of urgent precision and inventiveness. This and his apprenticeship in James Brown's employ qualified him for the house band at the trend-setting Sigma Sound complex, from which had emanated Philadelphia's feathery soul style earlier in the decade.

All three writers of 'Fame' were present at a Grammy awards ceremony at the Uris Hotel in New York on 1 March 1975. John was sporting a lapel badge that read "ELVIS" – who, back on the concert platform, displayed ardour for little but the most conservative post-Beatles pop. Moreover, in an amazing and ramblingly respectful letter to President Nixon, he had requested enrolment as a federal agent in order to fight "the Hippie Element".

Unconscious of his boyhood hero's reactionary tendencies, John Lennon – who evidently typified all that he detested – was seen at one of a dismayingly portly Memphis Flash's grandiloquent pageants at 20,000-capacity Madison Square Garden, where the King included songs that had fuelled the ex-Beatle's adolescent imaginings. His stock-in-trade, however, was mainly country pop ('Kentucky Rain', 'Sweet Caroline' *et al*) plus bursts of patriotism like 'American Trilogy' and just plain 'America' – and the last that John, like most people, would ever see of him would be in the white garb of a rhinestone cowboy *sans* stetson.

As regressive in its way as seeing Presley was Lennon's growing collection of Beatles bootlegs – dating as far back as rehearsals in early 1960 with Paul, George and Stuart – and recording 1975's non-original *Rock 'n' Roll*, its content telegraphed on the sleeve by a photograph of 1961 Hamburg vintage and the artist's own sentiment: "You should have been there".

Its spin-off single – which rose to Number 20 in the States, 30 in Britain – was another stab at 'Stand By Me'. As well as the Ben E King prototype from 1961, Lennon was also up against moderately successful covers later in the 1960s by Kenny Lynch and Cassius Clay (Muhammad Ali). Viewers of BBC 2's *Old Grey Whistle Test* on 18 April 1975 were treated to an *in situ* film of Lennon at the microphone in New York's Record Plant, delivering both an exaggerated broad wink at the camera and 'Stand By Me' with its curiously stentorian vocal. Neither were very appealing.

Having gone full-cycle professionally with this plus other favourites that The Beatles may or may not have performed in the Hamburg era, and a greatest hits collection entitled *Shaved Fish*, Lennon chose to take a year off to master his inner chaos and take professional and personal stock. At a press conference back in 1964, he'd answered a question about retirement with a rhetorical "Who'd want to be an 80-year-old Beatle?"[90] Well, he was nearly halfway there now.

Reunited with Yoko – who'd been with him at the Grammy Awards at the Uris Hotel – John was finally granted US residential status. His and his wife's happiness was completed by the arrival of their only surviving baby, Sean, by caesarian section on John's 35th birthday. The very proud father judged this to be an appropriate moment to extend the "year off" indefinitely to become Yoko's quasi-incommunicado "house husband" in the apartments they'd purchased in New York's snooty Dakota block. This retreat was, he felt, the "karmic reaction" to the holocaust of pop, summed up by his much-quoted, "Don't bother trying to make it, because when you do there's nothing to make".[91]

Besides, the gang had broken up long ago. Having gained no contentment from following John and Ringo to California, Mal Evans's slaughter on 5 January 1976 by gun-toting police – after a woman alleged he'd threatened her with what turned out to be an air-pistol – was said by some to have been a form of suicide.

While Mal's extinction was unexpected, few were caught unawares entirely on 7 September 1978 by Keith Moon's body's final rebellion after a lifetime of violation. As he drifted away on the tide of twice the recognised lethal intake of a potion to combat his alcoholism, his last utterance was to tell his girlfriend to get lost.

However, with remarriage and the birth of his eldest son, Harry Nilsson – as heavy a drinker as Moon – was perhaps the first of the Santa Monica clique to pull back from the abyss. Artistically, he proved capable still of the odd startling moment, such as the composition of 'Easy For

'Me', the strongest track on Ringo Starr's *Goodnight Vienna,* but his living rested mostly on earlier achievements, exemplified by a 1978 stage adaptation of *The Point* in London's West End starring former Monkees Mickey Dolenz and Davy Jones.

Nilsson continued to grind out one album per year until the RCA contract expired. On 1980's *Flash Harry,* he was to mobilise illustrious contemporaries again, among them John Lennon – though their friendship had cooled because he was regarded by then as the proverbial "bad influence" by Yoko. Indeed, he passed much of the next decade jet-setting whilst nursing debilities not unrelated to the stimulants that had been common currency amongst the "superstar" elite in the 1970s.

A proposed 1993 album contained a revival of The Platters' 'Only You' – a rediscovered duet with Lennon, *circa* 1974 – and a huge helping of comic songs like 'UCLA', 'All In The Mind', 'Try' and 'Animal Farm'. Now dried out, Nilsson was making the most of whatever new opportunities came his way whilst looking forward to the past as a regular speaker at Beatle conventions where, before his death in 1994, he engaged in question-and-answer sessions and, surprisingly for one once well known for *never* singing in public, even performed a couple of numbers onstage.

Meanwhile, Lennon had elected not so much to settle cosily into middle age on the consolidated fruits of his success, but to find out what else awaited him on the other side of the Santa Monica interlude, when he'd been unable to make long-term plans. Whatever was wrong appeared to be righting itself. The intolerable adulation, the smash hits, the money down the drain could be transformed to matters of minor importance compared to the peaceful life he felt he deserved, the potential for domestic stability, and providing young Sean with the best of everything, especially more paternal attention than most – certainly far more than John ever had.

It was enough as well to be on the way to tolerable health after all the physical and mental vicissitudes his 35 unquiet years had sustained. In the title track to a 1979 album, *Rust Never Sleeps*, Neil Young, an *après*-Woodstock bedsit bard, was to whinge lines like "It's better to burn out than to fade away", which seemed to laud the banal live-fast-die-young philosophy involuntarily played out by Jimi Hendrix, Jim Morrison, Janis Joplin, Keith Moon, Sid Vicious and like unfortunates chewed upon and spat out by the pop industry. "For what?" inquired John during one of his last interviews. "So that we might rock? If Neil Young admires that sentiment so much, why doesn't he do it?"[21]

Every day he still lived was a bonus now that John Lennon had let go, stopped trying to prove himself – though if he had abandoned the world, the world hadn't abandoned him, not while his work was kept before the public via, say, The Damned's high-velocity overhaul of 'Help!' in 1976, or a revival of 'Working Class Hero' by Marianne Faithfull in a voice grippingly bereft of any former soprano purity on 1979's *Broken English*, an album that was as much a fixture in student halls of residence in the late '70s as a poster of Che Guevara's mug had been years earlier.

A centre-page *NME* article pleaded for if not a full-time return, then Lennon's blessing on the burgeoning punk movement, but it elicited no immediate response from one no longer preoccupied with cooking up marketable food of love and sprinkling it with cheap insight. Nothing from John Lennon, not even another repackaging, would show its face in the charts from a belated appearance of 'Imagine' in the UK Top Ten in November 1975 until '(Just Like) Starting Over' in November 1980. Neither would a solitary new melody or lyric be heard commercially from him after 'Cookin' (In The Kitchen Of Love)', a self-satisfied donation to *Ringo's Rotogravure* in 1976. What right had anyone to expect more? He said as much in a brief and reluctantly granted press conference in Japan a year later.

Lennon's was almost as sweeping an exit from public life as that of the great Belgian *chansonnier* Jacques Brel, who chose to "stop once and for all this idiotic game"[92] – in 1975 too – by fleeing to the last bolt-hole his fans and the media would expect to find him, namely the remote Pacific island where the painter Paul Gauguin had lived out his last years.

Brel and Lennon weren't the only ones to fling it all back in their faces. An unnerving spell of ballroom one-nighters – which included a date at the Star-Club – had caused Twinkle, a swinging London dolly-bird who scored a UK hit with 1965's 'Terry', a 'Leader Of The Pack'-like "death disc", to retire as a full-time pop star at the age of 17.

Once as famous for composing John Leyton's chartbusting 'Johnny Remember Me' in 1960 as Twinkle was for 'Terry', Geoff Goddard was depressed over a messy legal dispute over infringement of copyright in 1964. This brought about his sudden if calculated withdrawal into anonymity in the catering department at the University of Reading, where workmates would deduce from the odd secret smile and what was left unsaid that Geoff had, indeed, Hit The Big Time long ago and far away. A rapid weariness of the shabbier aspects of the record business also led to guitarist Brian Pendleton leaving The Pretty Things in 1965 when he got off a train *en route* to some dates up north. "We went round to his flat afterwards," said Phil May, "and it was like the *Marie-Celeste*."

The *ultima Thule* of pop hermits, however, is Syd Barrett, whose departure from The Pink Floyd in 1968 was on a par with John Lennon, unable to cope with being a Beatle after 'From Me To You', scurrying back to Woolton to dwell in seclusion with Aunt Mimi, or – as actually happened – Chris Curtis washing his hands of The Searchers in 1966 for the security of the civil service.

Hearsay painted the likes of Scott Walker, The Move's charismatic bass player Chris "Ace" Kefford and no less than three Fleetwood Mac guitarists – Peter Green, Jeremy Spencer and Danny Kirwan – in similar hues. They seemed to live outwardly unproductive lives in which nothing much was calculated to happen, year in, year out.

All these examples are the tip of an iceberg of pop artists who, on growing to adulthood in the hothouse of pop's turbulent and endless adolescence, made deliberate attempts to jump the gun and become nobodies again before their time in the limelight was up.

Yet they never quite became nobodies. Self-deception, genuine belief and the balm of ignorance become jumbled as such a recluse's enigma deepens. A legend takes shape, bringing out the strangest yarns. As with the Loch Ness Monster, there'd be purported sightings – of Spencer as a street-corner evangelist, Kirwan as a down-and-out, a brain-scrambled Green as a grave digger. Now something in the City, Brian Pendleton stonewalled a Pretty Things train spotter who accosted him in a Virgin megastore. Someone insists that, wild and pathetic, Walker was prowling an otherwise uninhabited peninsula in the Hebrides like a mad Robinson Crusoe, and that Kefford had revealed his identity during a death-bed confession after spending his final world-weary years in spiritual contemplation. Someone else swears that Jacques Brel had been observed plucking guitar in a cocktail jazz combo as customers chattered in a Hawaiian bar.

Thus it was that, in the teeth of a possibly dull truth, John Lennon continued to fascinate the English-speaking pop world as much as Brel did the Gallic one. Mention of Lennon during his so-called "house husband" years still brings out strange tales of what alleged "insiders" claim they heard and saw.

The mildest of these were that he had albums of The Goons on instant replay, and that he was also "into" new age, the only wave of essentially instrumental music to have reached a mass public since jazz rock in the mid-1970s. You hear it today in hip dental surgeries. Is it merely aural wallpaper or low-stress "music for the whole body" to ease the ravages of modern life? Do you buy it with the same discrimination as you would three pounds of spuds?

A wholesome diet figured prominently in Lennon's new life too. When filling in the *NME*'s "Lifelines" questionnaire early in 1963, George, Paul and Ringo had all chosen chicken, lamb and steak cuisine as their favourite foods while John went for non-committal "curry and jelly".[93] He had acquired such a comparatively exotic taste via Pete Best's Indian mother and, later, in a Britain where most restaurants that served a late-night square meal were Indian or Chinese. Otherwise, during that year's travelling life of snatched and irregular meals, The Beatles' palates had been coarsened by chips with everything in wayside snack bars. It had been the same back in meat-happy Hamburg, where menus in establishments like Der Fludde, Harold's Schnellimbiss and Zum Pferdestalle (which translates as "the Horses' Stable") favoured horsemeat casserole, *Labskaus* (a *mélange* of corned beef, herrings, mashed potato and chopped gherkins, topped with a fried egg) and *Deutsch bifsteak*. A search for a nut roast would be fruitless as all over Europe in the early 1960s vegetarianism was an eccentricity and an inconvenience for dinner-party hosts.

None of The Beatles had, therefore, ever seriously considered adopting vegetarianism, even when they had the means to order more than beans on toast. On the run around the world, gourmet dishes with specious names – *trepang* soup, veal Hawaii, *furst puckler* – pampered stomachs yearning for the greasy comfort of cod and chips eaten with the fingers.

Nevertheless, after the decision to quit touring, Lennon was the first, apparently, to at least try a meat-free diet – though Cynthia and Julian didn't then. Later, he backslid, justifying himself in 1980 with "We're mostly macrobiotic – fish and rice and whole grains – but sometimes I bring the family out for a pizza. Intuition tells you what to eat."[21] Nowadays, he was studying cookery books and baking bread, monitoring Sean's meals with a detail that dictated how many times each bite was to be masticated, and undergoing long fasts when only mineral water and fruit and vegetable juices entered his mouth.

A story leaked out later that he was also swallowing temazepam-like relaxants. Among the side-effects were stream-of-consciousness monologues, directed as much to himself as anyone listening, and mood swings from I'm-a-dirty-dog self-reproach to rhapsodies of peculiar exaltation. Straight up. A mate of mine told me.

By thus internalising, was John Lennon running away from himself in a place where, in his heart of hearts, he didn't want to be? What seems to be true is that, encouraged by his wife, he began spending lonely holidays progressively further afield – Bermuda, Cape Town, Hong Kong, anywhere that was the opposite of the Dakota, where life with Yoko wasn't exactly Phyllis and Corydon in Arcady.

Yoko had become quite the astute business person, ably representing John at Beatles business meetings and investing particularly wisely in properties and agriculture. What he called "work" was attempting to write a third book – "about 200 pages of *In His Own Write*-ish mad stuff"[21] – and now and then tuning his acoustic guitar after breakfast. After strumming and picking for a while, all the fragments of music he was struggling to turn into a composition would sound flat. Then his fingers would start barre-ing the old, old chord changes from when the world was young. Languor would set in and he'd let out an involuntary sigh. Maybe he'd knuckle down to it properly tomorrow. What was the use, in any case, of continuing to mine the same worn-out creative seams over and over again from new angles in wrong-headed expectation of finding gold?

When his former songwriting partner, six-string in hand, attempted to visit the Dakota one day, Paul McCartney was sent away by a harassed John via an intercom message: "Please call before you come over. It's not 1956, and turning up at the door isn't the same any more. You know, just give me a ring."[21] Neither could Lennon bring himself so much as to put his head round the door when McCartney, with Harrison and Starr, met Yoko in the same building to discuss further the division of the empire.

Yet belying a growing legend of Lennon as "The Howard Hughes of Pop", both Mike McCartney – Paul's brother – and Gerry Marsden were able to reach him. "I didn't see John for many years when he was in the States," reminisced Gerry, "or hear much about him other than what I read in the papers. Then once when I was appearing in New York, I called him after a gap of nearly a decade of not communicating, and it was just as if the days of the Seamen's Mission in Hamburg hadn't gone." Moreover, a chance encounter with Lennon in some Bermudan watering-hole caused one journalist to report that not only did the myth-shrouded John stand his round but that his songwriting well wasn't as dry as many imagined. This was confirmed in August 1980, when he and Ono recorded sufficient new material to fill two albums.

The first of these, *Double Fantasy* – which could almost be filed under "Easy Listening" – was issued that autumn, when, from Rip Van Winkle-esque vocational slumber, a fit-looking 40-year-old was suddenly available for interviews again with the unblinking self-assurance of old. He was even talking about a return to the stage, now that such innovations as programmable consoles and graphic equalisers were doing battle against adverse auditorium acoustics. He'd understood too that in sports stadia and exposition centres – especially in the States and Germany – a performance by a pop Methuselah could enthrall Cecil B de Mille-sized crowds. Framed by sky-clawing scaffolding, giant video screens and lighting gantries like oil derricks, you'd be louder and clearer than ever before.

Some of the faithful might have preferred John's to remain an ever-silent "no return" saga rather than him perhaps trying and failing to debunk the myth of an artistic death. However much they might have gainsaid it, they didn't want a comeback from someone who would thrive on goodwill with a side-serving of morbid inquisitiveness, a Judy Garland among Swinging '60s pop heroes. Let's keep the memory of a jewellery- rattling 'Twist And Shout' at the Royal Command Performance and a bow-legged profile defined by an *Ed Sullivan Show* arc light. Otherwise, the sweet mystery will rest in pieces.

It appeared, however, that John Lennon meant business, and maybe, like his pal Elton John, was set to enter middle life as a fully integrated mainstay and wanted party guest of contemporary rock's ruling class. Though May Pang was to maintain that most of the "new" material had been written long before, he seemed rejuvenated as a composer too, as there were plenty of numbers left from both the two albums and stark demos of songs – like 'Free As A Bird' and 'Real Love' – which he'd taped as far back as 1975. There were, indeed, enough for for him to present Life Begins At 40 and three more to Ringo when, in November 1980, the two ex-Beatles spoke for the last time, and parted as good friends.

John Lennon and Mark Chapman were more than good friends – at least, in Mark's mind. Something enormous if perverse had taken place, possibly as a sublimation of the depression brought on by parting with his girlfriend, an unhappy espousal on the rebound, his parents' divorce and a general psychological malaise. With everything else in his life now stripped away, the old Beatles craving had reared up with a vengeance. This time around, however, Mark was perceiving directives from them – to the degree that he was certain that he'd been sent a telepathic message from John. "I know you and you know me," it read. "We understand each other in a secret way." They had become as one.

Chapman was, therefore, no longer someone not far removed from a rabid supporter of a football team. He had evolved too strong a need to affiliate himself to a world of fantasy from which he would never emerge unless he received regular psychiatric monitoring, even residential care – which, in a manner of speaking, he would do, albeit too late.

During the autumn preceding that eerie Christmas in 1980, Mark David decided that the chief Beatle's control of his life could not remain remote, hence, he finished his last shift as a security guard in Hawaii – signing off as "John Lennon" – and appeared in New York as if from nowhere early in December. The needle was in a big haystack, but it was the right haystack.

He was in high spirits, despite the body pressure and the chatter when being jolted from the airport by internal railway to the city centre. It was a moment of quiet joy when he stood at last outside the Dakota, looking upwards, paying muttered homage and wondering what was busying those rooms at that very minute. For hours daily, he stood on that pavement with all his soul in his eyes, totally desensitised to the stares of passers-by as he continued to gaze at what he could make out of outlines that seemed to dart across the Dakota's windows. He felt endlessly patient and vaguely enchanted that his vigil might last forever.

Then something incredible happened! Twilight was falling on Monday 8 December when John – with Yoko – strolled out of the building. Of the few pop stars Mark had ever seen close up, nearly every one had disappointed him. Bob Dylan, for example, had looked like someone who looked a bit like Bob Dylan. However, for all the sunken cheeks and expected ravages of middle age, the person who was crossing the sidewalk, with a slightly pigeon-toed gait and hair frisking in the cold breeze, was 100 per cent John Lennon. The Quarry Bank school tie he'd taken to wearing in recent photographs wasn't in evidence, but he wasn't that much different from the way he'd appeared in "The Beatnik Horror!".

What do you say when you meet God?

Mark did not assume an instant intimacy with one who'd opened a door to his psyche, even though no one knew Lennon like he did. For a split-second, John stared at Mark, almost with dislike, as if he resented his adoration. Obviously, he was suffering from shock and could not grasp the magnitude of the encounter.

Then, in one soundless moment, that adoration was extinguished like a moth in a furnace. After assuming that all he had to do was autograph another copy of *Double Fantasy* – "Is that OK? Is that what you want?"[5] – John Lennon sort of smirked like Billy Fury had when signing his name for a Silver Beatle in 1960.

That was all. It came and went in the blink of an eye. Yet in that instant, Mark saw a stranger. Had they always been strangers? Had there never been anything special between them in the first place? Lord, I believe: help thou my unbelief. But that was when the being Chapman had worshipped for three decades mutated before him into just The Man Who Used To Be John Lennon.

He sauntered off, and Hell's magnet began to drag Mark David Chapman down. Before the day was done, Mark would be standing on the same spot with a smoking revolver in his hand. Yards away, The Man Who Used To Be John Lennon would be grovelling and open-mouthed with his life's blood puddling out of him.

13 "The Look Of Fated Youth"

In common with everyone else who cared, Gerry Marsden remembers the very moment he received the news. In his house on the Wirral, he was wrenched from sleep at 5am that mind-boggling Tuesday by a call from Liverpool's Radio City. With phlegmatic detachment, Gerry "went back to sleep. It wasn't the kind of information I expected to turn out to be true."

When the world woke up, John Lennon had not recovered from being dead. Marsden decided that "the only thing to do was to carry on with some kind of routine to get rid of the shock". He chose not to cancel a business meeting in Bradford in the face of constant attempts to reach him by the media. Yorkshire Television landed the biggest scoop by persuading Gerry to sing 'Imagine' on *Calendar*, an early-evening magazine programme.

As it was with the early death of Hollywood heart-throb Rudolph Valentino in 1926, the slaying of Lennon had sparked off suicides by mid-morning – though there were to be no reported deed-poll Lennons, bedroom shrines, séances and letters written to him years after 8 December 1980. Furthermore, his death was too public for anyone to manufacture a survival story. John was never to be spotted behind the counter in a Dagenham fish-and-chip shop, moustached and crewcut in a Canberra suburb or opening a bank account in Copenhagen.

Conspiracy theories, nevertheless, had been flying up and down when flags were still at half mast and the wireless was broadcasting the dead man's music continuously in place of listed programmes. Was it an Art Statement more surreal than anything John and Yoko did post-*Two*

Virgins? Had Yoko reneged on an elaborate suicide pact? Was John cursed with "the look of fated youth",[94] as suggested in a *Daily Express* editorial (which thanked fate the next day that it hadn't been the "much more talented"[95] Paul McCartney instead)?

How about a rite by which the kingdom of the "Beatle generation", now with paunches and punk children, was rejuvenated by the sacrifice of its leader – well, one of them – in his prime? The same had happened to certain Greek, Roman and Norse fertility gods as well as King Arthur, Harold Godwinsson, William Rufus, Charles I – beheaded in his climacteric seven-times-seventh year – and John F Kennedy. The Victim's awareness of his role is irrelevant. The point is that the common people – some of them, anyway – believed that he had been slaughtered for them and their land. It said as much in *The Golden Bough*, and it was visible on general release in *The Wicker Man*, a 1973 B-feature that Lennon – and Mark David Chapman – may well have seen, in which a far-flung Scottish island reverts to pagan ways in hope of rich harvests.

For all the mystical, arty and political analogies that went the rounds, most people reckoned that John Lennon had been killed simply because Chapman, who'd also been sighted sniffing around Bob Dylan, was as nutty as a fruitcake – though he was to be confined not to a mental institution but gaol after he pleaded guilty, saying in effect, "I insist on being incarcerated for at least the next 20 years."

In New York's Attica Correctional Facility – the setting of Lennon's 'Attica State' from *Sometime In New York City* – Mark served his sentence, spending most of it separated from other prisoners for the sake of his own safety, particularly when he seemed to be becoming something of a celebrity as the focal point of a video documentary and numerous magazine features.

However, eligible for parole again, an apparently remorseful and rehabilitated Chapman is, if freed, likely to become, advisedly, as reclusive as his victim was during the "house husband years". In prison, he'd refused written requests for autographs, remarking, "This tells you something is truly sick in our society. I didn't kill John to become famous, and I'm horrified by these people."[5]

When Mark Chapman first began amassing this supposedly unlooked-for immortality, John's side of the tragedy had bequeathed unto *Double Fantasy* and its follow-up, *Milk And Honey*, an undeserved "beautiful sadness" – with particular reference to tender 'Beautiful Boy', which told five-year-old Sean Lennon of "what happens to you when you're busy making other plans", and 'Hard Times Are Over' with its line about "you and I walking together round a street corner".

Elsewhere, 'Watching The Wheels', 'Nobody Told Me' – which borrowed the tune of 'Mama Said', a Shirelles B-side – and the remaindered 'Help Me To Help Myself' were riven with an amused, grace-saving cynicism, while the first *Double Fantasy* single, '(Just Like) Starting Over', hinted at Lennon's Merseybeat genesis.

Overall, however, both *Double Fantasy* and *Milk And Honey* were bland, middle-of-the-road efforts musically – with the former's 'Woman' reminding me vaguely of Bread's slushy 1970 hit, 'Make It With You'. As for the lyrics, smug, slight statements were made by a rich, refined couple long detached from the everyday. Once, their antics had been wilder than those of any punk rocker, but with 1981 approaching, John and Yoko had been derided by punks and hippies alike as indolent, Americanised breadheads.

Be that as it may, Lennon's passing was a boom time for those with vested interest – who regarded his absence as no more of a hindrance than Elvis Presley's stint of square bashing in Germany had been for Colonel Tom Parker. Indeed, when the King died suddenly in 1977, record-store windows had bloomed with his splendour. He was scarcely off Top 40 radio and was swamping many national charts six or seven repromoted singles and albums at a time.

Likewise, universal grief and an element of ghoulish Beatlemania was to reverse the fall of *Double Fantasy* and '(Just Like) Starting Over' from their respective listings as Christmas petered out, and John Lennon would score a hat-trick of British Number Ones within weeks, an achievement that matched that of his Beatles in the dear, dead Swinging '60s. Out of sympathy too, Yoko engineered her only solo Top 40 entry – with 'Walking On Thin Ice' – in February 1981, thus lending further credence to the cruel old joke: death is a good career move.

The next time her poor husband made the charts, however, was in 1982 when 'Beatles Movie Medley' reached the Top 20 in both Britain and the States. Always it boiled down to The Beatles. Yet, in interview, George Harrison in particular underlined his boredom with the ceaseless fascination with the group – a fascination that was to escalate with the runaway success in 1994 of *Live At The BBC*, a compilation of early broadcasts.

This prefaced an official proclamation of a coming anthology of further items from the vaults. These were to be hand picked by George, Paul and Ringo themselves for issue over the period of a year on nine albums (in packs of three) as appendant commodities to a six-hour documentary film to be spread over three weeks on ITV, and presented likewise on foreign television.

Then came talk of the Fab Three recording new material for the project. The general feeling, however, was that it wouldn't be the same without Lennon. Yet, after a fashion, a regrouping of Harrison, Starr and McCartney in the later 1990s wasn't without him. Their labours in George's and Paul's respective private studios yielded the grafting of new music onto John's voice-piano tapes of 'Free As A Bird' and 'Real Love', provided by Yoko after much negotiation.

With Harrison's producer, Jeff Lynne, rather than elderly George Martin, at the console, 'Free As A Bird' took shape as near as dammit to to a new Beatles record, complete with a guitar break from George, Ringo's trademark pudding drums and Paul emoting a freshly composed bridge as a sparkling contrast to John's downbeat verses. The result was certainly better than 'Can't Buy Me Love' and 'The Ballad Of John And Yoko', A-sides released by The Beatles when Lennon was still alive.

For me, however, 'Free As A Bird' wasn't as piquant as either a briefly reformed Sex Pistols on *Top Of The Pops* in 1996, or the launch of *Zombie Heaven*, a four-CD retrospective, at London's Jazz Café that November. Trooping onstage at 10:45pm in this nicotine-clouded club were, yes, organist Rod Argent, bass player Chris White, singer Colin Blunstone, drummer Hugh Grundy and, still jet-lagged after flying in from the USA, guitarist Paul Atkinson. Rough and ready they may have been for their first performance in 28 years, but like Lennon in Toronto in 1969, it was sufficient that the original Zombies were merely there.

All the same, I was among the multitudes willing 'Free As A Bird' to leap straight in at Number One as Beatles singles were supposed to – and as a verification of the lost value of the performance of a song as opposed to the producing of a production. Yet for all the amassing of anticipation via no sneak previews, and a half-hour TV special building up to its first spin over a remarkable video, it stalled in second place in Britain's Christmas chart. The 'Real Love' follow-up reached the UK Top Ten more grudgingly.

Who could not understand Paul, George and Ringo's mingled regret and elation when the *Anthology* albums shifted millions, affirming that almost but not quite reaching the top in the UK singles chart was but a surface manifestation of enduring interest in The Beatles that made even this abundance of out-takes, demos and other leftovers as much of a joy forever as *Zombie Heaven* and similar produce issued around the same time by The Beach Boys and The Doors?

In deference to the years before the coming of Ringo, the first *Anthology* package contained tracks with Beatles who'd left the fold one way or another. Such inclusions were of no use to Stuart Sutcliffe, mouldering in a Liverpool parish cemetery for 35 years – or John Lennon. The group's sacked drummer, however, could foresee that the attention would enable his Pete Best Band to broaden its work spectrum. Thus a busy 1996 schedule covered 18 countries as well as bigger UK venues than before – Barnsley Civic, Margate Winter Gardens, London's Bottom Line, Southport Floral Hall, you name 'em.

Assisted by Bill Harry, Pete recovered further scrapings of his stolen heritage through *The Best Years Of The Beatles*,[96] a timely second memoir just over a decade after his long-awaited *Beatle!*.[97] The other living ex-Beatles covered their respective tenures with the group with the publication of the pricey *Anthology* autobiography in 2000. Several years in gestation, it was a "Beatles story told for the first time in their own words and pictures".[98] Whereas Ringo, George and Paul's were from turn-of-the-century taped reminiscences, with no anchoring narrative, John's were from media archives and, therefore, not influenced by the fact of being observed: *litera scripta manet*.[99] He came over, therefore, as less of a straightforward, unspoilt Merseyside lad than any of the other three.

JOHN LENNON

If an engaging and sometimes courageous account – and a thought-provoking companion to this one – it was aimed at fans who prefer not to learn too much about what kind of people their idols are in private. Too many illusions will be shattered, and the music may never sound the same. The more salacious amongst us were, therefore, to be discomfited: Though you'd think that, like a fisherman boasting about a catch, the stories (particularly about Hamburg) would get more eye-stretching with each passing year, the sex and drugs were actually played down.

On other matters, however, there were not so much new twists in the plot as further snippets of detail. Finally, while the Swinging '60s are hardly the Schleswig-Holstein question (the most complex matter ever to perplex European politics), *Anthology*, despite an unavoidable subjectiveness, was certainly a more palatable way to at least scratch the surface of what the fuss was about than 1,000 Open University treatises.

With its weight on a par with that of a paving slab, *Anthology* amassed enough advance orders to slam it straight in at Number One in *The Sunday Times* book chart, a feat duplicated across the world. It was still doing well while EMI co-ordinated its biggest-ever marketing campaign. Eight million copies of *1*, a compilation of The Beatles' 27 British and US chart-toppers, were shipped around the world. The fastest-selling CD ever, *1* reached that number in the charts in Britain, Japan, Germany and Canada within a week of its issue.

What victory was John Lennon's? "The leader of the band's arrived!" *NME* reader's letter had bawled back in the aftershock of 8 December 1980, presuming that John was being conducted to the table head in some pop Valhalla. A spiritualist *au fait* with Lennon's afterlife adventures knew of his affair with a long-departed Hollywood screen idol – intelligence that might have inflamed his volcanic widow whose *Season Of Glass* album sleeve in 1981 had depicted a pair of bloodstained spectacles – while the following year's *It's Alright (I See Rainbows)* employed trick photography whereby a spectral John stood next to her and Sean in what looks like a recreation ground.

Even before the necessarily hasty cremation, although a Coalition To Stop Gun Violence – of which Harry Nilsson was an active supporter – was inaugurated, less altruistic was the bursting of a commercial dam of such force that John Lennon's name would continue to sell almost anything. Publishers liaised with biographers that included a team who had a life of Lennon – entitled *Strawberry Fields Forever* – in the shops inside a fortnight and Albert Goldman, the US journalist whose brief was to portray Lennon as being as certifiable a lunatic as Chapman.

Needless to say, there were also individuals thick skinned enough to start work on a tribute disc within minutes of catching the first bulletin on 9 December. With a bit of luck, it'd be in the shops and on radio playlists in time for mourners to spend their Christmas record tokens on it.

Totally eclipsing efforts like 'Elegy For The Walrus' and 'It Was Nice To Know You, John', George Harrison's 'All Those Years Ago' was the promotional 45 from his *Somewhere In England* album, and the reason why George by association was to end 1981 seven places behind Lennon as tenth Top Male Vocalist in *Billboard*'s annual poll. Regardless of this singalong canter's mediocrity, another incentive for buyers was the superimposed presence of Ringo and Paul, who, with Wings, had taken a break from another project in George Martin's Monserrat complex to add their contributions when the unmixed 'All Those Years Ago' arrived from Harrison.

It's futile to hypothesise about John's beyond-the-grave verdict on George's first big hit since 'Give Me Love (Give Me Peace On Earth)' in 1973, but I like to think that he would have preferred Roxy Music's go at 'Jealous Guy'. Lennon was, after all, an artist with whom the group's Bryan Ferry, via a *Melody Maker* article, expressed a wish to collaborate. Bryan may have told the man himself when, in 1974, he dined with John, George and Ringo in New York. Touring Germany with Roxy Music the week after the slaying, Ferry suggested closing the show with 'Jealous Guy'. A German record company executive ventured that it would be a sound choice for the next Roxy Music single, but Bryan felt it might appear tasteless. Nevertheless, after further deliberation, the outfit tried an arrangement during an exploratory studio session. With the oblique message "A Tribute" on the picture sleeve, the sole reference to its main purpose, 'Jealous Guy' scudded all the way up the UK charts, the only Roxy Music 45 to so do, by March 1981.

Sean Lennon's godfather, Elton John got no further than Number 51 with his 'Empty Garden' tribute in 1982. Though he procrastinated for even longer, Mike 'Tubular Bells' Oldfield – with sister Sally on lead vocals – slummed it on *Top Of The Pops* with 1983's 'Moonlight Shadow', which addressed itself to the horror outside the Dakota on the night it happened. Waiting a decent interval, more deserving of a chart placing was the title song of The Downliners Sect's *A Light Went Out In New York*, a 1993 album that mingled remakes of some of the reformed British R&B combo's old tracks and Beatle obscurities. Dare I suggest that the Sect actually improve upon 'I'll Keep You Satisfied', 'That Means A Lot' *et al*? Also, that 'A Light Went Out In New York' – composed by the Sect's own Paul Tiller – may be the most moving Lennon oblation ever released, knocking the likes of 'All Those Years Ago', 'Empty Garden' and po-faced 'Moonlight Shadow' into a cocked hat?

The principal subject of Mike Oldfield's ditty was not John but Yoko Ono, who was to sanction and partly compère 1990's televised and international concert tribute to John at Liverpool's Pier Head. Since 1980, Yoko has not retreated from public life. As recently as summer 2002, she endeavoured to re-invent herself as a disco diva with a remix of 'Open Your Box', her self-composed flip-side to 'Power To The People'. While this was still being advertised via posters in London underground stations, Ono was presented to the Queen during Her Majesty's golden jubilee visit to Liverpool's John Lennon – formerly Speke – Airport. It's likely that I've got Yoko all wrong but, to me, she gives an impression of hurrying her duties by John out of the way in as bombastic a manner as possible while simultaneously using him as leverage to further her own artistic ends: kind of "Yes, he was quite a guy, but listen…"

The ease with which Yoko's step-son secured a British Top Ten hit in 1984 might be the most renowned instance of affinity to The Beatles kick-starting a musical career. In April of the following year, Julian Lennon also played three nights in a theatre in New York. During this brief residency, he and his mother Cynthia were spotted at a dining table, sharing the proverbial joke with his half-brother and Yoko Ono. "It was after Julian's first appearance in New York," Cynthia elucidated, "and he and I, Yoko and Sean were there – so for the photographers, it was a classic coup, but though we both wed the same man and both had a child by him, we were and still are worlds apart."

A more convivial repast was eaten by Cynthia with Maureen, Ringo's late ex-wife, at Lennon's, Cynthia's short-lived Covent Garden restaurant, which bored journalists made out to be in fierce competition with ex-Rolling Stone Bill Wyman's Kensington eaterie, Sticky Fingers. The two well-dressed, "liberated" divorcees might have hardly recognised their younger Merseyside selves. "We'd remained best friends through thick, thin, births, deaths and marriages," smiled Cynthia. "I happened to be staying with Maureen when Ringo rang at dawn with the news of John's death. She was also my last link with The Beatles. I'm out of their social orbit completely now."

Though Cynthia had gained a lucrative design contract in 1984 on the strength of her Art College qualifications, her memoir, *A Twist Of Lennon*, had done brisk business when published in 1978. Another account may follow "because so much has happened since then. It would be very easy to get in a ghost writer, but, because the first one was all my own work, it'd have to be in the same vein, in the way that I saw it – not the way other people want to see it. In the film *Backbeat*, I was a simple girl who wore tweed coats and head scarves, and that all I ever wanted in life was marriage, babies and a house – which was totally untrue. I was training to be an art teacher for four years, and it was only when I became pregnant that marriage followed, and The Beatles followed after that.

"People think of The Beatles in terms of millions of dollars. I don't see those dollars. What dollars I see are from my own damned hard work since I was out on my own after the divorce. From being so protected by millions that I never saw, and having a secure family, it was desperate really."

Yoko held the purse strings of John's fortune, but, after much to-ing and fro-ing of solicitors' letters, Julian Lennon received assorted – and, according to him, long overdue – monies. There was, therefore, no love lost between him and his father's relict. While noting that she and Sean attended 88-year-old Aunt Mimi's funeral in December 1991, another of John's blood relations felt the same as Julian about Yoko Ono. "Dad bought his half-sister Julia and her family a house to live in," snarled Julian by way of example. "As soon as Dad passed away, Yoko went and took their home that had been given to them by him, and then gave it to charity with no compensation for them."[5]

The second Mrs Lennon didn't appear to be very popular with John's former workmates either. On 27 April 1981, Yoko had been conspicuously absent from Ringo Starr's wedding to film actress Barbara Bach. Furthermore, George Harrison was to have nothing to do with Ono's Pier Head shenanigans and, while Paul and Ringo each sent a filmed piece, they declined to show up in person.

No Merseybeat groups "who'd got drunk with him"[100] had been invited even to warm up for Kylie Minogue, Christopher "Superman" Reeve, Roberta Flack, Hall And Oates, Cyndi Lauper and the rest of Yoko's star turns. Some, however, paid their respects that same year in a John Lennon Memorial Concert at the Philharmonic Hall. Blowing the dust off their instruments, many of those on the boards on that night of nights were belying daytime occupations as pen pushers, charge hands and captains of industry.

Old friendships and rivalries had been renewed likewise in May 1989 at the Grafton Rooms, scene of many a rough night in the early days, during the inaugural evening of Merseycats, a committee formed by Don Andrew, once of The Remo Four, to facilitate reunions of Merseybeat groups in support of KIND (Kids In Need and Distress), an organisation that provides activity holidays for seriously ill and handicapped local children.

Brian Epstein, "John Lennon of The Beatles" and "Stuart Sutcliffe of The Beatles" were pictured amongst "absent friends" in the souvenir programme. The latter two were also central to *Backbeat*, the 1994 bio-pic from the makers of *Letter To Brezhnev* – set in Liverpool – and *The Crying Game*. The action took place against the background of the *vie bohème* of Liverpool and Hamburg and concentrated on the often volatile relationships between John, Stuart and Astrid (and, to a lesser degree, Cynthia).

Backbeat's commercial success helped Sutcliffe close the gap on John as the most popular dead Beatle – at least, until George Harrison was taken by cancer in 2001. During the early 1990s, small fortunes changed hands for both a letter to Stuart from George and a Sutcliffe oil painting, not in the murmur of a museum or art gallery committee rooms but the bustle of a pop-memorabilia auction – for, regardless of how regrettable a loss he was to the world of Fine Art, as a figure in time's fabric Sutcliffe's period as a Beatle remains central to most considerations of him.

Conversely, their own merits, more than their association with The Beatles, have enabled Gerry Marsden and Billy J Kramer to be among the few of the old Merseybeat school who have managed to cling on to recording careers. In 1998, they delivered respectively Take That's 'A Million Love Songs' and REM's 'Losing My Religion' with more guts than the originals on *Sixties Sing Nineties*, an album on which hits by callow apprentices were given the masters' touch.

Tidy-minded (or lazy) journalists were mostly responsible for the habit of finding 1960s opposite numbers to Britpop acts that bestrode the UK Top 40 in the mid- to late 1990s. It was, however, too black and white to categorise, say, Oasis – whose 'Don't Look Back In Anger' was covered by Dave Dee on *Sixties Sing Nineties* – as the day's Beatles. Nevertheless, a few similarities are noticeable. For instance, their Liam Gallagher seems to have inherited a singing style that crosses that of John Lennon – after whom his eldest child is named – and Allan Clarke, once of The Hollies.

Yet Britpop belonged to a radically different economic, sociological and technological climate than the decade in which a provincial youth's decision to grow his hair even *With The Beatles* length, prefaced years of incomprehension, lamentation, deprivation, uproar, assault and oppressive domestic "atmospheres". At Aldershot Magistrates Court in 1965, a soldier accused of beating up a total stranger offered the plea, "Well, he had long hair, hadn't he?" Men don't have periods and can't get pregnant, but pillars of women's liberation might note how difficult the issue of hair could be for boys in the 1960s. You had to fight every literal inch of the way.

As a result, those who suffered this and other repressions were much more liberal when, as former Mods, Rockers and hippies, they became parents themselves and bought MIDI equipment for 16th birthday presents. More insidiously, the notion of the two-guitars-bass-drums line-up of a self-contained group was instilled from the cradle for many of their offspring. This was partly why 1960s outfits still operational in what was no longer such a nostalgia netherworld began drawing a remarkably young crowd that, not wanting its 1960s medicine neat, mouth the words of what little new songs are performed as accurately as the ancient smashes.

The latter, however, had dominated proceedings at the John Lennon Memorial Concert. Gerry Marsden was present but not participating beyond a brief cameo at the end. Nonetheless, the Philharmonic Hall's resident orchestra helped him do his bit in 2001 with Much Missed Man, a remarkable CD that, clocking in at just over 20 minutes, hung on a title requiem for Lennon with lyrics by Joe Flannery, once Brian Epstein's friend and business associate.

Within weeks of 8 December 1980, Flannery had written 'Much Missed Man' with Marsden in mind. "I felt it was too soon for a tribute from me then," thought Gerry. "However, when the anniversary of John's 60th birthday was coming up in 2000, Joe rang and asked me to give it another listen as he felt that the time might be right for me to record it – and he was right. The words said what I thought about John. People who like John will like the record."

Most of the playing time, however, would consist of a chronologically illogical collage of John holding forth amid a recitation of one of his poems and interruptions by Yoko and persons unknown (among them a "street corner evangelist" that I suspect might be McCartney). There's fun to be had dating these excerpts, which seem to stretch from final interviews back to the "Jesus" press conference in Chicago in 1966.

As for 'Much Missed Man' itself, a fragment of dialogue by Lennon and an 'Imagine'-esque piano figure sequed into a lush and adventurous arrangement behind a serenade that is on a heartfelt par with 'A Light Went Out In New York'.

To a greater degree than The Downliners Sect, Gerry Marsden still earns good money as an entertainer. He certainly has as warm a rapport with the audience as he did way back when, even if the rehearsed jokes told by both him and the latest edition of the Pacemakers about his age, weight and love life are received nearly as well as 'How Do You Do It', 'Ferry 'Cross The Mersey' and all the rest of them.

Getting laughs was more important than the music for Ricky Richards, albeit as "Rick Hardy" nowadays, though his act as a singing comedian betrays hardly any link whatsoever with the rock 'n' roll he, Tony Sheridan and the other Jets punched out in Hamburg. A decade on, a similar chicken-in-a-basket circuit was interrupted for The Searchers by two well-received albums of new material for the new-wave label Sire. Since then, The Searchers have split into two separate factions, each claiming to be the most *bona fide* line-up.

The still-functioning Merseysippi Jazz Band bloomed again too and, as demonstrated by the very existence of locally published *Sweeping The Blues Away*, a "celebration" of their first half-century by BBC Radio Merseyside's Spencer Leigh, the unit have become as much of a Liverpool institution in their way as the long-lost Beatles – and, once upon a time, Lord Woodbine.

He, however, was all but lost to the archives of oblivion, although daughter Barbara was to surface as a playwright whose work includes episodes for Channel Four's Merseyside soap opera, *Brookside*. If well-placed to grow fat on Beatlemania, her father chose instead to continue living on his wits around Toxteth. Yet, before he perished with his wife Helen in a house fire on 5 July 2000, Lord Woodbine sold a rather bitter story to *The Observer*, but – perhaps surprisingly – he never guested at any Beatles conventions and, unlike others less entitled, resisted further incentives to cash in on The Beatles ticket.

Who could begrudge Lennon's ex-wife from doing so with unprecedented abundance? A 1999 exhibition of her paintings at the KDK Gallery down London's Portobello Road was only part of it. Was I attending a preview or a cocktail party? White wine, please. Red gives me heartburn. Do those canapés contain meat? Don't look now, but wasn't that fellow with the camera once in The Troggs? Is that Mick Hucknell or one of Kula Shaker? That bloke I can't quite place: I'm sure he played Lennon in some play or other?

Actually, he *was* Lennon. Julian was there supporting his mother and Phyllis McKenzie, friends since student days in Liverpool when they breathed the air around others occupying that wide territory between realism and abstract expressionism: Phyllis leaning closer to the latter form than Cynthia – who freighted *A Twist Of Lennon* with her own illustrations.

The originals were on display in KDK for most of the summer, along with further visual mementos of her life at the storm centre of 1960s pop as well as later pictures bereft of such reference.

Cynthia Lennon was not nominated for that year's Turner prize. Nevertheless, her work had a charm that begs the question: does only the surname prevent her from being an artist in her own right? Maybe, but in such matters, your opinion is as worthy as mine, and beyond both of us, the only approbation KDK, McKenzie and Lennon need really are those whose time is utilised interestingly in an experience that, through my eyes, was as much aesthetic as historical.

Three years earlier, while it may not have reactivated the Cynthia Lennon Fan Club, the release of a debut single, a revival of Mary Hopkin's chart-topping 'Those Were The Days', had precipitated a more far-reaching reassessment. Produced by Isle of Man neighbour Chris Norman, formerly of Smokie, for his own Dice Music label, Cynthia's was not one of those discs that you buy for the wrong reasons – not like her former father-in-law's unmelodious 'That's My Life' in 1965.

Fifty-five-year-old Cynthia turned in a surprisingly appealing vocal – though perhaps not so surprising considering that "from the age of 10 until I was 14, I was in the Hoylake Parish Girls' Choir, and I ended up as soloist. "As an adult, I had no aspirations to be a singer. I didn't even sing around the house or in the bath, but a fax came through from a German record company who wanted to get in touch with Julian. So Jim, my partner, phoned back and said sarcastically, 'Julian's not here, but you can have his mother' – a throwaway comment that they answered in all seriousness, 'We can't do anything unless we know whether she can sing.' My voice had dropped about two octaves – probably because of all the cigarettes I smoke – but I'm game for anything nowadays, so

I taped a selection of songs *a cappella*. Chris asked to hear it out of curiosity and said, 'Let's give it a whirl.'

"Chris thought 'Those Were The Days' would be a good song for a person of my age, and very pertinent, looking back – though I resisted a temptation to sing, 'Once upon a time, there was a *Cavern*' on disc. For weeks after the session, I was on cloud nine. I was so pleased with it – and it was so creative for me. Six months earlier, if somebody had told me a record of mine was going to be on the radio, I'd have fallen about on the floor in hysterics, but – what's John's expression on *Double Fantasy*? – 'Life is what happens when you're busy making other plans.' At nearly every interview I've done, I've got one of the same two questions. 'Don't you think you're jumping on the bandwagon?' 'Won't people think you're cashing in?' I've tried for intelligent answers that don't sound aggressive, but no one other than me will ever understand. 'Cashing in' is earning a living as far as I'm concerned. Why should you feel guilty for working?"

With this in mind, Cynthia took the show on the road as novelty headliner of With A Little Help From Their Friends, a revue that you shouldn't have missed but probably did, judging by the half-capacity audience at any given theatre *en route* around Britain. Other "insiders" on the bill were more hardened to both poor turn-out and general stage exposure than Cynthia – notably The Merseybeats, who appeared with her ex-husband's group more times than anyone else.

Subtitled "a celebration of The Beatles by those who were part of the story", this package was not a convention-like evening of selective reminiscences, but a musical spectacular coalesced by scripted patter and short cameos like Cynthia's then-boyfriend Jim Christie scuttling on as "Brian Epstein" during a spot by the soundalike Silver Beatles', who focus on their namesake's apogee as a local attraction. The fab-gear winsomeness was flawless, but ropey mouth-organ blowing from "John", "Ringo's" too plummy vocal on 'Boys', and, the most common problem of the clone groups, a right-handed "Paul", might have been distracting for some. For me, however, these were of no more account than, say, the real Lennon's loosened tie, Paul's frequent five-o'-clock shadow – and, of course, the wavering tempos and fluffed riffs that the Fab Four themselves delivered onstage.

The Silver Beatles captured the required ramshackle grandeur. Other With A Little Help From Their Friends antics, however, appear lame or peculiar in cold print today – such as a sketch in which matronly Cynthia was embraced by The Silver Beatles' Andy Powell as youthful "John" in his high-buttoned suit – but they made sound sense in the context of proceedings that closed on an emotional high with the assembled cast joining The Merseybeats and a jubilant audience, blasting up chorus after rowdy dah dah chorus of 'Hey Jude'.

It seemed that, the older you were, the louder you clapped and shouted, the more you waved your arms about. Everyone whose life has been soundtracked by The Beatles should have attended, but the Congress Theatre, Eastbourne, on 14 March 1996 was the last opportunity to do so as cancellation of the remaining dates was the only way to staunch the financial losses that the trek had suffered since opening in February.

At the last hurrah in Eastbourne, a palpable wave of goodwill had washed over Mrs Lennon the instant she walked centre-stage before a backdrop mock-up of the graffiti-covered Cavern wall. From being a softly spoken outcast after the world and his wife were confronted with a John they'd never known before in 1968, Cynthia, if no Ken Dodd, proved a self-assured, likeable MC. Moreover, the former chorister also dropped sufficient reserve to open the second half with 'Those Were The Days'. Shorn of the Welsh soprano's incongruous maidenly innocence, Cynthia's pining for past times was as poignant as 'Free As A Bird'.

The customers, typically English, loved Cynthia for being a survivor – and for reaching her half-century in such great shape, too. The same applied to another lady on the bill, Twinkle, who couldn't let the evening go without giving 'em a stirring 'Terry', which had left the charts 31 years ago almost to the day.

On a *Ready Steady Go* nostalgia tour two summers earlier, Twinkle has been accompanied by her 1965 Top 20 contemporaries, The Four Pennies – who weren't quite the full shilling, containing only one original member, bass player Mike Wilsh. Perhaps mitigating this shortfall for 1960s purists was the onstage presence of a certain John Charles Duff Lowe, the selfsame pianist with The Quarry Men. He was combining Four Pennies duties with an attempted relaunch of if not *The* Quarry

Men, then *a* Quarry Men. A 1994 debut album, *Open For Engagements*, mixed items from the 1958 edition's repertoire with some startling originals, more *Sgt Pepper* than 'In Spite Of All The Danger'.

"In 1975, I'd moved to Bristol," John explained. "We always had a piano, and I used to play a lot, so I never lost interest in music. In 1991, I received a call from Mike Wilsh, who until then hadn't realised that I lived only two miles away from him. I was rehearsing with The Four Pennies within three or four days. I spoke at a *Merseybeatle* convention in Liverpool in 1992, and the following year we played at a party at the Cavern as 'The Quarry Men'. Later that year, were asked to do a recording by a producer named Tony Davidson, who had done one with The Four Pennies.

"That all came to nothing, but early in 1994, John Ozoroff, The Four Pennies' guitarist, wanted to do a solo album in a Bristol studio. Three tracks were done with me on keyboards, and we decided to turn it into a Quarry Men album, to be put out on my own Kewbank Records. It was mastered at Abbey Road by Nick Webb, who, incidentally, was assistant engineer on *Yellow Submarine*, the 'White Album' and *Abbey Road*. Of the new songs on *Open For Engagements*, there's a tribute to John Lennon, 'John Winston'.

"Rod Davis came over from his home in Uxbridge to play rhythm guitar on the sessions, but I took over the mantle of The Quarry Men. A number of other people could have done it. They didn't; I did – therefore, I run the present-day Quarry Men. I've got plans for another six Quarry Men albums."

It was to be The Quarry Men's task to kick-start With A Little Help From Their Friends with a brief skiffle prelude before Lowe swapped washboard for his more customary state-of-the-art keyboards for the remainder of the longest half hour of the show. Olde-tyme rock 'n' roll was adulterated by Lowe's synthesiser and Ozoroff's guitar solos, which reacted to underlying chord patterns rather than the melodic and lyrical intent of any number.

Yet there was a clever Cajun arrangement of Chuck Berry's 'Sweet Little Sixteen' with programmed accordion and Rod on inaudible fiddle; a daring 'History' from *Open For Engagements*; a competent rendition of 'Woman', with quotes from The Searchers' 'Don't Throw Your Love Away'; and an *a cappella* finale with 'In My Life', taken from *Rubber Soul*.

Theirs was an almost scholarly recital, which provoked clapping rather than screams. More agreeable a venture was when Rod Davis and others still alive from the Woolton fete line-up were heard 43 years after the event on *Get Back Together*, 15 tracks of rocked-up skiffle from the opening 'Mean Woman Blues' through to the apposite 'Lost John' valediction. As lead singer, Len Garry coped better with, say, Bing Crosby's 'Have I Told You Lately That I Love You' than Eddie Cochran's 'Twenty Flight Rock', but, on his solitary vocal, 'When The Sun Goes Down', Rod – hedging his bets – was as uncannily close to the Donegan template as John Lennon was with 'Putting On The Style' on the rediscovered tape from the day when the Lennon–McCartney partnership began.

On the whole, there wasn't as much grit as I'd have liked – but perhaps that's not the point for incorrigible old rockers with no other cards left to play. If nothing else, *Get Back Together* – with a teenage Lennon in pride of place on the front cover – sounds like it was fun to record, even if that particular brand of fun isn't a thing that money can't buy anymore.

Epilogue

"And Now, Thank Christ, It's Over"

How different could John Lennon's life have been? This is probably a senseless hypothetical exercise, but let's transfer to a parallel dimension for a few minutes.

Sean Connery has failed his screen test for *Dr No*; Cassius Clay didn't beat the count when knocked down by Henry Cooper, and, in summer 1966, Dave Dee, Dozy, Beaky, Mick And Tich top the US Hot 100, the first British act to do so since The Tornados.

Around the same time, John Lennon quits The Beatles, an also-ran beat group, for a hand-to-mouth existence as a jobbing commercial artist back in Liverpool. For a while, he's on the periphery of the Liverpool scene, a mixed-media aggregation, before a supplicatory chat with Arthur Ballard lands him a post as technician in Ballard's department at the college.

As his marriage to Cynthia deteriorates, John becomes a fixture in Ye Cracke, still a student pub, where he often rambles on with rueful and misplaced pride about The Beatles' meagre achievements. On one maudlin evening, he brings in his photo album – "us with Tony Sheridan", "me and George with Ringo Starr in the Top Ten. Ringo was in Georgie Fame's Blue Flames later on, you know..." Most regulars find both John's reminiscences and the pictures mind-stultifyingly boring.

For beer money and a laugh, Lennon reforms The Beatles for bookings in local watering-holes. They became as peculiar to Liverpool alone as Mickey Finn, a comedian unknown nationally but guaranteed work for as long as he can stand on Merseyside. A typical engagement is providing music after Finn's entertainment at a dinner and dance at Gateacre Labour Club on 8 December 1980. The group's personnel on that night of nights consists of Pete Best, deputy manager at Garston Job Centre on drums; George Harrison, a Southport curate, on guitar; Paul McCartney, a Radio Merseyside presenter and amateur songwriter, on bass; and Lennon, his singing voice darker and attractively shorn of 1960s ingenuity, now a slightly batty art lecturer who'd wed a Japanese performance artist he'd seen at a 1967 "happening" at the college.

The four leave a dancing audience wanting more after a finale of a 1965 Oriole B-side, 'I'm A Loser', during which Lennon accommodated suitable – and often amusing – gestures and facial expressions as well as wailing an endlessly inventive harmonica. He also displayed a commendable sense of historical perspective during humorous continuity. Meanwhile, George delivered workman-like solos, and Paul sent frissons through middle-aged female nervous systems with his pretty 'Till There Was You', but a more unsung hero of the night was Pete, ministering unobtrusively to overall effect and, in his way, a virtuoso.

Brought back for an encore, The Beatles affirm their staying power once more. None of their few records ever sold much beyond Merseyside but, as an eminently danceable live act, they've outlasted most of their local rivals – and there's every reason to suppose that they'll still be around in the next millennium.

Unreal life isn't like that – at least, it wasn't for John, whose unmeasurable fame had accorded unto him a magnificently god-like certainty about everything he said and did for invisible armies of fans, old and new, whose adoration will never dwindle. As pressured denizens of the media cobbled together hasty obituaries on the morning of 9 December 1980, one of the more memorable comments any of them reported was by the recently retired Arthur Ballard: "I think his death is more significant than that of a leading politician. Like Michelangelo has never been forgotten, neither will John Lennon be."[101]

Shall we try again with an interview with John Winston Lennon,

MBE, retired musician and composer at Fort Belvedere, Sunningdale, Berkshire, on 9 December 2002...

To the click-clack of his own approaching footsteps, the former Beatle sings what sounds like "Softly, softly spreads the grunion/thinner thorn our saviour's feet..." to the tune of 'Johnny Todd', title theme to the old BBC television series Z-Cars.

"Welcome to the inner sanctuary," he begins. "Better not shake hands. I've just given the old feller a swift dekko at the scenery. My MBE's on the wall in the bog, y'know. Best place for it. I only asked the Queen for it back to cheer up my auntie during her last illness.

"Do I seem larger than life? Don't worry. That'll change as this chat progresses. I'm ordinary, modest, boring and all too human since that arsehole winged me outside the Dakota in 1980. Quite spoiled Christmas, it did – though it was that other gun-slinging get who did for Reagan in '82 that finally put the tin lid on my 'American period'.

"I miss New York sometimes, and I got pissed off recently with Berkshire County Council or whoever they are, when they turned their noses up at the plans to modernise this place. Used to belong to Edward and Mrs Simpson, don't-ye-know? All the same, I'm unlikely to live out of England ever again – especially since getting back together with Cyn and his Holiness down in Sussex, even if the old chart-busting magic isn't there any more.

"Never mind, we made our contribution to society a 100 times over in the '60s, and I reckon now that the four of us should have been put out to grass as soon as we split up the first time. But the game dragged on, didn't it? And now, thank Christ, it's over. Live Aid was a laugh, but all it proved was that looking forward to the past isn't healthy for any bunch of musicians, let alone John, Paul, George and Pete. Anyway, I wouldn't want to be an 80-year-old Beatle..."

Author's Note

While John Lennon's deeds and personality have become more ambiguous and nebulous in retrospect, care has been taken to define as widely as possible the myriad social, cultural, economic, environmental and other factors that polarise and prejudice what is generally known about him already, and the new and rediscovered evidence and information that recent research has brought to light. Often pop biography – and that is all this account is – has tended to shy away from these areas, even though they form a more tangible basis for investigation than, as I said in the prologue, treating the subject's most flippant public remarks as gospel.

Those whose lives are devoted to collating facts about The Beatles may pounce on mistakes and omissions while scrutinising this work. All I can say to them is that it's as accurate as it can be after the synthesis of personal memories and interviews with some of the key *dramatis personae* – not to mention a filing cabinet of Lennonia, and exercise books full of doctor's prescription-like scribble drawn from press archives – some of them quite obscure.

Please put your hands together for Penny Braybrooke, Iain MacGregor, Michelle Knight, Laura Brudenell, Chris Harvey, Alan Heal, Chris Bradford and Michael Wilson and the rest of the team at Sanctuary, who went far beyond the call of duty from this biography's sluggish genesis to its final publication.

I am also grateful to Rod Davis, Rick Hardy (Ricky Richards), Bill Harry, Cynthia Lennon, John Duff Lowe, Gerry Marsden, the late Harry Nilsson and Tony Sheridan for conversations and interviews that took place before this project was commissioned.

Whether they too were aware of providing assistance or not, let's have a round of applause too for these musicians: Frank Allen, Ian "Tich" Amey, Don Andrew, Roger Barnes, Alan Barwise, Cliff Bennett, Dave Berry, Colin Blunstone, Barry Booth, Clem Cattini, Don Craine, Tony Crane, Dick Dale, Trevor "Dozy" Davies, Rod Davis, Dave Dee, the late Lonnie Donegan, Vince Eager (Roy Taylor), Freddie Garrity, "Wreckless" Eric Goulden, Keith Grant, Mike Hart, Brian Hinton, Donald Hirst, Tony Jackson, Garry Jones, Billy Kinsley, Phil May, Jim McCarty, Mike Pender, Brian Poole, Mike Smith, Norman Smith, Mike and Anja Stax, the late Lord David Sutch, the late Vivian Stanshall, Dick Taylor, John Townsend, Paul Tucker, Fran Wood and Twinkle.

Equally invaluable was the clear insight and intelligent argument of my principal researcher, Ian Drummond.

It may be obvious to the reader that I have received much information from sources that prefer not to be mentioned. Nevertheless, I wish to thank them – as well as B & T Typewriters, Bemish Business Machines, Stuart and Kathryn Booth, Maryann Borgon, Eva Marie Brunner, the late Ray Coleman, Kevin Delaney, Peter Doggett, Katy Foster-Moore, Ann Freer, Gary Gold, Louise Harrison, Dave Humphries, Rob Johnstone, Allan Jones, Graham Larkbey, Spencer Leigh, Russell Newmark, Mike Ober, Mike Robinson, Mark Stokes and Ted Woodings – plus Inese, Jack and Harry Clayson for letting me get on with it.

Selective Bibliography

Such is the volume of literary spin-offs after his death that someone ought to write a book about books about John Lennon. These have ranged from scurrilous trash to well-researched, scholarly works that any historical figure of his stature would warrant. There have also surfaced countless volumes containing raw information that only the most crazed devotee would not find too insignificant to be interesting.

Therefore, rather than attempt a long – and probably incomplete – list of dry titles for further reading, it makes more sense to compile a selection with brief commentary of items that either I found helpful or are prototypical of specific aspects of John Lennon and The Beatles.

BADMAN, KEITH: *The Beatles After The Break-Up* (Omnibus, 1999). This reference work provides comprehensive facts about Lennon's life as an ex-Beatle.

CLAYSON, ALAN and SUTCLIFFE, PAULINE: *Backbeat – Stuart Sutcliffe: The Lost Beatle* (Pan-Macmillan, 1994). Ostensibly a film tie-in, this serves as an insight into the social and academic atmosphere from which The Beatles emerged.

COLEMAN, RAY: *John Winston Lennon, Volume 1 1940–1966* (Sidgwick & Jackson, 1984); *John Ono Lennon, Volume 2 1967–1980* (Sidgwick & Jackson, 1984). The antithesis of the Goldman job, these are very much the sort of books of which John himself might have approved. Take that how you like.

GOLDMAN, ALBERT: *The Lives Of John Lennon* (William Morris, 1988). Intricately researched muck-raking, this must be read on the understanding that the good doctor disliked Lennon, The Beatles and pop, and that he did it for the money.

HARRY, BILL: *John Lennon Encyclopedia* (Virgin, 2000). A vast and detailed tome by an art-school crony of John Lennon, editor of *Mersey Beat* and pal of The Beatles up to and beyond their disbandment.

NORMAN, PHILIP: *Shout! The True Story Of The Beatles* (Elm Tree, 1981). Despite factual errors, this is still accepted by most as the standard work on the group.

SEAMAN, FREDERIC: *Borrowed Time* (Xanadu, 1991). One of the more compassionate "insider" efforts.

SHEFF, DAVID (with John Lennon and Yoko Ono, edited by G Barry Olson): *The Playboy Interviews* (New English Library, 1982). One of the final interviews, and perhaps the lengthiest ever, it delves into many important areas, including memories of nearly every song he ever composed.

SHEPHERD, BILLY: *The True Story Of The Beatles* (Beat Publications, 1964). Neither a triumph of linguistic ability nor a penetrating insight into the human condition, this assignment was, nevertheless, the first of more Beatles biographies than anyone in 1964 could ever have comprehended.

Notes

In addition to my own correspondence and interviews, I have used the following sources, which I would like to credit:-

1. *Today*, BBC Radio Four, 9 December 1980
2. *Lennon Remembers: The Rolling Stone Interviews* by J Wenner (Penguin, 1980)
3. *Six O'Clock News*, BBC 1, 9 December 1980
4. Richmal Crompton was to be short-listed for inclusion on the *Sgt Pepper's Lonely Hearts Club Band* montage.
5. *The John Lennon Encyclopaedia* by B Harry (Virgin, 2000)
6. *Record Mirror*, 21 January 1956
7. *Backbeat: Die Stuart Sutcliffe Story* by A Clayson and S Sutcliffe (Bastei Lubbe, 1994), a translation of the original manuscript of *Backbeat – Stuart Sutcliffe: The Lost Beatle* by the same authors (Pan-Macmillan, 1994)
8. *Arthur Ballard* by P Davies (Old Bakehouse, 1998)
9. By coincidence, a photograph of another 1960s pop-star-in-waiting, Dave Berry, was published that same week in the *Daily Mirror* above a non-story about his big feet.
10. 1975 letter to Stuart Sutcliffe's mother
11. *Liverpool Daily Post*, 19 March 1964
12. *Disc And Music Echo*, 6 November 1970
13. *Trinity Parish Magazine*, August 1960
14. Renamed "The John Lennon" in 1964, during the Rickenbacker firm's period of greatest prosperity – because Lennon was still picking at his Model 1996 at the height of world-wide Beatlemania. If employed but rarely for soloing, it was unique for its jangling effect as rhythm *arpeggio*.
15. *Hamburg: The Cradle Of British Rock* by A Clayson (Sanctuary, 1997)
16. *The Beat Goes On*, February 1992
17. *Let's All Go Down The Cavern* by S Leigh and P Frame (Vermilion, 1984)

18. And later butt of Lennon's paraphrasing of a 1967 B-side hook-line – "baby, you're a rich man too" – as "baby, you're a rich fag Jew", a dig at the public school undercurrents of anti-Semitism and homo-eroticism that helped make Brian Epstein what he was.

19. *Brian Epstein: The Man Who Made The Beatles* by R Coleman (Viking, 1989)

20. *Serge Gainsbourg: View From The Exterior* by A Clayson (Sanctuary, 1998)

21. *The Playboy Interviews* ed G Barry Golson (New English Library, 1982)

22. *The Beatles: The Authorized Biography* by H Davies (Heinemann, 1970)

23. Once, Brian Poole And The Tremeloes were said to have been the ones Decca chose instead of The Beatles when, allegedly, both groups auditioned on New Year's Day 1962. According to Brian Poole himself, however, "Our studio test took place sometime in 1961 – not the day The Beatles did theirs. How did that story get around? Maybe one of our publicists made it up.

    "You check the release dates. Our first LP was *Big Big Hits Of 1962* – the first ever party-dance compilation mix, by the way – so we had to have been recording quite a bit before that to be allowed to do an album in those days. Also, George Martin told me later that The Beatles were still in Germany when we were recording as a backing vocal group for Decca – at EMI Studios."

24. *Peterborough Standard*, 7 December 1962

25. Lennon's sleeve notes to *Off The Beatle Track* by The George Martin Orchestra (Parlophone PC5 3057, 1964)

26. *Melody Maker*, 31 March 1973

27. *Lennon* by R Coleman (McGraw Hill, 1984)

28. *New Musical Express*, 1 February 1963

29. *Radio Luxembourg Book Of The Stars No 2* ed J Fishman (Souvenir Press, 1963)

30. *Tribute To The Big O*, BBC Radio Two, 5 January 1989

31. *Melody Maker*, 7 May 1963

32. *Melody Maker*, 9 March 1963

33. With a title borrowed from Walt Disney's *Snow White And The Seven Dwarfs*, 1937

34. *Mersey Beat*, 29 November 1963

35. *Melody Maker*, 3 August 1963

36. *Andover Advertiser*, 3 January 1965

37. Not the Johnny Sandon And The Remo Four number.

38. Third track, side two of *Memphis Beat* by Jerry Lee Lewis (Philips, 1966)

39. *Mojo: The Psychedelic Beatles: Special Edition*, 2001

40. Quoted in *Heroes And Villains: The True Story Of The Beach Boys* by S Gaines (Grafton, 1986)

41. *Playboy*, 19 October 1964

42. Even in the light of John Lennon's laddish comment to Brian de Courcy, Melbourne concert promoter: "Christ, Brian! You've got a grip like a fucking bear. I bet you're

not a poofter." (Quoted in *The Spinning Wheels: The Story Of A Melbourne Rhythm And Blues Band* by D Hirst, published by Park Fraser, 2002.)

43. *X-Ray* by R Davies (Viking, 1994)

44. Quoted in Alex Palao's booklet to *Zombie Heaven* CD box set (Big Beat ZOMBOX 7, 1997)

45. To Ray Coleman

46. *Paul McCartney: Many Years From Now* by B Miles (Vintage, 1998)

47. *New Musical Express*, 25 June 1966

48. *Don't Let Me Be Misunderstood* by E Burdon and J Marshall Craig (Thunder Mouth, 2001)

49. *Frank Zappa In His Own Words* ed B Miles (Omnibus, 1994)

50. *National Rock Star*, 18 December 1976

51. *Revolution In The Head: The Beatles' Records And The Sixties* by I MacDonald (Fourth Estate, 1994)

52. *Melody Maker*, 7 August 1971

53. *Rolling Stone*, 14 December 1967

54. *Time Out*, 4 September 1988

55. *Sunday Times*, 27 February 1983

56. Published by Pierian Press, 1983

57. *Disc And Music Echo*, 16 December 1967

58. Excerpt from Yoko Ono's opening address at her exhibition at the Everson Museum of Art, 9 October 1971

59. *Disc and Music Echo*, 12 August 1968

60. *Beatles Monthly*, July 1968

61. Adapted in the USA as *All In The Family*

62. *Ginsberg: A Biography* by B Miles (Viking, 1996)

63. Quoted in *Loose Talk* ed L Botts (Rolling Stone Press, 1980)

64. *Daily Express*, precise date obscured, 1969

65. *Chicago Tribune*, March 1981

66. *Rolling Stone*, 27 August 1987

67. *Rolling Stone*, 15 February 1969

68. *Rolling Stone*, 22 January 1981

69. *Rolling Stone*, 30 April 1981

70. *The Observer*, 27 November 1968

71. Sleeve note to *Let It Be* (Apple PXS/PCS 7096, 1970)

72. *Beatles Unlimited*, February 1977

73. To Giovanni Dadamo

74. *Daily Express*, 3 May 1969

75. *Disc And Music Echo*, 22 March 1969

76. To Michael Wale

77. *Daily Express*, 5 May 1987

78. *Musician*, November 1987

79. *Melody Maker*, 19 July 1969

80. *Zabadak* No 7, July 1994

81. *Disc And Music Echo*, 9 November 1969

82. *Henley Standard*, 30 August 2002

83. *Record Mirror*, 14 February 1970

84. *Melody Maker*, 27 April 1974

85. *Stereo Review*, November 1969

86. Covered in Britain by Frankie Vaughan

87. *Arena*, BBC2, 27 November 1989

88. To be issued in mass-market paperback by Simon & Schuster, 1988

89. *Time*, 21 May 1976

90. *New York Times*, 20 December 1964

91. Quoted by Chris "Ace" Kefford in *Record Collector*, No 179, July 1994

92. Translated from *Jacques Brel: Un Vie* by O Todd (Robert Laffont, 1984)

93. *New Musical Express*, 15 February 1963

94. *Daily Express*, 10 December 1980

95. *Daily Express*, 11 December 1980

96. Published by Headline, 1996

97. Published by Plexus, 1985

98. *Anthology* by The Beatles (Cassell, 2000)

99. "The written word remains"

100. *Sunday Times*, 6 May 1990

101. *Reading Evening Post*, 9 December 1980

Index

George Harrison

Printed in the United Kingdom by MPG Books Ltd, Bodmin

Published by Sanctuary Publishing Limited, Sanctuary House, 45-53 Sinclair Road,
London W14 0NS, United Kingdom

www.sanctuarypublishing.com

Distributed in the US by Publishers Group West

ISBN: 1-86074-489-3

George Harrison

Alan Clayson

Sanctuary

"*Like most clever young men, hurrying home with a pile of books and glowering at the passers-by, he magnifies the gulf between men of genius and ordinary stupid people... He cannot believe that stockbrokers may have strange dreams, that butchers cutting off chops may be touched with intimations of mortality, that the grocer, even as he hesitates over the sugar, may yet see the world in a grain of sand.*"

JB Priestley on Colin Wilson's The Outsider

November 2001

George Harrison could not permit himself the luxury of hope after a syndicated photograph from Tuscany reached the media. He smiled his old smile, but, ashen-faced and grey-haired now, he seemed to have aged shockingly. Those well-wishers in closest contact – including Ringo and Paul – became as uneasily aware as George was that there might be less than six months left.

As if blowing sparks of optimism, he marshalled enough energy to record "Like A Horse To Water", a new opus by himself and Dhani. Yet outward evidence of respite from gathering infirmity ended when a brain tumour developed, requiring weeks of chemotherapy in a specialist clinic in Switzerland. Prescribed a course of drugs and avoidance of stressful situations, he convalesced in Kuppaqulua – where he continued to practice guitar and tease songs from nothing more than the ghost of a lyric or melody.

Being awash with medications for a debilitating illness wasn't the soundest footing from which to consider another Cloud Nine-sized comeback. A final desperate strategy was an admission to New York's Staten Island University Hospital for what George had been convinced was a "revolutionary" new radiotherapy technique that had bought time for other cancer sufferers. There was, however, little that could be done.

Coming to terms with what was inevitable, George resigned as director of Harrisongs, and, with characteristic black humour, created "RIP Ltd.", an outlet for "Like A Horse To Water" and other latter-day compositions. He also affirmed a wish to be cremated without ceremony, and for the ashes to be scattered on the Ganges.

A further onslaught of symptoms brought him to UCLA Medical Centre in Los Angeles for care rather than cure. The light was fading, but he discharged himself and took refuge in the house of Gavin de Becker, head of the most proficient Hollywood security service money could buy. As it had been in Switzerland and New York, there wasn't a newspaper editor on the planet who wouldn't promise a fortune for a Harrison exclusive or an up-to-date picture. Nevertheless, de Becker's home was as off-limits as Howard Hugues's Las Vegas penthouse. For George Harrison, it was there, with imposition on his treasured privacy as low as it could be, that the light went out in the early afternoon of Thursday, 29th of November 2001.

About The Author

Described by *The Western Morning News* as the "AJP Taylor of pop", Alan Clayson is the author of many books on music, including the best-selling *Backbeat*, subject of a major film. He has contributed to journals as disparate as *Record Collector*, *The Independent*, *The Beat Goes On*, *Mojo*, *Mediaeval World*, *The Guardian*, *Folk Roots* and, as a teenager, the notorious *Schoolkids Oz*. He had also written and presented programmes on national radio and has lectured on both sides of the Atlantic.

Before he became better known as a pop historian, he led the legendary Clayson And The Argonauts and was thrust to "a premier position on rock's Lunatic Fringe" (*Melody Maker*). Today, his solo cabaret act remains "more than just a performance; an experience" (*Village Voice*). "It is difficult to explain to the uninitiated quite what to expect," adds *The Independent*. There is even an Alan Clayson fan club, which dates from a 1992 appearance in Chicago.

Alan Clayson's cult following continues to grow, along with demand for his production skills in the studio and the number of versions of his compositions by such diverse acts as Dave Berry – in whose Cruisers he played keyboards in the mid 1980s – and (via a collaboration with Yardbird Jim McCarty) Jane Relf and new age outfit Stairway. He has also worked with the Portsmouth Sinfonia, Wreckless Eric, The Pretty Things and Screaming Lord Sutch, among others.

Born in Dover in 1951, Alan Clayson lives near Henley-on-Thames with his wife, Inese, and sons, Jack and Harry.

To Alan Peacock

Contents

Prologue
The Invisible Man

I'm not certain how many people know this, but George Harrison – along with Paul McCartney, John Lennon and various others – used to be a member of a Merseyside pop group whose act went down well with local teenagers. Later, quite a few of their gramophone records got into the hit parade. George was the readiest of the four to venture beyond pop music through his explorations of Indian culture and, after the group disbanded, the underwriting of HandMade Films, now a pillar of British cinema. More subtly than John Lennon, he rode out the 1970s as the most self-contained – and oddest – ex-Beatle. Nevertheless, despite a career blighted with stimulant abuse, marital ructions, religious obsession and proven artistic plagiarism, muckrakers would be hard pressed to ravage a distinguished, charitable and humorous middle-aged musician whose character – in contrast to those of John, Paul and Ringo – was rooted in a secure family background.

Following the success of 1989's album, *Cloud Nine*, fans await George Harrison's next album with more anticipation than at any time since the celebrated *All Things Must Pass* triple LP of 1970. His growth as a composer was one of the pressures that caused the sundering of The Beatles in that same year, notably when his 'Something' – along with McCartney's 'Yesterday' – emerged as one of the most covered songs of all time.

Harrison's sojourn as a Beatle and its repercussions will always remain central to any consideration of him as a figure in time's fabric. Unlike in a biography of some Dark Ages king, we are embarrassed with too much information – an idle afternoon in 1968 when George and Klaus Voorman painted a friend's 1966 Citroën 2CV was deemed worthy of a half-page of speculation in one Beatle fanzine in which no piece of information was without value, no item too insignificant to be interesting. As the Bible can prove any religious or moral theory, so the millions of words chronicling and analysing his every trivial act (to which I shall be adding) can warp the Harrison saga to any purpose.

In one empty moment, I thought of writing it as a calypso, but, as I'd arrived at many (although not all) of the same conclusions as other Beatle-related authors, I decided it would be misleading to be too "original" or to disguise nostalgia as social history. With a bit of perverted logic, I could have been mischievous enough to intimate that George indulged in bondage sessions with Dora Bryan or that he paid a Mafia hit-man to bump off Roy Orbison. One of Lennon's biographers did worse.

Lately, many well-known heroes have gone down. Richard the Lionheart, Robin Hood and Bonnie Prince Charlie are three who have been transformed respectively into a sadistic homosexual, a non-existent thug and a wife-beating alcoholic. Edward the Confessor, apparently, turns out to be A Right Bastard. Indeed, if one American author is to be believed, there is a case for Adolf Hitler to be re-assessed as Not Such A Bad Bloke After All. A similar reappraisal has been applied to the notorious pop manager Allen Klein, "the Robin Hood of pop", whose questionable financial machinations were excused by Rolling Stone Keith Richards as "the price of an education".[1] Nonetheless, it is feasible that more "new and rediscovered" evidence may prompt a restoration of earlier assumptions until they are again amended.

While the deeds and personalities of the illustrious become more nebulous and ambiguous in retrospect, I have taken care to define as widely as possible the myriad social, cultural, economic, environmental and other undercurrents and myths that polarise and prejudice what we know about George Harrison and The Beatles. Often, pop biography has tended to shy away from these areas, even though they form a more tangible basis for investigation than treating a subject's flippant remarks as gospel or squeezing a few paragraphs from, say, an encounter between Paul McCartney and Dave Dee, Dozy, Beaky, Mick And Tich in a Cromwell Road pub: "All he said," recalled Dozy, "was, 'I've seen you lot on the telly,' and we said, 'We've seen you on the telly as well.'"[2]

This is a fair example of the depth to which those who happen to be in the same profession know each other, although in showbusiness it's easy to get a different impression. Entering a Southsea hotel bar one evening in 1988, a puzzled Dave Berry was embraced by Gerry of The Pacemakers, who'd become buoyant with rose-tinted enthusiasm for the Swinging '60s. Dave hardly knew Gerry then. "People can only see each other from their own state of consciousness," expounded George Harrison. "The press' state of consciousness is virtually nil, so they never get the true essence of anything they write about."[3] During The Beatles' only Australasian tour, was George "outgoing and friendly", as the singer Johnny Devlin found him, or "deeply introspective and hard to know",[4] the view of radio personality Bob Rogers?

As Horace reminds us, "*quandoque bonus dormitat Homerus*" – even the wisest can make mistakes. In his own autobiography, George is guilty of factual error, such as when he states that his family was living at Mackett's Lane when he first visited Hamburg. (A recording agreement that he signed during his second trip to Germany clearly gives his home address as 25 Upton Green, Speke.) Those whose lives are devoted to collating information about The Beatles could alight on lesser mistakes and omissions, as they might while scrutinising *The Quiet One*. To them, I can only say that it's as accurate as I was able to make it.

They might also take into account that I'm the sort who has to screw himself up before talking to complete strangers at a moment's notice. My nerve failed completely when I noticed Jane Asher, McCartney's former girlfriend, two seats to the left of me in a London theatre. During the interval, it didn't seem the time or place to actuate a dialogue with her about Paul's ex-colleague. At times, I was riven with self-disgust when wheedling an interview from someone who only wanted to crawl away and hide. I spent a lot of time while in Liverpool wandering the streets with pangs of muttered nostalgia for locations to which I'd hitherto never been but only drunk in second hand as germane to The Beatles' legend – Litherland, Penny Lane, the ferry 'cross the Mersey, *et al*. In 1977, my group Clayson And The Argonauts played at Eric's, a club in Mathew Street where the spirit of '77 faced the ghost of '62. While The Argonauts busied themselves in the adjacent pub – the Grapes – after our usual harrowing soundcheck, I crossed the road and climbed through a gap in the fence to pay my respects on that patch of unofficial countryside that had surfaced on the site of the Cavern. If it had been a film, you'd have heard the ranting abandon of 'Twist And Shout' as a spooky drift, as if through a seashore conch.

Ten years later, Merseyside, in recession, had fallen back on its cradling of The Beatles, just as it had so long fed off its past as a great port. While it was entirely fitting that the city's university should have founded Britain's first Institute of Popular Music, other by-products of The Beatles weren't as anxious to foster research. A "Cavern" had been reconstructed down Mathew Street next to Cavern Walks shopping mail. Propping up the bar in the John Lennon pub opposite, tourists on the scent of The Beatles might have been regaled by John's late Uncle Charlie or, more reluctantly, former Beatles "manager" Allan Williams with endless reminiscences about what Ringo said to Rory Storm down the Blue Angel in 1962.

In the aftermath of Albert Goldman's infamous portrayal of Lennon, I could understand why Williams and others either refused to talk altogether or demanded payment for so doing. According to his secretary, The Beatles' record producer George Martin was sick and tired of retelling the old, old story. Many of Harrison's former employees were legally bound not to discuss life in the offices of HandMade Films or at Friar Park, George's estate in Oxfordshire.

After weighing every word of it, I delivered a letter to Friar Park by hand. Requesting George's co-operation, it assured him that I wasn't a scum reporter but an *artiste* like himself. *The Quiet One* was to be a respectful account, concentrating mainly on his professional career and artistic output. Unlike certain other tomes about musicians with whom he was (and is) associated, it would not peter out after a rehash of Those Fabulous '60s. I wanted him to like it. Six weeks later, I received a charming reply from California. It advised me that "Mr Harrison does not have the least interest in having his biography done again".[6]

By then, however there was no turning back. I'd accumulated a filing cabinet of Harrisonia, exercise books full of scribble to decipher, interview tapes to transcribe and a deadline I'd never meet. More material was arriving with every post. To get closer to him, I'd attended a Hare Krishna evening and waded through numerous religious tracts that led me to research myself as much as George Harrison.

His not granting me just one little interview was galling with me living "just up the road", so to speak, but this isn't a scissors-and-clippings job; I've drawn a lot of information from press archives – some of them quite obscure – because we can learn a lot from verbatim accounts that recreate the feeling of being there. Unlike people, they are not influenced by the fact of being observed – *litera scripta manet*[7]. For most of my secondary research, I went first and last to my good friend Ian Drummond, who, as a scholar and observer of The Beatles and George Harrison, commands the highest respect. I wish to express my deepest gratitude to him for his encouragement and practical help with this project.

I'd like you all to put your hands together for Peter Doggett, who saw me over the final hurdle. I am also grateful to Brian Cresswell, Pete Frame, Spencer Leigh, Steve Maggs, Colin Miles and John Tobler for their faith and very real assistance, especially as consultants over apparent trivia. For example, dear sub-editor, I'm told it's HandMade rather than Handmade or Hand Made. I also owe a particular debt to Dave and Caroline Humphreys for accommodating me whenever I was on Merseyside, and for Dave being Dr Watson to my Sherlock Holmes.

Special thanks are in order, too, for Susan Hill, Amanda Marshall, Carys Thomas, Helen Gummer and the rest of the team in Museum Street, plus a special "hello" to my original editor, Hilary Murray. Let's hear it too for Penny Braybrooke, who authorised this reissue, as well as Jeffrey Hudson, Eddy Leviten, Alan Heal, Dan Froude, Chris Bradford and especially Michelle Knight, whose patience and understanding went beyond the call of duty.

For their advice and for trusting me with archive material, let's have a big round of applause for Phil Cooper (of Radio 210), Ron Cooper, Lesley Dibley, Mark Ellen, Ann Freer, *The Henley Standard*, David Horn (of the University of Liverpool Institute of Popular Music), David Humbles, Allan Jones (of *Melody Maker*), Fraser Massey, Steve Morris, Darrell Paddick, Jill Pritchard, Charles and Deborah Salt, Jonathan Taylor-Sabine and Michael Towers.

I have also drawn from conversations with the following musicians: Ian Amey, Don Andrew, Roger Barnes, Andre Barreau, Alan Barwise, Cliff Bennett, Dave Berry, Barry Booth, Allan Clarke, Terry Clarke, Frank Connor, Eric E Cooke, Tony Crane, Daniel D'Arcy, Spencer Davis, Dave Dee, Wayne Fontana, Freddie Garrity, Gary Gold, Eric Goulden, Mike Hart, Rick Huxley, Garry Jones, Billy Kinsley, Graham Larkbey, Kenny Lynch, Stephen MacDonald, Kevin Manning, Jim McCarty, Zoot Money, Adrian Moulton, Sandy Newman, Ray Phillips, Ray Pinfold, Brian Poole, Gail Richards, Mike Robinson, Twinkle Rogers, Jim Simpson, Larry Smith, Norman Smith, the late Vivian Stanshall, the late Lord David Sutch, Mike Sweeney, John Townsend, Paul Tucker, Chris Warman, Norman Warwick, Val Wiseman and David Yeats. Invaluable too was a long chat with Bill Harry.

It may be obvious to the reader that I have received much information from sources that prefer not to be mentioned. Nevertheless, I wish to thank them.

Thanks are also due in varying degrees to Veronica Armstrong, B&T Typewriters, Robert and Janice Bartel, Colin Baylis, Stuart and Kathryn Booth, Carol Boyer, Rob Bradford, Eva Marie Brunner, Gordon and Rosemary Clayson, Hilary Cresswell, Greg and Debi Daniels, Doreen Davidson, Nancy Davis, Kevin Delaney, Tim and Sarah Fagan, Kathi and Rick Fowler, Caroline Freyer, Ian Gilmore, Stanley Green, Tom Hall (of the Spinning Disk), Louise Harrison, Virginia Harry, Paul Hearne, Martin Hockley, Matt Holland, Graham Humphreys, Oliver Johnson, Sarah Knake, Graham and Yvonne Lambourne, Mark and Carol Lapidos, Brian Leafe, Bill Mielenz, Coy Ness, Russell Newmark, Sarah Parish, Carolyn Pinfold, Evan and Lyn Reynolds, George Rowden, Steve Rowley, Steve Shiner (of the Reading Hare Krishna Society), Maggie

Simpson, Andrea Tursso, Kathryn Varley and Ted Woodings – plus Inese, Jack and Harry, who are now more knowledgeable about George Harrison and The Beatles than they ever needed to be.

Alan Clayson, July 2001

1 *The Rebel*

With middle-aged candour, he'd insist, "I'm just an ordinary fellow."[8]
Certainly, the occupations of George Harrison's immediate forebears
were the kind you'd expect an ordinary fellow to have. Merseysiders
all, they came and went and in between they earned livings as joiners,
able seamen, bricklayers, engine drivers and similarly honourable if
unlettered professions. Edward Harrison, George's great-grandfather,
had inscribed a mark rather than a signature on the parish register
when he wed Elizabeth Hargreaves, a carter's daughter, in 1868 when
both were under age. As well as bearing the stigma of his illegitimacy,
Edward had been launched into life at the height of a cholera
epidemic that had struck Victorian Liverpool.

From peasant stock with such solid-sounding tributary surnames as
Shepherd and Thompson, the Harrisons had lived in the
predominantly working-class South Liverpool district of Wavertree for
perhaps two centuries when Edward's grandson, Harold Hargreaves
Harrison, was born in a house off one of its main junctions in 1909.
By the time 17-year-old Harold threw in a job selling mangles to go to
sea as a White Star Line steward, new tangles of terraces – raw red
brick rather than ancient sandstone – were beginning to impinge upon
the area's surviving parks and tree-lined avenues. The largest patch of
green, Wavertree Playground, had long been slashed along its western
side by the clattering railway connection to Lime Street Central, three
miles away in the heart of the city.

To outsiders, Wavertree was already becoming indistinguishable
from any other Merseyside suburb when Harold Harrison began a
two-year courtship of Louise French, a greengrocer's assistant and

daughter of the uniformed commissionaire at New Brighton's grand Tower Ballroom, the most capacious seaside dance palais in the northwest outside Blackpool. Within a year of their marriage in 1931, Harold and Louise were blessed with their only daughter, who was named after her mother, as their eldest son, born three years later, was named after Harold.

His job being the only impediment to family stability, Mr Harrison left his ship to take a chance on finding work in the mid-1930s' recession. For months, he drew dole money until taken on as a Corporation bus conductor in 1937. By the outbreak of the Second World War, he'd been promoted to driver and was also an active member of his depot's union and social committee. In 1940, Goering's Luftwaffe pounded the Liverpool docks, and Louise gave birth to another child, Peter, in the two-up/two-down family home along a small, neglected cul-de-sac within the clang of the High Street fire station.

With its front door opening straight onto the pavement, 12 Arnold Grove had no garden, apart from a minuscule square of flower-bed that was less prominent in the paved back yard than the outside toilet and the zinc tub that was carried indoors and set down before the fireplace in the lino-floored kitchen whenever sufficient hot water had been accumulated for the family to bathe. Water was boiled either on the open coal fire or a gas cooker that boomed when lit. It was generally lukewarm by the third immersion in the tub. Babies were washed in the sink. The kitchen apart, the house in winter was cold enough for the windows to ice up and goose-flesh to rise on those who'd neglected to warm their freezing sheets with a hot-water bottle before retiring.

Into this household of shared bedrooms and bathwater, plumpish 33-year-old Mrs Harrison's final confinement would produce the remarkable George – named after King George VI – on 25 February 1943, a mild, dry night.[8.1] The worst of the war was past, although barrage balloons still hung over the docklands where giant chimneys and cranes were trained on the sky like anti-aircraft guns.

Both Peter and George took after their father, with his slim build, jug-handle ears, angular features and eyebrows that, thickening towards the nose, tinged their lopsided smiles with gravity. George inherited some Irish blood from Louise, and there was the hint of a leprechaun about him, but one that carefully deliberated its impishness. Growing from babyhood, his blond hair darkened to brown, and he caught and held a dry and "common" Scouse drawl that would be with him always, rendering "care" as "cur" and splitting "bringing" into "bring-ging".

His earliest memory was of the buying of three chickens to fatten in a back-yard coop for Christmas. He also recalled the hard wooden kneelers in the church down nearby Chestnut Grove, where he'd been baptised and where his Roman Catholic mother would take her youngsters to Mass. George has said, "[Although] I almost became a Catholic when I was eleven or twelve, I couldn't relate to Christ being the only son of God. The only things that made an impression were the oil paintings and the Stations of the Cross." Reacting against "the Catholic trick" of indoctrinating young minds, he also questioned the motives of adult communicants: "They go to church and it's all that thing about, you know, Tommy Jones has got a brown suit on, and here comes Mrs Smith with her new hat. It's a bore."[9]

None of the Harrison offspring were forced to attend church. In any case, Harold was a lapsed Anglican. Neither he nor Louise pressured the children to do well academically, either, although Harold was pleased when "Our Kid" (as youngest Merseyside siblings were often nicknamed) passed the Eleven Plus examination to gain a place at a grammar school rather than a secondary modern where Peter went. Perhaps to beef up a self-image of one streetwise beyond his years, George has told tales of being allowed, while still at primary school, to "stay out all night when I wanted to and have a drink when I wanted to".[10] Such excessive licence seems at odds with both George's later destruction of unfavourable school reports before they reached his parents' eyes and the moderation and hard work incumbent upon Mr and Mrs Harrison to keep their young family fed and clothed.

Harold was the firmer of the two, but in practice the Harrison household was more liberal than might be expected in an age when "spare the rod and spoil the child" was still a much-quoted maxim.

Nonetheless, until the age of 13, when he was hospitalised for seven weeks with nephritis,[11] George's upbringing was as undramatic and free from major traumas as that of any other "ordinary fellow" from Liverpool.

"It is one big family," Jimmy Tarbuck, one of Liverpool's many famous comedians, would say. "No matter where a Scouser goes, he never stops being a part of it."[12] Liverpool looks after its own. The Saturday after the Hillsborough disaster, I just happened to be there when the entire city, with every traffic light on red, observed a silence for those crushed to death in the bulging stadium during a Liverpool football team away match. The quiet was so absolute you could almost listen to it. When the two minutes were up, a Salvation Army band pierced the heavy air at the crowded Anfield ground, from where a symbolic chain of football scarves stretched across to Goodison Park, home of Everton, the rival club in this city formed of overlapping towns.

Southern settlements in Britain lack the fiercer sense of regional identity and loyalty – even fair play and compassion – peculiar to areas like Liverpool, Glasgow and Newcastle. There is a common unconsciousness that bonds Liverpudlians more strongly than, say, the inhabitants of Dover or Guildford. I would dare to hint that tolerance towards minorities is more pronounced than elsewhere in this, one of the most cosmopolitan of cities. As well as containing the largest Chinatown in Europe, Liverpool is referred to facetiously as "the capital of Ireland". This is traceable to the ingress from across the Irish Sea and through the murky sweep of the Mersey that led to Irish dockers becoming the foundation of the 19th-century merchant prosperity when a third of Britain's exports went through Liverpool.

Prosperity was thin on the ground when George Harrison and those born in the war years came to consciousness. Food and clothing continued to be rationed well into the 1950s. To further alleviate the plight of poor families – of which the Harrisons were typical – the government introduced "Utility" goods. Although not expensive, a garment or item of furniture thus marked was deemed to be functional and hard wearing. The same could not be said of the homes in which many Utility consumers on Merseyside had to dwell, however. It hadn't been practical to erect more than the most essential buildings during the war, and in peacetime a lot of those still standing cried out for modernisation. Even in 1960, thousands of Liverpudlians were still living without bathrooms and hot water in dark terraces with front rooms cold and tidy for funerals, and grim side passages leading to outside lavatories.

As an economic base, Liverpool had been overlooked since the gouging of the ship canal to Manchester. To the affluent south, it had become a corner of the map where penury and unemployment clotted. It was assumed that the further north you voyaged, the more primitive the natives, just as the Roman historian Tacitus had stated. Past Birmingham, people still wore clogs, didn't they?

Disregarded by the rest of the country, "the pool of life" – as Jung had tagged it – had bubbled in its isolation and built-in resilience. "A good cry and a good laugh were never far apart,"[12] playwright Carla Lane wrote of her home city. What else can you say about a place where, beneath a hoarding inquiring, "What would you do if Jesus came to Liverpool?" a hand had taken the trouble to scrawl "Move St John to inside right."[13] Liverpool spawned a crop of that strain of comedians who relied on cheeky forthrightness to get laughs and conveyed the feeling that everyone knew him and he them, although most were compelled to go south for national acclaim.

More buffoons than other types of artists emerged from the city, but festering in the streets to the immediate east of the unfinished Anglican cathedral was a Scouse bohemia teeming with poets, painters and the like eking out a living or feeding off college grants in studio flats within crumbling back-to-back Victorian town-houses with peeling pillars, off-white window ledges thick with pigeon droppings, thunderous door-knockers and rubbish clogging behind railings. One day, the adult George Harrison would be asked if Liverpool was like New York's vibrant beatnik district, Greenwich Village. "No," he replied, considering the area as a whole. "It's more like the Bowery."[14]

From the perspective of poky Arnold Grove, you could appreciate the comparison with the Big Apple's most run-down corner. For the Harrisons, things could only get better, and during the family's 18th year on the council housing list they did. Assisted partly by the Luftwaffe, an urban renewal programme was under way, which was evidenced by the erection of churches like dental surgeries and the box-like dwellings that spread across slum overspill estates like that in Speke, where the Harrisons moved when George was six.

25 Upton Green was unquestionably an improvement, with a hallway, bathroom and extra bedroom. The prospect of a refrigerator replacing the meat safe did not seem as far fetched here as it had in Wavertree. Not so remote, either, were such luxuries as a washing machine and a telephone. However, while Our Kid, in his excitement, "just ran round and 'round it all"[15] that first day, his mum soon missed the cosier domesticity of Arnold Grove. She felt uncomfortable in the terrace circling the roundabout of scrappy grass where the forlorn side road came to its dead end. Some neighbours glared with gormless menace as the newcomers unloaded their furniture. Louise blamed their brats for the nocturnal theft of shrubs she planted in the small front garden. Such was the consequence, she concluded, of the council mixing "the good and the bad families together, hoping the good would lift the rest".[10]

Thrust to the city's outskirts, the Harrisons' home was in the middle of what had once been fields but was now a sprawling peninsula of residential streets built by the book for those who had no choice. To the south and west, Liverpool airport droned by the windswept mudbanks of the river, while the A561 ran along the northern border, lined with belching chimneys. Chemical waste fouled the air and waterways. Harold Harrison had to pass through this industrial zone to reach Speke Bus Depot.

Harold's youngest sons were prevented from enrolling at Alderwood Junior School, directly opposite Upton Green, because its roll was full. Instead, Peter and George were bussed five miles back towards Wavertree to Herondale Road, where stood Dovedale Church of England Primary, the only school with vacant desks, when the gaberdine-raincoated and short-trousered brothers' formal education began.

Under the unimaginative regime of chanted multiplication tables and spelling tests, George made steady progress. To his father's fury, he was once caned for quite a minor misdemeanour, but headmaster Robert "Pop" Evans and his teachers had to struggle on termly reports to write anything that made Harrison Minor remotely extraordinary. He was sound enough in most subjects, his retentive memory and methodical tenacity facilitating a mature and sometimes encyclopaedic understanding of people and places, interactions and outcomes. As well as a solid grasp of mathematics, there were also indications of a flair for art and creative writing, although he was loath to take literary risks for fear of getting into trouble. For the same reason, he was rather a shrinking violet when obliged to approach the teacher's desk with his exercise books. However, George was talkative enough with his playground pals and needed little coaxing to participate – and even to sing solo – in class assemblies.

A younger child asserting himself, George also loved to entertain at home. Louise remembered her husband giving him glove puppets on the Christmas before his tenth birthday and how, "from that day on, whenever we had visitors, he always insisted on giving a little show kneeling behind the settee. George was always full of fun when he was a child. He never caused any big trouble, and even the neighbours liked him a lot, which is unusual with a little boy."[15]

A different George had cringed with embarrassment when, after delivering him for his first day at school, Louise had lingered outside with the other mothers. The next morning, he implored her to let him and Peter walk the mile from Arnold Grove to school unescorted. Even at five, he resented any personal intrusion that her gossiping at the gate with other parents might precipitate.

Yet another George would later turn his back on the Speke estate to roam the farmland, woods and marshes of the Cheshire plain to the east on foot or bicycle: "There's a part of me which likes to keep quiet, and I do prefer wide, open, quiet spaces to traffic jams."[15]

He endured plenty of those after he started at Liverpool Institute High School For Boys in September 1954. Self-conscious in the regulation uniform of black bomber shoes, grey flannels, blazer, white shirt and tie, the first-former boarded the number 86 bus to school from the stop on Speke Boulevard for a trek which, in the morning rush hour, took just under an hour to reach the dropping-off point in Mount Street, within earshot of the cathedral bells. A compensation for living so far away from the school was that he was generally able to secure a seat before the vehicle filled to standing room only. He quickly came to detest this cramped, jolting commuting, with its banal chit-chat, body pressure and "some old man breathing down your neck".[16] For the return journey, he discovered that other pupils from Speke preferred to walk through the bustling city centre to catch the bus home from the Pier Head terminus.

From the outset, the long journey to and from the Institute dogged George's involvement in the extra-mural activities that the school offered. To attend a swimming gala at the usual venue in Walton meant hanging about for hours after the 4pm dismissal. Unless they were held during the lunch break, attending meetings of the many worthy societies devoted to chess, modelling, archaeology *et al* meant arriving back at Upton Green in the middle of the evening, ravenous, tired and with homework to do. That Peter's mixed secondary modern was only a ten-minute dawdle from home made up for any intellectual inferiority he may have felt through Our Kid going to a grammar school. Needless to say, the family's limited finances forbade a week in Ireland with the Canoeing Club and school trips further abroad.

Because his participation was so restricted, George nurtured a resentment of the Institute's hearty clubbism, with its slide shows, "eminent speakers" and patronage by masters who either dressed down in cardigans or, to drill those daft enough to enlist in the Combined Cadet Force, donned dung-coloured regimentals. Yet, at a time when many English grammars were a cross between daytime borstals and homosexual dating bureaux, the Liverpool Institute wasn't too bad, although you might not have thought so at first glance. Old enough for Dickens to have given readings there, the building behind the imposing Greek façade was in poor repair, despite having escaped major damage by enemy action. An ink-welled desk mutilated with the initials of comedian Arthur Askey was still in general use 40 years after he had collected his leaving certificate.

The Institute was adjoined by a sister school, the Dance and

Drama Academy and the grimy looking Art College. Perhaps its proximity to these establishments and the city's Bohemian oasis bestowed upon it an attitude less shrouded in the draconian affectations and futile rigmarole prevalent in newer Merseyside grammars such as the Collegiate or Quarry Bank over in Calderstones, nicknamed "the Police State". Nevertheless, academic streaming was in full force and, rather than a cry of "Quiet!", the Latin "*Cave!*" would hush a noisy classroom when a gowned master was sighted. Religious education was of the Old Testament persuasion and, technically, the tone-deaf could get by in music lessons by adhering to quasi-mathematical rules of harmony. Prefects were permitted to cuff recalcitrants for such ghastly crimes as entering the school via its main door. Other than masters, that privilege was reserved for sixth formers, a select number of whom were allowed to attend life classes next door and watch "art" movies under the aegis of the Film Society. Moreover, an Institute pupil wasn't automatically threatened with expulsion for talking to a girl.

The headmaster in George's day was Jack Edwards, a round-faced Oxbridge type who stared appraisingly at whoever spoke to him. "In his own work," so it was written, "only excellence satisfied him. The second rate wasn't good enough."[17] Though his school cradled an impressive number of university graduates, the perfectionist Mr Edwards did not neglect – so his valediction in the Institute magazine attested – "its traditional quota of competent, hard-working but less brilliant boys, as well as some slower people. Mr Edwards kept a watchful eye on all three groups and, from time to time, he was minatory as seemed appropriate."[17]

With more than 1,000 "Liobians", as pupils were dubbed, under his wing, Edwards was "minatory" more often than his anonymous hagiographer implied. He was, however, amused despite himself when Ivan Vaughan, a gifted classical scholar, spent a morning impersonating a new boy at Quarry Bank. Other eccentric japes were also excused, including Vaughan's appearance at the Institute with his shoes painted yellow.

George Harrison was little more to the headmaster than a name in a register. As a second former, George was remembered by another master as "a very quiet if not even introverted little boy who would sit in the furthest corner and not even look up. I'm not saying he was unintelligent, but Harrison hardly ever spoke."[18] In the previous year, George had settled down almost eagerly to schoolwork, proud to be the brainiest member of the family. Two terms transformed him into a capable but uninvolved student, unblinking in the monotony of, say, geography teacher "Frankie" Boote's chalky exposition of Latvia's inner waterways.

Next came homework copied shakily off someone else on the bus, orders to spit his chewing gum into the classroom litter bin, even more passive disinterest in school and a report that concluded that he "seeks only to amuse himself".[10] The signature on the chit supposedly confirming that his parents had received the report was forged by the obliging mother of Arthur Kelly, a friend in the same class. As well as Arthur and, intermittently, a bespectacled boy named Charlie Shaw, George's circle of Institute ne'er-do-wells included Tony Workman, who'd tried to pick a fight with him on first acquaintance. With such allies in delinquency, George "found the wit, not the brain"[19] to cheek even the head boy, "Pontifical Pete" Sissons – later a well-known television broadcaster[20] – during Sissons' harassed efforts to enforce school rules in lunch queue and quadrangle.

Workman, Kelly and Harrison became known as truants, sharers of smutty stories and initiates of a caste who'd graduated from the innocence of tooth-rotting Spangles to the lung-corroding evil of Woodbines. Not standing when he could lean, that Harrison boy, with his bad attitude, "would not have wanted to be a prefect" in the understated opinion of Jack Sweeney, head of modern languages, "because he was against everything. I think George may have felt lost in the academic environment."[21]

His extra-curricular pursuits had little bearing on what he was meant to be learning at the Institute. To afford them, he'd taken on a Saturday morning delivery round for Quirk's, a local butcher. For George, the longest lasting of his diverse hobbies was motor racing. Attracted by a poster advertising the 1955 Grand Prix at the Aintree circuit, he journeyed by bus and internal railway almost twice as far as school to see the great Argentinean driver Fangio and his team-mate Stirling Moss dominate the event. Soon, he would be as ever present at Aintree as other boys were at Anfield: "I had a box camera and went 'round taking pictures of all the cars. If I could find an address, I wrote away to the car factories, and somewhere at home I've got pictures of all the old Vanwalls, Connaughts and BRMs."[22] With help from his father and eldest brother, driving was second nature to George and Peter long before they were officially entitled to take a car on the public highway.

George's enthusiasm also extended to motorcycle scrambles, and as far as he ever had a boyhood sports hero, it was Geoff Duke, perhaps the best professional biker of the 1950s. If short of cash, George would watch the kick-starting panorama from the railway embankment adjacent to the race course with a packed lunch at his side.

In most of his pastimes, he was a spectator rather than a doer. Throughout the 1950s, he and a million other children would queue for Saturday-morning cinema sessions and a weekly diet of Walt Disney, cowboys and injuns and swashbuckling "historical" epics. Though he was never as keen on films as he was on racing, "It was just nice to get out of the house and go somewhere where there were all nice golden lights and goldfish swimming in the foyer."[23] It was always fun there – the convulsions of laughter at the same joke; telling yourself that they're only acting in the sad bit; the lump in the throat giving way to giggles at mawkishness; the Pearl & Dean commercials; the involuntary dip into the rustling packet of Murray Mints or popcorn; the choc-ice; the Kia-Ora; and the muted buzz as the house-lights dimmed before the main feature.

When truanting, George's gang would frequently seek refuge at the Jacey Cinema in Clayton Square. They were particularly fond of the more escapist horror flicks about outer space "things". This period also saw the apotheosis of Hollywood's film noir and its Ealing Studios antithesis of hello-hello-hello policemen, monocled cads, kilted Scotsmen and happy endings. "I liked the way things looked in those 1940s films," said George, "when the streets weren't crowded and the chemist shops had nice signs over them."[24]

In a haze as rosy, he would hark back also to the time "when I used to go to the Liverpool Empire. It used to be ninepence up in the back upstairs, and I'd watch all the variety shows – whatever came in there."[25] The Harrisons went regularly to the city's most ornate theatre, whether to Christmas pantomimes or to those presentations that marked the passing of the music hall. To perform at the Empire was nearly as high an aspiration as Drury Lane for any up-and-coming juggler, ventriloquist and feathered dancing girl. There, too, onlookers like the Harrisons could shut off – however fleetingly – the nastier realities of post-war economies – the repellent housing estates where they'd been put, the dingy jobs they had to do. George could forget about school in the reverie of a magician sawing his buxom assistant in half and Max Miller telling the one about his wife and the nudist come to use the telephone.

It was called "music hall" because each artist was expected to make use of the pit orchestra, if only for a rumble of timpani as a rabbit was produced from a top hat. Usually the bill would contain an entirely musical act – a singer, more often than not. In those days, you'd be less likely to be serenaded with 'Danny Boy' or 'The Road To Mandalay' than 'How Much Is That Doggie In The Window?', 'Mambo Italiano' or something else from the newly established *New Musical Express* record and sheet-music sales charts.

"That was my contact with the musical or entertainment world," said George of the Empire, "because it was before the days of TV – *before* we had TV – and the only other thing was the radio."[25] Most of the music heard on the BBC's three national radio services before about 1955 was directed at the over 30s. Otherwise, there was *Children's Favourites* – record requests aired by "Uncle Mac" – on the Light Programme. For the adolescent listener, there was *Quite Contrary*, a show built around the light operatic style of Ronnie Hilton, a former apprentice engineer form Leeds, who, for want of anyone better, was cited by the *NME* as the most popular British vocalist of 1955.

Disturbing Uncle Mac's red-nosed reindeers and Davy Crocketts as that year drew to its close was a disc by Bill Haley And The Comets, a North American dance band. Like all but the most serious-minded children of the 1950s, Peter and George Harrison were superficially thrilled by the metronomic clamour of 'Rock Around The Clock'. A more profound impression was created by Elvis Presley's hillbilly-blues shout-singing that the USA only dared televise from the waist up. Presley was not married and paunchy like Haley, but, as the first photograph of him published in Britain[26] testified, a hoodlum type whose brilliantined but girly cockade was offset by sideburns down to his earlobes. Garbed in outrageous "cat" clothes – pink socks, hip-hugging slacks, checked shirt and box jacket – this "unspeakably untalented and vulgar young entertainer" (as a US television guide described him) made adult flesh creep. Unlike Bill Haley, he made no apologies for his on-stage frolics, which involved hip-swivelling, doing the splits and rolling about as if he had a wasp in his pants.

How could he miss? "At school, there was all that thing about Elvis," George enthused. "You never wanted to go to school; you wanted to go out and play or something. So when some record comes along like Elvis' 'Heartbreak Hotel' and you had this little bit of plastic... It was so amazing. Now, it's hard to realise that there are kids like I was, where the only thing in their lives is to get home and play their favourite record."[27]

It went without saying that George's growing record collection did not conform with Institute dictates of what was "good" music. Infinitely less meaningful to him than the heart-stopping second guitar break of 'Hound Dog' was the Music Club's "appreciation" of Brahms' *German Requiem*, its outings to hear the Liverpool Philharmonic play Beethoven and, for light relief, a master choosing *Desert Island Discs*, like real celebrities did on the Home Service. In Upton Green, "classical music" meant string-laden Muzak sometimes oozing from the Light Programme by the orchestras of Mantovani or Geraldo: pruned-down arrangements of Handel's 'Largo', 'Tales Of Hoffman' and the *Lone Ranger* theme.

Even wilder than Presley was shrieking black Little Richard in billowing drapes, beating hell out of a concert grand in the movie *The Girl Can't Help It*, which arrived in Liverpool in 1957. Every week seemed to bring another American rock 'n' roll wildman into the British hit parade – Chuck Berry, with his crotch-level electric guitar; Jerry Lee Lewis, a piano-pumping fireball from Louisiana; crippled Gene Vincent, "the Screaming End"... Britain hung onto the new craze's coat-tails with strict-tempo supremo Victor Sylvester's sanitised "rock 'n' roll" sequence, and certain jazz musicians forming contingent groups in the Haley image. More attractive was 'Sweet Old-Fashioned Boy' by Terry-Thomas Esq and his Rock 'n' Roll Rotters, notable for the distinguished character actor's haw-haw interjections of "dig those crazy sounds, Daddio", "see you later, *alma mater*", *ad nauseum*. Liverpool was represented by Clinton Ford's rocked-up 'Nellie Dean'. As pathetic in its way was the Best Guitarist category in a *Melody Maker* popularity poll being won by Tommy Steele, England's answer to Elvis, who was "just as talented or just as revolting, according to the way you feel".[28]

Thus spake *Everybody's Weekly* in an article entitled, "Are we turning our children into little Americans?" Still a principal port of embarkation for the Americas, Liverpool was more prone to such a metamorphosis than other cities. Many teenagers within the Merseyside hinterland knew transatlantic seamen – "Cunard Yanks" – who would import Davy Crockett caps, otherwise unobtainable records, checked cowboy shirts and other treasures long before they filtered even to London. George's source was Arthur Kelly's sister, Barbara, whose fiancé, Red Bentley, was a ship's engineer.

For a while, a crew-cut like Red's bristled on George's scalp, but eventually he adopted a closer-to-home look. On desolate estates like his and down in the docklands, pedestrians would cross streets to avoid fearsome clusters of hybrid Mississippi riverboat card sharps and Edwardian rakes out for more than boyish mischief. The first Teddy Boy murder had taken place in 1954. Less overtly violent was the secretive slitting of cinema seats with flick-knives while young women jived in gingham to the musical interludes in Presley's movies. Thanks in part to Elvis, the word "teenager" had been coined by the media to denote all 'twixt twelve and 20 who were deciding whether or not to grow up. However, although teenagers had become a separate target for advertising since the war, a girl still wore socks well into her teens, and a sure sigh of growing up was when she pulled on nylon stockings held up with a suspender belt.

At the Liverpool Institute, boys were still supposed to dress like little men, men like English master Alfred J "Cissy" Smith, very smooth in his 1950s "quiet" style of dark business suit with baggy trousers. Mr Smith's white hair was thin, matted and actually quite long at the back, which is why it was odd that he should poke fun at Harrison of the Fourth's lavishly whorled Teddy Boy quiff. Actually quite short at the back – cut in a "Boston" – George's oiled coiffure was not the sole butt of teachers' sarcasm. Just short of openly flaunting school rules, he'd customised his uniform to seedy-flash Ted-cat standards. He seemed top-heavy on thin legs that, from a distance, gave the illusion that they'd been dipped in ink.

His father had eventually seen the funny side of George's enterprise in drainpiping a pair of new flannels on Louise's sewing machine. For a blazer, he'd dyed one of his eldest brother's cast-off box jackets black, although to his glee the check pattern was still discernible. From Harold, too, came a custard-yellow waistcoat that alternated with a black double-breasted one with drape lapels. With his Quirk money, George bought a white shirt, as ordained, but it was pleated down the front and was stitched with black embroidery. On his feet were winkle-pickers of dark-blue suede and, costing nine shillings and sixpence ($47^{1}/_{2}$ pence), fluorescent socks with a rock 'n' roll motif.

In all his finery and with his lips curled in an Elvis half-sneer, he'd slouch last into class. Oblivious to the jibes of both wrinkled senior master and trainee on teaching practice, he lounged in the back row, dumbly insolent and indifferent to logarithms and the Diet of Worms. In reciprocation, he was ignored by most teachers now, as long as he didn't disturb other pupils. Relieved when he was absent, they were as anxious for him to leave the Institute as he was. About the only master to warm to Harrison was Stanley Reid, head of Art. Significantly, art was the only subject in which George did not fail among the few GCE "O"-level examinations he was considered able to sit.

Academically, George may have coped better with the comprehensive system's concept of "education for all", then so new that schools of this ilk were comparatively unknown north of Birmingham. Combining elements of both grammar and secondary modern, these skirted around the Eleven Plus and, theoretically, enabled children to follow what best suited their inclinations and abilities as they developed. So open-minded was the outlook in some comprehensives that skiffle – a British offshoot of rock 'n' roll – was seen not as a plague but as a more effective means of arousing adolescent interest in music than Brahms and his *German Requiem*.

Although it was derived from the rent parties, speakeasies and dustbowl jug bands of the American Depression, skiffle had never gripped the imagination of young America. Rockabilly, its closest American equivalent in primeval rowdiness, employed conventional rather than home-made instruments. While retaining a thimbled washboard for percussion, even those British skiffle outfits that made the hit parade tended to abandon the makeshift, too, thereby adulterating the form for purists, who were still divided over the policy of London's Chris Barber Jazz Band, in which an ex-serviceman named Tony Donegan had been allowed to sing a couple of blues-tinged American folk songs

With his very stage name lifted from that of Lonnie Johnson, a black blues singer, "Lonnie" Donegan was, more than Tommy Steele, a British "answer" to Elvis in his vivacious processing of black music for a white audience. Sung in an energetic whine far removed from the gentle plumminess of other British pop stars, his first hit, 'Rock Island Line', was from the repertoire of walking musical archive Huddie "Leadbelly" Ledbetter. As exemplified in the titles of later chart strikes such as 'My Dixie Darling' and 'Battle Of New Orleans', Donegan delved deeper into Americana to embrace also bluegrass, spirituals, Cajun and even Appalachian music, which in its minimal melodic variation was the formal opposite of jazz. Backed by his Skiffle Group, Lonnie bossed the form throughout its 1957 prime as he brought a vigorous alien idiom and transmuted it into acceptability onto an impoverished and derivative UK pop scene.

George Harrison had been aware of pop since his infancy but, Elvis apart, had had no real allegiance to any specific star (although particular records, like Hoagy Carmichael's 'Hong Kong Blues', twisted his heartstrings now and then), but "Lonnie and skiffle seemed made for me."[29] Like punk after it, anyone who'd mastered basic techniques could have a go: "It was easy music to play, if you knew two or three chords, and you'd have a tea chest as a bass and a washboard, and you were away... [sings] 'Oh, the Rock Island Line is a mighty good road...'"[29]

The idea was to find an individual style, even with well-known material. Hence Dickie Bishop and his Sidekicks' 'Cumberland Gap' deviated from that of Donegan and his Skiffle Group in its substitution of slashing acoustic guitar with a jigging fiddle. Most such outfits were formed for the benefit of performers rather than audience, but nationwide there were thousands of skifflers thrumming tea-chest-and-broom-handle basses, tapping washboards, singing through nostrils, rasping comb-and-paper, clanking dustbin-lid cymbals and thrashing the E chord on finger-lacerating guitars for all they were worth.

Once the guitar had been associated mainly with Latinate heel-clattering, but now it was what Elvis and Lonnie played. In April 1957, *The Daily Mirror* cracked "Springtime Is Stringtime" as 'Cumberland Gap' became Donegan's first Number One and a London musical instrument firm with 2,000 unfilled orders for guitars indented a West German manufacturer for a further 6,000 One found its way (via several owners) to the hands of Peter Harrison for the knockdown price of five shillings (25p). "Some of the lads," believed leading guitar tutor Ivor Mairants, "are buying them just to hang on their shoulders."[30] Groups often had an embarrassment of guitarists, most of them just strumming chords, but this rudimentary rhythmic impetus could be overlaid by a "lead" guitarist, sometimes crudely amplified, plucking obligatos and solos.

There also evolved vague regional shades of skiffle. Birmingham leaned towards jazz, while in the West Country groups like The Avon Cities Skiffle and Salisbury's Satellites – led by a youth who would assume the stage name "Dave Dee" – betrayed roots in Morris dance bands in their respective uses of mandolin and piano accordion.

Merseyside, meanwhile, had more of a country-and-western bias, which was understandable, because within the area abounded more such artists than anywhere outside Nashville. On any given weekend, you could guarantee that plenty of the 300-odd venues affiliated to the Liverpool Social Clubs Association had booked The Dusty Road Ramblers, The Hillsiders, The Ranchers or any other band from a legion of outfits also playing the kinda music folk like a-tappin' their boot-leather to. Notable among young skifflers favouring a C&W

approach were The Red Mountain Boys, who adapted the "hard" style of the legendary Hank Williams. From Oak Hill Park, sporting cowboy suits, The Texan Skiffle Group acquired local eminence by winning a Butlin's Holiday Camp contest. A Wild West influence was also felt by The James Boys, featuring Edward "Kingsize" Taylor, a singing guitarist whose powerful build and knockout punch was a reassuring asset at more unrefined engagements.

The city's thriving folk tradition left its mark, too, as skiffle groups began to plunder its motherlode of sea shanties, like 'The Leaving Of Liverpool' and 'Maggie May'. From the ashes of The Rivington Ramblers rose The Gin Mill Skiffle Group, which was later to mutate into The Spinners, a professional folk quartet for almost 30 years.

Some of the chaps that George knew at school had been bitten as hard as he by the skiffle bug. Two older lads with guitars, Don Andrew and Colin Manley, had their own group, The Viscounts. With "Ive the Jive, the Ace on the Bass" painted on his tea chest, even madcap Ivan Vaughan was among the mutable pool of players that made up The Quarry Men, formed by his friends at Quarry Bank. They were a cut above a lot of groups, in that they had a drummer with a full kit.

While appearing casually knowledgeable, George drank in accounts of his contemporaries' progress. Fired by envy, he'd turned over an idea of starting a skiffle group with Peter. As his brother had a guitar, George wondered aloud about the humble washboard while trailing along with Arthur Kelly and his grandmother on a shopping expedition in the city centre. Passing through Cazneau Market, Arthur's soft-hearted grandma paused at a hardware stall to hand over a threepenny bit for George Harrison's first musical instrument.

This kind gesture was much appreciated, until his mastery of the washboard surpassed that of Peter's with a guitar now in the evening of its life. George wished that he had a guitar and expressed his longing by tracing its shape in the condensed vapour on windows and in illicit doodlings at school. Through overspending on his provocative clothes, George had nothing saved up when someone at the Institute offered him a second-hand guitar with f-holes and a movable bridge for half its cost price of £5.

His mother came to the rescue with the required cash transfusion, and he brought home a battered, stringless model with a damaged neck. Trying to mend it, he removed a connecting screw that he then failed to re-insert. Dismayed, he thrust the disjoined instrument into a cupboard, hoping that Louise would forget what had been rather a Jack-and-the-Beanstalk episode. For nearly three months, the guitar gathered dust in a darkness broken only when George opened the door to peer wistfully at it. Finally, he begged Peter, now an apprentice welder, to see if it could be fixed.

George then made two depressing discoveries. Firstly, the repaired guitar – ill made, anyway – could only be restrung so high above the fretboard that holding down a barre chord was painful and single-note runs were impossible on high frets. Secondly, like the rest of the family, George was no natural musician. He was, however, handsomely endowed with a capacity to try, try again. Boosted by his mother's jocund encouragement, he laboured over his guitar late into the evening, to the detriment of even that modicum of homework necessary to avert a detention the next day. Positioning yet-uncalloused fingers on the taut strings, he'd pore over 'When The Saints Come Marching In' (sic), 'Simple Blues For Guitar', 'Skiffle Rhythms' and other exercises prescribed in *Play In A Day*, a tutor book devised by Bert Weedon, guitarist with Cyril Stapleton's BBC Show Band and on Tommy Steele's records.

After commendable effort, George moved on to a more advanced manual. His fingertips hardened with daily practice, and it occurred to him – and Louise, egging him on over the ironing – that he'd become a better guitarist than Peter. He might even be not that far behind Colin Manley and Don Andrew, or even Johnny "Guitar" Byrne of The Texan Skiffle Group, whom he'd seen in action at a dance in Garston, a grim Liverpool suburb a couple of bus stops from Speke. Both George and his mother saw that the next step was the purchase of a worthier instrument. Between them, they scraped up enough for an electric model from Hessy's, a central Liverpool music shop that boasted "our easy terms are easier". Compared to his first guitar, George's new £30 Hofner Futurama cutaway was as a fountain pen to a stub of pencil.

From a kit advertised in *Melody Maker*, it was feasible to solder together an amplifier "with a ten-watt punch" that was transportable in a school satchel. Neither was it laughable for a skiffle group warily magnifying its volume to wire guitars into the workings of a record player. George fed his semi-solid Hofner through an amplifier of unspecifiable make mounted on an unpainted chipboard speaker cabinet when the skiffle outfit he'd dreamed of leading made its first public appearance.

He, Arthur Kelly and Peter were the guitarists, with the remaining personnel being two other lads on mouth organ and an inaudible tea-chest bass decorated with wallpaper gnomes. Rehearsals took place either in a Harrison bedroom or back at Arthur's in Wavertree, where Mrs Kelly served percolated coffee, a rare treat to the Speke contingent. They called themselves The Rebels, a name duplicated by other groups throughout the country, including one in South Wales containing future political leader Neil Kinnock and another that recorded for Parlophone, a subsidiary of EMI, one of London's four major record labels.

George's Rebels had no such aspirations, but with two songs at their command they began at the bottom by procuring an audition at a British Legion club on Dam Wood Road, a few hundred yards from Upton Green. On that night of nights, the quintet assembled at number 25. In honour of the occasion, the word "Rebels" had been daubed in red across the front of the tea chest. At the moment of departure, George advised that they sneak from the house, crouching with their instruments behind the hedge before dashing down the road one after another. In case their debut was a flop, he wanted the least possible number of people to know about it.

At the Legion Hall, a surprise awaited them: the booked act hadn't materialised. Clutching at straws, the social secretary bundled The Rebels on stage and hoped for the best. Courageously, they stretched out their limited repertoire for the whole evening, the bass player's fingers bleeding by the finish. Cheered for their youthful nerve, The Rebels tumbled through the Harrisons' front door afterwards, wild with excitement, each recounting the eventful engagement at the top of his voice and flourishing the ten-shilling note he'd been given from the grateful club's petty cash.

The first time was the only time, however, and The Rebels didn't spoil the greatest night any of them could ever remember with a repeat performance. Besides, Peter was fed up with the guitar, and Arthur's parents didn't want him to think of skiffle as a career. Even George conceded that it had lost its flavour on the bedpost overnight. Among the nails in its coffin was growing approval by grown-ups. "Never before have so many young people made their own music,"[31] chortled one aged television pundit on the BBC's *Six-Five Special* magazine programme, in which self-improving features on mountaineering, ornithology *et al* were slotted in between the pop items.

A hastily assembled skiffle group at Scott Base went to town on 'My Bonnie Lies Over The Ocean' to greet Dr Vivian Fuchs after his historic trans-Antarctic trek in 1958. With this *Boys Own Paper* incident as the spur, Sunday schools and youth clubs saw skiffle as a potent medium for instilling the Lord's Holy Word into teenagers. However, bored silly by ping-pong, "Brain Trusts" and now abominations like a Camberwell vicar's "Skiffle Mass", formerly tractable adolescents had taken to either loafing about the streets or frequenting coffee bars that, although thickest in the city centres, had penetrated even the furthest-flung suburbs.

Even Donegan, the genre's figurehead, had hacked "Skiffle" from the name of his Group, and in the teeth of much criticism was broadening his appeal with 'Knees Up Mother Brown' and other music-hall gems, scoring his third Number One with an adaptation of the Liverpool folk ditty 'My Old Man's A Fireman On The Elder-Dempster Line'. Lonnie Donegan and his Group also included a comedy routine in their act when they topped a variety bill at the Empire. Yet, if he did nothing else, Donegan made skiffle homogenously British by fusing black rhythms with pub singalong and folk music, the ripples of which spread across decades of British pop.

At the end of skiffle's brief but furious reign, some of its exponents turned to traditional jazz. On Merseyside, however, there was a greater tendency to backslide via amplification to classic rock and an increasingly more American Top 20. "I think a lot of people dropped the idea of being musicians," commented an ex-Rebel, "but the ones who didn't, like the washboard players, progressed into snare drums, and the tea-chest players bought bass guitars."[25] To reflect their new leanings, groups re-emerged with new handles – The James Boys, for example, were now Kingsize Taylor And The Dominoes and Gerry Marsden's Skiffle Group evolved into Gerry And The Pacemakers.

The remnants of The Texan Skiffle Group wasted no time in relaunching themselves as just The Texans, and auditions for new members had been held at leader Alan Caldwell's home. In this tidy Victorian house in West Oakhill Park, Caldwell's parents, Ernie and Violet, backed his activities with a zest that even Louise Harrison may have thought excessive. Alan's group was, therefore, welcome to rehearse there at all hours, despite moans from the neighbours.

When George Harrison came to try for The Texans, he was already a familiar figure to the Caldwells. After his first girlfriend, Ruth Morrison, moved to Birmingham with her family, he had paired off with Alan's sister, Iris. This became a foursome when Arthur Kelly dated her best friend. Violet Caldwell apparently nicknamed the two boys "Arthur and Martha".

It was her duty to tell 14-year-old Martha that, for all his experience as a Rebel, he was too young to quit school and go professional, as The Texans intended to do at the earliest opportunity. This had been a foregone conclusion for her son and Johnny Byrne, no matter how well George played and sang the ballad 'Wedding Bells' – Gene Vincent's 1956 arrangement – for them. Another disappointed hopeful was Graham Bonnet, a singer destined for modest fame ten years later as a member of The Marbles and then Ritchie Blackmore's Rainbow.

George was less concerned with The Texans' impression of him than with Jack Edwards' testimonial, which each leaver received as he filed out on his last day at the Institute. An inkling of what George's would say was detectable in Edwards' acidic remark that he'd "made no contribution to school life". Sure enough, George read on the bus home that the headmaster "cannot tell you what his work is like because he hasn't done any". A play that captured George's imagination later was David Halliwell's *Little Malcolm And His Struggle Against The Eunuchs*, in which an expelled student gets his own back on the headmaster.

A postscript to George's bursting free of the Institute was his return in September to repeat the "O"-level year, so some mortified teachers assumed. Only an hour in class, however, convinced him that slacking until the following summer among boys a year his junior was an uninviting prospect that would give him no more time to find an opening as a musician than if he followed his father's advice to get proper work.

The War Office, anxious about the stalemate in North Korea, had sent for Harold Harrison junior. Although Harold completed his National Service without complaint, the regular army figured nowhere in his unqualified youngest brother's vocational stock-taking. Our Kid was, nevertheless, contemplating travel of some kind, perusing job opportunities in Australia, Malta and Canada. After all, sister Louise had emigrated, following her marriage in 1954 to an American named Caldwell. Waiting, like Mr Micawber, for something to turn up, George stayed where he was as month succeeded jobless month, playing for time, in every sense of the phrase, until, to placate his displeased father, he submitted half-heartedly to a written test for eligibility to work for the Liverpool Corporation. Botching this, he then underwent a humiliating interview at the Youth Employment Centre.

The YEC sent him to Blackler's, a largish department store opposite Lime Street Station, where there was a vacancy for a window dresser. While George was sauntering over there, however, it went to someone quicker off the mark. It was probably just as well as, in order to publicly adorn dummies in sober clothing, you have to dress soberly yourself. Nonetheless, he was found a job under Mr Peet, Blackler's maintenance supervisor, as a trainee electrician. Dusting strip-lights with a paintbrush wasn't exactly showbusiness, but it would do for now. Although George had failed at the Institute, his Dad was delighted at his respectable overalled apprenticeship. In George's stocking that Christmas was a magnificent set of electrical screwdrivers. With young Harold a mechanic, Peter a welder and George an electrician, Mr Harrison's daydreaming ran to a family business – a garage, maybe.

Window-gazing in Blackler's, George realised how far removed his own notion of self-advancement was to one who'd borne the brunt of the Depression. Rigging up Santa's Grotto in December or laying cables in the firm's Bootle warehouse had been among few highlights of a workaday routine as dull as school. Already he'd absorbed habits of his idler co-workers, stopping the service lift between floors for a quiet smoke or enjoying rounds of darts on a board hung in the basement. During an under-age drinking session one lunchtime, he showed the others what a hell of a fellow he was by managing – so he bragged later – to hold down two hamburgers, three rum and blackcurrants and 14 pints of ale.

2 Carl Harrison

The audition with Alan Caldwell's Texans hadn't been George's only attempt to "be in a band, as opposed to having a job".[32] Along Hayman's Green, a leafy thoroughfare in West Derby Village, was the Lowlands, a skiffle club in uncertain transition, where he'd scraped acquaintance with some lads more his own age who were forming a group. One of its guitarists, Ken Brown, was committed enough to invest in a Hofner and a new ten-watt amplifier. He and George became the instrumental backbone of The Les Stewart Quartet, with Les taking most vocals and hacking a third guitar. General factotum – mainly percussion – was his friend Geoff Skinner. With a tuneful if rather bland voice, George came to the fore to sing only for a prescribed time, as Lonnie used to with Chris Barber.

Regular bookings at the Lowlands seemed to be the fullest extent of the Stewart combo's ambitions. Therefore, while religiously attending rehearsals, George had no conscience about playing with other musicians whose outlook might prove more attractive. Around the time that his school career began its decline, he'd discovered that another boy who boarded the number 86 at Speke also had a guitar. This Paul McCartney was in the year above George, but could exculpate himself from criticism of hob-nobbing with a younger pupil as Mrs Harrison had once met him on the bus and had lent him the money to pay his forgotten bus fare. From then on, Paul felt obliged to be civil to her son George.

Because of the academic gulf between co-operative pupil and form captain McCartney in the A stream and C-stream hardcase Harrison, Institute masters were surprised later that the two even knew each other, although Frankie Boote had expressed his disapproval of Paul's interest in skiffle. Unheeding, Paul had seen Donegan at the Empire and begged his father to buy him a guitar.

A cotton salesman by trade, Jim McCartney had taken his place on many a local palais bandstand during the 1920s with his own Jim Mac Jazz Band. After family commitments and the war effectively put paid to his charlestons and square tangos, he relived the old days in anecdote and seated at the upright piano in his house on Western Avenue, to the west of Speke estate. Of Jim's two sons, dark-haired Paul, the eldest, was the more fascinated listener. Sensibly, neither Jim nor his wife goaded the boys to formalise their innate musical strengths.

When Paul was 13, the family moved to Forthlin Road on the more up-market council estate of Allerton, which bordered on the mock-Tudor colonies, golf courses and boating lakes of Woolton, a village-like suburb that aligned itself more with Lancashire than Merseyside. After only a year in the new semi-detached, Mrs McCartney died suddenly. Various aunts and neighbours rallied around to help Jim cope with housework and what remained of his sons' childhood.

Jim was glad enough to give a few pointers when Paul took up the guitar. Skiffle, even jazz, was harmless, as long as it didn't interfere with school. Jim, like Arthur Kelly's parents, understood that, unless you'd been born into showbusiness, it was unwise to see it as a viable career. This rock 'n' roll was all very well, but it wouldn't last, any more than previous crazes, like the Jitterbug or the Creep. Presley, Vincent, Donegan – they'd jumped the gun, because, by Jim McCartney's book, popular musicians were generally well into their 30s before achieving worthwhile recognition after servitude in an established band who played the good old ones, such as the silent-movie classics 'Charmaine' and 'Ramona'. His son would recall that "My dad gave us some of the worst advice ever. 'It's all right on the side,' he'd say, 'but, Paul, it will never last.'" "Remember," added George, "he always wanted us to sing 'Stairway To Paradise'."[33]

After the McCartneys left Western Avenue, Paul and George's friendship lapsed until George consulted the older boy about a manual exercise by jazz guitarist Django Reinhardt. Cycling over to Speke that evening with his guitar on his back, Paul, with his greater theoretical insight, was able to make sense of the piece. He in turn was stunned by his host's advanced fretboard expertise. Either at Upton Green or Forthlin Road, the two began practising together, frequently truanting to do so. They even lugged their guitars with them when, on the spur of the moment, they disappeared on a three-week hitch-hiking expedition along the south coast one summer holiday.

Usually, Paul sang to his acoustic as George picked at his Futurama. Discussions during these sessions drew to light George's liking for Carl Perkins, a rockabilly artist from Tennessee whose harsh guitar style was as cutting as his singing on his best-remembered hit, 'Blue Suede Shoes'. Much admired, too, was Duane Eddy, a New Yorker who'd pioneered the "twangy guitar" approach by booming the melodies on his instrumentals solely on the bass strings. Jauntier, but still highly regarded, was Chet Atkins, heard on countless Nashville country-pop recordings, including some by Elvis Presley.

As far as he could, chubby Paul modelled his appearance on Elvis, although he was also fond of The Everly Brothers, a quiffed duo with delinquent-angel faces whose double-edged bluegrass harmonies had propelled them into charts beyond their native America. Repeated listening to 'Bye Bye Love', the *risqué* 'Wake Up, Little Susie' and subsequent smashes brought home to Paul how rock 'n' roll could be simultaneously forceful and romantic.

He and George were in complete agreement about Buddy Holly, a singing guitarist from Texas, who dominated his group, The Crickets. George was the later convert, through borrowing Holly singles from Tony Bramwell, son of a family to whom he delivered meat. Making up for a manifest deficit of teen appeal, gangling Buddy possessed other creative talents, not least of which was an ability to compose – with various Crickets – simple but atmospheric songs tailored to his elastic adenoids.

Of all the elements that coalesced to produce the British beat boom of the 1960s, perhaps the single most influential event was when fated young Holly and his Crickets – second guitarist, double bass and drums – undertook a British tour in March 1958. "How these boys manage to make such a big, big sound with such limited instrumentation baffles me,"[35] remarked a reviewer after the Holly outfit closed the show at a Kilburn cinema with a loud half-hour mixture of their own and rivals' hits. Among those schoolboys of George and Paul's age who found Buddy's stage act and compact sound instructive were Mick Jagger, Dave Clark and Brian Poole, who, from Kent, London and Essex respectively, caught The Crickets at Woolwich Grenada. At the Manchester stop were two Salford boys, Allan Clarke and Graham Nash, who sang together as Ricky And Dane. Reading of Buddy's death not quite a year later, a member of Dave Dee And The Bostons, Trevor "Dozy" Davies, "cried all the way home. Yes, he was a big hero."[2]

After The Crickets had played the Empire, Paul suggested to a less enthusiastic George the idea of writing their own songs. Paul had already made up a few on his own. To George, nothing could be up to American standards, but he didn't mind being Paul's sounding board.

A study of chord charts on sheet music revealed that three basic structures recurred in rock 'n' roll: the "three-chord trick", the twelve-bar blues and the I-minor VI-IV-V ballad cliché. More often than not, these were complicated by a "middle eight" or bridge passage. This understanding was the foundation of Paul and George's first efforts at composition. A collaboration that survived into 1960 was 'Hey Darlin'', a doctored twelve-bar piece much in a lovelorn Everly Brothers mould.

Through Ivan Vaughan's sponsorship, Paul had joined The Quarry Men in July 1958. Nonetheless, despite this and George's fealty to Les Stewart, George and Paul may have toyed with the notion of being a double act, like The Dene Boys, The Allisons and other Britons who imitated Don and Phil Everly. When they performed during the lunch hour of George's last full day at school, Charlie Shaw remembered only "the vibrant sounds of electric guitar"[34] as George gave 'em his party piece, 'Raunchy', a morose jogalong by Bill Justis and covered for the British market by The Ken Mackintosh Orchestra.

Such syndication was anticipated, even welcomed, by US pop stars, as it brought their music, if not their performances, to another country full of teenagers with money to waste. Rather than pre-empting Elvis, wiser British acts gave themselves a more sporting chance by mechanically reproducing records by lesser-known Americans. On the radio, these could sound virtually identical to the originals. There were no takers for the medley of nursery rhymes by canine vocal group The Singing Dogs, but a veritable pack of Britishers fought over Marty Robbins' 'The Story Of My Life'. The war was won by Liverpool-born Michael Holliday, who, with Robbins on the other side of the Atlantic, was better able to promote his version in concert and on television. Tommy Steele had a more unfair advantage with his 'Come On Let's Go', originally by Ritchie Valens, who was killed in the same aeroplane crash as Buddy Holly.

After a controversial tour in 1958 by Jerry Lee Lewis, Sir Frank Medlicotte, MP, pointed out in Parliament that "We have enough rock and rollers of our own without importing them." In quantity, at least, Britain had more than enough duplicates of almost every US pop sensation.

After Tommy Steele abdicated by appearing on the *Royal Variety Show*, the role of English Elvis was assumed briefly by Cliff Richard, until he shaved off his sideburns at the behest of producer Jack Good, who'd also insisted that Gene Vincent array himself in biker leathers before setting foot on the inspired Jack's ITV pop showcase *Oh Boy!*. With a more electric atmosphere than *Six-Five Special*, its pious predecessor, *Oh Boy!* was a parade of vocalists following each other's spots so quickly that the screaming studio audience, urged on by Good, scarcely had pause to draw breath – although screams became cheers for the resident Vernons Girls, a troupe of choreographed singers recruited from employees of the Liverpool Football Pools company.

From the *Oh Boy!* stencil came more televised pop: *Drumbeat, Cool For Cats, Boy Meets Girls*. Implied in the last title was the emphasis on male stars. Most were studs from the stable of the celebrated manager Larry Parnes, who tended to give them names which juxtaposed the run of the mill with the descriptive, hence Vince Eager, Dickie Pride, Marty Wilde and so on. As expected, these specialised in American covers plugged on the "scream circuit" package tours of Britain's cinemas and theatres.

A regular spectator whenever such a show hit Merseyside, George Harrison noted the similarity in presentation to *Oh Boy!*: "They'd have ten or 15 different people on the show [who'd] all just go on and sing a couple of tunes each."[25] Backstage, there'd be squabbles over who'd do Ray Charles' 'What'd I Say', wherein a vocalist could, over ten minutes, take it down easy, trade "heys" and "yeahs" with the audience, build the tension to raving panic and finally sweep into the wings, leaving 'em wanting more. Time limitations truncated such exhibitions on television and the Light Programme's new *Saturday Club*, a two-hour pop show hosted by Brian Matthew, who was as "with it" as an ex-announcer in his 30s could be without being called to task by his staider superiors.

Saturday Club was recorded in Birmingham, which in 1959 was where the motorway from London terminated. It was also the geographical limit of the pool from which the entertainment industry centred in the capital was usually prepared to fish for its talent. Although Manchester, with its radio and television stations, was "entertainment capital of the north", it had still been necessary for the likes of Clinton Ford, Michael Holliday and The Vernons Girls to head south to Make It. "In the noise and heat of a tailor's shop," cooed *Everybody's Weekly*, "a 19-year-old negress from Liverpool thinks of crooning in a West End night club."[36]

The same impossible visions appeared before George, Paul, Alan Caldwell, Ted Taylor, Gerry Marsden and scores of other Scouse rock 'n' rollers as Cliff Richard's image flickered from *Oh Boy!*. Spurred on by his mate Jimmy Tarbuck, an unemployed Mersey tugboat hand by the name of Ronnie Wycherley cut corners by insinuating his way into Marty Wilde's dressing room at Birkenhead's Essoldo Theatre. There and then, he played songs he'd written to Wilde and Larry Parnes. Enthralled by Ronnie's prominent cheekbones and restless eyes, Parnes squeezed him into the show. Wycherley's knees knocked and his voice was tremulous with terror, but the girls all thought it was part of the act. An overnight sensation, he joined the tour as "Billy Fury". Next, Parnes dressed him in gold lamé, and his metamorphosis from nobody to teen idol was set in motion. Billy-Ronnie rarely spoke to fans. Apparently, he was ashamed of his "yobbish" accent.

John Lennon was very much the opposite. As leader of The Quarry Men, he was given to brutalising his Lancashire intonation to facilitate a "common touch" at bookings in districts rougher than Woolton, where he'd been brought up in middle-class comfort. His father had deserted the family when he was an infant. While John's mother would visit him daily, her complicated domestic arrangements made it more convenient for him to grow up in the semi-detached villa of her childless sister, Mary, whom John would always call by his cradle articulation "Mimi".

Lennon, too, might have fared better at a comprehensive school, for, like George Harrison at the Institute, he left Quarry Bank an academic failure and with a reputation as a square peg in a round hole. He was also an incorrigible rock 'n' roller in appearance, in attitude and in the musical style of his Quarry Men. In character, however he resembled the unique Ivan Vaughan, his friend at the Institute. On an annual holiday with Scottish cousins, Lennon, affecting a piping Highland trill, went shopping in Durness clad in a kilt he'd found in a chest of drawers. That he wisnae a *bona fide* Scot became obvious when he forgot to take his change in a tobacconist's.

More so than Harrison and McCartney, Lennon and Vaughan were fans of BBC Radio's *Goon Show*. Starring Spike Milligan, Peter Sellers, Michael Bentine and Harry Secombe, its parodies – 'I Was Monty's Treble', 'Bridge On The River Wye' *et al* – and incongruous connections not only made it different from other comedies like *The Clitheroe Kid* and *Hancock's Half Hour* but also ushered in the "offbeat" strata of humour that was to culminate in *Monty Python's Flying Circus*.

A habit of Lennon's that intensified with exposure to The Goons was scribbling lines of nonsense verse and surreal stories, supplemented by cartoons and caricatures. As Aunt Mimi wouldn't hear of him entering the world of work without qualifications, she fastened onto John's skills as an illustrator to get him into the Art College. There he matured not so much as an artist but as a would-be hardened Teddy Boy in an establishment where girls, hiding their figures inside baggy sweaters annexed from "existentialist" boyfriends with bumfluff beards, were more likely to be "sent" by Lewis, Meade Lux than Lewis, Jerry Lee.

Moreover, the new student was a lecture-disrupting wit, made more aggravating by an illusion of perpetual mockery in the short-sighted eyes that he was then too vain to protect with spectacles. His tutors' names were inserted irreverently in 'When You're Smiling' (sung in a Goon voice) and other items by The Quarry Men, whom he'd brought with him from school. Regarded as the college band, they were heard often enough in both midday sessions in the Life Room and dances in the main hall. Sometimes, they'd support one of the traditional jazz outfits that were nowadays finding favour with intellectual types living in the shadow of the Bomb – or, more precisely, of the Anglican cathedral.

For longer than he could possibly have anticipated, George Harrison would live in John Lennon's shadow. At Dovedale Primary, John had been in the same form as Peter Harrison (as well as Jimmy Tarbuck and Peter Sissons), but George was first aware of him as a rather sharp-featured boy who lived in one of the posher houses on his meat round. They were formally introduced by Paul in February 1958 at a Quarry Men engagement at the same Garston hall at which George had seen The Texan Skiffle Group. If out of context in Ted attire, George was still only the errand boy, and so was granted only an irresolute nod as John turned away to continue chatting with someone else.

The turnover of personnel within The Quarry Men had abated, and in the more fixed set-up Paul had surfaced as John's lieutenant. He was therefore well placed to champion George as Ivan Vaughan had championed him. The group's next booking was on 13 March at the Morgue, a club run by Alan Caldwell in the starkly-lit cellars of a large semi-derelict house in Oak Hill Park. If George brought his guitar along, Paul would do what he could.

In the Morgue, George lifted his Futurama from its case. It was a splendid instrument, compared to any owned by The Quarry Men and other local combos entertaining that night. Lennon was among those who gathered around in admiration. Feeling obliged to do a turn,

George was too overwhelmed to sing before older lads bunched so closely around him like friendly if over-attentive wolf hounds. In a quandary, he picked out 'Raunchy' and a Bert Weedon number that some listeners recognised from the harder tutorial book. As his notes hung in the musty air, even Lennon was impressed by this pale slip of a lad's virtuosity, lowering himself to actually speak to George. The display was not, however, sufficient for the great Lennon to consider George as an official Quarry Man, but he became a reliable understudy whenever the regular lead guitarist, Eric Griffiths, didn't turn up.

Neither did John object much when George came too whenever Paul cut classes at the Institute to attend rehearsals in the Life Room. Like Scullion of Tom Sharpe's *Porterhouse Blue*, George knew his place and tried not to put his foot in it with some inane remark that showed his age. "With George, you'd get virtually nothing going between you," observed Bill Harry, one of Lennon's cronies. "I think George was just extremely shy. He kept in the background so much in those days, he was almost the invisible man." Tagging behind when the Lennon gang went lunaticking around central Liverpool, his reserve would drop when John's butterfly concentration alighted on him. One remarkable Rag Week stunt had George and Paul garbed as vicars who, with Lennon as referee, would start a wrestling match on tables in chain-store restaurants until staff intervened.

Before he realised that John was making fun of him, George would pluck 'Raunchy' at his request in the oddest setting. Quoted most frequently by Beatle biographers was a performance on a bus. "Knowing John," reflected Bill Harry, "I can imagine him taking the mickey out of George mercilessly in private. He'd try it on you, and if you stood up to it, fine. If you put up with it, he'd keep on." Although he learned rejoinders, nothing in George's eyes could belittle John, even when it transpired that he was related to Cissy Smith by marriage. "Living with good and bad," he'd write later of Lennon, "I always looked up to you."[37] George was enchanted to be in the court of a fully-fledged rock 'n' roller who'd had sex and was on the verge of moving into a flat in beatnik Gambier Terrace, fount of wild parties, stolen street furniture, afternoon trysts and bare floorboards. John might have been less able as a guitarist than he, but he was a marvellous Presley-derived vocalist with instinctive if indelicate crowd control.

Then more Lennon's disciple than friend, George was sometimes a bit of a pest with his "Look! I've worked out this new chord" and his guileless arrival at Aunt Mimi's doorstep to ask her nephew to go to the pictures with him. Wishing that the floor would swallow him up, John pretended to be too busy. Still some inches short of his adult height of just under six feet, George was conscious that John, mature enough to have luxuriant sideburns, was "a bit embarrassed about that, because I was so tiny. I only looked about ten years old."[32]

George's hero-worship and machinations to be a Quarry Man also encroached on Lennon's amour with Cynthia Powell, another art student. Because John liked her, so did George – although, as he confided to John, man to man, "She's got teeth like a horse."[38] With the insensitivity of puberty, he'd wait outside the college portals for the couple to emerge after lectures. At first, he'd follow at a distance as John and Cynthia quickened their pace, intending to get up to he knew not what. When he caught up, neither had the heart to tell him to get lost. Growing bolder, he'd greet them with a trademark piercing whistle and once more, with their hearts in their boots, they'd be stuck with George for the afternoon. Cynthia's patience finally broke when she was hospitalised with an ill-humoured appendix. Anticipating an hour of sweet nothings during John's first ward visit, she burst into tears when he approached the bed with his admirer in tow. This time, George was told to go away.

An only child, John couldn't appreciate how much lack of privacy was the way of things at the Harrisons'. Young Harold and his fiancée, Irene, understood during their courtship that there'd nearly always be someone sewing, practising guitar or sweating over homework, should they choose to canoodle on the front-room settee at number 25. Fortunately, Irene had a soft spot for Our Kid. Although four years his senior, she and he had "hung out together"[39] while Harold was in the army. She'd even accompanied him to some pop shows at the Empire. Naturally, George was called upon to entertain with one of his groups at her and Harold's wedding reception.

For this and similar family functions, George preferred The

Quarry Men to the more dour Les Stewart Quartet. With fond pride, he was gratified that his mother and John got on so well, despite an inauspicious start when Mr Harrison entered to find his wife and Lennon seemingly entwined on the sofa. About to shake her hand, John had tripped and fallen towards her.

Although less eventful, George's first meeting with strait-laced Aunt Mimi had been frosty. However, her disapproval of his "common" manner and mode of dress was a point in his favour, as far as John was concerned. He was also touched when George – admittedly forced by Louise – went around to commiserate with him after his mother was killed in a road accident on 15 July 1958.

There were more pragmatic reasons for Lennon to finally accept Harrison as a Quarry Man. As Paul sensibly pointed out, "George was far ahead of us as a guitarist...but that isn't saying very much, because we were raw beginners ourselves."[15] In addition, George's training at Blackler's ensured that overloaded amplifiers with naked wires would be rendered less lethal and less likely to fall silent midway through a number. Of equal importance was the availability of Upton Green as a place to rehearse, where Mrs Harrison's welcome sometimes extended to tea and beans on toast. Furthermore, George's dad was such a power on various depot social committees that he could swing it for The Quarry Men to play in clubs like the one in Wavertree where he and Louise taught ballroom dancing. Indeed, some of these clubs were quite prestigious, and tin-pot skifflers considered themselves lucky if booked for a bill that also included The Merseysippi Jazz Band, that side-splitting Knotty Ash comic Ken Dodd, The Hillsiders and local speciality dancer Lindsay Kemp.[40]

Even with George in their ranks, however, such engagements were few and far between, despite The Quarry Men's willingness to perform for as little as a round of drinks. In the months before they disbanded, bookings were confined mainly to "a few parties at night. Just silly things – John, Paul and I, and there were a couple of other people who kept coming and going."[32] Going for good was Eric Griffiths, very much a spare part after the more skilled George joined. The job of telling him was assigned to drummer Colin Hanton, his best pal. Shortly after a foolhardy expedition to Manchester to audition for a spot on television, Colin himself packed it in after some beery unpleasantness at Picton Lane social club. And then there were three.

Len Garry, the most consistent of their bass players, had long departed through illness, agreeing, as everyone did, that groups who still used instruments made of household implements looked amateurish nowadays. At a Butlin's camp ballroom, Alan Caldwell had seen a band called Rory Blackwell And The Blackjacks using one of those new-fangled electric bass guitars. A few weeks later, Alan's singing bass player, Lou Walters, had bought one on credit from Hessy's. Not only did it have an infinitely greater volume and depth of sound than a broomstick bass but, as George noted, "it was much easier to get around. [You could] do more gigs and carry it in a case."[25]

All local groups not wishing to be anachronisms now had to have a bass. However, John's proposal that George switch to one had as much effect as if he'd suggested an Indian sitar. As a compromise, George dangled the carrot of a place in The Quarry Men before Arthur Kelly, as long as he could muster up £60 for an electric bass.

This was a dubious carrot, now that the group were so desperate for work. George was better off with Les Stewart, even if the Lowlands, like the Morgue, was about to close. Through Ruth Morrison, the Quartet had become known to the brothers Peter and Rory Best, who, with a team of helpers, had spent most of the summer of 1959 converting the spacious basement of their family home into a coffee bar-cum-club.

At 8 Hayman's Green, just up the road from the Lowlands, the club was to be like the Gyre and Gimble, the 2I's and like London venues where Harry Webb and Reg Smith used to sing before changing their respective names to Cliff Richard and Marty Wilde. "As certain sections of the adult population go to the public house for relaxation," sniffed *Liverpool Institute* magazine, "so the younger generation goes to a coffee bar to contemplate the weird and exotic vegetation."[41] These new havens made it possible to sit for hours, conversing with other teenagers, for the price of a transparent cup of frothy coffee. Entertainment was usually coin operated, but, as a change from the juke box, some bars would book a live act. Sunday-press condemnation of such houses of ill repute, where boys smoked and

girls were deflowered, may have been justified in the case of the
Morgue, where neighbouring gardens were receptacles for cigarette
butts and used rubber johnnies.

Peter and Rory would not have their mother, invalid grandmother
or any of the lodgers so offended. This was West Derby Village, not
Oak Hill Park. Their father was almost permanently away, and the
atmosphere in the Bests' 15-room Victorian property – with its
enamelled Hindu goddess depicted in the hall – reflected their mother
Mona's upbringing in India, where Peter had been born in Madras in
1941. From voluptuously handsome Mona had come his own sultry
good looks, similar to those that had made Cliff Richard so popular.
Girls who initiated conversations with Peter were further charmed by
his modest bemusement at their interest in him. The impression that he
was the strong-but-silent type was enhanced by his broad shoulders and
slim waist of an athlete, which were evident when he posed for the team
photograph during a football season at Liverpool Collegiate, where he
also distinguished himself academically. With hardly a murmur, he went
along with advice to apply to teacher training college after the cache of
"O"-levels his teachers expected him to pass.

Whatever the school thought he should do, Mrs Best would
support with all the vivacity of a Violet Caldwell any more glamorous
ambitions that could be teased from her reticent son. When he and his
friends began spending hours listening to pop records in the basement,
it was she who suggested turning it into a club. It was Mona, too, who
christened it "the Casbah Coffee Club".

Partly because Ken Brown and, less often, George Harrison had
assisted in the redecoration, The Les Stewart Quartet were asked to
play for £3 – a generous fee in 1959 – on the Casbah's inaugural
evening on Saturday 29 August, when a huge attendance was
expected. A week prior to this engagement, the four met at Stewart's
house to run through the set. A tense mood came to a head when Les
rounded on Ken for missing rehearsals. The accused guitarist
protested that the group would have nothing to rehearse for if it
wasn't for the time he'd put in at the Bests'.

Lines were drawn as the quarrel boiled down to Stewart washing
his hands of the Casbah. Keeping his peace throughout, George

elected to side with Ken. Outside Stewart's banged front door that afternoon, he tried to assuage worries about letting Mrs Best down with the idea of amalgamating with "two mates I sometimes play with".[42] For two hours, Ken fretted in the Casbah until George reappeared with Paul, John and Cynthia. After casing the joint, Lennon decided that The Quarry Men, augmented by Brown in his Buddy Holly glasses, would perform in front of the juke box. To save dragging more than their guitars over to Hayman's Green, they'd all plug into Ken's pristine amplifier, as he lived nearest. Entering the discussion, Mona pushed paint-brushes on the new arrivals and energetically put them to work.

Paul's brother, Michael, was spectacularly sick after swigging some noxious liquid from a bottle marked "lemonade" when The Quarry Men played before a full house of 300. Except for the guitarist whose turn it was to sing, the group were seated rent-party style in deference to Ken, who was a skiffle purist. Drawing protracted salvos of applause were Paul's race through Little Richard's 'Long Tall Sally' and John's growled insinuation in The Coasters' dolefully comic narrative 'Three Cool Cats'.

What Les Stewart's unit had been to the Lowlands The Quarry Men were to the Casbah for several weeks, until a dispute with Mrs Best and Ken Brown – present but unable to perform through illness – over the division of one night's £3. Ken had been the key to the Casbah, but musically he was as superfluous as Eric Griffiths had become. He wasn't missed when the remaining three took their brief turn under the Empire's proscenium in a "Search For Stars" talent contest organised by Carroll Levis, spiritual forefather of fellow Canadian Hughie Green, of *Opportunity Knocks* fame. In an earlier heat, the ubiquitous Alan Caldwell and his group, Al Storm And The Hurricanes, had scrambled to second place, and even if they weren't able to seize the ultimate prize of a spot on "Mr Starmaker" Levis' ITV series, at least they'd come out of it with a fuller, more lucrative date-sheet.

Although it's debatable whether or not The Quarry Men's decision to change their name made a difference, the fact remains that Johnny (Lennon) And The Moondogs qualified for the next and then final round of the contest, which was held at the Manchester Hippodrome. Up against such disparate acts as a blindfolded knife-thrower and Three-Men-And-A-Microphone comedy impersonators, the Liverpool trio went down sufficiently well to eat their hearts out when obliged to catch the last train back to Lime Street before they could be judged by volume of applause in the finale. The winners, so they learned later, were Ricky And Dane, who had played an Everly Brothers number.

Although John let George duet with him on Buddy Holly's 'Words Of Love', Johnny And The Moondogs' principal asset was the vocal interplay between Lennon and McCartney. Fans attempting to describe it found it simpler to say that it sounded like The Everly Brothers. That power structure, in which George was subordinate to John and Paul for as long as they stayed in the same group, was founded not so much on vocal compatibility as the handshake that had formalised the Lennon-McCartney songwriting partnership during John's last term at Quarry Bank. Between the two older boys, it was understood that, should the group fold, they would make a go of it purely as composers.[43] After all, jobbing tunesmiths were staples of the record business. In New York's Brill Building, there was even a songwriting "factory" where such combines as Goffin and King, and Mann and Weill churned out assembly-line pop for the masses. Although musically untrained, a London printer named Lionel Bart and actor Mike Pratt had together written hits for Tommy Steele and Cliff Richard. Why too couldn't a pair of Liverpudlian schoolboys called McCartney and Lennon?

While Johnny And The Moondogs survived, songwriting was more of a sideline. Paul's 'In Spite Of All The Danger', with slight help from George and sung in shooby-doo-wah style, had been recorded on a demonstration disc by The Quarry Men. This had been the tide-mark of McCartney's collaboration with Harrison, for whom composing was incidental to his artistic self-image. Made to feel intellectually (as well as chronologically) inferior to Paul – who was soon to sit his "A"-levels – and Art School John, he felt he had neither the knack nor the inclination to compose. Where did it get you, anyway? The Dusty Road Ramblers' 'Sweet Liverpool' was a rare example of a band performing an original in public, but, as George and everyone else knew, if anything more than the familiar was attempted, dancers would be inclined to either sit it out or go to the toilet. It just wasn't done.

However pointless it seemed, the increasing exclusiveness of his two friends' creative alliance must have been a wellspring of emotional confusion for George. Where it had once been George and Paul, it was more Paul and John. During 1960's summer holiday, those two had spent a week down south in Paul's married cousin's Berkshire pub, even performing as a duo in its bar. It wasn't as easy to absent himself from his job at Blackler's as it had been from school, but when he could, George would accompany the two students on similar expeditions and sit in, as their lyrics and melodies took form. All the same, as Cynthia concluded, "George, being younger and not writing songs, didn't have the same communication with them, but John and Paul couldn't stop playing together."[44]

For an audible but private gauge of John and Paul's efforts alongside that of professionals, they and George committed 'Hello Little Girl', 'The One After 9.09', 'You Must Lie Every Day', 'I'll Follow The Sun' and others into McCartney's Grundig tape recorder, rigged up in Forthlin Road living room. On a muffled tape of one such session, the three guitarists are anchored by the plonk of a simplistic bass line supplied by Stuart Sutcliffe, a gifted painter in John's year at college whom he had befriended. With dress sense peculiar to himself and a beard that hadn't really taken, Sutcliffe's yardstick of cool was Modigliani, rather than Presley. Although all were the most heterosexual of males, George was anxious and Paul frankly jealous of the vice-like grip that slight, sensitive Stuart appeared to have on John. Lennon in turn fascinated Sutcliffe because he wasn't like most of the others at Art College. Therefore, it wasn't surprising when Stuart bought an electric bass and John told a consternated Paul and George to welcome a new Moondog. At John's decree, too, George and a student called Dave May took turns in teaching Stuart the rudiments of his new instrument.

Prior to Sutcliffe's arrival, Paul had thought of taking up bass himself, as, no matter how contrasting his and John's chord shapes could be, the group had one rhythm guitarist too many. On the likely conjecture that the greater number of lead vocals, the higher a member's rank in the group hierarchy, Paul was several cuts above George, who was well ahead of Stuart, who had only 'Love Me Tender' to sing. As well as a handful of Perkins, Holly and Presley favourites, George – with a voice not long broken – was now carrying the tune of 'Three Cool Cats', a gift from John, who, with Paul, just harmonised on key lines. Lennon had gone off the song after the trio of Marty Wilde, Cliff Richard and Dickie Pride had massacred it on *Oh Boy!*. Later, John nobly surrendered his lead-guitar *pièce de résistance* – Duane Eddy's 'Ramrod' – to George.

Much as he professed to despise the synchronised footwork with which Cliff Richard's backing quartet, The Shadows, decorated their instrumental airs on stage, Lennon would admit that, as a guitarist, he'd "vamp like Bruce Welch [of The Shadows] does".[44] Recording in their own right, The Shadows would become nearly as famous as Richard himself, especially when their tune 'Apache' was voted Top Record of 1960 in the *NME* readers' poll. Although a butter-finger phrase on their follow-up, 'Man Of Mystery', went unchanged to EMI's pressing plant, The Shadows' Hank Marvin remains the most omnipotent of British lead guitarists, given those fretboard heroes like Jeff Beck and Ritchie Blackmore, whose professional careers started in outfits who copied The Shadows.

While their line-up – lead, rhythm and bass guitar plus drums – consolidated the pop group stereotype, few assumed that there were openings for The Shadows and their imitators beyond instrumentals and accompanying some pretty boy like Cliff. The main attraction of being in a group was, perhaps, the implied camaraderie, whereby – in the words of Jimmy Page, then a guitarist backing Cliff soundalike Neil Christian – "some of those Shadows things sounded like they were eating fish and chips while they were playing".[45] Also, glancing at four-eyed Hank and stunted fellow Shadow Jet Harris, you didn't have to be a Charles Atlas to join a group.

Other group leaders might have done, but Lennon did not entice Stuart to peroxide his hair like Jet's or cajole George into sporting lensless Marvin horn-rims. Nonetheless, sniffing the wind, he and his

Moondogs began rehearsing more instrumentals. In the forefront of these was George, loud and clear on 'Ramrod', Weedon's 'Guitar Boogie Shuffle' and faithful old 'Raunchy'. Trickier, but with as little scope for improvisation, were several group originals like 'The Guitar Bop', developed from a passage in Chuck Berry's 'Brown-Eyed Handsome Man'.

Almost as strong an influence as Berry was Eddie Cochran, a multi-talented Elvis from Oklahoma. His 'Summertime Blues' and other singles that outlined the trials of adolescence had already garnered a plenitude of British covers when, co-starring with his pal Gene Vincent, his first "scream-circuit" tour of the country reached Liverpool's Empire in March 1960. Although all of Johnny And The Moondogs attended, George – with his working-man's wage – was able to follow Eddie to other northern cities to learn from a distance what he could of the American's terse, resonant lead-guitar technique. Joe Brown, an English intimate of Cochran's, later told George about Eddie's practice of using an unwound, extra-light third string. This was the secret of his agile bending of middle-register "blue" notes.

The indigenous supporting bill included Billy Fury and other charges of Larry Parnes, and it was through Larry's contact with Allan Williams, a local agent, that Vincent and Cochran were scheduled to return to Merseyside on 3 May to head a three-hour extravaganza at a 6,000-seat sports arena near Prince's Dock. The rest of the bill would be filled by an assortment of Parnes acts and two Liverpool groups: Cass And The Cassanovas and Rory (formerly Al) Storm And The Hurricanes. Williams added Gerry And The Pacemakers and four more bands to the bill after Eddie Cochran couldn't make it, incapacitated as he was by his death in Bath's St Martin's Hospital on 17 April.

Pulled from the same car crash was Gene Vincent, who, despite broken ribs and collar bone, plus injuries to his already callipered leg, insisted with characteristic obstinacy on honouring existing British dates. Using the microphone stand as a surgical support, Gene paid tribute to Eddie with a mournful 'Over The Rainbow', which in Liverpool only just upstaged Gerry Marsden's equally plaintive 'You'll Never Walk Alone' and Rory Storm's riveting 'What'd I Say'.

With his aversion to signing groups, Larry Parnes abstained from leading more Scouse musicians to his stable that night, but he was sufficiently awed by both the local boys' impact on the frenzied audience and former plumber Allan Williams' competence as a promoter to discuss a further – albeit less ambitious – joint venture. After the show, he'd been invited back to the Jacaranda, Williams' late-night coffee bar a stone's throw from Central Station. Watching them from an outermost table were Johnny And The Moondogs – minus Paul, usually the most willing to picket on the group's behalf. None of the other three summoned the courage to approach Parnes, but in the cafe two nights later John lodged a plea with Williams to "do something for us".[46] Thick-set and black-bearded Allan had known them as customers before realising that they were also a pop group of lesser standing locally than those he'd procured for the Gene Vincent spectacular. Mainly because he was something of a curt agony aunt to Stuart and his artistic sufferings, he there and then began acting for Johnny And The Moondogs in a quasi-managerial capacity, in exchange for whatever non-musical services he felt that they could provide. Under Stuart's direction, they painted murals in the Jacaranda basement, which had a dancing area and a space for groups to set up their equipment.

Before Lennon's outfit reached a high enough standard for Williams to let them perform there, a steel band played alternate evenings to Cass And The Cassanovas, whose leader, Brian Cassar, allowed Lennon to sit in on the night of his negotiation with Allan Williams. John mentioned that his group was thinking once more of changing its name. Buddy Holly had his Crickets and Gene Vincent had been backed by The Beat Boys, so he and Stuart had come up with Beetles, Beatles or Beatals. An adherent to the 'Somebody And The Somebodies' dictate of the 1950s, Cassar howled with derision, and with Robert Newton's role in the film version of *Treasure Island* (lately extended into a television series) in mind suggested Long John And His Pieces Of Eight. Warming to his theme, he next put forward Long John And The Silver Beetles. Cass stopped being facetious long enough to help secure John the drummer that the group – whatever they called themselves – had been lacking since Colin Hanton's exit.

A forklift truck driver at Garston Bottle Works, Tommy Moore started rehearsing at the Jacaranda with The Silver Beatles, although it was understood that, with his heart in jazz, 26-year-old Tommy would never quite fit in among arty youths whom certain of the Cassanovas derided as "posers". Chief among them was drummer Johnny Hutch, who nonetheless saved the day for Lennon *et al* on occasions when Moore and the sticksmen who came after him were unavailable.

Hutch first stepped in when Tommy was late for the group's make-or-break ten-minute spot during auditions held a week after the Vincent show for Larry Parnes, who was after an all-purpose backing combo for his solo stars. It was assumed that the singer he had immediately in mind was Billy Fury, now with a hat-trick of modest hits to his credit, who accompanied his manager that afternoon to the auditions. These were held in premises that Williams would open as the Blue Angel night club later that year.

Their drummer's tardiness exacerbated The Silver Beatles' collective feeling of inadequacy as the other groups that Allan had called up to play for Parnes tuned their Hank Marvin Stratocasters, positioned gleaming cymbals on pearly drum sets and brushed non-existent specks of dust from costumes that gave each a neat, professional identity. Despite a pep talk from Williams, The Silver Beatles were too aware of being the least probable contenders. Over in Derry Wilkie And The Seniors' corner, Howie Casey adjusted the reed in his lustrous silver saxophone to the purring note of a two-tier Hammond organ. In another recess, Gerry and his Pacemakers chatted idly. They were saving up for "GP"-monogrammed blazers. Over there lounged Rory Storm, a blond Adonis in hair lacquer and Italian suit, as much a star on Merseyside as Fury was in the Top 20. He and the Hurricanes were shortly to begin a residency at Butlin's in Pwllheli for £25 a week each – not a bad deal when £500 a year was thought to be a good salary for a young executive.

After Mrs Kelly had refused to let George have the silver-grey curtains of her French windows as material for The Silver Beatles' stage outfits, they performed for Larry Parnes in two-tone plimsolls, jeans, black shirts and cheap pendants. Prudently, they concentrated mainly on instrumentals and, while they toed no conventional line with fancy dance steps, at least they weren't slick to the point of sterility, like other bands that Parnes surveyed that day. "Silver Beetles – very good," he jotted on a pad. "Keep note for future work." He recalled the sensation at Bradford Gaumont recently when Marty Wilde experimented by taking the stage with The Wildcats, who'd backed him when he was still Reg Smith, rather than the "corny and square" session musicians foisted on him by his record company. "It takes youngsters," he'd announced, "to play and feel the rock beat." Apart from their drummer, The Silver Beatles, with George just turned 16, were young enough. Furthermore, they weren't encumbered with a flamboyant non-instrumentalist who might agitate to get in on the act.

"Future work" came sooner rather than later. On 14 May at Lathom Hall, a dilapidated Victorian monstrosity in Seaforth, they'd completed their first true semi-professional engagement. Less than a week later, group and equipment were hurtling from Lime Street to an eight-day tour of Scotland, beginning in Alloa. It wouldn't be Billy Fury they'd back there but a square-jawed hunk on whom Larry Parnes had bestowed the *nom du théâtre* Johnny Gentle. A-twitter with excitement and childish swagger, the three youngest Silver Beatles straightaway gave themselves stage names too, George's being "Carl" Harrison, in recognition of Carl Perkins. While the stratagems Stuart "de Stael", Paul "Ramon" and John Lennon used to obtain release from college and school were not entirely honest, all Tommy had to do was take an early summer holiday from the bottle works, while "Carl" – who'd never acknowledged that he'd one day be a department supervisor like Mr Peet – went the whole hog by resigning altogether from Blackler's.

Only the swiftest rehearsal was feasible before star and group trooped on at Alloa Town Hall to entertain with mutually familiar rock 'n' roll standards, plus the simpler side of Gentle's four singles, such as self-penned 'Wendy', a four-chord ballad – "Wendy, Wendy, when? Wendy, Wendy, when?" *ad nauseum* – that must have made Paul and John wonder what they were doing wrong. Whatever they thought of him, Johnny was delighted with The Silver Beatles as musicians, especially George, and said as much when he called

Parnes with progress reports. The story goes that he presented George with one of Eddie Cochran's old shirts.

The light-heartedness of such a gesture was atypical of the prevalent atmosphere of the tour, which after Alloa zigzagged along the north-east coast with its brooding sea mists and dull watchfulness when the van in which the party huddled stopped at lonely petrol stations. In the grim digs where The Silver Beatles would repair late each night, Lennon would authorise who slept where, ensuring that he had the least crowded bedroom. Good-natured Tommy or the acquiescent Stuart would sleep on the floor if ever they were a bed short.

Stuart and Tommy were also the prime targets for abuse when the spurious thrill of "going professional" gave way to stoic cynicism as each man's £18 for the week's work dwindled. Rumbustious repartee became desultory and then suddenly nasty as, led by John, Paul and George – swimming with the tide – poked ruthless fun at whomever of the other two seemed likelier to rise to it. With malicious glee, Sutcliffe and Moore would be snubbed as the rest sat on a separate table for breakfast.

Well, it helped pass the time as they trudged around Scottish venues where Gentle's past appearances on *Drumbeat* guaranteed top billing over a diversity of local acts, from tartan-clad *ceilidh* bands to Alex Harvey, "Scotland's own Tommy Steele". The most northerly engagement, Fraserburgh Town Hall, was notable for the estranged Moore drumming with his head in bandages, fuzzy with sedatives and missing several teeth. He'd been the sole casualty when the van had crashed into a stationary Ford Popular earlier in the day. Not of Gene Vincent's "the show must go on" persuasion, Tommy had been semi-conscious in hospital when the group and hall manager barged in as showtime approached. They weren't laden with grapes and sympathy either.

Larry Parnes had a homily that ran, "Take care of the pennies and the lads can take care of themselves." Well before they steamed back to Liverpool after the final date, Tommy Moore – with only £2 left to show for his pains – had had more than his fill of being a Silver Beatle. They all had.

3 Das Liebschen Kind

"The Germans were just coming to the end of their jazz era," remembered Dave Dee, "and the American rock 'n' roll thing had really taken off. For the Germans to bring in all these stars from America would have cost a fortune, and there they had, just across the Channel, these English blokes that were copying the Americans and doing it very well. So it was easy to bring them in for 20 quid a week and work them to death, so all the English bands were in Germany doing two- or three-month stints."[47]

Britain in 1960 was in the thick of its own jazz era, which to the man in the street meant a bowler-hatted Somerset clarinettist called Acker Bilk, plinking banjos and "dads" who'd boo if a "trad" outfit deviated from defined New Orleans precedent by corrupting their toot-tooting with amplification. In the Cavern, Liverpool's principal jazz stronghold, proprietor Ray McFall would dock the fee of any band who dared to launch into a rock 'n' roll number within its hallowed and rather mildewed walls. With trad jazz's stranglehold on such venues and classic rock denounced as kids' stuff by most collegians, it was small wonder that Dave Dee's Bostons and others keeping the rock 'n' roll faith were open to offers from abroad.

One of the first West German impresarios to put action over debate was an ex-circus clown called Bruno Koschmider, who in spring 1960 set off with his interpreter for London and the Soho coffee bar that seamen visiting his Hamburg clubs had assured him was still the shrine of British pop. From the 2I's, Herr Koschmider raked up a ragbag of out-of-work musicians to transport across the North Sea for re-assembly as The Jets on the rickety stage of his

Kaiserkeller, a nightspot down a side street of Die Grosse Freiheit, a main thoroughfare of the Reeperbahn area, an erotic Blackpool notorious as the vice capital of Europe. A hitch over work permits caused a delay on the Dutch border, but with Bruno's unbothered string-pulling they were on their way.

Although pianist Del Ward was The Jets' nominal leader, they were licked into shape by the better of their two singing guitarists, Tony Sheridan, an ex-art student who'd flowered momentarily on *Oh Boy!* before being consigned to an obscurity largely of his own making. Twenty-year-old Sheridan's self-destructive streak did not, however, tarnish his ability as a performer. His wanton dedication to pleasing himself rather than his audience resulted in a sweaty intensity rarely experienced in British pop before 1960. Seizing songs by the scruff of the neck and wringing the life out of them, Tony and the other Jets were an instant and howling success with a clientèle for whom the personality of the house band had been secondary to boozing, brawling and the pursuit of romance.

Rival club owners cast covetous eyes on Koschmider's find, and soon Tony and his boys were administering their rock elixir at the Top Ten, a newer and bigger night spot, where they were protected by its manager's henchmen from any reprisals for deserting the Kaiserkeller.

When he'd calmed down, Bruno returned to London armed with a cast-iron contract for any attraction likely to win back the many customers who'd followed Sheridan to the Top Ten. Through one of those chances in million, he and Allan Williams froze in mutual recognition across the kidney-shaped tables of the 2I's.

Earlier that year, the Jacaranda's steel band had been seen by a German sailor, and it was on his recommendation that, with Deutschmarks and mention of affectionate *frauleins*, the West Indians were poached by a Reeperbahn club agent. Quite unashamed of their perfidy, letters from them arrived at the Jacaranda, telling of the recreational delights of Hamburg. The opportunist Williams found himself soon afterwards on the Grosse Freiheit, sampling an evening of music and loose money. With amused contempt, he listened to the inept Kaiserkeller band who were destined to be displaced by The Jets. Before the night was out, Williams and

Koschmider, entrepreneur to entrepreneur, had had an exploratory talk about the possibility of bringing to Hamburg some of the Merseyside outfits held in esteem by no less than Larry Parnes. The discussion ended on a sour note, however, when a tape of the fabulous groups in question that Allan proudly threaded onto the club recorder had been rendered a cacophonous mess through demagnetisation, probably as it passed through customs.

Back in Liverpool, Williams shrugged off this embarrassing episode to concentrate on the possible. A group without a permanent drummer was no use to anyone, and so after Tommy Moore's disgusted resignation from The Silver Beatles it had fallen upon Cass And The Cassanovas to trek up to Scotland for the next leg of the Johnny Gentle tour and another with Duffy Power, whose second single had been an arrangement of the ragtime standby 'Ain't She Sweet', whereby he'd planted unfruitful feet in both the trad and rock 'n' roll camps.

It reached Larry Parnes' ears that Brian Cassar had been prone to pushing off the star that his Cassanovas were backing in order to commandeer the central microphone himself. A tarring with the same brush may explain why Derry Wilkie And The Seniors' forthcoming summer season in Blackpool was cancelled by Parnes just as the gentlemen concerned had given up their day jobs and spent a loan on new stage uniforms. Looking for a scapegoat, they marched to the Blue Angel, from whence all their woes had emanated. "Well?" demanded burly Howie Casey of its owner. Thinking fast, the intimidated Williams threw a slender lifeline. The next day, he drove Derry And The Seniors the long miles down to the 2I's. To his amazement, room was made for them to do a turn that very evening. Even more incredible, Koschmider was there. The group showed London what Scousers could do with such unbottled exuberance that three days later they were on their way to Germany.

To Reeperbahn pleasure-seekers, Wilkie And The Seniors proved a comparable draw to Sheridan. With the Kaiserkeller thriving again, Bruno's thoughts turned to the Indra, his strip club at the dingier end of the *Strasse*. With only a few onlookers there on most nights, it could only be more profitable to put on pop.

Of a like mind was Les Dodd, who ran "21-plus" nights in two dance halls in the Wirral, on the opposite bank of the Mersey to Liverpool. For half a crown, adult dancers could savour Tuesday evenings with (as Dodd's advertisements stressed) "No Jiving! No Rock 'n' Roll! No Teenagers!" Yet it would be these undesirables that would give his profit graph an upward turn when, grudgingly, he began to promote Saturday night "swing sessions" with "jive and rock specialists" like The Silver Beatles, who appeared last after busier groups – like those led by Gerry Marsden and Kingsize Taylor – finished and left to play further engagements elsewhere on any of the given evenings.

Maybe middle-aged Dodd excused his cashing-in on the grounds that it was a moral crusade to bring the scum to the surface in order to dissipate it so that decent music could reign once more. At the Grosvenor Ballroom, especially, there was immediate trouble, with youths pushing their way in *en bloc* without paying, usually just after closing time. Narrow-eyed bouncers were hired to keep order, but if delegations from rival gangs showed up then there was at least the threat of a punch-up. Fighting and vandalism outside the premises was a matter for the Merseyside constabulary, who started paying routine calls towards the end of Grosvenor swing sessions.

Fists often swung harder than The Silver Beatles, who felt compelled to maintain ghastly grins as their music became a soundtrack for beatings-up. At Neston Institute, Dodd's other concern, a boy was half-killed before their eyes and beneath kicking pointed shoes. Musicians weren't immune, either, and a table was hurled at Paul McCartney during one enbattled evening. The provocation would be either catching the eye of some roughneck's girl or not playing enough slow ones (or fast ones) to facilitate the winning of a maiden's heart. There were a few close shaves but, mercifully, only one serious assault on The Silver Beatles, when, at Seaforth's Lathom Hall in the following February, the gentle Stuart received head injuries that were at first be thought to be minor.

Certain agents weren't above using stink bombs and hiring strippers to disrupt proceedings at a rival venue, thus blackening its reputation with local burghers, but it was an exposé in a local newspaper that led to Dodd resuming his earlier policy of strict tempo only. As if the rowdiness of the patrons hadn't been enough, what wasn't reported was the trouble he'd had with groups turning up with only half their equipment or a player short. The Silver Beatles had been the limit, with their shabby amplifiers and no drummer for most of their bookings. *In extremis*, Paul bashed away with bad grace, but once a hulking Liscard gangleader had volunteered. Not liking to say no, they'd let him inflict untold damage on Tommy Moore's kit, which was still in their possession, even if Tommy himself wasn't. When they'd lost Moore's successor, Norman Chapman, to the army after only three weeks, Allan Williams was forced to pass the chance of another Parnes tour – backing Dickie Pride – to another group.

With the end of their employment with Les Dodd, all that The Silver Beatles' future appeared to hold was Jacaranda nights for one fizzy drink and a plate of beans on toast per man, plus odd engagements at less public Williams venues. "Odd" was the word for the week in which, twice nightly, they tried to keep their minds on their job of accompanying the cavortings of a Mancunian stripper at Allan's new Cabaret Artists club, a well-concealed ledger in his accounts. Allegedly, the lass took a fancy to George ("that nice boy with the bony face"[46]) as, without looking up, he fingered the smoochy melodies of 'Begin The Beguine' and Gershwin's 'Summertime'.

Because they'd so gamely gone through with this tasteless assignment, Williams was finally convinced that the group, now defiantly trading as plain Beatles, were no longer, as George would say, "hopefully messing around".[32] When Rory Storm, Brian Cassar and other possibilities with a full complement of musicians demurred, the Indra contract was theirs, if they could enlist a drummer.

The Beatles' campaign for work had driven them back to the Casbah, where, about to disband, was the club's resident quartet, the Blackjacks – nothing to do with Rory Blackwell but formed by Ken Brown with Peter Best, whose adoring mother had bought him an expensive drum kit with skins of calf-hide, rather than plastic. No more was Pete harbouring thoughts of being a schoolmaster. The news that he wanted to drum for a living provided the answer to The Beatles' dilemma over Hamburg. Following a cursory audition at the Blue Angel, Best became a Beatle and, to many who heard him play with them, would always remain so.

Pete packed his case with Mona's blessing. John, Paul and Stuart's guardians and teachers raised quizzical eyebrows but, after grumbling about the opportunities they were wasting, didn't stand in their way either. With no ties, academic or otherwise, George met hardly any opposition from his parents for this, his first trip abroad, although Harold was still a little reproachful about his losing a chance to Make Good at Blackler's. Unlike his big brother on National Service, George would have no old job waiting for him when he got back to the real world. His mother, who'd seen the group play, felt that, if he kept at it, he might just make a reasonable living as a musician.

Hazy impressions of a Germany of bomb sites and lederhosen were rudely shattered on entering Hamburg, a port that had recovered more thoroughly from the war than Liverpool ever had. They climbed from Allan Williams' exhausted minibus outside the Kaiserkeller, vaster and plusher than any club or ballroom they'd seen on Merseyside. It was therefore a disappointment when Mr Koschmider showed them around the tiny Indra, which had the tell-tale signs of having known better days: the dusty carpeting and heavy drape curtains; the padded wallpaper peeling off here and there; the depressed forbearance of its staff.

Ist gut, ja? Nein, not really. Worse were the three windowless holes at the back of a cinema where they were to sleep – coats for blankets, naked light bulbs, shampooing in a washbasin in the moviegoers' toilet and waking up shivering to Stuart snoring open-mouthed on a camp-bed a yard away. Until now, George's only taste of roughing it had been a fortnight at Gambier Terrace in the first flush of his wonderment at John. "It was us living in squalor with things growing out of the sink," he said. "'Where's my share? Why can't I have some?' That sort of attitude."[24]

With martyred nobility, The Beatles let themselves be pushed in whatever direction fate, Williams and Koschmider ordained. The living conditions of Derry's Seniors were as poky, but they were talking of staying on as a strip-club band when their contract with Bruno was up. The Beatles, therefore, could hope to step into their shoes at the Kaiserkeller. There was token sullen mutiny when the season began, but, forgetting the misery of their position, they perked up, quite tickled when anyone cried encouragement to them.

The Beatles endured the Indra for seven weeks, six hours a night, an hour on and 15 minutes off. Up at the Kaiserkeller, Derry And The Seniors' intermissions caused patrons to drift away, Bruno presumed, to the hated Top Ten and entrapment by Sheridan for the rest of the evening. It was a bit unreasonable to expect Wilkie's group to work around the clock without a break, but, discontinuing the juke box, Koschmider bridged the gaps with an instrumental group he created by extracting Sutcliffe from The Beatles and Howie Casey and pianist Stan Foster from The Seniors and luring a German jazz drummer from another club.

This quartet's disparity, plus the related umbrage of the depleted Seniors and Beatles, combined with complaints about the noise and change of programme at the Indra, but it was the situation's false economy that led Koschmider to reconstitute the two groups and move The Beatles uptown to the Kaiserkeller.

Not a word of moral protest was raised when the Indra's gartered erotica was restored. Striptease, clip joints and brothels were to the Reeperbahn as steel was to Sheffield. Naked before their conquerors, Germans of all sexes would wrestle in mud, have sex with animals and perform all manner of obscene tableaux, frequently inciting their audiences to join in the fun. "Everybody around the district," George would recount fondly, "were homosexuals, transvestites, pimps and hookers, [and I was] in the middle of that when I was 17."[32] Back home, he might have fled if accosted by a prostitute in a dark doorway, but with Mum not looking a young Merseysider might abruptly lose his virginity in the robust caress of a bawd who'd openly exhibited her seamy charms in a bordello window. "They usually arrived knowing it all, poor sods," sighed Iain Hines, one of the Jets, "taking no advice that I offered them and, sure enough, would return to the good old UK with crabs, pox, 'Hamburg Throat' – you name it, they had it."[48]

More knowingly self-inflicted were the headaches, rashes and other side-effects of stimulants swallowed to combat exhaustion during the last sets of the night. "The only problem with that," warned Dave Dee, "was that, when we finished work, we couldn't sleep and went through the next day waiting for the pills to wear off. Of course, we were knackered again at four o'clock, so we asked for more pills."[47] Lennon might have crowned this with, "What with playing, drinking and birds, how could you find time to sleep?"[49] He and Stuart had been introduced to benzedrine – a stimulant extracted from Vicks inhalers – through the beat poet Royston Ellis, whose declaimed verses The Beatles had once framed musically at the Jacaranda. New to both of them, however, were Preludin tablets, amphetamice-laced appetite suppressants that, although recently outlawed in Britain, were easily available over counters in German pharmacies. A supply of Preludin was stocked for employees' use in every all-night establishment along the Grosse Freiheit for purposes other than fighting the flab.

In the Kaiserkeller, Bruno's musicians could also avail themselves of a nightly quantity of free beer and salad. A virtue of both was that they could be consumed in instalments on stage if need be. Outside working hours, breakfast was *"Cornflakes mit Milch"* in Freiheit cafes. At the British Seamen's Mission along Johannis Bollwerk in a dockside suburb of Davidswache, lunch was something with chips. For young George, at least, this unvaried diet was a psychological link with home.

On hot afternoons, there were excursions to Timmendorf on the North Sea, where The Beatles would recharge their batteries on the beach for the night's labours. Otherwise they might take pot luck on a tram to an unknown part of Hamburg and whatever diversion it might hold. From a bric-à-brac shop in one such district, John and Paul returned to the Reeperbahn with jackboots and Afrika Korps *kepis* decorated with swastikas.

The less extrovert George was, however, the first Beatle to walk on stage in cowboy boots and a lapel-less leather windcheater bought from a club waiter, garments that became central to the group's look for the next two years. At the Indra, their uniform black had been broken by grey winkle-pickers and mauve jackets, but on transference to the bigger club they earned the nickname "Little Black Bastards"[48] from the Top Ten's UK contingent. In acquiring black-leather trousers, too, they certainly became very beetle-like in colour and texture, but their precarious pompadours, glistening with grease, caused more of a stir at a time when veterans of both the Somme and Dunkirk still wore their hair shaved halfway up the sides of their skulls.

Also worth seeing now was The Beatles' stage act. After a week's petrified inertia on the expansive Kaiserkeller podium, they had slipped into gear when Allan Williams' exasperated yell of "Make a show, boys!" was taken up as "*Mach schau!*" by club regulars. This chant – later corrupted to "Let's go!" – infused each of the group's front line with the desire to outdo each other in cavortings and skylarks. John made the most show of all, with much bucking and shimmying, like a composite of every rock 'n' roller he'd ever admired, an act that – so they and other outfits observed – always elicited a wild response. "They go in for movement," The Spencer Davis Group's leader said later of Reeperbahn patrons. "Musical ability doesn't matter so much."[50]

Suddenly, The Beatles found themselves home and dry as involved onlookers rushed towards the stage or clambered onto crammed tables, worrying when the five flagged, cheering when they rallied, glowing when they went down well. Driven by the new fans' enthusiasm, as well as the fizz of amphetamines, The Beatles' last hour each morning was often as energetic as the first had been at 7pm. Now that they had the knack, there was no stopping them, although, as George would recall, "All we really were was thump-thump-thump."[27] Abandoning his instrument, McCartney might appeal to dancers to clap along to Pete's bass drum, snare and hi-hat, now simultaneously stomping every beat in the bar.

The most active participants were male "Rockers" in uniforms of real or imitation leather jackets, jeans, motorbike boots and T-shirts. The girls sometimes dressed the same, but more frequently it was flared skirts, stilettos and beehive hair-dos. Had they been British, the boys' Brilliantined ducktails would have been in direct descent of the Teds'. Their taste in music and hostility towards interlopers into the Kaiserkeller certainly were.

In comparison, the Grosvenor in the Wirral was a vicarage fête. While up to a dozen waiter/bouncers hacked and struck at single *Schlager* – a chap actively looking for fights – amidst upturned furniture and shattered tankards, a ragged cheer would ensue when Koschmider himself bounded from his office with his ebony truncheon to pitch in, too. *Pour encourager les autres*, the unresisting, blood-splattered victim would then be raised aloft, weight-lifter style, and chucked into the street. A man once staggered from the Top Ten with a stevedore's baling hook embedded in his neck. More conventional aids to keeping the peace could be purchased from a Reeperbahn store called simply "the Armoury" which – as well as the usual coshes, flick-knives and pistols – once displayed a submachine gun, a bargain at 350DM.

All this was a trifle unsettling to a youth of George's temperament, for, guest workers or not, The Beatles' well-being depended on their standing among "all these gangster sort of people".[32] With fear spreading from them like cigar smoke, a midnight *demi-monde* of Mr Bigs and the wealthier madames clumped table-tops to Pete's *mach schau* beat rather than demean themselves by dancing among the Rockers. This fortunate and unquenchable partiality for Bruno's new band was manifested in crates of liquor and even trays of food being sent to sustain them while on stage, or as prepayment for requests.

The Beatles all knew better than to show less than the fullest appreciation of these gifts. In between reprising some parochial Capone's favourite song seven times, they each swigged liberally at a bottle of champagne. An advantage of being so frighteningly honoured was extra-legal protection if ever they ran into trouble within such an admirer's sphere of influence. Descending on a clip joint that had fleeced another approved British group, a *polizei* squad smashed every bottle, mirror and tumbler in the place before boarding it up.

Through Koschmider, George was unofficially exempted from the curfew regulation that forbade those under 18 from frequenting

Reeperbahn clubs after midnight. Bruno had noticed a placard daubed "I love George" – the first of its kind – being hoisted as a fair cross-section of Kaiserkeller females, and males, shouted for *das liebschen kind* – "the lovely child" – to take a lead vocal. Waved in by Lennon, George would evoke desultory screams with Presley's throbbing 'I Forgot To Remember To Forget' or Carl Perkins' 'Your True Love', singing close to the microphone with concentration on every phrase lighting his face.

Sending frissons through more nervous systems was Pete Best, toiling at his kit, his eyes not focused on anyone. He kept in trim by denying himself Preludin and too much booze, and his need for natural sleep emphasised a gradual isolation from the others. Although an improvement on Tommy Moore, Pete's hand in The Beatles' on- and off-stage frolics was dutiful, rather than hedonistic. They'd remember later the longer conversations he had with fellow drummers such as The Seniors' Jeff Wallington or, from the group who replaced them, Ringo Starr of Rory Storm's Hurricanes.

Although George was initially indifferent, even antipathetic, to Ringo, "the nasty one with this little grey streak of hair",[10] as he'd rhyme more than 20 years later, "Dislike someone and will not bend/Later they may become your friend."[51] It was hardly Ringo's fault, either, that his group, direct from Butlin's, received a higher wage than The Beatles. With this intelligence, John immediately solicited Rory to lend him the balance for a new guitar.

Fraternising more with the Storm combo than they had with the rather supercilious Seniors, George, John and Paul gladly helped out when Allan Williams financed Lou Walters' recording of a couple of numbers in a minuscule studio behind Hamburg's central station. Able to reach a bass grumble and falsetto shriek with equal precision, Walters – another who borrowed from the Buddy Holly pin-up aesthetic – was backed by Ringo and the three Beatles (with Paul on bass) on a version of 'Summertime'.

By this time, the Kaiserkeller's stage, creaky in The Jets' day, had become downright unstable, and the two groups conspired to damage it beyond repair and force Bruno to buy a new one. Much stamping and jumping during a spirited performance by Rory And

The Hurricanes did the trick, but rather than provide a new stage Koschmider felt entitled to deduct an amount from the culprits' pay. He'd grown somewhat leery of these British imports of late and, although he couldn't prevent The Beatles from paying their respects to Tony Sheridan, he was damned if any Top Ten defectors were going to pollute the Kaiserkeller. Two Jets got as far as a front table disguised as matelots in false moustaches and striped jerseys before they were frogmarched out. The Beatles had spotted them from the playing area and Lennon, with perverse humour, had announced them ceremoniously and, for the benefit of the knuckle-dustered waiters, in pidgin German.

Pete and Paul knew some schoolboy German, but all of them picked up enough to get by, despite that insular arrogance peculiar to certain Britons abroad that would come to a head in the soccer hooliganism of the 1980s. John was at the forefront of the on-stage cursing, mock-Hitlerian speeches and jibes about the war to an audience uncomprehending, disbelieving or shocked into laughter. Although tittering behind him, George would cry off at the last fence of his hero's habitual shoplifting sprees and one ineffectual attempt to mug a drunken marine who had been sufficiently impressed by the group to stand them a meal.

Mention of The Beatles in Hamburg still brings out strange stories of what people claim they heard and saw. Many of the escapades later attributed to them had taken place under the alibi of a stage act, were improved with age or were originated by others. More shocking than a nauseated memory of a Beatle loudly breaking wind in a Top Ten dressing room is a member of Johnny Hutch's new group The Big Three stepping onto a club stage in nothing but pinafores or one of The Undertakers donning a gorilla suit and emptying several Freiheit bars.

However much The Beatles made themselves out to be frightful pranksters and desperados, to Tony Sheridan, "They weren't that rough at all."[52] As bigoted a southern chauvinist as ever walked the planet, Norwich-born Sheridan gave them credit as "brighter, more intelligent then most of the northern Liverpool people, who are not famous for their intelligence".[52] In corroboration, George would suggest that The Beatles resulted from an English grammar-school interpretation of rock 'n' roll, and who could have disagreed in 1960, when all five were products of such establishments? Although clothed as Rockers, that they were of the so-called academic elite may have been a subliminal lure for the "existentialist" element, who were afraid of Rockers (with good reason) but dared to trespass into the Kaiserkeller to see The Beatles. "Up north, we'd be reading *On The Road* and they'd be reading *On The Road*,"[53] noticed McCartney. "We'd be looking at the same kind of things."[54]

Thanks to the prevalent atmosphere at Liverpool Art College, The Beatles were aware of existentialism. Lennon, especially, was a fan of Juliette Greco, one of its icons. *The Rebel*, a period Tony Hancock film vehicle, represented its adherents as pretentious, middle-class beatniks – all berets, ten-day beards, white lipstick and old sweaters – going about their action-painting, free-form poetry and scat-singing in Paris, the traditional home of bohemianism.

The first German existentialists – nicknamed "exis" – to stumble on The Beatles were an illustrator named Klaus Voorman and his photographer girlfriend, Astrid Kirchherr. It's tempting to imply that they fell for the group like the mock-up "Parisian set" did for abstract artist Hancock's Infantile school, but it was more likely that the Hamburg students were tacitly bored with the coolness of Dave Brubeck, The Modern Jazz Quartet and other hip music-makers whose LP covers were artlessly strewn around their pads. Exposure to the uproarious abandon of the English groups and their trashy rock 'n' roll in the Reeperbahn mire inspired in the city's young intellectuals a horrified urge to reject coolness altogether. Beyond specific songs, all that counted was the rhythmic kick. *Mein gott*, let's dance.

Slumming it at first, sombrely garbed exis cowered near the sanctuary of the stage, hiding behind the piano when, squinting their way now and then, the Rockers commenced their nightly brawl. Little by little, the exis sat more comfortably in the Kaiserkeller and, later, the Top Ten, partly because they'd adopted Rocker dress but mainly because of the friendship they'd struck up with the musicians. "They wanted to know what made us tick," said Tony Sheridan, "and we found them entertaining. Rather than associating with the real tough characters, we just sort of fell together. They showed us the ropes and a lot of things we otherwise wouldn't have seen."[52]

For Klaus and Astrid, the most enigmatic Beatle was not Pete but Stuart, the tortured artist whose eyes were usually hidden behind sunglasses unnecessary in the overcast German autumn. It was no coincidence that bass guitar was the instrument that Klaus began to teach himself. He also felt no loss of face or admiration for Stuart when Astrid and the younger Stuart became lovers.

Astrid's disarming Teutonic directness might have put him on his mettle, but the intelligent rather than intellectual George was also drawn to her. Part of the fascination was her daunting independence – her own car, a separate annex in her parents' house, the ease of her switching from Voorman to Sutcliffe. Her refusal to be an adjunct to Stuart, like Cynthia was to John, was very different to what George had known of women in northern England, who overcooked the cabbage for their dart-throwing husbands.

Like everybody else, including the lad himself, Astrid acknowledged that George was the "baby" of The Beatles. After she presented John with an edition of the works of de Sade for a Christmas gift, George enquired whether his contained comics. A decade later, however, Astrid would express the opinion that the baby had become the most talented Beatle.[29]

As Astrid and Stuart's affair blossomed in 1960, George – not so naïve now – didn't hover around them to the obtrusive extent that he had with John and Cynthia. Of his own age among the exis was another photographer, Jurgen Vollmer, who was also the maker of the "I love George" sign. Vollmer's most abiding memory of the youngest Beatle was of adolescent narcissism, after George had to be roused for an afternoon's boating on a Hamburg lake. While understanding his guest's need to stay dry, Jurgen was amused at how much persuasion was required before, in order to stabilise the vessel, George would remove his long winkle-pickers, stuffed with cardboard so that they didn't curl up. Back on shore, he carefully combed his wind-blown hair into place before he and Vollmer caught the tram back to the Freiheit evening.

Jurgen, Klaus and Astrid's *pilzenkopf* ("mushroom-head")

hairstyle, commonplace in Germany, would be emulated by Stuart and then George during a second trip to Hamburg, although it would be restored to its old shape before George went home. Even if Adam Faith, a new British pop star, was the darling of the ladies with the similar Henry V cut, a male so coiffured would be branded a "nancy boy" on the streets of Speke when even a Presley quiff was still regarded as a sure sign of effeminacy. Funny looks from Kaiserkeller Rockers and open laughter from the other musicians were bad enough, but within a year, said McCartney, all of The Beatles bar Best would get Vollmer "to try and cut our hair like his".[53]

Questions of haircuts may have been as yet unresolved, but at the club George reckoned that "We got to be very good as a band because we had to play for eight hours a night [sic]. We got together a big repertoire of some originals, but mainly we did all the old rock things."[55] A bouncer's typical recollection of the group's Freiheit period was of John and Paul composing in a backstage alcove while George drank his pay, chatted up girls and let the exis lionise him. Few, if any, Lennon-McCartney compositions were then unveiled publicly, but the monotony of stretching out their Merseyside palais repertoire up to four times a night at the Indra had been sufficient impetus to rehearse strenuously even the most obscure material that could be dug from their common unconscious.

The hoariest old chestnuts were tried, though preferential treatment was given to those covered by artists they rated, such as 'Over The Rainbow'. However, bearing a closer likeness to Duffy Power's treatment than Gene Vincent's was The Beatles' 'Ain't She Sweet'. Also, because it had been recorded rock 'n' roll style by US comedian Lou Monte in 1958, The Beatles even had a go at the vaudeville novelty 'The Sheik Of Araby', with Harrison on lead vocal. Neither had they inhibitions about deadpanning standards such as 'September Song' and – an eternal favourite of George's – Bing Crosby and Grace Kelly's 'True Love', from the 1956 movie *High Society*.

In the days when vocal balance was achieved by simply moving back and forth on the mike, the three-part harmonies of John, Paul and George were hard won but perfected in readiness for what lay ahead. Even John's rhythmic eccentricities were turned to an advantage. "We learned to live and work together," said George, "discovered how to adapt ourselves to what the public wanted and developed our own particular style – and it was our own. We developed along the lines we felt suited us best."[56]

Musical progress didn't correlate with personal relationships within The Beatles, however. Once amusing but now annoying its target was the ragging of "baby George" about notices forbidding minors from entering certain red-lit streets. More serious than this and the imperceptible alienation of Pete was Paul's furious jealousy of Stuart as John's closer intimate – so close now that Lennon's inner ear ignored the hard truth that his best friend's bass playing hadn't got far past the three basic rock 'n' roll forms after all these months. Had Paul acquired a bass before Stuart had had the chance, the group would have been less cluttered, Sutcliffe might not have gone to an early grave and the more musical McCartney wouldn't have felt so redundant, often just singing and dancing about with a disconnected guitar around his neck or impersonating Little Richard at the abused Kaiserkeller piano, from which irritating Stuart would snip wires to replace broken bass strings.

A short-lived opportunity for Paul to contribute more would occur sooner than any Beatle contemplated, when history repeated itself. In the face of Bruno's reprimands, the group's visits to the Top Ten had gone beyond merely watching The Jets. When The Beatles joined them on stage during Kaiserkeller breaks, Top Ten proprietor Peter Eckhorn heard not casual jamming but a new resident group, after The Jets' stint ended on 1 December. As well as higher wages, Eckhorn also offered bunk-bed accommodation above the club that, if plain, was palatial compared to the dungeons of Koschmider. Furthermore, The Jets found Peter an affable employer from whom bonuses and other fringe benefits could be expected when business was brisk. Also, rather than racketeers, sailors and tearaways, the Top Ten tended to cater for tourists and *Mittelstand* teenagers.

After he'd secured Sheridan, Eckhorn had next charmed away key members of Bruno's staff, including his formidable head bouncer, Horst Fascher. Reading Eckhorn like a book – and an avaricious publication it was – Koschmider acted swiftly. Firstly, The Beatles were given a month's notice and reminded of a contractual clause that forbade them from working in any other Hamburg club without his permission, which he withheld. Aware that Eckhorn could grease enough palms to circumvent such legalities, Bruno struck harder by withdrawing whatever immunity he'd arranged concerning the youngest Beatle's nightly violation of the curfew.

With less than a fortnight to go at the Kaiserkeller, The Beatles were ordered to present their passports for police inspection. As George was a good three months short of his 18th birthday and had so flagrantly disregarded the law, he was to be deported from West Germany forthwith.

He spent much of the day before his exile giving Paul and John a crash course in lead guitar the Harrison way, as they seemed quite willing to continue in his absence. Indeed, after a month at the Top Ten, there were prospects of playing a season in Berlin. Another possibility was a stint at Le Golf Drouot in Paris, after the departure of its British house band, Doug Fowlkes And The Airdales. Despite government efforts to ban subversive rock 'n' roll, a Gallic species of Rocker – *le yé-yé* – had bred entertainers such as Les Chats Sauvages, Les Chausettes Noires and a Parisian Presley in the form of 17-year-old Johnny Hallyday.

Because the French weren't as rigid about youngsters up past their bedtimes, perhaps George could rejoin The Beatles if they went to Le Golf Drouot. This hypothesis was cold comfort, however, as he gathered his belongings for the voyage back to Upton Green. He also carried with him the heart-sinking conjecture that the others were managing without him. Eric Griffiths had been dumped by The Quarry Men, so what would stop The Beatles recruiting another lead guitarist, if need arose? There were plenty to choose from among the many Merseyside groups now flooding into Hamburg. "A lot of really good guitarists came over from Liverpool," estimated Bill Harry. "Nicky Crouch of Faron's Flamingos...Paddy Chambers – he could have stepped in."

Only Astrid and Stuart saw him off from Hamburg railway station. Bewildered, subdued and very young, George flung his arms around the couple before heaving his suitcase, amplifier and guitar into the second-class compartment of the long, high, foreign train. An inexperienced traveller, he wouldn't be reckless enough to get out to stretch his legs as others did during the painfully slow disembarkations from stops *en route* to the Hook of Holland. Babble penetrated from outside as he stared moodily at the flat landscape, where the exposed cold from the Westarweg hit like a hammer.

The pallor of dawn gleamed dully as he walked stiffly from the ship with his luggage across the concrete desolation of the customs post at Newhaven. After the connection to Liverpool jolted forward, he may have slipped into the uneasiest of slumbers, now that he was more assured of getting home. Hours later, George Harrison climbed down into the vastness of Lime Street's glass dome. Near the taxi rank, an elderly pipe-smoking road sweeper pushed a broom along the gutter. A newspaper vendor in his kiosk barked the headline of Tuesday 22 November 1960's edition of *The Liverpool Echo*.

4 The Cave Dweller

Over a few days' convalescent sloth, George pondered. With every reason to believe that The Beatles would remain indefinitely in Europe, who could blame him if he joined another group? Since he'd been away, the Merseyside music scene, while not yet exploding, had grown immensely. From The Pathfinders in Birkenhead to Ian And The Zodiacs in Crosby, each vicinity seemed to have a group enjoying parochial fame. Either active or in formation were outfits of every variety and size, including sextets and octets. Some were all female, others all black. A couple were even all female and black. Most were in it (as The Quarry Men had been) for beer money and a laugh with a "Bert-can-play-bass" attitude. However, as their hire-purchase debts at Hessy's demonstrated, some meant business, among them The Remo Four, who, emerging from Don Andrew and Colin Manley's Viscounts, were recognised as Liverpool's top instrumental unit.

No more an amateur, George might have been welcome in a band of like standing, perhaps Lee Castle And The Barons, which contained his old colleague Les Stewart. Nonetheless, such a consideration proved academic as, by the second week of December 1960, all of The Beatles except Stuart Sutcliffe – by now betrothed to Astrid – had come home, their Top Ten enterprise scotched when Best and McCartney were ordered out of the Fatherland on a trumped-up charge of arson, courtesy of Herr Koschmider.

With ex-Blackjack Chas Newby deputising on bass, The Beatles regrouped for an exploratory booking at the Casbah, followed by another on Christmas Eve at the Grosvenor, cautiously re-opened for pop business. Because of their sojourn in Hamburg, the "successful German tour" of pre-engagement publicity, they were an unknown quantity locally, but not for long. They were a last-minute addition to a bill at Litherland Town Hall on the 27th, and John Lennon would recall The Beatles "being cheered for the first time"[57] in Liverpool after a casually cataclysmic performance that their spell in Hamburg had wrought. Whereas the customers had jived to The Searchers and the two other groups engaged, there'd been a spontaneous rippling stagewards when the curtains swept back a few dramatic bars into The Beatles' first number. As Sheridan would, they behaved as though they couldn't give a damn about the audience and were just up there having fun amongst themselves. "And so many people really dug the band," exclaimed George, "and they were coming up to us and saying, 'Oh, you speak good English.'"[32]

The Beatles' Litherland wipe-out was food for thought for many of the hip Merseysiders who witnessed it. One of Kingsize Taylor's Dominoes, Bobby Thomson, "could see that they were going to be big and I wanted them to be. It was a funny feeling for blokes to want that. Everybody loved them."[58] Actually, it wasn't quite everybody, because to some The Beatles were a scruffy lot who smoked on stage and made, in Don Andrew's view, "a horrible, deafening row". You couldn't deny their impact on the crowd, yet musically they were a throwback, now that pop was at its most harmless and ephemeral. "In England," recounted George, "Cliff Richard And The Shadows became the big thing. They all had matching ties and handkerchiefs and grey suits, but we were still doing Gene Vincent, Bo Diddley...you know, Ray Charles things."[32]

At this time, most of the fiercest practitioners of classic rock were either dead (Buddy Holly), gaoled (Chuck Berry), disgraced (Jerry Lee Lewis), in holy orders (Little Richard) or otherwise obsolete. The Everly Brothers were less than a year off enlisting as marines when Elvis was demobbed, now a sergeant and "all-round family entertainer". The hit parades of North America and everywhere else became constipated with insipidly handsome boys next door, all doe-eyes, hairspray and bashful half smiles, matched by their forenames (mainly Bobby) and piddle-de-pat records. If they faltered after a brace of Hot 100 entries, queuing around the block would be any number of substitute Bobbys raring to sing any piffle put in front of them.

However, in this twee morass, there were few sparkles. Without compromising their rhythm and blues determination, Ray Charles and Fats Domino were still chart contenders, while a Texan named Roy Orbison transformed 'Only The Lonely' – a trite Bobby exercise – into an unprecedented epic with a voice that combined hillbilly diction with operatic pitch and breath control.

No Beatle would equal Orbison's *bel canto* eloquence, but John, George and Paul together could produce distinctive vocal arrangements of The Marvelettes' 'Please Mr Postman', Barrett Strong's 'Money' and other records on Tamla-Motown, a promising black label from Detroit that had manoeuvred its first fistful of signings into the Hot 100. Of all Tamla-Motown acts, George listened hardest to The Miracles, whose leader, Smokey Robinson, had an "effortless butterfly of a voice"[59] that he would never bring himself to criticise.

John was fonder of Chuck Berry, whose celebrations in song of the pleasures available to American teenage consumers would remain prominent in the repertoire of almost all young vocal-instrumental groups on Merseyside, with Berry's incarceration and lack of major British hits only boosting his cult celebrity. Although more popular Yanks dominated British pop, groups within Liverpool's culturally secluded hinterland – as well as those outside the region who went to Hamburg – didn't lean as obviously as others on chart material. Unless specifically requested, most of them scarcely bothered with numbers by British stars, as only a few were up to US standards.

Although Gerry And The Pacemakers prided themselves on embracing everything in each week's Top 20 in their act, they were as competitive as any other professional Merseyside group in seeking out more obscure numbers. "If a rhythm and blues record – say, something by Chuck Berry – was issued, then I'd rush down to the shop and buy it straight away, and chances were I'd see somebody like Paul Lennon [*sic*] of The Beatles in the same queue. Then there'd be a big rush to see who could get their version of it out first."[60] In exchange for the words to The Olympics' 'Well (Baby Please Don't

Go)', John Lennon scribbled the ones to Gene Vincent's 'Dance In The Street' for The Big Three.

Tony Sheridan praised The Beatles' "great talent for finding unusual records",[52] as did Bill Harry and Chris Curtis, The Searchers' drummer. Some musicians and disc jockeys were on the mailing lists of untold US independent record companies, many of which, said George, "were not even known there".[59] A goldmine of such erudition for The Beatles and Gerry was the collection of Bob Wooler, a master of ceremonies on "jive nights" at Wavertree's Holyoake Hall. Along less exclusive avenues, groups might tune in to some static-ridden rarity on the BBC's overseas service or, more often, on the late evening programmes in English on the continental commercial station Radio Luxembourg.

The Searchers and The Beatles were particularly adept at adapting songs by American girl groups to a different set of hormones. Both tried The Orlons' 'Shimmy Shimmy' (less far-reaching a dance craze than Chubby Checker's Twist variations), while The Beatles' 'Boys' from The Shirelles' catalogue was a favourite with the ladies, because it was one of Pete Best's infrequent vocal outings. In Rory Storm's Hurricanes, it came to be sung as a duet by Ringo and Swingin' Cilla, a typist by day who'd made her debut as a chanteuse at the Iron Door, a former jazz club that had cautiously readjusted itself to pop after the trad boom declined. This was paralleled in a wider world via Dick Lester's film *It's Trad, Dad!*, in which performances by Gene Vincent, Chubby Checker and schoolgirl pop star Helen Shapiro were juxtaposed with those by Acker Bilk and other jazzmen.

As a solo by some New Orleans dotard would be revered as definitive by trad dads, so a certain song might be so worthily executed by this or that Liverpudlian pop outfit that it would be shunned by rivals. Few, for instance, were assured enough to take on 'You'll Never Walk Alone' after Gerry had brought the house down with it at the Vincent show, and similar criteria applied to such diverse items as The Merseybeats' gauchely sentimental 'Hello Young Lovers' and black vocal group The Chants' arrangement of The Stereos' 'I Really Love You'.

Only fractionally more than just a name than The Stereos was James Ray, a New Yorker whose 'If You Gotta Make A Fool Of Somebody' was among those numbers that became Merseybeat standards. Another was Richard Barrett's 'Some Other Guy'. While Jack Good *protégés* Little Tony And His Brothers – expatriate Italians – would simply mimic Chan Romero's 'Hippy Hippy Shake', the intention in Liverpool was to make that song, 'Money', Larry Williams' 'Slow Down', The Clovers' 'Love Potion Number Nine' and all the rest of them sound different to any other group's version. Hence the calm precision of The Searchers' rendering of The Isley Brothers' 'Twist And Shout' and The Beatles' frantic work-out of the same, just one step from chaos. Sometimes a song like 'Up A Lazy River' or Brook Benton's 'Hurtin' Inside' would be heard all over Merseyside before being dropped quite inexplicably, never to be played again.

Allegedly, it wasn't until Paul noticed Earl Preston's TTs performing a self-penned song that The Beatles risked any Lennon-McCartney originals in their stage repertoire. Other Mersey Beat musicians – such as The Zephyrs' Geoff Taggart and ex-Liobian Stuart Slater of The Mojos – also came up with items superior to some of their respective groups' non-originals, while The Big Three knocked together 'Cavern Stomp', immortalising the club that, taking its cue from the nearby Iron Door, had allowed pop and trad bands to share the same bill before hosting its first all-pop event in May 1960.

Despite an essence of disinfectant and cheap perfume in its subterranean rankness, to Liverpool footballer Tommy Smith, the Cavern was "the dirtiest place on Earth",[61] with its arched bricks, sweating with slippery mould, and the suffocating heat growing by the minute as more teenagers descended its narrow stone steps toward the metallic beat of either a group or a record spun by one of the club's resident disc jockeys, be it Billy Butler, who occasionally sang with The Merseybeats, or Bob Wooler, uttering his catchphrase: "Hi there, all you cave dwellers. Welcome to the best of cellars."

This sodden oven in a ravine of lofty warehouses would become as famous a Liverpool landmark as the Pier Head. All manner of future worthies, from government minister Edwina Currie to television actress Sue Johnson, would proudly recall how they'd been among the massed humanity bobbing up and down in the blackness as The Beatles entertained on its wooden stage beneath white light-bulbs. The infrequency of the violence that still marred or supplemented pop evenings elsewhere said much about the Cavern's clientèle. Hatchet-wielding hooligans with grievances against Derry Wilkie converged on the Iron Door while his new group were on stage. Of the same mentality were those who wrecked Knotty Ash Village Hall the night on which The Big Three appeared.

At the Cavern, "It wasn't just kids going to a thing with music in the background," explained Bill Harry. "They were interested in the individual musicians. 'I liked the solo Johnny Guitar did on "Doctor Feelgood".' 'Isn't so-and-so a good singer?' They used to compare the abilities of the different musicians and talk about the tunes they used to play. They were quite an intelligent crowd."

Devoid of the complicity of Mona Best or the anxious disapprobation of Aunt Mimi, Louise Harrison was as fanatical about The Beatles and Mersey Beat as any cave dweller young enough to be her grandchild. Frequenting the Cavern even after The Beatles ceased playing there, she accepted honorary membership of the fan club created for The Hideaways, who performed at the Cavern more times than any other ensemble. Without embarrassment, she'd be down there, clapping and cheering, foremost among those blamed by John's tight-lipped auntie for encouraging "the stupid fool" and his so-called group.

As a "rock and dole group" – Wooler's words – no obligations to regular employment had hindered The Beatles making their Cavern debut in February 1961 during one of the new lunch-time sessions that were further maximising the club's profits since it had gone pop. It was still predominantly a jazz venue then, and its main concession to pop was a weekly off-peak evening with The Swinging Blue Jeans, who walked an uncomfortable line between trad and the blandest of pop. Their days as the club's resident pop group were numbered, however, when The Beatles were rebooked on 21 March as the Jeans' guests. By loudly voicing their preferences, 60 extra customers abused this hospitality. In their striped blazers and pressed denim hosiery, the swinging combo failed to see how anyone could respect a group whose lead guitarist had almost been refused entry for his slovenly turn-out.

The Beatles performed there more than 200 times over the next two years, as much a fixture at the Cavern as The Searchers at the Iron Door, The Undertakers at Orrell Park ballroom and, later, Michael McCartney's Scaffold at the Blue Angel. All Mersey Beat groups that counted had a full work schedule. On the evening of George's 18th birthday, The Beatles crammed in two separate engagements, which was a common undertaking now that hard-nosed promoters had smelled the money to be made from all these young bands happy just to have somewhere to make their noise for the many silly enough to pay to hear them.

On one chronicled occasion, George slipped Cavern doorman Paddy Delaney a few shillings – "but don't tell her I gave it to you"[62] – to pass on to an impoverished fan loitering with vain hope outside. George must have been unusually well heeled that day, because his average turnover was only "a couple of quid a week".[22] Typical, too, was one midsummer evening at Orrell Park when, of the net takings of £67, only £19 was split between three groups.

Church halls, social clubs, village institutes, pub function rooms, ice rinks and even riverboats now offered beat sessions. Eventually, there would be a Junior Cavern Club on Saturday afternoons. The managements of larger places, such as the Locarno and the Grafton Rooms (both in West Derby) and the New Brighton Tower Ballroom, were capitulating to older teenagers. After tussles with the Municipal Parks Committee, open-air promotions catered for pop, too, commencing with an event featuring more than 20 groups amid the playing fields of Stanley Park.

George Harrison's earliest remark in the national music press was, "You know, we've hardly done any touring in England. Working in and around Liverpool keeps you busy throughout the whole year."[63] Other areas couldn't duplicate that unique brand of pop enthusiasm that was Liverpool's, but, other than a smattering of venues like the Beachcomber in Bolton and Cardigan's Black Lion, nowhere else in Britain engaged Mersey Beat outfits. Each locality felt a certain territorial superiority towards other bastions of beat. One agency was "formed with the sole intention of stopping Brum groups playing at Worcester venues".[64] However, such embargos were relaxed for visitors of qualified fame like Screaming Lord Sutch And The Savages or Johnny Kidd And The Pirates, on the understanding that local heroes were to be given support spots.

For The Beatles, that left only Hamburg. Thanks largely to Mrs Best's badgering and Peter Eckhorn's assurances of their good behaviour, the West German Immigration Office allowed firebugs Paul and Pete back so that The Beatles could begin a four-month season at the Top Ten in March. Paul had transferred to bass guitar at last because Stuart – now a student at Hamburg's State Art School – had for all practical purposes left the group. His last duty on their behalf would be to write to Allan Williams, repudiating their professional association with him. The grounds for this schism were that, since The Beatles' ignominious return to Liverpool in December, Williams had negotiated only two bookings for them; the rest had snowballed from those found by either themselves or by Mona Best. Saddened by what he saw as the group's disloyalty – although they'd never really been his – Allan found it in him to offer to take them back, after making token legal threats.

What wounded them more was his barring them temporarily from the Blue Angel, where the bands were inclined to congregate after an evening's work while the rest of Merseyside slept. Johnny Hutch would brag of Paul McCartney's face draining of colour when The Big Three supposedly "blew off" The Beatles one night, but rivalry would dissolve into ribald camaraderie as musicians small-talked and had a laugh or a cry if the booking had gone badly – even if most, so it was frequently put about, were triumphs in retrospect. George's propensity for gossip was as profound as the next guitarist's, but, remembering how The Silver Beatles had borne disdain from other groups, he tended to champion those in need of a break. It was through his recommendation that dexterous barrelhouse pianist Terence O'Toole became a Mojo. George was also sincerely loud in lauding fellow Cavern regulars The Roadrunners.

The best-known example of Mersey Beat's *ésprit de corps* was a merger of The Beatles with Gerry And The Pacemakers, as The Beatmakers, one evening at Litherland Town Hall, but it wasn't unusual for, say, Rory Storm to leap on stage for a couple of numbers with Faron's Flamingos or Gerry to deputise for John Lennon at a Beatles Cavern bash, where it was noticed that, like John and The Searchers' John McNally, he had copied Tony Sheridan's high-chested guitar stance.

Back at the Top Ten, the most piquant memory of The Beatles' first, truncated residency was an extra-long extrapolation of 'What'd I Say' with Sheridan's departing Jets. For their second coming, the Liverpudlians would be replacing Dave Dee And The Bostons, whose leader, on receiving this information, said, "'And what are they called?' The Beatles. 'What a bloody silly name that is.' You make a statement like that and you always remember it. Then, of course, we ended up with a name like Dave Dee, Dozy, Beaky, Mick And Tich."[47]

In the Reeperbahn's bierkeller jollity, Dee And The Bostons had evolved from a clumsy Wiltshire group into perhaps Hamburg's most popular attraction. Crucially, they'd become celebrated exponents of the pounding *mach schau* beat that years later would underpin 'Hold Tight', their first big hit under their more ludicrous name. Now that links with the UK had been established, the Freiheit provided training for other British hit-parade contenders among the many streaming in to serve its clubs. "Germany boosted our morale," said West Drayton vocalist Cliff Bennett. "For the first time, we seemed to be making a solid impression on our audiences." As well as a Merseyside faction so pronounced that the bar staff's English was infused with Scouse slang, from further afield came the likes of Birmingham's Rockin' Berries, Bern Elliott And The Fenmen from the ballrooms of Kent and, sons of Weybridge, The Nashville Teens, with no fewer than three gyrating lead singers.

Although the undisputed Presley of the Reeperbahn, Tony Sheridan faced tough opposition whenever British stars of the same vintage were brought over. Prevented by their stage images from going Bobby-smooth were Lord Sutch with his cartoon horror, Johnny Kidd, and Hounslow's king rocker Vince Taylor – although, during one unhinged evening at the Paris Olympia, the latter floated on stage in atypical white vestments to preach a repent-ye-your-sins sermon to a mystified and then furious *yé-yé* audience.

More formidable than any Limey rock 'n' roller, however, was Gene Vincent, then domiciled in England. When asked by the Kentish instrumental sextet Sounds Incorporated what Hamburg was like, he replied, "Oh, it's OK there. I had a nice band backing me up. They're called The Beatles."[65] As well as signing an autograph for Lennon, the Screaming End also recalled "how desperately they wanted to make records!"[65] There was, however, a single recorded during their second stay in Germany, for which they'd been merely Tony Sheridan's accompanists. They weren't even credited as "The Beatles" on the label because, as George informs us, it was too close to "*die pedals* – whatever little kids' terminology would be for it – that's German for 'prick'."[32]

With Sheridan, they'd shared the Top Ten's skylit bunkroom. In order to reach the lavatory, four floors below, they risked an affray with Asso, Eckhorn's truculent boxer dog, whose teeth had sunk into the ankles of both Paul McCartney and Alex Harvey, among many others. Since The Jets' farewell, Tony had had no fixed backing band, using instead whoever happened to be also playing the club. Most felt honoured to be on the same stage, learning the tricks of the trade from one nicknamed "the Teacher" – although David Sutch likened him more to "a sergeant-major. He was really snappy towards them." Throughout the spring of 1961, the Teacher's class featured Rory Storm's Hurricanes, The Jaybirds (the Nottingham group who preceded them) and his star pupils, The Beatles, who'd been on stage with him when they were heard by Alfred Schlacht, a publisher associated with Deutsche Grammophon, with whom Sheridan had signed in Germany.

At Schlacht's urging, Bert Kaempfert, a power on Polydor, the company's pop subsidiary, invited the thrilled Beatles to be one of two groups – both to be called The Beat Brothers – who'd cut tracks with Sheridan from which a single and probably an album could be selected. Thirty-six-year-old Kaempfert was best known for conducting 'Wonderland By Night', a million-selling orchestral sound-painting of Manhattan, and although his music might not have been to The Beatles' taste he had co-written Presley's recent bilingual Number One, 'Wooden Heart', which they'd prudently included in their club set when Bert came by.

One May morning, after snatching a little rest from the night's Top Ten shift, Tony and The Beatles were transported to their first session. With a Deutschmark sign over every fretful crotchet in a proper commercial studio and a minimal budget, the taping took place on the stage of an infant school (the children were on Whitsun holiday) with equipment that Sheridan reckoned "was a leftover relic of the British Army occupation from some sort of radio station they had".[66]

Each number was punched out in three takes, at most, but the mood was sufficiently relaxed for Kaempfert to lend critical ears to some of Paul and John's songs and an instrumental that George – with John's executive clearance – had constructed to fool Rory Storm into thinking that it was the latest by The Shadows. Homing in on a simple phrase, and with generous employment of the tremolo arm – the note-bending protrusion on some electric guitars – George's joke sounded much like a Shadows out-take. As it was more in keeping with current trends than anything Lennon and McCartney had on offer, Kaempfert allowed The Beatles to record it as one side of a possible single in their own right. Given a title and enlivened with barely audible background yelling, 'Cry For A Shadow' – or 'Beatle Bop', as it was informally known – thus became the first Beatle original to be released on record, appearing in June 1962 on Sheridan's *My Bonnie* LP, named after the 45 that had taken him high up in the German charts. Unhappily for them, The Beatles had settled on a standard session rate rather than a stake in Sheridan's royalties.

As shown in its use by Dr Fuchs' skiffle group and Ray Charles' 1958 recording, 'My Bonnie' was one of those semi-traditional songs that never go away. (I remember being forced to pipe it out in an uncertain treble at a primary school concert in 1961.) Like 'Up A Lazy River', it was more in the air than actually popular that year. The same applied to Sheridan's B-side, 'The Saints', and the tearjerking 'Nobody's Child', which, with 'Sweet Georgia Brown' and two other numbers, was taped a week after the first session.

Producer Kaempfert also spared time to record The Beatles' 'Ain't She Sweet' to go with George's instrumental, but neither track was issued outside Germany until they acquired historical interest. When the group's time came, Bert would recount, "It was obvious to me that they were enormously talented, but nobody – including the boys themselves – knew how to use that talent or where it would lead them."[67]

Although he was persuaded in 1963 to re-record his vocal to 'Sweet Georgia Brown', inserting Beatle references, Tony Sheridan didn't exploit his connection as others less qualified would later. He all but crossed paths with three of his former colleagues in 1964, when all were benighted in the same Australian hotel, but he claimed to the one journalist who asked him why there'd been no reunion that he "wasn't trying to jump on their bandwagon".[68] Yet he continued to look up individual members, as he did Pete Best in 1978, when both chanced to be in Los Angeles, Pete there to talk about the old days on a television show.

A sadder Beatle casualty was Stuart Sutcliffe, who'd been a spectator at the Kaempfert sessions. Within a year, he would die at the age of 21 in a Hamburg ambulance of a cerebral haemorrhage that lay opinion would trace to the night he'd been worked over outside Latham Hall in 1961. After he quit the group, Paul's and – to a lesser degree – George's animosity towards him had diminished, both issuing an open invitation for him to sit in with The Beatles whenever they were in Hamburg.

'My Bonnie' appeared in German shops in June 1961. The final weeks at the Top Ten became very long, simmering as The Beatles were to get back to Liverpool to impress everyone with their marvellous achievement. Calling on Arthur Kelly, George and Paul had literally danced with excitement, leaving footmarks on the freshly scrubbed kitchen floor. To Barbara Kelly's deflationary scolding, Paul's riposte was that she'd regret her blunt words when he was famous. With John assuming Tony's lead vocal, The Beatles rubbed it in on stage. Bob Wooler plugged 'My Bonnie' relentlessly, for all it signified rather than its sound. He'd received his copy from George, who'd made sure his relatives and friends got one as well, even if Red Bentley, among others, wasn't that struck with it.

For the Harrisons, home would shortly be 174 Mackett's Lane, a council house again but this time the other side of Woolton from the McCartneys and a more select area than Speke. That three of the group lived so near each other was handy for the van pick-up for bookings. The Beatles' first true road manager was Frank Garner, who doubled as a Casbah bouncer. He was also their official driver, but, since both Harrison and McCartney had gained their licences, they would clamour for a turn at the wheel, the older Paul bullying his way most often into the driver's seat.

This unpleasantness was representative of the discord and intrigues that make pop groups what they are. The Beatles' history was and would be punctuated with unresolvable rows, prima-donna tantrums, *ménages a trois* and bouts of sulking. In spite of his 'Cry For A Shadow' coup, George was still not sure enough of his position within the quartet to impose unsolicited ideas upon the status quo established by John and Paul, who were so hand-in-glove that the two blew a birthday cheque from John's rich Aunt Elizabeth on a fortnight in Paris while the other two cooled their heels. When the chief Beatles came back with *pilzenkopf* haircuts, which they wore boldly around Liverpool, George nerved himself to do likewise.

Unspoken as yet was the desire of all three to be rid of Pete Best as soon as someone more suitable came to light. His dismissal in August 1962 may be ascribed to an inability to conform to the mores of his peers, shown by his maintenance of a shaped cockade instead of what became known locally as a "Beatle cut". More serious was his continued refusals of the amphetamines consumed by the rest during their Reeperbahn residencies. Neither did he contribute much to the group's studentish restricted code, superstitions and folklore.

Almost as much part of the act as their music was The Beatles' informal knockabout clowning, directives to the audience to shut up, coarser language in heated moments, private jokes and, for the girls, Pete's Brooding Intensity and film-star handsomeness. "Pete was the most popular member of the group," recalled Bill Harry. "Fans used to sleep in his garden. He was in such demand that they finally had to give way to all the girls' wishes and put Pete right at the front." With McCartney on drums, pensive Best would sing and demonstrate the Peppermint Twist, but "all the kids came up and dragged him from the stage".

Pete didn't have to try as hard as the less well-favoured Paul, scuttling to and from microphones, and John, who, scoffed Bob Wooler, "gave the impression of being so hard".[44] Brought forward for his 'Sheik Of Araby', George might have cultivated a Cheeky Chappie persona, but, loquacious as he was in the van, at the Cavern, said his mother, he "never used to say anything or smile. George used to say that it was because he was the lead guitar. If the others made mistakes through larking about, nobody noticed, but he couldn't make any." Nevertheless, the concept of John cementing George's runs with rudimentary chord-slashing had become rather a mistaken. Nowadays, lead and rhythm guitars often merged in interlocking harmony, evolved over hundreds of hours on stage. As Lennon elucidated, "I'd find it a drag to play rhythm all the time, so I always work out something interesting to play, [although] I never play anything that George couldn't do better – but I like playing lead sometimes, so I do it."[44]

The interaction of Harrison's *Play In A Day* virtuosity and Lennon's good-bad rawness was compulsively exquisite, even to more proficient guitarists like Colin Manley And The Roadrunners' Mike Hart, who could hear what was technically wrong. "George was regarded as a good guitarist," disclosed Bill Harry, "but he didn't rank with Adrian Barber and, later, Brian Griffiths [both of The Big Three]. People like that were rated and talked about."

Most of them also gilded their fretboard skills with a grinning vibrancy. George didn't always look glum but he was no natural show-off. His main and most imitated stage gesture came to be "the Liverpool leg", a rhythmic twitching of the said limb as if grinding a cigarette butt with the heel. All the same, John McNally affirmed, "You'd think somehow George would get left behind, but he didn't, and he developed his own style – a bit shy – and the girls really liked that."[58]

A perk of being a Beatle was readier access to female flesh than most of the blokes who'd paid admission to shuffle about in the gloom past the burning footlights. A kind of *droit du seigneur* prevailed as short-skirted "judies" with urchin faces and pale lipstick fringed the stage front, chewing, smoking and ogling. In the days before the birth-control pill, pre-marital sex was a bigger step to take than it was when the '60s started swinging, and The Beatles and other famous groups were showered with paternity suits. Many of them emanated from the Freiheit, where bartering in sex was less sheepish than in Liverpool. Giving in to nature's baser urges, free-spirited *frauleins* would simply lock eyes with a selected musician up on stage and point at him while flexing a phallic forearm. Do you reckon he got the message?

The Beatles' third Hamburg season would pass at the new Star-Club, which had given no quarter during a ruthless campaign to outflank the Top Ten as the district's premier night spot. When American pop stars of the calibre of Jerry Lee Lewis and Fats Domino began including the Star-Club on their European itineraries, a desperate tactic of the Top Ten was to bill a Glaswegian duo who impersonated The Everly Brothers as the genuine article.

During The Beatles' seven weeks at the Star-Club, they warmed up for three visiting US idols: Ray Charles, Little Richard and the ubiquitous Gene Vincent. At first, they were starstruck, but, "Backstage afterwards," Charles recollected, "we would sit and bullshit and say we loved each other's music, the typical thing that people in our musical brotherhood all do."[69] George hit it off straight away with Billy Preston, Little Richard's organist. Although only 15, Billy had been performing in public from his earliest youth in Texas and then California. He was a scion of a showbusiness family, and his prodigious command of keyboards led to his playing with many eminent black gospel artists. It was during a television show with Mahalia Jackson that the ten-year-old was spotted by a film producer, who cast him as the juvenile lead in 1958's *St Louis Blues*, which also starred Nat "King" Cole as blind "father of the blues" WC Handy. However, acting was incidental to Billy's chosen vocation. As well as his gospel work, he also ran his own dance band, which was much in the Nat "King" Cole/Ray Charles milieu. On leaving school, he joined what was supposed to be a gospel tour of the world, but with Little Richard and Sam Cooke involved it had become a straight pop presentation when it reached Europe, where Richard's band plugged a gap in the tour with dates at the Star-Club.

Neither Billy nor his new-found friend George knew the extent to which their careers would interweave. As far as George was concerned, they were only likely to meet again if Preston found himself on Merseyside or the Reeperbahn – which, for The Beatles, was all there was. Of the two stamping grounds, Hamburg seemed the better financial bet. Virtually resident in the Fatherland now, Kingsize Taylor, Ian And The Zodiacs and even obscure Liverpool outfits like The Georgians were making a good living there. Both Adrian Barber and Nashville Teens singer Terry Crowe had opted to pursue secure jobs in Freiheit clubs rather than waste a lifetime back in Britain trying to become stars.

Rather than modestly coming into their own on foreign soil, The Beatles preferred to return to Liverpool, even if some groups there had overtaken them on certain fronts. Fontana had just released The Seniors' debut single, while The Remo Four had broken into the US air base circuit and Rory Storm still had Butlin's, and The Beatles almost envied their Quarry Men past, when there was far less to prove. McCartney's forecast in reply to a fan letter – "the first one I had" – was founded in wishful thinking: "We will be making some records soon and will get them released in Liverpool as soon as possible."[70]

There was also a strong argument that self-contained groups were on the wane. You only had to look at Merseyside's crop of outstanding showmen like Rory, Freddie Starr, Lee Curtis, Ambrose Mogg or Bill "Faron" Russley, dubbed "the Panda-Footed Prince of Prance". All Liverpool girl singers like Barbara Harrison (no relation) and Beryl Marsden needed was to be in the right place at the right time. Although Swingin' Cilla had absented herself on the day through stage-fright, she had landed an audition with Kenny Ball's Jazzmen, then in the middle of their four-year chart run. Perhaps The Beatles ought to find themselves a female Johnny Gentle?

On the plus side, they were "the biggest thing in Liverpool", as Ringo Starr testified. "In them days, that was big enough."[57] In concurrence, George added, "We were recognised there, too, only people didn't chase us about."[56] Fans had no qualms about telephoning them at home to request numbers to be played during Cavern sets that would veer fitfully from the merry 'Sheik Of Araby' to Paul's torchy 'September In The Rain' to a stomping, elongated 'Money'. Copying their repertoire and off-hand stagecraft were units like the younger Merseybeats, who, as their Tony Crane admitted, hired a second guitarist "to make the band more like The Beatles".[2]

As unaware as his interviewers were of The Beatles' distant thunder, Roy Orbison – in London in 1962 – conjectured that "you don't seem to have the kind of rhythm groups that we have in the States, and I'm sure that is what the kids want: strong, beaty rhythms that make them jump".[71] Nobody at Roy's press conference could predict that soon native British "rhythm groups" would be jumping up the hit parade in abundance. One of them would end 1963 as arguably more popular than Cliff Richard And The Shadows, with records as competent and attractive but played with guts, like.

5 The Mersey Beatle

With The Beatles as principal carriers, the bacillus of Mersey Beat had spread down river. Touted as "Manchester's Beatles" were The Hollies, a quintet built around Ricky And Dane. The music-hall element of The Beatles' Cavern act was to have a beneficial effect upon another fan, a certain Peter Noone, who also regularly negotiated the 36 miles from Manchester to catch this Scouse group that everybody was talking about.

Before he became the Herman in Herman's Hermits, young Noone found work as a television actor. One of his more celebrated parts was that of Len Fairclough's son in ITV's *Coronation Street*, a gritty soap opera set in a fictitious northern town. An episode in late 1961 had "Eddie", a local rock 'n' roller, performing at the social club, while besotted teenager Lucille Hewitt incurred parental wrath by having his name tattooed on her forearm.

How aware were the scriptwriters of locally produced alternatives to mainstream pop? Like provincial football teams, artists like Eddie would acquire a tremendous grass-roots following of those who'd recount bitterly how, with chart success, this singer or that group later betrayed them by defecting to London. As far geographically from the Cavern as he could be, George Harrison would one day explain to Australian journalists, "When rock 'n' roll died and ballads and folk music took over, we just carried on playing our type of music. When at last we succeeded in cutting a record, the people were ready for a change, and we clicked."[72]

Before the storm broke, puppyish American Bobbys were not as easily hoisting their discs above the Number 20 mark in the UK hit parade. Nonetheless, although The Shadows ruled 1962's spring charts with 'Wonderful Land', their reliance on massed violins to do so buttressed record moguls' theories that groups with electric guitars were *passé*. Almost the only groups worth fussing over we those like The Kestrels – "Britain's *ace* vocal group" – and The King Brothers, whose records were glutinous with orchestration and their producers' ideas. Their moderate chart entries were regarded as secondary to earnings in variety revues.

Other outfits specialised in commercial folk. The best remembered of this bunch were The Springfields, whose panda-eyed singer, Dusty, achieved spectacular solo success when the trio split up. Of the same ilk were Peter, Paul And Mary, a product of New York's Greenwich Village, where the civil rights movement had fused with folk song to be labelled "protest". This trio first intruded upon the UK singles chart with 'Blowing In The Wind', an anti-war opus written by another Village protest singer, Bob Dylan, whose plaintive debut LP was acclaimed in the *NME* as "most exciting".[73] George, however, expressed little enthusiasm for Dylan's down-home intonation, untutored phrasing and eccentric breath control, until John proclaimed himself a convert.

Harrison and Lennon were also the keenest of The Beatles on the record productions of a weedy young New Yorker named Phil Spector, who was hot property in the music business for his spatial "wall of sound" technique, whereby he'd multi-track an apocalyptic *mélange* – replete with everything, including the proverbial kitchen sink – behind ciphers who'd submitted to his master plan. Styled "the Svengali of Sound", Spector was known in the early 1960s for hits with beehive-and-net-petticoat female vocal groups The Crystals and The Ronettes, the latter of whose lead singer, Veronica "Ronnie" Bennett, he would marry.

George swore by him: "He's brilliant. There's nobody who's come close to some of his productions for excitement."[57] Others – me included – ranked British console boffin Joe Meek far higher for inventiveness in his striking juxtaposition of funfair vulgarity and outer-space aetheria. From his Holloway studio in 1962 came 'Telstar', the quintessential British instrumental, by Meek's house band The Tornados. Unbelievably, it topped the US Hot 100, where no Limey group – not even The Shadows – had made much headway. Although a capitalising tour of the States by The Tornados was unwisely cancelled, 'Telstar' played Eric the Red to the British Invasion of America's charts in 1964.

Three years before, there were signs of resistance to the USA's domination of British pop. At large were Mark Wynter, Jess Conrad and Craig Douglas among a mess of blow-waved UK heart-throbs in the Bobby mould. Owing less to Americana, Joe Brown and his Bruvvers swept into the Top 30 with a blend of rock 'n' roll's country end and gorblimey Cockney music hall. On Parlophone, staff producer George Martin had scored his first Number One in 1961 with The Temperance Seven's period recreation of a 1920s dance tune with a stiff-upper-lip refrain from "Whispering" Paul McDowell, who was briefly George Harrison's favourite vocalist. A year on, Parlophone did it again with 'Come Outside', sung in Cockney by Mike Sarne and "dumb blonde" actress Wendy Richard.

Striking back harder was British television. Quickly shutting down *Wyatt Earp* and *Route 66* in the ratings war were home-produced serials. Most popular was *Coronation Street*, but close behind was *Z-Cars*, which was also as ingrained with northern working-class realism as censorship would allow. From the same environment rose playwrights such as Stan Barstow and Shelagh Delaney, novelist John Braine and others with names as uncompromisingly stark. On celluloid, Delaney's *A Taste Of Honey* was shot on location in Merseyside dockland, while the new young turk of British cinema was Liverpudlian Tom Courtenay as *Billy Liar*.

Charming some and sickening others with his "swinging/dodgy" thumb-sign mannerisms, in 1962, fellow Scouser Norman Vaughan had taken over as compere on ITV's long-running variety showcase *Sunday Night At The London Palladium*. A long way from bus workers' social clubs, now, was shock-headed Ken Dodd, "Squire of Knotty Ash" and a television fixture since 1960. With the coming of Richard Hamilton and David Hockney dawned the realisation in the spheres of fine art that, as Royal College student Vivian Stanshall commented, "Clever people could have Geordie and Mancunian accents." Indeed, they could have Liverpudlian ones, too. To crown it all, why not a northern pop group?

With boys combing their hair like John, Paul and George and iron-bladdered girls arriving ridiculously early in the front row at the Cavern to better gawk at Pete, The Beatles had taken local impact to its limit. They were becoming as peculiar to Liverpool alone as Mickey Finn, a comedian unknown nationally but guaranteed well-paid work for as long as he could stand on Merseyside. As one of the area's key pop attractions, The Beatles' triumphs and tribulations were chronicled in *Mersey Beat*, a fortnightly journal edited by Bill Harry. That the first edition sold out within a day demonstrated the strength of demand for its venue information, news coverage and irregular features, such as John Lennon's Goonish "Beatcomber" column. For the publicity it gave to deserving groups, *Mersey Beat* also served as a stepping stone between rehearsing in front rooms and playing the Cavern for the myriad amateur groups bending over backwards in their hyperbole.

Even the professionals they revered stooped to bulk-buying December 1961's edition, with its voting coupon for a poll to find the region's most popular group. By means as fair and as foul as other contenders, The Beatles came out on top in this tabulation, as they would every year.

An obtuse speculation is that, if, in some parallel universe, The Beatles hadn't gained record company interest, they might have been superseded in *Mersey Beat* stakes by younger acts such as The Riot Squad or The Calderstones. By late 1961, the four must have been aware that they were either the same age as or older than those already famous, like Phil Spector, all those Bobbys and Cliff Richard, who'd been just 17 when first he donned his pop star mantle. Was it time to thrust aside adolescent follies and settle down to a steady job, a mortgage, maybe wedding bells? The consolation of a full workload within easy reach was wearing rather thin.

If there was a storm centre of The Beatles' operation, it was surely the house in Hayman's Green, where promoters would telephone Mona Best to book her son's group. She was even organising Beatles showcases herself in halls in the suburbs of Tue Brook and Knotty Ash.

"Mrs Best wanted to manage the group," reflected Bill Harry. "She'd send the letters to get them on the radio and all the rest of it. She was one of those people born to manage, have control, do the business."

Campaigns for engagements beyond Merseyside yielded little but a further Hamburg residency and a Saturday one December in the Palais Ballroom in Aldershot, where all 18 patrons stayed until the last number, transfixed by The Beatles' racket, their funny dialect and endearing lack of arranged routines – quite unlike Aldershot's own top group, Kerry Rapid And The Blue Stars. This expedition had been the brainchild of Sam Leach, a maverick among Merseyside impresarios, who had hoped that what had enraptured Scouse teenagers would prove as alluring to those nearer the heart of the UK music business. However, continuation of the Aldershot project was aborted, even though over 200 turned up at the Palais the following week, via word of mouth, to see Rory Storm And The Hurricanes, another of these here Liverpool groups.

The lesson of this statistic was that there was a potential market for The Beatles beyond Merseyside and Hamburg. Groups in other areas who drew from like influences thought that the same applied to them. So parochial was provincial pop that there seemed to be no halfway between obscurity and the Big Time. From Mansfield, Shane Fenton And The Fentones had managed the quantum jump to a regular spot on *Saturday Club*. Also yet to make a record, Essex quintet Brian Poole And The Tremeloes would garner some national recognition on this programme when its producer, Jimmy Grant, sounded them out in a Southend ballroom.

As no one that The Beatles knew had the clout to enchant Grant and his sort north of Birmingham to catch them at the Cavern, they mailed a tape of one of their recitals over the edge of the world to the BBC Light Programme. Although John – and, by implication, George – disliked the galloping propulsion of Joe Meek's first chart-topper, 'Johnny Remember Me', sung by John Leyton, a package was also dispatched to the great man's Holloway address. However, no summons to report for audition came from Grant, Meek or any other big shot. They'd had quite enough guitar groups already, thank you.

It wasn't back to square one, however, because The Beatles'

undimmed ring of confidence had caught the eye of Brian Epstein, a local businessman, shortly before their poll victory in *Mersey Beat*. The eldest son of prominent Jews, Epstein had had a sheltered upbringing in which, from car windows, he'd noticed but never spoken to rough boys and girls hopscotching and footballing in grey streets and catcalling in that glottal accent you could cut with a spade. From his birth in 1934, and throughout a public school education that he endured rather than enjoyed, he knew nobody who lived much differently from his own family in the genteel Liverpool suburb of Childwall, with its weeded crazy pavings leading across gardens full of daffodils to front doors with silver letterboxes, where the bell would chime and an aproned maid might answer. Eminently satisfactory to Brian was the orderly way in which his mother kept house – the sugar in its bowl, the milk in its jug, the cups unchipped on their saucers on an embroidered tablecloth.

Before every home in Childwall had them, the Epsteins had long possessed a refrigerator, television and overhead bathroom heater as a requital of the family firm which had grown into a respected Merseyside department chain, specialising in furniture and electrical appliances. Brian followed his father into I Epstein & Sons, beginning as a trainee salesman. Apart from a term of National Service and a happier period at the Royal Academy of Dramatic Art, he stuck it out in the family business. 1961 found him in charge of the record department of the city-centre branch of NEMS (North End Music Stores), named after a smaller suburban shop taken over by the firm during his grandfather's time.

While Brian might have despised his own innate and fastidious talent as a shop-keeper, older employees regarded him as a chip off the old block, a hard-working supplier of sound goods. Straight as a die was young Mr Brian. Old Mr Epstein had run a tight, old-fashioned ship, but when his grandson inherited the firm he would drag it into the 20th century. Through his imaginative administration and absorption of modern techniques of commerce, Brian had already turned NEMS into what he could justifiably advertise in both the *Liverpool Echo* and *Mersey Beat* as "The Finest Record Selection In The North". Although he wasn't particularly enamoured with pop *per se*, the 27-year-old had an instinct for a hit, as shown by his bold requisitioning of 250 copies of 'Johnny Remember Me' when rival dealers, hearing a flop, didn't order any. Sometimes the chart performance of a single would be the subject of a small bet between Epstein and his sales assistant, Alistair Taylor.

Along with other central Liverpool stores that sold records, NEMS was on Bill Harry's *Mersey Beat* delivery round. When a gross of them disappeared like hot cakes from NEMS' counter, Brian – "an inquisitive bugger," according to Bill – invited its editor to join him in a sherry in the back office. After expressing his amused astonishment, he heard himself agreeing with Harry's proposition that he, Brian, should write a record-review column in *Mersey Beat*. While perusing consequent editions, he must have noticed the frequency with which The Beatles' name recurred, if only in the banner headlines.

One Saturday afternoon in October 1961, a couple of customers independently asked for 'My Bonnie'. They'd read about it in *Mersey Beat* and heard it down the Cavern in nearby Mathew Street. As a sealed batch of 25 was the minimum that Polydor could profitably export, WH Smith and other dealers couldn't be bothered with either the financial risk or the paperwork. Could the finest record selection in the north help? On one of his hunches, Brian ordered 200.

While these wended their way across the North Sea, Brian, intrigued, decided to investigate these Beatles. Far from thinking of records as mere merchandise, he was more conscious than he needed to be of the artistic and entrepreneurial aspect of their creation and marketing. As a teenager, he'd been privileged – through family connections – to be a fascinated spectator at a recording session by Geraldo's Orchestra. He'd also been interested enough in the spectacle and presentation of pop to pay exploratory visits to two or three "scream-circuit" shows. During an intermission, he'd encountered Larry Parnes, who, warming to the Liverpudlian's enthusiasm, had led Brian backstage to meet Marty Wilde and Billy Fury.

Through Bill Harry, it was arranged that Mr Epstein would be spared the giggling indignity of queueing for admission to a Beatles lunch-hour session with Cavern regulars ten years his junior. With the grace of a palace courtier, Paddy Delaney indicated the worn, slippery stairwell to the approaching gentleman in his conservative suit, sensible shoes, briefcase and "square" haircut. Only Brian's age set him apart, superficially, from many youths – among them absconded Liverpool Institute pupils – also milling about in the semi-darkness. Their appearances, too, were governed by work conditions. Clusters of girls in fishnet, suede and leather studied Brian as they did every reasonably good-looking newcomer. Assessing that he was a bit mature, they resumed their excited chatter until Bob Wooler announced The Beatles.

Merging into the shadows, Brian was torn between the sordid thrill of being out of bounds and a desire to flee the enveloping fug and sticky heat, never to go there again. He was still procrastinating when a thunderous cheer and squeal of feedback heralded the start of The Beatles' performance. Much has been written about Brian's homosexuality and his erotic attraction to The Beatles, especially John, but what struck him first was the volume that precluded conversation and the show's ragged dissimilarity to the slick Parnes presentation he'd seen. The four louts up there in their glistening leathers sounded like nothing he'd ever heard. Marty Wilde had indulged in a little scripted playfulness but this lot were downright uncouth in their verbal retaliations to bawled comments from the crowd.

Hitting all their instruments at once at a staccato "Right!", they'd barge into a glorious onslaught of pulsating bass, spluttering guitars, crashing drums and ranting vocals. Then the one addressed as "Paul" lunged into a sentimental ballad which Brian recognised as coming from the soundtrack of a musical he'd reviewed in *Mersey Beat*. Next they tried a song that Paul said he'd written with John, the guitarist with the loudest mouth. Between Paul and John stood the other guitarist, who spent most of the time between songs fiddling with the controls of his own and the other's amplifiers.

Brian, over his initial shock, tuned into the situation's epic vulgarity as The Beatles walked what seemed to him to be an artistic tightrope without a safety net. Dammit, they were great! When they stumbled off after exacting their customary submission from whoever hadn't wanted to like them, what could Brian do other than struggle through the crowd to congratulate them?

After the second set, Brian had a spot of lunch. With the Cavern odour in his clothes and temporarily deaf to even cutlery on plate, he pondered the laconic question that a Beatle – George, it was – had put to him when he'd poked his head into the bandroom: "What brings Mr Epstein here?" He'd know why when he was drawn back to another Cavern sweatbath a few days later. For reasons that included vocational boredom and frustrated aspirations to be a performer himself, Brian wanted to be The Beatles' Larry Parnes.

The group weren't as nonchalantly indifferent as they appeared to the intensifying and obsessive overtures made to them by this "executive type". Three had arrived late but arrived all the same when, after researching the professional history of his would-be clients, Brian suggested a formal discussion with them at NEMS after one Wednesday half-day closure. Finally, all four assembled for a second meeting – the day after the Aldershot fiasco – where Brian was informed by leader Lennon that he was the man for them. He lacked the know-how of a Parnes or even an Allan Williams, and there was also the likelihood of conflict with the volcanic Mona Best, who still saw herself as patroness of the group, but they were willing to trust his personal abilities and contacts to at least get them off the Liverpool-Hamburg treadmill.

As Harrison and McCartney were minors, Epstein had to secure the signatures of their respective fathers for the official contract that he drew up a year later, in October 1962, when he'd formed NEMS Enterprises as a management company for The Beatles and – not putting all his eggs in one basket – the other acts that he'd subsequently taken on. Until then, a makeshift agreement would suffice, but, determined on the utmost correctness, Brian called on each Beatle's parents to affirm his own sincerity and faith in the group. The Harrisons had fewest reservations about him, reassured that such an elegant, nicely-spoken gent was taking their youngest in hand. In The Beatles' present state, George would be the least of Epstein's worries.

As Larry Parnes would have advised him, Brian's first task was to make the group altogether smoother pop entertainers. They had to become what a respectable London agent or recording manager in those naïve times expected a good pop outfit to be. They had to be compelled to wear the stylish but not-too-way-out uniform suits he'd bought them. Playing to a fixed programme, punctuality and back projection were all-important. Stage patter must not include swearing or attempts to pull front-row girls. They weren't to eat or smoke on the boards any more. John was not to sing, "Oh me, oh my, I've got infection" to rhyme with, "Cast an eye in my direction" in 'Ain't She Sweet'. Paul was to stand nearer the razor when he shaved.

When George followed John's lead in loosening his matching tie during a performance, he'd be ticked off afterwards, as John would be for setting a bad example. Weren't they aware that, beyond the scruffy jive hives of Liverpool, there were strict limits of "decent" behaviour imposed by town councils upon places of entertainment in a prudish Britain that had compelled Billy Fury to moderate his sub-Elvis gyrations before he could be allowed on television?

Their new manager scuttled about like a mother hen, bringing about and enforcing the transformation, being met with irritated shows of resistance. These lessened after Epstein's string-pulling as a major retailer caused Dick Rowe, Decca's head of A&R, to send his second-in-command, Mike Smith, to the Cavern in mid December 1961 to judge The Beatles. It was the first occasion that any London A&R man had visited Liverpool for such a purpose. Smith thought them a lively enough act in their natural habitat, but only his boss could decide whether they'd come over on vinyl. Could the boys come down for a test in Decca's west Hampstead recording studio? Shall we say 11am on New Year's Day?

A quorum of A&R chiefs at EMI – Brian's first choice – hadn't been prepared to go that far after dutifully listening to 'My Bonnie'. According to company chairman, Sir Joseph Lockwood, the attitude was, "Well, we've got plenty of groups, and how can you tell what they're like just from the backing?"[74]

Decca it had to be, then. On 31 December, The Beatles crawled down south, some with amplifiers on their laps to make more room in the overloaded Commer van. At the wheel was Neil Aspinall, a ledger clerk and ex-Liobian who lodged with the Bests. The further he drove, the thicker the snowfall, the duller the wit as the cold and anxiety about the audition took its toll. After checking in at the Bloomsbury guest house where Brian had booked beds for them, the group and Neil ventured out to see the New Year in around the fountains of Trafalgar Square. It was flattery of a kind, they supposed, when two fellows eyed them up and decided they looked disreputable enough to know what pot was. The pair wondered if the Liverpudlians would care to join them in sampling some. It was packed into a large cigarette called a reefer and smoked communally in a hidey-hole like, say, Neil's van. The Beatles were all too aware of Preludin and other stimulants, but pot sounded a bit too cloak and dagger. Besides, they had to be fresh for the Big Day.

Nonetheless, The Beatles weren't at their best when, for a tardy Mike Smith, they ran through 15 songs selected by Brian to demonstrate their versatility as "all-round entertainers" rather than their individuality as a group. As he would later, in an unimagined future, George stole the show by default from John and Paul. Crippled with nerves as Smith issued commands from his glass-fronted booth of tape spools and switches, McCartney seemed too eager to please with misjudged extemporisations, while Lennon executed his lead vocals with a cautious politeness far removed from the bloodcurdling dementia with which he'd invest 'Money' on the boards at the Cavern.

Blotting out the solemnity of the occasion, George was inspired to sing Bobby Vee's latest hit, 'Take Good Care Of My Baby', with an edge that was missing from the original. He also injected the required humour into 'The Sheik Of Araby' and, after all these years, 'Three Cool Cats'. For the most part, his guitar playing – on a new Gretsch Jubilee model – was accurate, if unadventurous, even when simultaneously lilting Buddy Holly's 'Crying, Waiting, Hoping', backed by Paul and John's chiming responses. Furthermore, while fright muted the others, garrulous George came across to Smith as the Beatle with most "personality".

With as many vocal showcases as John, George might have been more of a prime candidate for election by Rowe and Smith as the group's figurehead, for, when British records charted in the early 1960s, it was usually with solo stars. Unless a hit instrumental unit like The Shadows, backing groups skulked in grey mediocrity beyond the main spotlight. Perhaps the compromise of "George Harrison And The Beatles" flashed across Smith's mind.

Such a suggestion proved hypothetical, however, as Dick Rowe, just back from a business trip to New York, reached wearily for the 1 January session tape while ploughing through the backlog accumulated in his absence. Among Dick's critical prejudices was that the last thing anyone – from a teenager in a dance hall to the director of the Light Programme – wanted to hear was a home-made song, and The Beatles had included three. Composers have to start somewhere, but, apart from B-sides of no real musical value, the possibility of a group developing songwriting to any great extent was unheard of. Even the exceptions, like Cliff Richard's 'Move It' and the climactic 'Shakin' All Over' from Johnny Kidd, began on the backs of either US cover versions or "professional" songs.

How, then, could Rowe appreciate how formidable the Lennon-McCartney partnership had become by 1962? After Decca joined EMI in turning them down, other companies offered The Beatles were just as blinkered.

Even without a record deal The Beatles were now a cut above most other Mersey Beat outfits. Although they weren't yet beyond the odd engagement back at the Casbah, Brian had moved them up to more salubrious venues with plush curtains and dressing-room mirrors bordered by light-bulbs (not all of them working). During a week dotted with Cavern bookings, there were now side trips to maybe a golf-club dance in Port Sunlight or on the bill with Rory and Gerry at Southport's Floral Hall, with its tiered seating. Lennon would spend the evening following his wedding to Cynthia Powell with The Beatles in Chester's Riverpark Ballroom.

No more were they changing in men's toilets or being paid in loose change. When supporting a hit-parade entrant, Brian ensured that his Beatles appeared second to last, as if to imply that they were only one rung below even Americans like Bruce Channel and Little Richard, as well as Emile Ford and Shane Fenton – who, incidentally, began a courtship of Iris Caldwell in 1962, after a period when she'd been "talked of" with Paul McCartney.

The next step up was to the ballroom circuits controlled by Jaycee Clubs and, even better, Top Rank, a leisure corporation that had belatedly clasped rock 'n' roll to its bosom. Reputations were made in these ballrooms, a link to recording contracts and nationwide theatre tours. Having scant seating on purpose, dancing was encouraged, and Top Rank expected its bands to provide action-packed music and the generation of a happy, inoffensive on-stage atmosphere.

Cleaned up, The Beatles rose to the challenge and became a dependable draw as their work spectrum broadened to Yorkshire, Wales and as far south as Swindon. Often they'd appear with other proficient groups who'd likewise broken loose of local orbits and compare notes, among them Sounds Incorporated, Sheffield's Jimmy Crawford And The Ravens, the diverting Barron Knights from Leighton Buzzard and The Rebel Rousers, whose X-factor, Cliff Bennett, could sing updated American R&B without losing the genre's overriding passion.

The same could be said of John Lennon and Paul McCartney, whose respective baritone and tenor were the Beatle voices heard most during the show. A hybrid of the two, George was no slouch on vocals now, either, although he was brought to the fore slightly less frequently these days. John and Paul still took most of the weightier material, leaving comic relief, Bobby drivel and no less than three Joe Brown numbers – including an embarrassed 'I'm Henery The Eighth I Am' – to George. When dancers wanted something from the charts, it would be George who'd give 'em passing joys like Tommy Roe's 'Sheila'. Nevertheless, John had handed him Chuck Berry's 'Roll Over Beethoven', and he'd been permitted to slow things down Paul-style with 'Devil In Her Heart' by The Donays, another obscure US girl group.

A reliable standby when McCartney and Lennon's voices needed a rest in the ballrooms, George was rarely allowed a lead vocal for less run-of-the-mill events, such as The Beatles' first radio broadcast, recorded before an audience at Manchester's Playhouse on 7 March 1962. Afterwards, the four were shocked when they were mobbed by libidinous females not much younger than themselves. Most were after Pete, who, pinned in a doorway, would lose tufts of hair to clawing hands while the other three bought their freedom with mere autographs. Despite himself, taciturn Pete was becoming a star. Watching the frenzy sourly was Paul's father, who would unjustly berate the drummer for stealing the limelight.

However, Mr McCartney couldn't have complained about George, who'd answered the knock of two girls at Mackett's Lane. Unrecognised, he'd been promptly left alone on the doorstep when they realised that it wasn't Paul's residence. Yet neither Paul nor rough diamond John would ever oust Pete as the ladies' dream Beatle for as long as he stayed with them. For a while, Best and his pushy mother had been unconscious victims of sardonic *bons mots* by the McCartneys and Lennon. Bill Harry "couldn't see him being at the root of it", but George joined in the underhanded dissection of Pete. To insiders like Harry, Best had long been a being separate from the others: "Pete would be right in the corner all by himself. George, Paul and John all mixed well. Paul was very smooth and easy to get on with. John was only abrasive if you let him be. George would be very polite, a very warm personality."

George's principal gripe was musical. Although Epstein might have been at fault in choosing the wrong material, Pete's unobtrusive but limited drumming at Decca became another focus for discontent. While Harry insisted that The Beatles were "a lot more raw and raucous with Pete Best", perhaps this was because, as Jackie Lomax of The Undertakers said, he "could only play one drum beat, slowed up or speeded up".[75]

Epstein, too, was a scapegoat. By mid 1962, he still hadn't landed that elusive record deal for his ungracious Beatles. EMI alone had signed up The Barron Knights and, via Joe Meek, Cliff Bennett. With John's wilful sarcasm pricking him, Brian embarked on one more traipse round the record companies of London, this time with a copy of the Decca tape as well as, for display only, a few 'My Bonnie' singles.

Two days after arriving, he had a lucky break. To gild his sales pitch, he decided to transfer the Decca session onto acetate reference discs at the cutting studio within EMI's busy Oxford Street record shop. There he'd arranged to see Robert Boast, its general manager, who he'd met at a retail management course the previous year in Hamburg, of all places. On learning what had brought Epstein to London, the genial Boast said that he might be able to help.

The next morning, in one of EMI's Manchester Square offices, Brian was sitting opposite George Martin, of the one EMI subsidiary that hadn't given The Beatles a thumbs down. Parlophone traded in comedy and variety rather than outright pop, and consequently it was less dogged with fixed ideas than other labels. Adam Faith and The Temperance Seven aside, it had produced few even marginally consistent hit-makers compared to rivals, but a number of Parlophone's records had done well enough without actually making the charts. Those that did were generally short-lived novelties by artists such as The Goons and Irish chat-show host Eamonn Andrews. Mostly, Parlophone ticked over on steady-selling LPs by Scottish dance bands, television spin-offs and light orchestral outings, some by George Martin himself, whose elevation to headship of the label in 1954, at the age of only 29, was no mean achievement.

One such as Epstein couldn't have guessed Martin's lowly origins in a north London back street, because service in the Fleet Air Arm during the war and, later, the BBC had raised his social standards and refined his elocution. A self-taught pianist, George gained a scholarship to the Guildhall School of Music that held him in good stead when he began on the ground floor at EMI in 1950.

Not letting personal dislike of teenage pop music deter him, Martin and his assistant Ron Richards had sought to provision Parlophone with some sort of equivalent to whatever sensations other labels threw up. Among those tried so far were Dean Webb (a dishwasher from the 2I's who resembled Marty Wilde) and Shane Fenton And The Fentones. As a musician, Martin had been more taken with Bill And Brett Landis, a duo who wrote their own songs. However, none of his finds could match Johnny Kidd And The Pirates on HMV or Columbia's precious Cliff Richard And The Shadows. Although a Parlophone artist, Adam Faith was someone else's production baby, and even he was waning when into George Martin's life came a chap called Brian Epstein.

What Martin heard of Epstein's group didn't excite him much, but they weren't obvious no-hopers and Brian himself was more believable than others who'd pressed their clients on Parlophone. It would do no harm, George supposed, to try The Beatles out in one of EMI's St John's Wood studios. As Ron Richards handled most rock 'n' roll, he could take charge of the session, which was set for 6pm on 6 June 1962.

The Beatles had been back from their third visit to Hamburg less than a week when, on that unseasonably cool evening, Neil Aspinall's white Commer bounced into the asphalt car park of 3 Abbey Road, after he'd ascertained that the building, with its Victorian *façade*, actually housed a recording complex. He and the group lugged in the equipment, which was even worse for wear – as were The Beatles themselves – after a seven-week beating in the Star-Club, shortly to be as well known in Germany as the Cavern was about to become in England.

In the crowded but cosy hotel accommodation laid on by the Star-Club, George Harrison had been the only Beatle awake when the telegram arrived with Epstein's news about Parlophone. Basking later on Timmendorf Beach, he seemed to have already counted his chickens as he outlined to Klaus and Paul all that he was going to buy with his share of the royalties from The Beatles' first hit – a house with a swimming pool for himself and a bus for his Dad.

After an eyeful of what other studio staff had told him was a funny-looking band with gimmick haircuts, George Martin sloped off to the Abbey Road canteen, only to be recalled to the console shortly after The Beatles began recording. Like Mike Smith before them, Richards and engineer Norman Smith wanted a second opinion. Taking over, Martin called the group into the control booth when they'd finished to hear a playback.

Towering over them as they lounged about the room, he then explained the technical functions of the studio and suggested that, before – or, rather, if – they returned to Abbey Road, they ought to invest in better amplification. The Beatles digested his words in unresponsive silence. Was there anything they didn't like? There was some fidgeting and poker-faced glances at one another. Suddenly,

George Harrison, lolling on the floor, piped up, "Yeah, I don't like your tie," and the ice broke.

More than their music, Martin was won over by the humour that nerves had suppressed that wintry morning at Decca. Unharnessed by Harrison's cheekiness, it was not unlike the ex-undergraduate satire that was infiltrating television. Martin had lately recorded an album with the team of BBC's *That Was The Week That Was*, a late-evening topical series that nurtured such future balusters of British comedy as John Cleese and Bill Oddie.

After The Beatles left, George Martin re-ran their tape. Cautiously, he decided to take them on for an initial two singles with an option on further releases if these gave cause for hope. All four songs on the tape were fairly mordant and at odds with the group's hilarious corporate personality. He'd have to grub around publishers' offices for a vehicle to project this. The notion of drafting in an outsider to be their Cliff Richard was dismissed.

When they returned to record their debut single in September, they'd done some structural tampering on their own account. The trickiest part of this manoeuvre hadn't been so much the heartless sacking of Pete Best – that they'd delegated to Epstein – but retaining the services of Neil Aspinall as general dogsbody, as well as his van. Not only was he one of Pete's best friends but he was also close to Mrs Best. He'd been disgusted by the cowardly fashion in which the group had cast out Pete, but, surprisingly, it was the drummer himself who convinced Neil that it would be in his best interests to stay on, as "The Beatles are going places".[76]

Because they were doing just that, their change of personnel couldn't be overlooked as simply another switchover in the Merseyside group scene, as incestuous a game of musical chairs as anywhere else. With the truth that Pete hadn't "left the group by mutual agreement",[77] as Brian had informed *Mersey Beat*, the vexation of his many devotees spilled over into "a lot of trouble",[78] as George wrote to a girl fan. This embraced damage one night to George's second-hand car, petitions calling for Best's restoration and an interrelated and very real riot in Mathew Street as The Beatles entered the Cavern with their new member.

George's appearance on stage that day with a black eye, however, resulted not from the Best affair but a jealous swain's vendetta caused by jealousy because of his girlfriend's inordinate fondness for The Beatles.

The bruise still hadn't healed in time for the publicity photographs taken during the group's second visit to Abbey Road, and he compounded this blemish with a sullen expression for the first that Britain at large would see of George Harrison. More welcoming was the wan smile on the homely visage of 22-year-old Ringo Starr, who'd been one of Pete's deputies and then his successor.

Equal to Best as a percussive aggressor but with neater hand-and-foot co-ordination, the ambidextrous Johnny Hutch had been headhunted for The Beatles but declined the post, mainly through loyalty to The Big Three. A requirement that he may have found burdensome was the lighter touch necessary to accentuate vocal harmonies more complex than those of his trio.

More pliant a character than Johnny or Pete, Ringo was prepared to look the part by brushing his hair forward and shaving off his beard. Unlike the hapless Best, Starr was "lucky to be on their wavelength when I joined. I had to be, or I wouldn't have lasted. I had to join them as people, as well as a drummer."[79] It has been said that, if Pete Best was the unluckiest musician in pop, the luckiest was Ringo Starr, even if Lennon later mused, "Ringo's talent would have come out one way or another."[80]

Born Richard Starkey, Starr had had an unsettled boyhood in the Dingle, a depressed Liverpool suburb backing onto the docks. Through his parents' marital unhappiness, he had spent much of his early years minded by other relations. Domestic conditions stabilised when his mother remarried, but long spells in hospital marred the sickly child's schooling. Nevertheless, despite his hangdog appearance, the solitary Richard remained cheerful, philosophical and blessed with a ready wit as guileless as John Lennon's was cruel.

Since rat-a-tat-tatting a tin drum in an Orange Day parade while at primary school, Richard discovered that he had a natural sense of rhythm. For occupational therapy while recovering from pleurisy, he'd bashed percussion in a ward band. This interest was encouraged by his step-father, who bought Richard a second-hand drum kit for his 16th birthday.

By then, British Rail had taken him on as a messenger boy, seconding him to Riverdale Technical College to complete basic education. Unimpressed by his prospects, he resigned to become a Mersey ferryboat barman until he was fired for insubordination. He was then persuaded by his Youth Employment Officer to start an apprenticeship at Henry Hunt Limited, manufacturers of school climbing frames.

With other joiners, he formed The Eddie Clayton Skiffle Group before drumming with other local outfits. With two of The Hi-Fi's, he amalgamated with Alan Caldwell and Johnny Byrne – after George Harrison's failed audition – in what evolved into Rory Storm And The Hurricanes. When the Butlin's offer came up, Richard was considering emigrating to the United States, but after much deliberation he collected his cards from Hunt's. On the rebound from a broken engagement, among other incentives beckoning him to The Hurricanes' booking at Pwllheli were increased opportunities to fraternise with girls.

It was then that he agreed reluctantly to adopt his stage name to facilitate Rory's introduction of a section of the set known as "Starr Time", which included a five-minute drum solo. He first noticed The Beatles when George was giving Stuart a bass lesson in the Jacaranda basement. Even after the shared experience of the Kaiserkeller, Ringo didn't feel that he knew them well enough to ask them to his 21st birthday party, although he became closer to The Beatles during that second Hamburg season, when, from that unfavourable first impression, George especially found him a bit of a card.

By January 1962, Ringo's worth as a drummer was such that, tempted by a huge fee and use of a car and flat, he left Rory Storm for Hamburg to back Tony Sheridan, re-enlisting as a Hurricane three months later for a tour of US military bases in France, followed by another few weeks at Butlin's in bracing Skegness. He seemed to be marking time, even debating whether to quit showbiz to finish his apprenticeship and settle down with Maureen Cox, his 16-year-old girlfriend. Another possibility was returning to Germany as either the Star-Club's resident drummer or as one of Ted Taylor's Dominoes. However, when Lennon and McCartney turned up at Skegness offering a fractionally higher wage, Starr gave Storm three days' notice and became a Beatle.

At the second session for the group's single, Ringo was dejected when George Martin hired a more experienced player to ghost the drumming. At Ron Richards' insistence, George Harrison left out most of the repetitive guitar phrases in an opus entitled 'Love Me Do', a harmonica-led Lennon-McCartney original that The Beatles preferred to the perky and "professional" 'How Do You Do It' that Martin thought tailor-made for them. 'Love Me Do' had been presented to their producer as, recalled John, "a slower number, like Billy Fury's 'Halfway To Paradise', but George Martin suggested we do it faster. I'm glad we did."[81] He later admitted, "We all owe a great deal of our success to George, especially for his patient guidance of our enthusiasm in the right direction."[82]

Perhaps they might have been better off with a remake of 'Like Dreamers Do' or another of the breezier items from the Decca tape. Nonetheless, 'Love Me Do' – still less than mid tempo – had an unusual atmosphere, with no obvious precedent. Not long after its release on 4 October 1962, a few scattered airings crackled from Radio Luxembourg. Tipped off about the night but not the time of the first of these, George sat up to listen. His mother waited, too, until she could scarcely keep awake. She rose from bed, however, at George's shout when 'Love Me Do' finally filled the airwaves. As his wife and son crouched downstairs, straining to hear the guitar work, Harold groaned. He had to be at the depot, fresh and alert for the early morning shift.

An avid surveyor of the hit parade, George was elated when, spurred on by plays on the Light Programme and the buzz from the northwest, 'Love Me Do' began its yo-yo progression to a tantalisingly high of Number 17 in the NME's Top 30. With nothing on file about this "vocal-instrumental group",[83] the newspaper made much of their hailing "from Liverpool, birthplace of such stars as Billy Fury, Frankie Vaughan, Norman Vaughan and Ken Dodd".[83] They'd done well, for first-timers, but who would assume that The

Beatles were anything other than a classic local group who'd caught the lightning once and would probably be back on the factory bench by this time next year?

The Beatles, you see, couldn't sing – not real singing, like Frank Ifield, a yodelling balladeer at the height of his fame, with no fewer than three singles concurrently in the Top 20. Already there'd been a sign that The Beatles were perishable, when the redoubtable *Peterborough Standard* reported that they'd "failed to please"[84] in the mismatched support spot Epstein had procured them to Ifield in that town's Embassy Cinema.

Responding to a request, The Beatles approximated Ifield's 'I Remember You' when, under protest, they disturbed their UK chart campaign by honouring two short seasons outstanding at the Star-Club. Into the bargain, as 'Love Me Do' had fallen from the hit parade, they were considered less deserving of the red-carpet treatment in Hamburg than Johnny And The Hurricanes – nothing to do with Rory Storm – on their first European tour.

It was noted that the American quintet had added vocal items to what had been a purely instrumental repertoire. Similar adulterations were taking place in Britain, as fewer instrumental units were making the charts. By the time The Beatles recorded their second single, 'Please Please Me', in November 1962, the swing towards vocal instrumental – or "beat" – groups had become permanent. This tendency was most keenly felt up north, where, charged Lennon, "other groups are pinching our arrangements",[85] but elsewhere local musicians were latching onto the concept that a group alone, without a featured singer, could be a credible means of both instrumental and vocal expression. In Birmingham, The Jaguars added a singer and became The Applejacks, while north London's Dave Clark Five – contracted to Mecca, Top Rank's rival – shifted their stylistic bias from sax-dominated instrumentals to vocals.

Younger groups sang in public from the outset. One formed by a lad named Kevin Manning was a typical case. Spending a school holiday in Liverpool with Irish relatives, Kevin's path became clear after an evening at the Cavern. On returning to his Hampshire secondary school, he was going to form his own group. They'd call themselves "The E-Types", because it wouldn't be just him and a backing group but a proper one, like The Big Three or The Beatles.

As Kevin carried the Olympic torch of Mersey Beat to his neck of England, its principal ambassadors' 'Please Please Me' was scudding up the charts, after they'd mimed it on *Thank Your Lucky Stars*, TV's main pop showcase. This prestigious slot was the ignition point for The Beatles' continued advancement, rather than a drift back to Merseyside obscurity. The change of colour of Parlophone's labels at this point from red to black was an apt herald of a new pop generation.

The studio audience had screamed indiscriminately at The Beatles, as it did at all male performers, but viewers, cocooned at home during that severe winter, would gauge more objectively from *Thank Your Lucky Stars* and later 'Please Please Me' TV promotions that The Beatles weren't like other groups. Musician Barry Booth, who was to be veteran of many a Beatles package tour, would reminisce, "One of the novelty aspects of The Beatles was that each member of the group was required to present a different identity, and they didn't have choreographed movements on stage. Each man's persona was different, so that John's movement would be up and down, Paul used to shake his head from side to side and George was a bit more still than the other two. Ringo was a law unto himself. There was a complete absence of any organised footwork and patter."

As dirge-like in embryo as 'Love Me Do', the arrangement of 'Please Please Me' had, on George Martin's instructions, been simplified and accelerated, with tight harmonies and responses behind John's lead vocal. Ringo was allowed to drum throughout the session this time, and the Harrison guitar – and voice – were more in evidence than before.

When Bob Wooler announced the momentous news that 'Please Please Me' had tied with Frank Ifield's 'The Wayward Wind' at Number One in the *NME* chart, the Cavern crowd – and, therefore, the rest of The Beatles' possessive Liverpool following – weren't particularly thrilled. After February 1963, "the newest British group to challenge The Shadows"[86] would never play another Cavern lunchtime session, as they were spirited even further away from the trivial round of local engagements. Driving, driving, driving to strange towns, strange venues and strange beds, with more bookings than they could possibly keep, they led what the economist would call "a full life". Five days spent pottering around Scottish town halls might be followed by four in Channel Island ballrooms and a one-nighter back on Merseyside. Often, they'd have to drop everything to fit in photo calls, press interviews and radio or television transmissions. So scrupulously hectic was their schedule that, caught off guard while snatching a quick snack, George spurted a mouthful of hot-dog on air when called to the microphone on an edition of *Saturday Club*.

More pleasant a shock were the considered ovations that unfurled into screams when the group were second billed to Helen Shapiro for an around-Britain tour that spring. By the final night, Helen was still closing the show, but the *de facto* headliners by then were The Beatles, with their "clipped negro sound".[86] She hadn't a prayer from the start. Her last two singles had flopped badly, while The Beatles, buoyed mid tour by their chart-topper, were, according to Barry Booth, "very new news. They'd just appeared from Hamburg. There were buzzes of conversation about this new quartet. The unusual spelling of 'Beatles' was causing comment."

Helen conducted herself with observed good humour when eclipsed by these Liverpool lads, who were as bewildered by their sudden fame as she'd been by hers in 1961. They'd been flattered but not quite comfortable when she chose to travel with the supporting bill in their coach rather than be chauffeured like the star she was. After a while, John became familiar enough with Helen to play practical jokes, while "George asked me lots of showbusiness questions. He is just about the most sincere of the four...and the most professionally intelligent. By that, I mean he's keenest to know all the mechanics of the music industry. Mind you, I was way out of my depth much of the time, because I don't get involved with royalties and things like that. I stick to my music, and so does George, most of the time."[87]

Space restrictions and the laugh-a-minute ambience of the tour bus circumscribed serious guitar practice for George and composition for John and Paul, although flashes of inspiration could be revised and developed in hotel-room seclusion. "The words are written down, but the music is never," elucidated Paul, "because we can't read music. We play it to each other and soon pick it up and fool around with it a bit. George suggests something extra, then John adds a new idea, and so on."[88] First refusal of the freshly-concocted 'Misery' was given to Helen, but it appeared in the shops by Kenny Lynch, another singer on the tour. "The song is very attractive," exclaimed the *NME*, "with a medium-paced beat."[89] It was also the first-ever cover of a Lennon-McCartney song.

The Beatles also left their mark on Kenny's own composing efforts, as exemplified by his 'Shake And Scream', modelled on 'Twist And Shout', soon to be regarded as their signature tune. This had been literally an eleventh-hour addendum to the overworked group's debut LP, issued to cash in on their 'Please Please Me' breakthrough. Legend has it that *NME* scribe Alan Smith, present with them for the "whole day"[90] it took to record, suggested 'Twist And Shout' to George Harrison during the last coffee break of the sessions, after hearing The Isley Brothers' version the day before. Just as the studios were about to close for the evening, the fatigued Beatles picked up their instruments and smashed out the raver that had stopped the show on their last night at the Star-Club, Lennon rupturing his throat with a surfeit of passion on what was, after all, only doggerel about an already outmoded dance.

It became one of those tracks that surface as being Worth The Whole Price Of An Album. The rest of the record was also of a high standard in a year when, geared for singled, LPs containing best-selling 45s were haphazardly programmed, short on needle time and padded with hackneyed chestnuts, stylised instrumentals and unoriginal "originals". As they always will be, good looks and "personality" were sufficient to sell sub-standard produce.

Compared to the electronic ventures of a less innocent age, The Beatles' early Parlophone recordings were crude affairs. "*Please Please Me* we did straight onto a two-track machine," Harrison had deduced from his comprehensive shadowing of George Martin's production methods, "so there wasn't any stereo as such."[32] A more complicated approach would have emasculated the raw drive of 'Twist And Shout', 'Boys' and other crowd-pleasers that George Martin had logged on a field trip to a Beatles bash at the Cavern.

Over half of the *Please Please Me* album was written by Paul and John, an extraordinary production choice when – as The Big Three would discover, to their cost – groups were forced to record material that bore little relation to their own musical inclinations. It was often presumed that, when an artist said he was recording all his own songs, his producer or manager had hired professional composers to come up with items exclusively for him. Even after they'd written dozens of hits for both The Beatles and others, Lennon and McCartney would still be damned by such faint praise as "reasonably good 'amateur' composers, greatly assisted by the poverty of British pop composing standards".[91]

Fusing industrious pragmatism with fertile imagination, John and Paul's originals on *Please Please Me* encompassed concessions to current taste. The melody of 'Please Please Me' itself was not unlike that of 'Charmaine', revived in 1962 by The Bachelors, while more than a touch of Frank Ifield prevailed in 'Do You Want To Know A Secret', George's only lead vocal on the album. Conscious that Lennon especially would knowingly warp the tunes of others to his own ends, it dawned on George that this particular opus was "actually a nick, a bit of a pinch"[59] from The Chants'/Stereos' 'I Really Love You'.

For all his sterling performances at the Decca audition, George was given 'Do You Want To Know A Secret' because, in Lennon's lordly estimation, "it only had three notes and he wasn't the best singer in the world".[80] Whereas Frank Ifield might have lustily yodelled its hookline, "I am in love with yoooooou," George got by with a thin falsetto, boosted with reverberation.

Only a slightly better job of it was made by Billy Kramer, the third act in Epstein's stable to reach the Top Ten, after Gerry And The Pacemakers. Lennon had advocated dividing "Billy" and "Kramer" with a non-signifying J and accepted a commission to provide him with another made-to-measure smash. Another beneficiary of Lennon and McCartney's creativity was Swingin' Cilla, now Cilla Black. Unsolicited covers from *Please Please Me* included a version of 'There's A Place' by The Kestrels' – less than Britain's ace vocal group, now.

They raised a few screams by association, but by 1963 The Kestrels and their kind were lost as The Beatles set the ball rolling for self-created beat groups. Tearing chapters from The Beatles' book, musicians in other outfits were having a go at writing their own songs. A personal triumph for Gerry Marsden was when his own 'I'm The One' was prevented from topping the hit parade only by 'Needles And Pins', The Searchers' third Top Ten single.

One of *Mersey Beat*'s many laudable aims was to foster group members' self-expression beyond merely hammering out 'Money' down at the Iron Door. As well as Lennon's prose, the journal's pages included others' cartoons and travel notes from home and abroad. Further extra-curricular activities encouraged by Bill Harry included a mini pantomime which The Roadrunners put on one Christmas.

On one evening in 1963, Harry fell in with George Harrison, who was just leaving the Cabin Club in Wood Street. The two strolled around the corner to the *Mersey Beat* office, where Bill invited his companion to climb its narrow stairs for coffee. Just in from Germany were review copies of a record by Kingsize Taylor. The conversation got around to The Beatles' Hamburg sessions with Sheridan. Bill recollected George's 'Cry For A Shadow'. Had he written anything else since? Why not? Had he thought about collaborating with Ringo?

From that day on until George actually wrote a song, Harry would embarrass him by bringing up the subject of songwriting each time they met. The steady drip of Bill's incitement impelled George to forego the Liverpool clubs on some of his few nights off to stay in and give this composing lark a whirl. For months, however, everything he tried sounded the same. He didn't have the confidence for the public trial and error that John and Paul endured without a thought when they pieced together The Beatles' third single, 'From Me To You', on the coach during the last leg of the Shapiro tour.

A bare week after this jaunt was finished, the group were thrust into another such trek. On the posters, their name was in smaller type than Tommy Roe and Chris Montez, Bobby-ish Americans both with singles currently in the UK Top 20. Assuming that they'd have a walkover, each went through the motions when the tour opened in east London with stock "wonderful-to-be-here" vapourings and, sneered one reviewer, "no semblance of a stage act".[92] What was a minor sales territory like England to them? Who needed its cold and the snow still on the ground in mid March?

Worse still, right from the first night, the running order was reshuffled as audience response had dictated that the home-grown Beatles play last, even on the three stops when they appeared as a trio, owing to John's absence with 'flu. To Paul's chagrin, the press were referring to Lennon as "lead singer" these days, but the group ably covered for him, with George manfully taking the lead in 'Please Please Me', as well as 'Do You Want To Know A Secret'. The Big Three managed without the almost-compulsory second guitar, so why shouldn't The Beatles? Besides, who could appreciate that a bit was missing in all that screaming?

The one-nighters that were The Beatles' bread and butter between tours were quite ticklish operations now. While Lennon was showering with sweat those crammed closest to the front of one low ballroom stage, "a fan grabbed hold of my tie and [laugh] the knot got so tight I couldn't take it off".[93]

Whether or not John was actually as benign about the incident at the time as he appeared, Beatle fans chose to believe that he was. They also didn't doubt George's humility when, at an engagement in Exeter, he apologised for the group's late arrival but hoped that "our fans were not disappointed with the show we put on".[94] To Jenny Walden, a teenager of the city, The Beatles were loved as "the most natural of all the groups, because they have not got big-headed and are just themselves. If they feel like putting their feet up, they do."[95] Bereft of the practised sincerity of a Bobby, their unabashed, light-comedy irreverence towards both girls like Jenny and music-industry bigwigs was as winsomely irrepressible as Ken Dodd's or Jimmy Tarbuck's, the latter of whom had become an established young comedian, now that he'd succeeded Norman Vaughan as master of ceremonies on *Sunday Night At The London Palladium*.

There was, apparently, no company in which The Beatles couldn't feel at home. The strangest booking of 1963 was at Stowe public school in Buckinghamshire, where 'Twist And Shout' *et al* precipitated only polite clapping from the seated pupils and their with-it headmaster. Noted photographer Dezo Hoffman's lens caught the four as they "talked with the Stowe boys as if they'd always mixed with people like that".[96]

During high tea, it was pointed out to The Beatles that school rules were so liberal that you weren't marched directly to the barber's if your hair touched your ears. Almost everywhere else, you'd risk suspension for cultivating a Beatle fringe, especially in grammar schools, where the formation of intellectually stultifying pop groups was regarded at best with malevolent neutrality – although, since Mr Edwards' retirement in 1961, treading warily at Liverpool Institute was a jazz club which dared to devote a meeting to "blues- and jazz-influenced pop singers".

A simple image – The Beatles in mid-air leap, like on the cover of the 'Twist And Shout' EP – could trigger a ten-year battle with Authority over hair. Back from school or work, you'd shampoo the combed-back flatness required to avoid persecution here and, with your sister's drier, restyle it as close to a Beatle moptop as possible. As he was the most androgynously hirsute, the ultimate objective was to look like George, whose dislike of haircuts went back to his thrifty father's cack-handed way with scissors at Upton Green.

Long hair wasn't a red rag to just teachers and parents. In Aldershot Magistrates Court in 1965, a labourer accused of assaulting a complete stranger offered the plea, "Well, he had long hair, didn't he?" as a defence. Even when it became acceptable for studs to have moptops, you could still get beaten up by members of the armed forces obliged to maintain short backs and sides. Nonetheless, it made your day if some Oscar Wilde bawled, "Get yer 'air cut!" from a passing car while his grinning mates twisted around in the back seat to register the effect of this witticism on you. You weren't insulted; you were proud to invite trouble. At last, you'd pulled wool over the eyes of parents and teachers long enough for it to show.

The Beatles visited the hairdresser more often than their detractors imagined. In Liverpool, the place to get trimmed was Horne Brothers, where the group were said to go on Epstein's recommendation. You'd sit before the mirror there as the wielder of the scissors would sculpt a Beatle cut from a gravity-defying quiff or a Bobby blow-wave. As it neared completion, your eyes would widen and your jaws would cease chomping their Anglo-Beatmint ("a real cool chew"). Such was the glamour of The Beatles and all things Liverpudlian that *Mirabelle*, a girls' comic, appointed as feature writer a lad named Pete Lennon (later a highbrow journalist), largely on the strength of his talismanic surname. From Mersey Beat slang, words such as "fab", "gear", "grotty" and even obscurities like "duff gen" (false information) spread across *Mirabelle* and similar literature and into the mouths of young Britons.

Even more influential were The Beatles' clothes on and off stage. Few teenagers did not adhere to prevalent fashion, various steps behind Carnaby Street (off Oxford Circus), that would soon become a wellspring of male Mod sartorial conformity, hinged vaguely on Cuban-heeled "Beatle boots", which looked like blunted winkle-pickers – high-buttoned jackets with narrow lapels or none at all, thigh-hugging drainpipes and either roll-necked pullovers or denim shirts with button-down collar and tie. The latter, being the cheapest, was the most variable, ranging from knitted plain to op-art slim-jim to – later in the 1960s – the eye-torturing kipper.

Except at set-piece bank-holiday clashes at seaside resorts, enmity between Mods and Rockers was never as virulent as newspapers made out. Usually they'd just congregate at opposite ends of a cafe. Mods dominated the beat boom, but The Beatles were "Mockers",[79] as Ringo quipped, Rockers in Mod clothing. As they and other Scouse upstarts thumbed noses at the wrong-headed London record business, some of the old guard began paying heed. Like Kenny Lynch, Johnny Kidd had seen what was coming and had injected his Pirates with a massive shot of rhythm and blues. Zooming in sharpish, Eden Kane and Adam Faith made smooth switches from lightweight ballads to ersatz Mersey Beat. Accompanied by visible beat groups – Kane with Earl Preston's TTs – their respective appearances on new BBC showcase *Top Of The Pops* was one in the eye for all these bloody bands who were making it just because they had the right accent and hairstyle. Adam had had his hair scraped over his forehead for the past four years.

Television commercials and episodes in serials like *Z-Cars* were given beat-group slants and negotiations began for The Beatles to top the bill on *Sunday Night At The London Palladium* – although, as John Lennon insisted, "We don't feel we are ready."[97] He was the first Beatle to pass judgement on the releases on BBC TV's *Juke Box Jury*.

The last was George, who, according to Barry Booth, was already coming across as "the most introspective of the group. He seemed diffident, shy. I wouldn't have thought he was overwhelmed, but he wasn't a looper. He was just very self-contained."

George was also the Beatle most inclined to oversleep. On the quartet's third major tour in four months, he shared this trait with a jet-lagged Roy Orbison: "George and I missed the bus a lot. They left without us."[98] Flattered to be told of Liverpool's Blue Angel club, named after one of his hits, Roy also enjoyed chatting about music with George. As his own style was "derived from true country music",[99] he was delighted that young Harrison was such an expert on the genre's obscurer trackways as well as sharing a spectator's enthusiasm for motorcycles.

Like his poorly received compatriots Montez and Roe, Orbison had embarked on a long-awaited British tour, understanding that he would be its foremost attraction. After the soundcheck at the Slough Adelphi, where the tour opened, Roy had just sat down in his dressing room when Lennon and Epstein asked if he'd got a minute. "They said, 'Who should close the show? Look, you're getting all the money, so why don't we [The Beatles]?' I don't know whether that was true or not, whether I was getting more than they were. It wasn't that much, and the tour had sold out in one afternoon."[58]

The source of this quick profit, 'From Me To You', would be at Number One for the tour's five-week duration. Just before screaming pandemonium greeted even compere Tony Marsh's attempts to keep order, Gerry Marsden presented The Beatles with a silver disc for this latest triumph. Not far ahead lay the first all-British Top Ten.

Relinquishing his bill-topping supremacy made sense to Orbison, as long as he got paid as per contract. Although aware of the chasm into which even he might fall, Roy, at 27 rather an elder statesman of pop, stood his ground to sustained and rabid cheering. Typifying the underlying affability of British pop's most optimistic period was Roy's initiation into its spirit. "I remember Paul and John grabbing me by the arms and not letting me go back to take my curtain call. [The audience] were yelling, 'We want Roy!' and there I was, held captive by The Beatles, [who were] saying, 'Yankee, go home.' So we had a great time."[58]

Roy was no lamb to the slaughter like Roe and Montez. Bar the remote Elvis, he came to command the most devoted UK following during a lean time for American pop stars, meriting respect for his unostentatious act and artistic consistency.

Headlining over him in 1963, The Beatles were relieved that they could still whip up screams that were growing louder every time they played. At first, Orbison considered them pretty rough and ready, "Just a rehash of rock 'n' roll that I'd been involved with for a long time, but it turned out to be very fresh and full of energy and vitality. So I recognised it at the time."[98]

Coming to recognise it too was an older British public in one of those periodic spasms when it would, as George put it, "get so bloody virtuous all of a sudden"[57] about indiscretion in high places. Throughout the summer, a flow-chart of immorality had unfolded via the trial of osteopath Stephen Ward and Fleet Street's intricate investigations of John Profumo, the unhappy cabinet minister whose disgrace and resignation had rocked the Tory government. His "sex romps" with a call girl who also enlivened the bedtimes of an official at the Russian Embassy in Park Lane led to another tearsheet and her upper-crust clientèle being winkled out. Soon, anyone connected with politics or the aristocracy was in danger of being accused of sundry corruptions, ranging from organised crime to a Pandora's box of kinky sex.

Next up were Congolese rioters ransacking the British Embassy in Leopoldville and, leading into autumn, further heavy headlines with the Great Train Robbery, in which a gang of thugs, since romanticised as 20th-century highwaymen, made off with swag worth more than £2 million.

Come September, adults were no longer failing over themselves from bedroom to doormat for first grab at the morning paper and its pungent disclosures. Saturated with wickedness, only a different kind of news could reactivate their interest. Anything would do, as long as it could hit. From their pop columnists, editors finally got to hear of

The Beatles, just as teenagers were wondering if the group had got into a rut, with 'From Me To You' having much the same overall sound as 'Please Please Me'.

Their tour with Orbison was causing scenes as uninhibited and contagious as those that had accompanied concerts by Johnnie Ray back in the 1950s. All pop music was rubbish but, by God, these Beatles were *British* rubbish. Theirs was a human-interest story of Poor Honest Northern Lads Who'd Bettered Themselves. Furthermore, they were good copy – plain speaking, coupled with quirky wit delivered in thickened Scouse.

John and Paul's comedy act had long been a diversion from the daily grind of road, dressing room, stage and hotel. George was on more solid ground when able to steer discussions with journalists away from "what's-your-favourite-colour" trivia to music, but there were moments when he exploded with succinct repartee. In fact, some of his backchat was even erroneously attributed to John. Joined by Ken Dodd for an interview on ITV, The Beatles were invited by Dodd to think up and earthy forename for him, as he wished to become a rock 'n' roller. "Sod?", suggested George the second the commercial break started.

A stooge-announcer was provided by the BBC to indulge their horsing around in *Pop Go The Beatles*, a radio series in which they held sway over such "special guests" as Johnny Kidd, The Searchers, and Brian Poole And The Tremeloes, who have been accorded an historical footnote – erroneous, as Brian himself told me in 1995 – as the ones that Decca chose instead of The Beatles. Every recording manager outside EMI was alighting with nitpicking hope on the remotest indication of The Beatles' fall. They'd surely had enough revenge on those who'd spurned them when at last they agreed to star on *Sunday Night At The London Palladium*. Could anyone get more famous than that?

Viewing figures were at their highest ever when, straight after the prescribed hour of religious programmes that October evening, The Beatles kicked off the next hour with a teasing burst of 'I Saw Her Standing There' during a single rotation of the Palladium's revolving stage. Before the four reappeared for five numbers that they could hardly hear themselves play, the seated majority of teenagers fidgeted through endless centuries of formation dancing, an American crooner, a singing comedian and the famed "Beat The Clock" interlude, in which a woman was scolded by Jimmy Tarbuck for producing a large toy beetle from her handbag, thereby setting off another orgy of screaming.

Parents in living rooms might have remarked how lowbrow it all was, but children noticed how their eyes were still glued to the set for the traditional finale, when the cast lined up to wave a cheery goodbye as the platform once more turned slowly while the pit orchestra sight-read the show's 'Startime' theme tune. Whenever The Beatles hoved into view, 'Startime' would be swamped in screams that would ebb abruptly as the group were carried off to the back of the stage.

The next day, the media was full of the "overnight sensation" and its aftermath as a police cordon with helmets rolling in the gutter held back hundreds of clamorous fans who'd chase The Beatles' getaway car into Oxford Street. A pressured journalist chronicling the mayhem came up with the word *Beatlemania*. The phrase stuck, but Beatlemania as a phenomenon was to have less to do with the group itself than with the behaviour of the British public, who, once convinced of something incredible, would believe it with an enthusiasm never displayed for mundane fact.

Before it had a name, the madness had rebounded on Liverpool, where those too young to have spent lunchtimes with The Beatles would huddle in blankets for days outside the Cavern to be sure of being first inside when the group came home. A few weeks before their final date in their old stomping ground, the four also played the Tower Ballroom for the last time. Their set over, they changed into casual wear – jeans and leather jackets – and were slipping unobserved through the dancers when, mere yards from the foyer, a female cavorting in the murk let fly a shriek and brought an adoring mob down on them before their pace could quicken.

The Beatles' old schools passed more coherent comment. In an article devoted to the doings of old Liobians, the Institute's termly magazine included a "less serious note" to the effect that "Mr G

Harrison (1956) and Mr P McCartney (1956) have found success as members of 'The Beatles' singing group and have had a number of television and local stage appearances. They recently made their second record to top the national Hit Parade."[100]

In the same publication, another stuffy compiler mentioned that CW Manley and DM Andrew were "displaying versatility in the realm of music",[99] too. The implication that The Beatles were more famous but no better than The Remo Four was also acknowledged by those Mersey Beat musicians who hadn't forgotten a callow group called Johnny And The Moondogs. Geoff Taggart of The Zephyrs had burrowed his way backstage at the Manchester Odeon to demonstrate some of his songs to Roy Orbison. Afterwards, he handed his camera to Paul McCartney to take a souvenir photograph of him with the great American. He didn't think to ask Roy to snap one of him with Paul.

There were at least five other Merseyside outfits that Geoff considered superior to The Beatles. Among these was Gerry And The Pacemakers, who, like The Beatles (and Billy Fury), were the sole subjects of a glossy monthly magazine. Matching *Pop Go The Beatles*, The Swinging Blue Jeans had their own Radio Luxembourg showcase every Sunday.

What, then, was so fantastic about The Beatles? For less than half the cost and discomfort of seeing them when they condescended to appear in Liverpool nowadays, you could scan *Mersey Beat* and amble over to Maggie May's, the Peppermint Lounge and any other of the new clubs that had sprung up. On the opening night at Warrington's Heaven and Hell, for instance, admission was half a crown for The Mersey Monsters, Rory Storm And The Hurricanes and The Pete Best All-Stars.

6 The Moptop

In the *NME*'s popularity poll for 1963, The Beatles would win the British Vocal Group section with more votes than everyone else put together. After 'From Me To You', 'She Loves You' shifted a million copies in Britain alone. In some overseas territories, it was retitled 'Yeah Yeah Yeah'. Succeeding it would be 'I Want To Hold Your Hand', with sufficient advance orders to slam it straight in at Number One. That Christmas, The Beatles occupied the first two places in both the singles and LP charts. Harrying the singles Top 20 too were no fewer than three EPs. Even re-promotions of their Sheridan recordings sold well. Such was anticipation for the group's second album that an ITV public information series warned of black-market copies under London shop counters a week prior to its release. The EMI pressing plant from which they'd been stolen could barely cope with demand for Beatles discs, anyway.

The only direction after that should have been down. By definition, pop stars weren't built to last, were they? With two smash hits in rapid succession since their record debut that summer, The Searchers, second in the *NME* ballot, were causing The Beatles nervous backwards glances. As Gerry And The Pacemakers had been the first Liverpool outfit to unarguably top all UK singles charts, so The Searchers were the first honoured with a gala reception by Merseyside Civic Council.

The figment of publicists' imagination, the "Mersey Sound" or "Liverpool Beat" had germinated in May, when 'From Me To You' eased Gerry's 'How Do You Do It' from Number One, while on their way up were debut singles by The Big Three and Billy J Kramer.

Waiting in the wings were The Merseybeats, who required police protection from the crowd killing them with kindness at Manchester's Oasis club. For the rest of 1963, Gerry, The Beatles, Billy J and The Searchers would slug it out for chart suzerainty, interrupted only by usurping Brian Poole And The Tremeloes, who – partly through the implications of Brian's surname – were promoted as the southern wing of the movement.

If this Mersey Sound was as transitory as any other craze, then as much of it as the traffic would allow ought to be marketed while the going was good. After an all-Liverpool *Thank Your Lucky Stars*, commercial expediency sent even the slowest-witted London talent-scout up north to plunder the musical gold. After all, The Beatles' lead guitarist had said that they were "typical of a hundred groups in our area. We were lucky. We got away with it first."[63] If this was true, why bother with positioning research? All you did was grab other peas from the same pod, groups with sheepdog haircuts who didn't temper their Scouseness and could crank out 'Money', 'Hippy Hippy Shake' and the entire Chuck Berry songbook. One of these could be recorded in a few takes – as was The Swinging Blue Jeans' definitive 'Hippy Hippy Shake' – and smacked out as a single. Why shouldn't it catch on like all the others? The Star-Club was concerned about customer complaints that all Liverpool groups sounded the same nowadays. Why waste resources trying to prove otherwise?

In the rush to the Holy City, unheeded was George Martin's cry that, "In my trips to Liverpool, I haven't discovered any groups with a similar sound."[60] Nevertheless, most of the groups signed were variations on the format of two guitars, bass and drums, such as The Undertakers and The Mojos, who substituted saxophone and piano respectively for lead guitar. Sticking out like sore thumbs were The Chants and three Toxteth schoolgirls christened The Orchids by Decca and proffered as a Mersey Beat "answer" to The Crystals.

Some behaved as though they were visiting another planet, but most A&R reps were discriminating enough to leave their scotch and Cokes half drunk in clubs after eliminating such-and-such a band from the running for, if not *The* New Beatles, then *A* New Beatles. Rory Storm was much loved, but how much studio trickery was needed to improve his dull voice? Like The Chants, Derry Wilkie was black, and in 1963 that presented marketing problems.

Most Mersey Beat groups with the faintest tang of star quality had at least a brief moment of glory as London – with little notion of how to project them – got in on the act. With mobile recording units, some record companies hired Liverpool ballrooms for a couple of days to tape as many groups from the region as could be crammed onto a cheap compilation album with a title like *This Is Merseybeat* or *It's The Gear*. Others cheated by using London session players, who probably bitched about The Beatles during tea breaks. As "Casey Jones", Brian Cassar – now based in the capital – actually moved south, where he assembled the short-lived backing group The Engineers to promote the single that resulted from his Scouse-talking his way into a one-shot deal with Columbia.

When The Hollies were snatched by Parlophone, the contract-waving host pounced on Manchester with the promptness of vultures. There, EMI also snared Freddie And The Dreamers, fronted by trouser-dropping singer Freddie Garrity, who figured, "We definitely succeeded on our visual appeal. We were on *Thank Your Lucky Stars* and just did a routine to take the mickey out of The Shadows. Next week, the record [a version of 'If You Gotta Make A Fool Of Somebody'] went to Number Three. We reckoned it must have been the dance, kicking our legs forward, so for our next record we did a routine kicking our legs back."[101]

More likely money-makers were processed for the hit parade in other northern towns. While Bolton's boss group The Statesmen were bypassed, Sheffield band The Cruisers backed spider-fingered Dave Berry and knocking 'em dead in Newcastle were The Animals. The pride of Nottingham, meanwhile, was the "Trentside Beat" of The Jaybirds, whose high-speed guitarist, Alvin Dean, was "considered by many the best in the Midlands".[102] Midway betwixt Liverpool and London, Birmingham was high on every grasping A&R chief's hit list. Not blessed with hits but adored locally, Mike *Sheridan* – like Brian *Poole* – had a negotiable Mersey Beat/Beatle-associated surname and a versatile backing group, whose ranks would include a teenage guitarist named Jeff Lynne.

Not for nothing would Lynne, Roy Wood, Steve Winwood and other precursors of the second city of pop's coming of age *circa* 1967 spend years mastering their assorted crafts in the ranks of outfits like Sheridan's Nightriders and The Spencer Davis Group. In late 1963, however, *Midland Beat* magazine – modelled on *Mersey Beat* – would bawl in an editorial, "Why has the Brum Beat failed to gain a place in the Top 20?"[103] Although Birmingham's beat boom was as unstoppable as the Black Death, it had mushroomed on the crest of a craze, growing in impact after rather than with Mersey Beat.

In all regions, whether they were deemed to have a "beat" or not, you didn't have to look far for the principal blueprint. The Grasshoppers were "Meridan's answer to The Beatles" while Church Crookham had The Termites. According to John Lennon, Gerry And The Pacemakers also suffered "terrible copying", but, infesting every borough, hundreds of groups had been formed in The Beatles' image, "and down to the last note at that".[84] While some used insectile appelations, others would work the word *beat* into their titles – Beat Ltd, The Beatstalkers, The Beat Merchants, and so on. Back-of-beyond youth club groups now wore moptop hairstyles and suits, and instead of a Hank Marvin lookalike they had an unsmiling guitarist with a Liverpool leg who – in imagination, at least – played a black Rickenbacker through a Marshall amplifier, just like George Harrison.

While grass-roots amateurs grappled with 'She Loves You', their older siblings might yearn for a return to the old ways. "Are you going to let Britain's king of talent be beaten by a flash-in-the-pan group like The Beatles?"[104] inquired a Cliff Richard enthusiast of *NME* readers. Apparently they were. Nevertheless, grinning indulgently, Cliff didn't bother to compete with the rearing four-headed monster.

Other old-timers beat a calculated retreat. Although he may have weathered the storm, Shane Fenton and his wife, Iris, metamorphosed into a song-and-dance act. In closer contact with The Beatles than most, he'd declined a management offer from Brian Epstein, who had used Lennon's 78rpm acetate of 'Do You Want To Know A Secret' as bait. In August 1962, he'd headlined over The

Beatles at the Cavern. Almost a year later, he was supporting them at a "Swinging '63" extravaganza at London's Royal Albert Hall.

In the front row sat The Rolling Stones, a group who'd sprung from an Ealing club as earnestly devoted to blues as other cliques were to yachting or numismatics. Aggressively untidy students and middle-class bohemians would come forth from the audience to thrash guitars and holler gutbucket exorcisms with house band Blues Incorporated, in which two future Rolling Stones were semi-permanent fixtures. Among the frayed jeans, beatnik beards and CND badges in the watching throng were subsequent Kinks, Yardbirds and Pretty Things, who would try to emulate the Slim Harpos, Muddy Waters and Howlin' Wolfs of black America. The results (especially vocal) were generally nothing like it but, after they – like the Stones – had sucked Chuck Berry into the vortex of blues, all three would appear on *Top Of The Pops* within a year of the Stones doing so.

No more a Blues Incorporated splinter group by spring 1963, the motley Rolling Stones were resident at the Crawdaddy, which convened in the back room of a Richmond pub. Descending on the club in droves were Rockers and Mods under a flimsy flag of truce, plus a *nouvelle vague* of "youths" and, half a class up, "young people". No longer appreciating blues with knotted brows, girls crowded around the front spotlight, their evening made if they caught the attention of Stones lead singer Mick Jagger, with his half-caste singing and grotesque beauty, or the general factotum, Brian Jones, who sported an exaggerated blond moptop. With both blues credibility and teen appeal, the group's cash-flow was such that Bill Wyman, their married bass player, was able to think seriously of packing in his day job as a storekeeper.

Through knowing Brian Epstein, club promoter Georgio Gomelsky engineered a visit to the Crawdaddy by The Beatles after they'd recorded a *Thank Your Lucky Stars* at nearby Teddington studios. It would be a fillip for the Stones if they impressed an act who, in April 1963, were bigger than Frank Ifield. Yet, though they attracted a small prattle of fans, The Beatles were not yet so well known around London that they couldn't be steered safely by Gomelsky through his crowded club to the side of the stage.

As Georgio had foreseen, their more revered peers took a shine to the Stones, and the cordiality between the two groups after the customers departed led to Jagger *et al* receiving complimentary tickets and backstage passes for the Albert Hall show. Less incidental to the Stones' future was George Harrison's judging of a "Battle Of The Bands" tournament at Liverpool's Philharmonic Hall a month later. On the panel, too, were Bill Harry and soul-tortured Dick Rowe. Decca seemed to be gorging itself with beat groups now in the hopes that one might be as successful as its failed Scouse supplicants had to teeth-gnashing effect with EMI. From Merseyside alone, Rowe had contracted Kingsize Taylor, The Long And The Short (with Les Stewart), The Big Three and – for who he was, rather than what he did – Pete Best.

Whispering to George sitting next to him, Dick thought that even the likely winners at the Phil – a group containing Ringo's cousin – were no better than any other Beatle-style group to be found anywhere in the country. Civilly, George agreed. Because Rowe had been honest in not over-justifying his mistake over The Beatles, George decided to help him out. There was, he said, this southern group he'd seen. Musically, they were "almost as good as The Roadrunners"[105] but far wilder, visually, and having the same effect on their audience in a provincial club as The Beatles had had on theirs at the Cavern. "Dick got up immediately," observed Bill Harry, "and caught the next train back to sign The Rolling Stones."

The Beatles' largesse extended from endorsement to a gift of – as the Stones' stabilising second single – a song by John and Paul, 'I Wanna Be Your Man', bestowed prior to its appearance on autumn 1963's *With The Beatles* album. Virtually every other track, too, was covered by another artist, from Mike Sheridan's 'Please Mr Postman' to 'Little Child' by a Billy Fonteyne. All were either Beatles' arrangements of non-originals from their concert repertoire or new Lennon-McCartney compositions. The one exception was 'Don't Bother Me', rehashed for Pye by Gregory Phillips with an "oo-aah" girlie chorus, the only digression from

Beatle precedent. This opus was the first published solo composition by George Harrison.

During an intermission at the Phil talent contest, Bill Harry had nagged George, as always, about songwriting. Backstage at Blackpool's ABC theatre, three months later, George would thank Bill "for keeping on and on about me writing songs. I would think about going out, but it was, 'Oh, Christ. I'll bump into Bill Harry and he'll go on and on about these songs.'" The week before, see, while suffering from influenza George had completed 'Don't Bother Me' from his sickbed at the Royal Spa hotel in Bournemouth during The Beatles' six nights there at the Gaumont. Its lyrics portrayed one still carrying a torch for an old love. His refusal of another's comfort may be reflective of George's ill temper that he wasn't unwell enough not to be hauled from fevered quietude for the evening's two performances.

With John as its main champion, the good rather than great 'Don't Bother Me' had been accepted as worth recording when, midway through the Bournemouth season, the group spent hurried daylight hours mixing those *With The Beatles* items already on tape. Even George Martin, who seemed to regard Harrison as a mediocre musician at most, would vary a diet of Lennon-McCartney with 'Don't Bother Me' on *Off The Beatle Track*, his LP of orchestrated Beatle tunes. In a prosy *Times* article that discussed Paul and John's "pandiatonic clusters" and "Aeolian cadence", mention was made of their lead guitarist's little number as "harmonically a good deal more primitive, though it is nicely enough presented".[106]

Against, say, nine takes for 'Not A Second Time' (the one with the Aeolian cadence), the less honed 'Don't Bother Me' needed 19. To pep it up a bit, Ringo, John and Paul overdubbed a loose polyrhythm of minor percussion. Although not an outstanding contribution to *With The Beatles*, a publishing division – Jeep Music – was created to gather its not-insubstantial royalties.

George didn't follow up speedily on this tentative exercise in composition, undeserving of inclusion in the stage act. Instead, he fell back to his accustomed role of being one of Paul and John's sounding boards, one whose advice wasn't taken as seriously as that of George

Martin. Nonetheless, they'd let him have three *With The Beatles* lead vocals to Ringo's one. "In The Beatles days, I was always very paranoid, very nervous, and that inhibited my singing,"[59] George said, but still he managed a painless 'Devil In Her Heart'. Although smoother than Lennon's might have been, his 'Roll Over Beethoven' emerged as a single – and hit, to boot – in many foreign parts.

It was a year when The Beatles could have topped charts with 'Knees Up Mother Brown'. Some listeners, however, weren't that snowblinded. At this most public and prolific phase of the four's recording career, it was easier for journalists and photographers to infiltrate the sessions regulated by the Musicians' Union that The Beatles were yet to challenge by running over into the small hours. When outsiders were scheduled to be present, George would forsake his usual jeans and open-necked shirt for clothes less casual. However, no amount of sprucing up for the cameras could prevent George Martin from stopping run-throughs to point out errors. In front of one scribbling reporter, he criticised the guitar tuning, "and you, George, should be coming in on the second beat every time instead of the fourth." "Oh, I see,"[107] replied Harrison, his hackles rising slightly.

Also noted were the jumbled solos that George would insert into some backing tracks. Those ignorant of advancing recording techniques might or might not be told that George had invented them on the spot for reference only. Later, he'd re-record the parts in less public circumstances, combining his and, most of all, George Martin's further thoughts about them.

Self-contained enough to disassociate the instrument from Martin's schoolmasterly perseverance, "A day doesn't pass without me having a go on the guitar."[108] His ambition, he said, was "to design a guitar myself and have it called 'the Harrison'. I'd like to play as well as Duane Eddy or Chet Atkins, and I wish I could compose like John and Paul."[109] George was, nevertheless, the Beatle whose musical competence was most questioned. Derided for the publicity stunt it was, an allegation that The Beatles used a substitute lead guitarist on recording dates was made by an expatriate Texan entertainer befriended by the group. The changeling was even named as session *wunderkind* Jimmy Page. Although such practices are common in pop, this suggestion can be refuted by documentary evidence that Page must have been in two places at once if he did play on Beatles discs. Moreover, the lead-guitar sections on sufficient Parlophone tracks are identical to those on extant early Beatles recordings, as demonstrated by consecutive hearings of the Decca release of "Til There Was You' and the 1963 treatment.

George also picked the song very prettily when it was second in the group's subdued four-song segment in the *Royal Variety Show* in November. On the boards, however, he wasn't generally so hot. It could be that his best moments were never immortalised on tape, and plausible excuses can be found for those that were. He'd been the worse for alcohol when Ted Taylor's tape recorder captured The Beatles' last stint at the Star-Club. Yet, although the intro was fumbled, George's solo on 'Roll Over Beethoven' was how it would be on *With The Beatles*, bar an unclean note or two. An indifferent improviser, he'd often double up with John, as plainly heard on 'I Saw Her Standing There' during five October days in Sweden, the group's first true overseas tour.

In his defence, however, it must be stated that, at that particular recital in Stockholm, George was about to be almost yanked offstage by rampaging fans as unrestrained as they'd be for The Beatles' first proper headlining tour of Britain. Setting the mood was the heroes' welcome accorded them on their homecoming from Scandinavia. Just over 1,000 teenagers on half-term holiday had ignored the heavy drizzle to converge on Heathrow Airport's upper terraces. From their morning flight, the baffled quartet were met by the unison banshee scream they'd mistaken for engine noise on touchdown.

All 4,000 seats for two shows at the Leeds Odeon had gone in a record three hours, with two 16-year-olds starting the queue four days before the box office opened. At every proposed stop on the tour, hundreds likewise ringed themselves around theatres, cinemas and city halls to guarantee admission. Those lacking such clubbable stamina recoursed to buying tickets from touts at up to eight times their market price.

As their respective Beatles nights crept closer, auditorium directors like Portsmouth Guildhall's David Evans grew "really alarmed at the prospect of getting The Beatles into and away from the hall in safety, because of the big crowds we anticipate. I shall call in every burly and able-bodied man on the staff to keep order and make a pathway, as well as extra police. I shall be glad when it's all over."[110]

Beatlemania was pop hysteria at its most intense. Even in sedate Cheltenham, streets surrounding the Odeon were closed to traffic as police, linked by walkie-talkies to the building, coordinated the group's admittance. Entrances elsewhere weren't as grand, as The Beatles smuggled themselves in through lofts and, in Plymouth, by groping along underground tunnels leading from Westward TV's studios two blocks away to a narrow lane beside the ABC. At a given signal, a fire exit was flung open and a support act ambled out to divert attention from The Beatles' dash across the passageway. Even so, they were still spotted, and a girl's fingers were crushed in the slammed door.

Once inside, they'd be incarcerated until, with the last major sixth of 'Twist And Shout' still reverberating in the pandemonium, they would bolt pell-mell to a waiting limousine in a back alley. They'd be halfway down the road by the end of the national anthem, when the crowd realised that there wouldn't be an encore.

The hours awaiting escape might have been passed carousing in the artists' bar, if there was one, or relaxing in the dressing room. Whereas the supporting programme made do with standard spartan facilities, The Beatles would often subside into freshly-redecorated rooms with television and, perhaps, individually-monogrammed hand-towels and champagne on ice. The comestibles laid on were edible enough for the four not to have to resort to the toaster and electric kettle packed as insurance against their ever being needed by Neil Aspinall's new assistant, Malcolm "Big Mal" Evans, ex-Cavern bouncer. When one venue's caterer read of The Beatles' humble dietary predilections in an *Evening Standard* exclusive about George's disappointment with his first mouthful of caviar, he uncovered for them a hugely appreciated platter of jam sandwiches cut in crescents, diamonds and other exquisite shapes.

Babbling like an idiot relation in the corner, *Take Your Pick*,

Dixon Of Dock Green or other early evening television programmes might be switched off and the Dansette record player plugged in. On instant replay throughout that autumn's jaunt was either the latest Bob Dylan LP or 'Do You Love Me' by The Contours, whose original Tamla-Motown version was pleasanter to George's ears than any of no fewer than three British covers. As they'd just left the Top Ten with a workmanlike 'Twist And Shout', Brian Poole's boys' version of 'Do You Love Me' had an edge over the hitless Dave Clark Five. Faron's Flamingos' adaptation was so vanquished that it was relegated to a B-side.

Other than themselves, no representatives of Mersey Beat were present on the tour, unless you count The Vernons Girls, who paraded their latest single, 'We Love The Beatles', on a nightly basis. An ex-member, Lyn Cordell, had just released a version of the jazz standard 'Moanin'', which was the most common number played during the post-soundcheck bashes that also occupied the time before the show. Although Paul seldom missed opportunities to jam, George was less ready to unwind that way with musicians of the exacting calibre of Peter Jay And The Jaywalkers or Sounds Incorporated. Apprehensive about showing himself up, he'd settle for rhythm guitar or simply rattle a tambourine. Neither was George that active in the off-stage larks during the show itself, such as John and Paul's tormenting interruptions of comperes' patter.

It was hard enough without smart-alec antics in the wings from the main attraction. As the announcement for her troupe was swamped in audience roar on opening night, Vernons Girl Maureen Kennedy panicked, "Oh, God, I can't face that. Them shouting for The Beatles, I mean. I think the boys deserve all this, but it's a bit rough on the other acts."[111] The Girls and other unhappy artists on the bill would soldier on as the eclipsing howls and chants for The Beatles welled up to a pitch where you drowned in noise.

Somehow, the already ear-stinging decibels climbed higher when The Beatles sauntered on, outwardly enjoying their work. The girls went crazy, tearing their hair, wiping their eyes, rocking foetally and flapping scarves and programmes in the air. The volume rose momentarily to its loudest, as if they'd all sat on tin-tacks, when Paul and George zoomed in on the right-hand microphone for the Isley Brother-esque "oooooo" in 'She Loves You'.

The circle stall buckled and the walls trembled, but no one was seriously hurt, as the havoc was tinged with good nature and British reserve. At Doncaster, a boy wriggled through the barrier of stewards to leap on stage for no other purpose than to dance self-consciously for a few seconds before meekly stepping down again. Somewhere further south, another buffoon yelled, "Down with The Beatles!" during a sudden lull between acts. His portly girlfriend swiped him with her handbag and everybody laughed. Girls would go into pretend faints after practising in the queue, their friends catching them under the armpits.

Still able to take greater celebrity in their stride, there was merriment rather than annoyance when The Beatles came upon two youths who'd hidden themselves in a hotel room for hours just to fraternise with the group when they flopped in after the show in Coventry. This wasn't the only such incident. More than once, roadside cafes served mixed grills on the house in exchange for autographs. An Exeter theatre manager's fawning was rewarded when all four Beatles scratched their signatures on a stairway brick for him to sellotape over for posterity. On the previous night, their Torquay hotel hideout had been rumbled and 100 or so fans – mostly truants – had collected in its lobby. Amused, the group had signed their books while strolling out to the limousine the following afternoon.

It was still possible for a Beatle to take the air after breakfast without public fuss, although, warned Lennon, "it's a bit dodgy if you all go out together."[112] Stopping at traffic lights would now attract the beginnings of a crowd, and certain factions desired more than autographs. Sheffield students planned to kidnap the group for a Rag Week stunt. Unwilling to play along, The Beatles cheerfully compromised with a donation to funds.

"At first, when we went on the road as a famous group, it was good fun,"[55] George would later remember. His main grumble was, "We could only sing our hits and none of the old rock things we'd loved doing in Liverpool and Hamburg."[55] Nevertheless, their music was being taken semi-seriously. Before *The Times* caught on, Derek

Taylor, northern showbusiness correspondent with *The Daily Express*, had seen the light and, after covering the Manchester stop on the Orbison tour, had become "very boring about it around the office".[74] When briefed to do a hatchet job on The Beatles' agreement to appear on *The Royal Variety Show* "for the middle-aged middle class",[74] Taylor could only praise them.

After Fritz Spiegl's Mozart pastiche, 'Eine Kleine Beatlemusik', a random B-side would be analysed as if it was a Beethoven symphony in highbrow *Music And Musicians* magazine. As it was estimated that more words had been written about them than about Shakespeare, newspapers no longer put sniffy inverted commas around their name, followed by "the Liverpool 'pop' group" or similar explanatory phrase. Soon, the first of more Beatle biographies than anyone in 1963 could ever have comprehended was in preparation.

The Socialist Worker might vilify Beatlemania, but overall a wider cross-section of the populace "knows how fab they are" – as The Vernons Girls sang – than any pop act before or since. Deb of the year Judy Huxtable was snapped entreating Ringo for his autograph, while swingin' radio vicars would slip them into *Five To Ten*, an incongruous religious broadcast linking *Uncle Mac* and *Saturday Club*. At a school speech day in Havent, Lady Nancy Bridge recommended, "If you feel you cannot do what is asked of you, think of The Beatles. They have got where they are by sheer hard work."[113]

As it had for Tommy Steele, so their fabled appearance in the 1963 *Royal Variety Show* rendered them harmless and lurched the weather-vane of adult toleration, if not approval, in The Beatles' direction. Short haircuts would still be imposed on sons of provincial Britain, and pop was not yet an acceptable career option, but parental blood had not run cold over Lennon's chirpy "rattle yer jewellery" ad lib to the royal balcony as it had over loutish excesses. When two Beatles shook their heads on the "oooooo" in 'She Loves You', it was like spun dishmops, but there was none of this hip-swivelling lewdness.

No distant Beatle could be imagined passing wind or urinating, any more than could a sexless cartoon character or teddy-bear. As a 1960s teenager, actress Kim Hartman – Helga in BBC's *'Allo 'Allo* –

fell in love with George, with his "suffering cheekbones, which made him look so poetic".[114] He was singled out as 'Gorgeous George' in The Vernons Girls' tribute, but Lancastrian comedienne Dora Bryan claimed "Ringo, John, Paul and George – they're all the same" in her 'All I Want For Christmas Is A Beatle'. Sung in a vile "baby" voice, the fact that even this yuk-for-a-buck made the hit parade exemplified the national obsession. Apparently beside herself with excitement, publicity-conscious Dora – no spring chicken – had pursued a terrified George after The Beatles' floorshow at a charity function at London's Grosvenor House Hotel. "Twist and shout! Twist and shout!" she kept yowling, clinging to him like a barnacle. However, other personalities weren't as demonstrative about their bandwagon jumping. Hoping that John and Paul might toss them a song, some would worm their way into the Beatle dressing room to pay artist-to-artist respects. Among the least transparent such visitor was the late Alma Cogan, whom the group liked enough to accept an open invitation to the liberty hall that was her Kensington flat. It was during a *soirée* there that George was introduced to Carl Perkins.

Alma was a mainstay of early editions of ITV's epoch-making pop magazine *Ready, Steady, Go!*, which, when it began in August 1963, was presented by a besuited interlocutor in his 1930s called Keith Fordyce and featured occasional send-ups of current hits by comics of the same age. The pruning of these unhip distractions kept pace with the series' elevation to the most atmospheric pop showcase of the decade. The programme also monitored the mounting isolation that their adoring public inflicted on The Beatles. In October 1963, they walked from make-up to the podium without hindrance to mime 'She Loves You', while on their second *Ready, Steady, Go!* appearance they needed an outside security force of 80 police and a headlong flight through the corridors of the adjacent London School of Economics. By their fifth and final booking, a separate and heavily guarded area would be set aside for the group's performance while the rest of the show took place in the usual Studio Nine.

Absorbing this accelerating adulation, George was initially the Beatle least unsettled by it all. For a while, he remained his old, selectively amiable self, although "old" was a little inappropriate.

Some of those reporters who'd figured out which one was which would refer to him as "young George". He didn't yet behave older than his years. To the group's long-serving publicist Tony Barrow, he lagged behind the other three "in terms of physical appearance and general sophistication".[15] He was the one sighted most often preening himself before dressing room mirrors, perhaps applying lacto-calamine lotion to spots that no hit record could prevent from appearing on an otherwise comely adolescent complexion.

With no steady girlfriend, he seemed perpetually on the look-out for an unsteady one. Fame is a powerful aphrodisiac, and to many within The Beatles' cabal George was something of a lothario on the road. Time which hung heavy between one concert and the next wasn't only killed with practising guitar and watching *Take Your Pick*. As *omerta* is to the Mafia, a vow of silence concerning illicit sex persists among bands of roving minstrels. A strong motive for a red-blooded lad to become a pop star is that, no matter what you look like, you can still be popular with young ladies. Look at Ringo and his nose. Look at spindly Freddie and spotty Herman.

Quite used to demure requests to meet a certain type of female admirer in, say, the romantic seclusion of a backstage broom cupboard, George wasn't quite so sure of himself with more ladylike judies. They were more likely to be won over by a Beatle who dropped names like Segovia or limp and tasteful Stan Getz than anything as coarse as The Isley Brothers or Duane Eddy. "I like most music if it's good" was a truism that George would qualify with "I like classical music on a guitar. I'm not so keen on classical music played on a piano."[115] At the Swinging '63 spectacular, he'd started chatting up a dashing young actress of good breeding named Jane Asher, but before the evening was out she seemed more taken with the suaver charms of Paul McCartney. "Society" Londoners like Jane were often intrigued to meet real "wackers" now that Liverpool was where more happened than just dock strikes. More fascinating was that some of them were suddenly rich enough, like George, to "get a Ferrari and bomb about".[116]

He could also afford well-deserved breaks in faraway places. With Ringo and Paul, he'd limbered up for the Orbison tour with twelve days in Tenerife. On 16 September 1963, the day after a second Albert Hall showcase, George was the first Beatle to set foot in the United States, when he and brother Peter flew via New York and St Louis to stay for a fortnight with their married sister, then living in Benton, Illinois. With a day in hand before the internal flight, they paid the seven-dollar fare from Idlewild to the Pickwick Hotel in New York, and to the taxi driver they were just another pair of long-haired Englishmen. They soaked up the sights like any tourists, and the highlight of the trip was a visit to the Statue of Liberty.

Benton was a restful interlude after the holocaust of Beatlemania. As his face hadn't been plastered over magazine covers in America for the past six months, as it had been at home, George was treated as Mrs Caldwell's youngest brother, some sort of musician. How unexpectedly pleasurable it was to be a nobody again, not to have to steal into a cinema – one of these "drive-ins" – after faded dimmers had guaranteed shelter from the stares and approaches of fans, to wander anonymously the boulevards of east St Louis or picnic on the cottonwood banks of the Mississippi. (See Appendix II.)

Professional interest found him in Benton's record store, thumbing through wares unreleased outside the States. Among albums that would return with him to England was James Ray's *If You Gotta Make A Fool Of Somebody*, which turned out to be "really terrible" on repeated listening, though he half enjoyed two tracks also composed by Ray's regular songwriter, Rudy Clark, 'It's Been A Drag' and 'Got My Mind Set On You Part One'/'Part Two'. Despite its title, the latter "didn't have a break in between. It was coming out of the old jazz/swing era, and it had these horrible screechy women's voices singing those back-up parts."[58] America was still taking saccharine sounds to its heart, but also clogging the ether was Californian surf music. Ruling this genre were The Beach Boys, who celebrated surfing and its companion sport, hot-rod racing, with chugging rock 'n' roll backing overlaid with a chorale more breathtaking than that of The Beatles.

Naturally, sister Louise had been kept posted about George's exploits with his group and had collected all of their Polydor and Parlophone records, plus the two or three issued in North American on labels of no great merit. Through her, some had been played on local radio, but these few spins had the impact of a feather on concrete in a continent whose wavelengths were overloaded with yapping disc jockeys with lurid *noms de turntable* – Wolfman Jack, Murray the K, Magnificent Montague – all unmindful of whatever was gripping a backwater like Britain.

"I don't know. What do you think?" was the spirit that pervaded the eventual unleashing of 'I Want To Hold Your Hand' by EMI's American outlet, Capitol. Although this ensured a better chance of airplay than earlier Beatles singles had with smaller companies, the group and Epstein could not yet assume that they'd be much more than a strictly European phenomenon, like Cliff Richard. Why should America want them? With The Beatles' deepest musical roots in US culture, it might be like taking coals to Newcastle. Besides, what about The Beach Boys, publicly as wholesome and all American as The Beatles were wholesome and British?

Why should The Beatles want America? George hadn't minded Illinois, but a lot of British musicians loathed what glimpses they'd had of the Land of Opportunity. "When The Dave Clark Five started," outlined their drummer/leader, "we used to play the American air bases in England. It was hell, because the American servicemen kept getting pissed. It was the only side of America I'd seen, and I didn't care for it."[117] Food for thought, however, were reports from the Star-Club of how well Dave Dee And The Bostons' medley of the entire *Please Please Me* LP went down with US ships' crews.

If the States were to be off limits, The Beatles had plenty to do elsewhere. They'd made sustained chart strikes in other parts of the world, from Eire to Australasia, although there were rare instances of local talent checkmating them with sly covers. Ray Columbus And The Invaders' single of 'I Wanna Be Your Man' sold more in New Zealand than those released there by both the Stones and The Beatles. Nevertheless, Brian Epstein was deliberating whether to commit The Beatles to a lengthy antipodean tour for as soon as September 1963. Hardly raising a liberal eyebrow then was another plan to send them to South Africa.

They always expected it to end. NEMS' general manager, Alistair

Taylor, recalled that the party line was, "If we can last three years, it would be marvellous."[118] To Pete Murray, Light Programme disc jockey and recurrent *Juke Box* jurist, their records "do not improve"[119] since they'd gone off the boil with 'From Me To You'. By 1964, preceding them on a British stage was less onerous "now that The Beatles have found their own level" – so said the most frequent of their guest stars, Kenny Lynch, in an article headlined "Is The Beatles Frenzy Cooling Down?"[119] Although a concert at the Prince of Wales Theatre – scene of their *Royal Variety* grand slam – had been standing-room only, everyone on a bill which included The Chants and a less fraught Vernons Girls "went down very well without interruptions by people shouting, 'We want The Beatles,' like they used to".[120]

This was London, where Kenny calculated, "The Rolling Stones may be just as big as The Beatles now."[120] Innocent of the capital's *sangfroid*, unabated screaming in the shires indicated that the Moptop Mersey Marvels were just as "gear" as ever. Many children had been as aghast as their parents at the Stones' transfixing androgyny, but in a nonplus of repelled bewitchment they also filled to overflowing venues starring "the Five Shaggy Dogs with a brand of 'shake' all their own",[121] as one local rag had it.

While 1963 was The Beatles' year, the Stones were still scrimmaging round the unsalubrious beat clubs that were now littering British towns – the Cubik in Rochdale, Swindon's X, or R&B night in Norwich's St Andrew's Hall to name but three. A shoal of Caverns abounded, too, from Leicester Square to Manchester to another in Birmingham that was lent an authentic sheen by dim lighting, an arched ceiling and The Searchers' presence at its inauguration.

The Searchers, Gerry and a few more Mersey Beat outfits were still able to take chart placings for granted, although, as Freddie And The Dreamers discovered, "There's only three ways you can kick your legs, and we never had another hit."[101] On Merseyside itself, there was a sense of impending hangover. As a beehive can function for a while after losing its progenitive queen, so did two-guitar-bass-drums combos continue to thrive in Liverpool. Clothed by London-style boutiques now operational in the city centre, the luckiest would gain a slot on the weekly *Sunday Night At The Cavern* broadcast by

Radio Luxembourg.

As the record companies weren't coming around so much any more, far-sighted Liverpudlian musicians realised that their very dialect was shortly to be a millstone around their necks. Too late to squeeze any blood from the Mersey Sound, more than one Scouse group attempted to dilute their accents and pass themselves off as Londoners.

The Beatles had become a London-based outfit when NEMS Enterprises uprooted itself late in 1963. Until then, they'd attended to their recording and broadcasting duties in the metropolis by commuting from wherever their concert itinerary found them. If benighted there, they'd bed down in hotels or avail themselves of the hospitality of old acquaintances like Ken Brown, who put them up the night before a *Saturday Club* recording in March 1963. A more regular port of call was the Shepherd Market flat of the programme's co-producer, Bernie Andrews, shared with George's friend and Beatles business associate Terry Doran. With a palate coarsened by chips-with-everything meals in wayside snack bars, and prevented by fame from frequenting such eateries in central London, George developed a fondness for egg and chips, as fried by Doran. "He didn't want to know about cooking it himself,"[122] recalled Andrews.

But a few streets from Shepherd Market, George began his London domicile by renting briefly a *pied à terre* in Green Street, just off Park Lane and handy for West End nightclubbing. By the time 52 sacks of mail were dumped on his parents' doorstep the day he came of age, he and Ringo were sharing what became an untidy flat beneath Brian Epstein's mews apartment in Whaddon House, Knightsbridge. Paul's billet with Jane Asher's family in Wimpole Street was not yet common knowledge, but Whaddon House and the Lennons' Kensington bedsit were targets for graffiti and marathon vigils by London fans.

Liverpool couldn't reclaim The Beatles, except perhaps if the bubble burst. Sniffing beyond northern counties now, EMI's opponents were still throwing down gauntlets – the laughable Severnbeats, "Hertsbeat" from Unit 4 + 2 and The Zombies, 'Blarney Beat' from The Four Aces, the "Solihull Sound" of The

Applejacks… It was a challenger from another EMI subsidiary that would seem to bring The Beatles to their knees and signal a finish to traipsing up north for pop news. Wowing 'em four nights a week at Tottenham Royal Ballroom, The Dave Clark Five went for the jugular in January 1964 when their sixth single, 'Glad All Over', ended The Beatles' unbroken seven weeks at Number One and sparked off a jubilant Fleet Street field day in which a prototypical headline was "Has The Five Jive Crushed The Beatle Beat?".

7 The Serious One

In foreign climes, The Dave Clark Five would rack up heftier achievements than their solitary UK Number One. Although hits at home didn't mean that much financially, Britain was about to become the world's prime purveyor of pop, and Liverpool – quoth post-beatnik bard Allen Ginsberg – "the centre of the consciousness of the entire universe"[123] after The Beatles instigated a large-scale re-run of British beat hysteria in February 1964, when 'I Want To Hold Your Hand' topped the US Hot 100.

A reason given for the Five's relegation to also-rans was "If you go off Dave, you're off the group".[124] As The Beatles had no obvious leader, fans could be fickle in affections towards individuals yet still maintain overall loyalty. The coherence of the group's image presented what had seemed at first glance to be a single focus for adoration, but by 1964 this Midwich Cuckoo regularity was balanced by the paradoxical realisation of inevitable differences between them – Ringo's harmless wit was especially benefical to the North American breakthrough.

"My part in The Beatles," figured George, "was I never wanted to be the one at the front."[52] This had indeed been acknowledged in a *Mersey Beat* headline, "The Quiet Beatle". He was also the Serious One, the Shy Beatle whose "replies might not be so memorable as Ringo's or John's but they often contain more sense".[125] Following some particularly pragmatic interviews, he also became the Money or Business Beatle, titles that would become more appropriate in the years to come. None of the group was markedly tight fisted, but all would pester Tony Barrow for minute-to-minute record-sales and chart information. "We'd be idiots," said McCartney, "to say that it isn't a constant inspiration to be making a lot of money."[57]

Certain contingency plans were already in force so that, should The Beatles' time be up, all four would recoup more than just golden memories. Harrison and Starr's main source of income was their quarter share apiece in Beatles Ltd, a budgetary receptacle for all net income from concerts. "Ringo and I are constantly being reminded that John and Paul make so much more money than us,"[126] snarled George, who didn't need reminding that the two songwriters each owned 20 times as many shares as he in Northern Songs, their publishing company. Although his eyes would glaze over during the quartet's quarterly meetings with its accountants ("confusing and boring and just like being back at school"[127]), it would be George who prodded most about where this percentage came from or why so-and-so had been granted that franchise. Indeed, it was his questioning that led to Brian Epstein re-examining the three-year-old German record contract. His vocabulary filling with phrases like "tax concession" and "convertible debentures", George's attitude was, "It's easy to get blasé and think we're making plenty and somebody's taking care of it, but I like to know how much is coming in, where it's being put, how much I can spend. I'm no more money mad than the others. I've just persevered and found out."[127] As the others made ready to go, George would stay put for a natter about his private investments, the most interesting of which was a stake in Sybilla's, a London night club. With Lennon and ex-Quarry Man Pete Shotton, he was also co-director of a Hayling Island supermarket until he resigned in 1969.

With most group earnings likewise tied up, George's wallet held little real capital, obliging him to borrow small amounts from Beatle menials, usually the road management. Larger bills were settled through the NEMS office. Like any backstreet lad abruptly rich, his consumption was more conspicuous than those for whom wealth was second nature. Though he'd later rein in his extravagance, purchasing a succession of flash cars was beyond rapture for a youth who for too long had had his nose glued to showroom windows. After an E-Type Jaguar came an Aston Martin DB5 and – motorised epitome of the 1960s – a Mini. When he spotted a maroon-and-black vintage model, he sold his Rolls Royce to Brian Jones. There was much bowing and scraping by a Hammersmith dealer as George paced up and down rows of gleaming Mercedes fitted with one-way windows and all the latest electrically operated gadgetry. Six days later, a black one was delivered, delayed by the personalising of the number plate and adjustment of driving-seat contours to George's – not his chauffeur's – measurements.

Because George had a Mercedes, Ringo and John had to have one, as George himself had earlier coveted Paul's Aston. Their uniformity before the public applied off duty, too: "We have the same number of suits in our wardrobes, and when we order new ones we order three, four, six at a time from the same tailor."[126] From nowhere, crazes would unburden themselves on all four. Cine-photography was one that lasted longer than most, and George's speciality was filming crowds as the group's limousine glided nearer each sold-out theatre.

On tour, they'd become practised at forging each other's signatures – as had Neil and Mal – to more rapidly dispose of the hundreds of autograph books left at stage doors for their attention. Back at the hotel, they usually doubled up in suites provided, George more often than not with John, whose sense of humour was closest to his own. "Sure, we all get on well together," Ringo has assured fans. "Most people call us offbeat. John writes a little poetry, which is the weirdest you ever saw, but it stops him going mental."[63] When Lennon was requested to collate his verse, stories and drawings for two immediate best-sellers, the second, A Spaniard In The Works, proved more difficult, as "it was starting from scratch. With the first book, I'd written a lot of it at odd times during my life."[44] As the completion date loomed, so he picked other brains. George, for instance, assisted with 'The Singularge Experience Of Miss Anne Duffield', an inventive corruption of Conan Doyle.

For reasons to do with the closed shop of his songwriting partnership with John, Paul saw George's greater social attachment to John as no threat. Nowadays, it was John and George – rather than John and Paul and Ringo – who were scrutinised through spyholes at the doors of clubs out of bounds to those not yet eminent enough to frequent them. It was George and John together who were interviewed on the first all-live *Ready, Steady, Go!*. With John taking the lead, their replies on these occasions sometimes had an antiphonal effect. When tackled about an inordinately high admission charge at one concert, John's "I wouldn't see anyone for five quid" was followed by a daring "I wouldn't see you for five bob." "Why don't you let the kids into the airport?" demanded John of a security officer after The Beatles landed in Adelaide. "Yes, we want to see the kids,"[68] echoed George.

In cold print, George's repartee often seemed inanely sarcastic or wantonly pedestrian. "Why aren't you wearing a hat?"[68] he cracked back when asked why he'd once dressed differently from the other three. His favourite meats? "Beef, pork...oh, mutton, yes."[68] In mitigation, a lot of questions he endured from ill-informed, patronising journalists were as banal and repetitious as a stuck record. At the New York press conference given after the group's tumultuous arrival on 7 February 1964 for their first US performance, when they were asked about how time passed when cooped up in hotel rooms, he said, "We ice skate." What would you have been if The Beatles hadn't become stars? "A poor Beatle." Do you guys think there'll be another war soon? "Yeah. Friday."

Chronologically, he'd grown to man's estate, but there remained a strong streak of the adolescent in him. At a party, he got so giggly over a quip about "pack up Mick Jagger in your old kit bag" that he had to write it down. In July 1964, at London's Dorchester Hotel, Princess Margaret laughed off as Beatle cheek his entreaty for her to leave so the company could begin the buffet celebration, following the première of The Beatles' first film, *A Hard Day's Night*. On an edition of *Juke Box Jury* showcasing the whole group, he switched the name plates so that, for years, my friend Kevin was under the misapprehension that George was John.

No Beatle was baited by the others as Stuart and Tommy had been, but George was often treated with less than respect by John and Paul. Sometimes he asked for it. One of his most irritating traits was butting into their conversations with some flat line as if trying to imprint his importance to the group on outsiders. Insecure and only

21, his ears strained to catch murmured intrigue and a glimmer of the more intense limelight in which McCartney and Lennon basked. "What are you talking about?" "Mind your own bloody business,"[128] barked John, helping himself to a cigarette from George's top pocket. Interrupting Paul and a *Melody Maker* interviewer, George "was thinking, 'How about something like Little Richard's "Bama Lama Bama Loo"?'" "You just write daft things, George," snapped Paul before turning back to the reporter. "As I was saying, about writing a rocker – I'd liken it to abstract painting…"[129]

Since 'Don't Bother Me', George had composed not a single "daft thing". Even Paul and John went through a bad patch in 1964 during the Australasian tour, which by many accounts was little more than a heavily subsidised debauch.[69] After the *Hard Day's Night* quota of 13 Lennon-McCartney originals, half of 1964's Christmas LP, *Beatles For Sale*, regurgitated old rock 'n' roll standards and songs buried since The Quarry Men. Striking an unfathomable chord for me, however, were the few bars of instrumental play-out on a minor track, 'I Don't Want To Spoil The Party', which somehow caught the essence of The Beatles.

George's undervalued guitar style was as rich a legacy for other artists as any other Beatle innovation. Because his solos and riffs were constructed to integrate with the melodic and lyrical intent of each song, they seemed unobtrusive – even bland – in contrast to those within the year's crop of groups who'd ditched Beatle winsomeness for denim taciturnity. Musically, the main difference lay in the lead guitarist, who, unlike Harrison, would step forward into the spotlight to react with clenched teeth and intellectual flash to underlying chord patterns rather than the aesthetics of the song.

Containing such an exquisite, The Yardbirds secured a support spot at The Beatles' 1964 Christmas season at Hammersmith Odeon. During their allotted ten minutes, they curtailed the extended instrumental "rave-ups" that had made them the toast of the Crawdaddy, where they'd taken over from the Stones. This streamlining cramped the style of their 19-year-old guitarist, Eric "Slowhand" Clapton, who'd briefly been one of Brian Cassar's Engineers. While sharing the self-immolatory tendencies of some of his black icons, Surrey-born Eric was steeped more than most in the note-bending dissonance of the blues. This distinction did not register with George Harrison, who passed the time of day with the Yardbird along backstage corridors "but didn't really get to know him".[32]

For as long as Clapton, Alvin Dean and other would-be virtuosi fermented hitless in the specialist clubs and college circuit, George would continue to win polls as top guitarist. Deservedly, he – and The Searchers – can be credited for introducing the twelve-string guitar to the common-or-garden pop group: "It's gear. It sounds a bit like electric piano, I always think, but you can get a nice fat sound out of it."[129] From an actor friend of Bob Dylan, he learned the rudiments of playing it finger-style, but he always reverted to the plectrum. While it was still a novelty at home, George had procured a Rickenbacker semi-acoustic model – with the four lowest sets of strings tuned in octaves – during The Beatles' first trip to the States. Limited as a solo instrument, its uniquely circular effect powered a flip-side, 'You Can't Do That', on which John played lead, although George's new twelve-string took the resounding bass passage in the title song on *A Hard Day's Night*.

Another American acquisition of George's was also heard in Abbey Road studios. Manufactured by Gretsch, the Chet Atkins Country Gentleman was also heard on the album *Chet Atkins Picks On The Beatles*, for which George was delighted to pen respectful sleeve notes. To his pleasure and embarrassment, a more venerated hero, Carl Perkins, chanced to be there during The Beatles' October evening session for Carl's own 'Everybody's Trying To Be My Baby', swamped in "flutter" echo. On *Beatles For Sale*, this constituted George's one lead vocal. The last Lennon-McCartney number he'd ever record was on *A Hard Day's Night*. Short and with the composers' backing "ooh-oohs" prominent, 'I'm Happy Just To Dance With You' was George's, because John "couldn't have sung it",[78] even though he'd been responsible for most of its lyrics. As a US single, it had sneaked to a lowly Number 95 for, although there was no serious sign of wavering, the impetus of The Beatles' conquest of America had relaxed slightly by late 1964. They'd been in France when Capitol had launched the 'I Want To Hold Your Hand' spring offensive on a Hot 100 rife with Bobby ballads and surf instrumentals. After the first night of their season at the Paris Olympia, they'd needed cheering up.

To a degree, the French way had been paved with Petula Clark's hit translation of 'Please Please Me' (rendered as 'Tu Perds Ton Temps' – "you lost your chance") and the inclusion of 'Money', 'You'll Never Walk Alone' and further Mersey Beat set works in the repertoires of Johnny Hallyday and other Gallic pop luminaries. Nonetheless, The Beatles got off to a bad start on a late-running bill, co-headlining with Trini Lopez and Hallyday's singing wife, Sylvie Vartan. Although he'd tried some nonsensical schoolboy French continuity ("John est sur le table"), George's remarks in English grew less jocular as the set wore on with equipment persistently malfunctioning and the outbreaks of barracking to which the yé-yé – nearly all male this time – were prone. A year later, after the Stones, Kinks and Animals had done well in France, The Beatles would be able to work up their accustomed pandemonium to justify closing the show two nights running at Le Palais de Sports.

By then, they had spearheaded what has passed into myth as the "British Invasion" of the New World, an eventuality predicted in May 1963 by Roy Orbison with English screams still ringing in his ears: "These boys have enough originality to storm our charts in the US with the same effect as they have already done here."[130] As British pop had long been regarded as merely furbished of nine-day wonder, like The Tornados, few believed him, However, even Roy would say, "As a male, I personally don't like feminine hair on men, and I imagine women don't like it either."[131] When a clip of a Beatles concert was shown on his nationwide TV chat show a month prior to their messianic descent on Kennedy Airport, Jack Paar – a US Wogan – wisecracked, "I understand scientists are working on a cure for this."[132] Not so amused, however, were factions in the crew-cut Bible Belt down south.[133]

Dallas, Texas was "a place not known for war", as Jerry Lee Lewis sang in 'Lincoln Limousine', his MacGonagall-esque requiem to president John F Kennedy, assassinated there in 1963 on the same November day that British pop papers proclaimed The Beatles' forthcoming US visit. Some would predicate that the four's American success was an antidote to the depressing Christmas that followed the Dallas tragedy. John Lennon's more forthright theory was "that kids everywhere all go for the same stuff and, seeing as we'd done it in England, there's no reason why we couldn't do it in America, too."[57] They could scarcely miss in a maternally-minded society that was later to indulge in the adoption of Cabbage Patch dolls.

Their confidence might have wobbled in Paris, but The Beatles were quite unruffled in New York. "If anyone dried up," said George, "there was always somebody else there with a smart answer. There was always a good balance, so nobody could quite nail us."[32] The Beatles were boys next door, but not like Bobby goo-merchants, who now couldn't get hits to save their lives. "I don't think they expected musicians playing rock 'n' roll to have any wit or repartee at all,"[134] reckoned Mike Smith of The Dave Clark Five, who likewise disgorged themselves from a Pan Am jet a few weeks later.

The Five would be televised on *The Ed Sullivan Show* – America's *Sunday Night At The London Palladium* – more times than any British group before or after, but it was The Beatles' pulse-quickening slot on 9 February that would be remembered more than that of any other Sullivan guest since Elvis in 1956. George hadn't made the dress rehearsal for the excellent reason that he was flat on his back in the Plaza Hotel, sweating out a high fever, his throat wrapped in a towel and cradling a portable wireless tuned to a commentary on the fans stationed outside. His increasing trepidation about flying may have exacerbated the illness – and sour mood – contracted in Paris. Not likely to improve his constitution either was bumptious Big Apple disc jockey Murray the K, who was trying to blag his way into rooming with George to tape his thoughts on waking and just prior to sleep. George conducted those interviews that couldn't be put off from his bed, but, spared Murray the K, he was able to go the distance on Sullivan's show, thanks to quick-acting medication and nursing by sister Louise, who'd extended her visit from Benton to so do. (See Appendix I.)

All About The Beatles, Louise's interview LP, was released in 1965. Another small label – the first of many – had got hold of poor old Pete Best. With his group, he was hauled over to milk his connection with The Beatles via a sell-out North American tour at odds with fading interest in him, even in Liverpool. Backtracking to 'Love Me Do' and the antique Sheridan tracks, so insatiable – and uncritical – was demand for anything on which The Beatles had ever breathed that, for one glorious week, they occupied nine places in the Canadian Top Ten and accounted for 60 per cent of record sales in the States over a twelve-month period. At home, each new Beatle release was, noted Derek Taylor, "a national event",[135] but with most of the Union's 50 states comparable in size to the British Isles it did no harm for US companies with rights to Beatle products to hurl at such a wide sales region singles of any album cuts that took their fancy. George therefore suffered no loss of prestige when the year-old 'Roll Over Beethoven' and the more ancient 'Do You Want To Know A Secret' hovered around the middle of the Hot 100. "Just about everyone is tired of The Beatles," groaned *Billboard* magazine, "except the buying public."[136]

Alighting in Midwest towns in the graveyard hours, The Beatles' aeroplane would still be greeted by hundreds of hot-eyed teenagers, many chaperoned by parents who had not chastised them for squandering their allowances on a six-dollar can of "Beatle Breath" or for neglecting their homework to ogle a TV "documentary" of the group's first US visit (with surreptitious hand-held shots of Ringo's ear for minutes on end). To less determinate purpose, invasions of privacy were enacted by such as "the Torpedo", one of an assortment of female fans notorious for skills in evading the most stringent barricades to impose themselves on The Beatles and other UK beat groups now being fully exploited in the States.

"Britain hasn't been so influential in American affairs since 1775," read the same *Billboard* editorial as fascination with all things from our sceptred isle peaked during that 1964 week, when two-thirds of the Hot 100 was British in origin, although one Capitol executive would caw, "I tell ya, Elmer, you heard one Limey group, you heard 'em all." Most of Britain's major pop acts – and some minor ones – succeeded to varying extents in the unchartered States, but, anticipating this, many Yankee entrepreneurs had crossed the

Atlantic to stake claims in the musical diggings, among them the self-important Phil Spector, who said he wanted to produce The Beatles. Years before they let him, his encounters with them left George with an idea of someone "a bit outrageous, but he was very sweet. He was like a giant person inside this frail little body."[137]

While such big shots were in Britain, a common complaint back home was that of Frank Zappa, of Los Angeles' Soul Giants: "If you didn't sound like The Beatles or Stones, you didn't get hired."[138] By 1965, a host of American groups had grown out their crew-cuts and cowlicks as much as they dared and seized upon whatever aspect of British beat they felt most comfortable with. In The Byrds' case, it was Beatle harmonies and the twelve-string sound pioneered by The Searchers and George Harrison. Moulded less successfully to breadwinning UK specification were the likes of The McCoys, The Wackers, The Remains, The Knickerbockers and, resident on Jack Good's networked *Shindig* show, The Shindogs. Although their debut 45, 'The Peppermint Beatle', was a miss, The Standells' Gary Leeds later drummed with The Walker Brothers, who found greater rewards in Britain itself.

Far behind all of them were The Sundowners, a Florida outfit formed after 13-year-old Tom Petty saw The Beatles on television: "I thought I could be a farmer or I could do that."[139] If teenagers like Tom had to emulate British beat groups, reasoned adult America, let it be ones like The Beatles and Herman's Hermits, as a palatable compromise to hairier monsters like The Rolling Stones and The Pretty Things. Demonstrating this acceptance of The Beatles as good, clean fun was an episode of *I Love Lucy* in which stooge Mr Mooney tries to book for $100 "that English combo everyone's talking about" for a firm's dinner and dance. Now that America had capitulated, the rest of the world was a pushover. Soviet Russia threw up a group, The Candid Lads, whom *The Daily Express* reckoned were The Beatles' opposite numbers. In the back streets of Hong Kong, you'd come across a local outfit with a set consisting entirely of deadpan Beatle imitations. Down Under, where even 'Cry For A Shadow' had made the Top Ten, New Zealand's Shadows clones, The Librettos, made the transition, as did The Bee Gees, regulars on

Australian TV's *Bandstand*. This was broadcast from Sydney, where, despite torrential rain, The Beatles were welcomed by the biggest crowd since aviator Amy Johnson landed there after her solo flight from England in 1932.

For much of this leg of 1964's world tour, The Beatles weren't quite the full shilling. Qualified mainly by his playing on *Beatlemania*, a budget LP of anonymous Beatles covers, freelance drummer Jimmy Nicol was thrust into transient stardom as temporary substitute for Ringo, then under the scalpel for acute tonsillitis. Paul and John had been amenable, but George had dug in his heels – if Ringo couldn't go, neither would he. As it turned out to be The Beatles' only visit to Australasia, it was fortunate for their distant fans – watching defiance, hesitation and final agreement chase across George's face – that Brian Epstein talked him around.

Brian had become accomplished at calming down unruly youths. He'd plenty of opportunity to practise these days as time ran out for many of his clients. Gerry, The Fourmost and Billy J had all borne their first serious flops, while other of his acts had never had hits anyway. After The Big Three's first set at the Blue Angel one night, another drummer took over when Johnny Hutch collected his pay and went home. While his Mersey Beat groups were cashing in what chips were left, Epstein had overloaded himself with trendier non-Liverpool signings like The Moody Blues, a Birmingham quintet who, under their previous handlers, had already topped the UK charts.

However manifold his other undertakings, Brian's primary concern would always be The Beatles. For his "boys" – his surrogate children – he did whatever energy and willingness could do to help their careers, to make him prouder of them and them of him. He took their gratuitous insults, their piques, their flagrant cohabitation with their lady-loves and their headline-making misbehaviour like the loving father he should have been. In language that George could understand, he'd unravel those complexities that still befuddled him after a session with the accountants. Knowing that George was generally grouchy first thing in the morning, Brian had been all sympathy when his "favourite son" (as he called George during a US press conference) had thrown orange juice at Brian Somerville, a publicist that neither of them liked much. As he'd once taken John on a Spanish holiday while Cynthia recovered from child-bearing, so George and a new girlfriend – a model named Pattie Boyd – accompanied Brian to the south of France. Solicitous as usual, he deferred to the couple's wishes about how they spent their leisure but could be relied upon to suggest diversions. A bull fight in Arles, however, wasn't a wincing George's notion of a pleasant afternoon.

When self-confessed Beatlemaniac Derek Taylor approached Brian with a view to ghosting a Beatle's day-to-day ruminations for *The Express*, it was thought that it would be "a nice thing for George, give him an interest in life because the others have their songwriting and Ringo is rather new".[74] In return for an agreed fee of £100 a week, all the newspaper wanted was permission to credit George with the column that Taylor was to submit for twelve Fridays.

Under the editorial lash, he hammered out the first article, but before handing it in Derek felt it was polite to show it to his subject. At Whaddon Court, he read it to Epstein, the Lennons and a bemused George. Uneasily tracing that fading Mersey Beat scent, Derek admitted that, "because the assumption was that George hadn't been to school, it was like a jolly docker would have talked".[74] One tortuous Scouse-ism, "big green job" (for Corporation bus), stuck in Taylor's throat as one that had never reached the lips of a Beatle or anyone else. As George had no wish to be portrayed as the definitive wacker (or, indeed, the definitive anything), he decided that the ghost had to be partly exorcised. He could string a sentence together as well as any ex-Liobian, couldn't he? Taylor and he would collaborate. Thus was laid the foundation of a lasting friendship, strengthened soon afterwards when Derek, a fellow Merseysider, was put on NEMS' payroll as Brian's personal assistant and then The Beatles' press officer after Somerville's outraged exit in October 1964, partly over stipulations in a contract of employment that he saw as implying a lack of trust.

The job was no picnic for Taylor, either, as his job often went *ultra vires* just answering telephones, writing publicity hand-outs and organising press conferences. At one US airport, he became embroiled in a running argument with security officials as The Beatles were bundled into limousines. Riled by his "girly" English accent, a guard punched Taylor in the stomach. Meanwhile, the group's motorcade slid away, leaving Derek gasping for breath on the tarmac.

After thuggish America, a tour of dear old England was a bagatelle. Patrolling round-the-block queues that had formed days before box offices opened, police kept eyes peeled for a girl runaway from Massachusetts believed to be following The Beatles. Otherwise, no bother was expected from the occupants of the sleeping bags that lined the pavements with their transistor radios and comics. Once they might have wrung their hands, but now mums and dads would bring provisions to their waiting daughters. Well, it was only The Beatles, ritualised and cosy.

Once inside, the girls let rip their healthy, good-humoured screams. Sure, there was fainting, and heightened blood pressure brought on nose bleeds. The odd tip-up chair would snap off its spindle, too, but after 'Long Tall Mandy', or whatever it was called, the screeching would cease for the national anthem, resuming half-heartedly before the audience filed quietly out.

Only fire-hoses could quell the riots at shows by those sinister Rolling Stones. A judgement on them was that among the 22 unconscious after one such fiasco lay their guitarist, Keith Richards, stunned by a flying lemonade bottle. On the sodden carpeting, auditorium cleaners would come across soiled knickers among smashed rows of seating.

Fun for all the family, The Beatles' TV appearances were always special, and Christmas wouldn't be Christmas without the "Fab Four" at Number One. Under parental pressure, some West Country headmasters reshuffled lunch hours so that senior pupils might rush to railway stations to glimpse The Beatles when they were shunted to and from Paddington and Devon for four days for some of the train scenes in *A Hard Day's Night*. Hell, they were an institution, weren't they? How could anyone old enough to have fought Hitler have guessed that The Beatles would be more than a passing phase? Like Tommy and Cliff before them, when they were overtaken by a newer sensation, they'd be set up in pantomime, cabaret, charity football matches and all that. Their unforced Scouse urbanity would be ideal for children's television, wouldn't it? "Who'd want to be an 80-year-old Beatle?"[140] laughed John Lennon. Being Liverpudlian, comedy was the obvious path to take. Any fool could see that in *A Hard Day's Night*.

The Beatles' celluloid career could have got under way with them headlining an all-styles-served-here conveyor belt of lip-synched ephemera linked by some vacuous story-line in the tradition of *The Girl Can't Help It* and *It's Trad, Dad*. In August 1963, more than 40 scripts considered had been of this disposition, but, although punctuated with musical breaks and concluded with a concert sequence, The Beatles were more than a monochrome sideshow in *A Hard Days Night*. With no highbrow pretensions, however, they were not required "to other be". That was left to the supporting actors.

Before co-stars were deemed unnecessary, among big names discussed was that of Peter Sellers, who so admired The Beatles – as they did him – that he'd recorded the film's main title as a cod-Shakespearian recitation and scurried into the Top 20 with it, too. A romantic sub-plot was on the cards briefly, until producer Walter Shenson realised how much the group's female following might resent it. Visualised for this role had been 16-year-old Hayley Mills, a pert, snub-nosed miss who'd been in films since the late 1950s. George was the Beatle who'd drawn the short straw for the pleasure of squiring her to the Regal in Henley-on-Thames for a showing of the Hitchcockian *Charade*. At this charity midnight matinee, he was as impressed with the cinema's art-deco interior as he was with *Charade* and Miss Mills.

A one-off date was enough to set tongues wagging about Harrison and Hayley, but rumours about him and Pattie Boyd had infinitely more substance. Pattie was then consistent with George's taste, which "runs to small blonde girls who can share a laugh with me".[141] Their backgrounds, nonetheless, were poles apart. The eldest of six children, Patricia Anne Boyd was born in Somerset in 1945, but one of her father's RAF postings obliged the family to move to Kenya four years later. When they returned to England after half a decade, Pattie was sent to boarding school. By 1962, however, anyone peering through the window of a certain Wimbledon hairdressing salon might have seen her putting the finishing touches to some aged crone's blue rinse. Noticing Pattie's willowy figure and avalanche of wavy hair, another customer – a writer for a women's magazine – asked if she'd ever thought of becoming a photographic model. This hadn't been the first such compliment paid to her, but it was the incentive for Pattie to broaden her horizons beyond shampoo and curlers.

When she met George, she was in the same mini-skirted league as Twiggy, Celia Hammond and Jean Shrimpton, the new face of *Vogue*, *Seventeen* and the fashion pages of Sunday supplements. With the relative girth of middle life, Pattie would later confess to possessing "a couple of minis which I still try on if I can get into them, but, God, I can never believe we wore them so short".[142] Mary Quant, Shrimpton's *haute couture* Diaghilev, noted how mandatory it had become for 1960s dolly-birds "to look like Pattie Boyd rather than Marlene Dietrich. Their aim is to look childishly young, naïvely unsophisticated, and it takes more sophistication to work out that look than those early would-be sophisticates ever dreamed of."[143]

It was fitting, therefore, for 20-year-old Pattie to land a bit part as a schoolgirl in *A Hard Day's Night*. Its director, Richard Lester, had remembered her toothy grin and lisp from an ITV commercial for Smith's Crisps he'd made a few months earlier. With her and three other uniformed and giggly girls as the audience, The Beatles mimed 'I Should Have Known Better' in a studio mock-up of a guard's van. "I could feel George looking at me," recalled Pattie, "and I was a bit embarrassed. Then, when he was giving me his autograph, he put seven kisses under his name. I thought he must like me a little."[143]

He liked her a lot, as did John, whose subliminal signals to her would intensify as his marriage deteriorated. At first, George, the unencumbered bachelor, came on as the rough, untamed Scouser, but even when this was moderated he was still very different from Pattie's previous *beaux* in London. Loyally, she clung to her latest boyfriend until his persevering Beatle rival – whose brash outer shell, she discovered, contained surprising gentleness and sensitivity – prised her away: "I said I was loyal, not stupid."[144] When her flat was burgled, listed on the police inventory was George's *A Hard Day's Night* gold disc.

This real-life courtship made up for the sentimental element that *A Hard Day's Night* thankfully lacked. Although it was, said Lennon, "The Beatles at their most natural",[141] Paul was self-conscious about many lines he had to utter. However, if no Laurence Olivier, the so-called Serious One coped so well with "acting" his big scene – making disparaging remarks about an array of "grotty" shirts – that Shenson demanded another, but the scene became John's instead of George's.

The Beatles' zany farce brought the curtain down on the old teenpics regime of neo-musicals full of cheery unreality. More dated a film than *A Hard Day's Night* was *Ferry Across The Mersey*, set in the fast-waning "Nashville of the North" and starring Gerry And The Pacemakers, whose evocative title song extended a Top Ten farewell for the Mersey Beat movement in January 1965. From the Cavern's battered stage, some musicians were fly enough to spot even those American tourists ungarlanded with cameras. It was a look in the eye, as though mentally ticking off a "gen-u-ine" Liverpool beat group from a list of attractions that also included the Changing Of The Guards and Morris dancers.

Nearing the end of its run, *Mersey Beat*'s saga aligned with that of a buoyant local scene singled out as a pop centre and then gutted of its principal talents by London predators. Like Liverpool itself, Mersey Beat was desecrated and the culprits pardoned. The Beatles could be exonerated from most of the blame, although a *Mersey Beat* editorial in April 1964 would complain, "Maybe we don't get many of our home-grown stars appearing too often these days."

Nevertheless, who wouldn't come out when, for the northern première of *A Hard Day's Night*, The Beatles passed in triumphal Rolls Royces through cheering streets from Speke Airport to a civic reception at the City Hall? Outside, a police-massed band pounded out 'Can't Buy Me Love', their fifth Number One.

At the Odeon, as the projectionist waited, they were brought on stage to say a few words. "All my people are here!" boomed George over the cinema tannoy, and so most of them were. Before he was famous, George didn't realise that he had so many relations and family friends. Although his mother's Australian pen-pal had been persuaded by a journalist with a cheque book to part with snapshots of George as an infant, no one had turned up with open hands like John's long-lost father. However, plenty of bogus cousins, neighbours who'd known him as a boy and the like had been refused entry at stage doors, and a *bona fide* uncle had been sent away with a flea in his ear from one Canadian theatre.

For his nearest and dearest, George was the indirect fount of gifts that fans parcelled to The Beatles' fan club to thank them for having him, including home-made "gonks", honorific plaques and childish daubs. Most were less than ornaments, but from those with more money than sense came complete dinner services and even silverware. Ideally, the most inquisitive among us would like to sample with our own sensory organs, say, the older Harrison brothers' feelings about Our Kid's popularity and wealth. Whatever the complicated emotional shades among them, neither could deny the material benefits of kinship to a Beatle. As well as expensive birthday presents, there were transfusions of cash for the asking. It was, however, the Harrisons' very stability as a family that forbade each from presuming too much upon George's good fortune. From sunning themselves on a Caribbean strand, Louise and Harold returned to Mackett's Lane, instead of spending more of his money by coming along for the ride on The Beatles' Australasian tour. This was in spite of Harry's earlier announcement of it "being good for George that we are going along. We will probably be able to take a load off his shoulders by dealing with fans out there."[68] Also figuring in their decision not to go, perhaps, was the fact that that Lennon's aunt – who'd never recanted some sharp words to Louise at the Cavern – had been invited along, too.

In crushed-velvet seats at the Odeon, the parents had listened to master of ceremonies David Jacobs' build-up to the film's unveiling. To spatters of applause, he'd popped in a couple of *bons mots* at the expense of The Rolling Stones. For weeks, 'A Hard Day's Night' and the Stones' 'It's All Over Now' had monopolised the first two positions in Britain's hit parade, necessitating the avoidance of such revenue-draining clashes in future. Although The Beatles would snipe at the Stones in the press (hardly ever *vice versa*), they'd send Mal

Evans out mid-session to purchase their competitors' latest LP and both groups socialised outside working hours; Jagger and Richards – the Stones' Lennon and McCartney – were among party guests after The Beatles' concert at New York's Shea Stadium in 1965.

In terms of attendance figures, this was to be The Beatles' zenith, but George at least was not so swollen-headed by it all not to drop in on The Merseybeats as they recorded a new single or gravitate back to Liverpool, albeit with decreasing frequency. Long a nightbird by vocation, he'd haunt the Blue Angel, with its anecdotes about what Billy Kramer said to Sam Leach in 1961. George was nobody's lion there but still one of the lads. Seizing the initiative, he ambled over to a Roadrunner with, "Hi, Mike, how's the band?" "Great, George," began Mike Hart's crushing riposte, "How's yours?"

When The Roadrunners ground to a standstill, Mike would be among the founders of that mixed-media aggregation known as "the Liverpool Scene" who drank from much the same pool as The Scaffold. By 1965, however, more and more Scouse artists were seeking their fortunes down south. An example was Gibson Kemp, Ringo's replacement in Rory Storm's Hurricanes, who became one third of Paddy, Klaus And Gibson with Paddy Chambers and Klaus Voorman. Before Voorman left in 1966 to join Manfred Mann, the trio were resident at the Pickwick on Great Newport Street.

The Pickwick was one of about ten fashionable London niteries from which the chosen few could select a night out, with "night" defined as around midnight to dawn. "Fashionable" meant that the supercool Ad-Lib would be "in" for a while, before the inscrutable pack transferred allegiance to the Speakeasy or the Bag O' Nails, off Carnaby Street, before finishing up at the cloistered Scotch of St James, within spitting distance of Buckingham Palace. Talking shop continually, pop's male conquistadores would hold court, with only their equals contradicting them. Close at hand would be a whiskey and Coke and, depending on their status, a variable abundance of skinny, Quant-cropped birds with double-decker eyelashes.

Since pairing off with Pattie, George became less of a West End clubman, but his record collection still reflected an advanced awareness of the American soul music that forever filled the downstairs disco's deafening dark at the Scotch. His record player would pulsate to the Betty Everetts, Don Coveys and Chuck Jacksons, as well as the better-known Marvin Gayes, Nina Simones and Wilson Picketts. Before saturation plugging on Britain's new pirate radio station put them into the charts' lower rungs, George had long been *au fait* with eruditions like 'Harlem Shuffle' by Bob And Earl, Edwin Starr's 'Headline News' and the originals of such British covers as The Hollies' 'Just One Look' (Doris Troy) and The Fourmost's 'Baby I Need Your Loving' (The Four Tops). George had persisted in his advocacy of Mary Wells, who was then Tamla-Motown's foremost female singer, touring Britain as The Beatles' guest star. Most nights, he clapped her three-song spot from the wings, even her unwise choice of the smoochy 'Time After Time', which was better suited for cabaret than a mob impatient for the Fab Four.

George imagined himself quite refined by now, but he would never be snooty about mainstream pop. His tastes again were largely American, running to the post-surf Beach Boys, The Byrds and New York's Lovin' Spoonful, who had roots in rural blues and Memphis jug bands. Both The Byrds and the Spoonful had been classified as "folk-rock", as was Bob Dylan, who'd also offended folk purists by going electric, *circa* 1965. Because it exposes a point of view, even 'Can't Buy Me Love' may be construed as political, but Dylan sang stridently through his nose about myriad less wistful topics.

Nor was he still going on about war being wrong. With The Beatles' Aeolian cadences, Dylan's rapid-fire stream-of-consciousness literariness was jolting pop's under-used brain into quivering, reluctant action. First of all, beat groups dipped into his stockpile of songs, with The Byrds, The Animals and Manfred Mann notable among those having hits. Next, the hunt was on for more Dylans, as it had been for more Beatles. In Britain, the job went to a crumpled Scot named Donovan who, with harmonica harness and nasal inflection, began on *Ready, Steady, Go!* as a more beatific edition of the master. Although it involved sweating a bit over lyrics, Tin Pan Alley composers put their minds to Dylan-type creations, thereby rendering 1965 the golden age of all-purpose protest songs like PF Sloan's 'Eve Of Destruction' for Barry McGuire, a former New Christy Minstrel.

Lennon and McCartney weren't in complete agreement on the issue of Bob Dylan. While Paul had reservations, John's moptop was often covered these days with a denim cap like Dylan's, and some of his newer songs – especially 'I'm A Loser', from *Beatles For Sale* – betrayed an absorption of the American through constant replay of his albums. Time would come when George would be even more hooked on Dylan than John. "Even his stuff which people loathe I like," he'd boast, "because every single thing he does represents something that's him."[145]

As an individual, Dylan was "the looniest person I've ever met".[145] The Beatles were first introduced to him in a New York hotel suite during their first North American tour, and when offered refreshment Bob asked for "cheap wine" rather than any finer beverage in the drinks cabinet. While Mal went out for the requested *vin ordinaire*, it transpired during the intervening chit-chat that The Beatles – contrary to their guest's assumption – had never had much to do with marijuana. "It's as if we're up there pointing down at us,"[118] tittered McCartney to Derek Taylor when Dylan passed round a rectifying joint laced with the narcotic that no longer terrified John, George and Paul like it had with those peculiar blokes the evening before the Decca audition. Paradoxically, if they'd still been worried after inhaling it, then it couldn't have been marijuana.

Dylan grew as heartily sick of explaining his songs as The Beatles were of answering questions about haircuts and how they found America ("turn left at Greenland"). "They asked one question eight different times,"[146] George snorted after another mind-stultifying press conference. What kind of a world was this, where hotel chambermaids would sell their stories to journalists before the group had even checked in? *Beatles Monthly* answered an enquiry about hairs on George's stomach. Actually worth writing about was The Beatles' harrowing visit to brighten the last hours of a Melbourne police chief's terminally ill niece, or the few savoured minutes of ordinary behaviour when, *en route* to a concert, the group's Austin Princess stopped outside a village shop in Devon while they purchased sweets.

It was less trouble to drive rather than walk the shortest distance now. When interruptive fans in restaurants spoiled too many meals, the four took to "ones where people are so snobby they pretend they don't know us".[146] Even an R&B jamboree in Richmond was no sanctuary, as an excursion by George and John to see The Animals there fired an outbreak of Beatlemania and the pair's hasty departure. George's rather optimistic summary of his privations is worth quoting at length: "This poverty of ours – if that's what it should be called – applies to the things we've been deprived of as a result of what we are. For instance, we can't go window shopping. We can't browse around a department store. We'll have this for four or five years or a few more. In the meantime, we'll wait, and it's not bad, really. We're making money while waiting."[126]

There are worse ways of making a living, but for George touring was becoming the most onerous obligation of Beatlehood. Some fans not close enough to maul him as he dashed past would resort to extreme emotional blackmail, threatening to jump off buildings, throw themselves under car wheels or swallow poison. Aspiring to an orgasm at the thrust of a Beatle, one single-minded woman actually slashed her wrists in frustration. Other girls had better luck, for, although admirable young men in many ways, The Beatles also had their share of young men's vices. A natural prudity discourages me from going into detail, except to say that the group's casual and unchallenging procurement of sexual gratification was not brought to public notice by a press who judged any besmirching of the Fab Four's cheeky but innocent image as untimely when no one wanted to know that they were any different from the way they'd been in *A Hard Day's Night*. Save the scandal for The Rolling Stones.

Dressing-room scenes were often how susceptible fans might have imagined them – a card or board game on the middle table, George tuning up, Paul shaving at the wash-basin. Sometimes, it really would be like *A Hard Day's Night*, when they cleared the decks to rehearse acoustically John and Paul's latest opus, with Ringo slapping the table or cardboard-box drums. Who could think ill of boys who, smothering inner revulsion, were charming to the chain of handicapped unfortunates wheeled in by credulous minders deluded that a "laying on of hands" by the four pop deities would bring about a cure? In Beatle parlance, *cripple* came to mean anyone they wished to be shooed from their presence.

Not everyone adored them. Priggish hoteliers would be at pains to stress that no minor was to be served liquor, their faces falling when George produced his passport. Armed with scissors, posses of manly yahoos would attempt raids on the group's quarters, assuming that they'd receive leniency from a regional justice who frowned on male hairstyles longer than a crewcut. None succeeded, but in such areas The Beatles were subjected to insulting placards and rarer peltings with decayed fruit, most of which were thrown by jealous boyfriends. As bullet-holes in the undercarriage of one Beatle chartered flight testified, some were sufficiently maddened to lie at the end of an American runway, shotguns at the ready.

With his nose in the aircraft company's digest, George had been blissfully unaware of the danger. Now and then, he'd be awed by the ego-dissipating effects of high altitude. Staring down on the Arctic's icy tundra, he was heard to mutter, "looking at that lot makes you feel very humble, somehow."[148] Nonetheless, some of the paint-peeling antiquities hired to lift them from A to B bolstered acute misgivings about flying. Billowing with tongues of flame, one such death-trap carried The Beatles and a retinue that included The Ronettes and Phil Spector over the Rockies to Seattle. Haunting George perhaps were the ghosts of Buddy Holly and Jim Reeves. As The Beatles continued to fly in the face of superstition, he fretted in royal plural that, "We've done so much flying without really any incidents that the more we do, the more we worry. If we can go by road, we do."[149]

The Beatles usually hurtled through the British countryside by train or in their Austin Princess, customised with headrests, radio, record player and extra seat. New driver Alf Bicknell had loaded the necessary tools to tackle problems from snowdrifts to overcharging alternators, but he had no remedy for George's Gretsch tumbling from an unsecured boot into the path of a lorry. Rather than bawl out Alf, George withdrew into a resigned silence. Later, he drifted back into the small-talk that always sprang up when the late-night radio station went off the air, disagreeing with Paul over the aesthetics of pylons. Even when too fatigued for deeper dialogue, they preferred not to fall asleep upright with the road roaring in their ears.

In concert, they heard the relentless screaming no more than a mariner hears the sea. As far as guesswork and eye contact would allow, they adhered to recorded arrangements, but, sighed George, "It was impossible to know which song they screamed for most."[150] Before stage monitors and mega-watt public-address systems, Ringo beat his drums without electronic assistance, while the guitarists' three 60-watt Vox amplifiers were less a sound than a presence. Virtually gulping the microphone, The Beatles' singing would strain against the horrendous barrage of noise. Even in Britain, hysterical fans were now subjected to arbitrary manhandling by a cordon of bouncers so exultantly brutal that Lennon reprimanded them from the footlights.

McCartney dealt with the bulk of the patter, which was becoming predictable to the syllable, although sometimes he'd appeal vainly for discontinuance of the rain of votive offerings cascading onto the stage. Because George had mentioned in *The Daily Mirror* that he was partial to them, jelly-babies would shower The Beatles in Britain. As different from these sweets as hailstones are to snow, their harder equivalents would hit them overseas. Through the medium of *Melody Maker*, George begged "a favour for us. Write down that we've had enough jelly-babies now. Thank the fans very much, but we'd like them to stop throwing them."[129] Almost as commonplace were toilet rolls inscribed with messages of undying love, but nothing that thudded onto the boards surprised them any more – cake, tubes of lipstick, combs, binoculars, even a hateful five-inch nail.

Up there, they endured the mixed blessings of their vulnerability by jesting amongst themselves. For devilment, they'd mouth songs soundlessly or slam deliberate dischords. For the wrong reasons, concerts could still be a laugh. "We must have been hell to work with," George would smile in another decade. "We'd always be messing about and joking, especially John."[151]

Who could keep a straight face in the madness? Socialites, civic dignitaries with their hoity-toity children and everyone who was anyone were failing over themselves to be presented to four common-as-muck Liverpudlians. At a famous-names-in-a-good-cause gala held in The Beatles' honour after their first show at the Hollywood Bowl, you could pass a dozen showbusiness legends on a single staircase. Cassius Clay and Ringo would spar playfully. Zsa Zsa Gabor would have her picture taken with George, who concluded, "Meeting everybody we thought worth knowing and finding out they weren't worth meeting, and having more hit records than everybody else and having done it bigger than everybody else – it was like reaching the top of a wall and then looking over and seeing that there's so much more on the other side."[152]

Soon to disappear was the jubilant youth who, clad only in a bath towel, waved at worshipping masses from a hotel balcony in Sydney. What had been the point of travelling so far and seeing nothing but what he could remember of, say, a stolen afternoon driving a borrowed MG sports car in the Dandenong Mountains or a bowling alley somewhere in Quebec, re-opened for his private use at midnight? He'd seen only glimpses of the places where his blinkered life with The Beatles had taken him. When asked what such-and-such a city had been like, he was damned if he could even find it on a map.

8 The Member Of The British Empire

George's prosperity granted Harold and Louise a dotage rich in material comforts. Indeed, nearly all Beatle parents were suddenly able to retire early. It was like winning the Pools. From Mackett's Lane, the Harrisons uprooted themselves to an isolated bungalow in three acres by a golf course in Appleton, where Merseyside bleeds into Cheshire. If short on neighbours, there were plenty of letters to answer, although by this time 1964's daily vanload had subsided to a steady couple of hundred a week. Mr and Mrs Harrison made the most of their second-hand celebrity, travelling as far as Wiltshire to open fêtes, judge beauty contests and, once, attend a fan's wedding. Most who wrote received some sort of response, usually one of the printed newsletters or signed photographs collected every month from Liverpool's fan club headquarters by Louise. She especially devoted tireless hours to answering selected fan mail. Her warm, chatty style often encouraged surprise visits, such as that of an American family whose daughter's whingeing caused them to interrupt a European holiday by flying from Paris to Manchester to be taxied to Appleton. Louise and Harold always made fans welcome. If not the fans, who else was responsible for their present ease?

Once, The Beatles' relations could slip quietly backstage after a show to exchange a few fleeting words in a bustling dressing room. Now the child you'd known all your life was influencing the minds of millions. He was no longer able to mooch down to the newsagent's without raising a riot, and seconds after finishing the last number his group's dressing room would be as deserted as the *Marie Celeste*. These days, you couldn't enter or leave a Beatles concert yourself without nicotine-stained fingers jotting down everything you said. It would be in the newspapers the next day, and The Beatles might or might not be annoyed.

Out in force when the group's 1965 tour of Britain reached the Liverpool Empire, waiting journalists were well rewarded when George's parents arrived with Pattie Boyd in tow. She was staying at Appleton until Tuesday – and George would be too! Did it mean he'd soon be making an honest woman of her? The world knew they'd been on holiday together, and some editors were itching to break the more distressing news that the shameless hussy had been living with him in his posh new house for months.

Indifferent to success rather than celebrating it, George had been seeking – as he'd articulate later – to "try to stop the waves, quieten them down, to make myself a calm little pool".[24] Rather than joining John, Ringo and Mr Epstein in their Weybridge stockbroker's estate, he'd chosen instead a place called Kinfauns, an exclusive property in wooded Claremont Park in Esher, a few miles nearer the metropolis. Surrounded by high walls, it was not as exposed to fans' attentions as his Knightsbridge flat, but George was, nevertheless, the first Beatle to equip himself with electronically operated gates. It was aggravating enough that the fans picked the roses he was cultivating along the inner driveway, but the last straw had come when he'd been startled awake one night when his arm dangled from the bed to touch one of two wretched girls hidden beneath the mattress. As they'd already stolen items of clothing as souvenirs, instead of fishing autograph books from handbags the pair wisely took to their heels as their idol switched on the light and yelled. Fright had become rage when he returned to bed after a pointless chase. Recovered from her own shock, Pattie indicated the window, left open for the Persian cat.

Little inside Kinfauns revealed its owner's profession, apart from the guitars and the juke box. With its pine furnishing, garden pond and home help, it might have been the bungalow of a young marketing executive so admired by his office superiors that he could get away with the Beatle fringe that would render slightly less able men ineligible for promotion.

Very much the junior partner in The Beatles, George's songwriting explorations thus far were of less value than the power he gave to Lennon and McCartney's patterns of chords and rhymes. Formidable even before the Parlophone contract, John and Paul's headstart had been a hard yardstick for Jagger and Richards, Ray Davies and other British beat composers. Nevertheless, artists were now courting Davies for numbers he felt were unsuitable for his Kinks, and, likewise, Jagger and Richards for Stones leftovers. As they'd found their feet as composers, the albums and demo tapes of The Yardbirds, The Who and even Unit 4 + 2 were searched for potential hits. No would-be Gershwin in a beat group would be able to equal the sales of Lennon and McCartney's chart-toppers for Billy J, Cilla and Peter And Gordon, but the 150 recorded versions of Ray Davies' compositions certainly put George's solitary 'Don't Bother Me' and its forgotten cover by Gregory Phillips in the shade.

Neither of the two albums that had passed since *With The Beatles* contained additions to the Harrison portfolio. He was under no commercial discipline to compose. "When I first started at it," he confessed, "I used to forget to keep going and to finish things off. It's like washing your teeth. If you've never washed your teeth before, it takes a bit of time to get into the habit."[153] If he lost heart, it didn't matter, as Paul and John's endlessly inventive and swelling stockpile could fulfil the group's contractual load many times over already.

All the same, as he'd struggled to teach himself guitar, so he strove to ensure that his one or two lead vocals per album would be songs of his own from now on. As much a part of his touring luggage as his cine camera was a transistorised reel-to-reel tape machine, a forerunner of the cassette recorder, on which he would note flashes of inspiration. In hotel-suite seclusion, he'd "play or sing phrases for perhaps an hour. Then I play it all back and may get three or four usable phrases or runs from it."[153] From these doodles, a song might grow, but sometimes he'd tinker into the night on a guitar that might as well have been a coal shovel. By 1966, however, he was able to work at home on less portable but more sophisticated equipment, "so what seemed on one machine to be a waste of time sounded possible when mixed and recorded and perhaps dubbed".[154]

Melodies came easiest. Lyrics were almost always "the hardest part for me. When the thing is finished, I'm usually happy with some parts of it and unhappy with others, so then I show it to John and Paul, whose opinion I respect."[154] He'd clear his throat and start chugging chords, take a deep breath and launch into the first line. When the song died, he'd blink at his feet before glancing up with an enquiring eyebrow. Sometimes he'd realise it was no good as soon as he opened his mouth. At other demonstrations, he couldn't comprehend his two listeners' amused indifference: "The hang-up of my playing my songs to John and Paul always used to hold me back, because I knew how it would sound finished and I had to try to convince them in one play. For that reason, there are a lot of numbers of mine that I decided not to do anything about. It was a shyness, a withdrawal, and I always used to take the easy way out."[153]

Lennon lent the most sympathetic ears when George presented two possibilities for inclusion on the soundtrack to the next film, *Help!*. A week prior to the recording dates in February 1965 (and, incidentally, the day before Ringo wed Maureen), John and George spent half the night polishing up 'I Need You' and, with a country-and-western tinge, 'You Like Me Too Much'. Much of George's adolescent awe of John would never fade. Although he could never hope to penetrate John and Paul's caste-within-a-caste, he loved occasions like these, when he had big John's solicitude. Utterances unamusing to anyone else would have them howling with hilarity on the carpet and waking baby Julian Lennon. Back to work, they'd cudgel an unshaven objectivity on 'You Like Me Too Much' as milk floats braved the dawn cold. "Well, it was 4.30 in the morning when we got to bed," enthused George, "and we had to be up at 6.30. What a fantastic time!"[155]

Much as George appreciated his help, John began to resent his tacit obligation: "He came to me because he couldn't go to Paul... I thought, 'Oh, no. Don't tell me I have to work on George's stuff. It's enough doing my own and Paul's."[156]

McCartney was the only Beatle still residing in London, but geographical inconvenience wasn't the reason why George "couldn't go to Paul". Partly it was his very familiarity with Paul since school that had provoked in George an attitude like that of a youngest child viewing a middle sibling as an insurmountable barrier to prolonged intimacy with an admired eldest brother. Since Stuart's departure, Paul had had no rival for John's attention, and such was their artistic alliance that The Beatles might have been as successful with any competent drummer and second guitarist. To John, anyway, George would be "like a bloody kid, hanging around all the time. It took me years to start considering him as an equal."[156]

To fans, George was as much the public face of The Beatles as John, and matters had gone far enough for any fears of him going the way of Pete Best to vanish. Although he was no match for John as a verbal intimidator or Paul as a diplomat, the concept of a Beatles without him or Ringo was now unthinkable. Nevertheless, the chemistry of the four interlocking personalities apart, he was expendable. In 1966, George could still be made to do as he was told.

In the studio, Norman Smith witnessed how Lennon and, especially, McCartney treated the other two as mere tools for their masterworks, "because George would have done two or three takes that seemed perfectly all right but Paul wouldn't like it and he'd start quoting American records, telling George to play it like it was such and such a song, like this Otis Redding riff for 'Drive My Car'. We'd try again, and then Paul would take over and do it himself on the left-handed guitar he always brought with him. Later I found out that George had been hating Paul's guts for this but didn't let it show. It says a lot for George that he took so much stick from Paul."

On 'Another Girl' from *Help!*, Paul on celluloid crossed what outsiders had understood as the group's demarcation line. As well as singing the cocky verses about "all the girls, and I've met quite a few", Paul hogged the lead-guitar role, eyeing its neck as if stupefied by his own dexterity. In the middle distance, George fretted staccato chords on the offbeat. Before this sequence had thundered from world cinema screens, none would have supposed that George hadn't played the main riffs and solos on other tracks, too. The promotional clips for television still paid lip-service to John on rhythm, Paul on bass, George on lead and Ringo on drums, even though the latest single, 'Ticket To Ride', had Paul on both bass and lead.

The single's B-side, 'Yes It Is', and 'I Need You', taped at the same session, were more taxing for George, as they kept his feet as well as hands and voice occupied. Mistaken in a *Music And Musicians* critique for a harmonica were the tearful guitar legatos achieved by George on both songs with a volume pedal. The precursor of the wah-wah effect, this device had been first employed by veteran session player Big Jim Sullivan in the previous autumn on Dave Berry's heartbreak ballad 'The Crying Game' and its follow-up, 'One Heart Between Two'.

Another absorption of a rival's idea was the dentist's-drill feedback that had introduced the previous Beatles 45, 'I Feel Fine'. This echoed its in-concert – although unrecorded – use by The Yardbirds and The Kinks. Rendering the circle unbroken, The Kinks would approximate the start of 'I Feel Fine' on a 1965 flip-side which also happened to bear the standardised title 'I Need You'.

Their camouflage nets sparkling with dawn dew, Centurion tanks guarded The Beatles as they mimed George's 'I Need You' for the film cameras on Salisbury Plain scrubland. Only a mild exaggeration of the protective bubble surrounding the group in real life, this scene was to be Harrison's big moment in *Help!*. Nothing of the magnitude of the shirt sketch had been written in for him, but if nothing else 'I Need You', for all its simplistic libretto and suspensions *à la* 'One Heart Between Two', was more immediately attractive than some of Paul and John's offerings on the *Help!* LP. While issued as a foreign single, its presence was felt by proxy in the Australasian charts, for which it was covered by the ubiquitous Ray Columbus And The Invaders.

No such synchronisation was applied to 'You Like Me Too Much', which was placed on the non-soundtrack side of *Help!*. Lyrically more substantial than 'I Need You', it might have described one of the tiffs that punctuated the otherwise happy domesticity at Kinfauns. Until it was resolved over the telephone, an argument with Pattie just before the outward flight had jaded the Australian tour for George, who was observed by Adelaide promoter Kevin Ritchie "wandering around the hotel feeling desperately homesick".[68] George felt her silence most when the other three rang home every night. Back in Esher, it would wound Pattie to give up her two dalmatians because they bothered the cat. Nevertheless, love rode roughshod over such differences, and most assumed that George – following fellow northerners John and Ringo – had settled down and that marriage was the next step.

The jealous character assassinations and physical threats that had fanfared Pattie's public entry into the Beatle "family" had abated by now. George's female fans still envied her but could now stomach Pattie's wasp waist, her lisping confidence, her finger on the pulse of fashion. She'd never be accorded a fan club of her own, like John's Cynthia, or be subject of a novelty record, like The Chicklettes' 'Treat Him Tender, Maureen'. Like Jane Asher, she wasn't a Liverpool "steady" from before 'Love Me Do' but an intruder daring to combine care of a Beatle with a separate career and income. In as late as 1968, she'd be consulted as "top model-girl Pattie Boyd"[157] by girls' annuals about clothes and make-up. Perhaps her advice on these was sound, for tolerance gave way to acceptance and, as George Harrison's girlfriend, she'd be commissioned to write a regular "Letter From London" for *16*, a US magazine that never probed deeper than her favourite colour, what food she served when the Lennons visited and whether she thought Ringo's smile was gorgeous. Pattie's report on her and George's evening cutting a rug with Mick Jagger in a London discotheque was also detailed by Mick's then-girlfriend, Chrissie Shrimpton, in *Mod*, *16*'s sister journal.

Their social circle extended beyond The Beatles and even pop, but, as Pattie discovered, "All wives and girlfriends were made to feel that we shouldn't leave the 'family' at all. We mainly went out with each other. It was just the eight of us and the people involved with The Beatles' company. We were cocooned."[44] Crucial to this insularity was the personal unity of the four principals. Never did it occur to The Beatles not to eat together in studio canteens. "We were good friends," said George, "though we were caged animals for most of the time."[158] Although they'd been within earshot of each other during every working day since 1962, blood ties counted for less than Beatlehood, then. No one, not even The Rolling Stones, could appreciate how the four's common ordeals and jubilations bound them, they supposed, for always. In qualification, George would add, "It's wrong to say we're inseparable. When we're on holiday, for instance, we may head for different places. But even then it could be two of us going together."[126]

Disguises, decoy tactics, false names and secret destinations were as essential as spare underwear when a Beatle and his missus decided to go on holiday. Without these precautions, today's deserted beach would become tomorrow's media circus. Curtains in hotel bedrooms would be drawn to reveal a sea of faces and camera lenses between the main entrance and the silver strand where palms nodded. Holed up in one such ruined paradise, Pattie and Cynthia had to be smuggled to the airport in a laundry basket.

Another vacation was cut short when the "quiet Beatle" and the "sexy Beatle" (as the local newspaper dubbed them) were run to ground and besieged in the Royal Hawaiian Hotel on Waikiki oceanfront. Pursuing an exclusive, one brazen disc jockey nosed through the babbling crowds in limousine, wig and affected Scouse accent in an attempt to breach hotel security by impersonating Paul McCartney. Finally, the Royal Hawaiian's advertising director put up the Beatle couples in his Oahu beach house, but three short hours of serenity there ended with a fresh onslaught of fans and reporters. Fleeing to Tahiti, George and John were delighted to wander the quayside streets of Papeete virtually unnoticed, possibly because the place was in the last throes of its monsoon.

Despite the interruptions, Pattie would recall "so many laughs".[142] The idiosyncratic humour that had sustained George and the others before she knew them was still potent. On the Madrid stop of the 1965 European tour, they pulled swimming trunks over their heads to greet ballet dancer Rudolf Nureyev, another hotel guest, who met fire with fire by deadpanning the subsequent platitudes. Such diversions were to George "always the best bit about being in a band, rather than like Elvis, who, being one, suffered things on his own".[158]

They might have been offhand with Nureyev, but The Beatles were speechless at first when brought to Presley in his Beverly Hills mansion late one evening in August 1965. A prelude to this had been an after-hours jam session with a group led by his ex-bass player Bill Black when both acts were in a Key West hotel a year earlier. There'd also been an exchange of presents when The Beatles dropped by at the Hollywood office of Presley's manager, Colonel

Tom Parker. Because of some now-forgotten quarrel that day, George was in a foul mood when he arrived with the others for the audience with the King. This, however, was put on hold when Elvis received them like deified Caesar had the Gallic peasants. It was Elvis who broke the silence, wondering whether The Beatles intended to stare at him all night. He'd met Herman's Hermits a few weeks before. They'd been shy, too.

Then followed an obligatory blow with Presley on bass, McCartney on piano and the rest (bar Ringo) on guitars. Three hours later, the visitors left, one clutching a signed boxed set of their host's albums. In the flesh, Elvis had been gracious enough. "We know Elvis is great," George said while bemoaning his artistic decline. "Basically he's got such a great bluesy voice." Fancifully, he went on, "It would be great if The Beatles and Elvis could get together for an album, it really would."[27] When Presley returned to the stage in the late 1960s, the group telegramed their felicitations, but in an astounding and ramblingly respectful letter to President Nixon in the early 1970s Elvis asked to be enrolled as a Federal Agent in order to combat "that hippie element" of which he then considered The Beatles to be a part.

Beneath it all, George would always believe that Elvis was on the same wavelength. According to Presley's stepbrother, David Stanley, in spite of mixed feelings about The Beatles *per se*, Presley thought, "George Harrison was all right. Harrison was a seeker of truth, just as Elvis was, and that gave them a special bond."[159] Oblivious to the idol's reactionary leanings, George would, in 1972, insinuate his way backstage to pay respects after an Elvis show in New York. The epitome of all that Nixon and, evidently, Presley loathed, "I had my uniform – the worn-out denim jacket and jeans – and I had a big beard and long hair down to my waist. He was immaculate. He seemed to be about eight feet tall and his tan was perfect. I felt like this grubby little slug and Elvis looked like Lord Siva."[160]

Lord Siva is a Hindu demigod. The journey to a George Harrison almost unrecognisable from the yeah-yeah-yeah moptop had started a few months before that first meeting with Elvis in 1966. The turning point had been an occasion when George and Pattie had, as usual, paired up with the Lennons. A mischievous dentist with whom George was friendly – "a middle class swinger",[155] reckoned John – concluded an otherwise pleasant evening around his house by slipping into his guests' coffee a mickey finn of LSD (Lysergic Acid Diethylamide), an hallucinogenic drug manufactured from *ergot* disease derivatives and known in the Middle Ages as St Anthony's Fire. Learning that they'd been spiked, the four left hurriedly in George's Mini. In the Ad-Lib an hour later, the mental distortions of the drug became all too hysterically apparent as they crossed from reality into a wild dream. His psyche boggling with paranormal sensations and surreal perceptions, George at the steering wheel was guided by street lamps flickering like never before as he inched back to a Kinfauns that was "like a submarine", gasped Lennon. "We were only going about ten miles an hour but it seemed like a thousand."[156]

LSD had been "turning on" factions within London's in crowd for about a year before it was outlawed for recreational purposes in 1966. The Moody Blues and The Small Faces knew it well. So did The Pretty Things, if the worst was thought of song titles like 'Trippin'' and 'LSD'. Its use had become so widespread that Dave Dee insisted to *Melody Maker* that, as far as the clean-minded lads in his group were concerned, LSD still stood for pounds, shillings and pence.

With the same exonerative intent, George eventually admitted to taking it unknowingly, while claiming, "I'd never heard of it then."[161] There is, however, speculation that Brian Epstein had indulged and that some of his charges had quizzed him about it prior to John and George's visit to the dentist. Brian could only elucidate in broad terms – it was a stimulating experience, but its effects varied from person to person, from trip to trip. Pattie had been in a nonsensical frenzy while coming down at Kinfauns. Cynthia surfaced from a quagmire of horror. For her husband, it was the start of a fantastic voyage that would carry him to untold heights of creativity.

George compared it to a mystic purging akin to an extreme religious reverie: "Up until LSD, I never realised that there was anything beyond this state of consciousness, but all the pressure was such that, like the man [Dylan] said, 'There must be some way out of here.' I think, for me, it was definitely LSD. The first time I took it, it just blew everything away. I had such an overwhelming feeling of well-being, that there was a God and I could see Him in every blade of grass. It was like gaining hundreds of years' experience in twelve hours."[162] On one hand was a George of whom he'd hitherto been unaware. On the other, the new profundities were already known – it was just that LSD "happened to be the key that opened the door to reveal them. From the moment I had that, I wanted to have it all the time."[3]

Full of their chemically induced glimpses of the eternal, he and John conducted themselves with smug superiority before Ringo, Paul and others yet uninitiated. However, in California, in the month they met Presley, Neil Aspinall and Ringo also "turned on" when George and John underwent a second trip. Joining them at the rented nerve-centre of this particular US tour were members of The Byrds. As The Beatles' dabbling in drugs was not yet public knowledge, Aspinall was instructed to usher another guest – a *Daily Mirror* reporter – from the premises.

The Mirror's principal source of pop news was through an agreement with *Melody Maker*, who, if they knew about LSD, likewise kept mum. Nonetheless, its interviewers couldn't help but perceive the change in George. Although his replies to questions were unfailingly to the point, any witticisms were oddly sour and would provoke but a puffy smile where there used to be a chuckle. After a facetious prediction that George, barely 22, would "probably end up being a bald recluse monk",[163] a scribe presumed that it was just a phase of growing up that would pass.

Whatever was left to enjoy about the screaming ecstasy, the luxury, the imprisoned larks in hotel-suite torpor – all seemed shallow and pointless now. In an as-yet unfocused spiritual quest, George took with him for idle hours on tour challenging literature co-related to his new mentality, Aldous Huxley being one favoured author. However, during bouts of self-loathing in this bandroom or on that chartered flight, it would occur to him that he'd scarcely peeked at any book during the entire tour and that the highlight of the day wasn't the concert any more but the building up and winding down.

Gourmet dishes with specious names – trepang soup, veal

Hawaii, *furst puckler* – pampered stomachs yearning for the greasy comfort of fish and chips eaten with the fingers. Wherever they were these days, local narcotics dealers were generally able to contrive a network from the outside to sell their goods to the group who'd puffed joints and giggled through the shooting of *Help!*. Varying strengths of marijuana had been imbibed as carelessly as alcohol since Dylan popped by in 1964. In a higher league (in every sense) with LSD, Harrison "started getting into thinking, actually saw what was happening. Before that, we didn't have time to think. We were just going from one gig to another and into the [recording] studio and TV studios and concerts."[164]

More than any in the entourage, George begrudged Beatlemania. Even before LSD worked its questionable magic, "I was fed up. I couldn't take any more but resigned myself to suffering it for another year."[165] To irregular fellow travellers, his hostility emerged almost overnight, giving vitality to a surliness towards both fans and media. He'd sign autographs with bad grace or refuse altogether. Worse still, a V-sign directed at a lucky photographer anticipated the loutish affectations of punk by over a decade. Revelling in his wickedness when the shot appeared in an American newspaper, Harrison ordered the tracking down of the negative – not so that it could be destroyed but so that it could be enlarged and displayed on the bathroom door at Kinfauns and on the front of a 1965 Christmas card. He seemed oblivious to the consequences of behaviour that would have been tantamount to professional suicide back in 1963. Speaking like some withered pedagogue from the Liverpool Institute, he was "by far the most difficult to deal with" to Tony Barrow, "and the most dangerous, because he was liable to say all the wrong things to the press and damage the clean image of The Beatles".[15] With no axe to grind, fledgling journalist Philip Norman was admitted to one backstage sanctum in late 1965, where he found the group "perfectly friendly and pleasant – all but George Harrison. He was rather withdrawn, but the others just talked away."[166]

Others mistook George's frequent brown studies for sullenness, but during this final tour of Britain those in the know might have attributed them to his longing for the sanctuary of Kinfauns and

Pattie. Just before Christmas, not so much a proposition as a discussion – involving Brian, too – led the couple to tie the knot as quietly as they were allowed at Epsom Registry Office on 21 January 1966. "I got married because I'd changed," George explained at the unavoidable press conference the next day. "Marriage didn't bring this about; I'd already changed." He didn't say how or why. That would come when Paul McCartney, one of the two best men, spilled the beans a few months later.

Winking at the camera in the wedding portrait, Paul proclaimed tacitly that he at least was still "available". Now and then, polls to ascertain who was the most popular Beatle were conducted in teenage magazines. Invariably, the results were arranged in ratio not to marital status but to each member's degree of commitment to performing and public relations: Paul first, George last. Ignorant of the imminent nuptials, one 1965 fan letter ran, "I'd like to love all four Beatles, but John's married, Paul is going out with someone and my friend loves Ringo. That leaves you. So I love you." Low vote counts and back-handed compliments were almost a cause for rejoicing for George, in that they might deflect some of the world's intrusive adoration from him.

The ambition to be unrecognised in a restaurant, unphotographed stepping from a lift and unchased out on the street now seemed more far fetched than getting rich and famous had been back in Liverpool. On rare moments, he got away with it because, in the flesh and minus his on-stage trappings, he looked like someone who looked like George Harrison. On a Los Angeles film set, years of unbroken press visibility later, he disguised himself successfully as a studio janitor for a joke by simply donning overalls and sweeping the floor. Ringo couldn't have managed it.

Beatlemania had not merely robbed him of privacy but had also stunted him artistically. As he cranked out the same 30 minutes' worth of stale, unheard music night after artless night, he weighed up the cash benefits of being a Beatle against his self-picture as a musician. While autumn leaves fell on the group's moptop period, the sound systems at some venues would be loud and clear enough for them to pull themselves together, but mostly they were taking numbers too fast;

transitions from choruses to middle eights were cluttered and lead-guitar breaks wantonly slap-dash. Once, George had taken the trouble to tune both his own and John's guitars. Now, he couldn't care less about the wavering bars of bum notes and blown riffs.

Box-office receipts remained astronomical, but by 1966 there was a perceptible falling-off in attendances, which were sometimes as low as half capacity. Although they'd pruned down their concert schedule ("doing a bit of a Presley",[155] said George) to mitigate over-exposure, they were becoming as common a forthcoming attraction in the States and Britain as they'd been on Merseyside in 1962. Like London buses, if you missed a show, there'd be another along soon, if you waited.

The momentum had slackened, but the screams hadn't. When Paul sang 'Yesterday' from the *Help!* album solo, the racket from the onlookers dropped slightly. Only his own strumming on acoustic guitar accompanied him, for no one saw any purpose in taking on the road a string quartet like the one that had been hired for the recording. Money was no object, but any subtleties crammed into the Beatle's short spot were lost on audiences who'd bought tickets for a tribal gathering rather than a musical recital.

'Yesterday' is an extreme example, but tracks from their newest LP, *Rubber Soul*, were also difficult to reproduce with the conventional beat group line-up, although some sections could be approached by using Paul or John's skills on the Vox Continental electric organ that now travelled with the guitars and drums. One that couldn't, however, was the sitar played by George on 'Norwegian Wood', John's smoke-screening of an extra-marital affair.

The sitar is a nine-stringed Indian instrument with moveable frets and vibrating under-strings. George had stumbled upon one among props strewn about the set of *Help!*. Messing about, he treated it as if it were some fancy guitar. As such, its wiry jangle was imposed on 'Norwegian Wood' as one of many funny noises to be heard nowadays on the records of The Beatles and other so-called beat groups. Some months before *Rubber Soul*, both The Kinks and The Yardbirds had invested respective singles with an Indian feel. The Kinks' 'See My Friends', from 1965, conveyed in pop terms a suggestion of somewhere in India without their lead guitarist, Dave

Davies, thrumming a hastily procured sitar. Centred on beat group instrumentation, The Who's Pete Townshend estimated it to be "the first reasonable use of the drone – far, far better than anything The Beatles did and far, far earlier".[167] Ray Davies' art-school friend Barry Fantoni would recall being "with The Beatles the evening that they sat around listening to ['See My Friends'] on a gramophone, saying, 'You know, this guitar thing sounds like a sitar. We must get one of those.' Everything Ray did they copied."[167] A seated sitarist had also been present on a Yardbirds session, but the group preferred the more exotic twang of Jeff Beck, the guitarist who'd replaced Eric Clapton. A deeper breath of the Orient would be exhaled by The Rolling Stones, with Brian Jones' masterful sitar obligato appearing on their third UK Number One, 'Paint It Black'.

With a seal of approval from The Beatles and Stones, the sitar, with its bulging gourd and quarter-tones, became as essential an accessory for certain harbingers of pop's fleeting classical period as a 'Yes It Is' volume pedal. Both Donovan and Dave Mason (from Steve Winwood's half-formed new group, Traffic) acquired a sitar after an exploratory hour or so on George's newly imported instrument, while Roy Wood of The Move – another up-and-coming Midlands act – invented the "banjar", which combined properties of sitar and banjo.

Beyond gimmicks, Eastern musical theories had long been a trace element in modern jazz and folk, becoming more pronounced in the mid 1960s via the work of British acoustic guitarist John Renbourn, John Mayer's Indo-Jazz Fusions and the "trance jazz" of guitarist Gabor Szabo, as implied in titles like 'Search For Nirvana', 'Krishna', 'Raga Doll' and 'Ravi'. The last was a salaam to Ravi Shankar, a sitarist who, in 1965, recorded an album which his record company released as *Portrait Of Genius* during his seventh tour of the USA.

Better known than Shankar at this time was Subbulakshmi, an Indian diva seen frequently on Western stages. However, it was Ravi who brought about the most far-reaching popularisation of Indian music, when, as he put it, "there was a sitar explosion all of a sudden. I become superstar [sic]."[168]

A rather solitary boyhood spent in Banares, holiest of Indian cities, was interrupted in 1930, when ten-year-old Ravi accompanied his family from this muddy arm of the Ganges to Paris, where his eldest brother, Uday, was leader of a Hindu dance company. Able to afford to continue Ravi's private education, his parents were pleased with their sensitive youngest son's balance of bookish excellence and the artistic leaning that, from infancy, had led him to "play with my brother's musical instruments, lose myself in thrilling stories or act out plays in front of the mirror".[169]

No coaxing from Uday was necessary to persuade Ravi to participate in the troupe's productions. As music was his strongest suit, on leaving school Ravi became a *shishya* – a cross between a student and a disciple – of Dr Baba Allaudin Khan, who was then the most venerable figure in Indian music and recipient of a *Padma Bhushan* (roughly the same as a knighthood). Under the *khansahib's* guidance, Shankar submitted to years of intensive tutelage, disciplining himself to practise his chosen instrument for up to twelve hours a day.

At 21, Ravi himself was a master musician and his teacher/guru's son-in-law. Through his cosmopolitan upbringing, he was well placed to return to the West to promote the performing arts of India. By 1965, his name might have been unknown to the European man on the street, but support from a substantial intellectual minority bound Ravi – now also a Padma Bhushan – to a fulfilling career of concerts, composing commissions and conducting university master-classes. After collaborating with the likes of the London Symphony Orchestra and jazz flautist Paul Horn, he was accused inevitably by purists of emasculating his art, but to most of those who'd heard of him he was respected (or at least patronised) as one of his country's leading musical ambassadors.

Shankar came into the life of George Harrison with deceptive casualness. *Portrait Of Genius* and other Shankar records had been recommended to George by Dave Crosby of The Byrds. As with LSD, one individual's reaction to Indian classical music can be markedly different to that of another. Some find it hypnotic while others are bored stiff. Its closest European equivalent is in the droning themes of the Scottish *pibroch*, for they, too, don't "go anywhere". Instead, single moods – many pertinent to particular times of day – are investigated undynamically and at length. More complex than the pibroch's pentatonic variations, the sitar's ragas never contain less than a scale of five notes, all reliant on varying ascending and descending patterns, but always in a set sequence.

George's discrimination about foreign music would always be acute. Once, in a Tunisian hotel, he'd manufactured earplugs from bread rolls to block out the wail of native musicians in an adjacent room. Indian music was, however, immediately transfixing. The subordination of the artist's ego to the music coincided with the spiritual decisions that LSD had thrust upon him and complemented his reading. As mere entertainment, too, the chasm between Ravi Shankar and rock 'n' roll was not unbreachable. The Duane Eddy instrumentals that had captivated the teenage Quarry Man were also based on folk tunes and repeated ostinati. Years later, under Harrison's supervision, Eddy would add a bridge to a Shankar melody, making the composing credit "R Shankar/D Eddy", surely the strangest – but perhaps not so strange – to be printed on a record label.

By chance, the Beatle and the middle-aged Indian virtuoso were first introduced at a mutual friend's London home in the late spring of 1966. Ravi was only vaguely aware of his new acquaintance's stature, but Harrison "seemed so different from the usual musicians I meet in the pop field. He was so simple and charming and kind, and he showed his desire to learn something."[170] Since *Help!*, George had been rending the air in the main living room at Kinfauns, trying to extend past the few notes that had lacquered 'Norwegian Wood'. Ravi put him right about the folly of teaching yourself sitar. Ideally, it was best to be accepted as a shishya under a master like himself. You'd never get anywhere without proper instruction.

Thus began a lifelong amity akin to that of a liberal-minded teacher and a waywardly earnest pupil. In his realisation that "through the musical you reach the spiritual",[171] George was beyond the first rung, but, insisted Ravi, he must visit India, not only for more intensive training but also to get the rhythm of life there under his skin and thereby slip more easily into his new musical tongue. As his Beatle duties beckoned until autumn, however, George would have to get by with Ravi's tape-recorded correspondence course.

His humility in Shankar's presence was not the same as his biting back on the exasperation of being told what to do in The Beatles. Nevertheless, the new LP, *like Help!*, contained two Harrison items. Furthermore, in a plethora of *Rubber Soul* covers, among the three that made the UK Top 20 – just – was George's 'If I Needed Someone' by The Hollies.

Second to The Beatles, The Hollies had survived Mersey Beat's collapse as the most distinguished northern group. If they recorded your song as an A-side, you could be in the money. During a vexing discussion in October 1965 about a follow-up to their last hit, their producer, Ron Richards, mentioned an acetate that he'd been given by George Martin of a Harrison number that The Beatles then regarded as unsuitable for *Rubber Soul*. The Mancunians' ill-advised 'If I Needed Someone' was issued on this understanding. However, the inclusion of this cascading *moderato* on the new album wasn't the only excuse for The Hollies' comparative failure. Disliked as a group by Lennon, they were further hindered by the composer's adverse and public criticism that they sounded like session players earning their tea break. While his frankness was commendable, this latest manifestation of George's bitterness hurt only himself through the resulting diminishment of his royalties. Not only that, but the fuss he made elicited praise for The Hollies in *Music Echo*'s argument that they'd salvaged one of the poorer selections on *Rubber Soul*, and one that had borrowed from the twelve-string figure in The Byrds' 'Bells Of Rhymney'.

In common with Bill Wyman, The Who's John Entwistle and other groups' second-string composers, less time was now spent on George's efforts than on those of the main fount of original material. His material was further undermined by being used as an avenue for loose experimentation. George's other *Rubber Soul* opus, the wordy 'Think For Yourself', hadn't a prayer from the start. It wasn't a terrific number, true enough, but its rehearsals had doubled as a session for ad-libbed banter for The Beatles' 1965 fan club flexi-disc. With the tape rolling throughout, the self-conscious mucking around was no help whatsoever during the few hours set aside for the song. Sound compression lent organ-like sustain to George's guitar, but 'Think For

Yourself' lived less in its oblique melody than in the searing trump of Paul's bass, which had been fed through a fuzzbox, then a newish device intended to make a guitar sound like a saxophone but which assumed a character of its own after its blackboard-scratching hoarseness had electroplated the Stones' million-selling '(Can't Get No) Satisfaction' that summer.

Outside the studio, George reaped some satisfaction by taking a firmer initiative in other matters. John was his principal ally in the campaign to stop touring. Bawling purgative obscenities in the teeth of the screams, his paranoia sharpened by drugs, Lennon had become, to Dezo Hoffman, "like a dog with rabies – you never knew when he would jump and bite".[96] He smiled and waved like he was supposed to, but it was anathema to John when he and the others, soberly attired, were driven through cheering masses to Buckingham Palace for investiture as Members of the British Empire on 26 October 1965.

Camouflaging vote-catching as acknowledgement of The Beatles' contribution to the export drive, the Labour government had awarded these decorations, seemingly taking to heart a March headline in *Melody Maker* that ran, "Honour The Beatles!" No honours list, before or since, has ever been as controversial. "I didn't think you got that sort of thing," exclaimed George, "just for playing rock 'n' roll music."[172] Neither did the disgusted senior civil servants and retired admirals who returned their medals to her Majesty. *The Daily Express* printed a suggestion that, if the group had to be honoured, they should subject themselves to a "decent" short-back-and-sides haircut before setting off for the palace. How many in this trickle of protesters would have held their peace, had they known how unwilling the chief Beatle had been to go through with accepting his MBE?

Nearly two years later, The Beatles would affix "MBE" after their signatures to lend respectability to a petition calling for the legalisation of marijuana. The only other use any of them made of the decoration was Lennon's renouncement of it as a political gesture in 1969.

If John was touchy about "one of the biggest jokes in the history of these islands,"[173] Paul was delighted with his MBE. He was still a cheerful stage performer, keenly rolling up for a behind-the-curtains jam session with The Paramounts, a support group when The Beatles last played the Hammersmith Odeon. Nonetheless, he was no glutton for punishment. Even the road crew had had enough. "I always look forward to tours," said Neil Aspinall, "but when I'm on them, they're a drag."[10] An unlikely scheme for a 1966 trip to Russia that might have re-awakened enthusiasm for the stage was thwarted by an immovable world tour in which The Beatles would visit many territories for the first – and only – time.

Along the way, too, was a Hamburg engagement, their first since that reluctant residency at the Star-Club in 1962. However, their old bunkroom above the Top Ten was vacated for a reunion party before they were driven in state to the city's Ernst Merck Halle in a fleet of glittering Mercedes with *polizei* outriders.

No home venues could yet compare with overseas sports stadia and exposition centres that could rake in the most loot with the least effort by accommodating thousands in one go. This policy also eliminated many (but not all) squalid hours in claustrophobic bandrooms and hotel bedrooms. Mr Epstein had cut down press conferences, too. No more were these interminable sessions of wry shallowness. "Epstein always tried to waffle on at us about saying nothing about Vietnam," John would later confide to a journalist's cassette recorder, "so there came a time when George and I said, 'Listen, when they ask next time, we're going to say we don't like the war and we think they should get out.'"[156]

Brian cringed as zany merriment about mini-skirts and debates about when Paul would marry Jane Asher swung in seconds to two-line debates about inflammable issues. He'd recently had to calm friction at Capitol over a record sleeve that showed The Beatles as white-smocked butchers gleefully going about their grisly business. It hadn't mattered that the limbs and heads of dolls were among the bloody wares when this picture appeared in Britain to advertise 'Paperback Writer', the quartet's new single. Such a scene was comic opera in a country that housed Madame Tussaud's Chamber of Horrors and Screaming Lord Sutch. However, with boy soldiers already blown to bits in Indochina, "the butcher sleeve" was hastily withdrawn from circulation in sensitive America. "All this means," said Paul, "is that we're being a bit more careful about the sort of picture we do." John, the instant pundit, had no time for tact. "Anyway, it's as valid as Vietnam,"[174] he quipped unfunnily as George, his young sidekick, sniggered beside him.

Backstage at the Ernst Merck Halle, someone passed around snaps from 1961 of George and John between quiff and *pilzenkopf*. The bunkroom party had become impractical, but a few old pals had been allowed past the stage-door security. Escorted by Gibson Kemp, Astrid was there to renew acquaintance with the "lovely child" who, big eared and woebegone, had once been exiled from Germany for staying up past his bedtime.

At the same station from which she and Stuart had waved him out of sight, The Beatles had steamed back to Hamburg in style on a train usually reserved for royalty. It was during this journey that they first listened to a test pressing of the successor to *Rubber Soul*. The running order was already decided – it would start with George's new song, 'Taxman', and end with the first song recorded during the sessions, 'Tomorrow Never Knows'. Still being bandied about was an album title. *Full Moon* and *Fatman And Bobby* were two possibilities put forward as The Beatles shot through the forests of Lower Saxony.

In the last weeks of The Beatles' most public journey, the privacy of the recording studio – where mistakes could be retracted – was a more agreeable location to contemplate than the ordeal directly ahead. Particularly dire in concert were the vocal harmonies and tricky guitar riffs on newer numbers such as 'If I Needed Someone', 'Nowhere Man' and 'Paperback Writer'. There'd lingered enough pride and concern for an eleventh-hour rehearsal in a hotel suite prior to the first show in Munich, but there wouldn't be any more.

Apart from a rendition of 'Long Tall Sally' smashed out literally at the last minute, the same songs in the same order were rattled off at every stop, despite John's assurance that, "Before we go, we get a list of hits in any particular country, so we try to include them."[174] On a similar premise, George should have warranted a greater share of the main spotlight in Japan, where he wasn't everyone's least favourite Beatle. His gruff taciturnity was translated as professionalism in a land where The Ventures, New Zealand's Peter

Posa and other old-fashioned or elsewhere obscure guitar instrumentalists were still popular.

Three routine performances in Tokyo preceded two more on Luzon, the largest island in the Philippines, as The Beatles traversed an Earth that was rapidly becoming less and less eye-stretching. A luxury hotel in Belgium was just like one in Tennessee – the Coca-Cola tasted exactly the same. Everywhere was the same. If it's Monday, it must be Manila.

Manila, however, would always be remembered. Unaware that they were required to pay a courtesy call on the family and friends of the Philippines' autocratic President Ferdinand Marcos, the group slept through the arrival and ireful departure of presidential lackeys who had been commanded to bring them to his palace. George recalled his bafflement when, over a late breakfast, somebody "turned on the television and there it was, this big palace with lines of people and this guy saying, 'Well, they're not here yet,' and we watched ourselves not arrive at the party."[175]

On the following day, the expected crowd of fans at Manila International Airport were puzzled that no security measures had been laid on. Close enough to be touched, their agitated idols lugged their baggage up static escalators a few steps ahead of an angry mob of adults who stopped just short of open assault when their prey threaded slowly and in a cold sweat through a customs area resounding with jack-in-office unpleasantness and every fibre of red tape that Philippino bureaucracy could gather. "They were waiting for us to retaliate," said George, "so that they could finish us off. I was terrified. These 30 funny-looking fellows with guns had obviously arranged to give us the worst time possible."[175] Out on the tarmac, The Beatles party scuttled for the aeroplane and escape, which was delayed when Mal Evans and Tony Barrow were summoned back to the terminal to be interrogated over some freshly unearthed paperwork.

This jubilant oppression had started the previous evening, when incessant interference contrived by station engineers had wiped out every word of Brian Epstein's televised apology for his Beatles' unknowing insult to the hallowed person of Ferdinand Marcos. The First Family's honour was further assuaged by vast tax deductions of concert receipts still in the grasp of accountants at the football stadium where the group had performed on the previous night. No one was ready to jeopardise his prospects, and possibly his freedom, by not co-operating with the President's harassment of these long-haired foreigners.

Sent on their way by boos and catcalls from the tyrant's creatures, never had George's arguments against continued touring made more sense, but even the Manila incident would be a trifle when compared to what awaited them on the final leg. Prophetic, then, was his flippant "we're going to have a couple of weeks to recuperate before we go and get beaten up by the Americans".[175]

A psychological rather than physical battering started when off-the-cuff comments about religion made by Lennon were reprinted out of context in *Datebook*, a US magazine in the same vein as *16* and *Mod*. Weightier journals picked up the story that Lennon had "boasted" that The Beatles were more popular than Jesus Christ. If anything, John in the original *London Evening Standard* article had seemed to be bemoaning the increasing godlessness of the times, but more sensational was the American interpretation of "blasphemy".

The most vocal supporters of this latter opinion were "redneck" whites from the Deep South, who laced their right-wing militancy with pious fear, not so much of "God" as of "the Lord". It was here, the heart of the Bible Belt, that thousands of Beatle records were ceremonially pulverised in a tree-grinding machine to the running commentary of a local radio presenter. Other mass protests were just as demonstrative. The group's new LP – finally titled *Revolver* – was removed from 22 southern radio playlists and hellfire sermons preached of the divine wrath that would fall on any communicants who attended forthcoming Beatles shows – although the casting-out of the pestilence by one Memphis station was as much in vengeance for Epstein's dim view of its exposure of a hush-hush – and subsequently cancelled – Beatles session at Sun Studios, where Elvis Presley's recording career had begun.

As the ripples of backlash and moral opprobrium spread, so did real fear of an assassination attempt on Lennon and perhaps the other three, too. Brian offered his personal fortune if only the US tour could be scrubbed. For most promoters, however, the possible in-concert slaughter of the artists was insufficient reason for cancellation. Instead, at a press conference hours before opening night in Chicago, John was trotted out to make a statement that most took as an apology.

Engagements in the north passed without incident, including a lacklustre return to Shea Stadium, where George stood stock still throughout with a face like a Merseyside winter. In the Southern states, counterbalancing the anti-Beatles ferment, "I Love John" lapel badges outsold all associated merchandise. Nevertheless, a firework that exploded on stage in Memphis gave all four a horrified start, following a telephoned death threat that afternoon. Recalling an evening in 1964 when "a kid in Brisbane threw a tin on stage and it freaked him right out", an eye-witness theorised that "George has an incredible fear of being killed—" who hasn't, sport? "—which possibly accounts for the shell he withdrew into".[68]

Even Paul was sufficiently unnerved to vomit with fear as The Beatles headed towards the last showdown at San Francisco's Candlestick Park on 29 August 1966, where they downed tools as a working band. No better or worse than any other concert they'd given on the tour, after two hours spent hanging around in a locker room backstage they ran through this final half-hour any old how, with Ringo forgetting the words to 'I Wanna Be Your Man' and George fluffing his guitar runs as Paul tried to make a show of it. Towards the end, the four posed for an on-stage photograph for a keepsake. "Nice working with you, Ringo," cracked John shortly before the four piled into the nostalgic finale, 'Long Tall Sally', which had been in and out of the set even before George had first tagged along with The Quarry Men.

George's would be the most quoted remark from the flight back to England. "Well, that's it," was his succinct and strangely dejected elegy. "I'm not a Beatle any more."

9 The Shishya

Pattie's modelling fees had escalated through her association with George, but by 1967 she all but gave up the catwalks, as she too identified more and more with Indian culture. While her husband grappled with his sitar, she furrowed her brow over the bowed dilruba. With her sister Jenny, she attended Indian dancing lessons garbed in some of the items that George had bought for her during a two-night stopover in New Delhi immediately after the scramble from Manila.

It must have been gratifying for George when John and Paul decided to follow his lead and join him there likewise to purchase native instruments, along with saris for Cynthia and Jane. Ringo also checked in at the BOAC hotel where a Sikh sitarist dropped by to give George a tutorial. In the interim before the last hurrah in America, Ringo and John sat through a recital at Kinfauns by Ravi Shankar and his tabla player, Alla Rakha. "They liked it," noticed George, "but they weren't as into it as I was."[32]

George's hard listening to Shankar came to the fore in 'Love You To' from *Revolver*. A backing track of himself on sitar and a certain Anil Bhaghat hired to tap the tablas set the mood with a slow *alap* ("introduction"), but rather than sustain this serenity, as Ravi would, they snapped into feverish tempo. Only the English lyrics and, down in the mix, the electric bass and fuzz guitar gave 'Love You To' any semblance of Western pop.

The common chord reasserted itself in other Harrison compositions, such as 'I Want To Tell You' and – with John's "few one-liners to help the song along, because that's what he asked for"[80]

– 'Taxman', the rhythmic bounce of which belied a libretto dark with dry fuming at the ravages of the Inland Revenue. George's tally of three songs on *Revolver* was the highest so far on any album. Delivered from the treadmill of the road, his consequent flowering as a songwriter contributed to The Beatles' eventual self-destruction, but on *Revolver* they were at their most effective as a team. Never again would each member work so fully according to his capacity. John may have bitten his lip when assisting George with 'Taxman', but he'd avow that George's presence had helped when he and Paul were putting together 'Eleanor Rigby', the 'Yesterday' of *Revolver*.

With the LP assured a gold disc before its conception, let alone its release, its creators could well afford the means to turn their every whim into audible reality. "In the past, we've thought that the recording people knew what they were talking about," generalised Harrison. "We believed them when they said we couldn't do this or we couldn't do that. Now we know we can, and it's opening up a wide new field for us."[174] Of all of The Beatles, George had become the most knowledgeable console buff, appreciating both Abbey Road's advancing technology and the reasoning behind seeming inadequacies, like the antiquated Altec playback speakers that "don't flatter the sound".[59]

Even on mediocre equipment, every groove on *Revolver* revealed that, in 1966, the group's three composers had been firing on all cylinders. Its programming squeezed the children's song for Ringo ('Yellow Submarine') and Paul's easy-listening 'Here, There And Everywhere' between the Harrison raga and 'She Said She Said', John's unsettling account of that second LSD trip. On paper, these juxtapositions seem inappropriate, but the liberal non-conformity within The Beatles' fundamental structure strengthened the clarity and balance of their rounded unity and gave them an unprecedented stylistic range. As yet, there were no cracks in the image.

From the verbose but confused 'I Want To Tell You' to the eerie omega that was 'Tomorrow Never Knows' there exuded evidence of half-understood Eastern mysticism and the "psychedelic" inner landscapes of LSD. With an electronically warped vocal, quotes from *The Tibetan Book Of The Dead*, a monotonous percussion *rataplan* and an aural junk-sculpture of tape-loops, 'Tomorrow Never Knows' defied adequate categorisation and stood little chance of superseding 'Yesterday' as the most recorded song of all time. "The Stones and The Who visibly sat up and were interested," said Paul. "We also played it to Cilla, who just laughed."[176]

"Everyone, from Brisbane to Bootle, hates that daft song Lennon sang at the end of *Revolver*,"[177] declared a horrified *Mirabelle*, whose schoolgirl subscribers were mostly opposed or insensible to shifts in parameters of musical consciousness as the watershed year of 1967 loomed. Most groups that carried any weight would be operating ambiguously with experimental fancies on albums and penetrating the singles charts with their most trite or mainstream cuts, as did The Beatles with 'Yellow Submarine' and The Yardbirds with the upbeat 'Over Under Sideways Down', from an LP that was praised by one critic as a "mini-*Revolver*".

The only *Revolver* cover to be a hit was Cliff Bennett's improvement on 'Got To Get You Into My Life', which was ideal for his soul-rock crossover, although his "let-me-hear-you-say-yeah" stage routines with The Rebel Rousers would be rendered *passé* in an era when even the bucolic Troggs would be singing about "the bamboo butterflies of yer mind". Others also either consolidated their abilities without developing them or else adjusted themselves to psychedelia without really getting the point.

Tellingly, The Beatles had been the only Mersey Beat group to play in 1966's *NME* pollwinners' concert, where they'd waved into the baying blackness and vanished from the British stage forever. That spring, too, Rory Storm had headlined at the Cavern hours before Authority closed the place. A telegram from The Beatles would be read aloud when the club was re-opened, with a facelift and proper sanitation, but the place would never be the same. That it hosted arty "events" and poetry readings now best exemplified the passing of the old order, while a few brave anachronisms like The Hideaways and Rory still did 'Money' and 'Some Other Guy' for the few who still remembered.

In an outer darkness of European dance halls, luckier brethren like The Swinging Blue Jeans and The Merseybeats staved off a drift back to whatever local venues were still standing. Although brought to their knees, such outfits maintained flashback dignity, even grandeur. By abandoning the Mersey Beat ferry at the first sign of a leak, other musicians had also clung onto a career in music. In the United States, ex-Undertaker Jackie Lomax had immersed himself in his new group, The Lomax Alliance, despite advice from Brian Epstein that he'd fare better as a soloist. Another ill-fated fresh start was made by former Searcher Chris Curtis in an unlikely role as lead singer with Roundabout, a band formed by his flatmate Jon Lord, ex-organist with The Flowerpot Men. Meanwhile, dying on its feet was The Pete Best Combo, whose figurehead was privately relieved to return to Straightsville from the treachery of showbusiness.

A more hard-nosed drummer/leader had taken a leaf from The Beatles' book by retiring The Dave Clark Five to the studio. Unlike the Liverpudlians, however, he didn't expand his musical horizons. Instead, the Five notched up two fast hits by the same songwriters who'd provided crooner Engelbert Humperdinck with the syrupy 'Release Me', which in February 1967 would keep The Beatles' double-A-sided *meisterwerk* 'Penny Lane'/'Strawberry Fields Forever' from Number One in Britain. Schmaltz, the antithesis of psychedelia, was very much alive.

It had been a waterfront covered on *Revolver*, but on 'Here, There And Everywhere' the melody had been potent enough for jazz flautist Charles Lloyd – resplendent in beads and kaftan – to extemporise it amid strobe lights in New York's Fillmore East auditorium. Other famous "underground" venues, such as London's Middle Earth and Amsterdam's Paradiso, also used lightshows among audio-visual aids meant to simulate psychedelic experience as bands – not groups – played on and on and on for hippies in a cross-legged trance and whirling dancers with eyes like catherine wheels.

A big draw on this circuit were Cream, a trio whose appeal hinged not so much on looks but virtuosity demonstrated in lengthy improvisations of selections from their debut album. The loudest cheers – not screams – were for the over-amplified flash of Eric Clapton, who had been the subject of graffiti claiming "Clapton is God" while with John Mayall's Bluesbreakers. The legend had first been scrawled in the Marquee, and one night in that celebrated Soho club's cramped bandroom, after watching The Lovin' Spoonful, Clapton nodded at George Harrison and John Lennon, who afterwards would only recall a crew-cut Yardbird low on the bill at a Beatles Christmas extravaganza. Eric was left behind when they drove off to a party at The Lovin' Spoonful's hotel. He would learn one day of a pang of remorse when George "remembered thinking, 'We should have invited that guy, because I'm sure we know him from somewhere'... He just seemed, like, lonely."[32]

Both *Fresh Cream* and *A Collection Of Beatles Oldies* were released in December 1966, but the former climbed higher in the LP charts than the latter, by which time George was no longer racking his brains to remember Clapton, who – with American newcomer Jimi Hendrix – was now the most worshipped of pop guitarists, while to *The Sunday Times* George was only "a passable guitarist (say among the best thousand in the country)".[90] Of no less import was an opinion given by a stranger during a concert by The Jimi Hendrix Experience who sidled up to Paul McCartney and, pointing towards Hendrix, muttered, "You ought to get a bloke like that in your band, mate."

Such implied slights on George as an instrumentalist were unfair, as The Beatles' stylistic determination left little space for any extensive extrapolations of the kind popularised by Hendrix and Cream – although, judging by unissued recordings of the four jamming to tedious effect at Abbey Road, this was probably just as well. Nonetheless, George must have warmed to Clapton, who in *Disc* magazine praised the lead-guitar playing on *Revolver*. This accolade was deserved, if only for the technical accomplishment demonstrated by George's idea of superimposing two backwards – and tuneful – guitar overdubs on top of one another to create the apt "yawning" solo and obligato on Lennon's 'I'm Only Sleeping'. This attractive enveloping sound was developed further by other guitarists, notably Hendrix on the title track of his LP *Are You Experienced?*.

It was pleasing to be liked and copied like this, but George wasn't to be as revered a guitar hero in the later 1960s as he'd been in the beat boom. Although he'd always see himself as a lesser guitarist, George was in a different rather than lower league to Clapton and Hendrix, whose fretboard fireworks were then heard night after night on stage.

For long after the armoured car had whisked George from Candlestick Park, his guitar had been played only sporadically. This wasn't because it symbolised all that he'd recently and gladly relinquished; it was simply that his concentration on learning sitar was comparable to that which lacerated adolescent fingers on his first guitar. As once he'd laboured over *Play In A Day*, so, from Indian script, he practised raga exercises hour upon hour.

Via the account that all four Beatles had at the hip Indica bookshop off Piccadilly, the Harrisons were digesting all manner of mystical and philosophical literature to do with the East. George found Paramhansa Yogananda's *Autobiography Of A Yogi* a particularly "far-out"[174] book, proving this to whoever was interested by opening it at random and reading aloud. One journalist was treated to the passage, "'I care not if all things are wrested from me by self-created destiny, but I'll demand of thee my own to God the slender taper of my love for thee'".[171]

Two weeks after Candlestick Park, George and Pattie had flown to Bombay, where they registered as "Mr and Mrs Sam Wells" in a lakeside hotel outside the city. Within a day, the alias was uncovered by local newspapers, who were informed by a rueful George that he was in India to study sitar under their own Ravi Shankar in Banares, 600 miles beyond their circulation area, over jungly valleys, jagged peaks and sun-scorched desert.

For much of this holiday-cum-cultural visit, the Harrisons were let alone. In loose robes and pyjama trousers, George was one of two hundred *shishya* studying under the master. Shankar delegated this day-to-day tuition to Shambu Das, his *protégé*, just as Shankar himself had been the Khansahib's. Looking in to check on his progress, Ravi found George to be "an enthusiastic and ambitious student because he realises that the sitar itself is an evolvement from Indian culture. It might take a lifetime of learning, but, if he progresses in the same way that he has been doing, his understanding will lead to a medium of greatness on the sitar."[178]

George would liken Indian music to "an inner feeling"[153] too intense for satisfactory verbal description: "It's like saying, 'It's soul, man!' You know? All this spade music that's going – it's just the first thing people get into, the soul kick, but when you really get into soul, then…it's God."[179]

To his *shishya*, Ravi Shankar was more than a music teacher; he was also a spiritual guide[180] and something of a father figure. He may not have cut much ice with a younger George in the fleshpots of Hamburg, but in holy Banares the refugee from Beatlemania was open to religious enlightenment. Nothing like an Institute RE teacher prattling on about Yahweh, Shankar's guru Tat Baba was straight out of a Victorian penny-dreadful: "They tell you about these yogis who just don't speak, and you ask them what it's all about and they give you a flower. Well, he's the only one I've seen like that. When we saw him, he sat for about two and a half hours and then just said, like, about four or five words, which [translated] is like a poem but so to the point."[171]

The Harrisons' Cook's tour of Hinduism took in religious festivals in temples towering over narrow alleyways and on the banks of the Ganges, the steps to which were worn as smooth as the the Blarney Stone by pious feet descending into the grimy but purifying bathing *ghat*s, each one dedicated to a different deity.

Rama and Krishna are Hindus' most popular manifestations of God, and they may regard Buddha, Moses and Jesus as others. The words to many of the sitar pieces prescribed for George's training were eulogies in Sanskrit to one or other of these avatars, as was 'Bhajan In Rupak Tal', which tells of a poet chanting Krishna's name every second in order to earn His blessings.

In Banares' Nepalese Temple, Pattie and George saw friezes depicting the 81 sins and their corresponding penances. Thus was illustrated the aspect of the Hindu law of karma, whereby all evil proceeds from antecedent evil and penalties must be suffered in each succeeding incarnation through which the soul must pass. "The living thing that goes on," explained George, "always has been, always will be. I am not really George but I happen to be in this body."[24] If you're godly, you might be reborn in a station better suited to self-realisation and eventual removal from the series of continuous transmigrations.

To keep themselves conscious of this aspiration and pre-empt future punishment, an army of ascetics throughout India devise ingenious modes of self-torture and – like LSD often does – humiliating destruction of the ego. Flocking to Banares, Allahabad and other points along the blessed Ganges are human pin-cushions, flagellants, loinclothed fakirs plastered head to toe with sacred cow dung and others whose fanaticism transcends not only self-inflicted pain and discomfort but also the heat, flies and filth that more common Hindus have to endure.

All good things must come to an end, and the Harrisons returned to Britain's unusually rainy autumn, George with a rakish Imperial beard and both with doctrines and perceptions of deeper maturity than before. Yogananda's was more than merely a far-out book. "Everybody has to burn out his karma," George was saying now, "and escape reincarnation and all that."[152] Values in the West were declining, he reckoned, because "discipline is something we don't like, but in a different way I've found out it's very important, because the only way [Hindu] musicians are great is because they've been disciplined by their guru or teacher and they've surrendered to the person they want to be".[179] The Beatles' wealth was "enough to show us that this thing wasn't material. We all get so hung up with material things, yet what they can give you is only there for a little bit and then it's gone."[181] Unlike John, George would never be rash enough to speak of giving it all away.

George and Pattie had both embraced vegetarianism, and George had even gone through a phase of eating with his hands, Indian style. As well as the expected nut roasts and meatless curries, the Kinfauns kitchen also served dishes that, while common in Banares, were exotic in Esher. On the menu might be pakoras (pasties stuffed with cauliflower and peas, deep fried in ghee), samosas or the consecrated prasadam. For dessert, you could tunnel into a rasamlai (a milk sweet) and wash this down with lassi (yoghurt diluted with rose water).

However scrumptious these meals were, the fact that a Beatle was tucking into them was splendid news for stockists of Indian goods in the West. In provincial Britain, where the 1950s hadn't ended until 1966, a Beatle fan might waste hours outside a record shop debating whether or not to spend three week's paper-round savings on Ustad Ali Akbar Khan's *Young Master Of The Sarod*, for which George had supplied sleeve notes. Youths whose short hair broke their hearts would board trains to London to buy joss-sticks. These would then fill sixth-form common rooms with tinted smoke and thereby lend credence to self-generated and false tales of a wild weekend among hippie friends in Swinging London, where nowadays a man wasn't asking to be beaten up by walking its streets with beads and bells around his neck, embroidered Indian slippers on his feet and an eyesore of tie-dyed kaftan and floral trousers. One hipper-than-thou Hampshire schoolboy, Stephen MacDonald, even came home with a sitar.

MacDonald was also the first at his grammar school to own the debut album by The Velvet Underground, an arty New York outfit in which Brian Epstein was "interested". Some of the sleazy perspectives on this record were underlined not by a bass guitar throb but by a noisy electronic drone that made a melodrama from what was merely implicit in Indian music.

Over in San Francisco, "raga rock" was an ingredient in the psychedelic brew being concocted by The Jefferson Airplane, The Grateful Dead and other acts in a city about to become as vital a pop Mecca as Liverpool had been. Like The Big Three's homage to the Cavern, hit records in 1967 by both Eric Burdon and Scott McKenzie paid tribute to San Francisco's new eminence. Each performed in June of that year at the Monterey International Pop Music Festival a few miles down the coast. There, The Jimi Hendrix Experience – at Paul McCartney's urging – was booked to make a spectacular American debut. Among many other highlights was an afternoon set by Ravi Shankar, which confirmed the larger public's acceptance of him and his instrument.

What had started as a gimmick on *Rubber Soul* now surfaced on vinyl as frequently as rocks in a stream. Dominated by sitar was Traffic's most famous song, 'Hole In My Shoe', also checkmated at a UK Number Two by the oily Engelbert. Record shops were also stocking an album of current hits by a certain "Lord Sitar", whose record company would not deny the erroneous supposition that it was George Harrison in disguise. Even if he hadn't originated Indian sounds in pop, George had definitely instigated what could be construed as a trend.

Ravi Shankar's association with The Beatles had done him a lot of good. Ticket sales for his concerts were guaranteed to pick up if there was a hint that George might be attending. As a recording artist in Britain, his destiny was then bound to the World Pacific label, who even tilted for a hit single with the Punjabi folk tune 'Song Of The Hills', from *Portrait Of Genius*. At first, Ravi took this unlooked-for attention in his stride, seizing the opportunity to publicise a new Indian music centre to be founded in Los Angeles, with George's assistance. A sizeable representation of Fleet Street lying in wait at Heathrow would disperse away happily after noting the amusing spectacle of George in flowing Indian garb greeting a disembarking Shankar wearing a Western business suit.

Although he owed his commercial bonanza to Harrison's patronage, Ravi admitted to disquiet when he and his Hindu musicians were placed on the same bill as loud rock bands with extreme stage antics. Especially appalling was Jimi Hendrix at Monterey: "I liked his music, but when he started being obscene with his guitar and burning it I felt very sad. We come from a different part of the world where we respect, almost worship the instruments."[182]

Hinduism is the most tolerant and gentle of faiths, advocating pacifism, rejection of materialism, kindness to animals and other qualities that had been absorbed by the blossoming hippie sub-culture with its "be-ins", "Flower-power" and, of course, its imported Indian exotica. Mantras were chanted *en masse* at San Francisco's Golden Gate Park, led on many occasions by visiting Indian yogi His Divine Grace AC Bhaktivedante Swami Prabhupada, who had topped the bill over The Grateful Dead at a "Mantra-Rock Dance" at the city's Avalon ballroom. The proceeds went towards the opening of the San Francisco Krishna Temple.

However, Shankar and Prabhupada were disappointed by the interrelated promiscuity and, worse, the currency of psychedelic drugs as an artificial means to greater awareness. "The aim of all Eastern religion is to get high," pontificated flower-power guru and disgraced Harvard psychologist Timothy Leary. "LSD is Western yoga." When Ravi had sat on the Monterey stage before beautiful people of like mind to Leary, his Beatle *shishya* and cohorts assembled at Lennon's house to join him in spirit: "We just took acid...and wondered what it would be like."[183]

That The Beatles were all users of LSD would soon become common knowledge after Paul, the last initiate, admitted as much to *Life* magazine – although some might have guessed already from 'Strawberry Fields Forever', which had issued from the radio with the spooky deliberation of a dream's slow motion. Garish psychedelic patterns had been painted all over the outer walls of Kinfauns and the bodywork of Lennon's Rolls, under the direction of four Dutch theatrical designers whose mediaeval fancy dress matched their work and tradename, The Fool. This amalgam also submitted a frontage that was turned down as too hackneyed for *Sgt Pepper's Lonely Hearts Club Band*, the LP that followed *Revolver*.

"I don't know how we met them," laughed Pattie. "They just appeared one day."[184] As part of The Beatles' perpetual small change of hangers-on, The Fool wormed their way into many of the group's private functions, including a party at Brian Epstein's country house, where Derek Taylor succumbed to George's request to try LSD. "Once you've had it," Harrison explained, "it was important that people you were close to took it too."[10] He and Pattie left Keith Richards' West Wittering lodge two hours before the famous drugs bust by the Sussex police in February 1967, their host believing to this day that he'd have been immune from arrest if George – a national treasure with an MBE – had stayed the night.

Sometimes seeming to be a bit gaga, George would talk openly about his psychedelic escapades, acknowledging no difference now between the straight press and underground journals like the fortnightly *International Times*. He'd mention the "magic eyes"[185] in the beads of his necklace or a grasshopper that only he could see jumping into a speaker cabinet.[171]

He'd also taken to quoting Bob Dylan lyrics, as if they were as unanswerable as proverbs. Illustrating what he meant by "karma" would be a couplet from 'Subterranean Homesick Blues'. With poker face and barbed-wire hair, Dylan had gazed from the sleeve of *Blonde On Blonde*, the odd album out among an otherwise all-Indian selection in George's suitcase for his expedition to Banares. Dylan's increasingly surreal symbolism had left its mark as far back as 'Think For Yourself', in which George had sung of "opaque minds" and "the good things that we have if we close our eyes".

By that time, no one was still booing Dylan for his use of an amplified Canadian backing group; in fact, very much the opposite. Off stage, he traded sillier answers for silly questions before he finally banned press interviews altogether, in self-defence, and stonewalled more earnest fans. Being so enigmatic was tiresome, and some cynics doubted that the motorcycle accident that ended this phase of his career in June 1966 had actually happened. He woke from a week's concussed oblivion with a broken neck, mild paralysis and amnesia. There wasn't a hope of any return to public life for at least a year.

During Dylan's enforced sabbatical, The Beatles acknowledged his influence on them – and, by inference, everyone else – by including his image in the photo montage of characters that festooned the fabled cover of *Sgt Pepper's Lonely Hearts Club Band*. Consisting mainly of each Beatle's all-time heroes, almost all of George's contributions were Eastern gurus and religious leaders. As John's choices of Hitler and Christ were vetoed by EMI, so was George's of Gandhi, although escaping the airbrush were Yogananda and Orientals even more unknown to the average Joe.

Just as erudite were those souvenirs of India with which George fairy-dusted passages of *Sgt Pepper*, among them tamboura and the swordmandel, a cross between a zither and an autoharp. From its mothballs came his electric guitar for instances such as the stinging solo on the title song. Otherwise, he remained as dispensably in the background of John and Paul's creations as Ringo. During the media blitz commemorating the 20th anniversary of the album's release, perhaps it was fortunate that George wasn't present to hear McCartney remark nonchalantly, "George turned up for his number and a couple of other sessions but not much else."[186]

It was true that George had absented himself once to attend a Ravi Shankar concert, but this could be excused as fieldwork for the orchestration of 'Within You Without You', his sole *Sgt Pepper* composition and, interestingly, the only one on which just one Beatle appeared. It was also the longest and most complicated piece on the album. Scored for an assortment of Indian instruments and superimposed violins and cellos, its three changes of time signature were unprecedented in a body of work that, since The Beatles' inception, had rarely deviated from straightforward 4/4.

Despite this gear shifting, 'Within You Without You' was as calmly devoid of surging climaxes as you'd expect from a piece based upon a raga exercise. However, it wasn't written on sitar at Kinfauns but on a harmonium in Klaus Voorman's Hampstead home following an after-dinner discussion of a metaphysical nature. More a psalm than a pop ditty, you could only dance to it if you were desperate, as George philosophised about walls of illusion, love, "the space between us all" and gaining the world but losing your soul. When replaying the LP, those as yet unacclimatised to pop as an egghead activity started to skip the ethereal 'Within You Without You' to begin side two with Paul's jaunty 'When I'm 64', dating from the Cavern days. Yet, however superficially boring it was, many stuck with George's opus, among them Steve Stills, leader of California's Buffalo Springfield, who said that he intended to have its entire libretto carved in stone for display in his garden.

After hearing 'Within You Without You', Juan Mascaro, a Sanskrit professor at Cambridge, was moved to write to George, expressing the hope that it would "move the souls of millions" and foretelling that "there is more to come, as you are only beginning on a great journey".[39] This aged academic enclosed a copy of *Lamps Of Fire*, an anthology of poems and maxims translated by himself, to aid religious self-education.

The Word made vinyl in the comfort of their own homes, many – especially in the States – listened to The Beatles' latest gramophone record in the dark, at the wrong speeds, backwards. Every inch of the cover and label was scrutinised for veiled but oracular messages, something that would turn listeners into more aware, more creative human beings truly at one with The Beatles. Nothing would be the same, not even the past. Thanks in part to *Sgt Pepper*, pop was upgraded from ephemera to holy writ. Although you'd have to look far for a Troggologist, one obsessed New Yorker advertised in an underground journal for a Dylan urine sample in order to prove a pet theory about his lyrics. By 1969, evidence traceable to *Sgt Pepper* supported a widespread rumour that Paul McCartney had been killed three years earlier and replaced by a *doppelgänger*.

Well before *Sgt Pepper*, however, others had also elevated the long-player to a product more than a pig in a poke, slopping with musical swill and a hit single. Inspirational to The Beatles were *Pet Sounds* by a Beach Boys estranged from the surf and the stunning pop-Dada hybrid – with snippets of Varèse, Stravinsky and Holst – that was Frank Zappa's Mothers Of Invention's *Freak Out*. Both groups had created a specific and recurring mood – a concept, if you like – that was more far reaching than simply stringing together a bunch of songs about cars (as The Beach Boys had done in 1963).

With McCartney and George Martin as prime movers, The Beatles had embarked on the next step, theoretically a continuous work with no spaces between tracks and teeming with interlocking themes, segues and leitmotifs. *Sgt Pepper* did indeed contain a reprise of the title number, plus various cross-fades and links, and yet only at its beginning and near the end were you reminded of what was supposed to be Sgt Pepper's show. Technically, it improved on *Revolver*, creating, said George Harrison, "new meanings on old equipment".[32] In this mediaeval period of recorded sound, the Abbey Road mixing desk would seem rather Heath Robinson by today's standards. "Well, we had an orchestra on a separate four-track machine in 'Day In The Life'," explained George. "We tried to sync them up [and] they kept going out of sync in playback, so we had to re-mix it."[32] For all its flaws, however, *Sgt Pepper* sounded stratospheric on 1967's shuddering monophonic Dansette machines.

It was almost the sound at any given moment that counted, rather than the individual pieces. Reduced to the acid test of just voice and piano, the raw material of *Sgt Pepper* couldn't hold a candle to the classic *Revolver*. With retrospective honesty, George would agree: "It was a milestone and a millstone in music history. There are some good songs on it, but it's not our best album." He preferred its two predecessors. "There's about half the songs I like and the other half I can't stand."[25]

He may have moderated this view if his 'Only A Northern Song' – which was about nothing in particular – hadn't been shelved at the last minute. Harrison songs in much lesser stages of completion included 'The Art Of Dying', which was another attempted summary of his newly acquired theological mores, although it intimated – albeit not obviously – that he'd also read relevant pages from the anonymous 15th-century tome *Ars Moriendi*. More topical was 'See Yourself', his reaction to Paul's free admission that he'd taken LSD. "And they asked the rest of us. We said yes, and there was a big outcry saying, 'You should have said no. It's your responsibility.' But it's not; it's the press' responsibility. So the song came from that. It's easier to tell a lie than tell the truth."[25] A further confidence to a gentleman of the very press was "That's how a lot of them work, you know. They just find... Well, rather than go into reality, they just cover over it."[25]

Perhaps The Beatles' least attractive trait was their habit of blurting out what their minds hadn't yet formulated in simple terms Like some Scouse Socrates, George was now going on about "these vibrations that you get through yoga, cosmic chants and things like that – I mean, it's such a buzz. It buzzes you right through the astral plane."[175] The music and underground papers in 1967 would be sodden with sentences just as groovy from George and similar victims of the same passion. One sweet flower from the lips of disc jockey and *International Times* columnist John Peel was, "There are sparrows and fountains and roses in my head. Sometimes I don't have enough time to think of loving you. That is very wrong."[187]

Before pseudo-mystical inanities like this were thought worth publishing, if the average guitarist in a beat group entreated the Almighty at all, it was as a sort of divine pimp with an amused tolerance of boozing and pill-popping, but with enough self-discipline to seldom indulge Himself. Piety had been considered a regrettable eccentricity in 1950s rockers like Jerry Lee Lewis and

Little Richard, who were prone to vigorous bouts of evangelism, while beneath contempt was married Pat Boone, who paraded his beliefs by balking at kissing the leading ladies in his films.

However, in tandem with its growth as a means of artistic expression, pop's contradictory merger with religion had reasserted itself. In as early as 1964, Cliff Richard had undertaken his first gospel tour, and a Salvation Army "beat group" called The Joystrings had used the devil's music to spread the word. Doing the reverse were The Small Faces, The Mastersingers and The Zombies, who in 1966 adapted the respective melodies of 'Ding Dong Merrily On High', the Te Deum and the Nunc Dimittis to secular purposes.

Orthodox pop is as devotional in its boy-girl way as sacred music, and, as George had discovered, the chasm between 'Don't Bother Me' and 'Within You Without You' was not unbreachable: "Singing to the Lord or an individual is, in a way, the same."[32] Although he'd been profoundly affected by Hinduism,[180] George's faith was evolving as a syncretic faith in which "the Lord has a million names". His studies had "brought me right back 'round to understanding Christ",[171] even if "my concept of spirituality isn't Cliff Richard and Billy Graham".[188] After "getting religion" in 1966, George's ideals would compound rather than alter. When the Kinfauns pond metamorphosed from clear tap-water to duckweed and wriggling animation, a visiting Alistair Taylor was drawn into a discussion that "veered off the subject of the pool... With George, everything leads to the cosmic meaning of life".[189] The cruel manner of an older Beatle's passing years later would hurt, but death itself "doesn't really matter. He's OK, and life goes on within you and without you."[190]

He wasn't always so beatific. "Cripples, Mal!" he bawled when The Pink Floyd were conducted in from the adjacent studio to see the masters at work on *Sgt Pepper*. Annoyance became contrition when their producer, Norman Smith, ambled in behind the young group. Although the protection of The Beatles' much-liked former engineer made them feel less like gatecrashers, after a few sheepish hellos the Floyd shuffled out. From this inauspicious beginning, however, after learning of their visitors' high standing in London's psychedelic clubs, George, Ringo and Paul returned the call early one evening when The Pink Floyd were recording their debut LP. "We all stood rooted to the spot," remembered Roger Waters, "excited by it all."[191]

Jaws dropped as well when George descended on Haight-Ashbury, the flower-power district of San Francisco, on a mid-week afternoon in August 1967. Here, more than anywhere else, *Sgt Pepper* was a code for life. "Beatle readings" were as much part of the pageant of its streets as mime troupes, palmists, dancers, painters, spiritual healers (who gave instruction on how to write to archangels), poets and vendors of journals such as *The Psychedelic Oracle*.

"Wow! If it's all like this, it's too much," George remarked politely as, flanked by Derek Taylor, Neil Aspinall and a hanger-on named Alex Mardas, he strolled self-consciously with Pattie and Jenny Boyd through "Hashbury" after parking the limousine a block away. Like a squire on a dutiful walkabout at a village fête, his easy smile did not rest on individuals but was diffused to the general populace. As his coming was unheralded, he was just another sightseer – "half like a tourist, half like a hippy"[161] – for a few yards, before someone cried out, "Hey, that's George Harrison!" As the beglamoured girl panted up to him with her tongue-tied laudation, other passers-by gathered around, "then more and more people arrived and it got bigger and bigger".[161]

A common touch was in order, so the most reticent Beatle borrowed a busker's guitar for an impromptu 'Baby You're A Rich Man', the B-side of the group's flower-power anthem 'All You Need Is Love', currently topping the Hot 100. Although he dried up with embarrassment, within minutes the community's edifice of cool shattered as even those who knew the dignity of labour hurried to Golden Gate Park's sloping greensward, where George had been followed by the buzzing crowd from the alleys. Most arrived too late, for, fearful of the growing commotion, he and his retinue had hastened back to the car with as much grace as they could muster after just over half an hour in the hippy capital.

Anxious to be off, George had extended an intimidated invitation to the president of the local Hell's Angels chapter for his boys to visit any time they were in London. Surely they'd never take him up on it in a million years. Despite their Nazi regalia, the dreaded motorcycle brotherhood then had a special rapport with the equally anti-establishment hippies. All this love and peace nonsense might be grasping the wrong end of the stick, but the stick still existed.

In his heart-shaped sunglasses, dry-cleaned denim jacket and psychedelic flares made to measure by The Fool, George had borne as much relation to the flower children he'd seen as dairy butter does to low-fat margarine. Cluttering the pavements in grubby floral tat, many seemed to be living out part of Timothy Leary's "turn on, tune in, drop out" slogan by begging from the very straights they mocked. "They are hypocrites," was George's gut reaction. "I don't mind anybody dropping out of anything, but it's the imposition on somebody else I don't like. I've just realised that it doesn't matter what you are, as long as you work. In fact, if you drop out, you put yourself further away from the goal of life than if you were to keep working."[160]

From London's den of illusion, he'd been the first Beatle to fly out to the Greek islands to investigate possibilities of setting up a private hippy commune there. This scheme had been mooted partly on the rebound from touring and partly in the euphoria of the Summer of Love. For a practical example of how a utopia could crumble, you only had to look at Hashbury, with its drug pedlars, teenage runaways and traffic snarl-ups as it was clogged with curiosity seekers and weekend ravers, who kept the freshly sprouted record shores, boutiques and restaurants in profit.

A look at the charts told you that the music industry had been at the forefront of this inevitable commercialisation of flower-power. When Richards and Jagger were acquitted of their drug convictions in July 1967, the Stones rush-released their double A-side 'Dandelion'/'We Love You', titles that reflected correctly a pixified musical scenario. Cashing in quick that same month with 'Let's Go To San Francisco' were The Flowerpot Men, who, garbed in chiffony robes, tossed dead chrysanthemums into the audience when appearing at London's Finsbury Park Astoria.

In the eyes of the world, the apogee of the Summer of Love was reached on 25 June, when The Beatles convened before the BBC's outside-broadcast cameras in Abbey Road's cavernous Studio One to perform 'All You Need Is Love' as Britain's contribution to *Our*

World, a satellite-linked transmission with a global viewing figure of 400 million. Even lead singer Lennon gnawed apprehensively at his chewing gum as the allotted time approached. On a high stool, George was more fretful as the amplifier that was to power his Stratocaster for the on-air solo buzzed into life. In the small orchestra that would augment the song, violinists tuned up and horn valves slid prelusively. At The Beatles' feet for the *omnes fortissimo* chorus was a turn-out of selected relations and fashionable friends, including Pattie, Gary Leeds, Mike McCartney and Eric Clapton, whose concert with Cream at Shaftsbury Avenue's Saville Theatre had been attended by all four Beatles. Both of the Harrisons had been impressed, and at a party at Epstein's afterwards it had struck Pattie that Eric's introspective on-stage image wasn't entirely contrived.

Now a periodic dinner guest at Kinfauns, Clapton had felt vague envy at George's apparent contentment with Pattie, "because I was certain I was never going to meet a woman quite that beautiful for myself".[43] In reciprocation, the presence of "God" Clapton a few feet away, rather than the unseen millions watching, drew an apologetic grin from George as he delivered a solo for 'All You Need Is Love' that he thought he'd fluffed but, played back, was safely adequate.

For Brian Epstein, George's uncertain hand in 'All You Need Is Love' encapsulated his role in The Beatles – nothing brilliant and in no danger of rocking the Lennon-McCartney ship of state. To paraphrase a disproved adage of Aunt Mimi's about her nephew's guitar, the sitar was all very well but, in Brian's estimation, George would never have made a living at it.

As Epstein had anticipated, the expiry date of his contract with the group in August 1967 meant a reduction of both his cut and his say in their affairs. There were also rumours of The Beatles bringing in a third party. Paul especially liked what he'd been told of Allen Klein, a cigar-chewing New York accountant – "like the archetypal villain in a film,"[166] according to Ray Davies – whose blunt stance in negotiation had done financial wonders for The Dave Clark Five, Donovan, The Kinks and, latterly, the Stones. Although no love was lost between them, Sir Joseph Lockwood said, "In fairness to Klein, I ended up doing deals that I have never regretted."[74]

One of many Goldwyn-esque homilies attributed to Klein was, "What is the point of Utopia if it don't make a profit?" Brian would never say anything like that, although Colonel Parker might. To Brian's mind, monetary killings were secondary to fair dealing and sound commodities. He'd made disturbing mistakes while learning his craft, but his painful commitment and often severely tested loyalty to his stable were assets more valuable than the ability to drive a hard and unrelenting bargain for Elvis to star in another awful movie.

On that score, The Beatles didn't want another *Help!*. While it was to be, as Lennon said, "a film vehicle of some sort to go with the new music",[192] they were adamant that the next one wouldn't portray them as Beatles. "No, we're not rushing into a film," said George. "We'll wait ten years, if we have to."[174] Two years after *Help!*, it looked as if they were going to do just that. While the Harrisons were in India, John had had a part in *How I Won The War*, a Dick Lester tragi-comedy. One up on the others, it was he who was mooted as main character in *Up Against It*, a rejected development by playwright Joe Orton of *Shades Of A Personality*, a script in which a single person has four separate personalities. Also thrust aside were *The Four Musketeers* and Tolkein's *Lord Of The Rings*, the hippy bible, with George as Gandalf. Another possibility particularly favoured by George – who'd been in cowboy gear for the *Rubber Soul* cover – was a screenplay derived from Richard Condon's western novel *A Talent For Loving*. Mel Brooks, then shooting *The Producers*, a black comedy appreciated only in retrospect, was considered as director.

Paul, meanwhile, came up with a plan to make something up as they went along. When in Haight-Ashbury, George had heard of The Merry Band Of Pranksters, an itinerant multi-media troupe whose press releases promised, advisedly, "a drugless psychedelic experience". They were also the ones who gave Beatle readings. Why not, said Paul, hire a coach and some film cameras and, like The Pranksters, just drive off somewhere – anywhere – and see what happens? Who needed a screenplay?

Group and manager also agreed to a full-length cartoon, *Yellow Submarine*, designed to be written off as a sop to United Artists, to whom a third Beatle film (in which they were required to physically star) was owed. Setting the wheels in motion for *Yellow Submarine* was Brian's last major service to The Beatles for a reason more absolute than a contractual termination. During his television chat-show appearances – frequent these days – his reports on the unseen Beatles' progress assured fans that he was as much the group's clear-headed mentor as he'd always been. To David Frost on ITV, he spoke more of the Saville Theatre in which he'd had a controlling interest since 1965.

The "Sundays at the Saville" pop presentations, which sometimes mitigated the poor takings for the drama and dance productions during the week, had been Brian's brainwave. When their turn came to top the bill there, it seemed entirely appropriate for Traffic to play amidst the cardboard ramparts left from the weekday set of a Shakespeare play. Other Sundays featured acts of such diversity as John Mayall's Bluesbreakers, The Four Tops and The Bee Gees.

Growing their hair and catching up with the latest psychedelic gear, The Bee Gees had arrived in London to be groomed for the big time by another Australian, Robert Stigwood, whose agency had merged with NEMS in January 1967. Also on his books were Cream, and it had been through this connection that George had "started meeting Eric and hanging out with him then at Brian Epstein's house".[32]

Brian had been the other best man at the Harrisons' wedding, and, although his feelings about George's musicianship were lukewarm, they were not indicative of any loss of affection for his "favourite son". Since LSD and India, George didn't ask as much about Beatle finances, but he and Brian – along with Eric Clapton and Pattie – had seen in the New Year together in 1967. Back at Kinfauns, after a later evening at Brian's, Pattie urged her husband to warn him of the dangers inherent in the over-prescribed tablets that he took compulsively to sleep, to stay awake, to calm his nerves and to lift his depressions. Pattie's concern was justified, because, so a coroner would conclude, Brian Epstein was killed by "incautious self-overdoses" on 27 August 1967.

One of the few outsiders present with the Epstein family at the interment in Liverpool was given a single white chrysanthemum by

George to throw in the grave. "Brian was one of us," was George's verbal valediction. "One of the boys, as you might say."[193] He'd have liked to have been. Instead, he was their safety net, a shoulder to cry on – faithful and reliable, so they thought. The Beatles had been far from the first to realise that Brian wasn't in the best of health. He'd been on standby for most of 1967, but still he'd waited, poised to serve his boys whenever they wanted him again.

The professional bond between The Beatles themselves had loosened since the abandonment of touring. Their solidarity over not playing themselves in the next film emphasised the separateness of their activities, now. George had his spiritual safari and John had his acting and Paul had written the soundtrack to the Hayley Mills movie *The Family Way*, while Ringo had been the titular head of his own building firm, before the credit squeeze forced its closure. On their records, even non-fans could differentiate between McCartney, Lennon and, nowadays, Harrison songs by musical and lyrical style, as well as through the simpler conjecture that the principal composer was also the lead singer. On the run around the world, Paul and John couldn't help but get together to work up hits from only a title or melodic phrase, but now John in Weybridge and Paul in London tended to present each other with songs in more advanced states of completion than before. The general polarisation was that Lennon's were the most way out, while the more prolific McCartney's sold more.

If not as inseparable as they once were, The Beatles still tended to keep pace with each other's caprices, being photographed at the same premieres, covering the same exhibitions and sampling the same stimulants. Following George, they were all sporting moustaches when *Sgt Pepper* was finished. Paul, Ringo and George also had to have "nothing boxes", mildly amusing but otherwise useless battery-operated what-d'-ye-call-its that this Alex Mardas chap – a high-born Greek, apparently – would knock up to keep in with John.

United in play, the four were also all determined self-improvers. Through Paul, the pioneering tonalities of Berio and Stockhausen were as likely to blast from their car stereos as Dylan or Shankar. It was George, however, who was to lead the others to transcendental meditation.

In San Francisco, George had surprised the hippies with his refusal of ingratiating tabs of LSD and tokes of marijuana as he strode past. Many of them had only "turned on" in the first place because they'd read that The Beatles had. As they were more than pop stars now, the group reacted to pressure from the world's youth to find "the truth", and, judging by the hollowed-eyed young derelicts that littered Hashbury and elsewhere, it wasn't LSD. "We're influencing a lot of people, so really it's up to us to influence them in the right way,"[178] admitted George. Although individually they either continued or resumed the habit, when The Beatles publicly repudiated the taking of illegal drugs, they never again made an issue of it.

George did not regret his experiences: "It showed me that LSD can help you to go from A to B, but when you get to B, you see C."[160] Notable junctures on his and Pattie's pilgrimage to C were a visit to San Francisco's Krishna Temple and a climb up a Cornish tor one night after digesting a book about cosmic communication. Several hours passed with no sign of any extra-terrestrials.

In February, a friend of Pattie's had persuaded her to attend a lecture at London's Caxton Hall on "Spiritual Regeneration". The novel-sounding doctrines advanced that evening were so imperatively appealing that Pattie became a convert, although the orator had stressed that his words were but a pale sketch onto which only the movement's founder, Maharishi Mahesh Yogi, could splash more vivid hues.

There remains bitter division about the Maharishi. Was he a complete charlatan or a well-meaning sage sucked into a vortex of circumstances that he was unable to resist? Definitely he was smarter than the average yogi. Born plain Mahesh Prasad Varma in 1918, he graduated from the University of Allahabad with a physics degree before spending the next 13 years studying Sanskrit and the scriptures under the renowned Guru Dev. Styling himself Maharishi ("great soul"), he travelled to London in 1959 to set up a branch of the International Meditation Society, which had garnered a British membership of some 10,000 by the time Pattie brought her intrigued spouse to a meeting. A gazer through the window of a passing bus might have discovered meditation on his own, but others needed guidance. Like a Charles Atlas course for the mind, the society promised increased productivity, less need for sleep, greater alertness and sharper distinction between the important and the trivial.

Deeper implications were inherent in the titles of some of its seminars, such as "Philosophy in Action" and the aforementioned "Spiritual Regeneration", and the overall aim – via short, daily meditation sessions – was to eradicate piecemeal all human vices and ego until a pure state of bliss was reached. Moreover, such washing of spiritual laundry was possible without forsaking material possessions (bar the society's membership fee) and, within reason, worldly pleasures. This seemed an excellent creed to a millionaire Beatle.

Practising what he preached, Varma stayed at the best hotels, commissioned the most up-market press campaigns and employed a full-time accountant. While he luxuriated in New York's Plaza before speaking at sold-out Madison Square Garden, handbills distributed by a one-man picket line outside railed against "capitalistic little devils within the holy man's robes". Cross-legged on a Louis XV chaise longue, His Holiness toyed with his silvery beard or a flower from the bouquets banking him while dealing with the North American media. "I deal in wisdom, not money," he replied in a gentle, high-pitched voice when some tried to bully him into talking finance. For all his disarming public attitudes – the tee-hee-hee chuckle, the mirth he invested into his expositions – there was no mistaking the steel underneath.

A few had been led to believe that a tutorial on 24 August at the Park Lane Hilton was to be his last before he disappeared back to his Indian fastness. Dragged along by the Harrisons, Paul, Jane and the Lennons stole into the hushed hotel functions room like children to Santa's grotto. He so lived up to George and Pattie's spiel that, directly afterwards, The Beatles buttonholed the Great Soul and wound up promising – as Pattie had already – to join him the next day at the Society's ten-day initiation course at a university faculty in the seaside resort of Bangor.

While packing, they telephoned others who might want to go.

Brian had made other arrangements for what chanced to be a bank-holiday weekend, but they could half-expect him later, although he wasn't sure he approved of this Maharishi. Also catching the mid-afternoon train from Euston to North Wales would be Jenny Boyd, Mick Jagger and Marianne Faithfull, all of whom had to shove through a crush of fans and journalists who had homed in on what one tabloid named "*The Mystical Special*". Although they'd secured first-class seats, it was an edgy, uncomfortable ride as the party, crammed eventually into the same compartment as the Maharishi, dared not risk a walk down the corridor.

For people who'd viewed the world from the Olympus of stardom since 1963, it was perhaps too much of an adventure. Unused now to actually paying for things with hard cash, they were at a loss the following night when handed the bill after a meal in a Bangor restaurant. George was the first to realise why the waiters kept hovering about the table, and it was he, too, who settled the matter with a roll of banknotes he happened to have about his person.

Neither this imposition nor the hard mattresses in their hostel accommodation on the late-Victorian campus could deflect the pop stars from their iron purpose. Yet, during the press conference that Varma's public relations agent had set up in the main hall, most journalists didn't appear to take The Beatles' preoccupation with meditation very seriously. It was worthwhile hanging around in Bangor, though, because the group still provided good copy, whether it was Lennon putting his foot in it or their cottoning onto another new fad.

One or two sick jokes started to circulate among the press corps awaiting them on Sunday afternoon, as they learned that a lonely life had ended in London. Inside the college, the Great Soul was consoling his famous disciples as the tragedy they'd initially refused to avow inflicted itself upon them. "The Maharishi told us not to be too overshadowed by grief," George reported. "I have lost only a few people who were very close to me. This is one of those occasions, but I feel my course on meditation here has helped me to overcome my grief more easily than before."[193]

As twilight thickened, The Beatles brushed past a pitiless

whoomph of flashbulbs, their mouths moving mechanically as they walked from the university building into a black Rolls Royce. Its interior was their last sanctuary before they would be obliged to respond more fully to their manager's death. "We didn't know what to do," shrugged George later. "We were lost."[29]

10 L'Angelo Mysterioso

Could Brian manage The Beatles from the grave? Time after time he'd turn in it as capital was wasted on too many Billy Bunters whose postal orders never arrived. To The Beatles, experience meant recognising mistakes when they occurred again.

Once, a heading emblem on a NEMS press release had been Epstein in a mortar board in the midst of his clients with their impudent schoolboy grins. Now that Sir had left the classroom, the children started doing whatever they liked. With adolescence extended by adulation, most of their ideas were more intriguing, conceptually, than in ill-conceived practice. In the end, their idyll was threatened not by any external danger but by their own inner natures and desires, and when it dawned on them that not everything they did was great. Long before their partnership was officially dissolved, each Beatle – however reluctantly or unknowingly – would be well into his solo career.

Brian's most tangible legacy was The Beatles' new deal with EMI, which gave them a royalty rate higher than that of any other recording act. All they had to do in exchange was produce 70 tracks for release before 1976. This they would do well within the limit, both as individuals and, to a diminishing degree, collectively.

Four were unloaded onto the soundtrack of *Yellow Submarine*, which, inspected halfway towards completion, had been a pleasant surprise. Without making The Beatles too cuddly, it portrayed them as Sgt Pepper's bandsmen in surreal encounters during a "modyssey" from Liverpool to Pepperland. So charmed were they with this epic cartoon that the real Beatles agreed to appear in cameo for the last scene.

However, as 1967's flowers wilted, so did their enthusiasm for

Yellow Submarine. Significantly, half of the cheapskate tie-in album consisted of George Martin's incidental music and the cancelled 'Only A Northern Song'. The only new items that The Beatles bothered to add were, as they realised themselves, just inconsequential fillers. Even Paul's 'All Together Now' was taped in one session. From George's less unwilling quill had dripped 'It's All Too Much', in which a wide-ranged melody and laughably pretentious symbolism stayed afloat amid a roughcast, noisy backing with a vignette from Purcell's *Trumpet Voluntary* chucked in for good measure. In 1975, it was to be revived by arch-hippy guitarist Steve Hillage.

If it seems twee now, *Yellow Submarine* was loved by Beatles fans, who, in obedience to the non-cartoon John Lennon's exhortation, skipped from cinemas singing 'All Together Now'. Once outside, however, they shut up. By 1968, if you carried on like that, sooner or later you'd get a kicking, even in San Francisco. In London, the likes of The Flowerpot Men had jumped on bandwagons new, and the prevailing gangster chic obliged even a cool cat like Georgie Fame to resuscitate a flagging chart career with 'The Ballad Of Bonnie And Clyde'.

Aided by pirate radio's demise and the cautious programming of the BBC's two new national pop stations, the British Top 30 became generally shallower and less subversive in content. The corporation had already banned two Beatles tracks from its airwaves – 'A Day In The Life', for its "I'd love to turn you on" line, and 'I Am The Walrus', for its sexual innuendo – even though a performance had been screened on the BBC's new colour network on Boxing Day 1967 as part of the group's hour-long spectacular, *Magical Mystery Tour*.

Favourable critical reaction to *Yellow Submarine* served to obscure memories of this laboured project, which wasn't perhaps suitable viewing for a nation sleeping off its Yuletide revels. Other than predictable plaudits from the underground press and the *NME*, the interesting-but-boring *Magical Mystery Tour* was universally panned, a first for The Beatles as artistes. As expressive as the most vitriolic review was discerning ex-Walker Brother Scott Engel's rise from his armchair to switch it off after 20 minutes.

It had been a development of McCartney's pretty idea of a journey with no known destination or outcome. "Everything will be spontaneous,"[194] revealed Tony Barrow when puzzled journalists rang to ask why a coach with "Magical Mystery Tour" emblazoned on its sides and alleged to contain The Beatles was trundling through the West Country with the holiday season still on. In trendy Al Capone suits, George, John and Ringo lent a passing uniformity, but inside the vehicle, too, was a hand-picked cast as variegated as a disaster movie's.

Among those described later as "a motley collection of uncouth and unlikable trippers" were a midget, a fat lady, a funnyman in a bow tie, a courier, a little girl, the omnipresent Alex Mardas, an actress playing Paul's girlfriend and Paul himself, who only needed the knotted handkerchief on his head to complete his parody of a holiday-maker coping with the meteorological whims of a British September. Picked up *en route* were minor characters of such diversity as Spencer Davis and bikini-clad truant Judith Rogers, who was roped in by McCartney because "I decided to use some glamour in the film on the spur of the moment".[195]

Judith was but one of hundreds who'd divined the hotels where The Beatles had been provisionally booked. As well as the chaos that their very presence summoned, the 40-seater bus – now divested of its too-distinctive trappings – failed to negotiate the twisty lanes, thus ruling out such potentially stimulating locations as Widecombe Fair and Berry Pomeroy Castle.

Although the bulk of *Magical Mystery Tour* was drawn from this troubled excursion, many interior scenes were filmed elsewhere, mainly back in London. Putting new moral objections on hold, George sat woodenly next to John in the front row of Paul Raymond's Revue Bar. Before him, a stripper entertained to the accompaniment of The Bonzo Dog Doo-Dah Band, whose eventual modicum of chart success was secondary to their alarming stage act, which earned them a weekly turn on *Do Not Adjust Your Set*, an anarchic children's comedy series on ITV

Not far from Raymond's palace of sin, The Beatles spent six weeks in a darkened room, wading through the formless celluloid miles of improvised dialogue and scenes that had seemed a good idea at the time. As Paul was less uncertain about the finished picture, George and John – uneasy about it from the beginning – and Ringo left him to it. Unless called in to give opinions, they whiled away hours in the adjacent office with such amusements as the clowning of 'Rosie', an old Soho vagrant who'd been immortalised in a hit record by a street busker called Don Partridge.

Magical Mystery Tour wasn't *Citizen Kane*, but its music was a winner. Proof of this was the grapple for UK chart supremacy between their latest single, 'Hello Goodbye', and a double EP for the film's six numbers, which cost three times more. Occupying a whole side of this novel package was George's repetitive 'Blue Jay Way', after the boulevard of the same name where the Harrisons stayed while in Los Angeles. As fog encircled their rented house, a still jet-lagged George had picked out its tune on a small electric keyboard to a lyric concerning a long wait for Derek Taylor and his wife, who were groping through the evening traffic. It wasn't much of a song, really, but when it was recorded the combined effect of guttural cello, monochordal organ and wordless responses behind George's phased singing conveyed the requisite misty atmosphere. So, too, did the clouds of incense that shrouded the 'Blue Jay Way' sequence in the film, with the composer squatting in a lotus position, his swirling image refracted as if seen through a fly's eye.

In *Yellow Submarine*, too, he'd been caricatured as a hazy mystic, and it was no surprise to Joe Public when George emerged as the most vocal supporter of this meditation caper. Although, like the Maharishi himself, he was criticised for plugging spirituality like a new record, George's exposition of his belief that "the world is ready for a mystic revolution"[196] on *The David Frost Show* – with witty asides from John – went down so well that he was invited back the next week: "So you can't say going on television and speaking to the press is a bad way to tell people about meditation."[3]

Since Bangor, a retreat for further study to one of the Maharishi's two *yoga-ashrams* ("theological colleges") in the forested foothills of the Himalayas had been on the cards. This trip had been postponed twice owing to *Magical Mystery Tour* commitments, but George had maintained contact with His Holiness, mainly by telephone, although he had taken a day trip to Sweden with Ringo to confer with him and, with John, accompanied the Great Soul to a Shankar concert in Paris.

The media uproar during The Beatles' curtailed sojourn in Bangor had brought home to Varma what a catch he'd made. Like Ravi Shankar before him, he'd been unaware of the group's stature, but, armed with the relevant records, he underwent a crash-course in their music and began to illustrate his talks with quotes from their lyrics. Flattered though they were, The Beatles were unconvinced by his argument that, if they were sincere about meditation, they ought to tithe a percentage of their income into his Swiss bank account. Because they hadn't actually said no, the Maharishi assured American investors that the four would be co-starring in a TV documentary about him. "He is not a modern man," explained George, as much to himself as anyone else. "He just doesn't understand such things."[197]

Shelving their stronger misgivings, Paul, Jane and the Starkeys followed an advance guard of the Harrisons and Lennons to India, in February 1968, where all were both relieved and disconcerted that, after a long and bumpy drive from New Delhi, the meditation academy was not a compound of mud huts but whitewashed, air-conditioned chalets fully equipped to US standards, with an attached post office, laundry and dining hall. The main lecture theatre was not unlike Bangor's. Across the Ganges stood the shanty town of Rishikesh, where hospitality was more frugal.

"It'll probably turn out like a Butlin's holiday camp,"[197] George had remarked to *Melody Maker* before he left, and so it did for Maureen and Ringo, who went home early. Among the 60 remaining seekers of nirvana were some of comparable renown, such as Mia Farrow, Donovan and – the only one to become a lifelong devotee – Mike Love of The Beach Boys, whose Dennis Wilson had been introduced by George to the Maharishi in Paris. Famous or obscure, all would assemble clothed against the morning heat in the open-air amphitheatre for lessons which included practical demonstrations, such as the apparent suspended animation that His Holiness induced in one of his staff. He also spoke of levitation, but no Beatle would be around long enough to witness any. Gradually, the talks became shorter and periods for individual contemplation lengthened. Later, George bragged of being entranced for a 36-hour period.

The balmy quietness of the campus yielded a long-denied if temporary peace of mind, as all of the day-to-day distractions that hindered creativity were on the other side of the planet. Relaxed and happy, new songs poured from the pop contingent, many of them observations of other students. Donovan dedicated his 'Jennifer Juniper' to Jenny Boyd, while Lennon's 'Dear Prudence' was about Mia Farrow's reclusive sister, who "wouldn't come out. They selected me and George to try and bring her out of her chalet, because she would trust us. She'd been locked in for three weeks and was trying to reach God quicker than anybody else."[80]

Shortly after the celebration of Pattie's 23rd birthday, Jane and Paul threw in the towel and returned to London. Alex Mardas, meanwhile, was torn between his own boredom with ashram life and his desire to maintain his position at John's ear. His problem was resolved three weeks later, when he'd accumulated enough tittle-tattle to speak to John and George of Varma's clandestine and earthly scheming for the downfall of an American nurse's knickers, propositioning her with the forbidden meal of chicken as other cads would with a box of chocolates. With the manipulative Alex urging him on, Lennon confronted the Great Soul with this infamy. Deaf to protestations of innocence, John announced his immediate departure, to the dismay of Cynthia, for whom the trip seemed an opportunity to save their marriage.

Not knowing what to think, the Harrisons chose to wash their hands of the Maharishi, too, although George preserved a vestige of regard for one who'd orchestrated "one of the greatest experiences I've ever had".[144] Still a believer in the soundness of the too-human guru's teachings, he confessed, "It's just that we physically left the Maharishi's camp but spiritually never moved an inch. We still meditate now. At least, I do."[3]

He broke the journey back to England to return a visit by Shambu Das to the ashram and to look up Ravi Shankar. At a press conference the previous August, he'd been addressed as "George" and Ravi had been "Mr Shankar". This was commensurate with the respect held for each as a sitarist. Starting too late in life, and with his pop career precluding daily hours of practice, Ravi admitted that George "realised it demands the whole time, like learning the violin or cello, but he still continues to learn from me as much as he can about Indian music, which he uses in his own work as inspiration".[170] George effectively gave it up one New York night in 1968, when "Jimi Hendrix and Eric Clapton were at the same hotel and that was the last time I played the sitar like that".[32] For years afterwards, "George Harrison (sitar)" would crop up in the Miscellaneous Instruments sections of music-press polls. "People put you in a bag,", he groused, "and nowadays all I've got to do is the slightest unusual rhythm and they say, 'There he goes, all Indian again.'"[145]

An electric sitar was the selling point on The Box Tops' 'Cry Like A Baby', which was in the Top 20 when the Harrisons finally got back to Kinfauns. Just as off-putting was session guitarist Chris Spedding's qualification that "nobody's trying to fool anyone about it being an Indian instrument. It's a sound effect. Every time I use it, I charge £10, apart from my session fee. It cost me £80. When they were new in the shops, they cost about £300."[74]

On BBC Radio 1, John Peel – not as "beautiful" as he'd been in 1967 – no longer inserted 20-minute ragas between progressive fare on his *Night Ride* programme. Instead, he bowed to frequent requests for "that boot-slapping thing" (Zulu step-dancing), "the Russian with the funny voice" (a singer from Azerbaijan, USSR) and further obscurities that he'd chosen from Broadcasting House's sound archives. A national pop station filling off-peak ether with nose-flutes, Romanian *cobzas* and further outlandish examples of what would later be termed as "world music" had been unthinkable three years earlier, when George Harrison had double-tracked the sitar on 'Norwegian Wood'.

Not as directly innovative were Brian Jones' explorations into the ethnic music of Morocco. Regarded as George's opposite number in the Stones, Jones was also admired for his weaving of quaint instrumentation into the fabric of their records. Another affinity with George was an artistic insecurity rooted in the near-monopoly of songwriting from a ruling team within his group. Neither were Jagger and Richards as receptive to the compositions of colleagues as Lennon and McCartney. An emotional disaster area, Brian wasn't as bold as George. However, he'd channelled part of his frustration by scoring the soundtrack for a German movie, *Mort Und Totschlag*.

Work of this kind had fallen into George's lap, too. After viewing its uncut rushes in October 1967, The Bee Gees had turned down the task of providing continuous music to an oddity of a cinema film entitled *Wonderwall*. George's name was brought up enough times during subsequent discussions with its backer that director Joe Massot – who'd met The Beatles during *Help!* – was elected to sound him out. George was more impressed with *Wonderwall* than The Bee Gees had been, but confessed that he hadn't a clue how to go about it. Aware of both the film's low budget and the publicity value of Beatle involvement, Massot felt that any old rubbish would do, as long as the words "George Harrison" could be printed on the credits.

Apprehensive about what he'd taken on, George started by "spotting" each sequence with a stop-watch. Back in the recording studio, he'd then "make 35 seconds, say, of something, mix it and line it up with the scene".[59] Within these tight strictures, he compiled an original soundtrack that many would cite as the saving grace of a film graphically condemned as "a right load of codswallop"[198] about an elderly scientist who spends his leisure hours peeping obsessively through a hole in his attic wall at the antics of a young model – played by Jane Birkin – in the flat next door. His new vista of her erotic mirror-posing, wild parties and athletic sex life is so alien to him that reality dissolves (as does the story-line), until his fantasies become concrete when he saves the girl from suicide.

Wonderwall faded from general circulation soon after its release in 1968. Too much for the ordinary moviegoer – although less so than *Magical Mystery Tour* – it only received occasional showings in film clubs and arts centres. Watching it was an intellectual duty rather than entertainment.

Issued some months before the film, the soundtrack album was worthy in its own right, regardless of imagined visuals and what George himself would dismiss as "loads of horrible mellotron stuff and a police siren", as well as the co-related blowing of mouth-organist Tommy Reilly, more famous for his theme to *Dixon Of Dock Green*.

A sympathetic reviewer mentioned that "the Harrison music replaces dialogue waxing almost vocal like a cinema organist from the silent days".[199] On 'Party Seacombe', a pointed reference to an expression in one of Lennon's books, George's schoolchum Colin Manley's wah-wah guitar indeed "waxes almost vocal" to the Pink Floyd-ish accompaniment of the rest of The Remo Four, who were still functional after years of backing various singers, including Gregory Phillips.

The Remo Four, Reilly and Clapton's parts in *Wonderwall* were taped at Abbey Road, but tracks like 'Gat Kirwani' and 'Guru Vandana' had come from an EMI studio further east. On the top floor of the Universal Building in Bombay, George had toiled for an intensive five days with old mono equipment and soundproofing so poor that it was impossible to record during the evening rush hour without picking up extraneous sounds of traffic and the exodus from the offices below. Nevertheless, these were fruitful sessions for George and the players gathered for him by Shambu Das. Under the Beatle's supervision, Das and his fascinated musicians obeyed Western rules of harmony as their contribution to a film most of them would never see quickly took shape – so quickly, in fact, that there was time in hand for George to produce several backing tracks for purposes that were then non-specific. "I was getting so into Indian music then," he'd recall, "that I decided to use the assignment as an excuse for a musical anthology to help spread it."[59]

As Joe Massot knew, George's Beatle status guaranteed the film some attention, but the soundtrack's elevation to Number 49 in the US album chart testified to more intrinsic virtues in an industry where sales figures are arbiters of success. An additional distinction was that it was the first LP to be released via EMI on Apple, The Beatles' own record label, which would be their most lucrative post-Epstein enterprise, almost despite themselves. It's name had first been tossed around during the *Revolver* sessions, to the extent of giving provisional fruity titles to tracks yet to receive one. 'Love You To', for instance, began as 'Granny Smith'.

Frank Sinatra and trumpeter Herb Alpért are off-the-cuff and all-American examples of performers who reduced the number of middlemen and increased quality control on output by founding their own record companies, albeit under leasing deals with parent firms. Neither, however, shared Apple's initial burst of world-shaking ambition, in which records would be only one division of an "Apple Corps", with tentacles in other spheres such as film, electronics and tailoring. After LSD moustaches and meditation, The Beatles had suddenly latched onto bourgeois greed. With their own struggles niggling still, "We had this mad idea of having Apple there," said George, "so that people could come and do artistic stuff and not have a hard time."[24]

In April 1968 – the beginning of the tax year – advertisements appeared in both national and underground journals soliciting the public to bring "artistic stuff" to the new Apple Foundation For The Arts in London. Not a postal delivery would go by without a deluge of demo tapes and manuscripts thumping onto the doormat. All day long, tongue-tied callers who'd found out Apple's ex-directory number would beg for their cases to be heard. Fingers calloused by guitar string and typewriter key constantly pressed the bell. "We had every freak in the world coming in there,"[24] groaned George.

That very month, I too sent Apple a bundle of my poems in the hopes that they'd want someone with imagination rather than ability. When the operation moved headquarters from Wigmore Street to Savile Row, I decided to pay a call to check whether the Beatle who'd read them had set a publication date yet. Well, I was only 16. Wondering what I'd wear on the dust-jacket photograph, I walked straight past the tall Georgian terrace containing Apple, not even noticing two or three girls hanging around the steps of what looked like a private residence. Its front door was wide open, so, unchallenged, I entered and explained my presence to a friendly receptionist on whose desktop was a tin labelled "Canned Heat". She was sorry no one could see me right now but promised I'd hear from Apple in due course. I should imagine that my teenage verse must be quite near the top of the pile by now.

No stranger could have bowled off the street into NEMS any more than they could have into Balmoral. I could have been some maniac out to get Lennon for shooting his mouth off about Jesus. "If you want George to listen to your tape, you're doing it all wrong," shouted one Apple employee when the first Beatle to arrive that day was smothered in kisses by some French-Canadian girl. Taking George at his word, a pair of particularly invidious Hell's Angels blew in from San Francisco to abuse without hindrance Apple's lavish facilities – and female secretariat – for two nerve-wracking weeks. Apple's house style was based on "complete trust", said Derek Taylor. "I now know that we were foolish."[200]

Because George had convinced, the others that Derek was "on the same trip",[199] Epstein's former assistant returned to the fold as Apple's press officer, but "I didn't realise the tensions underneath until George came back from Rishikesh and reacted with real horror to what was going on in the building".[199] A doorman was appointed to keep out riff-raff like me, although certain moneyed young Americans, glad to breathe the groovy air around The Beatles, were let in to act as unpaid and unrecompensed minions.

Behind that closed door, no one Beatle felt responsible for straightening out a venture that had taken a mere two months to snowball into chaos. To see what it was like, he might commandeer a room at Savile Row, stick to conventional office hours and play company director until the novelty wore off. He might (as George did) hammer at a partition he disliked at one of Apple's two unprofitable boutiques, but bigger policy decisions were more likely to be guided by a hired astrologer of the kind who warned George about the danger of wearing sapphire before August 1975.

As no one actually objected, John put Alex Mardas in charge of Apple Electronics, a post that rapidly became a sinecure as, one after another, the wondrous patents involving force-fields and robotics progressed no further than Alex talking about them. Lennon formulated a plan for ex-Quarry Man Ivan Vaughan (now a Cambridge graduate) to set up a school for The Beatles' children and those of their friends to attend. Meetings were arranged, various properties inspected and the skeleton of a steering committee established before Apple's accountant argued that it was not a viable proposition.

George's jobs-for-the-boys were less impeachable. Terry Doran had landed on his feet as George's general factotum, his face now framed by a beard and Hendrix frizz, and Astrid Kemp (*née* Kirchherr) was commissioned to photograph George for the *Wonderwall* cover. A seat had also been found for Tony Bramwell on the executive board, headed by Neil Aspinall.

With no speaker cabinets left to hump, Mal Evans' donkey-work now extended to minor instrumental roles on records. Once, he was asked by Paul – to John's chagrin – to pen some lyrics for a *Sgt Pepper* track. A lowlier office was travelling with the luggage to the Indian ashram. He was enough of an old comrade to be invited to join his masters on holiday, as he and his wife did with the Harrisons for three days in Corfu.

An even older pal, Pete Shotton, had left his Hampshire supermarket to manage the main Apple boutique in Baker Street. No worse than any other trendy store, it was remarkable only in the manner of its closure in July 1968, when The Beatles decreed that all remaining merchandise was to be given away to the public, who predictably pounced on even the shelves and hatstands like hags at a jumble sale.

All fittings, decorations and stock had been either requisitioned or designed by The Fool through a six-figure float from The Beatles, who'd also hinted that the Dutch clothiers could record an LP. The Fool weren't as daft as they looked. After castigation by Apple Retail for removing "a considerable amount of items as yet unpaid"[201] from the boutiques, they departed from The Beatles' court as mysteriously as they'd arrived, having first secured a contract with Mercury Records, for whom they made their album.

The Fool's album was produced by Graham Nash, now rehearsing in a Kensington flat with Dave Crosby and Steve Stills. Their warblings weren't everyone's cup of tea, but Nash ended up a sight richer than if he'd stayed a Holly. Styled as a "supergroup" by the music press, Crosby, Stills And Nash were approached in 1968 by George Harrison, who wanted to sign them to Apple Records. As none in the trio could extricate himself from existing contracts, the deal fell through, as did Apple's negotiations with another promising group, Fleetwood Mac, whose publicist happened to be Bill Harry. A lesser star in embryo, James Taylor, was taken on, but 20-year-old David Bowie slippèd through The Beatles' fingers after an interview with Paul McCartney.

When the first Apple recordings were pressed, in August 1968, no one could pretend that any other division of the organisation was either a money-spinner or of scientific or cultural value. No more qualified to run a business than Brian Epstein had been to play guitar, George was the Beatle least interested in any Apple function beyond making records. Nonetheless, he'd show willing now and then, poking his nose in at the first boutique's launch party, attending a charity showing of *Yellow Submarine* in Los Angeles and appearing on the Smothers Brothers TV show to introduce the film clip of The Beatles miming their inaugural Apple single, 'Hey Jude'.

As they and Gerry had held the UK Number One spot for NEMS in 1963, so it was in microcosm for Apple when, bearing the catalogue number Apple 2, Mary Hopkin's 'Those Were The Days' succeeded 'Hey Jude' at the top. A Welsh soprano with an aura of schoolgirl innocence, Mary had been conspicuous among entrants on several editions of ITV's *Opportunity Knocks*. Keener on her voice than he'd been on David Bowie's, Paul McCartney selected and produced 'Those Were The Days' and most of Mary's subsequent lesser hits. Though she wasn't his *protégé*, her singing so enchanted George, who listened in on one of her album sessions, that he sent Mal out to buy her a better acoustic guitar than the one with which she was accompanying herself. He also submitted songs from his growing portfolio for her and Paul's consideration, two of which were tried out by Marianne Faithfull, under the supervision of George, who perhaps saw her as a more worldly Hopkin.

Another Harrison composition was actually heard by the public as the A-side of the third Apple single, although not as often as 'Hey Jude' and 'Those Were The Days', both of which had more radio play and more appetising titles than 'Sour Milk Sea'. With George at the console, this jittery rocker, taped at a "glorified jam session",[202] was sung by Jackie Lomax, back from the States now that his Alliance had fallen apart there. An acquaintance rather than a bosom buddy, he'd supplicated George via Terry Doran for an Apple contract just as The Beatles were leaving for India.

Looking him up and down, George had decided that it might be worth taking trouble over Jackie. Lean and handsomely hatchet faced, his rock-star potential was supplemented by a lithe if tight-throated singing style, which was much in vogue just then. He also composed a bit, although nothing he played to George was markedly commercial. Agreeing with Lomax that an up-tempo A-side was more his line than a ballad, George returned to Britain with 'Sour Milk Sea', its lyrics inspired by a picture in a religious textbook that he'd understood to mean "if you're in the shit, don't go around moaning about it; do something about it".[38] Expressed more delicately in the verses of 'Sour Milk Sea', it was a similar sentiment to that expressed in the Maharishi's dubious maxim that "people are in poverty because they lack intelligence and because of laziness".[203]

None of the records that he cut with George made Jackie rich. Still, they plodded on, with George sparing no expense. An artist of Jackie Lomax's calibre deserved nothing less than publicity photos by Justin de Villeneuve, a full orchestra if he needed one and even the oscillations of one of these new-fangled Moog synthesisers. McCartney, Starr and Clapton were among the famous musicians namechecked on the sleeve of Lomax's only Apple LP, dog-eared copies of which spoke to casual browsers of deletion racks through its title, *Is This What You Want?*. Few did, however, despite Jackie's most professional vocal projection and George's competent – although occasionally cluttered – production.

Hardly any of Lomax's work on Apple was exceptional, but, paralleling George's kindness to Mary Hopkin, Eric Clapton gave him a relic to guard for life, the Gibson SG heard on Cream's double album *Wheels Of Fire*. Since *Fresh Cream*, the trio had gone from their native turf to grander, more impersonal venues in North America, where their musical sensitivity and subtle ironies were warped by high-decibel *diddle-diddle-diddling* and "endless, meaningless solos", reflected a perplexed Eric. "We were not indulging ourselves so much as our audiences, because that's what they wanted."[105] As long as customers went as ape over strings of bum notes as they did over the outfit's most startling moments, Cream in stagnation broke box office records once held by The Beatles in Uncle Sam's concrete colosseums and baseball parks. The band's calculated disbandment in November 1968 was no surprise to George, who'd arrived at a similar artistic impasse in 1965.

Cream had planned a final LP, *Goodbye*. Most of it consisted of in-concert tapings from the last US tour, although each member also agreed to donate a new composition. Songs had never come as readily to Clapton as they had to bass guitarist Jack Bruce and drummer Ginger Baker. Under pressure because the other had finished their *Goodbye* numbers, Eric now felt close enough to George to seek his assistance. Aid was rendered with none of the reluctance that John Lennon had evinced when helping with 'Taxman'. George was only too pleased to collaborate with "one of those people I get on so well with it's like looking at myself".[204] As well as sharing his Beatle friend's depilatory caprices and dress sense, Clapton wasn't "a leader sort of person. It's the same with me. I need someone to encourage me to do things."[204] With the purchase of Hurtwood Edge, a Surrey mansion, Eric was also on a par with George materially.

The two guitarists had similar tastes in women, too, as Eric's squiring of Paula Boyd for three months appeared to prove. Her big sister "wondered why he'd done it, but it became obvious later on".[44] A line towards the end of the number he composed with George implied a portent for the Beatle-ologist: "Talking about a girl who looks quite like you..." Whatever Clapton may have been trying to say, for his co-writer, "that whole song was quite silly. Ringo was sitting around drinking. We were amusing ourselves."[58] Its bridge reiterated the lyrical thrust of 'Sour Milk Sea', but the verses were merely syllables strung together to carry the tune. Its very title, 'Badge', came from misreading the word *bridge* on Harrison's scribbled draft.

In Cream's hands, 'Badge', with its pseudo-cryptic words, was the nearest *Goodbye* came to a straightforward pop song. It always reminded me of 'Love Potion Number Nine'. As the LP's promotional single, it grazed the lower echelons of Britain's Top 20 over spring 1969, and then three years later it almost repeated this modest triumph when reissued by Polydor as a stop-gap 45 during a period when Clapton had retreated from pop.

Other than a plain chord strummed after each verse, 'Badge' had no discernible hook line; much of its appeal lay in the interplay of Bruce's bass lope and the chopping of guest rhythm guitarist George Harrison, under the *nom de guerre* "L'Angelo Mysterioso" – Clapton's idea and used because such moonlighting on a rival label was frowned upon by EMI. Nonetheless, the mysterious angel's identity was a secret so badly kept that his inaudible presence on one track was a minor selling point for canny Jack Bruce's first solo album.

Baker and Clapton, meanwhile, had amalgamated with Steve Winwood and Rick Grech, the bass player from "progressive" group Family, to form Blind Faith, who, so a letter to *Melody Maker* wrongly predicted, would achieve "almost Beatle status".[205] Rather than an expected stylistic hybrid, there'd be strong evidence of Eric's fondness for an LP of insidious impact, *Music From Big Pink* by The Band, a group from upstate New York. The album demonstrated a True West blend of electric folklore that had been nurtured over many a rough night spent in hick Canadian dance halls before the musicians landed a job backing Bob Dylan.

As John's enthusiasm for Dylan had rubbed off on George, so did Clapton's for The Band. "They had great tunes," concurred George, "played in a great spirit and with humour and versatility".[58] Their professional relationship with Bob Dylan, however, had not ceased during his convalescence, as they recorded with him in the basement of their communal pink house in West Saugerties, not far from Bob's own rural home in Bearsville.

Throughout 1967, Dylan had been as unreachable an object of myth as Elvis. Until a water-testing re-emergence in the following year, he was incommunicado to all but his immediate family, The Band and perhaps a dozen or so of those who were his equals in the hierarchy of pop. They alone appreciated why he remained in seclusion even after he was fit enough physically to hold down another album-tour-album sandwich.

Beginning with an invitation from Band guitarist Jaime Robertson to call on Big Pink, George became the most frequent

Beatle guest at Bearsville during Dylan's shadowy refuge from fame. George had found him as initially aloof as John had been in The Quarry Men, although Bob was closer to him in age and outlook. Sleeping at the singer's manager's house for the first visit, he spent his waking hours at the Dylans', where the paterfamilias "hardly said a word for a couple of days. Anyway, we got the guitars out and it loosened up a bit."[24] Bob emerged – so George liked to think – as a kindred spirit, in that his supposed stand-offishness was no more than diffidence. When you got him on his own, he was quite chatty. Furthermore, as George fought an inferiority complex over lyrics, Bob struggled with melodies, even borrowing that of 'Norwegian Wood' for *Blonde On Blonde*'s 'Fourth Time Around'. With a vague music/words delineation, the youngest Beatle and Dylan formed a desultory songwriting team that would bear sparse, half-serious fruit.

George's cultivation of Dylan's friendship may have been interrelated with the behaviour of Lennon since his confrontation with the Maharishi. Shortly after their return to England, John had left Cynthia and Julian to move in with Yoko Ono, a Japanese-American who was to art what Screaming Lord Sutch was to politics. As some mug with a pocketful of money, John had been first introduced to her in 1966 during a preview of her "Unfinished Painting And Objects" display at the gallery attached to the Indica bookshop. Charmed by the all-white chess set, the apple with the £200 price tag and other puzzling exhibits, he'd funded Yoko's next event, taking a benevolent interest in her activities past and present – for example, her film of naked human buttocks in tight close up, or her "happening" in Liverpool's Bluecoat Chambers, where she'd had different members of the audience picking up pieces of a jug she'd just smashed. It was an Art Statement, like.

Yoko had also tried to make it as a pop singer, actually submitting demos to Island Records, who went in for oddball ethnic material. Her vocal flexibility was not dissimilar to that of Subbulakshmi, but she found a niche in the more distant extremes of avant-garde jazz, walking a highly-strung artistic tightrope without a safety net. In the company of respected figures such as Ornette Coleman and drummer John Stevens, she used her voice like a front-line horn, interjecting screeches, wails, nanny-goat vibrato and Nippon jabber into the proceedings.

Her vocal gymnastics actually owed much to stubbornly chromatic *seitoha* (Japanese classical music) and the free choral babbling and odd tone clusters present in the works of post-serialists like Schoenberg and Penderecki. This knowledge did little to soften a critique of a performance with Lennon and Danish saxophonist John Tchcai in which Lennon was squatting at her feet with his back to the audience and holding an electric guitar against a large speaker to create ear-splitting feedback.[206] Later, he elucidated, "I can't quite play like Eric or George, but then I gave up trying and just played whatever way I could to match her voice."[207]

After nature had taken its course one Weybridge night when Mrs Lennon was out, a writer to *Beatles Monthly* expressed the widespread view that Cynthia and John's subsequent divorce eroded The Beatles' magic even more than the absence of the usual Christmas single in 1966. Annihilating completely any cosy illusions such traditionalists had left was the first of a trilogy of non-Beatle albums by Lennon and Ono. The unmelodious avant-garde ramblings of *Unfinished Music No 1: Two Virgins* might have been anticipated, even tolerated, but the ordinary fan's shocked reaction to its cover photographs – of the couple unclothed – was best articulated in the topical disc 'John, You Went Too Far This Time' by Rainbo, alias Sissy Spacek, who was then a struggling starlet. Her love, she sang, would never be the same. Well, he had a penis, didn't he? Who'd have thought a Beatle could ever possess one of those?

Nakedness closed the first half of the Broadway musical *Hair*, but many of Lennon's blushing peers sought to talk him out of releasing *Two Virgins*, conjecturing that he'd finally flipped his lid. More forbearing than most was George, who was about to be an indirect victim of censorship when EMI refused to distribute a single by one of his discoveries, Brute Force, a one-man-band consisting of New Yorker Steven Friedland. Although 'The King Of Fuh' had been allocated an Apple matrix number, EMI were discountenanced by its tension-breaking chorus that ran "I'm the king of Fuh/I'm the Fuh King".

The company washed its hands of *Two Virgins*, too. However, it didn't mind the next Ono-Lennon LP as much – at least, not the non-controversial sleeve. *Unfinished Music No 2: Life With The Lions* was one of but two albums that appeared on Zapple, Apple's only subsidiary label. Intended as a platform for the spoken word and experimental music, "It seized up before it really got going," sighed George, "as with so many other things at Apple."[59] Zapple's charity did not begin at home, as shown by the preponderance of Americans lined up to declaim *vers libre*, read prose and crack jokes in hip restricted code. A few acetates of 'Listening To Richard Brautigan' by *Rolling Stone* magazine's resident rhymer were actually pressed, but whither the gems of Allen Ginsberg, who, drunk and naked, had met George and a disgusted John at a London party in 1965? Or Ken Weaver, a more permanent member of Greenwich Village's burlesque poetry rock group, The Fugs? Whatever happened about the "street diary" of Ken Kesey, mainstay of The Merry Pranksters? Foundering too was a 24-album retrospective of Lenny Bruce, a man who, to most of those outside the States who'd ever heard of him, was remembered as some sort of blue comedian.

George was especially keen for Zapple to acquire extant recordings by another American, the self-ennobled Lord Buckley, a night-club raconteur admired by Dylan for his unorthodox use of language. George also treasured hopes of a Zapple LP of children's stories related by daffy film actress Hermione Gingold and enhanced by effects from the monophonic synthesiser newly installed in a room at Kinfauns that he'd had converted into a cramped four-track studio.

With commendable honesty, George has said that "both of the albums that did come out are a load of rubbish".[58] Alongside Yoko and John's second soul-baring episode was George's own *Electronic Sounds*, which were exactly that: "All I did was get that very first Moog synthesiser with the big patch unit and keyboards you could never tune, and I put a microphone into a tape machine. Whatever came out when I fiddled with the knobs went on tape."[59] Although these haphazard bleeps and flurries were as far from Mersey Beat as he'd ever be, one side's worth of noise was given the title 'Under The Mersey Wall', after another George Harrison's column in the *Liverpool Echo*.

This opus was realised in February 1969 on George's synthesiser, probably the first to be privately purchased in Britain. Previously, such a device could only be hired domestically from US dealers, which is why the earlier half of *Electronic Sounds* – 'No Time Or Space' – evolved during an exploratory twiddle in a Californian recording complex three months prior to 'Under The Mersey Wall'. Later, engineer Bernard Krause would protest that George had stolen his demonstration performance on this synthesiser for issue on *Electronic Sounds*. This may not have been true, as Krause didn't press any claim for whatever scant royalties could be scraped from an album that, that even by a Beatle, rose no higher than Number 191 in the US chart. Mantovani would never cover 'No Time Or Space'.

Self-indulgence by individual Beatles had infiltrated their collective vinyl output on an unprecedented scale through the eight challenging minutes of 'Revolution 9', the longest track on the group's first LP – a double – on Apple. In a year in which "serious" modern composers like Terry Riley and Steve Reich were being promoted like rock stars, this patchwork of noises not usually thought of as musical was justifiably lauded in the *International Times* as a send-up of John Cage's 'Fontana Mix', a classic of its kind. In evidence on 'Revolution 9' and in other ditties during this round of sessions was Yoko Ono, who had now replaced Paul as John's creative partner, just as she had Cynthia in his affections. So too had commenced John's deviation from the spiritual pathway that George had been testing for him since 1966.

The last two to leave the Maharishi, John and George's appetites for mystical edification were more voracious than those of Ringo and Paul. Such a hunger was not unique to The Beatles, although other pop figures may not have looked to their souls' welfare if the likes of George hadn't been "so thrilled about my discoveries that I wanted to shout and tell it to everybody".[152] Nowadays, Radio 1 disc jockeys were "into" Zen macrobiotic cookery and yoga. Another sign of the times was the pragmatic opportunism of records such as The Lemon Pipers' 'Love, Beads And Meditation' and an inspired adaptation of George Formby's 'Hindu Meditating Man' by Birmingham's Alan Randall. Less superficial were the conversions of guitarists

"Mahavishnu" John McLaughlin and "Devadip" Carlos Santana to the doctrines of Bengal holy man Sri Chinmoy. Adopting the Sabud creed in 1968, Jim McGuinn of The Byrds had also assumed a new name. Purportedly, Gene Vincent had embraced Buddhism. Not committing themselves, Eric Clapton and Manfred Mann's Tom McGuinness would, nevertheless, gather some thoughts on religious matters in the respective hymns 'Presence Of The Lord', on Blind Faith's only album, and 'I Will Bring to You', which found a place in British primary school hymnals.

When united into their search for faith, Harrison and Lennon had alighted on an album that the former had brought back from the States. *Krishna Consciousness* featured the chanting of disciples of Swami Prabhupada, who, under commands from his own guru, had arrived in New York from India in 1965 to bring the maha-mantra to the West. Although disadvantaged by poverty and advanced age, he worked up a small following of acolytes dedicated enough to wear the order's citrus-coloured saffron robes, mark their faces with the white clay *tilak* sign of a servant of God and, if male, plane their scalps to a bare stubble, bar a dangling hank at the back. In crocodile procession, these *bhaktas* would jog the main streets of the Big Apple and, with finger cymbals keeping time, chant their endless mantra, "Hare Krishna, Hare Krishna, Krishna Krishna, Hare Hare/Hare Rama, Hare Rama, Rama Rama, Hare Hare," to a four-note melody that was millions of years old, according to the pamphlet they distributed *en route*. Continual repetition of Krishna's name, it read, would build up the chanter's identification with God, thereby drawing upon divine energy.

"Silent meditation is rather dependent on concentration," so George would learn, "but when you chant, it's more of a direct connection with God."[151] It could be practised even when the mind was in turbulence. Similar to what he'd gleaned from Varma, "I didn't get the feeling that I'd have to shave my head, move into a temple and do it full time."[151] Reaching this conclusion while The Beatles were still dazzling themselves with LSD were those who joined the charismatic Prabhupada and his devotees in the call-and-response group chanting that took place when their daily march terminated in Lower East Side Park. Another regular attendee was Allen Ginsberg, who sometimes accompanied the chanting on harmonium and would later lead The Fugs through a version of the mantra that appeared on their 1968 album *Tenderness Junction*. Back in the nearby temple, Prabhupada's sermons would be punctuated by stories of the all-pervading Krishna's personal incarnations taken from the *Bhagavad Gita*, the Hindu scriptures that predated the Bible. Underplaying his own later contribution, George would "see now that, because of [Prabhupada] the mantra had spread so far...more than it had in the last five centuries".[152]

As the Krishna Consciousness whirled for the first time in Kinfauns, "It was like a door opened somewhere in my subconscious, maybe from a previous life."[151] George began chanting himself, once keeping it up non-stop while driving from France to Portugal. When he listened to George's new album, John didn't go that far, usually chanting only when he was with George. When The Beatles were island hopping in Greece, the two "sang for days with ukulele banjos. We felt exalted. It was a very happy time for us."

The group's authorised biographer, Hunter Davies, blamed "the arrival in John's life of Yoko Ono"[208] for the end of The Beatles. To the general public, Lennon certainly seemed much changed since he'd taken up with her, and funny peculiar rather than funny ha-ha. Yet, although I might have dreamt it, because Yoko — small, bossy and no Madame Butterfly — obviously looked a fair old bit to John, the later 1960s brought an influx of good-looking boys hand in hand with girlfriends not conventionally beautiful onto the dance floors.

It may have been a boom time for wallflowers, but other Beatles may have hoped that, if they ignored Yoko, she would go away. In reciprocation, and contrary to John's jealous imaginings, "She wasn't particularly interested in us, anyway,"[188] said George. Through Yoko, Lennon was out on a limb, and The Beatles were less to him now than the artistic bond with her that was making him a laughing stock.

One day at Savile Row, George could no longer contain his resentment of Yoko's intrusion. Seeing red over a jibe at the other Beatles – "some of our beast friends" – in John and Yoko's contribution to 1968's fan club flexidisc, he burst into the couple's office and came straight to the point. "You know, that game of, 'I'm going to be up front, because this is what I've heard',"[156] sneered John later. Naming Dylan among those with a low opinion of uncool Yoko, Harrison went on to complain about the present "bad vibes"[155] within The Beatles' empire that were co-related with her coming. "We both sat through it," said John. "I don't know why, but I was always hoping that they would come around."[156]

Having let off steam, George did try to come around. Although, like Sissy Spacek, his love would never be the same, he and Pattie of all the other Beatle couples were most supportive of John and the soon-to-be second Mrs Lennon. George's *Electronic Sounds* could have been a gesture of artistic solidarity for John and Yoko's *Unfinished Music* series, while – with all pretensions of the Beatle four-man "brotherhood" gone – Pattie joined Yoko at the microphone for backing vocals on 'Birthday', a track destined to open the third side of the long-awaited successor to *Sgt Pepper*. George and John were the only Beatles heard on Lennon's unreleased 'What's The New Mary Jane', which, though it had lyrics and a tune, was closer to 'Revolution 9' than 'Birthday'.

Abbey Road staff were quite accustomed to half and, sometimes, only a quarter of the group being present at any given session. The Beatles didn't seem much of a group these days. "Except on disc," predicted *The Sunday Mirror*, "they will split up in 1969."[209] *Sgt Pepper* had opened floodgates for concept albums, rock operas and other questionable works requiring months in the studios, and its originators debated whether to make this next effort even more complete an entity. One proposal had been to hang each song on the idea and title of *A Doll's House* – a bit like *Wonderwall*, see, this girl and all the different characters, right, who visit her, kind of thing...

Although it encompassed the odd segue and reprise, all that the new record did was spotlight the talents of each separate Beatle. There had been a taste of this on *Revolver* and *Sgt Pepper*, but now it was out in the open. Perhaps they'd have been wiser to have divided the needle time in four and be damned, as The Pink Floyd planned to do. Instead, they functioned as each other's sessionmen, staying away if they weren't needed. "And that," said George, "was when the rot started setting in, really."[164]

It had become "Lennon and McCartney" rather than "Lennon-McCartney". George would deny it, but he was entering the lists as prime contender for their atrophied suzerainty: "I was starting to write loads of tunes, and one or two songs per album wasn't sufficient for me."[164]

Already, Paul and John had unbent enough to allow a Harrison number to grace a Beatles B-side. His last "Indian" song for the group, 'The Inner Light', parcelled a delightful melody over one of the Bombay backing tracks and a marginal adaptation of a Chinese poem from *Lamps Of Fire*.

The fact that he'd so freely lifted lyrics from another's work fuelled George Martin's long-held and deflating view that "an awful lot of George's songs do sound like something else. There actually was a song called 'Something In The Way She Moves', a James Taylor song, and that was written a long time before [Harrison] wrote his 'Something'."[210]

'Something' was also the name of a John Mayall composition for Georgie Fame that leaked into the UK Top 30 in 1965, but this track bore no more resemblance to the Harrison 'Something' than Taylor's number did. If Martin wanted to nitpick, why didn't he mention 'I'm So Tired', in which John had the gall to quote from James Ray's 'Got My Mind Set On You' or, further back, 'Run For Your Life' off *Help!*, which began with a line from Presley's 'Baby Let's Play House'?

Most of 'Something' had occurred to George when time hung heavy during one of Paul's overdubs for the double album and months, incidentally, before 'Something In The Way She Moves' was released. "I sort of just put it on ice," he'd recall, "because I thought, 'This is too easy. It sounds so simple.'"[211] With 'The Inner Light', an Abbey Road tape operator reported that he'd had "this big thing about not wanting to sing it, because he didn't feel confident that he could do the job justice".[212] So it would be with 'Something'. Momentarily, George considered passing it on to Jackie Lomax, although he felt that it was more the meat of Ray Charles, who'd lately made a gristly meal of 'Yesterday' and 'Eleanor Rigby' and was soon to tour Europe with his *protégé* Billy Preston, the youth from the Star-Club days.

One of the few British vocalists who came close to Ray's strangled vehemence was windmill-armed Joe Cocker, an ex-gas fitter from Sheffield who'd wrenched Mary Hopkin from Number One with a funereal overhaul of 'With A Little Help From My Friends' from *Sgt Pepper*. Figuring that it'd stand a better chance with a hit act than a lost cause like Jackie, George put 'Something' Joe's way "about a year before I did it, and then it took him that long to do it".[212]

The workshop ambience of Abbey Road permitted George to tape demos of 'Something' and other new compositions that were now streaming from him, such as 'Old Brown Shoe', 'Isn't It a Pity' and, from a stay at Dylan's, 'All Things Must Pass', which was inspired by the "religious and country feel" of The Band's 'The Weight'. Not meant for public ears, these weren't much more than guitar-and-voice sketches, but their very starkness often captured a strange beauty, a freshness that was invariably lost when they were reshaped by the group. Superior to the issued version was such a take of 'While My Guitar Gently Weeps', rated by many as George's greatest recording. This haunting melancholia was possibly thrust aside because Paul had just taped 'Blackbird', which was likewise sung to a lone guitar.

George's muse for 'While My Guitar Gently Weeps' appeared through a chance operation, his finger landing on the phrase "gently weeps" in a book opened at random at his parents' house. Back down south on 5 September 1968, he expected an enthusiastic response to his new song from John and Paul but "went home really disappointed".[59] There, he concocted an answer to this and future instances of artistic frustration. He was going to humbug the lads into giving his creations a fairer go. As well as the wives, more guest musicians than ever before were allowed increasingly less minor roles on Beatle recordings, from Jackie Lomax loud and clear on 'Dear Prudence' to Nicky Hopkins of The Jeff Beck Group hammering the 88s on 'Revolution'. George intended to bring in an outside party of such eminence that – like a vicar in a BBC situation comedy – his mere presence would compel the other three to bite back on their nonsense.

This would require delicate handling, though, and so, after

mentally rehearsing what he would say, George telephoned to ask Eric Clapton if he'd mind giving him a lift to the next evening's session. Taken aback by his friend's next request, Eric's gut response was, "I can't come. Nobody's ever played on Beatle records. The others won't like it."[211] Nevertheless, turning a thoughtful steering wheel as they neared Abbey Road, he relented, but still felt a gatecrasher as George escorted him into Studio Two. Within minutes, he realised that there was something rotten in the state of the group. Nothing was seen of John during the entire seven hours that Eric was there. On the previous night, Ringo had returned to The Beatles after resigning a fortnight earlier with more than his fill of sitting on the fence, as the shirtiness and provocative indifference mounted up. Yet he and Paul "were as good as gold",[213] smiled the crafty George as they and their distinguished visitor laid down a version of 'While My Guitar Gently Weeps' that he deemed satisfactory. A bonus – and a sure sign of esteem – was Clapton's gift of "Lucy", his beloved cherry-red Les Paul on which he'd delivered solos that were to be among the high points of the collection that they'd now decided to call nothing as ambivalent as *A Doll's House* but just *The Beatles*.

A more dubious accolade for Eric on *The Beatles* was George's 'Savoy Truffle', which – paling beside the storming 'While My Guitar Gently Weeps' – was notable for its raucous saxophone section and the purpose for which it had been composed, which had been "to tease Eric. He's got this real sweet tooth, and he'd just had his mouth worked on. His dentist said he was through with candy, so, as a tribute, I wrote, 'You'll have to have them all pulled out after the Savoy Truffle.'"[59] It wasn't so peculiar to Clapton, however, that it couldn't refer to any chocolate addict with self-inflicted toothache.

Why did 'Savoy Truffle' – stuffed with the latest slogans – and, as much of a muchness, 'Long Long Long' make it onto *The Beatles* when stronger Harrison material didn't? Possibly a green-eyed monster whispered to McCartney and Lennon, when he thought about it nowadays, that George – heaven forbid – might catch up on either of them as The Beatles' most self-contained and commercial force. And why not? "He was working with two brilliant songwriters," reasoned John, "and he learned a lot from us. I wouldn't have minded being

George the invisible man."[80] Of the new, clever music coming from inside the old Harrison, George Martin justified his previous condescension towards the baby of the group: "He'd been awfully poor up to then, actually. Some of the stuff he'd written was dead boring. The impression is sometimes given that we put him down. I don't think we ever did, but possibly we didn't encourage him enough."[210]

Whereas John could get away with 'Revolution 9' and Paul with the sugary reggae pastiche 'Ob-La-Di-Ob-La-Da', George, like a travelling salesman with a foot in the door, had to make a pitch with his most enticing samples: "The numbers I think are the easiest to get across will take the shortest time to make an impact [and will] sound the nicest tunes."[213] One that struck the right note for a while – especially with John – was 'Not Guilty'. "Even though it was me getting pissed off with Lennon and McCartney for the grief I was catching during the making of the album, I said I wasn't guilty of getting in the way of their careers and of leading them astray in our all going to Rishikesh to see the Maharishi. I was sticking up for myself, and the song came off strong enough to be saved and utilised."[59] But not on *The Beatles*, despite ear-catching qualities like odd spasms of syncopation, insistent heavy-handed drumming and the low-down guitar riff that broke into fading canon on the coda.

Glancing up from a newspaper, George Martin pressed the intercom button to warn Harrison that, if he put it up a key, he'd have even greater difficulty with the falsetto bit. It was feasible that everyone at Abbey Road could stand only so many fantastic versions of 'Not Guilty', which ran to a marathon 100 takes.

At least George couldn't complain that this song hadn't had a fair hearing. Now he was being treated more like an equal than a servant. A few months after *The Beatles* at last made the shops, the rocking 'Old Brown Shoe' became his second Beatles flip-side. Was it so unreasonable for George to hold in his heart the exciting hope that one day his would be the composition chosen to be the hit, like 'All You Need Is Love' or 'Hey Jude'? Only then would he no longer be an also-ran in the eyes of the world, lucky to have gone the distance with John and Paul. 'Wah-Wah', a song he wrote in 1969, said as much: "You've made me such a big star/being there at the right time." 'Don't Bother

Me' had been teased from a shy, ponderous boy by Bill Harry, who still bumped into a "completely different" George Harrison who had "confidence in himself where it wasn't so obvious before. He wasn't under the domination of the others. He wasn't a passenger any more."

11 *The Gravedigger*

Assessing the decade of which he'd be forever an archetype, George Harrison said, "At the beginning of the '60s, people would think you were a freak if you did yoga exercises, but now a huge percentage of the world does yoga exercises. I think the '60s did help to broaden understanding. When someone [male] liked long hair, people used to think he was from a zoo, but now a lot of barriers have been broken."[214]

Middle-class fathers in breakfast rooms would comment disparagingly about them, but by 1969 hippies were common enough, even in English country towns and the American Midwest.

Better late than never, *New Zealand Truth* reported that a group called The Underdogs had 'Gone To Pot' by performing 'The Inner Light' on prime-time television wearing flower-power get-up at least two years past its sell-by date. With more dignity, Frank Sinatra – the jackpot of all songwriters – was feeling his way through a "contemporary" album of numbers by the likes of Judy Collins and Glen Campbell. More pertinent vinyl artefacts of the year in which Neil Armstrong took his small step were David Bowie's 'Space Oddity' and Don Partridge's 'Breakfast On Pluto'.

There wasn't much to get worked up about any more. On the six o'clock news, terrorised Palestinian children, bombings in Belfast, a stabbing at a free Rolling Stones concert near San Francisco and the Sharon Tate bloodbath now horrified viewers as much as a shoot-out in a spaghetti western. The "death" of Paul McCartney was a mere amusement, with morbid Beatle-ologists seeing the cover of the group's *Abbey Road* LP as a funeral march, with John as the Priest,

Paul the Deceased, scruffy George as the Gravedigger and Ringo as the Sexton. Who Killed Cock Robin? Moptop McCartney Manslaughter Mystery!?

Had it been only the previous October that *The International Times* had exclaimed, "Charlie Manson is just a harmless freak"?[215] He and his "Family" had had *The Beatles* on instant replay as they'd prepared for the Tate murders, having heard revolutionary messages in Paul's 'Helter Skelter' and George's 'Piggies', an attack on clichéd targets "in their starched white shirts". Translated by Manson as a call to arms was the throwaway line "what they need's a damn good whacking", originally suggested by George's mother to rhyme with "there's something lacking".

"Revolution is this year's flower-power"[216] – so Frank Zappa had summed up in 1968, when, with Vietnam the common denominator, kaftans had been mothballed as their former wearers followed the crowd to genuinely violent anti-war demonstrations and student sit-ins to protest against "all these old fools who are governing us and bombing us and doing all that".[178] That was what George Harrison called them in *Melody Maker* last week, wasn't it? Still seen as founts of wisdom, The Beatles had chewed over a Zapple interview album with Daniel Cohn-Bendit, organiser of the New Left *événements* in France that May, even though a screening of *Wonderwall* in Cannes was disrupted by a political rally stoked up by "Danny the Red". Bluestocking girls went cow-eyed over Cohn-Bendit, but not as much as they did over the late Cuban *guerrillero* Che Guevara, who was, said George, another who wanted "to change the outward physical structure when really that automatically changes if the internal structure is straight. Christ said, 'Put your own house in order,' and Elvis said, 'Clean up your own back yard,' so if everybody just fixes themselves up first instead of trying to fix everybody else up like the Lone Ranger, then there isn't any problem."[3]

Although the United States took them as seriously as ever, The Beatles had become less pin-ups than favourite – if slightly dotty – uncles in Britain. Nevertheless, they weren't so far above the adoration of schoolgirls that they didn't have recent group photographs available on request for *Jackie* and *Fabulous 208*. The folded arms and unsmiling demeanour of each detached individual reflected the mood that had permeated sessions for *The Beatles*, which to the critic still snowblinded by *Sgt Pepper* were "joyful music-making which only the ignorant will not hear".[178] More privy to the outfit's internal rifts, *Beatles Monthly* was soon to cease publication, not through falling readership – far from it – but "because they are not The Beatles but four separate personalities. It is comparatively rare to find them together."[217]

They couldn't even manage to be in the same room to tape fan-club flexi-discs any more, hence John's annoying "beast friends" dialogue of 1968, unheard by the others until it was mastered. George could hardly spare time for this annual formality now. All he did that year was introduce a 'Nowhere Man' by the late Tiny Tim, an American entertainer whose castrati warble and doe-eyed eccentricities George found endearing enough to relay the heartening message, "You are a gas," as that exquisite was about to make a UK debut at the Albert Hall. George wasn't even in the country when Lennon and McCartney recorded 'The Ballad Of John And Yoko' as The Beatles' final British Number One – and their worst since 'Can't Buy Me Love'.

Paul and John's congeniality as they piled up this single's overdubs had been at odds with "the most miserable session on earth"[156] – Lennon's words – a few months earlier. This vain endeavour to get back to their Mersey Beat womb had been precipitated by McCartney's raising of the subject of touring again. The quickest to forget how dreadful it had been in 1966, he saw it partly as a means to stop the group's disintegration. George was not so averse to such a scheme now. "I agree with what John says about the old days. We were really rocking. We had fun, you know? We really had fun."[32] In as far back as 1967, he'd expressed hope that "The Beatles will tour again, but...I just couldn't stand all the police and crowds and helicopters in Shea Stadium and the scene that goes with it".[218]

Their rejection of a six-figure sum for 13 American dates in 1969 indicated that maybe a tour wasn't the answer to "the idea of being up there, not knowing what you're doing in front of a lot of people which is the fun of it".[218] George liked the notion of a residency like the one they'd had in Hamburg. "Then you've got your amps and drums set up and got used to the one sound."[218] Shortly after an announcement of Presley's televised comeback over Christmas 1968, *Melody Maker* was first with news of three Beatles concerts before the cameras at London's Roundhouse. There were even stranger stories circulating of impending engagements at what was left of the Cavern, on the steps of Liverpool cathedral, in an asylum and aboard a ship. All that was certain was that, on The Beatles' next LP, there'd be nothing that couldn't be reproduced on stage. "It's the old guitar, bass and drums bit again," explained George. "After going through all those things with *Sgt Pepper*, it'll be a regular simple single LP with about 14 tracks."[219]

Tiring of psychedelia sooner than The Beatles, the Stones had dug down to a raw three-chord bedrock with 'Jumping Jack Flash', perhaps their most enduring single. On *Beggar's Banquet*, the album that followed, it was clear that they – like most of The Beatles – had fallen under the spell of Bob Dylan and The Band's recordings, in which unvarnished arrangements and lyrical directness had steered pop from backward-running tapes, sitars and self-conscious symbolism. Rock 'n' roll revival was in the air as Bill Haley and Buddy Holly reissues sneaked into the charts and classic rock medleys closed the shows of "nice little bands" whose names – Tea And Symphony, Audience, Puce Exploding Butterfly – implied musical insights less immediately comprehensible. Entertaining a truer underground than these denizens of the college circuit were up-and-coming provincial combos led by actual Teddy Boys such as "Crazy" Cavan and Shakin' Stevens. Across the Atlantic, others such as Sha Na Na, Flash Cadillac and Cat Mother were also carrying a torch for the 1950s.

Now George was enthusing about Little Richard again ("that's who I'd love to record"[22]), just as he had about Ravi Shankar. Despite its prosaic title and plain white cover, the music of *The Beatles* suddenly seemed over-produced and too clever. "It's like 'Revolution'," said George. "I still think the best version is the one which we did on a Ampex four-track machine with acoustic guitars and Ringo just bashing on maracas."[220] From the perspective of security and experience gained since 'Love Me Do', he and the other mellowed Beatles hoped to "get as funky as we were in the Cavern".[219] Instead, they only hastened their sour freedom from each other.

They spoke less often of where it would take place, but rehearsals for a concert began in January 1969 in Twickenham Film Studios. Killing two birds with one stone, a film crew was on hand to document every unforgiving minute. If the worst came to the worst, the best bits could be stuck together for the movie still owed to United Artists. Most would watch it to the bitter end, whatever it was like, as they had *Magical Mystery Tour*, although you couldn't help wondering if they'd have been as committed if it'd been Dave Dee, Dozy, Beaky, Mick And Tich bickering, playing old songs and hitting trouble as soon as they tried anything new.

George breezed into Twickenham fully re-adjusted to Greenwich Mean Time after a leisurely crossing from New York just before Christmas. This most productive visit to the States had been principally to record sessions for the Jackie Lomax LP at Western Recording Studios in Los Angeles, where he'd also found time for Tiny Tim's 'Nowhere Man'. With this ineffable gentleman in tow, he and Pattie were the most famous among celebrities who looked in at a Frank Sinatra session, also at Western. Impressing George more than the middle-of-the-road material that the venerable Sinatra was tackling was how much was accomplished in one evening, compared to the months of remakes and scrapped tracks that had had to be endured for *The Beatles*. After only two takes, Frank and his orchestra had 'Little Green Apples' in the bag – no arguments, no overdubs – and on to the next number. At 11pm, they wrapped up. Maybe one of his entourage had had to remind him which Beatle had just been chatting to him, but the photograph of them together might do for the back of the album to show that Ol' Blue Eyes was hip.

On the way home, the Harrisons stopped off at Bearsville, where Bob Dylan was also readying himself for an album interspersed with recent easy-listening standards. Assisting him on this atypical venture – misleadingly titled *Self Portrait* – was guitarist David Bromberg, a Columbia University graduate who, like Dylan, had been drawn into the Greenwich Village folk scene. Before leaving, George supplied a melody for 'The Hold-Up', a song for Bromberg's debut album.

Fresh from this pleasant interlude, George returned to The Beatles with favourable memories of the easy but respectful professionalism of the US session musicians under his command for is *This What You Want* and Sinatra's brisk finesse. So, on a winter's morn, he faced the cameras, his three colleagues and the immovable Yoko in a draughty film set-cum-rehearsal room for Paul's latest wheeze. "Straight away, it was back to the old routine. Being together for so long, one of the problems became that we pigeon-holed each other."[211] Since school, he'd been the guitarist who had been at Paul and John's beck and call, along with their dogsbody drummer.

In every sense, they warmed up every day to whatever anyone – usually Paul – began to play. Like Pavlov's dogs, they reacted instinctively to the prelusive "Weeeeeell" that had pitched them into countless twelve-bar rockers back in the Star-Club. Spanning 15 years, numbers with all the standard chord changes and others long learnt by rote accumulated on footage and tape, most of them resurfacing on numerous bootleg recordings but otherwise unreleased. Sometimes they'd peter out, if bedevilled by a forgotten middle eight or words that the vocalist couldn't be bothered to la-la any more. George led them through a fistful of Dylan songs, but less predetermined was the looser jamming in which Yoko played a leading role. Anything went – 'Three Cool Cats', 'The Harry Lime Theme', 'Michael Row The Boat Ashore', 'You Can't Do That', 'Love Me Do'. Even the once-detested 'The One After 909' now had period charm.

Any euphoria that these ambles down memory lane had wrought would fade when they came up against each other's new compositions. Even Ringo had one. In keeping with both the flagrant spirit of self-interest and the uncluttered production choice, anything that needed thinking about got a thumbs-down. George could only get past quality control with 'I Me Mine' – a dissertation of egocentricity that took longer to explain than write – and 'For You Blue', a straight twelve-bar. The lyrics to 'For You Blue' bore out a recent and extraordinary remark of his that was either tongue in cheek or a vainglorious attempt to align himself with Dylan: "I now want to write songs that don't have any meaning, because I'm a bit fed up with people saying, 'Hey, what's it all about?' It's still all 'Within You Without You', but I don't want to go into that any more, because now I'm being a rock 'n' roll star."[27]

If George was full of himself after his American trip, Paul was there to take him down a peg or two. The self-appointed and barely tolerated leader of The Beatles since John's tacit abdication, McCartney was so purposefully confident that, "when he succumbed to playing one of your tunes, he'd always do good, but you'd have to do 59 [sic] of Paul's songs before he'd even listen to one of yours".[52] Sooner than either could guess, Paul would inform his solicitor that Harrison had actually quarrelled with everybody during these sessions. George actually appeared to derive supercilious amusement as Ringo ran through his little 'Octopus' Garden', and his frankness about Yoko still rankled with John, but it was the Beatle he'd known the longest who drove him over the brink: "The very first day, Paul went into this 'you do this, you do that, don't do this, don't do that', and I thought, 'Christ, I thought he'd woken up by now.'"[221] Frustrated to the point of retaliation, George was no longer prepared to studiously avoid confrontation or continue to be Paul's artistic pawn.

His would be one of the quieter departures that aggravated the absolute one. After the worst *had* come to the worst, the film did come out. Entitled *Let It Be*, after Paul's magnum opus, it contained "a scene where Paul and I are having an argument and we're trying to cover it up. Then, the next scene, I'm not there."[32] Not knowing why this was, the reviewer for *The Morning Star* had still been aware of "George Harrison's shut-in expressions".[222] Up until his temporary disappearance, George's glowering huff at Paul's subtle harangues had welled to overflowing. "You're so full of shit, man,"[223] was his rejoinder to Paul's proposal to play a show amid desert ruins in Tunisia.

The last straw was when it transpired that McCartney had already ordered an aeroplane to be put on standby to carry The Beatles to Tunis. The assumption that they'd bend to his will was but one aspect of – as George's court statement would attest – Paul's "superior attitude". Of course, if it hadn't been Paul, he might have focused his resentment on the early starts, Yoko's screech-singing, John's passiveness or a film technician who hummed all the bloody time. It took a week for him to up and quit the chilly encampment with mains leads fanning out in all directions across the hollow chamber. "I didn't care if it was The Beatles," he said. "I was getting out."[59]

After slamming his car door in Kinfauns' forecourt, he immediately directed his anger to a creative end: "Getting home in the pissed-off mood, I wrote 'Wah-Wah'. I had such a headache with the whole argument."[59] None of the others thought to either remonstrate or plead with him to return, although Ringo called with a reminder of the following week's business meeting. With a less specific grievance, Ringo had been the same during *The Beatles*, and George's walk-out, like Ringo's, was viewed as a registered protest rather than boat-burning.

Although he was over-boisterous, Paul was trying at least to whip the group into action. Who else would? Certainly not George, who, in his self-imposed exile, polished up the epigram, "Resistance to dominance does not determine fitness for leadership."[224] Ringo's meeting was not, however, conducted as if nothing had happened. Paul could no longer believe that he held The Beatles in the hollow of his hand. He and John looked at George with new respect. Who'd have thought it? This was George with an unprecedented glint in his eye, George making a stand, George without his thumb in his mouth.

The disagreement's most beneficial outcome was a transfer to the half-finished but cosier studio in the Savile Row basement. The strained atmosphere, however, could only be alleviated by George employing his 'While My Guitar Gently Weeps' strategy, "because having a fifth person there, it sort of off-set the vibes".[211]

Instead of a guitarist, George's eyes fell on Billy Preston, whom Ray Charles had predicted "will follow in my footsteps".[225] Preston's first LP, *Sixteen-Year-Old Soul*, and a recommendation from Sounds Incorporated had led to a regular spot on *Shindig*, where his jovial personality and energetic keyboard dexterity impressed Charles, with whom he recorded another well-received album, *The Wildest Organ In Town*. This spawned a modest US hit, 'Billy's Bag', and the appreciation by other artists as a "musician's musician".

It was after a Royal Festival Hall concert with Charles that Billy renewed his acquaintance with George Harrison. There was an amicable exchange of telephone numbers and an invitation from George to drop in at Savile Row. On 22 January, he and Paul were about to descend into the Apple basement when "Billy walked into the office. I just grabbed him, and brought him down to the studio."[211]

Preston's coming did, indeed, lift the strike-happy depression. On their best behaviour, the group were more receptive to each other's new material. Constructive advice was offered as the three principal composers demonstrated nascent arrangement of songs destined for either one of the two albums left in The Beatles, or on those that began their lives apart. However, although Paul was keen for it to be the next single, his saccharine 'Maxwell's Silver Hammer' was derided as "granny music" by John and "so fruity"[59] by George. First refusal on some of George's items would be given to Billy, whose catalytic effect on the *Let It Be* sessions was about to earn him an Apple recording contract.

The ideal conclusion to the film had to be some public spectacle. Therefore, with less than a day's notice, cameras and sound equipment were made ready for a Beatles performance on Apple's flat roof. Unannounced, they and Preston shambled onto this makeshift stage to impinge upon the hearing of those as far away as Oxford Street with three-quarters of an hour of 'Get Back', 'The One After 909' and other Lennon and McCartney numbers hatched in the bowels of the building. For this, their last-ever performance, The Beatles reverted to type, John and Paul carrying the show with George and Ringo labouring away behind them. To the many that rapidly clotted along the pavements below, The Beatles were invisible and their unknown music muffled by an icy wind. Lennon, especially, was bouncing with backchat between songs, but those watching from windows opposite couldn't pretend that this was what it must have been like down the Cavern around lunchtime 1961. Some within earshot were less aware than their younger employees that they were being treated to something they could tell their grandchildren about. They weren't square, but there was a time and a place for this sort of row.

The breach of the peace was curbed, the crowds moved on, and

The Beatles wondered what poor sod they could bludgeon to edit, tart up and mix the frayed miles of *Let It Be* tapes for an album to go with the film. Throughout the project, The Beatles had subjected George Martin – no longer the awesome figure he'd been in 1962 – to much the same oafish discourtesies they rendered each other. He'd become as sick of *Let It Be* as they were, and they were tempted to ditch everything to do with it altogether. After perhaps re-reading *Shades Of Personality*, George – under duress – supplied one journalist with news containing less substance than hope. The group, he said, were soon to get their teeth into a film that would be "at least as big as *2001*. It's based on an idea we had a year ago but which fell through because of a lot of technicalities at the time. We've agreed to let each other do exactly what he wants to do with it." To this, he attached the enigmatic addenda: "We've got to a point where we can see each other quite clearly, and by allowing each other to be each other we can become The Beatles again."[226]

Quotes like this and events like the rooftop bash gave few cause to doubt that the group would continue. Like the monarchy, they were part of the national furniture. *Let It Be* had cleared some of the air and, if anything, their drifting apart seemed less inevitable than it had during *The Beatles*, when the mayhem that was Apple had been at its most uproarious. As well as the incompetents and losers they'd taken on board, rampant larceny and embezzlement by unscrupulous staff went undetected or was overlooked. Not that far from the truth would be a scene from 1978's spoof Beatles film biography *All You Need Is Cash*, in which a thinly-disguised Apple Corps' is pillaged by its employees while, in the foreground, its press agent chats to a television news commentator (played, incidentally, by George Harrison).

Enough of the Money Beatle of old remained for George to worry about drainage of the company economy. On legitimate business at Savile Row on the afternoon of the *Let It Be* finale, a freelance publicist chanced to share a lift with Harrison and Billy Preston. Smiling with his palm outstretched, he was momentarily embarrassed when George "wasn't prepared to shake hands and get another Beatle fan out of the way. He wanted to know who I was and what I was doing in Apple."[227]

A letter from the group's accountant disabused George that his financial means were infinite. His overdraft on the corporate account of over £30,000 was light against those of John and Paul, whose composing royalties admittedly gave more leeway for extravagance. Although Pattie hung onto her shares in Northern Songs, George had sold his small stake to form a separate and more personally lucrative publishing division, Singsong Ltd. He was therefore well out of it when ATV – amid impotent howls of rage from McCartney and Lennon – managed to buy a majority shareholding of Northern Songs in the late spring of 1969.

Since the loss of Brian Epstein, some of The Beatles' antics – particularly John's – had given Northern Songs' executive founder, Dick James, pause for agonised wonder, but the root cause of his selling his percentage to ATV was what he saw as their supreme folly: the appointment of Allen Klein as their business manager on 3 February 1969. Former clients were caustic about this American go-getter with a brain that spewed forth estimates at a moment's notice; his Tony Curtis haircut atop a boyish face and Barney Rubble frame; his golf-course clothes; and his forward-thrusting gait. Once so pleased with Klein's bellicose interventions on the Stones' behalf, Mick Jagger now took the trouble to call at Apple to dissuade The Beatles from signing with one he suspected of sharp practice. Klein, however, was already there, spieling in top gear.

Mick later rang John, but, following the latter's lead, George and Ringo had already melted into Klein's contractual caress. Although he'd been the first to champion the new administrator, Paul was now the only dissident. To disentangle Apple's disordered threads, he'd advocated his own father-in-law, who'd turned out to be not Sir Richard Asher of Wimpole Street but a New York lawyer named Lee Eastman.

The Harrisons had been unable to attend Linda Eastman and Paul's wedding celebrations on 12 March. If he'd finished a Jackie Lomax session on time, George had intended to meet Pattie at the reception at the Ritz Hotel. That afternoon, however, he was summoned to the studio telephone. Trying to keep calm, Pattie told him that Kinfauns had been invaded. This time, she wished it was only fans under the bed. Armed with a search warrant, a squad of Scotland Yard officers and Yogi, a sniffer dog, had reason to believe that the premises were being used for the consumption of controlled drugs, contrary to the provision of the 1966 Dangerous Drugs Act, section 42. Unconvinced by Pattie's air of fluffy innocence, Yogi and his colleagues executed their duties under the direction of plain-clothes Sergeant Norman Pilcher, who had busted John Lennon in the previous October. National treasures or not, The Beatles weren't above the law any more.

By the time George's engine died on Claremont Drive, the hunt was over and Pattie was most hospitably serving coffee as her persecutors relaxed in front of the television or listened to records. "It was like a social club,"[144] George thought as he and his wife were charged with possession of 570 grains of cannabis and a quantity of cocaine. Most of this, Pilcher of the Yard would inform Walton-on-Thames Magistrates Court, was uncovered in a wardrobe, a shoe box and Mrs Harrison's handbag. Years later, after Pilcher had been jailed for corrupting the course of justice, George felt at liberty to protest, "I'm a tidy man. I keep my socks in the sock drawer and my stash in the stash box. Anything else they must have brought."[144]

Pleading guilty, nonetheless, he and Pattie were fined £250 each. Then followed a minute of comedy when George asked for the return of a Crown exhibit, an ornamental peace pipe on which had been found traces of illegal resin. It was a present, he added, from the Native American Church of Peyote Indians. The judge couldn't see why not, as long as "Mr Harrison doesn't mind if we first remove the drugs".[228] The more trivial tabloids also stressed the irony of a dog called Yogi bringing the most spiritual Beatle to book.

"You are a very holy man!" a lady in a fur coat had shouted at Lennon as he and Yoko had emerged from their court appearance. Although he was lapsing, John was still seen by many as The Beatles' "official religious spokesman",[57] as George had once called him; the Aaron to the less loquacious George's Moses. To say things most people didn't want to hear, the Lennons had made their lives an open and ludicrous book now that they'd started week-long bed-ins for world peace in posh hotels, holding press conferences from inside king-sized white sacks and engaging in further bewildering pranks too indecent for a family newspaper.

After a new angle as a change from weeks of Lennon's headline-hogging outrage, some journalists wondered if George wasn't just as screwy on the quiet. On the afternoon following his court sentence, he'd received a conveyor belt of press in his Savile Row office after changing from a sober blue suit to jumper and jeans. During his audience, the *Music Echo* correspondent logged the presence in the white room of both an unnamed "weird American woman gibbering incessantly" and "members of a quasi-religious cult calling itself the 'Khrishna [*sic*] Consciousness Society'".[299] As far as *Music Echo* could see, this Khrishna lot were no different from any other in the passing show of lunatics that infested Apple.

These days, it was understood by the receptionist that shaven-headed chaps dressed in orange sheets had something to do with George. Often, he and they would be heard on the roof chanting their unremitting maha-mantra. Even when they left, he'd continue *sotto voce* about the offices, sometimes dirging other bhajans by way of variation. Devotees were welcome at Kinfauns, too, for vegetarian feasts, with such occasions concluding (as was proper) with a bout of Hare Krishnas to synthesiser accompaniment by either their host or Billy Preston. As they didn't squander their appetites on stimulants, George was also striving – with incomplete success – to eschew soft drugs, cigarettes, caffeine and alcohol.

When Prabhupada's movement had extended a feeler into England, it was, to George, "just like another piece of a jigsaw puzzle that was coming together to make a complete picture".[152] His first practical response was to co-sign the lease for the Radha Krishna Temple (named after the avatar's closest earthly consort) in Holborn, which, if rather dilapidated, was handy for the regular-as-clockwork chanting processions up and down the principal thoroughfares of central London, mainly Oxford Street.

"I was never with the Hare Krishna movement," George would insist later. "I was just friends with them."[230] In 1969, however, a tale went the rounds that he'd almost become a full-time *bhakta*, bald head and all, but had cried off because Prabhupada himself had soundly advised that he'd be more useful as a pop star. On his death-bed in 1977, the swami would twist a ring from his finger and instruct it to be delivered to George, whom he called his "archangel". There were reasons aplenty for the expiring Prabhupada's gratitude. From George's purse had poured the means for founding and provisioning many temples and yoga-ashrams, as well as the printing of Krishna books, some of which contained Harrison forewords and interviews. "All part of the service,"[152] he reckoned of his astounding feat of steering the mantra into the Top 20 in September 1969.

As much a freak hit as those of The Singing Dogs or, more appropriately, The Singing Nun, The Radha Krishna Temple's accelerando 'Hare Krishna Mantra' on Apple was a smoother affair than The Fugs' version, with most of its accompaniment – harmonium, guitar, percussion and bass – manufactured by George just before a session for *Abbey Road*, The Beatles' next album. The strangest act ever invited to be on *Top Of The Pops*, the devotees nonetheless held their own amid the likes of Creedence Clearwater Revival, The Bee Gees and instrumental duo Sounds Nice, who were particular favourites of Pattie's.

Some chuckled incredulously when the chanters flashed into their living rooms, but thanks to George the irrepressible 'Hare Krishna Mantra' had encroached on public consciousness to a degree that Prabhupada could never had imagined in 1966. The milkman whistled it, it became fodder for comedians' gags and even a vinyl spoof in Harry H Corbett's 'Harry Krishna'. A rendition was a punch-line in a *Crackerjack* sketch on BBC's children's television.

More satisfying than these dubious accolades were the full houses at the movement's initiatory evenings. Admission was free, but some attendees arrived in anticipation of a pop show or of seeing George Harrison. After the talks, the slide shows, the Indian dancing and the performances by The Vedic Ensemble For Dramatic Arts, they were mollified when the Temple band played the hit – an audience-participation number – and hearty refreshments were served at the end. Nevertheless, there were many new converts and an even bigger increase of sympathisers who no longer regarded a line of Hare

Krishna chanters down Oxford Street with sidelong scepticism or contemptuous amusement.

Doing no harm either was the follow-up single, 'Govinda' – Krishna reincarnated as a shepherd boy – which was an actual verse-chorus song rather than a repeated chant. Its Sanskrit lyrics aside, with its muted but driving beat 'Govinda' didn't sound out of place on the juke box in the greasiest cafe. Although they'd made the charts and Jackie Lomax hadn't, The Radha Krishna Temple weren't pop stars any more than The Joystrings had been. As His Divine Grace would expect of them, it was *Top Of The Pops* today and back on the streets tomorrow.

Teaching by example, the ascetic Prabhupada, author of more than 70 profitable theological books, didn't stint on a vigorous global schedule of lecture tours, allowing himself only the barest minimum of material wants. The "humble servant of the servant of the servant of Krishna"[151] made money but had no wish to own it. In 1969, he and his closest disciples were in England, where they were put up in an annex on Tittenhurst Park, the Lennons' newly-acquired 80-acre estate between Ascot and Sunningdale. It was in these quarters on a cold and rainy afternoon that George, John and Yoko were conducted into the master's presence. Well into his 70s, he was a squat, brown, rather ugly old bloke whose lined features were relieved by an underlying humour. Where the Maharishi might have cackled, Prabhupada only twinkled. He and Yoko did most of the talking, enabling George to note that, although he sometimes lapsed into Sanskrit, "He never came off as somebody above you. He always had the child-like simplicity"[152] His Divine Grace had a feeling that, during his Calcutta boyhood, he had known the unborn Lennon in a previous existence as a businessman/philanthropist. Yet, in his self-inflicted poverty and his devotion to the purity of his ancient creed, Prabhupada seemed more plausible to the wary Beatles than the Westernised Maharishi.

At first, the new guru impressed John more than George, until "I realised later on that he was much more incredible than what you could see on the surface".[152] Whatever the rumoured zenith of George's personal commitment to the Krishna movement, his perspective just prior to Prabhupada's death was, "He is my friend. he is my master, who I have great respect for. It's like, if you want to learn how to ski, you go to somebody who'll teach you how to ski. I accept Prabhupada as qualified to teach people about Krishna."[32]

"Better than Disneyland"[152] was the Society's Bhagavad Gita museum in Los Angeles, from which the Harrisons ordered a life-sized fountain/statue of the demigod Siva to be delivered to their new home when they found it. There wasn't space at Kinfauns either for the four-poster bed, still to be collected from an antiques shop. From a vocational viewpoint, too, "The house isn't really big enough to have a proper studio. I've got all sorts of equipment together, but there's hardly room to move."[231] Whatever building George chose was less important than its surroundings. Although he'd recently roamed New York backstreets virtually unrecognised in non-descript denims and crêpe-soled work shoes, he – like John – required abundant grounds, "because I am seeking the absolute peace of complete privacy. I am also insisting on a private lake, because water is very peaceful for the mind."[231]

All four Beatles had been house-hunting of late. As well as being subject to supertax in the "one big Coronation Street"[231] (George's phrase) that was Britain, a problem facing all four was that of greedy estate agents forcing up asking prices for those they assumed had wealth beyond calculation. The Harrison solution was to send an Apple subordinate masquerading as a prospective buyer to look around and report on likely-looking properties on the market. On one occasion, an ivy-clung manor from the pages of Country Life was so intriguing that they had to inspect it in person. The plan was for Alistair Taylor and Pattie – in untrendy twin-set and pillbox hat – to pose as a newly married couple, with George as the liveried chauffeur of his own white Mercedes. His neglecting to open smartly its doors for his passengers implanted instant suspicion in the pile's lady owner. This grew with the frequency of Pattie and Alistair's scarcely suppressed giggles as they kept contradicting each other. Back at the front door, she glanced again at the driver, his hair pinned under a peaked cap, staring fixedly ahead. A great light dawned and she turned to Pattie to ask whether Mr Harrison wanted to see the house as well.

While George and Pattie's search continued, the Starkeys had moved from Surrey to Highgate after purchasing the home of a friend, Peter Sellers, with whom Ringo was co-starring in *The Magic Christian* in his first major film role. A fascinated observer, George looked on at several location shootings, which varied from Henley-on-Thames railway station to an Atlantic crossing on the *QE2*. This excursion was marred when, intending to stage another bed-in on arrival in New York, the Lennons were denied a visa because of John's drug conviction. Less notorious, the Harrisons had already understood that their own police record "means restrictions on where we travel in future".[228] Sellers' commiseration with them confirmed George's opinion that the distinguished comedian/actor was "a devoted hippy, a free spirit".[59] As a guest speaker at an Oxford Union debate, he'd been applauded for his honesty in admitting that he'd smoked cannabis.

Assisting Sellers with *The Magic Christian* screenplay were fellow humorists John Cleese and Graham Chapman, who were on the team of *Monty Python's Flying Circus*, then in the midst of its maiden series on BBC2. Their humour had similarities with that contained in Lennon's own slim volumes in its casual cruelty and stream-of-consciousness transmogrification, and seemed to be the culmination of all that had tickled George about fringe comedy since The Goons. Watching the first show in the company of Derek Taylor, "I couldn't understand how normal television could continue after that."[188] As was his expensive habit then, he sent a telegram straight away to Broadcasting House: "Love the show. Keep doing it."

Although he wasn't one of those people who re-enacted the Dead Parrot Sketch or the Five-Minute Argument at work, he took to quoting lines from Monty Python as frequently as those of Bob Dylan. Advantaged by his celebrity, he came to mix socially with the outfit that – so it was whispered – were to comedy what The Beatles were to pop.

George's enjoyment of this programme was a minor comfort during a year beset with more than just Beatle traumas. Pattie had been his muse for 'Something' and the beginnings of a song entitled 'Beautiful Girl', but the marriage had floated into a choppy sea. Her absence at that first audience with Prabhupada was a symptom of an increasing disinclination to play Yoko to George's John. Her personality precluded as deep an engrossment in spiritual pursuits as her husband. She wanted a bit of frivolity, for a change – and there were others after a bit of frivolity, too. George – console midwife to 'The King Of Fuh' – had become rather sanctimonious about certain London theatre presentations since the abolition of stage censorship in 1968. Nevertheless, Pattie took her seat in the Roundhouse on the opening night of *Oh! Calcutta*, a musical with much nudity and explicit language. With George's blessing, male companions such as Derek Taylor or Eric Clapton accompanied her on this and like occasions almost like 18th-century *cavaliere servantes*. Clapton, however, tired of always meeting her in public.

While Pattie resisted being alone with Eric, stray mutterings about her spouse's extra-marital picayunes filtered around Savile Row's offices, but the later memoirs of former Apple associates offer scant evidence that George was ever unfaithful to his wife. However, Lennon's confessions to *Rolling Stone* in 1970 about The Beatles' amatory adventures on tour may have provoked some frank exchanges in the Harrison living room. George himself was as indiscreet in 1977, attributing Clapton's coveting of Pattie to "trying to get his own back on me. I pulled his chick [*sic*] once."[32]

George confided the dilution of his marriage to a favoured "Apple Scruff", his nickname for a constant loiterer around its steps. No ordinary fans, some Scruffs were nomads from other continents, mainly America. A handful had clogged the pavement for so long that, in this less hectic phase of The Beatles stardom, they'd understood how privately ordinary, even boring, were the icons they'd once worshipped from afar. Some felt oddly disappointed when George began offering conversation as a preferred alternative to irritably signing his autograph while hurrying from kerb to doorway. Adoration, however, would be years a-dwindling. In February 1969, after George's tonsillectomy at University College Hospital, its switchboard had been jammed with requests for the gruesome excisions.

Through daily contact with the Scruffs, George's presumptions about fans had altered. No longer a screaming mass as amorphous as frogspawn, "their part in the play is equally as important as ours".[226] If he was in the mood and Savile Row was quiet, he'd reserve a little attention for certain Scruffs that he knew by name, asking after their families, noticing whether they'd had a haircut and bringing them up to date with progress on Abbey Road. Somehow, these familiarities were closer to the spirit of the Cavern than *Let It Be* had ever been.

Harrison was still as prone to idolatry as the most devout Scruff. Nonetheless, although he rarely missed Monty Python and played over and over again the same records by Electric Flag, Stoneground or whatever new US combo had briefly captivated him, he was always drawn back to Bob Dylan. As John had been fixated in 1965, so Dylan cropped up in Harrison's music – here a *Blonde On Blonde* chord progression for 'Long Long Long', there a *Highway 61 Revisited* chug for 'Old Brown Shoe'. Most heartfelt a homage was 'Behind That Locked Door', a new number about "the tales you have taught me" and George's apprehensions and hopes for Bob's first major concert since his motorbike calamity.

This comeback was to be a 60-minute set with The Band at the second Isle of Wight Festival on 1969's August bank-holiday weekend. A fortnight earlier, The Band had been among those entertaining the half-million drenched Americans who'd braved the larger outdoor gathering at Woodstock just over the state border from Big Pink. From a distance of years, Woodstock would be viewed as the climax of hippy culture, a vote of no confidence in square old President Nixon and the rest of George's "old fools who are governing us".

By Woodstock standards, the three days of music on the downs above the Isle of Wight's Woodside Bay were quite well organised, in that there were a few more portable toilets, washing facilities and vendors of over-priced food and tepid soft drinks than there were at Woodstock. On the Sunday afternoon, the Harrisons, the Lennons and the Starkeys arrived by helicopter in time for John Mayer's Indo-Jazz Fusions and subsequent acts who primed the massed tribes for the main event. In a special compound before the stage, The Beatles and lesser pop aristocrats sat comfortably apart from the common herd beyond the crash barriers. In the dying minutes before Dylan,

George was taken aback when the strains of 'Hare Krishna Mantra' effused from the disc jockey's turntable. Had Bob himself paused in his backstage pacing to request that particular record for his closest Beatle friend? Mattering almost as much perhaps was whether John believed he had.

As arranged, when the show was over, Dylan boarded the Beatle helicopter to spend the night at Tittenhurst Park. His performance had been more adequate than the festival's lavatory provision and, for many, it was enough that he appeared at all. Minstrel to a generation though he was, no one had really expected the waters of the Solent to part any more than those of the Serpentine in June when Eric Clapton's Blind Faith had made its concert debut free of charge in the Cockpit, Hyde Park's natural arena.

A few weeks later, at the same venue, The Rolling Stones hosted the largest assembly for any cultural event London had ever seen. Supported by Alexis Korner, Family and new sensations King Crimson, the Stones' buckshee bash became a memorial for Brian Jones, who had drowned in his swimming pool two days earlier. George was told of the tragedy while on holiday in Sardinia. "I don't think Brian had enough love or understanding,"[233] he said.

A cohort of Brian's even before the formation of The Yardbirds, Eric Clapton was touring the States with Blind Faith. Those six weeks on the road effectively finished off "the supergroup of a time".[234] The "gentle surprise"[235] of their Cockpit performance was perverted to blaring, ham-fisted resignation when "Acclamation By Riot!" became a typical headline summary of US audience conduct.

There were enough rest days on the tour for the band members to risk flights back to English peace and quiet, but Clapton preferred to kill time by purchasing vintage American cars and shipping them back to Surrey. After dark, he began loafing around with the package's small fry, seeking the particular comradeship of a workmanlike group led by Deep South guitarist Delaney Bramlett, a former Shindog, which also included his wife Bonnie, ex-Traffic guitarist Dave Mason and a faction of Los Angeles session musicians nicknamed "the blue-eyed soul school". That faintly sickening word *funky* was used to describe the economic tightness of their rhythm section.

"They were such down-home humble cats," said Eric. "I started a rapport with Delaney and saw ahead that I didn't want Blind Faith."[236] Eric's disenchantment with the Blind Faith routine and his pleasure at bashing tambourine while hidden in the larger ranks of the preceding Delaney And Bonnie And Friends may have been kindled by press criticism aimed directly at him. By the time "the ultimate supergroup" threw in the towel at the LA Forum in August, half of its number – including Ginger Baker – were slumming it in the Bramlett tour bus.

From Clapton's own pocket came the necessary outlay for the aggressively friendly Friends' European tour in December. He'd be their lead guitarist and, they hoped, a passport to fame. A highlight of the intervening months was Eric's recruitment by John Lennon into the *ad hoc* Plastic Ono Band for a hastily rehearsed performance at a festival in Toronto of old rock 'n' roll classics and Yoko's improvisations. They also had a go at 'Cold Turkey', the second hit single that John's new group had recorded as "an escape valve from The Beatles"[173] – so he put it – from whom he'd cast his net furthest.

Back at Savile Row, George was most sarcastic about the Lennons' latest venture. He didn't care for Yoko's Plastic Ono Band input, but nonetheless felt that John had cold-shouldered him by inviting Clapton to Toronto instead. Once, it might have seemed more of a betrayal, but now The Beatles – like his marriage – were held together only by habit. "When we actually split up," George would later remember, "it was just the relief. We should have done it years before."[211] While none of them were yet brave enough to deliver the *coup de grâce*, they prepared for the eventuality, after their individual fashions, with Ringo consolidating his then-promising film career and, like Paul, recording a solo album; John with his new band and espousal of various causes; and George, apparently, attempting to compose a stage musical with Derek Taylor and the soundtrack to *Zachariah*, a western staring Ginger Baker(!), neither of which came to fruition.

Whatever else he may or may not have had up his sleeve, from 1968 George had been "getting more and more into"[201] record production, which he saw as "psychologically trying to get people to do their best without imposing on them and without letting them freak out".[201] Under his aegis, Billy Preston's 'That's The Way God Planned It' had equalled the 'Hare Krishna Mantra' high of Number Eleven in the British hit parade, although his next smash would be a long time coming. George couldn't repeat Billy's success with Doris Troy, a former *protégé* of "godfather of soul" James Brown. Her early singles had been much-demanded spins on the turntables of the "in" nightclub-discotheques that George and Pattie had frequented in their first flush of romance. Even with stirling backing from Preston, Starr, Clapton, Steve Stills and other top-notch musicians assembled by her new producer, much the same impasse loomed for Doris – no big hits but fine-quality disco fodder. Her first for George, 'Ain't That Cute', would be 1970's Soul Record Of The Year in *Melody Maker*, not far ahead of its double-sided follow-up, fiery versions of 'Get Back' and the traditional 'Jacob's Ladder'.

In hard financial terms, George may have been barking up the wrong tree with Doris, just as he had with Jackie Lomax. As Decca had passed on The Beatles, did he miss something when auditioning and rejecting Bamboo, a Swedish band that would connect genealogically with 70s chartbusters Abba? The Hollies thought highly enough of Bamboo to shanghai its lead vocalist in 1971, when Allan Clarke briefly flew the nest.

Noticeably influenced by The Hollies were The Iveys, a Liverpool-Welsh group who were renamed Badfinger by Paul McCartney. With Paul and George among their producers, they were the only Apple band other than The Beatles to enjoy any measure of chart longevity. Badfinger had descended from The Masterminds and The Calderstones, two minor Mersey Beat acts formed by lads who'd coughed up the one-shilling membership fee to catch The Hollies – and The Beatles – time after time at the Cavern. Amalgamating as The Iveys, they were managed by Bill Collins, who'd rubbed shoulders with Jim McCartney in a dance band and was father to Lewis, a latter-day Mojo and future television tough guy. For a while, the Iveys backed a Scouse operatic tenor turned pop singer who, as "David Garrick", had twice penetrated the UK Top 30 in 1966. However, it was without Garrick that they were spotted by Mal Evans and, with their pedigree an asset, groomed for greener pastures.

The fact that Apple didn't throw down a line to better-qualified supplicants like Freddie Garrity – who was interviewed by Yoko – and The Remo Four may have been because their very names were too directly associated with dear, dead Mersey Beat. Nevertheless, when the latter – shedding Colin Manley – mutated into one-hit-wonders Ashton, Gardner And Dyke, George lent an apt hand on 'I'm Your Spiritual Breadman', a track from their second LP

George also had a tinge of complacent snobbery about who was or wasn't worthy of Apple's attention. Only pop's upper crust were really suitable, by which he meant "The Beatles, Stones, Bob Dylan, Eric Clapton and Delaney And Bonnie and that's it. Who needs anything else? Oh yes, Billy Preston's very good, and eventually he'll get through to the people."[224]

Work on the *That's The Way God Planned It* album had been postponed while George also abetted the Bramletts in their projected rise to superstardom. With Ringo, he'd watched Clapton strutting his stuff with his new-found Friends when the British leg of their tour began at the Albert Hall. A little blinded by Eric's hyperbole, he remembered thinking, "That's a great band. I'd love to be playing with them,"[188] as Delaney *et al* punched out their shrill, simple and neatly dovetailed repertoire, which included club soul in the Doris Troy vein, a Little Richard medley and a sexist original entitled 'Groupie'. Buoyed by big-name approbation, they then commanded the stage of the Speakeasy in the small hours and did it all over again. George was overwhelmed by their freewheeling Southern ebullience and drove home wondering how seriously they'd been when they'd said, "OK, we're coming to your house in the morning,"[59] when he'd spoken his thoughts about their earlier performance. For that matter, how serious had *he* been?

He took the plunge after breakfast, when "they pulled up the bus outside my house and said, 'Come on!' I just grabbed a guitar and an amp and went on the road with them."[59] The last time he'd played Bristol's Colston Hall was just over five years earlier. Beatlemania might as well have been five centuries ago as the adult

Moptop took the stage at the same auditorium amongst Bramlett's rank and file in his re-grown beard, drab denims and lank hair centre-parted like John's and splayed halfway down his back. Delaney And Bonnie's name was on the poster, but it was Clapton that the customers had paid to see. No one in the crowd knew who the extra guitarist was until he was introduced near the finish. Only then was he the cynosure of all eyes. This wasn't a record cover, television or a pin-up; George Harrison of the superhuman Beatles was actually there. Not everyone grasped the magnitude of the moment that they'd been fated to witness as the pale figure continued strumming, partly obscured by those drawling exuberantly into the front microphones.

Because the show could have gone on without him, George's return to the footlights wasn't as earth-shattering as Dylan's and Lennon's had been, and yet he was solidly at the music's heart, unobtrusively ministering to the overall effect. Moreover, so little was expected of him by the band that the trek started to be quite fun, as it progressed up England's spine to engagements in Sheffield, Newcastle and, on 5 December, the Liverpool Empire, where he couldn't prevent himself from addressing the audience with the mutual truism, "This certainly brings back a lot of memories."

Diners in motorway service stations stared at him, but it was Eric who was more often accosted for autographs as he laid into a greasy but obviously satisfying fry-up. Gazing at his chum with benign fascination across the formica table, George picked at baked beans and toffee-coloured chips with less enthusiasm. The rest of the band weren't as down home or humble as Clapton had made out, and their detailing of the previous night's carnal shenanigans and stimulant intake could prove monotonous, but otherwise they were good company. Nearly all were now using the Bramletts as a springboard for better-paid, more prestigious employment. Within weeks, most would stop being Friends to enter the ranks of Joe Cocker's cumbersome big band Mad Dogs And Englishmen. The horn section of Bobby Keyes and Jim Price found it convenient to take up British residency, commuting to fulfil a work schedule that blossomed from pot-boiling sessions with comparative unknowns like Audience and Third World War to proudly augmenting The Rolling Stones. Not so openly on the make was drummer Jim Keltner, who paradoxically emerged as the most in demand of these "super sidemen", as they became known. Also, of all the Los Angeles studio crowd, he was the one with whom George felt most at ease.

While crossing the North Sea for dates in Scandinavia, Delaney And Bonnie crept into the UK Top 30 for the first and only time. Strongly in evidence on 'Coming Home' was the departed Dave Mason's bottleneck-guitar obligato. It made sense to plug this single *en route* round England, and George was asked to supply the missing element: "Delaney gave me this slide guitar and said, 'You do the Dave Mason part.' I'd never attempted anything before that, and I think my slide-guitar playing originated from that."[59]

Tuned to any open chord, the guitar's strings were fretted with a finger-sized glass or metal cylinder around the finger. From sustained shiver to undulating legato, its resonant effects are most commonly heard in the contrasting spheres of blues and Hawaiian music. Although the dobro and pedal-operated steel guitar were instruments manufactured specifically for the slide technique, money-conscious non-specialists generally made do on ordinary guitars with test-tubes, bits of piping and, in George's case, a piece hacksawed from an old amplifier stand by Mal Evans: "I had some glass slides made, also. I find the glass slide tends to be a warmer sound, whereas the metal one is more slippery and is brighter, but I couldn't tell you which one I've used where."[58] Lest we forget, 'Old Brown Shoe' had an undercurrent of bottleneck, and there had been traces of it as far back as *Rubber Soul*. However, like the sitar on 'Norwegian Wood', it had been an inappreciable novelty played on either John's Hawaiian model – bought on a whim – or on his own retuned Stratocaster.

The bottleneck or slide guitar is difficult to play creatively and well, and during the earlier week of the Delaney And Bonnie jaunt George had confined himself to a passable solo on 'Coming Home' before dropping back to hack rhythm for the rest of the set. Gaining confidence, however, he gradually inserted more bottleneck and less rhythm. After this practical experience, he continued to teach himself at home, "thinking maybe this is how I can come up with something half decent".[59] With no Shankar of the slide to instruct him or even a worthwhile manual, he was in virgin territory, but he learned what he could from records and trial and error, just as Brian Jones had in 1962. However, rather than a direct absorption of Elmore James and other black bluesmen, he favoured the almost academic approach of Los Angeles-born bottleneck exponent and music archivist Ry Cooder, with his "good touch and good ear for melody".[59]

Although he copied Cooder by winding his guitar with heavy-gauge strings and heightening its bridge, George's slide playing would become musically as distinctive a signature as the mark of Zorro. Ethnic blues had entered his stylistic arsenal too late. It had been the same with his struggles with the sitar, but to these he'd attribute a quality in his post-Beatle guitar work "that you can't put your finger on".[59]

In Sweden, during the Friends tour, he'd written his first bottleneck song, 'Woman Don't You Cry For Me' (with meagre assistance from Delaney and Eric), which strode a tightrope between skiffle and the country-and-western end of pop. During the band's three nights in Copenhagen, he started another opus, 'My Sweet Lord', in which he imagined "corresponding guitar harmonies to the bedrock slide parts"[58] and East-meets-West backing responses that cleverly alternated hallelujahs with *hare krishna*s. As all artists do sometimes, he borrowed from and disguised his source of inspiration, in this instance by tampering with the chordal accents of 'Oh Happy Day', an 18th-century traditional spiritual that had itself been overhauled to chart-climbing effect in the previous summer by US gospel choir The Edwin Hawkins Singers. Although George removed it many degrees from 'Oh Happy Day', something else about 'My Sweet Lord' remained infuriatingly familiar.

Present in Scandinavia at George's invitation, another temporary Friend, Billy Preston – now a born-again Christian – liked the finished 'My Sweet Lord' enough to want to record it when he got back to London. The Edwin Hawkins Singers, of all people, were available to help with Billy's call-and-response interplay, although nearly all of them were ignorant about what this 'Hare Krishna' bit meant. Perhaps because the final result bore too much of a melodic resemblance to 'He's So Fine', a 1963 hit by US girl group The Chiffons, it was released as a single only in Europe, where it became a medium-sized hit. It might have spared George much grief if the 'My Sweet Lord' saga had ended there.

As there would never be enough room for them on Beatles records, George was foisting more and more of his songs onto his production clients, giving the new 'You' to Ronnie Spector while Preston cut 'All Things Must Pass', but he turned his nose up at the freshly concocted 'What Is Life'.

During The Beatles' last weeks, a new face around Apple was often seen beside George at the mixing desk. Phil Spector and George were to have "a lot of good times, but I had a lot of bad times as well".[164] Although past his best, Spector had been unfortunate enough to be reeled in to cobble together an LP from the *Let It Be* tapes.

Under the Klein regime, Apple had been more inclined to fire than hire. So chilling was this new realism that those employees who'd so far survived the purge dared not clock in late or pilfer so much as a paperclip. Out had gone the luxury items and dead wood like Zapple and Apple Electronics. Jackie Lomax's small retainer was discontinued and Ronnie Spector's 'You' was cancelled. Even the faithful Alistair Taylor – not yet over glandular fever made worse by overwork – was called back to the office midway through a business lunch to be cast adrift with three months' salary. Determined to tell The Beatles of what must surely be some mistake and somehow seek their protection, Taylor and others in the same boat were at a loss to comprehend why all four were "too busy" to come to the telephone or answer letters.

McCartney's deafness to these casualties' pleas, however, was not a sign that he'd accepted Klein, even if the American's radical pruning of staff and the huge royalty deal he'd struck with Capitol for The Beatles had amassed millions within months. Thanks to Klein, too, Paul was no longer flummoxed when someone like Frank Zappa rang to ask him if The Mothers Of Invention could parody the *Sgt Pepper* cover for their next album. The problem was that Paul didn't *want* to trust Klein, a feeling partly expressed in his *Abbey Road* songlet 'You Never Give Me Your Money'. Therefore, why should he excuse the seemingly concrete proof put before him by his in-laws of Klein's frauds, low cunning and high-handedness?

Indirectly, Klein was also blamed for the hash made of *Let It Be* by Spector, who, in the pungent words of engineer Glyn Johns, "overdubbed a lot of bullshit all over it, strings and choirs and yuck".[74] McCartney didn't like it much, either, but his written demand to Klein (not Spector) that the damage be repaired had little effect. Adding insult to injury, the release of *McCartney*, his solo album, was to be held back in order to give *Let It Be* a clearer run. Only by bawling out Ringo – sent to mediate by John and George – was he able to ensure that *McCartney* was issued as first scheduled.

When Paul served his writs to dissolve the group, Ringo took it hardest, but John's private announcement of his own resignation many months before had been hushed up for fear of it cramping Klein's bullying of Capitol. As fatigued as everyone else of the fraternal animosity, Lennon was flunking out of more Beatle commitments as The Plastic Ono Band, his peace mission and his life with the Wallis Simpson of pop took priority. He was even missing at the final Beatles recording session, convened on 3 January 1970 to tie up a *Let It Be* loose end. In skittish mood between takes, George indulged in a little verbal tomfoolery at John's expense: "You all will have read that Dave Dee is no longer with us, but Micky, Tich and I would like to carry on the good work that's always gone down at Number Two."[237]

During an Abbey Road session, a digestive biscuit he'd left on top of a speaker cabinet which was found and eaten by Yoko had been the pretext for George to air again his pent-up exasperation with John. Just before Christmas, John and Yoko trawled what a reviewer would describe as "a jamboree of pop talent"[238] to constitute a sprawling Plastic Ono Supergroup for a charity knees-up at the Strand Lyceum. Joining in the impromptu racket was an artillery of drummers, including The Bonzo Dog Band's "Legs" Larry Smith and The Who's Keith Moon, plus pianist Nicky Hopkins and most of the Bramlett Friends, among them Preston and a cynical Harrison. Like Dylan at the Isle of Wight, it was sufficient that two Beatles were simply there, but after a lengthy and headache-inducing 'Cold Turkey' came Yoko's 'Don't Worry Kyoko'. As it stretched into its

20th howling, cacophonous minute, the jamboree of pop talent exchanged nervous glances.

A stone's throw from the Strand, Messrs Harrison, Lennon, McCartney and Starkey were disassociated formally as a business enterprise one morning in 1971 within the stained-glass High Court, where Mr Justice Stamp presided over their mud-slinging before declaring in Paul's favour and delivering Apple's finances to the official receiver's scrutiny. Although it didn't seem so then, this last measure was a boon to the defendants when they too grew disenchanted with Allen Klein, because, said George, "nobody could spend it".[239]

Back in the winter of 1969, however, George for one was not unhappy with his manager. As Bill Harry said, "It took Allen Klein to get him his first A-side." Its six-note instrumental hook too understated, the arrangement of 'Something' that framed Joe Cocker's tardy belly-aching was but a skeleton of what it had become on side one of *Abbey Road*. That hook alone drove me to distraction when it was whistled by a fellow employee during my sojourn as an office cleaner in the following summer, when it was given a second lease of life in the British Top Ten by Shirley Bassey in one of nearly 200 cover versions. Almost as durable a standard as 'Yesterday', 'Something' was heard as supermarket muzak, in the tinklings of Liberace, Smokey Robinson, Elvis, Bert Kaempfert, Booker T's MGs and, yes, Ray Charles. Of them all, George's favourite was the re-invention by James Brown, who masked the hook with a hollered "I got to believe in something" before burying the song in one of his anguished raps. 'Something' was also the only Beatles number to be recorded by Sinatra, who hailed it as "the greatest love song of the past 50 years".[240]

George would cite later compositions as equal in quality, "but they might not be as popular, because it was The Beatles who made 'Something'".[210] This blueprint had been trimmed down from an eight-minute take, losing a long instrumental fade and – like 'While My Guitar Gently Weeps' – an entire verse. None the worse for that, it sliced to Number One in the States like a wire through cheese. Pop, however, obeys no law of natural justice, which is why, in the UK, 'Something' – coupled with John's 'Come Together' – was stopped in its tracks during the usual Yuletide silly season.

Perhaps Paul was right about 'Maxwell's Silver Hammer', for 'Something' was the first Beatle 45 since 1962 that didn't infiltrate the UK Top Three. This petty dampener on George's triumph could be ascribed to Allen Klein's adherence to US procedure of issuing a single off an already successful album. In the week it came out, *Abbey Road* barged its way to a gold disc, outstripping the latest by pretenders like Led Zeppelin, Ten Years After and the defunct Blind Faith. Also swallowing dust was another hot property, Fleetwood Mac, whose 'Albatross' instrumental had triggered one *Abbey Road* track – John's lush 'Sun King' – as outside sources had triggered George's recent songs, "just to get going. ['Sun King'] never really sounded like Fleetwood Mac, just like 'All Things Must Pass' never sounded like The Band, but they were the point of origin."[59]

The atmosphere during the making of *Abbey Road* had been, if not genial, then more co-operative than it had been during *The Beatles* and *Let It Be*. It was as if the four protagonists had agreed – at least, subconsciously – that *Abbey Road* was to be the last LP and so they might as well go out under a flag of truce. Fanning dull embers, George would proffer the press the faggot of a follow-up to *Abbey Road*, on which "we're going to get an equal rights thing so we'll all have as much on the album". He hedged his bets with talk of "doing an album of my own, mainly just to get rid of the songs I've got stacked up."[220]

These days, he was "doing it a lot. I just get the compulsion – like the other week, when I suddenly had the desire to write a country and western song and I didn't have any idea of its shape, but I just had to do it."[241] The outcome of this urge might have been 'Sunshine Life For Me', a countrified hoe-down written and forgotten about when holidaying at Donovan's Irish cottage while the litigational storms gathered. Its subtitle, 'Sail Away Raymond', referred to one of Klein's legal advisers.

Although not as overtly as on Paul's 'You Never Give Me Your Money', Apple's interminable board meetings also had a bearing on George's second *Abbey Road* composition, 'Here Comes The Sun', One morning in early summer, Harrison awoke nauseated with the thought of another spell in the office. Like a truant, he found a bolt-hole at a friend's house. In Eric Clapton's garden, "it was sunny, and it was obviously a release from the tension that had been building up. I picked up the guitar for the first time in a couple of weeks, because I'd been so busy, and the first thing to come out was that."[211]

'Here Comes The Sun' encapsulated more than the relief of a day off work. In the sparkle of its finger-picked acoustic Gibson and light-hearted verses about melting ice and smiling faces, it caught the moment of emergence after a winter cocooned indoors. "You can almost feel the rays of the sun,"[241] *Melody Maker* exclaimed of the *Abbey Road* original while damning with faint praise its cover by a chap called Paul Munday, who was poised to trouble the forthcoming decade as "Gary Glitter". A younger glam rock executant than Glitter, Steve Harley's better timing would put his version of 'Here Comes The Sun' into the British Top Ten during 1976's extraordinarily warm July.

That George's *Abbey Road* songs were subjected to the most widespread syndication reflected both his commercial peak as a composer *per se* and his ascendancy over both Lennon and McCartney. Although John – with sound reason – continued to ridicule Paul's "granny music", he would demonstrate an alarming capacity for tweeness himself, although he would never reach the depths of McCartney's *Abbey Road* vignette 'Her Majesty', surely the most sycophantic lines ever unleashed on a record. The duo that had soundtracked the swinging '60s wouldn't be able, as solo songwriters and ex-Beatles, to so minister to the '70s. The illusion of reconciliation that was *Abbey Road* still fooled the public into believing that The Beatles had saved not the world, perhaps, but themselves. It was, as Debussy said of Wagner's *Das Rheingold*, "a glorious sunset mistaken for a dawn".

12 The Ex-Beatle

The most emphatic twitch in the death throes of The Beatles was 'Something'. Of its singer, George Martin predicted, "I think it's possible that he'll emerge as a great musician and composer next year. He's got tremendous drive and imagination, and also the ability to show himself as a great composer on a par with Lennon and McCartney."[237] This was praise indeed from the one who, almost to the last, had rated George Harrison midway between lowly Mal Evans and the high command of Paul and John. To the world at large, too, Harrison had been no more than merely half of the Other Two.

George's eleventh-hour victory and the hip circles in which he now moved had left him with a firm footing on which to begin a new career. Little could capsize the supposition that he'd continue as a successful recording artist, either solo or as part of a supergroup like Blind Faith or Crosby, Stills And Nash, who were now the toast of the "Woodstock generation".

On the very release date of 'Something' – 31 October 1969 – George had been at Olympic Studios in Barnes recording with what was, in theory, a supergroup drawn from other supergroups. Heard with him on the since-destroyed tapes were Eric Clapton and Rick Grech from Blind Faith; Alan White, one of The Plastic Ono Band's drummers; and Denny Laine, former leader of The Moody Blues. Whatever the quality of the music realised that day, further development of this contingency plan was thwarted as its participants involved themselves in other projects. Laine, for example, joined Wings, Paul McCartney's new group. Nevertheless, like the Delaney And Bonnie episode, this endeavour had fuelled

George's contention that, "Having played with other musicians, I don't think The Beatles were that good."[239] Perhaps they weren't, but a non-member – even if he could sing like a nightingale or make a guitar talk – couldn't guarantee the same attention as the most ill-judged folly of an ex-Beatle.

While McCartney and Lennon's first post-Beatle offerings were either barrel scraping, slap-dash or uxoriously self-centred, to George was afforded the luxury of sifting through a backlog of around 40 songs – "and some of them I think are quite good"[242] – for a new album, a double if he felt like it. Although he was always inclined to function best within the context of a group, George had decided by 1970 to go it alone. Rather than submit his work to the quality control of equals, he'd work with hired assistance as hand-picked as the songs had been. Although stalwarts like Ringo, Mal and Klaus Voorman presented no difficulties, to call the shots to other of the proficient musical practitioners he knew meant fighting giant inhibitions about his own abilities. Warming up for the next backing track, someone might kick off an instrumental jam and extrapolate it at considerable length. With the likes of Ginger Baker dropping by to indulge in these meanderings, it was thought prudent to keep the tape rolling: "Just blowing, having a ball," to quote a contemporary sleeve note. "What a gas, just blowing, blowing, blowing..."[243] As the other participants immortalised their own arrogance, George confined himself mainly to accompaniment, as he had in the post-soundcheck sessions during The Beatles' package tours.

He was particularly in awe of Clapton, because "there's things Eric can do where it would take me all night to get it right. He can knock it off in one take because he plays all the time."[244] However, if not on equal terms technically, George had plucked the heart-strings harder by integrating his talent to his old group's general good with a supine subtlety untried by flasher Eric.

As a singer, George was no Scott Walker. Even Procol Harum's Gary Brooker (an ex-Paramount) and some of the others he'd enlist for the album outclassed him vocally. Nevertheless, his inability to stray far beyond his central two octaves reinforced an idiosyncratic charm peculiar to certain personable vocalists who warp an intrinsically limited range and eccentric delivery to their own devices. George would be one of this oligarchy, as were androgynous Adam Faith, wobbly Ray Davies, laconic Dave Berry and mesmerically ugly Bob Dylan. A Caruso-loving fly on the wall may well have blocked his ears during a secret twelve-hour Harrison-Dylan recording session, after a special dispensation from the US State Department had allowed drug fiend George to visit New York on, ostensibly, a business trip in May 1970. The nadir of his knockabout musical stumblings there was accompanying Dylan groaning a funereal 'Yesterday'. However, with musicians who'd back Bob on his forthcoming *New Morning* LP, George sang two pieces for which he would find room on his own album, a sketchy 'If Not For You' – that Bob had set aside for *New Morning* – and 'I'd Have You Anytime', complete with pattering bongos, one of their joint composing efforts from a stay in Bearsville.

In common with other British rock 'n' rollers, George was discovering that, mere pop star that he was on native turf, he was considered an Artist in enthusiastic North America, where "there's still more chance of picking up on something fresh, interesting. Maybe because it's a much bigger industry, there's not so much tendency for them to get in cliques. England does tend to get very cliquey, as far as I can see."[145] Every pop generation throws up an inward-looking, privileged in crowd, the innermost of all being Presley's Memphis Mafia and, once, The Beatles' retinue. No cabal, however, was so insufferably smug as that of the early 1970s, which "traded licks" during sessions for George Harrison's new LP, mostly at the Trident complex in London's Soho.

Exchanging smirks over the console were Bobby Whitlock, Bobby Keyes or any combination of those interchangeable "funky cats" from Delaney And Bonnie, plus a smaller handful of "heavy friends" from Britain. It was as if George couldn't work in any other way or with any other people than the self-absorbed elite whose only contact with real life out in Dullsville was through managers, runarounds and narcotics dealers.

Leaning against the wall opposite Trident in dawn drizzle that summer, Apple Scruffs sank into a languid daze induced by the fixity of gazing at the studio door. Inside, while George, the engineers and sometimes Phil Spector were head to head in the control booth, the guys toked marijuana, swigged Southern Comfort and discussed who they were going to "ball" later on. In bad shape, Spector "used to have 18 cherry brandies before he could get himself down to the studio. I got so tired of that, because I needed someone to help. I was ending up with more work than if I'd just been doing it on my own."[59] Drafted in to co-produce with George, after applying his spent "genius" to just under half of the backing tracks, Spector's sudden mood swings and absences became more trouble than they were worth. Although he reappeared for the mix, the ailing Svengali of Sound's principal contribution to the outcome was that he could be included among all the other big names credited on the sleeve on what would be – after the Woodstock soundtrack – pop's first triple album, named after one of the songs George had previewed in the *Let It Be* film – 'All Things Must Pass'.

Other than "Old King Log" Spector's maladies, the completion of *All Things Must Pass* was interrupted by the serious illness of George's mother, which involved constant journeys to the Liverpool neurological hospital, where a brain tumour requiring an operation had been diagnosed. "When I went up to see her," said George, "she didn't even know who I was."[58]

Some of the *All Things Must Pass* personnel also embarked on other projects during its pre-planning, Mrs Harrison's infirmity and the four months' recording time booked. Unperturbed and flattered that they should ask, George was delighted to assist his friends, often appearing on their albums under a weak pseudonym, such as "Hari Georgeson" or just "George H". Most of the Bramlett faction and, briefly, Dave Mason had enrolled in Eric Clapton's new band, but its leader's greater commitment to *All Things Must Pass* was such that Dave would sneer, "Eric would be in London doing George's album and nothing was really happening."[245] It has to be said that Clapton wasn't the easiest person to rub along with since contracting a heroin dependency, as some of his group had already, during rehearsals for the outfit's first concert. Events and Eric's own admission would show that an indirect but major cause of this addiction was George Harrison.

Digging the vibes backstage on the June night of Clapton's debut at the Strand Lyceum, George was among those whose brains had been picked for a name for the group – who were due on an hour ago, but that was cool. Let 'em wait. Finally and facetiously, Derek And The Dominoes sauntered on to unacknowledged acclamation by an unreasonably patient audience who'd aped their inconsiderate heroes and their chicks by dressing down in a flurry of pre-faded Levis embroidered with butterfly or mushroom motifs, clogs, long print dresses, cocaine-spoon earrings, Joe Cocker grandad vests and stars-and-stripes singlets revealing underarm hair. Chatter during the long wait embraced misinformed mention of fads – heroin, Jesus, Stoneground, Buddy Holly B-sides – that the condescending Anglo-American superstars were "into". "I can sing better after shooting smack in both my arms,"[246] boasted Linda Ronstadt in an issue of groovy *Rolling Stone* which reached London one month after its publication in High Street, America.

The petrification of British pop since 1968 led to the top of its singles chart bracketing 1970 with what many heard as the undiggable sounds of faceless session group Edison Lighthouse and 'Grandad' by Clive Dunn, who ended the six-week reign of Welsh guitarist Dave Edmunds' trundling 'I Hear You Knocking'. Better exemplifying the dearth of new original talent was Free's 'All Right Now', *the* hit song of 1970, which had been influenced by the Stones' 'Honky Tonk Women' of the previous year. Its central riff was logged by George for later use: a rehash of a rehash. Beyond *Top Of The Pops*, from college juke boxes would moan other album-enhancing 45s plugging albums by Humble Pie, Black Sabbath and their ilk, whose "heavy" excesses appealed to male consumers recently grown to man's estate. With Deep Purple as the link, this category stretched towards the "techno-flash" pomp rock in the ELP/Yes vein.

Infesting the university bedsit rather than its bar juke box were LPs from the other end of the spectrum. Reaching out to self-doubting adolescent diarists rather than headbangers was the early-1970s school of singer/songwriters, which was called "self-rock" if you liked it, and "drip rock" if – like *Melody Maker's* Allan Jones in a scathing article[247] – you didn't. The genre's ethos was of being so bound up in yourself that every trivial occurrence or emotion was worth telling the whole world about in song.

Most of its perpetrators' drab uniformity was but another symptom of the hungover morning after the Swinging '60s. With all the charisma of sacks of potatoes, solemn James Taylor, sweet Melanie or Linda Ronstadt – a singer/songwriter type, except she didn't write many songs – would whinge "beautiful" cheesecloth-and-denim banalities in sold-out stadiums. No Mick Jagger cavortings were necessary; all you had to do was sit on a stool, sing to your guitar and beam a small, sad smile now and then. More than gruff heavy metal or pomp rock, drip rock epitomised the bland tenor of a decade that, to George Harrison, "seemed a bit grumpier than the '60s".[248] With Simon And Garfunkel's 'Bridge Over Troubled Water' its anthem, 1970 was a re-run of 1967 without colour, daring or humour.

When Joe Average first slotted it onto his stereo on 27 November 1970, *All Things Must Pass* seemed to have caught the overall drift of the early 1970s. Even to its creator, it was modern enough to sound dated and in need of a remix within years. As non-hippies were hardly aware of *Wonderwall* and *Electronic Sounds*, *All Things Must Pass* was the first time George had truly shown his head as a soloist. From both detailed demos and half-formed ideas computed on his mind, it was like "being constipated for years, then finally you were allowed to go. I had 17 tracks and I didn't really want to chuck any away, although I'm sure lots of them, in retrospect, could have been. I wanted to get shot of them so I could catch up on myself."[164]

Unfettered as he was by obligations to the most objective and critical of familiars, George had needed a Lennon, McCartney or Martin to suggest paring down *All Things Must Pass* to a lean single album and reserving the best of what remained for a follow-up. The insubstantial 'I Dig Love' could have been ditched without any hardship. As well as including two takes of 'Isn't It A Pity' (one over seven minutes long), much on the package's first two records was blighted by not so much gratuitous soloing as repeated choruses and extended fades which put some in a mantric (or stoned) trance, while others wondered, "How much longer?" Like many latter-day Beatle tracks, constant replay was necessary to comprehend trifles like what sounded like a motor changing gear in the final seconds of 'Wah-Wah'.

Most fans found that the third record remained in pristine condition while its companions acquired scratches and surface hiss. Although it was a free gift to offset a high retail cost, *Apple Jam* – with one exception – made tedious listening. If anyone was expecting a continuation of ersatz Beatle magic, all they heard were edited highlights – if that is the word – from the interminable jamming that consumed time as late arrivals set up their gear or engineers twiddled. Despite intriguing titles – such as 'I Remember Jeep' – bestowed on these extemporisations of twelve-bar blues and two-chord riffs, the clouds parting on the gods at play revealed nothing more remarkable than any idle session crew's ramblings not intended for public ears. However, I must add the raw information that 'Thanks For The Pepperoni' was among the "amazing sounds"[249] beloved by neil, a hippy-drippy anachronism from the 1984 BBC series *The Young Ones*.

Rick, neil's flatmate – and Cliff Richard admirer – would have preferred the only vocal item on *Apple Jam*, the quirky and brief 'It's Johnny's Birthday', which borrowed the melody of Cliff's 1968 Song For Europe entry, 'Congratulations'. Although an in-joke, with its unusual tonality and wandering varispeed, 'It's Johnny's Birthday' was the most musically adventurous offering on *All Things Must Pass*.

The "Johnny" it celebrated was John Lennon, rather than orchestral arranger John Barham, who'd also worked on *Wonderwall*. As the poly-synthesiser was yet to become common in studios, Barham had to notate the required scoring for *All Things Must Pass* as the composer – who could barely sight-read – *dah-dah-dahed*. A backwash of strings gnawed at many selections either as fairy dusting or, as on 'Isn't It A Pity', assuming a part that could have been allocated to lead guitar or saxophone. There were fierce moments – 'Let It Down', for instance – and a few weird shudders, but *All Things Must Pass* was generally easy on the ear and suited to a year when the likes of James Taylor and Crosby, Stills And Nash still held sway. Because some hip names – including Klaus Voorman's – had been printed on one of his LP jackets, it was cool to dig even a purring Mister Wonderful like Andy Williams, who could have adapted with ease most of *All Things Must Pass* to his style, in which was absorbed just enough of prevailing trends not to turn off older fans. Without making any such concessions, English balladeer Matt Monro covered 'Isn't It A Pity', hoping to repeat the Top-Ten success he'd had with 'Yesterday' in 1965.

However much the predominant blandness may have affected his music, George's contributions to albums by Bobby Keyes, Leon Russell, Jesse "Ed" Davis and his other Bramlett pals left less of a mark than you might imagine. While he may have shared these opportunists' prolixity, he forwent, thankfully, their lyrical preoccupations with snorting cocaine, balling chicks and other overworked myths of the rock-band-on-the-road lifestyle. He devoted several libretti to his intensifying religious explorations, rather than to frustrated eroticism. Updating JS Bach's artistic tenet, he'd decided that "music should be used for the perception of God, not jitterbugging".[250] Of greatest antiquity was 'The Art Of Dying' and – with the Billy Preston versions as helpful demos – the title track and 'My Sweet Lord'. The latter was elongated and given a fatter production, but more uplifting was 'Awaiting On You All', a semi-litany and one of the few *All Things Must Pass* numbers with a succinct ending.

From the overt 'Hear Me Lord' to veiled allusions in 'Beware Of Darkness', George invited mockery by so persistently superimposing tracts about Japa Yoga, meditation, karma, maya[180] and the like onto a pop framework. Much later, it was sent up as *All Things Must Fart* in *neil's Book Of The Dead*, a paperback spin-off from *The Young Ones*. Next to some tortuously rhymed doggerel concluding with "a whiff of friendship, love and lentil", neil's mournful visage was pasted over Harrison's in a reproduction of the album cover. As hirsute as he'd ever be, the artist sits in pastoral contemplation, like a spaced-out Farmer Giles, a posture which seems to amuse mildly four garden gnomes – possibly an allusion to The Beatles – sprawled on the grass around him. A box set, *All Things Must Pass* was a handy working surface for rolling a joint in hip student hostel rooms, where it was as much a fixture as Che Guevara's mug had been.

As an old trouper, George must have gauged that the intangible buzz that had been in the air for months would push *All Things Must Pass* to the top of the album lists for reasons other than still-potent loyalty to the Fab Four, whose regrouping was seen then as inevitable by even the most marginally hopeful outsider to whom the concept of collecting every record The Beatles ever made was not yet economically unsound. It wouldn't be too sweeping to say that religion – especially Christianity – was a turn-of-the-decade craze, just as the Twist had been. In corroboration was a trio who seemed to be approximating The Jimi Hendrix Experience for an appearance at Reading University one evening in 1971. Cutting through their noise were half-heard phrases such as "bless the Lord", "mend your ways", "come to Jesu". Some driven to dance were even crossing themselves and bawling hallelujahs that weren't taking the mickey. Seeking more temporal amusement, I headed for the exit, thanking Christ I'd got in without paying.

In *The Liverpool Echo*, Edward Patey, the dean of the cathedral, lauded the new coalition of religious sentiment and pop as "the best partnership since the mediaeval duetting of clowns and folk singers",[251] even if those responsible were, like George Harrison, not aligned to orthodox Christian worship. With politicians envying the pop star's easy manipulation of young opinion, surely the new fad could cajole more teenagers from pot-smoking depravity into Matins, or at least to God? George, too, was "sick of all these young people just boogying around, wasting their lives".[152] Of the same opinion was Dean Patey's fellow Liverpudlian John Lennon, whose perky but reproachful 'Instant Karma' entered the charts in February 1970 and prompted a *Top Of The Pops* appearance, the first Beatle to do so in four years.

After 'Oh Happy Day', 'Spirit In The Sky' answered the prayers of its singer, Norman Greenbaum. While this song was a worldwide smash in the spring of 1971, Diane Colby's 'Holy Man' was huge in Australia, if nowhere else. With at least three renditions of 'Amazing Grace' about to ascend hit parades in major territories later that year, Tin Pan Alley's quick appraisal of the situation led to abominations like 'The Man From Nazareth', mimed on *Top Of The Pops* by John Paul Joans (*sic*), a bearded herbert dressed in bedspreads.

Past the crap, many consumers and artists found the vogue for saintliness reassuring, a relief almost, stuck as they were between the supposed drug-crazed sensuality of rock 'n' roll and their own stolid compliance to middle-aged values. Born-again fervour saw evangelical marches up high streets and the Scriptures being quoted at parties. The Bible, the Koran and *Chant And Be Happy*[152] now had discreet places on hip bookshelves. Mostly, this was just for show as a reefer was passed around during a conversation pocked with words like "mantra" and "karma" while James Taylor's *Mud Slide Slim*, Deep Purple's *Machine Head* or *All Things Must Pass* poured from the stereo. Behind school bike sheds a few years earlier, it had been "gear" and "grotty" over a Woodbine.

This shallow spirituality tipped the balance for many who were then ripe for religion. In as late as 1982, George would "still get letters from people saying, 'I have been in the Krishna temple for three years, and I would never have known about Krishna [if you hadn't] recorded the *All Things Must Pass* album.'"[152] As the Portsmouth Sinfonia would bring popular classics to those who otherwise wouldn't experience them, so George brought Krishna Consciousness. With lines like those in the crass bridge of 'Beware Of Darkness', George might not have been touched with the same gift for hymnology as, say, Charles Wesley, but he closed the gap on Tom McGuinness' 'I Will Bring To You', when 'My Sweet Lord' became accepted as a *bona fide* gospel song.

The first and biggest-selling 45 to be lifted from the album, 'My Sweet Lord', pulled Clive Dunn off the top in Britain within a fortnight of its release. By February 1971, it was Number One virtually everywhere else, too. From newly converted rock groups murdering it on God-slot television to a rendering by Johnny Mathis for the supper-club market, 'My Sweet Lord' would be that year's most performed work.

Every silver lining has a cloud, however, and both the Harrison re-tread of Preston's blueprint and the vast exposure of 'My Sweet Lord' threw the song's stomach-knotting similarity to The Chiffons' 'He's So Fine' into sharper focus. Allen Klein brought to George's notice a revival of The Chiffons' opus by Jody Miller, onto which was faithfully grafted every detail of the 'My Sweet Lord' arrangement, even the plainly strummed acoustic guitars that had replaced Billy's jazzy keyboards on the introduction and the background chants where The Chiffons' *doo-lang-doo-lang-doo-lang*s had been.

Worries that this was litigational ammunition for Bright Tunes, publishers of 'He's So Fine', brought the same questions up again and again as George groped for reasons why such a case would or would not be pursued. Bouncing his thoughts off Klein, he would build up a damning case against himself before concluding that Bright Tunes either couldn't be bothered or hadn't enough evidence to justify making a fuss. However, with no word from Bright Tunes as the months slipped by, perhaps George was panicking unduly. "Maybe he thought God would just sort of let him off,"[80] John Lennon would laugh after He didn't.

This bad karma, however, was at arm's length as the falling 'My Sweet Lord' collided with the catchy 'What Is Life' (the one turned down by Billy Preston) on its way up. Belying its pensive title, this second single from *All Things Must Pass* seemed to be a straight, lovey-dovey pop song. Driven by Mal Evans' tambourine, 'What Is Life' renewed craftily the simplistic tonic-to-dominant riff cliché. Unissued as an A-side in Britain, where it had already appeared on the flip of 'My Sweet Lord', the rise of a version by Olivia Newton-John – pulchritudinous, middle-of-the-road vocalist from Australia – into the Top 20 was, like Shirley Bassey's 'Something', a wooing of a parallel dimension of pop turned off by all this religious nonsense that hippies liked. George's infiltration of this area by proxy continued with 'Isn't It A Pity', which, when sung by Ireland's Dana as the storm brewed in Ulster, was more poignant than either his own or Matt Monro's version.

Olivia's 'What Is Life' had been preceded by her song 'If Not For You', based on the smoother *All Things Must Pass* rather than the *New Morning* treatment. While George's own multitracked vocals ("The George O'Hara Singers"), blaring horns and battalions of strings bloated many other *All Things Must Pass* tracks, those written by, with and about Bob Dylan veered towards the understated production aesthetic of the latter's comeback album, *John Wesley Harding*, even employing its steel guitarist, the late Pete Drake, for the waltz-time 'Behind That Locked Door'. Appropriately, little more than huffing mouth organ and Spanish guitar accompanied 'Apple Scruffs', in a manner closer to Don Partridge than Dylan. The Scruffs themselves – after having "stood around" for years – were actually invited into the control room to hear a playback of the most intrinsically valuable if belated recognition of a vigil soon to end with adulthood and the realisation that The Beatles as a 1960s myth would long outlive the mere mortals that constituted its *dramatis personae*.

Eric Clapton was human now, too. After his guitar divinity had peaked in Cream, only miracles could have rescued his subsequent projects, even if media build-up forestalled an instant backlash. He either couldn't or wouldn't play like he had in Cream, and neither was he an outstanding singer or composer. Nonetheless, he'd always find sufficient buyers to guarantee a good turn-out for his concerts and chart placings for most of his records. Among the rarest of these was a withdrawn single taped during an *All Things Must Pass* furlough. With producer Spector half-seas over, Clapton served up 'Tell The Truth' in a hoarse smoker's monotone. Content once to fret chords under his mate's soloing, George now felt that it was a feather in his cap when he was allowed a bottleneck obligato on its flip-side, 'Roll It Over'. Still earnestly finding a way with the non-standard tuning and slithering left hand, for George to be so rated by even a below-par Clapton was such that, "for me, if Eric gives me the thumbs-up on a slide solo, it means more to me than half the population".[243]

Before 1970 was out, Clapton's heroin odyssey brought about The Dominoes' dismissal midway through their second album together. He'd made no long-term plans. How could he? His descent into this abyss was hinged on what had now become an infatuation with Pattie Harrison. So far, she'd spurned his advances, which even his friendship with her husband would not rein. Not surprisingly, Eric's muse on several tracks on the first Dominoes album was romantic frustration, notably in the hit single 'Layla', in which he howled about comforting the object of his desire "when your old man let you down".

The Harrisons' marriage muddled on because neither partner had enough motivation to finish it. Yet, although her flirting with his friends didn't appear to bother him, George showed her small fondnesses as he and she posed for an Apple Scruff's camera, smiling like they were happy. Why shouldn't the world at large assume that 'What Is Life' was another lovingly crafted paean to Pattie, rather than something dashed off "very quickly, 15 minutes to half an hour"[39] while driving to a Billy Preston session? As neither was yet the sort to wash dirty linen in public, nothing substantial suggested that the childless couple's life together was less than tolerable.

Pattie's hopes for raising a family were impeded by George's reservations about adoption and his months on end of sexual abstinence. While there was less lust in him now than when he'd first clapped eyes on her toothy charms, his restraint was dictated by a more rigid adherence to religious tenets whereby the purpose of sex was for procreation only. "I think if you do something and you don't really like doing it," he would affirm, "then you're a hypocrite about it. In a way, we all have desires; we must learn either to fulfil the desires or terminate those desires. If you can do it by being celibate and it's easy to handle, it's OK. You can either lose certain desires you had when you were younger or the thing that you have to watch – particularly the sex and things like drugs, too. The problem is, you can go, 'Oh well, I'll just have a bit, then I'll be fulfilled,' but it doesn't work that way. First you have a bit and then you want more."[32]

This well-argued point could as easily have come from a street-corner evangelist warming to a pet theme amid jeers from the few stopping to listen. As common a sight in Oxford Street as the Hare Krishna chanters was ex-civil servant Stanley Green, who paced daily back and forth in a sandwich board that declared his creed of "Less Lust From Less Protein". If asked, he'd tell you, "Protein wisdom changes your whole life, makes it easier. Passion can be a great torment. I've seen some remarkable changes in people. The first thing a woman does when she takes up protein wisdom is change her hairstyle." All the lonely people, where do they all come from?

George's incentive for rising at dawn was not the same as Mr Green's. When an interviewer suggested that it was to avoid wet dreams, George laughed and explained that Krishna devotees regarded sleep as the "little death. Prabhupada sleeps an hour or two hours a day. These yogis don't need sleep at all. The don't need food. They're living on the Divine Energy."[32] After a nice cold bath, he'd settle down to a study of the Bhagavad Gita. At given moments, he'd break into the maha-mantra. As Roman Catholics keep count of Hail Marys, so George would tally his *hare krishnas* with a string of Japa Yoga beads kept in a small bag slung over his shoulder. Unlike Stanley Green, who'd "spoiled my life by being too honest", George found it easier to say he'd shut his fingers in a door. The depths of depravity nowadays were three filter tips per day.

George was accorded considerably greater space and luxury for what were regarded as his eccentricities than Stanley Green in his one-room flat in Harrow. For hours at a stretch, George would meditate in his own temple in the grounds of Friar Park, which Ringo Starr would describe in song as "a 40-acre house he doesn't see".[253] Its purchase in January 1970 had concluded the Harrisons' year of searching for a dwelling that would combine privacy without imprisonment, and close proximity to London.

Catering similarly for other famous names, the region where Berkshire dissolves into Oxfordshire – Hollywood-on-Thames – was centred around the Windsor-Ascot-Henley triangle, throwing together the most disparate of neighbours. Thespians such as Michael Caine and Susan George would fill petrol tanks at the same garage as comedian Ernie Wise or Sir James Carreras, retired head of Hammer Films. Fête-opening "personalities" like Rolf Harris, Freddie Starr or Vince Hill might be vaguely impressed when told that the guffawing drinkers in the next bar of the local pub were members of Deep Purple.

Most of the rock 'n' roll elite ensconced themselves in the rural calm of Hambledon, Middle Assenden, Skirmett and other olde worlde hamlets buried in the woods surrounding a reach of the river where no cascading pylons blighted grassy downs and where sheep nibbled on Saxon battlegrounds. While Ten Years After's organist or Deep Purple's drummer might attend village bazaars in undisguised anonymity, seeing an ex-Beatle dipping into the bran tub might be as profoundly disturbing as finding the Prince of Wales using an adjacent urinal in the gents. George, therefore, was hardly ever seen in Henley, whose town square was two minutes' walk down Gravel Hill from the gatehouse of Friar Park, the estate that was to be as synonymous with his name as the Queen's with Windsor Castle.

Unseen from the Peppard Road, this spired and turreted mansion of 120 rooms on Henley's western outskirts was the creation of Sir Frank Crisp, a prominent and astute City of London solicitor. When completed in 1889, the architectural manifestation of Crisp's personality was dismissed by one contemporary journalist as "a bizarre folly"[254] and lauded by another as "a beautiful example of high-Victorian architecture in the style of Pugin".[255] In as late as 1978, *The Henley Standard* was still discussing "Friar Park: beautiful or a monstrosity?"[246] It depended on whether you shared Sir Frank's sense of humour. In deference to its founding on the site of a 13th-century friary were the many intricate carvings of a monastic nature on its red brick and yellow low-stone exterior. Over the legend "Two Holy Friars" is a friar with a frying pan with holes in it. Get it? Visitors' eyes would pop when they saw that, instead of a conventional light switch, there was a wooden friar's face with a moveable nose.

In 1905, one disgruntled guest, Lady Ottoline Morrell, wondered whether Crisp "was colossally simple and really thought these vulgar and monstrous jokes amusing and beautiful".[257] To his offspring, Friar Park was as tangibly grotesque as a Gothic scenario, "Full of surprises. Around every corner, you could come across a quirky statue, an arbour with a seat inscribed with one of my grandfather's special quotations, a summerhouse sited to obtain a certain vista, and numerous little tucked-away gardens, each with its separate identity."[257] What child of this Coca Cola century would not be deliciously chilled by the three artificial caverns with their wishing wells, distorting mirrors, model skeletons and glass grapes, from which you paddled into the Blue Grotto and out into the lowest of the three split-level lakes. Then there were the mazes, the secret passageways and, dominating the Alpine rock garden, a 100-foot-high replica of the Matterhorn constructed from trainloads of millstone grit.

By the mid 1950s, the manor had returned to the Church. Its new proprietors were nuns of the order of St John Bosco. Among minor adjustments in the mansion's conversion was the overpainting of underpants on naked cherubs depicted on ceiling tableaux. Falling rolls, however, depleted the establishment's resources, causing a gradual withering of the estate, so that even Crisp Street – with houses built from Yorkshire stone left over from the Matterhorn – lay outside its environs when the hard-pressed nuns were forced to sell up in 1969. There were woefully few prospective buyers, too, and the one who looked like Rasputin embodied, at first sight, all that the Catholic Church detested. While being shown round, he deposited a four-armed and pagan poster of Vishnu in an empty fireplace and "it sort of freaked them out a bit".[152]

Trailing along behind their guide, the Harrisons pondered the neglected splendour. The topiary, on which thousands of different varieties of flora, shrubs and trees had bloomed, had been strangled by couch grass and creepers and was littered with broken lavatories from a building site. The house itself was in such a state of dereliction that demolition contractors had been readied, should it be taken off the market. Nonetheless, some instinct intimated to George that the high asking price and the money he'd surely have to lay out on renovations might be cash well spent: "It's like a horror movie, but it really doesn't have bad vibes. It's had Christ in it for 16 years, after all."[258]

Money talks in any religion, and by March 1970 a labourer's cottage sufficed as temporary abode for Pattie and George while the main edifice was an unserviceable no man's land of rubble, planks and tea-drinking artisans. While being restored to near enough its former glory, the mansion was customised to the new owner's specifications. A tweaked nose still flooded a room with light, and the cherubs' pants stayed on, but alien to a Victorian baronet, if not a nun, were the juke box, the cinema, the Tiffany lamps and, ultimately, the recording studio that replaced a suite of two bedrooms, bathroom and dressing room.

Freeing him of the restraints of a hired studio, this electronic den enabled George to potter around with sound, tape the wackiest demos, invite friends around to play and begin a day's recording with nothing prepared. Eventually, every note of his public output would also be hand tooled there. Although he graduated from 16-track to digital 48-track and beyond, playbacks were still heard through crude Altecs, as at Abbey Road, because, "when you play it back anyplace else, it sounds fantastic".[58] The latest transistorised toys came and went. "People were talking about quadraphonic sound, and while I didn't think it'd catch on, I figured I'd better have that, just in case."[59] His instructions to engineers came to be dotted with jargon like "pan pots" (stereo-channel potentiometers), "EQ" and "carbon faders". Often technological steps ahead of even Abbey Road, George's FPSHOT (Friar Park Studio, Henley-on-Thames) was recognised as the world's most sophisticated private recording complex.

While this proved a worthwhile investment, he took less detached pride in marshalling a team of gardeners to do battle against the weeds that had ruined Sir Frank's careful landscaping. However, although bellbine and thistle perished by hoe and bonfire, the rabbits that overran the fields continued to multiply. Left alone, too, were the quaint homilies inscribed in the Park's nook and crannies. Around the sundial, for instance, was the legend (in Latin) "Shadows we are and shadows we depart", but more peculiar to Crisp was the phrase "Herons will be prosecuted". His "Don't keep off the grass" had a meaning other than horticultural in 1970, when a fiver persuaded a London butcher to surrender to Dave Crosby a cardboard "All joints must be weighed" sign.

Such jive-talking inanity might have been stonewalled by one such as Sir Frank Crisp. Nevertheless, as more of his domestic idiosyncrasies were uncovered, the 19th-century knight began to walk a tightrope between craziness and heroism – as John Lennon did – for the Harrisons and their house guests. George's particular friend from the Monty Python crowd, Eric Idle, began researching Crisp's career for a biography, while 'The Ballad Of Sir Frankie Crisp' was a breath of fresh air amid the dicta and aimless jamming on *All Things Must Pass*. Couched in mediaeval expression as it was – "through ye woode, here may ye rest awhile" – George had resisted orchestrating this most Beatle-esque of his new songs with tabor and crumhorn. Instead, a sense of the mysterious was conveyed with 1970s rock instrumentation. Other carved Crispisms would inspire further compositions.

George also took it upon himself to perpetuate the founder's good works, which included financing the erection of Christ Church steeple in Duke Street and more anonymous donations to the upkeep of Henley's churches and listed buildings. He was no Little Englander, but, while some aspects of the late 20th century could be welcomed, the town's wealthiest addressee sought to conserve an older aesthetic. From the five-arched bridge, constructed in 1786, the main street has an oak-beamed gentility that overflows onto the art galleries and olde tea shoppes along the waterfront, where the Thames has straightened for a clear mile and motorboats bump in their moorings. The annual Royal Regatta fills the towpaths and meadows that frame this marina with Henley's most noticeable influx of debutantes, yuppies and sightseers.

On the rim of the old town, new housing estates with concrete garages were beginning to intrude upon the countryside. People have to live somewhere, but disquieting to the Harrisons and other residents were those prongs of modern enterprise – supermarkets, car parks *et al* – that pierced Henley's very heart, to the detriment of its elegant past. George, however, would not immediately put action over debate, even though, "during the time I've been here, one old building after another had been torn down".[259]

It would be years before he risked mingling with the few thousand souls who lived in the town beneath his eyrie. Whereas in Sir Frank's day the grounds had been open to the public every summer Wednesday, a sign in ten languages outside Friar Park's tall, iron-barred gates read "Absolutely No Admittance". Razor-sharp barbed wire crowned the outer walls. Now known more for its pop-star incumbent, British trippers would say "cheese" outside that forbidding boundary and Americans would train cine cameras up the drive before ambling down to the Thameside promenade for an ice cream.

Ringo Starr's less grandiose spread in Compton Avenue, Highgate, was less of a magnet for fans. Most at a loss after the break-up, the "straightest" ex-Beatle had been the pliant executor of others' ideas, until renewed confidence teased from him a plethora of original songs, among them his first solo single, 'It Don't Come Easy', which, in the spring of 1971, outsold current offerings by John, Paul and George. The latter had emerged as Ringo's most willing helpmate, producing and twanging the wires on both 'It Don't Come Easy' and its follow-up, 'Back Off Boogaloo'.

This repetitive opus was registered as a "Richard Starkey" composition, but some made the waspish allegation that it was actually the work of Marc Bolan, who was pioneering a swing back to the cheap thrills of the beat boom. This was encapsulated in *Born To Boogie*, Ringo's first essay as a film director, which used footage of Bolan's group, T Rex, at a British concert deluged in screams. Behind the cameras at stage front, it must have been strange for Ringo to find himself ignored as hysterical girls clambered to get at Marc. Their elder sisters might have fancied George Harrison or James Taylor, but, light years away on *Top Of The Pops*, T Rex, Slade, Alice Cooper and other newcomers – who'd never mean half as much in laid-back America – were paving the way for the greater musical and sartorial excesses of David Bowie, Gary Glitter and Roxy Music. Also in the ascendant in the UK charts was a mascara'd Shane Fenton, who, borrowing from Glitter's name, had been exhumed as "Alvin Stardust".

Most ex-Beatles embraced different elements that were anathema to glam rock. Rather than George's *ad hoc* aggregations of semi-famous names, Wings favoured a permanency as cosy as Paul and Linda's "simple life" on their Sussex farm among a growing family. Vinyl reflection of this contentment was Wings' cloying 'Mary Had A Little Lamb' – yes, the nursery rhyme – which nestled uneasily in a British Top Ten in which T Rex's 'Metal Guru' had just toppled a version of 'Amazing Grace' by a Scottish military band. An Hibernian outfit of more mercurial stamp was The Sensational Alex Harvey Band, whose bombastic leader – no longer styling himself as "the Tommy Steele of Scotland" – enquired, "Do you think Paul McCartney makes records just to annoy me personally, or does he want to get up everybody's nose with his antics?"[260]

"Everybody" meant those sickened by Paul's developing Mr

Showbusiness image, which seemed bourgeois when set against his former songwriting confrere's more cathartic projection of himself, which involved singing the f-word twice in the primal scream that was his Plastic Ono Band LP. After Lennon regurgitated his lot in 'Working Class Hero', the artistic gulf between him and McCartney widened, and the sibling rivalry intensified so that they were sniping at each other in the press and even in record grooves. Of these attacks, John's were the most malicious. Not content with airing grievances against Paul in the pages of *Rolling Stone*, further insults effused from 'Crippled Inside' and, nastier still, 'How Do You Sleep' (with a few lines suggested by Allen Klein) from *Imagine*, Lennon's winter album of 1971.

In as much as he'd sided with John in the desperate hours of 1969, so George endorsed on slide guitar and dobro these diatribes and other *Imagine* cuts: "I enjoyed 'How Do You Sleep'. I liked being on that side of it, rather than on the receiving end."[59] Although *All Things Must Pass* had shut down The Plastic Ono Band commercially, George would remain a rank outsider to John in the sense of the artistic competition that forever persisted between the ex-Beatles. In *Rolling Stone*, the snigger was almost audible in Lennon's claim that, to the "rubbish"[156] of McCartney, he preferred *All Things Must Pass*. The fact that he was needling Paul rather than praising George was inherent in the qualification, "I think it's all right, I suppose. Personally, at home, I wouldn't play that kind of music, but I don't want to hurt George's feelings."[156]

John's own feelings were hurt when an incident shortly after the *Imagine* sessions instigated George's gradual isolation from his old idol. However, Lennon was "openly pleased I came"[59] when Harrison's car pulled up at Tittenhurst Park. Although he'd helped on 'Instant Karma', George was relieved that John so beholdenly conducted him into the eight-track studio where *Imagine* was taking form, because "very strange, intense feelings were going on. Sometimes, people don't talk to each other, thinking they're not going to be the one to phone you up and risk rejection."[58] *All Things Must Pass* had conditioned George to dozens of retakes and overdubs, so it was with mild apprehension that he tuned up in a playing area where the exhilaration of the impromptu was prized more than technical accuracy. When his lead break came in 'How Do You Sleep', George, bereft of preconception, "hit a few good notes, and it happened to sound like a solo. We did all that work in one day."[59]

On bass was Klaus Voorman, who, gone from Manfred Mann, had been like the stock Hollywood chorus girl thrust into a sudden starring role with the first of countless spurious rumours concerning The Beatles' reformation. See, as Paul was *persona non grata*, the other three were going to try again with Voorman. "New Beatle Klaus Goes Into Hiding!"[261] *Melody Maker* had bawled that spring when he and his wife spent a few days at Friar Park.

A stronger presence around George's gaff was that of Swami Prabhupada and some disciples who'd outstayed their welcome at Tittenhurst Park. Although devotees had been featured on The Plastic Ono Band's first single, 'Give Peace A Chance', their chanting hadn't been peaceful enough when it recurred at regular intervals on the Lennons' own doorstep. Far from finding Prabhupada's louder devotions disturbing, their new host gladly extended his invitation into 1972, when they were able to decamp to Pickett's Manor, the mock-Tudor theological college – renamed Bhaktivedanta Manor – in Hertfordshire that was to become the most popular Hindu rallying point in Europe. Footing the bill for these 17 acres near Letchmore Heath, not far from the Maharishi's stately meditation centre in Mentmore, was George, who felt "fortunate enough to be able to help at the time".[152]

The faith that had prompted such beatific generosity would never exempt him from the odd loss of cool. Unprepared to bite back his annoyance, he steered his Mercedes slowly but threateningly towards a singularly intransigent traffic policeman in Westminster. Pleading guilty to driving without due care and attention, the sentence – a year's ban – was postponed because the defendant had forgotten his driving licence.

Off the public road, his increased leisure had facilitated the resumption and assiduous pursuance of his long-dormant interest – "apart from watching the odd bit on TV or reading magazines" – in motor racing. Nowadays, rather than perch on a railway embankment to goggle illicitly at distant Vanwalls and BRMs, he could luxuriate in the VIP enclosure at Monaco. It was at such a meet that he was introduced to Jackie Stewart, who'd just regained the sport's world championship. A critical thorn in the flesh of his more staid racing comperes, long-haired Stewart had been admired by George, because "he always projected the sport beyond just the racing enthusiasts".[22]

Partly through Jackie, George came to compound his enthusiasm for circuit dare-devilry, but it was Peter Sellers who "was a considerable influence on my getting into the film world".[59] After dinner at Friar Park, Sellers and Harrison would pass pleasant evenings slumped before the silver screen. The discerning Peter's favourite picture, Mel Brooks' *The Producers*, soon became George's, too, as his understanding of which films were worth seeing and which weren't became more acute.

Tightening the bond between the former Beatle and the ex-Goon was that Sellers was "into" Indian culture to a deeper extent than his oft-mimicked part as a Punjabi doctor in *The Millionairess*, a 1960 film starring Sophia Loren. Under George's influence, he was now wearing kaftans, practising yoga and burning incense. During a frightening account of a high-altitude engine mishap, Peter assured a rapt dining room that only his chanting of 'Hare Krishna' had prevented a crash landing. George might have capped this anecdote by recalling a similar scrape with death as a passenger on a transcontinental aeroplane in 1971, when, after two hours of buffeting, the craft had plummeted, the lights had fused, explosions had rocked the fuselage and "I ended up with my feet pressed against the seat in front, my seat belt as tight as could be, gripping on the thing and yelling 'Hare Krishna' at the top of my voice. I know [that], for me, the difference between making it and not making it was actually chanting the mantra."[152] This terrible journey took George from Los Angeles to New York to co-ordinate what would stand as his finest hour: The Concerts For Bangladesh.

Like most occidentals, he was "not interested in the politics of the situation"[262] which had emerged from the division of East and West Pakistan by both geography and 23 years of worsening antagonism.

In March 1971, four months after East Pakistan – now Bangladesh – had been devastated by a cyclone, General Yahya Khan amassed a Moslem army mighty enough to eradicate the Hindu majority who opposed his military dictatorship in both regions. Prostrated by the tempest's aftermath of homelessness, lack of sanitation, cholera and starvation, the East Bengalis were further traumatised by this reign of terror. Carrying their pathetic bundles, millions of refugees stumbled towards the safety of India, which had received hardly a tenth of the foreign aid needed to cope with the disaster.

Ravi Shankar's own family and friends and those of his guru were among the ceaseless fatalities and exiles. In California, during these unhappy months, from Ravi's distraught helplessness came the notion of a modest fund-raising concert. When George arrived in Los Angeles in late June, a better answer clicked in Shankar's mind like a key sliding into a lock. "He wanted to do something which would make a little more money than he normally made. He gave me all this information and articles on what was going on in Bangladesh, and I slowly got pulled into it. I started getting carried away with the whole idea of doing something good, maybe making $10 million."[211] Officially, he'd flown in to produce Badfinger and to negotiate the release of *Messenger Out Of The East*, an Apple Film study – two years in the making – of Shankar and the land that bore him. When this duty was done, George made his giant leap for Bangladesh.

He held at bay misgivings about treading the boards again and instructed Allen Klein to book no less a venue than New York's 20,000-capacity Madison Square Gardens, where no Beatle had gone before. The most convenient date was Sunday 1 August, which left George just enough time to recruit and rehearse whatever musicians he could muster to support him. "We had to get this together quickly, so I had to put myself out there and hope for friends to support me."[262] The coup of the decade, meanwhile, would have been the regrouping of The Beatles. Contacted in Spain while playing a bandit in a Klein-produced western, Ringo was game, but over in Sussex Paul declined, as 'How Do You Sleep' and the legal turmoil at Apple were still sore points. Although in the midst of promoting a book by Yoko, John seemed keen, even when, despite Klein's assurances to the contrary, there'd be no place for his wife on stage that evening. Exercising his novel power of veto, George wouldn't hear of it – 'Don't Worry Kyoko' at the Lyceum was too hard to forget.

Yoko might have been of greater notoriety than Jim Keltner, Carl Radle and the rest of the West Coast minions that George now gathered about him, but she obviously wasn't boring enough. Neither did she know *All Things Must Pass* – the show's principal source of repertoire – backwards. The rank and file would also include a small choir, three members of Badfinger on acoustic guitars and a horn section, led by Jim Horn. When the call came, all had been only too pleased to help. Bigger names were, however, "terribly difficult. It took me three months [*sic*] on the telephone, really, night and day, trying to con everybody into doing it."[211] Some problems were administrative. Newly domiciled in France, Mick Jagger was prevented from taking part because his visa couldn't be cleared in time. Busy with the post-production of *Being There* in Hollywood, Peter Sellers couldn't make it, either. During a trip to Disneyland made by the odd but amicable trio of Harrison, Shankar and Sellers, the latter had been suggested as an ideal compere. Instead, the task fell to George.

To share his lead guitar functions, who better than Eric Clapton? Unfortunately, Clapton's drug habit had now reduced him to spending many lethargic hours between fixes either asleep or before the television, nourished by fast food. As testimony to his regard for George, however, Eric dragged himself from this pit to cross the Atlantic to do his bit for East Pakistan. He found this no easy job. Hours passed at Kennedy Airport for those appointed to look after him. Plane after British plane would land and Clapton would still be shuttered in Hurtwood Edge. Giving up, they missed him when he finally touched down the night before the reckoning. Dazed and ill, he festered in his hotel room while the poor girl he'd brought with him scoured the city for heroin.

Just as doubtful a participant as Clapton was Bob Dylan, whom George had had in mind to be the 1970s equivalent of "featured popular vocalist". Although unnerved by headlines such as "Dylan's Midnight Flop!"[263] after his Isle of Wight re-emergence, he was nevertheless intrigued enough to turn up with his guitar at George's hotel suite to find out exactly what was required of him. While mulling over the more recent of his songs, Bob's rejoinder to Harrison's earnest proposal that they dredge up 'Blowing In The Wind' was to wonder why they didn't try 'I Want To Hold Your Hand' as well. George seemed to have talked him into appearing, but, "right up until the moment he stepped on stage, I was not sure that he was coming".[210]

With sales of *All Things Must Pass* approaching three million, George alone could have sold out the concrete-and-glass amphitheatre many times over. From the onset, an extra performance had had to be crammed in. In order to mollify further demand (and to battle bootleggers), both shows were to be captured on tape and celluloid. Now there was no turning back, as George stole nervous glances at the increasing depth into which he might plunge should he not live up to the selfish public's expectations.

Rather than Blind Faith's self-conscious iconoclasm or The Plastic Ono Band's pandemonium, George's scrupulous rehearsals in a studio on West 57th Street, near Carnegie Hall, aimed at a slick, professional show with few avenues for excessive improvisatory excursions. There'd be nothing in the set that hadn't been a hit for someone on stage or wasn't well-known enough for applause to burst out and subside over its introduction, whether this was the circular riff of 'Wah-Wah' or the backing harmonies prefacing Ringo's vocal entry in 'It Don't Come Easy'. No matter what his musicians got up to elsewhere, George emphasised punctuality and discipline and provided wholesome Indian dainties when some might have expected beer and hamburgers for meal breaks.

Of the principals under his metaphorical baton, only Billy Preston and Ringo could be relied upon to attend as George drove the band through the umpteenth attempt at 'Beware Of Darkness'. Very much in charge, he'd decided to do that one as a duet with Leon Russell, whose star-studded album credits and production of Dylan's latest single during his stint with Mad Dogs And Englishmen indicated his elevation to hip omnipresence after years of anonymous studio work. This reputation had also earned him a solo spot in George's show, although this could be withdrawn if and when room was needed for Dylan, Lennon or Clapton. On standby, too, was Clapton's understudy Jesse "Ed" Davis, whom Klaus Voorman had subjected to a crash-course of the set.

There was still no sign of Eric during the final run-through on the Saturday. Into the bargain, as the evil hour when her husband was actually going to walk onstage without her crept closer, Yoko Ono's rage had exploded in a tantrum of such violence that her other half, after crushing his spectacles in his fist, slammed out of their hotel to catch the next flight home. Dylan got as far as the auditorium but, pausing in the dusty half-light beyond footlight still being tested, "He freaked out...and he was saying, 'Hey man, this isn't my scene. I can't make this.'"[211] He was persuaded to at least soundcheck, but who knew how seriously his stage fright was to be taken?

At around noon the next day, even those without tickets began milling round the huge lobby entrance to Madison Square Gardens. Bestowing each forehead with pinpricks of sweat, the humidity was what The Lovin' Spoonful had sung about in 'Summer In The City'. And yet, despite the leaden skies and touts richer by 1,000 per cent, the mood of the wilted flower children in the queue was light and friendly. When the audience settled down, rumours were as rife in the euphoric atmosphere as frisbees and balloons. Clapton had been seen, guitar case in hand, panting along the dingy passages of nearby Pennsylvania Station. McCartney was stuck in a traffic jam on Seventh Avenue. Even as the customers filed in, Harrison was outlining the set to Dave Clark amidst the wearisome blues jams, prima-donna piques and the usual dressing-room squabbles.

With credulity stretched to the limit, some were weeping with anticipation when the lights dimmed and George steeled himself to face facts. He needn't have worried. The whole extravaganza was a triumph, because everybody wanted it to be. The vogue for spirituality had already provoked philanthropy in other pop stars. Fleetwood Mac's Peter Green, for example, had commanded his accountant, on pain of a punch on the nose, to redirect incoming monies to the coffers of the needy. Cliff Richard had even made a field visit to Bangladesh in as early as 1968 – although, by his own uncomfortably honest admission, this patronage of the Evangelical Alliance Relief Fund "was to give me a sense of satisfaction and fulfilment, and I don't pretend I felt any heartache for the people in the Third World or anywhere else, for that matter".[264]

Even the humblest equipment-humper would be namechecked on the subsequent album and film, but, whatever the motives of those George Harrison had assembled at Madison Square Gardens, "The whole vibe of that concert was that it was something bigger than the lot of us".[262] The onlookers thought so, too. They had a glimmer of how much George had, did and would have on his plate, and so loved him for wanting to please them before he'd even plucked a string. On the radio for the past week had been his new single, 'Bangla Desh' (sic), written after Shankar came "to me with sadness in his eyes".[265] A slow recitative broke into rushing feverishness as George, singing like he might mean it, appealed for "bread to get the starving fed".[265]

'Bangla Desh' was to be the finale of both shows before George vanished stage left. Descending the escalators to the lobby afterwards, most of the customers would agree that they'd participated, however passively, in making history. If nothing else, it had been a diverting evening's entertainment. Opening the show, Ravi and his three musicians' long 'Bangla Dhun' raga had garnered a fidgety respect as their affinity to the main event ensured an almost palpable wave of goodwill – reminiscent of Monterey – washing over them.

Polite clapping for Shankar gave way to barrages of cheering, whistling and stamping when George and his cohorts attacked song after familiar song. A reluctant interlocutor, the bandleader – in matching white suit and Stratocaster – restricted himself largely to announcing the boys in the band six numbers in, building up the lesser-known of those he'd let take a lead vocal and bringing on his one surprise guest. Via nods and eye contact, he conducted a punchy set in which some All Things Must Pass items were actually rattled off in less time than the studio originals, in what might have been an opportunity to correct oversights. Headed by Claudia Linnear, the nine-voice chorale fermented with a passion above and beyond that of The George O'Hara Singers. Wisely, a creaky 'Hear Me Lord' was dropped for the second house, but even so, "We were very lucky, really, as we didn't have full rehearsals, as a lot of people had just come in from England or were on tour in the States. It worked out pretty good, considering."[188]

To many, the essence of the show was Harrison and the thrillingly unrehearsed Clapton breaking sweat on duelling guitars during 'While My Guitar Gently Weeps', one of the rare "blowing" numbers. Extricating himself from his Hammond organ, Billy Preston enlivened his one hit with a flickering dancing display that prodded the right festive nerve, while Ringo's singing was endearing in its distracted clumsiness during 'It Don't Come Easy'. Unlike Ringo, George didn't forget his words, but his larynx hadn't switched immediately into gear. Through either trepidation or a blunder at the PA desk, it had been less conspicuous than the accompaniment during the first minutes of the matinee, but, as the sound balance evened out, his voice shimmered like full moonlight over the sea of heads. He was in good form, edgy and without the irritating embellishments that vocalists like Leon Russell are prone to produce in a concert setting.

For longer than Billy and Ringo put together, The Concerts For Bangladesh became The Leon Russell Show. George's band introduction had purposely enabled an instrumental switchover, whereby minstrels in better accord with Russell's Southern-fried flamboyance could get on stage, with grizzled Carl Radle's throb considered preferable to Klaus Voorman's Teutonic elegance. With no hits of his own, Leon offered a medley of 'Jumping Jack Flash' and The Coasters' 'Young Blood', once a Harrison lead vocal with The Quarry Men. To the relentless snappy jitter that typified the "funky" oeuvre, Russell's up-front encroachment was the epitome of the self-satisfied sexism of the Delaney And Bonnie super-sidemen. In a slobbering Dixie whine, abetted by Claudia Linnear's strident responses, a raunchy monologue that was the pinnacle of male chauvinist piggery segued into the lascivious 'Young Blood', which culminated with the cocksure high velocity of Russell's regular guitarist. The most that can be said for this aberration was that it made a change from the piety of 'My Sweet Lord' and 'That's The Way God Planned It'.

Getting back on course after indulging Leon, George took it down with a 'Here Comes The Sun', in which only he and Badfinger's Pete Ham – each on acoustic six-string – were heard. George was unsure what would follow this lull. On the set list sellotaped to his guitar, "Bob?" had been written, "so I just looked 'round to see if there was any indication if Bob was going to come or not, and he was already there. He was so nervous, and he had his harmonica on and his guitar in his hand, and he was walking right on stage. It was, like, now or never, and so I had to say, '[I'd] like to bring on a friend of us all – Mister Bob Dylan.'"[262]

The timid songbird was backed by a relieved Harrison and Ringo on tambourine and Leon Russell (that man again) on bass through a 20-minute slot that, yes, did include hoary old 'Blowing In The Wind'. Feeling almost as jumpy as Bob, George picked his obligatos without the safety net of the big band's blast. Nevertheless, any apprehension was lost in the mob's silent disbelief as Bob Dylan – the single most reclusive and messianic symbol of hipness – swept aside like dust all that had gone before. What else could come after but The Beatles' last US chart-topper, 'Something?'

After the 'Bangla Desh' playout, the company repaired to a celebratory party at which merry-andrews from The Who and Grand Funk Railroad queued for the buffet with swamis and sarod players. Roaring drunk at the piano, Phil Spector pounded out 'Da-Doo-Ron-Ron' and more from his voluminous back catalogue. Once again, he'd been commissioned by Harrison to co-produce a triple album, and once again the twitchy Spector couldn't abide more than a few hours in the studio as the *soirée* – from 'Bangla Dhun' to 'Bangla Desh' – was readied for vinyl. Starr, Dylan and others who'd been put in the spotlight had been promised that they would not be incommoded "if it turns out lousy".[262] All, however, gave their approval, bar Russell, who insisted on a remix of his bit.

Although the artists involved were contracted to different companies, this was less problematic than the unseemly antipathy preceding the album's release. Blaming Capitol's president, Bhaskar Menon – who happened to be Indian – for unwarranted delay, George passed the prestigious task of its distribution to CBS,

Dylan's label, whose television outlet broadcast concert highlights. The world outside North America would have to wait until the following spring, when the film went on general release via 20th-Century Fox.

In collusion with the director Saul Swimmer, George had compiled excerpts of the night's travail. Adding to his technical knowledge of film as faults were ironed out, he noted "about twelve cuts in the film. Nine of them were fake. We had to get a long shot of me where you couldn't see my mouth moving, because they didn't have the opening segment."[188] Meanwhile, Bob Dylan, present at the editing, got his own way over "not changing camera angles, and it is all grainy, but that was because Bob wanted it like that. It was great to have him in it at all."[262]

The flick would win no Oscars, but the album – out in time for Christmas – earned a Grammy and spent most of 1972 in the Hot 100. More self-interested was a band who nipped in sharpish with a French cover version of 'Bangla Desh' and another who cloned every last lecherous gurgle of Leon Russell's medley in a "Battle Of The Bands" tournament at Reading University. Harrison's 'Bangla Desh' had been only a middling hit, while missing completely was another tie-in single, Ravi Shankar's 'Joi Bangla', which translated as "Be Triumphant, Bangla!" It was more melodiously uplifting than any other of George's Indo-pop productions.

The LP's picture sleeve mentioned the Bangladesh Disaster Fund organised by UNICEF, for whom was earmarked the $243,418.50 generated by the show plus the greater amounts accrued by record, film and other by-products, such as George's Material World Charitable Foundation, created to "encourage refugees to start growing their own food and thereby make the cash go further than it would in outright purchases".[262] However, although record companies might have waived royalties theoretically owing to their artists, George discovered that "the law and tax people do not help. They make it so that it is not worthwhile doing anything decent."[262] The show might have been over, but "just that one decision to help Ravi, it took two years solid of my life",[211] as turgid bureaucracy on both sides of the Atlantic dissected the Bangladesh millions with unhelpful slowness. As George hadn't registered the event as a charity, most of the cash would remain at the mercy of the IRS in Washington until – via a conversation between his hip son and George – President Ford began "to try and help it go through the normal channels and get it solved".[210]

In London, even personal appeals by George failed to reduce purchase tax on the album, although the Exchequer's chief financial secretary, Patrick Jenkin, was "glad to talk with a man who has gone right to the top and has stayed there so long", and who put his case so "very eloquently".[266] Eventually, George had to sign a cheque for £1 million to the British government after he had been quoted "sections, schedules and all the other bullshit which is so much part of the game of politics. Until the [politicians] became human, we must do our service to others without their help."[267]

The only gleam of hope had come from the House of Lords, when Lord Harlech met Allen Klein over a meal. Since hosting a reception for The Beatles at the British Embassy in Washington in 1964, Harlech had taken on – among other posts – the chairmanship of Shelter, the campaign for the homeless. With a daughter lately moved in with Eric Clapton, he was, if not "with it", then more conscious than other upper-class do-gooders that The Beatles were just the tip of the pop iceberg that had made more fortunes than had ever been known in the history of entertainment. When George stepped off the QE2 from New York, he did not deny the Harlech-Klein summit nor further talks with Tory MP Jeffrey Archer, who arranged George's luncheon date with Patrick Jenkin. Some newspapers even named the day – 10 October 1971 – when Harrison would repeat his Madison Square miracle on a grander scale in Britain for Shelter. Not reported, however, were the impossible conditions that Klein had stipulated as *quid pro quo* for this deed. One would require a revision of British law so that Harrison and Lennon's drugs convictions would be quashed.

In one throw, George had outshone all John and his wife's bed-ins, John's repudiation of his MBE and more mystifying tactics to right the wrongs of mankind. Perhaps in a spirit of one-upmanship, Lennon spoke for a while of a Wembley showcase for a worthy cause with him, Yoko and their sort of people, instead of George and his Bangladesh gang.

With no such axe to grind, cells within the general public – not only the young – had taken up George's challenge. "There were a lot of people who gave a lot of money and collected on the streets and were hanging on UNICEF's door saying, 'What can we do to help?' A lot of people don't do anything unless they're inspired, and on that it is important, I suppose, that I inspired a lot of people to do something. I mean, I didn't really want the task in the first place."[262] However unwillingly he'd shouldered the burden, George – as the representative of common folk – contemplated riding roughshod over official interference by travelling personally to India to ensure delivery of what he'd describe in a 1973 B-side as "the rice that keeps going astray on its way to Bombay".[268] Composed the day after the concert, his naïve 'The Day The Word Gets 'Round' had smouldered from the angered question of why a mere pop star rather than a governing body was obliged to pinpoint iniquities.

With The Concerts For Bangladesh shipwrecks as his sea markers, Bob Geldof would be knighted for Live Aid after 1985, but, further back on pop's road to respectability, George's efforts had been rewarded by an elevation to *Playboy*'s "Musicians Hall Of Fame". He'd received an MBE for less. Live Aid was still two years away when he presented a cheque for a fraction of the concert's net proceeds to Hugh Downs of the US committee for UNICEF on an American chat show. Accepting a special citation in return, George told the viewers, "It's nice to know you can achieve these sorts of things, even though the concert was ten years ago and the public has forgotten about the problems of Bangladesh. The children still desperately need help and the money will have a significant impact."[269] It was beneath him to vilify those who, in frozen ledgers and computer run-offs, had super-taxed the starving, the diseased and the huddled masses fleeing from terror.

13 His Lectureship

The Bangladesh spectacular was the George Harrison moment, never to return. During the 15-month hiatus between the film's première and his next album, no time would have been better for a world tour. With its appetite whetted by *All Things Must Pass*, The Concerts For Bangladesh and associated hit singles, the public awaited a carnival of the same magnitude as a Fab Four tour, albeit, as Brian Epstein once said, "not in the context of the previous terms".[270] George was now the most respected and, seemingly, the most capable ex-Beatle. Already the first fan club devoted to him alone – the Harrison Alliance – had sprung up in Connecticut. Dollars danced before his eyes, but the so-called Money Beatle, his own man at last, "wouldn't really care if no one ever heard of me again".[271]

His fortunes were by no means secure, but after a decade on the run he chose the stink of fertiliser to dressing-room fug. While growing to manhood in the hothouse of the beat boom and its endless North American sequel, he'd been treated like a food pigeonhole in a self-service cafeteria. No more could it be taken for granted that George Harrison existed only to vend entertainment with a side-serving of cheap insight. The world wouldn't let him stroll unmolested in a public park, so he'd had to buy one of his own. Unobserved, he'd stride forth on a clear, dew-sodden morning across his lake, whose stepping stones made it look like you were walking on water, and into the woods and pastures of his acres. At one with nature, all of the intolerable adulation that his life contained – the Number Ones, the money down the drain – could be transformed to matters of minor importance.

In the first of many hibernations, he watched Friar Park's flowers bloom again, ended a joyless marriage and was conducted by the head waiter to the best table in the restaurant. Of his celebrity, he'd admit, "There are perks, but it all balances out."[272] Although it wasn't downhill all the way, George's popularity on disc was eroded by an overloading of his artistic canvas with the religious preoccupations that were besetting his private life. Once a real cool cat, he was derided by hippies as one more bourgeois liberal with conservative tendencies, a fully paid-up subscriber to what neil would call "the Breadhead Conspiracy". The economic potential of a damaging re-emergence on stage would outweigh its creative merit. They'd find him out.

His fall was not perceptible in 1971, as 'Bangla Desh' was waved out of sight after a reasonable chart run. Some juke boxes had been more inclined to wear away its B-side, 'Deep Blue', which – sung with veiled resignation – was an articulation of Louise Harrison's final illness. Sent home after her operation, "She recovered a little bit for about seven months and, during that period, my father – who'd taken care of her – had suddenly exploded with ulcers, and he was in the same hospital. So I was pretending to both of them that the other one was OK."[59] That sick-room smell was still in their youngest son's nostrils when 'Deep Blue' came to him "one exhausted afternoon, with those major and minor chords. It's filled with the frustration and gloom of going in those hospitals, and the feeling of *disease* – as the word's true meaning is – that permeated the atmosphere."[59]

For all the dicta that he'd absorbed that trivialised death, George was still shaken by the manner of his mother's wasting away. Although a pitiable invalid, Louise had remained to the end the cheerful, patient ally who'd been unmindful of the din as his youthful fingers had striven to emulate Carl Perkins and Chuck Berry into the witching hour. She'd been his biggest fan, but she'd never had favourites among her offspring. Nevertheless, George's immediate kin had continued to be recipients of his largesse. Taking over from Terry Doran in managing Friar Park for Our Kid was brother Harold, in whose gatehouse office had been installed electronic screening for surveillance of the vast expanse of gardens. Meanwhile, overseer of a squad of full-time gardeners plus a botanist was Peter, who'd also been persuaded to turn south. In a bungalow on the same road as the school established by the recent cowled occupants of Friar Park, his wife cooed over Mark, who, in 1972, had been the latest addition to the Harrison brood.

The new baby's Aunt Pattie grieved for the children that she'd never have – not by George, anyway, as he'd purged himself of all things carnal. An inattentive spouse is apt to provoke extreme strategy in his partner. Thumbing her nose at George's spiritual pursuits, Pattie lowered the Om flag that flew over Friar Park and replaced it with a skull and crossbones. George's behaviour was not so funny after he and Pattie sustained minor injuries when, within days of him regaining his licence, the car skidded off the A4 through Maidenhead. Pattie took to her bed on medical advice, but her recovery was impaired by George's pounding on a drum-kit that he'd set up in the next room.

Worse still would be the embarrassment when, during dinner at the Starkeys', the company almost leapt out of their skins when George suddenly declared his deep love for Maureen. Calculated to wound his wife rather than compliment a bright-red Mrs Starkey, this bombshell would reverberate beyond the tense dining room as Pattie rushed out in tears to lock herself in the bathroom. Although Ringo's knuckles had whitened after George's outburst, Maureen's later reciprocation of her guest's affection wouldn't pain him as much as he'd thought it would. It might have hurt more if Harrison had been underhanded about it. What did it matter? Ringo and Maureen were washed up, anyway. If anything, John – as self-appointed Beatle paterfamilias – was more annoyed, apparently chastising George for this "incest".[273]

Although he "always had a sense of humour, even during my really heavy religious period",[151] his displays of devilment were more skirmishes than jokes as he and Pattie drifted into open estrangement. Alone in New York's Park Lane Hotel, George composed 'So Sad' as a requiem for his marriage.

Almost all of George's next LP was cut at Apple, but he and Ringo were spending increasingly longer spells away, mainly in the ego-massaging environs of Los Angeles, where George maintained a

Beverly Hills *pied à terre* with obligatory swimming pool and tennis court. Living on the West Coast unavoidably affected his vocabulary, although other Englishmen in the Hollywood Raj were more pliant in drawling "can" for toilet and "sidewalk" for pavement. Among them was Dave Mason, who reeled in George to pick guitar on his new album. Further affirming his standing in this firmament of hipness, George's played on an LP track by hippy comedians Cheech and Chong, whose humor (*not* humour) wrung dry what it could from drugs and balling chicks.

Turning out for other sessions, he'd be greeted by familiar faces amidst the many British musicians now seeking their fortunes in California. Badfinger had been over there when George's sure-footed production of their third LP was abandoned when all decamped for Madison Square Gardens. Salvaged from his ministrations was the hit single 'Day After Day', which was propelled by a guitar introduction too singular to have been played by anyone else but the producer. In a more creative role, George left his mark on an eponymous album by Ringo that would temporarily allay the ghost of "the downtrodden drummer. You don't know how hard it is to fight that."[260]

Ringo was the closest The Beatles would ever come to an artistic reunion, embracing as it did compositions of all four, with Lennon's semi-autobiographical 'I'm The Greatest' utilising by chance the Klaus-instead-of-Paul line-up, plus Billy Preston. Both 'I'm The Greatest' and Paul's contribution could have been written asleep, but of greater substance were three by George. As a trailer for the album, his 'Photograph' – co-written with Starr – sold a million. Sweeter, however, was John's affable telegram to Ringo to "write me a Number One tune".[274]

The session for 'I'm The Greatest' had started with only John, Ringo, Klaus and producer Richard Perry grouped around a piano figuring out the unfinished song's bridge when George telephoned to invite himself along. Their concord when recording was so jovial that he was emboldened to suggest to John that they ratify the old rumour by forming a permanent group with the others present. Still peeved, perhaps, over the Bangladesh business, John floored George with a sleight of social judo by shrugging off this idea as a *faux pas* and artlessly changed the subject, pretending not to notice George's pride twist into a frown. Despite the glaring commercial pragmatism of a continued solo career, to be on equal footing with John in a new group had been too sorely tempting for George. Although the idea had been scorned, just as his friendly overtures had been when he had first known John, for a while George would champion Lennon's music and confess, "I'd join a band with John Lennon any day, but I couldn't join a band with Paul McCartney. That's not personal, but from a musical point of view."[275]

Wings' *Red Rose Speedway* and George's *Living In The Material World* – only a single album this time – were both released in summer 1973 and were poles apart. The catchy jingles that were *Red Rose Speedway* only confirmed that McCartney's wispy capacity for "granny music" was bottomless. Always a weak link nowadays were his lyrics, churned out with much the same nonchalance with which Ernie Wise wrote plays.

Whereas *Red Rose Speedway* was starved of intellectual depth, there was no shortage on *Living In The Material World*, on which all of the songs were "about" something – the transience of fiscal cares, the inevitability of death or 'The Light That Has Lighted The World'. Although 'Don't Let Me Wait Too Long' betrayed that George's sublimation of lust was by no means total, its consummation was, nonetheless, "like it came from above". With two numbers inspired by Prabhupada's teachings, buzzwords like "om" and "Krishna" blended with Scouse parlance – world leaders acting "like big girls" – and references to The Beatles. However, his verbosity was offset by humour that was not always obvious, the stodgy arrangement of 'Be Here Now' masking a lyric born of a funny story. George was unable to bottle his mirth on the in-joking 'Miss O'Dell' – written after an Apple employee – which, interspersed with Dylan-esque harmonica, let fly such eruditions as Paul's old Liverpool telephone number.

'Miss O'Dell' hadn't suited the LP, and so was consigned to the B-side of its promotional 45, 'Give Me Love (Give Me Peace On Earth)', which had flowed from George with an ease as devoid of ante-start agonies as a Yoko Ono "think piece". It had been one of those lucky creative accidents in which monetary gain – largely from a US Number One – was out of proportion to basic effort. The line "help me cope with this heavy load" might have touched a raw nerve or two in Britain's dole queues, even if the publishing royalties from 'Give Me Love', along with all but one other album track, were assigned to the Material World Charitable Foundation.

The exception was 'Try Some Buy Some', which was left over from the Spector era. Rather than re-record it, George had simply substituted his own vocal for that of Spector's wife, whose version was now mouldering on deletion racks. Although its lyrics mattered less than the general effect, 'Try Some Buy Some' fitted the ethereal mode of *Living In The Material World*. However, its heavy-handed orchestration was at odds with a self-production criterion closer to the style of George Martin, in that it was much less concerned about inflating songs with gratuitous frills. The looser abundance of *All Things Must Pass* was stripped away in favour of a sparser ensemble from which Jim Horn's solitary saxophone might honk a counterpoint that Spector would have saturated with massed strings. Two thumps of timpani would enliven a middle eight all the better for not being buried in grandiloquence.

This moderation resulted in arrangements flexible enough for the title track to flit smoothly from a verse rocking with clipped guitar and Nicky Hopkins' jangling ivories to its quiet "spiritual-sky" sequence made celestial by tabla and flute. As well as ending with a syncopated blues run-down, this number also contained an interlude in which tenor sax intermingled with George's now quite distinctive bottleneck.

"George is king of rock 'n' roll slide guitar"[164] was the opinion voiced by a musician of such sagacity as Jeff Lynne, of the just-launched Electric Light Orchestra. Others wouldn't rate him as highly as that, but in 1973 George was certainly a contender. With controlled grace, he was as inventive in subtle careen on the downbeat hootenanny of 'Sue Me Sue You Blues' as he was in shinning up the octaves for 'The Light That Has Lighted The World', composed originally for Cilla Black to record. George's new niche was once described as "country and eastern",[275] but his most exotic exploit on *Living In The Material World* was the decorative fingering and harmonics of 'Be Here Now', which was on a par with the acoustic virtuosity of John Renbourn.

Harrison himself applied a flattering comparison to his own singing which unfurled a hitherto unprecedented audacity as he tackled the album's more oblique metaphysics without affectation. In swerving from muttered trepidation to strident intensity in 'Who Can See It', you could appreciate why George would later avow that "it reminds me of Roy Orbison".[39] He may have lacked the Big O's operatic pitch, but 'Who Can See It' was among George's most magnificent performances on record. Veering cleanly into falsetto on other tracks, too, never had his pipes been so adept.

The virtues of George's latest did not prevent some scribes – in Britain, especially – from pulling it to bits, their strongest objections being its preachy overtones. "They feel threatened when you talk about something that isn't just be-bop-a-lula," George countered, "and if you say the words 'God'…or 'Lord' it makes some people's hair curl."[210] With the merest mental athleticism, some lumped *Living In The Material World* with the outmoded works of Deep Purple, ELP and James Taylor. Its mystic flavour was somehow too familiar. Wasn't that "spiritual-sky" bit like 'Baby You're A Rich Man'? Only the most hooked Beatle fan had the time to decipher the concealed messages in the cover shot of George proposing a toast to the other musicians on a Friar Park lawn. Was it a comment on the Last Supper? Among objects positioned in the middle distance were a pram (Mark?) and a wheelchair (his mother?). Further back, a woman dangled her bare leg out of a window, but so what?

Unimpressed by this symbolism (if that's what it was), a British teenager might have still dug the gear worn by Krishna in his chariot on the inner sleeve. Androgynous in beaded kaftan, jewelled fez and peacock feather, and strikingly pretty, the Supreme Personality of Godhead was not unlike some of the new breed of theatrical British chartbusters. On *Top Of The Pops*, a commercially expedient toy windmill twirled on Jeff Lynne's hat when he lip-synched The Electric Light Orchestra's debut single. If the art-college camp of Roxy Music and David Bowie – who'd dressed as a lady for one LP cover – appealed to intellectuals as The Beatles had to Hamburg "exis", The

Bay City Rollers – all bow ties and half-mast tartan trousers – were hyped as "the new Beatles", and for a few months Rollermania was rampant among schoolgirls.

The newcomers' many chart strikes guaranteed that they were despised by the whiskered, denimed buyers of Leon Russell's new live triple album. As one who'd "never read the pop papers now and never listen to Radio Luxembourg",[271] George was unable to comment, because, even in as late as 1975, "I've still never heard The Bay City Rollers."[275] Bowie's clothing might not have been for George, but he must have approved a musical taste which led Bowie to revamp The Merseys' 'Sorrow' in autumn 1973. With a nod to Ringo, he agreed that Marc Bolan had come up with "good commercial songs",[271] as had fellow singer/composer Gilbert O'Sullivan, but the impact of these was adulterated by O'Sullivan's being "made to look a dummy by his management".[271]

The shorts and pudding-basin haircut might have been contributory to Gilbert having more hits than more conservatively-attired Peter Skellern, a Lancastrian whose wittily observed love songs were in the same bag. Skellern, George's favourite of the current crop ("he reminds me of Harry Nilsson, full of potential"[276]) and a former pianist for Billy Fury, was honoured with more than mere praise when his fellow northerner popped in with a guitar to lend a hand on his sixth album, *Hard Times*.

George's assistance on the over-rated Nilsson's unpleasant 'You're Breaking My Heart (So Fuck You)' was a more accurate indicator of preference. British pop had nothing on the more traditional exactitudes of laid-back Yanks like The Allman Brothers Band, who were to New York what the Bramlett mob had been to Los Angeles. As well as such contemporary Americana, a concert by reggae apostles Bob Marley And The Wailers was the "best thing I've seen in ten years".[276] Once ignored by most of the so-called intelligentsia, West Indian pop was now outflanking even blues as the new "twisted voice of the underdog" and student disco accessory. Marley reminded George "so much of Dylan in the early days, playing guitar as if he's so new to it. And his rhythm – it's so simple, and yet so beautiful."[276] For the same reason, George was "still basically in favour of the things I liked in the old days – Smokey Robinson, Stevie Wonder, those sort of things".[276]

So were The Carpenters, the States' major singles export of the 1970s, who hit in 1975 with an overhaul of 'Please Mr Postman'. David Bowie and Roxy Music's Bryan Ferry had cut entire albums of oldies, as Lennon also did in 1975. To a lesser degree, George too would succumb. A lot of his pals, including Klaus Voorman and Delaney Bramlett, were among those invited to London to record with Jerry Lee Lewis. At around this time, also, many artists released tracks with "rock 'n' roll" in the title. Seeing the transparency of it made many pop consumers scour jumble sales, junk shops, deletion racks and charity stalls for overlooked artefacts from past musical eras. At the Parisian grave of The Doors' Jim Morrison, a mourner reasoned that these and later seasons of revivals were because "the '60s' music was much better than stuff now".[277]

At the table head in the Valhalla of the lamented decade's youth culture sat The Beatles. By proxy, their presence was felt still in vinyl respects paid by the likes of Elton John and Eric Burdon's new group, War. That glam rock did not bear the same us-and-them parallel to pop's elder statesmen as punk would was implied in a reverential treatment of 'Tomorrow Never Knows' by 801, an offshoot of Roxy Music. Beatle compilations sold briskly, too, with two double volumes of "greatest hits" qualifying for a gold disc two days before release in 1973.

Timely, then, was a Stuart Sutcliffe art exhibition in a Greenwich gallery and *John, Paul, George, Ringo – And Bert*, a musical play by William Russell which shattered box office records at Liverpool's Everyman Theatre that summer. Its stylised portrayal of The Beatles' fable through the eyes of Bert, a fan, was uncannily close to the bone. Contrasting with Pete Best, sacked and alone beneath the proscenium, was a comedy scene of George – played by Philip Joseph – trying to blow into a sitar when still new to Oriental music. When it reached the West End, the proper George looked in, primarily to see his old friend Arthur Kelly, who was playing Bert. "George found it hard to watch," perceived Derek Taylor, "and I found it hard work sitting with him. It was a genuine form of suffering for him."[276]

The drama's climax was Bert, who'd grown up to become a Gary Glitter-ish performer, deputising for the disbanded Beatles who'd just chickened out of a reunion appearance at the Philharmonic Hall. George didn't see this scene, having shuffled out during the interval, but he knew of all sorts of old groups trying their luck again recently. Rebirths had been attempted by The Byrds, The Small Faces, The Temperance Seven, Dave Dee's lot, The Spencer Davis Group, you name 'em. As if they'd never been away, The Walker Brothers rematerialised in the UK Top Ten after eight years apart. Stranger – and infinitely grander – things could happen.

It had only been George and Ringo at Madison Square Gardens, but still the headlines had shrieked, "Beatlemania Sweeps A City!"[278] and even, "The Beatles Are Back!".[279] Since then, monetary inducement for the whole group to play together just one more time had multiplied until for the taking were millions for half an hour at Shea Stadium and even more for an outdoor show at Aintree racecourse. On top of that would be advances for television coverage, merchandising and closed-circuit cinema by satellite.

The four were still embroiled in the financial horrors of Apple, but socially the ex-Beatles were on friendlier terms with each other. George traipsed along with Ringo to a Stones concert in New York. On another night, John had joined them for dinner with Bryan Ferry. Even George and Paul had been photographed together at a Wings press party and, crucially, John had kept a civil tongue in his head when he and Paul had met for a drink in Los Angeles.

Time had healed, but there lingered memories of the struggle back in Liverpool and the unbelievable outcome. The old days had passed, but, no matter how much they'd feigned indifference, neglected to send birthday cards and traduced each other, each Beatle had stayed in the picture by making circuitous enquiries about the other three's activities. George's mask had slipped during the 'I'm The Greatest' session, and Paul – in a dark hour, professionally – had mentioned that he wouldn't mind working with John again on a casual basis. John was now saying how wrong it had been for the group to have split so decisively.

With hormones raging in a premature male menopause, Lennon

had just left Yoko to fling himself into a 15-month "lost weekend" in the company of hard drinkers like Nilsson, Spector and Keith Moon. With divorce from Maureen pending, Ringo too was sucked into this woozy vortex.

For all the hail-fellow-well-met bonhomie, that all four were losing their grip one way or another wasn't the soundest foundation for a second coming of The Beatles. Pressed on the subject, Gary Glitter hit the nail on the head: "They'll have to come back as a bigger creative force than they did before, which would be very difficult indeed."[280] It had been just as difficult for Muhammad Ali to regain his world heavyweight title in 1975. Possibly The Beatles might have regained theirs, even though the world had become wiser to their individual weaknesses. Inevitably, too much would be expected of them, but whether their first new record was good, bad or – worse – ordinary wasn't the issue. As would be proved by a 1980 event more shattering than any one-off concert, Beatlemania was for life. While 'She Loves You' spun on Radio 1's *All Our Yesterplays*, Mr and Mrs Average became Swinging '60s teenagers again, lovestruck and irresponsible.

The objects of their distant adoration did not, after all, amalgamate once more. Their very vacillation over the matter indicated neither destitution nor any real enthusiasm. "You can't reheat a souffle,"[246] concluded McCartney. Instead, you could – as Wings did – take the market that carried the fiercest torch for the departed Fab Four for every cent.

Oddly, it was the Beatle least addicted to the limelight who, in winter 1974, was the first to undertake a coast-to-coast trek across North America as a solo attraction. Balancing George's dislike of the road was restlessness and a resolution to cover as many prestigious venues as possible to give his forthcoming LP, *Dark Horse*, an extra boost – although, with *Living In The Material World* doing as well as its bulkier predecessor, he was still on much of a winning streak, as demonstrated by a huge turnout for the pre-tour press conference. Set in a Beverly Hills hotel, it was like a parody of some Hollywood B-feature: cameras click like typewriters at the star's tardy arrival in a flash Mercedes; no autographs, please; media hounds circle the star, thrusting stick-mikes at his mouth as he deadpans their usual inane and damned impertinent questions. Mr Harrison, are The Beatles getting back together? How did you find America? Turn left at Greenland. Everyone cracks up because Ringo said that in 1964. Are you getting divorced? No, that's as silly as getting married. Why isn't Eric Clapton in your backing band? Tell us why, George.

It wouldn't take long for the scum press to flesh out the Harrisons' domestic upheavals. Clapton hadn't been the first to cuckold George, had he? One Sunday much later, *The News Of The World* teased some sleazy column inches from Krissy, once the bride of Ron Wood, the newest Rolling Stone. In arm-chaired languor after their roast lunch, many Britons found her tale of Beatle-Stone wife-swapping a soothing read. Across two hemispheres, the Woods and Harrisons had flaunted their shame – Krissy and George on holiday "on a very serious and spiritual level"[281] in Portugal and then Switzerland; Ron and Pattie were in the Bahamas. "If anyone was jealous, it was me,"[281] protested Krissy. No one else was. George and Ron tinkered on guitars and wrote songs together and Pattie hadn't minded when the paparazzi named another of her husband's paramours, a Kathy Simmons, whose previous boyfriend had been Rod Stewart, singer with Wood's old group, The Faces.

Two old friends who used to be lovers, Pattie and George made light of each other's infidelities, understanding that sooner or later one of them would find – in the words of 'So Sad' – "someone who can fill the part of the dream we once had". When at last Eric confronted George with his feelings about Pattie, there was less anger than amusement, with George offering to swap her for the latest of Clapton's long-suffering girlfriends. Because George's disarming wit and rationalisation had defused what might have developed into an ugly showdown, the path to a formal dissolution of the Harrisons' dead marriage on 7 June 1977 began on a summer's day in 1975 in the hallway at Hurtwood Edge during some light banter between the parties. As if watching a tennis match, Pattie's eyes flickered from husband to lover. First it was George with, "Well, I suppose I'd better divorce her," then Eric's, "Well, that means I've got to marry her."[44]

Eric's best-selling solo single thus far had been a version of Bob

Marley's 'I Shot The Sheriff', and he'd been annoyed that George and not he had met the great Marley, who died in 1981. This was checkmated by Eric being in thicker with Bob Dylan than George was then. Despite their continued amity, a striving for one-upmanship persisted between Harrison and Clapton. With retrospective honesty, Eric would discourse to his eulogists of his winning of Pattie's hand. Verified by friend and actor John Hurt is a story of Harrison challenging Clapton to a guitar duet over the woman, trading licks rather than using them as clubs, although this may have been one of George's little jokes.

A combination of fame, wealth and religious education had rendered unto Harrison a greater certainty than before about everything he said and did. Longer and more discursive these days were his stern dissertations about living a godly life. Pottering round the garden, he'd go on about karma – often using floral metaphors – and likening working with the soil to meditation. Gravely, he'd present those he considered spiritually inclined with sacred texts. Once he'd lived for cars, girls and records, but 1974's most exciting experience had been an Indian pilgrimage to the holy city of Brindaban to seek Krishna.

Old at 31, a crashing bore and wearing his virtuous observance of his beliefs like Stanley Green did his sandwich board, he was nicknamed "His Lectureship" behind his back. Visitors to Friar Park tended not to swear in his presence. In deference to their vegetarian host – who, since Pattie's departure, had learned to cook his own meals – some would repair to Henley restaurants to gorge themselves with disgraceful joy on steak and chips, mocking over dessert George's proselytising. Back up Gravel Hill, the place smelled of incense and righteousness. Along corridors where portraits of bearded gurus gazed haughtily, you would just as often bump into a robed ascetic as a *Dark Horse* session musician.

"Compared to what I should be, I'm a heathen"[276] seemed, therefore, a strange admission. Morally, some of his guest appearances on the albums of others – Cheech and Chong, Nilsson, *et al* – had been a bit shaky, and there had been rare excursions to catch prurient films like *Last Tango In Paris*, but the greatest paradox during this most cerebral phase of his life was that George was boozing quite heavily. His consumption became so immoderate that for years small tabloid paragraphs would hint falsely of private clinics where blue devils had been sweated out of him.

When tequila and brandy worked their short-lived magic, they stayed the phantoms of paranoia, mounting business difficulties and personal desolations. There were more fatalities, all of them sudden. Most saddening to the Beatle "family" was that of faithful Mal Evans. Dividends from the investments that Mal had made had been disappointing, and, missing the activity and reflected glory of his previous post, he'd left his wife and children for sunny California, where perks of his Beatles connection included an honorary sheriff's badge, which permitted the carrying of sidearms. Thinking that they needed him, he fell in with Ringo and John on the next barstool. He'd also got in on George's act again, even co-writing 'You And Me (Babe)', one of the Harrison contributions for *Ringo*.

More and more often, he'd wake in his Los Angeles bedroom feeling groggy, having salvaged no contentment from following his former masters. The end came when a girl he'd allegedly invited to his apartment told the police that he'd threatened her with a gun. By the time the squad car arrived, he'd barricaded himself in. The cops bashed the door down and the ex-bouncer faced them with the supposed weapon in his hand. Rather than listening to what he might have had to say, they opened fire. At Mal's cremation, some theorised that it had been a kind of suicide.

That had already been the official verdict on Badfinger's Pete Ham, also riven with vocational frustrations, while yet another deprived of the acclaim he may have merited was Ringo's old boss, Rory Storm, who'd expired after tablets prescribed for a chest complaint had been washed down with an injudicious quantity of scotch. No Beatle attended the funeral or the Stormsville wake, Ringo's excuse being that "I wasn't there when he was born, either".[282] Rory's more fortunate brother-in-law, Alvin Stardust, echoed the general opinion, "Rory was very unlucky. None of us could really sing, but some got the breaks and some didn't."[58]

One that did was Cilla Black, now a middle-of-the-road media personality. Their paths had diverged, but her Beatle mates had kept in touch with Swingin' Cilla, with John and Yoko sending a telegram when she wed, Paul writing a theme song for her first TV series and Ringo guesting on another such show, their rehearsed patter far from that of the 1960s, when she'd had to lean over his kit to share the mike for the 'Boys' duet in the Iron Door.

Ringo's drumming – and Clapton's guitar – figured on Cilla's abortive recording in London of a song written and produced by George Harrison in 1972. 'When Every Song Is Sung', once intended for Shirley Bassey, had already exhausted a provisional title ('Whenever') and attempts by both Ronnie Spector and Leon Russell. Although she'd sacrificed her day off from a summer variety season in Blackpool, Cilla had squeezed in a painful dental appointment earlier in the day and "wasn't in the mood to record, and it was a very hot Sunday".[58] Still, she thought that George's lyrics were "super" and tried again in 1974 with another producer, "but even then it didn't have the magic it deserved. It should have had a 'Yesterday'-type arrangement."[58] Melodically, it was more like 'Something'. Cilla remained keen enough to discuss having another go during a chance meeting with the composer in a Chinese restaurant in London, even after it had been re-titled 'I'll Still Love You' for burial on Ringo's *Rotogravure* in 1976

Not a note had been played or written by George on Ringo's previous LP, *Goodnight Vienna*. Under pressure both to complete *Dark Horse* and to prepare for its attendant tour itinerary, scheduled to begin in Vancouver's Pacific Colosseum on 2 November 1974, George didn't have much time for anyone else's music. Another reason for this came to light at the Beverly Hills palaver, when he spoke of attending preliminary *Goodnight Vienna* sessions with John in 1974 "and we all ended up here, fighting Allen Klein".[275]

Gone were the days of open-handed conviviality around Allen's desk. As Mick Jagger had said they would, the three ex-Beatles were – to put it politely – having doubts about the Robin Hood of pop. He was increasingly less available since the Bangladesh shows, and headlines like *Rolling Stone*'s "Did Allen Klein Take The Bangladesh Money?"[238] were not reassuring. "Some guy in New York got onto the idea of Klein," explained George. "You know, 'Well, if Klein is involved with it, it must be a rip off,' and started the whole thing."[275]

However unfounded the story, it sparked off an intense and unwelcome interest by Messrs Harrison, Lennon and Starr in their manager's handling of their affairs. With sufficient music-industry experience for glibness to defer to probing suspicions, the three mustered legal forces to enlighten them as to precisely how much fiscal wool the *de facto* controller of the lumbering Apple empire had pulled over their eyes. No wool was so white that a dyer couldn't blacken it. The instigator of many such investigations himself, Klein's dogged streamlining had, indeed, recouped a fortune from disregarded record-company percentages to the smallest petty-cash fiddle, but where was it – and Klein – when George was challenged with a tax bill that had snowballed over 15 years of international stardom?

Like never before, George "needed someone to organise me out of all that mess. I wanted someone to help me with my present and future, but unfortunately he would have to get involved with my past."[284] Such an apparent paragon materialised in the form of an American who was temperamentally and physically everything that the portly, brash Allen wasn't. A bald, bespectacled beanpole of a man, Denis O'Brien seemed every inch the stereotyped financier. Retiring and besuited, his methodical approach to his university studies in law and accountancy had led to a favoured position in Rothschild's merchant bank. By the early 1970s, a bluffer, battle-hardened Denis emerged with enough cautious confidence to strike out on his own as a Los Angeles financial consultant.

His first showbusiness commission was to superintend Peter Sellers' *Being There*. Although he'd appreciated that The Beatles had been a cut above the usual bilge, he'd never been crazy about pop, "and the stories I'd heard of record people, I thought they'd crawled out of the gutter".[284] Whatever his disinterest in its artistic worth, he understood that pop's growth as an industry meant that deals between entrepreneurs and artists could no longer be mapped out on a serviette over lunch, as Brian Epstein's had been with Billy J Kramer.

It became prudent for O'Brien to lay aside his preconceptions when George Harrison was brought to him in 1973. As George explained, "a Hare Krishna friend of mine discovered this ruby mine in India and was wondering how he could use it to support the temple. He'd met Peter Sellers, who put him in touch with Denis, and the Krishna guy put us together."[284] Whether or not O'Brien and his new client anticipated more than a practised but detached professional relationship, there grew between them a friendship as each came to know what made the other tick. They had a shared sense of humour, and George respected Denis' good sense: "In 20 minutes, he gets more from a budget sheet than most people do in 20 hours."[284] Recounting their first conversation, O'Brien gushed with rare passion, "The chairman of Shell, of RTZ, of IBM, of Ford – I've met all these people and I've never met anyone as together as George."[284]

Outsiders might have assumed this mutual admiration to be a collision of opposites. Even Eric Idle generalised that it was "a balance between George as an amateur saint and Denis an amateur devil".[285] As Harrison wasn't a drug-crazed boor nor O'Brien an unsmiling pedant, there was enough common ground between the Money Beatle and his business advisor for each to be prone to both thrift and extravagance, as well as frequent distribution of alms to outstretched hands.

Although overshadowed by the Concerts For Bangladesh, a not-inconsiderable percentage of the takings and all proceeds from programme sales for the long-awaited *Dark Horse* tour were annexed for all manner of charities, from the Ethiopian famine to community hospitals in the Mississippi Delta. At the beginning, nothing seemed too much trouble for George, who was always uneasy at the possibility of accusations of arrogance or parsimony, – vices for which the Stones had been denounced by *The San Francisco Chronicle* in 1969. Aggrieved, they had responded with the disastrous free concert at Altamont, an hour's drive from the city. Learning from this corrupted endeavour, George confined himself to a guided visit to Haight-Ashbury's Free Medical Clinic, recipient of that night's profits from the Cow Palace, the same venue at which The Beatles had kicked off their first frenzied tour of the continent.

Ten years on, there was only one Beatle and no screaming. However much George had loathed the uproar that had degraded his musicianship, at least he'd been spared the unsettling hush of those who'd shelled out good money specifically for an evening with George Harrison. However demonstrative his giving, the purpose of his sold-out tour was the same as that of any other rock singer. As such, he was to be judged and, by some, found wanting.

The only *bona fide* pop star joining him this time was Billy Preston with his array of assorted keyboards. No more a one-hit-wonder since signing to A&M in 1972, Billy was fresh from his third US Number One, 'Nothing From Nothing'. If not as well known or as conspicuous on stage as Preston, the other players in George's band had impressive *curricula vitae*. At the core was The LA Express, a sextet led by trumpeter and flautist Tom Scott. A crack session team, Scott's boys had been tempted to hit the road from studios where they were equally at ease reading dots for Frank Sinatra as Frank Zappa. Their pricey but blithe dedication to their craft was refreshing after the shiftlessness of some of those on the Bangladesh shows.

Rehearsals on a soundstage at A&M studios didn't run as smoothly as expected. Since leadership had been thrust upon him after The Beatles split, George had never been out on a longer limb. As well as sweating blood over his LP and attending to day-to-day matters during the Klein-O'Brien interregnum, he'd also been organising a Ravi Shankar Music Festival at the Albert Hall, "and the time I'd allowed myself was too tight to allow for a rest between the album and the Ravi Shankar thing and the tour of the States".[276] Unaccustomed to singing for so long and having to instruct The LA Express, for whom the material was new, his vocal cords weakened to a tortured rasp. "I had no voice for the road and I was knackered. I had a choice of cancelling and forgetting it or going on and singing hoarse."[59] Like a trouper, he took the latter course, after supplementing the band with two old retainers, Jim Horn and Jim Keltner, at the last minute but not in the nick of time.

As the tension built on opening night, a backstage security guard might have glanced at a set list that promised an equilibrium of

Beatles numbers, Harrison hits since and a couple of tunes from *Dark Horse*. With that in mind, it looked like George didn't intend to renege on his past, even if – as Billy Preston informed a nosey-parker from *Rolling Stone* – "George didn't want to do 'Something' at all. I knew he was going to have to do it, and he started rebelling against it by doing it in a different way, rewriting the lyrics."[286] Still vying for John's attention, he'd also coarsened 'In My Life', Lennon's *pièce de résistance* on *Rubber Soul*, imbuing it with oppressive horns and squittering wah-wah from Robben Ford, the Clapton of The LA Express. Over where there'd been baroque wistfulness, Billy's Hammond B-3 now rolled like treacle. Perhaps to counteract the continuing 'He's So Fine' debate, George hustled a not immediately recognisable 'My Sweet Lord' out of the way at breakneck speed.

From the instant criticism detectable in the audience's reaction, there was less eagerness whenever he launched into the three *Dark Horse* numbers. 'Maya Love' had perfunctory lyrics but – like the 'Hari's On Tour' instrumental – was a vehicle for its writer to show off how much he'd improved on slide guitar. More piquant was the title track, if only for the hoarse lead vocal, which, although bubbling with catarrh, was a not unattractive cross between McCartney and Rod Stewart. Half-finished in Henley with help from Starr and Keltner, it had become less amorphous with each succeeding run-through with the tour ensemble. "I decided, because I had to teach the band the song anyway, that we'd mic up the soundstage and record it live. If you listen now, it's sort of OK."[59]

"Sort of okay", too, was the first three-hour show, where matches were lit in trendy approval and a girl in the front row sobbed noisily throughout what she'd convinced herself was a recreation of the Bangladesh magic. At every stop was a faint scent of Beatlemania, as in Oakland, where the stage was aswarm with maverick fans adding to George's heavy load during 'Give Me Love'. "It is really a test," he'd predicted. "I either finish the tour ecstatically happy or I'll end up going back into my cave for another five years."[275]

On the minus side, discomforted snarls had replaced 1971's peace sign as everyone with the same-priced tickets grappled for a good view when the stadium doors were flung open. The "festival seating" at many venues, you see, meant no seating. In another of pop's slow moments, there was no overt focus for adoration in North America in 1974, nothing hysterical or outrageous. With Bowie only a marginal success then, glam rock was but a trace element in the Hot 100. While precedents were being forged by the likes of The Ramones in New York's twilight zone and The Sex Pistols, conducting exploratory rehearsals in London, teenagers and post-psychedelic casualties had to make their own amusements. Spirituality was forgotten like last year's grandad vest. Cheap spirits, Mandrax, head-banging and streaking were among the desperate diversions that caught on during that apocryphal year.

At roughly the same mental level was the high-energy blues-plagiarised brutality of minstrels like Rush, Grand Funk Railroad, Led Zeppelin and Bachman-Turner Overdrive, whose sound pictures of Genghis Khan carnage were ideal for US stadia designed originally for championship sport. Meanwhile, lower on the scale were the likes of The Climax Blues Band and Supertramp. If no one went particularly wild over them, at least they were an excuse for a social gathering, an opportunity for friends to get smashed out of their brains together and hurl urine-filled beer-cans stagewards if the band didn't boogie. However, few of these odious projectiles landed within the spotlight's glare, where matchstick figures with V-shaped guitars and double drum-kits cavorted, oblivious to the squalor before them.

Where did George belong in this? After the fifth show, a flight connection variable obliged him to hang about for two hours. Alone, he ambled round Long Beach Arena, deserted but for a bulldozer scooping residual tons of broken whiskey bottles, cigarette packets, discarded garments and other litter left by the rabble who, at one juncture, he'd admonished, "I don't know how it feels down there, but from up here you seem pretty dead."[286] When animated and volatile, some had bawled for the good old good ones played in the good old way and just plain "boogie!". He'd done neither, because "Gandhi says [to] create and preserve the image of your choice. The image of my choice is not Beatle George. If they want that, they can go and see Wings. Why live in the past? Be here now. Whether you like me or not, this is what I am."[286]

His own enquiries and observations told a different story, but a cutting article in that mighty Cerberus *Rolling Stone* implied that a good few hadn't liked him. George protested, firstly that, from the original critique of the tour, the magazine had "just edited everything positive out".[211] Next, "a lot of people who came, without any preconceived ideas, really loved the show. And it really wasn't that bad. Every show was a standing ovation."[211] Naturally, he wrote a song about it, the first of his "sequel" compositions. "'This Guitar (Can't Keep From Crying)' came about because the press and critics tried to nail me on the 1974-5 tour. [It] got really nasty."[59]

From bootlegs and the one officially issued live recording from the tour, it actually wasn't really that bad, and the rottenest reviews he'd ever had didn't diminish George to loyal fans, who lapped up his mistakes and deficiencies as the prerogative of glamour. Even John Lennon – not then on the best of terms with George – opined, "George's voice was shot, but the atmosphere was good and George's performance was great."[44]

The star's pensive stroll around Long Beach Arena was after a harrowing recital, during which every battered inflection had been dredged from an inflamed throat. No medication or enforced silence could forestall the cruel caption "Dark Hoarse" appearing in newspapers local to the itinerary. When the going got especially tough, up to three instrumental items could be stretched out to give George's voice a few minutes' relief, but "rest was the only answer, and there's no way you can rest in the middle of a seven-week tour. I might have been the odd one out, but I quite liked my voice – it sounded like Louis Armstrong a bit, [and it] got better toward the end of the tour."[276] Putting on the agony for sometimes two feverish shows a night, he certainly got better at capitalising on – rather than shrinking from – his temporary inability to pitch past a gruff vocal compass without cracking. Rather than try and fail to hit that high G in the coda of 'In My Life', he extemporised huskily like a soul singer, as though its sentiment couldn't be expressed through expected melodic articulation.

What many would be unable to pardon, however, was his fracturing – perhaps with one word – of the emotive intent of some of the most nostalgic songs ever recorded, including "something in the way she moves it" and, most vexing of all, "while my guitar gently smiles". "In myyyyyy life," he loved *God* more. For those out for a good time, George's milking the audience with hi-di-hi exhortations to chant the name of God was similarly unendearing. "Krishna! Christ! Krishna! Christ!" he kept hollering as best he could, throwing in the odd "Allah!" and "Buddha!" now and then. Some responded, because they understood it was part of his image, but – hell, what had all this Krishna crap to do with heads-down, no-nonsense rock?

More enraging to bigots and racists was the support act, usually brought on after a musical taster from the headliners. Concert promoter Bill Graham advised that advertising it as "George Harrison and Ravi Shankar" would confuse people, although he conceded that both could have equal space in the programme notes. "I even wanted the ads to read, 'Don't come if you don't want to hear Indian music,'" George later insisted. "I thought it would give people another kind of experience other than just watching Led Zeppelin all of their lives."[221]

As a master of ceremonies, Harrison was no Ken Dodd, and he did Ravi no favours by imploring spectators to "be a little patient"[286] before they'd even heard a note from the 16-piece Indian orchestra. He'd then greet his former sitar teacher with a ceremonious *pranum*. Once, less meekly, he swore that he'd die for Indian music. "But not for this," he continued, tapping the sunburst Stratocaster held to him with a strap adorned with a button badge of a yogi.

It might have defied Led Zeppelin to go down well after a build-up of such priggish solemnity. Although he couldn't win, Ravi steered his musicians as close to Western pop as he'd ever gone with the jazzy 'Dispute And Violence' and his latest single, the toe-tapping 'I Am Missing You (Krishna, Where Are You?)'. However, his reappearance in the second half snapped much of the patience that the audience had been asked to have and they began chattering restlessly amongst themselves or heading for the toilets to partake of various soft drugs on offer. "It's a pity that a lot of people missed out on something that went above their heads,"[211] sighed George.

For this faction, Billy Preston had already stolen the show by then. By injecting his trio of recent million-sellers with fancy footwork and soulman exhibitionism, only Billy – up-front in his sequined suit – was able to give 'em what they knew and wanted to dance to, after a monotony of bamboo flutes and sitars. When they'd let their hair down for Preston, George's return to the central microphone to croak 'Dark Horse' or 'For You Blue' was rather an anti-climax.

Upstaging provoked no friction. Like a managing director doing the twist with a voluptuous typist at an office party, George – in checked trousers and raffish moustache – joined in Billy's frolicking, high stepping like a Tiller Girl and messing up the synchronised hand gestures in 'Will It Go Round In Circles'. During a post-mortem of the Vancouver show, said Tom Scott, "No one wanted Ravi to come out to a hostile audience."[286] Among enacted remedies was George coming on to growl a harmony on 'I Am Missing You'. Rather than ask for trouble after the intermission, Ravi's orchestra combined with the rock band, after a mid-tour rehearsal had produced satisfactory re-arrangements of Shankar pieces.

Another restorative ploy was George's open invitation to Dylan and Lennon – then enjoying his first solo US Number One – to do a turn as a surprise treat for the fans. Each turned up at one or two stops but declined to tread the stage. Also along for the ride was Peter Sellers, who provided George with much-needed hilarity when he was in the mood. "When Peter was up," said George, "he was the funniest person you could ever imagine. So many voices and characters. When he wasn't up, he didn't know who he was."[59] By this time, Harrison and the unpredictable Sellers had less in common. Through Denis O'Brien, they had remained bound by mutual investments (mainly in property development), but Peter's mystical phase had fizzled out, the last straw being when he requested Ravi Shankar to arrange a private recital. As he'd assisted Shankar financially in the past, he was astounded by the huge fee demanded by Shambu Das – now Ravi's business manager – for this service. Soon to die, Sellers was never as close to Ravi and George again after the 1974 trek wrapped up, on 20 December at Madison Square Gardens of blessed memory.

At the post-concert party in a Manhattan club, George, Ringo,

Maureen and John chatted amicably enough. The tour had encapsulated every extreme of what had become, in Lennon's estimation, "a love-hate relationship".[79] John had been the only ex-Beatle to send George a bouquet of first-night flowers at Vancouver. George attempted to more than reward this kindness when hip Jack Ford prevailed upon his father to receive the Harrison party – which included George's own father – at the White House on 13 December, the day of the Washington show. Amid the cocktail platitudes, George asked President Ford if anything could be done for Lennon, whose efforts to settle permanently in the States after leaving England forever in 1971 had been hindered, purportedly, by ceaseless official harassment. As recently as November, he'd been in court to battle yet another deportation notice. Like fellow marijuana miscreant Harrison, he had to keep re-applying for an extension of his H-1 visa to remain on US soil.

Their residency status was not the only topic discussed when, two days after the White House chin-wag, George subjected John to a tongue-lashing in a dressing room at Long Island's Nassau Colosseum. Annoyed because John had procrastinated over signing documents pertaining to The Beatles, George had withdrawn his invitation for Lennon to take part in any of the concerts. More relieved than chastened, John had, nevertheless, attempted to bury the hatchet when he and Yoko popped by to congratulate George on the show. In the Colosseum's backstage disarray, the resulting row was of the where-were-you-when-I-needed-you variety, culminating with Harrison whipping off Lennon's glasses and hurling them to the floor. No more the tough guy that he'd never been, John "saw George going through pain, and I know what pain is, so I let him do it".[44]

Exhausted and foul tempered through being too long out of his depth, George fled to his Henley fastness – after first making his peace with John – to assimilate what good had come from this, the most harrowing public ordeal of his solo career. "You either go crackers and commit suicide or you try to realise something and attach yourself more strongly to an inner strength."[32] If he'd had the inclination, he might have regained lost ground at home, where both

Dark Horse singles had faltered outside the Top 30, the first solo Beatle products to do so. The logistics of shunting the show across the ocean for Christmas dates in Britain was discussed with dwindling enthusiasm until, within a day of the New York finale, the troupe had scattered like rats disturbed in a granary. Although 'I'll Be Missing You' had sold well in Europe, how would Ravi have gone down during the second house at the Glasgow Apollo? For that matter, how would George have fared? His name was sufficient to fill the Albert Hall, but how long would it be before some smart-alec of a reviewer compared him and his "Krishna! Christ!" routine to Vince Taylor's sermon at the Paris Olympia back in 1961?

If *Rolling Stone*'s faint praise hadn't been enough, the now-radical *NME* was making up its mind about whether to categorise George's retinue with dinosaur bands as either over the hill, like The Grateful Dead, or wholesomely Americanised, like Fleetwood Mac, who were as far removed from the rough-and-ready blues quartet they once were as George was from 'Roll Over Beethoven'. The street-level acclaim granted to pub-rockers such as Kilburn And The High Roads, Ace and Dr Feelgood was a reaction against the distancing of the humble pop group from its audience. By definition, "pub rock" precludes stardom and its isolation from the everyday. Instead of paying to see whether the Harrison spectacular was really as terrible as *Rolling Stone* made out, how much more gratifying it was to spend an evening in the warm, jolly atmosphere of licensed premises, where – with no religion, Indian music or lyrics that made you embarrassed to be alive – a band would play with more dignity than any remote supergroup with an ex-Beatle in it, forever in America. With *Dark Horse* joining its singles in British bargain bins, who cared about a born-again millionaire like George Harrison any more?

Some *Dark Horse* tracks had been infected by his laryngitis and not all had the sandpapery appeal of the title song. Like Judy Garland, George could elicit anxiety rather than contempt whenever he was obviously struggling, as in the expiring falsetto in 'So Sad'. Another worry was that the LP contained only nine tracks, which included a non-original and an instrumental that went in one ear and out the other. As with *Living In The Material World*, he'd delved into his portfolio for items first given to other artists. Although his sources were less transparent than before, he admitted later that the refrain of 'It Is He' was a syncopation of a devotional *bhajan* that he, Ravi and a spiritual master had chanted *ad infinitum* when in Brindaban. At the heart of 'Ding Dong Ding Dong' were a few Crispisms, while other libretti fused the obscure, the earnest and the slap-dash, as in 'Far East Man', partly composed as George hurtled from Henley to Ron Wood's house in Richmond Hill. After clearing the decks with *All Things Must Pass*, he'd assumed that his muse – like Allen Klein – wouldn't let him down.

However, his writer's block didn'ot prevent more than a little off-hand breast-beating to intrude on *Dark Horse*, as – like Lennon's – his output tended to be more autobiographical now, one man's vision of his immediate world. Most blatant was his liberty-taking with The Everly Brothers' 'Bye Bye Love'. With its 'Badge' bass sound and sly lyrical digs at Pattie and "old Clapper" – neither of whom were present on the session, in contradiction of the album-sleeve notes – he justified what some saw as a rebuttal to 'Layla' as "just a little joke".[211] In a bluer mood, he emoted 'So Sad' with more compassion than had Alvin Lee (formerly "Alvin Dean" of The Jaybirds and the leader of Ten Years After) in the previous year on an album with Mylon Lefevre. In their less fussy rendering, however, this duo made more of the song's oblique riff.

Dark Horse in general would have benefited from a leaner approach to arrangements. Would the absence of trilling flute on 'Dark Horse' itself have spoiled it? On 'Simply Shady', there were what Frank Zappa might call "redundant piano triplets". "Phil Spector nymphomaniacs"[287] was George's own term for the choir, bells and brass layered onto the guitar-bass-drums bedrock of 'Ding Dong Ding Dong', the single that he hoped would reap a similar harvest as that of 'Merry Christmas Everybody', Slade's seasonal Number One twelve months earlier. 'White Christmas', 'Christmas Alphabet', 'Blue Christmas' – no one had cornered the New Year yet.[289]

'Ding Dong Ding Dong' was a brittle basis for optimism, however. "Repetitive and dull"[289] wrote reviewer John Peel in a column that also accused George of complacency. Two years later, Jethro Tull would be luckier with the only record to celebrate the winter solstice. With a chirpy-chirpy-cheapness worthy of *Red Rose Speedway*, 'Ding Dong Ding Dong' had all the credentials of a Yuletide smash but none that actually grabbed the public.

Despite its non-Christian slant, George might have fared better with the wonderful 'It Is He (Jai Sri Krishna)'. Over an accompaniment with pulsating wobble-board to the fore, the repeated chorus was so uplifting that it scarcely mattered that it was sung (without laryngitis) entirely in Hindi – no more, anyway, than McCartney breaking into French on 'Michelle' off *Rubber Soul*. Just as joyous was the decelerated verse which (in English) dwelt on the glories of "He who is complete".

Programmed to precede it on the album was 'Far East Man', one of the fruits of George's musical concurrence with Ron Wood. From just the title, none would guess its far stylistic cry from 'It Is He'. Recorded by Wood, too, it conjured up – intentionally, on *Dark Horse* – a band winding down for the night in some after-hours cocktail lounge. Although featuring altered lyrics and not as torpid as his co-writer's treatment, Harrison's 'Far East Man' adhered to the same sluggish tempo, underpinned by Andy Newmark, the same drummer who'd serviced Wood.

Dominating the artistic texture of *Dark Horse* was the nonchalant proficiency of Newmark's Californian contingent. It was as if they couldn't accomplish what the rowdier Beatles or Plastic Ono Band – for all their casually strewn mistakes – committed to tape instinctively. Even the tracks that included the old firm of Starr and Voorman were overwhelmed by the squeaky-clean, dispiriting neatness behind George's hit-or-miss singing. Given the circumstances under which it was made, these craftsmen kept pace with their employer's physical weariness rather than his emotional and vocational turbulence.

It was a record of a condition more serious than just a sore throat. Apart from a couple of passable numbers and the startling 'It Is He', *Dark Horse* was a comedown after the less derivative sophistication of *Living In The Material World*. Nonetheless, beneath the premeditated carelessness, the hurried meticulousness and yawning ennui was a non-Beatle, as well as an ex-Beatle in uncertain transition. For that reason alone, *Dark Horse* – an artistic *faux pas* – is worth a listen.

Adapted from the logo of an Indian paint firm, a seven-headed dark horse had reared up throughout the tour – on the stage backdrop, on the T-shirt George presented to US Secretary of State Henry Kissinger, on belt buckles and on necklaces. As well as the album, it also signified Dark Horse Records Limited, a label founded by George in May 1974. As EMI had buoyed up Apple, so Dark Horse was under the aegis of A&M. George and Ringo had considered briefly the possibility of buying up Apple and putting it back on course, "but it seemed logical to get more involved in my own set-up."[209] George's nine-year contract with EMI/Capitol wasn't due to expire until 1976, but he doubted that he'd re-sign, owing to what he saw as the company's avaricious dithering over the Bangladesh album and certain royalty discrepancies. Needless to say, EMI/Capitol refuted this sullying of its good name. Swallowing its ire at his accusations, its representative joined the queue of other major labels submitting their bids to Harrison, who at that time was still hot property. Looking for a new record company was as chancy as looking for a new girlfriend. Partly because Billy Preston got on well with A&M, George tested the water by leasing to the label via Dark Horse "a lot of things I was working on".[209] This liaison was rewarding enough for George to add himself to Dark Horse's roster when his time came, "because of the relationship we were, supposedly, going to have [with A&M], which it turned out we never did."[211]

Before it ended in tears, George's mere endorsement of Dark Horse's output as figurehead and pseudonymous record producer ensured exposure, if not chart success. Like Apple in microcosm, more demo tapes than could possibly be heard piled up in the in-trays of Dark Horse's office in London, Amsterdam and within A&M's block in Los Angeles. From the start, George attempted to be more discriminating than Apple had been. "We'll stick to a few," he declared, with his corporation president's hat on, "and we'll work hard on them. No act we sign is going to get hidden away."[290]

Chief among rescued projects from Apple was a narrative ballet composed by Ravi Shankar that had been performed in the Albert Hall and on continental Europe just prior to his joining George for the US tour. Ravi's Dark Horse LP, *The Shankar Family And Friends*, was a refinement of items from his work with both his usual musicians and an augmentation of what George called "the loony band"[211] – the East-West amalgam formed to placate those unwilling to endure two Shankar sets in one concert. With Ringo's paradiddles blending with sarod and swordmandel, *The Shankar Family And Friends* was a likelier commercial proposition than neater medicine on the soundtrack to *Messenger Out Of The East*, now retitled *Raga*.

Shankar merchandise was a reliable potboiler, but the jewel in Dark Horse's crown was Splinter, a duo from South Shields and another discovery by Mal Evans, who'd been on the look-out for an act to play in a night-club scene for another intended Apple movie. Beginning with George's production of their ' Lonely Man' for this sequence, Splinter came to sound as much like mid-period Beatles as Badfinger had. One member of Splinter, Bill Elliott, had already had a brush with Apple, featuring as a singer on John Lennon's production of The Elastic Oz Band's 'God Save Us', a 1971 single to help raise the defence costs of the celebrated *Oz* magazine obscenity trial.

Whatever their feelings about the end result, Splinter seemed in awe of George's working "for 24 hours straight"[291] at FPSHOT sessions for their debut album. Their mentor played at least four superimposed instruments, including the calculated handclaps on their hit 'Costafine Town', which – with a nagging chorus, further accompaniment by Harrison's heavy friends, the fullest distribution network and publicity that included a press photo of them standing on either side of George – scrambled to Number 17 in the UK hit parade, the same position as 'Love Me Do'.

No 'Please Please Me' equivalent was forthcoming as Splinter's follow-up, 'Drink All Day', slumped well outside the Top 50. Some blamed lack of daytime airings on Radio 1 on account of the fact that it contained the world *bloody*. Although as raggedly carefree as, say, Mungo Jerry's chart-topping 'In The Summertime', 'Drink All Day' was not a masterpiece of song. Neither were Splinter the new

Beatles – or the new Badfinger, for that matter. In a letter to a British pop journal years after Splinter's third and final Dark Horse LP, Peter Coulston judged them one of the worst outfits he'd ever heard.[292] However, far from deserving this accolade, they were appropriate to the mild, harmless nature of mid-1970s pop.

So too were other Dark Horse signings, their deals acquired mainly from either knowing George or though the lobbying of someone who did. Even Jiva, whom George had taken on during a genuine talent-spotting expedition, had once backed Donovan. They had a classic two-guitars-bass-drums line-up, and George noticed "a lot of influences from the '60s",[290] but theirs was more a soul than a Mersey Beat calling. Concentrating on creating a party atmosphere, Jiva were roughly the southern Californian counterpart of Geno Washington's Ram Jam Band, which had been popular on Britain's club circuit in around 1966. Although Dark Horse stumped up a Splinter-sized budget to launch Jiva, they were dropped after a solitary album failed to set the world alight.

Henry McCullough's spell as a Dark Horse artist followed a similar pattern. A veteran of several respected British progressive bands, Irish singing guitarist McCullough had never been short of work. After playing in Joe Cocker's Grease Band, he joined Wings during the *Red Rose Speedway* sessions. In 1973, a tiff with McCartney led to his dismissal. He wasn't prepared to play precisely what Paul ordered. George didn't have to be told what Paul was like, but he listened carefully to both Henry's tale of woe and *Mind Your Own Business*, a self-financed LP the artist had just recorded. Because he'd wanted to like it, George decided to put out the album on Dark Horse. After all, it would've been one in the eye for Paul if it'd made Henry a star. By 1977, McCullough was back on small UK stages as a hireling of the likes of Carol Grimes and Frankie Miller.

Simply to let off steam after tapping out take after take of someone else's song in the drum booths of LA, Jim Keltner decided to lead a casual weekend combo of other session musicians. The Dark Horse supremo only "got to sign Keltner's band from meeting the piano player, which is slightly crazy, when you consider the friendship between Keltner and me".[144] Christened 'Attitudes', not so humble were the aspirations of the group when Dark Horse underwrote and issued two of its albums and a pestilence of singles, the third of which, 'Sweet Summer Music', actually climbed into the 90s of the Hot 100 – but, come 1977, Jim and his pals were once performing for their own amusement in local venues.

Encouraged by Billy Preston, Dark Horse had acquired in 1975 an established act, a black vocal quartet calling themself The Five Stairsteps, who had cut their teeth as regulars at Harlem's famous Apollo Theater and, on Buddha Records, in the US R&B chart. In 1970, they were casting their longest shadow with the million-selling 'Ooh Ooh Baby'. Maybe Billy had given George his very own Isley Brothers. A family affair, too, the group were the children of manager Clarence Burke. When sister Aloha left in 1974, her four brothers chose not to replace her, preferring the simpler expedient of continuing as Stairsteps. The title of Stairsteps' only Dark Horse LP, *Second Resurrection*, was, however, only wishful thinking. Leaving his siblings to fend for themselves, lead singer Keni Burke tried again with what chanced to be the penultimate album by Dark Horse, which by then was no longer affiliated to A&M.

At A&M Studios when it was still all smiles, George had fulfilled his last commitment to EMI/Capitol, as well as the final album release for Apple as *Wonderwall* had been the first. Like a tenant paying overdue rent with bad grace, he turned out "a grubby album in a way. The production left a lot to be desired as did my performance."[59] Even so, his fickle public bought as many copies of *Extra Texture (Read All About It)* as it had of its predecessor. In Britain, of all places, it lasted a month in the LP chart, which was a month more than *Dark Horse*.

Credit for its title – wordplay on a line from Edwin Starr's 'Headline News' – was Attitudes bass guitarist Paul Stallworth, who'd been among the highest quota of slick LA studio casts to figure on a Harrison project, and it showed. Their infallible polish suited the large helping of 'Far East Man'-type lethargy that begged critics to rubbish *Extra Texture*. It was a bedsit record rather than a dancing one, with close-miked vocals floating effortlessly over layers of treated sound. There were touches of Motown here and there, but the backbone of *Extra Texture* dabbled in the more feathery emanations from Philadelphia by the likes of The Stylistics and Jerry Butler. He wouldn't capitulate to the limpid mush of "Philly soul" at its most soporific, but you'd be forgiven for thinking that old George was trying to make it as a "quality" entertainer like Sinatra, whose flop singles were excused as "too good for the charts".

Extra Texture, however, wasn't Harrison's *Songs For Swinging Lovers*. In its contradiction of enjoyable depression, only 'Tired Of Midnight Blue' passed muster. Otherwise, the long, dull melodies on *Extra Texture* were, as far as I'm concerned, on a slushy par with those of Bread and, in the 1980s, the equally smooth Style Council, both studio-centred groups who had moderate success with moderate records of uniform blandness. Some of George's tunes were almost watered-down flashbacks to The Beatles, particularly 'Grey Cloudy Lies' and 'This Guitar (Can't Keep From Crying)'. There was also a 'Badge'-style rhythmic lope in 'Tired Of Midnight Blue'. George later argued, "If something's good, you tend to remember it, and sometimes if it's bad, too. I don't think you can get away with your past, if you want to put it like that."[59]

'This Guitar' and 'You' – the oldest and most up-tempo song of the collection – were the soundest choices for singles. 'You' was even Radio 1's Record Of The Week, but such approbation couldn't crank it above Number 38 in Britain, although it tickled the Top 20 in the States. As with 'Try Some Buy Some', George had grafted his own singing onto the original backing track for 'You', hence its high key and indelible traces of Ronnie Spector's vocal. On some other tracks, he'd chosen to sing straight from the nostrils, as if trying to recapture the inadvertent vulnerability of *Dark Horse*, but in better accord with the material was a melting warble reminiscent of Smokey Robinson, who was then never off the Henley juke box.

The music on *Extra Texture* could not be rescued by the words, which, if sparser than before, were either cursory or in restricted code. Even so, although simplistic, 'You' and 'Can't Help Thinking About You' were the only lyrics that took on a breadth of gesture that was immediately universal, as well as personal – apart from the archaic parlour poetry of 'The Answer's At The End', lifted from semi-legible quotes etched above Friar Park's entrance hall.

'His Name Is "Legs"' was a tribute to "Legs" Larry Smith, who, seldom seen since the Plastic Ono bash at the Lyceum, had re-entered George's life via mutual friend, Terry Doran. So charmed was he by Larry's quaint turns of phrase and dress sense – which embraced toy cows grazing on his shoes – that a song about these idiosyncrasies grew as George doodled on a piano one morning. Smith's officer-and-gentleman tones cropped up intermittently on the recording, but, as the composer acknowledged, "really, you have to know him to find it funny".[59]

It was indeed "a piece of self-indulgence, like some other of my songs about things that nobody else knows or cares about, except maybe one or two people".[39] Did that magazine's editor care because George could "climb *Rolling Stone* walls" in 'This Guitar'? When the stereo arm lifted at the close of side two, the lasting impression for most listeners was that of a man as self-obsessed as any drip-rocker. Only the most zealous Beatle-ologists were bothered about covert vinyl revelations by ex-Beatles, and even some of them listened *before* purchasing, these days. Although few were prepared to disconnect them with their previous incarnation, the days of instant Number Ones had passed with 'The Ballad Of John And Yoko'. Whether the latest by John, George, Paul or Ringo made the charts now depended entirely on its commercial suitability.

Six years after disbandment, John had effectively retired; Paul was basking in rave reviews for Wings' US tour; and Ringo was about to rise up the American Top 30 for the tenth consecutive time. Too far out for the commonweal and not cool enough for hipsters, George had become the laggard of the pack. On the eve of punk, a widespread feeling was summarised by King Crimson's Robert Fripp: George Harrison was "a talented bore".[293] His newest alias, "Ohnothimagen", intimated that the self-denigrating creator of *Extra Texture* was of like mind.

On the album, his artistic nadir could not be divorced from the weighty personal misfortunes that split his concentration. 'Grey Cloudy Lies', for example, "describes the clouds of gloom that used to come over me, a difficulty I had". It slopped over into media interviews, too. On Radio 1, he intoned dolefully, "People who were never really keen on me just really hate my guts now. It has become complete opposites, completely black and white."[294]

He was inflicted with such inflexible polarity himself. Once a hero, Allen Klein was now a villain of the darkest hue. The auditors appointed by the three Beatles had unravelled enough evidence of "excessive commissions" from Klein's mazy balance sheets for a court case. Going in fighting, Klein counter-sued for an eight-figure sum, with a cunning card up his sleeve for the specific trumping of George. Mr Klein, George would discover, was not a gentleman – but perhaps he never had been in the first place. It would take until 1977 for the blizzards of writs to settle into complicated but fixed financial channels whereby the assorted and incoming monies could be divided and sent to the sometimes disgruntled parties.

With Klein on the way out and The Beatles not even a legal partnership now, there was no tangible barrier to prevent Lennon, McCartney, Harrison and Starr from forming a group. Since 1970, hardly a day had gone by without somebody asking one of them when they'd get back together. "No one ever asks me about Rory Storm And The Hurricanes or The Eddie Clayton Skiffle Group," moaned Ringo. "They were good bands, too."[295] With all but Paul flying EMI/Capitol's nest, 1976 was a big year for re-promotion of Beatles singles. In Britain alone, seven had breached the Top 40, all from the second half of their career.

Although he was "always pleased when the other three do something good",[276] who could blame George for eating his heart out when even his old music with them was more acceptable than his current solo offerings? As he seemed to be the only one sagging on the ropes, he was struck by the unreasonable notion that, rather than Paul, it might be he who'd have no place in any plotted Beatles of the 1970s. "The way it sometimes comes across is that there is Paul and John and Ringo, and they are very much together, and there's this fly in the ointment called George Harrison" ran one extraordinary press statement that he felt driven to make. "It's put about that I'm the one who is always missing when the talk is on. What I want to say is this:

if Paul, John and Ringo get together in a room, I just hope they invite me along."[290]

He seemed so defeated that it was fanciful to look to future victories – and, in some ways, the worst was yet to come. However, from this, George Harrison's lowest ebb, the tide, with majestic slowness, had already started to turn.

14 The Jewish Man In The Kitchen

During one of his last interviews, John Lennon sighed, "Well, he walked right into it. He must have known, you know. He's smarter than that. George could have changed a few notes and nobody could have touched him, but he let it go and paid the price."[80] Found guilty of "subconscious plagiarism" on 7 September 1976, John's former colleague had been ordered to pay the aggrieved party just over half a million greenbacks – and in days when half a million was worth something.

The plaintiff was Bright Tunes, rather than Richard Self, the composer of 'He's So Fine'. The Grim Reaper had come for Richard in 1967, but the Self-serving accountants of the record company and its British outlet, Peter Maurice Music, remained on the look-out for royalties that they felt were owed to their client's estate, ie his mother, who was suing Bright Tunes for non-payment when the writ against Harrison was served.

Such matters were settled out of court, more often than not, as had been a pay-off to Bill Martin and Phil Coulter for 'It's Johnny's Birthday'. Witty Mr Justice Slade suggested that he should sing 'Congratulations' to the parties[296] when Peter Maurice Music and George decided on such a course over 'He's So Fine', and it seemed once – said the defendant – that "the lawyers in America were going to give the people some money to shut them up".[25]

The two factors that provoked the extremity of Bright Tunes' proceedings were the howling success of 'My Sweet Lord' and the intervention of litigation-loving Mr Klein, who, scenting a financial killing, had "brought the case"[211] from Bright Tunes. When he'd been

George's manager, it had suited him to say that 'My Sweet Lord' had "nothing to do with this other song, and now its the other way 'round, just to get some money off me".[211] As well as Jody Miller's 'He's So Fine', Bright Tunes' objection had been hammered home with a 1975 Chiffons rendering of 'My Sweet Lord' rearranged to stress its affinity to their ancient hit.

At the three-day hearing before Judge Richard Owen, star-struck legal staff employed elsewhere in the building came to watch the fun during coffee breaks. They were delighted when the harassed ex-Beatle was obliged to demonstrate on guitar his counsel's argument, which boiled down to the first three notes of the verse and four – "really want to see you" – in the chorus. Among audio-visual aids used were huge wall-charts of musical staves. An ethno-musicologist under oath even questioned the definitions of the items concerned as "songs", if their central riff was subtracted. Both, he further pontificated, were derived in any case from the chorus of 'Oh Happy Day', which had become public domain – ie "traditional" – 50 years after the death of its composer, Paul Doddridge. However, victory was Klein's, who, it would be pleasant to think, ensured that the bereaved Mrs Self got her cut.

This conclusion to perhaps the best-known civil action of the 1970s exacerbated the music industry's icier ruthlessness where there had once been indolence. Whereas The Lovin' Spoonful had got away with imposing the 1940s melody 'Got A Date With An Angel' onto their 'Daydream' smash in 1966, the outcome of *Bright Tunes versus Harrison* led Little Richard's publisher to claim for breach of copyright in a track on the twelve-year-old *Beatles For Sale* album. In 1981, the music press intimated a howl of artistic ire from Rolf Harris when Adam And The Ants' UK Number One, 'Prince Charming', borrowed the tune of one of his (apparently not so) forgotten singles, 'War Canoe'.

Although his bile may have also risen, George had not taken Roxy Music to task when part of their Song For Europe melody bore an uncanny resemblance to 'While My Guitar Gently Weeps', nor The Jam when someone suggested that this Surrey trio had leaned too heavily on 'Taxman' for their chart-topping 'Start'. Later, George would likewise overlook what he considered to be Madonna's heist of the salient points of 'Living In The Material World' for a best-seller of similar title. That George was so forgiving was demonstrative of how much the 'He's So Fine' affair had agitated him. "Look," he said, "I'd be willing, every time I write a song, if somebody will have a computer and I can just play any new song into it, and the computer will say, 'Sorry' or, 'Yes, OK.' the last thing I want to do is keep spending my life in court."[297] He was unable to listen to pop radio or months before and after without nitpicking vigilance. There was 'Hello Goodbye' in ELO's 'Telephone Line'. Didn't you hear 'Food, Glorious Food' in that Stevie Wonder number? "One of them that drove me crackers," he said, "was 'Tie A Yellow Ribbon Round The Old Oak Tree',"[211] in which he perceived both 'April Showers' and a Gilbert O'Sullivan song.

For a while, too, "it made me so paranoid about writing that I didn't even want to touch the guitar or piano in case I touched somebody's note. Somebody may own that note."[297] You could understand his attitude. Surely every combination of even the chromatic scale must have been used by now. The other day, I detected the melody of 'Simon Says' by The 1910 Fruitgum Company in 'Help Me Make It Through The Night'. By rights, the inventor of the twelve-bar blues ought to be richer than Croesus. Should a plumber receive a royalty every time a toilet he has installed is flushed?

Fortunately, George was able to home in on the humorous aspects of what had been a humiliating episode. After all, it wasn't the only song he'd ever written or would write. Who could weep for a composer for whom 'Something' would always provide a regular and substantial income?

Not as big a hit, yet a hit all the same, was the therapeutic 'This Song' and its one-take B-side, 'I Don't Care Any More', penned in the aftershock of the lawsuit. 'This Song' unburdened itself with lines like, "This song ain't black or white and, as far as I know, don't infringe on anyone's copyright", and "This tune had nothing Bright about it" – a play on words, like. The backing laid it on with a trowel, too, in its Leon Russell-type descending piano inversions and gratuitous instrumental work-outs. No sooner does it occur to the listener that the underlying ostinato sounds familiar than the thought is acknowledged on record by Harrison's court jester, Eric Idle, in his "ratbag" guise, wondering whether it's been lifted from The Four Tops or Fontella Bass.

As strained as 'This Song' itself was the accompanying video, shot over one night in a borrowed Los Angeles courtroom. Perhaps it was trying to mirror the Stones' promotional film short for 1967's 'We Love You', Mick and Keith's riposte to their brush with the law. With Ron Wood cast as a lady juror, director Michael Woodleigh's 'This Song' clip had a bewigged Jim Keltner pounding his gavel at George, handcuffed in the dock. During its editing, as Harrison fired suggestions about rhythm, pacing and camera angles, Woodleigh was astounded by his knowledge of film technique.

'This Song' was the first of two moderately successful US singles and one flop to be taken from the delayed new LP *Thirty-Three And A Third* (George's age, see). The album kept that territory's FM radio in tasteful focus, and at its bedrock were the defiantly spare bass lines of Willie Weeks, veteran of many a velvet-smooth Philly soul recording. Willie had recently worked on David Bowie's "plastic soul" LP, *Young Americans*, and with Steve Winwood, and his was a voguish name to print on your album sleeve. *Thirty-Three And A Third* also conceded to the drowsy "country rock" wafting from California by such artists as John Denver, the ubiquitous Linda Ronstadt and The Eagles,[298] whose *Greatest Hits* collection was ensconced in the North American album lists for most of 1976. Less plausible a setting for the Harrison bottleneck swirl was the discreetly jazzy 'Learning To Love You', the reggae jerk of 'Crackerbox Palace' and a couple of nods towards disco fever – a form that he generally disliked – that was then sashaying its way towards its John Travolta zenith. Bemoaning the predictability of George's pool of hip session players, Dark Horse hopefuls and half-famous friends, an English reviewer dismissed it with "Of course it's not rock 'n' roll. Whatever gave you that idea?"[299]

American progressive radio was amenable enough to *Thirty-Three And A Third*, but in Britain artists of George's stamp were despised by journalists, who fawned to someone called Johnny Rotten, 19-year-old chief show-off with The Sex Pistols. The punk rock thunderclap had resounded, and a disaffected adolescent in Speke or Bognor Regis was more likely to go for the Pistols' 'Anarchy In The UK' than a disc about George Harrison's legal hassles in New York.

The Beatles at the Star-Club might have been as excitingly slipshod, but what counted about 'Anarchy', The Damned's fast version of 'Help!', 'Wild Youth' from Generation X and other bursts of self-conscious racket was that, more so than George's beloved skiffle and rockabilly, anybody could do it. As punk fanzine *Sniffin' Glue* elucidated, all you needed were three chords. Not a week went by without another hot "new wave" group ringing some changes, even if most of them looked and sounded just like The Sex Pistols, whose stage entertainments were notable for gobbets of appreciative spit from the audience rather than Beatle jelly-babies.

In August 1977, news of Elvis Presley's death drew a malicious cheer in a basement club frequented by London punks. Benignly, some Grand Old Men refused to bitch back. Roy Orbison, for instance, saw only "a bunch of fresh, new people trying to do their thing like we did".[300] To George, however, it was "rubbish, total rubbish. Listen to the early Beatles records – they were innocent and trivial but still had more meaning than punk music, which is destructive and aggressive."[214] Punk was also the start of his own – albeit temporary – farewell to pop.

No incentive for any withdrawal was apparent, however, when the new Harrison album qualified for a golden disc within weeks of its release in time for Christmas 1976. Most of the sales were in the States. Although it found enough home buyers to flit briefly into the LP charts, "I get the impression from time to time that England is not particularly interested".[25]

Masking an encroaching creative bankruptcy had been George's more pronounced rummaging through his back catalogue than on *Extra Texture*. As well as 1969's 'Woman Don't You Cry For Me' and 'Beautiful Girl' – related to a new "constant companion", Olivia Arias, whom he intended to marry as soon as his and Pattie's decree absolute was accorded – he'd delved even further back for 'See Yourself'. More telling was 'True Love', the first solo Harrison cover version to be issued as a single – but only in The Sex Pistols' Britain. On the premise that the opposite extreme of the day's dominating force is never completely submerged, his overhaul for Grace Kelly and Bing Crosby's funereal duet – with introductory organ sweep, muted funky twitch and altered chord sequence – soundtracked a weakly humorous video, directed by Eric Idle, capturing an Edwardian mood with the artist in boater and false handlebar moustache.

'Crackerbox Palace', another 45rpm extract, failed in the United Kingdom, too (although it sold more than 'This Song' in the States). Dedicated to hep-cat Lord Buckley, George had scrawled its title – the name of Buckley's Chicago home – after meeting the late monologist's manager, George Greif, in January 1976 at the MIDEM music publishing convention in France. On the preceding *Thirty-Three And A Third* track, Harrison had thanked the Lord – God, not Buckley – "for giving us pure" Smokey Robinson, thus expanding on a homage already paid in 'Ooh Baby You Know I Love You' on *Dark Horse*. In so doing, George was at the forefront of a later tendency for pop stars to buttress their own positions with tributes to credible influences on record. In that same year, Bruce Springsteen had slipped a line about "Roy Orbison sings for the lonely" into one of his songs, while just beyond the horizon was Orbison's own 'Hound Dog Man' to the departed Elvis. These would be only the tip of the iceberg.

John Citizen had even less idea what hero George was on about in 'Dear One' than he had been in 'Pure Smokey'. In a press hand-out, however, it was revealed that 'Dear One' was in praise of Yogananda. George had written it on a guitar tuned to an open chord, whereby – other than its bridge – it rose from a drone more Gaelic than Indian. In straying from habit, he'd arrived at the boldest arrangement and most attractive piece on *Thirty-Three And A Third*.

Like 'Dear One', 'It's What You Value' – with the 'All Right Now' riff – was both a product of a holiday in the Virgin Islands and confusing to those unknowing of its lyrical source. As far fewer had the inclination to plumb the depths of his songs these days, they'd wait for his explanation in a newspaper article that its motor-car allusions were to do with the Mercedes 450 SL that was the price that Jim Keltner had put on his participation in the 1974 tour in lieu of a lump sum. That was what Jim valued, sort of thing. Not as sodden with Aesop's fable imagery was 'Learning To Love You', which closed the album. Another religious tract, this song dwelt on unconditional spiritual love, in which "the goal is to love everyone equally, but it doesn't necessarily work out that way."[301]

To a more worldly end, George had been commissioned to pen an item for consideration by Herb Alpert – the A in A&M – as one of his occasional vocal excursions. That the resultant 'Learning To Love You' came home to roost on an LP by Harrison rather than Alpert was not among the principal causes of discord between Dark Horse and its parent company's high command that had led to the sudden release of *Thirty-Three And A Third* not by A&M but the mightier Warner Brothers conglomerate in Burbank. Although George was finally free to sign himself to Dark Horse in January 1976, this did not mitigate the comparative insolvency of the label's other acts. George blamed A&M's distribution set-up and lack of faith while, having ploughed nearly $3 million into Dark Horse, Alpert and partner Jerry Moss had hoped that, by cross-collateralisation, *Thirty-Three And A Third* would transfuse what had become a disappointing investment. Stipulations in Harrison's contract forbade such a ploy, so they sought to recoup what they could, even if it meant losing their ex-Beatle, who – if *Extra Texture* was anything to go by – was past his best, anyway.

Expected in July 1976, George's album master tapes arrived three months late. Symptomatic of the erosion of rapport between artist and corporation was, first, a remonstrative letter from Moss and then an eight-figure writ against Harrison for "non-delivery of product". George's explanation in a depressingly familiar court – in Los Angeles, this time – was the plain truth, that for most of the summer either his bowels had been exploding or he'd been heaving his guts up with what had been initially diagnosed as food poisoning. When his skin turned yellow, his doctors concluded that it was hepatitis, necessitating a long stay in bed and, for the sake of his liver, total abstinence: "I needed the hepatitis to quite drinking."[274] He called it 'hippy-titis'. When I was poleaxed by this disease myself in 1970, a Department of Health official – damn his impudence – called to ascertain whether I was a junkie who'd caught it via a dirty syringe.

George finally vacated the chilly A&M building with the *Thirty-Three And A Third* artwork already in Warners' clutches. As Warners' out-of-court reimbursement of A&M's Dark Horse money was part of the deal, he was delighted to announce, "We're very excited about our new affiliation."[302] To show willing, he'd subjected himself to an extensive publicity blitz, which included an open-ended interview recorded for radio use – a device particularly favoured by Warners – and a five-city promotional tour of the States, accompanied by Gary Wright, another artist who'd also defected from A&M to Warners, and had played keyboards on *Thirty-Three And A Third*.

More than ever, now, it wasn't sufficient merely to mail a pre-release copy of a Harrison album to *Rolling Stone*; you had to yowl it from the rooftops, despite some who still insisted that there was an unbreachable chasm between rock – which only the finest minds could appreciate – and vulgar pop. Patiently puffing a Gitane, George gave the media unblinking copy, clarifying the album's more obscure lyrical byways, justifying his stand in the Bright Tunes bother and retelling the old, old story of The Beatles for the trillionth time, tormenting some questioners with mischievous hints of a reunion. Recuperated from his illness – thanks, he said, to herbs prescribed by a Californian physician – the subsequent weight loss and beardless pallor made him look for all the world like Dave Davies, the youngest Kink. George's shoulder-length hair was kinked and centre-parted, too, and his teeth freshly capped. There was no doubting it – the boy meant business.

Yes, he'd pencilled in a world concert tour for summer 1977, "but I would pace it better."[299] It would embrace, he promised, neglected markets in Japan and Europe, "because they keep shouting about it."[302] When the campaign actually reached Europe, he wasn't so sure. He didn't wish to "compromise himself".[301] No, he wouldn't even entertain a one-off event on a Bangladesh scale, because it would lack intimacy. At the Hamburg stop, a reunion with Tony Sheridan – over from his San Fernando home for a Star-Club anniversary show with Cliff Bennett and PJ Proby – was one of the less onerous incidents of an itinerary which reawakened George's nausea for the dazzle of flash bulbs, the scratch of biros on autograph books and, even now, screams (which may or may not have been ironic). In Los Angeles, a virago had badgered him to boogie on down with her in an adjacent disco, and a lift door in Boston had opened on a wild-eyed, Beatle-fringed youth grinning as if he had a mouthful of salts. "I play guitar," he'd spluttered, "in a band." Within that awe-struck – and possibly dangerous – gleam, George smothered a likely annoyance, playing Mr Nice Guy with an affable "Keep playing, man! Stay with it!" as a nervous Warners publicist shepherded him away. By recoiling, he might have lost a fan.

As unexpected as the encounter in the lift was, the thrusting-together of former Prime Minister Edward Heath and George for a photograph at Manchester's Television Centre. During this British leg of the *Thirty-Three And A Third* marketing quest, George's most significant plug was as a guest on BBC2's "progressive" pop showcase, *The Old Grey Whistle Test*, on 30 November.

Ten days earlier, he'd done more than simply chat when his pre-recorded appearance with Paul Simon on NBC's satirical *Saturday Night Live* in New York had broken the programme's viewing record. As well as putting up with facetious enquiries from the studio audience, George had hunched over a hollow-body Gretsch to sing 'Dark Horse' in dim blue light. From the shadows, Paul Simon had then joined in for 'Here Comes The Sun' and his own 'Homeward Bound', for which his temporary partner required an idiot card. Thus satisfying public presumptions, the pair indulged themselves with 'Bye Bye Love', an unsteady 'Rock Island Line' and Presley's 'That's All Right', all of which had been common to both The Quarry Men and the pre-Simon And Garfunkel duo, Tom And Jerry.

As the show's producer, Lorne Michaels, had once offered a sardonic $3,000 bucks for The Beatles to regroup before his cameras, George called his bluff by asking for his quarter of the fee. By coincidence, in the following month all four ex-Beatles happened to be in New York. As all enjoyed *Saturday Night Live*, American cousin of Monty Python, "they decided to rebound on us," revealed its host, Chevy Chase, a pal of Eric Idle, "and appear on the show. I never dreamt they'd actually take up our offer."²³⁰ Unfortunately (or not) Lennon's chauffeur drove to the wrong studio, thereby capsizing what would have been, had they kept their nerve, the ultimate practical joke.

The ceiling of more serious incentives was now an appeal from the United Nations on behalf of the Vietnamese boat people and from an American who offered $50 million for one Beatles performance. Beyond hard cash were pleas on vinyl like that of an act called People – Americans again – with 'Come Back Beatles'. The solo produce of each former Beatle intimated that what you'd hear might not be magic, just music. Yet, admitted George, "The Beatles was bigger than the four personalities separately – not like The Bee Gees. They make good records, but they don't have whatever it was that The Beatles had."²¹⁴

This was best demonstrated by the brothers Gibb's starring roles in a 1978 musical film based on all of the *Sgt Pepper* songs, minus 'Within You Without You'. George "heard it was dreadful and wouldn't bother watching."³⁰³ No Harrison compositions were included, either, in an earlier Beatle-inspired movie, *All This And World War Two*, which contained among its Lennon-McCartney works two tracks by Jeff Lynne, whose ELO had also reworked 'Eleanor Rigby' in concert. George's role in The Beatles' history was also belittled after post-production on the made-for-TV *Birth Of The Beatles*, for which, according to one bizarre report, Pete Best would play the teenage Harrison. Actually, the sacked drummer had been engaged as the project's unheeded factual advisor. The part of George had gone to a professional actor named John Althan.

Another slight on the Quiet One was when the suit he wore in *Help!* – although a suspected fake – did not fetch its reserve price in an auction at one of the Beatle conventions that had started in Western continents. George had donated saleable artefacts to such a function in Los Angeles, where Jackie Lomax was a guest speaker. On the *Thirty-Three And A Third* campaign trail, however, George shied away from a gathering at London' Alexandra Palace, fearing that, in Britain, at least, "the media are not interested in me as a person. They are only interested in The Beatles."³⁰⁴ In the Fab Four's footsteps, foreign visitors – mainly Japanese and American – were pouring vast amounts into the English Tourist Board's coffers for conducted treks round London and Liverpool to such golgothas as the Abbey Road zebra crossing and 25 Arnold Grove.

After doing his *Thirty-Three And A Third* duty, George, with Olivia Arias – formerly his personal secretary at A&M – and Gary Wright, had embarked on a pilgrimage of his own: four days in southern India for the wedding of Kumar Shankar, Ravi's nephew, and a Hindu festival, where Olivia feared losing the other two when the sexes were segregated. On to Los Angeles, George and his girlfriend looked in on Prabhupada, then at the city's Krishna centre. Having had no qualms about exalting His Divine Grace even in hard-core rock magazine interviews, George in 1976 had also found it in him to vindicate the Maharishi: "I can see much clearer now what happened, and there was still just a lot of ignorance that went down. Maharishi was fantastic, and I admire him – like Prabhupada – for being able, in spite of all the ridicule, to just keep on going."[32]

When her future husband had first spotted her at a Los Angeles party, Olivia Arias – five years younger than George – had been a devotee of Maharaj Ji, a moon-faced Perfect Master with an adolescent moustache whose sermon before the multitudes at 1971's Glastonbury Fayre had been punctuated by indiscreet glances at his gold watch. Among his thousands of followers was a sound engineer that I knew. In many a shabby hotel room, I would wake to find him cross-legged in meditation beneath the counterpane of an adjacent bed. Such a habit formed common ground between Olivia and George. The fancy-free Harrison had been attracted instantly to the self-possessed, California-reared Mexican whose easy smile showed off her fine teeth. Despite her Aztec forebears, she was not unlike her Liverpudlian suitor, both facially and in her slim build.

George and the second Mrs Harrison plighted their troth on 2 September 1978 in an unpublicised ceremony at Friar Park. Among the few witnesses was their son, Dhani, who had been born the month before in a Windsor nursing home. Called after the notes *dha* and *ni* from the Indian music scale as much as for the name's phonetic proximity to the English "Danny", the infant would be so removed from public gaze that, when he was older, he would be able to walk around Henley unnoticed.

Appropriately clad in a Union Jack coat, Dhani's father had dared a sortie down the hill to a street party during 1977's Royal Jubilee. For greater distances, it was safer to drive. Nevertheless, George was sighted on more than one occasion knocking back a quiet brown ale in one or other of South Oxfordshire's more far-flung pubs or eating in a favoured Indian restaurant in Caversham Park Village, on the outskirts of Reading. Out of the blue, he'd even rolled up with his guitar to jam with an *ad hoc* combo assembled by Jon Lord to the disbelief of the yuppie patrons of a hostelry in the whimsically named hamlet of Pishill.

On a more makeshift stage at Hurtwood Edge, he'd do likewise at the wedding reception of his ex-wife and Eric Clapton on a May evening in 1979. Also among the stars up there to blast out a pot-pourri of classic rock and old Beatles numbers were Paul McCartney and Ringo, plus various Rolling Stones, Jeff Beck, percussionist Ray Cooper – who'd accompanied Elton John as one of the first of Western pop's ambassadors to Russia – and, for one night only, the reunited Cream. It says much for George's self-confidence that he was able to tread the boards with the outstanding Beck, who – more deserving of guitar deity than Clapton – displayed eclecticism and unpredictability in compatible amounts.

Terming himself Eric's "husband-in-law", George went along for the laugh on Clapton's European Tour that year, sitting in for a couple of shows. Through Eric and Elton John, who came too, he'd got over his aversion to organised sport, particularly cricket, as they, with ex-Traffic drummer Jim Capaldi, "got me going to the matches in this nice little English town, drinking beer, laughing. I think we've all had similar times and experiences, and because of that we can just make fun and have a real laugh. You can't ask for much more than that, really."[75]

Rubbing shoulders with professional cricketers such as Ian Botham and Mike Gatting, George's spectator's interest grew, although he was never to be as enthusiastic as Mick Jagger, Bill Wyman – or Phil May. As a Pretty Thing in the 1960s, May had been a social pariah, but, having won the heart of a Stuart and trimmed his girlish tresses, he was among those attending Prince Charles' wedding in 1981.

The Beatles' MBEs had been the turning point in impressing the upper crust that pop was a generator of vast financial power. At first, its younger fledglings had appalled staider swells by dropping into small-talk references of this or that long-haired rock star they knew. Soon, lads like George and Eric came to inhabit a world more exclusive than even that of the Bangladesh superstars. The new pop squirearchy began taking up pastimes recommended by those born into privilege. Steve Winwood, born in a Birmingham semi-detached and owner since 1970 of an ivy-clung manor house not far from the ancestral Cotswolds home of the Mitfords, had an open invitation from one of his monied neighbours to take part in the disgusting aristocratic passion of stag hunting.

Huntin', fishin' and shootin' didn't appeal to the Harrisons, but George dabbled once more in motorcycle scrambling, sponsoring champion Steve Parrish – although in 1979 he declined an approach for £185,000 to run a BMW M1 in the Procar series. Parrish and Harrison had met through both knowing Barry Sheene, who had transferred his allegiance from bikes to racing cars in 1976. Always stimulated by the celebrity of others, George had been introduced to Barry at a 1977 meet at Long Beach. Later, he readily consented to appear on an edition of ITV's *This Is Your Life* that honoured Sheen, on which he'd recall his first circuit of Brand's Hatch when "Barry persuaded John Surtees to let me have a go."[22] In a borrowed helmet and overalls, an apprehensive Harrison followed Surtees' shouted instructions while "just hanging on for dear life. I hadn't even remembered to close my visor. Still, it was a great feeling, [although] I didn't go very fast. I just signed the chit saying that, if I killed myself, it wasn't John's fault."[22]

After this cautious spin, George took part in many celebrity meets, such as a 24-hour run at Silverstone organised by Maltin's, Henley's sports car concessionaires, in aid of a cancer foundation to the memory of Swedish driver Gunnar Nilsson. For the same charity – to whom he'd also donated some record royalties – George, in Stirling Moss's famous Lotus 18, swallowed dust behind the terrifying Jackie Stewart. As they ambled to the royal enclosure afterwards, Stewart in his mandatory corduroy cap commented, "I don't know why I dress like this," to which Harrison replied, "Because you're a twit."[15]

Stewart's chuckling along to such familiarity didn't solely stem from his personal liking for the track's most renowned amateur. Repaying the VIP treatment that was automatically his, George publicised the sport with almost the same fervour as he had meditation. An expected presence at Grand Prix events around the globe, the ex-Beatle resigned himself to "getting too well known at motor races now"[22] as he was besieged by journalist and fans who had just rushed past the victor of the last race. With Stewart in Brazil, where no Beatle had gone before, he was blinded by flashlights the second he stepped off the Concorde at Rio. Only police intervention allowed a safe passage to a waiting limousine. Amid the droning excitement of the Formula One tournament at São Paulo the next day, his tormentors' persistence drew from him a cornered "You should photograph the cars. They're more important than I am."[214] When probed, he spoke with jaw-dropping authority about oversteer and gear ratios, while tipping Jody Scheckter to be 1979's world champion, because he was ready: "It would be good if Grand Prix racing was like the music business, where you can have a Number One hit and then get knocked off by your mate – but, unfortunately, it isn't like that. There is a point where you are just 'ready' to be world champion, and if it doesn't happen it could be all downhill from there."[22]

Like a dog to a bath, George steeled himself for the press conferences and other media slots that he could have sidestepped during what was meant to be a private visit. However, with an eponymous new album imminent, it would do no harm to go politely through the motions. Yes, he liked Brazilian music – "more wild music...rumba, samba, conga drumming, that type of thing"[214] – and intended to tour there real, real soon. Words are cheap.

"We heard your latest record is dedicated to racing," prompted one correspondent. "Only one out of ten," corrected George. "It's called 'Faster', and I think the words are good because it's abstract. It could be about anyone, and not just about cars and engines."[213] With its title taken from Jackie Stewart's 1973 autobiography, 'Faster' was inspired by the injured Niki Lauda's return to racing, although "his wife held back her fears". Like The Beach Boys' more erudite '409' of 1963 or Jan And Dean's 'Dead Man's Curve', buzzing carburettors – from 1978's Grand Prix – riddled 'Faster', but George was right, the lyrics could as easily apply to the Grand National or the Tour de France, and the line "he's the master of going faster" was adapted from Apollo Creed's nickname in the film *Rocky*. The orchestration effortlessly tracks George, who, with his jogalong acoustic guitar and overdubbed bass, catches listeners off guard with unpredictable phrasing.

The first reference in song to his racing mates had been to Elf Tyrrell's six-wheeler in 'It's What You Value', but the attractive 'Blow Away' – the first 45 from *George Harrison* – if nothing to do with the sport was still "a song that Niki, Jody, Emerson [Fittipaldi] and the gang could enjoy".[39] Barely teetering on the edge of Britain's Top 50, 'Blow Away' showed class as a US Number 16 in March 1979. In 1960s' journalese, it might have been described as a "blues-chaser", but shackled to this elevating opus was a Beatle-esque guitar riff that irritated the memory, just as – if you want me to be pedantic – Irish songstress Enya would in her unconscious integration of the 'Blow Away' hook into her 1988 hit 'Orinoco Flow'.

As Enya's rarefied Gaelic *lieder* were forged in the "wild country" of Donegal, so items on *George Harrison* were as referential to their composer's surroundings. Although the album was mostly recorded at Friar Park, a good half was written at George's new home from home on Maui, midway across the northern Pacific. Named after the demigod whose fish-hook wrenched up the ocean floor to form the Hawaiian archipelago, Maui, with its tropic-softened terrain, ranges from lunar-like desert to a lush eastern coastline where a moustache of surf lashes petrified lava cliffs from the vomitings of the extinct Haleakala. Much of Maui – comparable in size to the Isle of Man – remains trackless jungle, particularly in the depths of the volcano's capacious crater.

From the stultifying humidity of a Thames Valley summer, the Harrisons could escape to the purer air of an opulent Maui spread called Kuppaqulua, separated by two miles of gravelled track from the fern-edged coastal road on which mongooses were flattened, as hedgehogs were on the A4155 through Henley. Secluded on this refuge were other stars, such as Dolly Parton, Kris Kristofferson and comedian Robin Williams – with whom George once hiked the Haleakala slopes. Escaping from the facile superficiality of showbusiness, it was most agreeable to mix with the 60 or so islanders who populated nearby Hana, where Hasegawa's General Store served the more immediate needs of stomach and household. Hana's only other major public facilities were a garage, a hotel and a plant nursery, whence George would furnish Kuppaqulua with silversword, poinsettia and other local flora.

Both 'If You Believe' and 'Love Comes To Everyone' on *George Harrison* were finished on Maui, as was the pretty-but-nothing 'Dark Sweet Lady' – dedicated to Olivia – which introduced the harp to Harrison's canon. More obviously born of Kuppaqulua was 'Soft Touch', which transmitted the blue curvature of the ocean via the swoop of a Hawaiian guitar, while the lengthy intro to 'Your Love Is Forever' had a subtler Polynesian flavour. 'Soft-Hearted Hana', however, screamed its origin, its background hubbub taped directly from Longhi's restaurant in Lahaini, only two miles from Hana.

The title was a warping of The Temperance Seven's 'Hard-Hearted Hannah', but from George's own arsenal came 'Here Comes The Moon', which – like the Hana number – came from a naughty-but-nice clifftop flirtation with hallucinogenics, his first in ten years. The Pacific sunset is spellbinding, "even when you're not on mushrooms",[59] but, dazzled by surreal colour formations and even the gambolling of some dolphins, "I was blissed out, and then I turned 'round and saw a big full moon rising. I laughed and thought it was about time someone – and it might as well be me – gave the moon its due."[59]

A tang of sitar, a few "oh yeahs" and a vaguely Dylan-esque vocal also harked back to a 1960s past in 'Here Comes The Moon'. While 'Not Guilty' was an actual artefact of that era, the chord sequences of 'Deep Blue' and 'Run Of The Mill' which had led, respectively, to 'Soft Touch' and 'Hard-Hearted Hana' were from only a couple of years later.

These revisions and leitmotifs may have been contributory to the relatively favourable critical notices for *George Harrison*. Without the niggling preoccupations that shrouded the previous outing, the LP had a more disciplined instrumental attack. George was in strong voice, too. The task of drawing these virtues from him had been assigned to co-producer Russ Titelman, "who was a great help. At that time, I felt I didn't really know what was going on out there in music, and I felt Russ, who was in music day by day, would give me a bit of direction."[59] Then on Warners' payroll, other professional landmarks in Titelman's past and future embraced albums by Ry Cooder (his brother-in-law), Christine McVie, Chaka Khan and, in 1985, his apotheosis, the award-winning 'Back In The High Life' by Steve Winwood, whose penchant for blood sports George had overlooked when inviting him to play on *George Harrison*. Other cronies likewise participated, among them Ray Cooper, Clapton, Wright and the newly wed Kumar Shankar. Anchoring most of the ten selections was Willie Weeks again and his usual rhythm partner, Andy Newmark. The detached and high-waged precision of these two, as Winwood had discovered, did not always reconcile easily with their paymasters' artistic intent.

Theirs, however, was no death touch. With the absorption of punk's more palatable performers into the music-industry mainstream, there'd been a move towards more melodic fare, of which there was no shortage on *George Harrison*. Whereas in Europe and Australia, it did only as well as its predecessor, its steady sales in the States overtook popular favourites of such middling chart variety as Frank Zappa's *Joe's Garage* and the latest from Herb Alpert and Smokey Robinson. Newer to the album list was another bandleader, former Sundowner Tom Petty, who'd grown up a blond stick-insect of a guitarist whose style had been determined by listening to The Byrds.

As his less intense media junket for *George Harrison* intimated, records were now less prevalent a concern. As other of his peers had diversified into back-room branches of entertainment – like, for instance, ex-Animal Chas Chandler into management and Dave Clark's exploitation of the *Ready, Steady, Go!* archives – so George looked beyond music for fun and profit. Scoring only one vote against Ringo's 60 in a 1966 *Melody Maker* poll[305] for best actor in

Help!, George always seemed the Beatle least likely to involve himself in films. However, a fleeting appearance in the specialist *Raga* apart, he'd first dipped his toe into that cultural pool by financing the shooting of the vengeful *Little Malcolm And His Struggle Against The Eunuchs* in the early 1970s. He had seen the stage version – starring John Hurt – with Mal Evans. The movie (also with Hurt) won awards but was rarely seen by the general public.

In netting a rich sponsor, the film's writer, David Halliwell, had been luckier than Eric Idle, who had a heap of original film scripts mouldering unmade in his filing cabinet. After the final series of *Monty Python's Flying Circus* in 1974, among the more successful ventures was Idle's own BBC2 series, *Rutland Weekend Television*, with Neil Innes. On one programme, in December 1975, George was roped in to back Idle on 'The Pirate Song'. Riddled with excerpts from 'My Sweet Lord', the track had an Idle-Harrison composing credit.

With his too-serious singing of the exploits of "Mrs Black" and "Captain Fantastic" while chopping at an electric guitar in *Do Not Adjust Your Set*, Eric Idle had already signalled that he was a frustrated pop star. This inclination was given its head when, as a spin-off from *Rutland Weekend Television*, a parody of The Beatles – The Rutles – was elongated for the silver screen under the direction of Gary Weiss. Premièred in March 1978, *All You Need Is Cash* ran the gauntlet, from an Arthur Scouse sending The Rutles for a season at Hamburg's Rat Keller, their rise to fame, *Sergeant Rutler's Darts Club Band*, formation of Rutler's Corps, and the split following *Let It Rut*. Get the picture? While Idle cast himself as the heart-throb "Paul" character, the part of "Stig O'Hara" (ie George) went to a musician, Rick Fataar, a latter-day Beach Boy. Mainly in cameo were other of Idle's pop-star pals, including George himself, Mick Jagger, Ron Wood and Paul Simon.

So began George's transition from maker of curate's-egg albums to paladin of the British film industry. In with the Python crowd, he'd stayed informed about he follow-tip to John Cleese *et al*'s feature film *Monty Python And The Holy Grail*. Originally called *Jesus Christ: Lust For Glory*, *Life Of Brian* – with Graham Chapman in the title role of the 13th disciple – trod on thinner ice with the scriptures than The Rutles had with the Fab Four. God might have been able to stand the joke, but during pre-production the film's nervous investors elected to wash their hands of it. Prodded by pangs of Lord Delfont's Jewish conscience, as well as a loss just incurred through signing and hastily dropping The Sex Pistols, EMI's withdrawal of financial support was on the basis of blasphemy – although, as George pointed out, "It's only the ignorant people – who didn't care to check it out – who though that it was knocking Christ. Actually, it was upholding Him and knocking all the idiotic stuff that goes on around religion."[59]

Rather than jettison *Life Of Brian*, the Python team investigated other possibilities for raising the budget required. Chief of these were Chapman's drinking buddy Keith Moon and Idle's bit-part player George Harrison. Moon's sudden death precluded that line of enquiry, but Idle's man was not so inconsiderate. Amused by Eric's ideas for the film, George considered EMI's *volte face* regrettable but by no means disastrous. A sceptical Idle, however, "didn't believe you could just pick up a film like that for four million. I didn't know how loaded he was."[23] Loaded or not, Harrison, in conjunction with Denis O'Brien, "pawned my house and the office in London to get a bank loan – and that was a bit nerve-wracking".[23]

Purchaser of the dearest cinema ticket in history, it was only fair that, as well as getting a credit as "executive producer", George should be fitted into the film somewhere. Thus, hanging around the set in Tunisia, he was persuaded to don Arab gear as an extra in a kitchen scene "among a bunch of incurables and women taken in sin" who are supplicating the mistakenly messianic Brian for his curative blessing. As Michael Palin noted, "For George, the shock of finding himself in a crowd mobbing someone else was just too much."[285]

With his own property as collateral, the "Jewish man in the kitchen" was mightily relieved when *Life Of Brian* grossed in excess of $15 million in North America alone. Thus heartened, George reconsidered a view expressed in 1974 that "the film industry is like the record industry ten years ago – very difficult to get a look-in. It needs a kick up the arse."[285] With the *Brian* speculation proving that conventional routes could be circumvented more effectively than anything attempted by Apple, O'Brien and Harrison then ventured further into the celluloid interior with the official formation of HandMade Films in 1980, named "as a bit of a joke"[23] following George's outing to the British Handmade Paper Mill at Wookey Hole in Somerset.

Denis, at least, looked like a movie mogul. Furthermore, apart from the statue of Buddha and a corridor lined with gold discs, HandMade's suite in Cadogan Square off King's Road was just how you might visualise a film company's headquarters: receptionist clattering a typewriter, crenellated wallpaper, glossy magazines under the waiting area's coffee table and workaholic O'Brien standing pensive at his office window, sun-blanked spectacle lenses flashing over Knightsbridge. Sprawled in a button leather armchair is George, his young partner.

The maverick firm developed an adventurous policy of taking on what a major backer would most likely reject or, at best, severely edit, just as the Grade Organisation intended to do with the gangster film *The Long Good Friday*. For its disgruntled male lead, Bob Hoskins, Eric Idle was again the catalyst for Harrison and O'Brien's rescue of a promising flick. Not as immediate a money-spinner as *Life Of Brian*, *The Long Good Friday* was, nevertheless, well received and also facilitated Hoskins' rise to an international plateau of stardom.

Such career opportunities were not extended to any old riff-raff. Unlike Apple, HandMade assured no theoretical glad welcome to would-be directors. It mattered that you could nurture a connection via, say, a friend of a friend to its inner sanctum. It was the time-honoured adage of "it isn't how good you are, it's who you know". Once over this hurdle, it was often easier to get a deal than might be imagined. For a start, you were advantaged by George being "on the other side to the artists, and it's a funny position for me to be in. I hope I can understand their problems and that they can see I do."[8] This praiseworthy sentiment was to be much tested throughout the shooting of *Shanghai Surprise* in 1986.

On the strength of a two-page synopsis, Monty Python's American animator, Terry Gilliam, got the go-ahead for the *Time Bandits* family fantasy, while HandMade's first US film, Tony Bill's

Five Corners, came about because Harrison "liked his restaurant in LA. We'd had a good meal there, and then he came up to the table and said he'd like to make a film for us."[306]

Economic potential rather than artistic worth led George to back *Black And Blue*, a 1980 movie featuring Black Sabbath and other heavy metal acts. With the most irrevocable veto in the organisation, George tended to exercise thrift by encouraging editing at approved screenplay level instead of in the cutting room, but he'd say with quiet pride, "Sometimes I have nothing to do with a film until the rushes."[306] In an age when Hollywood underwriters would fork out $20 million for the average picture, HandMade managed *Time Bandits* on five. The fact that Palin's *Bullshot* was a tale too damn British for the colonials was mitigated by an even lower bill of less than two million.

It wasn't all roses, however, as exemplified by Monty Python defecting elsewhere for *The Meaning Of Life* – the cabal's least pleasing work – evidently through a falling-out over O'Brien's over-ambitious monetary propositions. Of all of the Python *dramatis personae*, HandMade was most at odds with Gilliam, who to George was "eccentric, bordering on genius",[285] just like Phil Spector. When an aghast O'Brien suggested nixing one particular *Time Bandits* sequence of jailed midgets eating rats, Gilliam said he'd burn the negatives of the entire feature. This threat could be tolerated when *Time Bandits* brought in more than $80 million.

HandMade's losses – such as that sustained for 1984's *Water* – were blamed on poor distribution and the faint hearts of many American buyers. At first hand, George pinpointed one US failure: "Everybody who hadn't seen *Withnail And I* was trying to find out where it was on. It had already been whipped off. That's the problem. If you don't pack out cinemas in the first week, that's it."[306] Most administrative functions were therefore doled out to bigger organisations like EMI, while HandMade retained its creative initiative and exploitation.

George put his own eminence at the disposal of HandMade's publicity department after implying to the tabloids that "three old friends *might* act in *Life Of Brian*".[307] He stirred up interest in

HandMade product less crassly on such key forums as BBC2's *Film '83* and, with Bob Hoskins, in a pre-recorded segment on *Good Morning America*.

Although his new position as movie Big Shot had novelty appeal, George was too long in the tooth to harbour pretensions far beyond that of money lender and lay advisor, as there were "some films I wouldn't have done that were really good",[282] such as *Mona Lisa*, a film about an ex-convict's entanglement with a lesbian prostitute. Initially, this film lark had been incidental to his music, because "I don't put in much time, not even into scripts. I can think of project to do and I can put people together, but I'm no good at saying, 'Here, give me five million dollars.' All this firing people and shouting, you know? I'm a sensitive artist."[282] He'd tool along to an odd day's shooting, but ultimately, "I'm just this lad who happens to be standing around watching them make a movie."[272] As with Alfred Hitchcock, the sharp-eyed viewer might espy George in minor cameos – for example, as a Mexican janitor in 1988's *Checking Out*, and singing in a night club band in *Shanghai Surprise*. More pertinent to his calling were soundtrack contributions, like 'Only A Dream Away' – with an insidious nonsense chorus – for *Time Bandits*. In *Water*, with Ringo behind the kit, George and Eric Clapton portrayed themselves in The Singing Rebels Band, sharing a microphone during a concert sequence. Through George, Larry Smith – now a resident of Hambledon and a lesser light in what was becoming known as the "Henley Music Mafia" – gained both a singing and a dramatic role in *Bullshot*.

Increasing respect for HandMade within the industry caused more illustrious thespians to be seen frequently in its productions. As well as Bob Hoskins and Michael Palin, other HandMade regulars included David Warner, Maggie Smith and Michael Caine. Also among those with HandMade service to their credit were Helen Mirren, Paul McCann, Frances Tomelty (first wife of pop-star-turned-actor Sting), the late Trevor Howard and Dennis Quilley, convincingly out of character as the openly homosexual leader of an ENSA concert party in *Privates On Parade*.

The engagement of such comic stalwarts as Leonard Rossiter and the scriptwriting team of Dick Clement and Ian La Frenais enhanced HandMade's image as a saviour of British comedy during its dullest period. In the late 1970s, only the likes of *Fawlty Towers* were oases of rampant hilarity in a desert of "more tea, Vicar?" home-counties sitcoms in which a moptopped and acrylically amiable young man muddled through a weekly half hour in, perhaps, a restaurant, hospital or shared flat, fraught with innuendo about wogs, poofs and tits. HandMade jokes from the Python team attacked these prejudices and often overkilled their perpetrators. Refreshingly tangential to the current vogue altogether were *The Missionary*, a lunge at Edwardian "muscular Christianity", and *Privates On Parade*, with Cleese as Quilley's Fawlty-esque CO. Blacker was the humour of *How To Get Ahead In Advertising*, with, promised director Bruce Robinson, "something to offend everybody".[285]

Films at other points of the HandMade compass were hardly any fun at all, among them the gloomy *The Lonely Passion Of Judith Hearne*. Still grimmer was *Scrubbers*, set in a girls' borstal and directed by Mai Zetterling.

As if in late consolation for his poor showing in *Melody Maker*'s *Help!* tabulation, the placing of *Time Bandits* at Number Three in its Film section was the sole Beatle-associated entry in the magazine's 1979 popularity poll. The only other Beatle still in the running was the irrepressible Paul, who – with or without Wings – was happy to bask in the limelight of what were often hit singles, especially in snug old Britain. At least Paul was no snob. Plugging 'Mull Of Kintyre' and appearing in a comedy sketch on BBC's *Mike Yarwood Christmas Show* were all part of a day's work. If rather subdued after a custodial drugs bust when Wings' world tour reached Japan in January 1980, Paul bounced back with 'Coming Up', which in April was high up international charts, thanks to a promotional video with him in various guises all over it.

As much Mr Showbusiness in his way was Ringo, who had actually been close to death in 1979 with an intestinal complaint. Those who read about it felt sorry for him but were no longer buying his records. The day would soon come when no British or US label was prepared to release his latest album, and his movie career was all but spent. Although in 1980 he met his second wife, Barbara Bach, on location in *Caveman*, this – his last major film – drew all of six customers the night after its London opening.

Until his final weeks, nothing as public could cajole John from his reclusive sojourn as Yoko's house-husband. Now blessed – like the Harrisons – with a son, the Lennons were based in New York's exclusive Dakota block, where they were systematically buying up additional apartments as other tenants departed. Of John's city, George had once observed, "Some of my best songs were written there. It's great, in that it gives you 360-degree vision, New York."[275] Events, however, would convince him that "the lifestyle I lead is more correct than the one [John] chose, to have some peace and quiet, rather than live in the middle of New York, which is – let's face it – a madhouse".[306] Lennon may have found his spiritual home there, but not one melody or lyric had been heard from him commercially since the appropriately premonitory 'Cookin'', a donation to Ringo's *Rotogravure* in 1976. What right had anyone to expect more? He said the same in a reluctantly given press conference a year later, adding that, when Sean was no more such a baby, "then we'll think of creating something else other than the child".[308]

The wanderings of the four ex-Beatles, even ten years after disbandment, did not prevent them from keeping in touch. With Apple finances set to occupy lawyers and accountants into the next century, George, Paul, Ringo and – wearing the trousers – Yoko were obliged anyway to convene on occasions to review progress. Old wounds were sometimes reopened, but at the end of the decade there was a protracted truce.

McCartney's arrest in Tokyo had been instrumental in establishing this concordat. The detainee's week spent pondering his folly in a Nippon gaol elicited a sympathetic telegram from George, even if – though in New York that same night – he had found no reason to attend Wings' show at Madison Square Garden. It also prompted Ringo's realisation that he no longer knew Paul's telephone number. Between Starr and Harrison, however, any bad blood had long been diluted, as shown by George's affectionate cameo in the drummer's made-for-TV spectacular *Ringo*. However, only the rare postcard filtered between George and John. Other than these, Harrison now knew Lennon only via hearsay and tales in the press of him as the Howard Hughes of pop. The same as any other fan, George was "very interested to know whether John still writes tunes and puts them on a cassette, or does he just forget all about music and not play the guitar?".[309]

A chance encounter with John in a Bermudan night club made one newshound report that the Lennon songwriting well was not as arid as might be imagined. This was confirmed a month later in August 1980, when John and Yoko booked sessions in a Big Apple studio to cut enough material for two LPs, the first of which was later scheduled for release in autumn. There were enough songs left over for John to present four to Ringo that November, when they met for the last time.

New records from George, however, were not big events any more. Maybe he also needed to absent himself from pop for years on end, for – as Ringo was already aware – an old stager's album was now less likely to be accepted without comment by a record company's quality control. 1977 had seen Warners' signing of The Sex Pistols and the company's farewell to middle-aged Van Morrison, much admired but tetchy and often long winded, musically. Not as drastic but still unnerving was executive reaction in October 1980 to *Somewhere In England*, George's proposed third album for the label. "If George wants a million-seller," moaned company president Mo Ostin, "it's not on here."[52]

Firstly, Mo didn't like the front cover: with a satellite shot of England superimposed over the back of his head, the artist in profile gazes westwards. As to the music, most of it was sufficiently "current", but some numbers would have to go, such as the opening one about "drowning in the tears of the world". That's a cheerful thought for short-listing on a radio playlist. Just as downbeat was 'Sat Singing'. Depression, however tuneful, didn't get airplay like it had during the drip-rock fad. Also axed from *Somewhere In England* were 'Flying Hour' and – surfacing years later on a B-Side – 'Lay His Head'. Like 'Writing On The Wall', which slipped through the net, both were pleasant but unexciting Harrison fare that he'd earmarked to end side two. What Ostin wanted instead was some up-tempo product to balance the mood. Until then, George's LP was to be postponed indefinitely. In any case, Lennon's *Double Fantasy* album was imminent. Even in 1980, the issue of two ex-Beatle discs within weeks of each other could still be detrimental to the sales of both.

More than anything, Ostin desired not a promotional single that might or might not chart but an unmistakable worldwide smash like 'My Sweet Lord' had been. George had had a good run since then, but now – even in the States – only by pulling such a stroke could he reverse what was an undisguisable downward spiral. Because so many cuts on his latest effort hadn't been up to scratch, this possibility was unlikely. As with Ringo, Harrison's previous handlers had been lucky in milking his calling-card Beatlehood when they did. Amid these glum reflections, an occurrence as the Yuletide sell-in got under way would give Warner Brothers a miracle.

With pride smarting at the company's rejection of the first *Somewhere In England*, George's return to the drawing board for four replacement tracks threw up two potential hits. While the words of 'Teardrops' were as lachrymose as those of 'Tears Of The World', no more did they convey socio-political tenets commercially unacceptable to Mo Ostin. To an ebullient backing and ear-grabbing melody in which the beat lifts for the chorus, George sang of a lonely man's need for love. However, although a stronger song, 'Teardrops' failed to shift a fraction of the units of the first *Somewhere In England* single, 'All Those Years Ago'.

A US Number Two, and placed in most other Top Tens, its lyrical connotations and the affinity of its writer to its subject had bequeathed unto this singalong canter an undeserved piquancy. 'All Those Years Ago', you see, was about John Lennon, who had been shot outside the Dakota in a travesty of legitimate admiration by Mark David Chapman, described in the song as "the Devil's best friend". "Are you John Lennon?" asked one of the cops in whose squad car the victim was rushed to hospital. "Yeah," gasped John. Then he died.

Everybody remembers the moment they heard. In our house the morning after, my wife shouted the intelligence up the stairs after catching it on the seven o'clock news. A few miles away in Henley,

George already knew. Olivia had told him after being wrenched from sleep by a long-distance call from her sister-in-law just before dawn. She shook George gently and came straight to the point. "How bad is it?" he inquired dozily. "A flesh wound or something?" With phlegmatic detachment, he turned over and "just went back to sleep, actually. Maybe it was a way of getting away from it."[306]

When the world woke up, John Lennon still hadn't recovered from being dead. Cancelling the day's recording session, George withdrew indoors with Dhani and Olivia. By late afternoon, he was collected enough to parry calls from the media with a prepared opening sentence: "After all we went through together, I had – and still have – great love and respect for John."[310] Paul's hiring of bodyguards on that strange day contradicted a flippancy of 1964 when asked about security by *Ready, Steady, Go!* compere Cathy McGowan. "What do we want to be protected for?" Paul replied. "We may be popular, but we're not china dolls."[311]

Paul and George had each suffered derogatory remarks from John during the promotion of *Double Fantasy*. His last published thoughts on The Beatles had been sugared with regretful affection, but, apparently, it might not have bothered him that much if he'd never seen any of them again. Among John's valedictions in print to George was some pot-calling-the-kettle-black self-righteousness about the Bright Tunes affair, which ignored his own melodic plundering of The Shirelles' B-side 'Mama Said' for 'Nobody Told Me', one of his final recordings.

His waspishness – as both his targets and John himself realised – could be shrugged off. "I don't want to start another whole thing because of the way I feel today. Tomorrow I will feel absolutely differently. It's not important, anyway."[80] George had been stunned not by the bald fact of John's passing but by the way he died. After catharsis and a dull ache, he wondered why this Mark lunatic had done it. Chapman had been photographed stalking Bob Dylan too. "John's shooting definitely scared all of us – me, Paul and Ringo," admitted George. "When a fan recognises me and rushes over, it definitely makes me nervous."[151] In as late as 1990, George was accompanied in public by a bodyguard, a six-foot-four-inch former

SAS crackshot, but any worries he may have had for his own safety in 1980 were unfounded. Like McCartney, Steve Winwood and Jeff Lynne, he didn't appear to be in the same vulnerable league then as Lennon, Dylan and other possessors of original genius rather than anything as common as mere talent.

On the "improved" *Somewhere In England* – as with George's other albums – it was vice versa. Technical advances – even since *George Harrison* – accorded greater clarity, particularly in the close-miked lead vocals, which blended Dylan-esque whinge with ingrained Scouse more than ever: "I've had my shur of cryin' bookets full of teardrops." Unruffled dispatch was tempered by details such as the slightly heavier snare drum on 'That Which I Have Lost', co-producer Ray Cooper's percussion frills and the oscillating degrees of wah-wah and other artifices on minor guitar sections throughout. All but blocked were avenues for flabby extemporisation of the kind instanced on the lengthy fade of the remaindered 'Tears Of The World'. Once he might have had licence to metaphorically blow his brains out, but now Tom Scott was limited to a fluid, one-verse solo in 'Unconsciousness Rules'.

In keeping with its title, the LP featured George's highest percentage of English musicians since *All Things Must Pass*. From The Albion Dance Band came drummer Dave Mattacks, while other natives included top session bass player Herbie Flowers and – summoned from his Godalming pub – landlord Gary Brooker, whose purring organ stood out on 'Life Itself', a slow waltz extolling George's religious liberalism.

Not as non-sectarian was 'That Which I Have Lost', which, countering its country and western-ish punch, was "right out of the *Bhagavad Gita*. In it, I talk about fighting the forces of darkness, limitations, falsehood and mortality."[151] A worldly ferocity pervaded 'Blood From A Clone'. That this was one of the substitutions was evidenced by nose-thumbing phrases about "beating my head on a brick wall", "nitpicking" (presumably by Mr Ostin) and being "nothing like Frank Zappa", whose drift towards lavatorial "humor" restricted mainstream airplay. However, because it had a popular ska rhythm and, less so, because he was George Harrison, he was excused. Otherwise, the ill-humoured 'Blood From A Clone' was in like vein to 'This Song'. Who but the most uncritical fan wants to pay out to listen to a singer getting his hassles with his record company off his chest?

Appealing more directly to common sensibilities was 'Save The World', the title of which said it all. As much an all-round protest song as 'Eve Of Destruction', any conservationist could appreciate George's laudable anxiety about our abused planet, if not his sometimes clumsy expression. With the impartiality of one long and, perhaps, guiltily isolated from the everyday, he railed against pollution, nuclear weapons, deforestation and other ills motivated by human greed. Driving it home are sound effects of bombs, a cash register, a wailing infant and similar noises when the quasi-reggae tempo slows down. According to the composer, 'Save The World' was "very serious but at the same time...hysterical. The lyrics have a lot of funny things about 'dog-food salesmen' and 'making your own H-bomb in the kitchen with your mum'."[59] Most amusing, I'm sure. As to the snatch of 'Crying' from *Wonderwall* on the play-out, he explained, "I just wanted to let the whole song go out with something sad to touch that nerve."[59]

More subtle a sign on *Somewhere In England* that George's heart was in the right place was the vicarious pleasure he gave many listeners through two chestnuts from his childhood which he sang more or less straight. Both by Hoagy Carmichael, George included these tunes partly because, prior to the pressures that spurred him to write 'Teardrops' *et al*, he'd been fresh out of ideas. Also, Carmichael was much in the air, then; Robin Sarstedt – younger brother of Eden Kane – had soared into the British Top Ten with 'My Resistance Is Low' in 1976, while, even as *Somewhere In England* was shipped to record stores, cool Georgie Fame was planning an entire Carmichael album in collaboration with Annie Ross, one of his smart jazz friends. Most significantly, if Hurtwood Edge was empty, Eric Clapton's Ansafone would croon a customised verse of 'Gone Fishin''. Rather than consume needle time with a pair of sub-standard originals, why shouldn't George – who'd been "nuts for him since I was a kid"[58] – indulge himself with 'Baltimore

Oriole' and a 'Hong Kong Blues', bracketed by the clashing of "old Buddha's gong"?

For all its overhauls and alterations, no one could pretend that George's higher chart position was down to any improved qualities within the grooves since *George Harrison*, which was coming to be regarded as the Serious Beatle's most compelling solo collection. However, ever since Buddy Holly's Number One with 'I Guess It Doesn't Matter Any More' in 1959, it had been understood that a death in pop tends to sell records. Before they'd even wiped away the tears, music-business moguls were obliged to meet demand kindled by tragedy by rush-releasing product while John's corpse was still warm. Indeed, ghoulish Beatlemania had already given the slain Beatle a hat-trick of UK chart-toppers within a month of his cremation. Out of sympathy, too, his widow finally made her Top 40 debut without him. For the first time since *Two Virgins*, Lennon's bum made the cover of *Rolling Stone*.

Inevitably, there were a rash of tribute discs. Head and shoulders commercially above titles like 'It Was Nice To Know You, John' and 'Elegy For The Walrus' and Lennon covers such as Roxy Music's 'Jealous Guy' was George's better-qualified 'All Those Years Ago', the main selling point of *Somewhere In England* and the reason why George – by association – was to end 1981 seven places behind Lennon as tenth Top Male Vocalist in *Billboard* magazine's awards. Another incentive for buyers was the overdubbed presence of Paul and Ringo, who, with Denny Laine and Linda McCartney, had broken off recording Wings' new album in George Martin's Monserrat complex to add their bits when the unmixed 'All Those Years Ago' arrived from Friar Park.

It's futile to hypothesise about John's beyond-the-grave judgement on 'All Those Years Ago'. However, I would submit that, in the same interview as the Bright Tunes barbs, he seemed wounded by the "glaring omissions"[80] of him from George's autobiography, *I Me Mine*, published earlier that year. The roots of what its author admitted was "a little ego detour"[39] lay in a conversation in 1977 with two representatives of Genesis, a publishing concern. Not any old publishing concern, Surrey-based Genesis specialised in beautifully made books of creamy vellum, coloured inks, gold leaf and hand-tooled leather bindings. Limited by cost, it was good going if an edition exhausted a run of a couple of thousand, as did a facsimile of *HMS Bounty*'s log, a snip at £158 apiece.

After the visit to Wookey Hole paper mill, George warmed to the notion of Genesis reproducing his lyrics as a joy forever, "because how it's made was almost more important than what's inside".[58] Derek Taylor, then HandMade's publicist, was commissioned to write a scene-setting introduction, but confessed, "I couldn't, though I'd known him for 15 years. I didn't know enough. I decided that the introduction should be the story of his life as he chose to tell it."[52] Interspersed with Taylor's narrative, therefore, were transcriptions of George's taped reminiscences.

This filled but 62 pages. A photograph section then led to Part Two, which took up the remaining two thirds of the "autobiography". Here, George's original scribblings of rhymes and chords are printed alongside his commentary on each. With a choice of three colours for the cover, the fly-leaf signed by George himself and – via some outlets – sold at a knockdown £116, what discerning fan could resist investing in *I Me Mine*? As only 1,000 were available in this form, its rarity enabled a London radio station to auction a copy for charity at over twice its recommended price.

Easier on the pocket in mass-market paperback, seven years on, its value in my research was not as great as you'd think – although it was more rewarding than a slim Harrison biography by Ross Michaels published in 1977.[312] Although the background to George's songs is quite intriguing, *I Me Mine* is not so much a serious study of his life as a good read. There's little space for in-depth estimation of motive or weighing of experience, but the surfacing of some unfamiliar anecdotes and the recounting of the old yarns in the subject's own laconic words is as relaxed as a fireside chat.

15 The Hermit

Throughout the 1980s, pop's history as much as its present was seized upon as a way of making money. No more the market's most vital consumer group, teenagers were outmanoeuvred by their Swinging '60s parents and young marrieds with high disposable incomes who'd sated their appetites for novelty. No matter how it was packaged – twelve-inch club mix on polkadot vinyl, or whatever – the pop single became a loss leader, an incentive for grown-ups to buy an album, hopefully on more expensive compact disc.

Incorrigible old Mods, Rockers and flower children didn't mind squeezing into the smart casuals that were the frequent norm in citadels of "quality" entertainment and on under-40s weekends where "Sounds Of The Sixties" nights would pull in capacity crowds. Rebooked at the same such venues time and time again, the likes of The Searchers, Herman's Hermits (now minus Herman), Gerry Marsden and The Swinging Blue Jeans – now with Colin Manley in their ranks – had opportunities to form genuine friendships rather than play backstage host to a residue of stargazers.

In the charts, it was often as if time had stopped. The sampler single for US albums would be an act's revamp of an oldie, like Tiffany's 'I Saw Her Standing There' or Van Halen's touching Number Twelve in 1982's Hot 100 with Roy Orbison's 'Oh! Pretty Woman', which the previous year had resounded as part of Tight Fit's 'Back To The Sixties' medley in a Britain that was even more awash with nostalgia for that decade. At one stage, every fourth record in the UK hit parade was either a re-issue or a revival of an old song. Contradicting Billy J Kramer's 'You Can't Live On

Memories' single of 1983, the culmination of this trend was The Hollies' windfall when the 20-year-old single 'He Ain't Heavy (He's My Brother)' shot to Number One in 1988 via the offices of Miller Lite lager, who'd worked it into a television commercial.

Not needing unsolicited snippet coverage, another re-promotion of The Beatles' back catalogue by EMI began well, with 'Love Me Do' and the spliced-up 'Beatles Movie Medley' both cracking the Top Ten. A year earlier, Dutch session musicians Stars On 45 – imitating the Fab Four – had done likewise, as would Siouxsie And The Banshees with 'Dear Prudence' in 1984.

The latter was a one-shot ploy to revive a flagging career, but there were other bands whose *raison d'être* was centred solely on impersonating The Beatles. Foremost among these were Abbey Road, Cavern and – most accurate of all – The Bootleg Beatles, formed from the cast of the West End musical *Beatlemania*. While "Paul" more resembled *Old Grey Whistle Test* presenter Mark Ellen, one Bootleg Beatle watcher was able to confirm to the real Harrison – at a Formula One meet – that actor Andre Barreau's "George" was authentic down to the Liverpool leg.

In that city's Kensington district, where they'd recorded 'In Spite Of All The Danger', a cluster of new streets had been named in the Beatles' honour, with George Harrison Way being the shortest cul-de-sac off John Lennon Drive. In similar ratio, Lennon ephemera drew highest bids among Beatle memorabilia on offer at Sotheby's and other top sale rooms. Although few bothered with *Dark Horse* items under the hammer, a letter to Stuart Sutcliffe from George fetched just short of £2,000 and his first guitar had appreciated by over 1,000 per cent by 1983. Even the Harrison family toilet, removed during modernisation of Mackett's Lane, was displayed and sold as solemnly as if it had been a Duchamp ready-made.

Although a gold 'My Sweet Lord' went for £2,750, comparative indifference towards other artefacts from George's post-Beatle years reflected his standing as a contemporary artist. The goodwill that had propelled 'All Those Years Ago' into the charts was not extended to 'Teardrops' or even to *The Best Of George Harrison*, a budget re-issue from 1968 with a cover photo. While McCartney was accorded

41 lines in the *Who's Who* social register, in 1981 George was stuck between Bill Haley and Noel Harrison in *Whatever Happened To...?*, a publication claiming to be "the great rock and pop nostalgia book".[313]

In commercial decline as a recording artist and with his very competence as a composer questioned by Warners, George had come to loathe public fascination with his "previous incarnation".[8] Ringo's tentative agreement was rumoured, but George would have nothing to do with a multi-million-pound bribe for a one-album collaboration by the Fab Three and the adult Julian Lennon. According to "Uncle George", Julian took most after Cynthia. Although his surname had opened doors and packed out Carnegie Hall for one of his concerts, Julian had become something of a "Tumbledown Dick" among pop stars. Nevertheless, the press produced another rumour – that he and his father's former confreres would perform together at the climax of Live Aid in 1985. Instead, Paul sang a gremlin-troubled 'Let It Be'. As an elder of pop altruism, an invitation merely to attend had been sent to George, but he confessed, "I was just a little worried in case somebody was trying to re-form The Beatles, trying to trick us all into being on it."[188] However, he contributed a vignette to a paperback published in aid of the associated charity, Comic Relief.

To no humanitarian end, George and the other Beatles were more lucratively exploited when an old recording was used to advertise Nike's "revolution" in footwear, supposedly with Yoko Ono's permission. A suit was filed by the surviving Beatles because, predicted George, "If it's allowed to happen, every Beatle song ever recorded is going to be advertising women's underwear and sausages. The other thing is, even while Nike might have paid Capitol Records for the rights, Capitol certainly don't give us the money."[188] To redress similar royalty grievances, a legal battle was joined by The Beatles against EMI in 1984. Four years later, the group slapped a writ for damages on old rival Dave Clark's video company for Beatles clips shown in Channel 4's re-runs of *Ready, Steady, Go!*. Minor matters included an injunction to stop an English independent company from releasing an album of their Decca audition.

In the ups and downs of George's separate business affairs, his rapport with Warners was even less cordial now. On top of the disheartening um-ing and ah-ing over *Somewhere In England*, he'd been miffed over an unimaginative – if justifiable – usage of Beatles stills and footage in the video for 'All Those Years Ago'. That he'd left the making of this to the company rather than intervene personally showed the extent of the disenchantment he'd spelled out in 'Blood From A Clone'. Moreover, like others his age, he concluded, "The Top 40 songs are so bland and trends like hip-hop or rap music are so tedious. I can't wait until we go back to the old days, when the charts were full of good songs by real musicians. These days, there's not an ounce of talent to be seen."[315]

The sweeping lack of sympathy with an ear of commodity over creativity was coupled with a realisation that he'd lost the knack of writing hits, even American ones. Quite simply, George was out of touch. He was not, however, unduly worried. No longer did he explore the same worn-out themes over and over again from new angles in the wrong-headed expectation of finding gold. He'd sit down to compose almost eagerly, but sometimes all he'd hear were vibrations hanging in the air. Glazed languor would set in, and his mind would wander to car-racing tracks, Friar Park gardens, Maui – anywhere but to the job in hand. His, however, was not the same malady that had crept up on John, who, unlike George, was basically lazy.

George had found a full life beyond either cheerful lassitude or the pursuit of hit records. By gripping tightly on the realities of past success and defining his motivations sharply enough, he had reached a level – both professional and personal – where another 'My Sweet Lord' would have been a mere sideshow. It was income from HandMade – which by now averaged three or four films annually – rather than royalty cheques from *Somewhere In England* that kept the wolf from the door nowadays. Despite heavy promotion, there'd still been a few damp squibs, and George had been alarmed by the movie industry's competition and occasional downright thuggishness: "A lot of cinemas down the eastern seaboard of America wouldn't pay over the box-office money. They held it for six or nine months, investing our money, but it's all Mafia connections, and there's nothing you can do about it."[315] Nevertheless, HandMade had gone from strength to strength, from Bob Hoskins' BAFTA Best Actor statuette for *Mona Lisa* to George and Denis receiving from the Duchess of Kent an award for HandMade's services to British film. Before millions of BBC viewers, a jubilant George planted a kiss on the royal cheek.

Such Fab Four-ish sauciness was absent on ITV a few months later, when *News At Ten* showed George among protesters at an anti-nuclear rally in Trafalgar Square. This was one of the less anonymous manifestations of his and Olivia's concern about pressing environmental and human issues that had passed him by during the ebbing bustle of the 1970s. As well as a generous financial gesture to float *Vole* – a green journal launched by Monty Python's Terry Jones – a re-recorded 'Save The World', with specifically adjusted lyrics, was donated to a fund-raising LP for Greenpeace, an organisation dedicated – like *Vole* – to the extirpation of iniquities like whale fishing and radioactive dumping. "As an ordinary member of humanity and of the British public," he explained, "the only vote I have ever cast is Green. The whole planet is operating on the waste of over-indulgence. It's just ridiculous. 'Money doesn't talk, it swears.' Bob Dylan said that years ago."[316]

An appeal from the Cancer Research Fund, who'd noted his involvement in the Nilsson foundation, fired George "to try and get something started"[317] in order to publicise the British leg of Canadian "13-million-dollar man" Steve Fonyo's marathon 'Journey For Lives' sponsored walk. *Leg* is a crucial word here, as one of 22-year-old Steve's had been amputated because of cancer. *En route* from Scotland to London in March 1987, he and his fiancée were joined along the towpath in Henley by the Harrisons. With his collar turned up against a chill spring breeze, George, Dhani and Steve posed in midstride before press cameras, and then all repaired to Friar Park and afternoon tea.

If seldom seen, George continued throughout the 1980s to function as town patrician and patron of Henley events and institutions. Among the pies in which he had a finger was the Kenton Theatre. He was not, however, present when I performed there in 1980, although he'd been sent a complimentary ticket and an invitation to bring his guitar along in case he couldn't prevent himself from joining The Argonauts and me on stage. Maybe he did turn up after all. Certainly, he saw fit to attend a reception for television gourmet Ken Lo in the restaurant above the Angel on the Bridge pub and present a cheque for a charity fun run at a local college.

Of all of George's interventions in parochial affairs, none were as intensely public as those concerning the threatened demolition of Bell Street's Regal Cinema, scene of his date with Hayley Mills and other assignations "long, before I lived in Henley".[318] From its grand opening in 1936 with *Take My Tip*, starring Cicely Courtenay, until its abrupt closure with *Back To The Future* half a century later, this 740-seater theatre had been a popular facet of the town's social life, its attendance figures increasing by almost half during the months preceding the declaration by its owners, Henley Picture Houses Ltd, that it had become "unprofitable" since the advent of video.

To the howl of rage from the 7,000 who signed an opposing petition, the Regal was to be levelled by the John Lewis Partnership's bulldozers in order to extend the adjacent branch of Waitrose supermarket and create a mall of 18 shops – and, if you like, a smaller cinema. "This is rape!"[318] yelled an affronted *Henley Standard* editorial. Furthermore, the turmoil of the proposed reconstruction would exacerbate the already critical traffic problem of – as George complained – "cars and lorries crashing through the narrow streets that were originally built for the horse and cart".[318]

As *éminence grise* behind some of the Regal's weekly offerings, George had needed little persuasion from borough councillor Tony Lane to join the Davids against the John Lewis Goliath in a star-studded show of strength outside the empty cinema on a busy Saturday morning in September 1986. "I'm not doing this for an ulterior motive," elucidated Lane's most powerful convert, raising a placard from the centre of the bunched local celebrities. "I genuinely want to preserve this town. These faceless people who made the planning applications and those who give permission should come out of the shadow. Let us see the faces of the assassins!"[318] Hemmed in by jotting reporters, George snarled further about Waitrose's "Orwellian cynicism" and "concrete monsters",[318] even evoking

Dylan and Liverpool during a debate that simmered on even after Environment Secretary Chris Patten decided against calling a public enquiry in October 1989. This was in spite of crowded Town Hall meetings (some attended by Olivia), offers to the Lewis firm of alternative sites, "Save The Regal" galas and Dhani joining in the booing as a children's protest march passed Waitrose. Lobbying the constituency's unmoved MP, Michael Heseltine, George's sarcastic suggestion of replacing Henley's antique bridge with a wider concrete model was met, allegedly, with a look "as if to say, 'Shut your mouth, you Liverpool git.'"[315]

Also pitching in were the likes of barrister/playwright John Mortimer, actors George Cole and Jeremy Irons and – from up the river, in Wargrave – Mary Hopkin. Others supporting George, among members of what was still technically his own profession, were Joe Brown from neighbouring Skirmett, Dave Edmunds and Jon Lord, who, as squire of the acres round Yewton Lodge, could well afford the thousand quid he put into the "Save The Regal" kitty.

They and other members of the Henley Music Mafia played together, either in the privacy of their own homes or on stages like those in Watlington's Carriers Arms or the Crown in Pishill, with a rambling selection sprung from "old twelve-bars, The Everly Brothers and the odd bit of Django Reinhardt".[187] From these casual unwindings came more palpable liaisons. While house-hunting in the area, The Hollies' Tony Hicks stayed at Kenny Lynch's place near Nettlebed, where owner and lodger wrote songs that would be unveiled on a consequent Hollies album. George composed 'Flying Hour' with Nettlebed guitarist Mick Ralphs – former mainstay of Mott The Hoople – and 'Shelter Of Your Love' with Alvin Lee from Goring. In 1985, he lent Mike Batt a hand on the Womble *führer*'s musical setting of Lewis Carroll's 'The Hunting Of The Snark'. For George, Jon Lord tickled the ivories in the Cascara band in *Water* and manipulated synthesiser on *Gone Troppo*. This album, so George disclosed two years after its release in November 1982, would be his last. He'd had his fill of the music business, thank you. "Once I'd got myself out of that star rat-race, I promised myself I'd never work again. Well I do work – but I want it to be enjoyable, not just a slog."[272]

As a farewell, if it was one, *Gone Troppo* was the sort of record you could leave on instant replay while you put your feet up. Although 'I Really Love You' was conspicuous, it was almost the sound at any given moment that counted rather than individual tracks. Working sensually more than intellectually, it was warm latitudes, dreamy sighs and an ocean dawn from the quarterdeck: a slow boat redirected from China to Maui. After the adulterated *Somewhere In England*, the new LP was a refinement and apparent culmination of the seam mined on *George Harrison* – which means that it was Harrison's most enterprising musical statement since The Beatles.

Pacific culture had been absorbed by George less self-consciously than his Indian studies had been in the 1960s. His slide-guitar playing was now closer to that of Hawaiian virtuoso Frank Ferera than Ry Cooder's. On one number, he even plucked a Javan *jaltarang*. Nowhere were there raucous and distorted-fretboard pyrotechnics, which were never his style, anyway. Instead, George's obligatos and solos were all the more rewarding for their semi-acoustic restraint in the overall elegance of *Gone Troppo*.

Opening the album was its most laboured song, 'Wake Up, My Love', which dwelt in a staccato unison riff and tension-building chorus, both of which marred by the snotty grating of a synthesiser. These extrovert qualities rather than gentler possibilities were presumably why 'Wake Up My Love' was selected by Warners as the trailer single, which peaked around the middle of the Hot 100 while slumbering in deletion in most other territories.

More deserving of even this slight chart placing was the US follow-up, the charming 'I Really Love You'. Blowing the dust off this favourite from The Chants' Merseyside repertoire, George didn't reconstruct it as he had 'True Love'. To a sparse accompaniment, which included the rhythmic clattering of Ray Cooper's feet – an idea from *Ringo* – George, in street-corner harmony with three other singers, conveyed both the despondency of abused infatuation and – largely through the "fool" grumblings of bassman Willie Green – the feeling that George and his accomplices had exploded with laughter the second that engineer Phil McDonald stopped the tape. More flattering perhaps than its fleeting visit to the US charts was Rocky

Sharp And The Razors' later cover of 'I Really Love You' in Britain.

Vocal interplay was also to the fore in less light-hearted *Gone Troppo* songs such as 'That's The Way It Goes' – another slant on the transience of worldly care – and the less complicated 'Baby Don't Run Away'. Although the melody of The Rolling Stones' 'All Sold Out' from 1967 was buried in the title track, George's tunes elsewhere had never been so wrought with quirks of phrasing and bar lengths. Particularly intriguing are 'Mystical One' and 'Unknown Delight', each serenely unpredictable and of a world more free of pain than could be imagined by a *Gone Troppo* consumer daydreaming through the vapour of a train window on the way to work.

Purposely listless was the performance of the finale, 'Circles', in which a sense of once more going through the old routine suited the world-weary lyrics. "I think you have to be a George Harrison fan to appreciate his music" had been Phil McDonald's excuse. "He does them the way he likes them."[319]

Even if the very president of Warners disliked *Gone Troppo*, George, at the end of his tether, would not brook any demands for amendment this time. There were no 'All Those Years Ago' Godsends on it, but maybe the repercussions of *Somewhere In England* and, of course, The Beatles would be enough to make this new Harrison project a practical proposition. Attractive though they were, the inclusion of a neo-instrumental ('Greece'), a non-original and the previously issued (if remixed) 'Dream Away' attested to the dryness of George's commercial fount. Still irked about *Somewhere In England*, wild horses couldn't drag him from his hideaway to utter the odd word on behalf of *Gone Troppo*: "I didn't want to end up like some famous people, always living in a goldfish bowl, so I just decided not to do all these television talk shows every five minutes and tons of interviews."[151] Besides, he had more important things to do.

If the artist wasn't going to co-operate, neither would Warners' press office. Left to fend for itself, the album – treasured only in retrospect – dithered in the lower reaches of the charts before leaving quietly. As the remaining pressings waited in vain for shipment, Warners' high command may have used its title among politer descriptive tags applied to George.

The phrase "gone troppo", meaning "gone crazy", is one of Australia's florid gifts to the English language. In New South Wales, six months before its release, the expression had been bandied about when George magnanimously invited staff at Warners' Melbourne office out to lunch. This wasn't the only reason for his visit. Since a hush-hush landing at Queensland airport and exit by helicopter to racing driver Bobby Jones' homestead on the Gold Coast, George had been house-hunting after drinking in glowing accounts of God's Own Country from Bobby and other racers, including world champion Alan Jones, another with whom the Harrisons lodged that March.

Unrecognised on a trip with Dhani to Sydney's Sea World, a clean-shaven sightseer with a "pre-Astrid Teddy Boy haircut"[320] also paid his respects at the city's Hare Krishna temple. Nonetheless, it would have been an incurious media that hadn't got wind of an ex-Beatle in their midst. Without revealing why he'd really come to the Antipodes for the first time since 1964, George granted an audience to *Australian Woman's Weekly* as well as a television interview on *Good Morning Australia* where he was most complimentary about the continent he'd dismissed with scant lines in *I Me Mine*. Before flying out, he instructed an estate agent to go up to two million notes for a "crash-hot pad" – as an Aussie might call it – on secluded Whitsunday Island off Repulse Bay and opposite the Great Barrier Reef. It was also close to Barry Sheene's villa on a stretch of Queensland coast known as Surfer's Paradise.

By coincidence, on the market then, for just under £200,000, were two houses on Friar Park manor where, for all the fluctuations of its owner's musical and celluloid undertakings, his toparian ventures had been an unqualified triumph. Recovering from overgrown neglect, the parkland had become once more a fairyland panorama of floral harmony, a unified blending of shape and colour. Dedicating his autobiography to "all gardeners everywhere", George loved "being close to nature; it makes me feel very peaceful",[321] although not when a tractor once ran over his foot. In the expert estimation of Beth Chatto, author of *The Damp Garden*,[322] *Plant Portraits*[322] and other classics, he had "the makings of a very good gardener. He's appreciative of good taste. He doesn't want a gaudy garden. He wants a sensitive garden where plants look natural."[322]

Because he'd taken a fancy to her yellow-flowered bog plant, George had sought out Mrs Chatto during his now-annual visit to the Chelsea Flower Show. Later, he'd drive to her Colchester nursery to purchase further unusual plants. It had been too late for George to become a master of the sitar, but it wasn't too late for him to become a master gardener. Soon he was fraternising as much with the craft's top echelon as he did with the Formula One *côterie*. A bouquet from Friar Park was arranged at Beth Chatto's bedside when she was recovering from an operation. Gardening correspondent Peter Seabrook was pleased to help George identify a white hardy perennial – an antirrhinum asarina, he reckoned – that had sprouted in the Park rockery, and, said Olivia, "We had someone visit us from the Soil Association to teach us how to upgrade the standard of our vegetables."[316] Whatever the field of expertise – music, sport, bookbinding or gardening – George enjoyed associating with those who were good at something and watching them doing it.

With him at an Everly Brothers concert in Adelaide were Ferrari drivers Michele Alboreto and Stefan Johansson, "with their nice clean clothes, such good little boys, and the next morning you see them come down the pit land at 120 miles an hour like these lunatics. That's what amazes me."[315] Contrasting with the quiet of wheelbarrows and hoes were George's ongoing weekends at the races, an enthusiasm now shared with nephew Mark – then a trainee motor mechanic – and Ringo. One Beatle fanzine bleated that he "lives more for car racing than rock 'n' roll",[247] but George wasn't that addicted: "If I had three million to give away, which I haven't, there's probably better things to give it to than motor racing – like the starving, for example."[22] Nonetheless, although a critic of Yoko Ono's apparent Nike error, he allowed the revitalised Chrysler auto corporation to avail itself of 'Something' for a TV commercial. Nobler was a cash incentive allegedly offered to the aging Barry Sheene not to risk death or maiming by racing again.

An older mate accepted a cheaper yet just as valuable present from George in the doleful 'Wrack My Brain', written for Ringo Starr's first album in three years, 1981's *Stop And Smell The Roses*. As songs by Paul and the late John had also been considered, it was possible to guess the identity of the "three brothers" thanked by Ringo on the LP cover. As financiers, however, Yoko, Paul, George and Ringo in 1983 would lock themselves away with champagne and salmon in an eighth-floor suite in London's Dorchester Hotel to talk again of the division of the empire. Also pertinent to the past was Harrison and McCartney's later mulling over the making of "the definitive Beatle story",[324] comprising home movies, scenes edited from *Help!*, *et al*, and new narration. After Dick Lester passed on the scheme, *Back To The Future* producer Steven Spielberg "was far more encouraging".[324] However, another schism between Paul and the others lay close ahead, thwarting for now this and further creative reconciliations.

Business turmoils apart, George was not averse to more sociable reunions. "Paul and I had not been friends for a number of years," he said, "but lately we spent a lot of time really getting to know each other again."[325] Ringo's marriage to Barbara Bach at Marylebone Registry Office in April 1981 was splashed across the front of *The Daily Express*. For the reception in a Mayfair club, a car-rental firm delivered instruments and amplifiers, but most of the conflicting reports intimate that the three former Beatles did not reunite on stage as they'd done at Hurtwood Edge two years earlier. When the party broke up, screams hailed the exit of Paul – still a chart contender – while George and Olivia shuffled out almost unnoticed.

Starring with David Yip in ITV's *The Chinese Detective*, even George's pre-Beatle pal Arthur Kelly was more likely to be accosted by starstruck British teenagers. George still had a lot of time for Arthur, respecting him for not profiteering from his Beatle connection as Allan Williams had done with a digitally touched-up tape of a rough night during the group's final Hamburg residency. As well as issuing this on disc, Williams also cashed in with *The Man Who Gave The Beatles Away*, a book which, if heavy on poetic licence, was an atmospheric chronicle of his *soi-disant* "management" of John, Paul, George and Pete.

Infinitely more acceptable to George was Derek Taylor's *50 Years Adrift*, an autobiography that would have been most odd if it hadn't also contained hefty segments of the George Harrison saga, especially as the lad himself was its editor. George couldn't help liking Derek, whose appointment as Warners' general manager in Europe had been a deciding factor precipitating Dark Horse's transfer from A&M. One of his more burdensome tasks in this post had been to bear the news of Mo Ostin's savaging of *Somewhere In England* to its originator. In the following year, Taylor's promotion to vice-president of Creative Services found him in Los Angeles, where the company honoured him with a *This Is Your Life*-type citation, with George, Ringo and many leading entertainers walking on to tell funny stories from the past.

By autumn 1979, the mercurial Derek had gravitated back to England when HandMade cried out for his unique skills. Happy with the result of both his work and the assistance with *I Me Mine*, George interceded to convince Genesis Publications that Taylor's idiosyncratic story of his first half-century would be viable. With facsimiles of such relics as his *Help!* première ticket physically stuck on the pages, 2,000 hand-numbered volumes of Taylor's prose – completed at tranquil Kuppaqulua in November 1983 – went on sale at £148 each. To the chagrin of Warners, who'd just deleted *Gone Troppo*, Harrison was much in evidence during Derek's promotion of *50 Years Adrift*. At his side at two literary luncheons in Australia, George had been tractable enough to autograph an entire collection of Beatle LPs and patiently request one ill-informed hack to rephrase his question, "Mr Harrison, what prompted you to write this book?"[326]

By letting their contractual option on one more album lapse, any anger at Warners about George's antics had dissipated to apathy. He hadn't a hope of getting back on his perch, had he? Let him do what he liked. To the confusion of those bootleggers still bothered, and what he regarded as Warners' cloth-eared ignorance, Harrison had started thinking aloud to anyone listening in 1985 about including an EP of the four recordings ousted from *Somewhere In England* with another planned *de luxe* exercise by Genesis. Illustrating *Songs By George Harrison* would be appropriate water-colours by Keith West, an artist who had lately entered the Friar Park circle.[327]

That George was contemplating tying up this loose end was one more indication that he had dumped his load, as far as the record-buying populace was concerned. Now that the pressure of making albums no longer loomed, there was just the perverse joy of creating uncommercial music: "I've never stopped writing songs, and I've made hundreds of demos."[328] He also added to a multitude of credits on the LP jackets of others. As well as Ringo's latest and film soundtracks, he was also heard on albums by Gary Brooker and Mick Fleetwood, drummer with Fleetwood Mac and husband for many years of Jenny Boyd. Harrison was at Alvin Lee's service, too, playing slide on his US-only *Detroit Diesel* LP.

A HandMade spokesman in 1982 had pleaded stage-fright "after all these years away"[329] in reply to a call for George to walk the boards again for charity. All the same, he sat in with his guitar when Sean Lennon's godfather, Elton John's world tour reached Sydney that year. On the day after a *50 Years Adrift* bunfight in the city, he was introduced as "Arnold Grove from Liverpool, New South Wales", winner of a competition to play an encore with Deep Purple. It took a minute of a Little Richard number with Jon Lord's reformed quintet before screams of recognition reverberated past the footlights. In contrast, George's was the slightly throaty vocal refrain – in Hindi – on the title tack of Ravi Shankar's eclectic *Tana Mana* album, which also contained a track entitled 'Friar Park'.

Confining such favours to fellow old soldiers, a meeting with Dave Edmunds in 1985 included George's only formal stage appearance in Britain since The Plastic Ono Band 16 years earlier. While producing a soundtrack for the US teen-exploitation movie *Porky's Revenge*, Edmunds was fishing around for contributors whose names would help sales of the tic-in album. Having procured Jeff Beck and Led Zeppelin's Robert Plant, Dave then sounded out George. That his friend had no suitable original material was no problem; he could do a cover. George whittled down his choices to 'I Didn't Want To Do It', one of two obscure Dylan numbers considered. Harrison's response to this humble summons encouraged Dave to prod him into allying with other guest musicians for a TV special he was co-ordinating. Fourteen months in preparation, it was to star one whose songs about clothes, lust and violence had captured George's adolescent imaginings – Carl Perkins.

Fifty-three-year-old Carl had been another of Edmunds' assistants on *Porky's Revenge*. While in Memphis to supervise the recording, Dave had been invited to a party at the much-modernised Sun Studio that climaxed with the taping of a roistering medley for *Homecoming*, an album conceived four years earlier when Sun released a 30-minute sing-song from 1956 supposedly involving the "Million-Dollar Quartet" of Perkins, Jerry Lee Lewis, Johnny Cash and Elvis Presley. This provoked sufficient interest for a premeditated 1980s reconstruction to be organised, with Roy Orbison filling in for the departed Elvis.

Implicit in the presence of Edmunds, Creedence Clearwater Revival's John Fogerty and other younger performers on *Homecoming* was the renewed veneration felt for pop's methuselahs. The 60th birthdays of Fats Domino and Chuck Berry were both sanctified before television cameras with back-slapping attendance by celebrities who'd grown up to their music. Roy Orbison's turn came in 1987 in a glittering extravaganza in Los Angeles with the likes of Ry Cooder, the over-valued Bruce Springsteen and Elvis Costello backing him.

Carl Perkins And Friends: A Rockabilly Special, broadcast on 21 October 1985, had some of the ingredients of a self-congratulatory disaster, but if any of the distinguished rank and file had sought to upstage Perkins this was edited out of the two hours of film before it hit British screens on New Year's Day 1986. On the cutting-room floor lay Harrison's attempt to lead the cast into Dylan's 'Rainy Day Women' and his plug for the latest HandMade movie. George was also very quick to criticise the audience for not clapping hard enough. Few of these sequences had impressed the Teddy Boys who'd queued in the cold outside Limehouse Studios amid London's dockland wharfs. Three hundred quiffs strong, they might have preferred a more typical Perkins recital, unimpeded by the contemporary stamp of approval of his illustrious helpmates. Carl was who they'd mob afterwards.

The Teds were appeased, however, by the homely pub-like

ambience as the players switched on small amplifiers. With grey-haired Perkins close enough for everyone to see, Dave Edmunds and his usual combo were stage fixtures, while among those waiting in the wings were Eric Clapton, two of the revivalist Stray Cats, Rozanne Cash (daughter of Johnny) and Ringo Starr, who was to rattle the traps while singing 'Honey Don't' and, with Carl, 'Matchbox', two Perkins items that had thrust him into the main spotlight with The Beatles.

No one was surprised when George ambled on in a baggy grey suit for 'Everybody's Trying To Be My Baby'. However, as his spot progressed with less familiar pieces from the Silver Beatles era, such as 'Your True Love' and 'Gone Gone Gone', many were struck by his animated enthusiasm and obvious pleasure in performing again. With an ear cocked on the tightly arranged rhythmic undercurrent from two days' rehearsal, George's hopping from shoe to unbearably excited shoe was belied not so much by his vocal confidence as his tough guitar soloing. His picking was certainly truer to the show's driving rockabilly spirit than that of slap-dash Clapton. Both, nevertheless, were delighted to sit with the others in a devout semi-circle at Carl's tapping feet in the finale.

George guaranteed himself a more pronounced stake in the proceedings when he booked Perkins as entertainment for a televised celebration of HandMade's first decade in business. As he was paying for it, George had no qualms about sharing the limelight with Carl. Backed by Joe Brown and Ray Cooper, among others, the pair rampaged through 'That's All Right', 'Boppin' The Blues' and further 1950s favourites while revellers cut a rug in the dancing area of the private sanctum within Shepperton Studios. Master of ceremonies Michael Palin's after-dinner speech had concluded with glasses raised to the founder of the feast. Following this toast, George's opening sentence, to sycophantic titters, had been, "Thank you all for coming. Now fuck off."[285]

A couple spared this amicable vulgarity were Madonna and her husband, Sean Penn. Since completing their roles in *Shanghai Surprise*, an adaptation of Tony Kenrick's novel *Faraday's Flowers*, George hadn't "seen them from that day to this".[315] Neither was he troubling to see Madonna's newest flick. This petulant little madam, you see, had been another pop singer who'd seen herself as a cinema attraction. Like Petula Clark and Cilla Black before her, Madonna was an ordinary-looking but competent female vocalist with a facial mole. Unlike them, she let you know she was a star. That's S-T-A-R! Star! Star! Star! Moreover, she'd saddled herself with a volatile spouse who resented being "Mr Madonna". He was also a competent film actor, albeit one with a face asking to be punched. On a short fuse, Mr Madonna's own fists had already landed him a spell in jail.

In deference perhaps to their hosts' more glorious pop pedigree, the Penns had been genial enough when sampling Friar Park hospitality. "The project got to within a day of being elbowed and then suddenly Sean Penn and Madonna decided they'd be in it. We didn't know all the trouble they were going to cause us."[24] Both had made earlier forays into film, but Madonna's cache of hit records tipped the balance. Although other actresses had been auditioned, George had agreed, "It was obviously good to have her in it, because it's better than having somebody nobody had ever heard of."[330] Nonetheless, after sinking £10 million into *Shanghai Surprise*, HandMade had been "damn lucky to get our money back and not lose our shirts."[151]

George blamed this close shave on "a combination of her thinking she's a star and the way the press was gunning for her".[8] Penn and his wife's Garbo-esque refusal to be interviewed was a provocation to Fleet Street, which disgraced itself from the moment the pair arrived at Heathrow *en route* to the filming location in Kowloon, Hong Kong. Even incarceration in their hotel brought the Penns no peace, as "creative" journalists disguised themselves as staff to get a scoop. Notebook at the ready, one muckraker loitered for hours in the ladies' in order to buttonhole seat-bound acolytes of the Penn entourage.

More than anyone, George could sympathise with the brusque Penns' plight and said so at a London press conference in March 1986. As at the *50 Years Adrift* lunch dates, most questions were directed at George throughout the 45-minute grilling, which ended with Madonna proclaiming, "We're not such a bad bunch of people, are we? Byeeeeee."[330]

Hoping the newspapers might agree, executive producer and stars then split like an amoeba, he to Henley and they to Kowloon, with the press in close pursuit. To the glee of breakfast-table readers everywhere, the situation worsened. Juxtaposed with misappropriated *Shanghai Surprise* stills were both true and untrue tabloid stories of "Poison" Penn's bodyguards assaulting a photographer; a make-up girl's sacking for asking Madonna for an autograph; and frightful quarrels that could be heard all over the set.

While appreciating how the smallest incidents could be embroidered, interruption in day-to-day shooting had become so serious by September that a despairing George was compelled to jet eastwards to sort out the mess. Later, he'd laugh off this "bloody nightmare",[151] even framing one front page – "George Harrison Emerges As A Movie Mogul To Take The Penns In Hand!" – alongside more tasteful prints in Cadogan Square; but, when first he reached Kowloon, "[Sean and Madonna] weren't being very nice to the crew. It's hard work [for the crew], dragging equipment 'round places where it's freezing cold for hours. And while she's in a warm trailer, the crew are trying to drink a cup of tea to keep warm, and a little 'Hello, good morning, how are you?' goes a long way in those circumstances. So when I got there, the crew hated them."[188]

The executive producer's descent into their midst stripped the Penns of enough hauteur for Madonna to propose humouring the malcontented underlings with a party. Disgusted, George had already gauged that such tardy sweetness and light wouldn't wash, "because, to tell you the truth, nobody would show up."[188] For the second time that year, he submitted himself to another paparazzi ordeal for Madonna's benefit. Although he bore himself with his accustomed self-assurance, clicking shutters froze a thunderous countenance in marked contrast to Mrs Penn's smirk.

George's last word on Madonna in *Shanghai Surprise* was, "She doesn't have a sense of humour, which is unfortunate, because it was a comedy."[188] Some had been astonished by his firm and stoical conduct during this episode as he mediated between journalistic malevolence and the Penns' prima-donna snootiness. "I never realised you had it in you,"[331] commented John Peel to George on an ITV chat show.

Harrison also rendered unto *Shanghai Surprise* a soundtrack, which went unreleased "because the film got slagged off so bad".[59] Other than elongated interludes, such as 'Hottest Gong In Town', much of it would reach the public when staggered over the next three years in either album tracks or makeweight flip-sides. Madonna had been mooted to duet with George on the main title theme, but the job went instead to the more affable Vikki Brown, ex-Vernons Girl, wife of Joe and cabaret star in northern Europe.

The song 'Shanghai Surprise' set her with George amid verses clustered with lines about rickshaws, Asia Minor and it being "a hell of a way to see China". Switching musically from the Pacific of *Gone Troppo*, the bright tone colours of *sheng*, *koto*, *erhu* and like instruments common to south-east Asia were simulated in George's Friar Park studio via synthesiser, effects pedals and Western session players. The opus was as accurate and attractive a pastiche as Bryan Ferry's 'Tokyo Joe' or John Entwistle's 'Made In Japan'. A more insidious dose of Yellow Peril, however, was contracted on 'Breath Away From Heaven', a softer-hued piece with fragile zither glissandos and George's "nice words"[59] about smiles and whispers at sunrise "in another life". Also wasted on Madonna's movie was 'Someplace Else', which wouldn't have been out of place on *Gone Troppo*.

In a night-club scene, the drama had continued over 'Zig-Zag', in which George's vocals played as incidental a part as they had in 'Greece'. Smeared with muted trumpet and clarinet, his combo shuffled away at the Kenny Ball end of traditional jazz. Of more long-term import was the attendance on 'Zig-Zag' of Jeff Lynne, whose bond with Harrison was to prove considerably more productive in the months to follow. Finding that, "when you write, perform and produce, there's a good chance of getting lost",[59] George had sought a console collaborator with as much objectivity as percussion aesthete Ray Cooper but with a background more in accordance with his own. He wondered "who would understand me and my past, and have respect for that, who I have great respect for – and then I hit on Jeff Lynne, thinking he'd he good if we got on well."[58] This he mentioned to Dave Edmunds, whose two most recent albums had been produced by Lynne. In Los Angeles, Dave passed on this matter-of-fact information to Jeff. With Edmunds as go-between, the bearded leader of the now-redundant ELO was invited to dinner at Friar Park.

As well as overseeing ELO's explorations of the more magniloquent aspect of The Beatles' psychedelic period, 39-year-old Lynne was a studio veteran with skills perfected from a Birmingham adolescence when he converted his Shard End front room into an Aladdin's cave of linked-up reel-to-reel tape recorders, editing blocks and jack-to-jack leads. Yet, for all the technical refinements since, Lynne's attitude towards recording seemed to have gone full circle. 1980s pop was full of short-cut records in which vocals glided smoothly over perfect time-keeping, sequencers, "twanging-plank" disco bass and other programmed sounds. The Japanese had even invented a drum machine that would make a deliberate mistake within bar lines every now and then to preserve some vestige of humanity. No such allowances had been made on a Steve Winwood album of 1982, on which more machines and sound laboratories received "special thanks"[105] than people.

With ELO, Lynne had never yielded to expensive electronic paraphernalia to anywhere near the same extent, which is why his work was admired by rock 'n' rollers of Dave Edmunds' discernment. George came around too when, while they were getting to know each other, he and Jeff "drank red wine for a year and a half".[332] After confessing to his new chum that a drum machine had been used to "toughen" *Gone Troppo*, George unburdened his own dislike of automation in music. He'd recently added "a few choice modules"[59] to FPSHOT, but admitted, "I prefer the old components and spending a friendly weekend getting the manual mix you want just as much as I prefer my ancient Fender Strat."[59] He wished for "all these whales stuck in ice – namely the music industry – to release all these people from feeling guilty for not using a synthesiser and not being able to programme it," which forthright Lynne crowned with, "Don't even bother learning; just play the bleeding piano."[333]

In Jeff, George found "the perfect choice", while if Jeff "could've picked one guy I wanted to work with, it would've been George."[168] With the compatible Lynne, George prepared to contradict his 1982 retirement statement with a new album – and, although Mr Average would not be made aware of this undertaking until the last minute, the wheels had been cranked into motion long before. Even the thought of publicising it was almost inviting enough to erase flashbacks of how ghastly such a duty could be.

This was all very well, but was a comeback actually tenable? Although George had been quite actively consolidating his other professional and recreational interests since *Somewhere In England*, when he'd materialised to defend Madonna it was as a ghost from the recent past, detached from a life where you got up, went to work, got home and went to bed. Symbolic of grass-roots disaffection with George was the downsizing of a Harrison fanzine from Glasgow that went by the title of *Soft Touch* to a generalised Beatles tract, because, wrote editor David Dunn, "I've found there is no real interest in George Harrison. I personally find the personality of George Harrison most unappealing and depressing. His inactivity has led me to the conclusion that it's just not worth doing a fanzine for him."[334]

Among the Bob Dylan homilies quoted by George was "I become my enemy the instance that I speak."[315] Fuelling rumours that were to paint him in the same psychotic colours as housebound Pink Floyd founder member Syd Barrett were reported remarks like, "I plant flowers and watch them grow. I don't go out to clubs and partying. I just say at home and watch the river flow."[335] Even brother Peter would "hardly ever see George socially these days".[304] Onto George's shoulder, therefore, was pressed Lennon's mantle of the Howard Hughes of pop. Instead of that noted recluse's bottles of urine and yard-long fingernails, bored tabloid hacks had Harrison defecating on a Kuppaqulua khazi customised to play 'Lucy In The Sky With Diamonds' whenever its seat was raised. In as late as 1990, a laughable "investigation" by one Sunday newspaper had George as a cocaine abuser who shied from appeals to help clean up the "floating sea of drugs" with which Henley was awash. Worthy of Peter Sellers was George's insistence on taking herbal remedies for a minor ailment, causing an orthodox MD to snap shut his black bag and storm off testily straight into a Friar Park broom cupboard. When the juke box malfunctioned, it was repaired by an artisan brought blindfold to the mansion by the secretive Harrison's minions. Rabbits would peer indifferently at squealing 140mph burn-ups in either a Porsche or Ferrari racer on a ten-mile circuit winding around the estate.

The latter distortion of a dull truth had grown from George's infrequent spins through the woods, but "It's all very slow speed around the garden, you know – tractors and wheelbarrows and things like that."[22] It was hard fact, however, that George had contested a £50 fine imposed by a Brentford magistrate after he was hooked in his lead-free Porsche 924 for speeding at "only" 84mph – police claimed that it had been over 90mph – on the M4 motorway to London.

Like the Loch Ness Monster, there were unofficial sightings, too, of George sipping tea in a Birmingham hotel lounge with Jeff Lynne, backstage at a Wembley concert by Simon And Garfunkel, and at the respective birthday parties of Elton John and Dot Mitchell, landlady of the Row Barge in Henley. At the height of the revels in this West Street pub, he bade the to hostess close her eyes and hold out her hand. "Have a happy birthday," he said, dropping three valuable rubies onto Dot's palm.

At his other domicile, *The Honolulu Advertiser* noticed his presence at the occasional art exhibition in Hawaii, but more uncaring were those organs in Queensland whose coverage went beyond paragraphs about George watching the Australasian Grand Prix. His comings and goings on Whitsunday Island would "become the world's worst secret. It seems everybody in Australia knows about it and they're starting to come down in droves to stare at it. it's turning into a wallyworld and there's no way I'm going to live in it."[336]

The sale of this retreat narrowed George's domestic options and reinformed the press-inspired concept of him as "the Hermit of Friar Park". Nevertheless, although his so-called seclusion had been aggravated in part by the horrible release of John's spirit, fear for his own safety had mutated to a blithe fatalism that enabled him not only to show up at Dot's party or a sculpture opening in Lahaina but also to pop out to shops around Falaise Square and even from HandMade's office to Chelsea emporia. The years away from the public at large had helped in that. "Thankfully, today's generation really doesn't know much about me or what I look like. Now I reckon I could walk down the high street and there would be very few people who would recognise me, and that's a great feeling."[258]

Prominent in a citrine pullover, he was conducted round Shiplake College, midway between Henley and Reading, by headmaster Peter Lapping. Until he was 13, Dhani had attended the Dolphin School, near Twyford. Representing the antithesis of his father's formal education, this Montessori establishment had a very broad curriculum, including the teaching of French at nursery level, as well as small classes, no uniform and an extremely child-centred set-up. Shiplake had been recommended by Jon Lord and Deep Purple drummer Ian Paice, whose children had gone there after finishing at the Dolphin School. Had Dhani's parents been of Paul and Linda McCartney's self-consciously homely bent, they might have considered one of Henley's state institutions, instead of such a slap-up, fee-paying seat of learning with vast grounds cascading down to a Thameside marina that swelled with supervised aquatic activity during jolly boating weather.

While providing their boy with the best of everything, George and Olivia hoped that "we can instil the right values in our son. It is his nightmare that he should grow up spoiled. No child likes to be singled out."[316] Nonetheless, although it wasn't stressed at home, Dhani couldn't help but become aware of his sire's celebrity, even if – as with John and Sean Lennon – George's "retirement" granted his handsome offspring more paternal attention than most. Most of George's familiars agreed that fatherhood suited him.

Best illuminating the balanced content of the Quiet One in middle life was his authorship of brief forewords to both *Chant And Be Happy*[151] – a learned history of the Hare Krishna movement – and Joe Brown's chirpy autobiography, *Brown Sauce*.[337] With the imposition on his privacy at its lowest level within the parameters of his fame and means, he had "gone about my life like a normal person. Every so often, I see a newspaper saying I'm this, that or the other, but, as Jeff Lynne says, 'It's tomorrow's chip-paper.'"[315]

16 The Trembling Wilbury

The 1980s would end with George as the most engaging and commercially operative ex-Beatle, although the opposition were admittedly both at a personal or artistic low by then. Sibling rivalry had abated with maturity, but it must have been sweet indeed for George not only to score over Paul in the charts but also to hear of his desire to compose with his old schoolmate. It had been a long time since 'Hey Darlin'. After Lennon and Wings, McCartney had teamed up with Elvis Costello, one of the first and most successful new wave ambassadors to make it over the Atlantic. Paul looked at it like this: "George has been writing with Jeff Lynne; I've been writing with Elvis Costello, so it's natural for me to want to write with George...and we're both quite interested in that idea, so if only we could get the shit out of the way and get a bit of sense happening."[338]

The shit to which he referred was the question of how big a chunk of the Beatle money each should receive. Dismissed by one Apple attorney as "a storm in a teacup"[339] was a lawsuit brought by Harrison, Starr and Mrs Lennon against Paul over a deal he'd made whereby six post-Beatle albums he'd delivered to Capitol had rewarded him with increased royalties from the company's Beatles stock. On the line to George in Maui, McCartney twigged that the plaintiffs were "mightily upset – in their minds, it's all for one, one for all."[339]

As well as finding his *Thriller* video "the squarest thing I've ever seen",[187] Harrison was also indignant that Michael Jackson – who'd once joined Paul for two singles – now owned most of The Beatles' publishing rights, feeling that it was "like owning a Picasso". "It was a bit off, the way Michael Jackson bought up our old catalogue when he knew Paul was also bidding. He was supposed to be Paul's mate."[152]

George, Paul and Ringo were also united with Yoko in condemning the ignoble Lennon biography by Albert Goldman, who, having previously dished the dirt on Presley, depicted John as barking mad inside the Dakota after a lifetime of incredible human frailty. Goldman was as twisted in his way as Mark Chapman, but morbid inquisitiveness nonetheless ensured a mammoth return for his *The Lives Of John Lennon*. This was in spite of protests from George – a better authority on Lennon – that its purchasers "don't realise it's the same old clap-trap. People's consciousness is stuck, and the Goldmans of this world can make a hell of a living, a lot of money, for slagging off someone who's dead."[340]

John was missed "because he was so funny"[187] whenever George or any of the others – without prompting now – spoke of past times. Beatle reunions were two a penny these days, not on stage or record but for dinner. Rather than a fashionable Knightsbridge restaurant like San Lorenzo, where whirring Nikons heralded the arrival of professional celebrities, George and Paul – environmental evangelists both – favoured Healthy, Wealthy and Wise in Soho, where plain-clothed Hare Krishna devotees served "proper foods, good balanced stuff – and it's fresh".[151] All three ex-Beatles would dine and chat more often in a Chinese restaurant down London's Finchley Road, where service had once been so much to Harrison's satisfaction that he'd left a tip of £200.

Sustained by what must have been an excellent table, the "reasonably sane"[190] survivors of perhaps the most unique human experience of the century would enjoy companionable evenings of matey abuse, coded hilarity and reminiscence. Removed from financial wrangles, George would "remember a lot of the good stuff. It used to be only the bad, but enough time has gone by for everything to be all right."[315] Everything had long been all right with him and Ringo, but George's relationship with Paul still blew hot and cold. Because he didn't give Paul a bear-hug when both attended an Italian music festival, George felt obliged to affirm on television, "We weren't avoiding each other. Neither of us knew each other was going to be there."[190] Obstructed by journalists when disembarking at Heathrow, George's finding Paul "definitely a bit too moody for me"[341] was more widely quoted.

Back at his place for coffee, Paul was able to fill curious gaps in George's understanding of the Lennon-McCartney pact. Idly singing 'She's Leaving Home' at McCartney's harmonium, George inquired which one wrote what bit. "Then I thought, 'This is stupid. I'm asking Paul about "She's Leaving Home" 20 years later. Who cares, anyway?'"[340] Since a rediscovery of more than 50 of the group's Light Programme recordings, the BBC calculated that there were enough caring listeners to make it worthwhile producing a 14-part Radio 1 series based on these relics.

With Paul and other 1960s icons, mainly American, George was drawn into a television documentary celebrating the anniversary of *Sgt Pepper's Lonely Hearts Club Band*, on which he read a relevant passage from Scott's 'Lay Of The Last Minstrel'. This coincided with the transference of Beatles LPs onto compact disc, on which you could almost make out the dandruff falling from Ringo's hair. The selling of these was but one aspect of the persisting demand for 1960s music and musicians. Beyond re-releases of oldies, there were also *Top Of The Pops* visitations – either on video or in the chicken-necked flesh – by elderly pop stars with their latest releases. As well as perennials like McCartney and Cliff Richard, such old faces as The Kinks, Beach Boys, Steve Winwood and The Bee Gees filled the screens. In 1987, some would try to will Tom Jones to Number One as a verification of the lost value of someone singing a song, as opposed to producing a production. A younger hopeful than that beefcake Welshman, George Harrison had his moment, too.

From the beginning of 1986, his re-emergence as an entertainer became more and more perceptible. A performance in Birmingham's National Exhibition Centre involving Jeff Lynne was a welcome break during sessions for his new album. During the soundcheck, George was hurtling up from Henley in his new black Ferrari to catch what would be no ordinary concert. Also on the bill were other Brum Beat denizens, such as Denny Laine and Robert Plant, all doing their bit for Heartbeat '86, a committee headed by ELO's Bev Bevan to raise money for Birmingham Children's Hospital. As George had discovered with Deep Purple in Sydney, "It's hard to go to a show and just watch it without someone hanging a guitar 'round your neck [and] pushing you on stage."[188] So it was that George – with Plant and Laine – stood stage centre during the finale, belting out 'Johnny B Goode', his fingers barring its over-familiar chord changes.

Not quite a year later, he was up on the boards again whilst on a business trip to Los Angeles in connection with his now-completed album, entitled *Cloud Nine*. Mixing work with pleasure, he and Olivia were in the company of Bob Dylan and John Fogerty, being serenaded by bluesman Taj Mahal in the Palomino Club on Sunset Strip. Emboldened by a few Mexican beers, the males in the Harrison party clambered on stage to delight the other 400 drinkers with an amused rendering of Creedence Clearwater hits, old time rock 'n' roll and Dylan's 'Watching The River Flow', the latter sung by George. A few months later, George was less sure of the words to 'Rainy Day Women' as he intoned them at Wembley Arena during a ragged encore on the last night of Bob's European tour.

George was no stranger to Wembley. On 6 June 1987, 25 years to the day after The Beatles' Parlophone recording test, he made a more formal appearance there among star acts assembled for a show organised by the Prince's Trust, one of the heir to the throne's charities. Contrasting with the processed frenzy of Curiosity Killed The Cat and other young chart-riders, George's spot was as nostalgic, after its fashion, as that of Freddie And The Dreamers on the chicken-in-a-basket trail. Endearingly nervous, in between 'While My Guitar Gently Weeps' and 'Here Comes The Sun', George saluted his *ad hoc* backing quartet of Eric Clapton, Jeff, Ringo, Elton John and Ultravox's Midge Ure on bass. A handshake from the Prince of Wales afterwards had possibly less intrinsic value than "You were good, Dad, you were good"[342] from a round-eyed Dhani, for whom the extravaganza was his first experience of his father as a stage performer. Rather deflating, however, was Dhani's enquiry as to why George hadn't played 'Roll Over Beethoven'.

This was one of the boy's favourite Beatle – and ELO – numbers, because it had been written by Chuck Berry, who'd been discovered obliquely when Dhani heard The Beach Boys' 'Surfin' USA' – derived from Chuck's 'Sweet Little 16' – in the film *Teen Wolf* Applauding his son's taste in pop, George had dug out the 1958 source from his collection while compiling a Berry tape for Dhani's further edification.

The Harrison adults continued to broaden their own cultural and spiritual horizons, respectively booking seats for a South Bank recital of Bulgarian music and a flight to an Indian retreat for deeper penetration into the disciplines of yoga and meditation. The reissue of George's 1969 production of the maha-mantra back in Britain had brought into sharper perspective the threatened closure of Bhaktivedanta Manor. Once on cordial terms with the college's hundred or so incumbents, Letchmore Heath locals had become increasingly uppity about the volume of traffic and noise, especially during the week-long spring festival of Holi. By the mid 1980s, Holi swelled the community by 20,000 worshippers – "But not all at once," protested the manor's president, Akhandadhi Das (Martin Fleming). "Most stay for only and hour or two."[343] When the district council rejected compromise solutions, such as a new approach road, George did not swoop as publicly to the centre's defence as he had over the Regal Cinema matter. His surreptitious intervention hindered but did not prevent the Environment Secretary from ordering the centre's dissolution, just as he had the closure of the Regal.

As well as the tithing of his time and high income to sacred topics, George shared with Cliff Richard a stake in a tax scheme that, launched in 1977, had attracted others in the top income bracket because it enable them to claim a loss of £4 for every £1 invested. Managed by the Southbrook Film Group, the idea was to put money into limited partnerships – called Monday and Tuesday Films – which, with the banks supplying the balance, provided 25 per cent of the finance for three major movies, including 1987 Oscar winner *Platoon*. However, despite appeals to the House of Lords, the Inland Revenue wouldn't allow the depositors to take credit for the entire loss made by the partnerships, thus reducing the chances of similar manoeuvres in the film industry succeeding. For many of those in on it, a decade's interest on the tax due more than doubled the Revenue's claim.

"I hate all the wheeling and dealing,"[272] shrugged George. Leaving more and more poring over figures to Denis O'Brien (who was to leave the company in 1993), he was also adding less creative input into HandMade, which, he'd concluded, hadn't of late "been enormously successful. We have big debts. We can't afford $25 million productions. HandMade Films will continue, but in order to get an audience you have to make one of these big budget blockbuster movies, like *Batman* and *Ghostbusters*, full of crash, bang, wallop."[316] He was nevertheless benevolent enough to accept an invitation to join O'Brien, Bob Hoskins and Michael Palin in a debate staged at the National Film Theatre during a "HandMade On Parade" film season in autumn 1988, although recording commitments necessitated his last-minute absence.[344] It wouldn't be long before George Harrison would wash his hands of HandMade altogether, after a falling-out with the departing O'Brien. However, the partnership was outwardly still a functioning concern when, together with Ringo and another old friend, Donovan, George was scheduled for a cameo in *Walking After Midnight*, a film starring Martin Sheen and James Coburn. Shot partly in Tibet, the Dalai Lama appeared unscripted in one scene.

Harrison and Starr's names cropped up more often in high-society gossip columns than in *Melody Maker* since their most recent albums had failed in the marketplace. With Viscount Linley, they, Steve Winwood, Roger Waters and actor George Hamilton were noticed at a shindig at the Café de Paris. The Queen's nephew was also there when the ex-Beatles were among the vetted guests at Elton John's wife's lavish birthday party in another London night club. However, the royal ears were not there to hear George's after-dinner laudation of Eric Clapton when Elton, Bill Wyman, Ringo, Phil Collins – all the usual shower – gathered at the Savoy Hotel on 7 June 1987 to celebrate old Slowhand's first quarter-century as a professional guitarist. George's best friend was, he enthused, "such a sweet cat. I caught one of his shows just before Easter last year. I stood at the side of the stage, holding up my cigarette lighter for the encore. Really! I love him that much."[59] Although Eric was now estranged from Pattie, both of her former husbands would remain friends with her.

Social diversions apart, George had been so busy on *Cloud Nine* that many exotic plants and shrubs in Friar Park that had been destroyed in an unforeseen hurricane were not immediately replaced. The console labours related to this marginal neglect were not in vain. Released in 1987, *Cloud Nine* was less offensively adult orientated than current offerings by Clapton, Winwood and Dire Straits – a group liked by George. Physically unmarred by baldness or podginess, he brought much of the aura of a fresh sensation to those young enough not to have heard much of him before – especially as, at Warners' request, he'd shaved off a scrappy beard. When he walked into a Burbank record shop, a teenager near the counter cried, "Look! There's that singer!" Turning their heads, her companions saw neither a dotard nor the oldest swinger in town.

Although they'd lately rejected the running order of a Clapton LP as they had *Somewhere In England*, Warners' executives had passed *Cloud Nine* as "a killer sequence of tracks".[162] Selections had been culled from 17 pieces, mastered mostly at FPSHOT. Among these were more "Oriental"-sounding remakes of 'Breath Away From Heaven' and 'Someplace Else'. The only cover version was an update of the James Ray number that George had heard when he visited his sister in Benton in 1963: "I did that song because Jim Keltner got this drum pattern going that was a cross between swing and rock. Gary Wright turned around and said, 'Hey, doesn't that remind you of "Got My Mind Set On You?"' I was so surprised that anyone had ever heard that tune."[59]

Keltner and Wright – who co-wrote 'That's What It Takes' – were but two old hands called to Henley when Harrison "started missing the whole thing of making a record and playing with my mates".[151] Rather than call all the shots, George wanted it to be a group effort, "where you can come up with all your own ideas, and you have other people's ideas and they all mix together and they become a different idea".[277] Also mucking in were comfortable comrades like Clapton, Winwood, Elton John, Ray Cooper, Jim Horn and Ringo, who was "like myself with the guitar. I don't play it that often. Ringo may not play the drums from one year to the next, but...he'll just rock and play just like he played in the old days."[164]

Of earlier antiquity was the Gretsch, dating from the Mersey Beat era, that George – in mirror shades and Hawaiian shirt – gripped on the *Cloud Nine* front cover. The words were not included, because the main writer thought the practice *passé*. This mattered little, however, for George's diction was clear enough. Vocally, he was more consistently strong than he had been before, delving into a hitherto unrealised bass register on the title track, although he still trotted out his Dylanish rasp for 'Devil's Radio'. If his backing singing was not sufficiently "depersonalised", unlimited studio time facilitated the honing of George's every nuance and vibrato as well as the disciplined structuring of instrumental interludes, such as the adroit break in tempo in 'This Is Love'. In its clean breadth of expression, Lynne and Harrison's production was not so pat that listeners were purblind to the quality of the album's raw material, nearly all of which stood tall as basic songs. There was also a healthy tendency for *Cloud Nine* to embrace definite endings rather than fading out.

Pulling from all elements in his musical past, George had come to terms with both The Beatles and his present situation. Other than one more obvious and calculated stroll down Memory Lane, you'd pick up on this "oh yeah", that ascending guitar riff from *Revolver*, a gritty *All Things Must Pass* horn section and a sweep of *Gone Troppo* bottleneck. On the opening track, there were traces of both Cream and a Temptations single from 1969, also entitled 'Cloud Nine', but who minded?

A brake had been applied to the religious lyricism that had hung over him like a mist since 'Within You Without You'. Only 'Cloud Nine' itself – setting human limitations against divine potential – is blatantly spiritual, its title an advance on "Cloud Seven", a pictorialisation of the Seventh Heaven, the abode of God Himself in both Mohammed and Jewish tradition. With the James Ray item and 'Breath Away From Heaven' were two other love songs, 'Fish On The Sand' – with rapid-fire verses – and the brighter 'This Is Love', which had come about when Harrison enlisted Lynne's help on a melody: "He came down with lots of bits and pieces on cassette and almost let me choose. I routined the song with him and we wrote the words together."[59]

Going along when the artist took a breather Down Under for the Adelaide Grand Prix, Jeff also contributed to an opus from a sketchy outline by George on a borrowed guitar with a broken string. The resulting 'When We Was Fab' was a happier invocation and exorcism of The Beatles than the selfish 'Ballad Of John And Yoko' or 'All Those Years Ago'. Unlike 'Blood From A Clone', it was as simultaneously personal and universal as 'Don't Cry For Me, Argentina', 'The Battle Of New Orleans' and other musical encapsulations of historical events both less and more far-reaching than Beatlemania.

To a backing track that included a count-in and period "pudding" tom-toms from Ringo, the composer/producers "overdubbed more, and it developed and took shape to where we wrote words".[59] Interweaved with false clues and negative symbolism – "caresses fleeced you in the morning light" – were odd lines from Dylan, Smokey Robinson and even 'This Pullover' by Jess Conrad, plus "fab! gear!" vocal responses. Musically, it leaned most heavily on the *Magical Mystery Tour* age, with its ELO cellos, a melodic quote from 'A Day In The Life', effervescent 'Blue Jay Way' phasing and a psychedelic coda of wiry sitar, backwards tapes and 'I Am The Walrus' babble. At the song's heart was an F augmented ninth chord common to both 'I Want To Tell You' and Lennon's 'I Want You' off *Abbey Road*. Fab Four trivia freaks will be fascinated to learn that these two numbers are adjacent if you list Beatles songs alphabetically. Moreover, the late Louise Harrison's maiden name was French, while that of 'When We Was Fab' pianist Steve Winwood's mother was Saunders. Like, there's this British comedy duo called French and Saunders. Weird, eh?

The mock significance of 'When We Was Fab' might have overshadowed companion pieces that had more to say, such as 'Devil's Radio', a swipe at tittle-tattlers by one who'd long been one of their victims. Driving Dhani to school, the words "Gossip! The devil's radio! Don't be a broadcaster!" had screamed at George from a church notice-board in Hurst. Another added ingredient as he frowned over the first draft of the song that morning was "that straight-from-the-gate force"[59] of The Eurythmics, a combo whose musical policy and subsequent chart entries had been founded on a truce between synthesiser technology and minor-key human emotion.

George's hook-line sentiment that "it's everywhere that you go/the Devil's radio" was quite sound. Doing most damage is the popular press, which he harangued as "poison penmen" in the middle eight of 'The Wreck Of The Hesperus'. In this musical resistance to dignified aging, George aligns himself to Arkansas blues crooner Big Bill Broonzy, who continued to mature as a working musician until the month of his death.

You wouldn't catch George trudging around European concert halls with an acoustic guitar like Broonzy, but an enthusiastic record company's generous budget guaranteed his active participation in the promotion of *Cloud Nine*. From pretending to be someone else whenever a journalist telephoned, throughout the winter of 1987/8 he – quite often with Ringo – never seemed to be off tabloid pop pages with quotable jocularities and scathing attacks on radio disc jockeys' yap and the latest Top 20. There he was on an ITV chat show with a ponderous quip about the vastness of Friar Park's acreage: "You can stroll 'round my garden in ten minutes – if you're power-walking. If you saunter, it could take half an hour. Swagger? Maybe 45 minutes."[190] He was just as congenial on *Countdown* in the Netherlands and when interviewed by BBC1's omnipresent Terry Wogan. Of more specialist persuasion was a natter about the merits of Rickenbacker guitars over on BBC2.

In America, headlines on the glossy pages of *Newsweek*, *Musician*, *et al*, proclaimed, "Quiet Beatle Finally Talks!" Patiently, he endured three hours of shooting to give 15 minutes' low-down on *Cloud Nine* for CBS television. Worse was an interview for inclusion in a morale-boosting promo clip for the annual Warners sales conference in Miami, where, as a Briton, his interrogator's running joke about baseball was lost on him. Over a beer and Marlboro cigarette after these tribulations, he'd sign and smile for the pushiest autograph-hunters, listening with a glazed expression to long-winded accounts of how they'd seen The Beatles once.

Cloud Nine was nudging the higher reaches of the US chart when George mounted the podium in New York's posh Waldorf-Astoria

Hotel after The Beatles had been inducted by Mick Jagger at the third Rock 'n' Roll Hall of Fame ceremony. Representing what was left of the group, too, were Ringo, John's widow and Julian Lennon. In the opening sentences of his speech, George made light of McCartney's glaring absence. Although he then assured everybody that "we all love Paul very much", he wasn't as friendly a fortnight later on Australian television, when, while acknowledging that the Capitol lawsuit was at the root of Paul's non-attendance, George railed at what he saw as his fellow Liverpudlian's inability to separate business from the citation. Paul should have made his way too onto the Waldorf stage, heaving with celebrities, for the "surprise" jam session at the end. Perhaps in his honour, Jagger, Harrison and Dylan bunched around a single microphone for a raucous 'I Saw Her Standing There'.

Paul also backed out of an apparent agreement to appear in videos for the *Cloud Nine* singles. George had been slightly disappointed that the non-original 'Got My Mind Set On You' was chosen as the first of these. Furthermore, Warners had so disapproved of its attendant monochrome video – a flirting adolescent couple in a amusement arcade with George, Jeff and Ray performing on a nickelodeon – that director Gary Weiss was instructed to film another in which Harrison was more prominent. Hurriedly, Weiss cobbled together a scenario in which furniture came to life around a seated George, who – with help from a stunt-man – seemed to execute gymnastic back-flips at one point. Admitting that teenagers might not identify so easily with this second attempt, Warners let programmers make up their own minds. *Top Of The Pops* used the "furniture" video, which was shown when 'Got My Mind Set On You' touched its British high of Number Two. Over in the States, it went one better, the first Harrison 45 to top a national chart since 'Give Me Love'.

Not as gigantic a smash was 'When We Was Fab', which, nonetheless, still did better than similar singles by less bankable contemporaries, such as Freddie Garrity with 'I'm A Singer In A '60s Band' and 'This Is Merseybeat', a medley from The Merseybeats (who also showcased 'Got My Mind Set On You' in their cabaret act). With greater resources and lingering hip sensibility, George could afford the expensive services of Godley And Creme to direct a video in which he and Ringo donned the *Sgt Pepper* costumes that the older Starkey children had been borrowing for fancy-dress parties.

Along with Elton John, Ray Cooper and a left-handed bass player dressed as a walrus, Jeff Lynne had had a cameo in the video for 'When We Was Fab'. With his part in steering the former Beatle back into the spotlight recognised, Jeff was much in demand these days. A considerable accolade for him was a contract to produce most of *Mystery Girl*, the LP that restored Roy Orbison to the charts. Even during the *Cloud Nine* sessions, he'd worked on an album by Duane Eddy, from the same pop generation as Roy, who'd re-entered the hit parade after a much longer absence than Harrison, thanks to a link-up with The Art Of Noise. For all their wrinkles, hair loss and belts at the last hole, old timers like Orbison and Eddy intrigued the young and artistically bankrupt. The Art Of Noise also had success with Tom Jones, and Marc Almond's duet with Gene Pitney was a UK chart-topper in 1989.

George Harrison needed no such affinity. Nevertheless, he was pleased to put both his musical skills and private studio at the disposal of Duane Eddy, whom he'd listed as "favourite instrumentalist"[345] for the *NME*'s "Lifelines" annotations in 1963. His was the good-measured slide touch-ups on two or three tracks cut by Duane Eddy in Henley. For those who hadn't heard much of Duane since the early 1960s, his Friar Park output – with twangy guitar high in the mix – was much how they may have expected him to sound in the 1980s.

As he'd postponed work on *Cloud Nine* in order to cater for the peripatetic Eddy, so Jeff had left off *Mystery Girl* – and his work on tracks by Tom Petty – to oversee one final and trifling detail of his prior commitment to Harrison, a bonus number for the European twelve-inch of 'When We Was Fab'. Roy Orbison was on the conversation's edge when the two Englishmen discussed this over luncheon in Los Angeles. That Roy was so well versed in the Monty Python genre of British comedy staggered George, with whom Roy had had only sporadic contact since the ravages of Beatlemania. The closest encounter of the 1980s had been when Orbison attended a

Sgt Pepper party at Abbey Road at which George did not show. George was elated, however, when the jovial balladeer volunteered to sing with him on this extra track. Well, it might be a laugh. Fun is the one thing that money can't buy. Anyway, it was doubtful whether anyone would bother playing a throwaway B-side.

It wasn't worth booking anywhere expensive, so George – impressing Roy with his proud familiarity – telephoned the Santa Monica home of Bob Dylan, whose "little Ampex in the corner of his garage"[333] was available the next day.

Duly rolling up late the following morning, Roy shook hands with Tom Petty, whom Jeff and – to a lesser extent – George had assisted in his production of a Del Shannon album in 1987, after Petty's group had backed Dylan on the tour that had terminated at Wembley.

From initially merely providing refreshments, Dylan later lent a hand when Harrison – with his B-side only half-finished – said, "Give us some lyrics, you famous lyricist."[340] To Bob's reasonable enquiry as to the subject matter, "I looked behind the garage door and there was a cardboard box with 'handle with care' on it."[340] At that instance, George may have had a mental flash that 'Fragile (Handle With Care)' had been the title of the first single by Mark Peters And The Silhouettes, with whom his far-distant Merseyside acquaintance Dave May had played.

By the evening, flesh had been layered on the skeleton of 'Handle With Care'. George had added what he called "a lonely bit"[333] for Orbison, who'd long been stereotyped as a purveyor of woe, while Dylan wheezed his trademark harmonica on the fade-out. Cemented with an ascending five-note riff, 'Handle With Care' – about a pop idol's personal vulnerability – could only have radiated from a caste thus cosseted and deprived. At this juncture, the gathering was not intended as any permanent "supergroup", that most fascist of all pop cliques. Fulfilling a suggestion made to George by chat-show host Michael Aspel for "getting a bunch of oldies together",[190] it was more like Roy's 'Class Of '55' on *Homecoming* – just the ancient gods at play over a long afternoon among the cedared slopes of the Hollywood hills. Roy spoke for everyone when he said, "We all enjoyed it so much. It was so relaxed. There was no ego involved and there was some sort of chemistry going on."[346] Apart from certain distinctive voices heard on it, none would suppose that 'Handle With Care' was special. Would they?

On the next day, Roy left for a one-nighter in Anaheim, near Long Beach; Bob carried on preparing for a summer tour; and George slipped over to Warners with the new tape. There it was pronounced too potentially remunerative to hide its light under a twelve-inch 45. In conference with Jeff afterwards over a quantity of Mexican lager, the idea of cutting a whole LP with the 'Handle With Care' quintet surfaced. When the two skidded up to his house with the plan, Petty jumped at the chance while, over the phone, Dylan's affirmative was blunter. That evening, Jeff, George, Tom and their wives drove down the coast to Anaheim to put it to the Big O. "Roy said, 'That'd be great,'" remembered Petty. "We watched Roy give an incredible concert and kept nudging each other and saying, 'Isn't he great? He's in our band.' We were real happy that night."[338]

When intelligence of this new combination spread, other musicians in the Harrison circle wondered why they hadn't been invited to join in, but the album, completed over the summer of 1988, "worked because it was so unplanned,"[346] estimated Orbison. Most of the composing took place at the hospitable LA home of The Eurythmics' Dave Stewart, then Dylan's producer. Nourished by a continuous running barbecue, George's team "would assemble after breakfast at about one in the afternoon and just sit around with acoustic guitars. Then someone would have a title or a chord pattern and we'd let it roll."[340]

With Tinseltown stretching as far as the eye could see under a rind of smog, fraternisation on Stewart's lawn would breed retrospection about the old days. The Beatles may have integrated Roy's 'Oh! Pretty Woman' riff into their concert version of 'Dizzy Miss Lizzie', but would Bob bring up the demo of his 'Don't Think Twice, It's Alright' that Roy had turned down in 1963?

The word "Wilbury" entered the five musicians' vocabulary. It had been an in-joke during *Cloud Nine*, referring to studio gremlins. First, "The Trembling Wilburys" was suggested as a name when, remembered Lynne, he and George had "this fantasy idea. We'd start inventing a group that would have all our favourite people." Ultimately, the vote went to "The Traveling Wilburys".

As its instigator, Harrison was the most avid Wilbury plugger, enthusing about the album at a Warners summit in Eastbourne(!) and on *Kaleidoscope*, a BBC radio programme usually more devoted to Etruscan pottery or Bach fugues. Later, he'd chew over the likelihood of a full-length movie based on the sleeve notes attributed to Michael Palin from a brainwave of Derek Taylor's.

Masquerading as half-brothers sired by the same philandering father – Charles Truscott Wilbury, Senior – the five appeared on the cover under chosen pseudonyms, George's being "Nelson Wilbury". Entering into the spirit of the elaborate prank, 50-year-old Orbison – as "Lefty", the eldest sibling – remarked, "Some said Daddy was a cad and a bounder, but I remember him as a Baptist minister."[340] As to the group going on the road, discussions only got as far as the order in which each member would walk out on stage. George made it clear that he'd "hate waking up in motels in Philadelphia. I'd rather be home." However, he added that, if the others wanted to tour, then "I'd be inclined to do something."[340]

Despite a "Volume One" tag on the cover, no second Wilbury LP was then on the cards, partly because, as Roy explained, "We couldn't repeat the ploy on the record companies the second time 'round."[346] None of the relevant labels had raised any fuss when *The Traveling Wilburys, Volume One* was foisted on them as a *fait accompli*. Nobody wanted to be unpopular. One executive simply muttered something about not standing in the way of history before hanging up on the Wilbury concerned.

Out of step with the strident march of hip-hop, acid house, *et al*, the release of *Volume One* was like a Viking longship docking in a hovercraft terminal. After the songs had been written, only ten days could be set aside for the taping, owing to Lucky Wilbury's forthcoming tour, but any lifting of this restriction might have detracted from the proceedings' rough-and-ready spontaneity and endearing imperfections. Close in execution to skiffle or rockabilly, the items on *Volume One* were for George a V-sign at all that he detested about 1980s mainstream pop: "They represent the stand against this horrible computerised music."[316] As producers, he and Jeff had respectively combined the adequate and the pedantic in the mix, with George recognising that his colleague was "a craftsman, and he's got endless patience. I tend to feel, 'OK, that'll do' and go on, and Jeff'll be thinking about how to tidy up what's just been done."[59] Although it was the product of gentlemen who could afford to lark about, minor experiments – such as hired drummer Jim Keltner's whacking a refrigerator's wire grille with brushes – reflected the LP's do-it-yourself air.

Orbison's only contribution as featured singer, 'Not Alone Any More', crystallised the tenor of the production by making its point without the cinematic strings, sombre horns and wailing chorale generally associated with 'Running Scared', 'It's Over' and other of his hits. The chugging guitars, Jeff's one-finger crash-diving fairground organ, some staccato sha-la-la-las and a secondary riff of unison piano and guitar were just as effective. On 'Dirty World', George got Roy to unloosen that querulous 'Oh! Pretty Woman' growl like a conjuror reproducing a popular trick to amuse children.

Not the most prolific of songwriters, the obliging Orbison had contributed least to the ten numbers selected. Nevertheless, these were credited to the Wilburys as a whole, rather than individual members. A study of UK publishing rights, however, reveals that to Harrison was allocated 'Handle With Care', the Beatle-esque 'Heading For The Light' and the appositely titled closing track, 'End Of The Line', which he described as "sort of like Carl Perkins says, '[sings] Weeeeeell, it's aaaaaall right!' If you're going to be an optimist, then it's going to be all right. If you happen to be a peg-legged old pirate who's trying to make an album, it's still all right."[333] Vocally, other than specific the lead singing required on 'Not Alone Any More' or Dylan's 'Tweeter And The Monkey Man', items were communal efforts, with verses, backing harmonies and bridges more or less doled out equally.

When *Volume One* was finished, the personnel returned to individual projects – although, bound by the Wilbury "brotherhood", each performed services for the others. *Mystery Girl* was completed at Friar Park, with George on acoustic guitar. He also assisted on both

Tom and Jeff's first solo albums. As for Bob, George noted that "people close to him say that, since the Wilburys, he's started writing really good songs again".[340] Among these, apparently, was an offering for the follow-up to *Mystery Girl* that was never recorded because of the ill-starred Roy's fatal heart attack in December 1988.

It was to be expected that the morbid publicity would boost the Top-40 placings of both the slipping 'Handle With Care' single and the LP. Whereas the video for 'Handle With Care' had had all five grouped around an omni-directional microphone, in the one for 'End Of The Line' Roy's spiritual presence was symbolised by a guitar propped up in a vacant chair. Certain media folk speculated on who would be the new Wilbury. In the running were Roger (formerly Jim) McGuinn, Carl Perkins, Jaime Robertson and Gene Pitney. "I hope there will be another Travelling Wilburys record," said George. "It was one of the most enjoyable things I've done. I don't really have a desire to be a solo artist. It's much more fun being in the Wilburys."[316] In April 1990, he, Lynne, Petty and Dylan were recording together in a rented house in Bel Air for what was presumed to be *Volume Two* but was actually entitled *Volume Three* when eleven selected tracks were issued later that year, after a mere three weeks spent in the studio.

Apart from a "best of" package yet to come, the Wilburys had seen out George's commitment to Warners. Hot property again, George contemplated options that only one of his means could consider. He could, for instance, sign up for no more than one album at a time, or – cutting out middlemen – press his own records and distribute them by mail order. In no hurry to snap at the heels of *Cloud Nine*, it could be years before the next Harrison album hit the shelves, reckoned HandMade insiders.

As a possible pointer to future methodology, shortly after Warners had released *Cloud Nine*, Genesis Publications quietly made available the long-scheduled *Songs By George Harrison*. This was limited to 2,500 copies, each in a leather box for Keith West's hand-lettered interpretations, with a pull-out wallet for a record of the three tracks axed from the *Somewhere In England* epoch, plus an in-concert cut of 'For You Blue' taped during the 1974 US tour. At over £200 a time, you wondered how anyone dared place a needle on it. "It's expensive, yes," conceded George, "but in a world of crass, disposable junk, it's meant to be a lovely thing."[59] Enough people thought that it was for West to mix his colours for a second volume.

With similarly unassuming commercial ambition, George – with Ray Cooper, The Bee Gees and Eric Clapton – had concocted some music for a BBC series based on a David English story about cricket-playing rabbits. A new composition with Tom Petty entitled 'Cheer Down', deemed unsuitable when put before Clapton, was recorded by George himself, to be heard over the closing credits of the Mel Gibson flick *Lethal Weapon 2*.

The first manifestation of George's post-Orbison Wilbury sessions had been the release of 'Nobody's Child', a cover of the ancient Tony Sheridan And The Beat Brothers standby. This was taped two days after Olivia had asked her husband to consider recording a number for the appeal she'd set up – with assistance from Maureen Starkey, Linda McCartney and Yoko Ono – after the Romanian earthquake in May 1990, which could be felt as far away as Moscow and Istanbul. With help from Joe Brown, George dug the first bit of 'Nobody's Child' from his memory but wrote a new second verse relevant to Olivia's shocked inspection of an orphanage 100 miles from Bucharest, "which had had no food for three weeks, building packed with small children often two to three to a bed, left naked because there is no one to wash or dress them."[349] She and George were to house a deaf Romanian orphan and his adopted British mother on Friar Park Estate. Hot off the press, copies of 'Nobody's Child' were on sale at Henley Regatta Bazaar on 28 July. "If you can't help your own wife," reckoned George, "then it's a pretty bad state of affairs."[349] In support of the compassionate Mrs Harrison's Romanian Angel Appeal was a compilation LP – with 'Nobody's Child' the title track – organised by George and featuring mostly his old musical confreres, among them Clapton, Starr, Dave Stewart, Elton John, Duane Eddy and Paul Simon.

Far less likely than a *bona fide* new Harrison album was George's full-time return to the stage, in spite of Cynthia Lennon suggesting that the remaining Beatles would re-unite for a concert at Berlin's Brandenburg Gate on 9 October 1990, the day on which John would have turned 50. Unlike Paul and Ringo, George had had nothing to do with an international tribute to Lennon at Liverpool's Pier Head in May 1990. Sanctioned and partly compered by Yoko, no Mersey Beat groups who'd "got drunk with him"[350] had been invited to warm up for the likes of Lou Reed or Australia's Kylie Minogue. With sound reason, George considered the event to be "in poor taste".[350] There were, however, plausible reports of the four living Wilburys playing unannounced acoustic floor spots in folk clubs in and around Los Angeles as "The Traveling Ovaries".

Such weapons as programmable desks and graphic equalisers in the war against adverse auditorium acoustics couldn't erase George's memories of touring in 1974 with "people...trying to shove drugs up my nose"[321] and the perturbing psychological undertow compounded by an admirer "going absolutely bananas"[321] feet from the stage at the Prince's Trust gig: "He was so fanatical and kept staring at me with this manic glint in his eye."[321] With gun-toting Chapman and his sort shadowing his thoughts, George had decided that, "even if I had been considering coming back to do large shows, the sight of this guy made me think twice."[321]

From a person or persons with an apparent grudge against Olivia, a series of poison pen letters – signed by "Rosalind" – began to arrive at Friar Park in 1989. As they threatened death – "Time you went", "Your time is up" and so forth – the matter was serious enough to call in the Thames Valley CID, whose Detective Sergeant Robert Harrington would "feel sorry for [George]. He is a recluse and just wants to be left alone."[351] Misinterpreting a 1989 Harrison biography, one of the letters implied that George was an admirer of Adolf Hitler. "The world is full of strange people who do stupid things like this,"[352] commented Peter Harrison, who'd been ignorant of the hate mail until the story was leaked by a London police officer to a national newspaper.

Similarly ugly occurrences of cold terror did not thwart Paul or Ringo, who in 1989 each chanced their first tours since John's slaughter. The show went on for others, too. The diverse likes of Jefferson Airplane, The Who, The Fugs, The Applejacks and the Stones were also poised to do it again. George, however, didn't "really see myself as being out there like the George Michaels or the Mick Jaggers. I'm not putting them down, but they have performing built into them. The most I ever did was the Liverpool leg. Well, I just don't have a desire to be a pop star, and acting – well, that's the most boring job in the world. I just want to be a musician, somebody who writes songs and makes music."[315]

On the telephone during the *Sgt Pepper* anniversary hoo-hah, George Martin – knowing his man – had re-assured him by saying, "Never mind, George. It'll soon be gone and we can go back into our shells."[315]

Cloud Nine and a spot on *Wogan* with Olivia (in connection with the Romanian appeal) had drawn out the agony, but in 'Just For Today', the slowest, saddest song from *Cloud Nine*, George poured out his need to escape these distracted times. At least he was free to run away to Maui, although he wasn't so far gone from the discontent festering on the claustrophobic streets of Brixton in the late 1980s not to comment, "It's terrible. It's like hell."[164]

His comments could also have applied to a seldom-visited Liverpool. Whereas once Daniel Defoe had praised "the fineness of its streets and the beauty of its buildings", boarded-up Georgian houses in its centre awaited flattening to make room for characterless skyscrapers, shopping precincts and multi-storey car parks. Many old haunts – including the Cavern – had either been demolished in the process or refurbished for re-opening as cabaret clubs or restaurants. More profitable than ever were the Merseyside Tourist Board's guided Beatle coach trips around suburbs where the "four lad who shook the world" had spent their formative years. Who'd have cared otherwise about a corporation terrace swallowed in Speke? In 1990, George Harrison was paying £300 less poll tax than pensioners Matthew and Edna Kermode, who moved to 25 Upton Green in 1983. This still-expanding overspill estate might have been home to the heroine of *Letter To Brezhnev*, a film of harsh, dead-end realism that, for George, "resurrected my original belief in the character of the Liverpool people. It is a fantastic example of how someone with no money and no hope can actually get through that."[188]

As always, Liverpool looked after its own. In the Anfield silence in the week after the Hillsborough tragedy, tears filled the eyes of elderly supporters. For some, Gerry's 'You'll Never Walk Alone' – the Kop choir anthem – had been the only pop record they'd ever bought. Their vigil was more widespread than that held outside St

George's Hall in 1980 for John Lennon, or at the Pier Head tribute a decade later that George had ignored. Partly, this was because the 95 ordinary people killed in the swollen away-match stadium had been closer to home than the Beatle spirited away to the New World. Lennon's three mates had long flown the nest, too. Although posters of Paul's 'My Brave Face' single were defaced with a day of their appearing in the city centre, McCartney was the only known Beatle "friend" of the University's Popular Music faculty and other local projects. He was also the only one to bother with a few words of printed encouragement in the souvenir programme for the inaugural evening in May 1989 of Merseycats, a committee formed by Don Andrew to facilitate reunions of Mersey Beat groups in support of KIND (Kids In Need and Distress), a group which provides activity holidays for seriously ill and handicapped local children.

The venue was the Grafton Rooms, scene of many a rough night in the early days. Old friendships and rivalries were renewed as groups and fans united in a common cause. Among those on the bill were The Undertakers, Faron's Flamingos and The Fourmost, each containing some if not all of their original members. Headlining were The Merseybeats, who, like The Beatles, had lost a player to the Grim Reaper. Taking their late drummer's place was Pete Best. After a quarter of a century's deliberation, he'd decided that one of Mr Epstein's suggestions following his ousting from The Beatles – that he join The Merseybeats – wasn't such a bad idea after all.

The ecstatic 2,000-strong audience – possibly the real stars of the occasion – included a high percentage of middle-aged Cavern dwellers rabidly recollecting lunchtimes spent underground. Mike McCartney and members of The Roadrunners, Mark Peters' Silhouettes and like 1960s beat combos were also spotted in the throng. A couple of the acts weren't as wild as they might have been owing, perhaps to years of cabaret taming, but, following the advent of monitors and high-tech PA systems, no Mersey Beat groups were ever so loud and clear. Neither were any seen so well, courtesy of giant video screens erected on either side of the stage, where they played before a mock-up of the graffiti-covered Cavern wall and, to their left, a ghostly photo enlargement of Rory Storm.

Pete Best smoked and chewed gum from a ringside table until his time came. I couldn't help wondering what that solitary mister was thinking as group followed group, particularly when The Undertakers were joined mid set by Lee Curtis, into whose All-Stars Pete had been absorbed immediately after he had left The Beatles. In the All-Stars, too, had been Beryl Marsden, whose unscheduled three-song spot at the Grafton confirmed that she should have represented Merseyside womanhood in the 1960s charts, rather than a lesser talent like Cilla. When the grippingly raw vocals of grey-headed Geoff Nugent brought The Undertakers within an ace of stealing the show, I was also questioning whether in Jackie Lomax they'd chosen the right man to be lead singer back in 1961. Closing the night's entertainment, the venerable "Panda-Footed Prince of Prance" led his Flamingos through 'Do You Love Me', the sure-fire smash that he'd let slip through his fingers in 1963 when, so the story goes, he dictated its lyrics to Brian Poole for the price of a double whiskey.

Hip-shakin' Faron no longer had the figure for such gyrations. He looked his age, even if he didn't act it. Nature had been kinder to Pete Best, however, who enjoyed the biggest ovation of the evening, even eliciting a few screams. Pop is unfair and erratic. Mersey Beat had hinted at a golden future for Best, Faron, Beryl Marsden and Lee Curtis, but, as Bill Harry gloomed, "The cream doesn't necessarily come to the top in this sort of business." Arbitrary isolations, a mislaid telephone number, Larry Parnes' extended lunch break, a drummer's hangover, a flat tyre – all of these unrelated trivialities can trigger changes affecting the entire course of the career of a musician, even one with the tenacity of George Harrison.

A brief chart entry, a one-shot record contract and even an encore were once sufficient to feed hope. Often, without vanity, mere awareness of your worth in the teeth of ill luck was enough, although with every passing day you were less likely to become The Beatles. You had the right haircut, clothes and accent at the wrong time. The bass player leaves. A band who used to support you turns up on *Top Of The Pops*. If only there hadn't been a power-cut when Brian Epstein was there. If only the singer hadn't had a sore throat at New Brighton Tower. If only we hadn't lost our way...

17 The Anthologist

After the Romanian Angel appeal, 'Nobody's Child' and an interrelated appearance by the Harrisons on BBC1's chat show *Wogan*, things went as quiet as they had during the post-*Gone Troppo* period. In the following years, George put his head above the parapet rarely, if memorably.

Yet if he'd never been seen again after *Cloud Nine*, George Harrison would still have continued to preoccupy countless devotees, despite certain of them considering that it was his misfortune not to have died after shedding what they could presume to be the bulk of his creative load. However, other believers would feel that he almost owed it to them to reappear as if from Rip Van Winkle-esque slumber, rejuvenated and contemporary, thus debunking the myth of either an artistic death or the spending of final world-weary years in religious contemplation.

Meditation, gardening, recording, watching *Brookside* or whatever else George Harrison gets up to in the privacy of his own home – as long as he doesn't break the law – and the length of time he spends doing it is no more everybody else's business than the activities of Joe Average outside working hours. If everybody else disagrees with that, then it's conceivable that George might envy not so much Mr Average as St Francis with his "hidden solitude where I can listen in loneliness and silence to the secret treasures of God's conversation".[356]

A pop star, however, isn't either a nameless gazer from a commuter train in the rush-hour or a mediaeval anchorite but one whose face peers at you from half-page newspaper advertisements graciously inviting you to worship him on the public stage. If he elects not to bother with in-person appearances, then he'll ensure that record-shop windows bloom with the splendour of every latest disc he deigns to issue – and for his fans, whether there from the beginning or 'Got My Mind Set On You' latecomers, every new George Harrison release remains a special event.

As the substance of these have become progressively more autobiographical, pundits and fans alike have been increasingly more intrigued about what makes him tick, even when he himself wouldn't tell them, as he didn't during the ripplings of *Gone Troppo*. Although Harrison had been a willing enough interviewee in order to allow *Cloud Nine* the best possible chance, he didn't have to be. He could have remained remote and still sold enough records to more than break even. He certainly didn't need the money Why should he have felt bound to give it some showbiz? Why should he have felt obliged to set himself up as a target for media snipers? Was it really incumbent upon him to justify his artistic conduct or clarify more obscure lyrical byways?

Why waste such effort when all you have to do is let someone like me do it for you? However, I can only go so far before the amount of space I've been allocated runs out. If you want any more, you can write it yourself – but if you think you'd derive deep and lasting pleasure from a study and comparison of, say, on-stage utterances of each stop on George's twelve-date Rock Legends tour of Japan in December 1991 with Eric Clapton, please write to a magazine called *Beatlefan* which caters for anyone with an insatiable appetite for all things Beatle as it uncovers the distant past whilst keeping as intricate a pace with the present.

Beatlefan is published in the States,[357] where Beatlemania lasts for all eternity, as opposed to the mere lifetime experienced by the British faithful. Thanks to my authorship of *The Quiet One*, *Ringo Starr: Straight Man Or Joker?* and *Backbeat* (a tie-in to the 1994 biopic of Stuart Sutcliffe), I have been an honoured guest at many US Beatlefests, every one dwarfing even the Merseybeatle event.

The Union's politicians got in on the act, too, during 1996, the year of the presidential election. A well-timed if incredible story was leaked about swingin' Bill Clinton as a University of Oxford student visiting a Liverpool pub and wading in when Ringo was attacked by a crowbar-wielding drinker. To counter this astute attempt at image-polishing, Republican candidate Bob Dole purportedly considered utilising a tape of 'Taxman' in his campaign meetings.

That North America loves the Beatles so demonstratively explains why both George and Ringo had separate cameo roles in the US cartoon series *The Simpsons* in the 1990s and why Starr's aptly-named All-Starr Band – embracing at various times Dr John, Todd Rundgren, Dave Edmunds and key members of bands such as The Who and The Eagles – covered the United States more extensively than any other territory. The troupe was formed in 1989 to join the likes of The Beach Boys, The Who and The Monkees on the nostalgia circuit – for, although the 1992 edition featured a couple of tracks from the new Ringo studio LP *Time Takes Time*, if I'd gone to an All-Starrs recital, what would I have wanted to hear? Ringo's excerpts from his album didn't make him a current challenger again, partly because his fans, old and new, will always clap loudest for the sounds of yesteryear.

In many respects, the future was the past all over again. Whether The Fourmost on the chicken-in-a-basket trail or Ringo Starr, cynosure of 20,000 picnicking eyes in some US stadium open to the sky, all that an act still intact from the 1960s needed to do was to be an archetypal unit of its own, spanning every familiar avenue of its professional life – all the timeless hits, every change of image, every bandwagon jumped.

Opening at the same sold-out Yokohama Arena at which Ringo's ensemble had been just over a year earlier, George Harrison's understanding of this was apparent when, at Clapton's encouragement, he sought to experience what touring was like nowadays by easing into his trek around Japan, a country second only to the USA in the intensity of its passion for the Beatles. This was reflected in gross ticket sales of around £10 million and a naming as International Tour of 1991 by subscribers to *Performance*, trade journal of the concert industry.

With no new record in the shops, the lion's share of George's part of each night's proceedings was fixed solely and unashamedly on nothing that wasn't in either The Beatles' or his solo portfolio of favourites – some, admittedly, re-arranged slightly – up to and including 'Cheer Down'. Into the bargain, Clapton – whose "name and likeness can be no larger than any other sidemen's", according to a memo from his record company – slipped 'Badge' and his 1977 paean to Pattie, 'Wonderful Tonight', into his four songs at the central microphone. "Here's another one of the old ones for you" was a sentence that seemed to recur (along with fragments of Japanese) during continuity by George that was more effusive, witty and relaxed than customers who recalled *The Concerts For Bangladesh* movie might have expected. He was supposed to be the Quiet One, wasn't he?

Although 'Love Comes To Everyone' and 'Fish In The Sand' were dropped by the third show, whatever else carried ovation-earning punch – 'If I Needed Someone' (in The Beatles' Budokan show in 1966), 'I Want To Tell You', 'Here Comes The Sun', 'Something' (with the word "jack" inserted *à la* Sinatra after "just stick around"), 'Isn't It A Pity' (which segued into the long coda of 'Hey Jude'), 'Give Me Love', 'All Those Years Ago' (usually prefaced or concluded with a reference to Lennon), 'Devil's Radio' – you name it, George, sipping herbal tea between each song, didn't miss a laser-lit trick. He was also in excellent form, both vocally and instrumentally, as evidenced not so much in what few reviews there were by Western media ("entertaining if unspectacular" said *Billboard*[358]) as in the subsequent *Live In Japan* double album, extracted from highlights of the Osaka and Tokyo stops.

There was to be no falling off in quality, either, during what amounted to his first full-scale UK concert as an ex-Beatle when it was announced on 1 April 1992 that he'd be heading a surprise extravaganza entitled "George Harrison And Friends: Election Is A Celebration" six days later at the Royal Albert Hall. The Beatles had played this venue only once, at the Sounds '63 bash in 1963. However, the questionable acoustics had been improved so much since then that a season there starring Eric Clapton had become almost as established an annual fixture as the Proms.

The actuality of George's show and its underlying purpose turned out to be no April Fool joke. He was doing it to raise funds for – and sharpen the profile of – the Natural Law Party (NLP), an organisation that had smouldered into form in the previous month after the Prime Minister had called a general election. Its manifesto promised "a disease-free, crime-free, pollution-free society", epitomised by transcendental meditation on the National Health and the cross-legged yogic flying that is the best-remembered sequence of the party political broadcast that delayed BBC 1's *Nine O'Clock News* one evening as the population prepared to cross its ballot papers.

In case you haven't yet realised, the proposals of the NLP were traceable to the Maharishi Mahesh Yogi, now in his 80s, and again in favour with George, whose testimonial on behalf of the party explained, "I want a total change, and not just a choice between left and right. The system we have now is obsolete and is not fulfilling the needs of the people."[359] Hear, hear! 60,000-odd people – including me – voted Natural Law when the time came. This was no mean feat for first-timers. Yet, because proportional representation would be harmful to the Conservatives – who were to continue to cling onto power for another five years – not a solitary one of more than 300 NLP candidates fielded was to make a maiden speech in the House of Commons.

Harrison declined an invitation to stand for a Merseyside constituency, perhaps recalling Swami Prabhupada's advice that he'd be more useful as a musician, and for those who slept outside the Albert Hall box office to be first in the queue, his first solo "home game", was more than just entertainment by a pop star. Veiled in flesh, George Harrison was to materialise before them like Moses from the clouded summit of Mount Sinai to the Israelites. Others were more level headed. However, although it took several days for it to sell out, for those who went or wanted to go, the extravaganza was on the scale of a cup final or Muhammad Ali's last hurrah in Las Vegas – even if George's first announcement on the night was, "It's not all it's cracked up to be." Nevertheless, a small army of his famous acquaintances – including Joe Brown, a couple of Beach Boys and TV-actor-turned-pop singer Jimmy Nail[360] – were out in force. His past life flashed before him, too, via the presence of such as Julian Lennon, Pattie Boyd and – soon to die of leukaemia – a remarried Maureen Starkey.

Against a backdrop of the NLP rainbow symbol and amid a heavy fragrance of joss-sticks, George was accompanied by personnel drawn mainly from Eric Clapton's backing group,[361] still warmed up enough by the Japanese expedition to need few rehearsals. Although it wasn't mentioned over footage of these in television news magazines, other media outlets were to note and speculate upon the non-appearance of Slowhand himself. Had he and George fallen out? During the final show in Japan, they'd seemed the best of wisecracking, bear-hugging mates, George hailing his ex-husband-in-law as *"saiko!"* ("the greatest!") and Eric replying, "You're not so bad yourself."

However, while the two may have been regarded as artistic and commercial equals in the east, the over-valued and more omnipresent Clapton had continued to sweep the board in British music-journal polls, with the underestimated George remaining conspicuously absent, as he was in Q magazine's photographic supplement of pop guitarists in 1990. Although there has been very recent reassessment, nothing seemed to have changed since the 1960s, when Eric was god of the Marquee and George only *The Sunday Times'* "passable guitarist (say among the best 1,000 in the country)".[90] In 1992, at Clapton's Albert Hall stomping ground, George may have been aware that there were some determined to originate a myth that his friend had upstaged him, even before the concert. On the other hand, maybe Eric was simply otherwise engaged that particular evening.

In the absentee's stead at the Albert Hall, Eagle and All-Starr Joe Walsh and – heard on the Wilburys' *Volume Three* – Gary Moore[362] – guitarists on a par with Clapton (and Harrison) technically, if not as revered – were to dominate the stage, one after the other, before the intermission, and then pitched in with the main event.

When first the lights went down, however, a short speech about a "new sunshine for the nation" by party leader Dr Geoffrey Clements had summarised both the musical and political significance of the occasion in a telling paragraph: "George's music is the crowning melody of every heart in Britain. Let us build a beautiful new country...to bring joy, just as George's music brings joy to everyone." Laying it on with a trowel, the good doctor then brought, on to a roaring ovation "one of the greatest musicians of all time" to introduce 20 minutes of Walsh and accompanists that included Ringo's eldest son, Zak, on drums.

Before an audience with a preponderance of over-30s – who nonetheless weren't above odd outbreaks of screaming – George, in a plain black suit and white shirt like he'd worn at Yokohama, gave as admirable an account of himself – and delivered virtually the same set – as he had in Japan, but with the additional spice of a dodgy moment at the beginning of 'My Sweet Lord' and spontaneous salvos of applause for specific couplets in 'Piggies' and 'Taxman', the latter's topicality emphasised with an updated libretto name-dropping notable national and world figures (and, like 'Piggies', an additional verse). Less political than sentimental, however, was a clearly moved George calling up Ringo ("a bit of a blast from all our pasts") from a balcony box for the encores, 'While My Guitar Gently Weeps' and a reprised 'Roll Over Beethoven', the latter of which incorporated a drum battle between the ubiquitous Ray Cooper and other percussionists on hand.

Among the next morning's critical dampeners were *The Times*' "middling performance by today's standards"[363] and, worse, *The Daily Express*' complaints about Harrison's "shouted" lyrics as he "massacred" some of the songs.[364] Nevertheless, the London *Evening Standard* reckoned it was "fantastic"[365] and, more cautiously, *The Daily Telegraph* agreed that it "lived up to the hopes of those who had waited 23 years for the moment."[366] However, another "Greatest Night Anyone Could Ever Remember" was, like The Rebels' recital at Speke Legion Hall or The Concerts For Bangladesh, not repeated, despite a still-overwhelmed George's regret expressed in an interview with *Musician* magazine two months later: "Everyone has rehearsed really hard and so much effort has been put into the production that it should be a proper tour." Why it wasn't to be may have had less to do with any disinclination on Harrison's part than the logistics of finding suitable short-notice venues while the other participants were still available.

Among the assembled cast for the finale had been Dhani, now very much a young adult. He had also become a proficient guitarist, so much so that he joined his nervous father for 'In My Little Snapshot Album' from the 1938 film *I See Ice* as a contribution to a George Formby Appreciation Society convention in March 1991 in Blackpool. (Allegedly, Formby songs filled the bulk of an impromptu performance by Harrison *père* to relieve the boredom of fellow passengers during a three-hour delay in a departure lounge at Kennedy Airport.) Moreover, shortly after the NLP recital, Harrison was also heard in nearly as improbable a setting, singing and plinking ukulele on 'Between The Devil And The Deep Blue Sea' in *Mister Roadrunner*, a Channel 4 documentary.

Places where Beatle-spotters would have been more likely to find George were on the stage at London's Hard Rock Cafe, where he sat in with Carl Perkins; on two tracks of *Alvin Lee 1994*, that included a reworking of 'I Want You (She's So Heavy)' from *Abbey Road*; and at Madison Square Garden, where, on 16 October 1995, he was prominent in the jubilee atmosphere of a Bob Dylan tribute concert, paying his respects with 'If Not For You' and 'Absolutely Sweet Marie' (from *Blonde On Blonde*) and then ministering to overall effect when ol' Lucky Wilbury came on in person.

Others with principal roles in the story of the Quiet One had not left its latter-day orbit, either. Far from it. The Shankar family holidayed with the Harrisons in as recently as 1995, and George instigated the resurrection of the Dark Horse label in the following year to issue *Ravi Shankar: In Celebration*, a lovingly compiled four-CD boxed retrospective spanning different aspects of the now quite elderly Padma Bhushan's recording career, from the post-war decade to 1995, and including previously unissued items, some taped at FPSHOT. "Most music-lovers will have heard of Ravi Shankar, the sitar and the classical ragas and talas of India," read George's notes in the 60-page book that came with it, "but how about Ravi the singer, the orchestrator, the innovator or the experimentalist?"

George also turned up at the Oxfordshire home of another innovator and experimentalist, George Martin, to be interviewed for a June 1992 edition of ITV's *South Bank Show* that marked yet another anniversary, marking the quarter-century of the release of *Sgt Pepper's Lonely Hearts Club Band*.

It always boiled down to The Beatles. Yet, nearly two years earlier on BBC2's *Rapido* pop series, George had not only poured coldest water on any idea of a Beatles reunion but had also underlined his boredom with the ceaseless fascination with the wretched group, a fascination that was to escalate with the runaway success in 1994 of *Live At The BBC*, a compilation of early broadcasts. This prefaced an official proclamation of a coming anthology of further items from the vaults. These were to be hand-picked by George, Paul and Ringo themselves for issue over the period of a year on nine albums (in packs of three) as companion commodities to a six-hour documentary film to be spread over three weeks on ITV and presented likewise on foreign television.

Then came talk of the Fab Three recording new material for the project. When asked to comment in a connected news bulletin for London's Capital Radio, I estimated that all they'd be doing was incidental music. Writing in *The Daily Mail*,[367] the late Ray Coleman[368] hoped that it wouldn't go further than this, arguing – with no-one contradicting him – that it wouldn't be the same without Lennon. Six years earlier, George, for one, had been of like mind: "What good are three Beatles without John? It's too far in the past."[355]

After a fashion, Harrison, Starr and McCartney's well-documented regrouping in the mid 1990s wasn't without Lennon. Their labours at Friar Park and Paul's studio in Sussex yielded the grafting of new music onto John's stark demos of 'Free As A Bird' and other numbers on tapes provided by his widow after Paul's conciliatory embrace of her at another Rock 'n' Roll Hall Of Fame extravaganza.

Isn't it wonderful what they can do nowadays? Precedents had been set by the respective superimposition of backing material onto musical sketches by Buddy Holly and Jim Reeves. In 1981, Nashville producer Owen Bradley's skills with varispeed, editing block and sampler had brought together Reeves and Patsy Cline on record with a duet of 'Have You Ever Been Lonely'. A decade later, there arrived a global smash with 'Unforgettable', a similar cobbling together of

Nat "King" Cole and daughter Natalie's voices over a state-of-the-art facsimile of Nat's original 1951 arrangement.

With Jeff Lynne as console midwife, 'Free As A Bird' took shape as near as dammit to a new Beatles record as could be hoped, complete with a bottleneck passage from George, Ringo's trademark pudding drums and both George and Paul emoting a freshly composed bridge as a sparkling contrast to John's downbeat verses. The result was not unlike that of a mordant 'We Can Work It Out'. It was certainly better than certain A-sides released by The Beatles when Lennon was still amongst us.

Yet, for all the amassing of anticipation via no sneak previews, a half-hour TV special building up to its first spin over a remarkable video and the multitudes willing it to leap straight in at Number One as usual, 'Free As A Bird' stalled in second place in Britain's Christmas list when up against 'Earth Song' by Michael Jackson and an easy-listening cover of Oasis' 'Wonderwall' from the amazing Mike Flowers Pops. The follow-up, 'Real Love', reached the Top Ten more grudgingly, having been dogged by exclusion from Radio 1's playlist of choreographed boy bands, chart ballast from the turntables of disco and rave and – despite glaring evidence that they had been fed Beatles music from the cradle – Britpop executants like Supergrass, The Bluetones, Ocean Colour Scene and, most pointedly of all, Oasis.

Who couldn't understand George, Paul and Ringo's mingled disappointment and elation when the million-selling *Anthology* albums paralleled the 'Something'/*Abbey Road* scenario in its affirmation that almost-but-not-quite reaching the top in the UK singles chart was but a surface manifestation of enduring interest in The Beatles that made even their out-takes[369] as viable as any young Britpop outfit's finest work?

Oasis, The Bluetones and all the rest of them were inclined to be more impressed by Lennon and McCartney compositions than anything by the Other Two. This was epitomised by the proud familiarity of Oasis leader Noel Gallagher – and Paul Weller – with McCartney when sharing vocals as The Smokin' Mojo Filters on an arrangement of 'Come Together' for a 1995 charity album for children in war-torn Bosnia.

Yet, for whatever reason, George's *Wonderwall* soundtrack LP caught on too. Oasis borrowed its title for their best-known song, but the influence of *Wonderwall* in particular and George in general was heard most blatantly in the grooves of Kula Shaker, the most exotic of all the new Top-40 arrivals of the mid 1990s, with items like 'Acintya Bhedabheda Tattva', 'Sleeping Jiva' and 'Temple Of Everlasting Light'. Moreover, this London combo's fourth single – issued in November 1996 – was 'Govinda', complete with Sanskrit lyrics and "interwoven through an ancient north Indian folk song", as it said in the press release. More than the stimulus of the Radha Krishna Temple hit on the A-side, the flip, 'Gokula', lived so obviously in a *Wonderwall* guitar riff (from 'Skiing') that permission to use it had to be sought by Kula Shaker from Northern Songs via a direct appeal to the composer himself

Kula Shaker were a further acknowledgment that, as both a Beatle and ex-Beatle, George Harrison's entries in *The Guinness Book Of Hit Singles* count for less than his inspiration for pop musicians from The Zombies to Malcolm McLaren to dip into non-Western cultures. In 1982, a British act called Monsoon had made the Top 50 with 'Shakti (The Meaning Of Within)' and other Indian-flavoured excursions. The impact of Oriental music only seems to hold less allure these days because of the fine line between its ear-catching extraneousness and the real danger of it sounding like a parody of George Harrison, a point driven home in the coda of 'When We Was Fab'.

Beyond pop, where would the Krishna Consciousness Society be without the invocation of George's name and money? Without him, how many of its tracts would be screwed up unread or perused with the same scornful amusement reserved for Flat Earth Society's pamphlets? In a mugger's paradise like Reading, why else is there enough interest for chanting *bhakta*s to process down its main streets on Saturday afternoons now and then and to hold weekly meetings in a church hall also used for judo and amateur dramatics?

From George's lips in 1987 had come a desire "to be able consciously to leave my body at will",[354] but, no matter how far his spiritual wanderings since leaving Liverpool Institute, fellow pupil Charles Shaw would always "see him back in the classroom at break time saying 'Gorra ciggie, Charlie?'". In fastnesses forever unreachable to a bloke like Charlie, George was still as eternally Scouse as any who'd mounted the stage on that ravers' return at the Grafton in 1989 and the other Merseycats functions that have come since. In creating "skiffle for the '90s"[333] in his last studio records, he may have been trying to reach an even earlier epoch. If ever he succeeded, he might just about recognise himself.

However, Harrison doesn't spend as many incognito hours as Paul McCartney in a maudlin haunting of his genesis, although he and Olivia strolled the corridors of the Institute one evening shortly before its conversion – with a massive financial injection by Paul – into the Liverpool Institute of Performing Arts (LIPA).

The one least cut out for showbusiness, George was nevertheless "thankful that The Beatles enabled me to be adventurous. It saved me from another mundane sort of life."[151] What as? An electrician at Blackler's? A "good, medium-weight business executive", as *The Sunday Times* once suggested? A pen-pusher alongside Pete Best at Garston Job Centre? A latter-day Swinging Blue Jean instead of Colin Manley?

I think that, if George Harrison hadn't been a Beatle, he'd have been in the Jeans or in some other Liverpool outfit that may or may not have had hits. At Don Andrew's request, he might have blown the dust from his guitar to belie, for one 1989 night only, some daytime occupation in an office or factory. His moment of glory might have reared up and then subsided until perhaps the next Merseycats function.

Just as fond of hypothesising is George himself, who "would've probably been a better guitarist than I am now, because the fame made me end up playing the same old stuff for years".[189] He'd tell you himself, too, that he "can't write brilliant lyrics – though occasionally some are half-decent – and I can half-decently produce something, but I've never really had any cards to play".[151]

18 The Alien

On Wednesday 29 December 1999, a chilly twilight fell on the small village that is Friar Park. Within the parameters of a remarkable life, it started like an unremarkable night for George Harrison.

All of the staff bar three were away for the Christmas holidays. Dhani was home with a friend from university. The two were staying in one of the lodges. In another still dwelt Dhani's Uncle Harold. George spent most of the evening there before returning to the main house. The mother-in-law had already gone to bed. He and the wife watched some video or other. Olivia lost interest and retired, too. George joined her just after two o'clock.

Whatever the nature of the film and its effect upon his nocturnal imaginings as he climbed the stairs, how could he possibly have suspected that, by dawn on Thursday, his own gore would be splattered and drying on the surrounding walls and carpets, that he'd be half dead in hospital and that Olivia would be raised to unlooked-for heroine status?

Suddenly and unwillingly, he'd be back in even sharper public focus than he'd been during the 'Free As A Bird' episode in 1995. Since then, he'd melted into the background again without quite retreating into neurotically self-conscious seclusion or ostentatious McCartney-esque domesticity.

At an Australian Grand Prix, he took the trouble to amble over to Jenson Button's grid to say, "Good luck" to the young driver for his first Formula One race. They chatted easily, and Button was surprised to be told later by his mechanic, "That was George Harrison, you know." The ex-Beatle was also amenable to speaking learnedly about motor-racing in a *Sunday Times* supplement, *Formula One Handbook*,[375] but "I wouldn't want to be financially involved because only crazy people put their own money into it. It's the many different amazing people and their on-going soap opera that I can view closely without having direct responsibility for. It beats *Coronation Street*." Utterances like this were nevertheless rare, and few apart from regular readers of *Beatles Monthly*, *Beatlefan* and the like could speak with any authority or interest about a seemingly untroubled existence in which nothing much seemed to happen, year in, year out.

As each one passed, the usual hearsay went the rounds. One of the more intriguing rumours was that George had approached Elvis Presley's estate for any unissued tapes of the King singing. The idea was for The Traveling Wilburys to add accompaniment to these as Harrison, McCartney, Starr and Jeff Lynne had to John's 'Free As A Bird' demo (and, since then, The Hollies to an album's worth of Buddy Holly items). Yet, via material given to George by the family, a more likely candidate for ghostly fifth Wilbury is Carl Perkins, taken by a stroke at the age of 65 in February 1998.

A few years earlier, Perkins had recovered from throat cancer. Stray paragraphs in 1997's national tabloids had hinted – correctly – that George had undergone medical examinations for the same malady. Nevertheless, the fragile substance of this particular story was indicated by *The Henley Standard*'s silence about it while chronicling the mundane saga of Friar Park's fraught negotiations with South Oxfordshire District Council about a proposed new swimming pool. Complete with changing rooms and sauna, it was designed to blend tastefully within the exotic waterfalls of the caves. A gesture of defiance against a nosy world was George's refusal to allow the planning committee to inspect the site in person. Why couldn't the application be judged on the basis of the architect's drawings, just as they would be for a householder whose physical presence wouldn't thrill them to the marrow because he was a pop star? Over in Goring, George Michael was up against more or less the same problem, but as a newer comer to both pop and the area he was more co-operative.

Michael also hadn't been famous for long enough to be annoyed rather than flattered by the presence of bootlegs. Despite George, Paul and Ringo's attempts to contain it, the industry of illicit Beatles merchandise thrived as if the *Anthology* albums had never been released. There was even a US magazine, *Belmo's Beatleg News*, devoted solely to unforgiving hours of everything – and I mean everything – on which The Beatles, together and apart, ever breathed. An example germane to this discussion is 1997's *12 Arnold Grove*, conspicuous for George's lead vocal on a demo of 'It Don't Come Easy', an alternative mix of 'Got My Mind Set On You' and 'Every Grain Of Sand', another go at a Bob Dylan obscurity.

At what sort of lunatic were such products targeted? Who had the patience to sit through six takes of the same backing track, a fractionally shorter edit of some Italian flip-side, a false start of 'I Want To Tell You', one more fantastic version of 'It Is He (Jai Sri Krishna)' and then spend infinitely less time actually listening to something like *12 Arnold Grove* over and over again than discussing how "interesting" its contents were?

The overall effect of eavesdropping on such conversations was akin to overhearing a prattle of great-aunts comparing ailments. Yet, to The Beatles' most painfully committed fans, the intrinsic worth and high retail price of a bootleg hardly mattered – and, displayed on the CD rack between, say, *Portrait Of Genius* and *Jacques Brel Is Alive And Well And Living In Paris*, it served as both a fine detail of interior decorating and a conversational ice-breaker.

Beatles talk became more animated among the faithful in 1998 when a borderline case, *The Beatles Live At The Star-Club, Germany, 1962* – the one that Allan Williams had released in 1977 on a vinyl double album – reared up again when Lingasong, a record label of no great merit, announced its intention to reissue it on CD. Reviewing it the first time around, the now-defunct UK pop journal *Sounds* had noted contemporary implications in the back cover photograph depicting 1962 teenagers congregating beneath the club's attributive neon sign, Treffpunkt Der Jugend ("Youth Rendezvous"), before concluding waspishly, "The Beatles couldn't play, either."

That's as may be, but Billy Childish, a leading light of a Medway Towns group scene of agreeably retrogressive bent, had considered it "their finest LP". The artists concerned, however, lacked Billy's objectivity about both the alcohol-fuelled performance and the atrocious sound quality – despite further expensive studio doctoring – of what Kingsize Taylor ("not a friend we hung around with," reckoned George) had taped with a hand-held microphone onto a domestic machine.

So it was that on a mid-week day in May 1998, George Harrison represented The Beatles and Apple in the High Court witness stand before Mr Justice Neuberger, who was to compliment the litigant upon the clarity of his testimony. Leaving his Southport butcher's shop to take care of itself for the duration, Kingsize Taylor for Lingasong had already sworn that he'd been given verbal permission by John Lennon to immortalise The Beatles' late shift at the Star-Club "as long as I got the ales in". Taylor had assumed that Lennon's go-ahead meant that it was OK by the others, too.

That was an easy mistake, smiled George, because "John was the loudest, the noisiest and the oldest [sic]. We didn't ask [Kingsize] to do it. We never heard [the tapes]. We never had anything to do with them – and that's the story. One drunken person recording another bunch of drunks does not constitute a business deal or the right to put out a record." Neuberger agreed, and the elaborate press packs of the CD that had been distributed by Lingasong in false anticipation of victory became instant prized rarities.

A less onerous Beatles duty for George was to be promoter-in-chief of a renovated *Yellow Submarine* in summer 1999 – including additional footage, remixed soundtrack CD, video and DVD, along with associated clothing, memorabilia and toys – to the extent of inviting Timothy White, editor-in-chief of *Billboard*, to Friar Park to hear the retelling of the old, old story. Harrison was to relate it in far more detail, and in doing so would earn about £5 million in a single tax year via the publication of *The Beatles Anthology* book[371] in 2000. Despite a cover price of £35, this title accrued enough advance orders to slam straight in at Number One in *The Sunday Times* book chart, a feat duplicated in other publications around the world.

Its weight on a par with a paving slab, this de luxe "Beatles story told for the first time in their own words and pictures" had been several years in gestation. Transcriptions of ruminations and fallible reminiscences dating from the *Anthology* TV series by Harrison, Starr and McCartney, along with archive spoken material by Lennon and a treasury of photographs, documents and further memorabilia were edited by Genesis in consultation with usual suspects of the ilk of Klaus Voorman, Sir George Martin and, prior to his death in 1997, Derek Taylor.

Overall, a likeable and sometimes courageous account – and an intriguing companion volume to this one – passed the litmus test of any pop life story in that it provoked a compulsion in the reader to check out the records. Nevertheless, it was flawed, mainly because there is little if any anchoring text for that Tibetan monk who still hasn't heard of the group; and, while the surviving Beatles were often painfully honest about events that occurred up to 50 years earlier, it was an autobiography aimed at fans who prefer not to know too much about what kinds of people their idols are in private life. Too many illusions are shattered, and the music may never sound the same.

Just as serious a fault was the fact that, like the televisual *Anthology*, it lacked the perspectives of other living key *dramatis personae*, such as Pete Best, Tony Sheridan, Bill Harry, Pattie Boyd, the Maharishi, Phil Spector, you name 'em. But where do you draw the line? By including all the acts on the same label? Everyone who ever recorded a Beatles song? The foresters who felled the trees to make the paper on which they were written?

Anthology remained a bestseller when, with 60-year-old Neil Aspinall still at the helm, a four-strong team at Apple – now run from one of the white townhouses encircling the central gardens in Knightsbridge – helped to co-ordinate EMI's biggest-ever marketing campaign. Its budget was between £1 million and £2 million in Britain alone and eight million copies of *1*, a compilation of The Beatles' 27 UK and/or US chart-toppers (titled originally *Best Of The Beatles*), were shipped around the world.

The fastest-selling CD ever, *1* was just that in Britain, Japan, Spain, Germany and Canada within a week of being issued in autumn 2001, with over 400,000 customers stampeding into Japanese record shops during the first day. At home, it outsold Oasis' *Standing On The Shoulder* [*sic*] *Of Giants* four to one.

Whether or not looking forward to the past is a healthy situation for any artist is open to conjecture, but it was hard fact that Joe Average was more intrigued by the corporate Beatles than George Harrison or any other individual locked in their orbit.* Ringo's acceptance of this was manifest in his preparation for his next US trek with The All-Starr Band. He contemplated daring some tracks from his 1992 album, *Time Takes Time*, but he knew he'd be lynched if the majority of the set wasn't principally the good old good ones played in, approximately, the good old way, like it was the last time, when *The New York Times* had lauded Ringo's as "the better kind of nostalgia tour".

George, however, wasn't ready to go so gently into that good night. If being only instrumental in setting up a Beatles website, he was more directly involved in www.allthingsmustpass.com, personally answering internet users' enquiries, which ranged from "Does Paul still piss you off?"† to the gauge of guitar strings he used in 1965 to the bleedin' obvious.

In this respect, George was friendly, patient and tolerant, but he derived greater pleasure from doing favours for old friends. In 1997, he joined Ravi Shankar on the VH1 television programme *George Harrison And Ravi Shankar: Yin And Yang*[370] to plug *Chants Of India*, the latest Shankar album. A thoroughly diverting production, what might serve as the octogenarian maestro's recording finale balanced sung lyrics as succinct as *haiku* and instrumental passages of a quirky complexity vaguely reminiscent of Frank Zappa.‡

"*Chants Of India* isn't really sitar music," George elucidated. "It's basically spiritual music, spiritual songs, ancient mantras and passages from the *Vedas*, which are the most sacred texts on Earth."[370]

As well as penning a foreword to Ravi's autobiography,[373] George guested on a Radio 2 series hosted by Joe Brown to discuss influential rock 'n' roll records,* and he would also slide some bottleneck for Bill Wyman on a revival of Kitty Lester's 'Love Letters' during a January 2001 session. Initially, he was less inclined to do so on 'I'll Be Fine Anyway' and the funereal 'King Of The Broken Hearts' on Ringo's latest effort, 1998's *Vertical Man*. "He wasn't in the mood," sighed Ringo, "Two weeks later, I phoned him up from LA just to say, 'Hi,' and, 'What are you doing?'

"'Oh, I'm in the studio, playing with the dobro.'

"I go, 'Oooh, a dobro would sound good on my album.'

"So he goes, 'Oh, all right. Send it over, then.' I really wanted that slide guitar. His soul comes out of that guitar. It just blows me away."[374]

As honorary president of the George Formby Appreciation Society, Harrison himself was impressed by Jimmy Nail's ukulele picking on a Formby-type version of 'Something' with another Friar Park visitor, Jim Capaldi, on bongos. Nevertheless, Jimmy chose a less adventurous brass-band arrangement for the version of 'Something' on *Ten Great Songs And An OK Voice*, a collection of cover versions (now a common vocational ploy).

While admiring Nail's way with a ukulele, Harrison was more seriously in awe of U Srinivas, an Indian who was to the electric mandolin what Shankar was to the sitar. George's recreational listening didn't really extend to much contemporary pop. While he contributed a bottleneck obligato to 'Punchdrunk', an album track by Rubyhorse, a young Irish combo of vaguely Britpop persuasion, he regarded Oasis as "pretty average" and rap as "computerised crap". Indeed, he was as unable to distinguish between different rap artists as a shopper dithering between wedges of supermarket Muzak. "I listen to *Top Of The Pops*," he snarled, "and after three tunes, it makes me want to kill somebody."[375]

This was an unfortunate turn of phrase, in view of the events

---

* This may be illustrated by the raw statistic that, of nigh on 200 Beatles tribute bands in Liverpool alone, only one, Harry Georgeson, pays homage to George alone.

† To which he replied, "'Scan not a friend/With a microscope glass/You know his faults/Then let his foibles pass' – old Victorian proverb. I'm sure there's enough about me that pisses him off, but I think we have now grown old enough to realise that we're both pretty damn cute (!)."

‡ Prior to his death in 1993, Zappa had established himself as a composer in the same league as his "classical" idols Varèse, Stravinsky and Shankar. "Frank was into Ravi Shankar," Mothers Of Invention drummer Jimmy Carl Black told me in May 2000. "'Help, I'm A Rock' [from *Freak Out!*] was a raga."

that followed later, culminating with the agitated oscillations of an ambulance siren two nights before Big Ben clanged in the new century. The horror came to Henley in the likely-looking form of Michael Abram, alias "Mad Mick", a 34-year-old paranoid schizophrenic – from Liverpool, of all places. The wild hair and staring eyes betrayed an inner chaos of delusion and nightmare hallucinations in one deemed "normal" by Lynda, his mother, during an upbringing in a three-bedroom council house.

At 16, he left the local Roman Catholic comprehensive with sufficient qualifications to enter the world of telemarketing. His intentions towards Jeanette, a girl from school, were honourable, in that he stuck by her when she became pregnant with the first of their two children. However, passers-by would hear the couple quarrelling, Michael blustering through rages that climaxed in a Hitlerian screech. There was also something intangibly odd about his behaviour in the streets of Huyton-with-Roby, a twin borough that had descended into seediness since the days when Stuart Sutcliffe had been head chorister in St Gabriel's. Now the church was dwarfed by tower blocks on estates like Woolfall Heights, where a now-jobless Abram lived in tenth-floor squalor after separating from Jeanette.

Their estrangement was traceable to his increased reliance on illegal substances as a form of self-medication. According to Michael, cannabis, LSD, crack cocaine and, especially, heroin helped stay "the spooks" that had been haunting him since he was 18. In collusion with Jeanette, Lynda had made an appointment for him with a psychiatrist at Whiston hospital, where, although diagnosed as psychotic, he remained an out-patient, his afflictions dismissed as curable as soon as he stopped malingering and found the self-discipline to cease his drug habit.

Helplessly, his nearest-and-dearest monitored Michael's accelerating envelopment by a world inhabited by witches, devils and sorcerers. Outsiders gathered that he thought that the Messiah was alive in Marseilles, arriving at this conclusion after poring over *The Holy Blood And The Holy Grail*. First published in 1982,* this

---

* For George, these included the expected set works of Jerry Lee, Elvis, The Coasters, Eddie Cochran and Carl Perkins, plus Richie Barrett's 'Some Other Guy'.

remarkable tome cast uncomfortable light on the origins of Christianity and the very identity of Christ.

Texts that buttressed further unorthodox beliefs included the Bible and the more topical *Centuries*, the 16th-century book of prophesies by Nostràdamus, who equated the forthcoming millennium with global calamity. Abram also received Charles Manson-like messages when replaying certain discs by Bob Marley, Cat Stevens and Oasis on his personal stereo. Then he borrowed his mother's Beatles tapes, and his destiny was taken from him.

"Mad Mick", or "the fifth Beatle", became a familiar and grotesque sight – and sound – in Huyton and further afield. Mocked by children, who dubbed him "Sheephead" because of his shocked, pale-yellow thatch, the local Mister Strange would sit chain-smoking for hours – sometimes naked – on an upturned plant pot on his dismal balcony or roam the shopping precincts ululating Beatles numbers to himself and lost in misery, paranoid self-obsession and lonely contemplation. Who were, he pondered, the four phantom menaces, spreading global consternation and plague, as predicted by Nostradamus? Clinging desperately to his fantasies, he attracted comparatively little hostile attention as a seemingly harmless if unsavoury part of the parochial furniture.

Nonetheless, by 1997 so many shreds of human dignity had been torn from Abram that he was admitted into a psychiatric ward, although he was cast back into the community after eleven days, just as he would be two years later, after allegedly assaulting a male nurse. In an advancing state of bewilderment and panic, he sought fleeting shelter with his poor mother, sobbing – with some justification – "Nobody can help me."

"Alarm bells went off," cried Lynda Abram, "but were missed by doctors and social workers."

If such a condition can be quantified, the solar eclipse in August 1999 correlated with gradually more profound insanity, although a perceived directive in a Lennon song caused him to cease use heroin. Conversely, Michael had convinced himself that he was possessed by McCartney, deconstructing the title of 'Let It Be', for example, as

---

* By Jonathan Cape, written by Michael Baigent, Richard Leigh and Henry Lincoln.

"L" for "hell", "et" for "extra terrestrial" – and "It Be" an indication that he (Abram) was about to contract tuberculosis.

By October, he was focusing his persecution complex on George, seeing the line "It's going to take money" from 'Got My Mind Set On You' – albeit not a Harrison original – as a reference to the £80,000 he understood that someone he knew owed a drug dealer. After the game was up, Michael informed his solicitor, "The Beatles were witches, and George was the leader, a witch on a broomstick, who talked in the Devil's tongue, an alien from Hell." Mark David Chapman had grasped the wrong end of the stick, too, but the stick still existed.

As the incarnation of St Michael the Archangel, Mad Mick had been sent to execute George Harrison by God, with whom he was overheard arguing in a police cell on one of the three occasions that he'd been arrested for minor public-order offences since the eclipse.

On 16 December, Mad Mick bought a railway ticket from Lime Street to Henley. Keeping his dark reflections to himself for now, he stood before a church next to a stonemason's at the Reading Road roundabout at the top of Station Road. He'd learned the whereabouts of Friar Park from a clergyman. Yet, like Richard the Lionheart within sight of Jerusalem but declaring himself unworthy to proceed further, Abram peered through concealing shrubbery over a section of disrepaired wall that was neither as high nor as thickly razor-wired as elsewhere and turned away. Down in Falaise Square, in front of the Town Hall and less than 20 feet from the police station, he burst into ranting song, hoping to stir up an uprising to lay "the House" to siege. "Which house?" asked a bemused onlooker.

"Which house?" or "Witch House"? Fixating on the latter, the wheels of the universe came together for Michael Abram, as one of the psychiatrists who were to testify at the trial deduced. "If he did not kill George Harrison," added the good doctor, "he would be sitting on an upturned plant pot in his flat and made a fool of every time he went out."

A man's gotta do what a man's gotta do. Roman Catholic to the bone and full of superstitious terror of punishment for breaking the "Thou shalt not kill" commandment, Mad Mick hoped that something would prevent him from boarding the train for his second and final journey to Friar Park. He carried about his person a two-foot length of cord, knotted in the middle, and a black-handled knife with a six-inch blade. While his prey's awareness of his role in the tragedy was irrelevant, Michael was certain that Harrison knew what was coming. As it had been with the Crucifixion, the world would be saved by the sacrifice of a divine victim in his prime, be he angel or demon.

Spurred on by a voice in his ear as clear as a bell telling him that "God is with you", Michael affected entry to Friar Park in the graveyard hours of 30 December, undetected by the infra-red sensors, the closed-circuit television cameras and further state-of-the-art installations.

Not long after three, Olivia was jerked from slumber by what she'd describe in court as "the loudest crash of glass imaginable". Had a chandelier fallen? In case it was something more sinister, she broke into George's dreams. He toiled groaningly out of bed and, clad in dressing gown, pyjamas and sockless boots, semi-groped his way down the two flights of a wide stairway. A whiff of cigarette smoke and a blast of colder air from the crack under the kitchen door told him that it was no shattered chandelier.

With throat constricting, skin crawling and heart pounding like a hunted beast – which he was – the head of the household hastened back upstairs, where Olivia was attempting unsuccessfully to telephone the entrance lodge, where the video surveillance equipment was supposed to be under constant observation. However, another member of staff was contacted and instructed to ring the police and try to activate the floodlights. Olivia then dialled 999 herself.

Venturing to the balustrades overlooking the hall, George, frowning with astonishment, caught the crunch of footsteps on shards of glass. With a stone lance from a statue of St George and the Dragon in the conservatory, Michaél Abram had smashed the double patio doors of the kitchen. Now, his leather-jacketed, black-gloved shape stood foursquare, glaring into the gloom above as his victim's face smouldered into form.

His voice should have been shrill with fear, but George asked almost matter-of-factly the identity of the intruder. In contrast came a bawled "You know! Get down 'ere!"

As he had in that hair-raising flight to New York in 1971 and other ugly moments, George let slip a "Hare Krishna" or two (although perhaps 'Help!' or 'Get Back' may have been more appropriate). For a split second, Abram was dumbfounded before interpreting these exclamations as a curse from Satan. Furiously, he breathed hard and charged onwards and upwards.

Aware of the peril a beat before an eerily silent and strong assailant fell upon him, "My first instinct was to grab for the knife," Harrison was to inform the Crown prosecutor. "I tried to get into a room, but the key was stuck, so I decided to tackle him by running towards him and knocking him over. We both fell to the floor. I was fending off blows with my hands. He was on top of me and stabbing down at my upper body."

The commotion drew Olivia out. Freeze-framed for the blink of a bulging eye, Olivia held her husband's bewildered gaze, "one I had never seen before". The slow moment over, she seized the nearest blunt instrument to hand, a small brass poker, and waded in. A snatch at his testicles sent Mad Mick into a unbalanced half-spin, but, boiling over with pain, he sprang like a panther at Olivia, who dropped the poker and fled vainly into the sitting room next to the sleeping quarters. Abram's grip on the back of her neck slackened as George leapt on her pursuer, "but he continued to strike out and he got the better of me".

George and Michael tumbled, wrestling, onto meditation cushions. Beyond the knobbles of the latter's spine, George saw Olivia grab a weighty glass table lamp and bring it down with all her force. "Even as I was swinging," she later recalled, "I was aware and amazed that I was doing so without a drop of malice in my heart."

"Don't stop!" yelled George. "Hit him harder!"

Heaving violently like an erupting volcano, Abram took a few more indiscriminate blows while fumbling for the light's flex, whipping it around the woman's hands and gashing her forehead in the process. Panting too, George "felt exhausted. My arms dropped to my side. I could feel the strength drain from me. I vividly remember a deliberate thrust of the knife into my chest."

Warm liquid welled up inside his mouth. Blood. Lower down, the knife had missed his heart by less than an inch, but a twice-punctured lung collapsed, and so did its owner. "I believed I had been fatally stabbed," he said later. But, even as the blade had penetrated his flesh, he understood that he would be genuinely mourned by Olivia.

With facial wounds that needed stitching, the fight had gone out of Abram as well. "He slumped over me," Olivia later recalled. "I again took hold of the blade of the knife and wrenched it from his grasp."

At that point, two Thames Valley constables – PC Paul Williams and, only six months in the job, 33-year-old Matt Morgans – turned up, not exactly in the nick of time. "The house was in total darkness," so Morgans related to both his sergeant and *The Henley Standard*.[376] "We jumped out of the car and PC Williams went up to the huge set of front doors while I went around the side to see if someone had broken in there. My first thought was that, in my training, we were told you shouldn't touch anything, but then I heard the screaming, so I shouted for PC Williams and went through the window."

There, in a red haze, a bruised and bloodstained Olivia was staggering to the bottom of the hallway stairs.

"I was so new in training, I just went into automatic mode," gasped Matt. "Since then, people have asked me why I didn't call back-up or put a stab-proof on. I met her, and she said the man was upstairs, trying to kill George. He was my immediate priority.

"I saw a guy running across the landing. I thought he was wearing a mask, but it was just the blood running down his face and in his hair from where Olivia had hit him. He was a bit streaky and wild. I shouted to the man to stay where he was and get down on the floor, which he did. I stood over him, and then saw the bedroom light and George Harrison lying behind the door. I left PC Williams to handcuff the intruder and restrain him.

"George was in a right mess. He had been kicked, punched and stabbed. He was conscious, but his main concern was for his wife. He thought the man thought he was finished and had gone after his wife. I put him in the recovery position and did enough first aid so that he didn't croak."

The officers then checked elsewhere for any accomplices, but there was only Michael Abram, whose ravings you could have heard down at the police station in Falaise Square. "You should have heard the spooky things he was saying, the bastard," he shrieked, before "I did it! I did it!" several times in succession.

Next on the scene was Dhani. He knelt by his prostrate father and was "immediately covered in blood". As well as the lung, the knife had left its mark in George's thigh, cheek, chest and left forearm. "He was drifting," noticed Dhani. "I honestly believed he was going to die. He was so pale. I looked into his eyes and saw the pain. Dad kept saying, 'Oh Dhan, oh Dhan.' He looked even paler in the face, and he was groaning and saying, 'I'm going out.' He made little sense, and I knew he was losing consciousness. It was about ten to twelve minutes – although it seemed like a lifetime – before the paramedics arrived."

Both victim and attacker were rushed to the Royal Berkshire Hospital in Reading. The truth that he may have refused to avow at first inflicted itself on Dhani at this point: "As [George] was taken away in a stretcher chair, he looked back and said, 'I love you, Dhan.' My father's spoken words were broken with coughing and spluttering. He said, 'Hare Krishna,' and closed his eyes. At this point, he drew a very strange breath. It was deep and what I would describe as a death breath. His mouth was puckered, his cheeks were drawn in and he sucked at his bottom lip. I shouted, 'Dad! Dad! You are with me? Listen to my voice. It is going to be OK. Stay with me!' His face was contorted and he had not taken a breath for some seconds. As I finished shouting, he breathed out and opened his eyes. I have never seen another human being, whether dead or alive – and I have seen my grandfather in his coffin – look so bad."

Sooner than expected, George was off the danger list by the following afternoon. He was then transferred to Harefield Hospital, on the edge of London, where he saw in 2000 AD. Gruesomely hilarious remarks and relayed witticisms* hid the shaken man beneath to everyone but Olivia and Dhani, to whom he still had every appearance of being seriously unwell, despite assurances that he was on the mend.

For Olivia, fright had turned to rage towards one who "owes us a thank you for saving him from the karma of murder. We do not accept that he did not know that what he was doing was wrong. We shall never forget that he was full of hatred and violence when he came into our home."

When George's old smile was back by mid January, she accompanied him on a brief convalescence in Ireland as a prelude to a longer stay with Dhani and a lately-widowed Joe Brown in a rented holiday home in Barbados, the expensive facilities of which were less important than the ex-SAS militia who patrolled the grounds around the clock.

From less exotic surroundings, Michael Abram, on remand, sent a letter of apology "for having to face a lunatic like me in their house". Via the Crown Prosecution Service, this reached Friar Park the day before his case came up the following November. Olivia, for one, was not impressed: "I didn't read it properly. What I did read sounded like it wasn't written by him. Given the timing, it sounded convenient."

The next day, in Oxford Crown Court, Abram was smartened up beyond recognition in a pinstripe suit and John Lennon swot spectacles, his hair trimmed to a short crop. A vision of poker-faced sobriety, he denied two counts of attempted murder, causing grievous bodily harm, unlawful wounding and aggravated burglary. Through the oratory skills of his barrister, the jury were persuaded that Society Was To Blame, and in measured tones the defendant was to thank Mr Justice Astill, after being found not guilty on the grounds of insanity. The summit of his life conquered, Mad Mick was escorted away by two male nurses for the first stage of a journey that would terminate in the medium-secure Scott Clinic, a psychiatric wing of Rainhill Hospital, out of harm's way in rural Merseyside. He was to be detained there indefinitely, meaning that he'd be eligible for release if ever a mental health review tribunal decided that he was no longer a risk to the public. The Harrisons' plea to be informed if this should happen was rejected, but Justice Astill intimated that there might be "other channels" they could try.

This was food for thought, as, flanked by bodyguards in the

---

* Such as, "He wasn't a burglar, and he definitely wasn't auditioning for The Traveling Wilburys," and a more measured, "Adi Shankara, an Indian historical, spiritual and groovy-type person once said, 'Life is fragile, like a raindrop on a lotus leaf,' and you'd better believe it."

building's forecourt afterwards, Dhani Harrison read a statement to the gentlefolk of the press. Its most crucial sentence was, "The prospect of him being released back into society is abhorrent to us."

Newspaper reports on what amounted to 22-year-old Dhani's first public address were accompanied by photographs that accentuated his close resemblance to his father at the same age.*

Dhani had preferred not to stand up in court, but his mother had resolved from the start to testify in her own voice rather than "have my statement read by a male police officer in a monotone". Via a half-page interview in *The Independent On Sunday*, she also expressed hopes that "the growing violence in society is controlled and ultimately replaced by the goodness of most people in the world" before putting a full-stop on the affair, with a dramatic "The line is drawn under it all when I hang up this phone."[377]

Yet it wasn't as easy as that. Death threats from other Beatlemaniacs continued to reach George Harrison and unfounded media speculation that he was planning to leave Friar Park because it now had "bad vibes" reawakened parochial opinion that he intended to offer the place to the Krishna Consciousness Society.

"Mr and Mrs Harrison are not merely victims but continuing targets" was the thrust of hired QC Geoffrey Robertson's argument on behalf of George when approaching Home Secretary Jack Straw, one of Judge Astill's "other channels". Straw assured Robertson that to "put victims back at the heart of the justice system has been my guiding preoccupation as Home Secretary. When I read and hear of the experiences of those like George and Olivia Harrison, it intensifies my determination. I believe victims of crime have a right to know that those who have offended against them are released and I propose to introduce new laws to do just that."

These fine words in the run-up to 2001's general election have been thus far the most far-reaching repercussion of the Michael Abram incident, although the amassed publicity did help to pave the way for the release schedule of re-mastered CDs of George's solo back catalogue, complete with tacked-on alternative takes and hitherto-unissued songs, beginning with the 2001 boxed set of *All Things Must Pass*.* Its full-colour variation on the original black-

and-white front cover reflected the 30 years' worth of technology that had been developed since 1971. With the audio fidelity of compact discs, rather than suffer the sweet torment of worn-out vinyl, fans might at last think that they could catch the whirring of George's nervous system. Into the bargain, the new *All Things Must Pass* was made flabbier, with different versions of 'Beware Of Darkness', 'Let It Down' and 'What Is Life', the baleful 'I Live For You' – with a riff too similar to that of 'I Got A Feeling' from *Let It Be* – and the previous autumn's remake of 'My Sweet Lord', featuring Joe Brown's pop-singing daughter Sam† and, less conspicuously, Dhani Harrison on acoustic guitar, along with the ubiquitous Jim Keltner on drums.

"I just made it in the same way as we made it back in the '60s," explained George, "which is [with] analogue tapes, microphones and guitars, bass, drums, piano. The world is going mental, as far as I'm concerned. It's speeding up with technology and everything that's happening. I just liked the idea and opportunity to freshen it up, because the point of 'My Sweet Lord' is just to try to remind myself that there's more to life than the material world. Basically, I think the planet is doomed, and it is my attempt to put a spin on the spiritual side, a reminder for myself and for anybody who's interested."[378]

Plenty were, and the double CD's topping of *The Henley Standard*'s Top Ten was reflected to a lesser extent in lists throughout a wider world. This boded well for CD re-promotions of the more attractive *Living In The Material World* and the Dark Horse catalogue, that had now reverted to its maker. Jumping to the front of the queue, however, may be an album of fresh material that has exhausted two working titles already, *Portrait Of A Leg End* and *Your Planet Is Doomed, Volume One*.

During his stay at Friar Park, Timothy White had listened to home demos of three earmarked tracks, 'Brainwashed', 'Pisces Fish' and 'Valentine'. Once, such a preview might have been an enormous scoop for *Billboard* or any pop-music periodical, but George Harrison's name is now a far less potent tool for holding the front

---

* Eight days later, Dhani was the central figure in a road accident at the wheel of his Audi S3 sports car, purchased from Motor World in Kidlington, some 30 miles northeast of Henley, three weeks earlier. Dhani escaped serious injury, but the 60mph crash tore off the front wing on the driver's side and burst all four tyres.

page, unless he pulls some eye-stretching stroke like nearly getting killed. That had been much bigger news than any new or recycled Harrison disc of which a journalist might or might not have been aware as he cobbled together an editorial tirade about the government's vacillation about curbing the increase of violent crime in these distracted times.

In the aftershock of Michael Abram's homicidal campaign, George had sent a grateful bottle of champagne to the police station in Falaise Square, and both Paul Williams and Matt Morgans had been awarded with commendations for bravery. "We're not heroes," shrugs Matt. "We just happened to be on the right shift. People did say to me afterwards, 'Weren't you the one at George Harrison's house?' I'd reply, 'Well, yes, I was. But you still get your parking ticket.'"

For George, the experience faded, and according to Nick Valner, his London lawyer, he was "in the best of spirits and on top form – the most relaxed and free he has been since he was attacked". This was part of a statement relayed to the press in May 2001, shortly after George Harrison underwent his second operation in three years to remove a cancerous growth on a lung. From his bed in the Mayo Clinic in Rochester, Minnesota, George blamed smoking – a habit he gave up when the condition was first diagnosed.

While George convalesced in Tuscany with Olivia, Valner assured the public that "the operation was successful and George has made an excellent recovery. Although All Things Must Pass Away, George has no plans right now and is still Living In The Material World, and wishes everyone all the very best."

---

* The title track had been used in the 1998 movie *Everest*, as were 'Here Comes The Sun', 'Give Me Love' and 'Life Itself'.

† Sam Brown's greatest hits at the time of writing were 1989's 'Stop' and a revival of Marvin Gaye's 'Can I Get A Witness'.

Epilogue
The Once And Future Pop Star

Between us on the desk is a copy of a new biography of Harrison, called The Quiet One *by Alan Clayson... "God knows why these people bother," he says picking it up gingerly. "To make some money, I suppose."*

The Times, *12 November 1990*

Within my own limits, I am a principled wordsmith. Firstly, I wouldn't have got enmeshed in showbiz life stories if the market for them hadn't been a legitimate creation by the fans who, indirectly, pay the subjects' wages. Secondly, disgruntled reissue specialists who have commissioned me to pen eulogistic sleeve notes will tell you that I never write anything I don't mean, no matter how high the fee. Most crucially, however, I have to feel an empathy with the artists concerned, and a lot of these are not considered potentially commercial enough by those publishers who have even heard of them.

Conversely, there are myriad more renowned pop figures whom I love to hate. Rather than offend their fans with disobliging observations, I prefer not to talk – let alone write – about them. That's why my books tend to hurry through unavoidable passages about...well, certain people. No doubt the fault for such prejudices is mine, but I'm as childishly editorial about the James Taylor/Melanie singing/songwriter school of the early 1970s and virtually all the major rap executants. Catch me in full philistine flood about some new boy band, too, and I sound just like some middle-aged dad *circa* 1966 going on about the Stones.

George Harrison, however, passes muster. While much of his output has been unexceptional, his thwarted ambition as an instrumentalist provokes sympathy, and for all his self-deprecation he has realised some extraordinary visions as a composer. Yet tune into an easy-listening radio station and the orchestral medley of Beatle tunes you'll hear will be all Lennon-McCartney.

The jury is, therefore, still out – and probably always will be – over whether he's a merely adequate musician who was lucky enough to have been a Beatle or, as Leonard Bernstein assured us, "a mystical unrealized talent".[253] He's probably been both, but I'm not convinced that he's the God-like genius that others have made him out to be. What is a genius, anyway? Among the many blessed with that dubious title are Horst 'A Walk In The Black Forest' Jankowski, dart-hurling Jocky Wilson and Screaming Lord Sutch. As often happens with a celebrity who, however inadvertently, catches the lightning and sustains the momentum of public favour, reputation and legend continue to grow with each succeeding year, far beyond what has actually been achieved.

Not helping, either, is an established but too-analytical form of pop journalism that intellectualises the simply intelligent, turns metaphorical perfume back into a rotten egg and tells you what Greil Marcus thinks about such-and-such an album and what Simon Frith thinks he means. Why should I have been any different by not including in this book self-aggrandising sections that dismantle Harrison's music and stick it back together again? Obviously, I wouldn't do so if I didn't feel that it was either a worthwhile cultural exercise, a way of trying to convince people that I'm clever (a genius, perhaps?) or a method of covering the number of words I'd been contracted to write.

Whatever the motivations, I hope that such parts of *The Quiet One* have utilised your time interestingly. But remember that, however I dress them up, they're only my opinions – and not always subjective ones, either – about items of merchandise available to all. Your thoughts about 'Don't Bother Me', 'Something', the 1974 tour, the Wilburys, *Cloud Nine*, *et al*, are as worthy as mine – and beyond either of us, the only true approbation an artist needs is from those who buy the records and tickets for the shows. As the two singles from *Cloud Nine* demonstrated, given the right song – his own or not – George Harrison's return to a qualified prominence as a pop star can never be ruled out. On his own terms, there's no reason why he shouldn't still be making records in old age at a pace that could involve further long periods of vanishing from the public eye.

Appendix 1
The Big Sister

In March 1995, I was a guest speaker at the New Jersey Beatlefest. One of the calmer periods during this eventful weekend was spent sharing a graveyard-hour pizza on a lighting gantry with Louise Harrison, a lady I'd met the previous August at a similar function in Chicago. We'd communicated in a shallow showbiz way then, but this time around we became friends during the relief that follows the switching off of a tape recorder after a formal interview earlier, in which a thought had flashed through my mind: *It runs in the family.*

"I have the same basic beliefs as my brother," she'd confirmed – and, despite Louise's Scouse drawl being all but vanished after 40 years in the Americas, it might indeed have been George talking. "We are all part of one energy or intelligence, if you like, and if enough of us are in tune with 'All You Need Is Love' and other principles that The Beatles put across, then some of the things that are happening politically could swing more in the direction of caring for each other than of greed, and tolerance for other religions without Spanish Inquisitions. Something my mum told us was about a church – symbolising God – on top of a mountain and all of us trying to reach it. We may all take a different path to get there, but we're all heading for the same goal. You don't have to be a this or a that as long as you care about the Earth and other Earthlings."

Unlike her youngest sibling, however, she is "not really geared for meditation. Like many others, I try to live every moment conscious of the Creator working through me. I know my role is an active one. I've been given the gifts of physical stamina, great determination and

461

a natural ability to speak to people about our problems and to look for sensible solutions."

Neither is Louise a strict vegetarian. "I hardly ever eat meat," she disclosed, "but if I'm in a situation where someone's cooked me a wonderful meal with meat in it, I'm not going to turn my nose up at it. Yogananda reaches non-fanaticism about any of your beliefs. Actually, I hardly ever eat at all. I mostly have a lot of vitamins, herbs and minerals for particular needs, and I never really feel hungry."

Yet this was no skeletal ascetic – although the angular Harrison cheekbones and appraising gaze are prominent in this robust grandmother who is also prime mover of the We Care Global Family, the non-profit-making organisation she founded in 1992 to promote environmental education. Among tenets outlined in its application leaflet is "Determination to Restore Our Planet for our children". The Germanic capitals are deliberate, for We Care members are referred to as "DROPs" in *Newsplash*, the quarterly newsletter, containing items with titles like "Rubbish Soul", a children's section ("Drop-lets") and editorials ("From Me To You") by Louise, known within the DROP hierarchy as "the other Queen Mum". "They were calling me President," she explained. "I remarked that I'd rather they called me Mum. One replied, 'That's a good idea, but in deference to your biological children, why can't we call you Queen Mum?' This humorous title caught on."

She's "Miss Harrison", however, in her office as roving We Care spokesperson to schools, colleges, solar-energy conferences, Earthday functions and university ecology workshops. She also broadcasts "Good Earthkeeping Tips" – a regular feature in *Newsplash* – on more than two hundred US radio stations, with George's 'Save The World' as background music. Another of Louise's concerns is negotiating finance and a suitable director for a We Care-related movie, *The Time Is Now*. Based loosely on salient points from *Yellow Submarine* and Dickens' *A Christmas Carol*, this musical fantasy has already attracted big names. Of Beatle associates, Neil Innes has donated a title song, and Victor Spinetti has given tentative consent to play the villain.

Louise Harrison has therefore travelled more than mere geographic distance from Liverpool where she was born in her paternal grandmother's house in the suburb of Wavertree on 16 August 1931 as the Harrisons' eldest child, twelve years older than George.

Like him, Louise passed the Eleven Plus examination and gained a place at a grammar school known as La Sagesse, which was attached to a convent that buttressed now-old-fashioned concepts of a woman's role in a wider world. "We were asked to draw what we were going to be when we grew up," recalled Louise. "I drew myself on stage in a spotlight. I wanted to be an entertainer. But back in the early 1950s, a woman didn't think of herself as having a career. The only options for a woman was to be a nurse, teacher or secretary. If you were lucky, you got married. You dreamed that some wonderful man would ride along on a charger and sweep you off your feet."

It was her mother's wish for a disinclined Louise to be a teacher. To this end, Louise won a scholarship to teacher training college at St Mary's in Fenham, Newcastle-upon-Tyne. Although specialising in English, Geography and PE, she demonstrated a flair for drama one December when a visiting Father Agnelus Andrews – house priest on BBC radio – heard Louise's soliloquy as Mary musing about the new-born Jesus. Impressed, Father Andrews offered to write a letter of introduction to the BBC Drama department, should the trainee ever wish to pursue this type of career.

To Louise's disappointment, parental disapproval of her living alone in London – because of concern about the then-widespread white slave traffic – nipped this notion in the bud. As her We Care work would prove, she had a talent for dealing with children, but, midway through the course at St Mary's, "I was so stressed about being in something that I didn't want to do that I came down with a series of abscesses on my face." After counselling by an understanding head nun, she went back to a dismayed mother and a job as chairside assistant to a Merseyside dentist.

In 1954, she wed Gordon Caldwell, a dour but gifted engineer from Dundee. Married life began in Scotland, but the couple were considering what might lie further afield. "My whole attitude throughout my life has been that each day is an adventure," Louise elucidated. "My parents didn't foster in us the feeling that we had to be tied to anyone's apron strings. They gave us a solid foundation of self-confidence and self-esteem. Therefore, I didn't feel any trepidation about emigrating. We really wanted to go to Australia, but it just happened that, after Gordon wrote off for jobs, it was one in Canada that came up first."

A son, Gordon, was born there in 1957, followed by his sister, Leslie, in 1959. Their father's vocation took the family to Peru and then back to Canada to Gagnon, a dreary settlement near the Arctic circle. By the time they arrived in Benton, Beatlemania was ravaging Britain and, said Louise, "Mum was sending me clippings from *Mersey Beat* and the national newspapers. I was thrilled for George and did whatever I could to further The Beatles, because it was something in showbusiness, something I would have wanted to do myself. I got their records played on a minor radio station and wrote dozens of letters to Dick James, George Martin and Brian Epstein. When the first record came out in the States, on Vee Jay, I went to a company address in St Louis, but there was nothing there. Swan, who put out the next one, was no better, so I studied magazines like *Billboard* and *Cashbox* and sent Brian the names and addresses of more major labels like RCA, Capitol and Columbia.

"When Del Shannon's cover of 'From Me To You' came out, I was calling all kinds of radio stations and plugging the original version, but the general feeling was that The Beatles were never going to go anywhere over here. Gordon thought I was wasting my time, too.

"Nevertheless, when 'I Want To Hold Your Hand' came out on Capitol, a representative, Vito Samela, called me that January [1964] to say that, in nine days, it'd sold a million in the States. I called George at the George V Hotel in Paris to tell him. Originally, he had been going to come back over to Illinois again between the two *Ed Sullivan Shows*, but everything went so crazy that there was no way in which he could get away. George suggested that I come to New York for the weekend.

"We were going to meet at the airport, but it would have been difficult for us to link up, what with all the media descending on it. George booked a room for me at the Plaza, but he had such a bad throat that the hotel physician, Dr Gordon, suggested that using the already present sister made more sense than hiring a nurse."

Thanks to Dr Gordon and Louise's ministrations, George was able to be seen on Sullivan's spectacular with The Beatles. "My first impression of the other three," recalled Louise, "was that I felt like I had an extra bunch of brothers. As the only daughter of four children, I'd gravitated more towards football with the lads than girly pastimes. As a result, I was very much at ease. Paul was the diplomat, very gracious. He'd been doing tape recordings on the plane, funny fake interviews. Ringo was delightful, too, and so was Cynthia, but I was scared of John, because of his sarcasm, his biting sense of humour. Really nasty. I mentioned this to Mum, but she said that basically he was OK. When he behaved like that, he was covering up for his own insecurities. It was an interesting lesson to me, because it made me better able to cope with a wide variety of people on the right level, because you can understand and empathise with their frailty and, consequently, they respond to you in a much nicer way."

Through her affinity with the Fab Four, Louise's radio career got under way in New York when she played along with a spoof kidnap stunt by "the Good Guys" – disc jockeys on station WMCA. She found herself on the air for an hour that included a call to George at the hotel, where he plucked a few obliging bars on his new twelve-string Rickenbacker.

She was also present in Washington at the British Embassy, "where someone snipped off a chunk of Ringo's hair. He was really furious. When this happened, I was drinking tea at the back of the room with Lady Ormsby-Gore. When I got back home, there was a news item alleging that Lady Ormsby-Gore herself had wrestled Ringo to the ground and cut a lock of his hair off. I was horrified, and I called up the radio stations I'd tried in 1963, because I was so concerned about Lady Ormsby-Gore being made a fool of. They invited me on to talk about it. Initially, I was reluctant, but two days later one station in St Louis, realising its mistake in refusing to play The Beatles in 1963, asked me to tell the truth about other rumours and press garbage. They wanted me to do daily 'Beatle Reports' – anecdotes and ongoing news – for a couple of weeks."

The initial fee for the Beatle Reports would cover costs of replying to the thousands of fan letters mailed to Benton. "George called from

Miami and I told him about this proposal," said Louise. "We made arrangements that I would call Mum each week and she'd tell me the latest goings-on so that I could put together these reports. I ended up doing them for 15 major stations across the country for the next 18 months. It did wonders for radio ratings. Sometimes, I'd travel to do live phone-ins as far away as Minneapolis. I had to hire a housekeeper and secretary to cope with it."

This second-hand celebrity also took in personal appearances, such as that before a crowd of 15,000 at Minneapolis/St Paul winter carnival, receiving the key to the city of New Orleans during 1965's Mardi Gras and a three-week tour of the Midwest as part of a *Dick Clark Caravan Of Stars*, performing a spoken ballad to musical accompaniment.

That wasn't all. "The head of STORZ Broadcasting, that covered five stations, compiled some of my answers to five live-on-air press conferences," recounted Louise, "and pressed them on vinyl. A prize in each of their competitions was attending a hotel press conference with me. These were recorded and edited. A couple of guys who owned a carwash put up the money."

Louise's consequent *All About The Beatles* LP (see Chapter Seven) was released in 1965 on the understanding that "I was going to get a third of the proceeds on sales, but it never came to anything, because there were too many people putting out records with the name 'Beatles' or 'Beetles' on the front, and Brian put some kind of blanket cease-and-desist. All of the pressings left stayed in a warehouse."

Yet, like her parents, Louise still devoted tireless hours to answering mail in her warm, chatty style, although 1964's daily vanload had subsided to a steady couple of hundred a week. Her radio exposure boiled down to hosting a chat show, *Sound Off*, for a station in southern Illinois. At last, Louise became a personality in her own right, because the programme's stock in trade was not The Beatles but sewage treatment plants, education committees and similar parochial issues.

Sound Off ran until 1970, when, following the trauma of her divorce, Louise and the children were invited to live in George's middle lodge at Friar Park. "I had everything packed," recounted Louise, "and our passage booked on the *QE2*, but my kids were scared of the idea of going to England, what with the education system there being so much more advanced. They were worried about being put in classes with younger children, and so we didn't go. I'd like to feel that, had I gone, I'd have worked with rather than for George."

Instead, Louise seemed as if she'd landed on her feet in New York when commissioned to be a co-presenter on the ailing *Dick Cavett Show*. "They felt that I could increase the listenership. It got as far as them asking me what colour I'd like my dressing room painted, but then ABC cancelled the series." Thus was lost a chance to escape further into a public trajectory separate from that of The Beatles.

Four years later, Louise bounced back as vice-president of a marketing firm owned by Walter J Kane, her new husband, 14 years her junior. A move to Florida prefaced an "amicable" parting in 1983 and the sad conclusion that "I wasn't very good at choosing men".

Financial support from George might have granted Louise a dotage rich in material comforts, but rather than retire she chose instead to resume work in radio in 1985, applying 20 years' experience in the medium to continuity, programming, compiling and writing copy, producing advertisements and reading news – not forgetting to sign off with "'Til next time, cheerio!", the catch-phrase from the Beatle Reports era.

She re-entered the Beatle orbit in 1993. "I was at one of Paul's concerts where he was trying to bring fans' attention to environmental problems," affirmed Louise. "I thought it would be nice for this ready-made audience to have their own holistic organisation which looked at the planet as a global family, but it wasn't until I started We Care that I started speaking at Beatle conventions.

"I now realise that these and We Care are outgrowings of my parents' dealing with fan letters in the 1960s, that they'd often sign, "Love from Mum and Dad." At first, I was jealous, but then I saw that, far from losing my parents to Beatle people, they had so much love within them to give freely that they were collecting a lot more goodwill for me, being a sister in this huge family."

For information about how to become a DROP, write to We Care Global Family, PO Box 1338, Tallevast, Florida 34270, USA.

Appendix II
The Fifth Vest

In 1994, Robert Bartel introduced himself to me at a Beatlefest in Chicago. If a business consultant and private investigator by trade, he also functions as a poet and Beatles historian. "They kept me alive in the '60s, when things were not always good," he says of the pop combo that launched a thousand fanzines. Through one of these, Bob Bartel met his future wife, Janice, in 1991, whom he wed on Lennon's birthday two years later. A room in their house in Springfield, Illinois, is a shrine to The Beatles, with every nook filled with neatly displayed memorabilia, including a 1964 bubble-gum card, an autographed limited-edition George Harrison songbook and a signed photo of Sean and Yoko with Santa Claus.

At an equidistant 200 miles from St Louis lies Benton, just Off Interstate Highway 57, where Bob travelled shortly before Christmas, intending to photograph 113 McCann Street, a two-storey residence with a broad front porch and bay window where George Harrison's sister Louise, her then-husband and their two children had dwelt for five years, and where George and his brother Peter had visited in 1963. "I drove by and noticed it was empty," relates Bob. "I did some inquiring and found that the Illinois Department for Mines and Minerals Rescue had purchased it for $39,000 and was intending to tear it down for a parking lot for a nearby administrative building. I feel that Benton is sitting on a gold mine. Beatle fans are very loyal and would love to tour the house that George Harrison stayed in for a month."

As you will have read in Chapter Six, it was much less than a month. Nevertheless, as Louise was to point out when we met in

New York in 1995, "That's the only experience any one of [The Beatles] had of living in this country as a normal human being without anyone trying to pull out tufts of his hair and buttons from his shirt. Nobody had ever heard of him."

During the spring prior to George and Peter's holiday, the Caldwells had moved from Canada to the Franklin County settlement of around 8,000 souls when Gordon, a mechanical engineer, was hired by the Freeman Coal Company. "We arrived by car on 10 March and checked into a hotel," remembered Louise. "Gordon had to go to work the next morning, and I wasn't really prepared to buy a house. All I had was a £5 note and a $2 bill."

Nevertheless, she made an appointment with an estate agent, and "one of the first houses he showed me was the one on McCann Street. He told me that all I needed was $500 down and I could move in that day. I went to the bank and borrowed the down-payment and started moving in. I had to call my husband at work and tell him the address to come home to. He didn't get mad, though; he was used to me doing things like that. The first day we moved in, someone brought us a truckload of firewood and Mrs Lillie Lewis – who lived across the street – brought us a big pot of chicken and dumplings. I will always remember the people of Benton being very nice and kind to me, before I was related to someone famous."

For George, Benton was impressive for a temperature sign in the town square that he filmed when it rose to 105 degrees. "He'd never seen a temperature that high in his life," explained Louise. In a crew-cut continent, he was only conspicuous for his moptop. "I'd never seen any man with so much hair. Everywhere we went, people stared at him," exclaimed Gaby McCarty of The Four Vests, Benton's boss group, who had actually heard (via Louise) the *Please Please Me* LP. With this as a conversational starting point, Gaby and Kenny Welch, the Vests' guitarist, befriended George and showed him around.

Inevitably, chat around a record player would develop into jam sessions, and George was invited to sit in when the Vests played at the VFW dance hall in nearby Eldorado. "Everyone was dancing, until he started playing," recalled Jim and Darryl Chady, friends of the Caldwells. "Then everybody just stopped and watched him play.

He was a great guitarist", to which McCarty – now a sheet-metal worker at Southern Illinois University – added, "I thought he was going to play some of those Beatles songs, but he played Hank Williams tunes."

He delivered them on Welch's particular make of Rickenbacker. "He had never seen one before," said Kenny, "and he liked it really well. He wanted to buy it." Welch wasn't selling, however, so George purchased one from Mount Vernon, a town a few miles north. Kenny remains "unsure whether he bought it from an individual or a business". Around Louise's, he was heard picking at this same instrument, which would be heard on 'A Hard Day's Night' and other Beatles recordings.

Dawn greeted George as the plane landed in London on 3 October. If not yet adjusted to Greenwich Mean Time, he still breezed into Abbey Road that afternoon to resume work on what would become *With The Beatles*. During a break, he may have told a funny story about the Eldorado bash when a man told him afterwards that he'd appreciated George's performance, and that, "if you had the right handling, you could go places".

The man's judgement proved correct, and the next the people of Franklin County saw of George was on *The Ed Sullivan Show* in the following February. "I couldn't believe it," gasped Kenny Welch. "I never mentioned it to anybody, because I didn't figure anyone would believe that I had played guitar with him. I just remember him as a nice guy."

"The next time [we met George]," recounted Jim Chady, "was when the Caldwells invited us to see The Beatles when they performed at Cominskey Park in Chicago on their first US tour. Over 50,000 in a stadium was quite a contrast from the Eldorado VFW."

As the group continued to spearhead what passed into myth as the "British Invasion", Louise undertook radio broadcasts – "Beatle Reports" – from number 113. For this purpose, she would liaise by telephone every day with Brian Epstein for updates. "Many of the news releases that were sent to the national media came from this house," Bob Bartel would remark. "That in itself makes it pretty historical."

That's as may be, but the demolition crew were still awaiting instructions while Bob tried to persuade state authorities that the place may be a lucrative tourist attraction. Seeing visions of "each house on that block as a boutique in four or five years", Bartel put the case to the region's Historical Preservation Society, but there persisted "some question in their mind about the historical value of the house. I think it would be more so than that of the old Franklin County jail. Why not work to save a place where someone famous stayed, rather than where someone infamous stayed?"

The tireless young bard had more luck with the Illinois Capitol Development Board, the state's construction management agency, who extended the 26 February deadline (by coincidence George's 52nd birthday) to allow Benton and Beatles fans time to "come up with whatever their plan would be", said spokesperson Mia Jazo.

The state itself suggested that, at a cost of up to $40,000, the house could be moved to another location, and almost immediately a fast-food restaurant chain offered a low-cost lease. Then there was attorney Gerald Owens' idea of drumming up cash to buy another building nearby that could suffer the wrecking ball instead. He also mentioned a willing local lady with the means to do so.

Further champions joined the fray, among them Envirowood, a company that recycles plastic into plastic wood. It pledged to provide tables for a picnic area, while WXRT-FM's Terri Hemmert – a sort of female Jimmy Saville of Chicago and MC of the Windy City's annual Beatlefest – promised to spread the word on the ether.

Most crucial of all was the support of Louise Harrison, now 64 and living in Sarusota, Florida. In 1992, she'd ventured back into the public spotlight as both a speaker at Beatle-related events and as figurehead of the We Care Global Family Inc. The McCann Street issue seemed to combine both her vocational and her personal interests. "I heard about the wrecking plans from some fans in December," she recollected. "They reminded me that this is a special place from a special time. I would like to see if the redbud tree I planted in the yard is still there." She doubted if George would approve of her involvement: "He'd probably think it's a lot of nonsense, but once we've done it and good things are happening, I'm sure he'll say, 'That's OK.'"

Louise's three-day stay in Benton embraced a few campaign meetings and a press conference attended by most of the St Louis Beatles Fan Club. Apparently, during one of Bob's frequent calls to Florida, Louise had thought aloud about acquiring the wherewithal to install her daughter, Leslie, at number 113, but if this was ever more than mere talk it has since been abandoned.

With and without Louise, Bob soldiered on with petitioning and his dogged badgering of the media – including the BBC – and schemes for a book and even a movie about George in Benton. After much soul-searching, he donated his precious Harrison songbook to a fund-raising auction. "It's a world thing," he contended. "It's in everybody's interest. I don't care if you're from Springfield, China or whatever. It's preserving a part of history."

In the centuries to come, the ghost of George Harrison is perhaps less likely to be observed wading and rattling chains around Benton than, say, the Speke council estate where he grew up. Yet, through Bob Bartel's tenacity, sentences with "museum", "guided tours", "souvenir shop" and "Gracelands" in them were put into the mouths of Benton burghers, and 113 McCann Street was saved. Three Benton couples – including Jim and Darryl Chady – clubbed together and bought the place. They turned it into a guest house – called A Hard Day's Night – with restaurant facilities. "We're naturally in it for the investment," insisted Cindy Rice, one of the speculators, "and to preserve it tastefully and not exploit it."

"Just think, this might be 'Little Memphis'," laughed Jean Chamness, president of both the Chamber of Commerce and the Society for Historical Preservation. "I always liked country music more, but I'm forward-looking enough to realise that this could really be a good thing for us. Our economy is stagnant, to say the least."

Notes

In addition to my own correspondence and interviews, I have used the following sources which I would like to credit.

1. *Arena* (BBC2) 27 November 1989
2. *Zabadak* number eight, July 1989
3. *International Times*, 11 September 1969
4. To Glenn Baker, Sydney radio announcer
5. Even good Homer sometimes nods
6. Letter from Clog Holdings, Burbank, California, 28 February 1989
7. What is written down is permanent
8. *Mail On Sunday*, 4 September 1988
8.1 Officially, George's birth took place on 25 February, but later sources calculated that he actually appeared shortly after midnight on the 26th. Who cares?
9. *Rolling Stone*, 30 December 1976
10. To Hunter Davies
11. An inflammation of the kidneys, sometimes called "Bright's disease". Its treatment includes an unappetising but necessary diet of gruel and tepid milk
12. *Sunday Mirror*, 23 April 1989
13. A reference to noted Liverpool FC footballer Ian St John
14. *Melody Maker*, 29 August 1964
15. *Beatles Monthly*, November 1986
16. *Melody Maker*, 1 May 1965
17. *Liverpool Institute Magazine* volume LXIX, number two, July 1961
18. Arthur Evans to Chris Salewicz
19. Peter Sissons to Chris Salewicz
20. Notably as a newsreader and host of BBC1's *Question Time*
21. Jack Sweeney to Chris Salewicz
22. *Motor*, 28 July 1979
23. *Reading Evening Post*, 7 January 1989
24. *Time Out*, 4 September 1988
25. *National Rock Star*, 18 December 1976
26. *Record Mirror*, 21 January 1956
27. *New Musical Express*, 28 September 1968

28. *Everybody's Weekly*, 3 July 1957
29. *Disc*, 6 January 1971
30. *Daily Mirror*, 8 April 1957
31. "A musicologist" on *Six-Five Special* (ITV), 18 January 1957
32. *Crawdaddy*, February 1977
33. *Melody Maker*, 17 October 1964
34. *Sunday Times*, 27 February 1987
35. *New Musical Express*, 7 March 1958
36. *Everybody's Weekly*, 23 June 1956
37. 'All Those Years Ago' by George Harrison (Dark Horse single, K17807, 1981)
38. *A Twist Of Lennon* by C Lennon (Star, 1978)
39. *I Me Mine* by G Harrison (Simon & Schuster, 1988)
40. Kemp's own dance troupe became prominent in "underground" circles in the 1960s. In their ranks for a while was David Bowie
41. *Liverpool Institute Magazine* volume LXVIII, number one, February 1960
42. *Beatlefan* volume two, number two, 1979
43. This collaboration began prior to George joining The Quarry Men. Until 1970, Lennon and McCartney agreed to take equal credit, even if a given song was the work of only one of them
44. To Ray Coleman
45. Quoted in *Call Up The Groups* by A Clayson (Sanctuary, 1997)
46. *The Man Who Gave The Beatles Away* by A Williams and W Marshall (Elm Tree, 1975)
47. Radio Bedfordshire, 29 December 1985
48. *Fiesta*, May 1975
49. *Greatest Hits*, February 1981
50. *Midland Beat* number 31, April 1966
51. 'Circles', from the album *Gone Troppo* (Dark Horse 923734-1, 1982)
52. *Beatlefan*, volume one, number three, 1978
53. A reference to the 1956 novel by Jack Kerouac, recognised as being among the foremost prose writers of the Beat generation
54. *The Times*, 24 September 1988
55. *Globe Magazine*, September 1969
56. *Melody Maker*, 23 February 1963
57. *Playboy*, 19 October 1964
58. To Spencer Leigh
59. *Musician*, November 1987
60. *Hit Parade*, June 1963
61. *Sunday Times*, 25 February 1990
62. *Apple To The Core* by P McCabe and R Schonfeld (Sphere, 1972)
63. *Disc*, 24 November 1962
64. *Midland Beat* number one, October 1963
65. Vincent's widow in an unidentified British tabloid, 1971
66. *Beatlefan* volume three, number two, 1981
67. Sleeve notes to *The Beatles Featuring Tony Sheridan* LP (Polydor 24-4504, 1971)
68. *Beatles Down Under* by GA Baker (Wild & Woolley, 1982)
69. *Rolling Stone*, 22 January 1981
70. Reply to a fan letter to a girl named Annie (sold in Sotheby's in 1986)
71. Westbury Hotel press conference transcript, 2 June 1962

72. Sydney press conference transcript, 19 June 1964
73. *New Musical Express*, 3 August 1962
74. To Michael Wale
75. *Beatles Unlimited*, February 1977
76. *Beatle!* by P Best and P Doncaster (Plexus, 1985)
77. *Mersey Beat*, 23 August 1962
78. Extract from letter auctioned at Sotheby's, December 1981
79. *New Musical Express*, 1 February 1964
80. To David Sheff
81. *Melody Maker*, 9 February 1963
82. Lennon's sleeve notes to *Off The Beatle Track* by The George Martin Orchestra (Parlophone PC5 3057)
83. *New Musical Express*, 26 October 1962
84. *Peterborough Standard*, 7 December 1962
85. *Melody Maker*, 3 August 1963
86. *New Musical Express*, 1 February 1963
87. *Beatles Monthly*, March 1983
88. *New Musical Express*, 31 December 1966
89. *New Musical Express*, 22 February 1963
90. *New Musical Express*, 19 July 1963. (NB A "whole day" – ie 14 hours – was considered to be a reasonable amount of time to record an LP in 1963. Over at Decca, Mike Smith had been aghast at the eight hours needed for Dave Berry and his nervous Cruisers to record their debut single that summer)
91. *Sunday Times*, 13 November 1966
92. *New Musical Express*, 16 March 1963
93. *New Musical Express*, 19 April 1963
94. *Western Morning News*, 29 March 1963
95. *South-West Scene* volume one, number three, undated (*circa* 1963)
96. *With The Beatles* by D Hoffman (Omnibus, 1962)
97. *Melody Maker*, 15 June 1963
98. Veronica TV (Dutch), 1982
99. *New Musical Express*, 22 March 1963
100. *Liverpool Institute Magazine* volume LXXI, number two, July 1963
101. *The Independent*, 8 February 1989
102. *Midland Beat* number 14, 1964
103. *Midland Beat* number three, December 1963
104. *New Musical Express*, 5 April 1963
105. Quoted in *Back In The High Life* by A Clayson (to be published by Sanctuary)
106. *The Times*, 27 December 1963
107. *Record Mirror*, date indecipherable (*circa* 1965)
108. *Melody Maker*, 21 November 1963
109. *Mirabelle*, 19 October 1963
110. *Melody Maker*, 26 October 1963
111. *Melody Maker*, 16 November 1963
112. *Western Morning News*, 13 December 1963
113. *Havant News*, 2 November 1963
114. *Annabel*, September 1988
115. Brisbane local radio, 28-30 June 1964

116. George Harrison quoted in *Best Of Smash Hits* (EMAP, 1984)
117. Worldwide Dave Clark Fan Club newsletter, summer 1984
118. *The Fab Four* (French magazine), March 1975
119. *Melody Maker*, 23 November 1963
120. *Melody Maker*, June 1964
121. *Watlington Gazette*, 11 March 1964
122. To Kevin Howlett
123. Quoted in *Ginsberg* by B Miles (Viking, 1990)
124. *Sunday Times*, 13 November 1966
125. *Ready, Steady, Go!* (ITV publication, 1964)
126. *Radio Luxembourg Record Star Book Number Five* (Souvenir Press, 1965)
127. *Melody Maker*, 1 May 1965
128. *Melody Maker*, 27 February 1965
129. *Melody Maker*, 17 November 1974
130. *New Musical Express*, 31 May 1963
131. *Melody Maker*, 13 August 1966
132. *The Jack Paar Show*, 3 January 1964
133. I Corinthians xi 14: "Doth not even nature itself teach you that, if a man have long hair, it is a shame unto him?"
134. *Goldmine*, February 1982
135. Sleeve notes to 'Long Tall Sally' EP (Parlophone GEP 8913)
136. *Billboard*, February 1964
137. *Rolling Stone*, 22 October 1967
138. *The Rolling Stone Interviews Volume One* (Straight Arrow, 1971)
139. *Q*, July 1986
140. *New York Times*, 20 December 1963
141. *Jackie*, 13 October 1964
142. *Daily Mirror*, 8 October 1979
143. *Quant By Quant* by M Quant (Cassell, 1966)
144. *The Illustrated Rock Almanac* edited by B Miles and P Marchbank (Paddington, 1972)
145. *Melody Maker*, 6 November 1975
146. *Fabulous*, 31 May 1966
147. George Harrison on *Top Gear* (Light Programme), November 1964
148. *Fabulous*, 6 June 1966
149. *Melody Maker*, 11 December 1965
150. *Melody Maker*, 11 February 1969
151. *Woman's Own*, 21 November 1987
152. *Chant And Be Happy* (Bhaktivedante Book Trust, 1982)
153. *New Musical Express*, 1 September 1969
154. *Melody Maker*, 16 July 1966
155. *Record Mirror*, 1 January 1966
156. To Jan Wenner
157. *Boyfriend '68* (Trend, 1968)
158. *Los Angeles Times*, 6 October 1987
159. *Life With Elvis* by D Stanley (MARC Europe, 1986)
160. *Creem*, January 1987
161. *Melody Maker*, 2 September 1967
162. *Rolling Stone*, 5 September 1987

163. *Melody Maker*, 27 August 1966
164. *Rolling Stone*, 22 October 1987
165. *Disc*, 19 April 1969
166. *Beatlefan* volume three, number four, 1981
167. To Jon Savage
168. Quoted in *Experimental Pop* by B Bergman and R Horn (Blandford, 1985)
169. 1974 concert programme
170. *Radio Times*, 21 May 1972
171. *International Times*, 3 May 1967
172. *Daily Sketch*, 12 June 1965
173. *Student*, May 1969
174. *Melody Maker*, 25 June 1966
175. *Disc*, 16 July 1966
176. *New Musical Express*, 25 June 1966
177. *Mirabelle*, 19 August 1966
178. Ravi Shankar in *New Musical Express*, 5 October 1967
179. *Melody Maker*, 30 December 1967
180. As a devout Hindu, Ravi Shankar's God was not the Western creator of the universe but the universe's very unity, in whose indivisible wholeness he was inescapably involved, rather like an Anglo-Saxon's "weird" – ie not as an infinitesimal cog but, potentially, the spiritual embodiment of the impenetrably mysterious One who is All, no more human than animal or angel – a "no-thing", or, in the truest sense, "nothing". A Hindu's aim is to see through the illusion ("maya") that any person or thing has a reality independent of the One, that everything in life would vanish instantly if no mind was aware of it. The whole purpose of life is to know nothing
181. *Melody Maker*, 31 September 1967
182. *Record Collector* number 120, August 1989
183. *50 Years Adrift* by D Taylor (Genesis, 1984)
184. *Rolling Stone*, 9 September 1967
185. *Disc*, 19 August 1967
186. *Making Music*, June 1987
187. *International Times*, 17 May 1967
188. *Q*, January 1988
189. *Yesterday* by A Taylor (Sidgwick & Jackson, 1988)
190. *The Aspel Show* (ITV), March 1988
191. Quoted in *Pink Floyd* by B Miles (Omnibus, 1980)
192. *Rolling Stone*, 14 December 1967
193. *Western Morning News*, 28 August 1967
194. *Western Morning News*, 12 September 1967
195. *Western Morning News*, 14 September 1987
196. *The David Frost Show* (BBC), 30 September 1967
197. *Melody Maker*, 9 March 1968
198. Elkan Allan in *Movies On Television* (Times Newspapers Ltd, 1973)
199. *Films And Filming*, March 1969
200. *Record Collector* number 108, August 1988
201. Letter from John Lydon, head of Apple Retail, to The Fool
202. *Melody Maker*, 28 September 1968
203. *Rolling Stone*, 9 March 1968

204. *Melody Maker*, 20 December 1969
205. *Melody Maker*, 12 April 1969
206. Cambridge University journal, March 1969
207. *Yoko Ono* by J Hopkins (Sidgwick & Jackson, 1987)
208. *The Beatles* by H Davies (Heinemann, 1968)
209. *Sunday Mirror*, 5 January 1969
210. *Melody Maker*, 4 September 1971
211. To Anne Nightingale
212. Jerry Boys to Mark Lewisohn
213. *New Musical Express*, 1 November 1969
214. Brazilian press conference transcript, January 1979
215. *International Times*, October 1968
216. *Village Voice*, September 1968
217. *Beatles Monthly*, December 1969
218. *New Musical Express*, 27 December 1967
219. *New Musical Express*, 12 September 1968
220. *New Musical Express*, 1 November 1968
221. *New Musical Express*, I December 1976
222. *Morning Star*, 21 May 1970
223. *Rolling Stone*, 9 July 1970
224. Quoted in *Wit And Wisdom Of Rock And Roll* edited by M Jakubowski (Unwin, 1983)
225. *New Musical Express*, 26 December 1969
226. *Disc*, 5 April 1969
227. Well-known British record-reissue specialist
228. *Daily Mirror*, 1 April 1969
229. *Music Echo*, 19 April 1969
230. *Beatles Unlimited*, March 1977
231. *Daily Express*, 11 October 1969
232. *Disc*, 26 December 1969
233. *Record Mirror*, 12 July 1969
234. KRLA radio concert poster
235. *Melody Maker*, 13 June 1974
236. *Rolling Stone*, 15 October 1970
237. *Zabadak* number seven, July 1974
238. *Disc*, 22 December 1969
239. *Melody Maker*, 2 November 1974
240. Sinatra's announcement during a TV special in the late 1970s
241. *Melody Maker*, 11 October 1969
242. *New Musical Express*, 20 September 1969
243. Vivian Stanshall's sleeve notes to *Gorilla* by The Bonzo Dog Doo-Dah Band (Liberty)
244. *Guitar Player*, November 1987
245. *Melody Maker*, 1 August 1970
246. Quoted in *Loose Talk* edited by L Botts (Rolling Stone Press, 1980)
247. *Melody Maker*, 20 March 1975
248. *Beatlefan* volume two, number four, 1980
249. *neil's Book Of The Dead* by N Planer and T Blacker (Pavilion, 1984)
250. *Daily Express*, 27 February 1971
251. *Liverpool Echo*, 16 March 1972
252. It was included in *24 Super-Great Gospel Songs* (Hansen, 1973)

253. Early 1970 single B-side by Ringo Starr (Apple R 5898-B)
254. Jennifer Sherwood in *Buildings Of England*, quoted in *Henley Standard*, 9 June 1978
255. *Sunday Times*, 29 April 1990
256. *Henley Standard*, 16 June 1978
257. Mrs Jean Broome (Crisp's granddaughter) to *Henley Standard*, 9 June 1978
258. *Sun*, 2 October 1987
259. *Henley Standard*, 29 July 1986
260. *Let It Rock*, January 1973
261. *Melody Maker*, 27 March 1971
262. *Melody Maker*, 30 July 1971
263. *Daily Sketch*, September 1969
264. *Which One's Cliff?* by C Richard (Coronet, 1977)
265. 'Bangla Desh' single by George Harrison (Apple R 5912)
266. Letter from P Jenkin to J Archer, 28 September 1971
267. Letter from G Harrison to Steve Shore, a New Yorker who offered to organise a petition against the tax on the *Bangladesh* album (22 October 1971)
268. 'Miss O'Dell' single B-side by George Harrison (Apple R 5988)
269. *Entertainment Tonight*, October 1982
270. Epstein to Murray the K on WORFM, April 1967
271. *Record Mirror*, 15 April 1972
272. *Today*, 20 March 1987
273. *Sun*, 15 July 1980
274. *Rolling Stone*, 30 December 1976
275. *Melody Maker*, 2 November 1974
276. *Melody Maker*, 6 September 1975
277. *Guardian*, 5 July 1989
278. *Sun*, 2 August 1971
279. *Evening Standard*, 2 August 1971
280. *Melody Maker*, 27 April 1974
281. *News Of The World*, 22 January 1984
282. *Special Pop* (French magazine), November 1972
283. *Rolling Stone*, 6 February 1972
284. To Tim Willis
285. *Movie Life Of George* (LWT), 8 January 1988
286. *Rolling Stone*, 19 December 1974
287. G Harrison in conversation on a bootleg record of a 'Ding Dong Ding Dong' out-take
288. Unless you include Freddie And The Dreamers quoting 'Auld Lang Syne' in counterpoint in 'I Understand' in the UK Top Ten in December 1964
289. *Disc*, 21 December 1974
290. *International Musician And Recording World*, March 1976
291. Bill Elliott in Splinter's Dark Horse press release
292. *Q*, September 1989
293. *New Musical Express*, *circa* 1976
294. BBC Radio 1, February 1976
295. *Beatlefan* volume four, number one, December 1981
296. *Music Week*, 6 July 1977
297. *A Personal Musical Dialogue* with George Harrison at 33$^1/_3$ conducted by M Harrison, October 1977

298. Not the Bristol group who, in 1963, recorded on Pye the imaginative rocking up of the Cornish Floral Dance
299. *Sounds*, 22 December 1976
300. *New Musical Express*, 10 December 1980
301. *New Musical Express*, 7 December 1976
302. Transcript of press conference held at Madison Hotel, Washington, 17 September 1976
303. *Beatles Monthly*, December 1983
304. *Sunday People*, 12 February 1984
305. *Melody Maker*, 14 August 1966
306. *Time Out*, 19 October 1989
307. *Evening News*, 11 March 1978
308. Transcript of press conferences held at Hotel Okura, Japan, 4 October 1977
309. *Songwriter*, May 1979
310. *Daily Mirror*, 19 December 1980
311. *Ready, Steady, Go!* (ITV) 20 March 1964
312. *George Harrison: Yesterday And Today* by R Michaels (Flash Books, 1977)
313. By H Elson and J Brunton (Proteus, 198 1)
314. *Sun*, 11 November 1987
315. To Mark Lewisohn
316. *Daily Express*, 29 July 1989
317. *Evening News*, 30 March 1987
318. *Henley Standard*, 29 July 1986
319. *Beatlefan* volume four, number five, 1982
320. *Beatles Monthly*, June 1986
321. *Sun*, 2 October 1987
322. *The Damp Garden* (Dent, 1982); *Plant Portraits* (Dent, 1985)
323. *Daily Mirror*, 24 January 1983
324. *Daily Express*, 20 August 1986
325. *Midday* (Australian TV), February 1988
326. Press conference transcript after a literary luncheon at Sydney Opera House, 28 September 1984
327. But not the same Keith West who sang 'Excerpt From A Teenage Opera', a British hit in August 1967
328. *People*, 9 October 1987
329. *Beatles Unlimited*, February 1982
330. London press conference transcript, 6 March 1986
331. *Last Resort* (ITV), 16 October 1987
332. *Guardian*, 5 May 1988
333. *Kaleidoscope* (BBC Radio 4), 30 November 1987
334. *Soft Touch*, September 1982
335. *Melody Maker*, 10 March 1979
336. *Daily Mail*, 3 May 1987
337. *Brown Sauce* by J Brown (Collins Willow, 1986)
338. *Q*, July 1989
339. *Sun*, 1 May 1989
340. *Guardian*, 3 May 1988
341. *Daily Express/Sun*, 16 February 1988
342. *Daily Mail*, 4 January 1988

343. *Guardian*, 5 April 1990
344. In May 1990, the HandMade film *Nuns On The Run*, starring Robbie Coltrane, was well-received by critics and moderately successful in general circulation
345. *New Musical Express*, 15 February 1963
346. *Time Out*, December 1988
347. *Sunday Times*, 1 July 1990
348. Olivia Harrison to *Henley Standard*, 22 June 1990
349. *Standard Times*, 10 June 1990
350. *Sunday Times*, 6 May 1990
351. *Henley Standard*, 4 May 1990
352. *Reading Evening Post*, 2 May 1990. In connection with the case, police swooped on a house in Battersea where dwelt an American hippy couple who alleged that they'd had an altercation with Olivia Harrison "on another planet" and felt snubbed by her
353. *Inside Pop: The Rock Revolution* (CBS television), early 1967
354. *Today*, 13 April 1987
355. *Evening Post*, 30 November 1989
356. *The Little Flowers Of St Francis* translated by W Heywood (CEFA, 1974)
357. The address is *Beatlefan*, PO Box 33515, Decatur, GA 30033, USA
358. *Billboard*, 1 December 1991
359. Royal Albert Hall concert flyer, 6 April 1992
360. George Harrison is heard on a track on a 1992 album by Jimmy Nail
361. Which included Andy Fairweather-Low, former frontman of Amen Corner and 1970s solo star. During the Japanese tour, he shared lead-guitar duties with Harrison and Clapton
362. The former member of Thin Lizzy had included George's composition 'That Kind Of Woman' on a recent album. This – along with another Harrison opus, 'Run So Far' – was also recorded by Eric Clapton
363. *Times*, 7 April 1992
364. *Daily Express*, 7 April 1992
365. *Evening Standard*, 7 April 1992
366. *Daily Telegraph*, 7 April 1992
367. *Daily Mail*, 24 June 1994
368. Former editor of *Melody Maker* and biographer of John Lennon and Brian Epstein
369. Significant among the lesser tracks unearthed was 'You'll Know What To Do', a Harrison opus from the *Hard Day's Night* era, remaindered possibly as much for it being "not the greatest thing George ever wrote" (Paul McCartney to *The Independent*, 16 July 1995) as its intrusion on an otherwise all Lennon-McCartney soundtrack LP
370. Transmitted on 24 July 1997. Harrison and Shankar were also interviewed on *This Morning*, CBS, on 12 July 1997
371. Published by Cassell (UK) on 3 March 2001
372. *Raga Mala: The Autobiography Of Ravi Shankar* (Genesis, 2000)
373. www.allthingsmustpass.com
374. *Q*, August 1998
375. *Sunday Times*, 19 November 2000
376. *Henley Standard*, 17 November 2000
377. *Independent On Sunday*, 19 November 2000
378. *Daily Telegraph*, 23 December 2000

Index

Davies, Ray 179, 191, 219, 288
Davies, Trevor "Dozy" 45
Davis (Group), (The) Spencer 72, 327, 136
Davis, Jesse "Ed" 293, 311
de Villeneuve, Justin 240
Dean, Alvin 135, 158
Debussy, Claude 285
Dee, Dave (And The Bostons) (Dozy, Beaky Mick And Tich) 13, 34, 45, 64, 71, 90, 149, 259, 282, 327
Deep Purple 290, 295, 299, 324, 397, 406, 410
Defoe, Daniel 426
Del Shannon 464
Delaney And Bonnie (And Friends) 275, 277, 278, 279, 280, 286, 288, 313
Delaney, Paddy 88, 106
Delaney, Shelagh 101
Delfont, Lord 371
Dene Boys, The 45
Denver, John 356
Derek And The Dominoes 290, 297
Dev, Guru 223
Devlin, Johnny 13
Diddley, Bo 83
Dietrich, Marlene 167
Dire Straits 413
Disney, Walt 28
Dodd, Ken 52, 101, 118, 125, 130, 339
Dodd, Les 67, 68
Doddridge, Paul 354
Dole, Bob 431
Domino, Fats 84, 96, 398
Donays, The 111
Donegan, Lonnie 33, 34, 38, 43
Donovan 171, 191, 219, 231, 347, 412
Doors, The 326
Doran, Terry 151, 238, 240, 319, 350
Douglas, Craig 101
Downs, Hugh 317
Dr Feelgood 342
Dr John 431
Drake, Pete 297

Duke, Geoff 28
Dunn, Clive 290, 295
Dunn, David 404
Dusty Road Ramblers, The 34, 56
Dylan, Bob 100, 143, 158, 171, 172, 186, 188, 211-2, 214, 222, 242-3, 245, 249, 251, 258-60, 271, 273-4, 277-8, 288, 296, 297, 309-11, 314-5, 322, 325, 329-30, 340, 368, 379-80, 388, 397-8, 404, 410, 415, 417, 419-20, 422, 423, 436, 444

Eager, Vince 46
Eagles, The 356, 431
Eapstein, Brian 109
Eastman, Lee 265
Eastman, Linda (see Linda McCartney)
Eastman, Paul 304
Eckhorn, Peter 79-80, 89, 91
Eddie Clayton Skiffle Group, The 117, 351
Eddy, Duane 44, 58, 140, 147, 193, 418, 424
Edmunds, Dave 290, 390, 397, 398, 399, 402-3, 431
Edwards, Jack 26, 39
Edwin Hawkins Singers, The 280
Elastic Oz Band, The 346
Elizabeth, (John's) Aunt 94
Elliot, Bern And The Fenmen 90
Elliott, Bill 346
Ellis, Royston 71
ELO 323, 324, 355, 409, 410, 415, 403
ELP 290, 324
Elvis, Presley 59
Engel, Scott 228
English, David 424
Entwistle, John 194, 402
Enya 367
Epstein, Brian 104-5, 106-7, 108, 110, 112-3, 114, 115, 119, 126, 136, 137, 149, 151, 154, 163, 164, 178, 186, 189, 196, 198, 199-200, 204, 209, 211,

219, 219, 220, 221-2, 224, 227, 235, 237, 239, 265, 318, 333, 427, 428, 464, 470
Eurythmics, The 415-6, 420
Evans, David 141-2
Evans, Mal 142, 155, 170, 172, 198, 238, 277, 279, 286, 287, 296, 331, 346, 370
Evans, Robert "Pop" 24
Everly Brothers, The 44, 45, 56, 83, 96, 343, 390, 394

Faces, The 329
Faith, Adam 78, 113, 127, 288
Faithfull, Marianne 225, 239
Fame, Georgie 228, 250, 381
Fangio 27-8
Fantoni, Barry 191
Faron's Flamingos 143, 427, 428
Farrow, Mia 231, 232
Fascher, Horst 80
Fataar, Rick 370
Fenton, Iris 136
Fenton, Shane (And The Fentones) 103, 110-1, 113, 136-7
Ferera, Frank 391
Ferry, Bryan 326, 327, 402
Finn, Mickey 102
Fittipaldi, Emerson 367
Five Stairsteps, The 348
Flash Cadillac 258
Fleetwood Mac 239, 284, 311, 342, 397
Fleetwood, Mick 397
Flowerpot Men, The 204, 218, 228
Flowers, Herbie 380
Fogerty, John 398, 410
Fontella Bass 356
Fonteyne, Billy 138
Fonyo, Steve 388
Fool, The 211, 218, 238
Ford, Clinton 31, 47
Ford, Emile 110
Ford, President John 316, 341